Romantic Paris

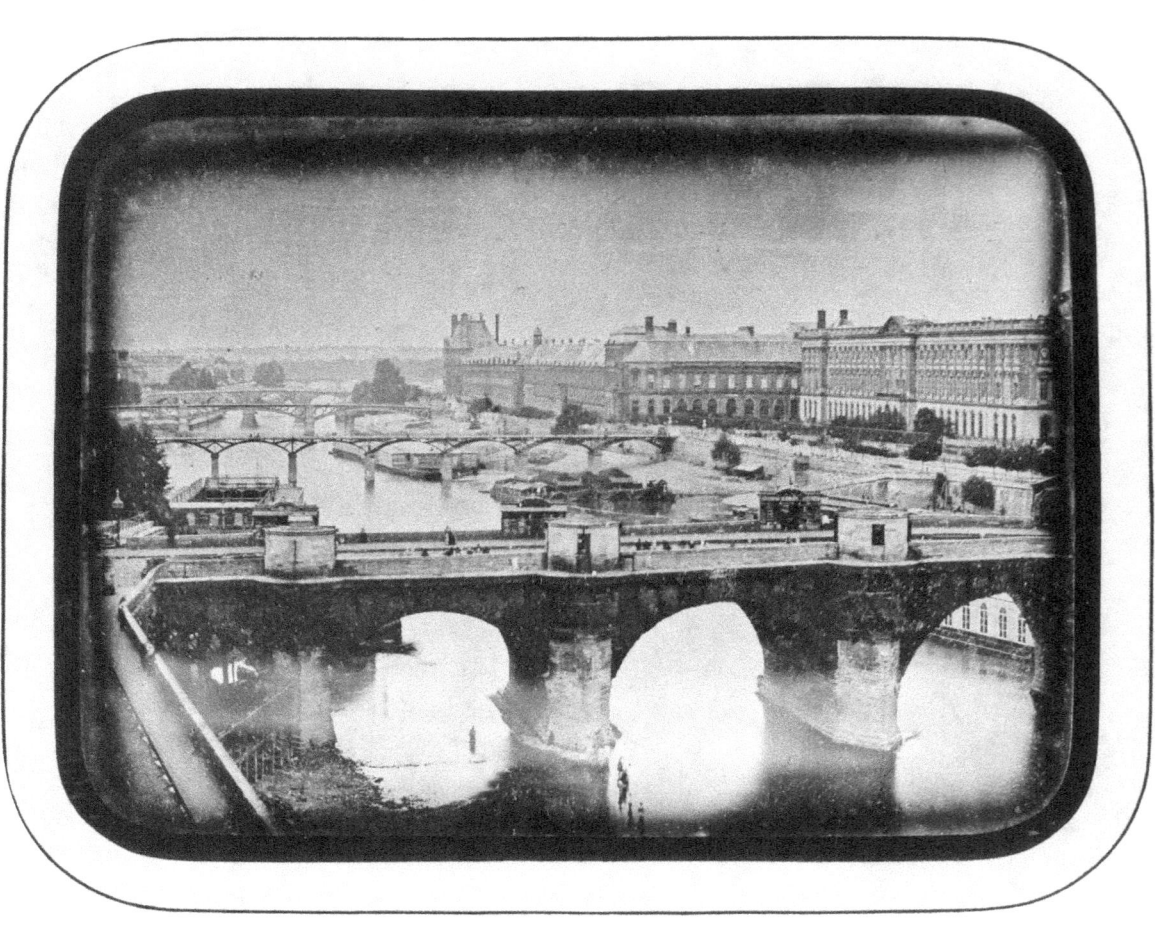

Romantic Paris

Histories of a Cultural Landscape, 1800–1850

❧ Michael Marrinan

Stanford University Press
Stanford, California

Stanford University Press
Stanford, California

Frontipiece: Anonymous daguerreotype, *The Pont-Neuf and the Louvre*, ca. 1845–1850. Herning, Collection of the Danish Musuem of Photography, courtesy of the Danish Museum of Photography.

Parts of Chapters 1 through 7 of the present work appeared in a different version in *The Art and Spirit of Paris*, vol. 1, pp. 675–867. © 2003 by Abbeville Press, Inc., and are published herein with its permission.

Paris, Les Paris: Words and Music by Paolo Conte, © 2000 Warner Chappell Music Italiana SPA (SIAE) and L'Alternativa Edizioni Musicali SRL (SIAE). All rights administered by WB Music Corp. All rights reserved. Used by permission.

This book has been published with the assistance of the Department of Art & Art History and the School of Humanities and Sciences, Stanford University.

Library of Congress Cataloging-in-Publication Data

Marrinan, Michael.
  Romantic Paris : histories of a cultural landscape, 1800–1850 / Michael Marrinan.
     p. cm.
  "Parts of chapters 1 through 7 of the present work appeared in a different version in 'The art and spirit of Paris', vol. 1, pp. 675-867"—T.p. verso.
  Includes bibliographical references and index.
  ISBN 978-0-8047-5062-2 (cloth : alk. paper) — ISBN 978-0-8047-6151-2 (pbk. : alk. paper)
  1. Arts and society—France—Paris—History—19th century. 2. Arts, French—France—Paris—19th century.
3. Paris (France)—Civilization—19th century. I. Title.
  NX180.S6M368 2009
  700'.1030944361034—dc22

                              2008020033

Designed by Bruce Lundquist
Typeset at Stanford Univerrsity Press in 10/14 Adobe Caslon

Oui, beaucoup d'paris
oui, tant de paris
tant de paris dans la tête d'quelqu'un
tant de paris dans la main d'quelqu'un
tant de paris dans le charme d'quelqu'un
oui, beaucoup de paris . . .
—Paolo Conte, *Paris, Les Paris*

Contents

Illustrations

Acknowledgments

MANY YEARS HAVE PASSED since I began to research this book, and many more while I wrestled with its text. During that time I have accumulated many debts, both to individuals and to institutions, for support and encouragement along the way. Although these brief comments will attempt to thank those who have helped me finish the project, I start with an apology to those I inadvertently might fail to mention. I am extremely fortunate to have a circle of friends and colleagues who never gave up on me, even in those moments when I believed I had run aground.

I must first mention material assistance. For several years I spent most of the summer months in Paris, working in the libraries and museums of the city. These excursions were funded in large part by two research endowments attached to the Department of Art & Art History at Stanford: the Ruth Halperin Fund and the Doris McNamara Fund. These two donors and good friends of the department understood fully the costs of research in the humanities. Without their enlightened gifts to our department this book would never have been finished. On two different occasions the dean of the School of Humanities & Sciences at Stanford awarded research monies: I thank both Keith Baker and Arnold Rampersad for their support at those critical moments.

I began this project in another form and context that eventually presented vexing legal complexities. Thanks to the unflinching efforts of two excellent lawyers—F. Kinsey Haffner and Carolina Fornos—these obstacles were negotiated so that I might continue work on the project. To both of them I express my very deep gratitude for all that they have done on my behalf. At Stanford University Press, Norris Pope, program director for scholarly publishing, saw the potential of a book that crosses the usual boundaries dividing art history, history proper, and cultural studies. He argued its merits to the publications board and demonstrated a bold confidence that was very inspiring. I hope the finished book meets his high expectations for it. Richard Gunde edited the manuscript beautifully and Judith Hibbard expertly guided it through production. I am grateful to both for their enthusiastic and close attention to the smallest details.

I have long been impressed by the professionalism and courtesy of colleagues working in the libraries and museums of France. One expects to be received with civility at large public institutions like the Bibliothèque nationale, and that is generally the case. Yet the kindness and welcome shown me every year by the staff of the Bibliothèque Doucet (officially now the library of the Institut National de l'Histoire de l'Art) goes well beyond civility and is especially noteworthy. I must also mention those museum curators who went out of their way to aid my research: Marianne Delafond (Musée Marmottan), Anne Gros (Musée Bouilhet-Christofle), Michaela Lerch-Moulin (Musée Baccarat), Tamara Préaud (Archives de la Manufacture de Sèvres), Béatrice Roussel (Musée de Valence), Bernard Terlay (Musée Granet), and Pascal Trarieux (Musée de Nîmes). Finally, I thank collectively those who helped me locate images in photographic archives: the Photothèque des Musées de la Ville de Paris, the Centre des Monuments nationaux, the Photothèque de la Conservation des Oeuvres d'Art Religieuses et Civiles, the Photothèque de la Réunion des Musées nationaux, and finally, Marta Fodor of Art Resource in New York.

When carrying around a long-term project like this book, one cannot avoid inflicting its vicissitudes upon colleagues and friends. I am very fortunate to have a circle of sympathetic listeners, on both sides of the ocean, who have responded tactfully and with patience to my frequent outbursts of despair or dismay. In Paris, the conversation over many dinners at the apartment of Marie-Cathérine Sahut and Régis Michel drifted to the subject of my long-overdue book, but always with encouragement and goodwill. Around their table I met others—including Jimmy and Nicole Bloedé and Abigail Solomon-Godeau—who have become friends and stalwart supporters of my faltering spirit. At Stanford, I owe much to the advice, encouragement, and wisdom of John Bender, my colleague from English, with whom I have collaborated on several other projects. John's good sense has often brought my own excitable temperament back to the task at hand, and for that I am grateful.

The trajectory of a person's life can change dramatically in the course of a long project like this one. I have had the good fortune of traveling this road with exceptional companions. At different times, and under different circumstances, Janet Jones, Claudia Einecke, and Davey Hubay have read this text, calmed my anxieties over it, and given me the courage to keep working. A much-loved border collie named Fergie has also done her part. Without falling prey to maudlin platitudes, I recognize that my best writing during these years has walked hand in hand with the well-being of a solid personal relationship. It may well be that this book did some damage along the way, but I never would have finished it on my own.

While thinking of life's trajectories, I should mention the book's dedication. My mother died many years ago when I was but a child. Her absence has haunted my life—and paradoxically affected its course—more than any other single event I can imagine. I was never able to take my mother to Paris, nor share with her my love for the city and its culture. Nonetheless, I like to think that she and I would have had a wonderful time there.

—Paris, July 2007

Romantic Paris

Introduction

My Paris is not some given monument or period of time. I loved this city before noticing any work of art in it. What is most beautiful about it is neither Notre-Dame, nor any such building, but the city itself. Even the beauty of buildings is of secondary importance to the beauty of a city. Walk along the quais and boulevards of Paris and you will sense, without looking at any specific detail, that you are in the capital of human sociability.

—Jules Michelet[1]

SOME PLACES JUST FEEL RIGHT. From my first impressions of Paris nearly thirty years ago—a backpacking graduate student tumbling off the night train from Nice into the glaring light of the quai at the Gare de Lyon—I have never ceased feeling a peculiar affinity with the city and her people. Naturally, I had been forewarned about the famous haughtiness of the Parisians, about their intolerance of French spoken badly, about their simmering hostility towards the hoards of twenty-something Americans who invade their beloved city every summer. But I found none of this in 1974, or at least spoke French so poorly that their sarcasms were lost in non-translation. I went on to write about French art, to spend many years in the libraries and archives of Paris, and to discover with each stay a bit more of the immaterial presence about which Michelet wrote so simply and eloquently. Some years ago it became clear to me that I would have to write a book about "my" Paris: not the one I actually inhabit from time to time, but the historical environment that I experienced vicariously through the documents, texts, and works of art that have been the ob-

ject my scholarly efforts in the history of art. This book has taken me far longer to write than I ever imagined; it is my attempt to give life and voice to a social space whose traces remain part of the city's fabric, but whose actors have long disappeared.

I USE THE TERM "SOCIAL SPACE" deliberately to indicate that this is not a guide to the streets and monuments of Paris. There are thousands of such books, written by authors of great erudition, that date, describe, and contextualize the cultural artifacts of the city. My goal has been to capture something of the sensation, "without looking at any specific detail," felt by Michelet when walking the boulevards and the quais of his Paris, even if doing so means paying attention to a great many details. To make my subject the ineffable of early nineteenth-century Paris responds to a challenge of the canonical work on "social space" written in 1974 by Henri Lefebvre.[2] His sketch of the concept both accords with Michelet's experience and endorses an approach across disciplines that I have tried to make the centerpiece of this book:

(Social) space is not a thing among other things, nor a product among other products: rather, it subsumes things produced, and encompasses their interrelationships in their coexistence and si-multaneity—their (relative) order and/or (relative) disorder. It is the outcome of a sequence and set of operations, and thus cannot be reduced to the rank of a simple object. At the same time there is nothing imagined, unreal or 'ideal' about it as compared, for example, with science, representations, ideas or dreams. Itself the outcome of past actions, social space is what permits fresh actions to occur, while suggesting others and prohibiting yet others. Among these actions, some serve production, others consumption (i.e. the enjoyment of the fruits of production). Social space implies a great diversity of knowledge.[3]

Lefebvre returns repeatedly to the idea that social space does not exist a priori; rather, it is produced continuously by its inhabitants. On his account, people and objects do not simply fill a space, but are engaged in a dialectic that joins separate components into particular configurations of lived experience [vécu]:

Vis-à-vis lived experience, space is neither a mere 'frame,' after the fashion of the frame of a painting, nor a form or container of a virtually neutral kind, designed simply to receive whatever is poured into it. Space is social morphology: it is to lived experience what form itself is to the living organism, and just as intimately bound up with function and structure. To picture space as a 'frame' or container into which nothing can be put unless it is smaller than the recipient, and to imagine that this container has no other purpose than to preserve what has been put into it—this is probably the initial error.[4]

Lefebvre writes at a high level of abstraction in order to unravel what he takes to be the dominant threads of Western thought: either to define social space as an abstraction that can be measured geometrically, or to subsume it under a general term—hence idealize it—for discursive purposes.[5] He wants to lodge the notion of social space in lived processes without relinquishing the power to speak of it as a concrete

thing—a position he rightly describes as riddled with paradox and hard to grasp:

Many people will find it hard to endorse the notion that space has taken on, within the present mode of production, within society as it actually is, a sort of reality of its own, a reality clearly distinct from, yet much like, those assumed in the same global processes by commodities, money and capital. Many people, finding this claim paradoxical, will want proof.[6]

Like money, which is both an abstraction and real, social space for Lefebvre is concrete and instrumental without becoming just another product or objectified form of knowledge. He calls for new modes of analysis that will attend to diversity and the multiple levels of meaning built up over time that nonetheless coexist in the present. To illustrate the point concretely, Lefebvre enlists a metaphor from the pastry-shop: "Thus social space, and especially urban space, emerged in all its diversity—and with a structure far more reminiscent of flaky *mille-feuille* pastry than of the homogeneous and isotropic space of classical (Euclidean/Cartesian) mathematics."[7] The image is appetizing: it registers Lefebvre's imagery of layers—time, events, past memories, current experience—present in every moment to the inhabitants of a social space.

What does a mille-feuille have to do with a book on Paris? First of all, the metaphor figures the impossibility of assuming the role of pastry-maker before the social space of Paris. It would be pointless to presume to know the recipe, the ingredients, and the gestures to replicate so complicated a *gâteau*. Consequently, this book does not offer a straight-line narrative that pretends to explain fully the Paris of early nineteenth-century France. Histories, the plural form of the book's subtitle, is meant to suggest that the reader will encounter multiple threads that intersect, interweave, and sometimes clash with one another. The chapters open several avenues of inquiry—political, literary, visual, urbanist, technological—that criss-cross and are cross-referenced. An urban metaphor appropriate to the general structure of this book would be a *carrefour*: although rendered in English as "crossroads," the allusion I want to enlist is when several streets cross within the city to form a space that belongs to none of them exclusively, to all of them at once, and yet carries its own name and identity.[8] A salient example is the irregularly-shaped space—today called the place Franz Liszt (Fig. 132)—formed where the rue Lafayette, the rue d'Abbeville, the rue d'Hauteville, and the rue des Petit-Hôtels intersect before the church of St-Vincent-de-Paul. Like that space, which becomes intelligible only to a person physically standing within it, my aim has been to open before readers something akin to Lefebvre's multi-layered social space, and to implicate them in its structure. The text does not presume a continuous reading from front to back. Chapters both stand alone and signal potential connections to others via cross-references. I have tried to break down the illusion of a mastering voice by inviting readers to explore the material in different sequences and by means of personalized zigzags.

Within chapters, the purview shifts from wide-angle to near view, from coarse grain to fine grain, from objects to texts more or less freely according to the task at hand. This should not be construed as authorial whimsy, but as my effort to manage with the linear tools of language the complexity of space evoked by Lefebvre:

Thus space may be said to embrace a multitude of intersections, each with its assigned location. As for representations of the relations of production, which subsume power relations, these too occur in space: space contains them in the form of buildings, monuments and works of art. Such frontal (and hence brutal) expressions of these relations do not completely crowd out their more clandestine or underground aspects; all power must have its accomplices—and its police.[9]

Lefebvre insists upon studying this complexity simultaneously on at least three levels. The first is spatial practice, "which embraces production and reproduction, and the particular locations and spatial sets characteristic of each social formation. Spatial practice ensures continuity and some degree of cohesion. In terms of social space, and of each member of a given society's relationship to that space, this cohesion implies a guaranteed level of *competence* and a specific level of *performance*."[10] I have tried to register spatial interaction in a couple of ways. First, by attending to accounts of how people actually behaved in public venues (arcades, theaters, restaurants, the street, the museums, the omnibus). Second, by foregrounding throughout the book many different voices

as recorded in several kinds of texts. While I do not believe naïvely that such voices are transparent windows to the past, they do register what Lefebvre calls *competence* and *performance* within a given lived situation. I have worked from the assumption that if one person has published a particular view about a situation or event it is likely that others shared the same view. At stake in this procedure is a level of plausibility more than absolute truth. Diligent researchers will surely find other voices who speak in terms diametrically opposed to those I cite: counter-examples in this case do not invalidate the fact of a recorded performance; on the contrary, they substantiate the complexity of lived space.[11] The second level of study concerns what Lefebvre calls "the representations of space, which are tied to the relations of production and to the 'order' which these relations impose, and hence to knowledge, to signs, to codes, and to 'frontal' relations."[12] This is the realm of monuments, museums, and similar projects of official high culture to shape, codify, and allegorize social space. Inversely, it is also the realm of so-called popular culture activities—caricatures, newspapers, boulevard theater, modes of dress—that cast events and experiences in idioms broadly understood throughout the social space, both up and down the social hierarchy. Finally, Lefebvre wants to attend to "representational spaces, embodying complex symbolisms, sometimes coded, sometimes not, linked to the clandestine or underground side of social life, as also to art (which may come eventually to be defined less as a code of space than as a code of representational spaces)."[13] This is a vast arena that encompasses works of art of all genres, paradigmatic performers (including virtuosi and media stars), self-styled exiles (bohemians), and the glittering windows of commercial shops filled with goods of all kinds. There are moments when I push hard on works of art, not necessarily to wrest from them a reading consonant with their place in the conventions of art history, but to make them speak as codings for "representational spaces."

Consonant with Lefebvre's theoretical requirements for the study of social space, individual chapters interleave, juxtapose, and interrelate these levels of study so as to cross-cut and distract the inexorable forward march of my written text.[14] The arrangement of chapters also responds to Lefebvre's call for a coexistence of differential analyses. Chapter One sets the stage by recounting the dramatic shifts of power bracketed by the rise and demise of Napoléon, and aligning these moments with the larger context of a nation that has just emerged from the turbulence of a profound revolution. Here, canonical works of art articulate the encodings of the social space of post-revolution Paris. Chapter Two traces the further history of political conflict from the return of the Bourbon monarchy to the founding of the Second Republic. Of special interest is the allegorical stature of Parisian monuments—and the long history they concretize—newly mobilized to immediate political ends. The terrain is both that of spatial practices—acts, gestures, and texts—and the pursuit of legitimacy via selective appropriations of the past. Chapter Three pursues this re-symbolization of Paris on two levels: first, by studying how a succession of governments worked to reshape spatial practices within the city by means of new streets, bridges, sidewalks, sewers, and cemeteries; second, by charting the re-allegorizing of existing monuments to support the status quo, thus exposing the battle being waged between living memory and politcal exigency over the representations of space. Chapter Four explores a more personal side of this re-symbolization by introducing emerging social practices of remembering tied to affect, sensibility, and nostalgia triggered by the chronicles and personalities of medieval France. Diffusion of these practices is traced from the private living chambers of educated and powerful women to the very public gesture of restoring the cathedral of Notre-Dame begun in 1843. Chapter Five returns to the spaces of representation and the world of art, where adherents of tradition and propriety cross swords with those committed to experiment and excess. The chapter is half of the book's centerpiece. The other half is Chapter Six, which explores some of the social practices accompanying developments in the world of art: bohemian lifestyles; literary cenacles and salons; the rise of portraiture; a revolution in drama and staging; the phenomena of virtuosi and stars. Chapter Seven returns to spatial practices by exploring shifts in comportment and dress in response to new urban experiences tied to the introduction of covered shopping areas and arcades, the mapping of entirely new neighborhoods within the city, and

the evolving social milieu of cafés, restaurants, and public transportation. All three levels of analysis are interweaved in Chapter Eight. First, by considering how the use of industrial materials in commercial architecture affected the evolution of social practices within those spaces. Second, by asking how adopting industrial techniques of production circulated new categories of goods within commercial spaces to trigger heightened levels of consumer desire. Finally, by tracing the effect of industrial forms of reproduction upon the creation, distribution, and criticism of fine art, culminating with the introduction and perfection of daguerreotype photography.

Subtending the sequence and focus of the last chapters are two interrelated transformations also discussed by Lefebvre. First, the distinction work–product. "A *work* has something irreplaceable and unique about it," he writes; "a *product* can be reproduced exactly, and is in fact the result of repetitive acts and gestures."[15] The shift from hand-worked silver or hand-blown glass to electroplating and molded crystal clearly registers Lefebvre's distinction, as does the shift from bespoke clothes to ready-to-wear garments cut in pre-determined sizes.[16] Differences between historical space and abstract space constitute Lefebvre's second distinction. On his account, historical space is "the space of accumulation (the accumulation of all wealth and resources: knowledge, technology, money, precious objects, works of art and symbols)."[17] Abstract space, by contrast, "functions 'objectally,' as a set of things/signs and their formal relationships: glass and stone, concrete and steel, angles and curves, full and empty. Formal and quantitative, it erases distinctions, as much those which derive from nature and (historical) time as those which originate in the body (age, sex, ethnicity)."[18] It is not difficult to map the disparaging criticisms of monotony and homogeneity in the new neighborhoods of Paris (Fig. 133) onto a realization—perhaps more intuitive than conscious—that the city was moving towards an increased level of abstraction. Lefebvre eventually argues that urban social space in the modern era sheds the quality of work [oeuvre]—historic Venice is his preferred example—to become ever more a product:

It is obvious, sad to say, that repetition has everywhere defeated uniqueness, that the artificial and contrived have driven all spontaneity and naturalness from the field, and, in short, that products have vanquished works. Repetitive spaces are the outcome of repetitive gestures (those of workers) associated with instruments which are both duplicatable and designed to duplicate: machines, bulldozers, concrete-mixers, cranes, pneumatic drills, and so on. Are these spaces interchangeable because they are homologous? Or are they homologous so that they can be exchanged, bought and sold, with the only differences between them being those assessable in money—i.e. quantifiable—terms (as volumes, distances, etc.)? At all events, repetition reigns supreme.[19]

Lefebvre is more properly describing tract housing built on speculation in our contemporary world than nineteenth-century Paris. My point is that the qualities he ascribes to the city-as-product—most of which became part of normal business practice during the building boom of the Second Empire—took root and began to germinate in Romantic Paris.

SOMETHING SHOULD BE SAID about the "Romantic" of the book's title. One option, the simplest and most circular reason for writing about Romantic Paris, would be to say that the time frame of this book happens to correspond to the working dates of most artists, writers, and critics associated with "romanticism" in French art. This does not get very far by way of explanation. Another option would be to posit a working definition or set of goals for Romanticism, and then set out to prove that the culture of Paris between 1800 and 1850 amply fulfills those criteria. That would be doubly counterproductive. First, because it has long been agreed that defining Romanticism is a fruitless enterprise rife with difficulties.[20] Second, because doing so would not simply

undermine, but completely obliterate, my efforts to suppress the mastering voice of an omniscient author.

Lefebvre holds out a third alternative by insisting that any revolution worthy of its name must create a new social space:

A revolution that does not produce a new space has not realized its full potential; indeed it has failed in that it has not changed life itself, but has merely changed ideological superstructures, institutions or political apparatuses. A social transformation, to be truly revolutionary in character, must manifest a creative capacity in its effects on daily life, on language and on space—though its impact need not occur at the same rate, or with equal force, in each of these areas.[21]

I happen to agree with Lefebvre that the French Revolution was not a failure. "Also among revolution's effects, direct and indirect," he notes, "was the definitive constitution of abstract space." The effects were not immediately apparent, for there followed a period of "taking stock and (to use a typographical analogy) for imposition."[22] This book chronicles the decades of taking stock, of clarifying and consolidating the triumphs and tragedies of the French Revolution. My understanding of the historical moment tends to accord with Lefebvre's own view: "Might not Romanticism be said to have lived through—even if it misunderstood—the transitional moment that separated abstract spatiality from a more unmediated perception? Was the Romantic movement not in fact shot through—and hence actuated—by this particular antagonism, even if it has been ignored in favour of more dramatic ones?"[23] Lefebvre's Paris of transitions—poised at the threshold of modernity—is my subject. For the historic capture of the term, and guided by my affection for the place, I have named this book *Romantic Paris*.

The Moods of Post-Revolution Paris

The simple title of French citizen is worth far more than that of royaliste, clichien, jacobin, feuillant, or any of those thousand and one denominations which have sprung, during the past ten years, from the spirit of faction, and which are hurling the nation into an abyss from which the time has come at last to rescue it, once and for all. This is the aim of my efforts.

—Napoléon Bonaparte in 1799[1]

DURING THE NIGHT of 22 August 1799 Napoléon Bonaparte, with a handful of trusted advisers and a small contingent of soldiers, slipped the English blockade of Alexandria in a hastily armed freighter to begin a six-week journey from Egypt to France. Bonaparte had been gone for more than a year, at the head of a French expedition to conquer territory in the Middle East, and Parisian newspapers had been filled with tales of military victories and archeological discoveries in Egypt that lent tremendous prestige to the general's name. By contrast, the dispatches he received from France were not good: French armies had suffered losses in Italy and along the Rhine; the Directory government seemed paralyzed by internal squabbles; malicious whispers suggested that his beloved Joséphine was carrying on with another man. Even more alarming to Bonaparte were reports that people thought he was dead, along with rumors of a brewing coup-d'état to put général Barthélemi Joubert in charge.

Bonaparte decided his political future was at risk and that he must reenter immediately the arena of Parisian power and intrigue. Although most historians agree his decision to leave Egypt precipitously and without orders was nothing short of desertion, so great was the prestige of his name that his arrival at Fréjus on 9 October was greeted by such public clamor that immigration officers were unable to hold him for the usual period of quarantine: six hours after setting foot on land he was headed for Paris. News of his return spread like wildfire and reached the capital by 13 October, three days before he actually entered the city. That evening, général Paul-Charles Thiébault was walking near the Palais-Royal when a growing, noisy crowd attracted his attention:

I hurried forward and wanted to question some of those coming from the gathering who crossed my path and hurried on their way. No one stopped; but one man, without breaking his stride, shouted out to me in a breathless voice these words, "général Bonaparte has just landed at Fréjus!" Military bands stationed in the city already criss-crossed Paris in celebration, carrying in their wake crowds of people and soldiers. As night fell, spur-of-the-moment illuminations were set up in every quartier, and this return—as much hoped for as unexpected—was announced in all the theaters to shouts of *Long live the Republic! Long live Bonaparte!*[2]

Once in Paris, Bonaparte was reconciled with Joséphine and cheered by the crowds: "Everyone waits for Bonaparte impatiently," wrote the *Messager*, "because to everyone he brings new hope."[3] He also began to meet with political leaders on all sides, including the Directors nominally in charge of government, army generals, his brother Joseph, and three key players: Joseph Fouché, the director of police; Charles-Maurice de Talleyrand, who was in charge of the Foreign Office; and the political philosopher Emmanuel-Joseph Sièyes, an early leader of the French Revolution and expert on constitutional law. By the first week of November plans were well advanced for the coup-d'état of 18 Brumaire that would dissolve the Directory government and install Bonaparte as First Consul.

The painter Jacques-Louis David had met Bonaparte in late 1797, a few months after the general's victory at Rivoli and prior to his departure for Egypt, when the young general agreed to a single sitting for a portrait originally intended to commemorate the treaty of Campo-Formio (Fig. 1). According to Étienne-Jean Delécluze, David deeply admired his sitter, and reportedly exclaimed to his students that "Bonaparte is my hero!"[4] Such an outburst of enthusiasm brought a smile to some of David's older friends who remembered his career as a Jacobin, his vote to send Louis XVI to the guillotine, the revolutionary festivals he had organized for Robespierre, his pictures of republican stoicism that had fueled the political struggles of 1789 (Fig. 2), and his unforgettable homage to the radical leader Jean-Paul Marat. But David's embrace of Bonaparte corresponds in time with his work on the great "reconciliation" picture of the *Sabines* (Fig. 3) and with David's attempt to forget his part in the public drama of the Terror.[5] David was not alone in this, of course, for many actors in those events were now struggling to find a place for themselves in the world of post-revolutionary Paris.

If there were doubts amongst David's friends about his sincerity, the picture put on public view in his studio during September 1801 put them all to rest, for *Bonaparte crossing the Saint-Bernard Pass* (Fig. 1) is nothing short of pure hero worship. The subject painted was inspired by a remarkable feat of arms from May of 1800, when a French army of thirty thou-

sand men, hundreds of canon, and tons of supplies crossed the Alps via the Saint-Bernard Pass to challenge the Austrian army operating in northern Italy near Genoa. Despite several tactical errors, Bonaparte eked out a great victory late in the day of 14 June at the battle of Marengo. David's picture speaks not a word of close calls or hardships, nor does it register the fact that Bonaparte crossed the pass on a mule rather than a great leaping horse. David may have been hampered by the general's refusal to pose for the picture and his admonition that "no one asks if portraits of great men are likenesses. . . . It's enough that their genius live in them," but he dutifully borrowed Bonaparte's uniform for the costume details and followed his patron's desire to be portrayed "calm on a fiery steed."[6]

David also invested the picture with visible admiration for the man and the exploit: Bonaparte looms large over the viewer and dwarfs the soldiers seen between the legs of his horse. Poised on a slightly tipped ground plane, astride the diagonal thrust of his rearing horse while gesturing both forward and up, Bonaparte seems driven by the same winds that whip his cape, the horse's mane, and its extraordinary tail into parallel vectors of forward energy. Amidst these repeated diagonals, the horizontality of Bonaparte's face marks a point of stillness and calm. He seems emotionally unmoved by the sublime vista of background mountains, and he holds the reins distractedly: although they float slack in the wind, the horse's great energy remains in check, tethered by the unflappable act of will working behind the general's icy gaze. Should the admiring visual rhetoric of Bonaparte's appearance be less than clear, David added useful "subtitles" along the picture's lower edge: shiny new letters that spell BONAPARTE are etched in rock alongside HANNIBAL and KAROLUS MAGNUS to remind us of the historical context of the general's achievement. David's picture encodes two aspects of the public mood that greeted Bonaparte's rise to

---

FIGURE 1. Jacques-Louis David, *Bonaparte crossing the Saint-Bernard Pass*, 1801. Oil on canvas. Malmaison, Châteaux de Malmaison et de Bois-Préau, inv. MM49.7.1 (259 × 221 cm). Photo: © RMN/Art Resource, NY/© Gérard Blot.

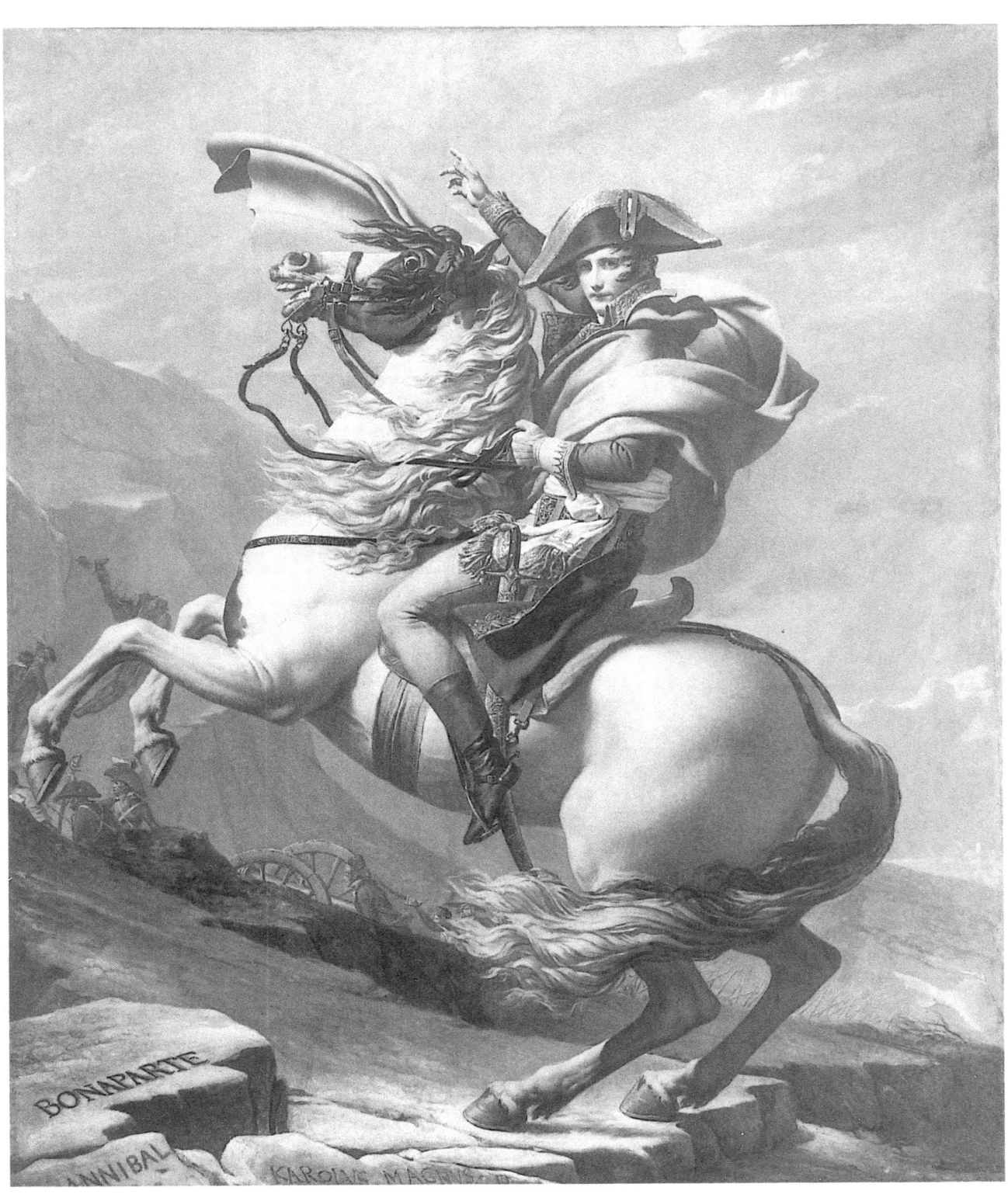

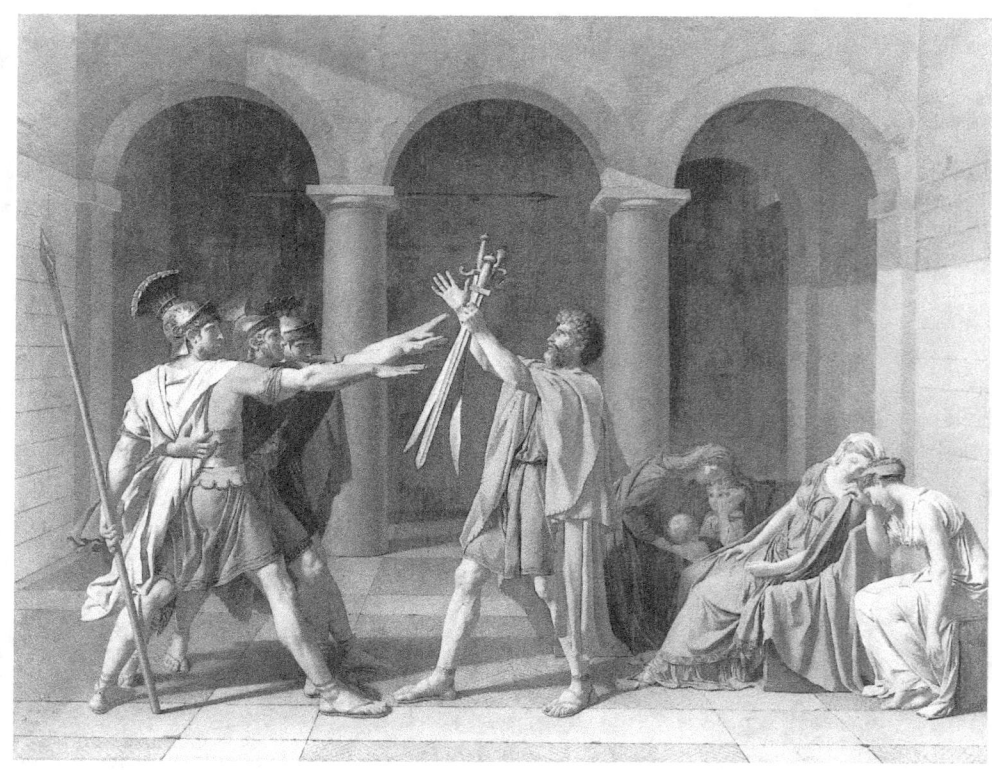

FIGURE 2. Jacques-Louis David, *Oath of the Horatii*, 1784. Oil on canvas. Paris, Musée du Louvre, inv. INV3692 (330 × 425 cm). Photo: © RMN/Art Resource, NY/ © Gérard Blot/Christian Jean.

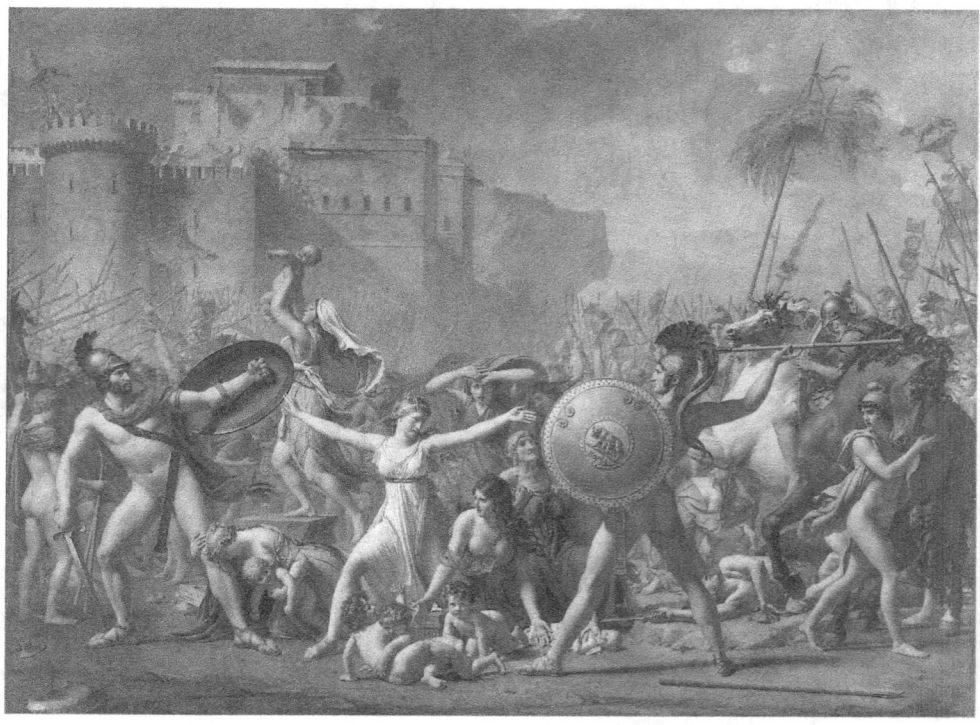

FIGURE 3. Jacques-Louis David, *Intervention of the Sabine Women*, 1799. Oil on canvas. Paris, Musée du Louvre, inv. INV3691 (385 × 522 cm). Photo: © RMN/Art Resource, NY/ © René-Gabriel Ojeda.

power: relief that the turmoil of revolution might soon end, along with acceptance of Bonaparte's project of enforced national healing, even if driven by the clash of arms.

A few months before David completed his portrait, Antoine-Jean Gros exhibited *Sappho at Leucadia* (Fig. 4) at the exhibition of contemporary art held every two years known as the Paris Salon, a picture that expresses a rather different mood of Parisian cultural life.[7] While David's picture surely participated in the circumstances of contemporary politics, it remained attached to the ideals of eighteenth-century Enlightenment thought—and to David's intellectual heritage—by celebrating the triumph of reason over sentiment: from the cold and even light that plays across the figure to the steely, unsensual colors of David's rendering; from Bonaparte's emotional indifference before the sublime splendors of nature to his unyielding commitment to an idea. Whatever Bonaparte's specific project, he fulfills the ideal of Kant's "enlightened prince" who sees clearly the road to betterment and boldly charts a path for his subjects to follow. Gros's *Sappho*, on the other hand, belongs to another world, one in which darkness triumphs over light and where the poetess—thinking herself abandoned by Phaon—throws herself from the cliffs of Leucadia. Like Bonaparte, Sappho is caught in a moment of frozen action, for she teeters above the abyss with one foot already slipped from her rocky perch, but hers is a flight into self-destruction, not a charge into destiny. Where Bonaparte's will was figured as an omnipresent force in David's picture, Gros depicts the *end* of will, as Sappho abandons herself to despair.

Today it seems normal that a critic for the *Journal de Paris* would say of the *Sappho*: "There is more poetry than truth in this painting—the scene is romantic, the color ideal. The subject could be presented to the imagination in this manner, but never to one's sight."[8] But to call a picture "romantic" in 1801, to say its color was "ideal" (meaning unlike the natural world), or to suggest its principal appeal was to "the imagination" located it in the orbit of an emerging challenge to the French tradition of reason and classical values. Gros's *Sappho* champions the individual's right to self-determination, dramatizes an extreme effect of melancholy, and recasts the Greek tale in the vertiginous landscape and lugubrious

light characterized by Madame Germaine de Staël as "the literature of the North."

Madame de Staël's essay, *De la Littérature considérée dans ses rapports avec les institutions*, was published in 1800 to great controversy and it quickly went to a second edition. In it, she praised the poetry of northern, Protestant Europe where the people "are less occupied with pleasures than with sorrows, and their imagination is only more fertile because of it. The spectacle of nature attracts them strongly."[9] De Staël's cosmopolitan and sympathetic view of other cultures was destined to clash with Bonaparte's long-range ambition to impose French taste and French laws on all of Europe. Moreover, she argued against Enlightenment reason and French classicism by suggesting that "melancholic poetry is the poetic form most in accord with philosophy. Sadness causes a more profound penetration of the character and destiny of man than any other state of soul." She described the "imagination of the North" in terms immediately relevant to any consideration of Gros's picture:

It takes delight, along the seacoast, in the sound of winds and the untamed heath; which, in the end, carries the soul weary of its destiny towards the future, towards another world. The imagination of northerners soars above this earth whose confines they inhabit; it soars amongst the clouds which rim their horizon, and which seem to represent the obscure passageway from life to eternity.[10]

In the words of cultural historian Frederick Hemmings, Madame de Staël's book seemed to map a cultural aesthetics deeply opposed to the political agenda of the newly installed First Consul:

The whole direction of Napoléon's policies and the whole ethos that underlay them were implicitly called into question in *De la Littérature*. Mme de Staël opposed a generous idealism to his hard-headed pragmatism, and an optimistic view of human nature to his cynical manoeuvring of men and their ambitions. She attacked the spirit of militarism and the idea of a disciplined society; she spoke up for literature as against science, claiming that writers, the best of whom work according to their own laws and sense of fitness, were the natural champions of liberty, while scientists were deplorably apt to accept any government, even a despotic one, provided it allowed them to pursue unhindered their inquiries into nature's laws.[11]

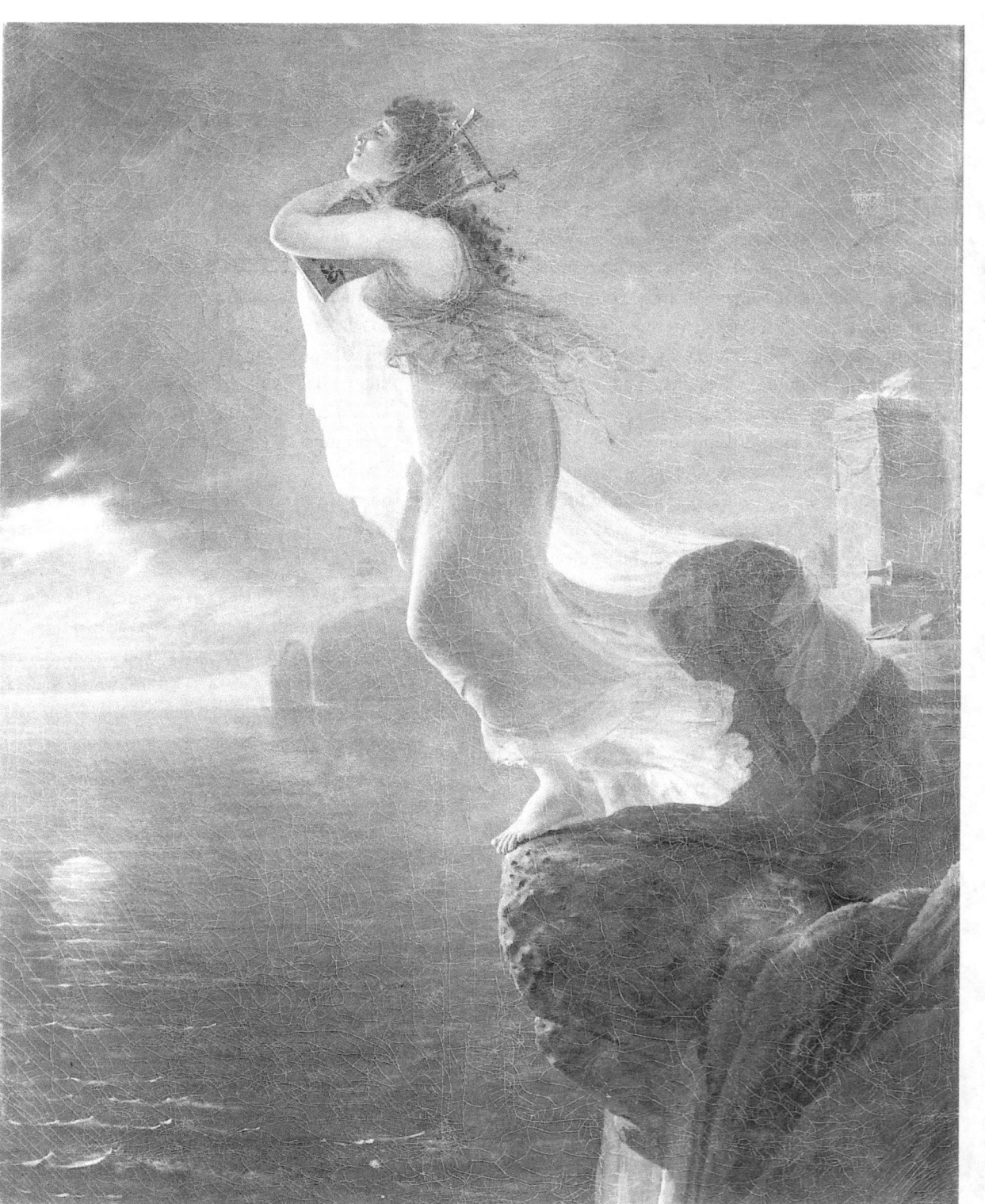

Not surprisingly, Bonaparte brushed off the attempts of Madame de Staël to ingratiate herself with his new regime. He found her novel *Delphine*, published in 1802, to be antisocial and unpatriotic, especially for its feministic defense of individual rights in matters of the heart. He is reported to have said, "I hope Madame de Staël's friends have advised her against coming to Paris; I should be obliged to have her conducted back to the frontier by the gendarmerie."[12]

This context helps to clarify the cultural stakes involved when some critics at the 1801 Salon attacked Gros's *Sappho* for its imaginative departures from usual expectations: "Oh! Dear me, it's so green!" exclaimed the author of *Arlequin au Muséum*; "How is it that Antoine Gros does not know that moonlight is not green?" asked another pamphleteer.[13] Or, as the semi-official and widely read *Journal des Débats* remarked:

Sappho is about to fall; she has already lost her balance, and we believe this moment is badly chosen. It seems to us . . . that the movement, properly so, is not at all within the bounds of painting. In order to fix upon the canvas any lively action whatsoever, the painter must seize an instant of tranquillity, and the imagination does not conceive of this instant in a body which falls.[14]

One might expect the same standard of judgment to apply to Bonaparte's leaping horse, improbably poised on the ice-slicked paths of the Mont Saint-Bernard. Yet it appears that no one raised this criticism before David's portrait. Why is this? One reason is that *Sappho* challenges—both overtly and subliminally—received notions of stoicism, masculinity, and virtue that were part and parcel of Parisian culture around 1800. Gros engages visually the critical terms mobilized by writers like Madame de Staël against the aggressive, militarist hero-worship that invested Bonaparte with the reins of power. Gros had long been interested in certain types of horrific themes—mainly English—that might predict a sympathy for Madame de Staël's ideas on literature. Does this mean that he was politically opposed to Bonaparte in the

way she was? Not at all, for we shall see that Gros became one of Napoléon's most favored painters. But our comments do suggest that works of art give shape to cultural meanings that need not be so explicitly stated as were David's in his picture of *Bonaparte crossing the Saint-Bernard Pass*. The point is worth making early, for it shall emerge as a recurrent theme in our wanderings through Romantic Paris.

Finally, between the hyper-ventilating energy of Bonaparte's charge into Italy and the rapture of Sappho's leap into space, a third painting—also exhibited at the Salon of 1801—allows us to deepen our grasp of Parisian cultural life at the start of the nineteenth century. Constance Charpentier's picture of *Melancholy* (Fig. 5) represents a woman dressed in the fashion of moment—a high-waisted garment of thin, clingy fabric and bared arms—and posed amidst a verdant green landscape. She sits slightly stooped, her arms fall limp and without purpose, and she stares blankly in the direction of her feet. The curves of the woman's negligent posture, echoed by her loosely tied chignon and the folds of her dress, are dramatized by an effect of lighting that bathes her figure in brightness without illuminating much of the surrounding area. The picture encourages us to grasp the visual parallels between the solitary, apparently distressed individual and the heavy, drooping branches of weeping willow [saule pleureur] that fill most of the background.

It has long been recognized that Charpentier's figure recalls that of Camilla, who weeps at the extreme right side of David's famous picture of stoic male valor, the *Oath of the Horatii* of 1784 (Fig. 2). The remark underscores how much feminine sentiment—kept at the margins of David's world—occupies center stage in *Melancholy*, and the shift rings true when we learn that a woman painted it. But the picture also engages other issues circulating in contemporary Parisian culture. Its suggestion of the expressive relationship between an internal, psychological state and the natural world, for example, links it directly to Madame de Staël's appreciation of northern European cultures. The image also acknowledges the rich tradition of melancholic ponderings of nature that flourished in the late eighteenth century. More specifically, the figure's solitude locates the picture within a thematic of isolation and loneliness characteristic

FIGURE 4. Antoine-Jean Gros, *Sappho at Leucadia*, 1801. Oil on canvas. Bayeux, Musée Baron Gérard (122 × 100 cm). Photo: © RMN/Art Resource, NY/© Jean Popovitch.

FIGURE 5.   Constance Charpentier, *Melancholy*, 1801. Oil on canvas. Amiens, Musée de Picardie, inv. 3213 (130 × 165 cm). Photo: © RMN/Art Resource, NY/© Droits réservés.

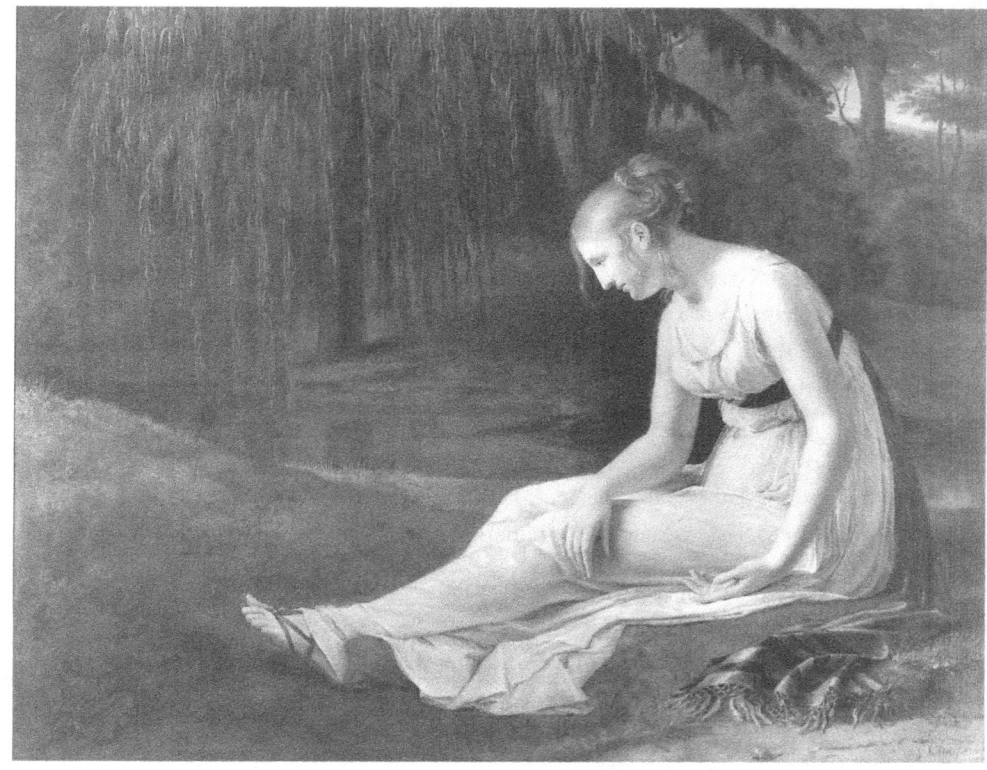

of contemporary writing by and about French émigrés: the approximately 180,000 professionals, aristocrats, and political opponents of the Revolution who fled France during the Terror. Bonaparte recognized that the émigrés, banished in perpetuity by a decree of 1793, constituted a national asset of human talent that could not be allowed to languish. As a gesture of reconciliation, he closed the official list of proscription on Christmas Day 1799 and established a commission to make it easier for those already on the list to regain their legal status. By the end of 1801, almost forty percent of the émigrés had returned to France.

What was it like to come home from exile? François-René de Chateaubriand, who returned from England in the spring of 1800, recorded of his impressions while traveling from Calais to Paris:

To the left and right of the road could be seen rundown châteaux: of their great forests, now clear-cut, there remained only a few chopped

up trunks upon which some children played. One saw broken paddock walls, abandoned churches from which the dead had been chased, belltowers without bells, cemeteries without crosses, saints in their niches pelted by stones and without heads. On the walls were scrawled those already dated republican inscriptions: LIBERTY, EQUALITY, FRATERNITY, OR DEATH. Occasionally someone had tried to erase the word DEATH, but the letters—black or red—reappeared under the layer of whitewash. This nation, which seemed to be on the verge of breaking up, was restarting from scratch, like those people who emerged from the darkness of savagery and destruction in the Middle Ages.[15]

Chateaubriand's melancholic musings on the countryside ravaged by revolution parallel exactly the emotions deployed in 1799 by Pierre-Narcisse Guérin's wide-eyed *Marcus Sextus* (Fig. 6), a picture taken to be a thinly disguised allegory of returning émigré meditations upon the ruined state of France. Melancholic reverie in 1801 was charged with contemporary import. Charpentier's picture—which seems at first glance to be about almost nothing—developed nuances of meaning and a complex resonance at the Salon among certain sectors of the Parisian public.

Finally, the fashionable dress of Charpentier's figure begs to be contrasted to the rather different contemporary fashion of modern military dress essential to the meaning of David's portrait of Bonaparte. Allegories in the guise of scantily dressed women were certainly not new. Even the morally strict leaders of the Revolution had championed a female (Marianne) as figurative emblem of the Republic. Among the several political factions of Paris around 1800—from die-hard radicals to those who welcomed Bonaparte, from die-hard royalist émigrés to the nouveau riche who hoped for a liberal and democratic constitution—the word of the moment was "reconciliation,"

and one way to represent it was to invoke the intercession of women. The most famous example was Hersilia, who throws herself between the warring figures of Romulus and Tatius in David's 1799 picture of *The Sabines* (Fig. 3). Similarly, Jean-François Ducis rewrote in 1797 his play *Oedipus at Colonus* to give Antigone a scene where she pleads for—and obtains—a reconciliation between Oedipus, her father, and Polynices, her estranged brother.

These role models of women as active agents of social reconciliation were not universally appreciated. Madame de Staël, for one, deplored the fact that "since the Revolution men have thought it politically and morally useful to reduce women to the most absurd mediocrity by speaking to them with an impoverished language lacking in delicatesse and spirit, so that women no longer have any

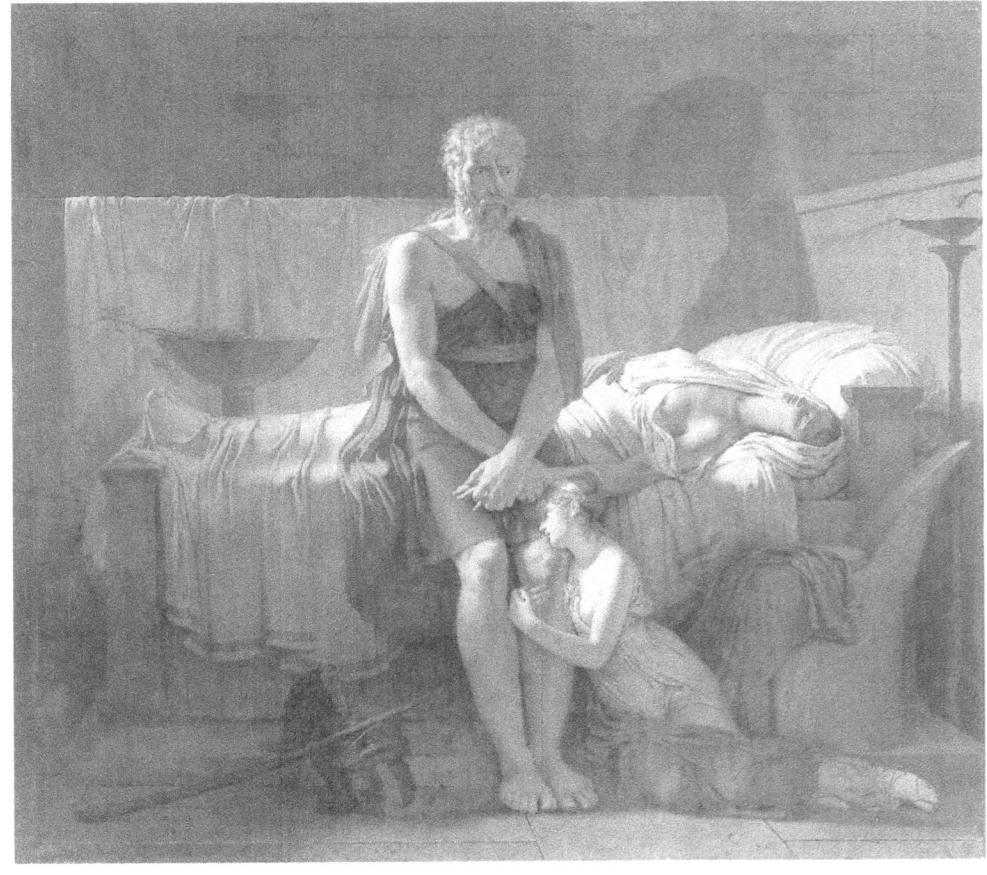

FIGURE 6. Pierre-Narcisse Guérin, *The Return of Marcus Sextus*, 1799. Oil on canvas. Paris, Musée du Louvre, inv. INV5180 (217 × 243 cm). Photo: © RMN/Art Resource, NY/ © René-Gabriel Ojeda.

incentives to develop critical thinking." She was convinced that "enlightening, instructing, perfecting women as well as men, nations as well as individuals, remains the key to a durable foundation for all the just goals, all the social and political relationships, one wants to ensure."[16] In fact, the revolutionary government had greatly relaxed divorce laws by making it possible to dissolve a marriage by mutual consent, so that in 1800 almost twenty percent of Parisian marriages ended that way. Bonaparte, on the other hand, wasted no time defining his hostility to the gains made by women's rights since 1789. Throughout the last half of 1800 a special commission worked on the draft of a new Civil Code. He personally participated in discussions of those sections dealing with family law: the final document specified that marriages must be approved by the families or parents involved, and limited divorce to cases of adultery, cruelty, or crime.

Bonaparte also showed little enthusiasm for the education of women: his reform of the school system in 1802 was uniquely designed for boys, and his thoughts on the subject—recorded in a note of 1807 about a proposed public school for girls at Ecouen—were thoroughly retrograde:

Religion is an all-important matter in a public school for girls. It is the mother's surest safeguard, and the husband's. What we ask of education is not that girls should think, but that they should believe. . . . I want the place to produce, not women of charm, but women of virtue: they must be attractive because they have high principles and warm hearts, not because they are witty or amusing. . . . But the main thing is to keep them all occupied, for three-quarters of the year, working with their hands. They must learn to make stocking, shirts, and embroidery, and to do all kinds of women's work.[17]

Clearly this was not the kind of education Madame de Staël had in mind, and it reminds us that the intellectual worth of a woman was not taken for granted. Understanding this context allows us to see that an allegory like Charpentier's *Melancholy*, whose meaning assumes the value of mental processes and private emotions, is a picture by a woman about a woman's psychic worth, although painted in a milieu—and for a public—where such worth was very much debated and

challenged. It presents a frankly feminine, contemplative, and personal activity thematically related to other forms of cultural resistance to the masculine ethos of aggressive military conquest central to Bonaparte's rule. We shall discover that an ethic of empowered femininity played a key role in the development of new art forms in Paris during the first decades of the nineteenth century.

PROFOUND CHANGES were wrought on the cultural and political map of Paris between 1801 and the opening of the 1804 Salon, where Gros exhibited *Bonaparte in the Pest-House at Jaffa* (Fig. 7). Perhaps the most important of them was that the French Republic had simply ceased to exist: Bonaparte was named First Consul for life in August 1802 and called to become Emperor of the French, with a right to hereditary rule, in May of 1804. Bonaparte had brokered his victory at Marengo, and that of général Jean-Victor Moreau at Hohenlinden (3 December 1800), to conclude a peace with Austria that ceded all of the left bank of the Rhine to France. He established a French vassal state in the north of Italy. Within two more years, and after long and difficult negotiations, France signed a peace treaty with England at Amiens (25 March 1802) that made it possible for commerce and travel to take root once again.

During this period of intense political maneuvering, Bonaparte opened discussions with the Pope to reconcile with the Roman Catholic Church the breach opened by revolutionary seizures of church lands and secularization of the clergy. By mid-September 1801 a compromise Concordat was ratified by Bonaparte and Pope Pius VII, but emotions in the legislature ran so strongly against the deal that the whole project seemed doomed to fail. To placate worries about papal meddling in domestic affairs, a group of detailed clarifications—the so-called Organic Articles—were appended to the Concordat: they mandated police control over the activities of church officials and guaranteed freedom of religion to French Protestants. Yet even these additional articles failed to quash opposition to the Concordat. Bonaparte was obliged to dissolve the lower house of the

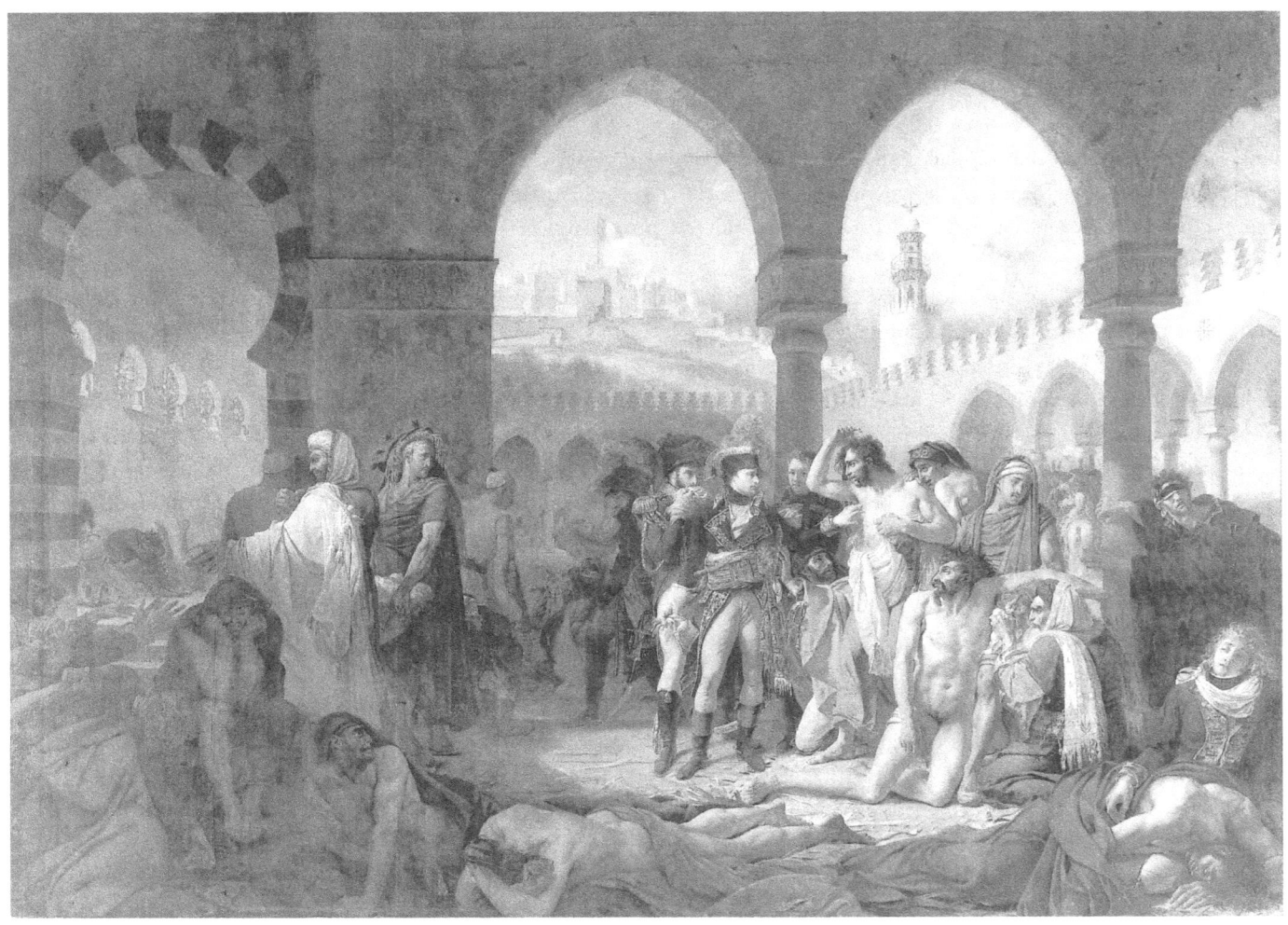

FIGURE 7.   Antoine-Jean Gros, *Bonaparte in the Pest-House at Jaffa*, 1804. Oil on canvas. Paris, Musée du Louvre, inv. INV5064 (532 × 720 cm). Photo: © RMN/Art Resource, NY/© Droits réservés.

legislature (Tribunat), purge the Senate of his political adversaries, and decree that all future laws would be reviewed by special councils he himself headed. Only after choking off democratic debate was Bonaparte able to obtain passage— perhaps "rubberstamp" is the better word—of the Concordat and its Organic Articles (8 April 1802).

Ten days later, on Easter Sunday, Bonaparte assisted at a Pontifical High Mass in Notre-Dame de Paris to celebrate peace in Europe (the Treaty of Amiens had just been ratified)

and to enact physically his reconciliation with the Church of Rome. The historian James M. Thompson summarized the moment:

It was—look at it as you will—one of the greatest moments, indeed the greatest, in Napoleon's career. . . . Here and now, in the building which for more than six centuries had symbolized the union of French monarchy and the Catholic church, and beneath whose roof had echoed the prayers and praises of

twenty-five generations of Parisians, he stood as the consumma-
tor of a nation's revolution, and the architect of its regeneration.
He had unified France; he had pacified Europe; he had reunited
the church. . . . Paris was to be embellished by the skill of its
architects and the plunder of Florence and Rome. Foreigners
were invited to see for themselves how France had recovered
from the poison of Jacobinism without recourse to the antidote
of Royalism.[18]

Now, after nine years of conflict and closed borders, thousands of English tourists visited Paris to rediscover the café
life and popular entertainments for which the city was famous. They found a Paris better lighted, better policed, and
cleaner than ever before (see Chapter Three), a Louvre filled
with new art treasures (confiscated war booty from Italy and
the Low Countries), and the Musée des Monuments français, a newly opened museum dedicated to the country's medieval past (see Chapter Four). The city's cultural life seemed
bursting with energy.

There was, however, a dark side to this bright picture of
political and economic success. Bonaparte suffered criticism
badly, and from the outset of his career as First Consul he
worked to muzzle freedom of the press: in January 1800
he shut down three-quarters of the newspapers in Paris and
ordered the national police to censor all that was printed in
the capital. A single newspaper, *Le Moniteur universel*, became the government's "official" voice. Censors encouraged
rival papers to avoid harassment by copying their news items
exactly from the *Moniteur*. By the middle of 1805 government surveillance of the press included handpicking editors
for all the newspapers in Paris. Journalists were not alone:
playwrights, book publishers, and theater managers were
held to the same standards of scrutiny by government censors. Even the pulpits were controlled because the Concordat
stipulated that salaries of bishops and parish priests were to
be paid by the government—any unseemly sermons could be
immediately and effectively reprimanded.

Neither Bonaparte nor George III considered the treaty
to be more than a respite in the larger, more desperate struggle for power in western Europe. Bonaparte, in particular,
pushed the Amiens accord to its limits on several fronts: by

refusing to open French markets to English goods; by annex-
ing northern Italy; by keeping French troops in Holland; by
invading Switzerland to impose a constitution; and by suggesting that France was about to launch a new offensive in
Egypt. This last threat especially alarmed Russia and provoked the English to postpone their withdrawal from the
island of Malta—a specific violation of the Amiens treaty.
In May of 1803 English warships began to seize French
merchant vessels anchored in British ports, and on 17 May
ambassadors of the two nations broke off all diplomatic relations. War had begun again.

Parallel to these foreign policy developments, Bonaparte
began to lay the groundwork for assuming total control of
the state as emperor. Eight days after the triumphant Easter
Sunday mass at Notre-Dame, he declared a general amnesty
for all but a handful of the most compromised émigrés, provided they return to France before 23 September 1802 and
submit to police surveillance for ten years. His gesture was
greeted coolly in the provinces, where the new owners of
confiscated lands feared lawsuits from former owners. By
contrast, the effect in Paris was to hasten the return of old,
aristocratic families and courtly lifestyles. In November 1802
Joséphine received an official rank and a retinue of ladies-in-
waiting drawn from the old nobility. Patterns of etiquette and
sociability based on pre-revolutionary models became the
daily routine of life at the Tuileries Palace. It seemed clear to
everyone that another change in the nature of government
was in the works: a plot to kill Bonaparte was the trigger.

Near the end of August 1803, Georges Cadoudal—a member of the Chouannerie royalist sympathizers based in the
west of France—secretly arrived in Paris to kidnap and kill
Bonaparte. Coincident with this murder, the comte d'Artois
would appear in France to claim power in the name of the
deposed Bourbon family. A fellow conspirator—a popular
general named Jean-Victor-Marie Moreau—was supposed to
rally the army. The British government provided one million
pounds sterling to finance the operation. Bonaparte's ever-
vigilant police intercepted two letters that revealed Cadoudal's presence in Paris and the expected arrival of an unnamed
Bourbon prince. A minor accomplice was arrested and revealed—apparently under torture—several of Cadoudal's hid-

ing places. Other arrests followed, including général Moreau on 15 February 1804 and Cadoudal himself on 9 March. The plot was destroyed, but Bonaparte worried about the mysterious prince expected in France: who might this be?

Bonaparte was convinced the duc d'Enghien, who lived at Bettemheim about 9 kilometers from the French border with Germany, was the culprit. He was determined to make an example of d'Enghien for others who might plot against his rule. On 10 March, in special council with his closest advisers, Bonaparte decided to kidnap the duc d'Enghien inside Germany and bring him to justice in France. The abduction took place on 15 March, and the prince was delivered to the military fort at Vincennes, just outside of Paris, on the 20th. A sham military hearing arranged at midnight delivered a verdict decided well in advance, even if no direct evidence linked the prince to Cadoudal's plot: he was found guilty of bearing arms against the Republic, of being in the pay of England, and of conspiring against the nation. At two o'clock on the morning of 21 March, d'Enghien was executed by a firing squad. Other members of the conspiracy came to trial in June: Moreau was sentenced to two years in prison (later commuted to lifetime banishment); Cadoudal and seven others were guillotined; twelve implicated nobles were sentenced to jail terms.

The harshness of Bonaparte's justice—and the injustice committed against the duc d'Enghien—raised new fears of retaliation against the First Consul. "The hate and vituperation aimed at the government have become as violent as ever I saw them in the time before the Revolution," wrote Pierre-Louis Roederer on 14 June.[19] How to preserve the state from further attacks? The answer seemed simple: place the government in the hands of Bonaparte, protector of the nation's well-being. On 18 May 1804 a *sénatus-consulte* entrusted the country to a new head of state called "Emperor of the French," offered the title to Napoléon Bonaparte, and added a crucial decree that "the imperial dignity is hereditary." A hastily organized plebiscite voted overwhelmingly in favor of the resolution. Napoléon Ier (as he was now called) began to organize his imperial court and to create a new class of aristocrats.

Gros worked on his picture of *Bonaparte in the Pest-House at Jaffa* (Fig. 7) during just these months of political intrigue.

The picture is signed "Versailles 1804" and must have been painted between 1 August 1803, when Gros began to use the indoor tennis court at Versailles as his studio, and 18 September 1804, when the Salon opened in Paris.[20] Gros originally moved to Versailles to paint a very large canvas (at least 24 feet wide) dedicated to général Andoche Junot's victory in April 1799 at Nazareth, but sometime in early 1804 that picture was cancelled. Perhaps the arrest of Moreau, one of Bonaparte's chief rivals within the army, made it seem inopportune to honor other generals who might challenge Bonaparte's authority. Nonetheless, Gros had a grand studio and a very large piece of canvas: what to do with them?

At this point Vivant Denon, director-general of the museums, enters the story. He had served with the French army in Egypt under Bonaparte, was known to have made copious notes and drawings of all that he had seen and experienced, and regularly supplied these documents to painters. Whose idea was it to paint the *Pest-House at Jaffa*? We will probably never know for sure, but it is unlikely that the idea came from Bonaparte, because Denon sent him a long note after the opening of the Salon that describes the picture, as if for the first time.[21] Although Denon had not been at Jaffa with the army, he probably supplied Gros with the account of Bonaparte's visit to the hospital written by Doctor René-Nicolas Desgenettes (visible in the picture behind the general). Denon was sensitive to issues of quality and posterity in the visual arts, and he pressured Bonaparte to ensure that commissions "not always be given as encouragements to painters who need work, but also to the best artists who would receive their glory from the government and make it that of their century."[22] Denon would have been able and willing to encourage Gros to transform a strict rendering of Desgenettes's story into something more: in the finished work, Bonaparte is bathed in a spot of bright light amidst the sick and dying, and he reaches out with his bare hand to touch the boil of an infected soldier. That gesture—hovering between tenderness and redemption—harnesses a visual tradition of miracle-workers and healing kings to invest the general's presence with an otherworldly grandeur, well beyond petty politics. In this way, the subject must be understood as a generalized reply to some of the blistering attacks mentioned by Roederer in June. It is also a specific response to reports of Bonaparte's cold-blooded killing of war prisoners at Jaffa, to rumors that he poisoned French soldiers afflicted with the plague to prevent its spread during the army's retreat, and to recurring doubts about the integrity of abandoning his army when he returned to France.

When the picture was put on display at the Salon, it was hailed immediately as a masterpiece. Admirers hung a laurel wreath on its frame, and a group of artists staged a banquet in Gros's honor where Anne-Louis Girodet read a eulogistic poem that sung the picture's praises. Keeping in mind that journalists were watched by police censors, it is probably significant that several of them praise *Jaffa* but also point out a peculiar tension within its formal structure: "It seems to me," remarked the *Journal des Débats*, "that those who die wracked by convulsions, and whom the author has relegated to the shadows, set up too much movement in this subordinate part of the picture."[23] A critic for *Le Publiciste* took up the theme in more detail:

General disposition noble and simple; principal group of very great interest and skillfully linked to its surroundings; very intelligent mix of French and Arab costumes and nude figures that announces a genuine feeling for picturesque effects and serves to conceal the meagerness and ineffectiveness of our clothing. However, it was perhaps unnecessary to use so much surface to express this action: the picture ends at the principal group and scarcely takes up half the image. The rest is little more than filler and one sees it too much, thanks to the care deployed by the author to sacrifice his foreground, where there are only dimly visible some wretches given over to the anguish of a horrible despair. Without changing anything, this part could be made into a picture of the Last Judgment, to which several of these figures seem to belong.[24]

Critics responded to the visual and emotional impact of the picture's "frame" of horrors, but could not articulate openly that this frame actually detracted from the rhetoric of Bonaparte's gesture. It may be—as some have suggested—that Gros and his critics suppressed their horror of the plague victims out of "a fear of powers that remain invisible: the capacity for the self, the heroic body, to be possessed by a force that cannot be seen and cannot therefore be fought."[25] Indeed, this psy-chological interpretation of the picture helps to explain the fact—already noted in 1804—that all of the victims in this plague seem to be French.

One might also suggest that Gros's picture of Bonaparte resplendent amidst the suffering and death of his soldiers, however much the spectacle moved him, refigures the basic premise of war itself: a commander, his troops—healthy or not—and the challenge of enemies both on and off the battlefield. Gros's picture took shape after the Treaty of Amiens had collapsed, when the specter of war was becoming ever more real. Having consolidated his political power, the new emperor was massing his army along the Channel coast, and was building a flotilla to invade England. Conscripts were called up, and a total blockade of English goods was reestablished. Against this background, Joséphine's version of a conversation with Napoléon just before the Coronation—although to be read with some skepticism—rings with an air of authenticity:

Peace now exists; and peace is in itself a thing so lovely that nothing ought to be omitted to preserve it, or at least the hope of it. Why sound the alarm? Why sow the seeds of distrust and excite animosities? Is it a sure method of preserving peace, to abdicate the modest title of consul, and immediately assume one more pompous? Is it, moreover, consistent and prudent, while you are setting forth the causes of war, to labor to show that all power is now lodged in the hands of the conqueror of Marengo? That he is ready to aggravate his provocations toward Germany, by seeking to demonstrate to her that all strength will henceforth be on one side, and all the weakness on the other and that she will probably find herself without resources to sustain the conflict? Hear me further: you well know that true valor detests butchery as much as it loves glory; does an enemy yield? she ceases to strike; she covets not blood, but honor, and even her enemy becomes dear to her if victory has cost her a great effort.[26]

The extraordinary part of this discourse, whatever form it had in fact, is that Joséphine dared to raise the issues of peace, valor, and butchery when similar questions were being asked about Napoléon's behavior at Jaffa, about his role in the death of the duc d'Enghien, and about his preparations for war.

While it may seem foolhardy to cite Joséphine's self-serving memory of a conversation with her husband when discussing a picture so seemingly masculine as Gros's *Jaffa*, the point gains credibility when we discover—by revisiting the archives—that it was Joséphine who commissioned the picture, apparently without Napoléon's knowledge or approval.[27] Placing the painting's rhetorical fissure alongside the terms of Josephine's harangue helps us to recognize that *Jaffa* operates in a richly layered manner: a piece of flattering political propaganda; an ominous reminder about the physical and psychological effects of war; an appeal from the heart of a woman to her husband that exhorts him to "heal" the political scene. This was not the only time that Joséphine resisted the official line of Napoleonic thinking (see Chapter Three), but it was perhaps the most secret—and most spectacular—of her initiatives.

The morbid fascination with death lurking at the edges of Gros's *Jaffa* came to center stage in a strange but compelling picture also exhibited at the Salon of 1804: Pierre-Auguste Vafflard's *Young and his Daughter* (Fig. 8). A man with closed eyes strides across a seemingly remote landscape as if in a trance or sleepwalking. His right arm grasps a shovel, but most of his energy is devoted to carrying the stiffened, wrapped corpse of a young woman. This funereal couple, whose bizarre geometric posture defies the laws of gravity, is bathed in an intense greenish light that bleeds the color out of things and renders the scene in an eerie, gray-green monochrome. Crisp, dark shadows powerfully etch folds of cloth and the contours of features to create odd, ghostly patterns of black that follow the couple on their journey. Who are they and what are they doing?

The subject of Vafflard's picture was taken from *Night Thoughts*, a long dramatic poem written by the Englishman Edward Young between 1742 and 1745. *Night Thoughts* remained enormously popular in France into the early decades of the nineteenth century. The pervasive sensibility of the poem's so-called graveyard school fascination with death and bereavement can be gauged by a letter of 1802 from the famed physicist André-Marie Ampère to his wife: "I have finally seen the church at Brou. I want to send a good description of it to my sister Julie, to make for her a superb

letter—tragic, melancholic, and funereal. I remember that she loves Hervey and Young."[28] Vafflard based his picture on a scene from "Night III," which describes the narrator's furtive, nocturnal burial of Narcissa in a foreign land. In fact, this part of the poem was inspired by a real death—that of Young's stepdaughter—in France near Lyon in 1736. Because she was Protestant, Young could not bury her in the local Catholic cemetery, but the incident became rather more bizarre in his poem:

For oh! the cursed ungodliness of zeal!
While sinful flesh relented, spirit nursed
In blind infallibility's embrace,
The sainted spirit petrified the breast;
Denied the charity of dust, to spread
O'er dust! a charity their dogs enjoy.
What could I do? what succour? what resource?
With pious sacrilege, a grave I stole;
With impious piety, that grave I wrong'd
Short in my duty; coward in my grief!
More like her murderer, than friend, I crept,
With soft-suspended step, and, muffled deep
In midnight darkness, whisper'd my last sigh.[29]

Some elements of the painting—its muted coloration and the man's awkward gait—respond directly to the poem's language, but so do its peculiar light and pronounced shadows that were evoked by the poem a few lines later:

To what compare we then this varying scene,
Whose worth ambiguous rises, and declines?
Waxes, and wanes? (In all propitious, night
Assists me here.) Compare it to the moon;
Dark in herself, and indigent; but rich
In borrow'd lustre from a higher sphere.
When gross guilt interposes, labouring earth,
O'ershadow'd, mourns a deep eclipse of joy;
Her joys, at brightest, pallid, to that font
Of full effulgent glory, whence they flow.[30]

The poem does not describe directly the actual scene of the Vafflard's picture in which Narcissa—loosely wrapped in a shroud—is physically carried to burial. For this motif it

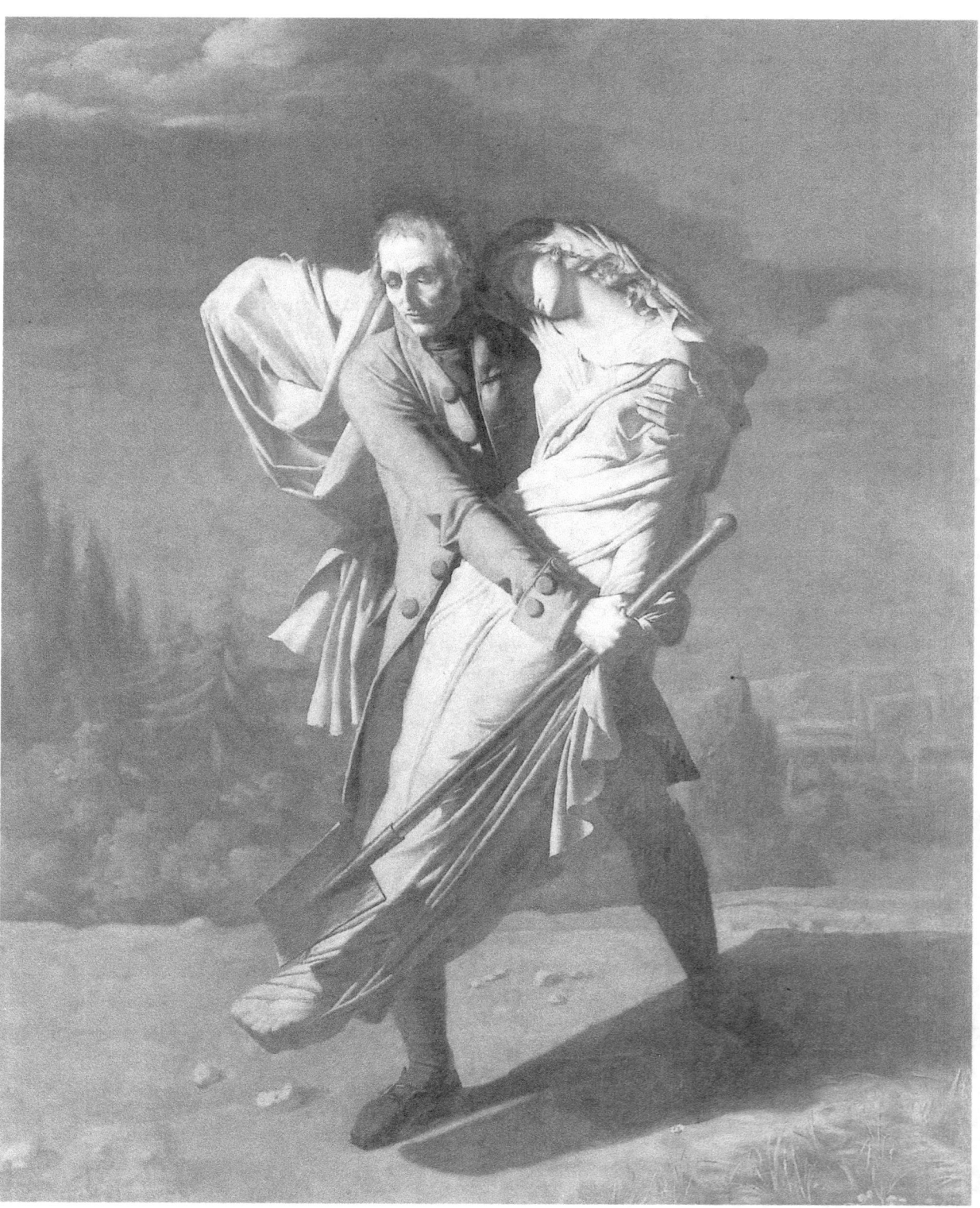

seems the painter dipped into François-René de Chateaubriand's *Atala*, one of the biggest "best-sellers" in the first years of the century.

Chateaubriand's romantic tale of a Native American girl, who was converted to Christianity and sworn to celibacy by her dying mother, ends in tragedy when Atala realizes she has fallen in love with a young man named Chactas. She takes poison rather than break her vow. Chateaubriand, who traveled briefly in America after fleeing the French Revolution, embellished this simple love story with elaborate descriptions of nature and exotic Indian customs—all of which thrilled European readers. Of special interest is the passage where Chactas and an old hermit prepare to bury the unfortunate Atala:

Towards evening we carried her precious remains to an opening of the cave that faced north. The hermit had wrapped her in a piece of European linen spun by his mother: it was his only remaining possession from his homeland, and for a long time he had kept it for his own tomb.[31]

The text goes on to describe the emotional effects of moonlight over the scene in terms that can be linked visually to Vafflard's picture:

The moon lent its pale torch to this funeral vigil. It rose in the middle of the night like a vestal virgin in white who came to weep on the coffin of a companion. Soon it spread through the woods this great mystery of melancholy that it likes to retell to old oaks and on the ancient beaches of the sea.[32]

Finally, at the first rays of dawn, Chactas carries Atala's body to its final resting place:

I lifted the body on my shoulders; the hermit, carrying a spade, walked in front of me. We began to descend from rock to rock; age and death both served to slow our progress. . . . Atala's long hair, toyed with by the morning breezes, often spread a golden veil over

my eyes; bending under the weight of my load, I was frequently obliged to lay it on the grass and to sit down, so as to gather my strength.[33]

In these passages we discover aspects of Vafflard's image not described by Young: the shroud-wrapped body, the shovel, the strands of golden hair, the melancholy effect of bright moonlight, and the physical act of carrying Narcissa to her makeshift grave.

What might be the significance of Vafflard's pictorial fusion of Young and Chateaubriand? On one hand, English-style "gothick" novels of horror were extremely popular in France just before 1800, so much so that French authors would take English-sounding pen names—such as J. H. Palmer or Miss Sharp—to lend an air of authenticity to their writings. The popularity of these stories, littered with old castles, bleeding corpses, and violent crimes, might be related to the end of the Terror, as if readers longed to move their immediate experience of revolutionary violence to the safer world of fiction. On the other hand, the supernatural effects characteristic of "gothick" novels did seem to fulfill a secret desire of readers for other-worldly mystery, a craving left by the secularization of French life during the Revolution. Interest in Young's graveyard poetry and "gothick" effects was probably propelled by the same psychological needs that showered success on Chateaubriand's lyrical account of Christianity among the natives of North America.

Yet the explanatory value of this general context is undermined by the critical failure of Vafflard's picture. It remained an idiosyncratic image—despite contemporary enthusiasm for *Night Thoughts* and *Atala*—that had no echo in French painting at the time. Some critics at the Salon of 1804 wondered out loud why Vafflard had bothered with the subject, while the *Critique raisonnée des tableaux du Salon* suggested that "the author would do better to handle subjects less somber and thankless."[34] The government showed no interest in buying the picture, which further suggests that Vafflard's large and ambitious project failed to speak to immediate programmatic concerns. That *Young and his Daughter* passed almost without notice teaches a valuable lesson about the multiple uncertainties circulating in Paris during 1804. Vafflard surely knew why Narcissa—a Protestant—could

FIGURE 8.   Pierre-Auguste Vafflard, *Young and his Daughter*, 1804. Oil on canvas. Angoulême, Musée National, inv. 383 (242 × 194 cm). Photo: © RMN/Art Resource, NY.

not be buried in a Catholic cemetery, and every Frenchman knew one of the most significant effects of the Revolution had been to break the political bonds between Church and State that supported such strictures. Napoléon's Concordat with the Pope proposed to reconcile those two powerful institutions, which led many to fear—despite the Organic Articles—that the old collusion between earthly and divine power would again signal special privileges for a few. Napoléon's amnesty for émigrés meant that nobles, whose lands had been confiscated during the 1790s and sold to the highest bidder, were returning to file lawsuits against the new owners for ownership or indemnity. Doubts spread about the government's resolution to uphold the post-revolutionary social order. Creation of the Légion d'honneur in 1802 seemed to verify Napoléon's desire for a return to monarchic forms of rank in a direct challenge to the revolution's "liberty, equality, and fraternity." His efforts culminated with the proclamation of Empire in 1804 and organization of an imperial court. The fragile Treaty of Amiens, which lifted briefly restrictions on travel to England, encouraged English literature and fashions to become all the rage. Vafflard's picture took shape at the crossroads of these social currents. From this intersection fraught with anxieties there emerged his troubling image of a somnambulist striding with a cadaver through an eerily lighted, deserted space. In contrast to the official line that touted a France poised on the edge of greatness under her new emperor, Vafflard's picture distilled from the situation a view more dark, more sinister, and far more pessimistic: small wonder that *Young and his Daughter* languished at the Salon without a buyer.

NAPOLÉON'S PLANS to invade England foundered forever on 21 October 1805 with the resounding defeat inflicted by Admiral Horatio Nelson and the British fleet upon a combined French and Spanish flotilla assembled at Trafalgar to protect the landing of troops. Moreover, the alliance of Russia and Austria menacing France from the east forced Napoléon to mount a lightning march to Vienna, where his stunning victory at Austerlitz (2 December 1805) broke the

coalition. France dictated the terms of Austria's surrender, but lasting peace did not follow: the wars ground on from year to year, straining the economy and human resources of an ever-expanding Empire. We need not detail the complex progression of battles, treaties, and annexations that filled the next four years, but a close look at Gros's profoundly unsettling work of 1808, *Napoléon on the Battlefield of Eylau* (Fig. 9), can help us to measure the effects of continuous warfare upon the spirit of the Parisian public.

The military campaign of 1806–1807 was opened when it became apparent that Prussia would not become a French vassal state or implement the Treaty of Schönbrunn signed after the battle of Austerlitz. Frederick William of Prussia, encouraged by his queen, began to ponder an alliance with Tsar Alexander of Russia, which France opposed because Russia remained an ally of England. The Prussian army was mobilized on 9 August 1806; by early October Napoléon and his army were in place to face them. When Alexander began moving west, Napoléon correctly calculated that he must defeat the Prussians before the Russians arrived: within two weeks, after stunning victories at Jena and Auerstädt, the Prussian army was in ruins. The French moved east to check Alexander and to skirmish the Russians outside Warsaw. Near the end of January 1806, Auguste de Bennigsen—the Russian commander—moved his troops north with Napoléon in hot pursuit. On 8 February 1807 the two armies squared off to do battle near the town of Eylau. The fighting raged all day and into the darkness of night amidst a blinding snowstorm, but the Russians held firm, only yielding under the shock of a massive cavalry charge led by général Joachim Murat. The Russian troops withdrew under cover of night and, by the light of dawn, Napoléon surveyed the bloodiest field of battle ever seen: more than 25,000 Russians and at least 18,000 of his own troops lay dead in the snow.

Bennigsen tried to claim victory, even if Napoléon occupied the field of battle, but it was clear that both sides paid dearly. News of the death toll, staggering even by modern standards, swept through a horrified Europe. Even seasoned veterans like Dominique Larrey, chief surgeon of the French army, were shocked: "Dear friend," Larrey

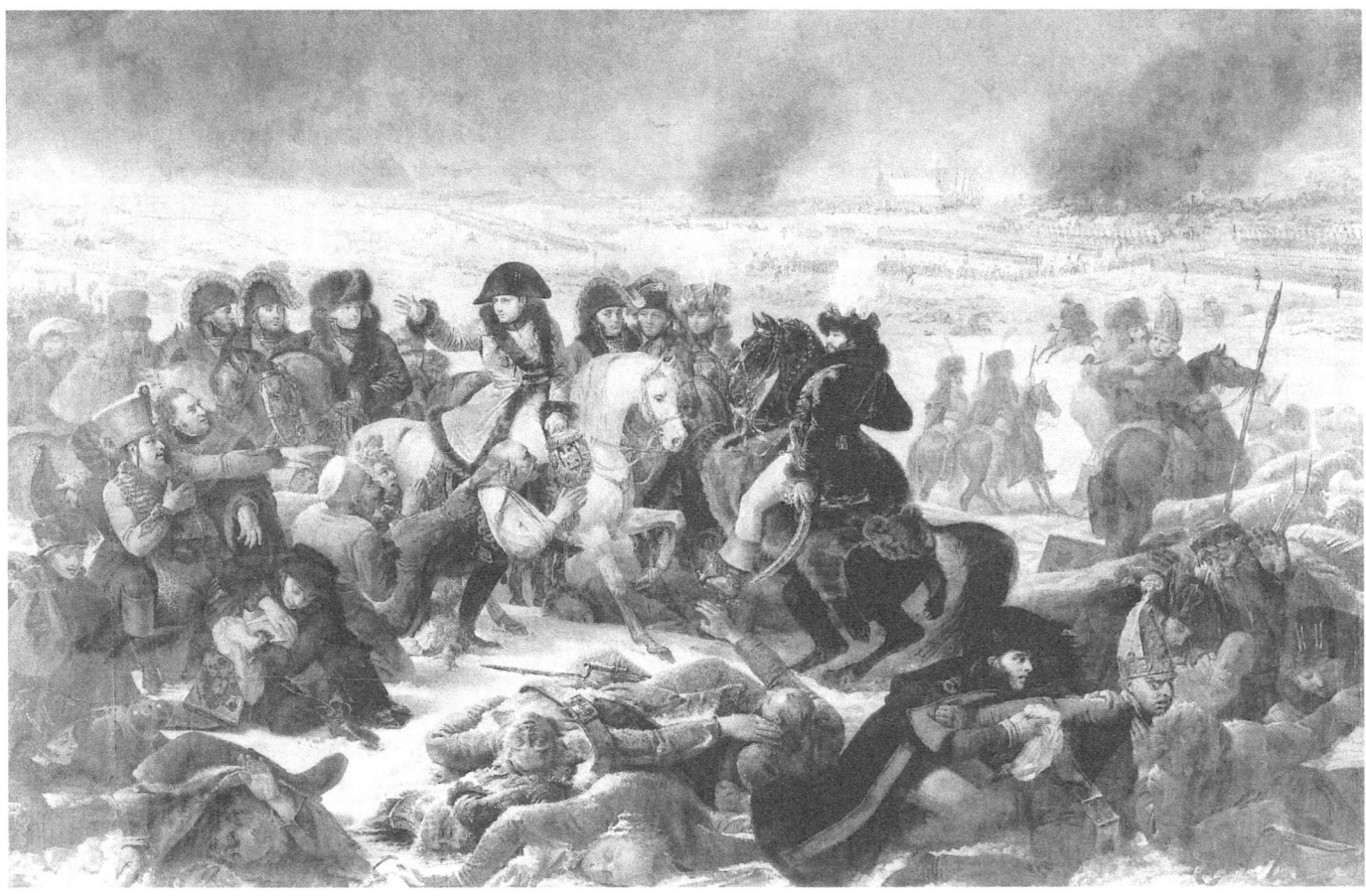

FIGURE 9.   Antoine-Jean Gros, *Napoléon on the Battlefield of Eylau, 9 February 1807*, 1808. Oil on canvas. Paris, Musée du Louvre, inv. INV5067 (533 × 800 cm). Photo: © RMN/Art Resource, NY/© Daniel Arnaudet.

wrote to his wife, "what sad and heart-rending scenes came before my eyes on that terrible and honorable day of the 8th. Never have I seen such a bloody aftermath of battle. The wounded who gathered together in a crowd behind the battlefield, their limbs mutilated, cried out with a single voice."[35] Much to Napoléon's chagrin, some Paris newspapers circulated rumors of exaggerated French causalities and inadequate medical support. To Joséphine, who alluded to such rumors in a letter, Napoléon wrote: "Many absurdities will be said about the battle of Eylau; the bulletin says it all, and generally exaggerates the losses rather than reduces them."[36] A sure sign of his concern,

Napoléon began a veritable media campaign to counter any lingering doubts about his victory at Eylau: Jean-Jacques de Cambacérès, who ran the government during Napoléon's absence, was ordered to "organize a great festival for the battle of Eylau" in Paris to celebrate the victory. A few weeks later Napoléon sent him "three plates of the battle of Eylau which give a clear idea of the combat," with orders to have them "engraved, printed, and distributed throughout Paris."[37] Finally, on 2 April 1807 all the major Parisian newspapers carried the announcement of a competition to select an artist who would paint a large picture of the Emperor on the battlefield of Eylau *after* the victory. Vivant

Denon wrote a carefully worded program for the picture and his cover letter informed interested artists:

In order to give a clear idea of the various positions, the Director-General has left a sketch of the battlefield at the offices of the Musée Napoléon. Each artist who wants to compete may consult this sketch by presenting themselves to the Secretary General, who will also lend them detailed notes about the site and the uniforms. The figural groups of the sketch, however true they might be, should not constrain artists in their compositions. Everything in the foreground that can be varied is left completely to the artist's discretion and to the choice he might make from among the situations outlined in the description.[38]

It was probably a surprise to no one that in June a selection committee awarded the commission to Gros, who had already worked with Denon on the *Jaffa* (Fig. 7); *Eylau* was specifically advertised as a pendant to that earlier work.[39] Gros finished his picture in time for the opening of the Salon of 1808, where it was reviewed by Napoléon. In a gesture of spontaneous admiration, the Emperor pinned his own Légion d'honneur on the artist's chest.

There can be little doubt that the entire enterprise of competition and commission around Gros's *Eylau* was a carefully orchestrated piece of political propaganda.[40] Gros accepted fully the task of faithfully illustrating the episodes outlined in Denon's program, thus furthering Napoléon's claim of victory: the Emperor on horseback oversees the treatment of wounded men and displays his compassion with a gesture lifted from the famous Roman statue of Marcus Aurelius; an abundance of fur or double-lined greatcoats proves that the army was well-protected against the cold; Russian prisoners are astonished when the French bind their wounds rather than kill them; a young Lithuanian pledges to serve Napoléon if he receives medical care, and so on.

Denon's covering letter exhorted artists not to feel constrained by his program but to pick from among its options. The program was quite explicit, for it evoked "the dead, the wounded, and the litter of weapons" left in the snow on the field of battle, the "traces of blood that contrasted against the whiteness of the snow," and the "great quantity of dead, dying, or abandoned horses in those places where the cavalry charges occurred."[41] If we attend to the way Gros situated these very real horrors relative to the leader and hero, the fabric of his picture registers an unraveling of France's enchantment with Napoléon and military conquest. The most obvious contrast is developed at the very front and center: in the immediate foreground a grisly pile of frozen cadavers; just behind, a wounded veteran reaches to kiss the imperial eagle of Napoléon's saddle; finally, the Emperor, who gestures in the direction of the wounded but lifts his eyes to heaven, as if not to see the dead men lying at the feet of his horse. In the very large picture (more than five by seven meters) Napoléon appears life-sized, but the corpses in the foreground are almost twice as large.

Many critics at the Salon faulted this excess: "One does not dare to stare for long at the sad remains of these cadavers sprawling in the snow," wrote one; "I greatly fear that women who might come to admire the picture will be seized by an attack of nerves."[42] These voices were responding to the interference established in the picture between its optimistic moral and propagandistic subject and the nihilism of those details necessary to render the whole "true" to the facts; an interference between life and death. More important, Gros offered no suggestion as to how these two incommensurate realms might be joined: they are simply present simultaneously, each describing what the other can never be. Although many glances and gestures traverse the space of the picture, none of them bridges the gap from life to death. Dead men cannot see. But neither is that gap bridged in the only other way that might matter, because Napoléon dares not look at those dead men, and he does not acknowledge their sacrifice; rather, his eyes are raised to heaven. Unlike the earlier picture of *Jaffa*, where Napoléon shared the space and touched the bodies of the sick and dying, the Emperor at Eylau is visible on the battlefield but psychologically detached from its carnage—a necessary distance if one dares to dispute victory surrounded by such butchery.

Gros's *Eylau* differs from his earlier picture in at least one more way. In the *Jaffa* the pictorial conceit that separates Bonaparte and his entourage from the diseased soldiers all around is a contrast between light and darkness: although the principal group where physical contact actually occurs is bathed in light, most of the suffering men are situated in shadow. The light articulating this difference falls through a regular space described by an architectural "box" in which the viewer is presumed to stand. Within this space the relative sizes of things and figures are consistent with one another, so that scale diminishes from foreground to background in a regular ratio as a function of distance and depth. By contrast, the *Eylau* exhibits no spatial structure of this sort: the foreground figures and cadavers are far larger than life, while kneeling figures at the left appear nearly as tall as a full-grown horse. Yet the viewer sees seamlessly across these difficulties, from the figures close at hand to the middle ground with Napoléon, and then on to the horizon across a vast space and thousands of tiny soldiers. If, while looking at the *Jaffa*, viewers can presume to be inside the pest-house, where are they at Eylau? We might say they are nowhere and everywhere at once, since what one sees is unhindered by the physical parameters of vision.

What holds together this visually illogical pictorial field? What makes sense of its impossible shifts in scale and vantage points? The answer lies with Denon's text, which not only provided Gros with details for *making* the picture, but also a way for viewers to *look* at it. If we face the picture and simultaneously read the text, our relationship to the image is no longer that of a fictive eyewitness inside the scene (as with the *Jaffa*), but a subject outside the frame who tests the truth of the written account against the evidence of the image. This was, of course, exactly what the painting was supposed to do: shore up Napoléon's version of the battle against rumors of extravagant losses and Russian claims of victory. In the meantime, something extraordinary happened. Gros worked to ensure the credibility of Napoléon's story, but his picture came to suggest inadvertently that the Emperor's tolerance for the butchery and excess of battle might lead to a policy of unending warfare. It comes as no surprise that at least one police report on the Salon of 1808 complained that "artists have collected every kind of mutilation, every aspect of a vast butchery as if they were required specifically to paint a scene of horror and carnage and make the war seem execrable."[43] Napoléon's ever-vigilant police censors were worried that the

trajectory of meaning made visible by Gros's picture—from overt partisan to surreptitious critic—might affect the population at large, for whom the glory of victory was wearing thin and lasting peace seemed to remain just beyond reach. Even Napoléon's trusted aides were beginning to grumble: "The Emperor is mad, completely mad," exclaimed the duc de Decrès, Minister of the Marine, to général Auguste-Frédéric Marmont; "he will turn us all head over heels: the end of it all will be utter disaster."[44]

Unlike Gros's *Eylau*, where the attempt to present a heroic military commander alongside the pathetic victims of war produced a visible strain in the image, Anne-Louis Girodet's *Revolt of Cairo* (Fig. 10)—one of the last great military pictures of the Empire—dispensed with heroes altogether. Girodet's skepticism about heroes had been suggested by a poem he wrote to honor Gros's *Jaffa* (Fig. 7) in which he paid greater tribute to "those warriors, emaciated, melancholic, wracked by pain" at the picture's edges than to Bonaparte.[45] In March 1809 Girodet was commissioned to make a work "representing the revolt of Cairo, or another episode equally related to the occupation of this town" from the annals of Bonaparte's Egyptian campaign of 1798.[46] The painting was destined to hang in the Galerie de Diane at the Tuileries Palace, and its subject revisits an important moment of the Emperor's youthful exploits. The choice is significant, insofar as the commission was awarded at a time when the tide of military conquest began to turn against Napoléon and France. Even as details of the commission were being finalized, the Emperor rejoined his army in the east to put down a new Austrian revolt against the yoke of French rule: victories at Essling, Vienna, and Wagram ended the threat, but French losses in men and material were again very high. The time was no longer ripe for images of dashing military genius like David's *Bonaparte crossing the Alps* (Fig. 1).

Girodet had to confront rumors and reports not unlike those that had poisoned the stories of Jaffa and Eylau. The event was almost banal: on 21 October 1798 a spontaneous revolt against Bonaparte's military rule erupted in Cairo that was put down by a full-scale attack with artillery on the Great Mosque. Napoléon's official report of the riot made little of its extent, and he described its end with a single

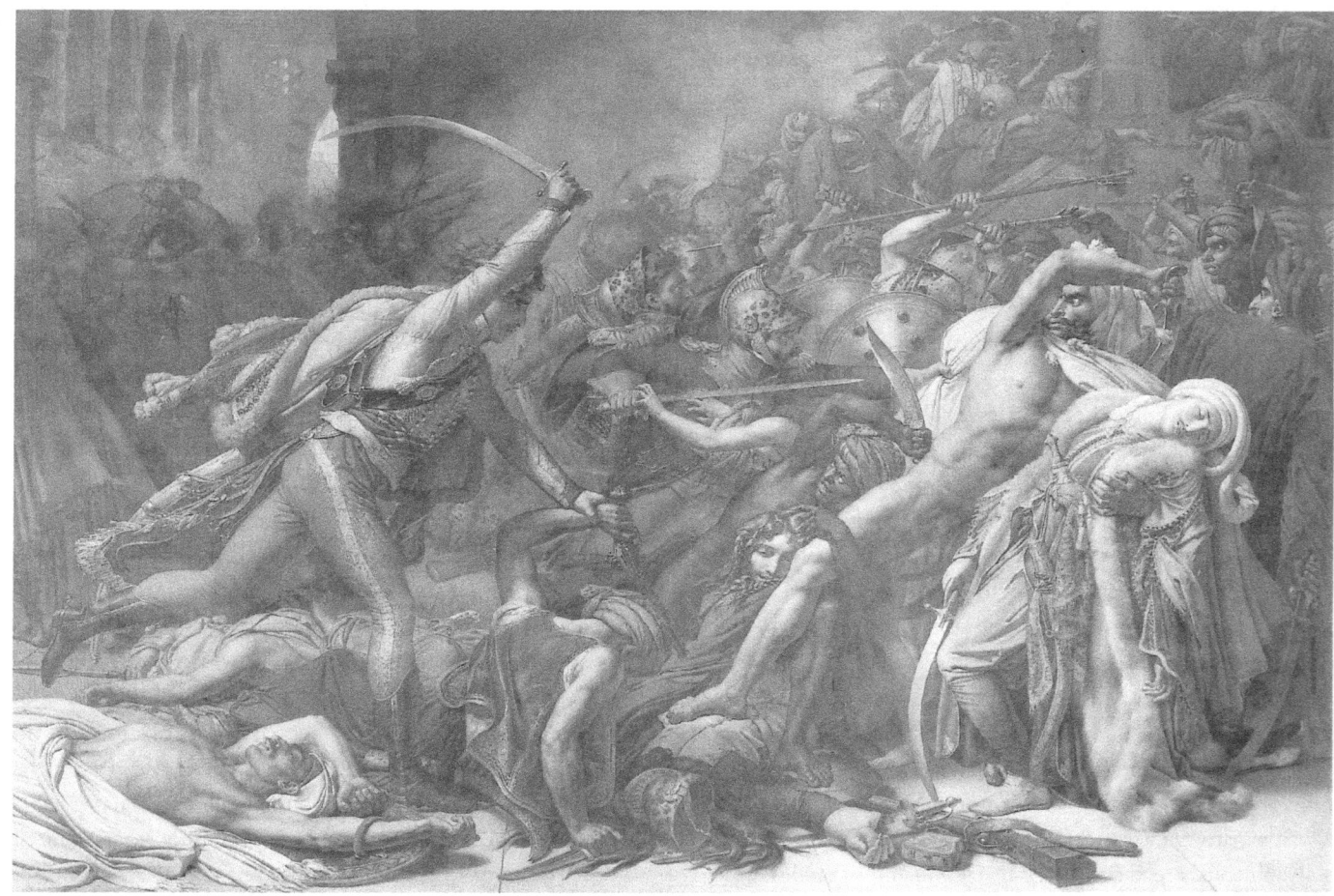

FIGURE 10.   Anne-Louis Girodet-Trioson, *The Revolt of Cairo, 21 October 1798*, 1810. Oil on canvas. Versailles, Châteaux de Versailles et de Trianon, inv. MV1497 (365 × 500 cm). Photo: © RMN/Art Resource, NY/ © Daniel Arnaudet / Jean Schormans.

line of flat prose: "in less than twenty minutes of bombardment the barricades were torn down, the neighborhood was evacuated, the mosque was in the hands of our troops, and perfect calm was reestablished."[47] There was, however, another side to the Cairo uprising which involved a savagery not part of the official story: Bonaparte's orders to kill anyone found in the street bearing arms; his command to burn immediately any house from which stones were thrown at soldiers; his approval to kill all the rebels holed up in the Great Mosque; his wish that the mosque itself be completely destroyed by breaking its principal columns. Equally sinister were his orders to général Alexandre Berthier: "Cut the throat of any prisoner taken with weapons in his possession. Take them tonight to the banks of the Nile between Boulâq and Old Cairo; their headless cadavers are to be thrown into the river."[48] Six days after quashing the revolt, Bonaparte reported to général Jean-Louis Reynier that he continued to have thirty or so prisoners beheaded each night, so that by dawn their bodies would be seen floating in the river through Cairo as a warning to local troublemakers.[49]

How familiar was Girodet with these atrocities? We shall never know, although Denon could have related some of them based on his first-hand experience in Egypt. What is certain is that Girodet—perhaps emboldened by rumors of this sort—made a picture that is singular in its savagery. French soldiers and Egyptian insurgents flail away at one another with swords drawn and muskets blazing. In the center foreground, a turbaned black man wields an enormous bloodied dagger in one hand; in the other, he grasps the fair-haired head of a French soldier, as if to take permanent revenge for the beheadings ordered nightly by Bonaparte. Girodet's setting is architecturally impossible, a space far too shallow for the many combatants who are jammed together and locked in mortal combat. Although the floor opens to the viewer, it yields almost no terrain upon which to stand, and no opportunity to determine aggressor from aggressee: both sides hold our attention and our sympathy here, and—most important—no hero appears to put the carnage in perspective.

Contemporaries sensed that something unusual was afoot in Girodet's image. Denon—who had directed the commission—criticized the picture in his report to the Emperor by suggesting that Girodet "was perhaps carried away by his subject; he has gone beyond the commotion of a revolt and the fury of revolutionaries. He has heaped up, rather than arranged, his resources and his means and—led astray by his exuberance and fervid imagination—his composition fails to make an impression."[50] Denon was surely being diplomatic in this critique of Girodet's work, because what he tactfully called a lack of "impression" was seen by others as a lack of order and narrative clarity:

The artist has encumbered his composition with needless figures; because the background planes on the viewer's right are overloaded with weapons, movement, and intermingled combatants, and are so crowded together that the eye gets lost, is worn out, and forgets to admire what is really admirable in the foreground sections. Unfavorably predisposed, the viewer finds the expressions exaggerated . . . and goes away unsatisfied.[51]

Girodet's picture enacts an ambivalence about the morality of violence and war that was becoming increasingly pervasive in Paris. Paradoxically, domestic changes in the imperial household were moving in the same direction: by the time Girodet completed his *Revolt of Cairo*, Napoléon had divorced Joséphine and married an Austrian princess, eighteen-year-old Marie-Louise, in the hope of producing an heir and linking by marriage the fortunes of France and Austria. Shortly after Girodet's picture was installed in the Galerie de Diane it was removed, for the new Empress "manifested a great loathing to look at it."[52]

NAPOLÉON'S AUTHORITY was built on military might but exercised, on a day-to-day basis, by a complex administration over a mix of annexed lands, vassal states, and semi-autonomous territories. As Napoléon tightened his personal grip on power, the Empire's administrative network was increasingly concentrated in Paris. The Emperor ruled directly through the Conseil d'État, and returned power to provincial administrative districts called *départements* by personally appointing the *préfets*. The criminal justice system was overhauled to centralize the naming of judges. Police were given broad powers of surveillance and detention to ensure that any opposition to Napoleonic policy would be known in the capital. The press was everywhere controlled by government-appointed censors. State finances were run by the Emperor and a handful of bankers and advisers. All the vectors of imperial power flowed from Paris. This concentration of responsibility in and around the capital made it the most important place to live and do business on the continent. Napoléon was concerned to make Paris a showcase of his rule with projects for new streets, public works, monuments, and museums (see Chapter Three). Parisians, who had a long history of taking pride in simply *being* Parisian, suddenly found themselves at the center of Europe's political, cultural, and intellectual life, inhabitants of a city whose physical state was constantly improving under the Emperor's watchful eye.

In the fall of 1811 Jacques-Louis David was asked by a rich Scottish nobleman, the Marquess Alexander Douglas, future Duke of Hamilton, for a picture of Napoléon (Fig. 11) to decorate the family palace near Glasgow. The commission was somewhat eccentric, since England and France were at

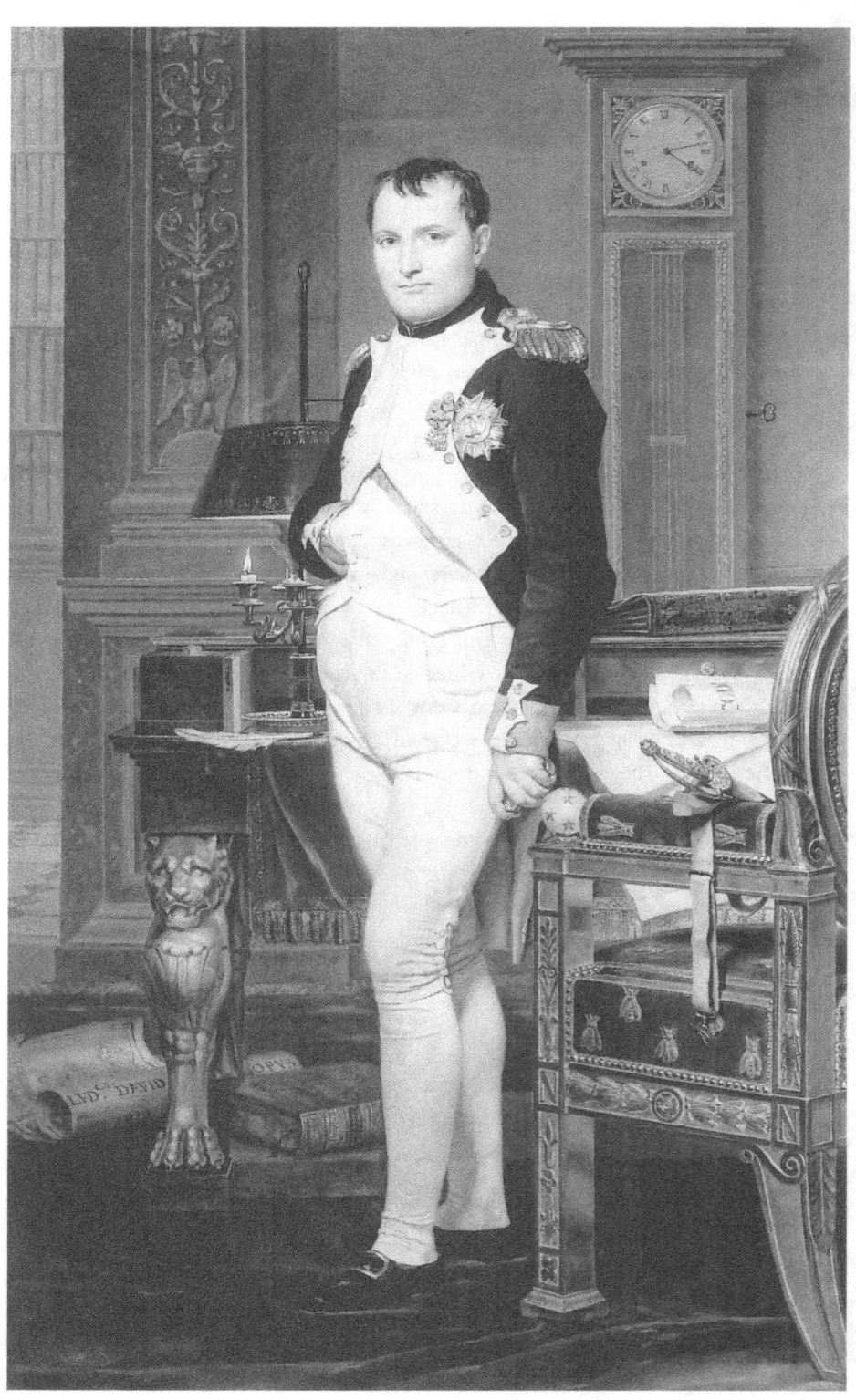

FIGURE 11. Jacques-Louis David,
Napoléon in his Study, 1812. Oil on canvas.
Washington DC, U.S. National Gallery
of Art (Samuel H. Kress Collection), inv.
1374 (203.9 × 125.1 cm). Photo: © 2004
Board of Trustees, National Gallery of
Art, Washington.

war and actively fighting on the Iberian Peninsula. Nonetheless, David was extremely pleased to be asked, and he hastened to write his acceptance:

The selection of me, coming from a person such as yourself, flatters me greatly, and so I do not hesitate, Monsieur the Marquess, to place this commission ahead of all the others I have received from foreigners without, however, trying to hide the difficulties of the task. This picture, I said to myself, will hang in the apartment of a man of taste, it will be seen by the elite of an enlightened nation, and it must represent a man about whom one's conception is always less than the truth. So, Monsieur the Marquess, these combined reasons compel me to undertake the work, and I intend to risk my happiness and all of my fame to respond to the favorable impression of my talents formed by a great gentleman and friend of the arts.[53]

Especially interesting in David's reply is his sensitivity to the fact that the portrait of Napoléon would be seen by the ruling elite of England. In a later letter to Douglas, which announced the picture was done, David restated his belief in its propagandistic mission:

I had the honor of writing to you [last September] that I was going to get busy immediately with all my forces so that my work might give to a nation, which has the habit of admiring great men, a clear idea of the person she would like to know. At that time I had only promises to offer you, but since my work has been finished now for six weeks, and because its extreme likeness of that immortal man attracts a huge crowd to my studio, I can assure Your Highness (by repeating the opinion of the general public) that no one has—to this day—produced a greater portrait likeness, not only the material features of his face, but also that appearance of goodness, composure, and perspicacity that never leaves him.[54]

The same letter informed Douglas that Napoléon was portrayed "in an instance of his life that is most characteristic: at work," in his study at the Tuileries Palace where, to cite the artist's own words:

Having passed the night composing the Napoleonic Code, he only becomes aware of the approaching dawn by the candles that burn down and flicker out, and by the mantle clock that has just sounded four o'clock in the morning. He rises from his desk to put on his sword and review his troops.[55]

The picture, as David was quick to point out, includes a host of incidental details rendered with a striking and intense realism: from Napoléon's signature-style uniform as foot soldier of the Imperial Guard to the carved gilt frame and embroidered Napoleonic bees of his chair; from the imposing lion's claw desk to an exact view into the neighboring map-room; from the characteristic gesture of tucking one hand into his vest to the snuff box he holds in the other.

David did not underestimate the propagandistic potential of his picture, because its compelling details are part of a carefully orchestrated fabrication that elides the imperial present of 1812 with a former time—back to March 1804—when the Napoleonic Code was adopted. For example, neither the particular chair so carefully described, nor the background clock, were actually in the Emperor's study, but both help to articulate David's allegory of a tirelessly working head of state: the clock sets a precise hour, while the chair—decorated with imperial emblems not yet invented in early 1804—conflates past and present under the disguise of material accuracy. Plopped on the floor under Napoléon's desk is a copy of Plutarch's *Lives*, an overt reference to the great men among whom the sitter is to be counted. There are also several sheets of paper nearby that appear to be maps or plans of battle, one of which David signed with his name and date. The double-edged effect of David's rhetoric can best be gauged by the Emperor's reaction to the picture: hearing it was on view in David's studio, and curious that it was commissioned by an Englishman, Napoléon asked to see the portrait. It is reported that he looked carefully at the picture and said to the painter: "You have found me out, my dear David; at night I am concerned with my subjects' happiness, during the day I work for their glory."[56]

In one sense, Napoléon was right: the picture for Douglas does present a leader who is at once general and lawgiver. What was unusual is the understatement of his military charisma, and that David pulled no punches when rendering the effects of work and age on the man himself: slightly balding, somewhat rounded in face and figure, even a bit disheveled after a long night with little sleep (note the unbuttoned left cuff and slightly sagging stockings). Compared to the magnificent energy and frozen time of David's equestrian portrait of Bonaparte (Fig. 1), this painting seems bound to time and physical constraints. The Emperor is no longer larger than life, but very much part of it, and he looks out from the picture to meet our eyes directly, as if to acknowledge that he lives amongst us, not over our heads. We might ask: why did David veer so dramatically with this picture from military valor into "everyday" life?

David was not alone. Several other artists exhibited pictures of a more human-scale and humane Napoléon at the Paris Salon of 1812, including four scenes of clemency and a visit to wounded soldiers at the Invalides hospital.[57] This alternate view of the Emperor was informed by a feeling that Napoléon should begin to pay more attention to the material needs of his empire than to the military goals of conquest. There were good reasons for this shift in public opinion: the economy was in deep crisis, and a poor harvest in 1811 forced such a rise in the price of bread that emergency purchases of foreign wheat for the Paris market were needed to calm the city. Napoléon's correspondence with the Minister of Police reveals that he did worry about the economy, for he suggests several "make work" schemes for the city's unemployed so as to keep them busy, able to provide for themselves, and out of political demonstrations in the streets.

Nonetheless, people were alarmed by the clear signs that the Emperor was planning to lead the army and the nation into another battle, this time at the gates of Moscow. Throughout the early months of 1812 preparations for war were everywhere apparent as huge stocks of supplies and munitions were gathered at depots in eastern Europe. An army of more than four hundred thousand men was assembled along the River Niemen. On 9 May 1812, Napoléon and Marie-Louise left Paris for Dresden, where he relaxed for eleven days amidst a continuous circle of courtly parties and festivals. Suddenly, at five o'clock on the morning of 29 May, Napoléon took leave of Marie-Louise and set out to join his army: the war with Russia had begun. David's idea to paint Napoléon as lawmaker and administrator took shape during the months that his sitter was preparing the largest, most expensive military campaign Europe had ever seen: it argued the greatness of peace to the Emperor as much as it argued Napoléon's greatness to the colleagues of Alexander Douglas.

In April 1812, one of David's students wrote to his parents that the painter was planning to make a replica of *Napoléon in his Study*, and in July he reported that David was busy at work on this second picture.[58] It is likely that David painted an almost-identical replica of his work with the hope of selling it to the government. His image of Napoléon the administrator—more involved with making laws than making war—failed to interest the Emperor, who burned with an ambition to conquer Russia. Meanwhile, complications with the export license required to ship David's original picture from France to England through the maritime blockade delayed delivery to Douglas until November 1812. By that time, David's entire conceit was hopelessly out of date, for Napoléon's Grand Army had fought its way to Moscow, only to find the city deserted, on fire, and without provisions. Forced to retreat through the Russian winter, the entire army was virtually destroyed by cold, famine, and disease. For the first time in his career, Napoléon returned from the army to Paris without a victory in hand.

The human disaster of the Russian campaign marks the turning point where Napoléon's dream of a vast European empire began to unravel. In its terrible wake came a profound crisis of confidence in the Emperor's judgment, so much so that his brother Lucien—long a stalwart supporter—wrote to his children: "We must not rebuke him, because I have seen the clouds of celestial anger accumulate around his head, from which will come the thunderbolt that cannot fail to strike him if he perseveres in his wickedness."[59] In this context of defeat and doubt, it is no surprise that David's replica—brimming with optimism about Napoléon's concern for the well-being of his subjects—remained unsold in the artist's studio. Only after the Emperor's own death, and well after France's final defeat on that day of 18 June 1815 known as Waterloo, did David manage to find a buyer for the second version of his homage to the leader he called, even after the retreat from Russia, "the man of the century."[60]

EMBOLDENED by the catastrophic end of Napoléon's campaign into Russia, the erstwhile allies of France—Prussia and Austria—joined forces with the Russians in the spring of 1813 to begin a concerted war against occupying French forces. By the end of the year, they stood poised on the borders of France itself, while the English—led by the Duke of Wellington—had driven the French army out of Spain. Napoléon managed to raise a defensive army, but money and supplies were sorely lacking, and the mood of the country was decidedly for peace and an end to foreign adventure. A resolution of the Legislative Corps spoke with an impunity unthinkable two years earlier:

Our suffering is overwhelming, our country is threatened on all its borders; we sense a destitution unexampled in the history of the state. Business is at a standstill. . . . Industry is dead. . . . A barbarous and purposeless war has regularly swallowed up our young men who have thereby been taken away from education, farming, business, and the trades. What we must do now is return within our own territories and bridle our ambitious impulses and activities, which have been, for the past twenty years, so disastrous for all the people of Europe.[61]

Alongside this internal discontent, royalists began to spread proclamations in favor of the king-in-exile, Louis XVIII. On 12 March 1813 the city of Bordeaux surrendered to an English landing force, hoisted the white flag of the Bourbon dynasty atop the cathedral, and welcomed the duc d'Angoulême and his wife with cries of "Long live the King!" For the first time since 1792, the tricolor flag of the Republic and Empire was renounced by Frenchmen on French soil.

Beginning in late January, Napoléon mounted an astonishing campaign of national defense against an Allied army many times larger than his own in which he scored several victories that stalled the Allied advance. But time was against him, and the Allies, who broke off all negotiations with Napoléon on 19 March, began to negotiate with the Bourbons for a transfer of power. A provisional government led by Talleyrand concluded an agreement with the Allies to surrender Paris without further fighting: on 31 March the Allied leaders and their troops marched through the city. One of their first concerns was to remove the Emperor's effigy from atop the Vendôme Column (see Chapter Three).

Within the week, Napoléon was forced to abdicate unconditionally. On 20 April he bid farewell to his troops at Fontainebleau and began a voyage—with a handful of followers and a few hundred loyal soldiers—into exile on Elba, a small island between the coast of Italy and Corsica. At about the same time, Louis XVIII began a reverse journey from exile in England to Paris: he arrived in the capital on 3 May to a warm, but not tumultuous welcome. Deep emotions simmered beneath a surface of calm, especially within the ranks of the army. Chateaubriand has left a chilling image of Napoléon's Imperial Guard, which was ordered to greet Louis XVIII along part of his trajectory:

It was an infantry regiment of the Old Guard that lined the route from the Pont-Neuf to Notre-Dame, along the quai des Orfèvres. I do not think that human faces have ever expressed something so menacing and so terrible. These grenadiers, covered with wounds, conquerors of Europe, who had seen so many thousands of bullets pass over their heads, who smelled like gunshot and powder; these same men, deprived of their captain, and watched over by an army of Russians, Austrians, and Prussians, were forced to salute an old king, disabled by time rather than war, in the occupied capital of Napoléon. Some, to demonstrate the scorn of their rage, wrinkled their brows so as to lower their busbies to the corners of their mouths; others, like tigers, showed their teeth beneath moustaches. When they presented arms, it was with a furious movement, and the clash of their weapons made one tremble.[62]

The more enthusiastic royalists—known as Ultras—and some members of the conservative clergy wanted not only to end the Empire, but also to erase the effects of the French Revolution: they pressed for a return of noble privileges, a repudiation of the Concordat, and restitution of lands seized during the 1790s. Although a new constitution, cobbled together in haste at the time of the Allied invasion, prevented such extreme measures, Louis XVIII was obliged to reward those who had stood by the throne for the past two decades. Many government administrators who had served Napoléon were dismissed and replaced by less-experienced men and women whose only claim to a job was a noble family name. Thousands of seasoned army officers were discharged at half pay and replaced by noblemen with little or no military background.

The political honeymoon between Louis XVIII and his people did not last for long: by June a major crisis developed when the king refused to ratify changes to the constitution he found too liberal. Paris, in particular, was torn by political differences. Working-class neighborhoods to the east exhibited a general loathing for the newly returned and privileged nobles along with deep and abiding affection for Napoléon, who was credited with dissolving class distinctions. In the wealthy western sections of the city, where most of the nobles lived, a strong and often haughty support for the king was the norm. The middle classes, many of whom abandoned Napoléon reluctantly in 1814, were increasingly worried by the rightward drift of government policy, especially a return to Sunday closing laws, efforts to muzzle press freedom, and the restitution of confiscated properties.

All of this was watched closely by Napoléon's spies, who sent him regular reports on the state of the nation. Who would have guessed that he would land again at Fréjus—almost a reenactment of his return from Egypt in 1799—and march in triumph to Paris? Yet that is exactly what happened between the 2nd and 20th of March 1815. As Napoléon and his little band of soldiers made their way to the capital, they were greeted by deputations of local officials, thousands of civilian supporters, and a cascade of soldiers who rallied to their leader and the tricolor flag. It quickly became clear to the king that the army could not or would not stop Napoléon's advance, so Louis XVIII and his family fled France once again, this time to the city of Ghent. The so-called Hundred Days of Napoleonic rule had begun.

The Allies wasted no time responding to Napoléon's bold gesture: meeting in Vienna on 13 March, they declared him an outlaw; by the 25th the military alliance was reconfirmed and an army of almost eight hundred thousand men began to move against France. To face this challenge Napoléon needed to rally the nation, but his old authoritarian habits were now held in check: a supplement to the constitution forced the Emperor to share his power with a bicameral assembly, guaranteed freedom of the press, and provided safeguards on individual liberties. Rather than the docile servitude to which he was accustomed, Napoléon was openly mistrusted by the legislature, and the task of raising an army was greatly complicated by the country's financial mess.

Undaunted, Napoléon cobbled together an army of about two hundred thousand men and left Paris on 12 June for his last campaign. Six days later, the main corps of his army—about seventy-five thousand men—launched an attack against Wellington's army at a place in Belgium called Mont-Saint-Jean, but which the English knew as Waterloo. By the end of the day, the entire French army had been dispersed or destroyed. Napoléon barely escaped capture before fleeing posthaste to Paris, where the city anxiously awaited news of the battle. He immediately invoked the need for new mobilizations, but legislators would hear nothing of it: they demanded a second abdication, which the Emperor was in no position to refuse. On 25 June he left Paris for Joséphine's house at Malmaison. Four days later he was on his way to the seaport town of La Rochelle. Napoléon hoped to obtain passage to America, but he ultimately surrendered to the captain of a British frigate. Once in their custody, the English treated Napoléon as a prisoner of war: his last days were spent under close guard far from Europe on the remote South Atlantic island of Saint Helena, where he died in 1821.

Meanwhile, the Allies continued their march on Paris as Louis XVIII made his way back to the capital. An armistice was worked out on 3 July to avert a military attack on the city, and the king officially returned on the 8th. But the Allies were far less tractable than they had been in 1814, and their terms of peace were harsh on France: territorial boundaries were reset to their positions of 1790, meaning that all gains made during the years of Revolution and Empire were taken away; the eastern and northern regions were to be occupied by Allied armies for five years at French expense; war retributions of 700 million francs were exacted; France was obliged to settle every debt incurred by any previous regime with any citizen anywhere in Europe. It is estimated that the annual cost of supporting the occupying armies amounted to 150 million francs a year, and that the outstanding debts exceeded 1,600 million francs. The Treaty of 1815 was clearly designed to punish France.

There were also scores to settle at home. Civil servants who refused to serve Napoléon during the Hundred Days demanded vengeance on those who had gone over to the Emperor's side. Lists were made of high officials and military officers susceptible to be tried or court-martialed. Violent and spontaneous reprisals broke out across France in what came to be known as the White Terror. Foreign soldiers, especially those stationed in Paris, requisitioned food and lodging with impunity, drank heavily, ransacked property, and attacked women. They also plotted to eliminate certain monuments to Napoleonic glory: General Gebhard Blücher, for example, wanted to blow up the Jena Bridge in Paris that commemorated Napoléon's 1806 victory over the Prussians; only after Louis XVIII wrote that he would personally sit on the bridge did the Prussian general renounce the idea. The odd spectacle of a Bourbon king defending Napoléon's bridge is but one example of how the symbolic and historic meanings of many Parisian monuments were fiercely contested arenas of ideological infighting during these years of swift and dramatic political change (see Chapter Three).

The second return of Louis XVIII did little to mend the rifts in Parisian culture that had been part and parcel of his first, short-lived reign of 1814. More than ever the faubourg Saint-Germain to the west remained a bastion of royalist sympathies, the cradle of Ultra extremism, and the seat of old-guard aristocratic power. Paradoxically, eliminating Napoléon as a viable political threat created a new kind of opposition that linked leading Liberals—bankers like Jacques Laffitte and politicians like Benjamin Constant—with former administrators and army officers of the Empire, such as général Maximilien Foy and Charles de Rémusat. This odd mix of talents tended to meet in the newly fashionable district near the Chausée d'Antin. Thousands of underemployed army veterans—the so-called *demi-solde* or half-pay officers—with plenty of time to grumble about the present and to lie about the glorious past gathered daily in the cafés, public squares, and social clubs of the capital. It is in the company of this informal sentimental public, steeped in Liberal and Bonapartist sympathies, that we encounter the painter Théodore Géricault.

DURING THE 1810S, most French adults probably lived some version of Géricault's convoluted personal trajectory through the labyrinth of national politics. The son of a prosperous family in the tobacco industry, and living in Paris since about 1795, Géricault attended the prestigious Lycée Impérial (today Lycée Louis-le-Grand). He was subject to the draft in the spring of 1811, at the start of Napoléon's military buildup for the campaign against Russia, but his father paid for a replacement, thus sparing him military service during the darkest hours of that disaster. Géricault enrolled at the École des Beaux-Arts as a student of Pierre-Narcisse Guérin (Fig. 6), with whom he had been studying informally since late 1810. French armies were entering Moscow when he finished work on his first picture for the Paris Salon, a large painting of an Imperial Guard cavalry officer in full charge (Paris, Musée du Louvre). Based on the evidence of this picture—which was awarded a gold medal by the government—we must assume that Géricault's efforts to avoid the draft were not a measure of his opposition to the policies of Napoléon, but simply an expedient (and a perfectly legal one) by which wealthy young men avoided the dangers of war.

Near the end of 1813, as the Allied armies tightened their noose on the capital, Géricault and his father rented a house in a developing section of northern Paris at 23, rue des Martyrs. Situated between the edge of the city and the hill of Montmartre, this was a neighborhood of small houses and private gardens: the property rented by the Géricaults, for example, included an outbuilding in the garden that Théodore used as his studio. Eventually so many literary and artistic salons met in the neighborhood that it came to be called Nouvelle Athènes (see Chapter Six). It was also home to many painters and a fair number of Napoleonic army officers discharged on half-pay.

Géricault's biographers all attest to his great skill and keen interest in equitation, but neither his love of horses, nor the milieu in which he lived on the rue des Martyrs, prepares us for his behavior after Napoléon's first abdication and exile to Elba. In the spring of 1814 Géricault enlisted in the cavalry of the National Guard of Paris, perhaps—like the artists Horace Vernet and Nicolas-Toussaint Charlet—to defend the city against the Allies. The surprising part is that when the National Guard cavalry was disbanded on 15 June, Géricault signed up for membership in one of the two new companies of Royal Musketeers that were being formed as part of the king's personal guard. From the seeming sympathy and support for Bonapartist adventure so evident in his early pictures, Géricault swerved into the company of young aristocratic royalists sworn to protect Louis XVIII. His action was too deliberate to be inspired, as some biographers have suggested, by simply the "love of military spectacles . . . the example of his royalist friends, his companions of society and relaxation; maybe too the brilliant and gallant red uniform of the musketeers."[63] Nor can we dismiss Géricault's stint in the king's guard as a passing fancy: he was part of the military contingent that accompanied Louis XVIII during his flight to Ghent at the time of Napoléon's return from Elba; he resumed his post in the Royal Musketeers in July after Napoléon's final exile; he served out his time until the Musketeers were themselves disbanded at the end of 1815. Géricault's career with the Royal Musketeers might suggest an attachment to the idea of a Bourbon monarchy, but it could also be understood as a gesture to indicate that he and his family—including the family's tobacco business—were ready to accept the new political realities of Restoration France.

Géricault belonged to the First Company of the Musketeers, whose commander—the comte de Nansouty—was a Napoleonic hero famous for a decisive cavalry charge at the battle of Wagram. Nansouty became one of three senior officials who represented the imperial past at the court of Louis XVIII. After Nansouty's death in February 1815, command of Géricault's company was given to the marquis de Lauriston, another imperial notable who had served Napoléon as aide-de-camp, ambassador, and general. Unlike the Second Company of Musketeers—commanded by the marquis de Legrange, a longtime royalist—Géricault's company was a place where prior service for Napoléon was reconciled with loyalty to the restored monarchy. In this light, Géricault's time in the Musketeers need not be dismissed as a passing fancy, nor taken as a moment of conversion to royalist politics; rather, it makes perfect sense as a not-so-unusual attempt to heal the wounds produced by the nation's defeat and the tumult of the Hundred Days.

Two other events of importance to Géricault occurred about the time the Musketeers were disbanded. The first is that Horace Vernet moved into Géricault's neighborhood at 11, rue des Martyrs. Vernet's garden connected directly with the garden behind Géricault's studio, so that it was possible to walk directly from one to the other. Horace Vernet was a popular painter of battle pictures who harbored strong Bonapartist sympathies. His studio was a notorious meeting place for a mix of artists, soldiers, and politicians united by their common disdain for the restored Bourbon monarchy. The second event concerned the Louvre. Beginning in July the Allies, spearheaded by the Prussians, posted soldiers in the galleries of the museum and began to remove all the works confiscated by Napoléon's armies in their march across Europe (see Chapter Three). The sculptor Antonio Canova arrived in August to negotiate the recovery of objects taken from the papal collections, and he began work—with the support of the British—in October. Many Parisians viewed the dismemberment of the Louvre's collections as a kind of second defeat, as we learn from this piece in the London *Courier*:

> The long gallery of the Museum presents the strongest possible image of desolation; here and there a few pictures giving greater effect to the disfigured nakedness of the walls. I have seen several French ladies in passing along the galleries break into extravagant fits of rage and lamentation; they gather round the Apollo to take their last farewell, with a most romantic enthusiasm.[64]

Emotions ran especially high among the city's artists for whom the Louvre had become a living reference book to the history of art. Taken together, Géricault's immediate milieu was strongly motivated to adopt an ever more pronounced opposition to Bourbon rule.

Related to the dispersal of Napoléon's war booty was the removal from public view of some of the most famous pictures of recent French painting. Because the Restoration government refused to exhibit in the Louvre any image of the deposed Emperor, many of the greatest pictures by living French painters, such as Gros's *Bonaparte in the Pest-House at Jaffa* (Fig. 7), were quietly moved from the galleries to museum warehouses—out of sight and, it was hoped, out of mind. Yet the memory of such pictures burned bright among young French painters and continued to shape their ideas about what a monumental image of modern life should hope to achieve. Géricault's own *Raft of the Medusa* (Fig. 12) is a picture whose ambition was driven by an unstated rivalry with those Napoleonic paintings of modern history that were vividly remembered, even in their absence.

The chronology of Géricault's great picture is complicated. He traveled in Italy for about a year beginning in late 1816, and returned to Paris with the intention of presenting a major work at the Salon of 1819. From our sketch of the politics within his immediate circle of friends, of the artistic climate in Paris following the dismantling of Napoléon's museum, and of his avowed ambition "to shine, to illuminate, to astonish the world,"[65] we can better understand how and why he was drawn to the idea of tackling a subject inspired by an event of contemporary life. His daily experience around Horace Vernet showed him that modern subjects generated wide interest and commentary, especially when treating events from the officially repudiated annals of the Napoleonic era. His regular contact with Liberal and die-hard Bonapartist political sympathizers made him realize that a subject even vaguely critical of the Bourbon government would provoke exactly the kind of attention he craved. Shortly after Géricault's return to Paris a little booklet provided him with the subject for his picture: it was the *Naufrage de la Frégate la Méduse* [Shipwreck of the Frigate *Medusa*], written by Alexandre Corréard and Henri Savigny, two men who survived the disaster they described.[66]

Their drama unfolded in July 1816, when a colony of soldiers and settlers was sent to Senegal (West Africa) to retake possession of the territory returned to France by the Treaty of 1815. The four-ship convoy was led by the *Medusa*, a fairly new frigate launched in 1815, under the command of Hugues Duroy de Chaumareys. The captain had served in the navy before the Revolution, but he joined the émigré army of the comte d'Artois during the 1790s and only returned to France under Napoléon's amnesty program. Chaumareys had been working in the Ministry of Finance when the restored Bourbons began to purge the military of Napoleonic officers. He successfully petitioned to be reinstated as a captain in the navy thanks to his record of faithful service to royalists during the Revolution. Nonetheless, when Chaumareys was ap-

pointed to lead the expedition to Senegal he had not been at sea for more than twenty-five years.

The convoy left France on 17 June. Chaumareys quickly demonstrated his lack of professional experience: despite the warnings of his junior officers, he raced ahead of the other ships in dangerous shoal waters off the coast of Mauritania and promptly ran aground. Although the crew was not able to refloat the vessel immediately, there was no real cause for concern; yet Chaumareys decided to abandon ship. Unfortunately, there were not enough life boats to evacuate all the passengers. Chaumareys committed the capital offense of placing himself and his officers in the life boats while relegating 147 passengers, soldiers, and sailors to a makeshift raft that would be towed to shore. The raft was so overloaded that its unlucky passengers stood in water up to their thighs and, of course, it was virtually impossible to pull. Panicked by the load, Chaumareys cut the tow lines and left the raft to drift at sea while he and his officers rowed to safety.

There were few provisions on the raft, almost no place to stand, and no means of navigation. A storm during the first night killed twenty-four passengers, and a vicious mutiny during the second night claimed sixty-five more victims. By the third day starved survivors were driven to cannibalism. On the sixth day—with only twenty-eight people still alive—the strongest fifteen threw the weakest of their colleagues overboard. These fifteen rather ruthless men survived seven days before being rescued by the *Argus*, another ship of the convoy, although five died soon after: only ten men survived the thirteen-day ordeal at sea.

News of the *Medusa*'s wreck was slow to reach France, and the Ministry of the Navy tried to suppress the most gruesome parts of the drama. Official announcement of the wreck in early September was a short, anodyne note in the *Moniteur universel*:

On 2 July, at three o'clock in the afternoon, the frigate *Medusa* was lost, in good weather, on the shoals of Arguin twenty leagues distant from Cap Blanc (in Africa, between the Canaries and Cap Verde). The *Medusa*'s six launches and lifeboats were able to save a large part of the crew and passengers, but of 150 men who attempted to save themselves on a raft, 135 have perished.[67]

Among the survivors who returned to France was Henri Savigny, the ship's surgeon. During his voyage home, Savigny prepared a detailed report of the wreck and the horrors he experienced on the raft. He dutifully submitted his account to the navy, but it was leaked to the press by the Minister of Police, who wanted to use the incident against the Ultra-royalist Minister of the Navy. On 13 September readers of the *Journal des Débats* were shocked to learn the lurid details of the raft's ordeal.

Liberal opponents of the Bourbon government dwelt on the captain's scandalous, unprofessional behavior. They denounced the fact that Chaumareys had obtained command of the *Medusa* because of his allegiance to royalist politics rather than his maritime expertise. The breaking story fanned the flames of a heated debate between Ultra-royalists and a coalition of Liberals and Bonapartists over the state of the armed forces: the former wanted a return to the pre-revolutionary practice of restricting officers' commissions to members of the nobility; the latter believed that experienced military veterans—including those who served Napoléon—should be first in line for promotions. Obviously, the incompetence of Chaumareys lent strong support to the Liberal-Bonapartist argument. Chaumareys himself was in no hurry to return to France or to defend his actions during the disaster; when he finally reappeared in late December he seemed surprised that he was arrested and held for court-martial. The facts had become common knowledge in his absence, and the public was in no mood for excuses.

Alexandre Corréard, who had been engineer of the *Medusa*, also returned to France. He teamed up with Savigny to petition the government to compensate the victims and punish the officers. The government responded haughtily with harassment, fines, and prison terms; eventually both men were dismissed from service. The two decided to collaborate on a more extensive—and far more melodramatic—account of their ordeal than Savigny's original report. This new booklet, and its tremendous public reception, inspired Géricault to take up the story of the raft at sea—a subject of modern life that stirred the hearts, minds, and political allegiances of nearly everyone.

Germain Bazin and Lorenz Eitner have each studied in detail the many drawings and sketches done by Géricault for the *Raft* to demonstrate the artist's long struggle to render the complex story in a single image.[68] His first ideas included a focus on the mutiny of the second night, rescue by the *Argus*, and even the horrors of cannibalism. He experimented with the moment when survivors of the raft hailed an approaching rowboat just before rescue, and of the moment when they first spotted the *Argus* on the horizon. In the end, he settled on a version of this last scene for its dramatic suspense between death and rescue: at one point the men on the raft spotted the *Argus*, but the ship failed to see them; when it sailed on, the survivors experienced a kind of final, terrible despair (Fig. 12). With this subject, Géricault realized he could combine a powerful range of expressions—from frantic excitement to hopeless resignation—in a single moment and simultaneously entangle us, who view the picture, in the emotional web of the story's drama.

The final picture's very large scale (nearly five by seven meters), the raft's steeply tilted orientation, and the powerful diagonal that runs from the nearest corner of the raft through the group of straining figures to the tiny ship on the horizon, produce the paradoxical effect of an action that seems both physically close and psychologically distant. Delacroix noted this when he wrote to a friend that "you feel like you already have a foot in the water. You have to see it up close in order to sense all its merit."[69] And yet, despite our proximity to the raft, we see little really terrible horror: although many figures are clothed in tatters, and some are already dead, Géricault did not linger on the physical afflictions of the men. Their bodies are full and muscled, with none of the wounds and sores described by Corréard and Savigny. The phalanx of their gestures towards the distant ship is a powerful movement far in excess of what the actual survivors were capable. All of which suggests that while working on his picture Géricault inched it away from simple illustration towards a more general expression: but of what?

"Picture, what do you want from me?" asked one critic, who complained that it seemed to avoid standard emotions to offer only the sight of "men jostled between life and death."[70] Unlike recent paintings of modern life that Géricault certainly had in mind, such as Gros's *Jaffa* (Fig. 7) or *Eylau* (Fig. 9), there is no hero on the raft: all are victims, and none dares to count on a savior who probably will not appear. Nor does this resemble Girodet's *Revolt of Cairo* (Fig. 10), a picture also lacking a hero that Géricault particularly admired, for the *Raft of the Medusa* makes explicit physical demands upon its viewer: where the soldiers of Girodet's painting flail away at one another in a shallow plane perpendicular to our line of sight, Géricault's work implicates the trajectory of our look within the desperate clamor of the raft's survivors to be seen by the ship. Géricault began

with the assumption that his picture would never replicate the horrors of lived experience, a point made clear in his reaction to what some critics had written:

This year our journalists have reached the height of ridicule. They judge every painting according to the *spirit* in which it was composed. You will find a liberal article praising some work for its truly patriotic brush, its national stroke. The same work, judged by a rigorous conservative, turns out to be nothing less than a revolutionary composition pervaded by a general tint of sedition; the heads of its figures are described as wearing expressions of hatred for the pater-

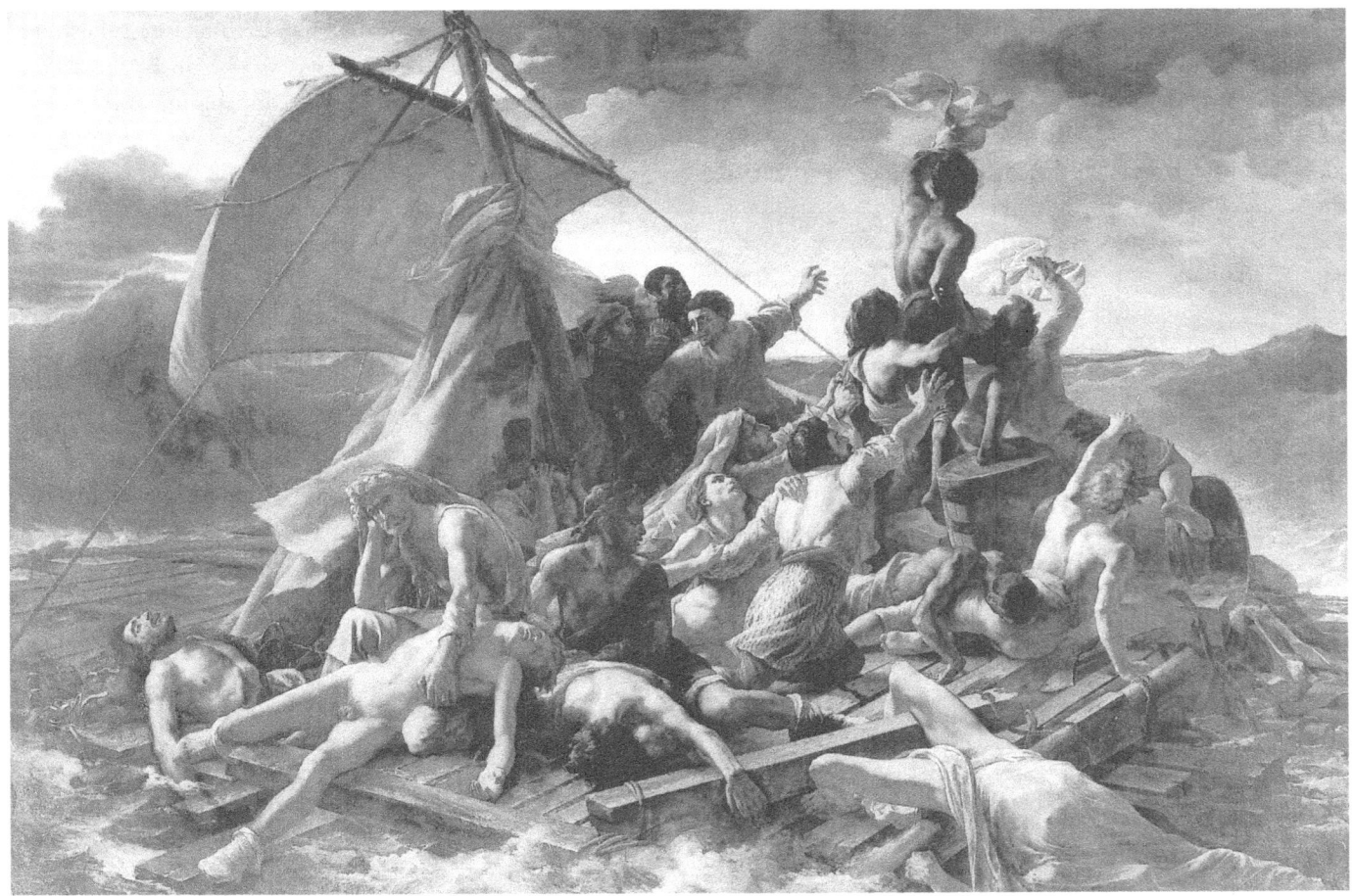

FIGURE 12.   Théodore Géricault, *The Raft of the Medusa*, 1819. Oil on canvas. Paris, Musée du Louvre, inv. INV 4884 (491 × 716 cm). Photo: © RMN/Art Resource, NY/© Daniel Arnaudet.

nal government. I have been accused by a certain *Drapeau blanc* of having slandered the entire Ministry of the Navy by the expression of one of the heads in my picture. The wretches who write such nonsense have certainly never gone without food for two weeks on end, otherwise they would realize that neither poetry nor painting can ever do justice to the horror and anguish of the men on the Raft.[71]

If very little of the graphic horrors of starvation appear in Géricault's picture, it is because his aim was to dramatize the psychological anguish of the survivors, not their physical suffering. His sarcasm about how the painting was read politically also makes clear that he knew well its potential to affect viewers, and that his subject lent itself to criticism of the Bourbon Restoration. So did the government: when printing the catalogue for the 1819 Salon, it did not allow Géricault to call his picture *The Raft of the Medusa*; rather, it was listed as *A Scene of Shipwreck*, although everyone knew perfectly well what could not be said in print.

It is but a small step to read the discouragement of those men on the raft who gesture wildly to a tiny ship on the horizon as an allegory of the nation itself: without a rudder, adrift at sea, perhaps even gesturing a frantic farewell to the ship that carried Napoléon into his last exile. Never had a nation risen so high, nor fallen so hard, as France between 1800 and 1819, and this weighed heavily on the minds and spirits of French men and women for the next several generations. Their discouragement, or *mal du siècle*, was much discussed and described by contemporaries. Géricault's own recent history—from Musketeer of the king to *habitué* of Horace Vernet's studio—was a kind of personal wandering on the sea of life shared by many of his countrymen.

Two minor details in the *Raft of the Medusa* allow us to link its enterprise of grand-scale painting to the expression of Géricault's more modest works from the same time. In the lower left corner lies a dead soldier, his head propped on a knapsack; near his hand we see a cartridge pouch and a shako. At the extreme right corner of the raft, almost swept into the water, is a soldier's cape decorated with gold epaulettes. Even if we grant that soldiers were amongst those on the raft, these identifiable items of military dress are oddly

anachronistic by their presence, their relatively good condition despite the chaos of the moment, and the way they anchor the extreme corners of the entire composition. We know the bearded man who posed for the dead soldier was named Gerfard, and that he was a veteran of Napoléon's Imperial Guard.[72] What were Géricault's thoughts while painting this veteran of the most elite corps of the imperial army—discharged and working as a model—in a picture that came increasingly to represent the plight of contemporary France? Among his fiercely Bonapartist friends and acquaintances from Vernet's studio, the answer would be clear: Gerfard had been humiliated by the Bourbon government, and so had the nation.

The extent to which Géricault shared a sentimental sympathy for the fate of the Grand Army is best illustrated by the *Return from Russia* (Fig. 13), one of the most moving lithographs he produced while planning and working on the *Raft of the Medusa*. The print was one of three that explored the stoic heroism of wounded soldiers left for dead when Napoléon's army collapsed in 1812.[73] These soldiers do not direct battles, but are the grist of warfare's mill; simple, ragged, and tenacious survivors very like those men who survived the ordeal of the *Medusa*. Here too Géricault invested his figures with a dignity in their suffering and a monumentality in their presentation: they are large in the image, visually isolated from the anecdotal context of the army in retreat, and seemingly oblivious to all but their immediate devotion to one another. The rider is blinded by his bandages and has one arm in a sling. His partner can see to lead the horse, but has lost an arm in combat. The one grips the reins tightly with his good hand while the other steadies himself by resting a glove on the shoulder of his companion. No words are exchanged, and none need be, for each knows that he can depend entirely upon the other in this moment of danger.

Although France breathed a collective sigh of relief at

FIGURE 13.   Théodore Géricault, *The Return from Russia*, 1818. Two-color lithograph. Paris, BnF, Estampes, inv. Dc 141b rés (1) (44.4 × 36.2 cm). Photo: BnF, Paris.

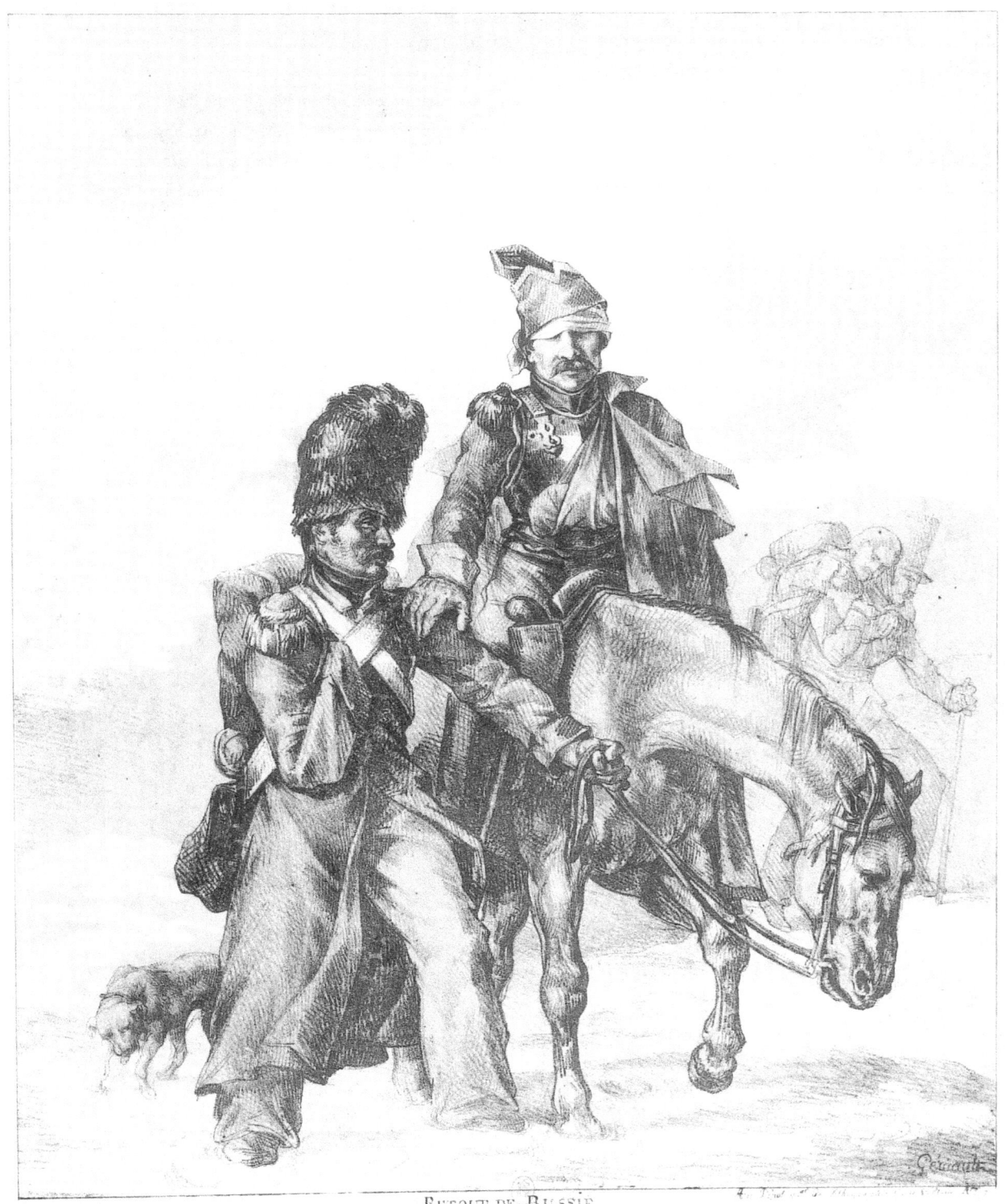

RETOUR DE RUSSIE

the end of Napoléon's wars, it was not long before the adventure of Empire was remembered as an age of lost greatness. In 1818, at the time that Géricault was producing his lithographs, Casimir Delavigne published a suite of poems called *Les Messéniennes*, whose title alluded to a thinly veiled allegory about the plight of France under Allied occupation. The book's first ode is about the death rattle of the imperial army—the battle of Waterloo—and contains a famous quatrain on the Imperial Guard:

One says that in seeing them lying in the dust,
With an afflicted respect impressed by so many exploits,
The enemy riveted his gaze on their warlike faces,
And saw them without fear for the very first time.[74]

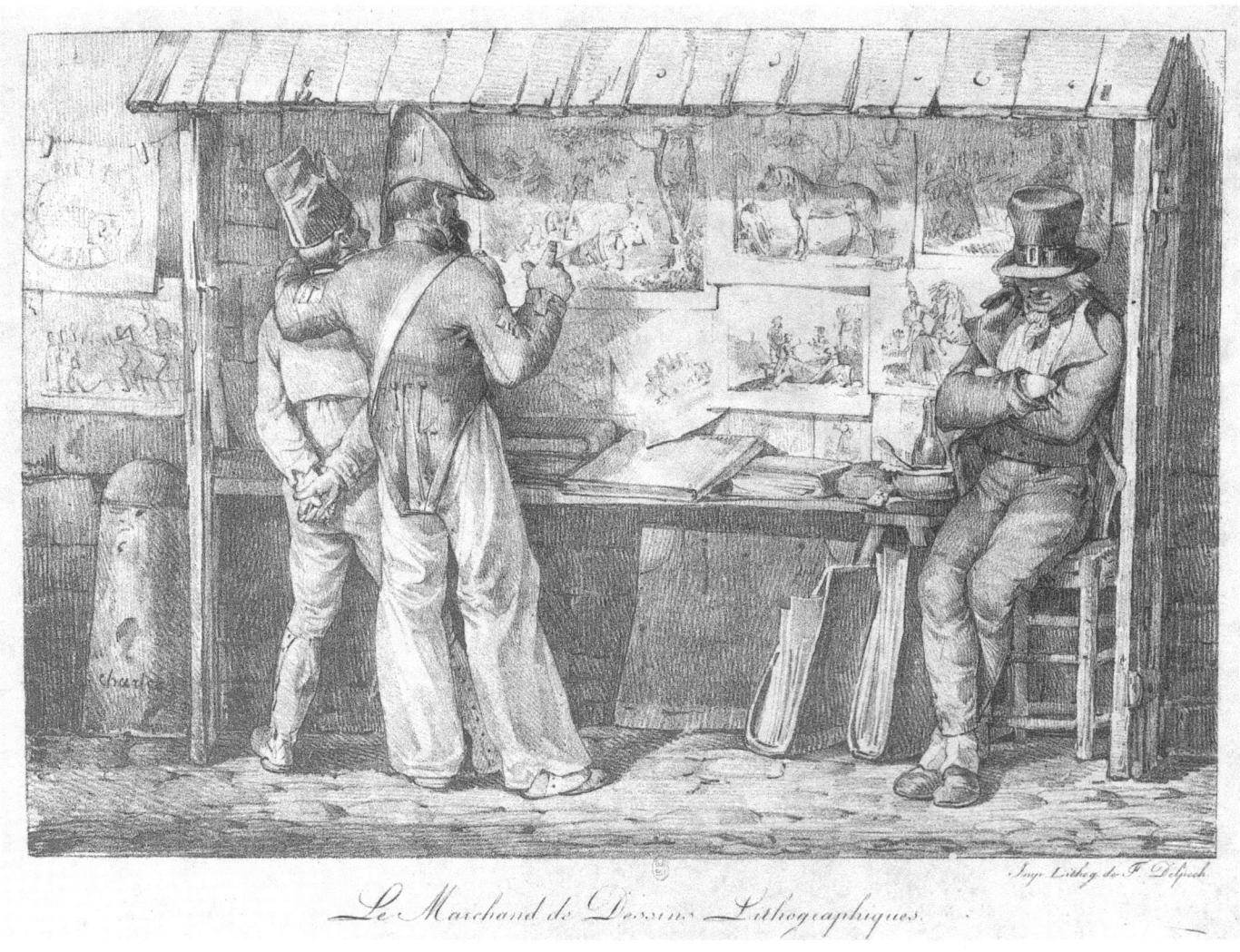

Le Marchand de Dessins Lithographiques.

FIGURE 14.   Nicolas-Toussaint Charlet, *The Seller of Lithographs*, ca. 1819. Lithograph. Paris, BnF, Estampes, inv. Dc 103k rés. Photo: BnF, Paris.

Delavigne's text was immensely popular. It was soon followed by many other manifestations of a sentimental and patriotic view of the common foot soldier who had carried the tricolor banner to the far corners of Europe: from the poems and songs of Pierre-Jean Béranger to the rowdy boulevard theaters of Paris, the painful memory of war and defeat became a mythic past of common glory.

To whom were the prints and lithographs, the songs and poems inspired by the Grand Army addressed? Obviously, to those many hundreds of thousands of veterans who returned to France, and their daily routines of city or country life, but for whom their exploits with Napoléon had been and would remain the great adventure of their lives. Charlet's lithograph of 1819 (Fig. 14), which actually depicts a seller of lithographs, speaks eloquently of the market for these images: an open-air stall with prints—mainly of horses and soldiers—tacked on the wall; thick folders of more prints to browse on the shelf; two soldiers—one old, the other young—looking, pointing, and talking about an image. They are discussing a lithograph by Horace Vernet that depicts some wounded French soldiers attacked by Cossacks during the retreat from Russia. Here is graphic evidence of how the experience of Empire acquired a second life in the realm of story, myth, and memory. The Napoleonic adventure remained a deep-rooted presence amongst ordinary people, one sufficiently potent for Napoléon's nephew—Louis-Napoléon Bonaparte—to be elected president of the Second Republic in December 1848 (see Epilogue).

DURING THE FIRST TWO DECADES of the nineteenth century governments and armies came and went, but Paris endured—a mute and elegant witness to the turmoil of revolution, conquest, and defeat. Yet the city was changed by these events in many different ways, for it was enlarged, embellished, and adapted to an emerging way of life that was both urban and modern. Through it all, and well into the second half of the century, the status and achievement of those years under Napoléon's rule—when Paris had been the capital of Europe—continued to haunt its painters, sculptors, and architects, and to inspire its composers, poets, and playwrights. Their story, and that of their city, is what follows.

CHAPTER 2

The City as Witness and Battlefield

Upon entering the Champs-Élysées I heard, to my great astonishment, the sounds of violins, horns, clarinets, and drums. I saw open-air cafés where men and women were dancing; further off, the Tuileries Palace appeared in the break between its two great clumps of chestnut trees. The place Louis XV was itself empty; it had the shabbiness, the melancholic and abandoned appearance of an old amphitheater. One passed it quickly; I was completely surprised not to hear wailing, and I was afraid of stepping in blood, although no trace of it actually remained. I could not take my eyes from the spot in the sky where the tool of death had been erected. I thought I saw my brother and sister-in-law, dressed in loose shirts and tied up near the bloodied machine: the head of Louis XVI had fallen there. In spite of the street's gaiety, the church towers were silent. I felt as though I had returned on a day of incredible sadness, a day like Good Friday.

—François-René de Chateaubriand[1]

CHATEAUBRIAND'S ACCOUNT of crossing the place de la Concorde in 1800, shortly after his return to Paris from self-imposed exile, was written in 1836, but it portrays vividly the troubled intersections of history and memory that were part and parcel of life in the city during the early years of the nineteenth century. On one hand, the city's great monuments, like the Tuileries Palace, were material signs of history—predictable, stable, and magnificently framed by the city itself. On the other, irrupting within the city's fabric without warning were the specters of memory left by the social upheaval of the Great Revolution: the stark machinery of the guillotine; the river of its victims' blood; the executioner's display of a severed head to the assembled throng. Pierre Nora's summary of the friction between the two primary processes of recovering the past—between memory and history—helps us to understand the underlying tension of Chateaubriand's commentary as it slips from description to hallucination:

Memory, history: far from being synonymous, we become aware that they are everywhere different. Memory is life, always sustained by living groups and, for this reason, is in a permanent state of evolution, open to the dialectic between remembering and forgetting, unconscious of its successive deformations, vulnerable to all kinds of uses and manipulations, susceptible to long periods of latency and to sudden revitalizations. History is the reconstruction, always problematic and partial, of what no longer is. Memory is a phenomenon that is always current, a lived link to the eternal present; history is a representation of the past.[2]

History and memory always coexist in the collective experience of a people, but these two projects were locked in an unusually intense struggle in Paris of the early nineteenth century, where former émigrés, former radical revolutionaries, and the many people who lived between those extreme political positions were forced to reconstruct the terms upon which they might once again live together. Nothing that had happened during the 1790s was so far in the past that it could be erased from one's consciousness, especially because many of the actors in the great social drama of the Revolution were still very much alive.

What had the Revolution meant? What had happened

to the nation since 1789? How did the Empire rise from the ashes of revolutionary fervor only to be swept away in its turn? These were the burning questions of the 1820s. Yet attempts to condemn or to whitewash events of the Revolution would have to square with the living memories of them, would be subject to challenge and correction, and would open the door to public debate and recriminations. It thus makes sense that the first comprehensive histories of the French Revolution were not written until the century's third decade. By contrast, the first two decades were marked by publications of personal memoirs, not so much to create a coherent history of the Revolution as to circulate myriad private memories and personal ruminations on what had happened. Alice Gérard summarizes the peculiar problem of writing the Revolution's history at this time:

With regard to the Revolution, whose memory was too virulent to be idealized, the first question was: how to acclimate it? Making documents accessible was one way in particular, and it was with the aim of calming tempers that Berville and Barrière undertook publication of the *Mémoires de la Révolution* (16 volumes from 1820 to 1826). From out of this synoptic confrontation, where the memoirs of the regicide Thibaudeau were next to those of Madame de la Rochejaquelein, truth would reemerge "the way learning follows from the mass of facts."[3]

Most of these memoirs tended to foreground events selectively in a process of self-justification that Pierre Nora's observation fully predicts. Their sheer number underscores the pressing cultural issue of how to reconcile the Revolution's moment of social rupture with a longer view of the nation's past and its historical continuity.

The conflicting aims of memory and history were also pitted against one another in and around the great monuments of Paris. Consider the Tuileries Palace seen by Chateaubriand from the place de la Concorde: at the time he returned to the capital it was the residence of Napoléon; eight years earlier it was where Louis XVI and Marie-Antoinette had been arrested; in 1814 it would be reoccupied by a Bourbon king, Louis XVIII; and, at the time Chateaubriand was writing (1836), the palace was home to King Louis-Philippe, himself installed by the Revolution of 1830. Despite its checkered history, the palace remained the seat of government and a fixture of the Parisian cityscape, both mute witness to political change and ever-present reminder that the nation's history—like its own—extended continuously across time. A similar geologic layering of events within the great monuments of Paris invested them with an aura of calm presence in the face of dramatic social ruptures. It gave them a special role in contemporary attempts to contextualize cataclysmic change. Thus Lady Morgan, writing from Paris in 1816 shortly after Napoléon's final defeat, was moved by a visit to the Tuileries to ponder how the monument's physical presence cut across and ultimately transcended political fortunes:

It was in the *Salle des Machines* of the Thuilleries, that Louis XIV celebrated many of his formal revelries, and danced, as *chef de ballet*, for the amusement of his court. It was there, also, that Voltaire was crowned, a short time before his death, at the representation of his own *Irene*. It was from its truly splendid chambers, that the unfortunate Louis XVI was dragged to the gloomy cells of the Temple;—there the National Convention held its assemblies;—there Robespierre resided during his reign of terror; and there Buonaparte dwelt, during the whole of his consular and imperial government.[4]

Ruminations of this sort are common in the literature of the time. They register the fact that during the opening decades of the nineteenth century the monuments of Paris were sites of ideological skirmishes between memory and history: much more than old stones in the city's fabric, they were the stuff of political legitimacy.

CHAPTER ONE sketched the contours of Napoléon's desire to bring the Revolution to a close. Part of his project included marshaling the immediate experience of military victory to displace—in a tide of nationalist pride—vestigial memories of the Revolution's factions and political infighting. It follows that a related strategy was at work in the way Napoléon used monuments to forge memories that would *shape* history, not simply challenge it. Perhaps the most striking example of this was the virtual monument erected for a triumphal entry into Paris with his second wife, Marie-Louise of Austria, on the day of their marriage (1 April 1810). Since the early days of the French monarchy, kings made ceremonial entries into Paris via the rue Saint-Denis, which was often decorated for such occasion with temporary triumphal arches (see Chapter Three). In the seventeenth century the Porte Saint-Denis—a permanent arch of triumph that commemorates the victories of Louis XIV along the Rhine—was erected at the city's limits to monumentalize the spot where arriving monarchs were greeted by the Paris town council (Fig. 42). Obviously Napoléon wanted to claim his place in this tradition of honorific entries into Paris, especially because his second marriage—politically arranged with an Austrian princess—was designed to bring a measure of bloodline legitimacy to his dynasty. But

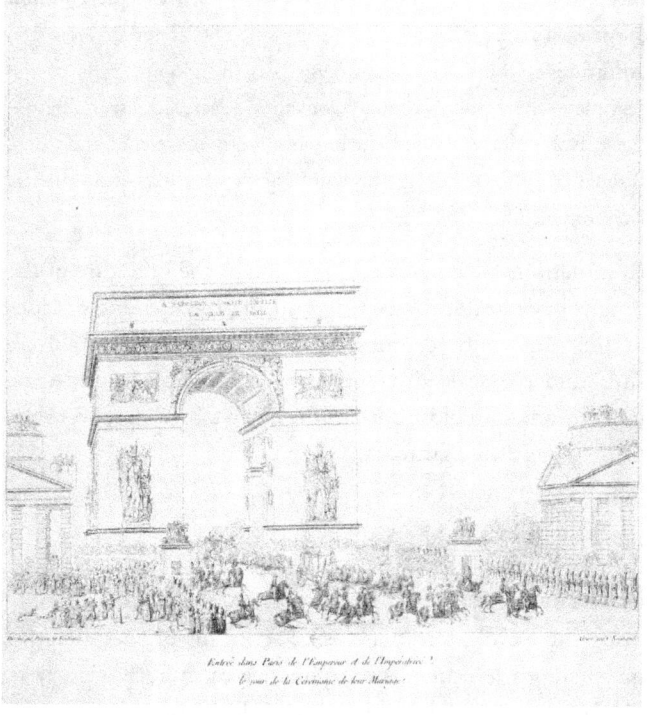

FIGURE 15.   Charles Percier and Pierre-François Léonard Fontaine (designers) and Charles Normand (engraver), *Entry into Paris of the Emperor and Empress on the Day of their Marriage, 1 April 1810*, 1810. Colored line engraving. Paris, BnF, Estampes, inv. Collection de Vinck, no. 8453 (28 × 28.5 cm). Photo: BnF, Paris.

it was equally clear that reusing the old rue Saint-Denis, and passing through the arch of Louis XIV, would not suffice, for the goal was not simply to appropriate emblems of the old monarchy but to surpass them in scope and grandeur.

Four years earlier, in 1806, Napoléon had imagined a colossal arch dedicated to the glories of the Grand Army for a site near the present-day place de la Bastille. By August of that year he had been persuaded to move the project to the far end of the Champs-Élysées at the Barrière de l'Étoile. Surely this would be a fitting gateway through which Napoléon and his new Empress might enter the city of Paris, but at the time of their marriage in 1810 work on the arch had progressed only to the point of laying the foundations. Under pressure to produce a symbolic entranceway where none existed, the project's architect, Jean-François-Thérèse Chalgrin, was forced to improvise: in the space of twenty days, and with a small army of more than five hundred workmen, he installed a full-scale, wood-frame and canvas facsimile of the projected arch.

An engraving from the official book of images designed by Charles Percier and Pierre-François-Léonard Fontaine to commemorate the imperial marriage, records the appearance of this ersatz structure (Fig. 15).[5] Contemporary witnesses in Paris for the wedding, such as Prince Charles de Clary-Aldringen of Austria, were duly impressed by the size and grandeur announced by the mock-up for the future monument: the prince realized the arch would be "the largest ever built" and admitted that it produced "a superb effect in every sense."[6] The point is that Napoléon wanted to ensure a great arch was part of the event's official history, which meant adjusting memories to include the monument years before its completion. Imagine if Percier and Fontaine had rendered an arch in their print when none existed: one might say the image practiced an appropriate political flattery, but that its representation was not historical. Chalgrin's stage-set mock-up of the *unfinished* monument meant that even unofficial images of the marriage would be obliged to include the arch if they claimed to offer a true account of the day. In this case, Napoléon staged memory in order to fix history: when work on the arch was finally complete, the wedding ceremony of 1810 was already part of its archeology of remembered events.

Napoléon's plans for the great triumphal arch were ultimately foiled by the fortunes of war. The main pillars of the structure stood only twenty meters high when he was forced to leave France in defeat, and the restored Bourbons showed little interest in working on a monument dedicated to the glory of their political nemesis. In 1823 Louis XVIII decided to complete the arch in honor of recent French military support for the king of Spain, but the project became bogged down in an argument among several architects as to whether one should follow Napoléon's original plans or make significant—and costly—changes to them. Although work progressed slowly during the 1820s, it was only after 1832, under King Louis-Philippe, that the sculptural program was given the form we know today. The final project's symbolism was significantly reworked, so that Louis-Philippe's conciliatory gesture of finishing the Empire's business actually became a battle for its monuments and their historical meaning (see Chapter Three).

When the Bourbon kings returned to power in France they were keen to reclaim for themselves monuments of the old, pre-revolutionary monarchy. In May of 1814 Louis XVIII consciously emulated his ancestors by reentering Paris—after twenty-three years of exile—via the Porte Saint-Denis. He followed the traditional route from the abbey of Saint-Denis (where the kings of France were buried) to Paris, thus claiming the triumphal arch of Louis XIV as his own. It is curious that an etching by Jean Duplessis-Berteaux (Fig. 16) records the day by nearly losing the king's carriage (at the lower center of the image) amidst a crowd of horsemen and spectators. What seems most important to the maker of this seemingly objective print was the looming presence of the arch itself—through which the cortège has just passed—and a view beyond of that uniquely Parisian landscape, the boulevard. The print seems to say subliminally to its viewers: Paris endures, and will ultimately transcend, the politics of a given moment.

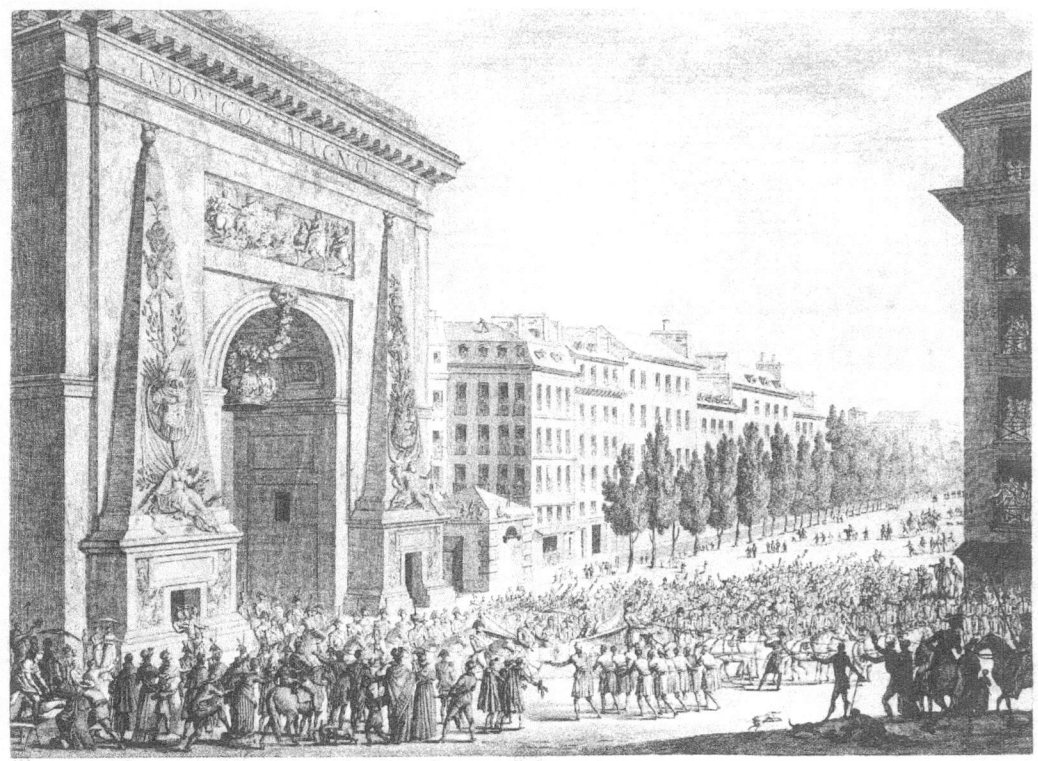

FIGURE 16. Jean Duplessis-Berteaux, *Entry of Louis XVIII into Paris through the Porte Saint-Denis, 3 May 1814*, 1814. Etching. Paris, BnF, Estampes, inv. Collection de Vinck, no. 9104 (23.7 × 32.2 cm). Photo: BnF, Paris.

Similarly, the entry into Paris of Charles X on 6 June 1825, as painted by Louis-François Lejeune (Fig. 17), situates us at the Barrière de la Villette—a locale specified by a glimpse, at the far right, of the eighteenth-century customs house designed by Claude-Nicolas Ledoux. Charles, who was Ultra-royalist well before his accession, insisted on being crowned and anointed in the manner of pre-revolutionary France with a religious ceremony at the cathedral of Reims. Guillaume de Bertier de Sauvigny, an historian generally favorable to the Restoration's legacy, remarks that "changes in the details of the ceremonies could not surmount the essential fact . . . this was the resurrection of the Old Regime in one of its most archaic forms and one most charged with religious significance."[7] In Lejeune's picture the royal carriage has just passed beneath a ceremonial canopy erected between a toll gate of the old Farmers-General wall, an enclosure originally built around Paris to facilitate the collection of taxes levied on goods entering the city. The eleven-foot continuous wall and its starkly massive toll houses were the most unpopular public projects of the 1780s and were, in the words of Anthony Vidler,

inextricably joined, in conception and realization, with the fate of the *ancien régime*. Erected in its last years, in secrecy and haste, they were inevitably seen as the visible emblems of fiscal tyranny, the overblown signs of the despised Ferme Générale; their monumentality and strange forms, exaggerating traditional architectural motifs in scale and placement to the point of caricature, seemed apt demonstrations of economic profligacy.[8]

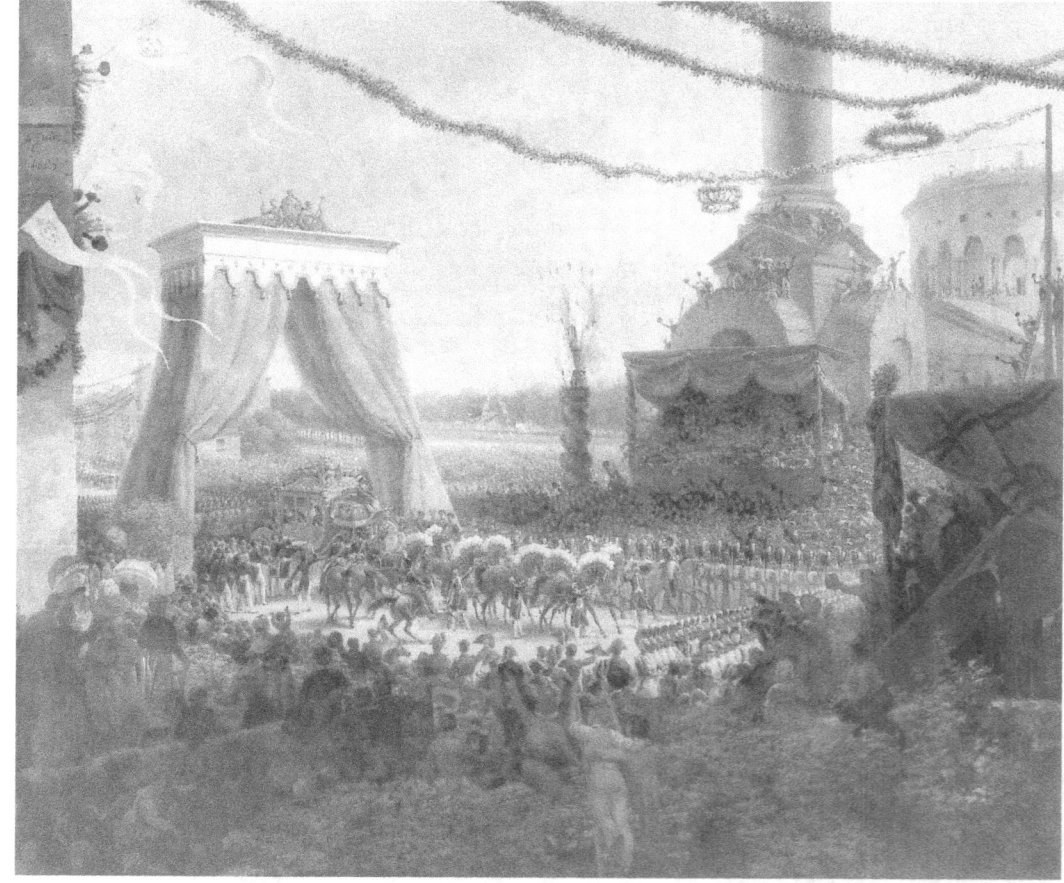

FIGURE 17. Louis-François Lejeune, *Entry of Charles X into Paris through the Barrière de la Villette, after his Consecration at Reims, 6 June 1825*, 1825. Oil on canvas. Versailles, Châteaux de Versailles et de Trianon, inv. MV1794 (154 × 179 cm). Photo: © RMN/Art Resource, NY/© Daniel Arnaudet.

Lejeune's picture includes an enormous column atop Ledoux's gatehouse that was never part of the original structure, perhaps to heighten the visual monumentality of the setting or to suggest the massive columns built by Ledoux for the toll gate on the road from Vincennes at the place known as the Barrière du Trone.[9] By prominently situating Charles's entry among such monuments, by alluding to the tax system that was part of daily life in pre-revolutionary Paris, and by recalling implicitly the royal privileges of its operation, Lejeune's picture of Charles X aligns the new king with a notorious past and its prerogatives. The painting encodes visually what everyone understood in 1825: Charles simply wanted to forget that the Revolution had occurred.

Thus, images that seem on the surface to be little more than "illustrations" of contemporary events actually deploy a visual rhetoric of historical interest. Do the three works (Figs. 15, 16, and 17) share qualities that could be called specifically *Parisian*? What are some of their common formal devices, in spite of their diverging politics? Each work massively displaces the principal narrative to represent the space, scale, and specificity of a monument (or, in the case of Napoléon's marriage, a future monument). In each image the fleeting and temporal passage of a miniscule cortège is witnessed by an imposing, highly detailed, seemingly permanent architectural presence. Finally, each image positions the viewer not on the street as an eyewitness, but above it; sharing the space, so to speak, of the monuments themselves. Our looking at the stories of each image mimics the way monuments witness the moment depicted. The visual rhetoric deployed in these works sublimates the fleeting, personal, lived experience of the event beneath a stable, public, and densely layered gaze of the monument. To return to the terms of Pierre Nora: each image transforms the shifting flux of eyewitness memories into the repeatable register of official history.

Unlike written histories, where the presence of monuments must be evoked or described in language, visual representations bridge the time difference between an event and its retelling in a unique and powerful way: the Porte Saint-Denis, for example, still exists in Paris. Seeing an image of Louis XVIII beneath that arch has a peculiar grip on us—even more than a century later—if we have actually visited

and experienced first-hand the monument's physical materiality. More than simple illustrations of the past, works of this type are visual documents that fuse a past event to contemporary life with a tight bond for those who inhabit the city and know it intimately. That a huge traffic in visual documents of this sort existed in Paris during the early decades of the nineteenth century comes as no surprise, for it was by and through such documents that the political drama sketched in Chapter One was symbolically reworked. With good reason, Maurice Agulhon describes the period as "a veritable civil war" in which

[a] series of political and—even more—philosophical battles unfolded in a climate still naïve, meaning a climate where political passion was less attenuated by a skepticism and relativism informed by a long history than today; a climate, as a result, in which the struggle over signs and symbols had an importance that we can hardly imagine. In short, a century of combating ideas where, among other forms of striking and emphatic propaganda destined to a new and rather simple public, a figurative and monumental didacticism was intensively employed.[10]

Agulhon's point helps us to appreciate how images about current events, a bit like television coverage today, both reported and shaped the news. If only for this reason we should attend to how the monuments and spaces of Paris were rendered in visual documents; doing so allows us to discover one of the principal arenas—amidst a shifting and uncertain political field—where battles for the minds and allegiances of Parisians were fought.

EXAMPLES FROM THE GREAT SWIRL of images that related and shaped the events of early nineteenth-century Paris provoke a few generalizations. The first is that newcomers to the political arena seemed compelled to legitimize their rise to power by invoking the monuments and spaces of history. Thus, a picture by Horace Vernet (Fig. 18) of Louis-Philippe d'Orléans on 31 July 1830—the day he was named caretaker of the throne after seventy-two hours of fighting in Paris—shows the duke starting a ride across town from his family

FIGURE 18.   Horace Vernet,
*The duc d'Orléans leaves
the Palais-Royal en route to
the Hôtel-de-Ville, 31 July
1830*, 1833. Oil on canvas.
Versailles, Châteaux de
Versailles et de Trianon, inv.
MV5185 (228 × 258 cm).
Photo: © RMN/Art
Resource, NY/© Gérard
Blot.

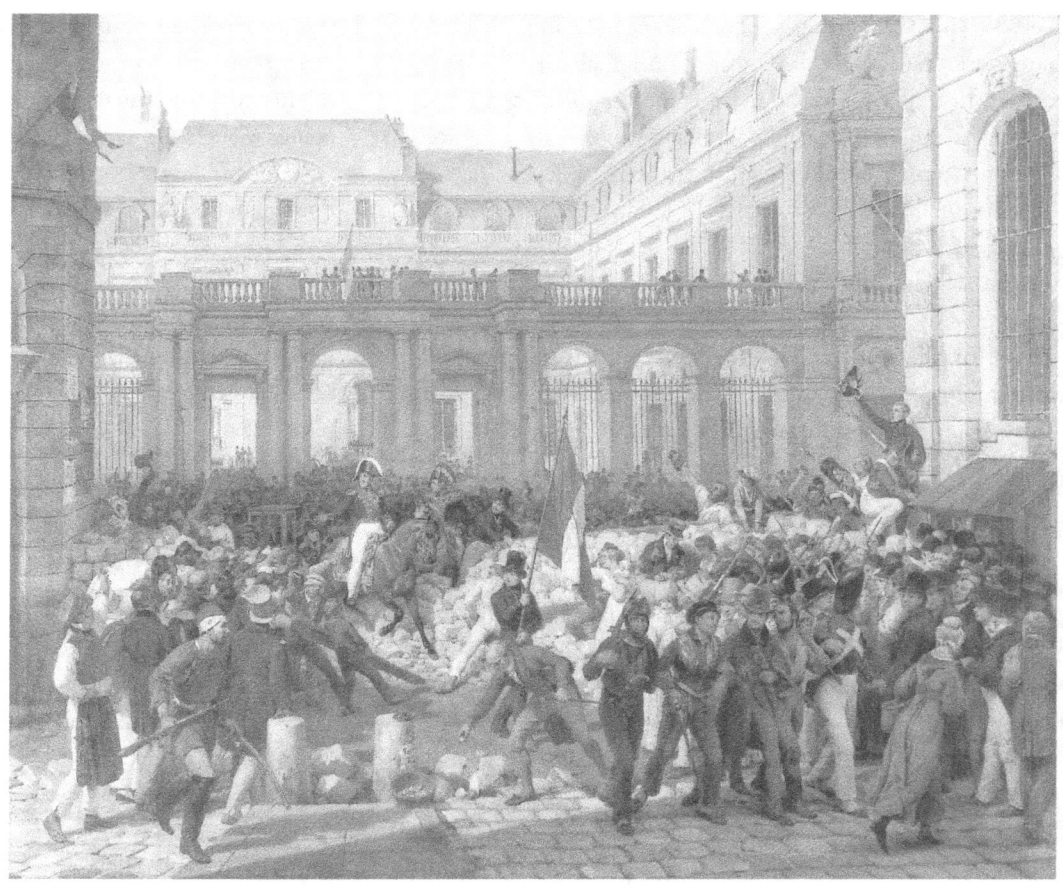

home (the Palais-Royal) to the Paris town hall (Hôtel-de-Ville). The principal action is again a cortège through the cityscape, while a major Parisian landmark, which was both the duke's ancestral home and a key monument in the history of Paris, fills the background. We again view the event from a slightly elevated vantage point, which tends to ally us psychologically with the city's facades rather than its cheering citizens. The duke's horse, gingerly picking its way across a barricade of paving stones torn from the roadbed, performs a gesture that signals the end of civil strife. The picture effects a complex mediation between the political newcomer, who seems to conquer a crisis that had literally torn the city apart, and viewers, who watch from front-row seats but remain offstage, part of a cityscape that seems to accept without question or emotion the turn of events. Critics who wrote about Vernet's picture at the Salon of 1833 often deplored this effect; witness the words of Gustave Planche:

Our memories of thirty months ago, still so fresh, so robust, so alive, as if the exile of a dynasty had occurred only yesterday; the image of dust-covered bloodstains; the ill-will that disappeared in a common and sympathetic hope: all of that is still so present. What has he made of it all? . . . [Vernet] can continue this kind of unhappy parody of our public events for many more years, but we will not give up our right to say publicly that he travesties them.[11]

Planche decried the picture's tendency to normalize the revolution by positioning the newcomer as simply the latest actor to play in the theater of history called Paris.

A slightly different visual strategy was deployed in a print (Fig. 19) inspired by an episode from the short-lived

Second Republic, itself founded by yet another revolution (February 1848) that forced Louis-Philippe to flee France for exile in England. In December 1848, against a background of the general confusion and competing politics of this fragile, fledgling democracy (including eruptions of violent civil unrest recorded in Fig. 27), a man with a famous name was elected president: Louis-Napoléon Bonaparte, nephew of the great emperor (see Epilogue). The print depicts the new chief executive traversing the boulevards in June of 1849, when Paris was in the grips of a cholera epidemic, and when Bonaparte's political opponents—mainly on the far Left—were challenging his administration with public demonstrations. True, the opposition was fueled by signs that Bonaparte was growing impatient with legislative democracy and planning a coup-d'état. Many people feared that Bonaparte resembled his uncle a bit too much. On the evening of 13 June, after a day of street demonstrations that saw protesters skirmish with the army and the arrest of several opposition leaders, Louis-Napoléon decided to test his popularity by riding through the city. He was rewarded by a generally warm reception. The print expends much energy to convince us of this public-relations victory by showing Bonaparte receiving the acclaim of a heterogeneous crowd comprised of men and women, workers in aprons alongside bourgeois in coats and top hats, soldiers and children. Unlike Vernet's earlier picture of Louis-Philippe, however, this image places us at street level, as if a participant in its cross section of ages and social classes, sharing the crowd's enthusiasm for its president, and looking up admiringly at Bonaparte as he passes. It is no accident that the viewer also glimpses, in the background behind Bonaparte, the Vendôme Column, a monument erected by the first Napoléon to the glory of his army and capped by a statue of the Emperor himself.[12] The print invites us to associate Louis-Napoléon Bonaparte with his uncle, and it appeals directly to the personal memories of those who had served the nation during the heady days of Empire.

This visual rhetoric, including the somewhat literal ploy of constructing our point of view from within the crowd, makes sense for an image designed to illustrate a popular and sympathetic biography of Louis-Napoléon Bonaparte published in 1853.[13] That is, two years after the president had engineered a successful coup-d'état that ended the Second Republic's experiment with democracy, established an authoritarian government, and prepared the way for Bonaparte's eventual installation as emperor. The print reconstructs a myth of social approbation for the president, restating visually the argument used in December 1851 to justify his usurping of the legisla-

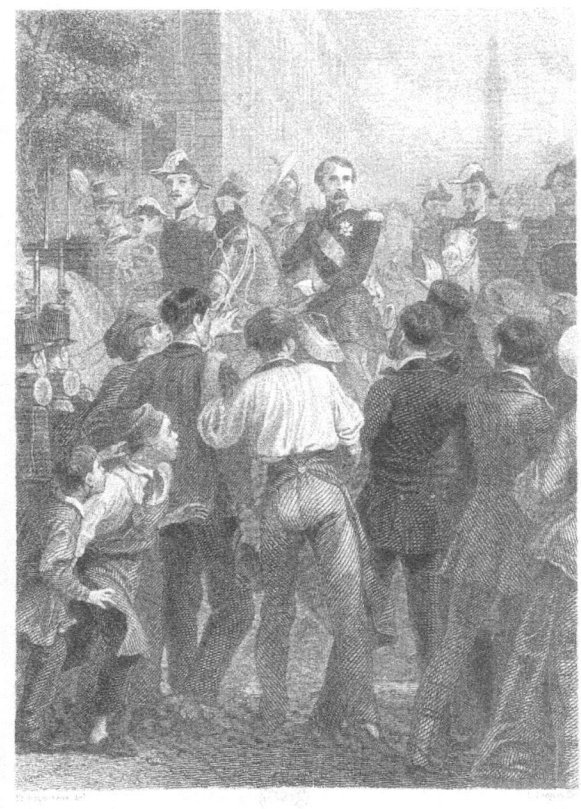

FIGURE 19.   Henri-Félix-Emmanuel Philippoteaux (designer) and E. Leguay (engraver), *Louis-Napoléon Bonaparte traversing the Boulevards of Paris, 13 June 1849*, ca. 1853. Steelplate engraving. Paris, BnF, Estampes, inv. Collection de Vinck, no. 15576 (13.9 × 9.9 cm). Photo: BnF, Paris.

ture's power. The point is not simply to underscore the skewed and self-serving version of history fabricated by this image, but to draw attention to the way its story is literally backed up by the presence of Bonaparte's famous and ever more mythic uncle atop the Vendôme Column. This rather humble visual document enlists the cachet of a well-known Parisian monument when attempting to displace contemporary memories of a sordid coup-d'état with the prestige of a glorious history.

A SECOND WAY OF SEEING how the spaces of Paris became implicated in the struggle between memory and history can be sketched in a sequence of images of public gatherings—staged over the course of several decades—on the Champ-de-Mars. This large open area between the École Militaire and the Seine, best known today as the site of the Eiffel Tower, was originally a parade ground for the military academy. It was the single most important ceremonial space in the early phase of the French Revolution: the outdoor theater for the

Festival of the Federation of 14 July 1790 where Louis XVI swore to uphold the constitutional monarchy (Fig. 20). Three years later, as if to physically displace memories of that early, monarchic phase of the revolution, a Festival of Reunion (10 August 1793) was held in Paris to mark the one-year anniversary of dissolving the monarchy. It culminated on the Champ-de-Mars with a collective public oath to uphold the new constitution. The following year, and in the same locale, Maximilien Robespierre—principal architect of the Terror's rule by guillotine—presided over a Festival of the Supreme Being (8 June 1794), where he declared the social utility of a new cult that would counter both atheism and traditional religions (Fig. 21).

The Champ-de-Mars was invested with tremendous symbolic and political capital by this string of revolutionary festivals. It was inevitable that the one person who had the most to gain by neutralizing such memories wasted no time appropriating the locale's symbolic value. Napoléon was crowned Emperor in the cathedral of Notre-Dame, but on the cold and rainy day of 5 December 1804 a new oath

FIGURE 20. Charles Thévenin, *Fête de la Fédération au Champ-de-Mars, 14 July 1790*, 1792. Oil on canvas. Paris, Musée Carnavalet, inv. P 2342 (127 × 183 cm). Photo: © PMVP/ Andreani.

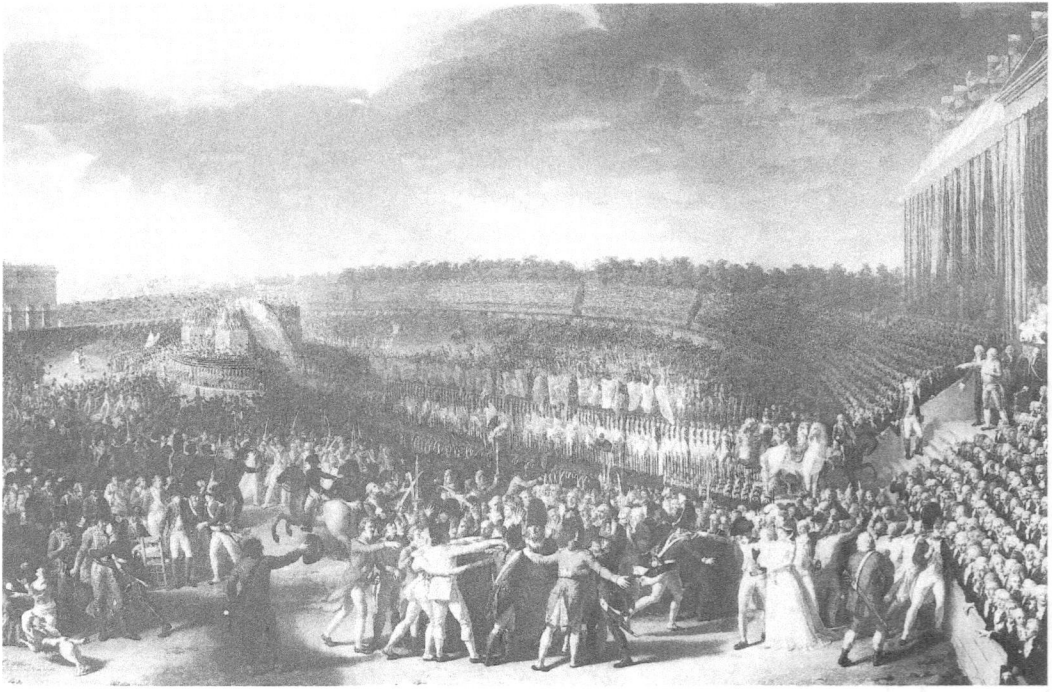

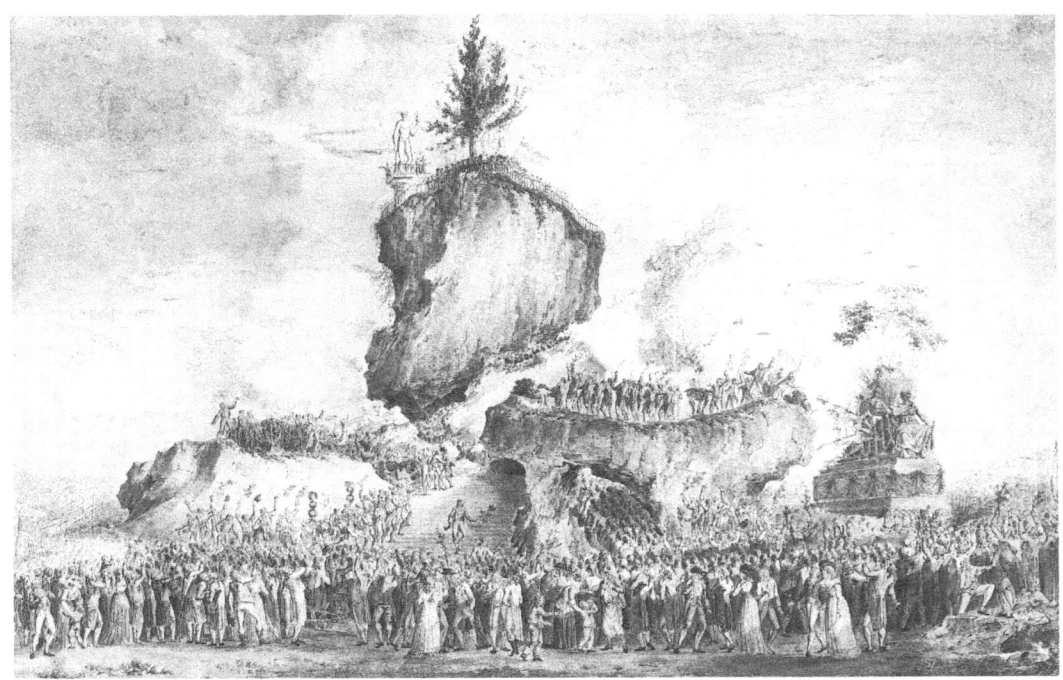

FIGURE 21.   Thomas-
Charles Naudet, *Fête de
l'Etre Suprême au Champ-
de-Mars, 20 Prairial II*, 1794.
Gouache and pastel. Paris,
Musée Carnavalet, inv.
D 05976 (47 × 73 cm). Photo:
© PMVP/Ladet.

was spoken on the Champ-de-Mars. This time, the French army pledged its loyalty to the Emperor and he, in turn, distributed the banners and eagles they swore to defend until death.[14] Far from collective dedication to fraternity and a republican constitution, far even from the half-hearted pledge of Louis XVI to support a constitutional monarchy, Napoléon's ceremony was designed to cement absolute dedication and subservience of the armies to their unquestioned leader and, parenthetically, to cleanse the space of its revolutionary past.

The irony in all of this is that while working on an enormous picture destined to commemorate the army's oath (Fig. 22), Jacques-Louis David could not have forgotten that he had orchestrated most of those earlier venues on the Champ-de-Mars. He had invented allegories for the Republic in 1793 and 1794, and was now painting the embodiment of their demise. It is, at first glance, astonishing to think that the same individual could have passed so easily from serving the Revolution to glorifying the Emperor, but David's trajectory was neither a straight line nor unique (see Chapter One). Part of the continuing historical interest in these years depends exactly upon the complexities and contradictions that riddled public life. David's passage from one regime to another did, in fact, leave material traces that register his private moments of doubt and self-reflection. Consider an almost-invisible detail in his picture of the army's oath to Napoléon: in the lower right corner of the image, between the gesturing figure of an Imperial Guardsman wearing a busby and the officer just above him on the stairs, we see through to the background and glimpse the upper body of a hatless soldier. The plumed hat dropped on the stairs just below this half-figure might even be a laconic visual clue left by David so that viewers would eventually take note of the man himself. What is this soldier doing? Against the grain of the army's clamor to climb the stairs toward Napoléon and the crowded display of their imperial standards, this man *descends* the stairs with a flag draped over his shoulder. Looking closely at his half-furled banner, we discover it is unlike all the others we see, for it is emblazoned with the words RÉPUBLIQUE FRANÇAISE. It is not a banner of Empire

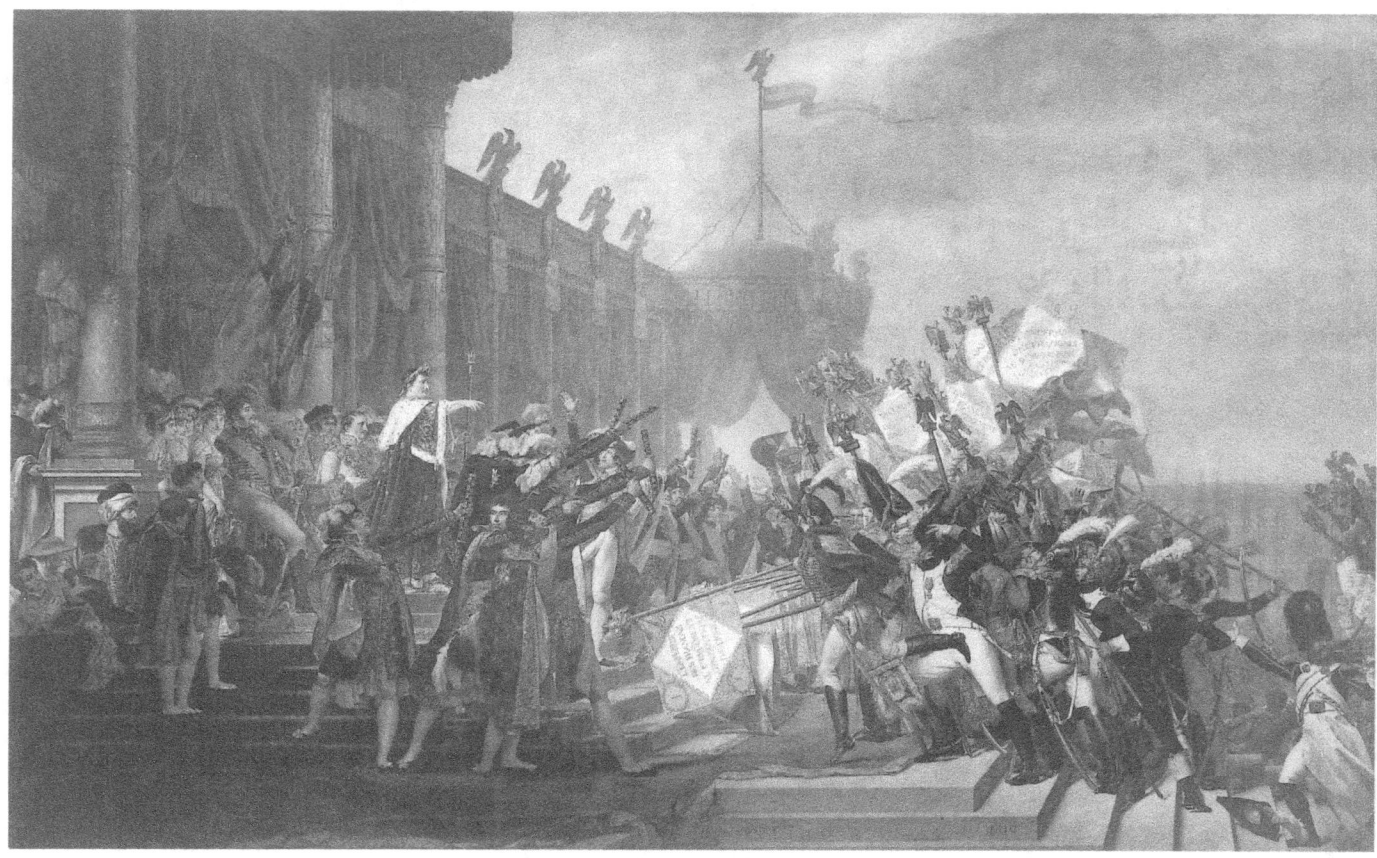

FIGURE 22.   Jacques-Louis David, *Oath of the Army to the Emperor Napoléon after the Distribution of Eagles on the Champ-de-Mars, 5 December 1804*, 1810. Oil on canvas. Versailles, Châteaux de Versailles et de Trianon, inv. MV2278 (610 × 931 cm). Photo: © RMN/Art Resource, NY/© Droits réservés.

but a tricolor flag of the old Revolution, a relic of those earlier gatherings on the Champ-de-Mars, and evidence that David could not completely forget his past. It is a material trace of the struggle between history and memory that gripped virtually every adult Parisian during these years, and a small reassurance that the renowned painter was—after all—only human.

There are other signs of David's personal struggle with the subject of this large canvas, including the very obvious fact that the picture cannot be read as an actual scene. It is not possible for so many massive bodies to be crowded into such a shallow sliver of space, nor do humans defy gravity

so effortlessly as does the figure at the top of the stairs who remains poised in forward motion on a single tip-toe. These internal contradictions were not lost on critics at the Salon of 1810, including François Guizot:

Once again we seem to encounter here [among the pictures of our most eminent painters] the influence on our school of studying sculpture. Our painters are used to studying statues of isolated figures but they too often ignore the art of grouping and placing them in space: their eyes are better at judging forms than distances and the effects of natural atmosphere. They have learned how to study each figure separately but, when they must bring together a large number of figures in a single place, their pictures remain marked by this piecemeal way of working. In general, they pass too quickly from the front planes to the background: look, for instance, at the picture by Girodet where, beyond the fourth spatial plane there is virtually no perspective; look, especially, at the figure of a sapper in the painting by David that represents the *Oath of the army after distribution of the eagles*. According to the picture's spatial gradations, the arm of this figure is more than six feet long. It seems clear that the painter, after having drawn his sapper in isolation, forgot to adjust him relative to those all around.[15]

Two things must be said about Guizot's observations. First, whether or not he is correct about the exact cause of the spatial trouble in David's picture, he is right to sense the visual tension between a great number of figures and a spatial box too small to hold them. The second concerns the way Guizot joins his discussion of the David to Girodet's *Revolt of Cairo* (Fig. 10). Recalling the conflicting facts and pictorial stress evident in that picture leads us to conclude that a related kind of stress—personal rather than historiographic—informs the strange visual configuration of David's *Oath of the Army*. In David's case, this clash pitted the artist against his own past: on one hand, as participant and shaper of the Revolution's historical legacy at the Champ-de-Mars; on the other, as painter working to liquidate that heritage in the visual glamour of Empire. While painting the army's oath David could not have ignored the flood of personal memories that wanted to keep the picture from happening—a secret reluctance to describe an event on the Champ-de-Mars that negated *by its very presence* a bit of himself. The odd, almost invisible appearance of the old order in this impossible space—that tricolor marked RÉPUBLIQUE FRANÇAISE—is material evidence of David's internal struggle and a clue to understanding the work's hallucinatory structure.

As in so many areas of public life, the scale and pageantry of Napoléon's symbolic appropriation of the Champ-de-Mars tended to overshadow its use well into the mid-nineteenth century. This was especially true during the months of the first Bourbon Restoration (1814–1815). Although the leading Bourbon princes—the comte d'Artois, the duc de Berry, and the duc d'Angoulême—staged regular military reviews to nudge the army's allegiance from Napoléon-in-exile to the new political order, Louis XVIII was reluctant to risk embarrassment before a hostile army corps. Germain Bazin's extensive search of the military archives in Paris uncovered only three occasions—twice in 1814 and once in 1816—when Louis met his army on the Champ-de-Mars, one of which inspired a splendid watercolor study by Théodore Géricault (Fig. 23). According to Bazin, and based on a detailed list of the review's components made by Géricault himself, the drawing represents a ceremony of 19 September 1814 when Louis XVIII distributed banners to the army's First Division.[16] If Bazin's date is correct (and it seems to be), it means that Géricault produced his watercolor when he was himself a member of the Royal Musketeers (see Chapter One). Since his military career suggests he might be interested to put a good gloss on the ceremony, we can ask: does his image meet the challenge?

A program for the activities of 19 September published in *Le Moniteur*, newspaper of record in Paris, stipulates that near the end of the ceremony "the general staff will execute a volte-face and will range itself in battle order facing the king while the regiments march past."[17] To judge from the animated disorder of the horses at the left of Géricault's picture, and from the riders who salute the king with sabers drawn, it was this final gesture that attracted the artist's interest. Louis is seated on the steps of the École Militaire, a posture dictated as much by his obesity and physical infirmities as by royal decorum. He is accompanied by his niece, the duchesse d'Angoulême, along with a contingent of officers. The king's carriage waits to the left of the porch.

The architecture of the École Militaire was apparently not drawn by Géricault himself, but was executed—according to the work's first owner—by someone with the expertise and patience for rendering the facades in correct perspective. Géricault was responsible for the tangle of riders at the left and the tentative placement of figures on the stairs. He apparently never attempted a more monumental or inclusive rendering of the day.[18] Amidst the riders that interested him are men wearing uniforms of several different regiments: hussars led by the duc d'Orléans, who is pictured in the left

FIGURE 23.   Théodore Géricault, *Review of Troops by Louis XVIII on the Champ-de-Mars*, ca. 1814. Pencil, pen and brown ink, with watercolor. Paris, Musée du Louvre, Département des Arts Graphiques, inv. RF1396 (28.8 × 35.5 cm). Photo: © RMN/Art Resource, NY/© Michèle Bellot.

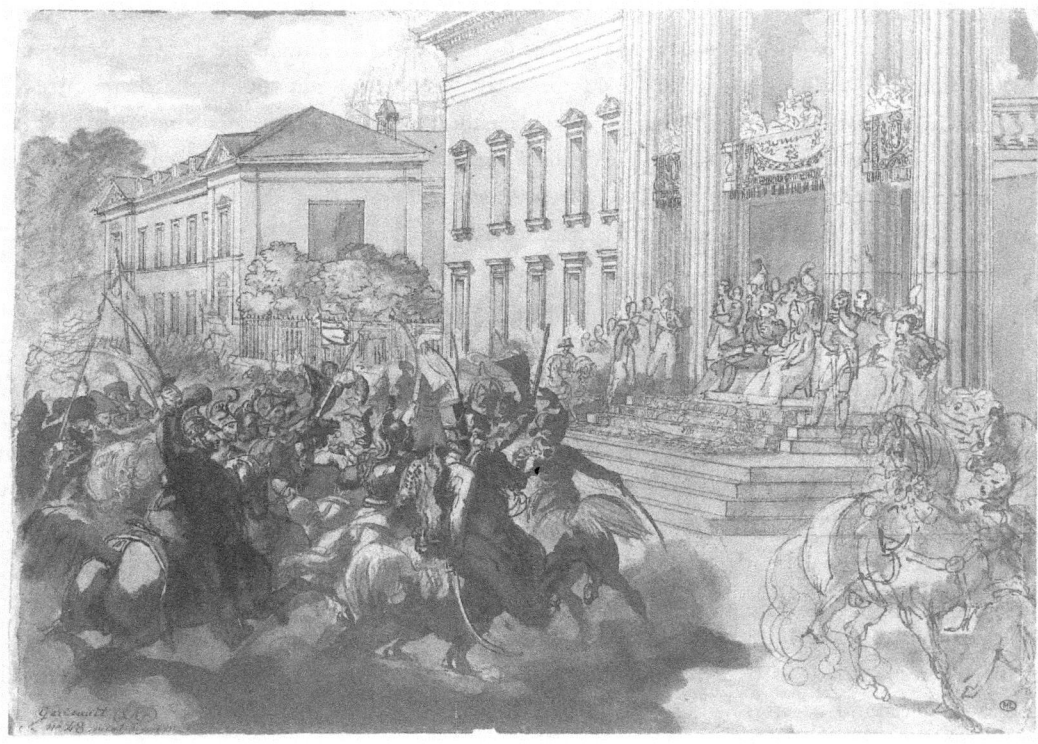

foreground; light cavalry lancers from the regiment led by the duc de Berry; light cavalry soldiers and Dutch lancers from the disbanded Imperial Guard of Napoléon. These last two are important to note, for Louis XVIII began his reign by keeping some of the elite corps of Napoléon's army on active duty. Later, after virtually all of these soldiers went over to Napoléon's side during the Hundred Days, Louis and his advisors realized their mistake: when the Bourbons returned after Waterloo the army was purged of all suspected Napoleonic sympathizers.

It is significant that Géricault focused most of his interest and attention on these groups of commingled soldiers. He spent relatively little time thinking about how to render the king, and he left the monuments to be drawn by someone else. The moment he describes is not when the king presented the army with its banners, but the end of the ceremony. Louis is about to turn his back on this display of excited camaraderie by a heterogeneous group of riders

that verges on chaos and disorder. Géricault seems not to believe that the Bourbon Restoration was about to reclaim the Champ-de-Mars from its Napoleonic past, for that symbolic space is almost incidental to his image. Rather, he seems keen to suggest that men of different histories will forge a new national solidarity from the broken remains of Empire—exactly the kind of experiment he was living out by joining the Royal Musketeers. Yet Géricault must also have sensed in September 1814 that the final act of the nation's drama had not yet been scripted: his project to paint a major picture remained unfinished, and most of the Napoleonic veterans in his watercolor would welcome the Emperor's return to France in March of 1815.

It was only much later, on 29 August 1830, that a real attempt was made to recapture the symbolism of the Champ-de-Mars for a new national agenda. On that day King Louis-Philippe (Fig. 24), ironically the same duc d'Orléans who figures prominently in the foreground of Géricault's watercolor, distributed standards to a new military force dedicated to domestic peace: the citizen-soldiers of the National Guard, who were regularly called up to do battle with rioters in the streets of Paris. Joseph-Désiré Court's picture registers the important role of ordinary citizens in this corps by placing the viewer in close proximity to the king, standing under the tent erected in the middle of the Champs-de-Mars. Eugène Delacroix, decked out in his new uniform of the National Guard, was among the participants that day. He

wrote an enthusiastic letter to his nephew about his experience of the collective energy:

At the review on Sunday 29 August there were already more than fifty thousand armed and newly equipped men, both infantry and cavalry, and it was really one of the most magnificent spectacles you could imagine. . . . In addition to the king's sincerity, of which everyone is convinced, the general situation will be protected by the truly admirable discipline and order of the National Guard.[19]

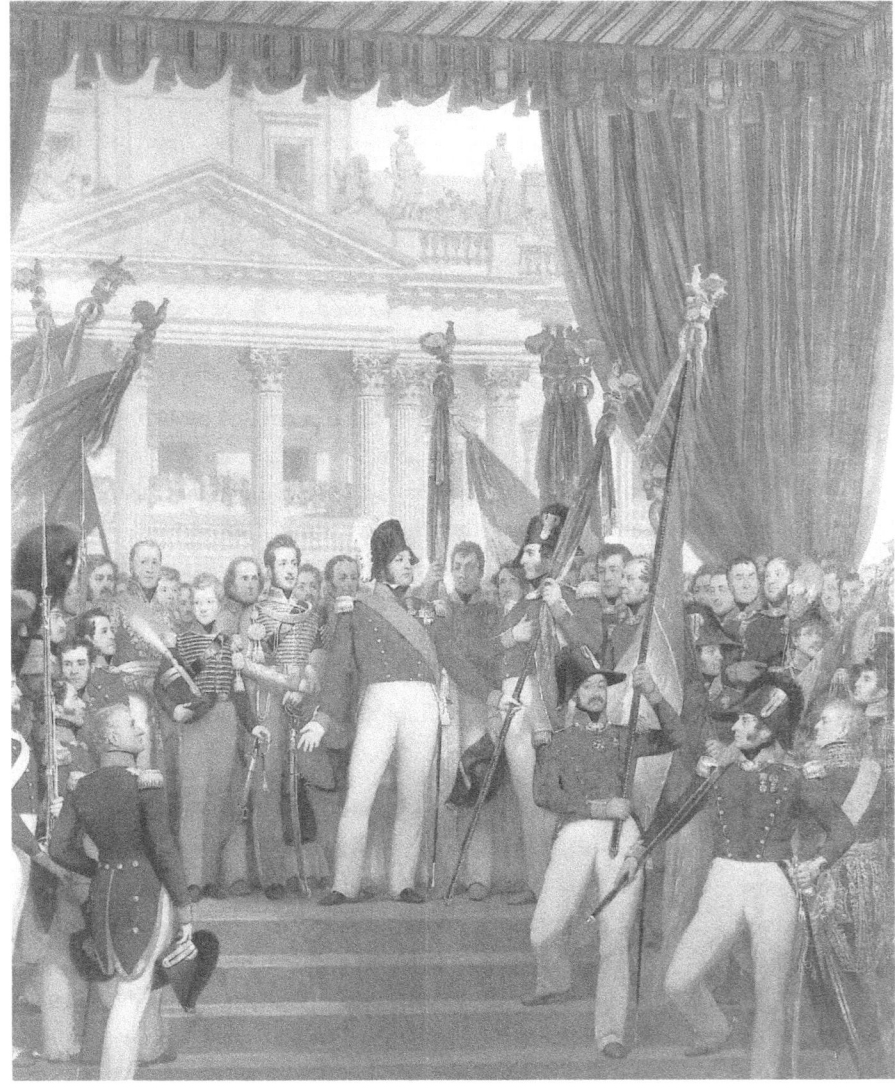

FIGURE 24.   Joseph-Désiré Court, *The King distributing Battalion Standards to the National Guard on the Champ-de-Mars, 29 August 1830*, 1836. Oil on canvas. Versailles, Châteaux de Versailles et de Trianon, inv. MV2789 (550 × 412 cm). Photo: © RMN/Art Resource, NY/ © Daniel Arnaudet/Jean Schormans.

Twenty-five years after Napoléon had laid claim to the space, it finally seemed possible to speak of a new beginning for the Champ-de-Mars.

DELACROIX'S ENTHUSIASM for the regime that emerged from the 1830 Revolution brings to mind one of the nineteenth century's most famous images of contemporary political strife, his painting of *28 July 1830: Liberty leading the People* (Fig. 25). The picture also introduces a third arena where memory and history often clashed: the streets of Paris. Delacroix seems not to have taken part in the actual street fighting of the so-called *Trois Glorieuses* [three glorious days] of July 27, 28, and 29, when the people of Paris successfully forced Charles X to abandon the throne. "I have undertaken a modern subject, a barricade," wrote Delacroix to his brother, "and if I have not won battles for the nation at least I will paint for it."[20] Delacroix's somewhat defensive turn of phrase—"if I have not won battles for the nation"—was entirely appropriate when writing to his brother who, as a former general in Napoléon's Grand Army, knew first-hand the heat of combat. By hedging his response to the recent revolution in this way, Delacroix defers to his brother's own lived experience—a vivid reminder of the tension between memory and history that permeated every level of social relations at the time.

Liberty leading the People participates fully in the political myth of the 1830 Revolution by suggesting that the citizens who defend fiercely their jerry-built barricade were drawn from every age and class: workers, young dandies in top hats, students of the École Polytechnique wearing their characteristic bicornes, and tough little street urchins are all joined in the picture to face the enemy. They are also joined by a striding, muscular woman with bared breasts who brandishes a large tricolor flag in one hand and a rifle in the other. Is she really there? Only the wounded young man at her feet seems aware of this figure who rallies the crowd, while her barefoot charge over the barricade tends to suggest she is more myth than reality.

Delacroix surely intended to honor the events of July by placing an allegory of Liberty on the side of the insurgents,

but the picture's mix of pictorial codes sparked a heated debate in the critical press. "I am rather annoyed that allegory is mixed up here with the factual," complained Augustin Jal; "instead of a Liberty, a goddess in phrygian cap with bared breasts, I would have liked to see in this fray one of those intrepid Parisian women who so honored their sex in our three-day war."[21] If Jal suggests that the events were in themselves sufficiently glorious to obviate the need for allegory, Charles Farcy fretted that Delacroix's Liberty appears to be physically unworthy of her allegorical mission:

The Liberty is a beastly woman, with dirty skin and coarse features, who wears a phrygian bonnet, brandishes a tricolor, and scales a pile of paving stones in such a way that one can surmise neither the movement nor the existence of her right leg. Moreover, one wonders—and the question is well worth asking—if this Liberty is a real woman or if she is an allegorical figure. Not a single viewer is equipped to solve this riddle.[22]

Even these few citations make clear that the debate about *Liberty* would never be resolved, for there were always partisans on one side or the other, and the issue of her existence was really one of personal temperament.

Yet the terms of the debate generated by Delacroix's picture were not simply about personal taste. Rather, they engaged head-on the two poles—memory and history—that thread through this chapter: those who decried Delacroix's use of allegory faulted the picture's departure from their memories of the events; those who agreed with the idea of an allegory faulted the picture's too visible physicality, a grittiness that should be edited from history. Gustave Planche, who was a great champion of Delacroix, put his finger on the problem:

At the Salon this year there is not one picture whose execution is more concise or complete than Delacroix's *Liberty*. He has struggled hand-to-hand with nature. One has faulted the grayish tone that reigns over the canvas, but I do not agree with this opinion.... Should one blame or praise the combination of allegory and reality that presides over this composition? We might fault the principle, but we praise its execution and its absolute success. . . . It adds to reality a character of idealism that was lacking, it adds to our

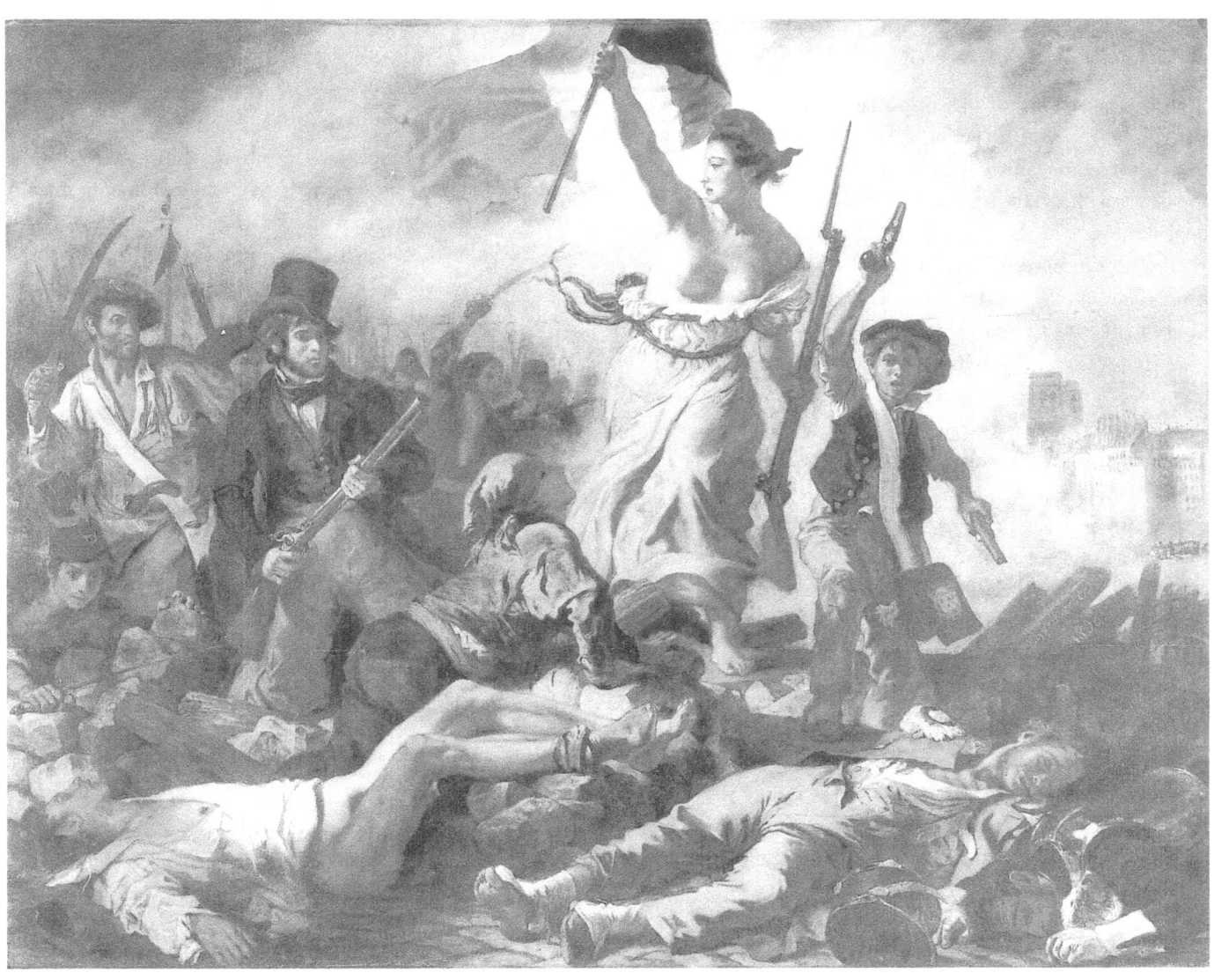

FIGURE 25. Eugène Delacroix, *28 July 1830: Liberty leading the People*, 1831. Oil on canvas. Paris, Musée du Louvre, inv. RF129 (259 × 325 cm). Photo: © RMN/Art Resource, NY/© Hervé Lewandowski.

memories of yesterday the majesty that only history—and the most distant history at that—masters and seems to reserve for itself.[23]

Planche realized that at stake in Delacroix's painting was the carrying-over of lived experience into a work of art that both told a story and claimed a place for itself in history: a place for itself in the grand tradition of painting; a place for its depicted event in the larger story of the nation. Delacroix wanted to do more than render a news item, and for that he needed a tool—an allegory—by which recent memories might be fused to a lasting history.

What was real about July 1830, and crucial to the development of groundswell support for the revolution, was the spontaneous reappearance all across Paris of the tricolor flag. The banner of Revolution and Empire had been outlawed since 1815 and replaced by the Bourbon flag of white with gold fleurs-de-lys. Unfurling the tricolor in the midst of the July Revolution was a gesture of defiance and memory that refused to forgive the Bourbons for returning to power in France by the force of foreign arms. Stendhal was in the midst of reading Napoléon's posthumous memoirs, the *Mémorial de Sainte-Hélène* (see Chapter Eight), when the revolution erupted. His response to the events was surely affected by his current reading:

I was carried away by the July Days. I watched the shooting from the colonnade of the Théâtre Français, and was never really in any personal danger. I will never forget the bright sunlight and the first sight of the tricolor banner.[24]

The thrill of the tricolor's return to the streets of Paris, and its symbolic power to galvanize the revolutionaries of the 1830 Revolution, were driven by a past they had been obliged to suppress but not forget. The charging figures of Delacroix's picture were not so controversial because of their outward appearances, but because they pictorialize a symbolic project of the revolution more profound than chasing Charles X from the throne: they fight to reclaim the *right to remember* within the historical spaces of Paris. This also explains why Delacroix's allegory was not sited very specifically within the city. Although the principal fighting of 28 July occurred around the Hôtel-de-Ville, *Liberty* strives to transcend any single event and to reach for the revolution's symbolic core.

Given our survey of Parisian monuments as markers and repositories of the past, it is no surprise that the tricolor's return to visibility—and the revolution's claim to remember its history—were inscribed in the background of *Liberty leading the People* on one of the city's most venerable buildings: to the right of the main group, and barely visible in the distance, a tiny tricolor flutters from a tower of Notre-Dame.

Episodes of conquering monuments are tropes for the successful wresting of Paris from the army of Charles X, and they are commonplace among the thousands of images produced in the aftermath of the July Revolution. Hippolyte Lecomte's picture of the fighting at the Porte Saint-Denis is one example (Fig. 26). The work takes up several themes informed by the revolution's mythic retelling that appear in Delacroix's *Liberty*. Foremost among these is the camaraderie of street fighters formed of different social classes, ages, and sexes: bare-armed workers fighting alongside men in top hats and suit coats; women who tend the wounded; army veterans who have donned parts of their old Napoleonic uniforms (another sign of reclaiming one's memory) fighting alongside children too young to have known the Empire first-hand; students of the École Polytechnique (the foremost academy of military engineering) supporting defectors from the army who have joined the revolution, and so on. All of these characters marshal their forces and face the army at the foot of the Saint-Denis arch, which has been occupied by the revolutionaries and flies the tricolor flag. Although the foreground skirmishes tend not to reveal which side has the upper hand in this neighborhood, that the monument has been taken suggests that the tide has turned to the insurgents' cause. When set alongside the generalized statement of Delacroix's *Liberty*, Lecomte's image can hardly be called heroic, for it seems not to strive for an expression larger than life. Rather, Lecomte's prominent attention to the monument focuses the immediate struggle, alludes to the people's eventual triumph, and reminds us that historical markers of the Paris cityscape were symbols of legitimacy open to appropriation by the shifting politics of revolution.

The legitimizing potential of Parisian monuments can be measured by their absence from the disturbing little paint-

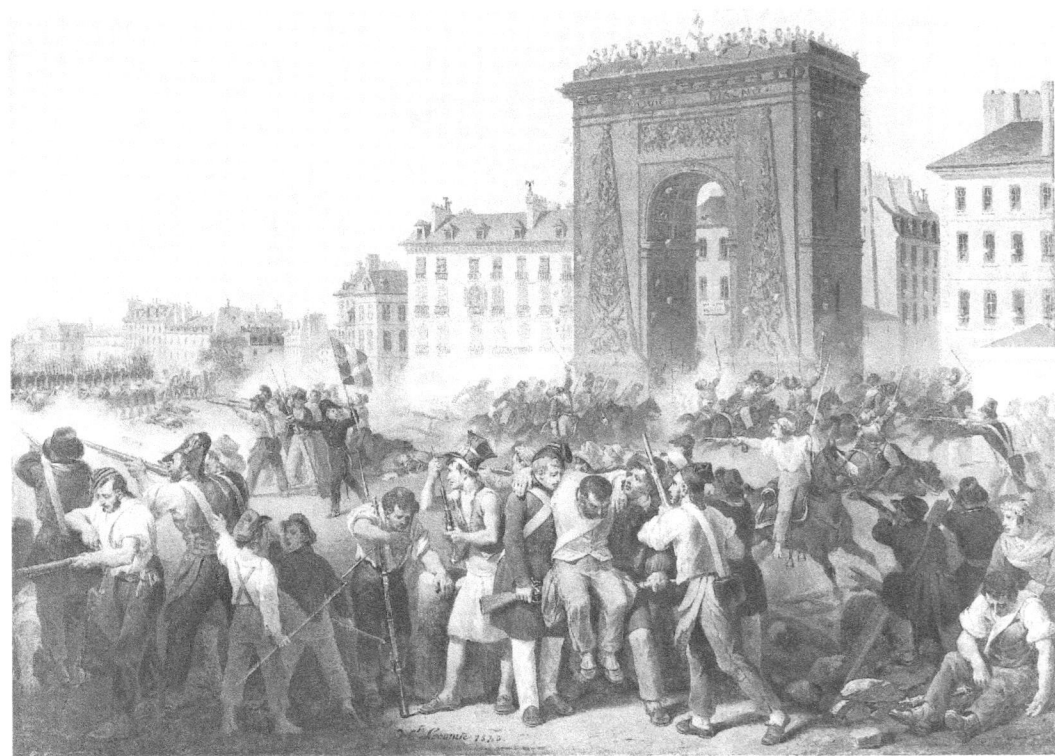

FIGURE 26.   Hippolyte Lecomte, *Fighting at the Porte Saint-Denis*, 1831. Oil on canvas. Paris, Musée Carnavalet, inv. P 0214 (43 × 60 cm). Photo: © PMVP/ Toumazet.

ing done by Ernest Meissonier in 1848 (Fig. 27). Although not publicly exhibited until 1850, the picture was the immediate result of Meissonier's participation in the five days of unrest that gripped Paris beginning on 22 June 1848. In February 1848, Louis-Phillipe was himself overthrown by a revolution, and the constitutional monarchy was replaced by an interim government aimed at founding a republic of elected representatives. Yet the new nation was as fragile as its Provisional Government was ambitious. Elections held in April 1848 were—for the first time in French history—open to every male adult, but the economy was in terrible shape: unemployment rising steeply, the stock market in free fall, and industry at a near standstill. To alleviate the desperate situation of workers without jobs or money, the government created "make work" public projects called National Workshops, but no one was prepared for the huge numbers of people who applied for aid. The elections yielded a very large National Assembly of almost nine hundred deputies with no

clear majority; in fact, many of the new representatives came from conservative regions of France that were openly hostile to expensive social programs in Paris like the National Workshops.

As their living conditions worsened, Parisian workers became ever more restless. On 15 May a large and unruly crowd invaded the National Assembly, declared it dissolved, and tried to establish a new provisional government. The crowd was dispersed by the National Guard and its ringleaders arrested, but the Assembly took the incident seriously. Plans were made to centralize military command under a single general, to position the army in and around Paris, and to strengthen a new peacekeeping force—called the Garde Mobile—recruited from the ranks of poor, young workers who would be willing to protect their pay of 1.50 francs per day. Paris seemed to be bracing for a final showdown.

The spark that caused fighting to flare again in the streets of the capital was the Assembly's decree of 22 June

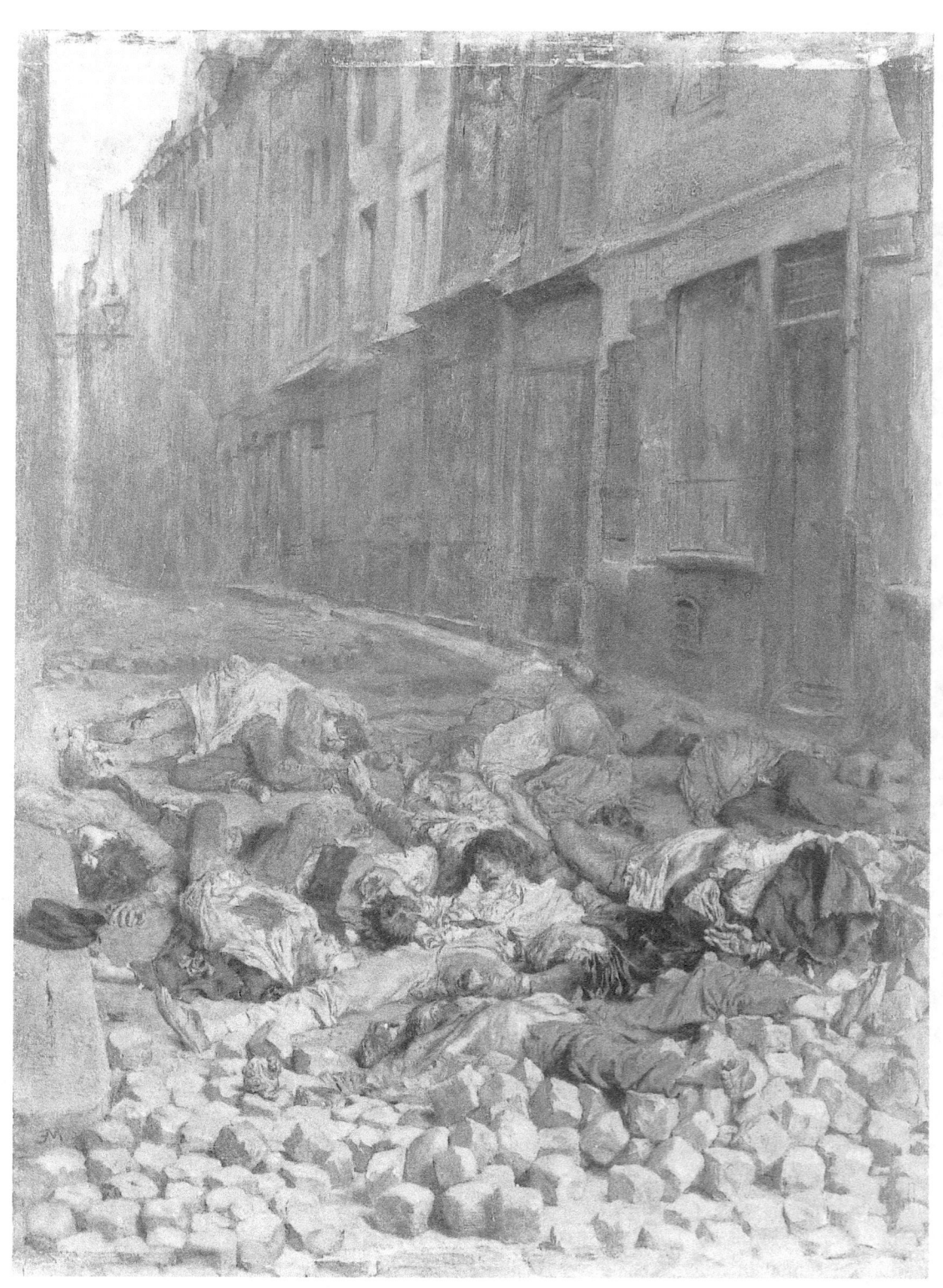

that announced gradual dissolution of the workshops, although bachelors were given the narrow choice of immediate dismissal or enlistment in the army. Affected workers interpreted the decree as an affront, a situation that seemed destined to pit rich against poor in a battle for survival. Karl Marx believed the tensions building within Paris were of epic proportions: "The workers were left no choice," he wrote; "they had to starve or start to fight. They answered on 22 June with the tremendous insurrection in which the first great battle was fought between the two classes that split modern society. It was a fight for the preservation or annihilation of the *bourgeois* order."[25] Marx was not alone in viewing the events of June as unlike earlier revolts in France; Alexis de Tocqueville also sensed a change:

Another point that distinguished it [the uprising] from all other events of the same type during the last sixty years was that its object was not to change the form of government, but to alter the organization of society. In truth it was not a political struggle . . . but a class struggle, a sort of "Servile War."[26]

During the day of 23 June thousands of barricades were built across the narrow, winding streets of eastern Paris, those neighborhoods in which most of the laborers, skilled tradesmen, and recent immigrants to the city lived in close quarters to one another. The National Guard was called up early in the day, but most of the civilian-soldiers of this crucial force refused to report for duty. By contrast, the Garde Mobile responded quickly to the alarm and took up assigned positions throughout the city. Units of the regular army began to sweep the boulevards in concerted columns. Perhaps it was inevitable that the first skirmishes occurred near the symbolically charged Porte Saint-Denis, and that the fighting was so fierce that army commanders had to call for reinforcements to dislodge insurgents from their entrenched and protected positions behind barricades.

FIGURE 27. Ernest Meissonier, *Memory of Civil War (The Barricades)*, 1848 (shown at 1850–1851 Salon). Oil on canvas. Paris, Musée du Louvre, inv. RF1942-31 (29 × 22 cm). Photo: © RMN/ Art Resource, NY/© Droits réservés.

Saturday the 24th of June was the most dramatic day, for it seemed briefly that the government might fall. The fear gripping Paris was palpable and graphically recorded by Tocqueville after encountering a group of workers while walking along the relatively calm—and extremely affluent— rue Saint-Honoré:

They wore blouses, which, as we all know, are their fighting as well as their working clothes; they were not actually carrying arms, but one could see from the look of them that they were pretty near to taking them up. With hardly restrained delight they noted that the sound of the firing seemed to be getting closer, which meant that the rebels were gaining ground. I had guessed before this that the whole of the working class backed the revolt, either actively or in its heart; this proved it to me. In fact the spirit of insurrection circulated from end to end of that vast class and in all its parts, like blood in the body; it filled places where there was no fighting as much as those that formed the battlefield; and it penetrated into our homes, around us, above us, below us. Even the places where we thought we were the masters were creeping with domestic enemies. It was as if an atmosphere of civil war enveloped the whole of Paris, and, no matter where one withdrew, one had to live in it.[27]

The most remarkable aspect of Tocqueville's account is the ever-increasing sense of paranoia: from workers who look the same whether on the job or in battle, to the spirit of revolution that courses through their class like blood, to the final image of no nook or cranny safe from the spirit of civil war. The slippage into chaos felt by Tocqueville could and did lead to extreme measures. The National Assembly declared a state of siege and placed all executive power in the hands of général Louis-Eugène Cavaignac, supreme commander of the government's troops. Cavaignac promptly closed all political clubs, seized a number of opposition newspapers, and appealed for support from National Guardsmen outside of Paris—an appeal to which almost a hundred thousand men responded. Throughout Saturday the tide of battle gradually swung to the government, as Cavaignac's forces moved methodically through neighborhoods. Facing intense pressure to give ground, desperate insurgents fought bitterly to the end. Cavaignac was determined to break the back of the revolt and refused any terms other than complete capitulation.

By the end of fighting, around 4:00 PM on the 26th, the army had lost over seven hundred men and distributed more than two million cartridges to its troops; the insurgents had suffered countless thousands of casualties.

The painter Ernest Meissonier was a captain in the National Guard who served the government loyally during the uprising. On Sunday the 25th he was stationed near the Hôtel-de-Ville, where he participated in the assault of a barricade in a nearby street. Some years later Meissonier described that day in a letter to the painter Alfred Stevens:

You ask me what I think of the drawing of a barricade that your dear brother Arthur owns? To speak of one's own work and to say all the good things that one thinks about it is never easy for an artist, but I have no modesty about this drawing and I do not hesitate to say that if I were rich enough to buy it back I would do so immediately, even ahead of the painting. When I made it I was still in the terrible grip of the spectacle I had just seen, and believe me dear Alfred, such things get into your soul so that, when you represent them, it is not simply to make a work but because you have been moved in your guts and you want this memory to last. I was at that time an artillery captain in the National Guard. For three days we had been fighting, I had seen men of my battalion killed and wounded. The insurrection surrounded the Hôtel-de-Ville where we were stationed, and when that barricade in the rue de la Mortellerie was captured I saw it in all its horror: defenders slaughtered, shot point-blank, thrown from windows, their cadavers covering the ground, their blood not yet absorbed by the dirt. It was there I heard that terrible phrase which speaks, more than anything, of how much men are outside of themselves in these frightening street battles. "Were all these men guilty?" asked Marast of an officer of the Republican Guard. "Monsieur the Mayor," he replied, "you can be sure that no more than a quarter were innocent."[28]

Meissonier was writing about a watercolor study (now in a private collection),[29] but it seems clear that his powerful impressions of the barricade and its carnage also informed his final painting of the event (Fig. 27). The picture's chilling lack of life, its heap of bodies mixed with paving stones, and its seemingly impassive rendering led one critic to say it had "the pitiless fidelity of a daguerreotype."[30]

Meissonier—like Tocqueville—was firmly aligned with the forces of order against the insurgents of June. In light of his picture's flat-footed literalism devoid of empathy, some historians have suggested that it be understood as a kind of warning to that "vast class" of workers about the consequences of rebellion. But *Memory of Civil War* is a very small work (about 29 cm by 22 cm) and hardly projects the public presence we would expect from so large a social warning. Rather, viewers must get close to the picture just to see it, and doing so forces them to confront its pathos intimately and at close range. The effect of this close-up encounter was described succinctly by a critic at the exhibition of 1851:

What is most cruel in this painting is that, because of the indecision and lack of energy or effects, we are obliged to look at it for a long time, detail by detail. It is not possible to see it in one glance and pass on. The flesh and the clothes are confused with the paving stones; the red and blue cloth seems to have been washed by rain for six months on end.[31]

Drawing the viewer into its restrained circle of encounter, forcing him or her to linger over its miniaturist rendering, Meissonier's image becomes a private—rather than public—experience. Its intimate and personal address is seconded by an almost complete lack of emblems or points of geographic reference. If, as Tocqueville's commentary suggests, many good bourgeois felt the terror of knowing no escape during the June Days from the great pulsing body of working-class fury, we might expect a sigh of relief to see that body—those bodies—so clearly defeated and lifeless. Yet Meissonier's letter dwells upon something else: that "terrible phrase" that assured the mayor "no more than a quarter" of the victims were innocent. The "atmosphere of civil war" engulfing Paris had caused perfectly good citizens—like Meissonier and Tocqueville—to think terrible things about the unnamed masses of their enemies. Finally, that cold calculation of "a quarter" was like a slap in the face: innocent people had died, and it must never be forgotten.

The critic just cited could not avoid seeing the blue cloth, the patches of red (which he also called cloth but are, in fact, bloodstains), and the flesh—pale, white and lifeless—of the victims sprawled in the street of Meissonier's picture. He seems on the verge of recognizing that the tricolor makes an appearance in the work, but it is a grisly, repressed appearance far from its triumphant unfurling in Delacroix's picture of *Liberty* (Fig. 25). What should we expect? In 1830, the tricolor had appeared on the barricades to replace the white field and gold fleurs-de-lys of the Bourbon flag with a banner steeped in the memories of Revolution and Empire. By contrast, both sides claimed the tricolor as their own in June of 1848: perhaps the greatest tragedy of any civil war is the collective realization that one's opponents are not fundamentally different from oneself—*at least one-fourth were innocent*—and this renders the violence and death of civil war all that more absurd.

Meissonier's veiled allusion to the tricolor in his picture of death in the streets of Paris, and our critic's inability to speak of it, are gestures of repression that register rather precisely the tenuous validity of symbols when a nation wages war on itself. Exactly parallel is the picture's lack of markers that might locate the scene within the city or its past: no monuments situate the murky, anonymous facade of Meissonier's street in a specific *quartier* or link the spectacle of death before us to some larger history. It is significant that while Meissonier's letter about his role in the June Days mentions an exact locale—the rue de la Mortellerie—he chose to exhibit his picture as simply *Memory of Civil War*. The key word here is "memory," and we must return to Meissonier's words to grasp its importance: "Such things get into your soul," he wrote, "so that, when you represent them, it is not simply to make a work but because you have been moved in your guts and you

want this memory to last." There are no monuments here, no symbols of the past, because the power of history to explain events can neither encompass nor contextualize the special horror and paranoia of civil war. Meissonier's picture implies that memories of civil war must be allowed to vanquish history because there is no excuse for the insanity of citizens bent on killing one another. One cannot accept impassively the specter of one's fellows left in a heap on the street.

ROMANTIC PARIS mapped simultaneously a geography and a volatile symbolic space. Within its borders, processes of history and memory clashed and did battle for the allegiances of a public whose lived experience was both historically determined and privately complex. Far from a neutral slate upon which contemporary events were inscribed, the spaces and monuments of Paris were freighted with an overlay of personal memories that submitted only with reluctance to the grand narratives of historical explanation. Coupled with the conflicted readings of the recent past outlined in Chapter One, it becomes clear that making art in Paris during this period, especially an art engaged in the shaping of a national identity, was never simply an enterprise of aesthetic delight, but a cultural practice of symbolic and ideological urgency. In the next chapter we shall sketch some of the ways that the arts—from grand architectural projects to the objects of everyday life—engaged the task of writing history in a specifically Parisian manner.

Writing History on the Cityscape

To find out if a monument is authentic, that is, if it belongs to the epoch, to the place, to the facts, to the individuals where you want to place it, you must compare it to many other monuments of the same type and include in this analysis all the known elements—chronological, geographical, and historical—with which it might be associated. . . . A second necessary condition for a monument to clarify, complete, and confirm history is that it must have a clear meaning, a fixed and incontestable significance.

—Pierre Daunou[1]

PIERRE DAUNOU'S REFLECTIONS on the historical truth and usefulness of monuments for writing history were not published until after his death in 1840, but they date from the inaugural lecture of his course in history given at the Collège de France in 1819. The time frame clarifies his concern to develop criteria for the evaluation of monuments because, during the years of Revolution and Empire, most of the monuments of Paris had been stripped of their original significations and, in many cases, given new ones that eradicated their heritage. The symbolism of some monuments, notably the Pantheon, flip-flopped several times between 1792 and 1819; small wonder that Daunou wanted to establish criteria for how to read monuments historically.

Daunou's caution characterizes that of many historians, writing in the wake of Revolution and Empire, who were driven by a need to understand the great upheavals they had witnessed. "My ambition shall be to speak of the age which we have lived as if it were already remote," wrote Madame de Staël in 1818, hoping to find a vantage point from which to make sense of the preceding three decades.[2] Prosper de Barante, who served both Napoléon and the restored Bourbons, explained his passion for history as a function of his life experience: "We had witnessed scenes so great, so diverse, so poignant, we had seen so much history made," he wrote, "that we wished to rediscover in the past something we had seen or experienced."[3] The point was not only to find historical precedents for the great dramas of the Revolution and its aftermath, but also to explain how radically different regimes could have followed one another in such swift succession.

Since some of the major players prevailed despite the tumultuous changes (Talleyrand is the most conspicuous example), one could not simply attribute the course of events to a succession of leaders; rather, Barante and his colleagues developed concepts like *epoch* and the *march of civilization* to guide their research:

The concern of history is the story of humanity, the march of civilization, the collective destiny of the human species. Each detail, each anecdote is attractive only as a characteristic sign of its epoch. To isolate them is to place yourself on the same level, or even below, that of novelistic fictions.[4]

Writing history became a more scientific enterprise, concerned with not only the life stories and experiences of great men or women, but also the miscellaneous artifacts of culture left by a particular epoch. This expanded range of interests was succinctly elaborated in the opening statement for the inaugural issue of a scholarly journal published in 1834 by the Société de l'histoire de France:

In fact, monuments of history are not only accounts written in metal and stone, but also those documents preserved by tradition that stamp habits, language, racial physiognomies, dress, and topographical names. All these monuments and these remains can shed upon historical narrative a light comprised not only of statements of facts and dates, like those provided in great number by coins and lapidary inscriptions, but also evidence of a specific social state of which they had been both elements and concrete effects.[5]

The passage codifies what became the modus operandi of the most influential group of historians to emerge during the first decades of the nineteenth century: François Guizot, Armand Thierry, François Mignet, Adolphe Thiers, and Prosper de Barante are but some of the members of the Société de l'histoire de France who believed that "spirit of an age" was a concept able to embrace and to organize into comprehensible patterns the myriad documents and monuments of the past.

Drawing attention to the enhanced role of physical objects in the work of early nineteenth-century French historians underscores the period's sensitivity to the power of monuments to shape one's image of the past. Leaders of the Revolution had understood this intuitively: witness their attempts to rename the streets and squares of Paris, to recycle major buildings to new uses, and to invent new symbols for the nation without a king. The following decades and governments were engaged in a struggle both to wrest monuments marked by the Revolution from the grasp of those years and to undo any intervening appropriations. Monuments taken over by the Empire were reinscribed with meanings—first by the Bourbon Restoration and then the July Monarchy—in a continuous battle for the memory of Paris and for the political legitimacy of history.

Something of this struggle was already visible in the streets of the capital in 1802, when the Englishman John Dean Paul

visited the city: "It is also worthy of remark," he wrote, "that on all the public buildings, nay in almost every street, the words *Egalité, Fraternité, ou la Mort*, were written up, or other words to that effect; and now, in all places belonging to the government, the words *la Mort* are scratched out, and *Justice*, or *Humanité* substituted."[6] Gradual effacement of the most extreme sentiments of the Revolution was an essential part of recycling a public building after 1800, just as the removal of Ancien Régime emblems during the 1790s had been part of turning the properties confiscated from nobles to other uses. In the course of a visit to Paris in the spring of 1802, Mary Berry spent one evening at the Hameau de Chantilly, "one of the many public gardens open most nights for dancing," which had once been "the hotel and garden of the Duchesse de Bourbon." Walking through the rooms which she had known before the Revolution, Berry noticed:

All the gilding and painting upon the walls, and the glasses remain just as they were in the time of Madame de Bourbon; and in one of the rooms are still the fine tapestry fauteuils that originally belonged to the house; we were struck also with the locks and fastenings to the doors and windows being much handsomer than usual, and found that the arms of France were carefully obliterated from every one of them.[7]

To echo the words of Prosper de Barante, those almost incidental emblems were exactly "evidence of a specific social state of which they had been both elements and concrete effects." Their systematic erasure was a small but eloquent commentary on the political upheavals in France since 1789.

If post-revolutionary Paris was a space of symbolic slippage, where monuments were loaded and stripped of signifiers with each change of government, what were the stable qualities that preserved the city as a center for the arts amidst war and political upheaval? One answer is found in the journal of Henry Milton, an Englishman who came to Paris in 1815, shortly after Napoléon's defeat at Waterloo:

For my own part, I much doubt whether I should have taken the trouble to visit France had it not been for this collection: certain it is, that the interest I felt at approaching Paris would have been much less vivid. Even the pleasure of hearing in every direction

English drums and bugles sounding triumphant on the boulevards of the capital of the Great Nation, was secondary to the delight of accomplishing the most ardent wish of many years—a delight not unmixed with anxiety, lest overwrought expectation should lead to disappointment.[8]

The collection which so interested Milton was the cultural plunder from the four corners of Europe that had been sent to Paris by the victorious armies of France. This assemblage, perhaps the greatest concentration of masterpieces ever seen, was open to the public at the Musée Napoléon. Like Milton, we must begin our tour of the arts of Paris at its door.

Spoils of Victory: The First Grand Louvre

You ascend to it (at present) by a commodious plain staircase, and first enter a large square room about twice the size of the exhibition room in Somerset House, lined with all the finest Italian pictures, very well placed as to the light. Out of this room you enter a gallery—such a gallery! But such a gallery!! as the world never before saw, both as to size and furniture! So long that the perspective ends almost in a point, and so furnished that at every step, tho' one feels one must go on, one's attention is arrested by all the finest pictures one has seen before in every other country.

—Mary Berry[9]

That Paris had a national museum may not seem unusual to visitors accustomed to the U.S. National Gallery in Washington, the Louvre as it is today, or any of the other great public collections of the world. But the idea of a gallery open to one and all was a novelty in the opening years of the nineteenth century, and a lasting product of the French Revolution. In November 1789, less than four months after the fall of the Bastille, the revolutionary assembly nationalized by decree all ecclesiastical property in France, including lands, buildings, and all works of art, books, or precious objects they contained. Obviously, portable items could not be left to languish in abandoned structures because looters would (and often did) spirit them away. Government commissions were established in 1790 to monitor, inventory, and eventually store the confiscated works of art. In the Paris region,

former Church property was deposited in the abandoned monastery of the Petits-Augustins, across the river from the Louvre (see Chapter Four). The gathering of art objects was well under way by the beginning of 1791.

The second event of capital interest to a history of the national museum occurred on 10 August 1792, when the monarchy itself was outlawed and the royal family sent to prison. Without digressing into the complicated politics of this time, abolition of the monarchy meant simply that the king's very large collection of paintings and sculptures now belonged to the nation. The Louvre—formerly the king's residence—also became national property. Jean-Marie Roland de la Platière, Minister of the Interior at the time, promoted the idea that circumstances favored founding a national museum in the Louvre, where the works of art formerly sequestered by the Church and the Crown might be exhibited for the benefit of every citizen. Not everyone supported Roland's plan. Administrators of the Petits-Augustins depot hoped to found their own museum, while some artists—notably the politically active Jacques-Louis David—opposed such a museum on the grounds that elitist cultural institutions had no place in the new republic.

Nonetheless, on 10 August 1793—first anniversary of the monarchy's demise—the national museum opened to the public with pictures installed in what was called the Grande Galerie: the long, barrel-vaulted wing along the Seine connecting the main part of the Louvre to the Tuileries Palace. Of the more than five hundred pictures on display, almost three-quarters came from the collections of the defunct monarchy (Louis XVI and Marie-Antoinette had been guillotined in January). Most of the others were confiscated from the Church. In keeping with the republican nature of its founding, the museum was open to everyone for three days of each ten-day week (the republican calendar having been recently inaugurated). Six days were reserved for special visitors and for artists to study or copy the collection. One day was set aside for cleaning and maintenance.

Thus, a national museum was established in Paris well before French armies scored any major victories against their European adversaries, and well before Napoléon Bonaparte was head of state. In fact, existence of the museum became the rationale for confiscating works of art from conquered lands. Already in May of 1794 the Directory government authorized and encouraged the army to forage for works of art in the newly conquered areas of Belgium. In June of that year it was decided that artists and learned men should secretly accompany the armies to supervise the selection, packing, and shipping to Paris of artistic and scientific monuments. A committee was established to "draw up with the least possible delay" instructions to be used by generals and officers "on the procedure for conserving and removing precious objects."[10] Time was not wasted: six days after the French army entered Antwerp (24 July 1794), a shipment of four capital pictures—including the central panel of the *Descent from the Cross* by Rubens—was on its way to Paris. About forty works of art were eventually taken out of Belgium, and this first campaign of selective pillage became the model for the next two decades of French conquests.

Writing in 1815, after the fall of Napoléon, the Englishman Henry Milton particularly deplored the informed and systematic nature of the French confiscations:

Bands of practised ruffians, their own land no longer furnishing them with the employment in which they delighted, were sent into other countries to continue their crimes under a less ignominious name. . . . But the usual and more general objects of plunder were not sufficient to satisfy the rapacity of the French. Troops of scientific robbers followed their armies; and either by forced treaties, or open violence, obtained possession of whatever they deemed excellent and valuable.[11]

Milton, as might be expected, lays the blame for this pillage of all the best things of European culture on Napoléon, even though it had begun and was institutionalized in 1794 when Bonaparte was merely a corporal in the artillery corps. During the spring of 1796, following a string of important victories in northern Italy, Bonaparte (now a general) received explicit instructions from the government in Paris:

The National Museum ought to contain the most famous monuments of all the arts, and you will take care to enrich it with those that are expected from the current victories of the army in Italy. . . . The Directory executive asks that you choose one or more artists for the purpose of seeking out, gathering, and shipping to Paris the

most precious objects of this type, and of issuing formal orders for the intelligent execution of these arrangements, about which you are asked to file a report.[12]

What emerges from this story is that the French policy of plunder was not driven by the private ambitions of Bonaparte, nor those of any individual, but the needs of a new institution: the national museum. As Cecil Gould has written, "if the Louvre and its sister institutions had not been in existence, above all if they had not been founded so recently as still to be very much in people's minds, it is very possible that the expert confiscation of masterpieces . . . might never have occurred. . . . The Revolution had set up an idol which itself demanded the offerings that were made to it."[13] General Bonaparte proved eager to fulfill his mandate, and even inaugurated a new subtlety in French policy. While negotiating a cease-fire with the Duke of Parma, Bonaparte stipulated that one of his conditions for peace would be the cession of twenty works of art for the Louvre museum.

Bonaparte's condition earned him such high praise in Paris that the practice became standard policy during the triumphant military campaign that overran the Papal States in June of 1796. Thus, Bonaparte's terms for an armistice with the Pope specified that one hundred works of art, selected by French experts, were to be handed over. Naturally, these experts did not hesitate to pick freely from the best works of art found in the museums of Rome: the *Laocoön*, the *Torso Belvedere*, the *Dying Gladiator*, and probably the two most famous objects in Europe—Raphael's *Transfiguration* and the *Apollo Belvedere* (Fig. 28)—were some of the treasures destined for the galleries of the Louvre.

It would be wrong to assume that the government's policy of organized confiscation was universally supported. Even as French commissioners in Rome were selecting works for shipment to Paris, Antoine Quatremère de Quincy, a leading historian and art theorist of the day, published a pamphlet against removing antiquities from the Eternal City. Quatremère argued that their removal would destroy the organic context upon which their appreciation depends:

To divide is to destroy. . . . Splitting up the museum of Rome would be the death of all learning based on the principle of its unity. What

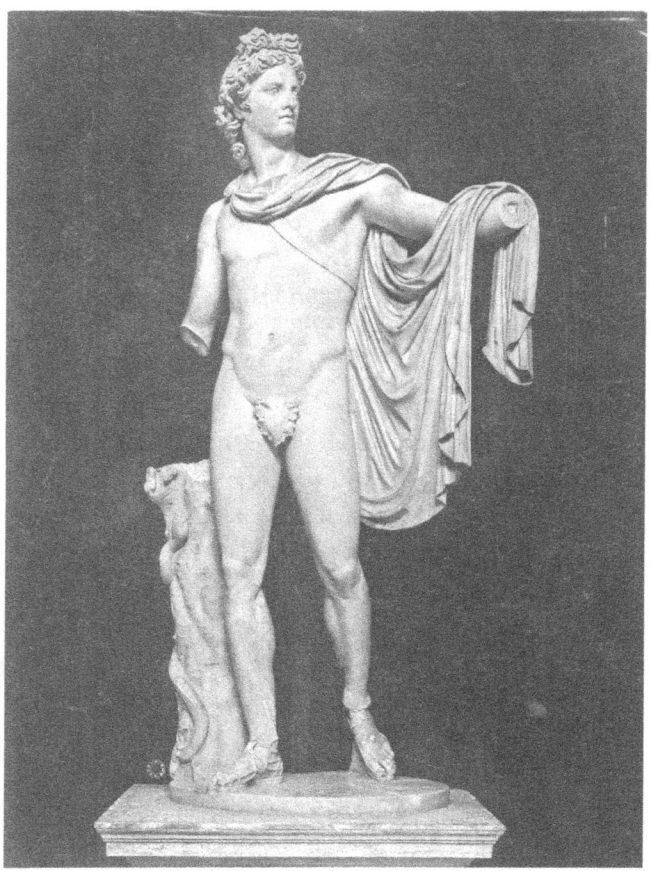

FIGURE 28.   Leochares (?), *Apollo Belvedere*, 4th century BC. Marble. Rome, The Vatican Museum (Cortile del Belvedere) (224 cm). Photo: © Alinari/Art Resource, NY.

is antiquity in Rome if not a great book whose pages have been destroyed or dispersed by time, and which modern research fills in the voids and mends the gaps every day? What would the Power who might select for export and appropriation a few of the most unusual of these monuments be doing? Exactly the same as an ignorant person who tears from a book the pages where vignettes are found.[14]

Quatremère's eloquent argumentation raised a few eyebrows, but failed to convince the authorities. The Directory was firmly committed to a policy of confiscation and so was Bonaparte: writing in February 1797 to the commissioners charged with looting the papal collections, he stated bluntly that "we will have everything of beauty in Italy, except for a small number of objects located in Turin and Naples."[15]

What prompted a military man like Bonaparte to be so interested in the best of Italy's artistic riches? The question is complicated by the fact that Jean-Antoine Chaptal, one of his closest advisers, left a rather disparaging portrait of Bonaparte's appreciation for works of art:

Napoléon did not like the arts. . . . It was odd to see him walk through the beautiful museum of his capital. He was always impassive before the masterpieces of any period; he stopped before none and, when his attention was directed to one of them, he asked coldly: "Who is that by?" without permitting any commentary and without revealing the slightest impression.[16]

We shall never know if Chaptal was exaggerating for dramatic effect, but his account tallies with the image of Bonaparte in a print from about 1804 (Fig. 29), which shows the general introducing the *Apollo Belvedere* to a group of dignitaries with a comment on the sculpture's market value. The enigma of Bonaparte's motives has led some scholars to argue that he was simply following orders from Paris, no more nor less than any other French general of the day. Others have suggested that his reading of Plutarch's *Lives* may have spawned the idea of rivaling Sulla, who returned to Rome with the treasures of Athens: bringing to Paris a rich bounty of books, manuscripts, and works of art would be a tangible sign of Bonaparte's Italian conquests. If that were true, why did he choose to be far from Paris and fully engaged with conquering Egypt when the objects he confiscated in Italy finally reached the capital, in July 1798, amid great fanfare and official ceremonies? Perhaps the best one can say about Bonaparte's motives during 1796–1797 is that he burned with an ambition to eclipse his colleagues at the head of French armies in other parts of Europe: if public policy advocated art plunder, then he must and would be its most prolific provider.

Chapter One sketched some of the reasons why Bonaparte left Egypt for Paris, where he engineered the coup-d'état that gave him vast executive powers as First Consul. On 1 December 1799, shortly after the coup, Bonaparte visited the Louvre only to discover that the artistic booty of the 1796–1797 campaign in Italy—*his* booty—was not yet on

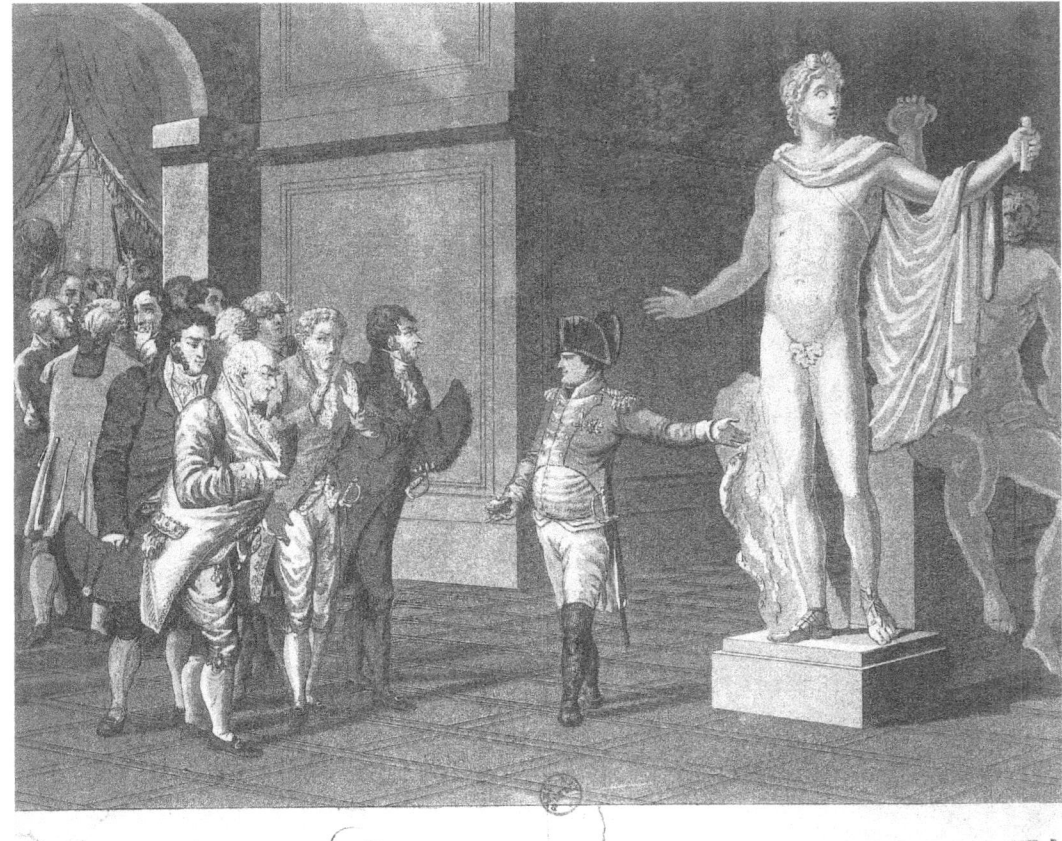

FIGURE 29.   Anonymous, *"And so Gentlemen! Two Million Francs!" remarks Napoléon as he points to the Apollo Belvedere*, ca. 1804. Aquatint engraving. Paris, BnF, Estampes, inv. Collection de Vinck, no. 6936 (16.3 × 20.9 cm). Photo: BnF, Paris.

public display. Hard questions to the museum administrators revealed there was no money to uncrate the works, much less to prepare spaces where they might be exhibited: incredibly, none of the museum staff, not even the guards, had been paid for fifteen months! Bonaparte immediately remarked that charging an entrance fee would offset most of the museum's financial woes, but this idea was vigorously opposed by museum administrators on the grounds that such a fee would not be democratic in the broadest sense. Bonaparte tried without success for more than a year to change the policy. Even in the midst of economic crisis museum officials vehemently opposed pay entry: their guiding principal was that the museum should be neither a project of personal prestige nor a money-making venture, but an institution of the Revolution open to everyone.

Eventually the museum's splendor did become associated with the name of a single person and his military conquests, but this was actually driven by the goal of keeping the museum free and open to the general public. Lacking their own assets, museum administrators were forced to look for a protector, and it soon became clear that the only possible candidate was Bonaparte. The museum's first official gesture in that direction occurred at the inauguration of galleries for the display of antique statuary brought from Italy. In the course of a gala private viewing for the elite of Parisian political and cultural life, Bonaparte was empressed to affix, on the pedestal of the *Apollo Belvedere* (Fig. 28), a bronze plaque reminding viewers that the sculpture before them "found at Antium at the end of the fifteenth century, placed in the Vatican by Julius II at the start of the sixteenth century, conquered in Year Five of the Republic by the Army of Italy under the command of General Bonaparte, was set up here on 20 Germinal Year 8, first year of his Consulat."[17]

Linking the museum's cultural prestige to Bonaparte's personal prestige began in earnest with the appointment of Dominique-Vivant Denon as director in November 1802.[18] It was largely complete by August 1803. In late July the Second Consul Jean-Jacques de Cambacérès, after making a preview visit to the newly rearranged sculpture galleries, wrote enthusiastically to the museum director that "the title that is best-suited to this precious collection is the name of the hero to whom we owe it. Thus, I think I express the nation's will by authorizing you to use for an inscription on the frieze above the entryway these words: Musée Napoléon."[19] The Englishman James Forbes happened to be in Paris at the time. His letter of 16 August bears witness both to the speed with which the recommendation of Cambacérès was implemented and to the fact that personal flattery now permeated the museum's rhetoric:

Another novelty to please the Parisians was the opening of Le Musée des Statues at the Louvre, which has been shut for some time to undergo various improvements; the scaffolding in front was removed, and over the new portal was inscribed in golden characters, *Musée Napoléon*. . . . The French catalogue informs us that the Apollo, after its destination in the Vatican by Pope Julius the Second, remained for three centuries near the banks of the Tiber, when a hero, conducted by victory, transported it to the borders of the Seine, and fixed it there for ever! So much for the Apollo.[20]

Public display of the museum's deference to Bonaparte is noteworthy on at least one other count, for the inscription was the first time that his given name—Napoléon—was used in the royal manner. Thus, renaming the museum prefigured by almost one year the fact that Bonaparte would eventually become Emperor Napoléon the First.

Like so many foreign visitors to Paris during these years, James Forbes viewed the collections of the Musée Napoléon with admiration tempered by a certain regret:

I never experience more mingled sensations than on entering the gallery of antiques. . . . The Apollo, the Laocoön, and many other masterpieces in sculpture which I had so lately beheld on classic

ground, excited many painful ideas, especially when I reflected on their unjust and insulting removal to Paris: at the same time, I must confess that the French have given them an honourable reception, and disposed of them in the best manner in six adjoining apartments, named after their most striking object.[21]

There were, nonetheless, some glitches. Many visitors to the museum complained that the lateral windows of the Grande Galerie produced an intolerable amount of glare on the pictures,[22] while others felt the ancient sculptures were placed too close to the walls and on bases too tall for optimal viewing.[23]

By contrast, the museum's generous visiting policies and—in particular—that it was open to the general public free of charge were very widely admired. Ann Plumptre's remarks on the subject are characteristic:

I must add my tribute of commendation to the French for the liberal manner in which these collections are thrown open to the use and entertainment of the public, and of foreigners in particular. They are all open twice a week for any one who chooses to visit them, while foreigners, artists, and literati, have the privilege of going in at any time: it must be observed that this is entirely without expense; not a servant, a door-keeper, or any one belonging to the establishments is ever permitted to receive the smallest gratuity. This is indeed worthy of a liberal and enlightened nation.[24]

Plumptre goes on to say that visiting the museum on the semi-private days reserved for foreigners is best for studying the collections, but that it is "worth while going sometimes on the public days" simply to watch the crowds:

The rooms are then thronged by a motley concourse of all ranks and descriptions of persons, all preserving the most exact order, and presenting the extraordinary spectacle of the most ignorant and the most enlightened uniting in equal notes of admiration;—of the ignorant beholding with as much reverence, and apparently with as much delight, as the scientific, works, the real excellence of which must be far above their comprehension. I question whether such a motley group in our own country would show the same respect for similar productions, or preserve the same order and regularity as the Parisian populace.[25]

Paradoxically, the museum's open-door policy tended to quicken identification of the growing collection with military conquest. Changing the name to Musée Napoléon instantiated a consensus best illustrated by the number of soldiers who flocked to the galleries on the weekend. "Saturdays and Sundays are open to everyone," remarked the German J. F. Reichardt with barely disguised malice; "on these days the crowd is so dense and so unwashed that Mondays have to be devoted to housecleaning. Amongst these crowds I have especially noticed many veterans and disabled soldiers, dressed in uniforms more or less in tatters."[26] What did these soldiers do at the Louvre? An English visitor pointed out that they went to see the fruits of their military efforts:

On our way home, we looked in again at the gallery of the Louvre, where we received at all times, the utmost gratification; it was one of the public days, and consequently very crowded; and it was a matter of great curiosity to see the soldiers (all of whom, when off guard, have free access to this place), possibly some of them the very captors of those pictures, surveying them with an air of triumph and witnessing the glorious acquisition which the power of their arms has brought home to their country.[27]

The museum's free and open access to the public, curious as it seemed to foreigners, was a lasting legacy of the Revolution that promoted development of a particularly Parisian arena for the exchange of ideas about art. The Musée Napoléon quickly became a center for study and learning and, to judge from eyewitness accounts, the galleries were used heavily by art students:

On the days appropriated to the accommodation of students, great numbers are to be seen in different parts of the museum, some mounted on little stages, others standing or sitting, all sedulously employed in copying the favourite object of their studies. Indeed, the epithet Central has been applied to this establishment, in order to designate a Museum, which is to contain the choicest productions of art, and, of course, to become the centre of study. Here, nothing has been neglected that could render such an institution useful, either in a political light, or in regard to public instruction. Its magnificence and splendour speak to every eye, and are calculated to attract the attention of foreigners from the four quarters of the globe; while, as a source of improvement, it presents to students the finest models that the arts and sciences could assemble.[28]

Another English visitor reports that during one of his trips to

the museum he saw "not less than twenty" students sketching in the sculpture galleries and "not less than fifty or sixty persons copying with easels and elevated stools quite close to the pictures" in the Grande Galerie; he too suggests that "these pictures and statues must prove a mine of wealth to Paris, as all the world will go to see them."[29]

Tourists were drawn to Paris by the lure of the museum's treasures, especially during the period of peace between England and France at the time of the Treaty of Amiens. It is estimated that during the summer of 1802 Paris welcomed approximately five thousand English tourists, and the number rose to almost twelve thousand during the single month of September.[30] This traffic fell to near zero when hostilities between the two countries were renewed in May of 1803. The final defeat of Napoléon in 1815 reopened the borders between France and England so that the Louvre once again drew visitors—like Henry Milton—to see the collection before it was dispersed by the Allies. The Grande Galerie became a fashionable meeting place:

From half past two o'clock till four the gallery is crowded. It is the general rendezvous of the English, and appears to supply extremely well the absence of Bond-street. The ladies sit on the benches, which are placed opposite the chief pictures, and look sideways at the gentlemen: the gentlemen walk up and down in long uncivil rows, and look full at the ladies:—and of the immense crowds of visitors from England who throng the Louvre, and doubtless would all assert that they came for the express purpose of studying its contents, it is laughable to observe how very few are really attentive to the treasures which surround them.[31]

For the more serious art lovers who came to Paris expressly to see the Louvre before its dispersal, the "troop of connoisseurs enter the doors every morning in fearful expectation that some of their favourites may have disappeared."[32]

Dismantling the collection began almost immediately. A contingent of Prussian soldiers entered the premises in July 1815 to take away by force the pictures that had been looted from northern Germany. Holland and several Italian states were quick to demand similar repatriations. The Duke of Wellington—head of the occupying Allied armies in Paris—sent British soldiers to the Louvre on 18 September 1815 to enforce removal of the Dutch and Italian pictures. Milton describes the ensuing scene:

This morning, the same rabble has been assembled to witness with astonishment and rage, the removal of the immense number of pictures which have been taken down during the last two days. It has long been certain that the collection would be broken up, but the Parisians, particularly the lower classes, could never bring themselves to believe that such an event was possible.[33]

Wellington's reasons for enforcing dispersal of the Louvre's collections were motivated by a feeling that it was an "opportunity of giving the people of France a great moral lesson." In his letter to the British Foreign Secretary explaining his decision, Wellington argued that the works had been "obtained by military concessions," and that "the people of France, if they do not already feel that Europe is too strong for them, should be made sensible of it; and that, whatever may be the extent, at any time, of their momentary and partial success against any one, or any number of individual powers in Europe, the day of retribution must come."[34]

Two weeks later the legendary horses from the cathedral of San Marco in Venice were removed from their perch atop the arc du Carrousel. A throng of spectators gathered in the courtyard and crowded the windows of the Louvre. Foreigners were allowed to approach the arch itself, but French citizens were held at bay along the quai by a contingent of Austrian cavalrymen who "shewed no backwardness in executing the task."[35] The sole vantage point for Frenchmen to watch the spectacle was from the windows of the Grande Galerie. Milton reports those on hand were "sullenly and ferociously attentive" until the moment that the first of the horses was suspended in the air:

The French could no longer bear the sights. Most of them drew back from the windows, and quitted the gallery, unable to suppress or disguise their feelings. Justice, policy, and good taste, all imperiously demanded that this ill-devised trophy should not be suffered to exist; but it was impossible at the moment not to feel some pity for the humiliation and misery of the French.[36]

The single greatest cultural monument of the Empire—the Musée Napoléon—ceased to exist, although the Louvre re-

mained, and remains to this day, one of the world's great museums. It may be true, as Cecil Gould suggests, that "the most unequivocal legacy of the Musée Napoléon is therefore the mere fact that for a few years it did exist, and that from that brief period enough traces survive to enable posterity, with a considerable effort of the imagination, to form some idea of its splendour."[37] Already in May of 1816, when Mary Berry revisited Paris, she wrote of the Louvre that "so many fine things still remain that they have certainly no right to complain. One can say the same thing of the statues; they are now working with great zeal to re-arrange them. The emplacement and decorations are superb. They have added many marble columns since I last saw it in 1802."[38] That work has continued unabated for almost two centuries. It seems safe to say that the Grand Louvre of today—from its pyramid by I. M. Pei to its renovated galleries and indoor sculpture courts—is an idea nourished, at least in part, by the memory and the prestige of the first Grand Louvre. Like then, today's Louvre is a mecca for lovers of the visual arts and the cornerstone of any discussion of the arts in Paris. Yet Paris was and remains a city of the arts: it is to the city itself that we now turn.

A City Beautiful: The Munificence of Rule

One of my recurring dreams was to make Paris the veritable capital of Europe. Sometimes, for example, I wanted her to become a city of two, three, or even four million people: in short, something fabulous, colossal, and never before seen, whose public institutions would have been able to support the population. . . . If the heavens would have given me but twenty years of rule and a bit of free time, one would have searched in vain for old Paris.

—Napoléon Bonaparte[39]

Writing from his exile on the island of Saint Helena, Napoléon vividly remembered his dreams for the city that he hoped Paris would become: capital of the Empire, political hub of Europe, the grandest urban space the world had ever seen. All the wealth, all the power, and all the ceremony of his empire were to be concentrated in Paris, veritable showpiece of his rule. Implementation of this grand scheme was thwarted by the cares and costs of constant war, and it was ultimately dashed by Napoléon's defeat in 1815. Nonetheless, the Empire set a benchmark for embellishing the capital unmatched until the team of Louis-Napoléon Bonaparte and Georges Haussmann, Prefect of Paris, initiated their program of dramatic, large-scale urban renewal in the early 1850s.

When Napoléon imagined a city of three or four million people, it was not simply an urban space dotted with monuments, but a total environment that would be safe, healthy, and clean. Some of his most important projects were improvements to the city's infrastructure: new quais (to control floods) and bridges (to foster commerce); new aqueducts and fountains (to improve hygiene); new markets and streets (to improve the distribution of goods); new cemeteries and slaughterhouses on the outskirts of town (to reduce the risk of disease and contamination).[40] There seemed to be such a buzz of activity everywhere in Paris that Prince Charles of Clary-Aldringen, visiting in 1810 at the time of Napoléon's second marriage, wrote to his mother in Vienna: "nothing can give an idea of the immense projects undertaken simultaneously in Paris. The incoherence of it is incredible; one cannot imagine that the life of a single man would be enough to finish them."[41] Many of Napoléon's utilitarian projects have more to do with urban history than with the arts of Paris, but some schemes did offer architects an opportunity to reshape the city's look in ways that have become synonymous with its visual identity. One such project was the rue de Rivoli.

Originally proposed in 1793 as a modest walkway along the Tuileries Garden to connect the Tuileries Palace with the royal stables, the rue de Rivoli really dates from 9 October 1801, when Napoléon authorized construction of a major artery connecting the northeast corner of the place de la Concorde to the place du Carrousel (Fig. 30). The project used several large plots of land north of the Tuileries Garden confiscated by the state from three different convents during the Revolution. It was decided in April of 1802—after reserving sufficient terrain for the new avenue—to sell the remaining parcels to developers. This large area was eventually subdivided by several new streets connecting the rue de Rivoli to the old rue Saint-Honoré and—via the present-day rue Castiglione—to the place Vendôme (Fig. 48).

Writing in 1804–1805, John Pinkerton recounted the work in progress and alluded to the project's symbolic meaning:

The street on the north of the Tuileries has been new paved, and the descent considerably lessened: several mean houses have here been pulled down, and a noble arcade or portico is actually begun, and is intended to be carried as far as the Garde Meuble, or whole length of the garden of the Tuileries. From this new and grand street, two others have been opened into the street Honoré and the Place Vendôme, the effect of the latter being particularly grand. It is hardly necessary to remind the reader who has visited Paris, that in order to open this street, along the north side of the garden, it was necessary to demolish, among other buildings, the famous Hall of the Convention, formerly the king's riding house, only a few niches of which remain in the garden wall.[42]

Pinkerton points out that the building which had served as meeting hall for the first three assemblies of the French Revolution—including the National Convention in the months before the Terror—has been literally erased from the fabric of Paris.[43] A few niches in the garden wall were the sole remnants of that stormy and chaotic site, and they were now to be seen from a broad, straight street of repeated arcades, aligned balconies, and restrained classical detailing that spoke of social order and master-planning.

The cut-stone facades of identical size and style that remain the hallmark of the rue de Rivoli were designed by Pierre-François Fontaine, Napoléon's favorite architect. Whereas the facades were erected at the government's expense, private investors were responsible for constructing buildings behind Fontaine's harmonious screen of elegant architecture. Despite the sizeable government investment, the project advanced very slowly. Near the end of 1810 Napoléon tried to stimulate investor interest in the area by according a thirty-year tax exemption on new buildings, but when Chateaubriand moved to an apartment on the rue de Rivoli during the winter of 1813 much of the street was still "only the arcades built by the government and a few houses erected here and there with their later denticulations of toothing stone."[44] Étienne Bouhot's 1808 picture of the rue Castiglione (Fig. 48) shows that some of the old convent buildings were still standing, even if the new cross-street was already in use.

FIGURE 30.   Giuseppe
Canella, *The rue de Rivoli in
Paris*, 1830. Oil on canvas.
Aix-en-Provence, Musée
Granet, inv. 903.3.003 (19.7
× 25.0 cm cm). Photo:
© Bernard Terlay CPA.

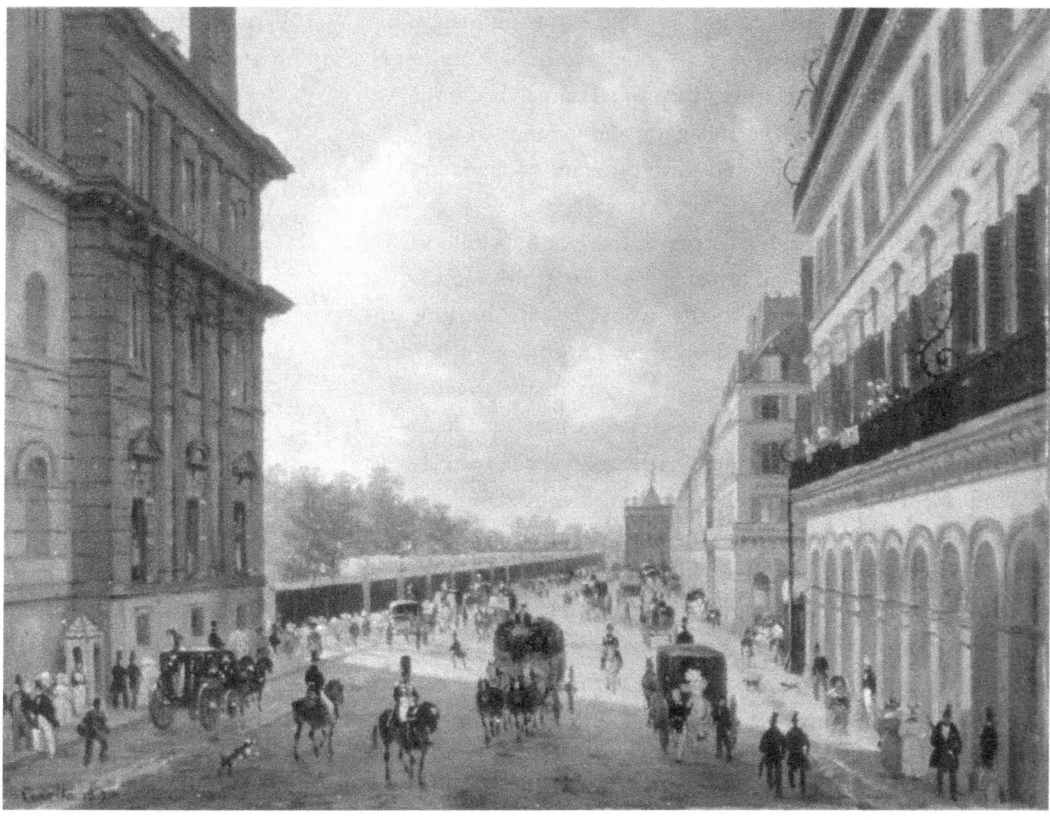

A tight money situation was partly to blame for the delay, but so too were the very strict limits placed on building use: no tradesmen working with hammers, no butchers, caterers, pastry or bakery shops, nor any business using an oven were allowed to settle along the rue de Rivoli. Shopowners were not allowed to hang signs on the exterior of the buildings, for that would disrupt the area's monumental scale and calm. Canella's painting of 1830 (Fig. 30) captures vividly the street's up-market character: the roadway is crowded with carriages and riders, the sidewalks are charged with pedestrians in elegant dress, but very few tradespeople are in evidence. The picture does not show that this world of order ends abruptly at the place des Pyramides, directly across from the Tuileries Palace (visible at the far left). Although the planned eastward extension of the rue de Rivoli to the Hôtel-de-Ville was not built until the Second Empire, the street's ensemble of straight trajectory, regular facades, and classical detailing re-

mained the prototype for the great boulevards cut through many parts of Paris during the 1850s and 1860s.

There were other, less spectacular urban projects initiated during the Empire, including improvements to the quais, clearing squares before the church of Saint-Sulpice and the cathedral of Notre-Dame, and constructing several streets in the neighborhood of Saint-Germain-des-Prés. None of these affected the city's daily life as much as the four new bridges that vastly improved circulation across the Seine: the pont Saint-Louis (1803), which connects the two islands in the center of town; the pont d'Austerlitz (1806), upstream near the Jardin des Plantes; the pont d'Iéna (1812), downstream at the Champ-de-Mars; and the pont des Arts (1803), which crosses the river at the cultural center of Paris by linking the Louvre to the Institut (Fig. 31).

The pont des Arts was designed as a pedestrian bridge that would allow individuals to cross the Seine without facing the usual dangers of carriages, horses, and commercial traffic. The bridge was also a technological curiosity, because it was the first in Paris to be built entirely of iron. "The curves which form the arches are gracefully arranged," remarked Henry Milton in 1815, "and as the piers are only the thickness of a pillar, the whole has a singularly light appearance."[45] The novelty of crossing this light and open structure, and the special beauty of its midstream panoramic view of Paris, ensured that the pont des Arts became a favorite destination of Parisian strollers. Although crossing was not free—pedestrians were required to pay a toll of one sous—it is said that sixty-four thousand people used the bridge on the day of its inauguration. Shortly afterward Ann Plumptre reported that it had already become "a fashionable lounge and promenade. . . . A coffee-house is erected at each end, and it is ornamented with orange-trees and other shrubs and flowers in pots."[46] A contemporary article in *Le Publiciste* waxed poetic on the special attractions of the new bridge:

It is a garden suspended over the water that pleases all the senses at once. On every side the eye wanders upon the most majestic buildings and then comes to rest with delight upon flowers from every region and every country. The air is gently freshened by that of the river, and sweetened by all the smells of heliotrope, rose, mignonette, jasmine, and orange blossom. Two rows of charming women complete the embellishment of this truly picturesque passageway which, on the whole, resembles that of a happy life: it is too short.[47]

This account reminds us that the pleasures of walking, a habit long nurtured by the city's boulevards, continued to shape the way Parisians adapted to changes in their environment: here, a utilitarian span quickly became a promenade; a few years later, the commercial spaces of glass-covered

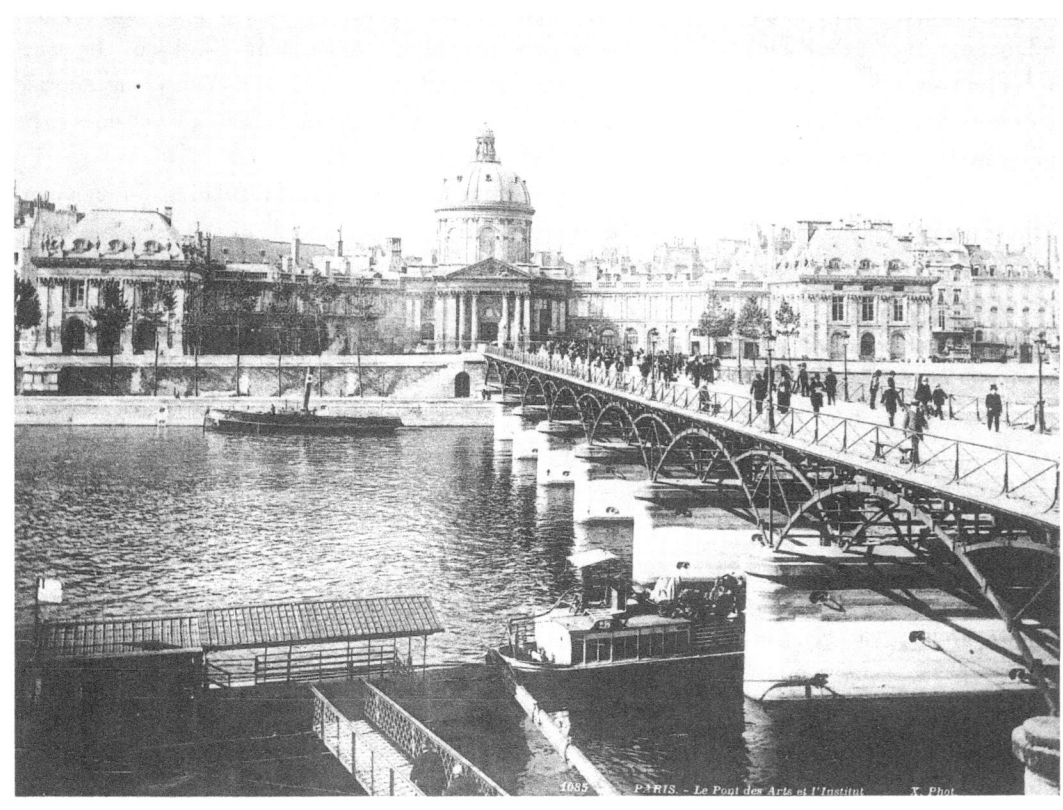

FIGURE 31. Louis-Alexandre de Cessart and Jacques Dillon, *The pont des Arts*, 1801–1803. Anonymous photograph, ca. 1900. Paris, BnF, Estampes, inv. Va 261a (18 × 24 cm). Photo: BnF, Paris.

passages would become arenas of highly stylized social encounters (see Chapter Seven).

THE PREDILECTION FOR STROLLING in Romantic Paris also informed the way cemeteries were transformed during the Empire from sinister enclaves of death and oblivion into public promenades of reverie and nostalgia. People had long been buried in small cemeteries close to parish churches scattered throughout the city: funerals were religious occasions and cemeteries belonged to the Church. Eighteenth-century city planners recognized that these urban cemeteries threatened the health of the living and must be treated as a municipal problem. Proposals were drafted in 1765 to close all of the city's cemeteries in favor of new ones beyond the city limits. Some of the most centrally located cemeteries—notably the Innocents near the church of Saint-Eustache—were shut down and their human remains transferred to new sites on the outskirts of town. Such projects were strongly opposed by the clergy, who feared that moving the dead away from churches—out of sight and mind—would jeopardize the substantial contributions they received from parishioners who paid for special prayers and masses in memory of souls languishing in purgatory.

The Revolution disrupted the established patterns of burial and remembrance by confiscating church property. Henceforth cemeteries belonged to the city, and the problems they posed became the business of municipal administrators. After 1789 the closing of cemeteries and moving their contents were accelerated because certain sites—deprived of surveillance by the local parish priest—became little more than open pits into which corpses were thrown, especially during the Terror of 1793–1794. At the time of Bonaparte's coup-d'état in 1799, the situation was not much improved, but corrective measures were soon forthcoming. In February 1801 the Prefect of the Seine, Nicholas Frochot, ordered construction of three large cemeteries outside of the city proper. That same year, Lucien Bonaparte—brother of Napoléon and Minister of the Interior—asked the Institut to open a competition on the following question: "What are the cer-

emonies to perform at funerals and the regulations to adopt for sepulchral spaces" if these are strictly laic and not attached to any specific religious practice?[48] The winning essay underscored the psychological need of survivors to demonstrate their sorrow, and the right to expect that corpses would be treated with respect by the authorities.

Philippe Ariès points out that the guiding principle of the Institut's discussion was "the affective relationship between the departed person and the survivors. It was in light of this *private* relationship that one discussed what steps to take."[49] A new set of rituals serving a "cult of the dead" came to replace the religious practices that had previously served the church: exposing the body, especially with the face uncovered; embalming the body to fix its appearance in the memory of survivors; enacting legal issues, such as proclaiming the death and reading the will, at ceremonies performed by civil officials; finally, transferring the body in a public cortège to the cemetery. In this scheme of civil and ceremonial display, the cemetery—itself a public space—became a final resting place, where each body has its own plot and each plot is marked and named by a monument or a stone. The cemetery was transformed into a place for remembering, a locale where periodic visits encourage memories of loved ones to be renewed and restored.

The government's final decree regulating funerals and cemeteries in Paris was announced on 12 June 1804. Most of the recommendations presented by the Institut competition of 1801 were adopted, including the important clause that no cemeteries were to be allowed within the city limits nor within forty meters of them. The decree stipulated that graves must be arranged side by side instead of being stacked vertically as in the past. It also specified the size of plots, the distance between them, the depth at which the coffins must be placed, and the time (five years) before which an ordinary plot might be reused. All these measures responded to health and sanitary concerns. The decree also endorsed the idea that cemeteries should be landscaped like gardens with pathways and trees, and—most important—included a provision for individuals to buy perpetual rights to a plot, thus removing it from the usual five-year rotation. In this way, it became possible for families to construct monuments to themselves, while the prescribed garden setting meant that visiting such monuments might even be pleasant.

At the time of Frochot's decree to build three new cemeteries, the city bought a large plot of land to the east that had been appropriated during the Revolution from the Jesuits. It had once been the residence of François de La Chaise, the Jesuit confessor of Louis XIV. The site comprised more than seventeen hectares (about forty-two acres), including a prominent plateau from which one can still see all of Paris. Alexandre-Théodore Brongniart was the architect chosen to design the layout for the cemetery known today as Père Lachaise. Brongniart proposed some monumental forms of geometric simplicity (Fig. 32): a massive portal signifying passage from the world of life to that of death; a large pyramid reminiscent of those admired by Bonaparte in Egypt. He also envisaged a network of meandering pathways and smaller structures scattered throughout the grounds, a formula patterned after the picturesque gardens of eighteenth-century England.

Preliminary landscaping of the grounds proceeded fairly quickly, so that the first burials at Père Lachaise took place in May 1804. By contrast, the more substantial architectural elements of Brongniart's plan were barely begun when he died in 1813. They were never completed. The pyramid was abandoned for a much smaller chapel built by Étienne-Hippolyte Godde in 1824–1825, and the entryway was finished on a much smaller scale than originally designed.

Père Lachaise was not an immediate success, for many Parisians felt it was too far from town and hard to reach. With only 110 burials registered during its first four years of operation, Napoléon began a campaign to increase the cemetery's appeal by insisting that officers killed in combat be buried there. Thus, Brongniart designed in 1810 a sepulcher for Guillaume Lagrange, an officer of the Imperial Guard who died in Poland: the monument was located on an alley leading to the plateau and became an extremely popular destination for melancholic ruminations. Soon this sector of the cemetery was the preferred resting place for military heroes and, in the following decades, for Imperial veterans who wanted to be buried amongst their comrades. During the Bourbon Restoration this same part of the cemetery was

a favorite pilgrimage for Parisians harboring a nostalgia for the Empire and its past glories. Such was the success of Napoléon's campaign to attract attention to Père Lachaise that it became a mark of prestige for civilians to be buried there. The program of perpetual concession, coupled with individual ambitions to leave a personal monument worthy of note, proved so successful that the cemetery was forced to expand in 1824. Expansions continued right to mid-century much to the dismay of the surrounding communities. When the Musée des Monuments français was disbanded in 1817 (see Chapter Four), its most popular attractions—monuments to the lovers Héloïse and Abélard and to the writers La Fontaine and Molière—were transferred to Père Lachaise, where they remained accessible to the public.

The popularity of Père Lachaise rested upon more than a few famous names, for it was propelled by the contemporary undercurrent of melancholy and retrospection already discussed around the pictures of Charpentier (Fig. 5), Vafflard (Fig. 8), and Géricault (Fig. 13). With its winding paths, shade trees, and monuments to greatness, Père Lachaise emerged as a preferred site for romantic reflections upon the past—made all the more poignant by its commanding view of the present city. Frances Trollope, an Englishwoman who visited the grounds in 1835, left a vivid account of the sensations elicited by remembering at Père Lachaise:

This mournful garden is altogether a very solemn and impressive spectacle. What a world of mortality does one take in at a glance! It will set one thinking a little, however fresh from the busy idleness of Paris,—of Paris, that antidote to all serious thought, that especial paradise for the worshippers of *sans souci*. . . . I do not remember any spot, either in church or churchyard, where the unequal dignity of the memorials raised above the dust which lies so very equally beneath them all is shown in a manner to strike the heart so forcibly as it does at Père Lachaise. Here, a shovelful of weeds have hardly room to grow; and there rises a costly pile, shadowing its lowly neighbor. . . . It is an epitome of the world they have left: remove the marble and disturb the turf, human nature will be found to wear the same aspect under both. Many groups in deep mourning were wandering among the tombs; so many indeed, that when we turned aside from one, with the reverence one always feels

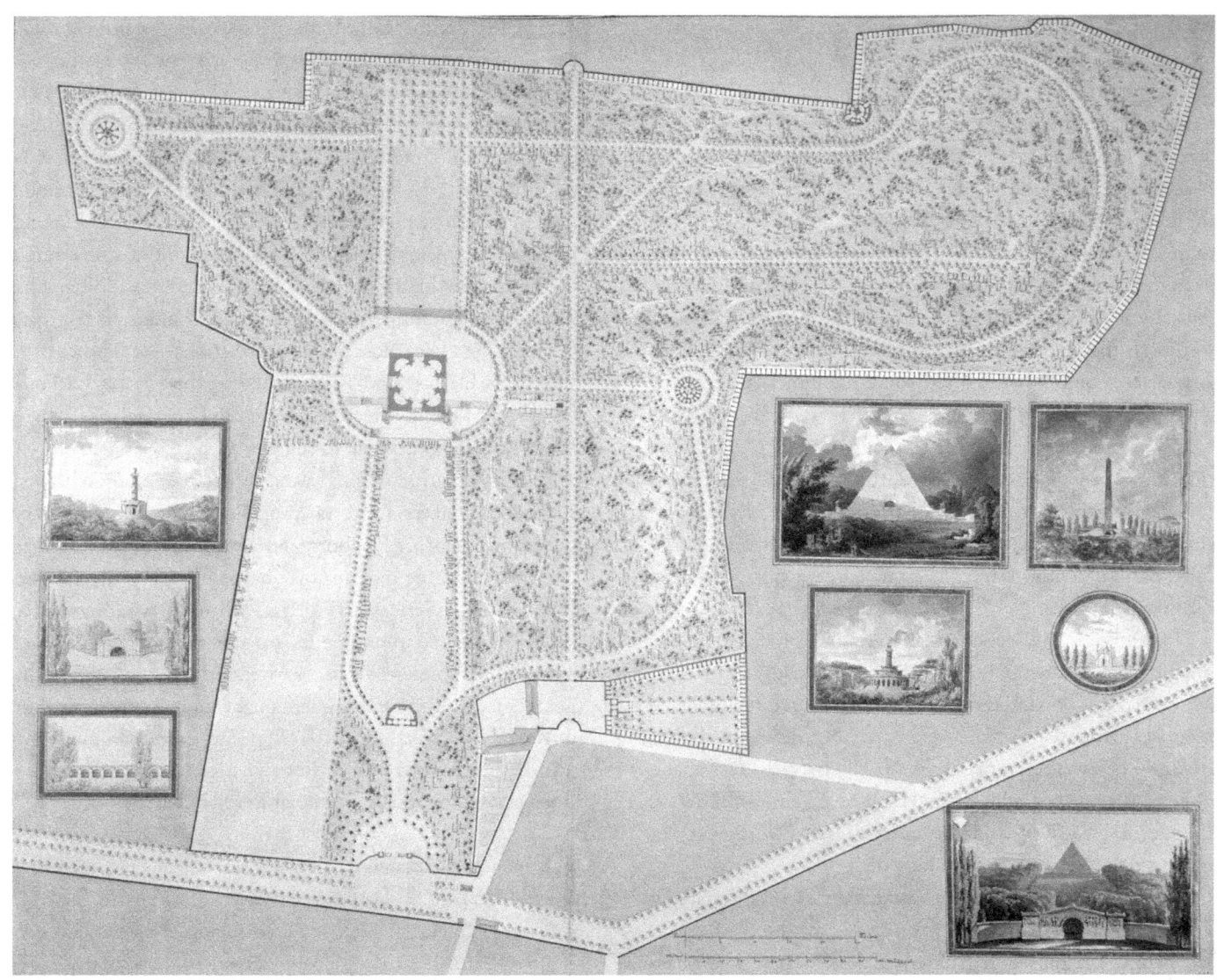

FIGURE 32. Alexandre-Théodore Brongniart, *Père Lachaise Cemetery (plan and vignettes)*, 1804. Ink and watercolor. Paris, Musée Carnavalet, inv. D 6701 (55.5 × 68.6 cm). Photo: © Centre des monuments nationaux, Paris/Alain Lonchampt.

disposed to pay to sorrow, we were sure to encounter another. This manner of lamenting in public seems so strange to us! ... It would, I believe, be more just, as well as more generous, instead of accusing the whole nation of being the victims of affectation instead of sorrow under every affliction that death can cause, to believe that they feel quite as sincerely as ourselves; though they certainly have a very different way of showing it.[50]

It is perhaps characteristic of the aesthetic complexity of these years that the garden of lamentation at Père Lachaise—where juxtapositions of wealth and poverty, pretense and sincerity formed an "epitome of the world" of the living—was designed by an architect simultaneously raising a temple to commerce in the heart of Paris, amidst a bustle of activity completely at odds with the reclusive sentiments of his cemetery. To appreciate fully this contrast brings us to the story of Brongniart's Bourse.

THE PECULIAR HISTORY of public finance in France during the eighteenth century tended to discredit a main premise of modern banking. With memories of the failure of John Law's bank in 1716, the financial troubles of the government's Caisse d'escompte in the 1780s, and the ephemeral worth of revolutionary *assignats* during the 1790s still fresh, Frenchmen were wary of paper money backed by a national bank. The Bank of England was founded in 1694 and flourished during the eighteenth century. By contrast, the Banque de France did not exist until January 1800, when First Consul Bonaparte joined forces with some of the leading money agents of Paris to establish a semi-public institution empowered to print paper money. His move coincided with an important evolution in handling the flow of goods and capital across Europe: single, centralized markets for all types of transactions were giving way to a specialization in which commercial products (such as wheat, corn, or coal) were traded in different physical spaces from stocks, bonds, and other forms of capital investment. This latter market was growing rapidly and several major European cities—notably Berlin and Saint Petersburg—erected splendid new

buildings especially suited to its needs. The Paris Bourse enjoyed no such permanence, but lived a somewhat peripatetic existence for more than a decade. Opened and closed several times during the Revolution, the Bourse was installed for a while in the Louvre, spent a few years in the Palais-Royal and, from the start of the Consulat in 1797 until 1802, was lodged in the disaffected church of the Petits-Pères, today Notre-Dame-des-Victoires. This last locale was much criticized. "Isn't it indecent and ridiculous," remarked the *Gazette de France*, "that Paris does not have what any commercial city calls a Bourse, and that traders are reduced to suffocating in the church of the Petits-Pères or to making deals in a public garden? The Revolution put so many buildings under the government's control that such an oversight is unforgivable."[51] In 1802 the Bourse was provisionally placed in a part of the former convent of the Filles-Saint-Thomas on the rue Feydeau that had long been used as a stage-set shop for the Paris Opera.

Napoléon could not ignore the fact that neither the Banque de France nor the Bourse were lodged in quarters worthy of the capital of a great empire. Yet his early thinking about a solution was singularly out of phase with emerging market practices, for he envisioned placing the entire financial community—Banque de France, Bourse, Tribunal de Commerce, Agents de Change, and Courtiers de Commerce—in a single, enormous structure. He was also keen to find a use for the unfinished church of the Madeleine, located just north of the place de la Concorde. His plan was to adapt that site for the new financial center. Pierre Fontaine, Napoléon's chief architect, tried to dissuade the Emperor from this course on the grounds that the Madeleine's completed foundations were too narrow for the kind of spaces required by a bank and stock exchange. Similarly, the chief of government buildings counseled against putting all the financial services in a single structure. Napoléon refused to budge: a decree of 21 February 1806 announced his plan to the public.[52] The project pleased no one, not the least being future occupants who felt the Madeleine was too far from the neighborhood of the Palais-Royal, which remained the banking and financial center of Paris.

Napoléon eventually had second thoughts about giving

one of the most beautiful sites of modern Paris to the banking community, for he changed his mind on 2 December 1806: the Madeleine would become a monument dedicated to the glories of the Grand Army.[53] Ten days later Napoléon wrote from Poland to Champagny, his Minister of the Interior:

It is, however, necessary to have a Bourse in Paris. My plan is to build a Bourse that might conform to the grandeur of the capital and to the amount of business that will one day be conducted there. Suggest some suitable locale. It must be vast so as to have promenades on all sides. I would like to have a detached site.[54]

For many years the financial community had pressed Napoléon to build a new Bourse on the site of the disaffected convent of Filles-Saint-Thomas, across the street from their temporary quarters. The terrain was large, centrally located in the financial district, and easily accessible to both the Seine and the boulevards. For these same reasons Napoléon resisted the move, because he wanted to sell that parcel to developers at a profit and use the proceeds for renovations at the Louvre. Finally, on 5 March 1808, Napoléon yielded to a complex deal: the Banque de France would buy from the state for two million francs the spacious old hôtel de Toulouse, near the place des Victoires, as its new home; half of this sum would be used by the government to start work on a Bourse at the convent Filles-Saint-Thomas; the remainder of construction costs would be funded by the business community and money agents of Paris. At the very least, these long and drawn-out negotiations for the Bourse remind us that Napoléon remained attentive to a project's bottom-line, regardless of his desire to have truly grand monuments.

During the more than two years of trying to close on a site for the Bourse, Brongniart remained in close contact with friends in the administration so that his own planning might shadow the Emperor's evolving views of the matter. When the decision was finally made to build on the site of the former convent, only Brongniart was able to present a fully developed project that was also attuned to Napoléon's symbolic aspirations for the building. Brongniart proposed a colonnaded temple structure that would be an architectural pendant to the Temple of Glory across town;

it is said that when his plan for an "Imperial Palace of the Bourse" was presented to the Emperor, the latter replied: "Mr. Brongniart, this is very fine! Put the workers on it!"[55] Yet it would be wrong to conclude that Brongniart slavishly plopped yet one more Roman imperial temple into the Emperor's capital city. The Bourse was part of a large urban-renewal scheme designed to clear a space for the new structure, provide adequate access, and open the vast promenades that Napoléon wanted. A rectangular space was carved out of the sprawling site of the former convent: in some cases, simply by altering facades; in others, notably along the north side, by constructing a block of houses to mask the meandering path of the rue Feydeau. New streets were cut through the neighborhood: the rue Vivienne was extended north to the boulevards; today's rue Notre-Dame-des-Victoires (behind the future building) was widened and extended both north and south; a street on-axis from the principal facade of the building was connected to the rue Richelieu. Courvoisier's view of the Bourse from about 1820 (Fig. 33) is much idealized and spatially exaggerated, but it provides a good idea of the structure's scale and compactness within its original site.

Those qualities are lost by later additions of flanking wings and an attic to the central core. Today the Bourse appears overly large for its space. By contrast, the Napoleonic building stood smartly away from its neighbors, and was further isolated by stands of trees suitable for shaded promenades. Moreover, Brongniart's original plan called for an Ionic-order temple more elegant and less grand than what was actually built. Several years into the construction— and well after the foundations and columnar spacing were complete—the future tenants decided that the upper story, which had been reserved as storage space, should be fitted up as full-fledged offices. This entailed raising the ceilings and heightening the columns, but doing so made them too tall and too closely spaced for the proportions of Brongniart's Ionic order. The entire temple was converted to the more ornate Corinthian order so as to mesh its taller profile with the proportional logic of a correct architectural idiom. Paradoxically, what appears today to be a hackneyed display of imperial ostentation was actually conceived with great tact

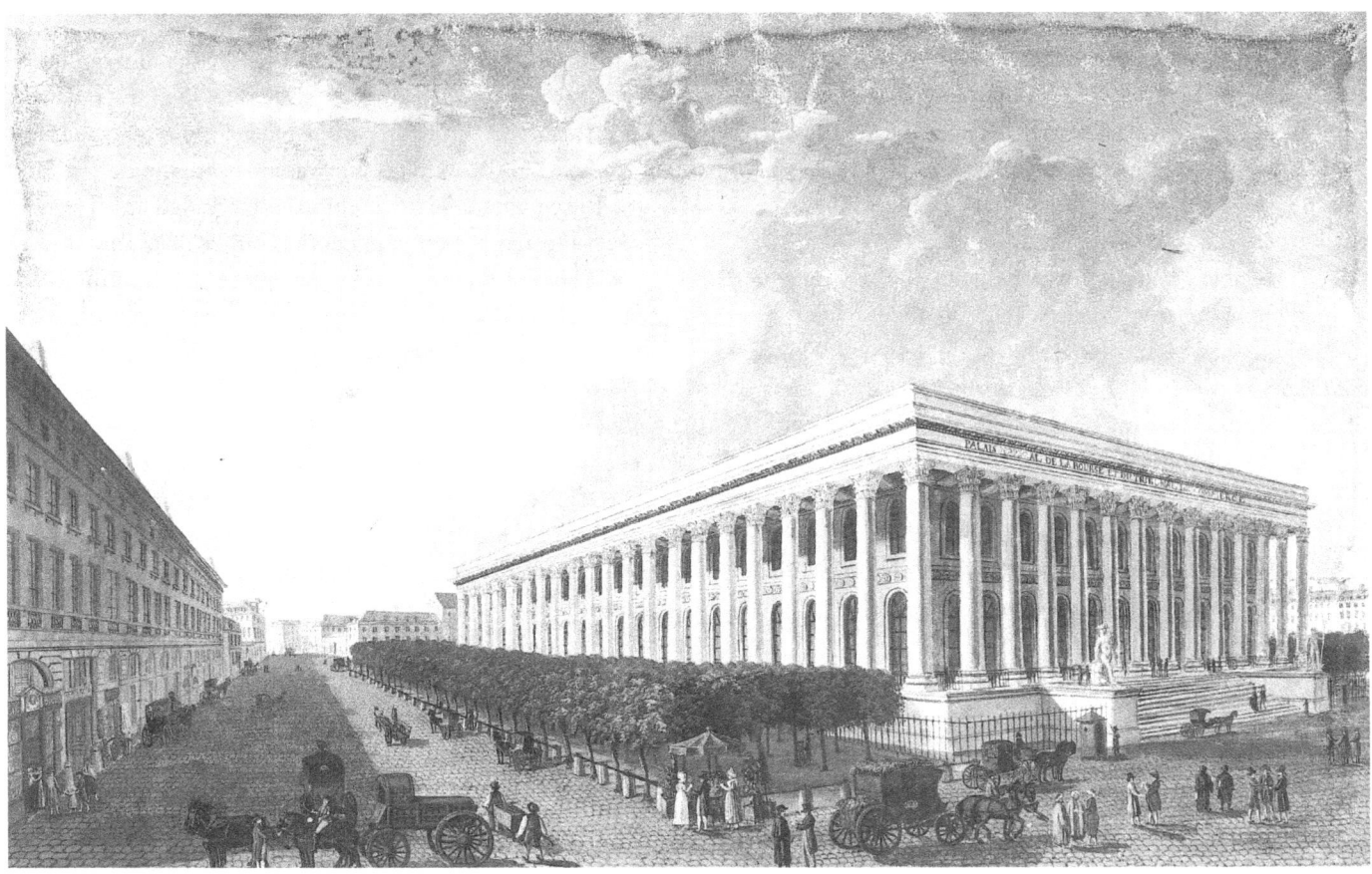

FIGURE 33.   Henry Courvoisier, *The Bourse and the place de la Bourse*, ca. 1820. Gouache. Paris, Musée Carnavalet, inv. D 03797 (50 × 78 cm). Photo: © PMVP.

and restraint as part of a complex project of urban renewal in this old *quartier* of central Paris.

Brongniart was not destined to see the completion of his Bourse: at his death in June 1813 the shell was finished only to the top of the columns. Yet the building's grandeur was already recognized. Pierre Fontaine remarked that "he [Brongniart] has left unfinished one of the most beautiful and most important monuments of the present reign."[56] Parenthetically, when Fontaine qualified the Empire as "the present reign" he betrayed his secret worries about the course of the war in 1813. Napoléon spoke of the Bourse with Fontaine on Christmas eve of that year, at the very last meet-

ing the two men would have to discuss the monuments of Paris. "Today," recorded Fontaine in his journal,

the Emperor, having gone by carriage to visit some of the new buildings under construction in Paris—such as the Bourse, the Madeleine, the markets of Saint-Martin and Temple, and the surplus grain storehouses—had me come to his dinner to talk about what he had seen. The Bourse, whose columns now rise to the height of the capitals, struck him as very beautiful. He wants the interior spaces, especially the large room, to match the magnificence of the exterior.[57]

Napoléon would never see the big skylighted main room, for the building was not inaugurated until November 1826, five years after his own death in exile on the island of Saint Helena.

Courvoisier's image of the Bourse, which certainly predates its inauguration, discreetly alludes to the demise of Napoléon: the original inscription on the entablature—*Palais Imperial de la Bourse et du Tribunal de Commerce*—has been partially effaced so that the word "imperial" is no longer legible. It is legible, of course, and would have been all the more so to contemporaries who knew full well under what regime the building had been commissioned and designed. This discontinuity between the Bourse's building history and its political context revisits the issues of monuments, memory, and the slippage of a monument's symbolism that opened this chapter. No one thought for a minute of demolishing Napoléon's Bourse because of the imperial connotations of its temple-form architectural style; it was far more expedient—and far less costly—simply to change its name.

BUDGETARY CONCERNS were among the main reasons why the Bourbon Restoration figures only marginally in the history of Parisian monuments during the first half of the nineteenth century. The country's financial situation remained precarious during the period 1815–1830 since the peace treaty imposed upon France by the Allies in 1815 exacted heavy war reparations and required full payment of all debts incurred by the government of Napoléon. There was little money for monuments. The Bourbons preferred to spend available funds on the twin tasks of reclaiming royal edifices expropriated by the Revolution and Empire, and restoring the lost splendor of churches that had been sacked, stripped, and left in ruins during anti-clerical years of the preceding decades.

The Restoration inherited a Louvre that had been the greatest museum in the world, but with galleries picked clean by Allied armies eager to recover the more than five thousand works of art looted by the Empire from the four corners of Europe. Already in July of 1816 Louis XVIII decided not to reinhabit the Louvre as a royal residence, preferring instead that it remain a museum—even if this meant continuing an

institution founded by the National Convention.[58] To fill some of the voids in the collection left by the dismantling of the Musée Napoléon, Auguste de Forbin, the museum's new director, gathered pictures from other locations—for example, the Marie de Medici cycle was moved to the Louvre from the Luxembourg Palace. Forbin also embarked on an aggressive campaign of purchasing entire private collections: in 1818 the Choiseul-Gouffier collection of ancient sculptures and the Tochon collection of Greek vases; in 1824 Edme-Antoine Durand's vast collection of Egyptian antiquities, Greek vases, and objects from the Middle Ages and Renaissance numbering more than six thousand items; in 1826 the Henry Salt collection of Egyptian antiquities; finally, in 1828, the collection of French antiquities assembled by the painter Pierre-Henri Révoil. In a report of November 1824—on the heels of the Durand acquisition and the memory of the Musée Napoléon hovering in the shadows—Forbin wrote to the Minister of the Interior that "since the time that the hazards of war plundered the museum, there has never been a more propitious moment to restore all the splendor of this great institution." He suggested that a section of the Louvre adjacent to the present museum be used to "bring together this immense collection, and that the most fitting name to give it would be the Musée Charles X."[59] An accomplished courtier, Forbin knew full well that the idea of a "museum within the museum" filled with new acquisitions, and named after the new king (Charles X was crowned in 1824), would be welcomed as a gesture of erasing memories of the Musée Napoléon.

Pierre Fontaine, who remained architect in charge of the Louvre after the defeat of Napoléon, designed a suite of eighteen rooms for the Musée Charles X (nine on the Seine side of the building and nine overlooking the Cour Carré). A separate entrance distinguished these new galleries from the picture galleries that belonged to the Louvre proper. Forbin commissioned a cycle of ceiling paintings for the new museum that opened with an homage to Charles X, *The King commanding the Musée Charles X* by Antoine-Jean Gros, that was removed from view after the 1830 Revolution. On the courtyard side, Forbin specified allegories loosely related to the antiquities exhibited in those rooms; on the river side, he chose subjects inspired by incidents from the history of the monarchy more or less contemporary with the objects on display. Thus, Eugène Devéria's picture, *Puget presents his Statue of Milo of Crotona to Louis XIV in the Gardens of Versailles* (Fig. 34), was destined for a gallery dedicated to a display of seventeenth-century drawings. The ceiling also refers indirectly to the fact that Forbin had recently brought Puget's sculpture of 1683 to the Louvre, where it went on display in 1819.

Despite Forbin's claim that the ceilings of the riverside galleries were "conceived historically,"[60] Gustave Planche could not resist the sarcasm that Devéria's picture was a "clumsy and false piece of flattery" because the event was a complete fiction:

It was not M. Eugène Devéria's job to leaf through biographies and learn that Puget never came to Versailles or that he saw the king only once at Fontainebleau, many years after his son had presented his masterpiece to Louis the Great; he was not supposed to read Lebrun's correspondence, or the manuscripts of Father Bougerel, so as to learn of the unsuccessful requests of the artist, who humbly explained to His Majesty that the sculpture bought for 15,000

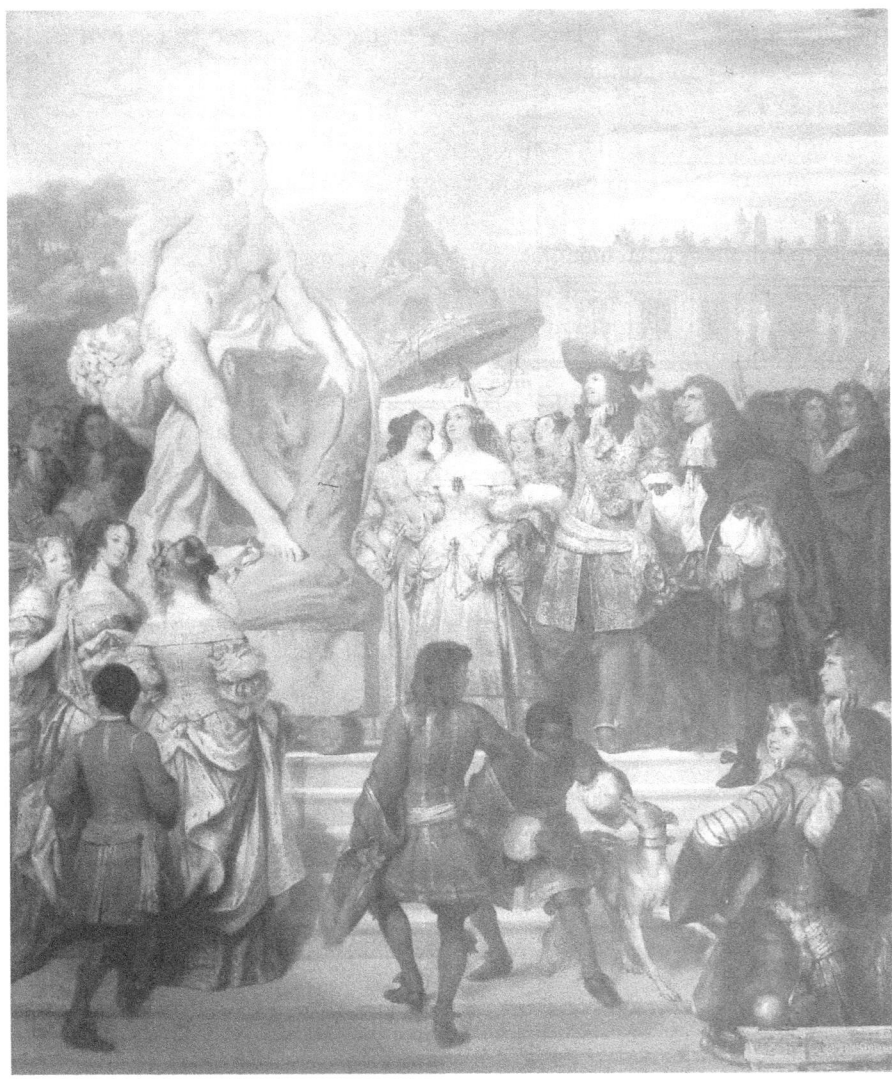

FIGURE 34.   Eugène Devéria, *Puget presents his Statue of Milo of Crotona to Louis XIV in the Gardens of Versailles*, 1832. Oil on canvas attached to ceiling. Paris, Musée du Louvre, Ceiling of the Third Gallery of Ancient Ceramics, inv. INV4074. Photo: © RMN/Art Resource, NY.

francs had actually cost him 14,500 francs to produce. It is up to the administration to look into these trifles, this loyal generosity, these lavish incentives.[61]

Apart from its historical fantasy, Devéria's picture, like all those commissioned for the Musée Charles X, is a kind of imposter, for it is actually a large-scale easel painting on canvas, executed in the studio, and glued to the ceiling. None of Forbin's commissions were "decorative" in a strong sense of the word, for they were not conceived for their specific architectural emplacements nor even as ceilings. Which is why Devéria's picture reads with a distinct top and bottom, and creates an illusion of space whose coordinates have little to do with the architecture of the gallery itself.

Forbin apparently sensed this lack of integration in the new galleries. He later commissioned *grisaille* paintings of decorative friezes for the gallery covings that were not part of his original project in an attempt to provide a visual and thematic bridge between the architectural elements and the ceiling paintings. But this was a jerry-rigged solution that only served to mask the real problem with the Musée Charles X commissions: artists were painting for spaces other than ceilings. Above all, they designed pictures to look good at the annual exhibition before the public and the critical press, because that was where reputations were made. The sculptor Pierre-Jean David d'Angers said publicly what many whispered in private when he proposed, in an article of 1838, that pictures destined to decorate public monuments be banned from the annual exhibitions. He believed this would "compel the artist to execute his work for the place it ought to be seen, without sacrificing the demands of monumentality to the futile honor of finding favor during the run of the Salon."[62] What were some of these "demands of monumentality"? The question raises critical issues about the renewal of monumental wall painting, one of the key developments in the art of Paris to emerge during the first half of the nineteenth century.

"MONUMENTAL PAINTING," remarked Gustave Planche in 1837, "by taking up several years of one's life, by making it pos-

sible for intentions to develop freely on lofty walls, greatly accelerates the training of an artist, and gives to his soul a peace of mind that doubles his forces. Endowed with a palace or a church, a salon or a chapel, the painter scales his ambitions to the size of his task."[63] A few months later Eugène Delacroix expressed something of that exhilaration when he wrote in a letter to his friend Charles Rivet: "I am on the trail of two or three intrigues . . . with the aim of painting a few feet of wall space, something that will surely not pay much more than I have already earned, but which will satisfy the need to work large, a need that becomes more pressing once one has tried it."[64] Delacroix's intrigues were rewarded—and his desire to paint large fulfilled—by the commission he received in the summer of 1838 to decorate the ceiling of the library in the Palais-Bourbon (today the National Assembly).[65]

The room is a long and narrow rectangle (42 × 10 meters), and the ceiling presents a complex surface of five cupolas and two half-domes (Fig. 35). Respecting the cardinal rule of monumental decoration argued by David d'Angers in 1838—that the work must respond to the shape and purpose of the architecture in which it is situated—Delacroix devised a sequence of paintings that "relate to philosophy, history and natural history, lawmaking, eloquence, literature, poetry, and even theology. Obviously, they recall the divisions used in every library, without however following exactly that system of classification."[66] The five domes organize these areas of knowledge thematically—Poetry, Theology, Legislation and Eloquence, History and Philosophy, and Science are arranged from north to south—but in a way that responds to the specifics of this particular library: the central dome of Legislation and Eloquence is above the entrance door, since they are subjects of special importance to the elected lawmakers who were the library's principal users.

Delacroix's presentation of human learning is bracketed historically by half-domes at each end. On the south,

FIGURE 35. Eugène Delacroix, *View of the ceiling paintings of the Bibliothèque du Roi*, 1836–1847. Oil and wax on plaster and oil on canvas attached to wall. Paris, Assemblée Nationale (Palais-Bourbon). Photo: © Centre des monuments nationaux, Paris.

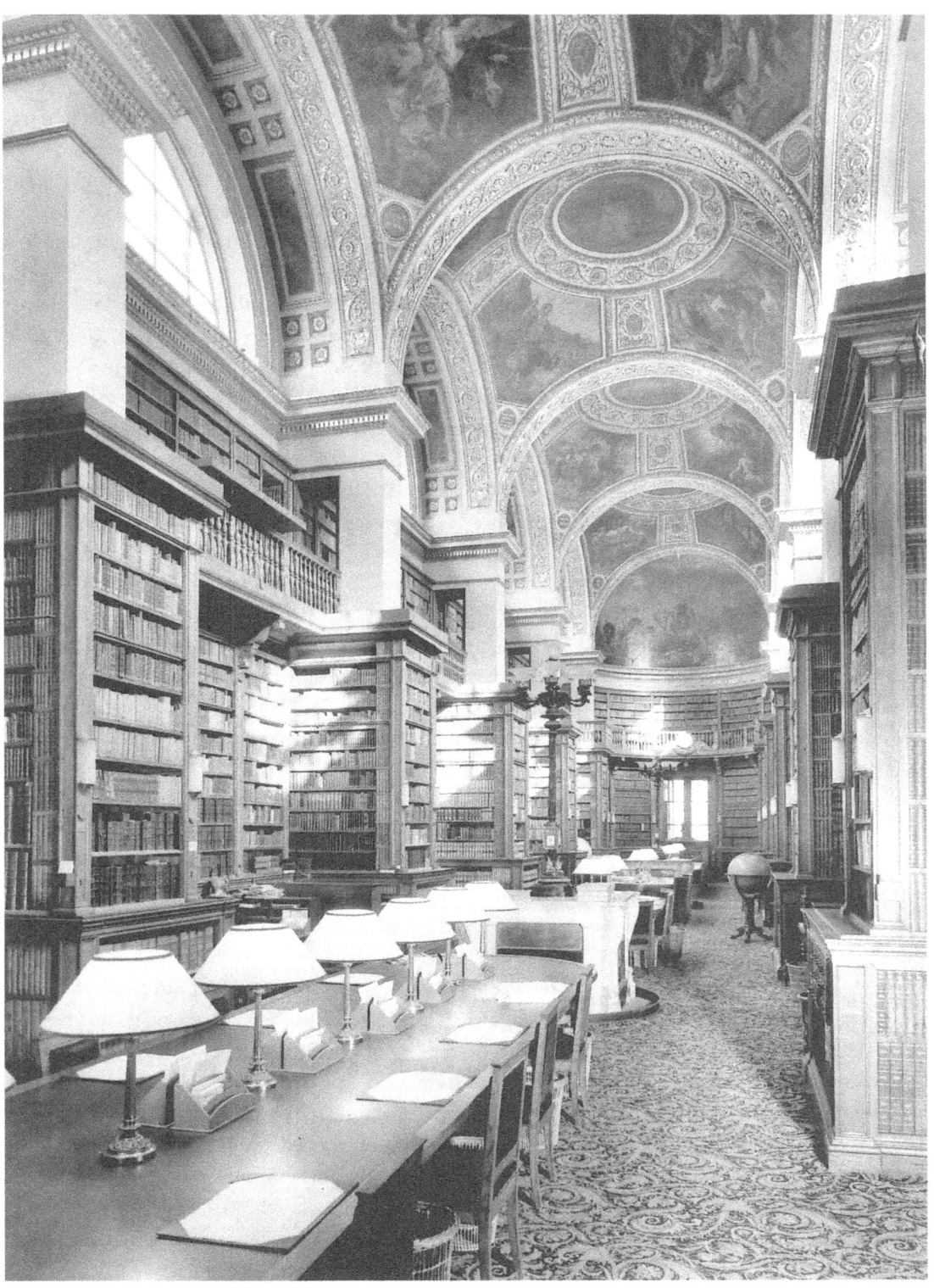

Orpheus brings to the Greeks the benefits of the arts and civilization while, at the north, Attila and his hordes overrun Italy and the arts. Lee Johnson aptly remarks that the Orpheus theme "quietly opens the era of ancient civilization" while the Attila episode

brings it to a violent close; bracketed between these epochal events and displayed for the edification of those politicians who care to look up is an array of exemplars of civilized conduct, of enlightened rule, of intellectual curiosity, and moral fortitude for which the price is sometimes shown to be death or exile.[67]

Delacroix's planning thus underscores a second trait felt to be an essential part of serious monumental painting; it must be morally edifying. "Monumental art," wrote Alexandre Descamps in 1836, "makes nations more powerful, more moral, and more enlightened."[68]

A project on the scale and complexity of Delacroix's ceiling for the Palais-Bourbon Library required assistants; indeed, many of the oddly shaped pendentive pictures for the five domes were painted by Louis de Planet or Gustave Lassalle-Bordes after drawings provided by their master. These works were executed in oil on canvas in the studio and touched up by Delacroix before being glued in place. Once installed, they were reworked again to balance colors relative to the natural light of the library.[69] Delacroix personally painted most of the large half-domes at each end of the room using a medium known as encaustic [peinture à la cire], which consists of applying oil paints mixed with wax directly on a wall prepared with a coating of wax. One of the most important motives behind Delacroix's use of encaustic was that it forced him to work in situ, thus emulating the practice of Italian Renaissance masters such as Giotto, Perugino, or Raphael, whose great fresco cycles remained the most revered exemplars of monumental painting. Genuine fresco—painting applied directly to a coat of wet plaster on the wall—is by definition architectural, its surface is matte and non-reflective, and its colors are more luminous than oil paints, which is a great advantage in the often dark spaces of a church. The disadvantages of true fresco are that it requires a large crew of master plasterers, painters must work quickly and cannot correct mistakes, and the damp climate of Paris is not particularly conducive to its conservation. Delacroix, like most of his contemporaries committed to working directly on the wall, adopted encaustic for several practical reasons: its formal qualities are similar to fresco, notably colors more pale and matte than oil paints; it can be retouched; it is fairly resistant to cold and damp. "[Encaustic] presents a thousand difficulties and delays," wrote Hippolyte Flandrin, "but it does not reflect light, which is its most notable advantage."[70]

Devéria's aesthetically self-sufficient picture for the ceiling of the Musée Charles X (Fig. 34) and Delacroix's suite of programmatic decorations specifically designed for the Palais-Bourbon Library sketch the general development of monumental painting in France during the Bourbon Restoration and July Monarchy. In the first years after the fall of Napoléon, it was felt that public spaces should be recuperated from the recent past as quickly as possible; the surest way of achieving that was to commission ordinary—albeit large—paintings that could be hung easily and even moved around if needed. This was especially true for churches stripped of their ornamentation during the Revolution, even though the circumstances of church decoration had been fundamentally altered by events of the preceding twenty years. According to the terms of the 1802 Concordat between Bonaparte and Pope Pius VII, the Catholic Church was reestablished in France but the state retained ownership of ecclesiastical lands and buildings. Obviously, Napoléon could not renege on the revolutionary seizures of church property without calling into question all the other seizures effected at the same time, many of which had since been sold to profit the state (for example, the parcel of land upon which the Bourse was built). The Concordat stipulated that the great cathedrals of France were owned by the central government, parish churches belonged to the city in which they were located, and salaries of local priests and bishops were to be paid by the state. Napoléon's intent was to harness the power of the Church as a tool of social control by making its material existence completely dependent upon the government.

Consequently, if the churches of Paris were to be readorned with paintings and sculpture after 1815, either the city or the central government would be obliged to pay the costs.

That is precisely what happened in Paris. In April of 1816 the new Prefect of the Seine, Gilbert-Joseph-Gaspard Chabrol de Volvic, set up a special committee of artists and municipal bureaucrats to oversee, in the words of one of its members, "the works of art that are going to be commissioned" so as to "erase the traces of vandalism of the 1789 Revolution, during whose stormy years the majority of objects that embellished the churches of the capital were destroyed."[71] Between 1816 and 1830 Chabrol's Fine Arts Committee commissioned 219 paintings and 125 statues for the churches of Paris. The committee's reporter, Joseph-Amable Grégoire, explained the raison d'être for this burst of patronage:

I ought to note that amongst all the public monuments, the churches of Paris are those that people can visit most freely: neither a dress code nor a membership card are required and, from dawn to dusk, the doors of these buildings are open to everyone. So one can honestly say that if the Church is the house of God, it is also the people's house. By embellishing it, by putting on view art-objects that are more or less valuable, one not only does something pleasing to the public, but also incites the foreigner to extend his stay in the capital and thus to spend more money, something that is always of profit to the populace.[72]

Grégoire's justification for the work of the Fine Arts Committee implies that the churches of Paris were free-entry museums and tourist attractions. In a text about the church of Notre-Dame-de-Lorette, he frankly admits that the committee's goal was to "make the churches of Paris, and those of the two arrondissements of Saint-Denis and Sceaux, into religious museums."[73]

Most of the works sponsored by the committee were what could be called museum pictures that happened to depict religious subjects and to hang in a church. Precisely this aesthetic detachment came to be regarded as unworthy of serious religious painting: by 1859 the well-known Roret manual for decorating churches reminded artists that "a church is not like a museum, a jousting yard open to egos eager to engage in battle, who come there looking for applause and critical viewers, but rather a solemn place where everything should be calm, modest, and full of reverence."[74] One can measure the shifting critical parameters for reli-

gious painting by comparing Grégoire's text of 1833 to the opening lines of Théophile Gautier's review of the ceiling mural in the apse of La Madeleine Church, completed in 1837 by Jules-Claude Ziegler (Fig. 36):

The first thing that strikes us about the work of M. Ziegler is the perfect harmony between its style and the architecture: the matte color of the cupola, strong and clear, accords perfectly with the chalky gradations of the stone and the tawny hues of gold leaf. We insist on this quality, because our painters generally worry far too little about the character of the buildings in which they work, and handle a fresco—a picture in situ—not much differently than an independent and moveable canvas. This is a great error, and Notre-Dame-de-Lorette is the proof of it.[75]

In fact, Ziegler's mural was not commissioned by the city of Paris but by the Interior Ministry as part of the government's commitment to complete the church. The site had been abandoned at the outbreak of the Revolution, and Napoléon's idea of 1806 to transform the structure into a Temple of Glory to the army never rose much higher than the foundations. The unfinished skeleton was an eyesore in a prestigious part of town, yet almost nothing was done to it during the Bourbon Restoration. Only in the early 1830s, under the government of Louis-Philippe, were the resources and the will to finish the church brought to bear on the project: by 1835 the building was ready for its final decoration.

The mastermind behind awarding the apse commission to Ziegler, who was a rather unknown artist at the time, was Adolphe Thiers, then Minister of the Interior. Thiers had been impressed by Ziegler's plan to paint a "History of Christianity" that would gather around the enthroned figure of Christ a host of ecclesiastical, historical, and artistic personalities: from the Apostles at his side to the repentant Mary Magdalene at his feet; from a pantheon of heroes of the Eastern church at the far left (roughly in chronological order from Constantine through the Crusades to Greeks persecuted by Turks in the 1820s) to its mirror-image of the Western Church (passing from Clovis to Henri IV by way of Charlemagne, Frederick Barbarossa, Joan of Arc, and Louis XIII). The gathering is interspersed left and right with artistic luminaries such as Homer, Dante, Raphael, and

FIGURE 36. Jules-Claude
Ziegler, *View of The History
of Christianity*, 1835–1837.
Mural painting. Paris,
Church of the Madeleine
(apse). Photo: © Ville de
Paris - COARC/Emmanuel
Michot.

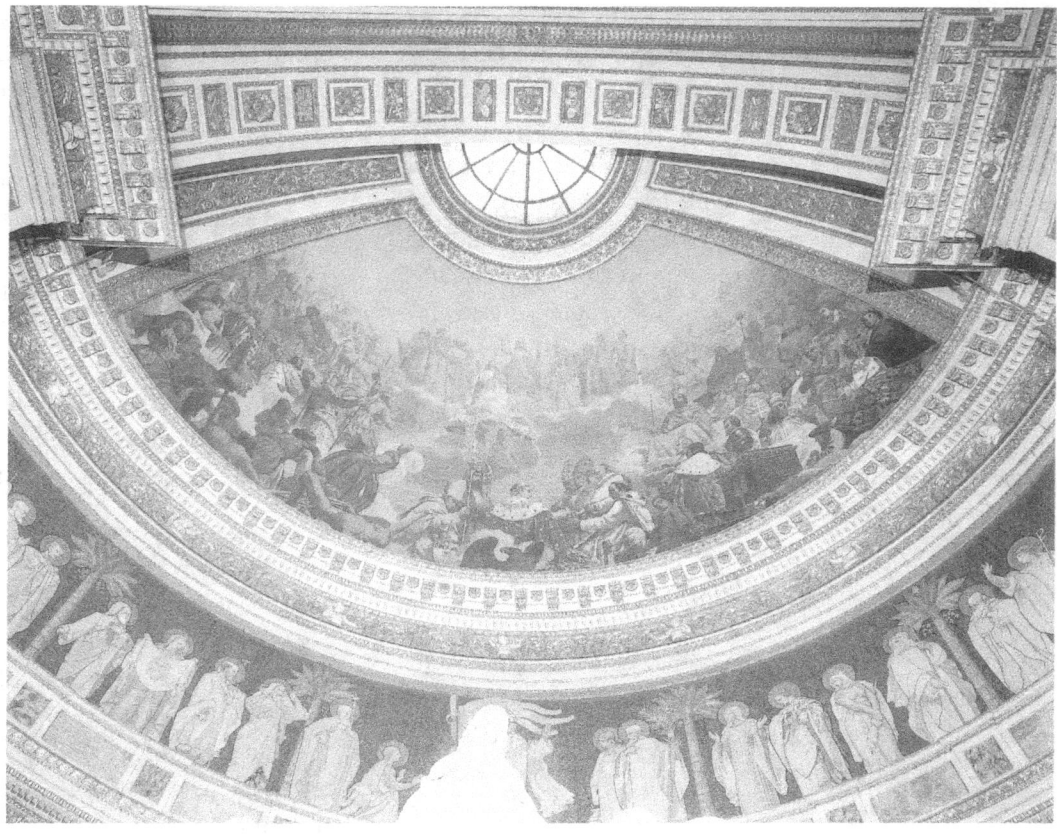

Michelangelo. Of particular historical interest is the front-and-center placement of Napoléon—seen from behind and dressed in the regalia of his coronation—taking the imperial crown from Pope Pius VII. Next to him, a bishop holds a plaque inscribed *Concordat 1802*: in Ziegler's image of this grand story, the balance of power established by Bonaparte in 1802 between Church and State—between papal authority and civil law—is positioned as the culminating point of the Christian epic. Consonant with contemporary ideas about monumental religious painting, Ziegler's work is both site specific and invested with a mission of serious moral instruction.

Today's sensibilities might not register the same thrill before Ziegler's display of complex erudition that Théophile Gautier experienced in 1838, when he exclaimed that the apse "is surely the most beautiful and the most vast bit of religious painting that we possess."[76] Nor are we likely to recognize that the emphasis Zeigler placed on the Concordat framed the sometimes volatile relationship between Church and State in complete accord with the politics of the July Monarchy and of Thiers himself: "The State protects the Church and its clergy," Thiers would say in 1845; "the Church must understand that there are laws governing it and that these laws cannot be bent."[77] Not everyone agreed with this assessment. In the course of a long address before the Chamber of Peers on the freedom of religion, Charles-René de Montalembert argued just the opposite:

The principles and the rules according to which the Catholic Church has been governed since its founding are incompatible with those that one wants to impose upon it today. The Church cannot and does not want to be a public service, subject to direction by the State. The Church is no more part of the State than the State part of the Church. They are two collateral, sovereign, and independent powers, each with its own domain. They can make mutual concessions to one another; this fact was the point of departure for the concordat, in which the Church made more concessions than at any other time in its history.[78]

Montalembert was one of the leading proponents of a social and political movement known as Ultramontanism that exercised considerable influence in France from about 1820 right to the end of the century.

The main thrust of ultramontanist thinking was that the long history of accommodation between the Catholic Church and the French state—initiated under Louis XIV but especially regimented by Bonaparte's Concordat of 1802—vitiated an essential part of Catholic doctrine; namely, the Pope's absolute power to direct the spiritual life of Roman Catholics. The ultramontane argument for subservience to the Pope (hence the name, which acknowledges that ultimate authority lies "over the mountains" in Rome) was first articulated by Joseph de Maîstre's polemical *Du Pape* of 1819. De Maîstre claimed that monarchy was "the only form of government that has suited mankind regardless of time or place,"[79] and that "for many centuries the Pope's authority was the real constituent power in Europe. It was responsible for making European monarchy a marvel of supernatural order that one admires dispassionately like the sun because one sees it every day."[80] According to de Maîstre, the French Revolution had been an episode of history "*satanic* in its essence," and he believed that "infallibility in the spiritual realm and sovereignty in the temporal realm are two perfectly synonymous words."[81] De Maîstre's political theory, in which the absolute power of popes marches hand in hand with that of kings, attracted fervent adherents in the early years of the Bourbon Restoration even if later writers—like Montalembert—gradually moved away from its extremism.

Montalembert's defense of religious liberty in 1845 demonstrates his commitment to the ideal of papal authority and ecclesiastical independence. For him, the Concordat of 1802 was a fatal compromise for the French Catholic Church and—more important—detrimental to the development of

a viable religious art. In an important earlier essay of 1837 Montalembert had written:

The clergy is no longer, as it once was, the absolute master of all religious buildings. By a ridiculous and illegal inconsistency that has become standard procedure in our bureaucratic habits, the clergy no longer has the exclusive right to accept or reject works of art to be placed in churches or construction to be done to them. It is no longer free to oppose municipal architects from plundering them. Nor can the clergy prevent the government from falling into the habit of thinking the churches are just so many galleries, where it has the right to exhibit permanently the so-called religious pictures that the support of some deputy, or the caprice of some minor bureaucrat, has gotten it to buy.[82]

As a result of the "system of methodical desecration" sponsored by the government, Montalembert saw churches invaded by ugliness, overrun by works of art inspired by the symbols of paganism, and executed by artists devoid of spirituality.[83] He placed a large part of the blame on members of the clergy, who accepted the government's intervention with too much docility. When Montalembert exhorts the clergy to "to take back its natural role, to reclaim this noble patrimony," he outlines a program of Catholic Revival founded upon ultramontane claims that the Church and its representatives must have the final say in both ecclesiastical issues and aesthetic matters related to church property.

In the same year that he published the essay on religious art, Montalembert wrote a lengthy and admiring review of Alexis-François Rio's *De la poésie chrétienne dans sa matière et dans ses formes*, one of the first significant studies of Italian trecento and early Renaissance painting to be written in French.[84] Exactly inverse to modern-day histories of Renaissance painting as the progressive mastery of realist illusion, Rio's book charted the period as a decline from a purely Christian or "sacred" art to one of pagan "naturalism." Montalembert summarized Rio's argument as the belief "that Christian painting is the most beautiful of all and that it renounces all that depends, directly or indirectly, upon materialism for expression or inspiration; in other words, upon the excessive cult of nature that has ruled art since the Medicis."[85] For Rio, the most potent Christian art, which he called the "mystic school," is devoid of naturalist illusion. It is an art of stasis, simplicity, and permanence that appeals to the mind by eschewing movement, color, and transient effects that seduce the senses.[86] Rio believed that Raphael and Michelangelo were corrupted by sensuality and a slavish imitation of antiquity. By his account, early Renaissance painters—notably Cimabue, Giotto, and Fra Angelico—were appropriate role models for the rejuvenation of nineteenth-century religious painting. Such masters painted from a genuine piety (Angelico was, after all, a monk) and they inherently respected the architectural integrity of the sacred spaces they were called upon to decorate. Their works seemed to offer both the moral fiber and formal principles that could reverse the decline of religious painting described by Montalembert in his essay of 1837.

Painters trained in the French academy, where the works of Raphael had long been regarded as the highest achievements of Western art, resisted many of the adjustments deemed necessary by this emerging program for a Catholic Revival art. In 1841, for example, Théodore Chassériau was commissioned to paint *The Conversion of Saint Mary of Egypt* for a chapel in the church of Saint-Merri. His first idea was rejected as out of character with the other works already under way in the church—a criticism that signals new concerns to unify the entire suite of decorations. The review committee felt his figures were invested with "a forced movement not sufficiently simple to be included in the decoration of a chapel of gothic architecture."[87] Chassériau responded by adopting a strict formal symmetry, banded registers, and a flattened space into which he placed fully frontal figures locked in frozen gestures (Fig. 37). His final work sufficiently fulfilled the brief of the Fine Arts Committee that he was awarded a second picture for the opposite wall of the same chapel. This work, *Saint Mary of Egypt carried to Heaven by Angels* (Fig. 38), reintroduces the criss-crossing diagonals, deep space, sweeping upward movement, agitated gestures, and complicated rendering of drapery folds characteristic of "museum" pictures exhibited in the Paris Salons of the 1840s. It might be that Chassériau willfully defied his patrons for having censured his first project. Perhaps he could not imagine an apotheosis beyond the models of Raphael. Maybe he was simply not enough of a believer to be convinced that the

spare, static art of Fra Angelico was up to the task at hand. Whatever the reason, Chassériau's second picture is far from the norms of religious painting extolled by Montalembert and Rio. Writing about the angels of the main panel, Théophile Gautier remarked: "The angelic types so often reused seem henceforth as rigidly fixed as the hieratic representations of an Egyptian temple. He [Chassériau] has made them into veritable ephebes, beautiful boys full of delicate energy and nervous elegance appropriate to beings entrusted with God's wishes."[88] In short, thoroughly infected with the pagan sensuality that Catholic Revival critics found anathema to serious religious painting.

Chassériau's resistance to the reformist discourse of Rio and Montalembert stands in sharp contrast to the trajectory of Hippolyte Flandrin, a devout Catholic who was determined to fulfill the spirit and the letter of Catholic Revival, ultramontane rhetoric. Nowhere is this more evident than in the great expanse of encaustic murals he executed on the choir walls of Saint-Germain-des-Prés between 1842 and 1848. The decoration of the south wall, which represents Christ carrying his cross on the road to Calvary, is characteristic—a stark image of stilled movement (Fig. 39). A solemn frieze of widely spaced figures extends the width of the composition. The impression of lateral spread is compounded by a simplified background architecture and a "sky" of an undifferentiated gold ground reminiscent of Byzantine mosaics. Since there is no deep space to contain or contextualize action, gestures and movement (such as the rearing horse) are slowed to the point of being frozen in place. The fabrics of garments are virtually undisturbed by the physical bodies they clothe; rather, they fall in sober, vertical folds or gently arcing curves as if weighted by the seriousness of the story. Faces of the main characters are seen in full-frontal or profile views, their bodies subject to a visual rigor consonant with the sobriety of the subject. Secondary characters are darkened silhouettes against the ground or shaded figures turned slightly in space. The colors are muted, the distinctions between areas of light and dark willfully manipulated, and the level of anecdotal detailing much reduced.

Flandrin's decoration includes two registers above the principal scene. Directly overhead, figures of the three moral

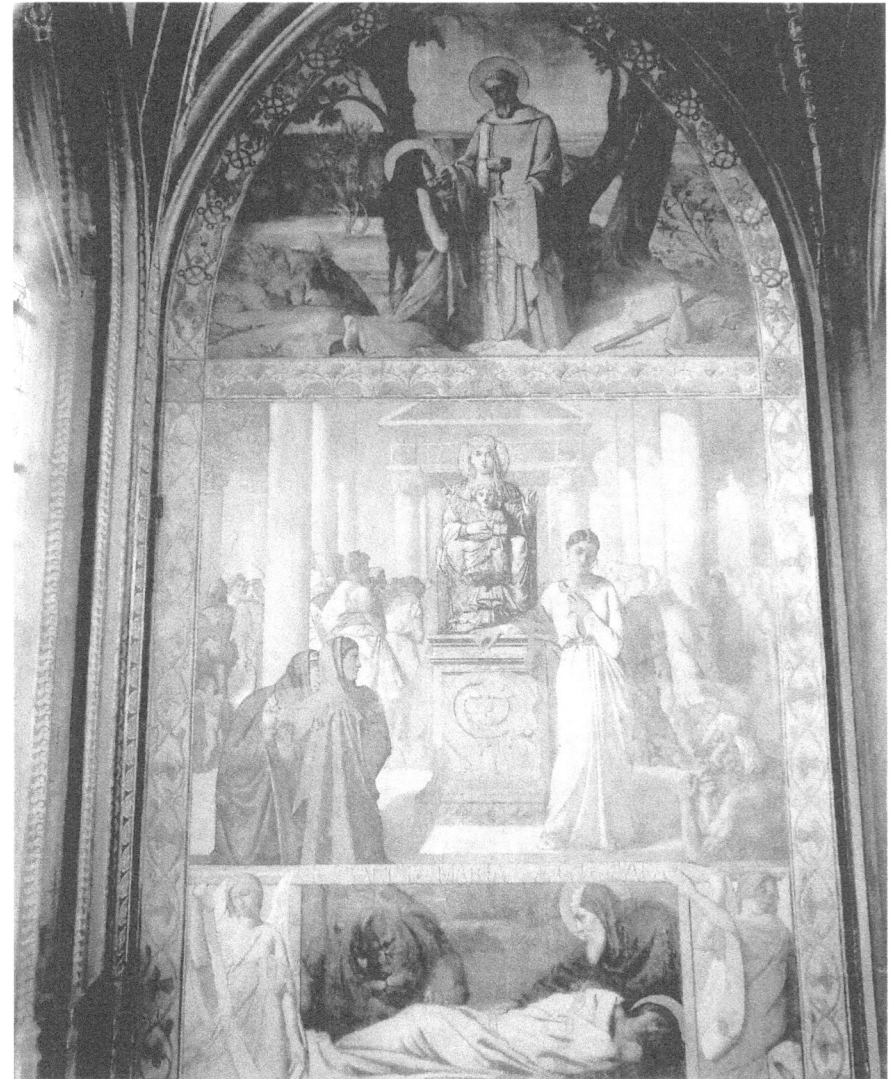

FIGURE 37.   Théodore Chassériau, *The Conversion of Saint Mary of Egypt*, 1841–1843. Mural painting. Paris, Church of Saint-Merri (Chapel of Saint Mary of Egypt). Photo: © Ville de Paris - COARC/Emmanuel Michot.

virtues (Force, Justice, and Prudence) are joined by a fourth (Temperance) to respond to the architectural exigencies of the pre-existing gallery. Above this, a third level includes four figures related to the history of the abbey that, to borrow a phrase from Gustave Planche's review of the murals, "speak to erudition more than sentiment in the strict sense, and so we need not stop to study them."[89] At the apex of the wall is a seated figure of Saint Vincent martyr, whose tunic had been the most revered relic of the church in its early history.

Throughout his extensive review of Flandrin's choir murals at Saint-Germain-des-Prés, Planche repeatedly tests them against critical categories of the Catholic Revival. "By treating two Catholic subjects in the manner of the Roman school at the start of the sixteenth century," writes Planche, "[Flandrin] has not feared the reproach of paganism and, to our mind, this is a sign of good sense on his part."[90] A few lines later he suggests that Flandrin "has wanted to reconcile the Catholic sentiment of Giotto with the pagan science

FIGURE 38.   Théodore Chassériau, *Saint Mary of Egypt carried to Heaven by Angels*, 1841–1843. Mural painting. Paris, Church of Saint-Merri (Chapel of Saint Mary of Egypt). Photo: © Ville de Paris - COARC/Emmanuel Michot.

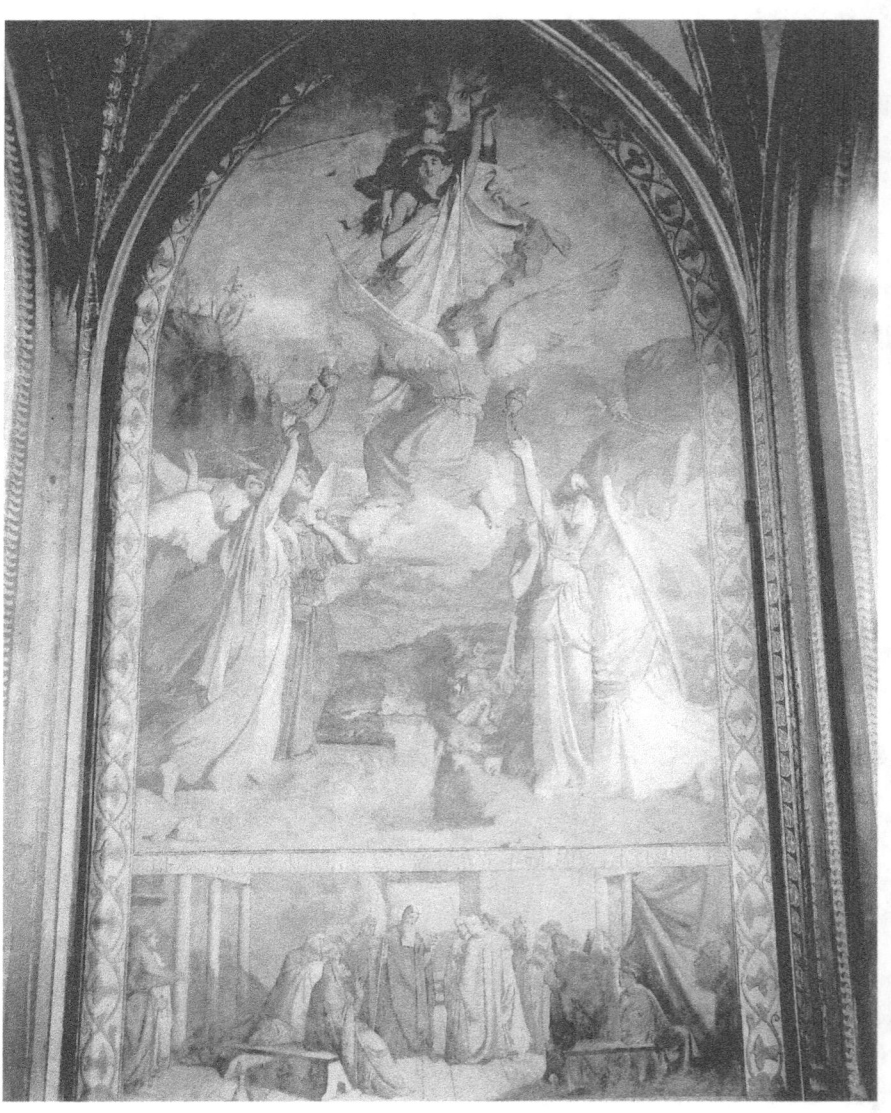

of Raphael. That's an endeavor that we approve of highly."[91] Planche's efforts to inoculate reception of Flandrin's murals from the most extreme forms of ultramontane criticism that viewed the "Roman school" of Raphael as the end of Christian art in Europe, registers the degree to which Catholic Revival ideas had moved to center stage in the debate about monumental religious painting.

Alongside his admiration for Flandrin's efforts to find a sincere compromise, Planche dismisses as "a childishness that does not merit discussion" those painters who "not understanding the real significance of history . . . believe in the pressing need to treat all Catholic subjects only according to the counsels of Giotto and Fra Angelico." He probably had in mind the servile imitation found in the work of artists like Eugène-Emmanuel Amaury-Duval. Amaury-Duval had stumbled upon the fresco cycle painted by Fra Angelico in the Noccoline Chapel of the Vatican while visiting Rome in 1836. "It struck me as sublime," he wrote; "one could do no

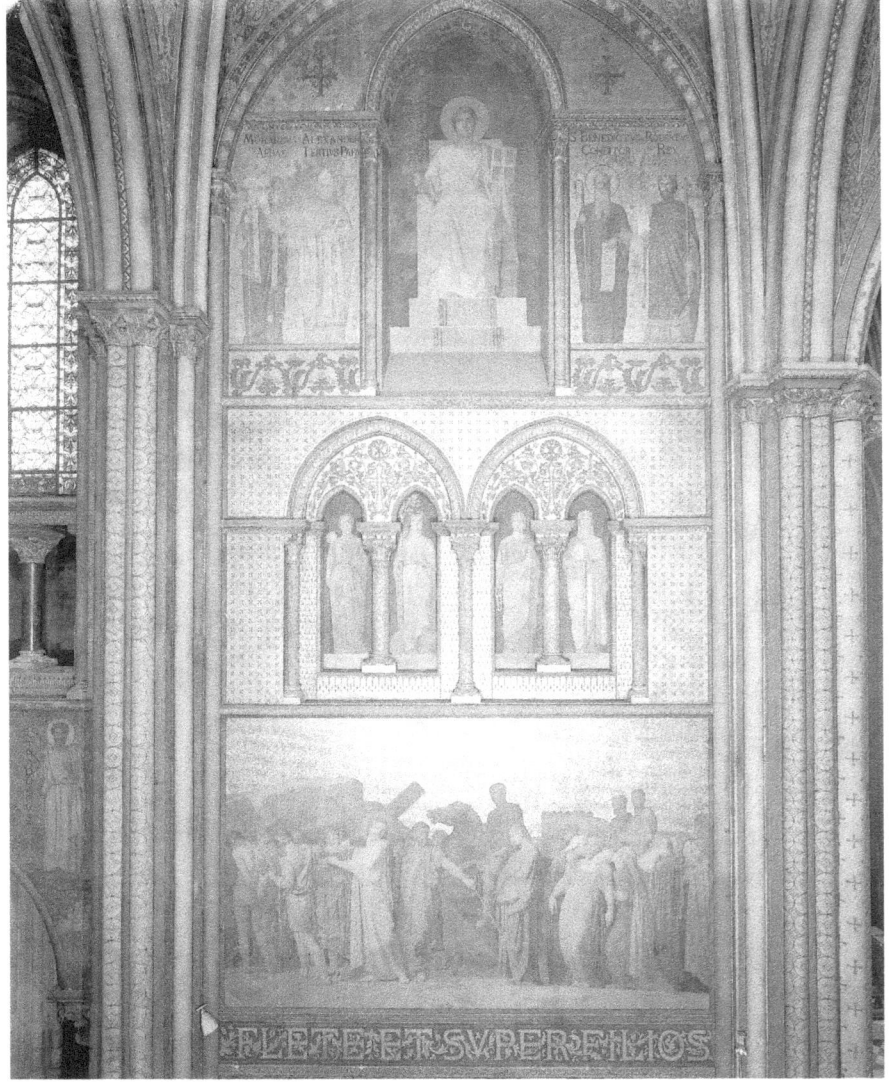

FIGURE 39.   Hippolyte Flandrin, *On the Road to Calvary*, 1842–1846. Mural painting. Paris, Church of Saint-Germain-des-Prés (choir). Photo: © Ville de Paris - COARC/Emmanuel Michot.

better. How beautiful it is, in both drawing and color! What simplicity! What a man, what a painter! I did not know his name."[92] If the works of Fra Angelico were a discovery to the young Amaury-Duval on his first trip to Rome, key theoreticians of the ultramontane movement—notably Rio and Montalembert—had long admired the monk's simplicity and piety. Writing about Angelico's frescoes in the same year that Amaury-Duval first saw them, Rio described the pictures as "so admirable that although next door to the famous rooms painted by Raphael, they do not elicit any less enthusiasm among true worshippers of Christian art; this work so simple, so pure, so free of all profane admixture, so superior to all that Ghirlandaio and Botticelli did in the Sistine Chapel."[93] The following year, in his review of Rio's book, Montalembert prefaced a long description of Fra Angelico's *Last Judgment* with the observation that "every Catholic should sense an unspeakable joy in contemplating these marvelous works in which God allowed the perfection of expression to match the

FIGURE 40.   Eugène-Emmanuel Amaury-Duval, *Crowning of the Virgin and other decorations*, 1844–1846. Mural painting and sculpted wood. Paris, Church of Saint-Germain-l'Auxerrois (Chapel of the Virgin). Photo: © Ville de Paris - COARC/Emmanuel Michot.

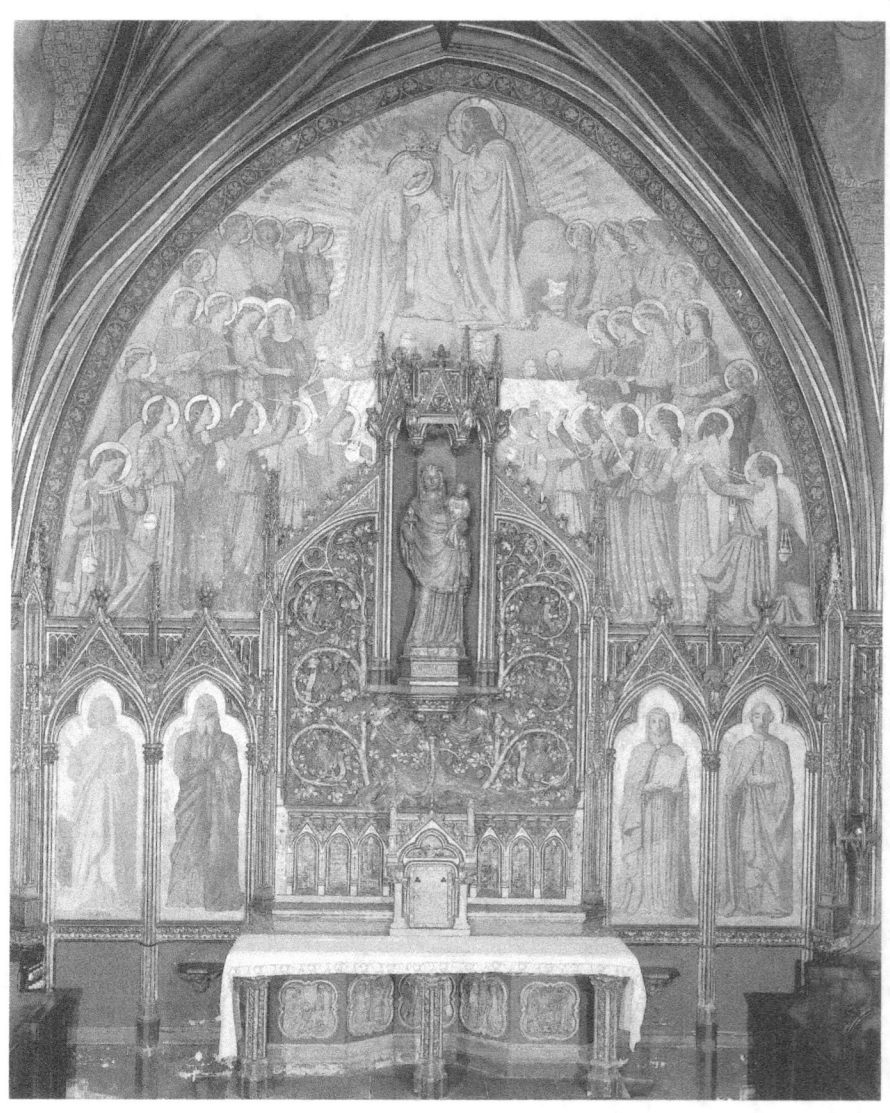

sanctity of purpose, and which are—one can say it boldly—the *nec plus ultra* of Christian art."[94] Both Rio and Montalembert remark that the Louvre was fortunate to own one of Fra Angelico's masterpieces, the *Crowning of the Virgin*. The picture had come to Paris from Fiesole as war booty of Bonaparte's Italian campaign, but remained in France after 1815 and had recently been placed on public view.

Commissioned in 1844 to paint a fresco for the Chapel of the Virgin in the church of Saint-Germain-l'Auxerrois,

Amaury-Duval basically lifted Fra Angelico's masterpiece from the Louvre and made it his own (Fig. 40). In the top-center of the image Christ crowns Mary: both figures are set in profile against a gold ground striated with rays of light emanating from a mandorla of glory. Symmetrically placed at each side are three tiers of angels, some in attitudes of prayer, others singing praises, and still others swinging incense burners. All of the angels wear haloes of golden disks arranged frontally to the picture plane, and most of the incense burners are frozen in place at the top of their arc through space. Nothing moves. The colors are largely unmodeled, since no natural light permeates the scene. The drapery material falls soberly in crisp folds, and—as Nicholas-Michel Troche was careful to point out in his booklet on the church—Amaury-Duval strictly followed the tradition of early-Christian hieratic representations by showing the feet only of Jesus, an unveiling taken to be a divine attribute.[95] Fresco-painted figures of the saints John, Joachim, Anne, and Joseph (also by Amaury-Duval) fill the four flamboyant gothic niches below the angels. Above the altar, a sculpted niche representing the tree of Jesse supports and frames the much-revered, polychrome wood sculpture of Mary holding Jesus that supposedly dates from the thirteenth century.

Two points should be made in defense of Amaury-Duval's seeming lack of personal invention. The first is that the commission was part of a massive restoration project. Saint-Germain-l'Auxerrois was closed for six years after being sacked in 1831 by a crowd protesting a group of Bourbon sympathizers who tried to hold a memorial service on the anniversary of the duc de Berry's assassination.[96] Working with the architect Jean-Baptiste Lassus, who designed the architectural divisions of the altarpiece and the tree of Jesse surround, Amaury-Duval accepted the brief of restoration by trying to make his frescoes approximate—in both style and material—an original of the fifteenth century. Second, the entire purpose of the chapel was to visualize and describe the "pious belief sanctioned by a very old cult and founded on feelings of piety and respect proper to the Mother of God, by which the blessed Virgin came back to life immediately after her death . . . and that her body, reunited with her soul by a special privilege, was received into Heaven."[97] Troche reminds visitors to the church that the story of Mary's death is a "genuine mystic tropology" comprising "hieratic" subjects. Both Rio and Montalembert had described such subjects as stock in trade of the "mystic school" of early Renaissance painters, among whom Fra Angelico was the archetype. This context tends to explain why Amaury-Duval quoted freely from the Italian master when designing his own work.

Troche praised the painter for knowing how to "give to his aesthetic arrangements the fragrance of chaste and sublime spirit that wafts from the works of Cimabue, Giotto, Orcagna, and Fiesole; true glories of Catholic art." He placed Amaury-Duval among

> that small number of artists today who, without renouncing the spirit of progress of our century, set the wholesome example of knowing how to go back to hieratic times to borrow the simple elements of a style that must be adapted to interpreting the Christian ideal, while still conforming to modern advancements in the arts and civilization.[98]

To modern eyes Amaury-Duval's frescoes at Saint-Germain-l'Auxerrois resemble pastiches lacking originality; to fervent Catholics of nineteenth-century Paris, they were sincere efforts to recover by archaeology and research the piety that seemed to live in genuine monuments of the past. They are also examples of how an erudite re-creation, informed by the history of art, was enlisted to forget the real violence done to the church in 1831: the history of art rewrites the history of politics. Examples of restoration of this sort are rare; it was much more common to rework the historical markers permanently attached to existing objects or monuments. The following sections explore how some of the city's most famous landmarks were retro-fitted to the march of time.

Contested Spaces: The Politics of Urban Memory

[Napoléon] wanted to use victory to glorify himself and, in the arrogance of his egoism, he placed his own image atop the trophies conquered by the Revolution, atop the melted-down canons of the column. Then the Germans came with a mission to avenge the Revolution and to hurl the Emperor from the heights he had usurped. Only the tricolor flag has a right to this place, and since the July Days it flutters there victoriously and full of promise. If one eventually reinstates Napoléon on the column of the Place Vendôme, he will no longer dominate it as Emperor—as Caesar—but as representative of the Revolution, absolved by misfortune and purified by death, as an emblem of the victorious force of the people.

—Heinrich Heine[99]

Heine's report on rumors to reinstall a statue of Napoléon atop the Vendôme Column reads like a thumbnail history of many Parisian monuments during the period 1800–1850. Although some projects related to the glory of the Emperor were recycled politically by the Bourbon Restoration during the 1820s, the largest number of them were given their present-day form between 1830 and 1848 under Louis-Philippe. As Heine points out, the July Monarchy was not much interested in reviving the Empire, any more than it was keen to relive the chaos of the Revolution; rather, the goal of Louis-Philippe's government was to effect a social and cultural healing that would accept the political patchwork of the recent past as the heritage from which an idea of the nation must be created. The motives behind such an enterprise are not difficult to imagine, for if the Revolution of 1830 swept away the Bourbon Restoration, the constitutional monarchy of Louis-Philippe was seen by many to have only postponed a true republic. With neither the bloodline heritage of the Bourbon family nor the test of a plebiscite to legitimate his rule, Louis-Philippe and his government were quick to adopt the mantle of closing an historical process that had begun with the fall of the Bastille. "Thanks to the conquests of 1789, the social state of France had been renewed," declared François Guizot, newly appointed Minister of the Interior; "thanks to the victory of 1830 her political institutions received in one day the principal reforms which they needed."[100] Alongside Guizot's self-proclaimed renewal of the country's political institutions, the July Monarchy took care to incorporate the events, the players, and the monuments of the recent past into a coherent story where—as Heine predicted—Napoléon would be simply one among many emblems of the "victorious force of the people" whose final act was the Revolution of 1830.

Consider the single largest construction site in all of Paris at the time of Louis-Philippe's investiture: the unfinished Arc de Triomphe de l'Étoile (Fig. 41). The arch, begun by Napoléon in 1806 as a monument to the Grand Army and a colossal portal to the city of Paris, was destined to be nearly fifty meters tall, forty-five meters wide, and more than twenty-two meters deep (see Chapter Two). The foundations for this enormous mass extend more than eight meters into the earth, and were barely complete for the Emperor's second marriage in 1810 when a prefiguration was erected in wood and canvas (Fig. 15). Work on the project progressed slowly: at the fall of the Empire the masonry stood only about twenty meters high and the site, strewn with abandoned blocks of uncut stone, was closed. The restored Bourbons were disinclined to spend money on finishing such an extravagant monument to the glory of Napoléon.

A complete sculptural program had never been designed for the arch, which is not so unusual if we remember that its decorative elements are little more than veneer attached to a principal mass. A program had been elaborated in 1810 for the temporary arch erected by Chalgrin that included components keyed to the imperial marriage, but it is unlikely that this design of circumstance would have carried over to the permanent structure. The general idea was to make the arch allude to imperial history using allegorical trophies on the large corner piers—similar to the arch at the porte Saint-Denis designed in the seventeenth century by François Blondel to honor Louis XIV (Fig. 42)—along with sculptural reliefs inspired by contemporary events.

Even if the arch was placed in limbo after 1815, the symbolic prestige of its site on the great axis through the center of Paris, and its visibility from nearly every part of the city, ensured that the project would not be abandoned for long. In 1823, following the duc d'Angoulême's successful military expedition in Spain to restore the rule of King Ferdinand VII, the Bourbon government hailed the event as worthy of celebration in both painting and sculpture. Some believed the unfinished arch at the Étoile could be wrested from the shadow of Napoléon by dedicating it to this most recent triumph of the French army. Louis XVIII authorized reopening the work site with a royal order of 9 October 1823. The architect in charge, Louis Goust, proposed a flattering sculptural program comprising four large allegorical trophies: for the facade overlooking Paris, France going to the aid of Spain and Spain throwing off her chains; on the

FIGURE 41.   Antoine Melbye (attributed to), *Arc de Triomphe de l'Étoile*, ca. 1848. Daguerreotype. Paris, Collection Société Française de Photographie, inv. 569/34 (10.3 × 8.3 cm). Photo: Société Française de Photographie.

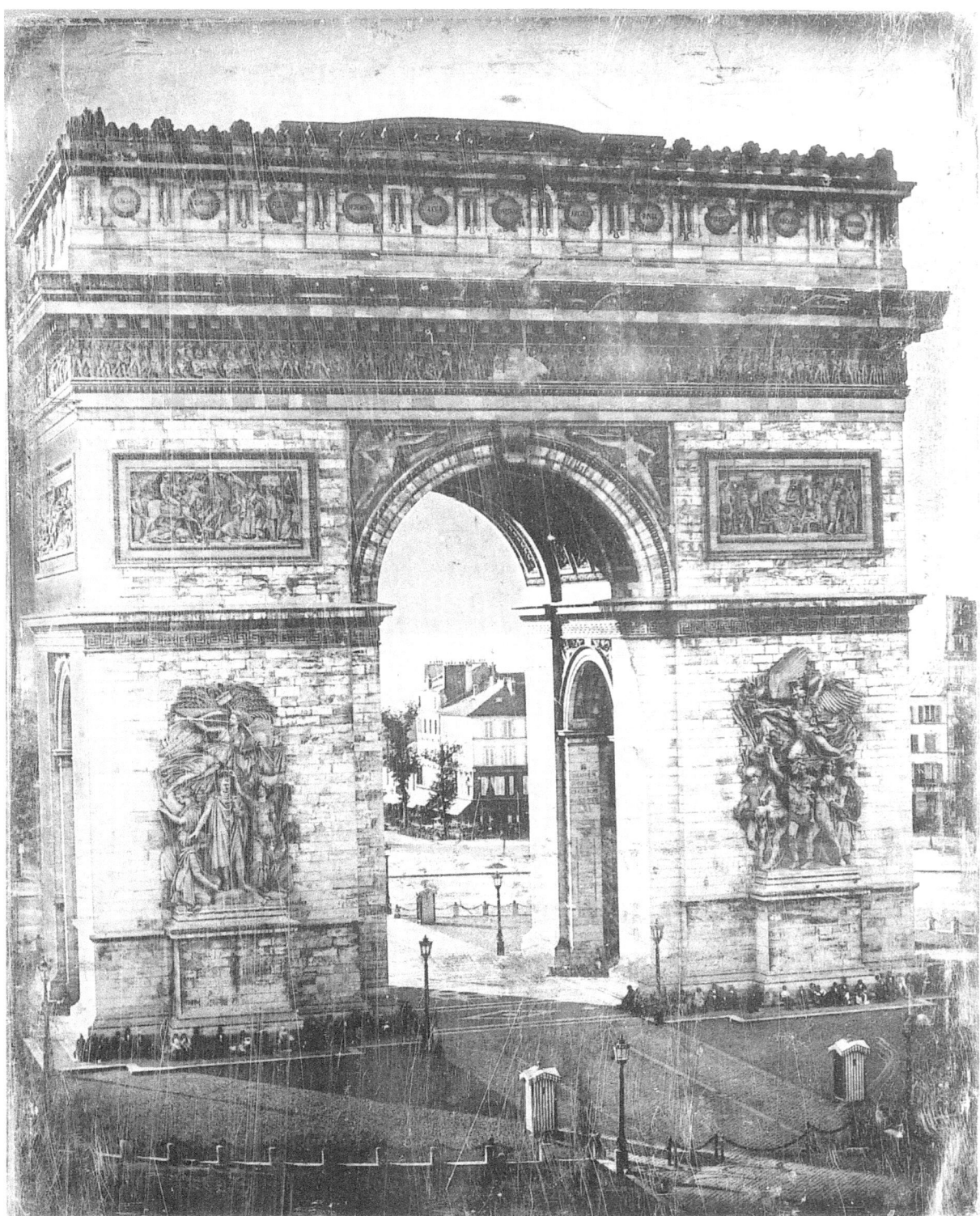

FIGURE 42.   Anonymous, *Porte Saint-Denis*,
ca. 1845. Daguerreotype. Private collection (18.5
× 14 cm). Photo: Sotheby's Picture Library,
London.

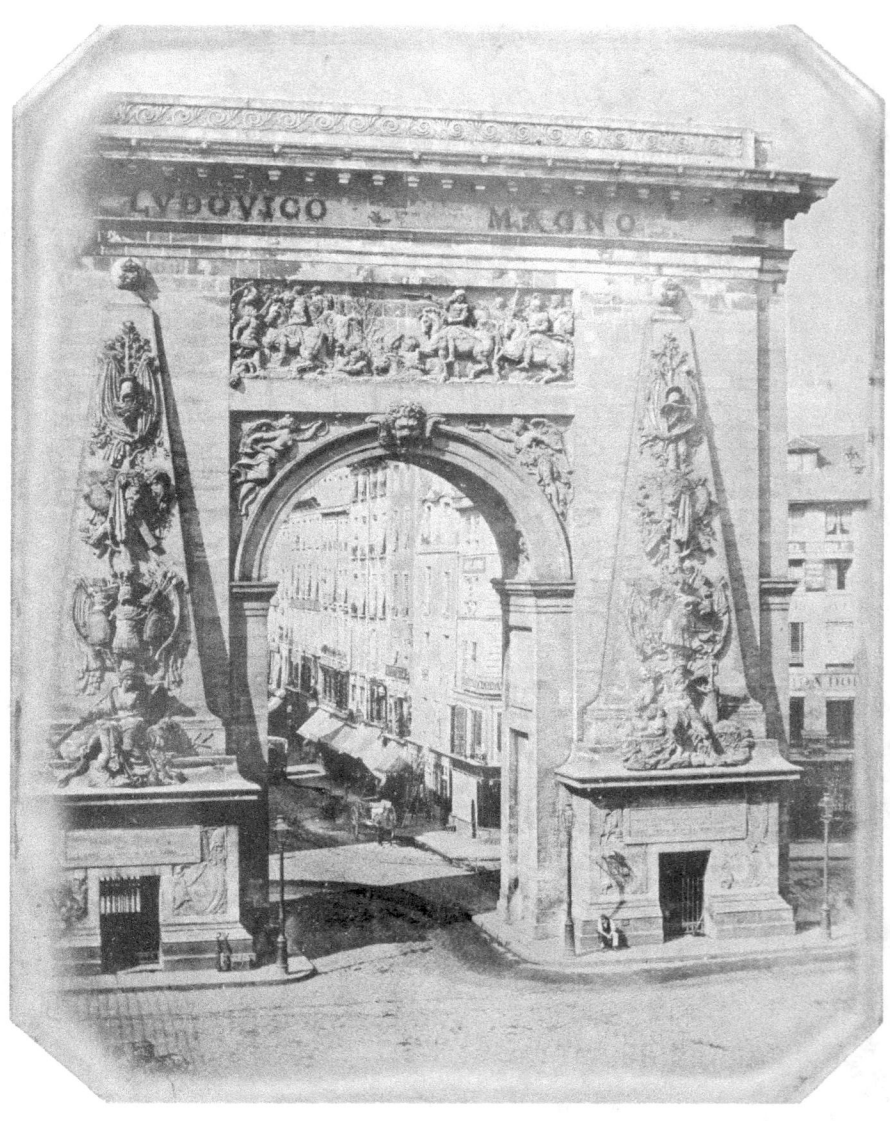

facade facing Neuilly, Victory and Peace. Six sculptural reliefs were to chronicle the events of the French engagement
in Spain, including two depictions of Louis XVIII: giving
thanks to heaven for the French victory; ordering completion of the arch itself. The point of Goust's proposal was
to reinscribe the meaning of the entire monolith within the
parameters of a minor military adventure and to take credit
for its construction. The obsequious sculptural program was
probably presented to Louis XVIII as an incentive to restart

work on the arch, with the idea that it would be several years
before any sculptures were needed; ostensibly, the program
could be modified at a later date.

   An identical symbolic exchange—replacing the exploits of Napoléon with those of the duc d'Angoulême in
Spain—was performed upon the arc du Carrousel at about
the same time (Fig. 43). Originally constructed in 1806 by
Napoléon's preferred design team of Charles Percier and
Pierre-François Fontaine, the arch was ceremonial gateway

to the military parade ground in front of the Tuileries Palace. It is remarkable for the richness of its decoration—including Corinthian columns of rose-colored marble with bases and capitals in bronze—and exquisitely carved detailing. Its Napoleonic incarnation included sculptural reliefs recounting the glorious campaign of 1805 (including the victory at Austerlitz) and standing figures at the attic level personifying various units of the Imperial Army. Eventually, the four bronze horses looted from San Marco in Venice, along with a chariot led by figures of Victory and Peace, were installed atop the arch (visible in Baltard's drawing). The horses were removed by the Allies in 1815 (see above), and the original reliefs were also removed and put into storage, although the soldiers were left in place. Sculptors were hired to recut the decorations so that every coat of arm and emblem referring

to Napoléon or the Empire was reworked into fleurs-de-lys of the Bourbon dynasty. The figure of the Emperor, who appeared in the apex of the main vault, was transformed into a faceless allegorical trophy of Victory. Full-scale plaster replacements for the original reliefs were installed on the arch by 1828, with subjects inspired by the duc d'Angoulême's excursion into Spain: facing the Tuileries, Angoulême consulted with Ferdinand VII and offered banners conquered in Spain to Louis XVIII; facing the Louvre, Angoulême accepted the keys to the city of Madrid and met the Spanish envoys at Cadiz. The lateral sides of the arch offered the capitulation of general Ballesteros to Angoulême at Campillo, and the surrender of Pamplona.

Obviously, if the much smaller but centrally located arc du Carrousel was dedicated to the duc d'Angoulême's

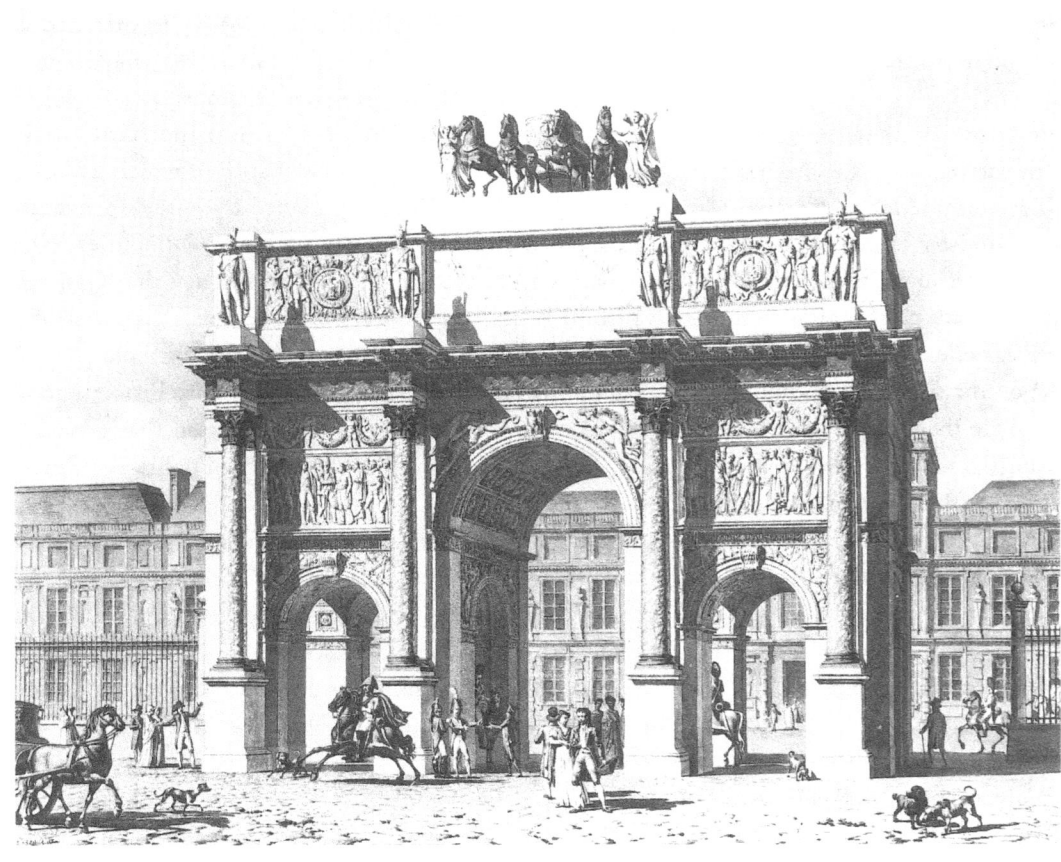

FIGURE 43. Louis-Pierre Baltard, *View of the Arc du Carrousel*, 1808–1815. Pen and ink with wash. Paris, Musée Carnavalet, inv. D 00036 (40.4 × 50.3 cm). Photo: © PMVP/Ladet.

Spanish excursion, it no longer made sense to commit the enormous monument at the Étoile to the same rather modest military foray. When the reworked arc du Carrousel was unveiled in 1828, the decorative program for the Étoile was rewritten in a manner both further removed from its original purpose and painfully flattering to Louis XVIII's successor, Charles X. In its new guise, the main pillars carried allegorical trophies, while the attic was to be adorned with thirty-two statues representing the principal cities of France. The sculpted frieze encircling the monument just below the cornice line would depict Charles X enthroned and surrounded by his leading generals (on the Paris side), the Dauphin receiving civil and military authorities (on the side away from Paris), and assorted units of the army on parade (on each of the short ends). In the words of a later historian: "Why these changes? Because one realized that glorification of the duc d'Angoulême did not call for a heroic display, and to substitute the effigy of Charles X for Louis XVIII. A real human trifle!"[101] The king's vanity was not to be denied: work continued on a plaster model of the new frieze right up to the outbreak of the 1830 Revolution.

The government of Louis-Philippe wasted no time canceling the frieze project before any carving was actually done to the monument. In November of 1830 Marthe-Camille de Montalivet, newly appointed Minister of the Interior, changed the program completely. His version of the sculpted frieze (the one on the arch today) memorializes the armies of Revolution and Empire: on the Paris side they march north and south (towards the corners); on the side facing Neuilly they return in triumph to Paris where they are crowned by "a regenerated France, accompanied by Public Prosperity and Abundance"; the short ends depict the army carrying to France objects of science (from Egypt) and art (from Italy) looted by conquest. Nowhere does Louis-Philippe or an emblem of his government appear. Characteristic of the July Monarchy's attempt to fashion itself as conciliator of recent French history, it moved the Revolution and Empire to center stage of the decorative program.

In February of 1831, during the same spree of vandalism that damaged the church of Saint-Germain-l'Auxerrois, the plaster reliefs on the arc du Carrousel honoring the duc d'Angoulême were attacked by insurgents and severely damaged. Louis-Philippe's government quietly replaced them with the original imperial reliefs but, not wanting to pander to the Emperor's personal cult, resisted calls to place a statue of Napoléon in the chariot atop the arch. In the same spirit, new subjects were designed for the six large reliefs on the upper story of the great arch at the Étoile to distribute the heroism of Revolution and Empire amongst several personalities. If Napoléon appears there twice (once as a young general leading the charge at Arcole, once as Emperor and master tactician at Austerlitz), so too do several of his contemporaries: the generals François-Séverin Marceau (killed at Altenkirchen in 1796) and Jean-Baptiste Kléber (wounded at Alexandria in 1798), who had teamed up during 1793 to quash a counter-Revolution uprising in the Vendée region of eastern France. The intrepid leader of Napoléon's heavy cavalry, général Joachim Murat, appears at the moment of his great lopsided victory at Aboukir. A more surprising presence is that of général Charles-François Dumouriez, who eventually defected and fled to Austria. Dumouriez is shown at the moment of his decisive victory over the Austrians at Jemmapes in November 1792—a battle in which a young officer of the Orléans family named the duc de Chartres participated and who appears alongside Dumouriez. Not incidentally, the duc de Chartres was none other than the youthful King Louis-Philippe. As an ensemble, the subjects of the sculptural reliefs suggest that intrepid patriotism on the field of battle is what matters to history and is worthy of honor—a devotion to the nation that precedes and overshadows the personal or partisan politics of Revolution and Empire.

The same theme was even more forcefully promoted by the four large sculptures placed on the corner piers of the great arch. Beginning with the first project of 1806, it was assumed that these would be sculpted groups of allegorical trophies, although nothing was decided and no commissions were awarded to sculptors. By December 1832 work had advanced to the point that Guillaume-Abel Bouet, the architect in charge of the project, began to press the Minister of the Interior to establish a sculptural program for the piers.

He continued to imagine them as allegories; witness his annual report about progress on the arch in 1832:

For the large trophies one could adopt either four large Victories surrounded by arms and banners captured from various powers, or four soldiers from the principal corps of the army, each the attributes that characterize his corps. But what I think would be more in harmony with the sculptural subjects presently being executed would be for the trophies to symbolize the four social divisions that support the prosperity of France: War, figured as Mars surrounded by modern weaponry; Science and the Arts, represented as Minerva along with the attributes that characterize these two domains; a Mercury with attributes to represent Commerce; and, finally, Agriculture in the guise of Ceres surrounded by farm implements.[102]

The minister to whom Bouet was writing at the time was Adolphe Thiers, who had played a central role in the decorative program for the Madeleine Church and was arguably France's leading historian of the Revolution.[103] Thiers was not impressed with Bouet's proposal for the large sculptures. He decided to anchor the program around four specific dates: 1792, year of patriotic fervor in which ordinary citizens rushed to defend the country's borders; 1810, the most resplendent year of the Empire; 1814, when Frenchmen faced the invading Allied armies as Napoléon's power crumbled; and 1815, year of the Empire's last hurrah at Waterloo and the start of a new era for the nation.[104] Commissions for the four large works were awarded to three sculptors in August of 1833: François Rude would create a *Departure of the Volunteers in 1792* (Fig. 44), Jean-Pierre Cortot was assigned *1810*, and Antoine Etex was awarded both *1814* and *1815*.[105]

The program sketched by Thiers stitches up the history of successive regimes and political ruptures in a narrative of collective struggle and national pride. The arch remained a monument to military prowess, but the leaders were several and the true hero was an enduring spirit of patriotism able to transcend the zigzag of specific events. Nearly three years later, when the arch was officially inaugurated, the ceremony was timed to coincide with the sixth anniversary of the 1830 Revolution (29 July 1836). An eyewitness account of the day published in the prestigious *Revue des Deux Mondes* under-

scores the idea that the July Monarchy was reclaiming for France both its revolutionary and imperial pasts:

It was as noble an idea as the one that resolved, after 1830, to finish the Arc de Triomphe de l'Étoile that it should be inaugurated on 29 July. In fact, what other day could be more appropriate for dedicating the monument? The 29th of July returned to France possession of that immense military glory of twenty-five years of Revolution and Empire. France will be grateful to the government that conceived this idea and realized it with such dignity and speed. . . . One is proud to come from a country that has done such exalted things in a quarter of a century, and knows how to establish so honorably the memory of them. What a history is given you to read in the solemn registers of those colossal vaults! What immortal pages left to posterity![106]

In the same vein, a broadsheet poster published to announce the inauguration reported that the War Ministry would issue special invitations to all those men presently living in Paris who had served in the armies of Revolution and Empire, and that they would be seated in places of honor close to the arch. "All the details of the festivities," remarked the broadsheet, "will recall as much as possible that they are meant to celebrate the military courage of Frenchmen, and to pay homage to the brave men who have honored our country."[107]

Nearly everyone at the unveiling agreed that Rude's *Departure of the Volunteers in 1792* (Fig. 44) was far and away the masterpiece of the arch. "The most important and best piece is that of M. Rude," remarked the *Revue des Deux Mondes*.

This is really '92. The border is threatened, but the enemy armies will not cross it. The entire population rises up as one and hastens to the fight. The genius of resistance guides our soldiers, soaring over them on large wings fully opened, eyes glittering, magnificently excited, sure of victory. Everything here is movement and enthusiasm; everything rises to the subject.[108]

Much of the attraction of Rude's group depends upon its extremes of expression and formal invention—the open-mouth cry, bodily extension, and dramatic turn in space of his winged figure—and the dynamic thrust of the whole, as if the figures are about to leap from the pedestal. Rude's rhythmic alterna-

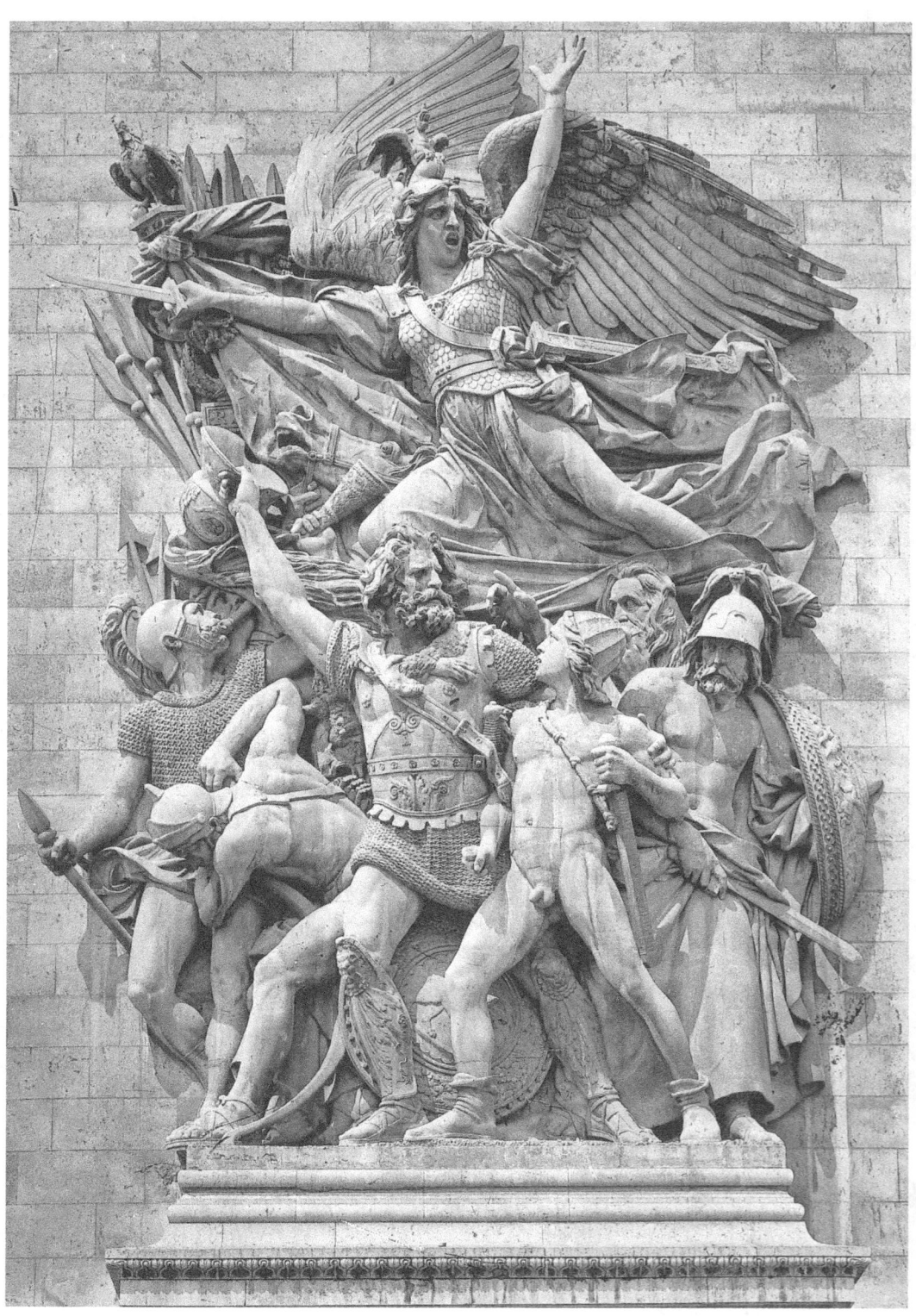

FIGURE 44. François Rude, *Departure of the Volunteers in 1792*, 1833–1836. Vintage photograph. Paris, Arc de Triomphe de l'Étoile. Photo: © Centre des monuments nationaux, Paris.

tion of heroic nudity that reveals muscles with heavy armor that cloaks the body, his centralized, arm-in-arm pairing of an older man with an admiring youth, and his dense stacking of props—banners, fluttering drapery, and an hysterical horse—all wedged into a narrow slice of background space, give plastic form to the mythic rallying of 1792 as a universal and somewhat chaotic élan. He also suggests, by the range of ages, physical types, and expressions, that it was a moment of profound consensus in which individual cares withered in the face of foreign invasion. This idea of a mythic accord, dramatically pictorialized by Rude as the nation finding its collective voice in the scream of his flying figure, was crucial to the July Monarchy's efforts to recuperate the Revolution and Empire. Consensus was at the core of its own myth of origins (see Chapter Two). Indeed, setting Delacroix's picture of *Liberty* (Fig. 25) alongside Rude's group on the arch (Fig. 44) reveals a shared visual vocabulary of dynamic movement, and the staging of a clash between generalized allegory and anecdotal detail that challenges norms of decorum and tradition. Both works mobilize a hybrid iconography that is characteristic of visual imagery striving to present recent history within the context of the fragile political framework peculiar to Paris of the 1830s.

The chronology of successive campaigns to rewrite the symbolic coding of the triumphal arch at the Étoile is paradigmatic of many Parisian monuments during the first half of the nineteenth century, although it differs from most in two key ways. First, because the arch was never fully completed until 1836, it had little prior history—apart from Chalgrin's prefiguration of 1810—to complicate the consensual nationalism of the final program. Second, despite the permutations of its decorative scheme, the arch was always a monument to militarism: its symbolic range remained constant across the several projects to alter its specific message. One might say that the arch had a rather short and uncomplicated memory of the recent past, so that the July Monarchy's deviation of its meaning from the personal glory of Napoléon to the national glory of France passed with little resistance. By contrast, some monuments were deeply implicated in the events of Revolution and Empire, and efforts to recast their meanings met the stiff resistance of an historical memory materialized

in stone and bronze: nowhere is this resistance more pronounced than at the Panthéon.

THE EMPIRE INHERITED a Panthéon heavily freighted with meaning by years of revolution (Fig. 45). The main structure of Jacques-Germain Soufflot's magnificent church of Sainte-Geneviève, its huge dome delicately floating on a dense forest of columns, had been completed in 1790, but most of the interior decoration was unfinished. The ecclesiastical life of Sainte-Geneviève was disrupted by the Revolution's suppression of religious orders (February 1790) and the law concerning the Civil Constitution of the Clergy (July 1790) so that, for all practical purposes, the great building had neither caretakers nor a purpose. A purpose was soon found. Two days after the death of Mirabeau (2 April 1791), the Constituent Assembly proclaimed that the building would be dedicated, in the words of the marquis de Pastoret, AUX GRANDS HOMMES LA PATRIE RECONNAISSANTE, and that Mirabeau would be the first "great man" to be buried there.[109] Funds to convert the church into a French Pantheon were voted on 16 May. Quatremère de Quincy (who later opposed looting artworks from Rome) was named architect in charge of the transformation on 19 July.

This is not the place to chronicle the many modifications effected by Quatremère at the Panthéon. The most dramatic measures included blocking up the thirty-nine windows of the nave, radically simplifying the decorations already in place, and eliminating all visual references to the monarchy and the Catholic Church.[110] The main body of the structure became a penumbral space, indirectly lighted and visually isolated from the outside world—a space of meditation and memory appropriate for monuments or statues to great men. Corpses of the elect were to be buried downstairs, in the full crypt that Soufflot had built beneath the church. Quatremère's separation of a person's monument upstairs from his or her body downstairs responded to the idea that the Panthéon was not a funerary space for the dead, but a place of living memory where role models for a new, revolutionary France would be forever part of present experience.

FIGURE 45. Charles
Chevalier, *The Panthéon
(Church of Sainte-Geneviève)*,
ca. 1842. Daguerreotype.
Bradford UK, National
Museum of Photography,
Film, and Television, inv.
1937-401 (33 × 24 cm).
Photo: National Museum
of Photography, Film, and
Television/SSPL.

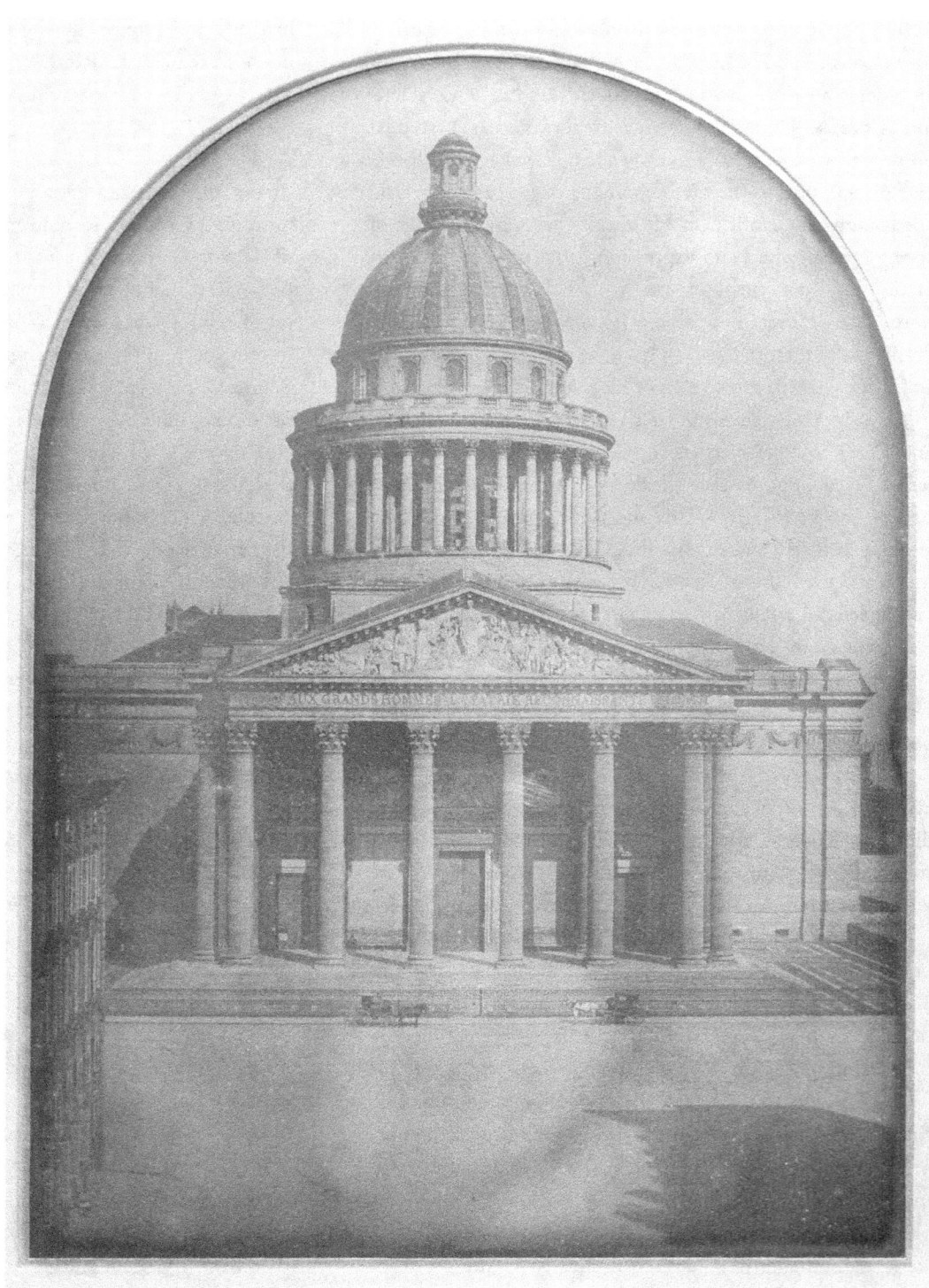

Mary Berry's comments upon visiting the Panthéon in 1802 sum up succinctly the building's physical state after a decade of revolution:

Went with Barrois to the Panthéon. The whole bas-reliefs of the facade have been altered from those of Ste. Geneviève to emblems of liberty, and between the six large columns which support the pediment, are four colossal figures in plaster, meant as models to be executed in marble, of Strength, Genius, the Republic and another figure which I did not make out. The inside, while intended for a church, was never finished. . . . In the lower church, or what in a Gothic church one should call the crypt, supported by Tuscan columns without bases, are the tombs, or rather cenotaphs, of Voltaire on one side and Rousseau on the other. In the middle had been placed Marat, but no trace of him now remained.[111]

Berry reminds us that many of the Revolution's heroes (such as Marat and Mirabeau) did not stay long in the Panthéon. Factional squabbles, personal denunciations, and the changing winds of politics were grounds for removing many of them within months after being acclaimed worthy of a place in the crypt. Her remark that she "did not make out" one of the large allegorical figures on the porch registers Quatremère's efforts to design a sculptural program that would invest the Panthéon with a symbolism resistant to the trials and tribulations of history. "This monument," he wrote, "although a work of the Revolution, was not specifically dedicated to it. . . . Here one should praise its effects more than its actions, and celebrate its influence more than its conquest."[112] Quatremère's recourse to allegory, even if sometimes so arcane as to be unintelligible, was the result of his reluctance to draw up a list of worthies and to make their effigies a permanent part of the monument. In light of the fluid historical situation of these years, it was both easier and cheaper to remove the tomb of a discredited person from the crypt than to replace his (or her) sculpted presence on the facade. So the Panthéon of the Revolution became, as Mona Ozouf remarks, "a place of collective memory outside of history" or, one might say, a monument to remembering with nothing to remember.[113]

Yet monuments will always remember, and the Panthéon was no exception. Its material intransigence is most appar-

ent in the story of the various pedimental sculptures executed for the building, beginning with the one carved by Jean-Guillaume Moitte under the guidance of Quatremère and completed in July of 1793 (Fig. 46 top). In accordance with Quatremère's insistence upon allegorical imagery, Moitte anchored the center of his composition with a figure of La Patrie, arms outstretched like a balance beam of Justice, who distributes laurel crowns to figures at each side. La Patrie forms a visual fulcrum between two distinct and clearly gendered spheres of civic life: at the left Virtue, in the guise of a young woman clad modestly in antique garb, waits for a crown to be placed on her head; to the right Genius, figured as a winged male in resplendent nudity, takes his own crown from the hand of La Patrie. The two figures flanking La Patrie set the theme for their respective halves of the pediment. At the left, as if following Virtue, a winged figure of Liberty carrying the palladium of France guides a chariot, laden with emblems of civic virtues, that leaves in its wake the conquered figure of Despotism. To the right, Genius is accompanied by Philosophy in the guise of a young cupid, whose oversized torch of Truth assures victory over a pair of griffons that stand for Error and Prejudice. Moitte's binary composition articulated the triumph of human values embraced by the Revolution without referring to specific contemporary events. Beneath this pediment were inscribed, in large letters of gilded bronze, the words from Pastoret's proposal to create the Panthéon: AUX GRANDS HOMMES LA PATRIE RECONNAISSANTE.

A number of great men entered and exited the Panthéon during the 1790s, but the building fell into disuse during the first years of Napoléon's rule—a neglect fueled by such startling shifts in the building's structure that many feared it might collapse. Mary Berry noticed in 1802 that "one of the great piers which support the cupola had given way (I think before the Revolution), and the whole arch between pier and pier is now filled up with a great charpente to support it."[114] Napoléon could not ignore for long the huge dome that rose above the Latin Quarter and was visible from all of Paris, while the Concordat of 1802 (see above) predisposed him to gestures of reconciliation with the Catholic Church. In a decree of 20 February 1806 he announced that "the

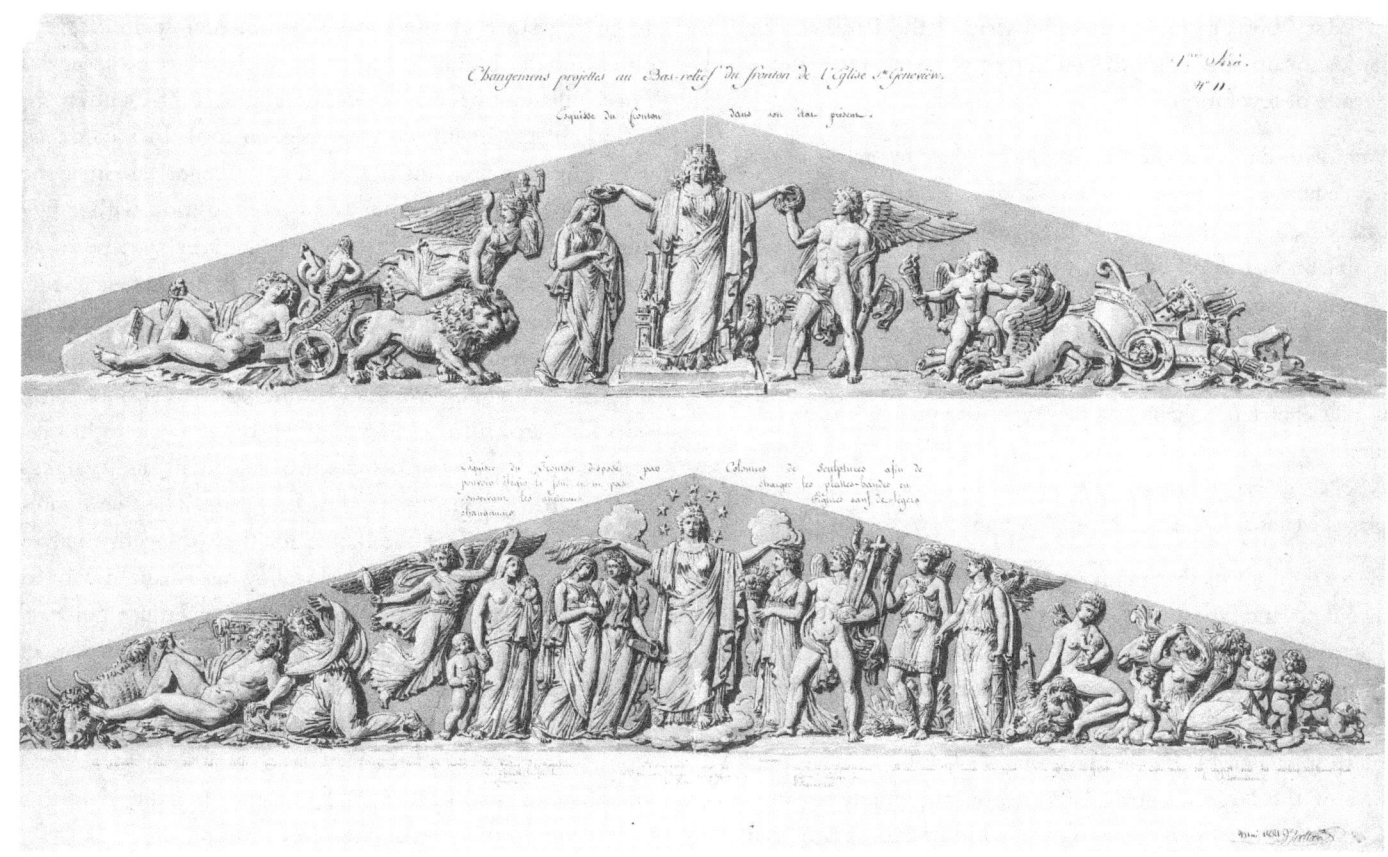

FIGURE 46.   Louis-Pierre Baltard, *Proposed Changes to the Reliefs on the Pediment of the Church of Sainte-Geneviève*, 1821. Pen and brown ink with color wash. Paris, Centre Historique des Archives nationales, inv. CP/VA 51/20 (61.5 × 97 cm). Photo: Atelier Photographique du Centre des Archives nationales.

church of Sainte-Geneviève will be finished and returned to the cult, according to the wish of its founder, under the protection of Sainte-Geneviève, patroness of Paris."[115] The curious part of this decision is that no one could forget the Panthéon's role in the history of the Revolution, and return of the building to ecclesiastical usage was curiously indecisive. The structure was not to become a church of daily use, because Napoléon specified that religious ceremonies within the building were authorized only four days a year: the religious feasts of Sainte-Geneviève and All Souls, along with two official feasts. All other purposes were subject to the Emperor's personal authorization. Nor was the build-

ing to be cleared of its revolutionary heritage, for Napoléon wanted the crypt to

keep the purpose it had been given by the Constituent Assembly, and will be committed to the interment of high dignitaries, grand officers of the Empire and the Crown, senators, grand officers of the Legion of Honor and—by virtue of our special decrees—of citizens who, in a career of military, government or literature, have rendered outstanding service to the country. Their embalmed bodies will be buried in the church.

To implement this plan, construction began almost immediately on a staircase leading to the crypt from a separate entrance at the extreme back of the building. The Panthéon of Napoléon was an odd schizophrenic structure where the monument's religious vocation clashed with the revolutionary heritage of its patriotic function. And what became of Moitte's allegorical pediment of civic virtue? It was covered by a sheet of gray canvas and kept hidden from public view right to the end of the Empire.

One of the first reports submitted in April of 1814 by Louis-Pierre Baltard, architect in charge of the Panthéon, to Louis XVIII's Minister of the Interior was an estimate for removing all traces of revolutionary and imperial emblems from the building.[116] The project was delayed by Napoléon's unexpected return during the Hundred Days (see Chapter One), but it was taken up in earnest with Louis XVIII's decree of 1816 that "the church of Sainte-Geneviève will be returned to the Catholic cult. Our Minister of the Interior will prepare and submit for our approval a plan of works that he thinks necessary to undertake in order to complete this monument that we owe to the piety of our august Grandfather."[117] Passing control of the church from the government to the archbishop of Paris opened a new phase in the building's life. Over the next few years Baltard developed several projects to correct the decorations of Sainte-Geneviève, including the pediment and its inscription. Because Moitte's sculptures were still in place, although hidden from view, Baltard tried to convince the authorities to recut the original in order to deflect its meaning. The project he submitted in 1821 argues that Moitte's work (Fig. 46 top) could be transformed into an allegory of France protected by religion (Fig. 46 bottom): to the right, acclaimed by Europe and the Genius of Christianity, and admired by the continents of North and South America, Africa, and Asia; at the left, attended by the theological virtues (Faith, Hope, and Charity) and a winged figure of Truth whose mirror turns back the cowering figures of Paganism.

The archbishop of Paris took a hard line. He would have none of Baltard's thinly disguised recycling of the Revolution's allegorical language and physical nudity. He insisted that Moitte's relief be destroyed and that the architect design a simple cross on a field of golden rays. He also insisted that the words AUX GRANDS HOMMES LA PATRIE RECONNAISSANTE be replaced with a Latin text erasing any allusion to the time between Louis XV's vow to build the church in 1744 and Louis XVIII's rededication of it in 1822. In a final irony, the letters of D.O.M. SUB INVOC S. GENOVEFAE LUDOVIC XV DICAVIT LUDOVIC XVIII RESTITUT were cast in bronze obtained by melting down the letters of the Revolution's inscription. The new words were installed on the building in 1823, exactly coincident with the most conservative moment of the Restoration—several months of political reaction triggered by the assassination of the duc de Berry known as the White Terror.

The new pediment of Sainte-Geneviève—indeed the entire project to make it again a church—was coded reactionary in the public mind. The street fighters of the 1830 Revolution were quick to reclaim the building: on 29 July an ersatz banner returned the Panthéon's revolutionary inscription to the pediment. When this expedient disappeared in mid-August, it was quickly replaced.[118] Louis-Philippe wasted no time appropriating this spontaneous public gesture as his own, and establishing his government's use of the building to contrast sharply with that of the Bourbons. A royal ordinance of 26 August 1830 specifically abrogated the decrees of both Napoléon and Louis XVIII to announce that the monument "will be returned to its original and legal purpose. . . . The inscription 'aux grands hommes la patrie reconnaissante' will be reinstalled on the pediment . . . and the remains of Great Men will be placed there."[119] The bodies of Rousseau and Voltaire, hidden away in a locked part of the crypt since the end of 1822, were returned to the vestibule, and Pierre-Jean David d'Angers was commissioned to carve a new pediment for the renewed Panthéon.

David d'Angers was an appropriate—if inadvertent—choice to create a sculpture that would reclaim Soufflot's building for the cult of great men established by the Revolution. He had fought as a young man in the armies of the Revolution alongside his father. He frequented the company of Liberal leaders, welcomed the fall of the Bourbon government, and professed his faith in the results of the 1830 Revolution. He wrote to the voters of Angers in 1834.

In spirit and heart I belong to the July Revolution. I accept without reservations the constitutional government of 1830; I accept it because I believe it conforms to the present state and future needs of France; I accept it because, if steadfastly understood and put into practice, it can guarantee the growth of all the seeds of civilization and well-being that are contained in the future of my country.[120]

David d'Angers was not an artist likely to challenge the motives or politics of the July Monarchy. What the sculptor could not predict is that even though he stayed close to the spirit of the 1830 Revolution with his design for the pediment, Louis-Philippe's government followed an increasingly conservative course. By the time David d'Angers finished his enormous project, its optimistic politics of consensus were hopelessly out of date.

The memory of Moitte's revolutionary allegory was still very much alive in 1830, so much so that David was originally asked to restore it.[121] But the sculptures had been so badly damaged when taken from the pediment in 1823 that it was decided an entirely new set would be necessary. In May of

1831 David received approval of his preliminary sketch from François Guizot, who was Minister of the Interior at the time, with the proviso that the sculptor would develop a more finished concept before actually beginning work. David apparently produced a fully elaborated plan by the end of 1832, but he was unexpectedly instructed by one of Guizot's successors to suspend all activity on the pediment. Not until April of 1834, when Adolphe Thiers—a figure already familiar as patron of the arts—became Minister of the Interior, was David authorized to take up the project once again. "Monsieur Thiers is extremely friendly with me," wrote David to a friend after meeting the minister, "he wants me to proceed with the pediment of the Panthéon. He is very pleased with the composition."[122] Why the delay of two years, and why did Thiers enthusiastically back David's project? To answer those questions requires studying the details of David's plan for the pediment (Fig. 47).

FIGURE 47.   Pierre-Jean David d'Angers, *Pediment of the Panthéon*, 1837. Contemporary photograph. Paris. Photo: © Davey Hubay.

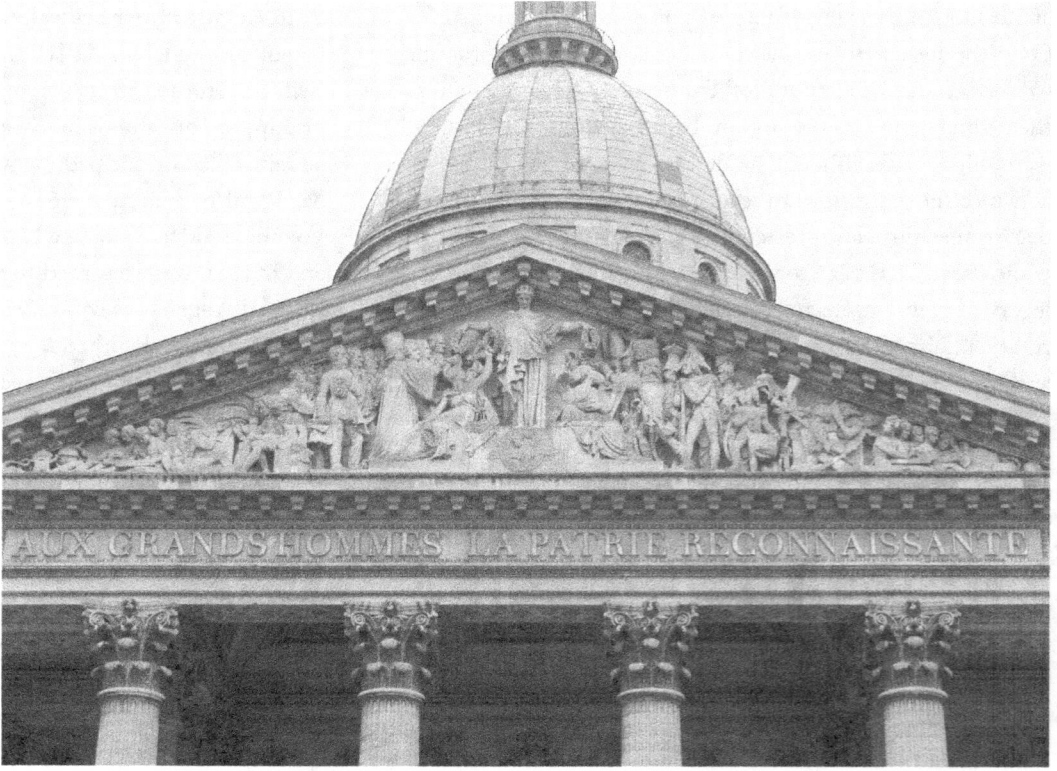

David adopted a binary division similar to Moitte's original by placing great men from civilian life at the left and military heroes to the right. A triad of allegorical figures occupies the center to separate these two spheres of patriotic life: at the apex, the standing figure of La Patrie extends her arms to offer laurel crowns to both sides; below and to the left, Liberty passes crowns to La Patrie; at the right, History inscribes the names of recipients in a great book. Hippolyte Fortoul, an art critic and friend of David, explained the overall division of the pediment as "a simple, popular idea that everyone can understand. On one side he placed civilian professions, on the other military groups. He put the former to the left, on the side of Liberty who, in fact, finds among them her safest refuge. The warriors are on the side of History, which great commanders have always preferred to brave."[123] David's innovation, Fortoul was quick to point out, was that instead of abstract allegories for the flanking figures

he characterized them by historical personalities, and he chose those that have been picked out in recent times by national instincts as the most reliable exemplars that one might hold up to future generations. In this way, he has written in the stone everything together: past glory, future hopes, and the general state of current thinking.

David produced a coherent reading of the recent past by deciding which characters, among many contenders, would be "the most reliable exemplars" to include. Quatremère de Quincy had hesitated to elaborate a list of great men amidst the political upheavals of 1791, opting instead for allegory as the Panthéon's principal mode of decoration. By contrast, David d'Angers made concrete choices, but the monument's checkered history ensured that his selections would be read politically. "He [David] saw in the pediment of the Panthéon the opportunity to express a political view, one exactly consistent with the hopes and the conduct of the French Revolution," wrote Gustave Planche; "conceived in this way, the subject narrows and loses the quality of impartiality that it ought to have; but if we criticize M. David's conception, we do not condemn it absolutely, because he has exercised his right to choose a fixed moment from our history."[124]

The politicians, intellectuals, and scientists assembled by David under the aegis of Liberty at the left were all firmly committed to Enlightenment principles of liberalism and reason: Rousseau and Voltaire sit together on a bench; Chrétien-Guillaume de Malesherbes (a backer of Diderot's *Encyclopedia* who defended Louis XVI and was himself guillotined), François Fénélon (Bishop of Cambrai who dared to challenge Louis XIV), the naturalist Georges Cuvier, and the mathematician Gaspard Monge are among the others nearby. Even more important, this group includes several leading figures of the French Revolution: Gabriel-Honoré Mirabeau, Lazare Carnot, and the painter Jacques-Louis David. They are joined by Jacques-Antoine Manuel, a Bonapartist politician allied with Liberals who opposed the Bourbons during the 1820s, and the marquis de Lafayette, whose long career embraced the entire saga of recent French history, from the fall of the Bastille to the 1830 Revolution. Lafayette, who died in 1834, played a crucial role in bringing Louis-Philippe to the throne in 1830, although his disenchantment with the ever more conservative tack of the July Monarchy eventually aligned him with opponents of the king.

To the right side of the pediment David d'Angers grouped a cross section of mustachioed soldiers from various branches of the armed forces. He included only one recognizable portrait among them: the long-haired, striding figure of young general Bonaparte leading the army of Italy at Arcole. David was much criticized for including only Bonaparte among the many military heroes that could be named. He defended his choice by arguing that he had specifically not represented the Emperor:

I had no other way of generalizing the idea of the army. Many of our great generals began as simple soldiers. Besides, I used général Bonaparte to represent the army's highest rank; that great military fame summed up all the others who have honored France. I did not represent Napoléon because, to my eyes, he is not grand and worthy of the gratitude of patriots, no matter how much he fought in the ranks of the defenders of liberty. I know the idea that presided over the conception of my relief is completely popular: it is to the people that I have devoted my artistic life; it is with them that the seed of truly noble and sublime sentiments is found.[125]

Finally, in both of the extreme corner angles of the pediment, David placed groups of young men assiduously applying themselves to their studies: they represent future generations of students in the Latin Quarter who will learn the way to greatness by emulating those being honored on the pediment and in the crypt.

There can be little doubt that the symbolism of David d'Angers's sculpture attempts to construct a continuous thread across the political fissures of recent French history, and that linking the men and deeds of 1830 to the liberal, Enlightenment tradition of the eighteenth century was consistent with the sculptor's own view of the period. It was also consistent with the early political rhetoric of Louis-Philippe, whose declaration of 26 August reclaimed the Panthéon in the name of its "original and legal purpose" established in 1791 by the Revolution: the king placed himself and his government in the tradition of revolutionary France that informed David's design of the pediment. Like Delacroix's picture of *Liberty* (Fig. 25), David used allegory to join historical facts—his pantheon of portraits—to the world of memory where shaded meanings of Revolution and Empire continued to shape the thinking of those who had lived them. In this way, David's pediment appears to be an honestly brokered document of its time. It is completely consonant with the hybrid program devised by Thiers for the monumental sculptures on the Arc de Triomphe de l'Étoile (Fig. 41), where four specific dates are treated allegorically even if they index historical episodes. These diverse visual projects of the early 1830s figured the nation's fractured past as a balancing act between history and memory—between lived events and one's mythic constructs of them—that required an imagery of discursive fissures rather than seamless certitudes.

What David d'Angers could not predict is that the July Monarchy soon became obsessed with forgetting its heritage of liberal politics and its revolutionary origins. In June of 1832, about the time David was enjoined to stop work on his sculpture, Paris was rocked by two days of street riots and armed revolt. The government of Louis-Philippe responded with an implacable show of military force and a zealous repression of the popular uprising that Victor Hugo later immortalized in *Les Misérables*. One of the politicians who encouraged the crowds in the early hours of the revolt was the marquis de Lafayette. Is it surprising that Louis-Philippe's government

objected to Lafayette's presence on the pediment of the Panthéon? In light of the recent violence among the same Parisians who had fought the July Revolution, is it surprising that Delacroix's painting of *Liberty* (Fig. 25)—where they appear so heroic—was removed from public view and placed in storage? In both cases, aesthetic choices map closely political events.

Two years later, under the protection of Thiers in the Ministry of Interior, David d'Angers returned to his pediment project. By the time he was finished, in the spring of 1837, the July Monarchy had moved even further from its founding myths. Louis-Philippe's eldest son and heir to the throne, Ferdinand-Philippe duc d'Orléans, was about to marry a German princess, Hélène de Mecklembourg-Schwerin, thus linking the fate of the relatively young French dynasty to an old-guard European monarchy. The wedding festivities in June 1837 included a gala celebration at the château of Versailles that was reopened, after four years of relentless restorations, as a public museum where "all the glories of France" were recounted in hundreds of history paintings. Not since the time of Louis XIV had Versailles shone with such royal munificence. On 8 May, in the context of these gestures of royal self-assurance, Louis-Philippe's government granted a general amnesty to "all individuals held for crimes or political offences." Four days later, the church of Saint-Germain-l'Auxerrois was returned to the Catholic Church and plans drawn up for its restoration (see above). Even hard-line aristocrats of the Ancien Régime had to admit that the July Monarchy seemed to be consolidating its power and prestige: "The bold measure of amnesty, the opening of Saint-Germain-l'Auxerrois, the marriage of the royal prince, the wonderful inauguration of Versailles," wrote the duchesse de Dino on 13 June; "all that has effected a change of decor that everyone takes advantage of for the moment, putting off the difficulties which, distant as they may be, cannot be thought of as destroyed. But, finally, we are on the sweetest, most brilliant, most magic honeymoon that can be imagined."[126] In the context of this display of monarchic prestige, David d'Angers's pediment for the Panthéon could not avoid anachronism—a document out of sorts with the present.

The comte de Montalivet, Minister of the Interior at the time, paid a visit to David on 19 July that appeared to go well.

David believed that official unveiling of his pediment would occur on 29 July during the anniversary celebrations of the 1830 Revolution. A second visit two days later seemed equally uneventful. Orders were given to begin dismantling the scaffold that hid the sculpture from public view. Work was suddenly halted on 24 July. Another meeting with Montalivet on the 27th apprised David that the government wanted not only to delay the unveiling but also to have changes made to the work. According to David's notes of this meeting, Montalivet feigned concern that only Bonaparte appeared amongst the soldiers, but the real issue concerned the figures of Manuel and Lafayette, Rousseau and Voltaire: the first pair was unacceptable to the government; the second to the archbishop of Paris, who still maintained that the Panthéon belonged to the Church.[127] David refused to consider making any changes and leaked his version of the meeting to some of his journalist friends. Throughout late summer the controversy was locked in stalemate but much debated in the press. The police placed the Panthéon under continuous surveillance to ward off any possible demonstrations. Finally, the government decided to unveil the pediment without fanfare or ceremony on the morning of 1 September.

Public reaction to the sculpture was immediate and deeply divided. The Catholic press was particularly harsh with David's use of allegory to paper over the past:

The Revolution is protestantism, deism, atheism, anarchism, the scaffold, despotism, corruption, pillage. But once again, since the Revolution dares not speak its name, it tries to allude and to hide itself behind a respectable signboard. Above all, its wish is to pass itself off as La Patrie: it traces the word *patrie* on its three-cornered hat, on its triangular pediment.[128]

The archbishop of Paris was so angry that he circulated a pastoral letter to every church in the diocese decrying "these emblems worse than profane that replace the radiant cross of Jesus Christ. . . . These images of impious, licentious, and corrupting writers substituted for that of the humble and chaste farm girl [Sainte-Geneviève]."[129] He asked that prayers of expiation be said throughout Paris during the third week of September. Political observers were not more charitable. "The glorification of skepticism in the person of Vol-

taire, of the people's sovereignty in that of Rousseau, of '93 in the sign of the red cap of revolution," asked the *Journal de Paris* mischievously even before the unveiling; "is this consistent with the September laws [of 1835], which forbid attacks on the fundamental institutions of society and the principle of constitutional monarchy?"[130] Rather than unifying the history of France between 1789 and 1830, rather than healing the breach between Church and State, the pediment of David d'Angers seemed to open old wounds.

Many years later François Guizot, the man who first approved David's design, remarked that "among the monuments upon which work was resumed at that time, only one—the Panthéon—was for me the occasion of a mistake, and it almost led to fairly serious troubles."[131] Guizot could take solace in the fact that he was not alone, for the riddle of the Panthéon had stumped both Quatremère and Napoléon. It continued to puzzle governments for many decades: the Second Republic of 1848 rededicated the building as a Temple of Humanity; it was reconsecrated a church in honor of Sainte-Geneviève in 1852; only in 1885, for the funeral of Victor Hugo, did it become the cathedral of modern France, the cold and eerily empty monument that one visits today. Perhaps the lingering problem of the Panthéon—its uneasy straddling of history and memory—has been most eloquently framed by Edgar Quinet:

Everything I could say implies a first Panthéon, a moral edifice of conscience, of ideal fatherland, of political liberty in the heart and house of each man. . . . So long as this edifice does not exist inside each Frenchman, let us not dream of reopening the town hall of civic glory and immortality. For as long as there is dogma in the human consciousness that says only the strongest are right, a Panthéon is impossible. It is quite certain that it will remain empty, even if filled to the top by a multitude of marble figures.[132]

THE ARC DE TRIOMPHE DE L'ÉTOILE and the Panthéon were among the most physical monuments of Romantic Paris, visible from afar and dominating their immediate surroundings. But solid stone is not the only way to invest urban space with a symbolic charge, especially in a city with a long tradition of royal squares that perforate the urban fabric. From the earliest of these squares—the place des Vosges and the place Dauphine built by Henri IV around 1610—to the last of them—the place Louis XV (Concorde) completed about 1775—the formula remained virtually unchanged: an open space defined by regularly proportioned architecture that is the setting for an effigy of the king. Marking Paris in this way expressed the idea of the city as royal property, which was partly true since only the king was authorized to shape, name, and thus claim the cityscape. None of the royal squares were spared the wrath of revolution. During the 1790s all of the royal statues in public—Louis XIV at the place Vendôme and place des Victoires, Louis XIII at the place des Vosges, Henri IV at the place Dauphine, and Louis XV at the place de la Concorde—were torn from their pedestals, melted down, and recycled as canons for the army. In some cases the Revolution reappropriated the empty spaces: witness the obelisk in honor of Louis-Michel Lepelletier de Saint-Fargeau, a lawmaker murdered by a royalist fanatic in 1793, erected at the place des Victoires. Elsewhere the past was liquidated by structures of everyday life, such as the restaurant and string of boutiques built where the statue of Henri IV had stood on the Pont-Neuf. Perhaps the most spectacular gesture of the Revolution occurred at the place de la Bastille where the old prison—site of the first insurrections of 1789—was completely demolished. An Englishman visiting Paris in 1802 reported that

scarce a vestige remains of that famous prison, and the space is converted into a faggot yard; the gate to the arsenal however yet remains. . . . It is interesting as having belonged to the Bastille, and imagination can picture the wretched victims that in former times were conveyed through this gateway to waste their lives in misery and chains.[133]

Only in the 1830s did the place de le Bastille recover a symbolic meaning (see below). Paris at the turn of the century offered several tabula rasa squares in high-visibility neighborhoods that the Consulat and succeeding regimes would attempt to make their own.

Bonaparte's intent to claim the symbolic voids of the city was expressed clearly in the course of festivities programmed for 14 July 1800. On this day, the first commemoration of 1789 to be celebrated under the Consular government, cornerstones were laid for two monumental columns on the former sites of royal statues: one, in the place Vendôme, would honor citizens from the department of the Seine (Paris) killed in the recent wars; the other, on the place de la Concorde, would be a national column celebrating the country's embrace of the Consular government. In both cases, the columns were to be raised on the exact spot (even reusing some of the foundations) where royal effigies had stood before the Revolution. A few months later, in September, Bonaparte ordered construction on the place des Victoires of a monument to the memory of général Louis-Charles Desaix, who was killed at the battle of Marengo in June—a project that entailed destroying the Revolution's monument to Lepelletier de Saint-Fargeau. Bonaparte moved quickly to occupy the terrain and to claim these important urban spaces for his government.

Neither of the columns inaugurated in 1800 was completed as planned. Design of the national column at the Concorde was awarded to the architect Charles Moreau: he proposed a tall shaft surmounted by a figure of the Republic, the whole poised on a large circular base decorated by reliefs representing all the departments of France. So many voices were raised against this project, which threatened to spoil the axial view from the Tuileries Palace towards the Champs-Élysées, that a full-scale mock-up was erected in wood and canvas during the spring of 1801 to test the effect. The mock-up was subjected to lively criticism, and when it was removed in the fall of 1801 the whole idea was shelved. The departmental column for the place Vendôme fared no better. The project was awarded to the architect Auguste Molinos, whose design included four fountains in a base supporting a simple shaft capped by a statue of Minerva. It too failed to excite much critical praise. His plan died quietly, along with the idea of honoring individual departments rather than champion a single, centralized state.

The place Vendôme was the center of a vast urban renewal project dear to Bonaparte that included the new rue de Rivoli and a connecting cross street, the rue de Castiglione. The intersection of these new streets, as depicted in

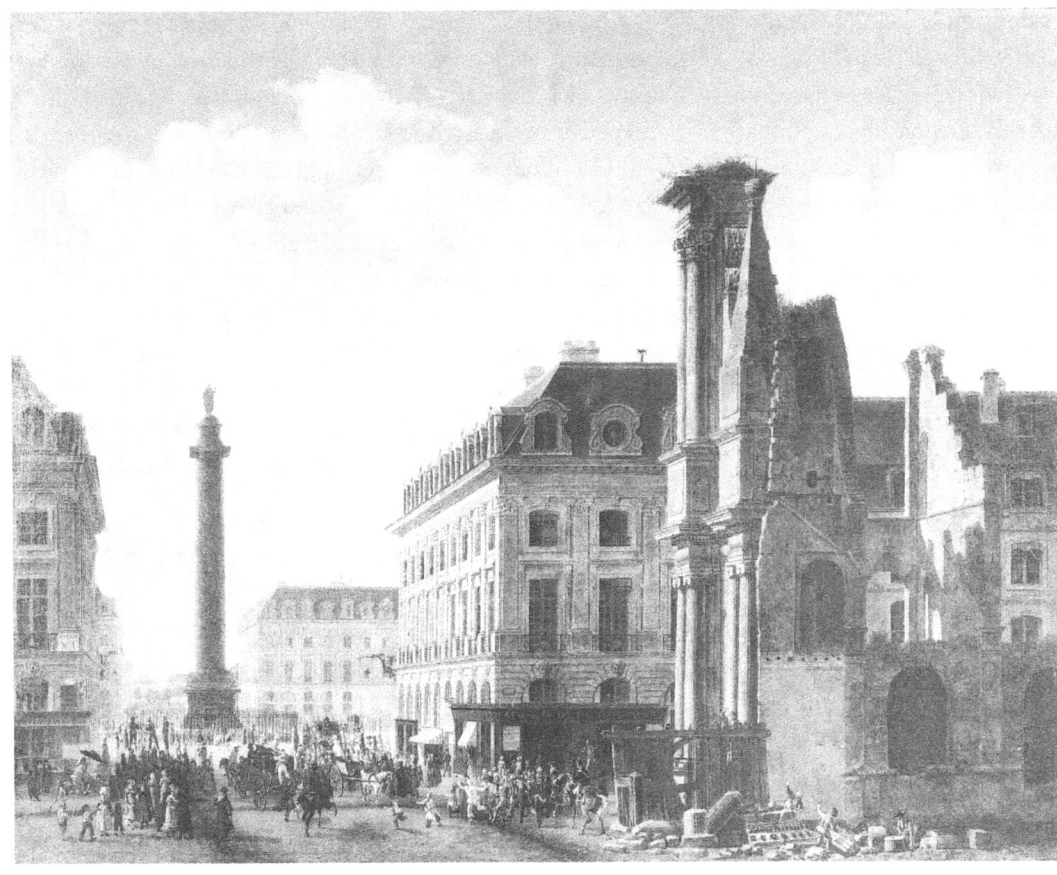

FIGURE 48. Étienne Bouhot, *View of the place Vendôme and the rue Castiglione*, 1808. Oil on canvas. Paris, Musée Carnavalet, inv. P 1285 (81 × 99 cm). Photo: © PMVP/ Lifermann.

Étienne Bouhot's picture of 1808 (Fig. 48), opens onto a magnificent vista of the place Vendôme. The space cried out for a central marker—something Bouhot anticipated by painting a column two years before anything was built. In the spring of 1803 Bonaparte proposed a monument for the place Vendôme to honor Charlemagne, founder of the Holy Roman Empire and an important role model for the First Consul in the months preceding his own accession as Emperor.[134] A declaration of 1 October 1803 specified Bonaparte's wishes for the new column: it would emulate the Column of Trajan in Rome; it was to be about three meters in diameter and stand more than twenty meters tall; its surface would be decorated with a spiral of one hundred eight allegorical figures in bronze relief representing the departments of France; it would be capped by a statue of

Charlemagne.[135] The general principle behind the symbolism of the column—that all of France supported the idea of an Emperor—was a thinly veiled allusion to the Empire soon to be declared.

Little work was actually begun on the Charlemagne project, although there was much discussion over several months about the plan submitted by a young architect named Savinien Thierry to construct an iron frame for the column upon which to hang the bronze reliefs. A review committee eventually rejected Thierry's proposal as too risky, preferring instead a core of masonry. The whole project was rethought after the French army's march through Germany that culminated in Napoléon's stunning victory over the Russians and Austrians at Austerlitz (2 December 1805). The very next day Dominique-Vivant Denon, director of the museum and point man for Napoléon's campaign of looting works of art, proposed that a column—clad in bronze forged from the hundreds of canons captured by the French at Austerlitz—be erected in honor of the Grand Army. Denon suggested that a spiral of reliefs could recount the recent string of victories. Although he did not dare to propose Napoléon's effigy for the apex of the column, few people doubted it would come to that. Napoléon was still asking in February 1806 about "the column that I have ordered raised to Charlemagne on the place Vendôme,"[136] but within a few days he decided to send the statue of Charlemagne to Aix-la-Chapelle. The stage was set for his own apotheosis.

Denon submitted an estimate on 10 March for a more generously scaled monument that would match the dimensions of Trajan's Column in Rome (almost four meters in diameter and forty meters tall), and be clad in a continuous spiral relief more than 260 meters long recounting the "memorable campaign against the Austrians." Two days later Jean-Baptiste Champagny, Minister of the Interior, reported that all of the details were in place, except one:

A purpose for the monument has yet to be determined. The wishes of the French people have designated one. Your Majesty had originally reserved the column of the place Vendôme to receive the statue of Charlemagne, but since then You have given this statue back to the city of Aix-la-Chapelle. May Your Majesty allow me to say that You would yield to the unanimous feelings of your subjects if You agreed that this column . . . would be used to perpetuate the memories of a campaign that has come to denote such a glorious epoch in the history of France, and that this column . . . would be surmounted by the statue of the Prince that the nation holds dear. What other statue could occupy the place left vacant by Charlemagne?[137]

Always mindful of the fate that had befallen the royal statues of Paris during the Revolution, Napoléon generally resisted placing his own effigy in public, but the Vendôme Column was simply too prestigious a site—and its subject too bound up with his personal glory—to refuse. Without directly responding to Champagny's initiative, Napoléon authorized the army to release a sufficient number of canons taken at Austerlitz to comprise the estimated one hundred fifty thousand pounds of bronze required to fabricate the column and its statue. Denon wasted no time getting the project underway. The architects Jacques Gondouin and Jean-Baptiste Lepère were selected to oversee construction of the foundations and the stone core. In August the site was cleared of the last remnants of Louis XIV's statue. A cornerstone for the column's base was laid on 23 September 1806.

Denon began working with a young painter, Pierre-Nolasque Bergeret, to develop the historical scenes for the long relief, with the idea that if one artist designed the entire suite the overall effect would be more unified. Bergeret was soon besieged by army officers who wanted their portraits placed more advantageously than events warranted:

After a very animated encounter with maréchal Lannes, who wants to be in the foreground, although nothing in the program warrants it [recalled Bergeret], I had the idea to have the Emperor decide which compositions would be executed. I talked to M. Denon about the plan, who adopted it, and who actually took to Napoléon a large quantity of drawings to be signed by the lion himself. This put an end to the entreaties that had become very hard to avoid.[138]

After being approved by the Emperor, working drawings for the 425 panels were distributed to a crew of sculptors: the Vendôme Column was a truly collective effort involving more than thirty-three artists. Where the column's reliefs were designed to relate the glorious facts of recent military history (although most are invisible from the ground), the statue for the top of the column spoke in another register. It was the work of Antoine-Denis Chaudet and depicted the Emperor Napoléon in the ceremonial robes of his coronation, a winged victory poised in one hand. Strictly speaking, historical fact informed Chaudet's statue, but the symbolic link between Napoléon of 1806 and the emperors of ancient Rome could not be missed.

Work progressed slowly. The masonry core was completed in 1808 and is probably why Bouhot painted the column into his picture of that year (Fig. 48). About half of the reliefs were mounted during 1809; by May of 1810 the column was complete except for some last-minute finishing. It was already something of a tourist attraction, as Prince

Clary-Aldringen reported in an enthusiastic letter of June 1810 to his mother. The prince writes that Denon gave him a ticket to climb the scaffolding that encased the column so as to view the reliefs:

Lots of people were going up and down the stairways. In two days the scaffolding will be demolished, and the column will be wrapped in canvas until 15 August, when it will be unveiled and inaugurated. The column is completely finished, except for cleaning and polishing. . . . The immense spiraling relief, which unfolds from top to bottom, appears to be very finely worked. Like all works of this type, it consists of a confusion of battles, entrances, and figures impossible to sort out, and that no one will see again once the scaffolding is taken away. . . . The statue of Napoléon, at the top of the column, is very beautiful in its form, costume, and draperies. . . . An interior stairway leads to the balcony that surrounds the statue and everyone wants to go up there because the view is extremely interesting. The Tuileries Garden, looked over from so close by, the parks of the hôtels on the place Vendôme, and everything else produces a charming effect. Because this vantage point is quite far from Notre-Dame and the Panthéon, its perspective on the city is completely different.[139]

Among all of the monuments planned by Napoléon, only the Vendôme Column was completed during his reign. Its inauguration on 15 August 1810 was the occasion for great celebration. But the joy of that day was mitigated by Napoléon's fear that too much ceremony around a column heralding his victory over Austria might offend his new bride: Marie-Louise was, after all, an Austrian princess. He cancelled publication of a sumptuous illustrated book explaining the reliefs in detail, and he changed the monument's official name from "the German Column" to "the Column of the Grand Army."

Napoléon's fears about the fate of his effigy were completely justified. Clary-Aldringen correctly noted that the Vendôme Column was visible from a large part of the city. When the Allied armies entered Paris on 1 April 1814 via the great boulevards, they could not avoid seeing the column, especially when crossing the rue de la Paix. If the victorious commanders raised their eyes with respect to the statue of the man they had finally defeated, a handful of young French aristocrats broke rank to attempt a decapitation of the column. An English eyewitness describes the spectacle:

To end this day of celebration, the viscount La Rochefoucauld, the marquis Maubreuil and a few other gentlemen had the idea to throw the statue of the great soldier of Austerlitz at the feet of the victorious enemy. A cask of wine and a few pieces of hundred *sous* coins were enough to recruit some willing workmen. They forced open the door of the pedestal, despite the resistance of several people, and reached the summit of the monument. Out on the platform, they pounded with hammers on the anchor-bolts of the statue. On the square below they pulled on ropes attached to the neck and torso of the statue. The figure leaned forward slightly. More drinks, new efforts: Napoléon remained standing. Then some wretch climbed onto the shoulders of the statue and slapped the bronze face two times.[140]

Unable to dislodge Chaudet's statue, the zealots had to settle for draping the Emperor with the Bourbon flag. The incident was not widely applauded and it worried the police, who feared that wounded national pride might incite some Parisians to fight for the column's safety. That evening a poster was affixed to the base with the announcement—signed by Étienne-Denis Pasquier, the chief of police, and Talleyrand, head of the provisional government—that the column would remain but that Napoléon would be replaced by a figure of Peace.

The next day brought attempts to arrange a more orderly removal of the irritating statue. The architects Lepère and Gondouin refused to cooperate with the authorities, as did the chief carpenter who worked on the column, a man named Lacasse. Finally, the man who actually cast the sculpture—a bronze founder named Delaunay—was forced to remove it under threat of military execution should he refuse to do so. A hoist was erected atop the column. Delaunay worked the entire day of 8 April to loosen the statue from its moorings. It was finally lowered to the ground about 6 PM before a crowd of curious spectators that included the German artist Georg-Emmanuel Opiz, who made a sketch later published as an etching (Fig. 49). The Bourbon flag was installed atop the column as an interim solution, although the promised statue

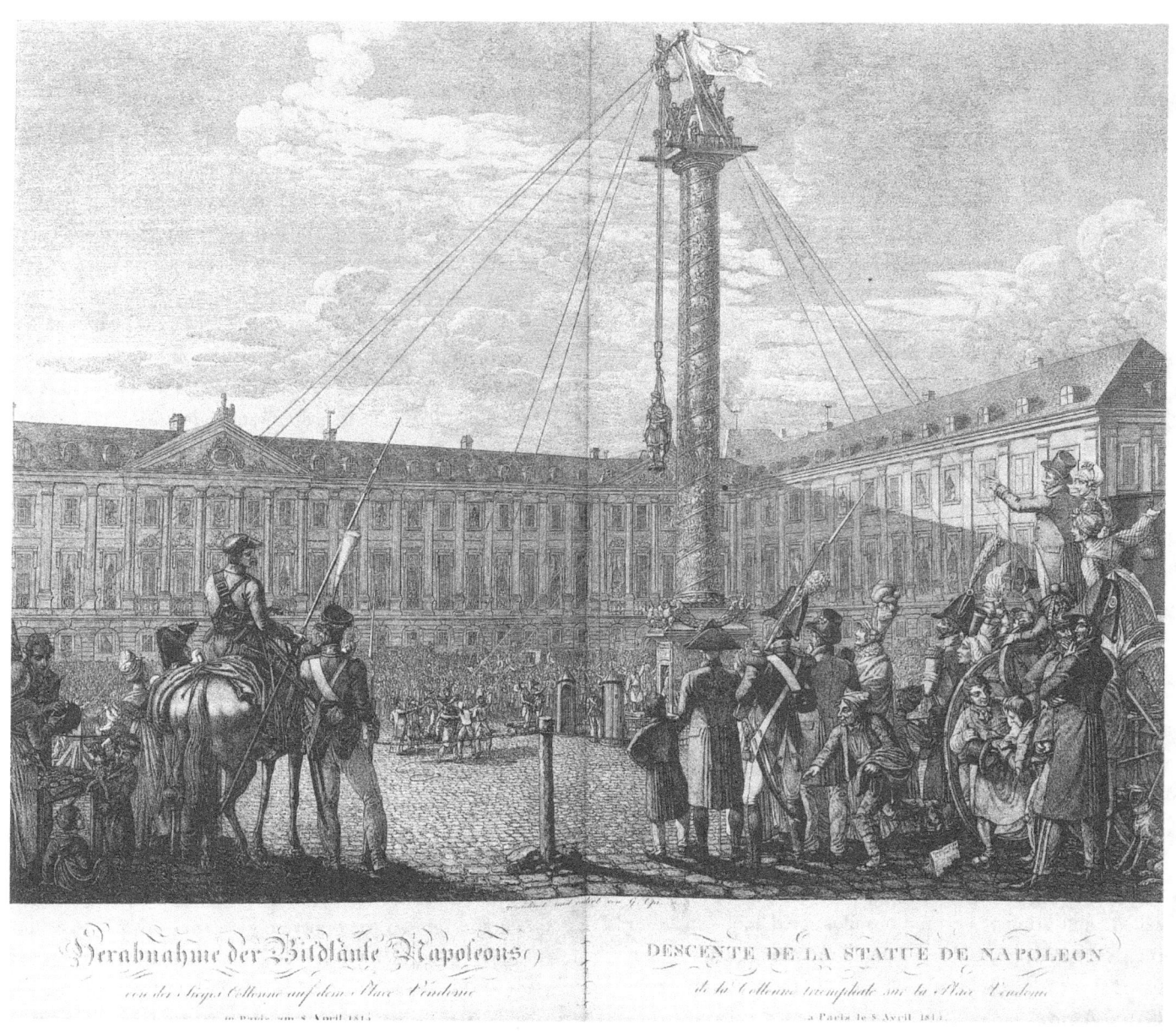

Herabnahme der Bildfäule Napoleons DESCENTE DE LA STATUE DE NAPOLEON

FIGURE 49. Georg-Emmanuel Opiz, *Removal of the Emperor's Statue from the Vendôme Column, 8 April 1814*, 1814. Etching. Paris, BnF, Estampes, inv. Collection Hennin, no. 13555 (42.7 × 55.3 cm). Photo: BnF, Paris.

of Peace never materialized. During the Hundred Days a tricolor fluttered from the column because Napoléon refused to replace his effigy, preferring instead to commission an allegory of the French People that was never executed. After Waterloo, the Bourbon banner was returned to the place of honor, where it stayed until 1830.

The Emperor was gone, but the column continued to elicit powerful sentiments of nationalism in the memory of French men and women both inside and outside of Paris. "Ah, one is proud to be French when one sees the column!" ran the refrain of a popular song of the 1820s called "La Colonne."[141] In October of 1830 Victor Hugo penned the famous lines that recall his impressions of the column's inauguration and celebrate the monument's staying power:

Oh! quand par un beau jour, sur la place Vendôme,
Homme dont tout un peuple adorait le fantôme,
Tu vins grave et serein,
Et que tu découvres ton oeuvre magnifique,
Tranquille, et contenant d'un geste pacifique
Tes quatre aigles d'airain;

A cette heure où les tiens t'entouraient par cent mille,
Où, comme se pressaient autour de Paul-Émile
Tous les petits Romains,
Nous, enfants de six ans, rangés sur ton passage,
Cherchant dans ton cortège un père au fier visage,
Nous te battions des mains.[142]

[And when, beneath a radiant sun,
That man, his noble purpose done,
With calm and tranquil mien,
Disclosed to view this glorious fane,
And did with peaceful hand contain
The warlike eagle's sheen.

Round thee, when hundred thousands placed,
As some great Roman's triumph graced,
The little Romans all;
We boys hung on the procession's flanks,
Seeking some father in thy ranks,
And loud thy praise did call.][143]

A few months earlier, in the first hours of the revolution that toppled the Bourbons and brought Louis-Philippe to power, the tricolor flag was once again hoisted atop the Vendôme Column in a spontaneous display of enthusiasm for the memory of Napoléon and the grand exploits of the Empire.

On 8 April 1831, exactly seventeen years after Chaudet's statue of the Emperor was removed by the Allies, Louis-Philippe approved a gesture completely in line with the cultural politics manifest at the Arc de Triomphe de l'Étoile and the Panthéon: a figure of Napoléon would return to the top of the Vendôme Column. Casimir Périer, who was Prime Minister at the time, suggested in his report to the king that the prestige of Louis-Philippe's newly minted dynasty could benefit from the gesture without embracing the politics of Empire:

The general and popular principles upon which the constitutional government of Your Majesty is founded permanently protect France from the evils associated with absolutism and the political program of conquerors. But, by honoring a great reputation, by re-erecting the monument that hallows a memory from which France derives great glory, the King forges, in a way, one more link between the country and the throne. I go so far as to believe that the proposal I submit for royal approval will be regarded both as a well-founded homage rendered to the public conscience, and as a striking and new proof of the power and justice of a thoroughly national government.[144]

Five days later Louis-Philippe approved a proposal from the Minister of Commerce and Public Works that a sculptor for the new Napoléon be selected by an open competition. Among the details of this proposal, article five is of special interest: "the figures on the bas-reliefs of the column being in French military garb, the statue should likewise be in military dress."[145] Without specifically forbidding artists from proposing designs of Napoléon as Emperor, the government let it be known that it expected an image of him as a military leader in modern uniform. The jury of selection was convened on 12 June 1831, and three days later—from a field of thirty-six entries—it declared Émile Seurre to be the winner.

Seurre's completed statue appears in a lithograph of its arrival at the foot of the Vendôme Column in 1833 (Fig. 50).[146] Napoléon is represented in the signature costume that remains part of his mythic persona even today: from the bicorne hat, greatcoat, tall boots, and colonel's uniform to the spyglass grasped in his right hand. Napoléon's gesture of tucking his left hand into the opening of his vest is paradigmatic of his appearance in popular prints and cult objects of the time; so too is the Legion of Honor medal on his chest and the sword of Austerlitz that he wore on the day of his greatest victory. Seurre modeled all of these costume details

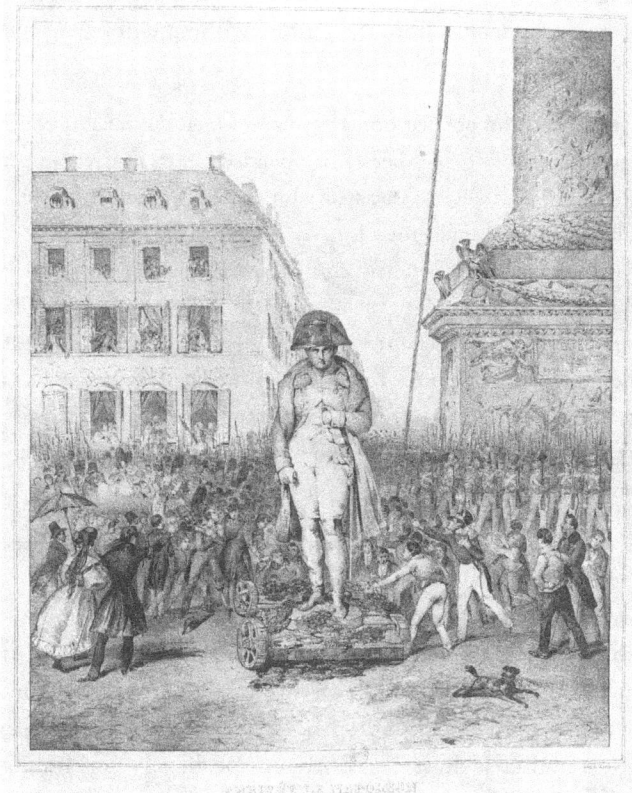

FIGURE 50.   Gabriel-Xavier Montaut (designer) and Alfred-Léon Lemercier (lithographer), *Arrival of the Statue of Napoléon at the Foot of the Vendôme Column*, 1833. Colored lithograph. Paris, BnF, Estampes, inv. Collection Hennin, no. 14596. Photo: BnF, Paris.

from the originals kept like holy relics by Napoléon's faithful companion-in-exile, général Henri-Gratien Bertrand. "The old soldier who happens, by chance, to pass the column will stop in ecstasy before the statue of M. Seurre and will exclaim several times: Oh! it's really him!" complained a critic in *L'Artiste*.

But do not look for any attempt at idealization in the statue of M. Seurre, for any trace of lofty expression of intelligence or force, for the least effort to achieve with the bronze one of those monuments of art that would be for all time the history of an epoch and a man.[147]

That was exactly the reaction of Frances Trollope to the sight of Seurre's statue when she first saw it in 1835:

The original statue, with its flowing outline of Roman drapery, was erected by a feeling of pride; but this portrait of him has the everyday familiar look that could best satisfy affection. . . . This *chapeau à trois cornes*, and the well-known loose *redingote*, have that air of picturesque truth in them which is sure to please the taste even where it does not touch the heart. To the French themselves this statue is little short of an idol. Fresh votive wreaths are perpetually hung about its pedestal; and little draperies of black crape, constantly renewed, show plainly how fondly his memory is still cherished.[148]

The sentimental reminiscence reported by Trollope was precisely what Louis-Philippe and his ministers hoped to manipulate by returning Napoléon to the Vendôme Column. Lemercier's lithograph (Fig. 50) suggests something of their immediate success: Seurre's statue is strewn with laurel wreaths and acclaimed by soldiers and workers, men and women, rich and poor in a rush of enthusiasm fueled by memories of their youth.

Ceremonies to inaugurate Seurre's statue were held on 28 July 1833 to coincide with the third anniversary of the July Revolution. For the unveiling Louis-Philippe, accompanied by his sons and aides, approached the column, gave a signal for the covering to be lowered, and saluted the effigy with a cry of *Vive l'Empereur!* The crowd responded with *Vive le Roi! Vive l'Empereur! Vive la Révolution!* and a military band struck up *La Marseillaise*. Here, for a moment, the July Mon-

archy seemed to achieve the elusive fusion of national identity in which distinct memories of Revolution and Empire
were joined to the present in exuberant celebration. Thirty
years later, during the reign of Louis-Napoléon Bonaparte
(nephew of the great man), Seurre's homespun effigy was
replaced by a replica of Chaudet's original that is still in situ,
but France was again an Empire and imperial allusions were
the order of the day (see Epilogue).

WHAT BECAME of Chaudet's original statue? In an odd
twist of fate, it was melted down and recycled to make François Lemot's equestrian statue of Henri IV that still stands
on the Pont-Neuf (Fig. 51). The reappearance of Henri IV
in the center of Paris was one of the few success stories of
the Bourbon Restoration's struggle to recapture some of the
city's public spaces for the old monarchy. The original had
been removed on 14 August 1792, even though Henri IV was
one of the most widely respected kings in French history.
"This king's virtues made us hold back for a time," reported a
spokesman to the National Assembly, "but we did not hesitate once we remembered that he had not ruled with the
consent of the people."[149] Later, a restaurant was built in the
open area between the spans of the Pont-Neuf where Henri
had stood. The restaurant was demolished in 1809 when Napoléon ordered construction of a giant granite obelisk, more
than one hundred eighty feet tall, to immortalize his most
recent military victories.[150] As with so many of Napoléon's
monumental projects, construction of the obelisk was suspended at the end of the Empire before even the foundations were complete.

After Napoléon's first abdication in 1814, the Municipal
Council of Paris was eager to demonstrate its devotion to
the restored Bourbon dynasty. In a meeting of 18 April it
decided that a statue of Henri IV should be reestablished
on the Pont-Neuf. By 3 May, the day of Louis XVIII's return to Paris, a hastily prepared plaster mock-up of Henri
greeted the king's passage. A public subscription to pay for a
bronze statue was opened so that all Parisians might demonstrate their enthusiasm for the new government. During the

Hundred Days, upon being informed that his original plans
for an obelisk were now supplanted by the project to honor
Henri IV, Napoléon replied:

I am pleased to see Henri IV honored. I too want to participate
in the homage paid to a ruler about whom France has preserved a
good memory and who alone, by his courage, knew how to gain the
right to govern the French, to their good fortune. I will add whatever money is lacking to the amount required to finish the work
that has been started.[151]

What Napoléon could not predict when he allowed the
project to proceed was that Henri IV would be made at
the expense of his own effigy and that of his good friend
général Desaix. In 1817, when Lemot's sculpture was ready

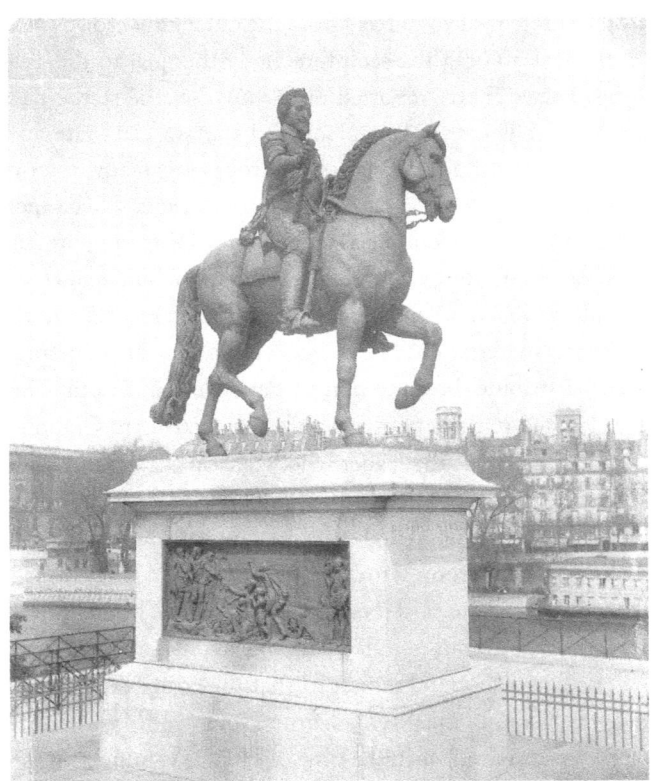

FIGURE 51. François Lemot, *Equestrian Statue of Henri IV*, 1818.
Bronze. Paris, Pont-Neuf. Photo: © Centre des monuments
nationaux, Paris.

for casting, the government of Louis XVIII donated the bronze obtained by melting down Chaudet's statue of Napoléon from the Vendôme Column and the sculpture of Desaix removed from the place des Victoires. The statue of Henri IV managed to survive the political flip-flop of the Hundred Days and, by bridging the turmoil of contemporary events, it became the first monument of post-Revolutionary France that might be called truly national in character.

The completed statue of Henri was ready to be moved from the foundry to its final site in July of 1818. A festive caravan was organized: "I went to see pass the bronze statue of Henri IV," wrote Mary Berry on 14 July, "enveloped in blue cloth covered with fleurs de lis, and drawn upon a sort of sledge by forty oxen in two lines."[152] So great was the weight of the bronze that the oxen faltered near the Champs-Élysées. Hundreds of volunteers from the onlooking crowd took up the task to drag the sculpture along the quai to the Tuileries Palace. Berry reported on 18 July that the statue had arrived safely at the Pont-Neuf, and that an elaborate apparatus of cords, pulleys, levers, and ropes was ready to raise Henri upon his base.[153] Louis XVIII was eager to channel some of the public enthusiasm for Henri IV to support his own, rather more shaky, political reputation. The choice of subsidiary reliefs attached in 1820 to the base of Lemot's sculpture materialized the king's ambitions: on one side, Henri distributes bread to hungry Parisians; on the other, he is welcomed to the city of Paris after converting to Catholicism and hailed as the leader who will heal the wounds of a long civil war. Benevolent father and conciliator of factions, Henri IV was a popular historical figure from within the ranks of the Bourbon family whose memory could burnish their claim to rule post-Napoleonic France. The historical analogy was a commonplace among apologists for Louis XVIII: Chateaubriand remarked that the crowds who came to greet the king on the road from Compiègne to Paris in April 1814 behaved "as in the time of Henri IV, hungry to see a king."[154] The inauguration of Lemot's statue on 25 August 1818 was a popular event that combined solemn and self-serving speeches with open buffets and free-flowing wine fountains for the enjoyment of one and all. For one day, at least, the restored Bourbon dynasty seemed willing to embrace the ordinary people of Paris.

THE LARGER TRUTH is that during the fifteen years of Bourbon rule, first by Louis XVIII and then Charles X, the kings never felt close to the milling energy and flammable passions of Parisian crowds. Both men remembered vividly what the Parisians had done to Louis XVI, Marie-Antoinette, and hundreds of other nobles during the Terror of 1793. Far more characteristic of their approach to remembering is Louis XVIII's decree of 19 January 1816 that instituted the 21st of January—anniversary of Louis XVI's execution—as a national holiday, and ordered construction of a monument to honor the martyr-king "as expiation for the crime of this unhappy day . . . in the name and at the expense of the nation."[155] One month later the king decided that statues of every Bourbon ancestor desecrated during the Revolution would be replaced on their original sites, which is why Louis XIII stands today in the place des Vosges and Louis XIV occupies the place des Victoires. Plans were also made to replace the statue of Louis XV on the place de la Concorde, newly renamed place Louis XV.[156]

This last was an especially troublesome locale. It was the place where the Revolution had violently purged itself of suspected traitors, and it remained haunted by the specter of the guillotine.[157] Chateaubriand imagined vividly the Revolution's "tool of death" when he returned to Paris in 1800, and for many years the power of that memory held sway. "Among the scenes of horror may be mentioned the square of Louis XV, now called that of Concorde," remarked John Pinkerton in 1802. He hastened to add that the former site of the guillotine was "in the centre, where stood the statue of Louis XV, and not in one of the corners, as asserted by a confident and careless German traveler. The spot is well known to all of Paris, and is enclosed with a rough wooden rail. It is visible from a great distance in all directions, a reason for its being chosen."[158] Napoléon had tried to reframe the symbolism of this place in 1800 by changing its name to Concorde and ordering a national column—complete with a figure of the Republic—that was deemed too tall for the site (see above). In 1806 and again in 1808 he entertained the idea of a monumental fountain that was never begun. The Concorde seemed to resist stubbornly all attempts to wrest it from its bloodied past.

Louis XVIII's plan to replace all royal effigies toppled by the Revolution included an equestrian statue of Louis XV for the Concorde. Pierre Cartellier, the artist selected to execute the work, waited almost a decade for a block of marble that never appeared. He was finally given approval to proceed in bronze, but on 27 April 1826 Charles X announced a new name and a new program for the square: henceforth it would be called the place Louis XVI and dedicated to the memory of the king executed in 1793. A statue of Louis XVI was ordered from Jean-Pierre Cortot (Fig. 52). Cortot proposed a pedestrian monument that offered a greater psychological proximity and pathos than a horse-mounted figure, even if coronation robes clearly signify the king's elevated social status. Louis XVI holds his last will and testament in one hand. He gestures towards heaven with the other to signal docile resignation to his fate. Cortot delivered a full-scale plaster of his sculpture to the bronze casters in November of 1829. The base carried personifications of the monarch's supposed personal virtues—Justice, Piety, Beneficence, and Moderation—and was completed by July of 1830. The nearly complete monument was a victim of the July Revolution: the insurgents of 1830 spared the pedestal but destroyed Cortot's plaster before it was cast in bronze. The new government of Louis-Philippe quietly dropped all plans of remembering the Bourbon martyr-king in the heart of Paris.

Charles X had also envisioned a redesign of the entire square. His government sponsored an architectural competition in August of 1828 to select an appropriate setting for Cortot's statue. The general idea was to define the space with four large fountains, although no final decisions were made and no work was begun before Charles was chased from the throne in 1830. In August of 1832 Jacques Ignace Hittorff was named architect in charge of the place de la Concorde with the immediate brief of developing a master plan for the ensemble. Hittorff produced several variants involving multiple fountains based loosely on ideas presented

in the 1828 competition, and he incorporated the entrance pavilions to the Champs-Élysées originally built during the Revolution. The goal was to consolidate prior work at the Concorde rather than beginning from scratch. Yet a large question remained: how to anchor the center in a way that would mitigate memories of the guillotine? What personality or theme might tie the ensemble together with the symbolism of national unity so dear to the July Monarchy?.

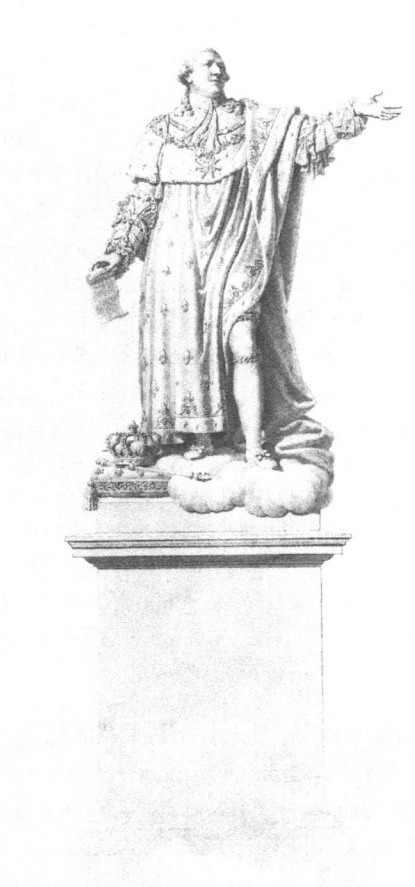

FIGURE 52.   Jean-Pierre Duvivier, *Drawing of Jean-Pierre Cortot's statue of Louis XVI destined for the place de la Concorde*, ca. 1826. Pencil drawing with sepia wash. Paris, Musée Carnavalet, inv. D 08915 (44 × 33.8 cm). Photo: © PMVP/Habouzit.

An expedient appeared in 1833 with the arrival in Paris of a solid granite obelisk after a long and technically complicated journey from Luxor in Egypt. The object was a gift to the nation from Méhémet-Ali, the pasha of Egypt and longstanding ally of France. The idea of erecting the obelisk at the center of the place de la Concorde opened a lively polemic among historians and scholars, especially with regard to how it was to be presented. In the months before a final decision was made, Jacques-Joseph Champollion-Figeac, brother of the erudite who first suggested that transporting the monolith was feasible, called for it to be installed in a public place where "this stone can be animated by illustrious memories, dedicated by a religious and national sentiment to the memory of those sons of France who died for glory in this same desert from which the obelisk has been uprooted."[159] Champollion-Figeac wanted to encode the obelisk with the memory and national prestige of Bonaparte's military and archaeological expedition to Egypt during 1796–1798. Not everyone agreed with him. Alexandre Lenoir, director of the Musée des Monuments français (see Chapter Four), deplored the idea of placing the obelisk on a high base in the middle of Paris where it would be impossible to study. Writing a critique in July 1833 of the wood and canvas mock-up installed in situ at the Concorde, Lenoir reminded his readers:

This monolith is not at all the fruit of our conquests in Egypt: it is a present for which we are indebted to the very great generosity of the Pasha. Thus, it is not appropriate to view it as a military trophy, and to use it to decorate one of our public squares. Would you set up the Venus de Milo, which was given to Louis XVIII by the marquis Rivière, in this way? Certainly not.[160]

Faithful to the pattern discovered in other July Monarchy monuments, no clear choice was made between the seemingly incompatible analyses of Champollion-Figeac and Lenoir.

The base of the obelisk still carries a textual anomaly that was much criticized by careful readers at the time of its installation. "What do we read on the pedestal of the obelisk?" asked Ernest Breton in 1840:

Monument of recent glory earned by our armies on the banks of the Nile; and the following line: Monument given to France by

Egypt herself. Who would not be struck by such a comparison? . . . If the monolith of Luxor had been carried to France aboard a ship covered with laurel crowns, then we would have been able to set it up in one of our public spaces and, with a noble sense of pride, to carve on the base: To the glory of the army of Egypt! But today, if we lack glory, at least let us have the courage to do without trophies. And, if we want to erect some to our past glory, let us not fashion them from gifts, even the ones that we want to dedicate to defeats, because, at that point, there is more at stake than vanity, there is ingratitude.[161]

Breton goes on to question the historical legitimacy of the entire operation, for if the inscription mentions the "recent glory" of the French army in Egypt the only date inscribed on the base is 1832. "Certainly there can be no doubt today," he notes; "but in a few centuries who will think that this recent glory already goes back in time nearly forty years? If you want glory, aren't the dates of 1798 and 1799 sufficiently brilliant to find a place on the pedestal of the obelisk?" Breton put his finger exactly on the vagaries of interpretation that appear when memory, monuments, and history intersect: contemporaries in 1840 understood perfectly that the July Monarchy was fudging historical truth; how many tourists visit the Concorde today and grasp that sleight of hand?

Nonetheless, installation of the obelisk went forward. On 25 October 1836 the granite shaft was tilted into place upon its prepared base before a large crowd of curious spectators (Fig. 53). François Dubois recorded the end of this complex and delicate operation with great fidelity, emphasizing the elaborate system of counterweights and winches used to raise the huge mass. He faithfully included the anecdotal episode of four men scaling the monument to plant tricolor flags and laurel wreaths at its summit. His picture also alludes visually and across time to the great throngs who had gathered in the square during 1793 to watch the guillotine at work. Behind the obelisk stands the shadow of the Revolution's fury: then, pulleys and ropes raised the bloodied blade to dispatch enemies of the state; now, they raise a monolith of stone that will remain forever still. The monument's heritage in ancient Egypt alludes to a stability across time. Materially embodying a physical and a temporal immobility, the obelisk was perfectly suited to displace and dispel memories of the restless movement—the incessant rise and fall—of the Revolution's "tool of death."

Hittorff's rearrangement of the place de la Concorde was not completed until 1840, well after the obelisk was set in place and after several years of running battles with Claude-Philibert-Barthelot Rambuteau, the Prefect of Paris, and the Municipal Council. Hittorff's final design includes two large fountains that flank the obelisk with extravagant displays of running water—a conceit felt by many to be especially appropriate for the imaginary "field of blood" left by the Revolution at the Concorde. "In the middle of the Place Louis XV," wrote Chateaubriand in an open letter of 1831,

"I would make a large gushing fountain, whose perpetually running waters, spilling into a basin of black marble, would sufficiently indicate what I want to wash clean."[162] Chateaubriand's letter is proof that even banal objects acquired loaded meanings when filtered through the layers of history and memory permeating the place de la Concorde. It also underscores the stakes involved in Hittorff's struggle to recode the square's symbolism. He eventually settled upon eight small pavilions built around the perimeter of the open space, each carrying an allegorical figure of a French town, and each located on its approximate compass direction from Paris. Thus, architectural markers for Lille, Strasbourg,

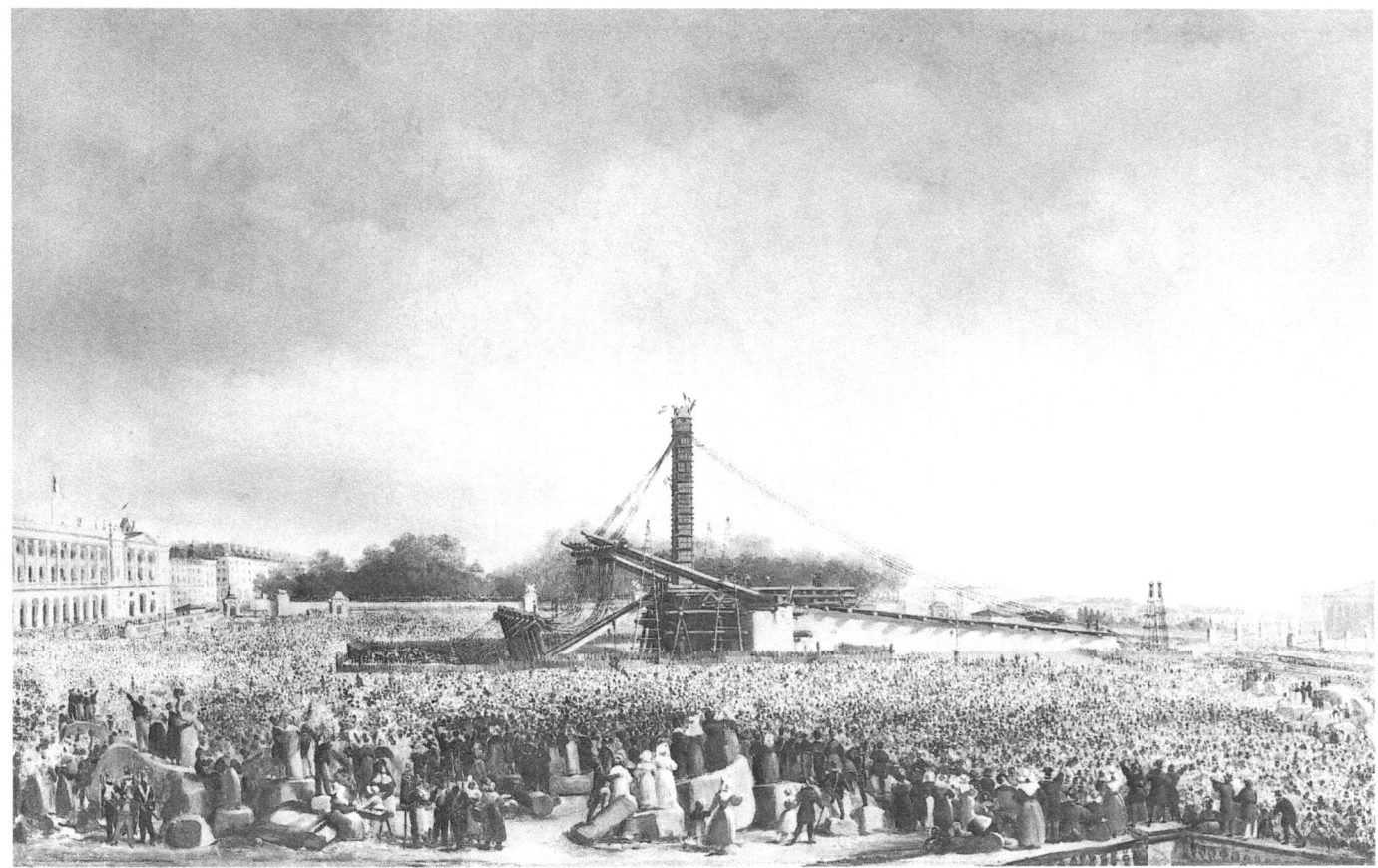

FIGURE 53.   François Dubois, *Erecting the Obelisk from Luxor*, 1837. Oil on canvas. Paris, Musée Carnavalet, inv. P 0107 (67 × 98 cm). Photo: © PMVP/Svartz.

Lyon, Marseilles, Bordeaux, Nantes, Brest, and Rouen delimit the square physically and situate it metaphorically within the geography of France in a system of mapping that both masks the historical notoriety of the Concorde and positions it as the symbolic center of the nation.

Several of Hittorff's pavilions are visible in the painting by Jacques Guiaud that represents the place de la Concorde on 15 December 1840 (Fig. 54). On this day Napoléon's body was returned to Paris and deposited under the dome of the Invalides Church so that the Emperor might rest amidst the aging veterans of his imperial army. The picture faithfully records the obelisk, the fountains, and the system of cast-iron light columns designed by Hittorff to articulate the space and illuminate it at night. Visible in the background, on the north side of the square, are the two buildings designed in 1757 by Jacques-Ange Gabriel for Louis XV (today the

Hôtel Crillon and Ministry of the Marine). Between them lies the church of the Madeleine, itself newly completed and decorated. Looking over this landscape, the Dominican theologian Jean-Baptiste-Henri Lacordaire left a vivid contemporary reading of the Concorde's layered meaning:

When the foreigner travels downstream on the river that divides Paris he comes across a space whose expanse and monuments incite his musings. On one side is the palace of the kings of France; in front of him, at the far end of a long avenue, a military arch of triumph. In a second vista that cuts the first cross-wise, two temples communicate with one another: one belongs to laws, the other to God. At the center stands an Egyptian obelisk, but it disappears behind an invisible monument that is on everyone's mind: the scaffold of Louis XVI. All of France is on this square: royalty, military glory, liberty, religion, revolution.[163]

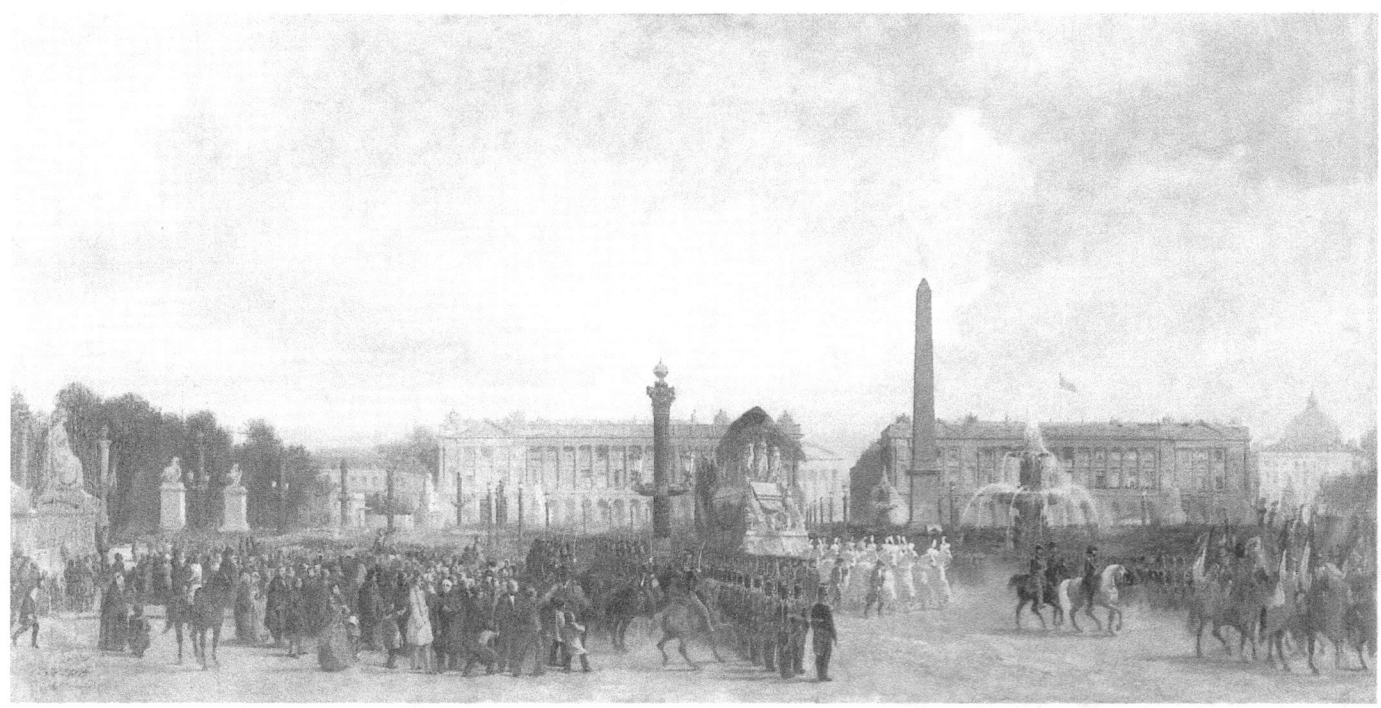

FIGURE 54. Jacques Guiaud, *Ceremony for the Return of Napoléon's Remains: The Cortege entering the place de la Concorde, 15 December 1840*, 1841. Oil on canvas. Versailles, Châteaux de Versailles et de Trianon, inv. MV5125 (105 × 117 cm). Photo: © RMN/Art Resource, NY/© Gérard Blot.

In Guiaud's picture, this terrain of accumulated history is traversed by the elaborate funeral wagon carrying the body of Napoléon—a final return to Paris engineered by the same Adolphe Thiers who sponsored work at the Madeleine, the Arc de Triomphe de l'Étoile, and the pediment of the Panthéon. Guiaud's picture provides more than an eyewitness account of a current event or the topography of a place, for it both diagrams and instantiates the efforts of July Monarchy politicians to forge a new political landscape of the nation from the splinters of a fractured past.

THE THEME OF NATIONAL RECONCILIATION recurs throughout the cultural politics of Louis-Philippe's government, but its most graphic expression is the monument erected in Paris by the July Monarchy at the birthplace of the 1789 Revolution: the place de la Bastille (Fig. 55). The site had long been little more than an open field, even though its symbolic prestige was undiminished by neglect and physical dilapidation. In December of 1803 Bonaparte ordered the Bastille cleared of rubble and loosely regularized around a central basin following plans adopted in 1792 but never carried out. Three years later, in the course of debates about where to place the colossal Arc de Triomphe (Fig. 41), Napoléon (already Emperor) preferred the Bastille but was persuaded that the Étoile was a more suitable site for so large a mass. He then entertained the idea of a large central fountain that would draw water from the canal being built between the Ourcq River and the Seine, especially because it was projected to pass directly through—or under—the Bastille. A decree of May 1806 authorized work on such a fountain and further suggested that it be decorated with scenes "taken first of all from the history of the Emperor, then in the history of the Revolution and the history of France. One must not, generally speaking, miss an opportunity to humiliate the Russians and the English: William the Conqueror and Duguesclin could be honored in these monuments."[164] Nothing came of this project to combine utility with political propaganda, but Napoléon remained attached to the idea of a fountain at the Bastille. Two years later he returned to the

scheme on a truly fantastic scale by ordering the Minister of the Interior to "draw up without delay the plans, drawings, and estimate for building a fountain on the place de la Bastille; this fountain will represent an elephant carrying a tower as in antiquity; one will be free to make this monument in bronze or in some other material."[165] Jean-Antoine Alavoine was named architect in charge. The cornerstone for this unusual addition to the cityscape was laid on 2 December 1808, fourth anniversary of the Emperor's coronation and third anniversary of his great victory at Austerlitz.

It was perhaps inevitable that many of Napoléon's advisers opposed the idea of a giant elephant in the heart of Paris. His resolve remained inflexible. "I presume that the elephant will be in the center of a large basin filled with water," he wrote from Madrid on 21 December 1808; "that it will be very beautiful, and large enough so that one could go inside the tower it will carry."[166] A decree of 9 February 1810 reconfirmed the project and suggested that the elephant be cast in bronze from canons taken in Spain. The following year (24 February 1811) Napoléon publicly humiliated Czar Alexander by specifying that Russian canons captured during the campaign of Friedland should be used for the elephant. Finally, in his impatience to see what the elephant would look like, Napoléon ordered confection of a full-scale model in wood and plaster that was unveiled in the summer of 1813.[167]

This huge elephant of painted plaster, sheltered in a special hangar at the edge of the Bastille, was never cast in bronze. The end of the Empire also marked the end of the fanciful project. Yet the plaster elephant was not immediately destroyed. Rather, it became a nostalgic emblem of Napoleonic ambition, its crumbling state vividly portrayed decades later by Victor Hugo in *Les Misérables*:

It was an elephant forty feet tall, built of wood and stone, carrying its tower on its back . . . painted black by the sun, rain, and time. At night, under a starry sky, in this deserted and exposed corner of the square, the large brow of the colossus, his trunk, his protectors, his tower, his enormous buttocks, his four feet almost like columns, cut a surprising and terrible silhouette. . . . It was gloomy, enigmatic, and immense. It was some kind of powerful phantom, visible and standing alongside the invisible specter of the Bastille.[168]

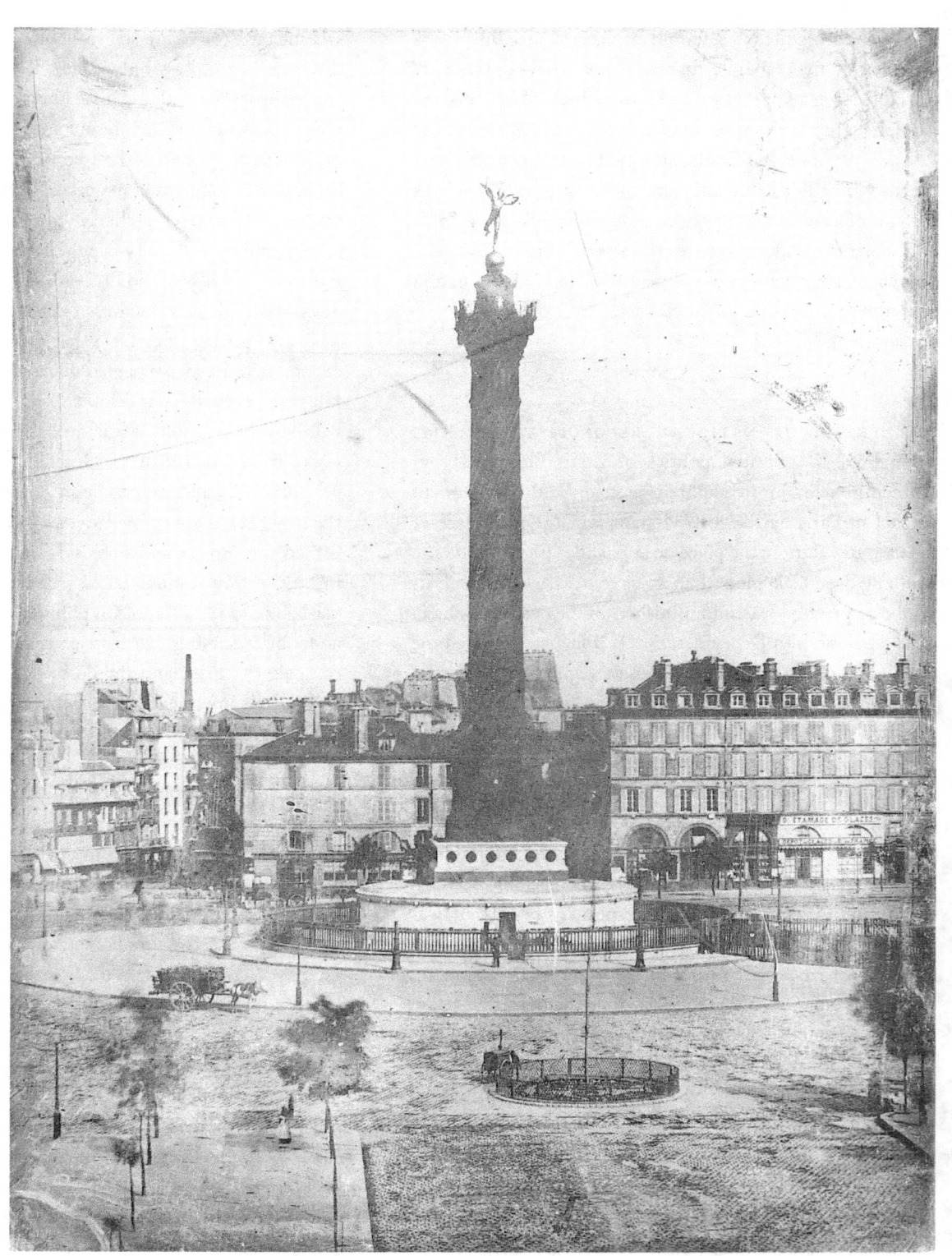

Hugo characterizes the ersatz monument as a catalyst for the layered histories of the Bastille—Old Regime, Revolution, and Empire—to become a volatile mix of memories and fantasies that trigger political action. Small wonder that Hugo set *Les Misérables* in 1832, the year of violent uprisings in the narrow streets of the surrounding neighborhood that nearly toppled the July Monarchy.

Incredibly, work on the foundations and basin of the fountain continued during the early years of the Bourbon Restoration. Alavoine tried desperately to save the elephant by arguing that "most people falsely attribute the idea for this monument to Napoléon."[169] His words fell on deaf ears. With orders to design a more appropriate centerpiece for the fountain, Alavoine proposed a colossal statue of the City of Paris flanked by figures representing the rivers Rhône, Garonne, Seine, and Loire. Commissions for this latest iteration were awarded to sculptors in January 1829 and materials were ordered, but nothing was finished when the revolution of July 1830 ended Bourbon rule.

The place de la Bastille inherited by the July Monarchy was something of a hodgepodge: in the center, a nearly completed basin for a large fountain; off to one side, a full-scale plaster mock-up of Napoléon's elephant. Two months into the new regime, Louis-Philippe's Minister of Public Works floated a plan to take up Napoléon's project and cast the elephant in bronze![170] But the euphoria after the July Revolution seemed to require that recent events have their own place in the city. On 13 December 1830 the Chamber of Deputies passed a law authorizing funds for a monument at the Bastille with a dual purpose: to honor those brave citizens killed in the recent revolution as well as those who died attacking the Bastille in 1789.[171] The July Monarchy's first project for the Bastille forged strong symbolic links between the two revolutions, a fusion exactly in step with the one proposed by David d'Angers for the

FIGURE 55. Antoine Melbye (attributed to), *The July Column, place de la Bastille*, 1848. Daguerreotype. Paris, Collection Société Française de Photographie, inv. 569/31 (10.3 × 7.6 cm). Photo: Société Française de Photographie.

pediment of the Panthéon and approved by the government in early 1831.

One might expect from the pattern established at the Panthéon that this fusion of historic moments did not last. In a report to Louis-Philippe dated 6 July 1831, the Minister of Public Works (comte d'Argout) outlined three days of ceremonies to celebrate the first anniversary of the 1830 Revolution, including an homage to those killed in the fighting. D'Argout mentions that Louis-Philippe "has wanted a commemorative monument, dedicated only to them, that would constantly remind France and posterity of their memory." He goes on to suggest that this cenotaph be raised on the place de la Bastille.[172] Article three of Louis-Philippe's response to the report stipulates that "a funerary monument in honor of the victims of the Three Days will be erected on the former site of the Bastille." The crucial point is that the king no longer draws a parallel between the events of 1830 and those of 1789: he describes a funerary monument for the Bastille dedicated solely to the victims of the recent revolution. When Louis-Philippe laid the cornerstone of this new project on 27 July 1831, a few old veterans of 1789 were seated at the ceremony in places of honor, but no part of the official program mentioned the taking of the Bastille.

Planning for the monument was entrusted to Jean-Antoine Alavoine, the same architect who had been charged with building the elephant-fountain for Napoléon. Over the next two years Alavoine submitted to the government several variations upon a freestanding column, an idea that recalled designs for the Bastille elaborated during the early years of the Revolution with which he was surely familiar. The older architect's attention to the Bastille's revolutionary past emerges in a letter written by his assistant, Joseph-Louis Duc, in December of 1831: "I am entrusted with building the column that is going to go up on the place de la Bastille in honor of the victims of the July Revolution," wrote Duc to a friend; "above all, I must not be banal, that defect of contemporary mediocrities, because it's a matter of glorifying '89 and 1830. May patriotic sunshine warm my heart and head!"[173] Although Duc refers to a column, plans for the project were not finalized and they remained in flux for several years. A law of 9 March 1833 appropriated nine hundred thousand francs for the project and speaks of a column, but in June of that year the Minister of Public Works described it to the Chamber of Peers in extremely vague terms: "Nothing is decided yet about the project that should be adopted," he reported, and he even suggested that Napoléon's elephant might not be such a bad idea since "there would be something emblematic in that image of a calm and unshakeable force."[174] The memory of an unbuilt monument proved, in this case, to be as persistent as the memory of an elephant, for Napoléon's beast refused to disappear. Eventually Alavoine's final design referred neither to the elephant nor to 1789: he proposed a simple Doric column set upon a sub-basement crypt where the remains of those killed in July 1830 would be deposited.

Alavoine's solution was announced in September of 1833 with absolutely no fanfare. A few lines of text inserted in the newspapers reported laconically that "the proposed monument for the place de la Bastille, upon which work is now in full swing, will consist of a bronze column similar to the one at the place Vendôme. . . . The monument is entrusted to the talent of M. Alavoine."[175] The announcement to build a column generated something of a polemic in the art world of Paris, not because the plan seemed flawed, but because the project had been decided in private by the government and its hand-picked architect. The journal *L'Artiste* asked incredulously:

How to characterize this decision, after the official commitment made to artists three years ago to hold a competition for the monument? Doesn't it insult the public conscience to break so boldly a promise taken seriously by those who received it? But everything related to the July monument has been handled behind closed doors in the offices of ministers, as if one feared that public opinion might be heard in the discussion.[176]

The point made by *L'Artiste* is probably close to the mark. Plans for the column evolved in the months following the armed uprising of 1832 that erupted in neighborhoods close to the Bastille. Eager to deflect the monument into a purely commemorative and funerary role, Louis-Philippe's government did not want discussions that challenged the gradual erasure of any references to political resistance or the memories of 1789.

The critic for *L'Artiste* was also quick to make the inevitable comparison between Alavoine's column at the Bastille and Napoléon's column at the place Vendôme. "We have in Paris the Vendôme Column, popularized as much as a monument can be by the great things it recalls and especially the great name of Napoléon," he wrote; "It is no doubt in the hope of stamping the new monument with an equal popularity that it has been given the form of a column; that would have been, on the contrary, a reason to give it a new and different form."[177] Indeed, the July Monarchy was about to reinstall the statue of Napoléon atop the Vendôme Column with great fanfare. Settling upon the Bastille monument as a column did cater to the popular fervor for all things Napoleonic that Heinrich Heine noticed in 1832. "For the French, Napoléon is a magic word that electrifies and dazzles them," he wrote; "a thousand canons sleep in this name as well as in the Vendôme Column, and the Tuileries will tremble if these thousand canons one day awaken."[178]

Despite the obvious formal similarities, the July Column differs importantly from the one at the place Vendôme. The Bastille Column is constructed entirely of metal, for it is supported by an internal framework of cast iron and sheathed in an outer skin of cast bronze. The shaft proper comprises twenty-one cylindrical drums, each a single bronze casting, that are stacked and joined by a complicated system of braces and latches. A similar configuration for the Vendôme Column had been rejected in favor of a traditional masonry core; by contrast, descriptions of the July Column consistently praise its modern technology as much as its art. The capital is nearly three meters tall, five meters in diameter, and weighs more than ten metric tons. It was the largest single piece of bronze ever cast in France at the time of its manufacture. The entire column, which rises to a height of just over fifty meters, required more than 174 metric tons of bronze. The July Column is not simply a monument to an event and its victims: it is also physical evidence of how modern French technology might serve the arts. In this respect it embodies the mechanization of art-making that was of great importance to the industrial growth of mid-century Paris (see Chapter Eight).

Work on the column began in February of 1834; by the end of the year all of the interior parts were molded, a scaffold was in place, and assembly was about to begin on the internal frame. At this point an important break occurred in the project's elaboration, for Alavoine died in November and Duc, who was promoted to head the project, completely redesigned the exterior skin. He transformed Alavoine's unadorned Doric order into a richly decorated composite style: a Corinthian capital, a shaft fluted near the top and bottom and divided by bands or "bracelets" into three midsections, and an elaborately decorated base. One critic, writing in 1840 shortly after the monument's inauguration, reports that Duc wanted

to find a system of decoration that would set off in a special way the metal upon which it had to operate. He wanted to invest the bronze with a life of its own, of the sort bronze would take by itself if, suddenly animated, it could bend and fashion itself in a manner consistent with its secret nature. . . . Crisp and elegant cut-outs of foliage comprise nearly all of the monument's ornamentation, and in this respect it is very different from sculpted columns that recall the working of marble.[179]

Construction of the July Column coincided with an expanded use of industrial materials in the design of architecture throughout Paris. Duc's changes to the column parallel the arrival of a generation of young architects—including Eugène-Emmanuel Viollet-le-Duc and Henri Labrouste—who consciously allowed new materials to be visible and openly expressed in the design of their buildings (see Chapter Eight).

The symbolism developed by Duc for the column does not differ in kind from the mix of historical motifs and allegorical figures employed in exactly contemporary projects like the Arc de Triomph de l'Étoile and the pediment of the Panthéon. The bracelets of the shaft divide it into three sections—one for each of the "Three Glorious Days" of the 1830 Revolution (27, 28, and 29 July). Each section is inscribed with the names of those who were killed on that day. The bracelets themselves are decorated with small lion heads, while a large lion in relief, modeled by Antoine Barye, stands guard over the door that leads to the crypt. The lion, which refers to the zodiac sign of Leo, became a standard emblem for the monarchy born in July. The same motif is repeated in the twenty-four bronze medallions mounted on the square marble base that forms a zone of transition between the large circle of the crypt and the column that rises above. Still more lion heads are intermixed with the foliage and cherubs that comprise the decoration of the enormous Corinthian capital atop the shaft.

Finally, at the very top, a striding male figure of Liberty breaks free from the chains of Despotism while holding aloft the torch of Civilization. He also seems ready to fly from his perch, which gave rise to the popular witticism that "France has trouble keeping Liberty at home, this one is always ready to get loose."[180] The figure was designed by Augustin Dumont and is loosely patterned on a famous Mercury sculpted in the late sixteenth century by Giovanni Bologna. Dumont's work is notable for its unusual departure from the visual tradition of Marianne—Liberty as a draped female—established during the French Revolution.[181] The Liberty atop the July Column is a slender male nude, about as far as one can imagine from a Marianne. He is also miles from the working-class heroine painted by Delacroix in 1830 (Fig. 25). Dumont's unusual figure suggests the difficulties set in motion by the July Monarchy's attempts to claim the politically loaded idea of Liberty, on the very site where the Revolution of 1789 was born, without awaking its volatile historical heritage or recalling its immediate eruptions in the civil strife of recent memory.

It is perhaps telling that for the inauguration of the completed column at the Bastille in July of 1840, Louis-Philippe's ministers feared the king's presence might precipitate an unfriendly demonstration. The Bastille is in the heart of eastern Paris, the cradle of working-class opposition to Louis-Philippe's ever more conservative government. The column had become a rallying point for demonstrations hostile to his rule even before its completion. "We were forcibly obliged to be left isolated for several hours on the outer boulevards and on the place de la Bastille, surrounded by an immense crowd," wrote Charles de Rémusat, Minister of the Interior in 1840, about the inaugural ceremonies; "and since it would not have been wise to mobilize the king, nor the princes and, so to speak, the entire government with them, it seemed to me that the Minister of Public Works, who had the monument built, and myself, who was entrusted with the completely political ceremony, should be present for everything."[182] Rémusat and his colleague led the convoy of coffins holding the victims of the 1830 Revolution from Saint-Germain-l'Auxerrois to the Bastille while Louis-Philippe watched them pass from the safety of a balcony on the Louvre. It is a sad, almost tragic postscript to the story of the July Column, one that underscores the tenacity of urban memory. The fortress of the Bastille was long gone, and the players in the Revolution of 1789 were a vanishing breed, but the place de la Bastille retained its potential for radical political action. Eight years later, on 24 February 1848, Louis-Philippe was himself forced to abdicate by a new generation of rebellious Parisians. His throne was dragged through the city from the Tuileries Palace to the Bastille and burned in public, at the foot of the monument he had hoped would close the era of Parisian revolutions. Three days later, leaders of the provisional government marched from the Hôtel-de-Ville to the Bastille in order to proclaim—at the foot of Louis-Philippe's column—the founding of the Second Republic.

NEARLY ALL OF THE MONUMENTS discussed in this chapter have alluded in some way to antiquity: from the Greek and Roman sculptures confiscated by Bonaparte and sent to the Louvre, to the Egyptian obelisk erected at the Concorde; from the mimicking of Roman imperial splendor in the arches and temples built (or at least planned) by Napoléon to the classical allusions of the July Column newly shaped by modern technology. The public spaces of Paris were written into history with a visual language borrowed from the ancient world. A walk down any of the city's great boulevards still makes abundantly clear that the formal language of classicism shaped Paris throughout the dramatic urban transformations of the later nineteenth century. Alongside this Parisian fascination with classical forms there developed a sensibility for a type of monument that Victor Hugo described in 1830 as a

vast symphony in stone, so to speak; colossal work of a man and a people, a single whole and complex, like the Iliades and Romanceros of which it is the sister. . . . A kind of human creation, in a word, powerful and teeming like the divine creation, from which it seems to have stolen the split personality: variety, eternity.[183]

Hugo was writing about a building whose claim to history is not etched on an arch or inscribed on a column, but is evoked by the very fabric of its being. He was writing about the cathedral of Notre-Dame de Paris—perhaps the quintessential landmark of Romantic Paris—whose physical presence embodies the past and speaks to memory with no allusions to classical culture. How monuments like Notre-Dame, and the epoch to which they belong, found a place in Parisian cultural life is the subject of our next chapter.

CHAPTER 4

Old Stones and Ruminations

The Musée des Monuments français

How many souls caught the spark of history there, the interest in lofty memories, the vague desire to go back in time! I still recall the emotion, always the same and always lively, that made my heart pound: when, still quite young, I entered those somber vaulted spaces and gazed onto those pale faces; when, full of intensity, curiosity, and fear, I went looking from room to room and epoch to epoch. What was I looking for? I don't know: probably life, first of all, and the genius of former times.

—Jules Michelet[1]

During the same years that the collections of painting and sculpture at the Louvre were growing with booty from French victories across Europe, another museum took shape in Paris on the opposite bank of the Seine. The Musée des Monuments français, originally opened in 1791 as a simple warehouse for storing works of art confiscated from royal and ecclesiastical buildings during the early years of the Revolution, became one of the most popular art institutions of early nineteenth-century Paris. Creation and elaboration of the museum was due largely to the unflagging energy of one man, Alexandre Lenoir, and his vision of how objects

from the past might become living documents in the present. The success of Lenoir's enterprise ultimately provoked a chorus of professional jealousies that forced the museum to close in 1816. But for the twenty-four years of its existence, and by adroitly adapting to the changing political climates of Revolution, Empire, and Restoration, Lenoir shaped a lasting model of how national history and its monuments were understood in French culture. "This visionary museum played an important role by exciting a 'romantic' sentiment that led to a definition of medieval patrimony at once theatrical and poetic," remarked André Chastel; "thanks to the impulsive and generous character of its founder, even if a bit mythomaniac, the Musée des Monuments français attracted, enchanted, and astonished people."[2] Michelet's enthusiastic memory of his experience in the galleries of Lenoir's museum underscores its formative role for a whole generation of historians.

In June of 1791 Lenoir was appointed guardian of the depot established on the grounds of a former convent known as the Petits-Augustins, located near the corner of the present-day rue Bonaparte and the quai Malaquais.[3] An erstwhile painter, writer, and art critic, Lenoir threw himself into the new post with gusto, carefully numbering, registering, and storing the works of art—many in fragments—brought to the depot during the height of the Revolution's iconoclastic fervor. Lenoir was firmly opposed to the wanton destruction of art objects by overzealous revolutionaries: in one well-publicized incident he was knifed while trying to prevent vandals from attacking the tomb of Cardinal Richelieu at the Sorbonne, a work later entrusted to his care. He was also extremely protective of his collection and was often reluctant to send sculptures to the Louvre, although in theory his job was to preserve objects that might find their place in the national museum.

Lenoir had another agenda, which was to arrange the depot's hodgepodge of objects into a coherent installation. As part of the festivities of August 1793 to mark the first anniversary of the old monarchy's demise, Lenoir received permission to open his depot to the public. His display was generally acclaimed, although some observers were surprised by the formality of a presentation that seemed to exceed the needs of a simple warehouse. Lenoir's superiors were caught short by the published catalogue that both guided visitors through the galleries and staked Lenoir's claim as its organizer. Not yet officially a museum, the depot looked very much like one in the making: "Work is underway on a serious and permanent installation of the marble monuments originally taken there for temporary safekeeping," remarked the painter Jean-Michel Moreau-le-jeune; "I have seen tomb monuments that have been almost completely rebuilt, and a large number of columns that have been reunited with their bases and capitals and placed upright against the walls."[4] In October 1794 Lenoir requested permission from the minister in charge of the arts to reassemble a group of major monuments, deposited piecemeal in his warehouse, by pleading that a work "left dismantled in a corner will slowly but surely deteriorate."[5] Significantly, he was refused permission.

Lenoir was not to be deterred. Within a year he was named "curator of monuments," and he took advantage of the new title to submit a proposal to the powerful Committee of Public Instruction for the creation of "a museum in Paris of French monuments."[6] In October 1795 the National Convention decreed that "the depot of the Petits-Augustins will be named the National Museum of French Monuments; and that there will be in Paris a museum of French monuments in which the monuments will be arranged in chronological order."[7] The Convention's declaration confirmed the most innovative aspect of Lenoir's proposal: objects were to be arranged in chronological order, which meant that religious, secular, royal, and civic monuments might find themselves cheek-by-jowl in the same galleries.

It is no accident that Lenoir's scheme to unite monuments of diverse social and political groups took shape in 1795 after the overthrow of Robespierre that ended the Terror. This was a period when the entire nation was trying to rationalize the violent upheavals and political purges of the previous two years and, in that context, the historical mix proposed by Lenoir became a catalyst for remembering and self-reflection. Sébastien Mercier's comments are characteristic:

All that had escaped the blind fury of a people who destroyed their own altars was brought together [at the Petits-Augustins]. What a source of reflections for the contemplative beholder. . . . The result is a unique spectacle, one that I found as curious and impressive as it was novel, and as striking to the eye as it was to the imagination. Saints and mythological gods, heroes, virgins, antiquities, cardinals, Etruscan vases, holy water basins, medallions, columns, colossal statues of Charlemagne and Saint Louis . . . all have been collected with care but dropped off, lined up, and tossed about haphazardly, so the whole gives this museum a peculiar but striking sensation of the centuries confused. It was the true mirror of our revolution: what contrasts, what bizarre juxtapositions, what twists of fate! What extraordinary chaos![8]

Mercier celebrates the sensation of chaos elicited by the debris of the Revolution's fury, and he laments that the objects are now arranged in chronological order. "Alas, today it's the display cabinet of a curious mind," he writes, "but no longer the universe of a dreamer."[9] To dispel the potential for musing on the chaos of revolution was precisely why Lenoir insisted on a strict chronological display. Only by reinserting his abandoned artifacts into a master narrative of historical time were they stripped of associations with the Church or the monarchy, and made objects worthy of preservation by post-Revolutionary France. Any other rationale would have been viewed as politically retrograde. At the same time, Lenoir's chronological exposition did preserve a mix of types and hierarchies that could be understood as a metaphor for the legacy of a revolution that swept away the social orders of Old France. Or so it seemed in 1795.

Lenoir's practical solution to the problem of how to present this material was to arrange a series of galleries in which the different epochs of French sculpture were "displayed in individual rooms, with each room decorated exactly in the style of the particular century."[10] In this sense Lenoir can claim to be the inventor of period rooms so common in modern museums, for his idea was to produce environments of a specific historical "feeling" using a combination of genuine monuments and reconstructed decors. The results can be gleaned from contemporary paintings of the museum's interior (Figs. 56 and 57). The introductory gallery, which was the first room a visitor entered, positioned the French Renaissance of the sixteenth century—embodied by the "reconstructed" tomb of Diane de Poitiers (attributed to Jean Goujon and visible in the foreground of Jean Vauzelle's painting)—as the centerpiece period of Lenoir's historical thinking. This in itself was significant, for it had been customary before the Revolution to think of the seventeenth century, and the reign of Louis XIV, as the golden age of French art. True to his mandate from the National Convention, Lenoir revised that story: on his account, artists who worked for the absolutist state of Louis XIV had inaugurated "an era of decadence in the fine arts"; by contrast, the Renaissance, with its emergence of distinct artistic personalities, was positioned as the acme of French achievement.[11] The effectiveness of Lenoir's installation is borne out by Mary Berry's remark at the time of her visit to Paris in 1802: "It is curious to observe the rapid decay of the art from the days of Francis I to those of Louis XIV."[12]

The introductory gallery established the historical breadth of the museum by including a range of works from Celtic altars to contemporary relief sculptures. It also contained Germain Pilon's *Three Graces* of 1560, Cardinal Mazarin's tomb by Antoine Coysevox from 1693 (visible in Fig. 56 against the back wall), and Jean-Baptiste Pigalle's 1776 monument to the comte d'Harcourt. In other words, the first gallery offered visitors an opportunity to compare and contrast the styles, technical facility, and subject matter of sculptures from diverse periods and places. The effect was a ready-made lesson in art history much appreciated by critics. "In spite of their change of place," wrote one commentator in 1807, "the learned man takes pleasure in these monuments that he might not have had the time or the means to see otherwise. Their gathering together even adds a kind of interest by setting up comparisons."[13]

The museum's period galleries were far more popular than the survey gallery at its entrance, and none more so than the room dedicated to Gothic art of the fourteenth century (Fig. 57). In a space outfitted with stained glass windows that replicated the diffused light of gothic cathedrals, Lenoir assembled "debris" (the word is his) from the cathedral of Saint-Denis and the Sainte-Chapelle in Paris within a fantasy environment of pointed arches and ribbed vaults as recorded in Bouton's painting.[14] Lenoir's archaeological license is nowhere more evident than in his arrangement of the figures standing in the arcade around the gallery's central space. Although originally reclining sculptures [gisants], Lenoir installed them upright to emulate the column figures usually found on the facades of extant gothic cathedrals. The gallery's central structure (visible at the extreme right of the painting) is equally fantastic: columns from Maubisson frame a monument that combines the statue of Charles V from Saint-Denis, another of his wife (Jeanne de Bourbon) from the Paris church of the Célestins, and a wooden coffer from the Sainte-Chapelle.

Ultimately, Lenoir's loose regard for historical accuracy was used against the Musée des Monuments français. Writers like Quatremère de Quincy, one of the museum's most virulent critics, condemned it as

a kind of cemetery of the arts in which works are crowded together pell-mell like useless materials, like the signs of some lost writing, whose marks are no longer of any interest to the intellect. . . . By losing their reason for being, they have lost their effect. The museum is the end of art. The lessons that artists receive there are dead lessons.[15]

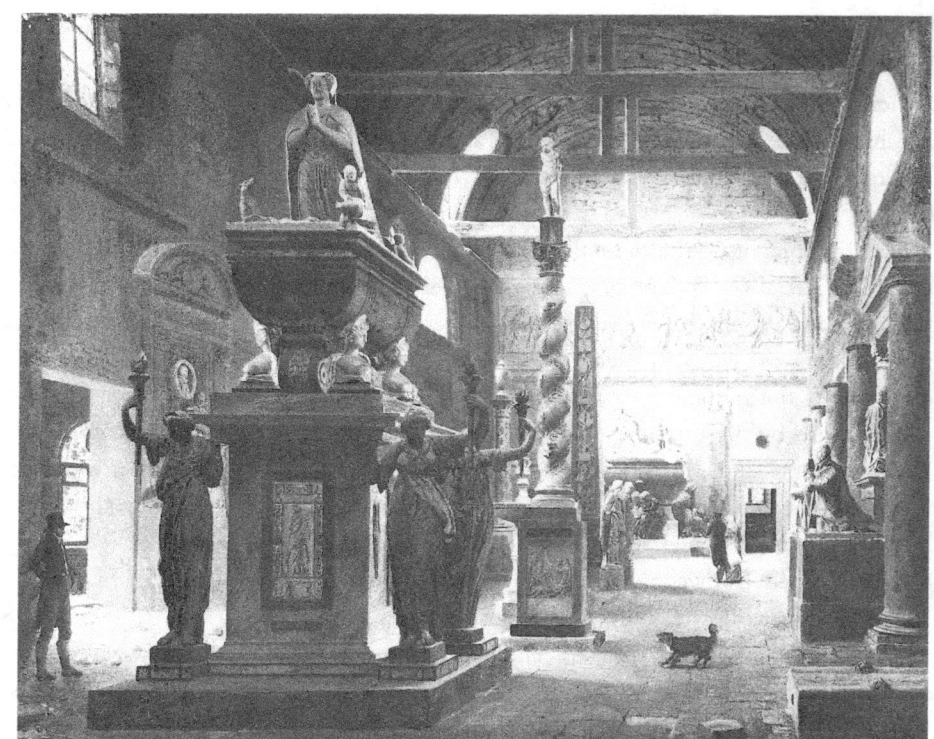

FIGURE 56. Jean Lubin Vauzelle, *Introductory Gallery at the Musée des Monuments français*, 1812. Oil on canvas. Paris, Musée Carnavalet, inv. P 2074 (60 × 74 cm). Photo: © PMVP/Degraces.

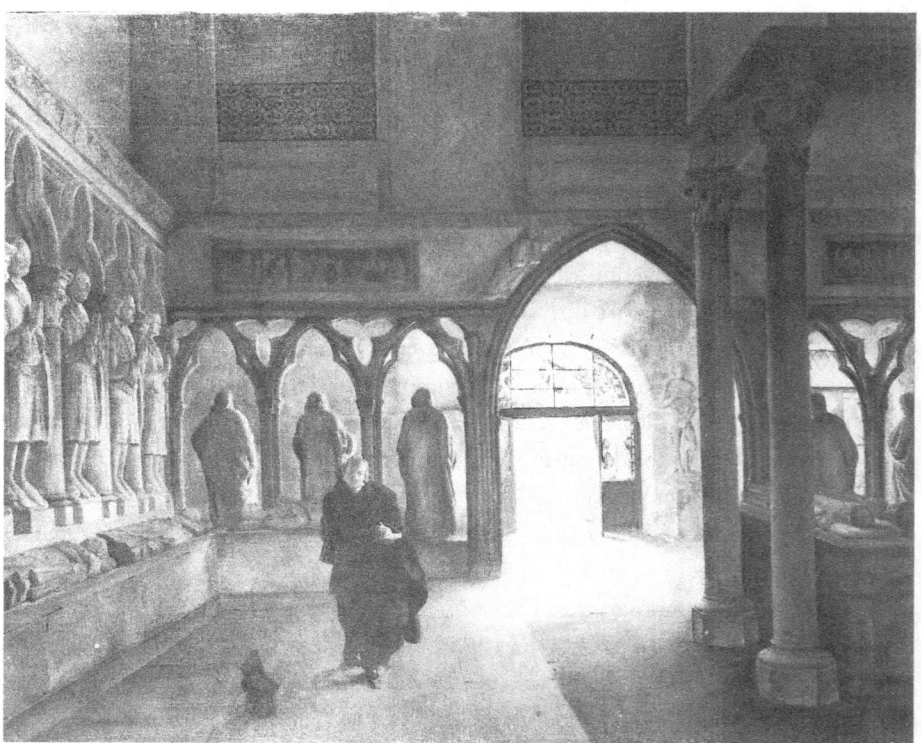

FIGURE 57. Charles-Marie Bouton (attributed to), *Gallery of the XIV Century at the Musée des Monuments français*, ca 1815. Oil on canvas. Paris, Musée Carnavalet, inv. P 1372 (60 × 75 cm). Photo: © PMVP/Ladet.

Quatremère's argument, like his opposition to pillaging the artistic riches of Rome (see Chapter Three), was rooted in the idea that a work of art and its context form an organic whole that must not be disturbed. But not everyone agreed with Quatremère's antiquarian rigor. Many contemporaries found Lenoir's museum compelling for its power to trigger memories and reverie, even at the expense of historical accuracy. The thrill of what Michelet later remembered as "the interest in lofty memories" and "the vague desire to go back in time" encouraged Lenoir to stage dramatic visits by torch-light. The Englishman James Forbes, invited to one such promenade in 1803, left an account worth citing at length:

A few evenings ago, when the moon was at the full, Mons. Lenoir invited us to meet the members of the National Institute on their first visit to the sepulchral chambers by torch-light, and view the sculpture with the solemn effect produced by such a circumstance. We joined the party about ten o'clock, and were introduced to several literary characters and their ladies. The company assembled in the hall, formerly the chapel of the convent, and now richly adorned with the choicest monuments: the effect was very striking. Mons. Lenoir and his attendants held the flambeaux, and by throwing the light on the principal objects, pointed out their beauties to his admiring friends. I had seen the Laocoön, the Apollo, and all the principal statues in the Vatican, in the same manner; but this was altogether a more curious visit; for on the company entering each chamber, musicians, prepared for the occasion, performed a funeral dirge; which, with the surrounding monuments, the numerous torches, and all the decorations of these sacred repositories, filled my mind with indescribable sensations.[16]

Forbes's experience documents how the Musée des Monuments français emerged from its origins as a simple repository of national history to become a place for private ruminations. Lenoir's torch-lighted tours capitalized on the evocative potential of the museum's galleries to rally support for his enterprise: for example, he organized a similar visit in April 1807 for the Empress Joséphine.[17] The Empress hardly needed convincing, for she was already an enthusiast of Lenoir's project, and she owned several pictures (Fig. 58) in which historical monuments were treated as sympathetic touchstones to the past rather than strictly factual documents. One of Joséphine's preferred painters—Fleury-François Richard—was also a great fan of the Musée des Monuments français.

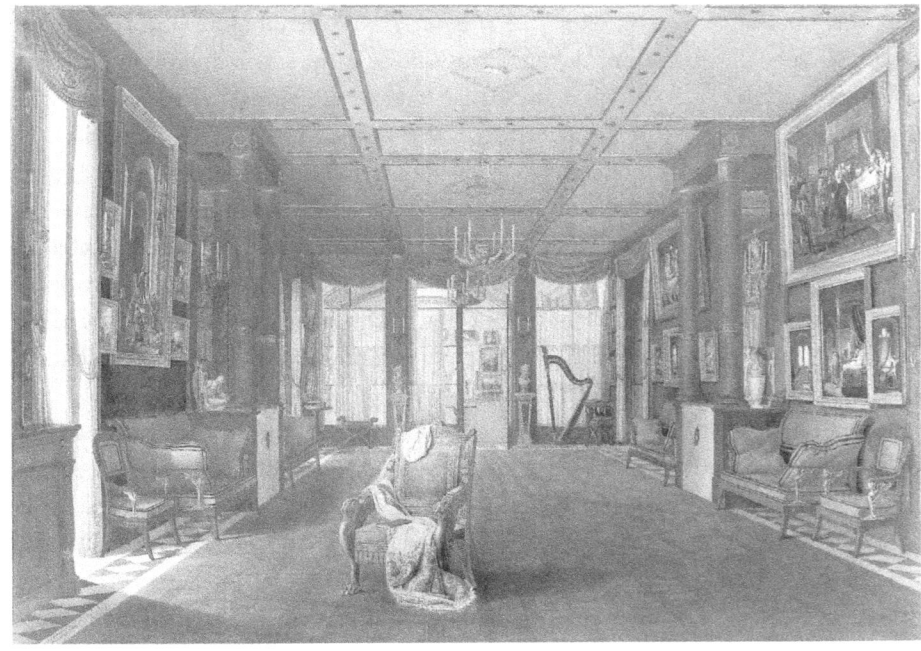

FIGURE 58. Auguste Garneray, *View of the Music Room at Malmaison*, after 1812. Watercolor. Malmaison, Châteaux de Malmaison et de Bois-Préau, inv. MM40.47.7215 (66.5 × 91 cm). Photo: © RMN/Art Resource, NY/ © Daniel Arnaudet/Jean Schormans.

The Troubadour View of the Past

Richard recalled that a visit to Lenoir's museum inspired one of his most famous pictures:

One day, in the course of my solitary reveries while walking through the monuments from Saint-Denis, at that time brought together in the Musée des Petits-Augustins, and trying to understand the gothic mottoes of these illustrious tombs, I was struck by the profound sentiment hidden in these few words engraved on the tomb of Valentine de Milan: *Rien ne m'est plus, Plus ne m'est rien* [Nothing more is left to me, More is nothing to me]. Spontaneously, I discovered there the subject of a picture.[18]

Richard's mention of "solitary reveries," his attempts to "understand the gothic mottoes," and the "profound sentiment" that struck him are all signs of the painter's individual and empathetic response to the museum's monuments. Paradoxically, the picture (now in the Hermitage Museum) generated by this experience is not very remarkable: Valentine is seated in a window box of the château at Blois, perpetually mourning her husband, Louis d'Orléans, who had been assassinated in 1407 by Jean-sans-Peur of Burgundy.[19] Yet the painting was a huge critical success at the Salon of 1802, precisely for its suggestive emotions. "Those who like to be affected gently are not able to look without a lively interest at this unhappy princess, weeping in solitude for her spouse so shamefully murdered," noted the anonymous author of the *Précis historique*.[20] Madame de Staël supposedly remarked that "Richard, with his *Valentine*, established a European reputation for himself."[21] An important testament to this reputation was the purchase of *Valentine* in 1805 by the Empress Joséphine, who hung it in a place of honor in her private picture gallery at Malmaison (visible at the extreme right edge of Fig. 58).

What kind of painting is *Valentine de Milan*? A closely related work painted by Richard in 1808 that also belonged to Joséphine can clarify matters. *The Deference of Saint Louis to his Mother* (Fig. 59, visible in Fig. 58 hanging second from the extreme right) takes us back to 1238 and the life of Louis IX, also known as Saint-Louis. Fearing the jealousy of his mother (Blanche of Castille), the sixteen-year-old king

makes a clandestine visit to his young wife (Marguerite of Provence) after she was left maimed and near death by a difficult childbirth. Guard dogs were supposed to bark if anyone approached their bedside tryst, but Blanche slipped by and orders her son to leave the room with the words: "Go away, you can do nothing here." In Richard's painting, Louis submits to his mother's words and heads for the door, while his bedridden wife exclaims: "Alas! alive or dead, you will not permit me to see my lord?"[22] Richard staged this exchange of admonition and supplication as a play of restrained gestures and criss-crossed glances set in period piece costumes and architecture.

The painter's notebooks reveal that many of the accessories—notably the bed and a statue of the Virgin and Child behind Blanche—are composite fabrications based on examples sketched while visiting Lenoir's museum. Nonetheless, contemporary reviews were enthusiastic about Richard's precise description of these accessories, his evocative handling of light that filters from an unseen window at the left, and his sympathetic characterization of the ailing young queen. "Persecuted, suffering, but noble in grief," wrote one critic about Marguerite, and all the more so in contrast to the king's ignoble air of "a schoolboy of sixteen who trembles before the rod of his master."[23] Pictures like *The Deference of Saint-Louis* offered a novel mix of stories from the annals of Old France rendered with an attention to authentic detail and an emotional range emphasizing personal feelings over public virtues. They tended to be moderately sized canvases and highly finished, so that their period piece re-creations were both intimate in scale and visually convincing. They were usually suffused in a complex play of soft light that critics likened to the works of Rembrandt, yet colored with strongly saturated tones in the manner of Dutch genre painters like Pieter de Hooch and Gerard Dou.

The tendency to focus upon evocative and sympathetic portrayals of historical characters, rather than historic events, closely parallels the ambitions and methods of personalizing the past deployed in the galleries of Lenoir's museum. Today such pictures are usually called troubadour style. They are important to the history of French art of the period because

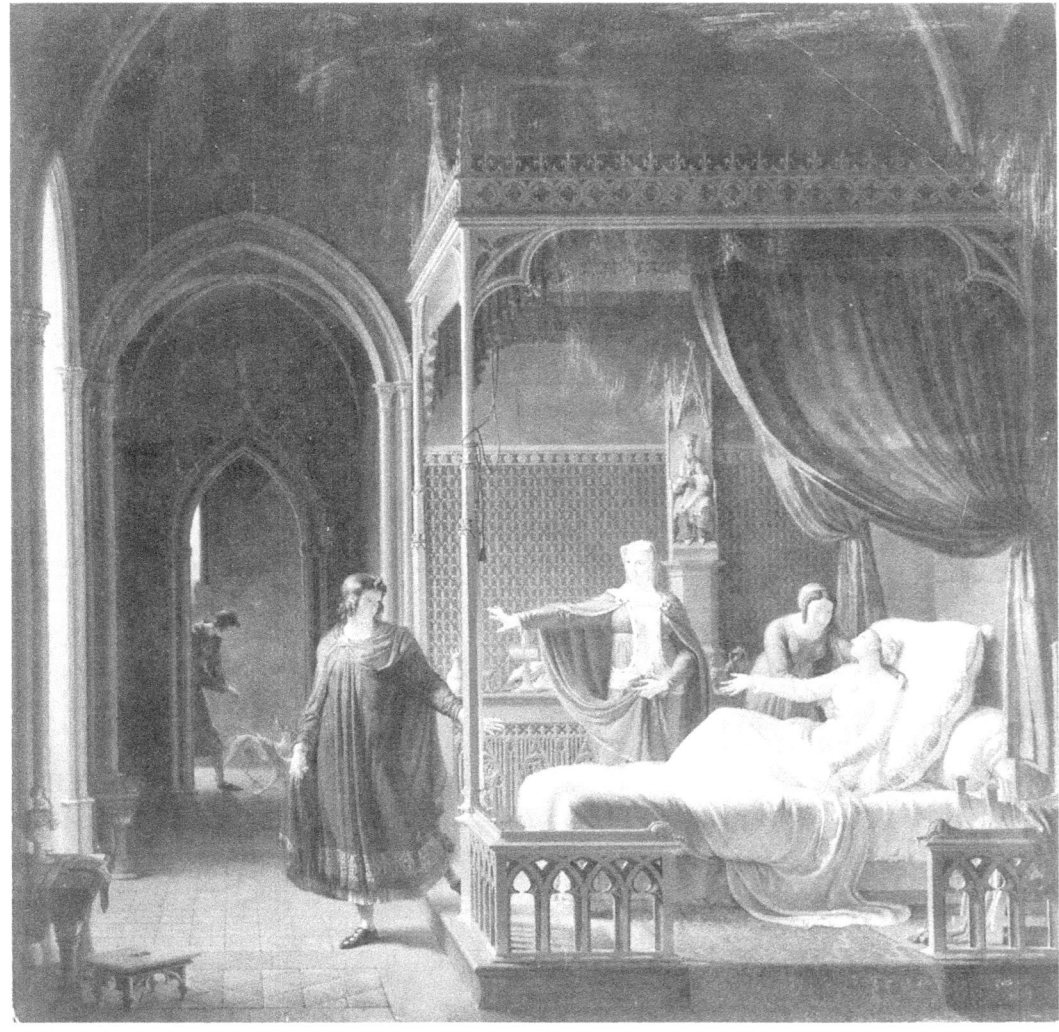

FIGURE 59. Fleury-François Richard, *Deference of Saint Louis to his Mother*, 1808. Oil on canvas. Arenenberg, Napoleonmuseum, inv. 1906/7, no. 123 (97 × 97 cm). Photo: Courtesy Napoleonmuseum, Arenenberg.

they sit uneasily between the traditional categories of history paintings—meaning heroic actions from antiquity in the manner of Jacques-Louis David (Figs. 2 and 3)—and genre pictures of everyday contemporary life. "A few artists have not been afraid to banter with the muse of history," remarked a critic in 1817; "they have presented us with kings in their interiors and made us see the man inside the hero. Simpler and closer to us, we like these historical personalities even more, and from this comes the anecdotal genre that is much practiced in recent times."[24] By turning away from ancient

history in favor of emotion-laden renderings from the history of France, troubadour pictures defined an entirely new critical category.

How and why did pictures so removed from heroic actions, and so often inspired by the lives of noble men or women of pre-Revolutionary France, come to be favored by Joséphine? Her predilection for the evocative historical settings of Lenoir's museum suggests a personal affinity for images treating the past in a parallel manner. Moreover, such pictures were not destined for the official galleries of the nation—such as the Louvre—but for Joséphine's private gallery at Malmaison (Fig. 58) where she amassed a collection of troubadour pictures that included seven by Richard.[25] Malmaison was a strictly private residence, open only to the most intimate advisers and friends of the imperial couple and subject to tight security. In August of 1802, for example, John Dean Paul passed near the château and reported that "there seemed to be a great deal of work going forward in the grounds, and a very strong guard at the gate. I wished to have a nearer view of the house, but we understood that no persons are, on any pretence, permitted to stop near the place."[26] Pictures of national history that stressed personal feelings and sentiments over the public virtues of heroic actions found a natural home in the private gallery and personal spaces of the first lady of France. If it seems anachronistic that Joséphine surrounded herself with images of the old nobility, one need only recall that by 1805 Napoléon had crowned her Empress, had begun to construct a new nobility around his throne, and was planning a column to honor Charlemagne at the place Vendôme (see Chapter Three). Joséphine's interest in the aristocracy of pre-Revolution France was very much in step with the political tenor of the times.

The fall of Napoléon and Louis XVIII's return to the throne brought a new effort to replace the effigies of kings, such as Henri IV (Fig. 51), destroyed during the Revolution. These same years witnessed the return to power of many aristocrats who joined the effort to revive public enthusiasm for the characters and events of the Ancien Régime. Pictures presenting sentimental, human interest stories of the old nobility in properly historical settings had a special appeal, since exhibiting them in Paris offered occasions to generate commentaries in the press sympathetic to the bloodline aristocracy upon which the Bourbon Restoration was built. The comte de Blacas is a case in point. An Ultra-royalist who was named ambassador to Naples by Louis XVIII, Blacas commissioned from Jean-Auguste-Dominique Ingres two small paintings of the troubadour type: *Leonardo da Vinci dying in the Arms of Francis I* and a pendant, *Henri IV playing with his Children* (Fig. 60).[27] Both of these works emphasize the humanity of the monarch. This is especially true of the picture

in which Henri is caught short by the arrival of the Spanish ambassador while playing "horsey" with his son. "Do you have children?" asked Henri. When the ambassador replied that he did, the king added, "then you won't mind if I finish making the round."[28] The picture invites us to smile at Henri IV, who suspends diplomatic decorum to fulfill the seemingly more important role of loving, playful father. Like Richard (Fig. 59), Ingres lavished attention on a fastidious and archeologically correct rendering of period costumes. He orchestrated a play of cold light that isolates each figure—and each psychological response to the touching scene—against a dark ground. Ingres references obliquely the grand tradition of painting he so admired by including a Raphael-like tondo of the Virgin and Child on the back wall: a gesture of remarkable restraint that reveals how troubadour pictures forced painters to rethink their usual preferences and working habits.

It turns out that Ingres was not the first to paint this anecdote from the life of Henri IV. Pierre-Henri Révoil, a friend and colleague of Richard, made a very similar picture in 1813 (now in a private collection) that he exhibited at the Paris Salon of 1817.[29] Blacas may have suggested the subject to Ingres after seeing Révoil's picture at the salon, but the point is that the earlier work also found its way into the collection of a high-ranking aristocrat. Révoil's picture was purchased by the duchesse de Berry, wife of a prominent leader of the Ultra-royalist faction. The duchesse, an avid patron of the arts and of troubadour painting in particular, continued to buy such works whenever possible: in 1819 she purchased Révoil's *Joan of Arc held Prisoner at Rouen* (Fig. 61). The drama of this picture is somewhat complicated. Joan has been arrested and jailed at Rouen, where she is visited by the Counts of Ligny (Jean de Luxembourg), Warwick, and Scanffort. They offer to pay her ransom if she promises to abandon her armed resistance to them and to the English. She replies:

Oh, good Lord, you are making fun of me, because I know perfectly well that you have neither the power nor the will. . . . I know full well that the English will kill me, believing that after my death they will win the kingdom of France. But should they be a hundred

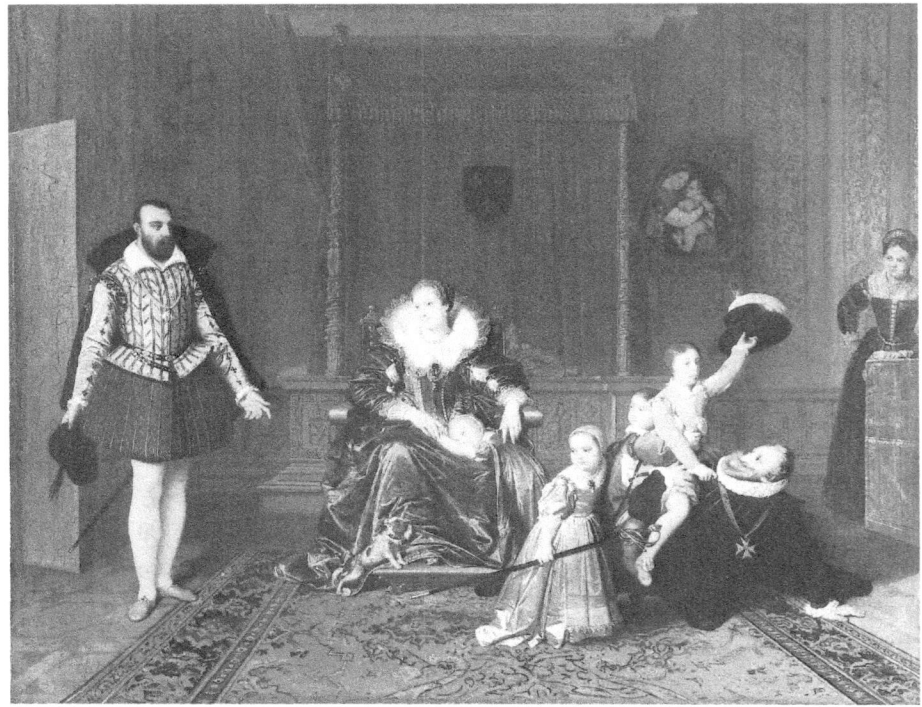

FIGURE 60.   Jean-Auguste-Dominique Ingres, *Henri IV playing with his Children*, 1817 (shown at the 1824 Salon). Oil on canvas. Paris, Musée du Petit-Palais, inv. P Dut 1164 (39.5 × 50 cm). Photo: © PMVP/Pierrain.

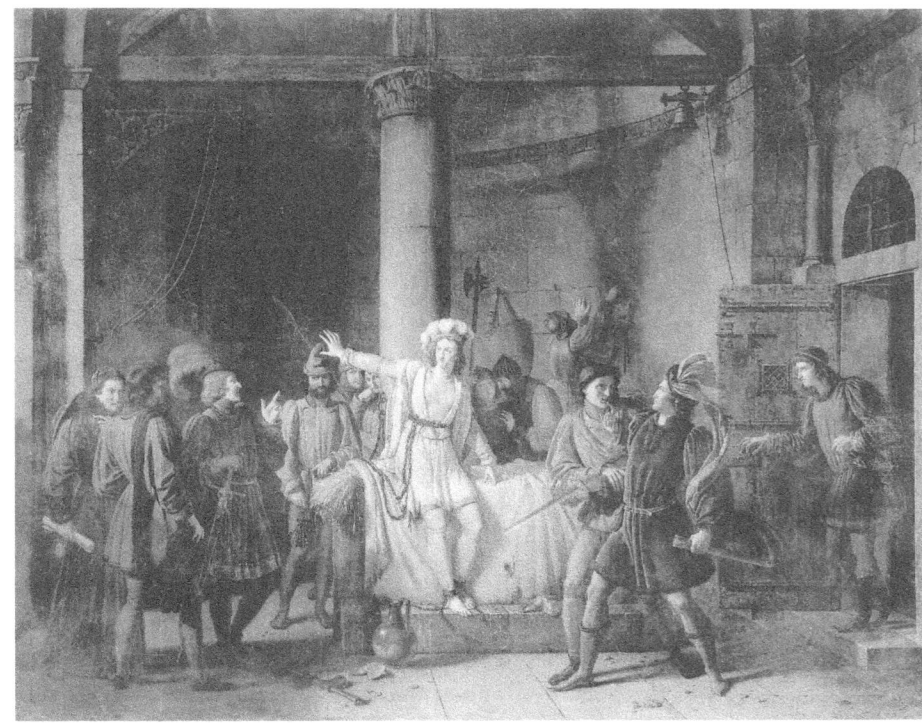

FIGURE 61.   Pierre-Henri Révoil, *Joan of Arc held Prisoner at Rouen*, 1819. Oil on canvas. Rouen, Musée des Beaux-Arts (Gift of Mme Léon Duvivier), inv. 931-16-3 (137 × 174 cm). Photo: © Musées de la Ville de Rouen/Catherine Lancien/Carole Loisel.

thousand more *godons* [pejorative slang for the English] than they are at present, they will not have this kingdom.[30]

Offended by her mocking tone and choice of words, Scanffort pulls his sword to strike the heroine but is stopped by Warwick (the two men scuffle in the right foreground). Joan, who ends her little speech with a sweep of her arm, is bathed in a pool of dramatic light, while the grim expressions of her guards and jailer signal the prophetic nature of her words. Like all good troubadour painters, Révoil wanted to make his image of Joan as archaeologically accurate as possible, so he copied her face, her dress, and her famous plumed hat from portraits of her on view at the Musée des Monuments français.

Even more important is the kind of story that Révoil relates. His saga of Old France involves historic figures, but their actions—the sharp-tongued retort of a woman chained to a column and the unchivalric response of a man who threatens to kill her—are neither heroic nor noble. What the picture does do is put viewers in touch with the pathos, the humanity, and the feelings of these characters, in the same way that Henri IV playing horse, or Louis IX meekly submitting to his mother's reprimand, foregrounds the human scale of historical actors. Such pictures offer a history unlike the declamatory chauvinism of recent military paintings (Figs. 7, 9, and 10), and a pathos more aligned with the tenor of post-Imperial France (Fig. 13). It is already surprising that pictures like these were first collected in the early years of the century by the political upstart Joséphine. It is even more unusual that they were also favored by arch-legitimists like the duchesse de Berry. Why is this so? Troubadour versions of history bridged the huge political divide between Empire and Restoration with an appeal to sentiment and ordinary emotions. They operated on a human scale more suited to the spaces of private apartments than the great galleries of the Louvre. Without being overly reductive, troubadour pictures opened the imagery of history to the patronage of powerful women, regardless of their politics. This observation is supported by a closer look at the evolving décor of those personal spaces where such pictures found homes.

Living with Power: Joséphine to Marie d'Orléans

Malmaison was a closely guarded retreat where Joséphine and Napoléon could be together in relative seclusion, where the most trusted political and military advisers could be convened, and where the public was kept at a distance. The small château underwent many cycles of renovation and redecoration that attest to its status as Joséphine's personal domain. Official functions certainly had their place at Malmaison: visitors today are reminded that Napoléon loved to work in the library where he eventually chose to sign his final abdication, and that a council room was fitted up like a field tent erected in the midst of a military campaign.[31] Other parts of the house, such as the picture gallery that no longer exists, were very much Joséphine's personal projects (Fig. 58). Her direct involvement is corroborated by Prince Clary-Aldringen's letter of 31 May 1810 to his mother in Vienna that tells how he and a friend were introduced to Joséphine in the gallery. The prince remarks that the space is "so well-built, painted with so much taste, so perfectly lighted from overhead, and so finely proportioned in every sense that one could not envisage a more beautiful room." He also reports that Joséphine was personally directing the rehanging of some pictures.[32] No less personal was the décor of Joséphine's bedroom, designed for her by Louis Berthault in 1812, three years after her divorce from Napoléon (Fig. 62). Perhaps motivated by a nostalgia for the pomp that was no longer part of her everyday life, Joséphine's new bedroom combined rich hangings with architectural elements that completely transformed the space. An arrangement of reflecting mirrors over the chimney and behind the bed established a setting for the bed itself—an elaborate ensemble of sculpted swans and a crown-shaped canopy all designed by François-Honoré-Georges Jacob-Desmalter. This imposing bedroom is where Joséphine received guests, although she usually slept in a much simpler room.

Joséphine's bed—a type known as *lit en bateau*—was probably inspired by one of the most famous beds of the epoch: that of Juliette Récamier, a legendary beauty who presided over one of the most brilliant salons of the Con-

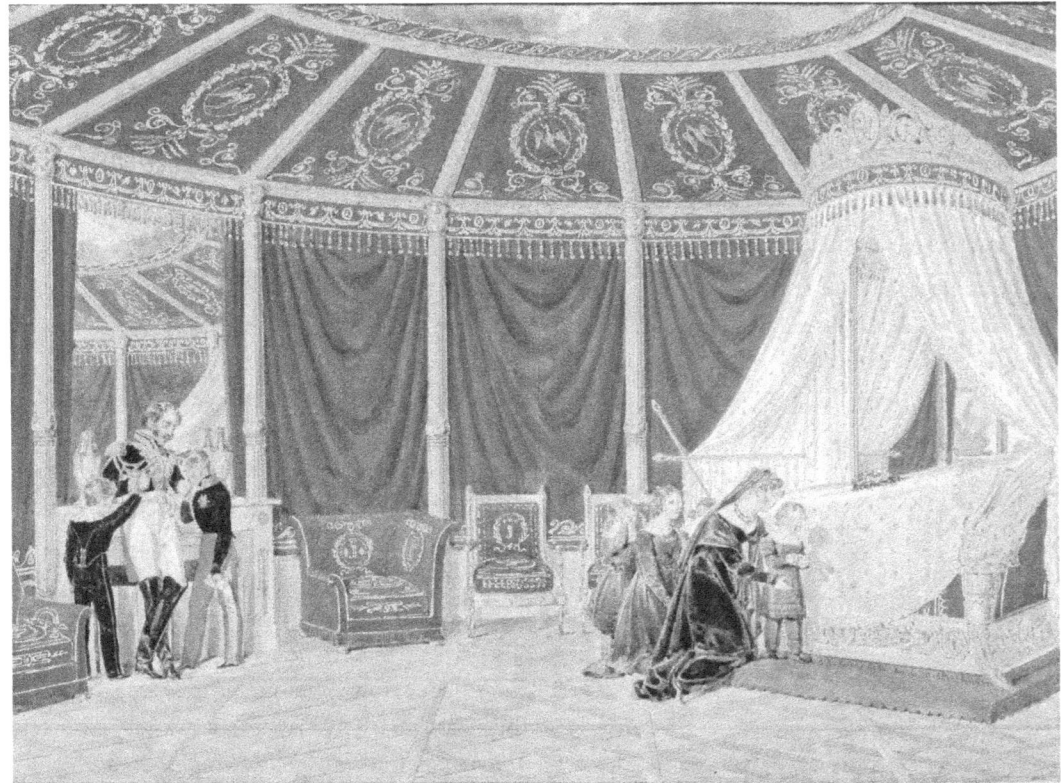

FIGURE 62.   Henri-Charles Loeïllot-Hartwig, *View of the bedchamber of the Empress Joséphine at Malmaison as arranged in 1812*, 1826. Watercolor. Stockholm: The Royal Collections, inv. MR 1303, sid 7. Photo: © The Royal Collections, Sweden/ Alexis Daflos.

sulat and early Empire. Récamier's bedroom no longer exists, but Mary Berry left a vivid description of it from her visit to Paris in 1802:

Went to the house of Madame Récamier. We were resolved not to leave Paris without seeing what is called the most elegant house in it, fitted up in the new style. . . . Her bed is reckoned the most beautiful in Paris—it, too, is of mahogany enriched with ormolu and bronze, and raised upon two steps of the same wood. Over the whole bed was thrown a great coverlid or veil of fine plain muslin, with rows of narrow gold lace at each end, and the muslin embroidered as a border. The curtains were muslin, trimmed and worked like the coverlid, suspended from a sort of carved couronne de roses, and tucked up in drapery upon the wall, against which the bed stood. At the foot of the bed stood a fine Grecian lamp of ormolu, with a little figure of the same metal bending over it; and at the head of the bed another stand, upon which was placed a large ornamented flower-pot, containing a large artificial rose-tree, the branches of which must nod very near her nose in bed.[33]

Like the later *lit en bateau* for Joséphine, Madame Récamier's bed was a miniature stage upon which she received visitors, even though situated in a room treated today as one of the most private parts of a house. Our divisions were not those of Parisian society in the early nineteenth century, for the bedchamber of a powerful woman was very much a public space and consequently decorated in the latest style to reflect her important social status.

The bed and alcove designed about 1803 by Jacob-Desmalter for Hortense de Beauharnais, Joséphine's daughter by a previous marriage, is a good extant example of the type (Fig. 63). An orchestrated play of mirrors behind the bed and to the right, along with architectural elements of classical forms, frame the bed itself. Rich hangings of heavy silk embroidered with Greek and Egyptian motifs echoing those of contemporary public monuments are all part of the ensemble. Another English visitor to Paris, this time Ann Plumptre, underscores the social importance attached to this peculiar hybrid of public and private space in Parisian social life:

As it is the fashion at Paris for madame's bedchamber to be one of the rooms the most seen of any in the house, the place where she often receives her company, nay even not unfrequently the passage-room to the drawing-room, so the taste in which it is fitted up is always a thing much studied. The newest fashion at this time was

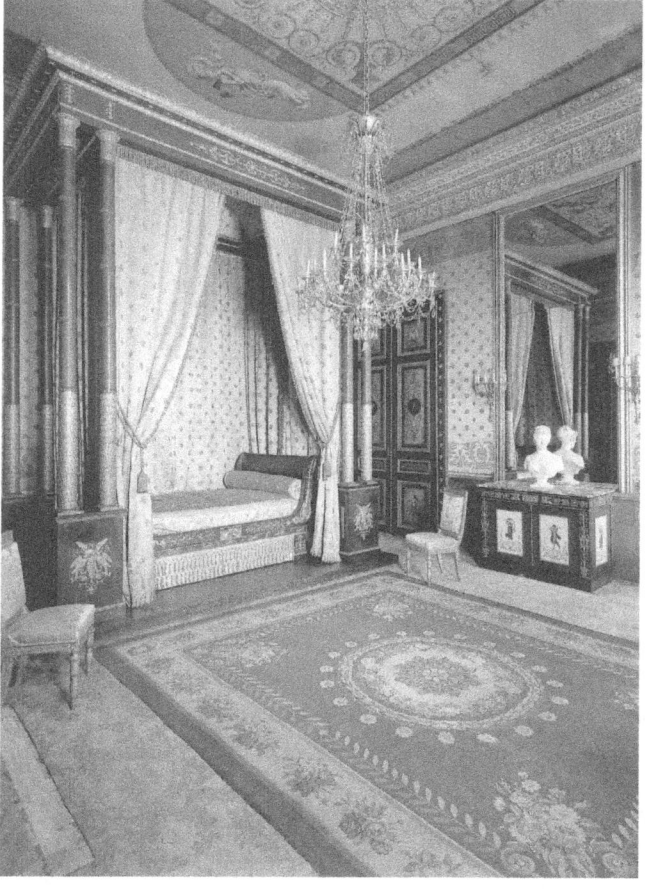

FIGURE 63.   François-Honoré-Georges Jacob-Desmalter and others, *Alcove and bed of Queen Hortense*, ca. 1803. Various materials. Paris, former hôtel de Beauharnais. Photo: © Centre des monuments nationaux, Paris.

.a mahogany bedstead *à la Grecque*, placed in an alcove, raised two or three steps above the room, so as to have the appearance of an altar. At the back and sides of the alcove were large looking-glasses, and in the middle of the ceiling a bronze eagle holding in its beak a large ring of or-moulu, through which the hangings of the bed were passed: these were united together so as to form one entire piece, and made of silk, or muslin lined with silk: in the day-time they were festooned up elegantly, and at night fell all around the bed, being supported only by the ring through which they were passed.[34]

The degree of stylistic continuity from private to public spaces—from bedroom to salon—within the confines of a grand house like the hôtel de Beauharnais can be appreciated by comparing the setting of Queen Hortense's bedroom (Fig. 63) to that of the sumptuous, nearly adjacent Salon of the Four Seasons (Fig. 64). The symmetry of both spaces, multiplied by strategic emplacements of mirrors, signals immediately the formal rigor of each room. Architectural elements—pilasters, cornice moldings, and door frames—are overlaid with gilded, low-relief patterns of stylized plant forms (acanthus, garlands, and rosettes), caryatids, sphinxes, swans, and the requisite profusion of imperial eagles. Yet this sculptural veneer tends to remain shallow and almost pictorial with respect to the rectilinear grid of the enclosing structure. One retains a strong sense that the intimate space belongs to the architecture of a larger, formal building.

The furniture designed for rooms of the imperial palaces was similarly architectonic. The best pieces were made of turned or sculptured mahogany and decorated with mounts of gilt bronze or ormolu worked in patterns similar to those used on the walls and ceilings. This is true even of furnishings for rooms devoted to care of the self, such as the dressing table [coiffeuse] and psyche mirror created by Pierre-Philippe Thomire about 1809 for the Empress's bathroom at Fontainebleau (Fig. 65). Each piece is a studied composite of separate parts. The flat, horizontal plane of the dressing table stands on legs of interlaced half-circles, while the circular mirror is supported by small, column-like forms comprised of bases, shafts, capitals, and pinnacle figurines. Similarly, the psyche glass is suspended in a robust frame rising from claw-feet supports to a cornice and pediment-like arrangement of volutes. The four-square structure of each

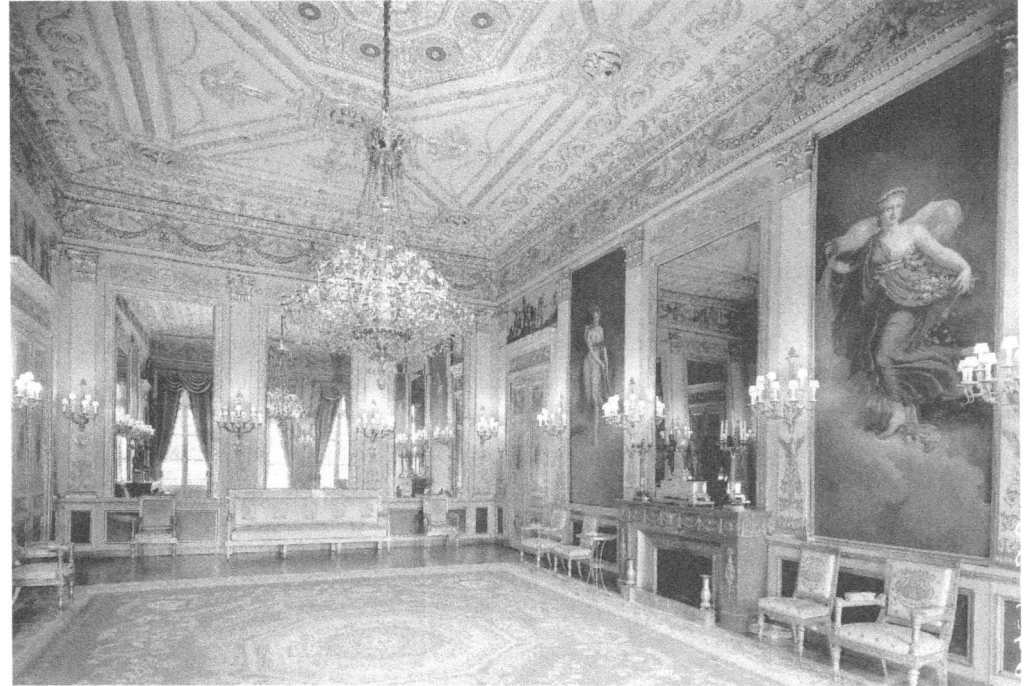

FIGURE 64. *Salon of the Four Seasons*, ca. 1803. Various materials. Paris, former hôtel de Beauharnais. Photo: © Centre des monuments nationaux, Paris.

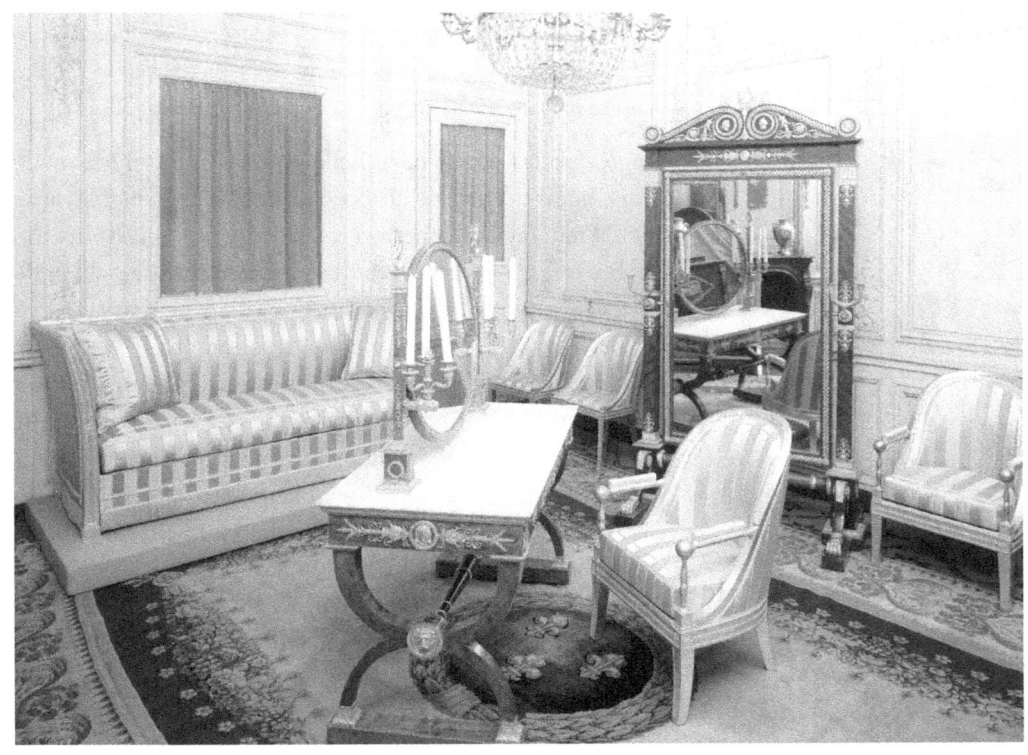

FIGURE 65. François-Honoré-Georges Jacob-Desmalter and others, *Bathroom for the Empress Joséphine*, ca. 1809. Various materials. Fontainebleau, Musée National du Château. Photo: © RMN/Art Resource, NY/© Gérard Blot.

piece echoes the rectangularity of the room itself, while the decorative elements—shallow linear patterns of arabesques, stylized foliage, and medallions—extend and continue the low-relief sculptural decoration of the walls. In spite of their luxurious materials, and the fact they were designed to be used while adorning one's body, the appeal of these works tends to be visual and rational rather than tactile or sensual. The same can be said for the dressing table made by Jacob-Desmalter in 1805 for Joséphine's use at the Tuileries Palace (Fig. 66). The legs, carved to resemble harps of the

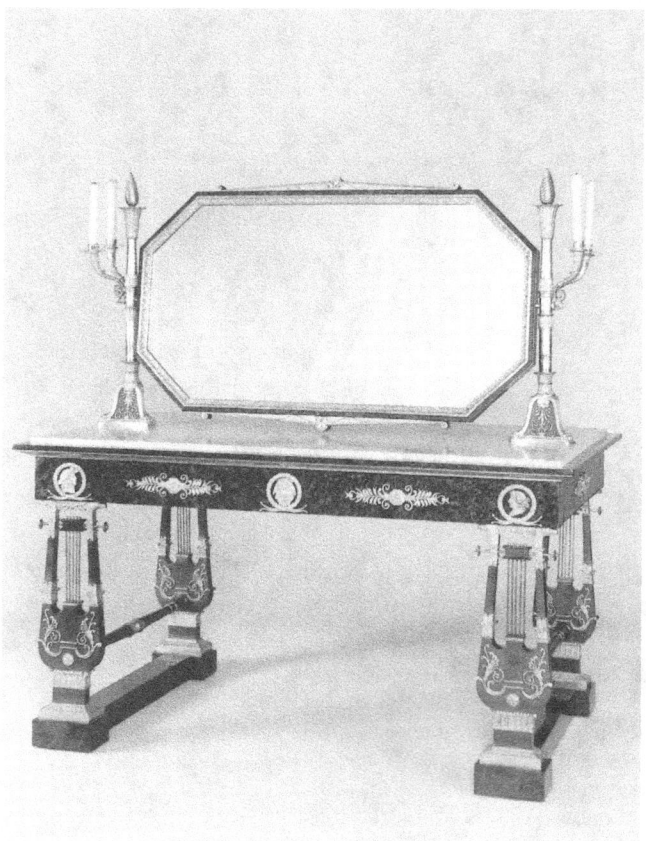

FIGURE 66.   François-Honoré-Georges Jacob-Desmalter, *Dressing Table of the Empress Joséphine at the Tuileries Palace*, 1805. Mahogany, gilt work, white marble, glass. Malmaison, Chateaux de Malmaison et de Bois-Préau, inv. MMD.28 (74 × 107 × 65 cm). Photo: © RMN/Art Resource, NY/© Daniel Arnaudet.

sort painted on Greek vases, produce an effect of fragility and seeming weightlessness. The motif nonetheless fulfills the brief that furniture for official spaces like the Tuileries Palace must always be in the latest style: at this time, as Ann Plumptre noted, the fashion was *à la grecque*.

The general enthusiasm for Greek forms—meaning an emphasis on silhouette, flattened arabesques, and motifs derived from vase paintings—also informed contemporary fashion. A case in point is Ingres's 1805 portrait of Mademoiselle Caroline Rivière (Fig. 67). The young woman's high-waist dress of thin white fabric, which both emulates antique types and offers the body a freedom of movement unencumbered by corset or bodice, was all the rage in the early years of the century and much commented upon by visitors to Paris. "I dined this evening at the Restaurateur's in the Thuilleries," remarked John Carr in 1802.

There were some beautiful women present, dressed after the antique, a fashion successfully introduced by David. . . . The women, though said, in point of corporeal sufferance, to be able to endure less than men, were enchanted with the design of the artist, and without approaching a single degree nearer to the sun, unmindful of colds, consumptions and death, have assumed a dress, if such it can be called, the airiness of which to the eye of fancy, looked like the mist of incense, undulating over a display of symmetry.[35]

Ingres portrayed Mademoiselle Rivière rather more modestly, but did bring to his portrait a high degree of stylization. From the nearly perfect circle of her face and symmetric arches of her heavy eyebrows—echoed by her almond-shaped eyes with large dark irises—to the long sinuous curve of her neck, we sense the presence of an abstracting force that reorders and regularizes her features. This impression of rhythmic linearity is subtly reinforced by the white-fur boa, interlaced in the young woman's arms and encircling her body with a seemingly unbroken curve, and by the flattening effect of her strong silhouette against the limpid sky. Like the designs of contemporary furniture, Ingres's picture makes few allowances for the physical materiality of Rivière's body, preferring instead to push, flatten, and reorder it to create an effect of visual simplicity and elegance thought to be Greek in character.

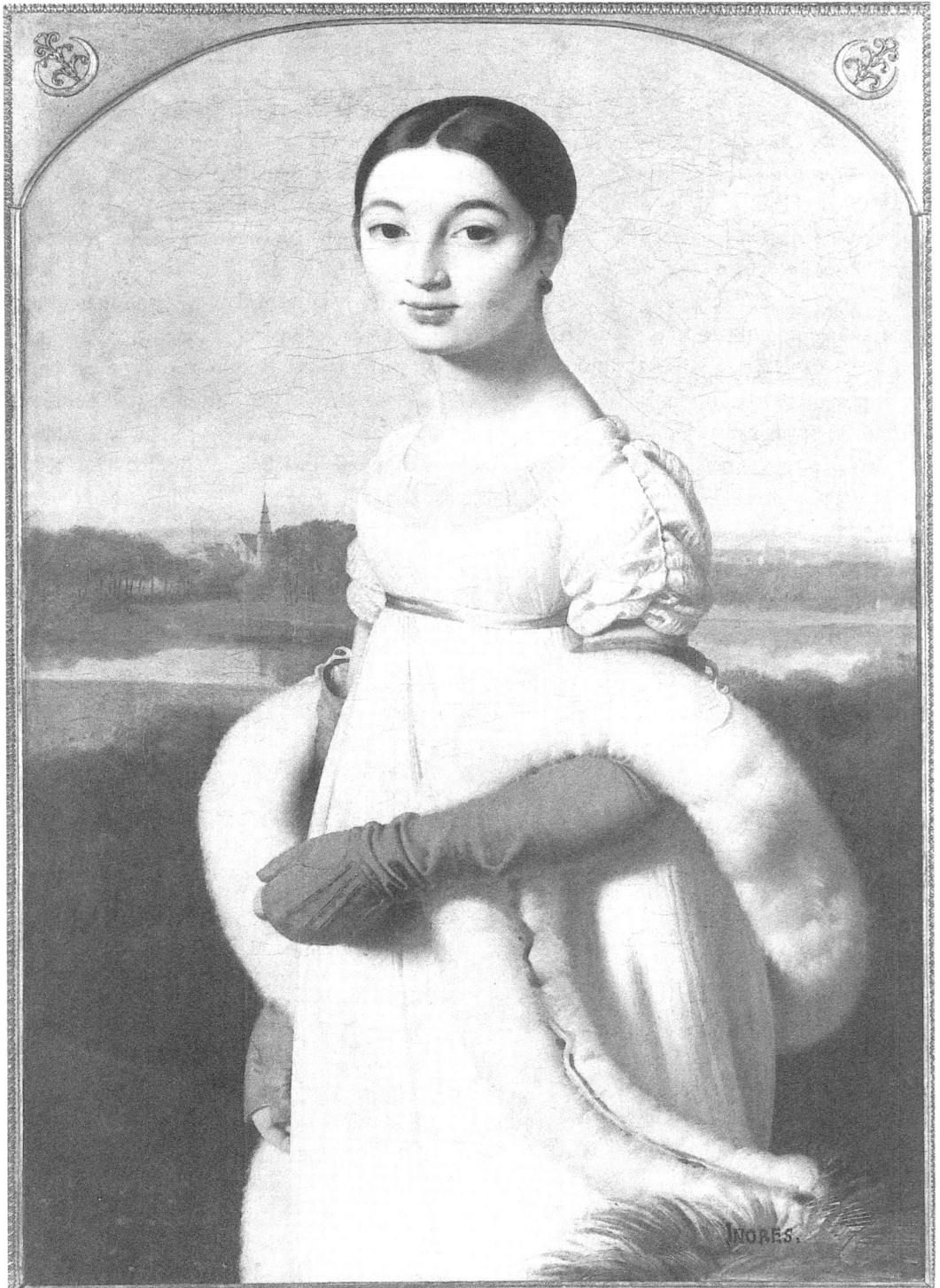

FIGURE 67. Jean-Auguste-Dominique Ingres, *Portrait of Mademoiselle Rivière*, 1805 (Salon of 1806). Oil on canvas. Paris, Musée du Louvre, inv. M.I. 1447 (100 × 70 cm). Photo: © RMN/ Art Resource, NY/© Gérard Blot.

Rarefied elegance inspired by antiquity was the hallmark of what came to be known as *style empire*. One senses its logic of restraint in even the most sumptuous objects, such as the large centerpiece of gilt bronze made by Pierre-Philippe Thomire for Lucien Bonaparte (Napoléon's brother) about 1815 (Fig. 68). Adorned with figures designed by the sculptor Pierre Cartellier and the painter Pierre-Paul Prud'hon, the ensemble reiterates the love of separate elements, regular spacing, and linear rhythms already noted in contemporary furniture and fashion. Nor was this conceptual clarity obscured when such works were used: John Pinkerton reports that contemporary taste dictated that "the *plateau* which decorates the middle of the table, is often strewed with fine sand, of various colours, in compartments, and decorated with small images, and real or artificial flowers. Images of porcelain seem particularly adapted for this purpose."[36] Designs drawn in sand are by definition two-dimensional, and the accessories, even when exquisite, tended to be small. The aim was not to clutter the table but to adorn it richly with a minimum of mass, a goal that seems perfectly reasonable but completely unlike the physically imposing table ornaments (Fig. 89) that became fashionable during the 1830s (see Chapter Five).

It was inevitable that the refined reworking of classical forms so closely associated with the reign of Napoléon would be viewed askance by the restored Bourbons after 1815. None of the rich furnishings commissioned by Napoléon were actually discarded following his demise. Rather, an entire branch of government—the Garde-Meuble du Roi—was devoted to the tasks of inventorying, maintaining, storing, and distributing the thousands of objects belonging to the state. During the early years of the Restoration the most pressing task was to remove from the furniture, wall hangings, and architectural details of royal palaces and public buildings all the emblems of the defunct Empire, from the initial "N" to imperial eagles and Napoleonic bees. The revival of court etiquette and ceremonies of pre-Revolutionary Paris—both major elements of the Bourbon program to forget the years of Revolution and Empire—fostered a gradual return to the

FIGURE 68.   Pierre-Philippe Thomire, *Large Table Centerpiece for Lucien Bonaparte*, ca. 1815. Gilded bronze and glass. Paris, Musée Marmottan (78 × 215 cm). Photo: Courtesy of the Museum.

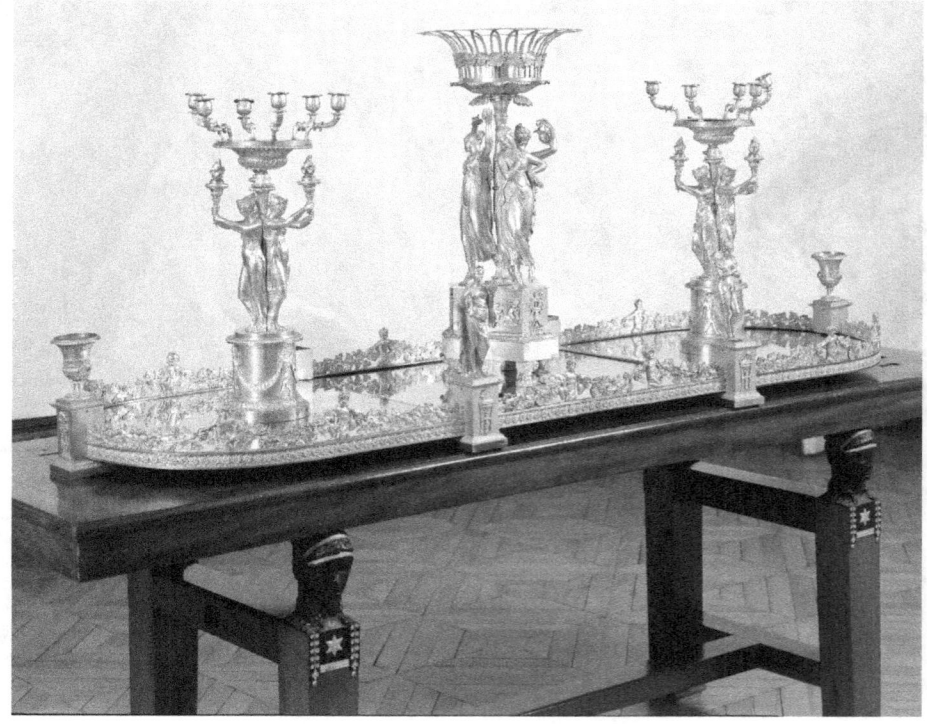

styles, fabrics, and colors of the Ancien Régime. When one of the large salons of the Tuileries Palace used by the duchesse d'Angoulême was outfitted in 1816 with new stools and a single armchair "according to court etiquette," the armchair selected from storage was one that had been made for Joséphine in 1807. The duchesse repeatedly complained to the Garde-Meuble that her chair was "distasteful in form and faded in color" and asked that it be exchanged for "an armchair and a footstool more suitable."[37] Joséphine's low-backed chair with arms in the shape of sensuous nude sphinxes was eventually replaced by an imposing and architectonic armchair of self-display [fauteuil de représentation] equipped with a high back that framed the duchesse under a miniature pediment to mark clearly her importance in the social hierarchy of the sitting room. None of this is surprising, for the duchesse d'Angoulême was one of the staunchest staunch royalists in the entourage of Louis XVIII. The only surviving child of Louis XVI and Marie-Antoinette (both guillotined in 1793), and married to her cousin (eldest son of the future Charles X), the duchesse d'Angoulême did not hide her desire to reinstate the formal etiquette of pre-Revolutionary life at court. Her apartments in the Tuileries Palace were redecorated to emulate the scale and luxury of the Ancien Régime. She much preferred a retrospective formality to experiments with style as an expression of personal taste.

That was not the case among the less important and younger figures at court, whose private apartments were reworked to reflect an aesthetic shaped by a sentimental historicism that parallels the popularity of Lenoir's Musée des Monuments français and the development of troubadour painting. A key figure in this transformation of taste within the walls of the Tuileries Palace was the duchesse de Berry, who was also an avid collector of pictures by Révoil (Fig. 61). Marie-Caroline de Berry, a Neapolitan princess, married the younger son of the comte d'Artois in 1816. Her husband, Charles-Ferdinand de Berry, was a leader of the Ultra-royalist faction at court that regularly opposed any policy of reconciling the Bourbon government with the country's revolutionary and imperial past. The duke's politics made many enemies: on 13 February 1820 he was assassinated while attending the opera. A widow at twenty-two years of age,

and expecting a child, the duchesse de Berry moved into an apartment at the Tuileries Palace—ironically the same suite of rooms that her husband had occupied before their marriage. In mourning, and waiting to give birth, the duchesse did little at first to alter the decorations or furnishings of these rooms: a watercolor by Auguste Garneray from about 1822 (Fig. 69) shows that her bedroom had changed little in two years. The canopied bed in the alcove at the left is a mahogany piece with pairs of small columns at each side and decorated with low-relief fittings of gilt bronze—a design simpler but in the same taste as the bed made for Queen Hortense in 1803 (Fig. 63).[38] The bedroom's wall coverings, part of a large stock of fabrics commissioned by Napoléon in 1812 but not used during his reign, were taken out of storage in 1820 for use by the duchesse de Berry.[39]

The young duchesse was not completely docile before the agents of the Garde-Meuble who supervised palace furnishings. Garneray's watercolor reveals that the clock on her mantle is a gothic design by Augustin-Michel Lepaute, a rather dissonant object amidst the classical forms of her furniture yet completely consonant with her patronage of troubadour paintings. The duchesse was particularly fond of plants, and to that end she commissioned two flower stands [jardinières] from Félix Rémond (visible at the right of Garneray's picture) that were singularly disliked by an inspector of the Garde-Meuble. "Mr. Rémond has made two flower-stands for Madame the duchesse de Berry," he wrote; "it is true that they are not pleasing to look at because of a surfeit of bronze fittings, but Her Highness finds them very much to her taste."[40] During the course of 1823 the duchesse de Berry began to exercise her own taste more forcefully. While visiting the Exposition des produits de l'industrie française of 1823 she was attracted to several of Félix Rémond's newest creations, including a psyche mirror and a dressing table made of indigenous woods—oak, elm, and burlwood—and richly decorated with mounts of gilt bronze (Fig. 70). The duchesse convinced the Garde-Meuble to purchase the pieces for her apartment. Soon after she commissioned a new bed and washstand made of the same light-colored oak with complicated wood veneers in very slightly contrasting colors.[41]

FIGURE 69. Auguste
Garneray, *Bedchamber
of the duchesse de Berry
at the Tuileries Palace*,
1822. Photogravure after
watercolor original.
Paris, Musée des Arts
décoratifs, inv. 15957. Photo:
© Photothèque UCAD/
Laurent-Sully Jaulmes.

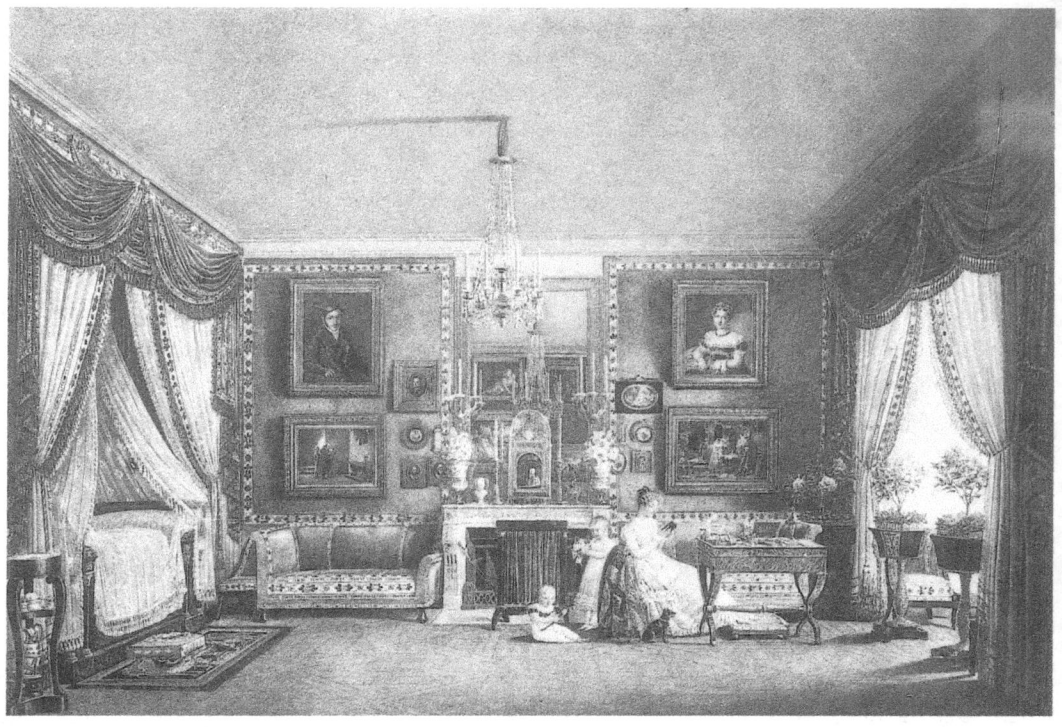

Within the course of two years, the duchesse de Berry completely replaced her dark furniture of mahogany and bronze fittings for a style both lighter in color and more delicate in ornament, since most of the patterning of the new pieces occurs within the surface of the wood itself. The dressing table she bought in 1823 (Fig. 70) was thus a work of transition: although constructed of indigenous oak, its system of decoration—exotic burlwood and oak veneers complemented by classical motifs of lion claws, rosettes, palm leaves, and winged tritons—mixes the sensual appeal of natural materials with established forms. Yet the direction of the duchesse de Berry's taste becomes apparent if we compare her dressing table to the one made for Joséphine in 1805 (Fig. 66): the robustness, sculptural presence, and inviting tactility of the former suggest a sensuousness rather foreign to the spare architectonics of the latter. The bed made for the duchesse de Berry in 1824 to match her dressing table stated the new aesthetic even more fully.[42] There are almost no decorative elements in bronze, yet the entire surface is subtly articulated with incrustations of ash into which bouquets of fleurs-de-lys, attributes of the arts, and assorted arrangements of leaves are delicately etched. Indeed, the duchesse de Berry's rejection of furniture inspired by classical antiquity exactly parallels a fierce debate at the Salon of 1824, which pitted advocates of decorum and restraint based on classical models against those favoring the simmering sensuality and expressive freedom of nascent Romanticism (see Chapter Five).

Because furnishings created for placement in royal residences involve huge investments of time and materials they are not always the most accurate barometers of changing taste. That the duchesse de Berry was able to replace completely the décor of her private apartment within a very few years suggests an official indulgence of her personal wishes, perhaps motivated by the untimely death of her husband. Yet even she was obliged to work with agents of the Garde-Meuble and to respect their annual budgets. Far more revealing of shifts in her personal taste are the small objects she could commission independently, such as the jewelry box [coffret] made for her in 1829 by the Manufactory of Sèvres.[43] This box of porcelain and gilt bronze was patterned on one of the four designs prepared for the duchesse by Jean-Charles-François Leloy of the Sèvres factory (Fig. 71). In October of 1829 she selected what Leloy called a "monumental form" that does resemble a small gothic monument: corner piers capped with tiny pointed-arch belfries; a roof with pointed crenellations and stylized gothic trophies; facades of running

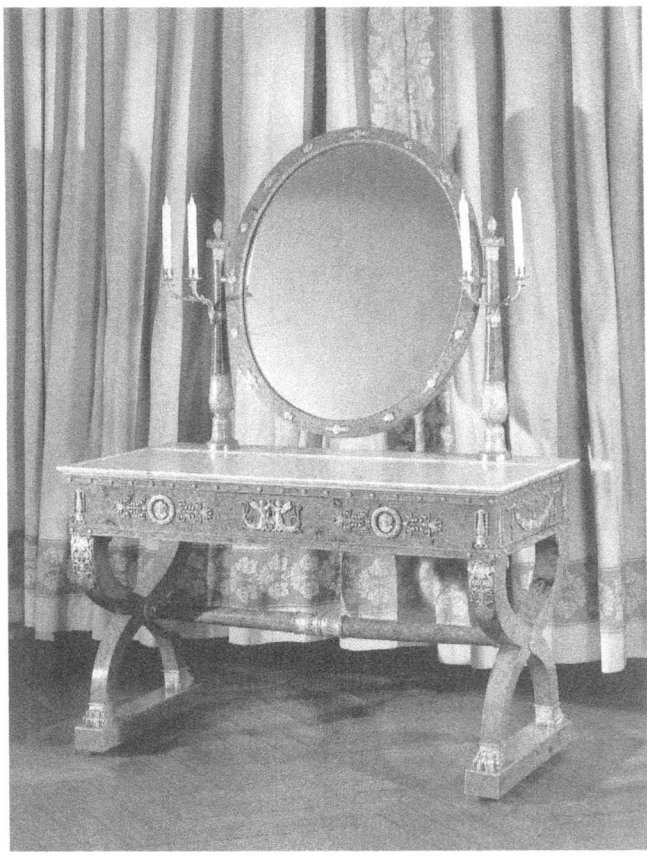

FIGURE 70.   Félix Rémond, *Dressing Table of the duchesse de Berry at the Tuileries Palace*, 1823–1824. Oak with veneer of elm and burlwood, gilded bronze, white marble. Paris, Musée des Arts décoratifs, inv. Mob. Nat. GME 4325 (154.5 × 115 × 52.5; mirror 70 × 61 cm). Photo: © Photothèque UCAD/Laurent-Sully Jaulmes.

arcades and bands of rosettes; a central arch that frames a miniature likeness of the duchesse herself.[44] The jewelry box was among the earliest objects produced at the Sèvres porcelain factory in a self-consciously gothic style. Its selection by the duchesse de Berry registers the rising critical fortune of gothic art in Parisian society.

The year 1829 is important to this reevaluation on at least three counts. First, on 2 March the duchesse de Berry hosted the Quadrille de Marie Stuart, a much-discussed costume ball set in a troubadour décor that cemented her reputation as a leading taste-maker of the gothic amongst the young generation of Parisian socialites.[45] Second, the social season of 1829 was the last in which the duchesse and her royalist friends held sway, because the revolution of July 1830 would sweep away their world with a new political order and an aesthetic even less indebted to the classical tradition. Finally, it was during 1829 that Victor Hugo was compiling research and notes for *Notre-Dame de Paris*, a book that would explode on the literary scene of 1831 and change dramatically how the general public thought about gothic art. Readers of Hugo's novel were quick to realize that the principal character of *Notre-Dame de Paris* was neither Quasimodo, nor Esmeralda, nor abbé Frollo, but the cathedral that seemed at times to seethe with a life of its own: "The restless brightness of the flame made things move before one's eyes. There were wiverns that appeared to be laughing, gargoyles thought to be heard yelping, salamanders blowing on the fire, tarasques immortalized in the smoke."[46] The art critic Gustave Planche wrote to Hugo that "you have sculpted our dialect, you have cut it into trefoils and lace-work, you have engraved in words the marvelous patterns of Moorish towers, Venetian palaces, and old Christian cathedrals that ravish us."[47]

Hugo single-handedly reanimated for a large reading public an empathetic and sentimental dimension of medieval monuments exactly parallel to what Lenoir's Musée des Monuments français had attempted more than fifteen years earlier. But now, prepared by a decade of Sir Walter Scott's troubadour novels and the sentimental history pictures of Richard and Révoil, the ground was far more fertile.[48] "Reading the novels of Walter Scott turned the imagination of many people towards those Middle Ages that not long

FIGURE 71. Jean-Charles-François Leloy, *Design for a Coffer in the Gothic Style for the duchesse de Berry*, 1829. Watercolor and pencil on paper. Sèvres, Archives de la Manufacture nationale de Sèvres, inv. D § 10 1848 No 7 (1er) (40.4 × 54.6 cm). Photo: Author.

ago had been disdainfully avoided," remarked the historian Augustin Thierry.

And if in our own time a revolution has occurred in the way one reads and writes history, those works, although frivolous in appearance, have contributed to it in some odd way. They have inspired, among readers of every class, a sense of curiosity about the centuries and men put down as barbaric, and it is to this curiosity that more serious publications owe their unexpected success.[49]

This empathetic side of history, of lives behind the documents, seduced even hard-nosed historians like Michelet, who mused over a pile of papers in the royal archives: "There was a movement there, a murmur that was not dead. These papers, these parchments were the lives of men, of provinces, of peoples; they all lived, spoke, and surrounded the author. Be patient, dead gentlemen, let us take things in order, if you please."[50] From our distance of almost two centuries it is hard

to imagine the excitement animating the rediscovery of gothic art and culture around 1830, a difficulty that contemporaries already predicted. "No doubt the turning back of certain of our contemporary intellects towards the institutions of the Middle Ages will become one day the subject of a genuine astonishment," wrote Étienne Delécluze; "in seeing . . . everyone muster their efforts to restore the intellectual and moral life of a world that no longer had a reason to exist, one will wonder what could have been the real goal that these utopians and passionate archeologists had set for themselves."[51]

Novels of contemporary life attest to the efforts expended by Parisians of the 1830s to fit up their houses in a gothic manner. Consider Balzac's account of Féodora's bedroom from *La Peau de chagrin*:

In a gothic bedroom, the doors of which were hidden by tapestry draperies, the fabric frames, the clock, the patterns of the carpet were all gothic. The ceiling, formed of carved, dark-brown joists, gave the appearance of being very elegant and highly original coffers, and the wainscoting was very artistically worked. Nothing destroyed the general effect of this pretty décor, not even the window casements, whose stained glass was colored and costly.[52]

It was a sign of the times that Balzac's description could be applied almost literally to the private apartment that Marie d'Orléans, the second daughter of King Louis-Philippe, arranged for herself on the ground floor of the Tuileries Palace (Fig. 72).[53] The retrospective painting made by Prosper Lafaye in 1842, three years after the untimely death of the princess, shows Marie studying intently an illustrated manuscript that rests upon an intricately carved gothic pulpit. Like

Féodora, Marie installed a sculpted and painted ceiling of coffers that emulated early Renaissance models. She also fitted the windows of her private quarters with stained glass, and she selected furnishings of dark, intricately carved wood. The softly filtered light, the historicizing décor, and the slightly theatrical arrangement of this room speak of Marie's full participation in a troubadour sentimentality. An anonymous biographer reports that after 1832, the year her older sister married King Léopold I of Belgium, Marie became increasingly reclusive, and that

to fill the void in her private life left by the absence of her beloved sister, she withdrew more and more from the constraining diversions of court life to devote herself with a real passion to her pencils and

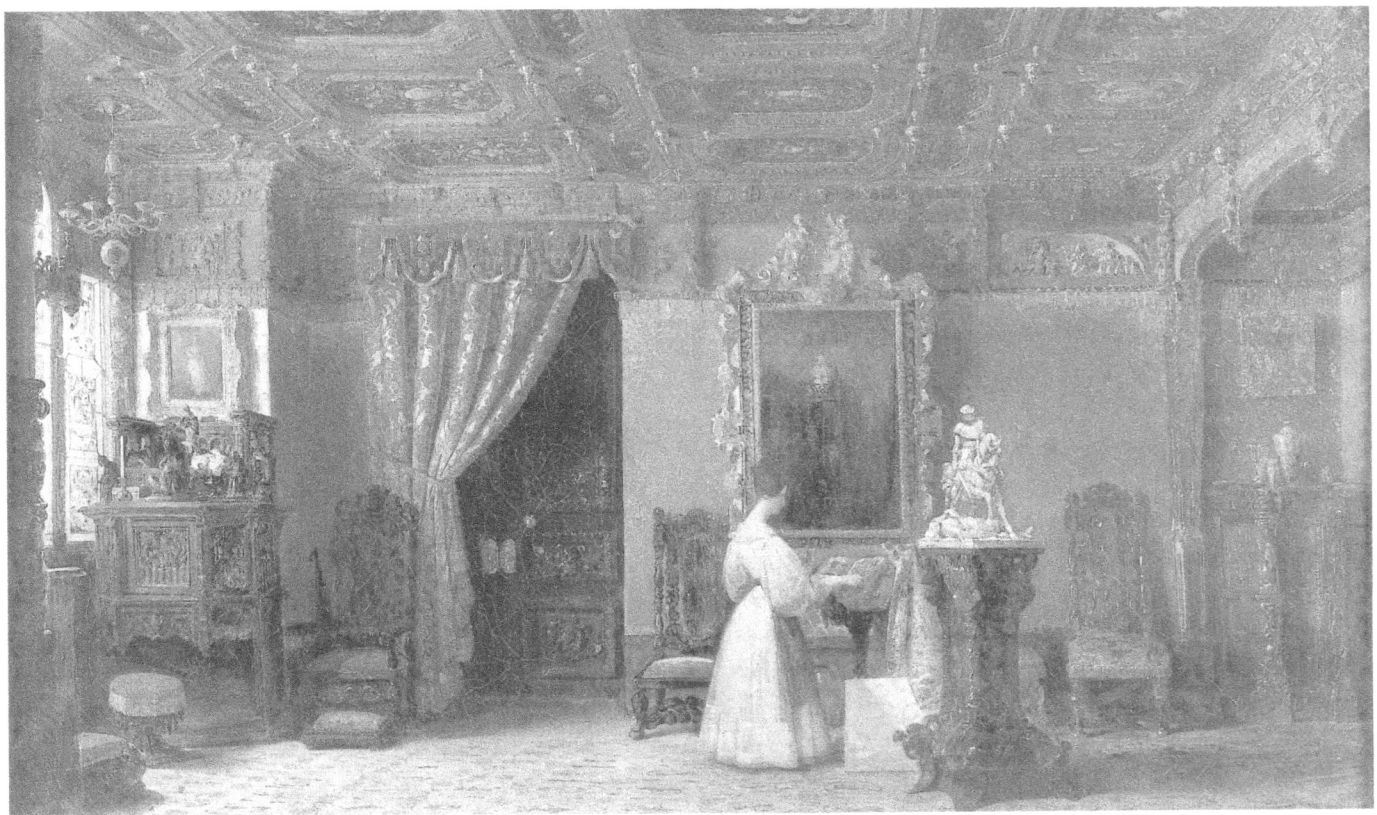

FIGURE 72. Prosper Lafaye, *Salon of the princesse Marie d'Orléans at the Tuileries Palace*, 1842. Oil on canvas. Versailles, Châteaux de Versailles et de Trianon, inv. MV6120 (55 × 87 cm). Photo: © RMN/Art Resource, NY/© Droits réservés.

her chisel, confining herself to the delightful studio in the apartment she occupied on the ground floor of the Tuileries that she had decorated with exquisite taste in the severe gothic style.[54]

Balzac's evocation of a gothic décor as the private retreat from an everyday world is here fully reiterated, but now at the highest levels of Parisian society.

Marie d'Orléans was an accomplished artist who studied with the painter Ary Scheffer.[55] The sculpture prominently displayed in her room on a neo-gothic pedestal is a work she made in 1834 that represents Joan of Arc weeping at the sight of soldiers wounded in battle—a melancholic and introspective rendering of the young warrior that accords well with Marie's own temperament.[56] Another sculpture, standing on the gothic dresser near the window, is very much a counterpoint: it represents *Charles VI in the Forest of Le Mans*, and was made for Marie by Antoine Barye in 1833 (Fig. 73). At his death in 1422, Charles VI left a divided kingdom partially controlled by England, which is why Joan of Arc attempted to rally Frenchmen against the foreigners. The moment depicted by Barye is far from the world of international politics; rather, it presents Charles in a moment of extreme personal agitation. Riding in full battle dress through the forest near Le Mans on a torrid day in August of 1392, Charles was suddenly accosted by a half-dressed highwayman who clutched the reins of the king's horse and cried "Stop good King! Go no further! You have been betrayed!" Charles, already feverish in the heat, was so startled that he threw his arms into the air. He soon fell prey to the first of many attacks of delirium that eventually made him unable to rule for months at a time and earned him the sobriquet "the mad" [l'insensé].[57] Barye's sculpture, which depicts the king's panicked reaction to his half-naked assailant, is organized as a dramatically interlocked composition of flaying limbs and exaggerated gestures that strives to give form to the confusion of the monarch's mental state.

The bizarre subject of a king gone mad found a place in the private, neo-gothic retreat of Marie's apartment, alongside her own pensive rendering of Joan of Arc, the young woman-warrior who was guided by mysterious voices that only she could hear. The pairing underscores how much contemporary interest in history had shifted from a strict concern for facts and dates to an imaginative reconstruction of the lives, personalities, and quirks of figures long dead. A few years earlier, when writing about his own book in which the exploits of Charles VI and Joan of Arc are recounted, Prosper de Barante remarked that

a picture [tableau] can inspire hate, love, or scorn. Certain marks and certain colors placed on a canvas are often a more subtle and complete judgment of a person's character than many, strung-out lines of prose. In this way, I have tried to paint the fifteenth century, I have wanted you to see its face rather than to hear a description of it.[58]

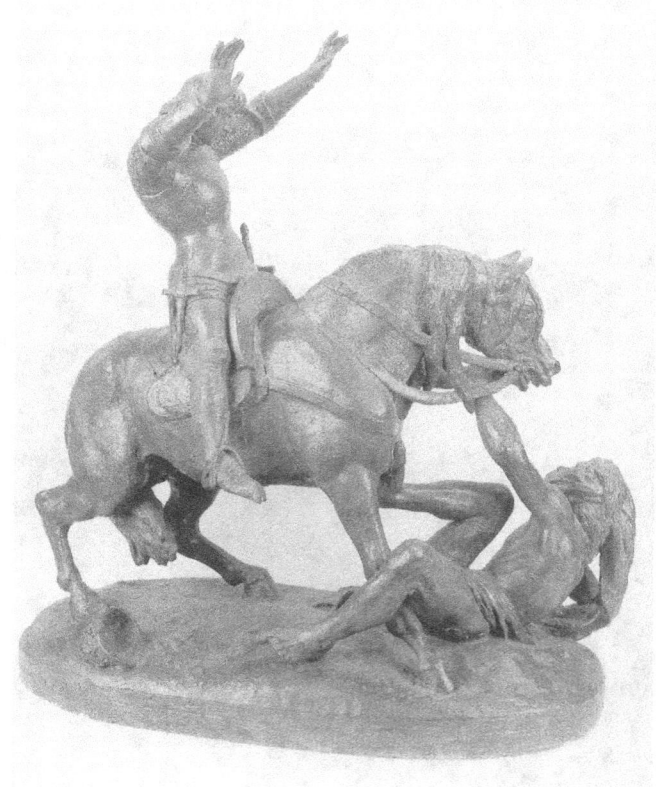

FIGURE 73. Antoine Barye, *Charles VI in the Forest of Le Mans*, 1833. Plaster and wax with bronze patination. Paris, Musée du Louvre, inv. RF1577 (50 × 45 cm). Photo: © RMN/Art Resource, NY/© Christian Jean.

Barante felt obliged to defend his narrative strategy in 1823. By the early 1830s it had become the norm for representing history: material objects—from Hugo's cathedral of Notre-Dame to fanciful environments like the apartments of Féodora or Marie d'Orléans—were the stuff of scenic recreations [tableaux] by which the past acquired an emotive force in the present.

The Gothic Revival

One of the more puzzling aspects of studying the art and culture of early nineteenth-century Europe is the energy and enthusiasm behind the odd fascination for late medieval and early Renaissance art and history now known as the Gothic Revival. This was hardly a Parisian phenomenon—the neo-gothic Houses of Parliament rebuilt in London during the 1840s by Charles Barry is an example familiar to many people—but the high visibility in Paris of genuine Gothic monuments like Notre-Dame and the Sainte-Chapelle especially stimulated the growth of revivalist ideas in the French capital. John Summerson, an historian of English architecture and no fan of the Gothic Revival, has perhaps best explained its contemporary attraction, and our indifference today, as the

conscious insistence on detail—not for its quality but for the excitement of displaying a historical trophy. . . . Whatever charm this architecture had vanished as soon as a deeper familiarity with medieval architecture prevailed—as soon, that is, as a richly traceried window ceased to be interesting *as such* and was judged by combined standards of archaeological and aesthetic taste.[59]

Summerson's distinction between "historical trophies" and a "deeper familiarity" with gothic forms characterizes precisely the trajectory of the Gothic Revival in Paris: from an early enthusiasm for bric-a-brac in the 1820s to the archaeologically driven projects of 1843 for restoring the cathedral of Notre-Dame de Paris.

The salon of the comtesse d'Osmond, recorded in a watercolor by Hilaire Thierry about 1820, gives an idea of the early, "historical trophy" phase of the Gothic Revival in Paris (Fig. 74). The comtesse and her husband lived in a mag-

nificent eighteenth-century hôtel (now destroyed) near the site of the present-day Opéra Garnier. She was an independently wealthy woman married to an aide-de-camp of the duc d'Angoulême. Frankly juxtaposed to the impressively colonnaded classical architecture of the main salon is an assortment of furniture and objects in various period styles, including a painting on the back wall to the right of the door that seems to be a troubadour picture of a vaulted gothic space. Through the doorway one glimpses an adjoining room fitted up in a neo-gothic manner: a freestanding table ornamented with small pointed arches, a chandelier in gilt bronze fashioned with vaguely gothic elements, and an hourglass perched on a chimney-piece ornamented with an arcade of pointed arches.[60] The door to this room, which opens into the salon, is decorated with a three-part arcade of pointed arches and thin supporting columns that emulate the interior elevation of a gothic cathedral nave.

Not visible in Thierry's watercolor is the pair of chairs in gilded wood that the comtesse d'Osmond commissioned from Jacob-Desmalter about 1817 (Fig. 75). Characteristic of the fantasy aspect of early Gothic Revival, the chairs freely combine architectural forms with a heraldic display of the Osmond family emblems. The somewhat stocky legs are fashioned as small columns—including stylized bases and capitals of the sort found inside Gothic cathedrals—but the added ornamentation of shallow arcades is pure fantasy. The upper part of the tall, straight back is handled like gothic tracery with elaborate cuspings—a quatrefoil centerpiece and two trefoil arches—but the whole is incongruously supported by architectural pinnacles festooned with crockets and capped by a stylized owl. Two facing unicorns—a motif adapted from medieval tapestries like the famous example now in the collection of the Musée Cluny—support the Osmond coat of arms and its Latin motto, *Nihil Obstat*. However stylish the pastiche of these chairs seemed in 1820, it is perhaps no surprise that the comtesse d'Osmond soon tired of them; by the 1830s she had placed most of her neo-gothic furnishings in storage.

The exquisite box given to Ferdinand-Philippe d'Orléans (eldest son of Louis-Philippe) by his wife, the duchesse Hélène de Mecklembourg-Schwerin, shortly after their

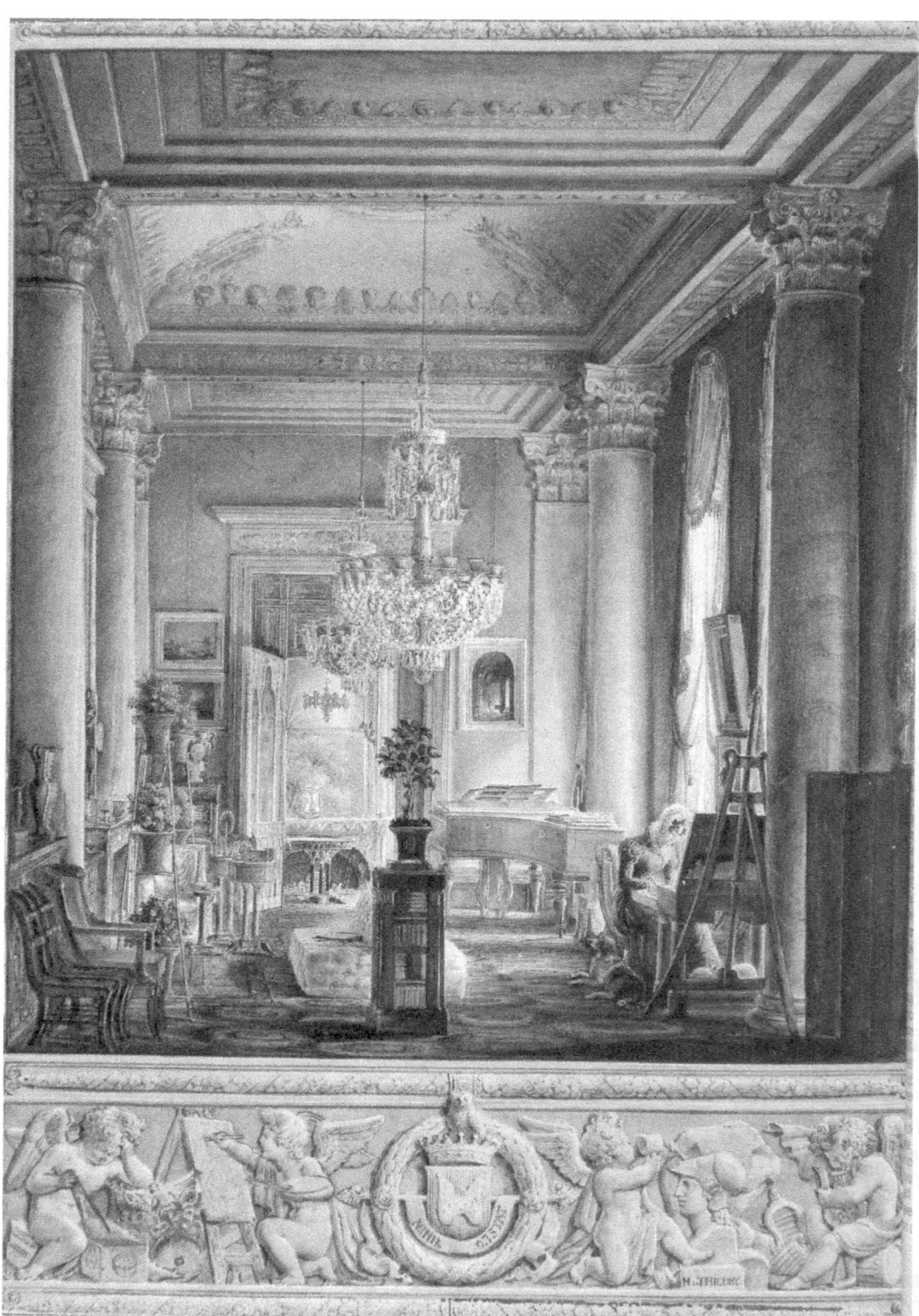

FIGURE 74. Hilaire
Thierry, *Salon of the
comtesse d'Osmond*, ca. 1820.
Watercolor. Private collection
(35 × 27 cm). Photo: Courtesy
La Connaissance des Arts/
© Droits réservés.

marriage in 1837 is a late example of combining gothic forms to elicit sentimental allusions that harks back to Lenoir's Musée des Monuments français (Fig. 76). Designed in the form of a reliquary and made of finely worked gilt silver with inlays of enamel, malachite, and precious stones, the box is fashioned with architectural niches at each corner where tiny soldiers mount guard. On the lateral sides, angels framed by tracery work carry a shield emblazoned with the initials of the duc d'Orléans. On the top, a reclining woman (which may be a portrait of the duchesse) holds a shield with the initials of Frederick-William III of Prussia, the sovereign who engineered the couple's marriage. The richness of its materials, its deeply personal meaning, and the fact that the duke prominently displayed this box on his desk register an appreciation for the fantastic and sentimental side of Gothic Revival well into the 1830s and at the highest levels of Parisian society.

Nonetheless, whimsical arrangement of formal elements plucked indiscriminately from the architecture, decorative arts, and sculpture of the Middle Ages was gradually displaced by a systematic archaeology based on documents—inventories, images, and written accounts—to produce more literal reconstructions of historic spaces. During the reign of Louis-Philippe many of the royal châteaux were restored with a concern for contextual accuracy and stylistic unity, so that interior ensembles were both recovered from neglect and reproduced anew in styles historically appropriate, or at least plausible, to their specific epoch. The latter tendency—to make new objects in the style of the past—is characteristic of Historicism in the arts. Indeed, the 1830s and 1840s mark a high point of historicist ambitions to recover the forms and spaces of the past.[61] At the château of Fontainebleau, for example, the salon of Madame de Maintenon (wife of Louis XIV from 1683 to his death in 1714) was completely redone with decorations and furnishings that either dated from the time of her life or replicated objects that did.[62] Similarly, the château at Pau, birthplace of Henri IV in 1553, was redecorated in a style characteristic of the mid-sixteenth century.

Historicist reconstructions of this sort produced an effect that is unusual in the decorative arts. "The evocative power of the place, its history, weighs with such a force that it imposes

a style of furniture," remarks Colombe Samoyault-Verlet; "up to this time, royal usage, etiquette, the sovereign's taste or even fashion could intervene in royal furnishings. The large-scale restorations of the Louis-Philippe period underscore the omnipresence of the past and of history."[63] The ambition of Louis-Philippe's historicist re-creations was to produce spaces with the power to evoke history, exactly

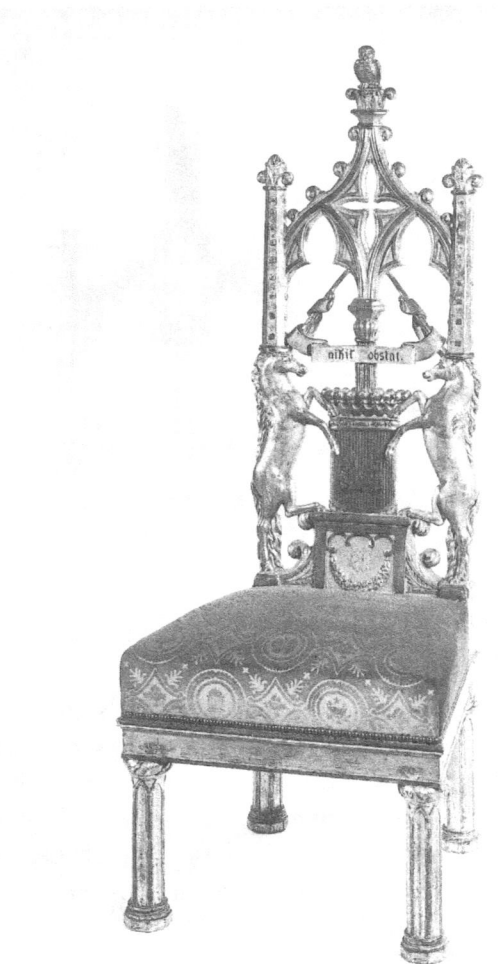

FIGURE 75. François-Honoré-Georges Jacob-Desmalter, *Chair for the "Gothic Study" of the comtesse d'Osmond*, 1817–1820. Sculpted and gilded wood. Paris, Musée du Petit-Palais, inv. PPO 3509 (146 × 54 × 52 cm). Photo: © PMVP/Ladet.

FIGURE 76. Jean-Baptiste and Jules-Jean-François Fossin, *Small Coffer given by the duchesse d'Orléans to her Husband as a Wedding Gift*, ca. 1837. Silver with gilding and enamel work. Darmstadt, Hessisches Landesmuseum, inv. KG 67:223 (16.5 × 18.5 × 13.3 cm). Photo: © Hessisches Landesmusuem, Darmstadt.

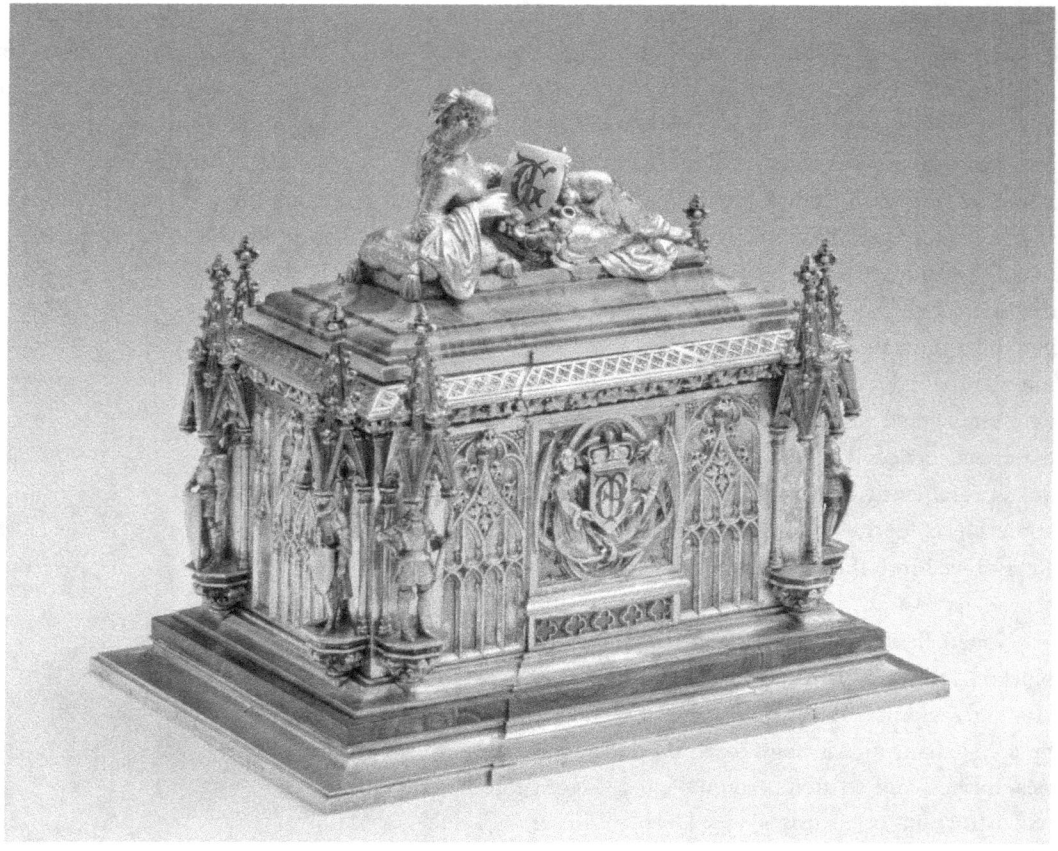

like the defunct galleries arranged by Lenoir had attempted three decades earlier, but now informed by an archaeological accuracy that Lenoir had almost completely ignored. The appearance of this tendency in the decorative arts marched exactly in step with contemporary developments in historical writing, where an emotional involvement of the reader was solicited by painstakingly reconstructed tableaux (to use the term of Prosper de Barante). Finally, the aesthetic goals of historicism were institutionalized in 1837 with the founding of the Commission for Historical Monuments under the aegis of the Ministry of the Interior. The mission of this new office was to survey the monuments of France, to rank their historical importance, and to oversee their safeguard and restoration. The first director of the new agency was a young man by the name of Prosper Mérimée.

The increasingly official context of historicism during the reign of Louis-Philippe sheds light on the polemic generated by the restoration of Notre-Dame de Paris, arguably the most famous landmark of mid-nineteenth-century Paris. We tend to forget that the centerpiece of Victor Hugo's novel was in a rather sorry state in 1830. While the material fabric of Notre-Dame was basically intact, the church was seldom used. Most of its external sculpture had been removed in the wave of iconoclasm that swept France in 1793. In 1830 insurgents burned down the bishop's residence and damaged the building's exterior. "Today, three kinds of devastation disfigure gothic architecture," wrote Hugo about the church;

wrinkles and warts on the skin, which is the work of time; assaults, brutalities, bruises, and fractures, which is the work of revolutions from Luther to Mirabeau. Mutilations, amputations, dislocations of the membrane, *restorations*, which is the work—Greek, Roman, and barbarian—of professors following Vitruvius and Vignoble. This magnificent art produced by vandals has been killed by the academies.[64]

Hugo laments the effects of time, political change, and especially the misguided good intentions of centuries of restorers who had altered the original gothic forms of the church with additions thought to be more correct, up-to-date, or functional.

Notre-Dame assumed an increased ecclesiastical importance as a result of the Catholic Revival in the 1830s and 1840s (see Chapter Three). In 1841, for example, more than twelve thousand faithful—including politicians like Guizot and Thiers and writers like Chateaubriand—crowded the church to hear the sermons of the charismatic priest Jean-Baptiste-Henri Lacordaire. The public attention directed to Notre-Dame at moments like this only served to highlight its dilapidated state, so that the question of restoring the cathedral become as pressing as how to do it. In 1841 the Ministry of Justice and Religious Rites [Ministère de Justice et des Cultes] opened a competition for the restoration of Notre-Dame, asking that prospective projects be turned in by 31 January 1843. Few architects participated in this exercise, perhaps because one of the competitors—the team of Jean-Baptiste de Lassus and Eugène-Emmanuel Viollet-le-Duc—seemed to have an inside track.

Viollet-le-Duc was a longtime friend of Prosper Mérimée, the energetic director of the new Commission for Historical Monuments, and a member of the selection board for the Notre-Dame project. Mérimée had recently appointed Viollet-le-Duc to supervise restoration of the abbey church at Vézelay, mainly because they shared a vision about the nature and scope of historic restoration. "By restoration," wrote Mérimée in 1844, "we mean the conservation of what exists, the reproduction of what had most evidently existed."[65] The key concept of Mérimée's historicism—like that noted in the redecorating of royal châteaux by Louis-Philippe—is that restoration includes both conservation and reproduction. Viollet-le-Duc and de Lassus reiterated that concept in the prospectus of their proposal for the Notre-Dame project:

We think that each part, added in whatever epoch, ought in principle to be preserved, strengthened, and restored in the style appropriate to it, and be done with a reverent discretion, even with a total abnegation of all personal opinion. The artist ought to remain entirely in the background, to forget his tastes and instincts in order to retrieve and follow the thought that presided at the execution of the work he wishes to restore. It is not a matter, in this case, of making art but only of submitting to the art of an epoch that is no longer.[66]

Like their contemporaries in painting who consciously designed murals in styles of the past (Figs. 39 and 40), these architects believed it was possible to "retrieve and follow the thought that presided at the execution of the work," and that one could actually get to know the deepest motives "of an epoch that is no longer." Their optimism about an ability to reach back in time lies at the heart of nineteenth-century Historicism.

The text presented by de Lassus and Viollet-le-Duc also inadvertently bared a paradox within the ambitions of historicist restoration. When dealing with a structure that was built and rebuilt over the course of several centuries, what epoch should the restorer accept as definitive? Nowhere was this dilemma more present than in their proposal for handling the south flank and windows of Notre-Dame (Fig. 77). The architects understood completely that the windows of the tribunes in the nave and apse had been changed between the twelfth and fourteenth centuries. They speculated that the windows were never built as originally planned, and that the makeshift solution using pitched roofs—still visible on the building—had been adopted as early as the twelfth century. They further surmised that fourteenth-century architects elected not to continue this ersatz solution in the apse. Thus, the question of restoration became three-fold: should one restore the fourteenth-century solution? should one restore the ersatz twelfth-century solution? should one reconstruct the tribunes and windows according to a system that one assumes the twelfth-century builders had intended to follow? When drawing the south flank for presentation of their project

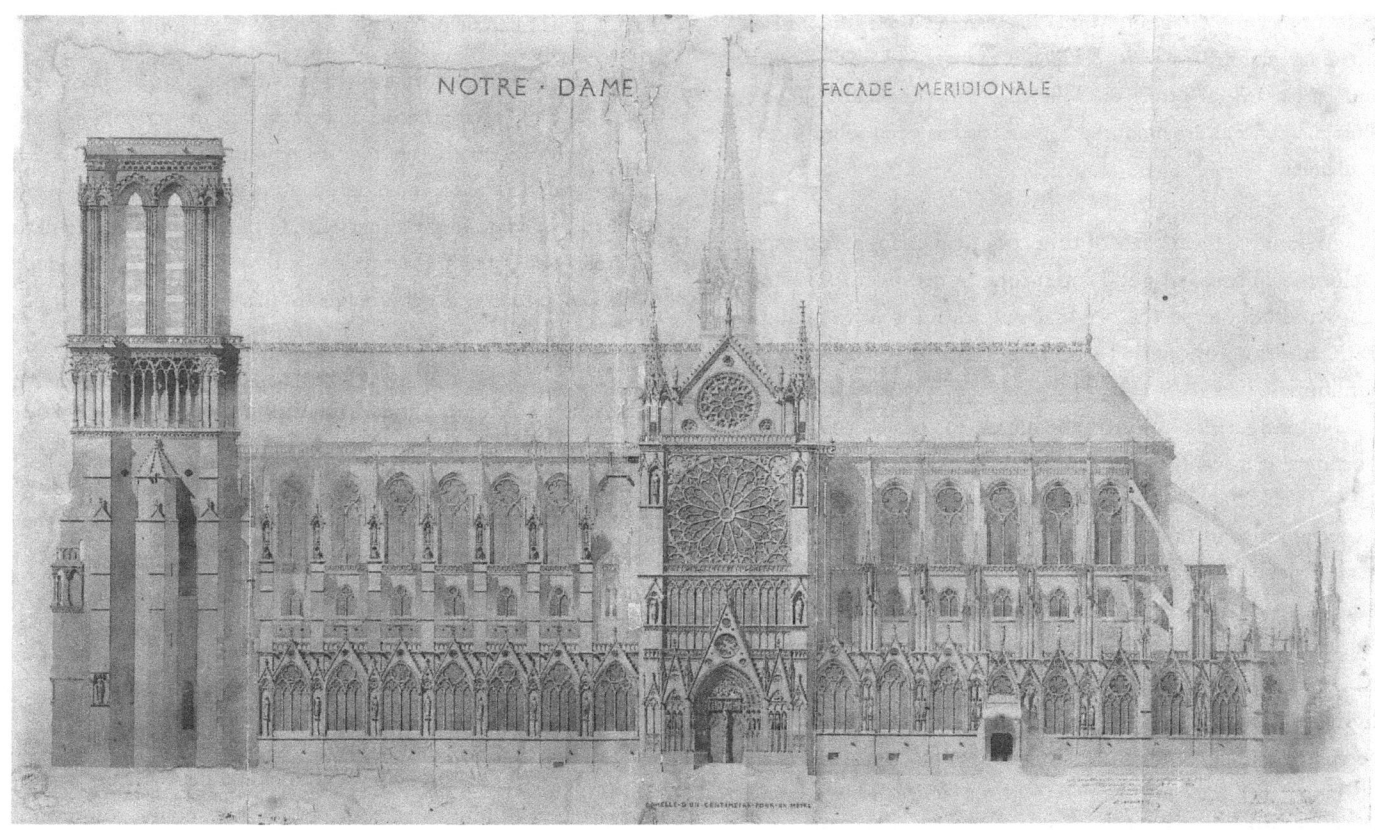

NOTRE · DAME   FACADE · MERIDIONALE

FIGURE 77.   Jean-Baptiste Lassus and Eugène-Emmanuel Viollet-le-Duc, *Restoration Project for the cathedral of Notre-Dame de Paris, Elevation of the South Flank*, 1843. Pen and ink with watercolor. Paris, Centre de Recherche des Monuments historiques, inv. MSC1840 (88 × 146 cm). Photo: © Centre des monuments nationaux, Paris.

(Fig. 77), de Lassus and Viollet-le-Duc thought "it would be appropriate to replace the ugly openings with windows in harmony with the general style of the facades, if only to facilitate the solution of this difficult problem."[67] Underlying their proposal is the idea that a harmony or unity of style should permeate the edifice, even if this meant inventing new forms. Their position, which exactly parallels contemporary practice for restoring the interiors of historical châteaux, was formulated even more pointedly by Viollet-le-Duc in a notorious article "On Restoration" published in 1866, just two years after the scaffolding had been removed from Notre-Dame: "The term restoration and the thing it-

self are both modern," he wrote; "to restore a building is not to preserve it, to repair it, or rebuild it; it is to reinstate it in a condition of completeness that could never have existed at any given time."[68]

Viollet-le-Duc's insistence on a "condition of completeness that could never have existed" is why visitors to Notre-Dame today will note that four bays—one in the nave, two in the transept, and one in the choir—do not match the rest of the church, for these sections have four levels rather than three. In the course of archaeological excavations at Notre-Dame, Viollet-le-Duc discovered that some parts of the gallery level of the nave had been aerated with round openings that looked a bit like spoked wheels. Wanting to incorporate this archaeological find into his restoration, Viollet-le-Duc sacrificed the cathedral's interior regularity to place a sample of this four-story elevation in each of the building's parts. He also altered the facts by transforming the openings into small rose windows, not simply blind openings in the gallery wall. "Here the restorer," remarks Bruno Foucart, "is betrayed by an archaeological intoxication and a passion for returning to origins that causes the most firm resolutions to waver, and he introduces into the organism [of the building] a youthfulness that is dangerous because it cannot be assimilated."[69] Foucart's criticism is mild in contrast to what others have written about the liberties taken by Viollet-le-Duc at Notre-Dame. "Above all," intoned Achille Carlier in 1922, "when you look at the lateral elevation of Notre-Dame, think neither of the twelfth nor of the thirteenth centuries: think of Viollet-le-Duc and only Viollet-le-Duc. Think of the nineteenth century and only the nineteenth century. There is next to nothing of the Middle Ages in it."[70] Ironically, the enemies of Alexandre Lenoir had used virtually the same argument when railing against his methods at the Musée des Monuments français:

How can one dare to say that one conducts a simple restoration of ancient monuments when four-fifths of the work is done with new materials shaped and worked by contemporary craftsmen? I imagine hearing a fool say in a perfectly reasonable tone: "Gentlemen, do you see this old body to which I have added pectoral muscles, a neck and head, arms, legs, and feet, accessories and a plinth? There you have it, an antique statue!" No learned men would be fooled by such fibbing, for they would recognize in both of these instances the imitation of ancient models of architecture and sculpture. Yet this is what happens at the Petits-Augustins, and it is called restoration.[71]

Viollet-le-Duc and his followers tried to avoid the pitfalls of Lenoir's projective fantasy by undertaking a systematic ar-

chaeological study of the monuments in their charge before attempting to restore them. That Viollet-le-Duc was himself targeted by critics for inventing new monuments underscores the peculiar tensions surrounding the nineteenth century's rediscovery of the Middle Ages. What separates the historicism of Viollet-le-Duc and his contemporaries from our grappling with it today is their optimistic belief in an ability to fully recapture the past, to "get the facts right" in both textual narratives and physical reconstructions.

Paradoxically, advocates on both sides of the debate—whether restorers like Lenoir and Viollet-le-Duc or purists like Deseine and Carlier—appeal to an idea of the gothic that clings mysteriously to the very material of its monuments. For all of them, to alter that material disturbs in some fundamental way the spirit of history that lives within the stone. One side might try to make that spirit more visible and cause the other side to decry its death. The point is that the old stones of the Middle Ages, lacking the written histories so often attached to monuments of classical antiquity, remained sites of historical ruminations whose past must always be invented, and thus always reflect the present. In 1914 the sculptor Auguste Rodin wrote: "the cathedral is a synthesis of the nation. . . . Rocks, forests, gardens, sunlight of the North, all of those are condensed in this giant body; all of our France is in the cathedrals."[72] Rodin's nationalist reading of the Gothic cathedral conveniently ignores the great German examples like Cologne, but his words make perfect sense under the specter of the First World War, when so many French Gothic cathedrals would be damaged or destroyed by German artillery. However time-bound and shortsighted Rodin's comments seem today, it is clear that his wonder before those great Gothic structures was not so far from what Michelet experienced in the galleries of the Musée des Monuments français: "What was I looking for? I don't know: probably life, first of all, and the genius of former times."

CHAPTER 5

An Aesthetics of Confrontation

The classic has imbibed in beautiful nature: he touches, excites and satisfies both heart and mind at the same time. The more he studies nature, the more beauties he discovers in it. He leaves it reluctantly and returns to it with pleasure. The romantic, quite to the contrary, has some inexplicable and unnatural urge that shocks at first glance and disgusts upon closer examination. The author in delirium needlessly combines dreadful scenes, spills blood, rips out entrails, paints despair and agony. Just as needlessly he achieves partial effects amidst a thousand extravagances, and he incites people to marvel at things they don't understand. Posterity will not admit works like this; contemporaries of good faith will tire of them, and they are already doing so.

—Auguste Chauvin[1]

CHAUVIN'S THUMBNAIL SKETCH of two clashing tendencies in French art at the Salon of 1824 is overly schematic, but it does echo a popular understanding of the rupture that seemed to resonate throughout Parisian culture at the time. A generation of young men and women schooled during the Empire began to challenge openly the direction of both art and politics plotted by the Bourbon Restoration, in particular the ever more conservative tenor of the official line after the assassination of the duc de Berry in February 1820. Pressed by the emotional heat of the moment, Louis XVIII heeded the advice of Ultraroyalists, such as the comte d'Artois, to dissolve the cabinet and to form a new, more conservative government under the leadership of the comte de Villèle.

Villèle moved quickly to impose strict censorship on the press and, in an effort to stamp out the glowing embers of republican or imperial sympathies amongst the young, he organized a purge of the university. Beginning in November of 1820 with the cancellation of Victor Cousin's lectures on philosophy at the Sorbonne, and culminating in 1822 with the closure of the elite École Normale, the government exerted

an unrelenting pressure to weed out professors thought likely to corrupt the political thinking of their students. In the words of Monseigneur Frayssinous, who was appointed grand master of the University in 1822, "he who had the misfortune to live an unreligious life and who was not devoted to the royal family should understand that he lacked what was required in a worthy teacher of the young."[2] Such precepts were not universally accepted. The period 1820–1822 was marked by a spate of student protests: in June of 1820, sparked by a debate over electoral reform that would reward the rich with double representation; in August of 1820, as part of an abortive conspiracy to overthrow the government. Student demonstrations at Grenoble in 1821 forced closure of its law school, and similar disruptions at the Faculté de Médecine of Paris in 1822 provoked the suspension of classes and a complete purge of the faculty. Finally, and most dramatic, the prestigious École Normale was closed in response to political protests by its student body. To many people, French youth—and especially Parisian youth—seemed permanently mobilized in a kind of inchoate conspiracy against the established order.

162

In Chauvin's summary, the classic is able to satisfy "both heart and mind" and savors the pleasures of beauty, while the romantic, victim of a "delirium" produced by "some inexplicable and unnatural urge," appeals to people who "marvel at things they don't understand." When Chauvin characterizes romantic as an extreme position of effect and naïveté, he aligns it with received ideas about youthful exuberance. Chauvin felt the picture best exemplifying the romantic at the 1824 Salon was Eugène Delacroix's *Massacres at Chios* (Fig. 78), and he worried about its effect upon young painters:

Indeed, one does not know which to reproach more, the appalling naïveté of all these slaughters, or the even more barbaric manner with which M. Delacroix has depicted them, with no regard for proportions, drawing, or the most accepted social conventions of art. If, as is rumored, a few young painters, seduced by a kind of audacious brushwork, stand in admiration before this butchery, I would say to them frankly: friendship leads you astray.[3]

What was it about Delacroix's picture that seemed so threatening? First of all, Delacroix painted the *Massacres at Chios* in response to an especially gruesome event. In April 1822 the Greek island of Chios was invaded by a Turkish army that methodically sacked or burned property, and slaughtered or sold into slavery its inhabitants over a period of two months. "The largest murder scene in the nineteenth century," is how one writer of the time described the disaster.[4] Lurid tales of rapes, murders, and pillage filled the pages of French newspapers sympathetic to the Greek cause. Delacroix surely followed such reports, and he expected his viewers to have done the same: the entry for his picture in the catalogue of the 1824 Salon includes the injunction to "see the various accounts and newspapers of the time."[5]

Delacroix entertained the idea of making a picture about the agony of Chios as early as May 1823.[6] However, it was not until the following January, after meeting a Frenchman named Olivier Voutier, who had served with the Greek army and recently published his memoirs about the experience, that Delacroix noted in his journal: "Thus, strictly speaking, it is today, Monday the 12th, that I start my picture."[7] We can be fairly certain that Delacroix had read Voutier's book, including the passage where a survivor of Chios reports that

"nothing had produced a more painful impression on his soul than the sight of a young woman's body whose withered breasts were grasped by the eager hands of an infant," a specific grouping that figures prominently in the right foreground of Delacroix's finished painting.[8]

Yet Delacroix did not imagine his picture to be the illustration of any single event recounted in the newspapers, for he was keenly aware of the expressive difference between images and words. "The writer says almost everything in order to be understood," he had written in October of 1822; "in painting, it is established like a mysterious bridge between the spirit of the characters and that of the viewer."[9] Later, just two weeks after starting work on the *Massacres at Chios*, Delacroix again remarked on the special advantages of pictures over language: "I recognize exactly in Madame de Staël the development of my thinking about painting. This art, along with music, *are both above thought*; from that point, by way of vagueness, comes their superiority over literature."[10] Although Delacroix was moved by accounts culled from newspapers about the slaughter at Chios, he was not interested in relating them anecdotally. Rather, he wanted his work to erect a "mysterious bridge" between viewers in Paris and the unfortunate victims so far away. His pictorial ambition was to generate a personal and directly affective viewing experience from the cold facts of the distant tragedy.[11]

This is a risky venture that can easily go awry. It is no surprise that hostile critics imagined the picture's history exactly backwards. "With all the best will in the world, I can't admire M. Delacroix and his *Massacre at Chios*," wrote Stendhal; "this work always makes me think of a picture originally intended to represent a plague, which the artist then turned into a Massacre at Chios after reading the newspaper reports. . . . A Massacre *must* have an executioner and a victim."[12] Stendhal objected to the picture's lack of a narrative thread that its title seems to require. His opinion was echoed by many other reviewers. "Here one finds only a confused collection of figures," lamented the conservative critic Charles Landon.[13] "Especially in dramatic scenes of poetry or painting, a leading idea should furnish the unique substructure," remarked another writer; "but, in the composition of M. Delacroix, I look in vain for this single idea, for I see

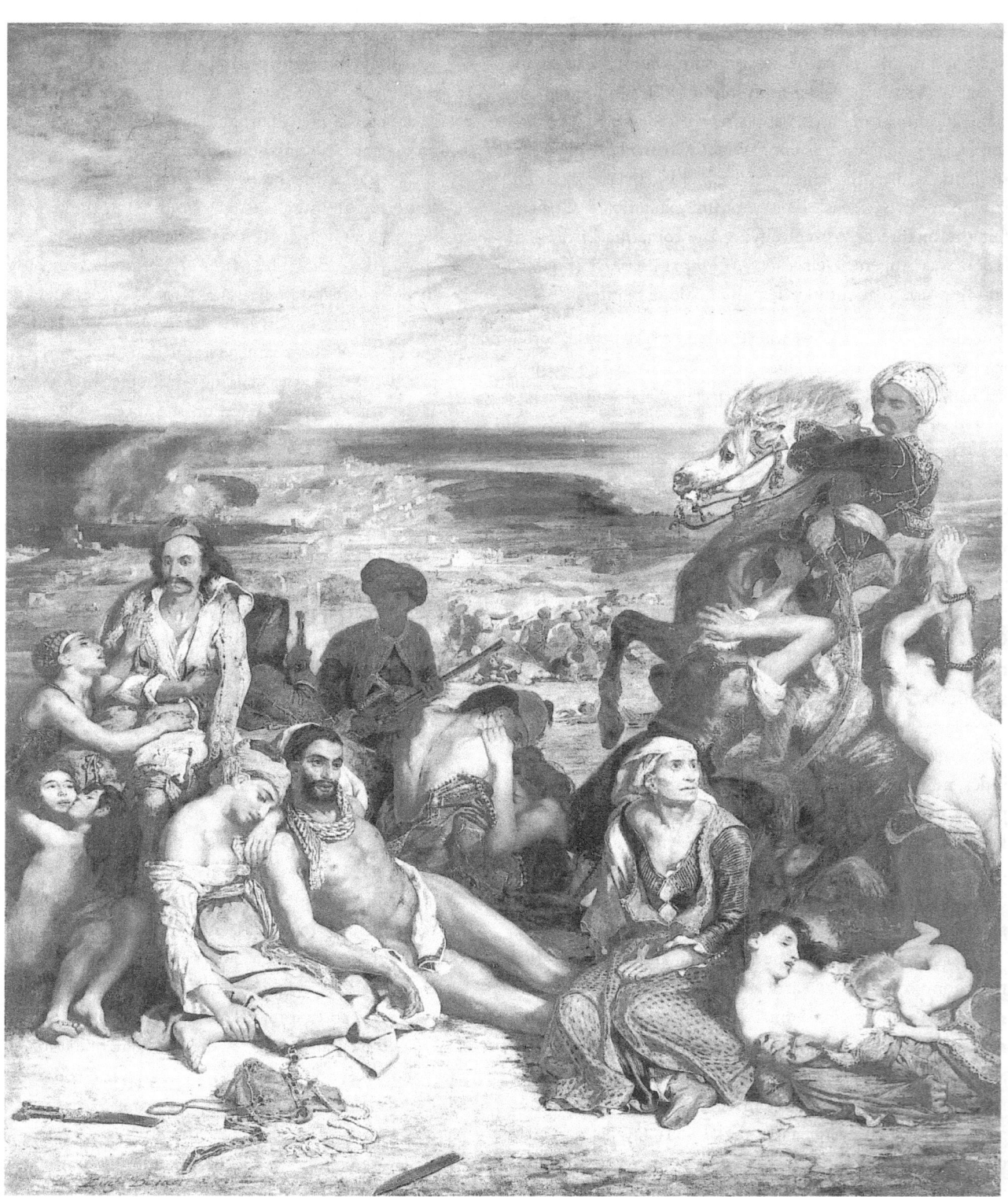

only a crowd of Greeks scattered about in confusion, who wait for slavery or death from only two Turks, stationed at each side, who proceed to enchaine or to massacre them."[14]

In fact, the picture is structured quite oddly. A foreground screen of large figures offers a range of ages and degrees of suffering: from the wounded and dying nude man at left center to the dead mother in the lower right; from the imploring children at the far left to the resigned old woman in the right center; from the seemingly lifeless male below the center—seen from the back and partially lost in shadow—to the writhing female nude bound and dragged by the Turkish horseman at the right edge. But the middle of the picture, where one might expect to find a visual integration of these disparate moments, offers no such closure. Rather, the screen opens to reveal a battlefield skirmish at some distance with figures drawn much smaller than those close at hand. Beyond them unfolds only an empty landscape. The aggressors, as one critic noted, seem too few in number to wreak such havoc, while their shadowy, profile presence in the image does little to justify "the weakness of the Greeks, who wait for death benignly and without hope."[15] Stendhal wanted to see "a fanatical Turk, as handsome as M. Girodet's, as they sacrifice divinely beautiful Greek women and threaten the aged father before he falls after his daughters."[16] Another writer suggested that Delacroix should have painted "a group of Greeks, wretched survivors of the carnage, struggling bravely against their larger enemy, and avenging the loss of their loved ones by inflicting countless casualties. This scene, if rendered well, would have had a very powerful effect."[17]

Delacroix's refusal to provide an organizing storyline to contextualize the *Massacres at Chios* meant that the picture's stark imagery of violence and physical suffering struck viewers as all the more shocking and gratuitous. "It must be recognized that one finds in it neither order, nor beautiful nature, nor a fine choice of forms; rather, everything is hid-

FIGURE 78. Eugène Delacroix, *The Massacres at Chios*, 1824. Oil on canvas. Paris, Musée du Louvre, inv. INV3823 (419 × 354 cm). Photo: © RMN/Art Resource, NY/© Hervé Lewandowski.

eous and the expression is pushed to the most repulsive level," remarked one critic.[18] Another, more disposed to liking the painting, argued that "if there is no order in his picture, there is a completely willful disorder. . . . All of that relates to a search for the terrible. This is another kind of classicism, whose models would be Shakespeare and Dante rather than Virgil and Racine."[19] The distinction is important, not only because it recasts Chauvin's sketch of the gulf between classics and romantics cited at the head of this chapter, but also because it helps us to see why Delacroix's work emerged as archetype for romantic painting at the time.[20] Partisans of traditional notions of beauty and decorum decried the picture's departure from those norms, while Delacroix's defenders claimed such departures comprised its virtue:

It would be difficult to say under what master he studied, but it is clear that he did not want to follow the method of any master of our school. Thus, he is accused of being a romantic, because today that word is used in painting, much as it has been used for some time in literature, yet without being able to define it precisely. It seems to me that the word is applied to those who have left the beaten path in order to achieve their goal by some undiscovered route that their audacity has forced them to discover. If this is so, instead of using it as a term of proscription, wouldn't it be better to applaud their efforts, especially when they are successful?[21]

The *Massacres at Chios* was a catalyst that organized the terms of an aesthetic battle between two competing schools of thought: on one hand, the stalwarts of tradition, reason, and decorum identified as classicists; on the other, the experimenters with improvisation, passion, and excess called romantics. It was, as Elisabeth Fraser has shown, due to a desire to demonstrate mastery of this battle that the government bought Delacroix's picture well before the Salon closed.[22]

Some years later, Delacroix admitted that *Massacres at Chios* had been a milestone in his career, the point where "I started to become for the school an object of antipathy and a kind of scarecrow."[23] Also in hindsight, but from the other side of the debate, Jean-Auguste-Dominique Ingres remembered the Salon of 1824 quite differently:

I had shown with pleasure only one of my works, the *Vow of Louis XIII*. . . . When comparing it to the paintings of our moderns who are the fever and epilepsy of art, to the *Massacre at Chios*, for example, I was happy to have respected the human form instead of dismembering my characters, of making them walk on their heads, or of changing the Holy Virgin and her good angels into Iroquois. I remained fiercely inflexible in my principles, which are true, in order to stop the invasion of the Barbarians.[24]

That Ingres pitched his *Vow of Louis XIII* (Fig. 79) as the last line of defense against the barbarians of "fever and epilepsy" unleashed by Delacroix is rather odd, because his picture stands far from the principles of truth he claims to cherish. Ingres admitted as much in a letter written shortly after receiving the commission to paint the altarpiece for the cathedral of his hometown of Montauban, in the southwest of France: "In my view, the vow of this king seems to be a second subject that can distract from the interest and unity of the main one, namely the Assumption of the Virgin," he wrote to the Prefect.

The first could, by itself, provide the material for an important picture. One consequence of my continuous study of Italian art, where these types of anachronistic subjects abound, is that I am always shocked by their unseemliness, especially when placed in a large temple where they should bring to mind only one deity.[25]

What bothered Ingres is that the commission asked him to violate the cardinal unities of time and space crucial to classical aesthetics since Aristotle.

Ingres was supposed to paint an image in which Louis XIII placed France under the protection of the Virgin Mary, an event of 1638 that fulfilled a vow made by the king in 1636, when asking for the Virgin's protection during a period of political and religious strife. Louis XIII also decreed that his gesture of submission to the Virgin should be commemorated yearly throughout France on the Feast of the Assumption. According to the original terms of the commission, the picture was to include a portrait of Louis XIII in 1638 and the Virgin being carried to heaven. Ingres's letter demonstrates his reluctance to elide this break in historical time and to fuse in a single image the ungainly mix of historical and religious genres. The painter apparently lodged his complaint about the commission before sufficiently weighing the reasons for why such a subject was important to the

Bourbon government in 1821. Louis XIII had prevailed as king in the face of religious and civil strife not unlike the challenges facing Louis XVIII, a point often made by historians of the Bourbon Restoration. "The reign of Louis XIII emerged, after the great commotion of the religious wars, almost into the same conditions where we ourselves are, in the wake of the double upheaval caused by the Revolution and Empire," wrote Anaïs de Raucou Bazin from the hindsight of 1840.[26] During the Revolution, the tradition of celebrating the vow of Louis XIII on the Feast of the Assumption had been scrapped but, as a sign of the event's importance to the restored Bourbons, the practice was reinstated shortly after Louis XVIII assumed power. Moreover, Louis XIII's gesture of placing his rule under the aegis of the Virgin was a strong precedent that linked Bourbon rule to the Catholic Church, a link that was the center of much debate in the months following the assassination of the duc de Berry and the rise of the Ultra-royalist faction. The subject of Ingres's commission for the cathedral at Montauban would articulate Bourbon claims of sovereignty as the union of throne and altar. That concept was the cornerstone of Ultra-royalist political thinking. Ingres's criticism of the commission suggests he did not grasp immediately its profound political significance.

About a month later, and without much warning, Ingres reports that "a few days after I had sent the letter to the Prefect, my thinking about the structure of the composition, some advice, and a more considered understanding of the *Vow of Louis XIII* finally convinced me to take it up."[27] We shall probably never know whose advice brought Ingres to a more "considered understanding" of the subject, but he was now fully committed to making the picture. He also offered a plan to fine-tune its rhetoric. Rather than a portrait of Louis XIII with the Virgin's ascent into heaven, Ingres proposed to paint the king partially turned away from the viewer, kneeling before an image of Mary and Jesus and offering his crown and scepter to them. This adjustment blurs the picture's fractured time frame, for it now reads as a reenactment of the king's dedication of 1638—a point underscored by the dated placard held by two little angels. The change also clarified the work's political message, because Louis XIII is vividly positioned as the linchpin between earthly and heavenly

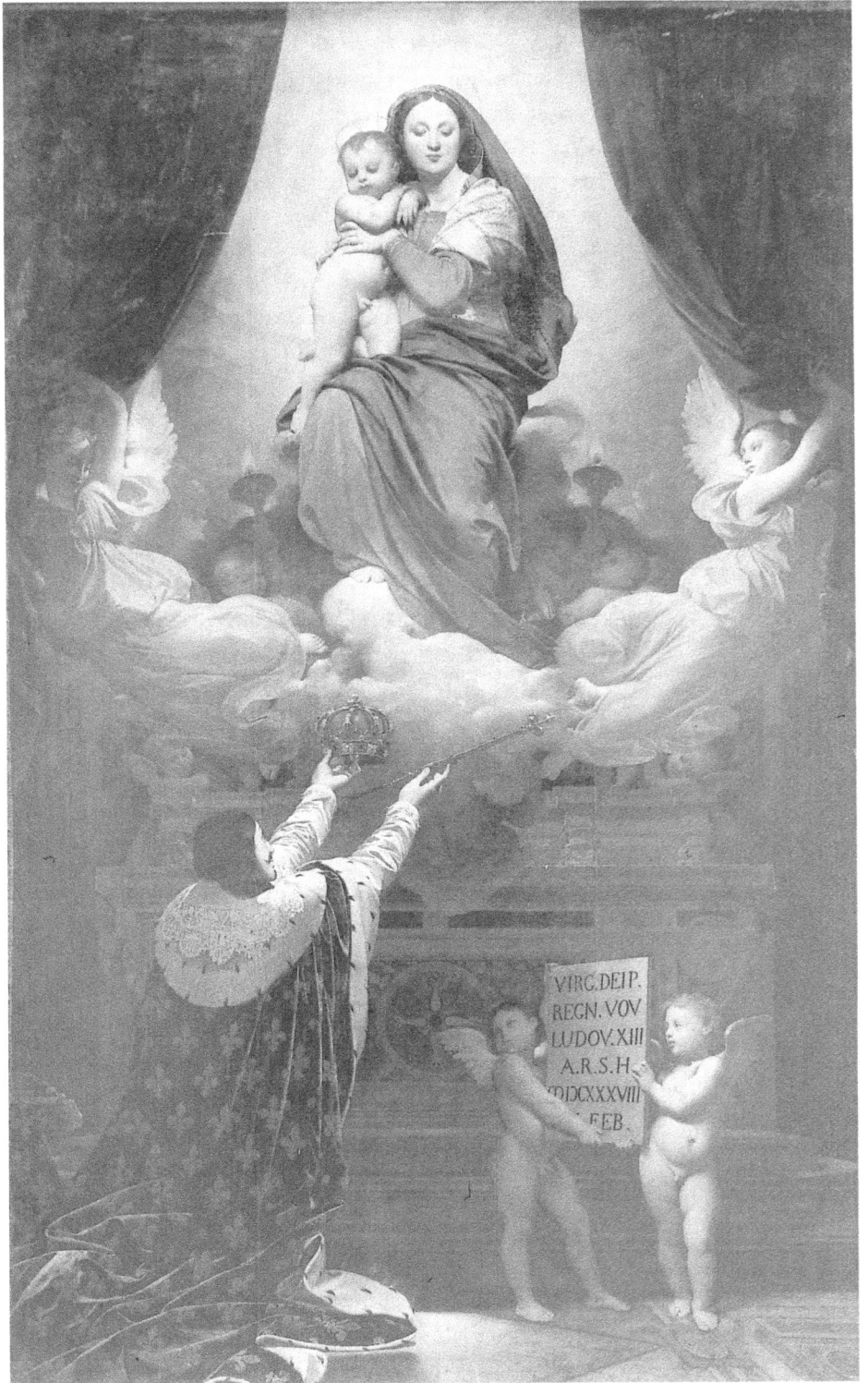

FIGURE 79. Jean-Auguste-Dominique
Ingres, *The Vow of Louis XIII*, 1824. Oil on
canvas. Montauban, Cathédrale Notre-
Dame (421 × 262 cm). Photo: © RMN/
Art Resource, NY.

power. The symbols of his rule—the proffered crown and scepter—make visible the alliance of throne and altar upon which Bourbon Ultra-royalists of 1821 staked their claim to rule France.

Ingres's strengthening of the picture's authoritarian politics was effected by directly invoking—some would say plagiarizing—the aesthetic authority of Raphael. Stendhal's first reaction to the *Vow of Louis XIII* was that it "is a very dry piece of work and, what is more, a pastiche of the old Italian painters," while another critic saw in it "a Virgin completely lifted from Raphael, and a pretty bad copy besides."[28] Ingres, for his part, freely admitted that all of his work (not only this picture) was deeply indebted to the art of Raphael, a point he had made in a letter written in April 1821:

Nevertheless, I want very much for people to know that for quite some time my works recognize no law other than that of the ancients, meaning the great masters who flourished in that renowned century where Raphael laid down the eternal and unquestionable limits of the sublime in art. I believe to have shown with my works that my only ambition is to resemble these predecessors, and to continue art by taking up where they have left off. Thus, I am a *custodian* of good doctrines, not an *innovator*.[29]

He repeated the idea shortly after his *Vow of Louis XIII* was hung in the Louvre at the Salon of 1824:

I cannot describe the flattering and respectful welcome that I am receiving here, nor the place that is ascribed to me. True believers say that this picture, which is completely Italian, has arrived by good fortune to stop bad taste. The name of Raphael (however unworthy I might be) is compared to mine. It is said that I, being full of his spirit, am inspired by him without copying anything.[30]

Ingres's insistence that "true believers" greeted his picture as a check on bad taste, and that they cheered his deference to Raphael, must be read alongside the painter's self-avowed conservatism as his response to critics who saw only servile imitation rather than inspiration. Moreover, Ingres conveniently overlooked the possibility that "true believers" were only peripherally concerned with the ravages of bad taste. It was no accident that his *Vow of Louis XIII* was hung in a place of honor in the most prestigious gallery of the Salon (see

Fig. 82), that the Ultra minister Villèle tried to buy the picture from Montauban so that it might stay in Paris, and that Ingres was nominated for membership in the Legion of Honor by two of the most influential Ultra-royalists in the court of Charles X. Although Ingres preferred to cloak the favorable reception of his picture in the terms of an aesthetic debate, he must have realized that Ultra-royalist politics affected its official acclaim as much as the peculiarities of its style.

Taken as a pair, Delacroix's *Massacres at Chios* and Ingres's *Vow of Louis XIII* defined the extreme terms of what could be expected from French painters in 1824: invention, material improvisation, and visual idiosyncrasy keyed to a theme of political struggle in the one; erudition, technical competency, and emulation of tradition to bolster conservative politics in the other. Yet most artists tended to work in the middle ground staked out by these two extremes, and critics at the Salon invariably wrote with great enthusiasm about works able to effect a compromise or hybrid between those poles. The 1820s are often characterized as fraught by running skirmishes between romantics and classics along the lines sketched by Chauvin at the head of this chapter. The art world of Paris in 1824 was actually far more complex, and gave rise to many works that do not fit Chauvin's neat binary.

One example, much discussed in 1824, is François-Joseph Heim's *Destruction of Jerusalem by the Romans* (Fig. 80). The subject, inspired by the *Histoire des Juifs* of Flavius Josephus, demonstrates a fascination with terribilità similar in many ways to Delacroix's *Massacres at Chios*. Foot soldiers and cavalrymen of the Roman army ravage the city and citizens of Jerusalem with a fury of violence and cruelty. Like Delacroix, Heim foregrounds the victimization of women and children. But here, unlike the resignation of Delacroix's Greeks, a muscular man struggles against horse and rider, and he braves the blows of a battle-axe to save the woman from a certain death. To the left, a young man pleads for his life before an armed Roman, while an older woman (perhaps his mother) claws and bites the aggressor in an attempt to stave off his hand. Behind this group, smoke from a burning temple obscures much of the combat, but we see that another soldier has grasped a woman by the hair and is about to strike her with his spear. At the right, partially screened

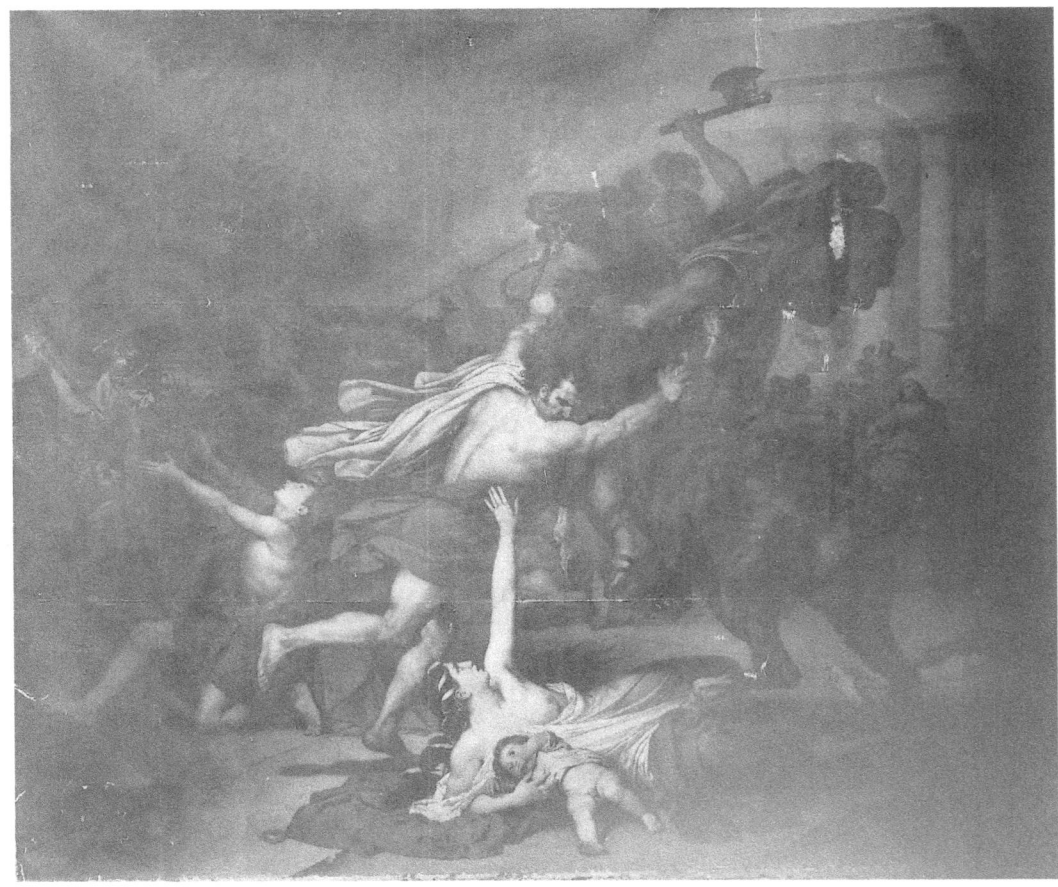

FIGURE 80.   François-Joseph Heim, *The Destruction of Jerusalem by the Romans*, 1824. Oil on canvas. Paris, Musée du Louvre, inv. INV5305 (392 × 460 cm). Photo: © RMN/ Art Resource, NY.

by the marauding central horseman, yet other crimes are visible, while a corpse—half out of the picture at the far right edge—reminds us of horrors left unstated in this scene of graphic violence and death.

Heim's picture is a vivid instance of works at the Salon of 1824 that elided the categories of classic and romantic in several ways. Although the subject was taken from the annals of the Roman empire, the picture's drama was too extreme for the classic camp. Heim's bright colors were much commented upon in the press, as was his tendency to orchestrate areas of light and shadow to maximize visual contrasts between figures and ground. "Perhaps he has also thrown too much light on the foreground," remarked one critic; "combined with the broken and clashing lines of the whole picture, this tires the eye. Many things still flicker there."[31] But if Heim eschewed the restrained color and penetrating light of contemporary classics like Ingres (Fig. 79), he also eschewed Delacroix's fluidity of line and plasticity of space (Fig. 78). Rather, as our critic went on to say, "the principal scene is not at all linked to the others, neither by dramatic interest nor by the lights and shadows; then, too, the main figures form a triangle, which is not terribly pleasing to see."[32] This last point calls attention to Heim's reliance—like many of his colleagues—upon shopworn academic devices such as compositional triangles to plot images of extreme expression or temperament. Where a painter like Delacroix, who was largely self-taught and inclined to improvise, rejected such formulas, Heim opted to stay within the parameters of his academic training, even when trying to raise the emotional temperature of his imagery.

Heim exemplifies the peculiar moment of painting in 1820s Paris when artists, trained by the generation of Jacques-Louis David during the First Empire (Heim had been a student of François-André Vincent from 1803 to 1807), reached artistic maturity. Filled with ambitions to rival the reputations of their teachers, but lacking the state patronage that had driven the agenda for all the arts under Napoléon, painters like Heim, Ary Scheffer (Fig. 112), Joseph-Nicolas Robert-Fleury (Fig. 87), and Xavier Sigalon (Fig. 81) produced works of a sometimes shocking impact without renouncing the formal conventions of the Academy. Later

generations of historians have tended to dismiss such pictures as merely weak hybrids between the strong personalities of Delacroix and Ingres. Yet simply to disparage these painters ignores both the huge reputations they enjoyed at the time, along with the particular conditions of the moment when emotional force displaced historical import as the principal term for the critical appraisal of pictures. Consider one of the most-discussed works at the 1824 Salon: Xavier Sigalon's *Locusta trying the Poison destined for Britannicus upon a Young Slave* (Fig. 81), inspired by Racine's *Britannicus* of 1669. Narcissus, the depraved and vicious counselor of Nero, is seated in a moonlit cave swarming with snakes. He has come to the lair of Locusta, renowned for her powerful poisons, to take

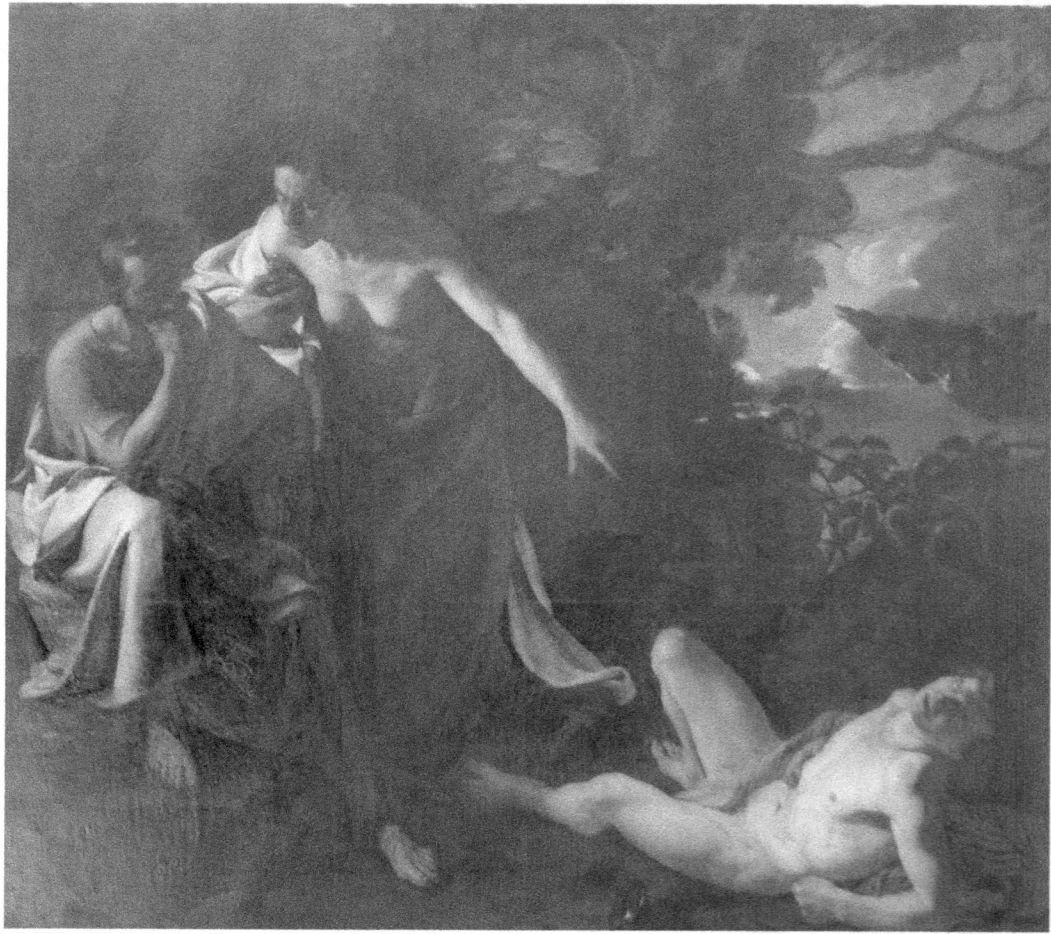

FIGURE 81. Xavier Sigalon, *Locusta trying the Poison destined for Britannicus upon a Young Slave*, 1824. Oil on canvas. Nîmes, Musée des Beaux-Arts, inv. IP 163 (220 × 290 cm). Photo: Courtesy of the Musée des Beaux-Arts, Nîmes.

counterpoint to the fair-skinned nude splayed across the king's bed. Anchoring this triad of attention is a shocking, nearly comic juxtaposition: a woman, nude from the waist up, looks out from behind the foreground victim; her face is paired with a huge elephant's head that also seems to look at us, but is actually part of the bed itself.

In many ways *Sardanapalus* asked too much of its audience all at once, a theme that runs through most of the critical commentary in 1827. "It is not enough to dazzle the eyes," complained Louis Vitet, "it is still necessary . . . that the intellect be able to understand that by which the eyes are amused."[45] Even Agustin Jal, who usually supported Delacroix, felt the painter had gone too far:

[he] has headed off in the direction of passion, of sentiment; unfortunately, in the delirium of his creation, he has been swept beyond all limits. . . . He wanted to compose disorder, yet he has forgotten that disorder itself has a logic; he wanted to frighten us with a spectacle of the voluptuous barbarisms that fill the eyes of Sardanapalus before closing forever, but reason cannot disentangle the chaos that surrounds and imprisons his idea. The destruction of so many living creatures on the funeral pyre of the most debased tyrant was a nasty horror. M. Delacroix was aware of this, but his hand let him down and the betrayal is complete. . . . Not only do the accumulated faults of this work carry the day over its beauties, but the beauties are not beautiful. Composition, style, drawing, coloring: I don't want to defend any of them.[46]

Delacroix recognized that his picture pushed hard on the usual viewing habits of his public. On 8 February 1828, the day *Sardanapalus* went on public view (it was sent late to the Salon and not installed until the end of January), he wrote to his friend Soulier that, upon first entering the gallery, "I was afflicted by a terrible sensation when arriving in front of it; I would hope the good public does not have eyes like mine for judging my masterpiece."[47] At least one influential member of the viewing public recognized the merits of Delacroix's picture, which a letter written by Victor Hugo in early April 1829 to his friend Victor Pavie makes clear:

Concerning great painters, I beg you not to believe, based on the strength of a few stupid pamphleteers—at whose head I place *The Globe* without hesitating—that Delacroix has declined. His *Sardan-*

apalus is a magnificent thing, and so huge that it escapes those who see small. Moreover, this beautiful work, as with many large and strong works, has had no success at all with the bourgeois of Paris: *the catcalls of fools are the fanfares of glory*. The one thing I regret is that he has not set the pyre on fire: this gorgeous scene would have been even more so if it had a basket of fire for its base.[48]

It may be unremarkable that Victor Hugo, arguably the leading figure of literary Romanticism, admired Delacroix's picture. But Hugo's enthusiastic support and scorn for the chorus of critical reprobation is more than incidental, for it alludes to an important convergence of the two men's thinking during the months that Delacroix worked on his canvas—a convergence that emerges from a close look at the picture's chronology.

Delacroix was billed on 12 July 1827 for the canvas and stretcher that would become *Sardanapalus*.[49] However, his correspondence with Madame Haro, from whom he ordered the pigments used for the picture, suggests that he began working in earnest only about the first of November.[50] The adjusted time frame is important, because it was during the month of October that Hugo wrote the preface to his play *Cromwell* that was destined to become a notorious manifesto of Romanticism. In a letter of 24 September to Victor Pavie, Hugo reports that *Cromwell* would be ready for printing in two weeks, because "all that remains for me to write is the preface and a few notes."[51] A few lines earlier in the same letter Hugo congratulates Pavie for two articles recently published, and he reports that "Delacroix is especially delighted and proud of the beautiful passage that concerns him. He has asked me to thank you." The comment proves that Hugo and Delacroix were speaking during the weeks when the former was writing the *Cromwell* preface and the latter was painting *Sardanapalus*. It also compels us to ask: what can we learn about the picture and its reception by reading it through Hugo's text?

Hugo fired many salvos at the established order in the pages of his preface, but perhaps the most shocking to contemporaries was his insistence upon the modernity of the grotesque and its place in the aesthetic debates of 1827:

So, in this way, a principle unknown in antiquity—a new type—is introduced into poetry and, just as a term added to a being modifies the entire being, a new form develops in art. The type is the grotesque, and the form is comedy. We must insist on this point, because we have just pointed out the characteristic feature, the fundamental difference, that separates, to our mind, modern art from ancient art, contemporary form from dead form, or—to use words that are less precise but more credible—*romantic* literature from *classic* literature.[52]

The general point of Hugo's essay was "to show that modern genius—so complex, so varied in its forms, and so inexhaustible in its creations—was born of the fertile union of grotesque and sublime types, and for that reason is completely unlike the uniform simplicity of ancient genius."[53] Hugo did not limit himself to examples from literature: when citing role models from the visual arts he mentions Murillo, Veronese, and Michelangelo—three artists also deeply admired by Delacroix.[54] Hugo's insistence on an interlocking relationship between the grotesque and the sublime in modern art dovetails exactly with the unsettling juxtaposition of those elements in Delacroix's *Death of Sardanapalus*, where the most beautiful of the king's treasures are systematically destroyed in deference to his unflinching resolve and under his impassive gaze.

The second aim of Hugo's preface was to attack the sacrosanct unities of time and place in the dramatic arts. He claims that crossing "the unity of time with the unity of place like the bars of a cage and, in the name of Aristotle, to fit in there all the events, peoples, and faces that in reality providence so expansively unrolls, mutilates both men and things, and makes history grimace!"[55] Hugo argues instead for a unity of action "which marks the dramatic point of view; taken by itself, it excludes the other two. . . . The unity of the whole [ensemble] is the theater's law of perspective."[56] By emphasizing the unity of theatrical action [ensemble] at the expense of a stable time frame or geographic place, Hugo promotes a form of representation specific to the dramatic arts. His larger point was even more radical:

Let's take a hammer to theories, poetics, and systems. Let's toss out this old plaster hiding the facade of art! There are neither rules nor models; or, better yet, there are no rules other than the general laws of nature that hover over all of art, or the special laws for each composition that result from the conditions of existence proper to each subject.[57]

Delacroix designed *Sardanapalus* in a kindred spirit of anarchy, aiming to invent a visual form for his subject that would provide a powerfully unified effect with little or no regard for the expected rules of space, time, or narrative. His disregard for those rules was registered by the disparaging remarks of critics like Vitet and Jal cited above, and the broadside fired by Étienne Delécluze from the pages of the prestigious *Journal des Débats*:

The *Sardanapalus* of M. Delacroix has not found favor with the public nor with artists. One has tried in vain to bring out the witty ideas that the author had when composing his picture, but the viewer's intelligence has been unable to penetrate a subject in which all the elements are isolated, where the eye cannot disentangle itself from the confusion of lines and colors, and where the first principles of art seem to have been violated on purpose. The *Sardanapalus* is a painterly error.[58]

Delécluze's final phrase echoes the words Delacroix would hear from the Minister of Fine Arts: his picture is an error and he must change course if he expects any further commissions from the Restoration government.

Hugo's preface to *Cromwell* set the critical terms of Romanticism as an aesthetic confrontation with tradition and the status quo, a position likely to raise the suspicions of the increasingly conservative Bourbon government under Charles X. Alongside this aesthetic recalibration, Hugo's politics were also in flux, as he shifted from generally supporting the Restoration to a more critical stance that included a growing admiration for the figure of Napoléon. In February of 1827 Hugo wrote "À la colonne de la place Vendôme" (see Chapter Three), and in December 1828 he wrote "Lui," a poem celebrating the genius of Napoléon and the tragedy of his death in exile. The critical alignment of Delacroix's *Sardanapalus* with the anti-establishment artistic program outlined by Hugo's preface, coupled with the praise garnered by the picture from Hugo's circle of friends, marked Delacroix—within the politically charged public space of the Parisian art world—as an emerging opponent of the Bourbon regime. Small wonder that the Minister of Fine Arts advised the painter to change course if he hoped to enjoy the government's favor.

Sardanapalus mapped the common ground between two giants of French Romanticism in 1827—Hugo the poet and Delacroix the painter—but it was not destined to be a lasting rapprochement. Perhaps it was Delacroix's lifelong admiration for classical literature that kept him from the inner circle of Hugo's cenacle on the rue Notre-Dame-des-Champs (see Chapter Six). Or, as Ernest Chesneau suggested long ago, perhaps there was nothing more to the strained and mutual disdain that developed between Hugo and Delacroix "than an equal and jealous pride, an equally prickly vanity, a sense of their own worth pushed to that stage of thin-skinned sensitivity that any bringing together, any comparison, any rivalry irritated each of them as a denial of justice."[59] Whatever the reasons, it was not Delacroix who emerged as Hugo's preferred painter but Louis Boulanger, to whom Hugo dedicated two poems in 1828 with the words "the author of this collection offers these two ballads as a sign of admiration, gratitude, and friendship."[60] Later, in May of 1828, Hugo wrote "Mazeppa"—a poem published in the collection *Les Orientales* of 1829—that was both dedicated to Boulanger and directly inspired by a picture shown at the same Salon where Delacroix's *Sardanapalus* had so challenged contemporary sensibilities.

Boulanger's *Mazeppa* (Fig. 84) shares many of the formal preoccupations of Delacroix's picture. Ivan Stepanovitch Mazeppa, a Ukrainian aristocrat, had actually lived in the mid-seventeenth century. It was his legendary punishment of being tied naked to a wild horse that was most familiar to nineteenth-century readers—a story greatly embellished and popularized by Lord Byron's epic poem of 1819. Byron invented the fiction that Mazeppa was punished by the husband of a woman seduced by the young hero. It was Byron who imagined Mazeppa's wild ride through forests patrolled by wolves, across raging streams, and running with a pack of wild horses until his own horse died of exhaustion. Especially after 1822, when a French translation was first published, Byron's "Mazeppa" was much discussed in Parisian literary circles. The poem tempted Delacroix for a moment in 1824, and Horace Vernet exhibited two small paintings of the theme at the Salon of 1827.[61] But far and away the most monumental and arresting rendering of the story was Boulanger's picture:

"Of the three *Mazeppas* now on view in the grand salon," remarked one critic in 1827, "we will be more than happy to say of M. Boulanger's that it reveals originality and energy."[62]

Enlisting a play of narrative and emotional contrasts very like those at the core of Delacroix's *Sardanapalus*, Boulanger depicted the moment just before the hapless hero begins his wild ride. Under the impassive eye of Count Palatin, whose honor Mazeppa supposedly compromised, the struggling and hysterical young man is lashed to a terrified horse. A pile of clothes in the lower right signals Mazeppa's indecorous stripping by the count's men. Their bulging muscles and grimly determined expressions emphasize the physical energy required to fasten their writhing victim to his rearing steed. Gradually the ropes will be drawn tight, the man standing to the right will whip the horse into a frenzy, and Mazeppa's crazed journey will commence. An overall darkness punctuated by the brightness of Mazeppa's body and the horse's streaming mane, the predominately diagonal arrangement of men and horse upward from the lower left corner, the complex criss-crossing of arms, legs, and glances all work to animate the image with a visual violence appropriate to the story and akin to that of *Sardanapalus*.

Boulanger's immediate friends were enthusiastic. Théophile Gautier remembered *Mazeppa* as "a great success . . . a hot-headed picture, full of daring and pride, superbly colored, with a very skillful brushwork—of the kind sought by Rubens and Titian—whose appearance dazzled eyes accustomed to the pale tones of the classic school."[63] Others, like Augustin Jal, challenged the artist's use of color and handling of paint, but were carried away by the picture's powerful effect:

The drawing generally needs more correction, but it has vigor; one or two heads in the left background recall the style of Géricault's *Raft of the Medusa*. The back of the slave in the middle of the canvas is strongly indicated, but not studied with enough subtlety. The figure of Mazeppa is done in a rather pallid tone; if it were more strongly colored, it would be more pleasing. The horse is not very well drawn, but I like it despite its faults. The local tones are of a colorist who will surely produce some remarkable things, provided he shakes off the systematic spirit to which he is now succumbed, out of a strong dislike for another, no less unreasonable system.[64]

FIGURE 84.   Louis Boulanger, *Mazeppa*,
1827. Oil on canvas. Rouen, Musée des
Beaux-Arts, inv. 835.3 (525 × 392 cm). Photo:
© RMN/Art Resource, NY/© Bulloz.

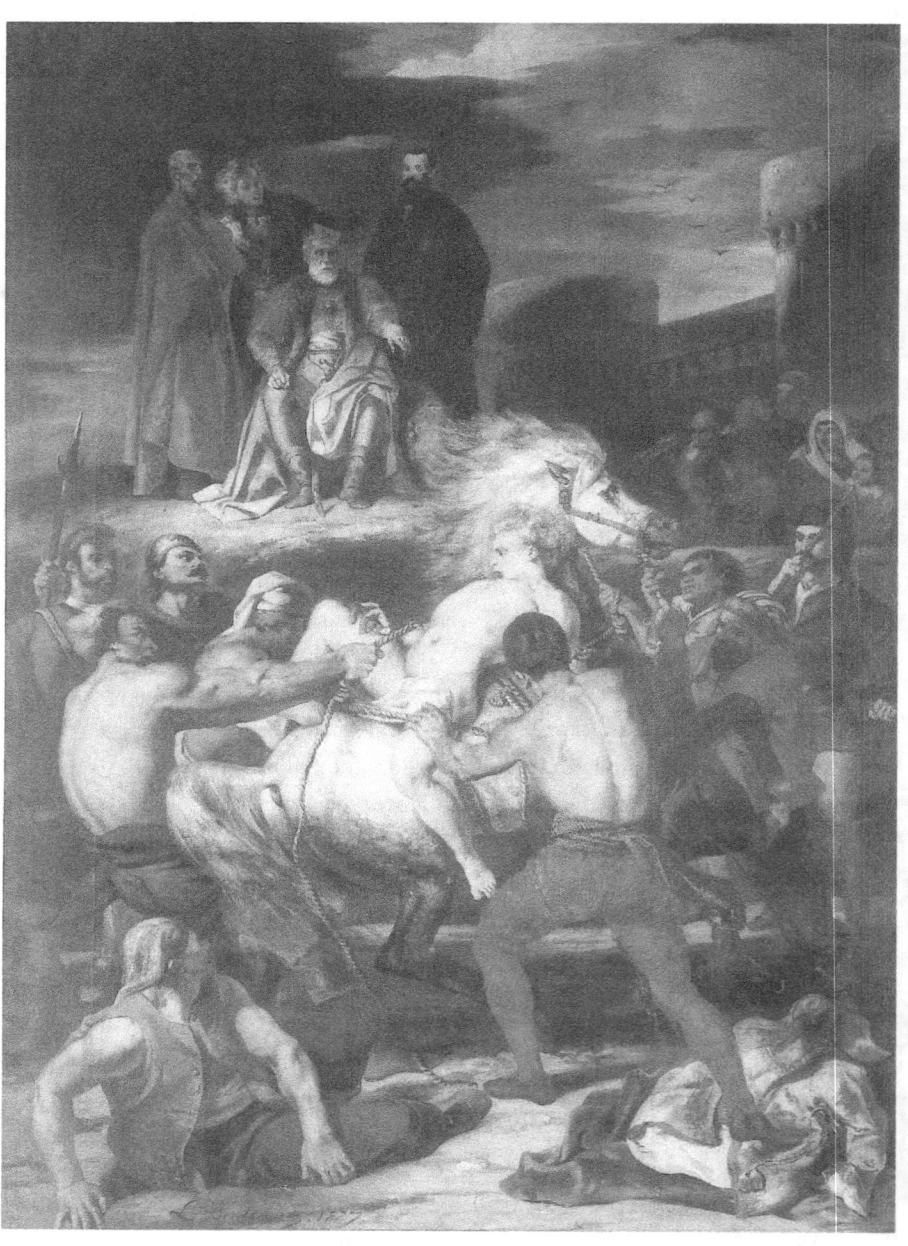

Jal's remark about shaking off a system was a veiled warning that Boulanger risked falling under the spell of certain partisans—namely the painters and poets around Hugo—who believed dramatic effect could and should eclipse received ideas of decorum and good taste. It was on these grounds that the most virulent critics chastened Boulanger: "This young artist," railed one staunch anti-Romantic, "needs a strict guide who will turn him away from the false route where he seems to want to follow the path of our so-called innovators. . . . He needs to be convinced that nasty and clashing tones are not at all *color*, and that romantic impropriety emphasizes impotence rather than genius."[65] Against such onslaughts, support for the visual experiments of Boulanger and Delacroix depended heavily upon the literary appeal of subjects that were patently transgressive. Both of their pictures accent the impassive infliction of physical violence and emotional abuse, so that the contrast set up between cause and effect is both grotesque and verges on the irrational.

Such extremes of expression were especially dear to the sensibilities of Victor Hugo and his circle. Hugo's poem "Mazeppa," for example, ignores the preparations painted by Boulanger to revel in details of shredded flesh, flowing blood, and a circling flock of vultures. The first part ends with the hero—newly chastened by his suffering—raised to a higher state of being:

Sa sauvage grandeur naîtra de son supplice.

Un jour, des vieux hetmans il ceindra la pelisse,

Grand à l'oeil ébloui;

Et quand il passera, ces peuples de la tente,

Prosternés, enverront la fanfare éclatante

Bondir autour de lui!

[His savage grandeur will spring from his ordeal.

One day he will don the mantle of the ancient Cossacks,

Huge to the bedazzled eye;

And when he passes, these tent-dwellers,

Prostrate, will send up a resounding fanfare

To swirl around him!][66]

In the poem's second part, Hugo transforms Mazeppa's physical chastisement into a metaphor for the artist's selfless pursuit of expression on the wild steed of genius: "Finally the time arrives. . . . He runs, he flies along, he falls, and he rises up as king!" The convergence of physical suffering and creativity distilled by Hugo from the story of Mazeppa is a recurring theme in his thinking about artistic production, one perfectly in step with his belief—as outlined in the *Cromwell* preface—that truly modern genius proceeds from a union of the grotesque with the sublime.

Hugo's ideas permeate the visual arts of 1830s Paris in subjects inspired by literature and history that celebrate physical suffering with an arresting explicitness. Consider the sculpture of *Orlando Furioso* (Fig. 85), a work in plaster exhibited by Jehan Duseigneur at the 1831 Salon. Théophile Thoré recalled—in an homage written after the sculptor's death in 1866—that the appearance of Duseigneur's piece at the Salon was "for sculpture, a kind of preface to Cromwell."[67] The work was inspired by Ariosto's text of the same name, in which Orlando goes mad when shown proof of Angelica's infidelity: he tears off his clothes, rips up trees, and embarks on a killing spree of any living creature—beast or human— within reach. After much effort, five of Orlando's colleagues managed to lasso his arms and legs with ropes and to tie him down, despite his almost superhuman efforts to resist. Duseigneur chose to represent the aftermath of this ferocious struggle. The hero's body is contorted in arrested movement, his muscles strain at the ropes, and he wears an expression of defiant resolution. Splayed diagonally on the rock to which he is relentlessly bound, Duseigneur's figure displays none of the "noble simplicity and calm grandeur" of figures from antiquity that inspired most of the works by contemporary sculptors.[68]

Ariosto's account also authorized Duseigneur to portray Orlando in heroic nudity. The result is an uneasy mix of ideal classical beauty with extravagant expression that parallels the peculiar hybrid of exaggeration and decorum already noted in the paintings by Heim and Sigalon at the Salon of 1824 (Figs. 80 and 81). Some critics, such as Victor Schoelcher writing in *L'Artiste*, ridiculed Duseigneur's attempted fusion:

Isn't this some eccentricity, this *Roland Furieux*? This knight, whom we have always imagined, ever since reading Ariosto, as sheathed and clad in steel from head to toe; M. Duseigneur shows him thrashing about like a poor traveler tied up by some robbers alongside a highway, after having stolen everything from him down to his most intimate piece of clothing.[69]

Avid partisans of Romanticism, by contrast, eagerly championed Duseigneur's break with tradition and—to judge from Théophile Gautier's extravagant ode of praise—were far more forgiving:

Roland la Paladin, qui, l'écume à la bouche,

Sous un sourcil froncé roule un oeil fauve et louche

Et sur les rocs aigus qu'il a déracinés,

Nu, enragé d'amour, du feu dans la narine
Fait saillir les grands os de sa forte poitrine
Et tord ses membres enchaînés.

[Roland the Palatine, foaming at the mouth
Under a knitted brow, rolls a wild and shifty eye
And on the sharp rocks he has pulled up,
Naked, crazed with love and nostrils on fire,
Thrusts out the ribs of his powerful chest
And contorts his enchained limbs.][70]

In these lines Gautier restates the two-pronged attraction of
Hugo's concept of the grotesque: on one hand, the fascinating horror of a body subject to extreme physical abuse; on the

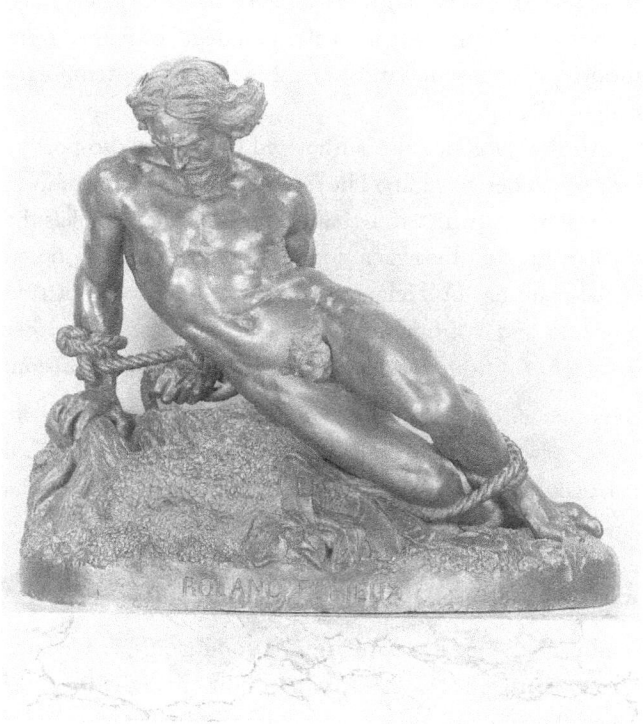

FIGURE 85.   Jean-Bernard (Jehan) Duseigneur, *Orlando Furioso*,
1831 (cast in 1867). Bronze. Paris, Musée du Louvre, inv. RF2993
(130 × 146 × 90 cm). Photo: © RMN/Art Resource, NY/© Gérard
Blot/Christian Jean.

other, the sublime beauty of Orlando's unconquered spirit in
the face of intense suffering.

Despite the recognition and immediate notoriety generated by his *Orlando Furioso* of 1831, Duseigneur was never able
to fulfill the promise of his auspicious debut. It may be, as Luc
Benoît suggests, that "the *Roland* was the product of a spontaneous and impersonal effervescence, something like the consequence of an overheated environment, the work of a collective
conviction," for the piece was long remembered as intimately
linked to the moment of high Romanticism in Paris around
1830.[71] In April of 1867, after visiting the exhibition where a
bronze cast of *Orlando Furioso* was on display, the sculptor Auguste Préault wrote to his lifelong friend, Théophile Gautier:
"Today I went to the exhibition on the Champs-Élysées. I saw
again *Roland Furieux*, the statue of our friend J. Duseigneur.
It's the best sculpture in the show. Friendship, 1830, dedication."[72] Préault's specific reference to 1830 when signing his
note not only alludes to the camaraderie and aesthetic quarrels
that remained a highpoint of his personal career, but also recalls the historical context of his own most famous and shocking work, *The Slaughter* of 1833–1834 (Fig. 86).

Préault was extremely impressed by the pictures of Delacroix and Sigalon at the Salon of 1824 (Figs. 78 and 81). By
1827 he moved freely in the same literary and artistic circles
as Delacroix, Hugo, and Gautier. He was among the claque
of supporters enlisted in 1830 to confront hostile critics at
the opening of Hugo's *Hernani* (see Chapter Six). Jules Janin
even suggested in a review of the 1833 Salon that Préault was
so influenced by the literary preoccupations of his friends
that his sculpture was beginning to suffer.[73] Nothing produced by Préault to date announced the radical formal innovations of the *Slaughter* (Fig. 86) he exhibited as a plaster
model at the Salon of 1834. By opting for a bas-relief, Préault
rejected the three-dimensional isolation of sculpture in the
round in favor of a two-dimensional pictorialism that permits a broader range of plastic and visual effects. He further
challenged established principles of contemporary sculpture
by presenting only body parts—heads, torsos, hands—that
are wounded, detached, and expressively exaggerated as if to
underscore his willful break with the classical tradition of
idealized bodies. Finally, Préault scaled the piece as if it were

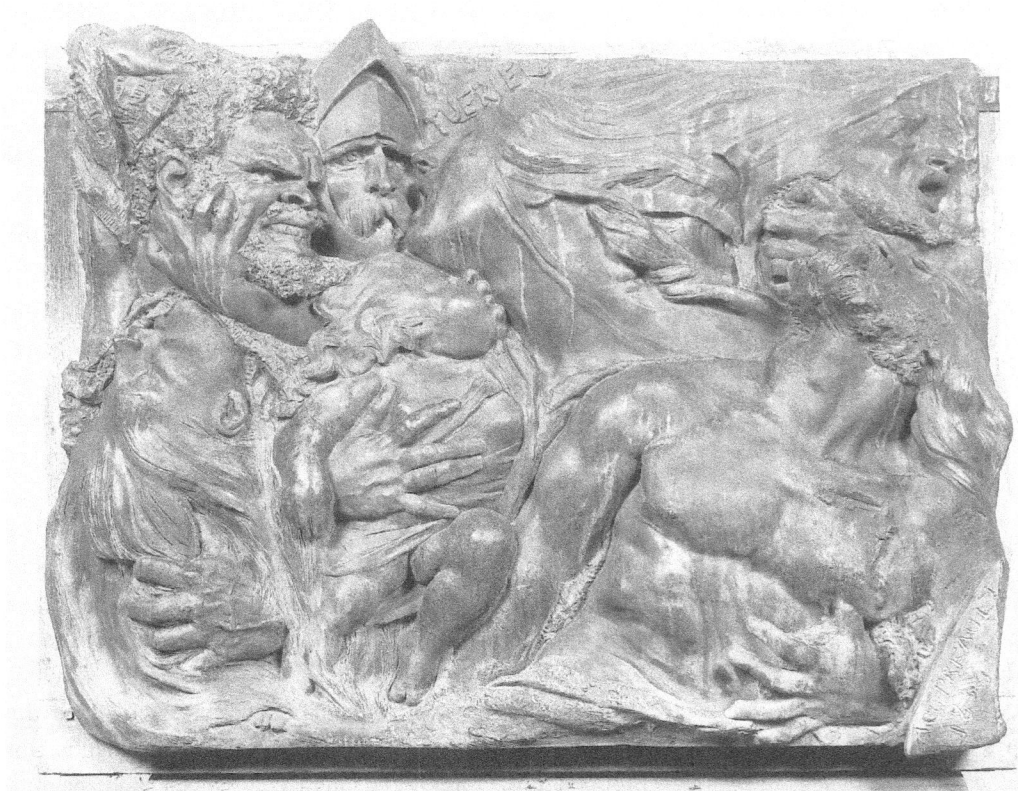

FIGURE 86. Auguste Préault, *The Slaughter [Tuerie]*, 1833–1834 (cast in 1850). Bronze. Chartres, Musée des Beaux-Arts, inv. 3264 (109 × 140 cm). Photo: © RMN/Art Resource, NY.

itself a fragment: individual elements are life-sized and everywhere cropped so that the work appears to be excerpted from a larger relief of colossal dimensions. In fact, Préault described his sculpture as "an episodic fragment of a large relief sculpture" when submitting it to the Salon.[74]

Freed from the constraints of narrative continuity, Préault compressed his figures into a compact mass where abrupt shifts in scale, sex, age, and expression produce a clash of unexpected power. "All these parts of bodies clinging and writhing together," were admired by Préault's friend Gautier along with the "frenzied vigor of all these heads carelessly thrown together."[75] Emulating the contrast between victims and victimizers of Delacroix's *Sardanapalus* (Fig. 83) and Boulanger's *Mazeppa* (Fig. 84), the intensity of Préault's foreground collage of body parts and expressions is both marked and measured by a mustachioed and helmeted face impassively

watching the carnage: who is he? what is his role? It may be, as some have suggested, that Préault's violent image of chaos and terror was inspired by his political sympathies for the plight of the urban working class, notably the worker-riots in Lyon squelched by the army in 1834.[76] Yet such references are left dangling and open-ended because, like his painter colleagues, Préault was less interested in recounting a specific event than producing a general effect. Gautier described the subject as "the battle at the height of its expression and fury; the warrior becomes a wild beast; one fights with claws and teeth like tigers."[77] Following the tack outlined by Hugo in his preface to *Cromwell*, Préault marshals our fascination with a grotesque show of violence to fuse the disparate parts of his relief into a complex emotional presence.

Préault's self-alignment with the romantics around Hugo was not free of risks. The sculptor Pierre-Jean David d'Angers, who generally supported Préault's works before the Salon jury, worried privately that Préault "had been killed off by the praises of literary men who often only write about what they see in their minds, rather than what they are looking at; moreover, they only used this young man as a mode of combat."[78] Despite the support of David d'Angers, the jury for the Salon of 1834 voted to reject Préault's *Slaughter* along with the four other works he submitted. The academic sculptor Jean-Pierre Cortot mooted the bright idea to permit exhibition of the *Slaughter* "like a criminal left hanging on the gallows, to scare the public about the disorders of the new school that, up to now, has not gone too far, but this time attains the frenzy of rebellion."[79] It was thanks to Cortot's gesture of feigned generosity that Préault's sculpture came to be seen at the Salon in Paris.

David d'Angers was right to suggest that Préault was a pawn in a larger battle unfolding in the Parisian art world, but neither he, nor Cortot, nor Préault himself realized that the new school had virtually won the day. The Romantics' attention to effect at the expense of decorum was already in full evidence amongst contemporary history painters of impeccable academic credentials. At the Salon of 1833 Joseph-Nicolas Robert-Fleury exhibited a picture (Fig. 87) in which extreme expressions and blood-curdling violence are rendered with none of the technical extravagances of a Delacroix or Boulanger. The subject had political resonance. The massacre of thousands of Protestant nobles in 1572, beginning in Paris on the feast day of Saint-Barthélémy (24 August), was openly supported by the Catholic Regent, Marie de Medicis. It was one of the bloodiest instances of religious intolerance in French history. Memories of it were awakened by the wave of anti-clericism that spread through France after the revolution of July 1830 ended the Bourbon Restoration's dream of forging a new alliance of throne and altar. The archbishop's house attached to Notre-Dame de Paris, and the church of Saint-Germain-l'Auxerrois in Paris, were among the religious buildings pillaged by unruly crowds (see Chapter Three). The new king, Louis-Philippe d'Orléans, signaled his distance from both the Catholic Church and Bourbon policies by naming prominent Protestant politicians, notably François Guizot, to key cabinet posts. There were compelling reasons to revisit the historical theme of Catholic intransigence with an eye to the present, and Robert-Fleury was not the only artist to do so.

What is surprising is the seeming delight with which Robert-Fleury staged the viciousness of the episode he depicts. In his picture a group of Catholic henchmen murder Brion, governor of the young prince de Conti, under the eyes of his young charge. Extravagant grimaces of hatred and delirium, especially notable in the ringleader at the right and the central figure about to thrust his dagger into the wounded teacher, are seconded by an unusual presentation of the victim's face. Brion's head is framed by the legs of a figure seen from behind, who is about to plunge an enormous lance into the old man's body. The victim's pathos and resignation are singularly isolated from the rest of the image. He stretches an arm to keep the prince away from danger in a final gesture of devotion, while the young man's open-mouth shriek of horror—adroitly emphasized by a pool of white light—pierces the scene. The saturated red of the bed canopy, the matching coverlet on a table under the window, and the bright red decorations of the manuscript dropped in the foreground allude coloristically and allegorically to the blood that will flow in the next instant.

Even more jarring than these markers of anticipated carnage is the frank juxtaposition of figures—victim, witness, and perpetrators—in a compact mass of tangled limbs, crisscrossed gestures, and conflicting emotions. This grouping far exceeds the norms of academic decorum, and registers how much the love of contrast and emotional shock had spilled over from Romantic theory into the practice of history painting—despite the glassy precision of Robert-Fleury's rendering. Ambroise Tardieu, who was not ordinarily a defender of Hugo's aesthetic, praised the painter's choice of subject taken from "this day of vile memory," in which a certain "exaggeration" of expressions was more than offset by a "truthfulness that makes the viewer shudder."[80] In the course of an imagined conversation before the picture, Augustin Jal justified the "savage joy" of the figure at the right on the grounds that the executioners were not paid professionals but "fanaticized bourgeois, murderers who worked for their own good with faith, enthusiasm and pleasure: they got rid

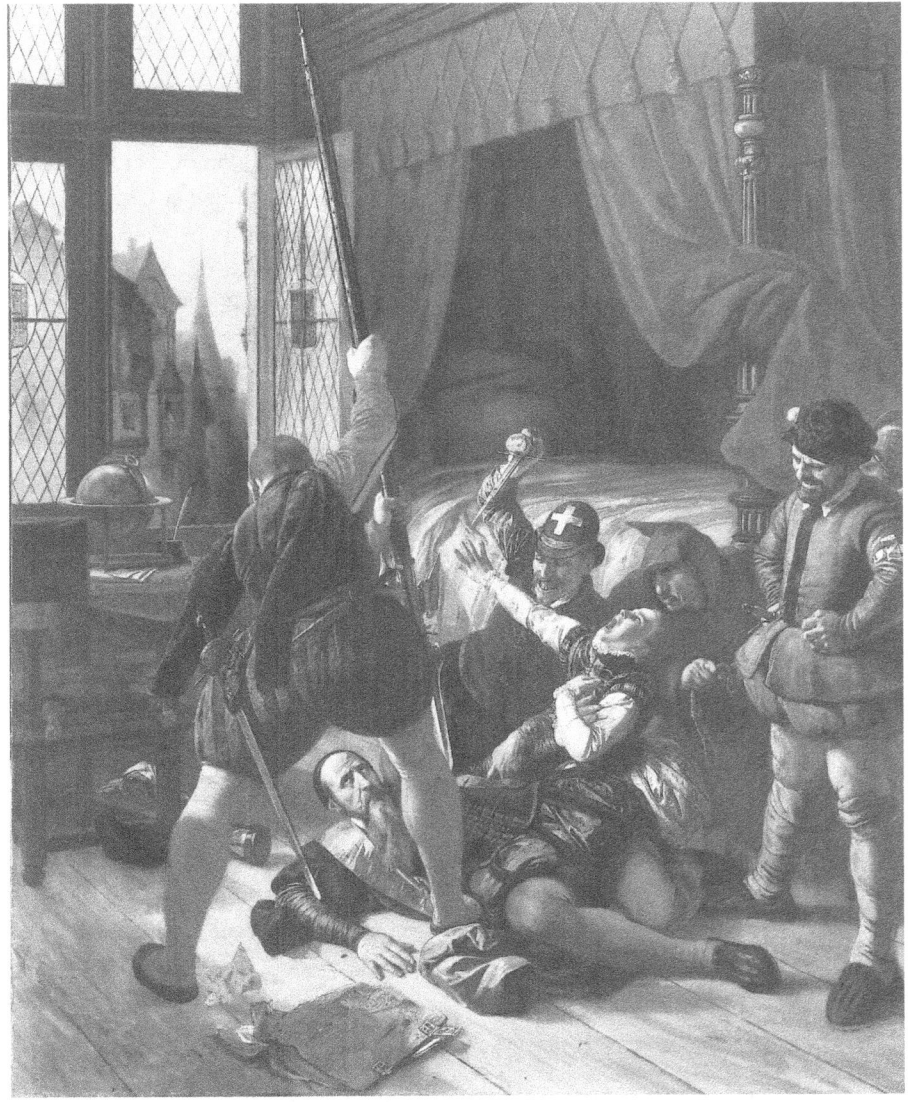

FIGURE 87.   Joseph-Nicholas Robert-Fleury, *The Assassination of Brion, Tutor of the prince de Condé*, 1833. Oil on canvas. Paris, Musée du Louvre, inv. INV7673 (164.5 × 130 cm). Photo: © RMN/Art Resource, NY/ © Droits réservés.

of Protestants they didn't know before entering the prince de Conti's house. . . . Thus, they cannot kill him calmly; they must be fierce and joyful. This barbarism rings true."[81] In each case, critical expectations of a picture's effect, especially when inspired by violent events of a timely political relevance, overshadow considerations of the decorum and style with which the representation has been mounted.

Of course effect might be nothing more than an aesthetic thrill, but it might also be a real social force—something con-

temporaries were beginning to discuss. Gabriel Laviron and Bruno Galbacio, two writers attracted to the social utopian ideas of Fourierist and Saint-Simonian thinkers, opened their review of the 1833 Salon on just that note:

So, leaving aside questions of form and the quarrels among schools that sour discussions without clarifying them, we will look for what might have individuality and power. . . . And, to state our thinking clearly, we will say that we know of only two ways to make art.

Artists can be divided into only two groups, and this is how we distinguish them. First of all, there are those who use the influence provided by the power they have acquired to move souls using words or color so as to effect society with their convictions, whatever they might be. Then, there are those who are thrown into the world amidst circumstances that do not allow for a fascination by any of the issues on the social agenda, and who make art for art itself because it allows them to see and to understand nature, and because they are tormented by a need to demonstrate their power.[82]

This distinction sketches an important shift in critical thinking, for what joins together the two purposes or functions outlined by Laviron and Galbacio is not a personal style, but an awareness of the social power of art either to move viewers or to translate nature. Discussion of value in the arts moves away from the polemics of form towards an evaluation of whether artists have responsibly employed their special gifts. In this emerging critical scheme, effect depends upon a peculiar artistic temperament and becomes the principal yardstick of aesthetic quality.

Lavrion and Galbacio isolate a move from the love of violent action and the explosive modes of representation dear to the early years of Romanticism towards less noisy and less idiosyncratic forms able to reach and to touch a large public. The wildly popular picture exhibited by Paul Delaroche at the Salon of 1834, *The Execution of Lady Jane Grey* (Fig. 88), illustrates vividly how the shock of violence—grotesquely celebrated in the *Sardanapalus* of Delacroix, the *Mazeppa* of Boulanger, and the *Slaughter* of Préault—was harnessed and tamed to send a shiver of polite excitement through the growing general audience attracted to the annual exhibitions of art in Paris. "The public gladly goes into raptures over the comportment of *Jane Grey*," reported Gustave Planche:

it admires her groping hands, the pathological whiteness of her shoulders; nothing, including her left knee, which is the only one resting on the cushion, fails to gain the approval of curious onlookers. I note carefully this peculiarity of public opinion, because it is related to similar peculiarities of public taste in music and poetry. It is clear that the painter wanted to interest us in Mary Tudor's victim by purposely exaggerating her pallor and her shakiness.[83]

Planche rightly emphasized that only one of Jane Grey's knees actually touches the pillow. It is an overt sign of the pathos orchestrated by Delaroche and duly underscored by the descriptive paragraph he inserted in the exhibition catalogue. The setting is England in 1554. Jane Grey, the young Protestant queen, has been imprisoned by her Catholic rival and condemned to death. Blindfolded for execution, and kneeling on a raised platform in the Tower of London, Jane Grey gropes for the place to put her head: "What shall I do now?" she asks, "where is the block?"[84] Touched by this pitiful spectacle, the Lieutenant of the Tower gently guides her hand. At the left side, two of the queen's attendants swoon in grief and turn away from the frightful scene. To the right stands the executioner, a muscular man in a rather mincing pose, whose fleeting look of compassion towards the victim is immediately checked by a bright glint of light on the sharpened edge of his axe.

Delaroche's preparatory drawings reveal that he reworked the executioner several times before arriving at what Stephen Bann has called "a finely judged compromise between the athletic disengagement suggested by some of the smaller sketches, and a sufficiently detectable involvement manifested in the half turned face."[85] It was this well-tuned balance, and the related counterpoint established by the painter's use of relatively bright colors against a somber ground, that Planche invoked when trying to explain why *Jane Grey* "threatens to be the biggest hit at this year's Salon." Planche certainly recognized that the picture's success was of a new kind:

His brand new figures please the greatest number of eyes. The patient stylishness of accessories, the shimmering colors, which are not clear and pure but at least have studied elegance and profusion going for them, receive an approbation whose sense and cause are not hard to figure out. With regard to any missing poetry, the public is quite indifferent; it worries very little that the *Jane Grey* of M. Delaroche is far more theatrical than dramatic.[86]

One might say that Delaroche exchanged dramatic movement and the graphic portrayal of violence for what Laviron and Galbacio had called the power "to move souls using words or color so as to effect society with their convictions." Delaroche's rendering of the scene moves us to sympathy for

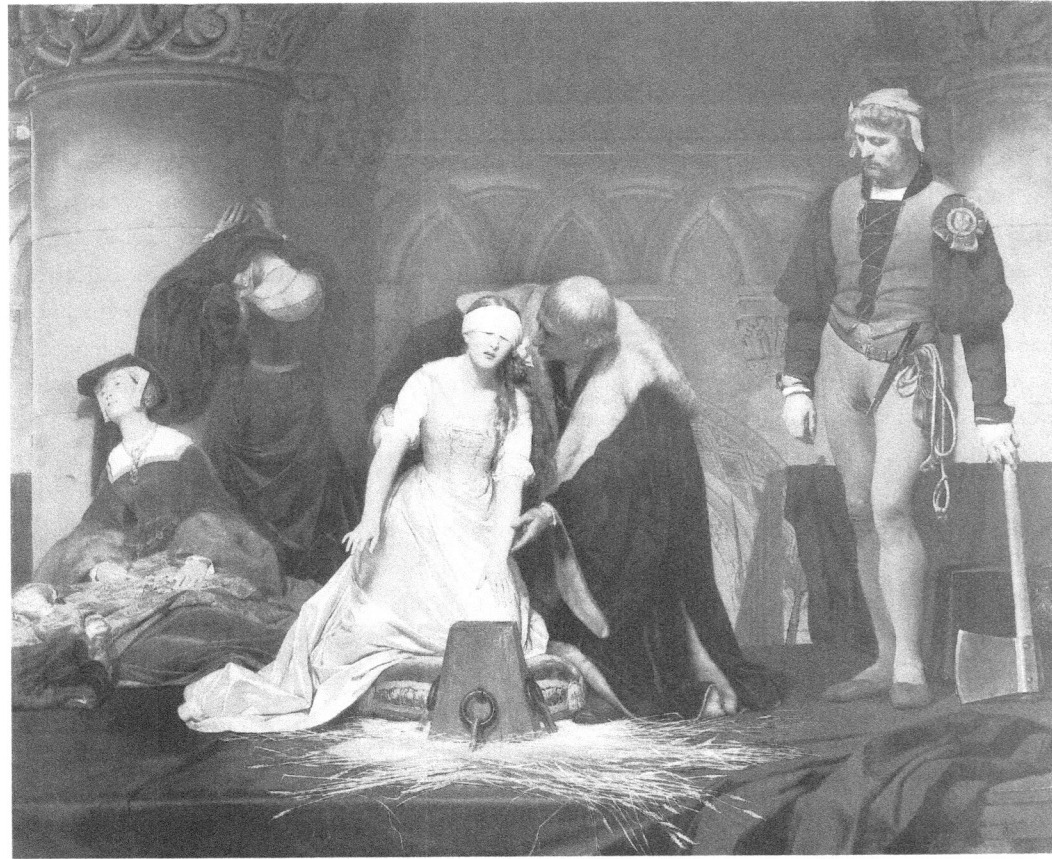

FIGURE 88. Paul Delaroche, *The Execution of Lady Jane Grey*, 1834. Oil on canvas. London, The National Gallery, inv. NG 1909 (246 × 297 cm). Photo: © The National Gallery, London.

the young girl who ruled England for only nine days, and yet—like the executioner whose emotional response resembles our own—we cannot arrest the course of events.

Many years later, the English painter William Holman Hunt expressed his admiration for Delaroche's attention to the drama of that moment before a scene of carnage, and for his ability to transform historical facts into what Martin Meisel describes as "something ephemerally psychological, the representation of a dawning apprehension."[87] The picture fuses fact to effect by a visually gripping, almost palpable presence of material things: from the sheen and fine pleats of Jane Grey's dress to the cold gray of the stone walls; from the soft fur of the Lieutenant's collar to the hallucinatory presence of golden straw carefully arranged at the picture's center to absorb the blood about to be spilled. The riveting

power of physical presence was frequently noted by critics. Where Planche called it "theatrical" in mild approbation, Alexandre Decamps used the same term to complain that pictures by Delaroche "resemble deftly arranged scenes of theater."[88] What these allusions to contemporary theater signal is the combination of psychological impact and immediate presence that pictures like *Jane Grey* brought to the world of painting with a newly focused intensity.

For many years historians followed the lead of Léon Rosenthal to dismiss Delaroche's easy intelligibility as a sign of aesthetic inferiority; his pictures, they claimed, demanded only a lowbrow sensibility because "the eye goes right through the painted canvas to the scene or object represented."[89] Rosenthal claimed that "the predominance of the subject is the most sure mark of inferiority. . . . The painting is only a support; the picture's interest depends not at all upon its aesthetic quality, but upon the scene represented: the painter should be a shrewd dramatist, a good costume designer, a clever director."[90] Painters like Delaroche were vilified because "the principle feature of their physiognomy is, perhaps, this absence of any clear-cut character," and they were pilloried for steering a predictably safe course between two powerful tendencies of the moment: an aesthetic "middle of the road" [juste-milieu] between the strong coloring and violence of the Romantics and the crisp drawing and idealized forms of the Classics.[91]

This simplified view of art history obscures the fact that *Jane Grey* and pictures like it were pushing in a completely new direction. Rather than being locked into the hermetic art world of aesthetic squabbles and personal styles, Delaroche boldly opened his work to experience outside the picture gallery—to boulevard theaters, waxwork museums, and the primacy of immediate perception—in a bid to place painting on a social footing supported by a large public of non-specialists.[92] "We were unable to fight off the immense number of admirers of this picture," recalled the painter Amaury-Duval; "the entrance door of the salon carré, close to where the work of Delaroche was exhibited, was completely obstructed by the crowd it drew."[93] Delaroche achieved this success by mobilizing a viewer's shock at the violence soon to befall this young woman. Ironically, his strategy was the legacy of Hugo's fascination with sublime qualities of the grotesque. Certainly the handmade painterliness of Delaroche's canvas all but disappears in an hallucination of immediate presence, but this need not be viewed as retrograde classicism. When asked in 1839 to comment on Daguerre's invention for fixing an image on glass, Delaroche enthusiastically described it as "being immensely useful for the arts" because "the process of M. Daguerre demonstrates by its achievements that it completely satisfies all the requirements of art, and it brings some essential conditions to such a point of perfection that it will become a topic of observation and study for even the most skilled painters."[94] From the vantage point of history, Delaroche's attention to the perfection of rendering things may be less a nostalgic retreat into idealism than the cutting edge of a forward-looking sensibility for the machine-made precision of photography (see Chapter Eight).

The contemporary fame of *Jane Grey* was no aberration. It responded effectively to the demands of a growing art-viewing public by refusing the highly personal pictorial extremes of Romanticism without abandoning a concern for effect. It adopted a mode of representation that mimics rather than challenges ordinary perceptions of the world. While this might constitute a middle-of-the-road strategy, it seems more fruitful to recognize that Delaroche negotiated the growing complexity of the Parisian art world with an eye towards the mass appeal of what are now called "soap operas" on television. "I am not afraid to be charged with exaggeration in saying that this composition profoundly moves the soul of the spectator," wrote Fabien Pillet in 1834; "I have seen, I have seen genuine tears!"[95] Should we be surprised, since its return from storage to the walls of the National Gallery in London, that the *Execution of Jane Grey* has become one of the museum's most popular pictures?

Parallel to Delaroche's trajectory of transforming the sublime violence and grotesques of high Romanticism into sentimental attractions for the general public lies another path, also sketched by Laviron and Galbacio in 1834. By this account, some artists turn their back on contemporary life to make "art for itself" because they are able "to see and to understand nature," and are driven by a need to "demonstrate their power." This second option developed most fully within a closed system of private patronage, insulated from the caprice of public opinion and debate. One of the most remarkable objects it produced was an elaborate centerpiece [surtout de table], designed for the duc d'Orléans by Aimé Chenavard in collaboration with Jean-Baptiste-Jules Klagmann and decorated with bronze sculptures by Antoine-Louis Barye (Figs. 89 and 90). Unfortunately, the complete ensemble has been dispersed and destroyed. It originally comprised eleven separate elements of various heights, the most spectacular being a triumphal arch in gilded bronze that supported a sculpted tiger hunt.[96] Barye represented an elephant being mauled by two tigers that are, in turn, attacked by three men riding the elephant. At the corners of this central component, which stood more than a meter tall, were four scenes of similarly violent animal combats: an eagle attacking a wounded ibex, a python strangling a gnu, a tiger gorging a nilgai, and a lion

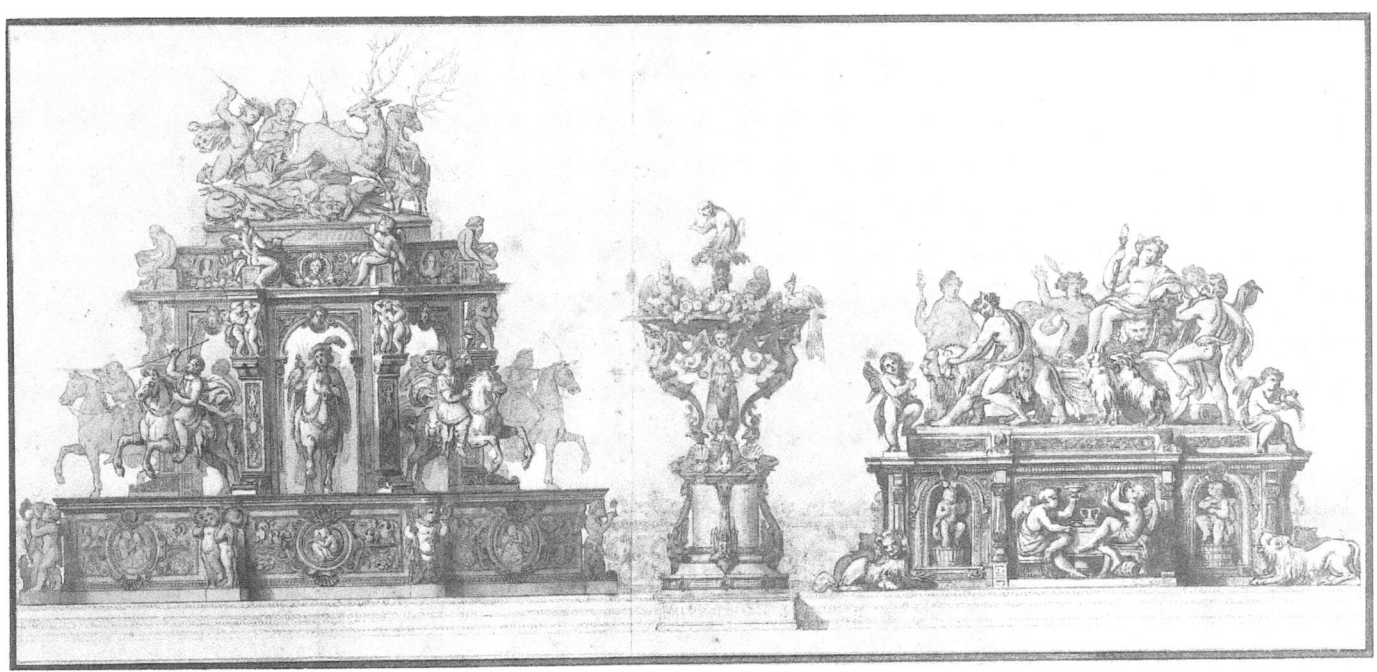

FIGURE 89.   Aimé Chenavard, *Project for the Table Centerpiece designed for the duc d'Orléans*, ca. 1834. Pen and ink with watercolor. Paris, Musée des Arts Décoratifs, inv. 26861 (30 × 65 cm). Photo: © Photothèque UCAD.

mauling a boar. Other sculptural groups dispersed throughout the centerpiece included lion, bear, and bull hunts of an equally gruesome tenor.

Barye's *Elk Hunt* (Fig. 90) exemplifies the animated movement and unsettling subjects of the entire set. One elk has already been killed, a second rears his head in a final death throe, and huge hunting dogs race between the legs of men and horses to mount a frenzied attack. Barye's human figures, described in an inventory as "mounted Tartars," place the action in some mythic Mongolia, a geographic locale seconded by traits of ethnographic shorthand that include shaved heads and pigtails, slanted eyes, and long mustaches.[97] The group violates a key principle of conventional sculptural design by literally overflowing its base with a flurry of limbs and gestures, as if hurled from the center by the centrifugal violence of the conflict. The chaotic layering of animal bodies—elks, dogs, and horses intertwined in a compact mass—recalls the visually violent, collage-like effect of Préault's *Slaughter* (Fig. 86), and

this physical confusion is both bracketed and accented by the grim-faced stoicism of Barye's hunters. The work's overall silhouette of spiky extensions and broken contours, and its complex cross-cutting of energy and movement, restate in three dimensions the fusion of grotesque and sublime championed by Hugo and painted by Delacroix in 1827 (Fig. 83), but which remained a rarity in contemporary French sculpture.

Barye was famous for his scrupulous and methodical study of animal anatomy, something his supporters were quick to signal as an essential part of his genius. "Since he had no money to pay for models," wrote Jules Janin in 1833,

he knew very well where to find some splendid ones that cost nothing: he set up in the Jardin des Plantes. He lived with the lions, tigers, and bears. He spent his life studying their features, their colors, their movements, and their habits. He became, like it or not, an artist, a sculptor of originality who reproduced in his art a whole part of the natural world.[98]

FIGURE 90.   Antoine-
Louis Barye, *The Elk
Hunt* (element of the table
centerpiece designed for the
duc d'Orléans), 1834–1838.
Bronze. Baltimore, The
Walters Art Museum, inv.
27.175 (52.9 × 52.3 × 37.9 cm).
Photo: Courtesy The Walters
Art Museum, Baltimore.

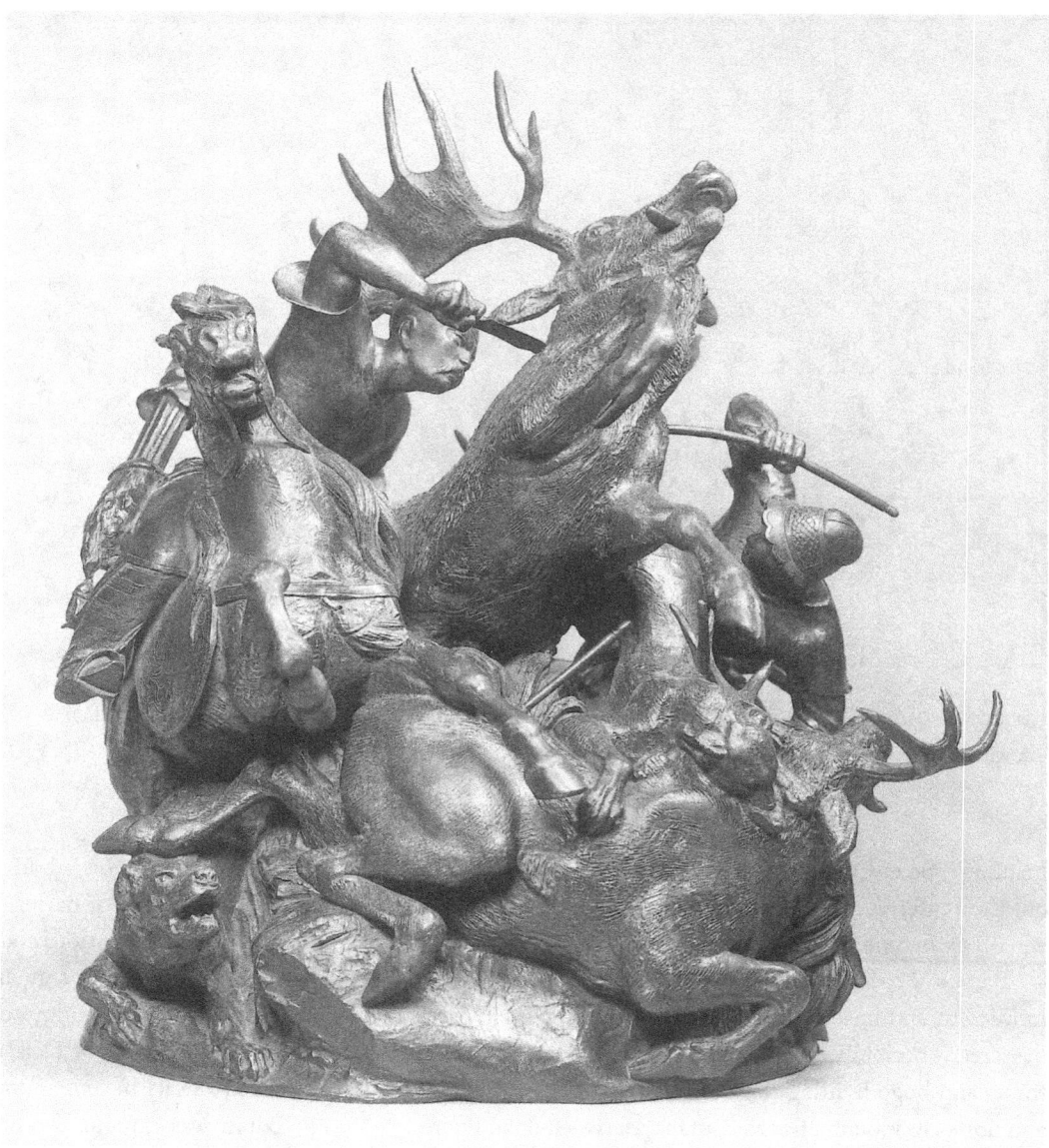

Janin was probably fictionalizing the effects of Barye's poverty, but the sculptor's working habits were certainly conditioned by a belief he shared with colleagues that the forms of art must be renewed by a firsthand study of nature. "The lion is dead. On the double. The temperature should speed us up. I'm waiting for you," wrote Delacroix to Barye on 19 June 1829 upon hearing an African lion had died at the Natural History Museum. The two enthusiasts rushed over to study the carcass and Barye made a set of *écorché* drawings of its anatomy.[99] In their eagerness to learn from the animal's death, both artists demonstrate their commitment to one of Hugo's rallying cries in the *Cromwell* preface: "Nature then! Nature and truth. Here and now, so as to show that the new ideas, far from ruining art, want only to rebuild it more solid and better grounded."[100]

Paradoxically, the settings created by Chenavard for the centerpiece of the duc d'Orléans completely removed Barye's groupings from anything like a natural context. Elaborately gilded, finely worked, and richly encrusted with precious stones, the supporting elements were architectural in design and heavily indebted to Renaissance models. Thus, two round temples—positioned about half way between the central tiger hunt and the ends of the table—showcased Barye's *Elk Hunt* and *Bear Hunt* but were designed as fantasy structures comprising six portals from which horsemen in Renaissance costume appeared to gallop in all directions (Fig. 89 left side). A profusion of architectural forms—pilasters, consoles, and entablatures—offered perches for nude figures that included "infant savages" of the Pacific Ocean, musicians, and cupids. Although nothing remains of Chenavard's originals, it is clear from his drawing that the prototype for this mélange of implausible architecture and oddly twisted figures was Michelangelo's Sistine Ceiling, a source far removed from the steppes of Mongolia where the drama of Barye's hunt claims to unfold. What might this odd juxtaposition of styles and times have meant to the duc d'Orléans? Why, in fact, would he want scenes of violent combat, struggle, and death on a dining table? To answer these questions means understanding how the elaborate centerpiece was used.

The duc d'Orléans died suddenly in 1842 while still quite young, the result of a carriage accident just outside of Paris. The great centerpiece, which was not delivered until 1839, seems to have been used only once in his lifetime, for a costume ball and dinner he hosted at the Tuileries Palace during the winter of 1842. The prince de Joinville, younger brother of the duke, was deeply impressed by the evening's festivities:

The elegant and artistic smart-set of Paris was there, dressed in historical costumes faithfully copied in our museums or in whimsical outfits that especially exploited the beauty of women. . . . The members of the diplomatic corps of both sexes, the foreigners, had in general dressed in costumes related to the history of their countries. Among the artists: Eugène Sue, Henriquel-Dupont, Tony Johannot, and Louis Boulanger took as their models the epoch of Louis XIII; Eugène Delacroix came in Moroccan dress; Horace Vernet as an Arab. . . . When we went to dinner, the band of my brother Aumale's

regiment—the 17th Light Infantry—turned into an Arab orchestra and played in the stairwell a whole series of Algerian tunes that the men had learned at Mouzaïa, at Médéah, in the Olivier forest, under the fire of the sky and the Arabs. Then the guests sat down at a table facing the famous centerpiece executed from the designs of Chenavard by Barye, Pradier, Klagman, Moine, my sister Marie, as well as Ary Scheffer and Paul Delaroche, who had abandoned their brushes for the moment to take up the chisel. . . . This feast was the highpoint of the winter season, one of those one-of-a-kind, original evenings that is remembered for a long time.[101]

Joinville's account underscores the importance of historical costuming to the evening, and it is worth noting that both Delacroix and Vernet came in the guise of North Africans (see below). The military band played songs learned while serving in Algeria with another of the host's siblings, the duc d'Aumale. During the 1830s all the sons of Louis-Philippe distinguished themselves in the military campaigns to colonize North Africa, and many of their exploits were celebrated in large paintings commissioned by the king for the museum of art and history at Versailles. The duke's wish to set his table with scenes of violent, life-or-death struggles that pit exotic animals against equally exotic hunters must have been motivated by his personal belief in the cultural and political value of colonizing North Africa. In this context, the centerpiece should be read as a richly ornamented allegory about the triumph of European civilization over the exotic Orient.

This neat interpretation of the centerpiece is complicated by its chronology and its physical expanse. Barye and Chenavard were awarded the commission at least one year before the duc d'Orléans actually went to Algeria. Although it is true that elaboration of the work marched hand in hand with French conquests in North Africa, Joinville's report that guests "sat down at a table facing the famous centerpiece" suggests another reading. The horizontal spread of the surtout's many components—each half of the table carried a round temple discussed above, a low platform with a scene of hunting wild animals, two mounted cups garnished with birds of prey or animals eating, an end piece related to hunting or fishing—and the considerable height of the central tiger hunt—more than a meter tall—meant that the table's sociability was divided lengthwise by a scenic horizon of violent action and expressive silhouettes. Joinville's remark suggests that guests facing this sculptural barrier of life-and-death struggles among humans and beasts were barely able to see, much less converse, with those across the table.[102] Thus, Barye's scenes of physical violence in far-off lands, even if presented within a thoroughly European architectural frame, would be not so much specimens of exotic culture under the concerted gaze of European masters than liminal images at the edges of the dinner party's sociability, existing at the horizon between immediate conviviality and a fantasy world of the imagination.

Why present any imagery of this sort on a dinner table? We might turn for direction to the question posed by Hugo in his introduction to *Les Orientales*, an immensely popular volume of poems published in 1828:

Why this subject? Don't you see that the first idea is horrible, grotesque, absurd (it doesn't matter!), and that the subject rides right over the *limits of art*? This is not nice, this is not seemly. Why not deal with subjects that please us and are to our liking? The strange whims you have there! To which the author has always firmly replied: that these whims are his whims; that he does not know what constitutes the limits of art, that he is not at all familiar with the precise geography of the intellectual world, that he has up to now never seen a road map for art with the frontiers of the possible and the impossible traced in red and blue; in the end, he made it like that simply because he made it like that.[103]

Hugo blazes a trail for contemporary artists to rethink boldly the limits of art. Barye followed that path when working on the his sculptures for the centerpiece, and it was invoked in 1834 by Laviron and Galbacio: "thrown into the world amidst circumstances that do not allow for a fascination by any of the issues on the social agenda, and who make art for art itself because it allows them to see and to understand nature, and because they are tormented by a need to demonstrate their power." Nothing could be further from the "social agenda" of 1830s Paris than the virtuoso naturalism of Barye's centerpiece sculptures. Privately financed by the young duke's personal fortune, the surtout was an experiment that pushed at "the frontiers of the possible" and expanded the "limits of

art" beyond the "precise geography" of the familiar and the everyday.

The most eloquent critical acknowledgment of the singularity of Barye's vision was the disavowal of his sculptures by the admissions jury for the Salon of 1837, despite the high patronage of the duc d'Orléans. "The jury refused the groups of M. Barye," reported Gustave Planche; "it did not hesitate to assert that these groups were not sufficiently accomplished, that this was not sculpture but artisanal metalwork."[104] It is said that Louis-Philippe, pressed by his son's dismay at seeing the works he had commissioned denied a place before the public, exclaimed in reply: "I have created a jury, but I cannot force them to accept masterpieces!"[105] For his part, Barye was stung but stalwart: he refused to exhibit anything at the Salon for nearly thirteen years. Hugo probably approved the sculptor's personal obstinacy, by which Barye placed himself squarely among the Romantics on the aesthetic battlefield of 1830s Paris.

The Exotic Other

Almost every day there is a crowd in front of the Mariner improvising on the Isle of Ischia *by M. Léopold Robert. All the people in this pretty picture are giving themselves graceful airs; it has none of that crude Neapolitan vigour which exceeds all possible accounts. The Neapolitan peasant is so valuable for artists precisely because he never play-acts, tries to look impressive, or imitate anybody.*

—Stendhal[106]

Stendhal's enthusiasm for the painting shown by Léopold Robert at the Salon of 1824—a picture bought by Louis-Philippe d'Orléans and badly damaged in the Revolution of 1848—is all the more striking when contrasted to his published dislike of Delacroix's *Massacres at Chios* (Fig. 78). Stendhal says little about Robert's manner of painting, but he was thrilled by the subject, for it seemed to reinforce his belief in the naïve authenticity of Neapolitan peasants as people devoid of pretense and affectation. Robert had begun the work in 1821 as a proper history painting based on the story of *Corinna at Cape Miseno*—a theme, unbeknownst to Robert, that François Gérard was also preparing for the 1822 Salon. Robert eventually decided the picture was not working: "My picture was so irritating me that I set it aside to make a few small ones that I am committed to deliver," he wrote to his friend François-Joseph Navez in April 1822.[107] The following March, Robert scraped off a large part of the abandoned canvas to eliminate Corinna. He transformed her former companions into a picturesque grouping of an old sailor/singer dressed in typical Neapolitan garb surrounded by young listeners in equally attractive attire. "I am finishing a fairly large picture that includes a dozen figures," reported Robert in the fall of 1823.

It represents some sailors near the sea listening to an old man sing; the sun is setting; I have mixed in a few young girls and some folksy women. Neapolitan costumes are complex, as you no doubt recall. When selecting them it seems possible to find some that are especially appropriate to painting.[108]

The painter did not haphazardly decide upon his transformation of *Corinna*, for he was responding to the extremely warm reception accorded several small pictures he had sent to the Salon of 1822 that represented scenes of Italian peasants.[109] Awarded a gold medal, Robert sold several similar works to dignitaries visiting Rome, including several to the king of Prussia. The latter so admired the scene of a brigand sleeping while his wife watched for soldiers that the king commissioned a number of copies to give as gifts. In light of this critical and financial success, it was entirely predictable that Robert reworked his troublesome *Corinna* into a similar picture for the next Salon.

Robert was recognized almost overnight as the inventor of an entirely new genre: charming pictures of idyllic Italian peasants living at the margins of "civilization" and civility. The *Mariner improvising*, as Stendhal's commentary demonstrates, was a great hit with viewers in 1824. Critics also praised its combination of a modern subject (albeit heavily freighted with nostalgia), its attention to detail without loss of picturesque charm, and its sympathetic ennobling of relatively ordinary, sometimes unsavory characters. The last point was especially true of the pictures of brigands and their women. "This is real life, passion in the raw, not trying to be elegant," wrote Stendhal about Robert's *Death of the Brigand*.[110] Strange as it may seem today, the bands of petty

criminals who thrived along the highways between Rome and Naples were heroized by contemporary writers—Lord Byron and Victor Hugo among them—as "incarnations of the romantic hero, the outlaw capable of killing but proud and loyal, standing up to authority and to society as the most desperate assertion of the individual."[111] Italian brigands were the mythic "Bonnies and Clydes" of the nineteenth century, and Robert's paintings of them pleasantly disrupted the expected critical categories of the Paris Salon. "I repeatedly ask," wrote an otherwise enthusiastic Étienne Delécluze in the *Journal des Débats*, "is this a genre painting? A history painting?"[112] Robert was keenly aware that he had stumbled upon—if not consciously invented—a completely new kind of image for the highly competitive space of the Paris Salon. Other painters were quick to jump on the bandwagon: in the 1824 Salon Jean-Victor Schnetz, Jean Alaux, Léon Cogniet, and Nicolas Robert-Fleury all showed works of Italian peasants very close in tone and style to those of Robert.

Robert was prepared to defend his turf. "Aurèle," he wrote to his brother in September of 1825, "you know about those who are making my kind of pictures, including Fleury, Roger, Bonnefond. They are going to do Neapolitan subjects for the exhibition: they must be *smashed*, as one says here."[113] Robert was about to embark on a trip to Naples to witness the religious festival at Santa Maria di Piedigrotta, with the idea of making a large-scale painting that would flatten his competitors. The resulting picture, *Pilgrims returning from the Feast Day of the Madonna dell'Arco* (Fig. 91), was the centerpiece of several canvases that Robert sent to the Salon of 1827. Paradoxically, the work does not actually depict the festival of Madonna dell'Arco. That celebration took place near the town of San Anastasia on the first Monday after Easter week. Pierre Gassier has shown, based on the evidence of Robert's own descriptions, that the artist recorded quite faithfully the landscape around Piedigrotta and the festival he attended in September 1825.[114] Robert apparently changed the name to another time and place (spring at Madonna dell'Arco) because he was nurturing a larger project to paint an allegorical cycle of the four seasons exemplified by real-life practices from four different parts of Italy. The ambition to paint such a cycle was not incidental to the question raised by Delécluze in 1824, for Robert wanted to shift appreciation of his pictures from mere genre subjects to a higher plane of interest and worth. Investing picturesque Italians with an epic allegorical meaning was part of Robert's plan to smash his emerging rivals.

The irony is that the principal attraction of Robert's imagery was its supposedly honest depiction of the rugged but noble life of Italian peasants. The figures of his *Madonna dell'Arco* were clearly arranged and staged with care: witness the nearly symmetric pyramidal grouping of their bodies and the careful orchestration of gestures that links them together. Critics repeatedly stressed the fine line walked by Robert between direct transcription and self-conscious idealization. Augustin Jal described the picture as having "grace without affectation, naturalness without triviality, characters with true and noble heads, charming poses, observation of the customs of the country, a firm touch, vigorous coloring, straight-forward effects."[115] The *Moniteur universel* reported that Robert's work

is one of those pleasant and instructive passages which reveal an experienced interpreter, respectful of the original meaning, and at

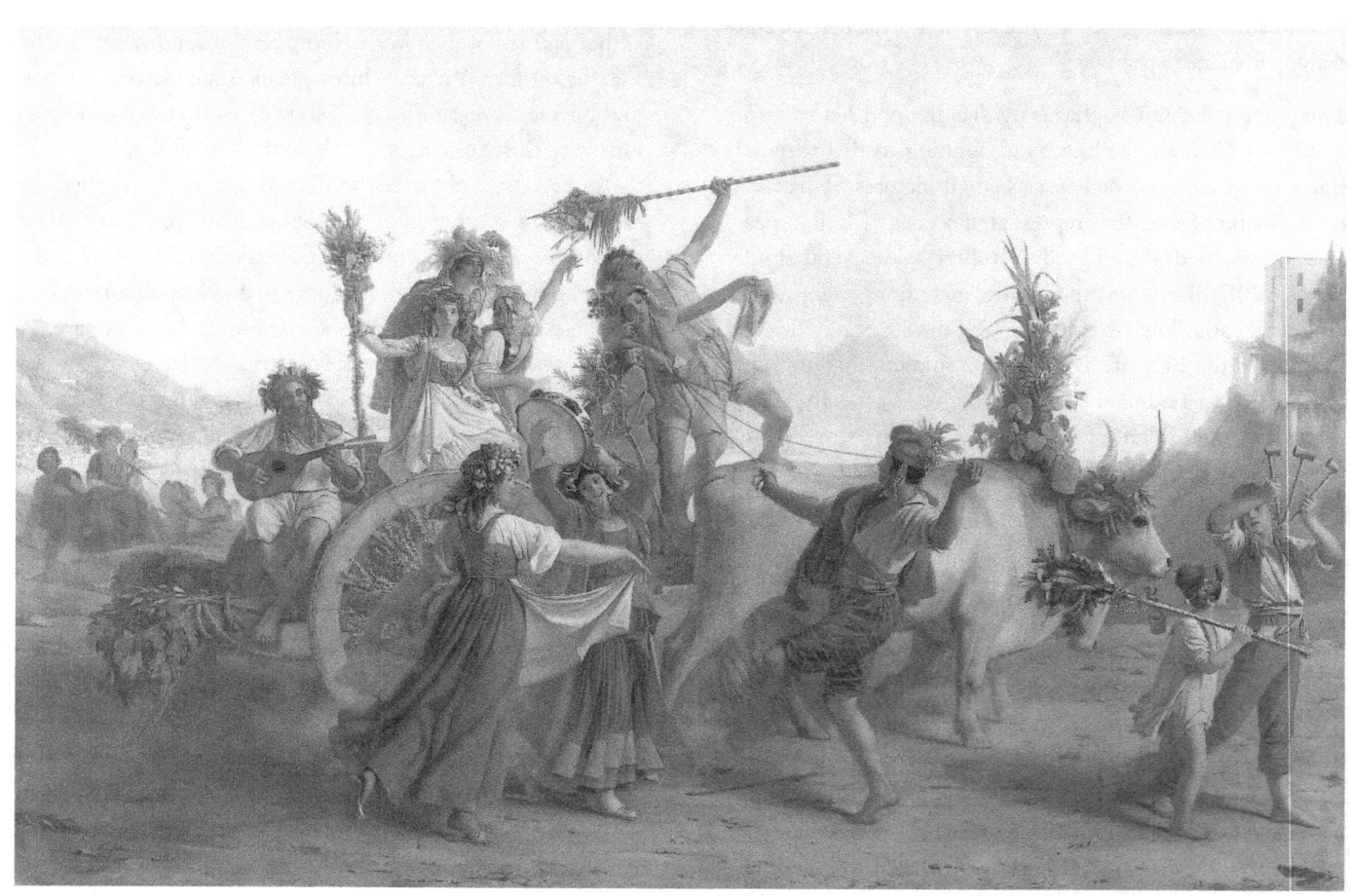

FIGURE 91.   Léopold Robert, *Pilgrims returning from the Feast Day of the Madonna dell'Arco*, 1827. Oil on canvas. Paris, Musée du Louvre, inv. INV7664 (142 × 212 cm). Photo: © RMN/Art Resource, NY/© Gérard Blot.

the same time free and proud in his style. It is not a servile copy, nor a fantastic imitation. . . . It is the intimate and mysterious union of nature and art which combines truth, the realm of the imagination and choice.[116]

Keeping in mind that Delacroix's *Death of Sardanapalus* (Fig. 83) was unveiled at the Salon a few days after the arrival of Robert's *Madonna dell'Arco* from Rome, helps us to appreciate why the latter was held in such high esteem by mainstream critics: although both works were inspired by exotic subjects, Robert dutifully avoided the excesses—both material and expressive—so rampant in Delacroix's painting. The golden light of Robert's background landscape, the peacefully puffing silhouette of Mount Vesuvius, the unbridled joy and impeccable cleanliness of his peasants belong to a world banished from the sullen mood and smoking chaos of *Sardanapalus*. The pitched battle for the aesthetic ground of Paris in 1827 ensured a predictable outcome for this public confrontation: the government admonished Delacroix to change his style, but it bought *Madonna dell'Arco* for the collection of the Musée du Luxembourg.

The interplay of power at stake when a social other is displayed for the delight of a dominant culture has become a mainstay of cross-cultural criticism, especially since the publication of *Orientalism*, Edward Said's important and influential book of 1978.

Orientalism can be discussed and analyzed [he writes], as the corporate institution for dealing with the Orient—dealing with it by making statements about it, authorizing views of it, describing it, by teaching it, settling it, ruling over it: in short, Orientalism as a Western style for dominating, restructuring, and having authority over the Orient.[117]

Said limited his study to "the Anglo-French-American experience of the Arabs and Islam, which for almost a thousand years together stood for the Orient." Do nineteenth-century Italian peasants actually qualify as cultural others in the way that Said means? To judge from Étienne Delécluze's account of his visit to Robert in 1824, the answer is yes. "Robert told us," wrote Delécluze, "that these oriental costumes were disappearing from Italy day by day and he thinks that in a few years they will no longer be seen. Only the old women still

wear them, and the priests prohibit their use as something coming from Turkish infidels."[118] Said's analysis surely resonates with the mastering gaze of cultural study taken for granted by the painter and his contemporaries.

Aesthetic diminutives were often used by critics to praise the *Madonna dell'Arco*: words like *charming*, *picturesque*, and *graceful* appear regularly in their reviews. That vocabulary might betray an unspoken project to feminize and subjugate the society made visible in Robert's canvas. But cultural domination seems too general and one-directional a concept to explain the great public excitement over pictures that strike us today as kitsch and amusing. Moreover, cultural domination fails to explain the ability of such images to challenge the expected categories of history and genre painting, and to effect a change in thinking about those critical categories in the art world of Paris. Robert's encounter with the exotics of Naples was first-hand, his contact with them was direct and personal, and he came away with an interest in specific details of place, costume, and physiognomy that shook the foundation of his classical training. His trip to Naples to research the *Madonna dell'Arco* might have been in part a mission of "describing . . . teaching . . . and ruling." It was also a voyage of discovery and regeneration peculiar to the time and place of high Romanticism. During these same months Hugo wrote:

At this moment when the equilibrium of Europe seems ready to break up, the European status quo, already worm-eaten and fissured, is thrown into crisis by Constantinople. The entire continent is favorably disposed to the Orient. We will see great things. Venerable Asiatic savagery is perhaps not so lacking in eminent men as our civilization wants to believe.[119]

Hugo's vantage point from a "worm-eaten" Europe is that the Orient is a source of renewal, not simply a terrain to conquer. Closer to home, but no less motivated to profit and to learn from contact with the others of southern Italy, Robert struggled to portray them with "a certain character all their own, one of nobility and truthfulness, of good taste and naïveté."[120] He ended by creating an entirely new kind of picture.

Romantic predilections for excursions to the margins of

Western culture as a means of rejuvenating the forms of European art are nearly lost on us today, because the frontiers that seemed so clear in 1827 have been permanently blurred by our technologies of travel, recording, and replication. So pressing was the call for renewal from outside that many artists felt obliged to synthesize the effects without actually making the voyage. Such was the case with Robert's contemporary François Rude, who exhibited a plaster model for the *Neapolitan Fisherboy* in 1831, and a highly finished marble version of it at the Salon of 1833 (Fig. 92). Unlike Robert, Rude never visited Italy. It is likely that his turn to a subject close

in spirit to the paintings of Robert was a response to the great acclaim with which Parisians greeted the *Madonna dell'Arco*. In a long article devoted to the *Neapolitan Fisherboy*, Charles Lenormant underscored the shared ambitions of Robert and Rude. He suggested they were

two sensitive artists methodically opposed to the icy daydreams of the ideal. By taking their models from the social classes closest to nature, by imitating what one sees every day rather than what is conceived by an overheated imagination, they have proven that the true superiority of the ancients consisted of living in a natural state more true and spontaneous than our own, and of imitating it with complete simplicity.[121]

Viewers today will surely struggle to find these lofty ambitions in Rude's life-sized sculpture of a naked adolescent boy dressed in nothing more than a knit cap, scapular medals, and a broad grin of amusement provoked by teasing a hapless turtle.

Lenormant's comments encapsulate the idea that the boy is to be envied for his uncomplicated proximity to nature. He goes on to suggest that Rude demonstrates

a figure can preserve all the grace, sweetness, and nobility imaginable without straying from the path of nature, from that timid, scrupulous, vulgar imitation for which the so-called followers of antiquity have never had enough scorn. . . . M. Rude has settled the lofty question of classics and romantics that we and other critics have been living on for almost ten years at the expense of a stupefied public: he reduces the exaggerations of the two sides to their proper value; he mixes them up in the same reproach of impotence and prejudice.[122]

By proposing that Rude's close study of nature sidesteps the aesthetic quarrel between classics and romantics, Lenormant critically aligns the *Fisherboy* with the paintings of Léopold Robert. Like Robert, Rude was handsomely rewarded: his sculpture was bought by the government and he was made a Chevalier of the Legion of Honor. The humble submission to nature praised by Lenormant ultimately announces a direction taken by a whole school of landscape painters in the 1830s, and only followed near mid-century by figure painters such as Millet and Courbet (see below). This prophetic dimension

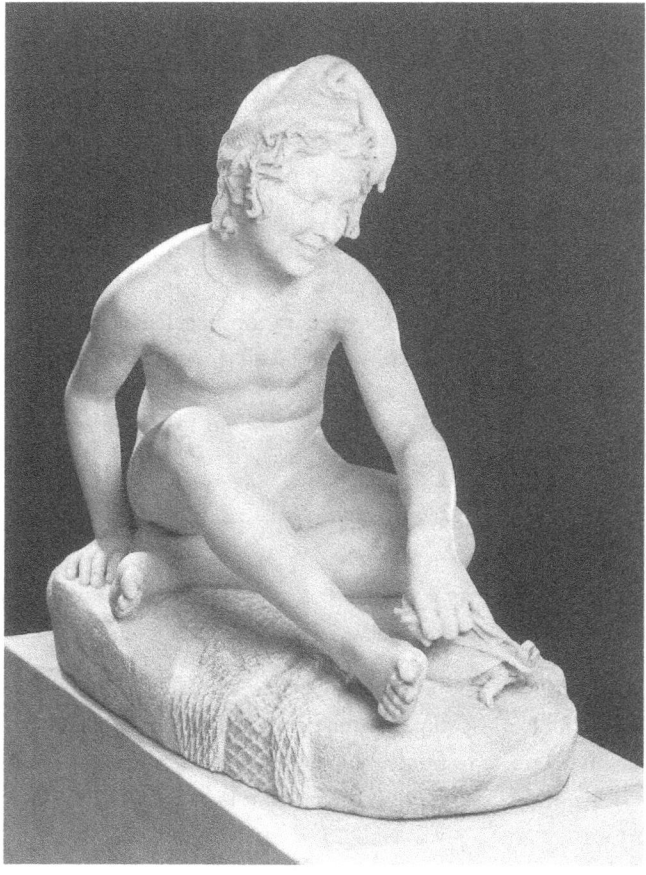

FIGURE 92. François Rude, *The Neapolitan Fisherboy*, 1833. Marble. Paris, Musée du Louvre, inv. LP63 (82 × 88 × 48 cm). Photo: © RMN/Art Resource, NY/© Christian Jean.

of Rude's *Fisherboy*—despite its maudlin sweetness—earns it a pivotal place in the history of French sculpture, one that belongs to this historical moment of shifting aesthetics as much as the *Jane Grey* of Delaroche (Fig. 88) or Barye's hunting groups for the centerpiece of the duc d'Orléans (Fig. 90).

Direct contact with a cultural other does not necessarily lead to representations of heightened naturalism. This is especially true in the fluid artistic context of 1830s Paris. A vivid example of the unpredictable intersection of cultural forces, personal ambitions, and direct experience during these years is Delacroix's 1834 picture of *Algerian Women in their Apartment* (Fig. 93). In December of 1831 Delacroix was invited to join a diplomatic mission to Morocco headed by comte Charles de Mornay, who had recently been appointed special ambassador of France to the Sultan of Mo-

rocco. Mornay's assignment was to repair relations between the two countries that had become seriously strained since the French capture of Algiers in 1830. A trip of six months was planned. Delacroix, who did not know Mornay personally, was recommended to the count as traveling companion and artist by Charles-Edmond Duponchel. Duponchel was an architect, a designer of stage sets, and future director of the Paris Opera. He was a long-standing friend of Delacroix and a regular in the social circle around the actress Mademoiselle Mars, who was also Mornay's mistress (see Chapter Six). Delacroix eagerly accepted Mornay's invitation to Morocco. The group left France from Toulon near the middle of January 1832 and landed in Tangiers. They went directly to Meknes where they were received by the sultan, crossed the Straits of Gibraltar to spend two weeks in Spain, doubled

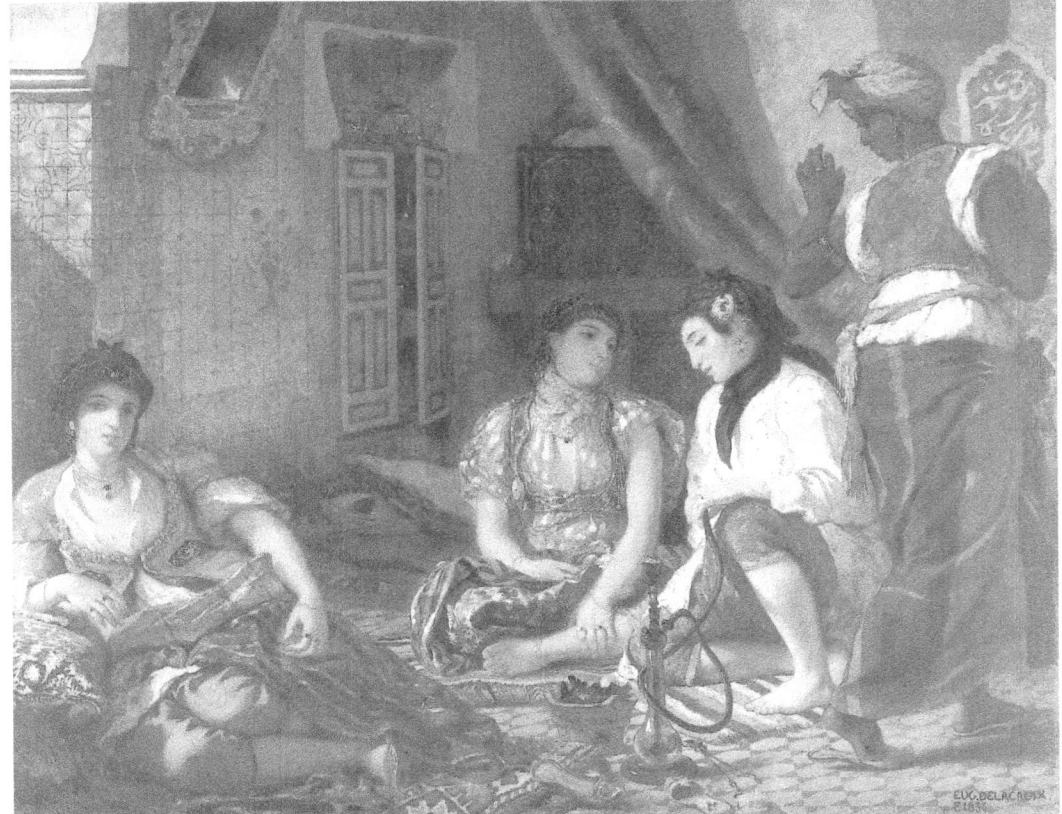

FIGURE 93. Eugène Delacroix, *Algerian Women in their Apartment*, 1834. Oil on canvas. Paris, Musée du Louvre, inv. INV3824 (180 × 229 cm). Photo: © RMN/ Art Resource, NY/© Droits réservés.

back for a journey along the North African coast by way of Oran and Algiers, and returned to Toulon in July.

During these six months Delacroix filled seven sketchbooks with watercolor renderings of people, places, and costumes that are copiously annotated in pencil and seconded by telegraphic phrases of written descriptions. Most are similar to this entry he made after walking through the streets of Meknes:

Went out about one o'clock. The city gate beyond the mosque when leaving the house. Another door in the street. Child with flowers in a twist of hair. Reached the market, looking behind into the dark passageway. Muslims squatting, brightly lighted. Man in his shop, walking sticks behind, dagger hung up. Man seated at the left, orange caftan, haik out of place that he readjusts. Black nude straightening his haik.[123]

Delacroix's staccato remarks read like a catalogue listing as he strives to enumerate all that he sees. Peering down narrow passages into dimly lighted interiors afforded glimpses of people, yet there is a sense he was not finding what he longed to see. Men were everywhere, of course, but Arab women were not. This was especially true of those women sequestered in mysterious harems about whom Delacroix had read—like most Europeans of his generation and background—in Antoine Galland's influential translation of *Thousand and One Nights*, in Lady Mary Wortley Montagu's *Letters* of her travels throughout the Orient, or in the fictive spaces of Lord Byron's poetry that the painter greatly admired. "To inflame yourself continuously," Delacroix had noted to himself in 1824, "remember certain passages of Byron; they suit me well."[124] It was, after all, Byron's poetry that had inspired the *Sardanapalus* of 1827.

Delacroix became one of those rare European male travelers who actually penetrated the protective barriers of a harem. Near the end of his Moroccan trip, and with the help of Victor Poirel (a civil engineer working for the Port Authority of Algiers), Delacroix was allowed to visit the private women's quarters of a house belonging to one of Poirel's Muslim coworkers. Charles Cournault, a friend of Delacroix, later recalled that "after long negotiations, M. Poirel got him [the *chaouch*] to escort Eugène Delacroix secretly into his own

house. The women, apprised of this, put on their most beautiful garments; Delacroix made from life watercolor sketches that were useful to him later when painting his picture of the *Women of Algiers*."[125] Three splendid watercolors (now in the Musée du Louvre) were apparently the fruit of Delacroix's clandestine excursion: two of the sheets depict figures used in the final painting with very few changes; a third watercolor is a view of the interior space itself.[126]

It is a commonplace, when writing about the *Women of Algiers*, to suggest that this immediate, physical, and highly unusual contact with harem life incited Delacroix "to raise it above mere documentary realism to the level of the highest traditions in European art."[127] Already, in his review of the 1834 Salon, Gustave Planche argued that Delacroix was very little affected by his personal experience of the harem because his ambitions were almost entirely formal:

To be interested in painting reduced to its own means without the aid of a subject open to a thousand interpretations, which almost always distracts the attention of superficial viewers so as to engage only their notion that rates the picture according to their dreams or speculations, is a difficult task; M. Delacroix has fulfilled it. In 1831, when he so felicitously framed historical reality in allegory [see Fig. 25], his pictorial power did not act by itself upon the minds of on-lookers. . . . In the *Women of Algiers* . . . it is painting and nothing more: honest painting, vigorous, vividly indicated, a thoroughly Venetian boldness that, nevertheless, owes nothing to the masters it brings to mind.[128]

Planche is surely stretching the point. His insistence on "painting and nothing more" masks Delacroix's unusual rendering of the harem behind a facade of art-historical references. How unusual is it? Unlike most of his contemporaries, Delacroix did not present his harem women in various states of undress that might signify sexual abandon or availability. On the contrary, it is said that while working on his sketches in the harem he exclaimed: "This is beautiful! It's like in Homer's time! Woman in her apartment busying herself with her children, spinning wool or embroidering beautiful fabrics. This is woman as I understand her."[129] Some writers focus on Delacroix's references to Homer and the houses of antiquity to argue that he rejected fantasy stereotypes from a "desire to convey a true image of the Orient," without neglecting "to link his work to the grand Western tradition, which the use of classical sources makes clear."[130] Yet Delacroix's recorded words suggest that he discovered in the harem a *type* of woman: what factors shaped his experience, filtered his memories, and helped him to define that type?

Billie Melman's study of the literature and imagery of harem life sketches an important difference between eighteenth- and nineteenth-century texts that turns on the issue of direct experience.[131] The earlier canonical texts were usually written by men who, according to Islamic law, were forbidden to visit harems: their accounts relied heavily upon hearsay, second-hand descriptions, and the occasional Arab willing to talk. Patched together, and largely shaped by fantasies of Oriental sexual promiscuity, these masculine accounts reveal more about their authors than their supposed subjects, and perhaps deserve being called exercises in "male voyeuristic pleasure."[132] By contrast, and beginning with Lady Montagu, women's descriptions of harem life differ importantly by being rooted in first-hand experience. This does not mean that women were inherently more truthful than their male counterparts, and Melman rightly observes that "women were as prejudiced as men travellers. . . . Participant observation often displays religious and racial prejudice."[133] But it does mean that women writers able to visit harems were faced with a different problem: how to select from a complex physical experience those telling details able to evoke the whole? Melman isolates four themes that characterize descriptions written by women travelers:

The first theme is the features of the *orientale* and her physique. The second is costume: dress and undress are used rhetorically and metaphorically as tropes and symbols of women's status and their position in society at large. Third is eating and table-manners, a particularly large category that comprises cookery, dietary habits, table etiquette, the nurture of infants and children, and so on. Fourth and last is hygiene, especially personal hygiene.[134]

What emerges from women's insider accounts of harem life is a cluster of attention and interest shaped by a different set of nineteenth-century European social codes. "The narrational language," writes Melman, "is middle-class language, encoding *bourgeois* sensibilities and *bourgeois* ethics of respectability and propriety. . . . The very selection of topics and themes is innovative, if not radical."[135] Radical relative to the long tradition of harem literature, yet inflected by a strong attachment to the order and hierarchy that organized and regulated contemporary European culture.

Keeping in mind Melman's four themes while looking at Delacroix's *Women of Algiers* makes it possible to see how much the picture resonates with the modes of eyewitness reporting formulated by women travelers. Consider the way Delacroix arranged vivid profile renderings of each woman, something completely absent from his on-the-spot watercolors. The reclining figure at the left is highlighted so that exactly half of her face is cast in shadow, leaving the bridge of her nose, full lips, and rounded chin etched crisply as forms of light against dark. The face of the half-kneeling woman is seen in brightly lighted profile against an almost black ground that reveals her physiognomy with astonishing clarity. Her companion, like the reclining woman, turns her head so that the viewer reads her profile clearly, despite a deepening shadow. Finally, the black servant woman seen from behind at the far right turns towards the central group to reveal her own, rather different profile against the lighter background wall. "The travel writers were not merely describing," remarks Melman; "they were physiognomists, that is, they used human features and expressions and the human physique to judge oriental 'nature', whether the character of individual oriental woman, or the moral state of Middle Eastern society."[136] Delacroix's carefully adjusted inventory of facial types is exactly physiognomic in its specific interests and mode of presentation.

Charles Cournault recalled that the women dressed in their finest clothes to meet Delacroix. He, in turn, lavished attention on the range of fabrics, embroideries, gold braids, and patterns of their dresses, the richness of their jewelry, and the care with which they arranged their jet-black hair. Delacroix penciled many notes onto his original watercolors in an effort to remember all that he saw. He also presented the women's bodies as strategically undressed: not voyeuristically for sexual display, but revealing just enough bare arms and legs to suggest the softness, slight plumpness, and undeveloped musculature of bodies that do not work. Melman is again instructive here when she remarks that for women travelers "physiognomy and synecdoche enabled the writers to imply what they could not in propriety explicitly say. Reference to the sensuality of Eastern women is indirect."[137] Delacroix's picture exhibits this type of indirect allusion to the luxury of the women's status and the indolence of their position relative to the society at large.

On the surface, Melman's third theme—that of eating and table manners—seems irrelevant to the Delacroix, for the women are not eating and no food is depicted. Nonetheless, there is a conspicuous form of consuming visible, for two of the women share the pleasure of smoking a water pipe. Smoking in Europe was mainly a masculine activity—usually associated with men's clubs, pubs and cafés, or private studies—but coded as a sign of dissolution when practiced by women. By contrast, women travelers discovered and reported that no such proscriptions existed in the Orient. Smoking was an integral part of harem social life. Here too, Delacroix breaks the expected European stereotype of dissolution: although his women smoke, they remain alert, they converse, and they handle the pipe with a familiarity that bespeaks regular use.

Did Delacroix broach Melman's theme of hygiene? Unlike most of the women travelers who wrote accounts of harem life, he surely did not visit the hammam where women bathed and manicured, gossiped, and transacted business in a world without men. Yet the picture does allude to practices of personal hygiene in two small but significant ways. First, Delacroix endowed all three of the principal women with very broad, smoothly arched eyebrows. It was not unusual for Oriental women to pluck their eyebrows, sometimes radically. "She had plucked out the whole of her eyebrows," wrote Julia Pardoe in 1836 about a young wife in Bursa, "and had replaced them by two strips of black dye, raised about an inch higher upon the forehead. This is a common habit with the Turkish women on great occasions."[138] Delacroix could not have known Pardoe's text, but his attention to the women's habits of makeup does betray his alertness to the fastidious eccentricity of their personal care. Second, we cannot avoid noticing the slippers that appear to have been dumped carelessly in the extreme front and center of the picture. Since no

slippers figure in the watercolor sketches prepared by Delacroix during his visit to the harem, it seems fair to interpret their prominent appearance in the final painting as a conscious addition. Was this simply because they add color and texture to the immediate foreground? Because they suggest a narrative and the passing of time? Or is Delacroix referring to a specific custom known in Europe since the 1786 publication of Elisabeth Craven's *Journey throughout the Crimea to Constantinople?* When women left their indoor slippers [çedik-pabuç] near the harem entrance it was to signal their desire for absolute privacy. No man—not even the master of the house—was welcome. The slippers were emblems of the harem dweller's control of her privacy and, by extension, of her sexuality. By introducing them into the foreground of his picture, Delacroix reinscribes personal freedom and propriety into a subject that had long been associated with male fantasy, voyeurism, and sexual submission. Delacroix's response to his first-hand visit is thus visually palpable: he distances his work from male stereotypes of harem imagery, and aligns it with the sympathetic and participatory accounts of those women travelers and writers who were his contemporaries.

The extent of Delacroix's innovations can be measured by comparing his *Women of Algiers* to the other canonical harem picture of the decade, *Odalisque with Slave* painted by Jean-Auguste-Dominique Ingres in 1839–1840 (Fig. 94). The juxtaposition reiterates the personal and artistic rivalry between the two artists that opened this chapter. It also clarifies how the distinctions of 1824 between romantics and classics had blurred by the end of the 1830s. Ingres might have been incited to paint a harem subject by the critical success of Delacroix's picture at the 1834 Salon—an exhibition where Ingres was personally stung by the harsh reception given his ambitious picture of the *Martyrdom of St. Symphorien* (today in the Cathedral of Saint-Lazare at Autun).[139] Ingres vowed never again to show at the Paris Salon, a promise he kept for many years. He left Paris in December of 1834 to take up directorship of the French Academy in Rome. However, a sketch of his first idea for *Odalisque with Slave* (now in the Musée Ingres) includes the name and address of a Parisian model, which suggests he was thinking of the subject before his departure and in the immediate wake of Delacroix's success.[140]

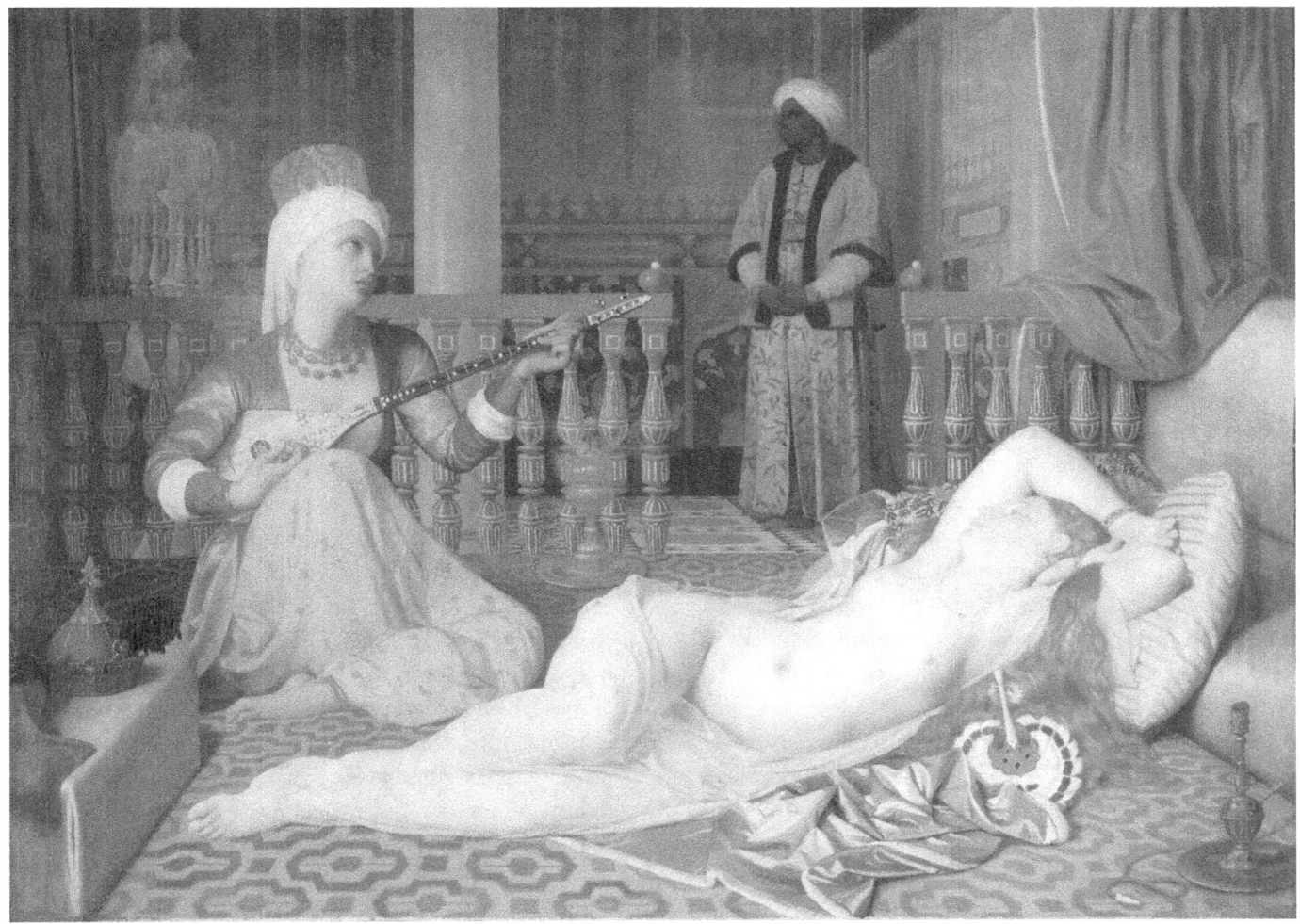

FIGURE 94. Jean-Auguste-Dominique Ingres, *Odalisque with Slave*, 1839–1840. Oil on canvas. Cambridge MA, The Fogg Art Museum, Harvard University Art Museums, Bequest of Grenville L. Winthrop, inv. 1943.251 (72 × 100 cm). Photo: © 2004 President and Fellows of Harvard College/Katya Kallsen.

Ingres was certainly familiar with the same literary texts that Delacroix had read about harem life. He copied the following passage from the *Letters* of Lady Montagu into one of his notebooks:

One entered into a vestibule paved with marble whose design formed the most beautiful mosaic. From there, one proceeded to a room surrounded by sofas, on which one could rest before entering the bath. . . . Around this bed there burned, in golden censers, the most agreeable aromatics of the East, and here several women devoted to this purpose awaited the sultana's exit from the bath to dry her beautiful body and rub it with the sweetest oils; and it was here that she subsequently took voluptuous relaxation.[141]

The rich décor, the bed prepared for "voluptuous relaxation," and the incense burners are all elements that appear in *Odalisque with Slave*. But where Lady Montagu spoke of female servants awaiting the sultana's arrival, Ingres places her sensual languor at the picture's center, along with a spectacular display of bodily curves and naked flesh, cascades of auburn hair, and a surround of rich satin fabrics. The female attendants mentioned by Montagu give way to a woman strumming the tar and a black male eunuch who guards the door. Montagu's vestibule becomes a closed, claustrophobic enclave of patterned surfaces. A water pipe stands ready for use—perhaps its overuse is responsible for the self-indulgent physical lethargy of Ingres's woman that is so unlike the lucid sociability of Delacroix's figures.

There can be little doubt that models from the grand tradition of Renaissance painting shaped Ingres's thinking: both Titian's *Venus and Cupid with Man playing a Lute* (Fitzwilliam Museum in Cambridge) and his *Venus of Urbino* (Uffizi Gallery in Florence) come immediately to mind as visual prototypes. Moreover, Ingres cites virtually every cliché consecrated by the tradition of men writing about harem life from the outside. His image constructs the kind of sensual/sexual fantasy graphically evoked by Théophile Gautier's response to the picture at the Universal Exposition of 1855:

A young blonde woman, overwhelmed by the debilitating languors of the harem and leaning her head upon her crossed arms amidst the torrents of her flowing tresses; her half-naked body writhes in a posture straitened by a spasm of boredom. Perhaps some secret, unsatisfied desire, some rash yearning for freedom troubles this beautiful creature, imprisoned alive in the harem's tomb, and makes her writhe on the mats and mosaics. A young Abyssinian slave, whose half-open vest reveals a tawny, bronze-like breast, kneels close to the white-skinned favorite and plays for her upon the tamboura some of those wild and strange melodies that numb suffering like a nurse's song, unless they still inspire strange pinings for unknown homelands. In the background, a black eunuch wanders about with a sullen and suspicious expression, either waiting for the end of the crisis or dreading it. All the details of dress and furniture have that scrupulous accuracy of place that is one of the virtues of M. Ingres. It is impossible to paint the mystery, silence, and suffocating atmosphere of the harem better than this: not a ray of sunshine, not a corner of blue sky, not a breath of air in this padded and stuffed room, imbued with the dizzying scents of tombac, amber, and benzoin where, far from all eyes, the most beautiful human flower wastes away.[142]

The airless clarity of Ingres's rendering, a perspective system that does not create space but compresses it, the abundance of disconcerting visual contrasts—the woman's undulating curves surrounded by hard-edge architecture, the whiteness of her skin juxtaposed to her colored servants, her visual brightness pitted against the dimly lighted depths—these are all interpreted by Gautier as symptoms of the harem's suffocating sensuality.

The picture reifies Gautier's male fantasy of captive beauty. Its principal attraction is a languid woman whose entire existence is devoted to pleasing her absent master with whom the (male) viewer is invited to identify. Ingres obviously orchestrated the presentation of female corporeality for the viewer's visual and carnal delight. She offers herself to us with virtually no restraints—even her garments are semi-transparent—and she averts her own eyes to allow ours a mastery without resistance over both her and the picture. *Odalisque with Slave* is certainly an image of "Orientalism" as Edward Said describes it: "a Western style for dominating, restructuring, and having authority over the Orient." Ingres's extreme statement of this dynamic led Charles Baudelaire to refer to the picture in 1846 as "that delicious, odd fantasy which has not a single precedent among the old masters."[143] "Odd fantasy" is just the right term. Ingres himself could not really articulate the peculiar power of what he had made. "My God, I don't dare to speak to you about this picture," he wrote from Rome to its future owner; "because, to tell the truth, I don't know what I've made."[144] A few months later, in a letter to Édouard Gatteaux, his longtime friend and confidante, Ingres expressed surprise at the picture's warm reception in Paris: "You were pleased with my *Odalisque*, even contrary to my expectations. So much the better; but . . . I will tell you in strict confidence that this extraordinary success astonishes me."[145] He reveals to Gatteaux that "many things in this picture, if not almost all of them, were painted from drawings without a live model (this is only between us)." Ingres reluctantly admits that the picture was mainly fiction, but he cannot embrace what Baudelaire sensed immediately: it is a highly personal fantasy, driven by male desires about which Ingres dared not speak.

Recognizing the role of fantasy in Ingres's work turns the tables on Auguste Chauvin's distinction between classic and romantic cited at the head of this chapter. For Chauvin, classics consulted nature to find beauty while romantics rejected nature in order to shock. Ingres had been a darling of the classicist and political reactionaries of 1824 with his *Vow of Louis XIII*, but his *Odalisque with Slave* of 1839 purposely convolutes nature at the expense of beauty. Théophile Thoré was not the only critic to fault the anatomy of Ingres's voluptuous woman, noting that "the modeling of the belly takes a lot of risks, and the navel seems wandering in the right side," but he alone drew the surprising, yet entirely appropriate, conclusion that "in the main, M. Ingres is the most romantic artist of the nineteenth century, if by romanticism one means exclusive love of form, absolute indifference towards all the mysteries of human life, philosophical and political skepticism, selfish aloofness from all common and shared feelings."[146] Meanwhile, Eugène Delacroix—the hot-blooded romantic of 1824—painted a harem that broke sharply with stereotypical male fantasies to confront the world of Oriental women directly, and with a scrupulous attention to detail fueled by his eyewitness experience. All of which suggests that the easy categories of style commonly used to frame the history of these decades—especially romantic and classic—were complicated and blurred by cultural forces unleashed in contemporary debates about exoticism and otherness, gender and class.

It is significant that Ingres admitted to Gatteaux how little of *Odalisque with Slave* was done from the model but insisted the information should be their secret. The hypnotic clarity with which he rendered minor details of the scene must be understood, following the lead of Linda Nochlin's seminal article of 1983, as a stylistic overcompensation for the fact that virtually all of it was fake:

Part of the strategy of an Orientalist painter . . . is to make his viewers forget that there was any "bringing into being" at all, to convince them that works like these were simply "reflections," scientific in their exactitude, of a preexisting Oriental reality . . . to make us forget that his art is really art, both by concealing the evidence of his touch, and, at the same time, by insisting on a plethora of authenticating details, especially on what might be called unnecessary ones.[147]

Nochlin was writing about pictures painted by Jean-Léon Gérôme during the 1860s, but her point about making us "for-

get that his art is really art" applies, at least partially, to Ingres's *Odalisque with Slave*. Certainly there are differences. Gérôme's seamless, pseudoscientific exactitude does not exhibit the passages of willful interventions that erupt within Ingres's picture as impossible anatomy, illogical perspective, or bright colors that resist modulation by light or air. Nonetheless, the overcompensation described by Nochlin was neither invented by Gérôme nor an innovation of the 1860s, for its roots extend back in time to the fluctuating and unstable rapports between imagination and observation of Romantic Paris.

If artlessness as marker of authenticity was secretly at work in Ingres's *Odalisque with Slave*, it became overt in an exactly contemporary work of sculpture: the *Seated Odalisque* by James Pradier exhibited at the Salon of 1841 (Fig. 95). Théophile Gautier had this to say about Pradier's piece:

You know what a happy feeling for sculpture M. Pradier possesses: marble is truly pliable in his hands; he kneads it and shapes it as others model in wax or clay. . . . He expresses the delicacy of flesh, the moisture and texture of skin effortlessly and without too much detail. But sometimes he replaces form by sensuality and the visionary ideal by desire. . . . This year's *Odalisque* gives the impression of an enlarged statuette, and the pose reminds one a little of a terracotta work by Clodion. . . . The torso, very well worked and well portrayed, is perhaps too artless and lacks nobility. . . . The *Crouching Venus*, whose pose is similar, could have served as an example for M. Pradier, who sacrifices too much to reality. His love of flesh sometimes diverts him from the purity of the Greeks, those sovereign masters of sculpture.[148]

Gautier's comments go right to the heart of the matter. Pradier carves marble with a facility that denies its hardness and grain so that it seems to take on the "moisture and texture of skin." If he occasionally crosses the line of decorum, it is because he has let desire take control of his work, and the result is sometimes "too artless." But what does Gautier mean when he associates Pradier's *Odalisque* with a statuette and compares her pose to the work of an eighteenth-century sculptor like Clodion?[149]

Unlike the odalisque of Ingres's picture, Pradier's woman appears to react to an intruder's presence. Her feet are entangled in the folds of cloth under her body to suggest that she has suddenly sat up. She turns her head to

FIGURE 95.   Jean-Jacques (James) Pradier, *Seated Odalisque*, 1841. Marble. Lyon, Musée des Beaux-Arts, inv. H.793 (105 × 94 × 61 cm). Photo: © RMN/Art Resource, NY/ © René-Gabriel Ojeda.

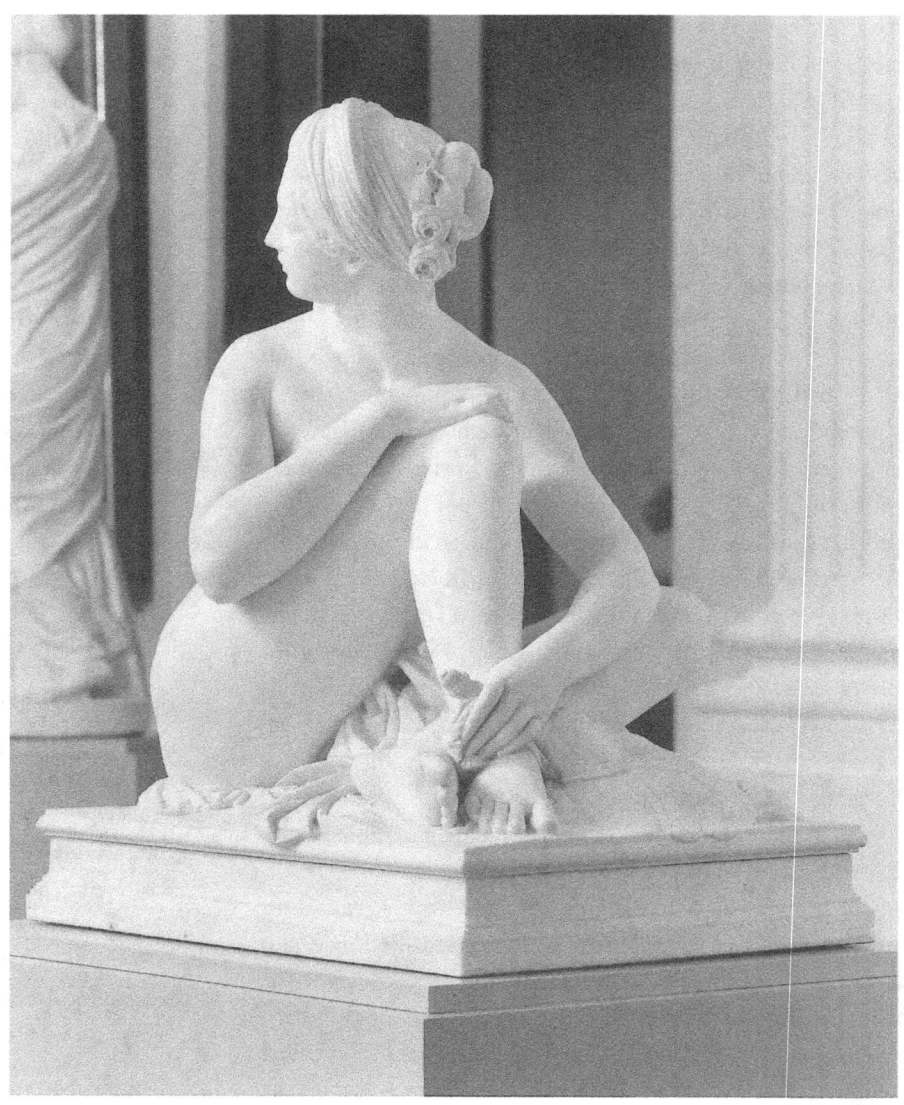

look over her shoulder in the direction of the supposed disturbance. Her pose energizes the surrounding space with a self-consciousness of being looked at—similar to the woman at the far left of Delacroix's *Women of Algiers*—with the key difference that Pradier's odalisque actually occupies three-dimensional space. Where Delacroix's painted image presumes a single viewing position, viewers can physically walk around Pradier's statue and experience it through time.

Indeed, the woman's twisted posture and interlocking limbs insist on being seen from several points of view, which is why Gautier mentions Clodion's small-scale sculptures.

When comparing Pradier's work to a statuette, Gautier was imagining a sculpture less than life-size that induces a precious, sensuous dimension to the experience and encourages the viewer's visual delectation. A life-sized figure designed to be seen from several angles produces quite a different effect: although Pradier's woman shares her space with her viewers, only *they* are able to move through it. She, by contrast, is locked into a single vector of attention. Moving around her, out of her angle of vision, a viewer suddenly feels the thrill of *seeing without being seen*, of taking delight in the woman's nudity without shame, of visually dominating her presence. Pradier's sculpture certainly restates "the Western style for dominating, restructuring, and having authority over the Orient" associated by Said with the cultural politics of Orientalism. It is not surprising that works of art instantiating Said's mechanics of domination characterize the years of French colonial expansion in North Africa.

Pradier's sculpture posits the odalisque as a specimen subject to study and thus forces us to shift from aesthetic debates about art to the social space of colonial rule. The cultural politics of viewing the exotic other came increasingly to be a fact of French political life during the 1840s. Thus, in September of 1844 Parisians were able to visit—as part of their Sunday stroll in the Tuileries Garden—an immense tent captured from the sultan of Morocco at the battle of Isly. The government's official paper described the tent as "a thing that in every respect deserves to be exhibited to an interested public."[150] It was taken for granted that material captured by force from exotic cultures should be placed on view for public comment. A parallel spirit of colonial thinking underpins the government's purchase of Pradier's *Odalisque* for display in a public museum: in both cases, the exotic other became simply one object of curiosity among many in the expanding political reach of Parisian cultural life.

The Other France

People who enjoy some sort of esteem in the provinces, and who encounter at every step a proof of their importance, are not at all accustomed to this complete and sudden loss of their worth. To be something in one's own region and to be nothing in Paris are two states that need transitions; those who pass too quickly from one to the other fall into a kind of annihilation.

—Honoré de Balzac[151]

Lucien, the hero of Balzac's *Lost Illusions*, has come to Paris from Angoulême with an older aristocratic woman, who promptly dumps him for the company of more sophisticated Parisians. Walking the boulevards of Paris, he is struck by the luxury, the activity, and the contrasts of rich and poor everywhere in evidence. He is also swept by a sensation of self-effacement. In fact, many of Balzac's novels are structured around the differences in lifestyles, ambitions, and levels of sophistication among those who live in Paris and those who live in the provinces of France. His characters often pass from provincial to Parisian, and dramas unfold when some try to make that transition too quickly. Lucien experienced this almost immediately when he spent the best part of his savings on the wrong wardrobe, one that served only to give him "the appearance of an apothecary's son, a veritable badly dressed store clerk!"[152]

Balzac was fascinated by differences between the conditions of life in Paris and everywhere else in France, differences that were being redefined even as he wrote (see Chapter Six). One of his ambitions with *Lost Illusions* was to map these shifting social frontiers onto traditional categories of class, sex, and generation, thereby dramatizing the dangers lurking within the immense allure emanating from the capital. "The relationships that exist between Paris and the provinces, its fatal attraction," he wrote in the preface to part one of *Lost Illusions*, "have shown the author a new face of nineteenth-century youth: all of a sudden he has reflected on the great evil of this century, of the journalism that consumes so many beings, so many fine thoughts, and produces appalling reactions from the moderate religions of provincial life."[153] Balzac never tires of exposing the exploitive world of the periodical press: impossible deadlines and skeletal pay; instant fame and equally quick oblivion; the triumph of mediocrity.

Perhaps inadvertently, the target of Balzac's wrath was one of the most powerful means by which Paris and the provinces learned about one another, and what each might expect when encountering the other. In the words of Nicholas Green, gossip columns in the newspapers of Paris, like Delphine Gray's "Lettres parisiennes," "opened the space for a perpetual light-hearted peroration on city habits and foibles. . . . To an audience outside of Paris, columns like this acted as a metaphorical eye through which to view the city, as a chaperone who taught the 'uninitiated' how to look and how to decipher urban space."[154] Conversely, reading about how city dwellers looked at landscapes—particularly how they looked at landscape paintings described in Salon reviews—offered provincials cues about how to market their regions to attract city visitors. "Here was a didactic discourse," comments Green, "spanning public and private which graphically encapsulated the new emphasis on a Parisian response to the countryside. For newspaper readers in the provinces as well as in the capital, here was a form of writing which laid down the law about how nature was to be consumed."[155] Obviously the visual arts had a special role to play in this cultural exchange across the frontier between Paris and the provinces.

An explosion of relatively inexpensive visual imagery, made possible by the perfection of lithography (see Chapter Eight), intersected in the early 1820s with a renewed interest in rural France to drive a brisk market for the illustrated volumes known as *voyages pittoresques*. The largest of these publishing projects, produced by the entrepreneurial genius of Baron Isidore Taylor, resulted in twenty folio-sized volumes of descriptive text about specific regions, each coupled with full-page lithographic images of its landscapes, its key monuments, and its sites of historic interest or picturesque attraction. How to explain this phenomenon? Why now this attention to rural France? One reason was the need—after the humiliation of Napoléon's defeat and foreign occupation—to rediscover the roots of the nation's identity. Writing in 1814 after the fall of Paris, Lazare Carnot exhorted his countrymen to

create a *national spirit*, because only great passions make great nations. For one, it's the passion of liberty; for another, that of conquests; for a third, religious fanaticism; for us, it should be love of the earth that has known us from birth, *love of the fatherland*. . . . France should govern itself by a love for its territory.[156]

Carnot did not need to spell out that the successive regimes of recent French history—Republic, Empire, Restoration—had opted in turn for one of the "passions" he describes, but he makes a clear case for recovering a sense of nationhood by returning to its soil. The popularity and proliferation of

illustrated *voyages pittoresques* during the 1820s were symptomatic of this return.

Where do higher forms of visual art fit into this scheme? Painted images of the French countryside suffered from a serious critical handicap. According to the time-honored categories of the French Academy, landscape painting was by definition an inferior form of imagery. History painting—the depiction of heroic actions and noble deeds of high moral interest—remained the pinnacle of academic achievement a century after André Félibien established its superiority in the preface to his *Entretiens*.[157] Because knowledge of nature is rooted in perceptions rather than ideas, Félibien argued that landscape painting cannot hope to match the lofty heights of reason and morality germane to history painting. During the course of the eighteenth century theorists modified and stretched Félibien's rigid categories. Roger de Piles suggested in 1708, for example, that three kinds of truth exist in painting, and he argued that one of them—what he called simple truth [vrai simple]—discovers "in all kinds of natural things the means of leading the painter to his goal, which is an imitation of nature so palpable and lively that the figures seem able to detach themselves from the picture, so to speak, in order to converse with those who look at it."[158] Near the end of the eighteenth century, Claude-Henri Watelet and Pierre-Charles Lévesque expanded de Piles's categories of truth to include three distinct kinds of landscape painting:

One can depict views of the country just as they present themselves to the eye; when painting a landscape one can use real views as a base, but take the liberty of making such changes that these representations are partly imitations of nature and partly idealized. Finally, one can paint the countryside without leaving the studio; the representation can be fashioned however one contrives it from the many compositions scattered over the earth's surface.[159]

The important innovation of this passage is the insistence upon a separate critical category for pictures of "views of the country just as they present themselves to the eye"— pictures that have no higher ambition than to record what is seen.

A few years later, in what would become the most influential treatise about landscape painting for the whole of the nineteenth century, Pierre-Henri Valenciennes fine-tuned these categories by ordering their importance. In his scheme, "historical landscape" retained pride of place because only it makes us

see Nature as it could be, the way a florid imagination represents it to a man of talent who has seen much, carefully compared, analyzed and reflected on the choices that must be made. . . . Thus, the artist does not make the lifeless portrait of a trivial and inanimate Nature; he paints it so that it speaks to the soul, has an affective force and a fixed expression easily communicated to any sensitive person.[160]

Alongside this ambitious type of picture, Valenciennes—like his predecessors—left room for what he called "landscape portraits," which claim "no distinct character other than being a likeness." He believed this type "strictly speaking, does not require very much talent, for only the eyes and the hand work at it."[161] While Valenciennes did treat pictures made on the spot as paintings in their own right, the paradox is that he always thought of them as nothing more than intermediate steps towards historical landscapes, not works to be exhibited independently.[162] Nonetheless, his treatise laid the critical groundwork for later painters to imagine landscape pictures with no greater ambition than to report what was seen, and to do so without idealizing; that is, to become visual equivalents in the high art of painting to what newspaper reports and *voyages pittoresques* offered to readers in print media.

The impact of Valenciennes's treatise cannot be overestimated. It became the planning document for efforts to establish a Prix de Rome fellowship reserved exclusively for landscape painters. Protocols set up in 1816 for the fellowship competition, which was to be held every four years, exactly mirror Valenciennes's distinctions between a direct experience of nature and the idealization of it informed by memory. The inaugural competition [concours] for landscape in 1817 first asked students to prepare in one day a sketch for an historical landscape. Those who advanced to the second round were given six days to paint from memory a chestnut tree seen against the sky. Finally, nine finalists were instructed to paint from scratch, within seventy-two days and without any

outside help or visual aids, a full-sized picture based upon the following written description:

Democritus retired near Abdera [a coastal city in Thrace] in rustic solitude where he devoted himself to anatomical studies with the hope of discovering the seat of human intelligence. The Abderites thought he had gone crazy, and begged Hippocratus to come and restore the sanity of a person they believed to be sick. Hippocratus, led by a few Abderites, arrives and surprises his friend while he is concentrating on the studies just mentioned. This moment should be the subject of the landscape. The landscape should be depicted in the morning, and it should represent a rustic site without settlements. The city of Abdera is in the distance.[163]

Students trained to prepare for such an assignment would recognize immediately the requirements for success: a background city with a view of the sea; a rugged surround for the hero Democritus; the broken, slightly veiled light of morning; and some trick of visual staging that would imply surprise.

The winning picture in 1817 was prepared by Achille-Etna Michallon (Fig. 96). It is easy to see why the jury felt his work merited the award, for it addressed every part of the assignment, including a clever alternation of light and shade to suggest the element of surprise. The two brightest parts of the canvas are the left middle ground and the enclave of space just in front of Democritus, who is lost in thought. Breaking up the light, which is not unusual for a morning sun, allowed Michallon to depict the group of villagers as shaded figures silhouetted against a brighter ground. They turn and call out to the figure of Hippocrates, who is caught by a patch of light in the middle distance, which causes his white tunic to stand out against the greens and browns of the surrounding foliage. Democritus, by contrast, is only partially revealed: his red cloak glows brightly in a circle of light, but his face and upper body remain in shade. Michallon's luminary drama unveils Democritus to the viewer with a start, and schematizes the narrative plot without recourse to declamatory gestures.

Michallon's picture exemplifies most of the principal traits of historical landscapes. Foremost among these is an apparent visual order that divides the canvas diagonally

FIGURE 96. Achille-Etna Michallon, *Democritus and the Abderites*, 1817. Oil on canvas. Paris, École nationale supérieure des Beaux-Arts, inv. PRP 56 (113 × 146 cm). Photo: © ENSBA, Paris.

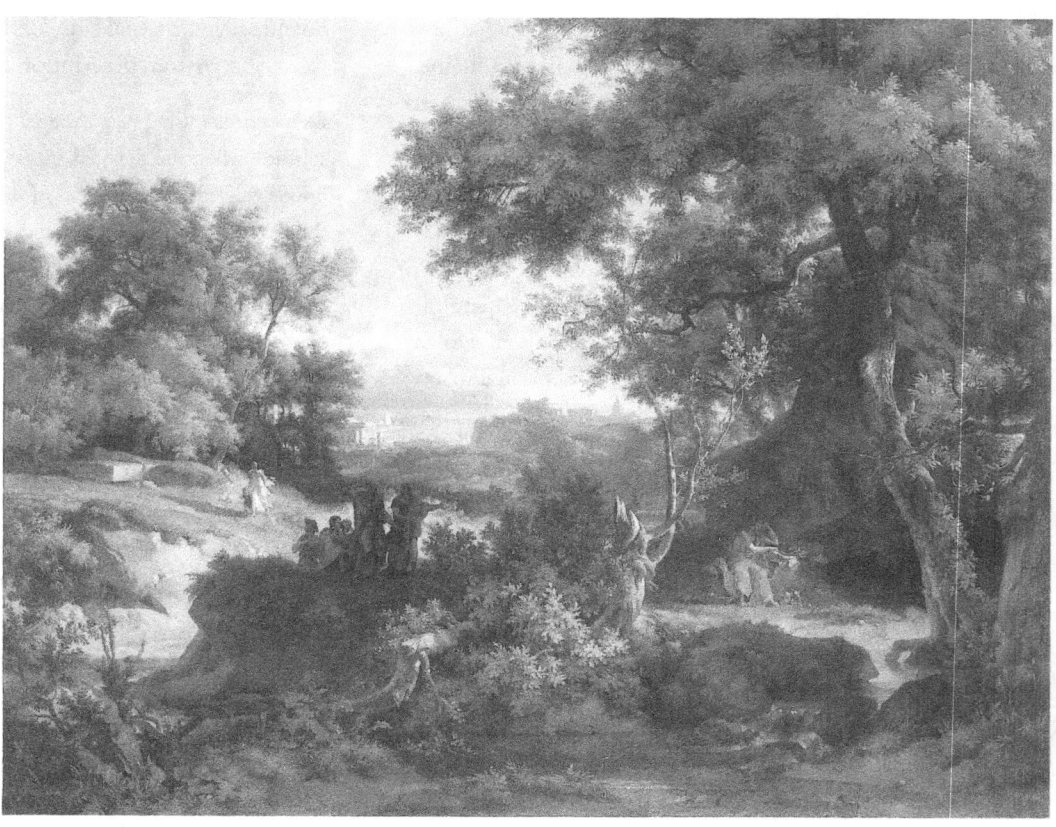

from lower left to upper right into separate regions of near ground and background to distinguish visually the rough and uninhabited terrain where Democritus has retired from the domain of civilization. Alternations of shade and light, first at the right and then to the left, move one's eye from the near foreground through space to the distance in a pattern of measured movements. A nearby tree at the far right hangs over the center of the picture, where its silhouette is matched and nearly continued by the middle-ground trees (at the left) and clouds in the sky. The gnarled trunk of a partially blasted tree near the center of the picture sprouts new branches: it functions as the portal to Democritus's little enclave and rhymes visually a pyramid on the distant cliff to draw a parallel between nature's cycles of renewal and the raising of man-made edifices. Taken together, Michallon's picture subtly underscores the Abderites' folly, because they

believed the flight of Democritus from culture into nature was a sign of madness, yet the story unfolds in a world visibly structured by reason, logic, and balance. "By the *historical style* of landscape painting," summarized Jean-Baptiste Deperthes in 1818,

is meant the art of composing sites from a selection of the most beautiful and majestic produced by nature, and of showing in them people whose deeds—whether recalling an historical event or showing an ideal subject—might be of great interest to the viewer, inspire noble sentiments in him, or cause his imagination to soar.[164]

In such pictures nature becomes culture and is everywhere dominated by human activities: land is tilled, animals are domesticated, buildings fill the distance, and even the weather remains forever pleasant.

The professional careers of most French landscape painters were marked by a fundamental rift between theory and practice that characterizes the first decades of the nineteenth century. On one hand, masters like Valenciennes encouraged their students to paint quick, on-site oil sketches, as he himself had done in Italy. On the other, students were admonished to forsake direct contact with nature when making finished pictures for public exhibition. Later theorists tried to negotiate this difficulty by redefining what was called pastoral landscapes [style champêtre] with a new and positive emphasis on verisimilitude. Here is Deperthes's formulation of 1818:

The pastoral style is understood as the manner of retracing exactly points of view taken from nature, of presenting the faithful image of the countryside in all its details; in a word, of fixing on the canvas, line for line, an expanse of land with the piece of sky rising above it, and illuminated by the light it receives at the very moment the painter busies himself with seizing its likeness. . . .

He can only offset the loftiness of the historical style by means of an extreme truthfulness when imitating the most picturesque natural effects.[165]

Nonetheless, Deperthes's injunction to "extreme truthfulness" convinced few of his colleagues to swerve from the path of historical landscape until they were challenged visually by the pictures of the Englishman John Constable.

It is probably coincidence that the Salon of 1824, where the rivalry between Ingres and Delacroix was drawn sharply for the first time, was also the occasion for French painters and critics to become familiar with Constable's work. In January of that year John Arrowsmith, an art dealer based in Paris, bought three pictures from Constable, including *The Hay Wain* (Fig. 97).[166] Arrowsmith planned to exhibit them as exemplars of the best in English contemporary art, which was a specialty of his gallery. He succeeded splendidly by placing two of his Constables at the Salon where they attracted considerable attention. Even a cursory look at *The*

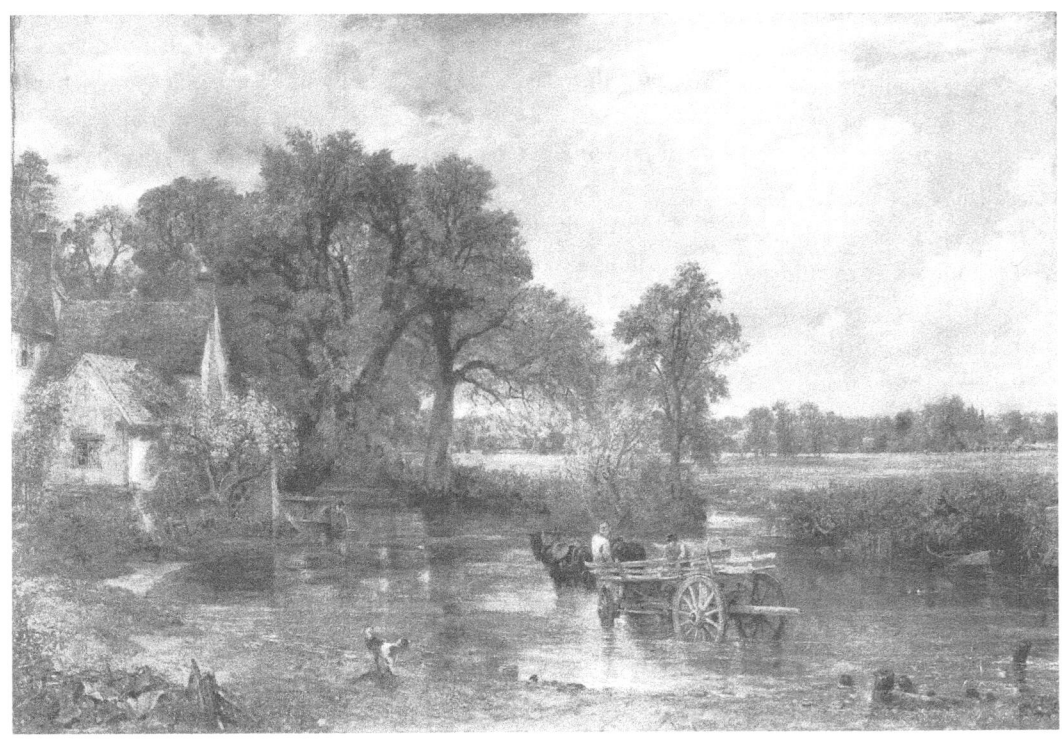

FIGURE 97. John Constable, *The Hay Wain*, 1821 (shown at the 1824 Paris Salon). Oil on canvas. London, The National Gallery, inv. 1207 (130.2 × 185.4 cm). Photo: © The National Gallery, London.

Hay Wain makes clear that Constable's vision of nature was far from the norms of French historical landscape. Constable's pictures seldom open onto vistas of deep space, but are closed off—as in *The Hay Wain*—by buildings and trees that elicit sensations of intimacy and proximity. Nor are they fictive composites assembled from views of several sites; rather, they represent actual places that can still be found in the English countryside. Constable's buildings do not belong to gleaming ideal cities, but tend to be slightly ramshackle structures nestled into their sites and overgrown with foliage. The figures in his landscapes of the 1820s are often shown working, but they perform everyday labors—like fording a stream with a hay cart—that are not freighted with allegories of mankind's civilizing presence. Both the sites and the subjects of Constable's paintings are rigorously modern, being rooted in the specifics of farming and commerce along the Stour River where he lived and painted.

All these qualities suggest that Parisian painters and critics should have been able to appreciate Constable's pictures at the 1824 Salon with the fairly well-defined critical parameters of *style champêtre*. Two important factors worked against such an appraisal. First was the physical size of the canvases: both *The Hay Wain* (Fig. 97) and *View on the Stour near Dedham* are very large, part of a series begun about 1819 that Constable called "six-footers" because they are actually that wide. "The series of six-foot landscapes," writes Ann Bermingham, "established Constable's reputation as a landscape painter. They are critical to the history of the rustic landscape—a history they culminate and conclude. Most simply, their monumentality, breaking with the traditional scale of the genre, gestures dramatically to call attention to themselves and their subject."[167] The sheer novelty of Constable's pictures made them even more striking in Paris than they had been in London. Stendhal remarked that "the English have sent us some magnificent landscapes this year by M. Constable. I doubt if we have anything to compare with them."[168] His assessment is seconded by a letter from Constable to his friend John Fisher, in which the painter reports gleefully that his pictures "have made a stir, and set the students in landscape to thinking."[169]

The second quality to complicate assimilation of Constable's pictures into the established categories of French landscape theory concerns how they were painted. A Constable landscape draws attention to itself as a material object worked manually. The entire curriculum of the French Academy was premised on an artist's mastery of his or her materials and the belief that a high standard of finish was essential. This was no less true for landscape paintings, which is why Constable's mixed technique and wide range of painterly effects were so difficult to accept. Consider this response of a fictive artist to *The Hay Wain*, from Jal's review of the 1824 Salon:

These waters are real, this cart is real, these boats are real; but the process that conveys this expression of truthfulness is very close to a mannerism. One might call it a ceaseless groping. This relief-like workmanship, these masses of brown, yellow, green, gray, red, and white flung upon one another, stirred up with a trowel, cut with a palette knife, and then glazed over to return some harmony and mystery to them: these things, I say, are less about art than technique and, moreover, this technique is graceless.[170]

Jal's artist particularly deplores the fact that Constable's technique—he calls it a "mannerism"—appears to proceed by trial and error rather than the discipline of learning. Stendhal echoed a similar mix of admiration and complaint: he admitted that "the truth of these charming works instantly strikes and delights us," but immediately qualified that praise by pointing out that "M. Constable's brushwork is excessively free, and the planes of his pictures are carelessly observed."[171] Not surprisingly, Constable's extemporaneous paint handling did not fail to attract less conventional artists. It is said that Delacroix repainted a large part of the background to his *Massacres at Chios* (Fig. 78) after looking long and hard at the Constables on display at the Salon.

French painters and critics did not know what to make of the extraordinary effect, but deplorable appearance, of Constable's paintings. This critical hesitation applies even to the professionals who organized the Salon. In the same letter to Fisher just cited, Constable reports that his works had originally been installed poorly because they were not properly understood:

My Paris affairs go on very well. Though the director, the Count Forbin, gave my pictures very respectable situations in the Louvre in the first instance, yet on being exhibited for a few weeks, they advanced in reputation and were moved from their original situations to a post of honour, two prime places in the principal room. I am much indebted to the artists for their alarum in my favour; but I must do justice to the count, who is no artist I believe, and thought that as the colours are rough, they should be seen at a distance. They found the mistake, and now acknowledge the richness of texture, and attention to the surface of things. They are struck with their vivacity and freshness, things unknown in their own pictures.[172]

Constable's example challenged the assumptions of French landscape painters by showing that the natural world—if rendered with vivacity and a kind of naïve directness—could support ambitious painting without classical allusions or ennobling baggage. His pictures proved that *style champêtre* need not be the poor stepchild of historical landscape. Forbin eventually came to understand that lesson. One mark of his admiration for Constable's achievement was that he tried unsuccessfully to buy *The Hay Wain* for the national museums. He also ensured that Constable was awarded a gold medal—ironically, the first official recognition the Englishman had ever received.

The ambivalence that greeted Constable's pictures in 1824 continued to be reflected in the work of most French landscape painters well into the 1830s. At stake in this reticence to adopt a Constable-like directness, whether in composition or technique, were basic assumptions about the relationship between a painting and the natural world. The cornerstone of academic theory and training was a control of one's perceptions and self exemplified by an ability to reorganize, reorder, and restructure the fleeting data of experience into a representation dominated by thought, reason, and timelessness. Constable showed that landscape painting could become a form of great interest to a wide public if freed from those timeworn formulas of idealization, but the academy remained committed to the idea that art must dominate nature. For many years French landscape painters vacillated between the rigors of theory and the pleasures of practice—a vacillation that is especially apparent in the early career of Camille Corot.

Corot originally failed to convince his father that the life of a painter was preferable to that of a cloth merchant. Only in

1821, upon the chance inheritance of a modest annual income, was he able to pursue his dream of an artistic career. Corot first enrolled as a student in the studio of Michallon (Fig. 96), who was already recognized as one of the leading landscape painters of the day. Following the example of Valenciennes, Michallon encouraged his students to study nature directly, but he also instilled in them a respect for historical landscapes. When Michallon died unexpectedly from tuberculosis in September of 1822, Corot transferred to the studio of Jean-Victor Bertin. The latter was a respected landscape painter but entirely committed—both in teaching and practice—to the superiority of historical landscape. After three years of study with Bertin, Corot left Paris in December 1825 for an extended trip to Italy. He remained there until the fall of 1828.

Although Corot was not officially a pensioner at the French Academy in Rome, his life and routine in Italy mirrored closely that of his fellow countrymen and students. During the summer he worked outdoors in their company, painting oil sketches at familiar sites of the Roman countryside preferred by students since the days of Valenciennes; during the winter he worked in Rome on sketches of the city and prepared composite landscapes in his studio. He incorporated the practice of making "landscape portraits," and he retained a deference for composite, historical landscapes. Corot lived out in Rome the tug-of-war between direct observation and ideal construction that had pervaded the career of Valenciennes three decades before. Upon returning to Paris, Corot launched his national career with a picture of *Hagar in the Wilderness* at the Salon of 1835 (Fig. 98). The work was painted without a commission. Its subject—based on the story from Genesis of Hagar and Ishmael wandering in the desert—demonstrates graphically that Corot still believed landscapes worthy of the Paris Salon must be historical in character.

Corot's training dictated that the broad landscape setting of *Hagar in the Wilderness* must be composed from disparate parts: the foreground rocks and the stand of trees at the center of the image were derived from oil sketches made during 1832–1833 in the forest of Fontainebleau outside of Paris; the rock cliff of the background was adapted from sketches painted about 1827 at Civita Castellana during his trip to Italy.[173] Into this vast, intensely lighted, and thoroughly fictive

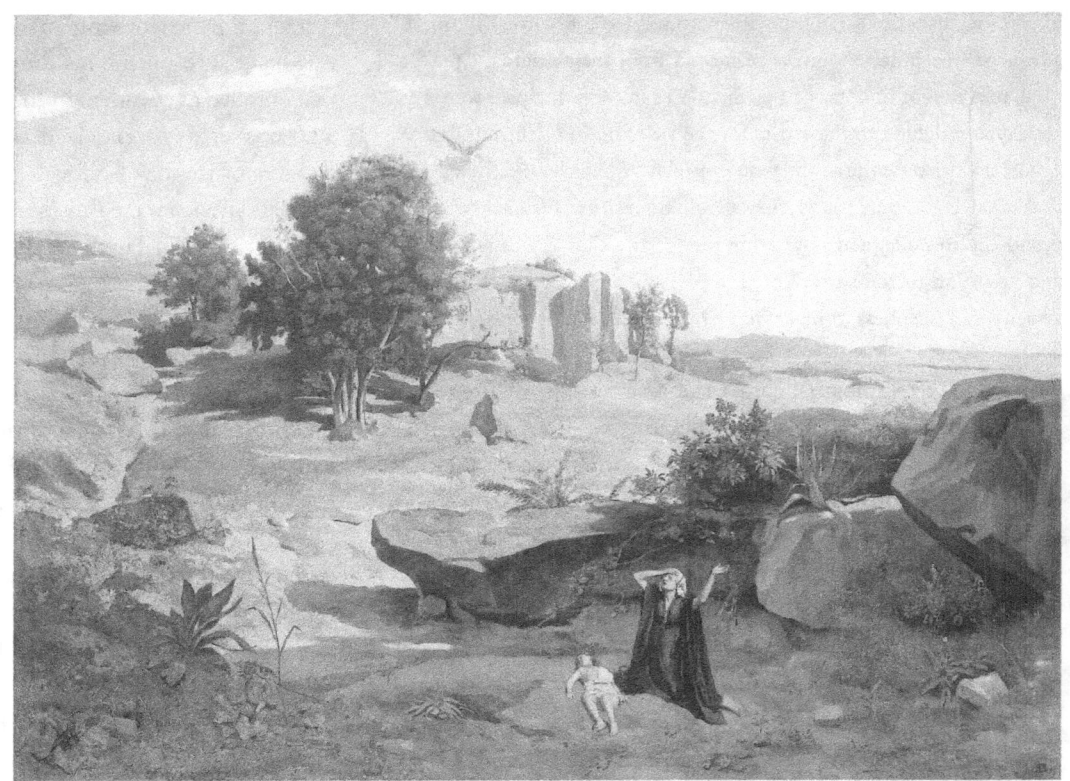

space, Corot rather awkwardly placed three small figures: in the foreground, Ishmael faints from thirst and Hagar gestures in despair; in the sky appears an angel inscribed in the arc of a rainbow. "One could say that he has had some difficulty covering his canvas," complained Louis Viardot.

We can accept that the clumps of bushes are scattered about, for we are not in the Bois de Boulogne. But the blocks of rocks should be grouped and arranged more agreeably. The angel, who responds to the mother's wailing in order to save the whole Arab ancestry of Israel, flies at a great distance and very high![174]

Where Viardot only intuits the bad fit between Corot's figures and his landscape, Charles Lenormant grasped fully the picture's internal tensions:

In some respects, M. Corot also speaks the language of landscape only by stammering. His touch is clumsy and dull; the suppleness, moisture, and charm of nature are foreign to him. For his talent to show itself brilliantly, he needs a subject like the one he has chosen this year: Hagar abandoned in the desert. In this case, the overall look can be neither too uniform nor too desolate. There is something heartrending about M. Corot's landscape, even before you discover the subject. Herein lies the peculiar value of historical landscape; that is, a harmony between the site and the passion or suffering that the painter wants to put in it.[175]

Lenormant situates Corot comfortably within the practice of historical landscape, but permits him only a "stammering" fluency in the formal language concerned with affects of the natural world such as suppleness, moisture, and charm. The critic signals elliptically that a rival standard has emerged, one ill-suited to Corot's talent. What was this rival?

Victor Schoelcher had published in 1831 a notorious and somewhat premature statement that announced a revolution in landscape painting parallel to the political revolution of July 1830:

A revolution has taken place in landscape painting as in the other branches of art. Conventional landscapes—respectable, well-swept and well-dusted landscapes lacking brambles or thorns—laid out in completely stilted and harmonized lines drawn with a compass, have almost completely disappeared from the Salon. Today, the landscapist tries to render nature as she is, and each work, instead of being cast in an unchanging mold and branded counterfeit by the seal of Poussin, bears the personal stamp of the painter's talent. In short, and in most cases, each work is a vein of ore worked more or less well in the extremely rich mine of true nature.[176]

Schoelcher was writing in the pages of *L'Artiste* about pictures being painted in the forest of Fontainebleau by artists living and working near the little village of Barbizon. For lack of a better name Schoelcher called this a "new school" of landscape painting, but today it is better known as the school of Barbizon. Four years later, pictures like Corot's *Hagar* proved that "conventional landscapes" had not completely disappeared from the Salon, but Schoelcher's claims for a new kind of landscape painting do tally with the imagery of living nature invoked by Lenormant in 1835. If the training program of most French landscape painters resembled the trajectory followed by Corot, we might well wonder from where Schoelcher's "new school" emerged. Constable would be one likely source. But even if Parisian painters and critics admired Constable's pictures in 1824, they were not convinced that his model of "natural painting" (as he called it) was sufficiently noble to support ambitious works of art. What seems to have happened about 1830 is that nature itself came to be regarded in new ways by the public at large. This in turn created a demand for new types of landscape paintings. To understand this development returns us to Balzac's interest in the differences between city and country.

The important market in travel prints and *voyages pittoresques* that flourished in the 1820s, and mentioned above, is one part of the story. Alongside this imagery appeared three related phenomena. First was the growing tendency for Parisians to escape from the city on weekends or summer vacations: not just the time-honored practice of going beyond the city's limits to eat and drink without paying Paris taxes on alcohol, but to make what Nicholas Green has called "extended promenades" that involved a "plunge into nature" as a source of enjoyment in its own right.[177] A second, closely related trend was the growing number of middle class merchants, bankers, and tradespeople who bought country houses [maisons de campagne] as secondary residences and places of relaxation. Green points out that advertisements for country houses stressed less the internal arrangement of the house than qualities of the site. "The *jardin anglais* or more modest *potager*, the lake or fountain, the well-filled fishpond, the comforting frame of gates and walls," he writes; "these were features to conjure up an intimate and private world. They promised safety, especially for women and children, and they implied *immersion* in your own sensations and experiences— here you could circulate unseen!"[178] Finally, by the late 1830s, these two developments were boosted by the opening of new railroad lines able to transport people quickly between Paris and the countryside.

Development of the industries of tourism and country real estate was accompanied by new ways of thinking and talking about the natural world. The goal was no longer to dominate nature, but to become lost in it. One index of the new value attached to sensations of immersion in nature was the contemporary craze for dioramas. Visitors to Louis Daguerre's Diorama in Paris literally entered a spectacle in which controlled lighting, a large visual field of changing imagery, and the viewer's physical placement inside the specially rigged auditorium combined to produce powerful physiological responses. Since Daguerre's technologies for portraying movement were fairly limited, it is not surprising that he favored landscape subjects. Some of the spectacles he mounted around 1830 included the eruption of Mount Etna, the interior of Canterbury Cathedral, and a view of Edinburgh. Daguerre did not situate his audience as detached observers before these phenomena, but immersed them in the experience. The shift is of great historical importance, because the Diorama's thrill registered on a popular level the idea that images of nature could be viscerally powerful without a superstructure of rational control. The lofty theories of landscape painting were being changed from the bottom up.

This conceptual transformation of nature—from a mass of raw material waiting for civilization into a geography of therapeutic escape—was a powerful force working against Academic doctrine. Its triumph by the end of the 1840s was perhaps best expressed by Théophile Thoré, writing in response to the landscape paintings of Narcisse-Virgile Diaz de la Peña at the Salon of 1847:

Long live life! Life everywhere: in the air you cannot grasp, in the endlessly varied landscape, in the flowers and animals happy to be in the world, in human beings stirred by so many passions! Dull painting is definitely not amusing! We all have enough troubles in our political and private lives to excuse the arts for reminding us of natural nature—*natura naturans* as the ancients called it—a nature eternally fertile and luxuriant that forms such a cruel contrast to our factitious morals and all the sad contrivances of a world upside-down.[179]

Thoré was a staunch advocate of the new school of landscape painting since the early 1830s. He was also a long-time friend of Théodore Rousseau, a painter who spent a good part of each year outside of Paris, and who increasingly lived immersed in the landscapes he depicted. One of Rousseau's pictures, *Alley of Chestnut Trees* (Fig. 99), inspired Thoré to explain succinctly the mechanics and poetics of immersion:

Stepping into the edge of the picture is like entering the wide end of a funnel from which there is no escape. But, in the deep background and very far away, you see the light of day in the distant aperture of this cavern of interlaced branches and thick foliage. You have no sky overhead, nor to the right or left; the trees planted trunk to trunk are entangled like climbing vines in a virgin forest, or like arabesques running along the wall decorations and

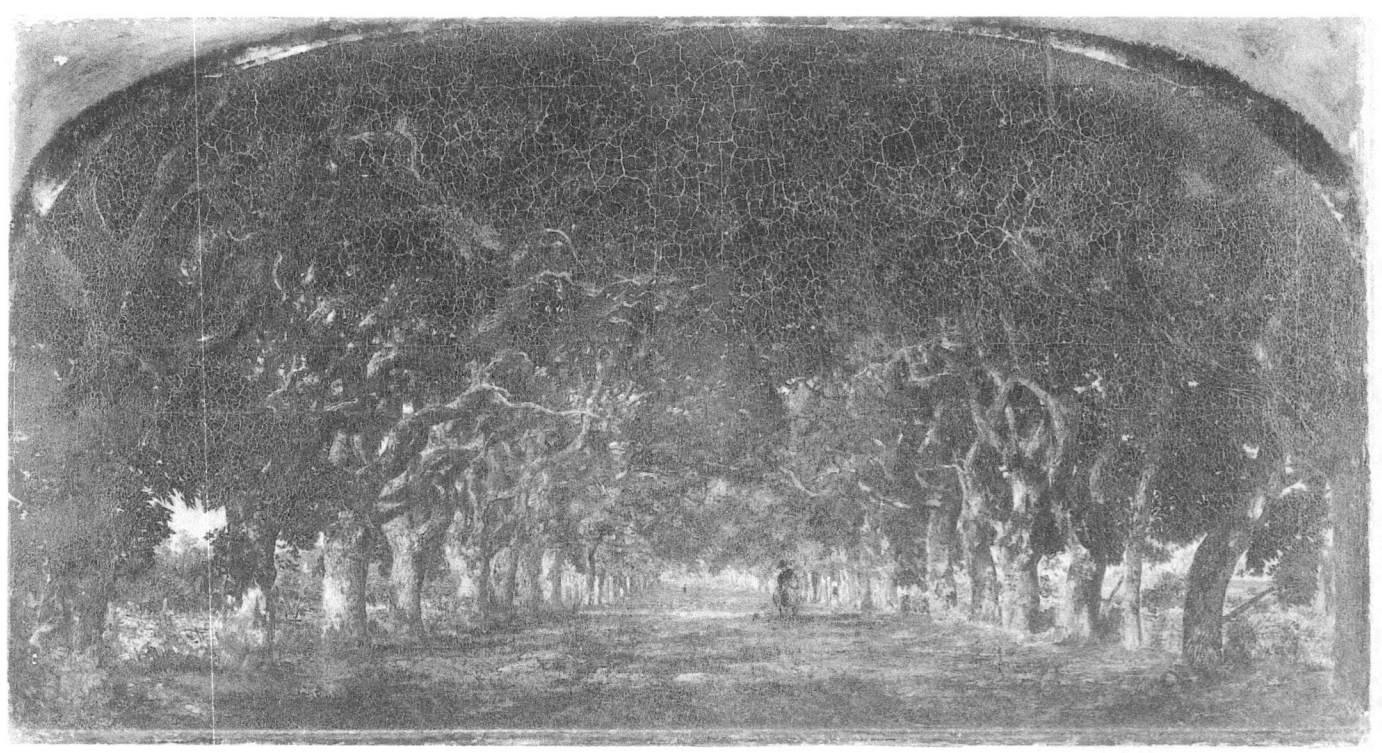

FIGURE 99.   Théodore Rousseau, *An Alley of Chestnut Trees*, 1837–1840 (refused at the Salons of 1838 and 1841). Oil on canvas. Paris, Musée du Louvre, inv. RF2046 (79 × 144 cm). Photo: © RMN/Art Resource, NY/© D. Chenot.

vaults of an edifice. . . . While pondering this beautiful painting, you experience the same feeling as when entering a vast gothic cathedral by yourself. . . . A picture like this is surely about an art for man, and not an art for art's sake. I am not saying that this poetry does not exist in nature; but only that one must feel it there and express it. . . . Nature is a voluptuous mother who provokes the passion of her lover, and art is the fruit of this union.[180]

The story of Rousseau's picture does not end with Thoré's praise, for the government bought it in May of 1840, after being pressured by Delacroix and Georges Sand.

Even that gesture of official favor failed to convince the Salon jury to accept *Alley of Chestnut Trees* for the exhibition of 1841. At stake in their refusal was not simply the thickly troweled surfaces or strident colors of Rousseau's painting (today much damaged by the corrosive effects of bitumen), but the relationship to nature it took for granted. Thoré understood that a profoundly personal, deeply immersive response—one might say a meditation—was at the core of Rousseau's vision. The jury understood perfectly that such a work ran counter to the Academy's sacrosanct principle that representing the natural world meant civilizing it visually and metaphorically. Rousseau's *Alley of Chestnut Trees* and pictures like it offered viewers a freedom to respond to art with no more nor less specialized training than they brought to their everyday encounters with the natural world—a freedom that challenged directly the Academy's position as premier institution of elite culture. People, newspapers, and pictures might be able to move freely from Paris to the provinces and back again, but the Academic painters who comprised the Salon jury clung desperately to their accustomed privileges as Paris-based arbiters of taste for all of France.

AESTHETIC ISSUES of moral authority and cultural power inevitably intersect with politics. This was especially true after the revolution of February 1848. One immediate consequence was a disbanding of the Salon jury so that the exhibition of 1848 was thrown open to all artists. An enormous number of works greeted visitors on opening day and the catalogue listed more than five thousand items. "The Salon of 1848 affords an extremely singular spectacle," remarked Théophile Thoré, who was somewhat disappointed by it all; "there are pictures in it that one has never seen in the shops of country glaziers. . . . The only thing that has changed today is the prodigious number of these eccentric images . . . and one hopes that the crowd's reception of several hundred daubed canvases will convince the daubers to take up another line of work."[181] After a short review of Delacroix's works, Thoré excused himself from a more fulsome discussion of the Salon by observing that "for us, politics holds more interesting spectacles. Today we are making more than art and poetry: we are making living history."[182] Talking about art had lost its urgency.

However brief his comments, Thoré tacitly assumed there was a qualitative difference between what one expects to find in the window of a country glass cutter and the galleries of the Salon. It was a difference that writers had exploited for decades by characterizing the countryside as a timeless background to the cosmopolitan modernity of Paris. Visual artists participated in this fiction by portraying French provincials with a vocabulary of picturesque ethnography identical to Léopold Robert's treatment of provincial Italians (Fig. 91). Adolphe Leleux's pictures of Brittany peasants and the images of rural life in the Limousin or Corrèze regions painted by Philippe-Auguste Jeanron are examples of this expansive genre. Moreover, when Thoré says "we are making living history," he does not mean to suggest that "we" are anything but Parisians. Thoré—like most of his colleagues—assumed Paris to be the mythic center of French political and cultural life: if Paris falls, so does the government (Fig. 16); if Paris makes revolutions, the country follows (Fig. 25); if the nation's history is to be inscribed in stone, it will be on the boulevards of the capital (Figs. 41–55).

This myth was shattered in June of 1848 when National Guardsmen from the provinces, responding massively to Cavaignac's call for support, quashed the uprising of Parisian workers and left the streets littered with corpses (Fig. 27). The provinces had imposed an agenda of "law and order" on the unruly capital. In the following months, especially after the establishment of universal suffrage, the provinces also began to exercise political clout at the ballot box. Provincial voters were largely responsible for the election of Louis-Napoléon Bonaparte to the presidency in December of 1848 against the advice of Parisian pundits and political leaders (see Epilogue). But in the legislative elections of May 1849, the provinces voted massively for democrat-socialist candidates of the Left. Suddenly and alarmingly, a huge swath of the French countryside turned against the conservative politics it had supported in June of 1848. "If only La Bruyère could see the peasant of today in all the splendor of his political, intellectual and moral progress," exclaimed one Catholic writer shortly after the legislative voting;

no longer heeding his priest, neither recognizing nor believing in God, strong-minded, reading M. Proudhon's or M. Thoré's paper in the taverns, and voting in the Red list at the polls, in the profound conviction that he will then be able to get his greedy paws on a good portion of other people's property.[183]

The ominous lesson was that the provinces were neither intellectually and politically inert nor especially predictable. With elections for president and the National Assembly scheduled for the end of 1852, Parisians understood that provincial voters might very well determine the nation's fate. "The new fact in the present situation," remarked Adolphe Blanqui in 1851, "is the political arrival of this rural population, who are called to set a great weight in the scales of our destinies."[184]

The provinces were beset by their own special problems. Land was changing hands more quickly than ever before as peasant farmers, faced with poor crops and low prices, were forced into debt and bankruptcy. "The bourgeoisie having sold their lands and being the peasants' creditor," reported the Prefect of the Drôme region at the end of 1849, "subversives have made peasants suspicious of the bourgeois by telling the former that the latter were opposed to what might allow the peasant to pay off his debts, in order to keep him in a kind of servitude. This is how war has been declared by the jacket against the dress-coat."[185] The prefect was describing a volatile local situation with troubling national consequences: how would the embattled peasants vote next time around? Behind whom would they throw their immense electoral support? No one seemed to know for sure. In this context of political uncertainty, to exhibit in Paris pictures of rural life was a sure way to become ensnared in controversy. Today, it is difficult to imagine the volatility of such imagery; it is also likely that neither Jean-François Millet nor Gustave Courbet fully anticipated the partisan debates that would be ignited by the paintings they sent to the Salon of 1850–1851.

Millet's *Sower* (Fig. 100) is certainly a powerful image. Although the picture is not physically large (about 100 × 80 cm), Millet's peasant almost entirely fills the frame with an imposing presence. Winter wheat is planted in the chill of November: Millet's sower has clamped his hat tightly to his head, his legs are wrapped in straw for warmth, and the low sun casts most of his features into an almost impenetrable shadow. The bleakness of Millet's dominant colors—muddy browns, muted blues, and blackened greens unrelieved by the hesitant pinkish tones of an evening sky—echo the bleakness of fields in late autumn. Yet the man's gestures are large, his stride is bold, and his body courses with coiled energy. A slightly tilted horizon line gives the impression that the sower marches downhill, thus joining the pull of gravity to his powerful and rhythmic forward motion. The man projects an energy that threatens to burst the picture plane and thrust him into the viewer's space. At the far left, distant crows scavenging for seed are easily mistaken as the seeds themselves, exploding into space from the clenched fist of the man's throwing hand. "Alone, in the middle of a naked and freshly plowed field, as if he seems to understand the grandeur of his task," remarked Albert de la Fizelière, "this man, minister of heaven, who holds in his hand and throws to the wind the riches of the earth with the faith of an apostle; and then, over there, under a cloud, this flock of greedy

---

FIGURE 100.   Jean-François Millet, *The Sower*, 1850. Oil on canvas. Yamanashi, Prefectural Museum of Art, inv. 3041 (99.7 × 80.7 cm). Photo: Courtesy of the Prefectural Museum of Art, Yamanashi.

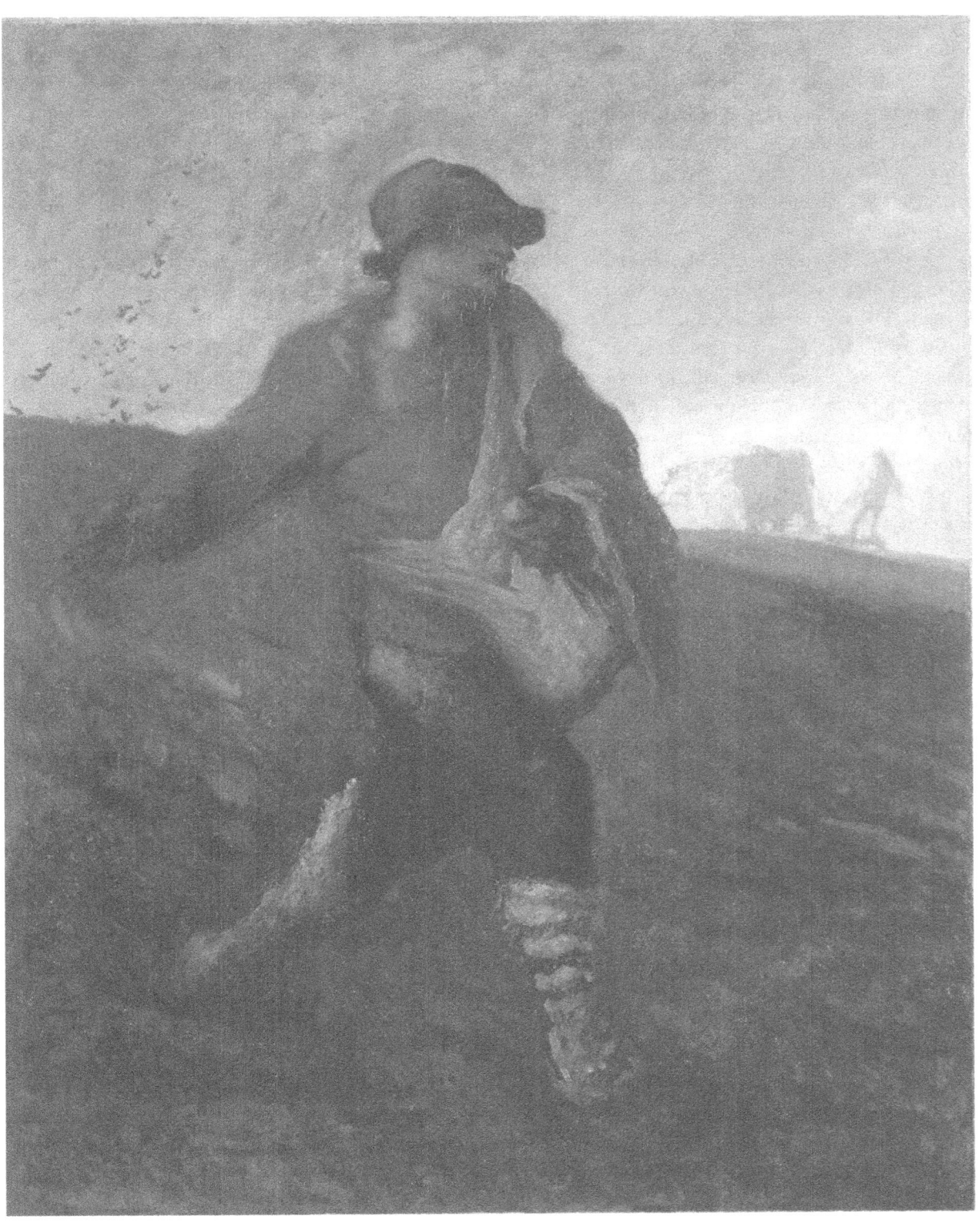

birds who screech with mockery and menace."[186] Fizelière strives to read the *Sower* in the biblical register that Millet probably intended, but he cannot avoid the sinister side of this anonymous, muscular peasant in the galleries of the Paris Salon. He cannot block out the menacing screech of those hungry crows.

Other critics acknowledged their apprehensions more openly. "Why this coarse countenance?" asked Auguste Desplaces in the pages of *L'Union*; "why these blackened and monochrome colors? Where has M. Millet met a worker with so grim an expression, a sky so gloomy, a landscape in sowing season so dreary?"[187] Desplaces questioned the accuracy of Millet's barely restrained violence, perhaps looking for assurances that the provinces and their people were not to be feared after all. His ambivalence before the *Sower*—recognizing its violence but not wanting to believe it—was characteristic of many responses to Millet's picture. In the uncertain months of 1851 Parisians longed for the provinces to remain pastoral spaces of mythic calm, and for peasants to remain mythic others who ignored politics. A critic named Dauger, writing for *Le Pays*, graphically expressed this longing:

In this realist school, we are familiar with a young man of talent who has a future . . . at least he has a poetry all his own, a wildness that commands respect, a staging that spurns his characters and keeps them at a proper distance. His name is François Millet, and he has sent to the Salon two canvases. . . . Always nature in the fields, but surely that is where one must look for it. The *Sower* is a rugged peasant who goes at it in earnest, and whose primitive coarseness has nothing to fear from his stay in the heart of Paris: he will always remain what he is, a rustic from head to foot.[188]

Timothy Clark correctly points out that Dauger—like most of his contemporaries—accepted the roughness and violence of the *Sower* precisely because Millet kept him in the country and insulated from change. A "stay in the heart of Paris" would not alter one bit of his "primitive coarseness." Dauger articulates what most Parisians wanted but could not say: provincials should remain unchanged "from head to foot" and be happy to take directions from the capital. The problem not addressed by Dauger was that the countryside of 1851 included not only peasants working the land but also—as the Prefect of the Drôme reported—a class of bourgeois landowners, moneylenders, and businessmen who increasingly controlled much of the local wealth.

Gustave Courbet brought this latter group to Paris on a monumental scale with his *Burial at Ornans* (Fig. 101). The subject is no surprise, because Ornans was Courbet's hometown and his family was solidly bourgeois. Courbet's father owned two houses (one in Ornans and the other in a nearby village), and a fairly large expanse of land. He was rich enough to qualify for voting privileges in the days before universal suffrage. Moreover, the picture was actually painted in Ornans, where many of Courbet's friends and family members posed for him: his father appears just to the left of the man weeping into a handkerchief, his mother is at the extreme right holding the hand of a young girl, and his three sisters stand just behind the dog. Yet the work is far from a family portrait, because Courbet's parents and siblings are interspersed with others from town in a ceremony that is both religious and civic—scholars now agree that the painting was inspired by the first use of a new cemetery located just outside the city's gates. In every sense the *Burial at Ornans* qualified as a genuine document of life in the provinces.

Courbet brought these outsiders to Paris in a big way. The picture is more than six meters wide, and the figures are life-sized. For viewers even to see the whole image means standing fairly far away or literally walking its width. In either case, experience of the picture is neither anchored nor centered. The figures do tend to coalesce loosely into three groups, but no single group dominates the others to organize or focus attention. At the center, where one expects a visual emphasis, there is only the empty hole of the defunct's grave.[189] To the right, individual bodies lose their definition and identity: faces, hands, and women's hats float as disconnected accents of light amidst an almost impenetrable field of black. To the left, the approaching procession of coffin and crucifix might generate a narrative thread if the priest was more attentive to its arrival, and if the two beadles did not defeat the moment's solemnity with their comic, red-nosed grimaces. "The family is pulled apart and reassembled in the context of a class, a community," notes Clark, but the

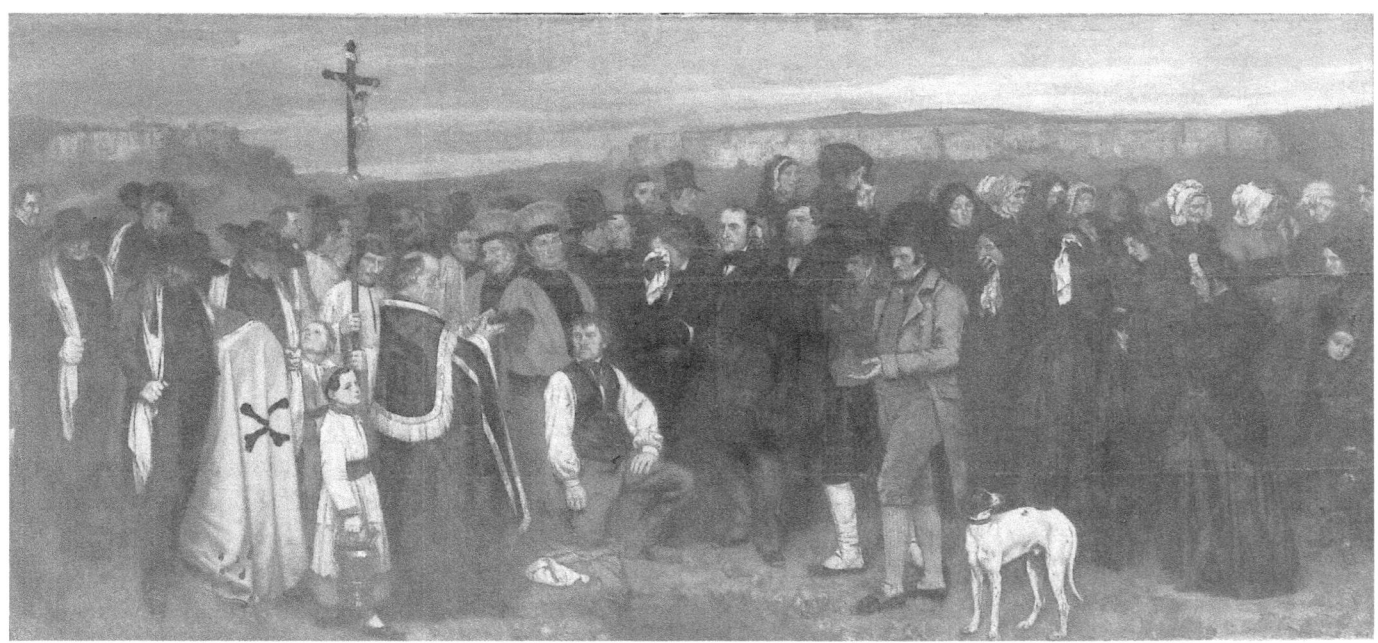

FIGURE 101.   Gustave Courbet, *A Burial at Ornans*, 1849–1850. Oil on canvas. Paris, Musée d'Orsay, inv. RF325 (311.5 × 668 cm). Photo: © RMN/Art Resource, NY/© Hervé Lewandowski.

oddest part of the picture was—and remains—the awkwardness of that reassembly.[190]

Courbet himself vacillated between an ambition to monumentalize his sitters and embarrassment before their slightly ridiculous naïveté. "Here models are for the asking," he wrote to Jules Champfleury in Paris.

Everyone would like to be in the *Burial*. I could never please them all, I would make quite a few enemies. . . . I had hoped to get by without the two precentors of the parish, but there was no way. Someone warned me that they were offended, that they were the only church people I had not included. They complained bitterly, saying that they had never done me any harm and that they did not deserve such an affront, etc.[191]

Clark argues convincingly that the picture's refusal to take sides for or against these earnest bourgeois of Ornans is also poignantly autobiographical, because Courbet was both one of them and desperately trying to be someone else, someone Parisian. In July, while making his way to Paris with his pic-

tures for the 1851 Salon (including *Burial at Ornans*), Courbet confessed to Francis Wey:

If I had to make a choice among countries, I admit that I would not choose my own. That is why I have begun with it. Besides, in life one learns above all from adversity. There is also a saying that one must try new things from time to time in order to be truthful, for you know that truth changes with the times.[192]

Courbet could not predict in July how much the truth of his pictures would change by the time they arrived in Paris.

The *Burial at Ornans* was simply too large to be ignored at the Salon, and it did not fail to elicit a throng of conflicting responses. Théophile Gautier was close to the mark when he wrote that the picture's effect "is hard to figure out: you don't know if you should weep or scoff. Was it the author's intention to make a caricature or a serious painting?"[193] In light of Courbet's own ambivalence about the subject and his models, Gautier's bewilderment makes perfect sense. His reference to caricature also echoes the many critics who scoffed at the picture's clunky form. "One sees men in black laminated onto women in black," reported Claude Vignon, "and behind them, ignoble figures of beadles and grave-diggers, four pall-bearers in black endowed with démoc-soc beards, Montagnard getups, and hats designed by Caussidière! Voilà!"[194] The subtle political references tucked into Vignon's description are worth decoding: "démoc-soc" beards alludes to the left-wing coalition of democrats and socialists who garnered so many votes in 1849; "Montagnard getups" refers to the revolutionary-epoch costume of the 1790s worn by the man just left of the dog; hats "designed by Caussidière" pillories the uniform imposed in 1848 by a former chief of police. Bubbling beneath the surface of Vignon's reaction to Courbet's rendering of bourgeois provincials is the specter of political strife, an undercurrent that exploded in the columns of *Le Constitutionnel*. "His painting is a revolutionary machine," exclaimed Louis Peisse; "to increase our fright, one even adds that this newborn art is the legitimate son of the Republic, that it is the product and manifestation of democratic and popular genius. Thanks to M. Courbet art becomes common."[195] Writing for the moderate liberal readers of *Le Constitutionnel*, Peisse lets slip that to "increase our fright" this art is lauded as "democratic and popular," meaning that "we" who hate the picture are not. How did critics move so far afield from a simple funeral in the provinces? Here we must return to Balzac.

One of the first sensations experienced by Lucien when walking the streets of Paris was an "incredible diminishing of himself" within the crowds of the city. For Balzac, trying to pass too quickly from provincial to Parisian provokes a kind of annihilation. Transitions are needed, he says, and nearly all the stories of Balzac's *Human Comedy* are concerned with the trials and tribulations of making those transitions. Paris in 1851 was a city of transitions. Many Parisians had made the passage from provincial to big-city bourgeois by hard work, sacrifice, and some guile. In most cases those years of struggle were not remembered as golden. Arrival and success were the moments of glory. Provincial origins marked the mythic starting point of the long trek towards achievement. The middle was

something to forget. Worst of all, Lucien discovers—being obliged to walk home in shame without a penny or a shred of fame—that success in Paris can be temporary and ephemeral. The lesson of *Lost Illusions* is that a similar fate might befall anyone. The specter of social or economic relapse hung heavy over the caprices of life in the capital. It also weighed on Courbet, since he too was one of the newly arrived. The *Burial at Ornans* put on public display the social origins of Courbet and those of many Parisian bourgeois. Its ambivalent message opened the door to a full range of commentaries and moments of self-reflection—from innocent ridicule to palpable fear.

Reversals of fortune might occur for many reasons. The June days of 1848 revealed all too clearly the underlying fragility of the Parisian social order. The electoral results of 1849 further challenged the city's illusions of political stability and moral authority. By 1851 the most immediate danger appeared to be the threat of political upheaval spearheaded by socialist principles: peasants rising up to avenge their economic plight; provincials marching on the capital to take control of the state; everything achieved by the bourgeois of Paris ruined and destroyed. It was enough to rally support for the idea of an enlightened despot (see Epilogue). In the midst of this maelstrom the embattled bourgeois of the capital needed a mythic provincial—a timeless and unchanging other against which they could measure themselves. Millet's *Sower* (Fig. 100), for all his implied violence, was no threat so long as he stayed in the fields. Courbet's countryside bourgeois (Fig. 101), for all their seeming inertia and comic presence, were at once too familiar and too ridiculous to praise. There was no recourse but to despise them. What better way to keep them at a distance—to fix their otherness—than to make them figures of what one feared the most? In this paradoxical and roundabout way, Courbet's image of the earnest and basically conservative inhabitants of Ornans was read in Paris as a harbinger of revolutionary socialism. Today, we are led to ask incredulously: what kind of cultural milieu was able to perform this odd and unexpected transformation? That is the topic of our next chapter.

˄ CHAPTER 6

The Art Scene

What a wonderful time! Walter Scott was then in his prime; we were initiated into the mysteries of Goethe's Faust that, according to the expression of Madame de Staël, comprised everything and even something a bit more than that. We discovered Shakespeare in Letourneur's rather patchy translation, and the poems of Lord Byron. . . . It was all so young, new, strangely colored, intoxicating and strongly flavored! We were all infatuated; it seemed that one was stepping into an unknown world. On every page we chanced upon subjects for compositions that we hastened to draw or sketch furtively, because motifs like that would not have been in the master's taste and, had they been discovered, would have merited a good thump on the head with the maulstick.

—Théophile Gautier[1]

GAUTIER'S MEMORIES of the early years of Romanticism probably overstate the impact of literature, especially the works of Goethe and Shakespeare, upon the artists who met in the studio of Jehan Duseigneur (Fig. 85) and came to be known as the *petit cénacle*.[2] The art historian Léon Rosenthal concluded long ago that cross-fertilization between literature and the visual arts was quite rare except in isolated cases like Louis Boulanger. Nonetheless, an appreciation of literary forms outside the canon of French masters affected both major players and minor participants in the cultural gatherings of 1820s Paris. Delacroix, for example, was an infrequent visitor to Hugo's salon, yet he entertained the idea of making a suite of works based on Goethe's *Götz von Berlichingen*, a project apparently inspired by conversations with his friend Jean-Baptiste Pierret.[3] While visiting London in 1825 the painter attended several productions of Shakespeare, including *Richard III*, *The Tempest*, *Othello*, and *The Merchant of Venice*. He regretted missing *Hamlet*.[4] Like most of his friends, Delacroix admired the extremes of Shakespeare's dark side. He wrote to Hugo shortly after an English troupe starring Thomas Kemble and Harriett Smithson opened a run at the Odéon theater in Paris:

Well! Generalized invasion: Hamlet raises his frightful head, Othello readies his dagger that is above all killer and subverter of every good dramatic policeman. Who knows what else? King Lear is going to tear out his eyes before a French audience. It will be the Academy's honor to proclaim that any importation of this genre is incompatible with public morality. Good-bye good taste! In any case, prepare a sturdy breastplate under your dress-coat. Fear the classicist daggers or, rather, sacrifice yourself courageously to our other barbarians for our amusement.[5]

Delacroix's language of combat, horror, and challenge to "good taste" was written in September of 1827, exactly contemporary with his *Death of Sardanapalus* (Fig. 83) and Hugo's preface to *Cromwell* (see Chapter Five). Delacroix understood the plays of Shakespeare to be catalysts that would unite painters and poets in their common struggle against the Academy.

Because theatrical productions are the most public form of making texts visible, they instantiate the intersection of literature and the visual arts during the 1820s.[6] While Delacroix was in London he saw *Faust* at the Drury Lane Theater. An actor named Terry was featured in the role of Mephistopheles, and James William Wallack played the hero. Delacroix was deeply impressed by this English production. It was "more diabolical than one could imagine," he wrote; "Mephistopheles is a masterpiece of personality and intelligence. It's Goethe's Faust, but rearranged: the main point is preserved. They have made an opera that mixes comedy with all that is blackest."[7] Here, too, the dark qualities of the performance stayed with Delacroix, a point he reiterated years later when recalling that "Terry, who played the devil, was perfect."[8] Delacroix later admitted to Philippe Burty that the lasting impression of this English production, much more than his familiarity with Goethe's text, motivated his lithographs for *Faust*.[9] Naturally, Delacroix studied carefully the French translation of Goethe's original in the course of his project. He also copied many excerpts into his notebooks while searching for potential subjects, and he experimented with a range of pictorial solutions in a visual dialogue with the text.[10] Delacroix eventually produced seventeen lithographs that were published by Charles Motte in 1828 to accompany Albert Stapfer's new translation of Goethe's original (Fig. 102).[11]

The most remarkable quality of Delacroix's lithographs is a visual inscription of the operatic darkness he so admired in the English production of 1825. Delacroix worked up his images using an unusual lithographic technique now known as the dark manner [manière noire], in which the artist begins with a field of black rather than the more intuitive blank sheet of white paper. Scratches in the prepared printing surface create forms by reserving areas of white within the black ground. Thus, the subject emerges from material darkness in a conceptual reversal that corresponds exactly to the dark mood of the stage production seen by Delacroix in London. His print of *Marguerite and Mephistopheles in the Cathedral* exemplifies the expressive potential of the manière noire technique (Fig. 102). Delacroix incised a regular and repetitive pattern of lines upon the field of black to describe the massive pillars of his imagined cathedral—a pattern that mimics visually the chisel strokes of the gothic

masons who cut the stone. Slight variations in the length, direction, and density of these scratchings elicit from the pervasive blackness the figure of a priest in prayer, an attendant crowd, and the frame of an image that seems to be the focus of their worship. The rustling, agitated fabric of a cape emerges from the same blackness using fewer lines, as does the contorted face of Mephistopheles, who screams hysterically into the ear of Marguerite. The raised right arm of Mephistopheles nearly disappears into the background, so that the accusing gesture of his hand floats in space as if detached from his body—a body actually visible to none of the participants.

Delacroix's print leads our eyes to the hapless figure of Marguerite, who is depicted with a whiteness that is all her own, as if bathed in a bright light that inexplicably penetrates the surrounding gloom. She appears to collapse under the weight of her guilt. Her neck—bent under the presence and words of the evil spirit—contrasts poignantly with the neck of a second young woman who is consoled by the words of a priest that Marguerite does not hear. Marguerite's emotional isolation from the group is indexed by her state of swoon and the inattention that allows her prayer book to slip from her hand. It is furthered by a juxtaposition of darkness and light that inverts the expected allusions of those terms: Delacroix's light is a metaphor for guilt rather than grace; the cathedral's space of religious fellowship is a cloud of darkness that keeps Marguerite at bay. Delacroix remembered vividly the church scene from the performance of *Faust* he had seen in London: in the same letter where he reports the play had "all that is blackest," he singles out "the church scene with the priest's singing and the organ in the distance. The impression cannot be surpassed on stage."[12] Music cannot be drawn, but it is fair to assume that Delacroix's memory of the deep, sonorous, and penetrating chords of the organ became the gloom of pictorial darkness that pervades his lithograph.

FIGURE 102.   Eugène Delacroix, *Marguerite and Mephistopheles in the Cathedral*, 1827. Lithograph. Paris, BnF, Estampes, inv. Dc 183 rés (4) (26.5 × 22.5 cm). Photo: BnF, Paris.

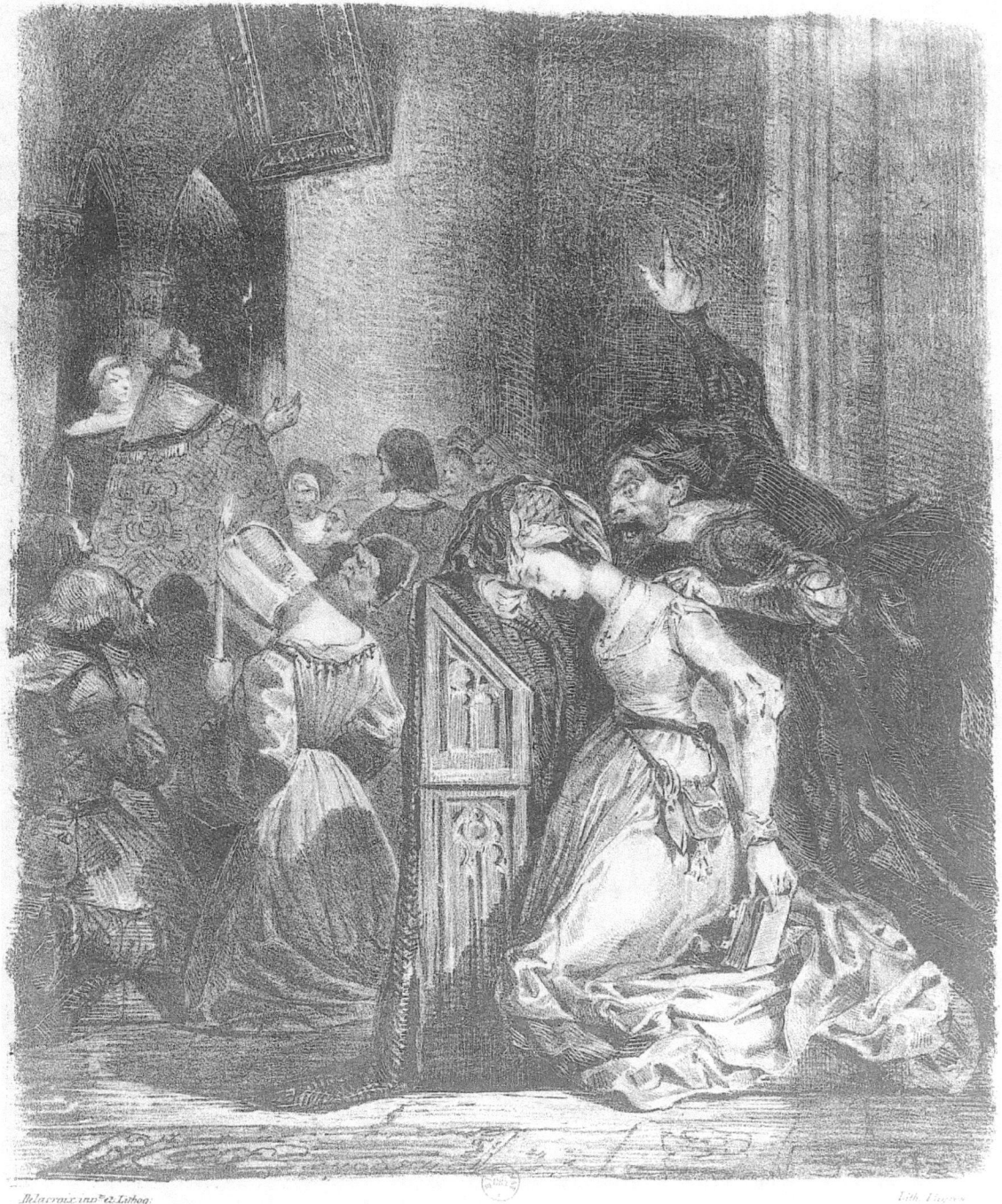

Delacroix inn.^t et Lithog.

Lith. Pagne

Marg.—Malheureuse ! ah ! si je pouvais me soustraire aux pensées qui se succèdent en tumulte dans mon ame et s'élèvent contre moi
Le mauvais Esprit.—La colère de Dieu fond sur toi ! la trompette sonne . . . . Malheur à toi.
Chœur.—Judex ergo cum sedebit,
Quid quid latet apparebit.
Nil inultum remanebit.

It is rare for the author of a literary work to record his or her reaction to its visual interpretation, but there is good evidence that Goethe was deeply moved by Delacroix's illustrations of *Faust*. In the fall of 1826, well before the series was completed, two of Delacroix's prints were sent to Goethe, who discussed them with his friend Johann Peter Eckermann in flattering terms:

Delacroix is a man of distinguished genius, who found in *Faust* the very aliment his mind needed. The wildness for which his countrymen blame him stands him in stead here. I hope he will illustrate all of *Faust*. . . . You see here the extensive experience of life, for which a city like Paris has given him such opportunity. . . . And, if I must confess, Delacroix has, in many instances, surpassed my own idea of the scenes which I myself originated.[13]

Delacroix may not have known about Goethe's admiration for those first prints, but he certainly was aware of Goethe's review of the new French translation and admiration for the plates. "Delacroix seems to have felt at home here," wrote Goethe in 1827, "as though on familiar ground, between the coarsest and the most delicate."[14] Exactly that contrast is drawn sharply in *Marguerite and Mephistopheles in the Cathedral*: the delicate, pale, and emotionally defeated figure of the heroine set against the coarse features, nearly invisible blackness, and triumphant evil of Mephistopheles. Delacroix later recalled that "the strangeness of the plates . . . increasingly positioned me as one of the chorus leaders of the *school of ugliness*."[15] The reason is clear. The character most interesting to Delacroix, and for whom he reserved the most daring pictorial inventions, was not the hero Faust, but the devil Mephistopheles. The illustrations incarnate Delacroix's ongoing fascination with the dark side of Goethe's story that had been so powerfully staged in London. Moreover, Delacroix's visual interpretation of *Faust* is perfectly in synch with Hugo's advocacy of the grotesque in the preface to *Cromwell* (see Chapter Five), and exactly contemporary with the flowering in Paris of the Gothic Revival (see Chapter Four).

Goethe believed that "the extensive experience of life, for which a city like Paris has given him such opportunity" was partly responsible for the peculiar insight of Delacroix's images. The German correctly sensed a link between the "wildness" of the artist and the ambience of Romantic Paris—an ambience that can be studied historically but not completely grasped. Today, we must struggle to understand the attraction of Jean-Jacques Feuchère's sculpture of *Satan* (Fig. 103), but Parisian viewers of 1833 accepted such subjects as completely familiar. Feuchère's nude and bat-like Satan might have been inspired by the first of Delacroix's *Faust* lithographs, in which a naked, bat-winged Mephistopheles flies above the

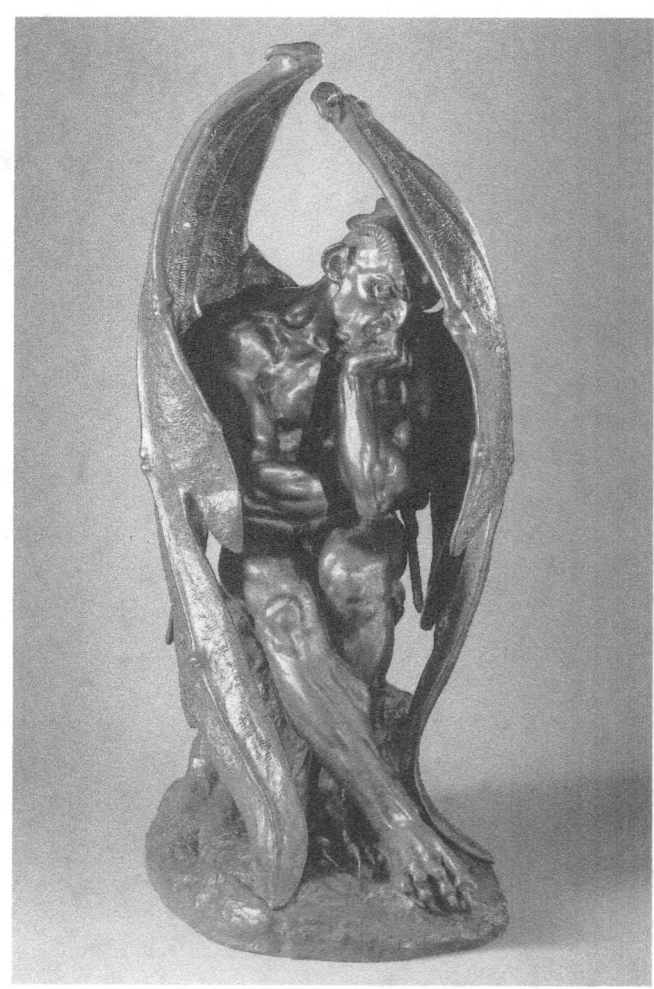

FIGURE 103.   Jean-Jacques Feuchère, *Satan*, 1834 (cast in 1850). Bronze. Los Angeles, Los Angeles County Museum of Art, inv. M.77.45 (87.4 × 53.3 × 31.7 cm). Photo: © 2004 Museum Associates / LACMA.

Paris skyline. Satan's posture also seems freely adapted from the figure of *Melancholy* in Albrecht Dürer's famous print, a copy of which Feuchère owned. Yet Feuchère's conception of Satan cannot be tied to any single literary source; rather, it resonates with allusions to several interrelated texts of great interest to readers of the early 1830s, including Goethe's *Faust*, Milton's *Paradise Lost*, Dante's *Inferno*, and the Bible. The most unusual and timely quality of Feuchère's sculpture is the psychological state of his figure. This is not evil triumphant, for Satan hides under his wings, rests his chin upon his fist, and gnaws at his own fingers. He holds a broken sword in his right hand. Isolation and dejection are written on the contortions of his face and his body language of self-enclosure. Feuchère imagines Satan after the fall, nursing the wounds of his anger, disappointment, and dashed ambitions. The sculptor's veiled allusion to Dürer's *Melancholy* makes good sense, for this outcast and vanquished Satan has much to ponder.

Feuchère's unusual *Satan* was originally cast as a small bronze (about 35 cm tall) and grouped with two vases, each rising from a base of coiled serpents. The vases were decorated with reliefs of flying bats and crowned by small winged devils similar to Satan himself.[16] Like the small Renaissance bronzes preferred by contemporary collectors, Feuchère's casts were not plated in gold or silver but finished in a dark patina perfectly in accord with their dark subject matter. The somewhat bizarre ensemble was reproduced on an intimate scale suitable for chimney mantles, curiosity cabinets, and similar displays within the domestic interiors of fashionable private apartments. As when confronting the peculiar table settings of the duc d'Orléans's centerpiece (Fig. 90), we must ask: what did a subject like this mean?

Satan in defeat was commonly associated with Romantic artists, whose soaring ambitions to break free of the material world often crashed on the rocks of mediocrity. The German critic Heinrich Heine, who was no stranger to Paris, described the plight of a modern and romantic artist in an essay exactly contemporary with Feuchère's sculpture. His terminology could equally apply to Satan's self-made fall from grace:

Even though it encounters no malignant enmity from without, genius will be sure to find within itself an enemy ready to bring calamity

upon it. This is why the history of great men is always a martyrology: when they are not sufferers for the great human race, they suffer for their own greatness, for the grand manner of their being, for their hatred of philistinism, for the discomfort they feel among the pretentious commonplaces, the mean trivialities of their surroundings—a discomfort that readily leads them to extravagances.[17]

The intersection of satanic melancholy with Romantic genius is a leitmotif among Feuchère's contemporaries. Consider the self-critique written by Delacroix a decade earlier: "I see myself in the mirror and nearly frighten myself with the wickedness of my features. Still, this is the person who ought to carry in my soul a fatal torch that, like candles to the dead, only illuminates the funeral rites for what is left of the sublime."[18] Odd as the subject seems today, Feuchère's *Satan* emerged from a set of shared values with wide appeal. The work reminds us that gruesome and morbid subjects were at the center of artistic life and polite conversation in Romantic Paris.

The fascination with picturing unreasoned violence owes much to a heightened exchange between Romantic painters and poets: Delacroix's *Death of Sardanapalus* (Fig. 83) was inspired by the poetry of Byron; Hugo's 1828 "Mazeppa" was a poem both inspired by and dedicated to Louis Boulanger's picture (Fig. 84). The dialogue between Boulanger and Hugo was especially intense during the late 1820s. Hugo dedicated to Boulanger two poems from the collection *Odes et Ballades* of 1828, in which he also singled out his friend as "in the forefront of this new generation of painters who promise to raise our school on a level with the splendid schools of Italy, Spain, Flanders, and England."[19] Hugo heaped praised upon Boulanger's picture of *Mazeppa* and the "colossal lithograph where he has added so much life, reality, and poetry to the *Witches' Sabbath*." That print (Fig. 104) is a milestone in the relationship between Hugo and Boulanger, for it is the first of many visual works produced by the painter directly under the spell of the poet's verse.

How to make visible the fantastic aspects of Hugo's poem? The simple answer is that Boulanger stayed close to the poet's imagery: the stroke of midnight in a darkened monastery, a rush of phantoms through the open roof, the

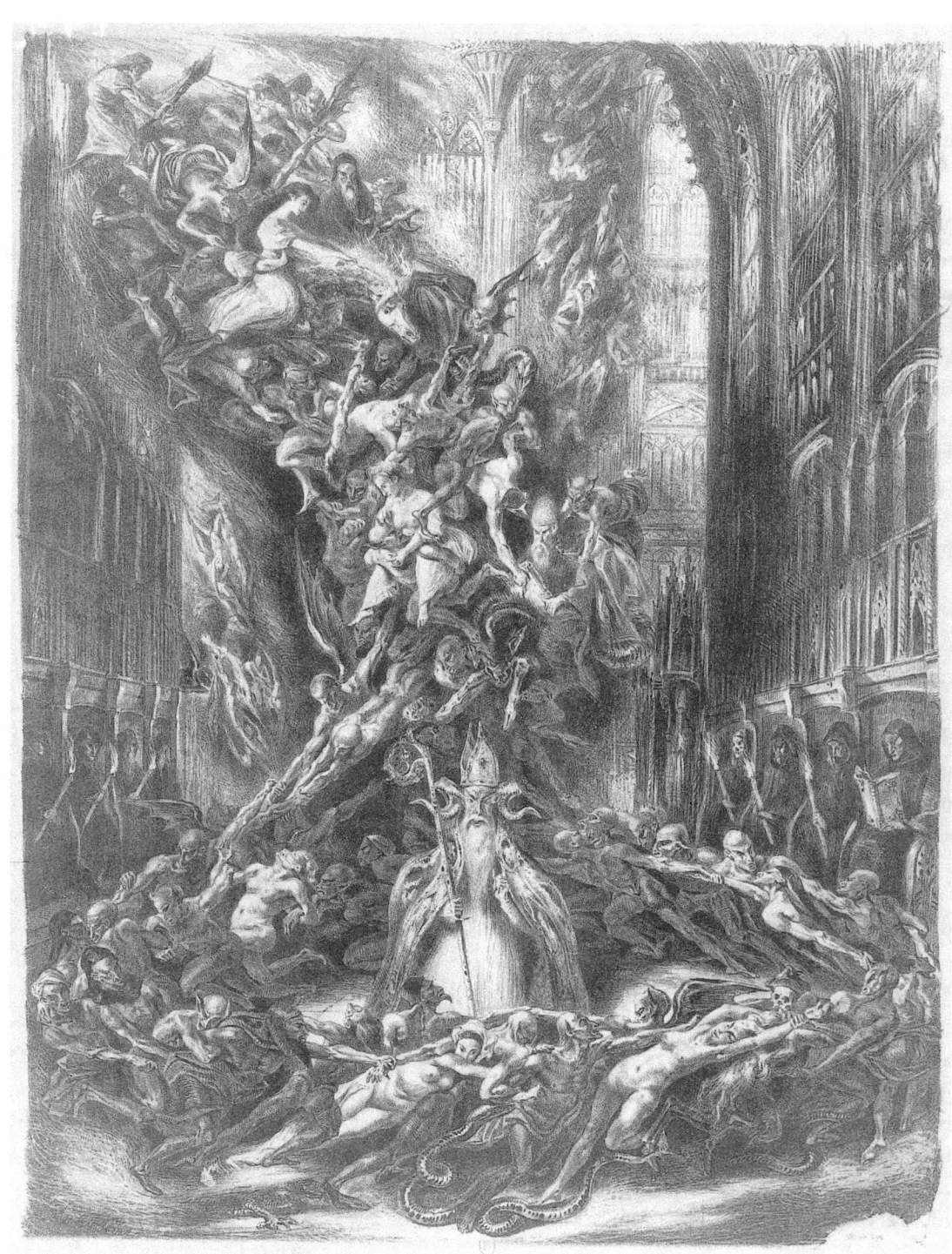

LA RONDE DU SABBAT

broken doors and smashed windows of an old cloister. Suddenly there appears a terrifying crowd:

Voilà que de partout, des eaux, des monts, des bois,
Les larves, les dragons, les vampires, les gnômes,
Des monstres dont l'enfer rêve seul les fantômes,
La sorcière, échappée aux sépulcres déserts,
Volant sur le bouleau qui siffle dans les airs.

[Behold! from every direction, oceans, mountains, forests,
Ghosts, dragons, vampires, gnomes,
Monsters whose phantoms only hell imagines,
The sorcerer, fleeing deserted sepulchers,
Flying on the birch that whistles in the wind.][20]

Boulanger rendered these horrors and their invasion of the darkened space as a tangled mass of bodies that tumbles from the sky and flows around the figure of Satan much as Hugo described him:

Debout au milieu d'eux, leur prince Lucifer
Cache un front de taureau sous la mître de fer;
La chasuble a voilé son aile diaphane,
Et sur l'autel croulant il pose un pied profane.

[Standing in their midst, Lucifer their prince
Hides his bull's head beneath a miter of iron;
The chasuble masks his translucent wing,
And upon the crumbling altar he places a profane foot.]

Boulanger also took literally Hugo's description of how the round begins: "Hands reach for hands. . . . Suddenly the immense ring, like a sinister hurricane, begins to whirl [Les mains cherchent les mains. . . . Soudain la ronde immense, Comme un ouragan sombre, en tournoyant commence]." In the print a circle of intertwined figures begins to form around Satan. Interlaced arms produce a continuous visual circuit that mimics the rhythm of the verse and the slowly building speed of the round. A two-line refrain controls the pace of Hugo's imagery: "And their steps, shaking the colossal arches / Disturb the dead resting beneath the paving stones of the hall [Et leurs pas, ébranlant les arches colossales / Troublent les morts couchés sous le pavé des salles]." Boulanger invests his print with an analogous visual pattern by imagining an

enormous gothic space in which repeated forms—arches and pillars, choir stalls and tracery windows—lead the eye from floor to roof in a convulsive, staccato movement. Our perception of the image mimics the rhythmic pounding of feet that shakes Hugo's abbey from bottom to top.

Hugo's enthusiastic praise for the *Witches' Sabbath* was surely motivated by Boulanger's respect for the poem's language and structure. The print marks the beginning of a close and lifelong relationship between the two men that became increasingly one-sided as Boulanger fell victim to Hugo's charismatic presence. Writing in 1845, Charles Baudelaire harshly dismissed the painter's works:

Behold the last ruins of old Romanticism. Behold what comes from a time when it is taken for granted that inspiration is enough to replace everything else. Behold the abyss into which the dissolute ride of Mazeppa leads. M. Victor Hugo has ruined M. Boulanger—after having ruined so many others. The poet has thrown the painter into the grave.[21]

Baudelaire's assessment might be ascribed to an outburst of personal spleen against a poetic rival, but his opinion was frequently echoed in private. A few years earlier, Gustave Planche had written to the painter Paul Huet:

The friendship of Victor Hugo, if this word still means anything to him, was disastrous for Boulanger. It was worth two or three tolerably resonant odes, and yet his name is spelled out only in the notes—the dedication calls him L.B., but it made him deaf to all advice, and prevented him from choosing once and for all a path he could follow steadfastly without looking back. . . . He does not know how to be himself.[22]

Planche worried about Huet's own relationship to Hugo because his friend occasionally seemed willing to embrace the poet's program without reserve. Two of Huet's pictures exhibited at the Salon of 1831 were accompanied by excerpts from Hugo's poetry, as if to suggest a direct relationship between image and text. The most important of these pictures was *Landscape: Sun setting behind an Old Abbey in the Middle of a Forest* (Fig. 105). It was listed in the exhibition catalogue with a few lines from Hugo's poem "Rêves" [Dreams].[23]

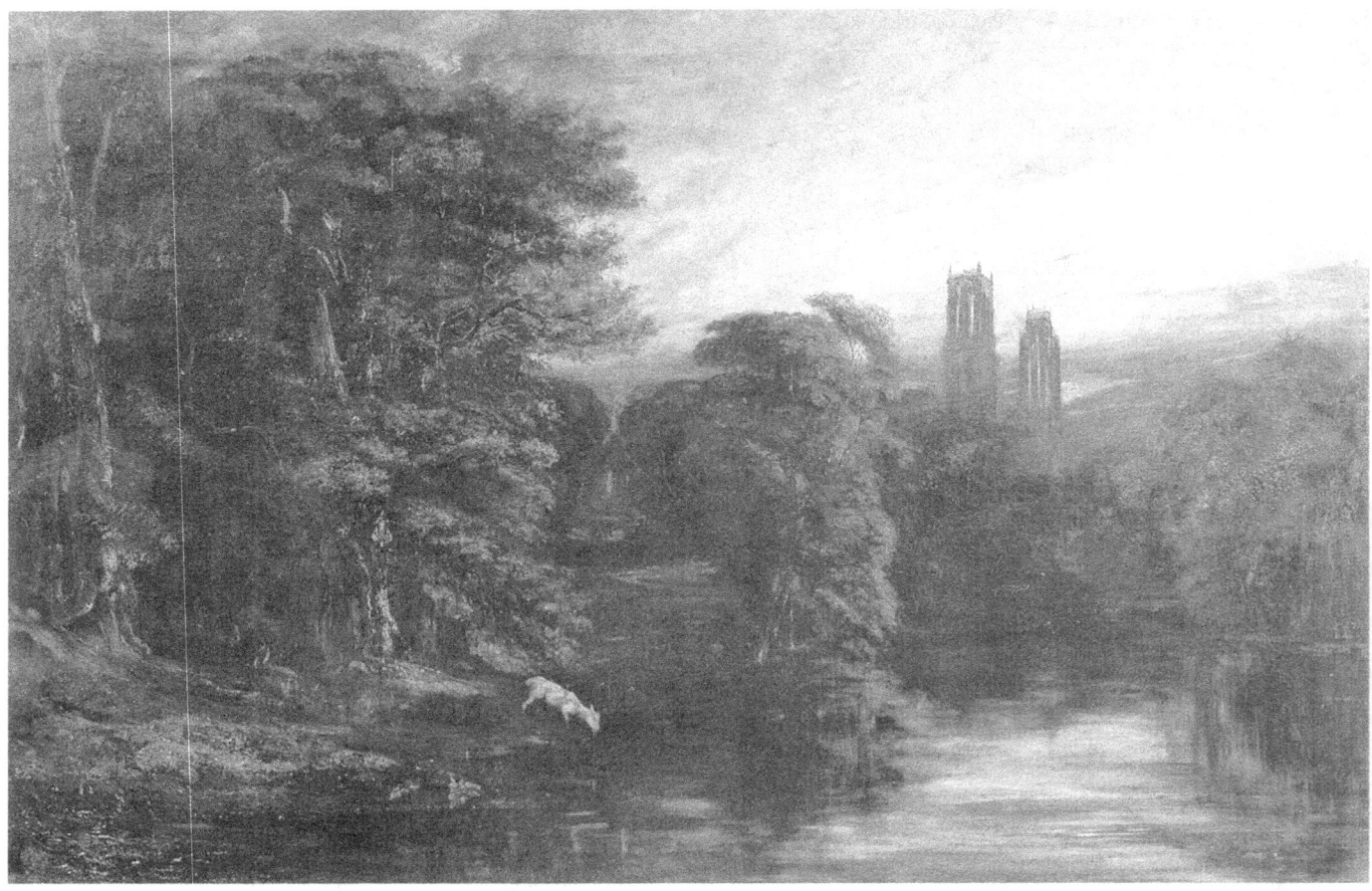

FIGURE 105.   Paul Huet, *Landscape: Sun setting behind an Old Abbey in the Middle of a Forest*, 1831.
Oil on canvas. Valence, Musée des Beaux-Arts (173 × 261 cm). Photo: © Musée de Valence.

Unlike Boulanger's *Witches' Sabbath*, Huet's picture does not attempt to illustrate Hugo's text. Rather, the painter strove to find a visual analogue for the poetic effects of verse. Contemporary critics were quick to appreciate his efforts. "Involuntarily, by a sudden and unavoidable recurrence of thought, the first appearances of M. Paul Huet recall the first *Meditations* of Lamartine," remarked Gustave Planche in 1831; "before his works, as when reading the *Meditations*, you experience the same feelings: the same vague and boundless reverie, the same temptation to solemn and undefined thoughts. You see opening before you the same distant and insuperable horizon."[24] Similarly, Victor Schoelcher wrote:

I can offer no higher praise than to say he has completely conveyed all the poetry, mysterious charm, and silence of Victor Hugo's peaceful thought. You hear the leaves rustle and the water running. M. Huet has a lot of imagination; he makes landscapes like a poet and so, to judge his works correctly, you must take care to look at them from quite a distance.[25]

The last part of Schoelcher's commentary is important. He suggests that there is a physical manner of looking at Huet's work—from afar—that responds both to its poetic generalizations and to the material qualities of the rendering. What were the technical innovations of Huet's visual poetry?

One way to gauge Huet's pictorial idiosyncrasies is to compare his painting to Michallon's classical landscape of 1817 (Fig. 96). Both Michallon and Huet divide the picture field into regions of light and dark: Michallon arranged them with a spatial logic to clarify near and far; Huet dispersed pockets of darkness within areas of brightness so that viewers experience a visual palpitation more than a spatial order. The viewer's relationship to the fictive space of Huet's landscape is further complicated by an immediate foreground entirely of water. Where is one to stand? Schoelcher suggests a plausible answer: viewers should not imagine themselves *within* Huet's painting, but at a distance *from* it. Severing the continuity between a picture's fictive space and a viewer's lived space undermines a fundamental premise of pictorial illusionism. It cuts the image free from literal transcription by opening a gap that elicits and requires an act of imagination or interpretation. This act, an essential component of visual poetry, is fairly easy to activate before a subject inspired by literature, allegory, or religion. Huet's achievement was to call it up before a rendering of nature.

Like many other French artists, Huet was deeply affected by the appearance of John Constable's pictures in 1824 (see Chapter Five). He later recalled that it was "by an effortless originality, supported by truthfulness and verve, that the two canvases of Constable stood out above all. . . . It was, perhaps, the first time that one perceived freshness, the first time that one saw a luxuriant and verdant nature without darkness, crudity, or mannerism."[26] In spite of his professed admiration for Constable, Huet's picture of 1831 (Fig. 105) displays little of the Englishman's clear light and vivid greens (Fig. 97). Constable strove to make portraits of the countryside where he lived and worked for many years. He wanted to re-create in viewers some of the sensations—both perceptual and spiritual—of his immediate experience of this familiar world. For Constable, a "natural painture" must break with hackneyed pictorial conventions and renew itself by attending to the nuances, textures, and effects of direct observation.[27] Although Huet recognized Constable's

work as an alternative to academic formulas for rendering nature, he never shared the Englishman's commitment to the transcription of place. Rather, Huet's aim was to produce a mood that might be incompatible with visual truth. Gustave Planche understood this dialectic perfectly when he wrote that Huet assumes

external nature is poetic and grand, able to impress and hold us, provided that it is perceived as masses and lines simultaneously arranged and coordinated so that some are obliterated and sacrificed, while others are left dazzling and embellished to further a desired effect. He loathes details and, with an eye to a higher purpose, is intentionally careless.[28]

In this scheme it may be necessary and appropriate to overlook descriptive lapses. The badly drawn trees at the left of the picture, and the oddly flattened alley that fails to open onto a credible middle distance, are two passages singled out by Planche where he felt Huet correctly sacrificed natural truth for visual poetry.

Other critics found Huet's pictorial reordering of the expected hierarchies among objects and things to be bothersome. Schoelcher admired Huet's poetry but deplored his technique: "His execution seems disagreeable to me. . . . It is heavy, affected. His pictures are embellished with precious stones: each touch is a ruby, a sapphire, or an emerald. His landscapes lack air. Everything in them is on the same plane, and the masses stick to one another."[29] The relative crudeness of Huet's painterly touch, the insistent materiality of his paint surfaces—especially notable in the yellow-orange sky of the 1831 landscape—and his suppression of details were all reasons to view his work from a distance. Seen from afar, the picture's overall effect [effet] emerged like a harmony from the otherwise crude and indefinite markings upon its surface.

Huet's ambition was to produce ephemeral effects with the materials of mimetic representation. To achieve this he was obliged to free his marks of paint from exact description. He must assume that his canvas is a field of contrived sensations rather than the fictive space of a microcosm. His studied disjunction between viewing near and far, between description and suggestion, between fictive space and point-to-point harmony generated a dialectic of viewing appreciated by his supporters as poetic. "He is the firstling of our lyric land-scapists," is how Philippe Burty summarized the painter's importance; "there was more precursor than revolutionary in him. By the episodes he introduced into his compositions, by leaning towards effect, he proved to be more literary than hard-core landscapist."[30] Critics like Burty were right to insist on the poetry of Huet's picture making, for his bold use of paint and perceptual contrasts found their natural allies in the unusual patterns of cadence and rhythm that poets like Hugo imposed upon the language of everyday life.

A convergence between words and images was central to Hugo's notion of language and his theory of poetry. Already in 1824 he had written:

Images are the foundation of every human language, and it would be as impossible to speak without images as to paint without colors. We can only conceive of what we have seen; we do not know how to invent imaginary forms that are not the product of some combination of real forms. The simultaneous work of thought and speech is a perpetual translation of realities into abstractions, and of abstractions into realities. In short, language itself, not just literature, could not be formed without images of the real world.[31]

Hugo's insistence on the interplay between words and images becomes apparent in his own watercolor drawings, of which *Mythen Mountain* is a characteristic example (Fig. 106). At first glance, Hugo's rendering appears to be little more than a traveler's occasional doodle. A note in the lower left-hand corner reports it was "drawn on the summit of the Rigi, on 11 November 1839 at sunset, 5676 feet above sea level." Hugo's specificity seems to leave little room for the imagination. By contrast, a letter written to his wife, Adèle, reveals the many levels of allusion at work beneath the surface of his immediate experience:

I climbed up to the observation point, and from there I drew the Mythen: prodigious cone of granite with a summit of reddish stone that gives the Mythen the appearance of having been patched with Roman cement, like the little pyramid atop the obelisk from Luxor. Seen from the Rigi, the Mythen has exactly the shape of the Egyptian pyramids. . . . The sun was going down behind the denticulated crest of the Pilate. It lighted no more than the extreme tips of all the mountains, and its horizontal rays perched on these

monstrous pyramids like golden architraves. All the wide valleys of the Alps filled with mist.[32]

Mental images of ancient monuments came to mind as Hugo looked at the mountain, and they informed his later retouching of the original pencil drawing with ink and brownish wash. In its final state, the summit emerges from a shroud of fog as a distinct pyramid of light, much as Hugo had reported in his letter and no doubt retained in memory.

Hugo pasted his drawing onto a larger sheet of paper when reworking the image. He also copied a stanza from a poem about poetry written in 1823. This later addition of text reveals that his letter to Adèle, in which he described the play of light on the mountain tops at day's end, was itself informed by the memory of his own verse:

Le poëte, inspiré lorsque la terre ignore,
Ressemble à ces grands monts que la nouvelle aurore
Dore avant tous à son réveil,
Et qui, longtemps vainqueurs de l'ombre,
Gardent jusque dans la nuit sombre
Le dernier rayon du soleil.

[The poet, inspired while the earth is unaware,
Resembles these great mountains that the new dawn
Gilds at its awakening before all else,
And they, longtime conquerors of shadow,
Retain until the darkness of night
The last bit of sunlight.][33]

Hugo's "finished" drawing thus pits two kinds of language written in ink (prosaic description and poetic verse), against an image (also done in pen and ink with wash) that is both different from the other two yet materially and expressively related to them.

Hugo's self-conscious collage of verbal and visual elements transforms the drawing into what Jean Gaudon has called "a veritable crossroads of the imaginary, a passageway between recollection and the thing seen, metamorphosed by poetic and pictorial vision, reworked by memory."[34] Although inspired by a lived experience, Hugo's drawing is far from a mimetic representation, for it entails a verbal-visual encounter in which the image both anchors words and is dispersed

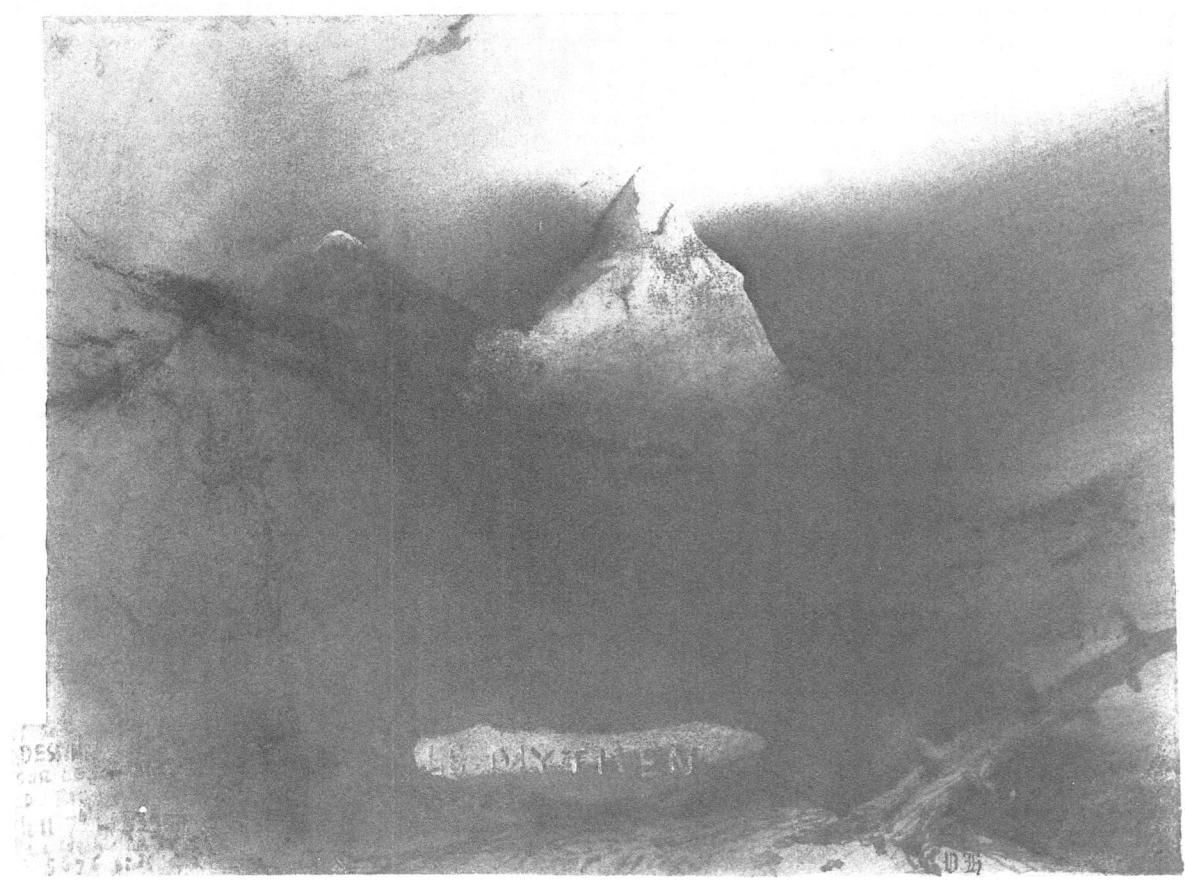

FIGURE 106.   Victor Hugo, *The Mythen Mountain*, 1839 (probably retouched about 1850). Pen and ink with brown wash. Paris, Musée Victor-Hugo, inv. MVHD 0921 (21.7 × 28.8 cm). Photo: © PMVP/Ladet.

by them. Exact meaning yields to a poetic play of layered meanings, an effect that pushes many of Hugo's drawings to the threshold of abstraction. In a famous essay about the drawings, Henri Focillon remarked:

They oppose an art of the unconscious—teeming with magic, astonishment, and vertigo—to an art of clear consciousness. To translate so many new notes, these amazing barbarians create for themselves tools, a material, and a technique, all perfectly coherent: still, every formal expression—even the most lyric and most free— is suited to the subject matter.[35]

Hugo's drawings were not abstract by intention (the idea would have seemed absurd to Hugo); rather, their forms emerged from the dialogue between words and images that constitutes the crux of Romantic poetry.

HUGO'S DRAWINGS can be viewed as precocious harbingers of a pictorial modernity developed and exploited by the Cubist painters and Surrealist poets of early twentieth-century Paris. They were, nonetheless, produced by specific configurations of individuals and interests peculiar to the middle decades of the nineteenth century. Tightly knit critical communities, such as the cenacle around Hugo, were proving grounds for the experiments in visual and verbal hybrids characteristic of the poetry and visual arts of Romantic Paris. How did such communities define themselves and their role in the cultural life of the capital? Those are the leading questions of our next section.

Staying In: The Culture and Cliques of Paris Salons

You own the city government, and that's fair because you are the force. But you must be fit for perceiving beauty; today, because no one among you can dispense with power, no one has the right to dispense with poetry. You can live three days without bread—never without poetry. Those among you who say the opposite are mistaken: they don't know themselves.

—Charles Baudelaire[36]

In the provocative and ironic opening to his review of the 1846 Salon, Charles Baudelaire flattered the bourgeoisie of Paris by acknowledging their social power. He chided them for believing that "a burning desire, a more active fantasy life, would make you renounce the activity of daily life." He suggests, by contrast, that "art is an infinitely more precious good, a refreshing and reanimating liquor that restores the natural balance of the ideal between the stomach and the spirit." Framing the utility of art in terms of bodily refreshment and natural equilibrium was no innocent gesture, for Baudelaire's argument cuts both ways. His appeal to material well-being simultaneously praises and pokes fun at the stereotypic bourgeois for whom physical comfort is the decisive factor in life.

Many of Baudelaire's colleagues eschewed irony for a blunt assessment of the gulf separating artists from their bourgeois public. "The tastes of the bourgeois are worthy of notice," wrote Théophile Gautier in 1836; "instead of loving what is beautiful, well made, elegant, spiritual or poetic, he prefers everything that is ugly, common, prosaic and stupid."[37] For Gérard de Nerval the ever more commercial interests of modern culture left artists and writers no alternative but to retreat into a world of their own:

The only shelter that remained for us was that ivory tower of poets, which we climbed always higher to isolate ourselves from the crowd. At those high altitudes to which our masters led us, we were finally able to breathe the pure air of seclusion, we drank oblivion from the golden cup of legends, we were drunk with poetry and love.[38]

Nerval's ideal of a separate society dedicated to art was a commonplace, although the actual gatherings of his cronies seldom reached such lofty heights. According to Théophile Gautier, their reunions over pasta in a rundown cabaret called Le Petit Moulin Rouge threatened over time to become

tasteless, bourgeois—yes, bourgeois—lacking surprise and vividness. Basically, there was nothing grandiose about eating macaroni in a cabaret, and the thunderbolts of the celestial arsenal should not have been roused by it. To give spice and pungency to this little feast would have required something risky, audacious, mutinous, byronic; in short, satanic.[39]

To that end, Nerval procured a human skull from his father, a former army surgeon. Gautier fitted it with a drinking cup. "The cup was filled with wine and passed around," he remembered, "and everyone brought his lips to it with a more or less well-concealed reluctance."[40] The drinking ritual not only tested one another's nerves, it also defined the group's social difference. Gautier sketched vividly its symbolic effect upon his thoughts during the ride home: "It's there, in that little red house, upright Joseph Prudhomme . . . sworn expert attached to the court, that I—your peaceful omnibus neighbor—drank from a skull like a pure cannibal, out of bluster, boredom, and disgust with your solemn stupidity."[41] But even here the social critique, like Baudelaire's, is double-edged, for Gautier's charade only develops symbolic clout in contrast to the established bourgeois values he is eager to flaunt. This reciprocity, as Jerrold Seigel remarks, was an essential component of fashioning oneself as an outsider:

Bohemia was not a realm outside bourgeois life but the expression of a conflict that arose at its very heart. Bourgeois progress called for the dissolution of traditional restrictions on personal development; harmony and stability required that some new and different limits be set up in their place. . . . Bohemia grew up where the borders of bourgeois existence were murky and uncertain . . . where social margins and frontiers were probed and tested.[42]

Nerval's ivory tower always required an unenlightened crowd over which it might cast its shadow.

The high altitudes for which Nerval longed were frequently a fact of real estate in Romantic Paris. Collective myths of bohemian artists were spun by writers like Henry Murger, whose *Scènes de la Vie Bohème* of 1851 summed up artistic life at the social and economic edges of Parisian culture. Murger's text offered his predominately bourgeois reading public a view onto a subculture that was largely fictional but certainly picturesque. Rodolphe, one of the book's heroes, was introduced to the reader after a long climb of stairs: "So, let's take the stairs and go up. Oof! one hundred twenty-five steps. Here we are. One more step and we're in the room; one more after that and we're no longer in it. It's small, but high; moreover, good air and a nice view."[43] Then, as now, one advantage of a mansard apartment (on the uppermost floor under the roof) is a view over the city. Perched simultaneously in town and above it, one can sweep through the urban landscape in imaginary flights of unfettered movement. One Sunday, while standing on his tiny balcony, Rodolphe passes from the "gilded balcony of a new house" to the "window of a little café" on the street; from a group of workers walking towards the city limits to the balcony just below where he meets Sidonia, a beautiful Spanish woman who shares her tobacco, her dinner, and eventually her bed with the young man.

Another reality of mansard life was that apartments in 1830s Paris, like those of every great city before elevators, were organized according to a vertical social scale (Fig. 107).[44] The best floor—in terms of high price and luxury appointments—was one flight up from the street. Rents declined proportionally as one moved to the fifth or sixth floor, but so did size and comfort. Balzac paints for us, through the eyes of Lucien, the stark realities of a room under the eaves:

Daniel d'Arthez's room, located on the fifth floor, had two wretched windows flanking a dark-wood bookshelf full of labeled cardboard boxes. A spare little bed in painted wood, a bit like those of a college dormitory, a night stand bought secondhand, and two chairs covered in horse hair filled up the far end of this room, which was covered with a Scottish wallpaper varnished by smoke and time. A long table, overloaded with papers, stood between the fireplace and one of the windows. Across from this fireplace was a wretched mahogany chest of drawers. A random rug entirely covered the floor tiles: this necessary extravagance saved on heat.[45]

When a young woman named Aurore Dudevant moved to Paris in 1831 to escape an abusive and loveless marriage, she had only a small monthly living allowance. Aurore rented an apartment on the top floor of a building in the Latin Quarter that was clearly better than Balzac's mansard, but no less artistic and sufficiently cheap:

I soon settled down on the quai Saint-Michel, in one of the mansards of the big building that forms the corner of the square, at the end of the bridge and facing the morgue. I had three very clean rooms opening onto a balcony from which I commanded a vast view of the Seine, and from where I contemplated face to face the colossal monuments of Notre-Dame, Saint-Jacques-la-Boucherie, the Sainte-Chapelle, etc. I had sky, water, air, swallows, and greenery above the rooftops; I did not feel so much in the Paris of civilization, which would have accorded with neither my tastes nor my resources, but rather in the picturesque and poetic Paris of Victor Hugo, in the city of time past.[46]

Living out the spirit of rebellion and experiment fostered by her newfound freedom among the bohemians of Paris, Aurore began to dress like a man in pants, greatcoat, hat, and boots. The disguise allowed her to pass for "an unimportant first-year student."[47] She began to write under the *nom de plume* of George Sand so that editors unfavorable to women authors could not discern her true identity.

Sand claims she never became accustomed to climbing five flights of stairs. Yet it was from the relative safety—whether real or imagined—of her mansard that she watched with horror the loading of corpses at the morgue during the cholera epidemic of early 1832, and with fright in June the raging battles between soldiers and insurgents in the winding, narrow streets of the Cité. Unlike Balzac's long-suffering young artists, Sand eventually fled the marginality of bohemian life. She left her

FIGURE 107.   Bertall, *Five Floors of the Parisian World*, 1852. Woodblock engraving from Texier, *Tableaux de Paris*, I, p. 65. Stanford, Stanford University Libraries, inv. DC707. T35 f (21.5 × 13 cm). Photo: © Davey Hubay.

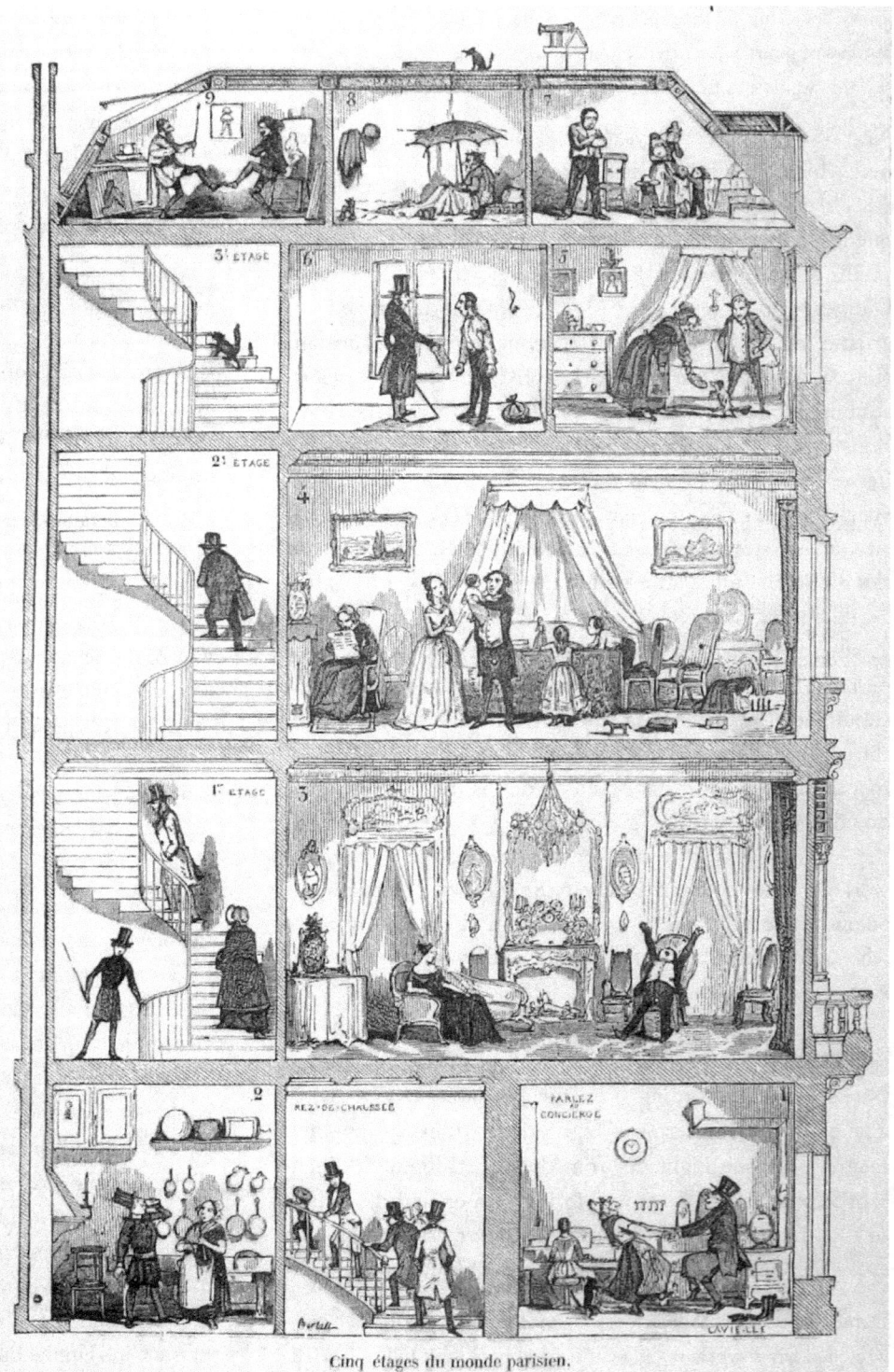

Cinq étages du monde parisien.

mansard the next year for an apartment a few floors lower that was "more spacious, comfortably equipped" and fulfilled her "pleasant daydream of a Prussian-style fireplace" to ward off the numbing cold. Critical acclaim for *Indiana*, Sand's first independent novel, signaled the debut of a successful literary career. She entered the inner circle of a prestigious periodical, *La Revue des Deux Mondes*, with a contract worth four thousand francs a year. In the same letter where Sand announces this good fortune she adds that her apartment is "so good and so warm; there is a lot of sunlight and such a profound silence that I am not able to tear myself away from it."[48] Whatever the romantic myths of a mansard apartment, it was good to escape bohemia of the fifth floor.

Some years later, in the fall of 1839, Sand rented two small pavilions in a secluded garden at 16, rue Pigalle. This section of Paris, known as "the new Athens" [la Nouvelle Athènes] since its development in the 1820s, was especially attractive to painters, writers, and musicians (see Chapter Seven). The neighborhood was designed as a collection of "private homes conforming to the needs of sundry fortunes," and with a concern to "preserve among them, and for all time, a considerable amount of air" so as to attract "people of quality, with established reputations in literature, science, or the military."[49] When Sand moved into the little pavilions nestled in a garden on rue Pigalle her neighbors were a star-studded cast: the actors Talma and Mademoiselle Mars (Figs. 123 and 124); the painters Horace Vernet, Ary Scheffer, Paul Delaroche, and Eugène Delacroix; the composers Gioacchino Rossini, Franz Liszt, and Frédéric Chopin—with whom Sand was living at the time. Her house, according to Balzac's close-eyed description, was clearly not bohemian:

She has a dining room with furniture of carved oak. Her small salon is the color of café au lait, and the salon where she receives guests is full of superb Chinese vases filled with flowers. There is always a plant stand full of flowers; the furniture is green; there is a sideboard filled with curios; pictures by Delacroix, her portrait by Calamatta. . . . The piano in rosewood is justly sumptuous and well-made.[50]

The bourgeois comfort of life in the Nouvelle Athènes quartier, and the cross-fertilization of ideas and talents that flourished in the salons held there, are captured in Josef Danhauser's contemporary—but probably imagined—picture of Franz Liszt at the piano in the company of George Sand and several other friends (Fig. 108). On the floor near Liszt is Marie d'Agoult, who had shocked the social world of aristocratic Paris in 1835 by fleeing France, her marriage, and her child to join Liszt in Switzerland. Seated on chairs at the left are George Sand and Alexandre Dumas. Standing behind them are Victor Hugo, Niccolò Paganini, and Gioacchino Rossini. A portrait of Lord Byron hangs on the background wall. Liszt plays while contemplating a bust of Beethoven. Danhauser portrayed each listener as if swept away in private rapture by the music, but an invisible bond among them is equally important, for each participates fully in the experience of heightened aesthetic sensation.

This sense of community among similarly attuned sensibilities—a highbrow remainder of the studied otherness of their bohemian roots—was essential to the spirit of experiment that flourished in the arts of Romantic Paris. It was also a well-established practice in the Nouvelle Athènes quartier to foster such communities: the studio of Jules-Robert Auguste, a painter and collector living at 11, rue des Martyrs, had been a meeting place of great importance to Delacroix during the early 1820s when he was working on the *Massacres at Chios* (Fig. 78). Many years later Ernest Chesneau still harbored vivid memories of those gatherings:

[Auguste] became acquainted with the young romantics, lured them to his house, and in his studio were created relations and friendships that only death could dissolve. During the day everyone worked on their own. In the evening, they gathered together and the night was passed in long conversations and discussions that cast such a fire in these ardent intellectuals that one of the cenacle's regulars—a painter of great talent—told me later that many a time, upon returning home, he sat down to work until dawn.[51]

The discovery of like minds, evenings filled with discussions, the excitement of sharing ideas across the usual boundaries of painting and literature, music and politics, are common threads in contemporary accounts of the cenacles that flourished in Parisian cultural life during these years.

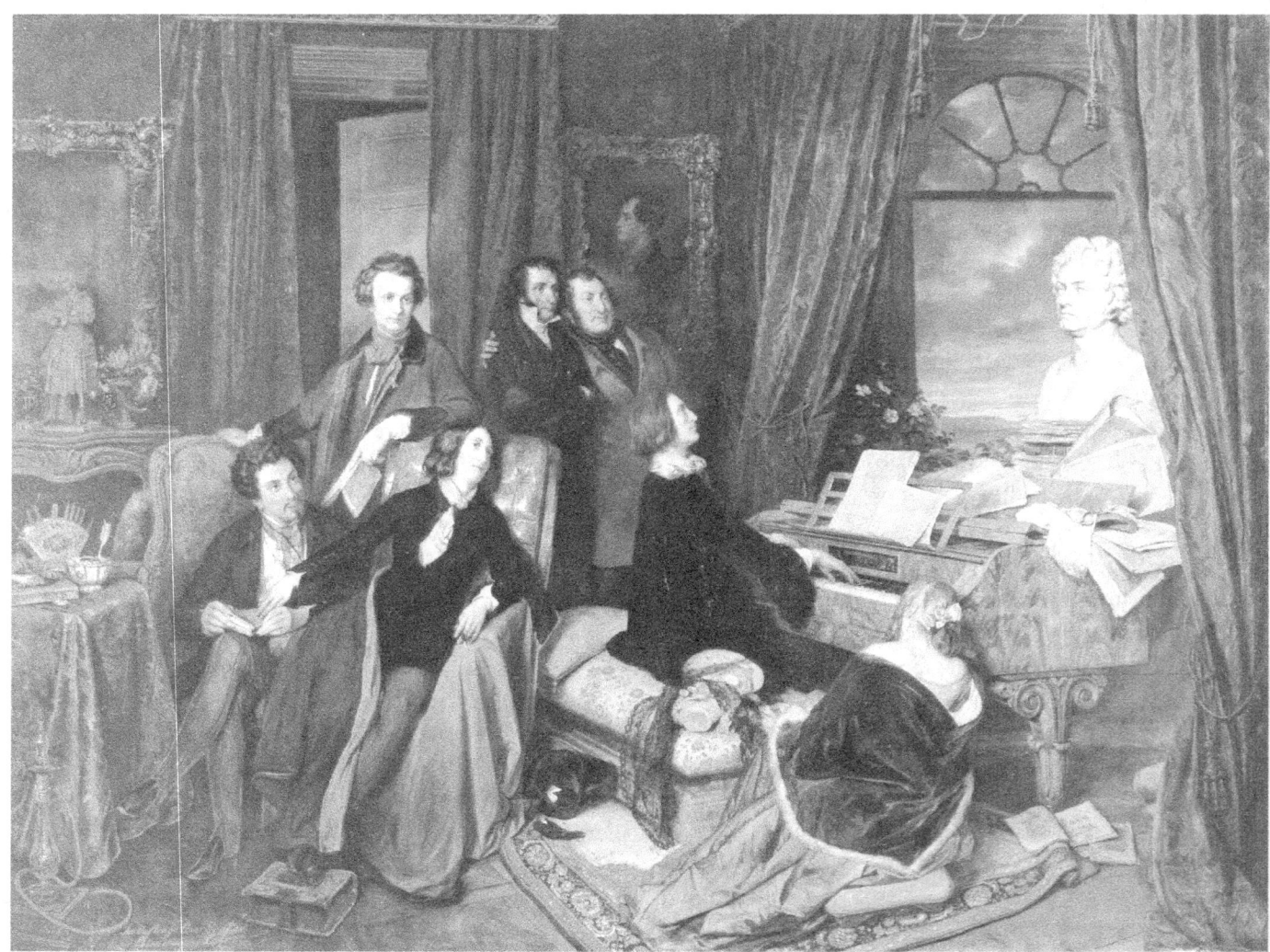

FIGURE 108.   Josef Danhauser, *Liszt at the Piano with Sand, Paganini, Rossini, Hugo and others listening*, 1840. Oil on canvas. Berlin, Nationalgalerie, inv. NG1968/54 (119 × 167 cm). Photo: © Staatliche Museen zu Berlin, Nationalgalerie/Jörg P. Anders.

Victor Hugo's gatherings, perhaps the most prestigious of all (see Chapter Five), were originally open to anyone who was a friend of the arts and willing to read his or her verse before the group. More selective evenings were hosted during the winter of 1836 by George Sand and Marie d'Agoult. The two women were sharing at the time a building on the rue Laffitte that had separate living quarters but a common salon. They wanted to arrange "a reunion of a select few" where one might "make wonderful music and, during intermission, teach oneself by listening to the talk."[52] Regardless of the social pretensions or exclusivity of their cenacle, Sand and d'Agoult were committed to quality conversation and the free exchange of ideas. Here, the ambitions of highbrow literary salons converged with those of bohemian gatherings by creating a space apart from the world at large, a place where opinions and sentiments were the yardstick of character. Lucien, the hero of Balzac's *Lost Illusions*, was impressed that among the nine members of his cenacle "esteem and friendship made peace prevail among the most contrary ideas and doctrines. . . . Everyone discussed without disputing. They had absolutely no vanity, since they were their own listeners. They shared their works with one another and counseled each other with the charming good faith of youthfulness."[53] In extreme cases, a cenacle might approach the mythic social utopia described by Henry Murger:

This long period of time passed in daily intimacy had brought about an accord of ideas without altering the clear-cut individuality of each of them, a harmony they would not have found elsewhere. They had their own manners and customs, a private language that outsiders could not decipher. Those who did not know them very well gave the name cynicism to their freedom of behavior. However, it was only sincerity.[54]

Murger's euphoric vision of a harmonious collectivity of distinct personalities occludes the frictions that inevitably arise between personal agendas and the demands of a group. Not surprisingly, most of the cenacles and related utopian communities that emerged during these years either succumbed to long-term paralysis or splintered into factional squabbling.

The history of Barthélémi-Prosper Enfantin's attempt in 1832 to found a working community based on the doctrines of social organization promulgated by the comte de Saint-Simon provides a spectacular example of this intrinsic dysfunction. Enfantin's program of social engineering and collective improvement accorded a large place to artists. If a high priest was destined to guide society to new levels of harmony and prosperity, the artist, in the words of Saint-Amand Bazard, "seizes the priest's thought, translates it into his own language and, incarnating it in every possible form, makes it universally understandable. . . . The Artist, in short, is the *word* of the Priest."[55] Empowering artists in this way assumes that plastic forms are able to mobilize masses of people. Artists are valued for their ability to orchestrate forms and to shape opinion. "His domain is the heart of other men, which he exploits

masterfully for society's benefit," is how Hippolyte Carnot described the artist's central place in the new world order.[56]

Members of the colony founded by Enfantin at Ménilmontant just outside of Paris embraced the concept of social utility for the arts. They donned special costumes to "efface the old hierarchy and establish a new equality," they engaged in collective singing at work and meals, and they staged festivals designed to attract a wider public following to their cause.[57] They consciously strove to integrate all forms of art into the colony's social life:

The fact dominating life at present is the foundation of our cult, or in other words the widespread introduction of art into our public and private activities; song before and after our meals, song when the *Père* meets the family in public, simple and standardized costumes, exercises done with ease—all this has great potential for taking root among the people and women. Women, artists, the people—they are the ones who will join us now.[58]

Pol Justus, a young painter deeply involved in Enfantin's community, emphatically sketched the reasons for his personal commitment to the group's project:

If one must work to create subjects, invent costumes, harmonize my ideas about art with doctrine and be inspired by yours to have sketches ready for use when the time is right, to make the principal events in the progress of humanity live again on canvas, to plunge into the future to conjure up a society by means of works that will carry it to fulfillment . . . then here is my life. Do you want it? I am giving it to you, my fathers.[59]

The paradox is that Pol's self-effacing enthusiasm is also symptomatic of why so few artists actually rallied to Enfantin's cause. In spite of the value Enfantin placed upon artistic creativity, in spite of the prestige he accorded artists within the community, his program seemed to discourage individuality and personal expression. Charles-Augustin Sainte-Beuve confided to Alfred de Vigny in 1830 that he detested Enfantin's religion because "it destroys the individual and spontaneity."[60] Émile Barrault, a notable defender of Enfantin, tried to neutralize such prejudices by arguing that "our religion does not stifle liberty nor subsume the sanctity of the individual."[61] He was not heard. No major artists ever showed more than a passing curiosity in the colony at Ménilmontant. Government officials, on the other hand, increased their surveillance of the commune, partly because of Enfantin's notorious advocacy of sexual liberation and partly because of a growing public interest in the group's festivals, an interest that might lead to social unrest. The colony was eventually evicted from their quarters in August 1832. Enfantin's experiment in living an artistic utopia came to an abrupt and inglorious end when he was tried and jailed for disturbing public order.

Nonetheless, many artists, intellectuals, and social reformers of Romantic Paris subscribed to the idea that aesthetic activity was capable of improving the world. The ambition to establish a subculture animated by the affective power of art ultimately links the large-scale social experiments of Enfantin at Ménilmontant to the private gatherings of like minds

hosted by Victor Hugo or George Sand. But, in contrast to the abundant textual documentation and theoretical treatises generated by Enfantin's colony, informal artistic cenacles tended not to leave much of an historical record. A rare exception is the fan painted by Auguste Charpentier in collaboration with George Sand (Fig. 109). Its otherwise arcane imagery offers a glimpse of how insider language and references developed in a circle of friends where familiarity and frankness suspended the usual formalities of social interaction.

Charpentier visited Sand during the spring of 1838 at her château in Nohant, where he painted the portrait of her exhibited at the Salon of 1839.[62] He also drew caricatures of the principal figures of her inner circle upon a fan she had decorated as a mythic garden of roses. It was an especially interesting spring at Nohant: Sand's romance with Félicien

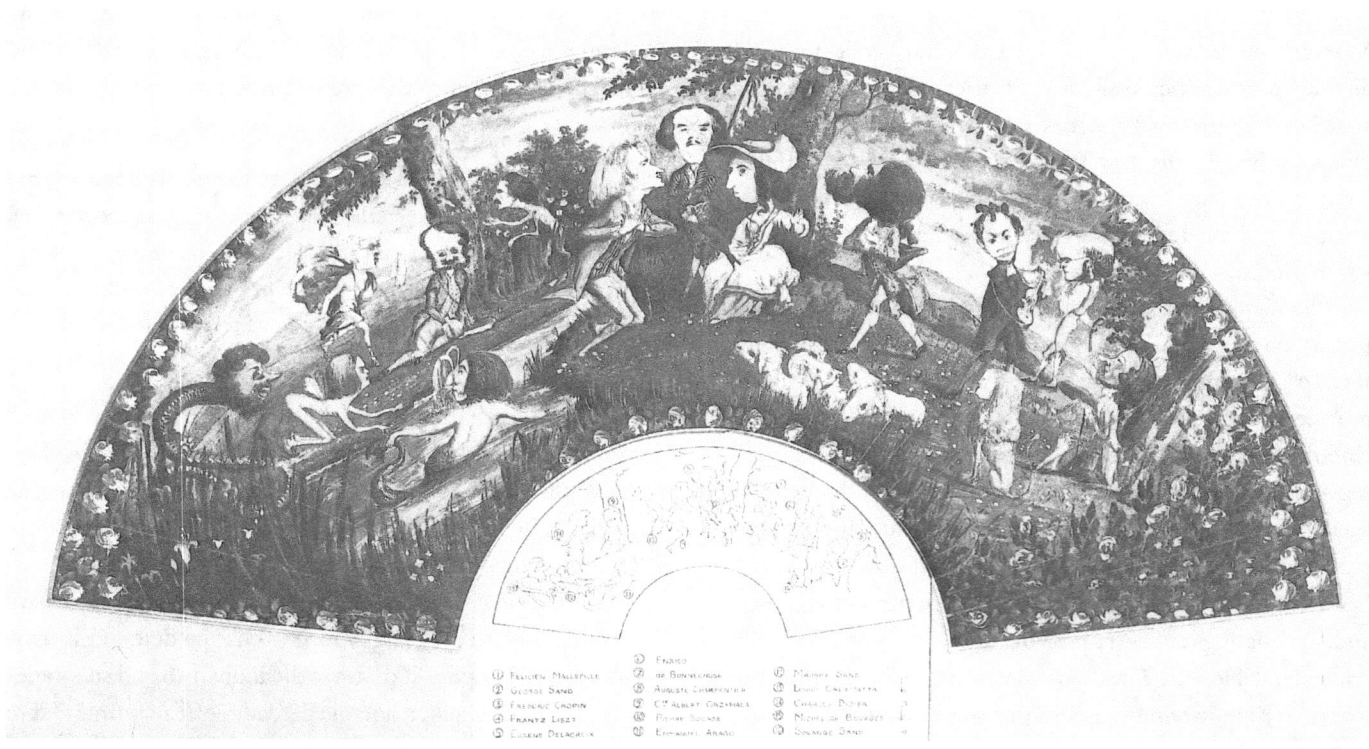

FIGURE 109.   George Sand (landscape) and Auguste Charpentier (figures), *Fan Painted with Caricatures*, 1838. Watercolor. Paris, Musée de la Vie romantique, inv. MVRD 89.105 (17.5 × 57 cm). Photo: © PMVP/Ladet.

Mallefille, her son's tutor, was cooling and she was newly smitten with Frédéric Chopin. Most likely in concert with his hostess (who composed a text to decode the fan's arcane imagery), Charpentier placed at the center of the composition "the incomparable nymph Sandaraque [George Sand] . . . disguised as a shepherdess named Piffoëlis."[63] On her hand is perched the "sacred bird Chopinois [Chopin] . . . whose wonderful singing heals colic and foot corns." Sand is surrounded by three other creative spirits. To the left, "the famous shepherd Lystil [Liszt] . . . describes a clarinet concerto he has just written." Just behind, and listening to Liszt's description, stands "the shepherd Croiseillas [Delacroix] who excels in the art of painting" and is inspired to make "a charming picture that will represent the clarinet concerto in oil paints." This synergy of creativity has inspired "a madrigal from the happy marquis de Malphilinte [Mallefille]," identifiable at center-right by his enormous beard. The painter Luigi Calamatta, represented at the far left as a "ghastly serpent," and Charpentier himself—at the extreme right in the guise of "the young sylvan Charpentis"—join this peculiar band of friends, lovers, and admirers in the "gardens of Paphos" that comprise George Sand's private world.[64]

Gatherings of talented, highly motivated individuals are seldom free of friction. It is no accident that Charpentier's fan reveals something of a darker side. Insiders would have noticed that all of the characters on the fan are men (except for Sand's daughter), and that one woman, Marie d'Agoult (Fig. 110), is conspicuously absent. There is no allusion to the literary salon run jointly by d'Agoult and Sand that had been a highlight of Parisian social life in 1836. By contrast, Franz Liszt, who was Marie's lover in 1838, prominently pays court to Sand. D'Agoult's erasure is doubly surprising because she and Liszt had stayed with Sand at Nohant on two occasions during the winter and spring of 1837. The women seemed to be close friends. Yet there was a deep and simmering rivalry between them: d'Agoult, the strikingly beautiful aristocrat who had abandoned her husband to join Liszt, coveted the acclaim of Sand's rising literary star; Sand watched with envy Liszt's deep affection for d'Agoult, was jealous of how other men were drawn to her beauty, and concluded that Marie was not fit to be the composer's mistress. D'Agoult indiscreetly

criticized the fickleness of Sand's love life in letters to a mutual friend who promptly passed them to Sand. Her revenge was swift. She took advantage of Balzac's stay in Nohant during January 1838 to disparage with juicy detailed reports the romance between Liszt and d'Agoult that Balzac immediately turned into a cruel and thinly disguised portrayal of Marie in the novel *Béatrix*.[65] Four months later, when Auguste Charpentier decorated George Sand's fan, Marie d'Agoult was nowhere to be seen. Such were the unspoken dangers lurking amidst the intellectual and artistic hothouse of a cenacle.

Marie d'Agoult did not literally disappear. Henri Lehmann painted a portrait of her in 1843 (Fig. 110), well after her liaison with Liszt was but a lingering play of intermittent intensity, and shortly after she began to publish under the pen name of Daniel Stern. During these years she established

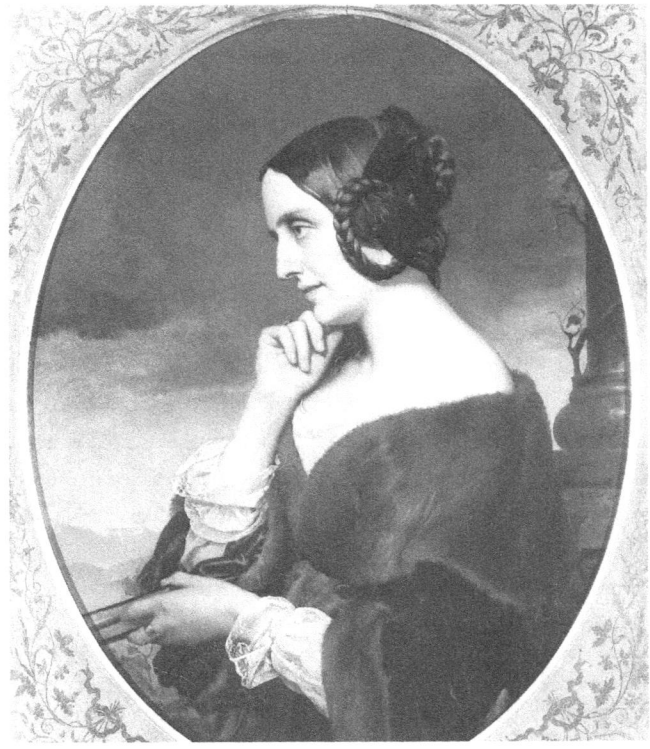

FIGURE 110.   Henri Lehmann, *Portrait of Marie d'Agoult*, 1843. Oil on canvas. Paris, Musée Carnavalet, inv. P 2170 (93.5 × 73.5 cm). Photo: © PMVP/Toumazet.

an important literary and political salon of her own that included Alphonse de Lamartine, Alfred de Vigny, Charles-Augustin Sainte-Beuve, Eugène Süe, François Ponsard, and the painters Ingres and Lehmann, both of whom she had met at the French Academy in Rome while traveling with Liszt. D'Agoult's circle of intimates included classicists of art and literature rather unlike the contemporary gatherings of romantic modernists around Victor Hugo or George Sand. Lehmann's portrait alludes to this orientation of d'Agoult's tastes by placing her in near profile, a cameo-like silhouette of sinuous contour set against the sky. His detailed rendering of the rich textures of her fur-trimmed dress, lace blouse, and perfectly braided hair contrasts with the pale smoothness of her skin—a juxtaposition very much in the fashion of the day. Equally flattering is the sitter's attitude. She has paused a moment from her book (a finger marks her place), and is transported by her thoughts. Her glazed, unfocused expression and gesture of hand to chin signal a distraction from her immediate surroundings provoked by the intense self-absorption of her response to what she has just read.

Lehmann's picture is the type of pleasing portrait whose modest ambitions were roundly dismissed by Charles Baudelaire in 1846:

In general, Messieurs Flandrin, Amaury-Duval and Lehmann have this excellent quality of a true and refined modeling. The piece is well understood in that regard, executed fluently and all in one breath. But their portraits are often tainted by a pretentious and clumsy affectation. Their excessive penchant for refinement plays a bad trick on them at every turn. One knows they search with an admirable good nature for elegant tonalities; that is tones, if intense, that would shriek like the devil and holy water, like marble and vinegar. But since they are excessively washed out and taken in homeopathic doses, the effect is surprising rather than painful: therein lies the great triumph.[66]

Baudelaire's disparaging comments echo more than a decade of critical fretting about the number and quality of portraits at the Salon.[67] Stendhal wrote to a friend in 1839: "my eyes were tired after an endless succession of reasonably good portraits. . . . On the whole, all these painters seem to me like skillful craftsmen, but devoid of intelligence, to say nothing of soul;

they see dignity in mere affectation."[68] Where Stendhal was looking mainly at paintings, other critics realized there was actually a social pecking order to the chaos. "The bourgeois who has his portrait in oil despises his neighbor with his portrait in watercolor," remarked Maurice Alhoy; "he does not return the greeting of someone who has his image lithographed."[69] For patrons living the bourgeois myth of self-actualized social identity, a portrait's material support was the most evident marker of the sitter's hard-won social standing.[70]

By contrast, patrons like Marie d'Agoult never wanted to be grouped amongst the bourgeois of Paris. The pressing problem of portraits appropriate to the rarefied culture of literary and artistic cenacles was how to project the intangible qualities separating an insider from the mass of ordinary people. Baudelaire put his finger on the "excessive penchant for refinement" that was a standard visual trope to signal that a sitter was special. As Gustave Planche wrote in 1838, the art of portraiture required more than optical data—the question was how to make visible those other qualities:

Although several thousand voices insist upon repeating it, it's not true that the entire task of a painter who undertakes a portrait reduces to copying literally his model; a portrait understood according to this single idea will be always inferior to reality. It's not within the power of the most talented brush to copy nature, and that's exactly why art should have in view—indeed, has in view—something other than the reproduction of nature.[71]

One year later, Planche's distinction between art and nature was drawn even more sharply when Louis-Jacques-Mandé Daguerre announced a photographic process able to reproduce nature so accurately that sitters were often terrified by its brutal rendering of their every quirk and blemish (see Chapter Eight).

None of what Planche writes is new. Portrait painters had wrestled for centuries with the relationship between a sitter's physical appearance and internal character. The most turbulent years of euphoric Romanticism involved expanding the parameters of expression for portraits of private individuals. One avenue of experiment, derived from the martial imagery of Napoleonic France (Fig. 1), transferred the implied movement, psychological alertness, and directed attention of heroic military leaders to civilian life. Thus, Horace Vernet's 1828 portrait of the painter Jean-Baptiste Isabey (Fig. 111) situates his friend in a dramatic light that accents the sitter's noble forehead, the studied disarray of his thinning gray locks, and his distinctive mutton chops. Isabey's head is turned sharply to the right. His face is framed by a collar of thick fur. A steady gaze upon some unseen person or object, the firm set of Isabey's mouth and chin, and the discreet but insistent presence of a Legion of Honor medal on his lapel all signal the sitter's nobility, his calm assurance, and his station in life. The expansive energy of Vernet's portrait seems somewhat out of character for a painter of miniatures, even if historically appropriate, given that Isabey had been a fa-

vorite of Empress Joséphine. Vernet, whose studio remained a gathering place for Bonapartist sympathizers (see Chapter One), rendered his friend's personal and familiar qualities with the visual rhetoric of dramatic action that references covertly Isabey's role in the glory days of imperial France.

A different kind of drama lies at the heart of Ary Scheffer's picture of his fellow painter Louis Hersent (Fig. 112). Unlike Scheffer, Hersent was not an intimate of the Romantic circle of Delacroix, Boulanger, and Hugo during the late 1820s. By 1830, when this portrait was painted, Hersent and Scheffer were working in almost diametrically opposed styles; nonetheless, Scheffer represents his colleague as a soul mate tethered in a psychological bond that ignores

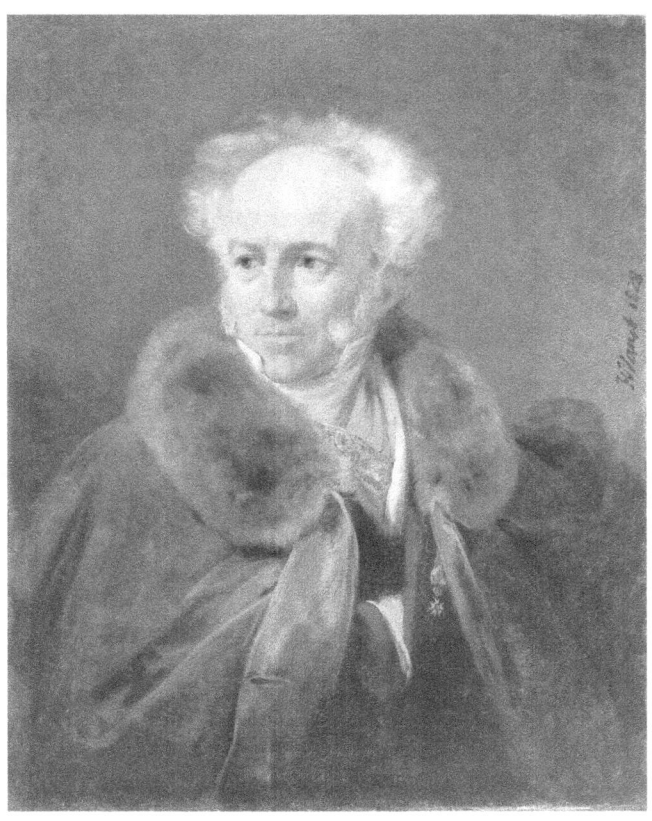

FIGURE 111. Horace Vernet, *Portrait of Jean-Baptiste Isabey*, 1828. Oil on canvas. Paris, Musée du Louvre, inv. RF661 (81 × 64 cm). Photo: © RMN/Art Resource, NY/© Daniel Arnaudet.

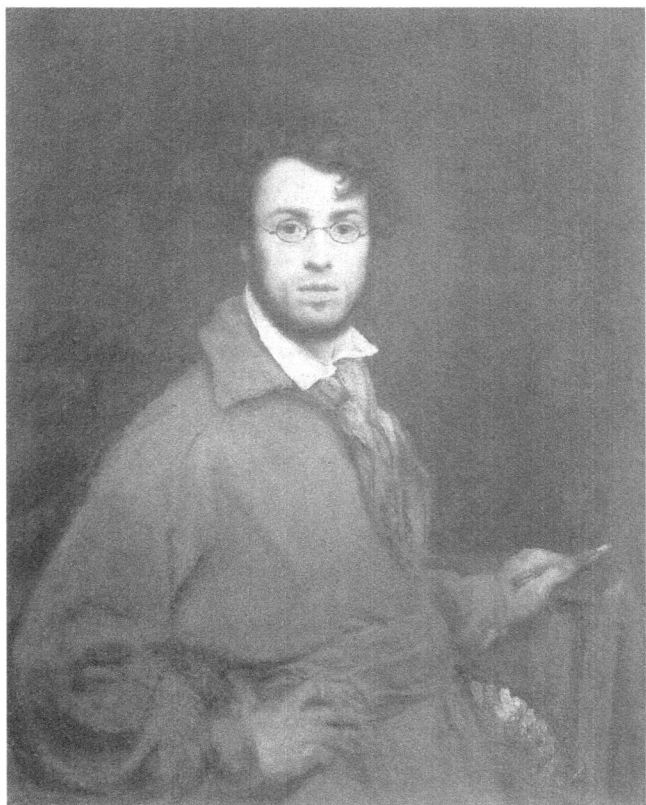

FIGURE 112. Ary Scheffer, *Portrait of Louis Hersent*, 1830. Oil on canvas. Grenoble, Musée de Peinture et de Sculpture (117 × 90 cm). Photo: © RMN/Art Resource, NY.

their professional differences. Hersent is at work (he grasps a pastel holder in his left hand) and dressed casually. His body language is equally casual: right hand on hip, he turns slightly into the picture while resting his left hand on a canvas propped against the background wall. Surrounded by darkness, and in stark contrast to the saturated reds of his dressing gown, the painter's face confronts us directly with an unblinking intensity. Eyes alert, an effect heightened by his wire-rimmed glasses, Hersent seems to study the viewer with rapt attention. His face edges into the shadow of a light beard, and his forehead, although smooth, is animated by an asymmetric lock of curled hair that only adds to the intimacy of our encounter with him. Scheffer's startling directness charges the picture with a psychological energy that invites us to enter the sitter's inner circle. The picture demonstrates what Delacroix believed to be the essence of portraiture: "It's the soul that speaks to the soul and not science speaking to science. . . . I have told myself a hundred times that painting—that is, the material of painting—was only the pretext, only the bridge between the painter's soul and that of the viewer."[72] Inspired by the friendship they shared, Scheffer's portrait of Hersent does speak soul to soul, and it continues to bridge with a compelling immediacy the expanse of time and space between ourselves and Paris of 1830.

Writing in 1831 for *L'Artiste*, the new art journal he helped to found, Jules Janin exclaimed:

So, if you point out to me, using the word "artist," a man over there in the palace, or up there in a garret, I salute him, I envy him in both places; he is among the happy ones of this world, a dreamer, a care-free philosopher who worries little about the material facts of life and who understands neither the import nor the danger of them.[73]

Janin's notion of the artist—a person apart, a dreamer, a figure relatively immune to the vicissitudes of material life—traffics in the myth that linked creative temperament to bohemian lifestyles and shaped the self-image of many young artists at the time. Théodore Chassériau's self-portrait of 1835 is a case in point (Fig. 113). The young man placed himself squarely in the center of the picture field before a drab gray-brown wall. He stands close to the viewer, one hand resting on a table rendered with a dull red that anchors visually the lower left corner of the picture. The other hand, tucked into his waistcoat, echoes a gesture made famous by Napoléon (Fig. 11), who was widely admired during the 1830s as the century's greatest Romantic hero (see Chapter Three and Fig. 50).

The intense blackness of Chassériau's outfit, relieved by only a few glimpses of white shirt, produces a dramatic visual presence without recourse to bright colors. This pictorial drama is focused and personalized by a strong raking light that strikes one side of the painter's face while casting the other in shadow. The brightness emanates mysteriously from some unseen source and seems to model only the face, so this part of the picture rivets our attention. What we discover is an impassive facial mask with eyes that seem to look both

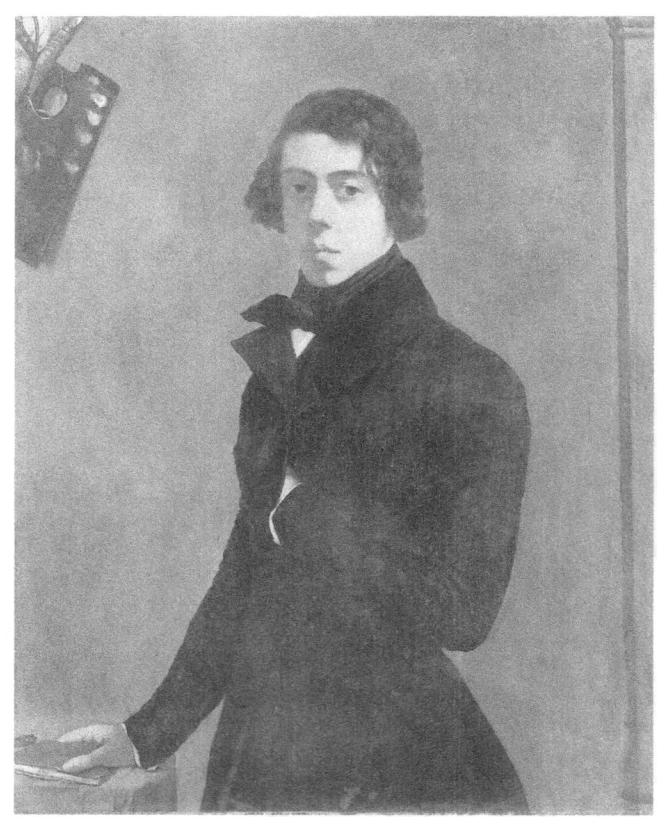

FIGURE 113. Théodore Chassériau, *Self-Portrait*, 1835. Oil on canvas. Paris, Musée du Louvre, inv. RF3788 (99 × 82 cm). Photo: © RMN/Art Resource, NY/© Christian Jean.

through and beyond us, as if the young man inhabits a mental world of his own creation. Only a few laconic markers signal his profession: a palette hanging from a nail at the upper left; a small book—perhaps a sketchbook—in his right hand. Significantly, he does not work; rather, Chassériau presents his energy as internal and spiritual. The spare setting furthers the idea that we have met "a dreamer, a carefree philosopher who worries little about the material facts of life."

The mythic artist's world of noble sentiments usually had a downside, namely a life of poverty and physical suffering. In *Lost Illusions*, Lucien's friends of the cenacle knew all too well the rigors of a marginal life: garrets without heat, meager meals on credit, boots worn through the soles. Lucien found it increasingly difficult to face such misery with stoic resignation. "I admit that I'm not as strong as you are," he told them; "I don't have the back or the shoulders to endure Paris, to struggle courageously. Nature gave us different temperaments and mental abilities, and you understand better than anyone that vices and virtues are mutually exclusive. Just between you and me, I'm already worn out."[74] What to do? Like many aspiring authors in Paris of the 1830s, Lucien came to believe that the career of journalist could be a way to earn a living while continuing to write poetry. His friends of the cenacle were horrified by the idea. "You have only too much the qualities of a journalist: brilliance and quickness of thought," exclaimed Fulgence; "you would never deny yourself a witty remark, even if it might make your friend weep. I see journalists in theater lobbies and they horrify me. Journalism is a hell, an abyss of iniquities, illusions, and treacheries that one cannot pass through, and from which one cannot escape pure."[75] Despite their warnings, Lucien threw himself into the whirlwind of contemporary journalism. Soon he was celebrated for his spirited reviews, he took up with an actress named Coralie, and he lived high on credit. Lucien saw less of his old friends. He now wondered if "those lofty spirits that he so admired two months earlier . . . weren't a little silly with their ideas and their puritanism."[76] Yet he could not resist inviting members of the cenacle to a grand dinner hosted by Coralie: when Lucien's new friends of the press baptized him a "genuine journalist" in a spray of champagne, his old friends left the party with sadness in their eyes.

Balzac's graphic depiction of an enormous gulf between the rarefied sentiments of artistic creativity and the crass materialism of hack journalism is surely exaggerated for dramatic effect. Moreover, the two worlds were inextricably intertwined in Paris of the 1830s. One of the great innovations in mid-century publishing, spearheaded by Émile de Girardin, was recognizing that the cost of newspaper subscriptions could be greatly reduced by charging higher prices for advertising. Girardin's successful launch of *La Presse* in 1836 established a business model for the entire newspaper industry that is still very much alive today. Because advertising rates and good profits were indexed to circulation figures, newspapers began to commission literary works from established authors—names like Alexandre Dumas, Eugène Sue, and Alphonse de Lamartine—for publication as installments over several weeks or months. Editors commissioned extensive reviews of theatrical productions and exhibitions of visual art to keep their readers abreast of the most current cultural affairs. The result was that the separation of art from ordinary life—the raison d'être of literary salons and cenacles—was actually undermined by highbrow authors who wrote for money, and by thoroughly modern professional journalists who wrote to demystify art for the general public.

In this new cultural environment, artists and journalists could not avoid meeting face to face. One of the most memorable records of such an encounter is the portrait of Louis-François Bertin painted by Jean-Auguste-Dominique Ingres in 1832 (Fig. 114). Bertin was not simply a newspaper man, but one of the most powerful in Paris. He owned and managed the *Journal des Débats*, a paper closely allied with the politics of King Louis-Philippe and the economic interests of the *grand bourgeoisie* that had brought him to power in 1830. Bertin was not easily intimidated: in 1801 he dared to challenge Napoléon and was sent into exile; he was jailed in 1829 for publishing an attack on Charles X. Ingres captured much of Bertin's implacable energy with a pose that, according to tradition, he agonized over to the point of tears. One evening, while watching his sitter's animated conversation with friends over an after-dinner coffee, Ingres spotted a gesture that struck him as the essence of Bertin's character: seated with knees spread; hands splayed on thighs

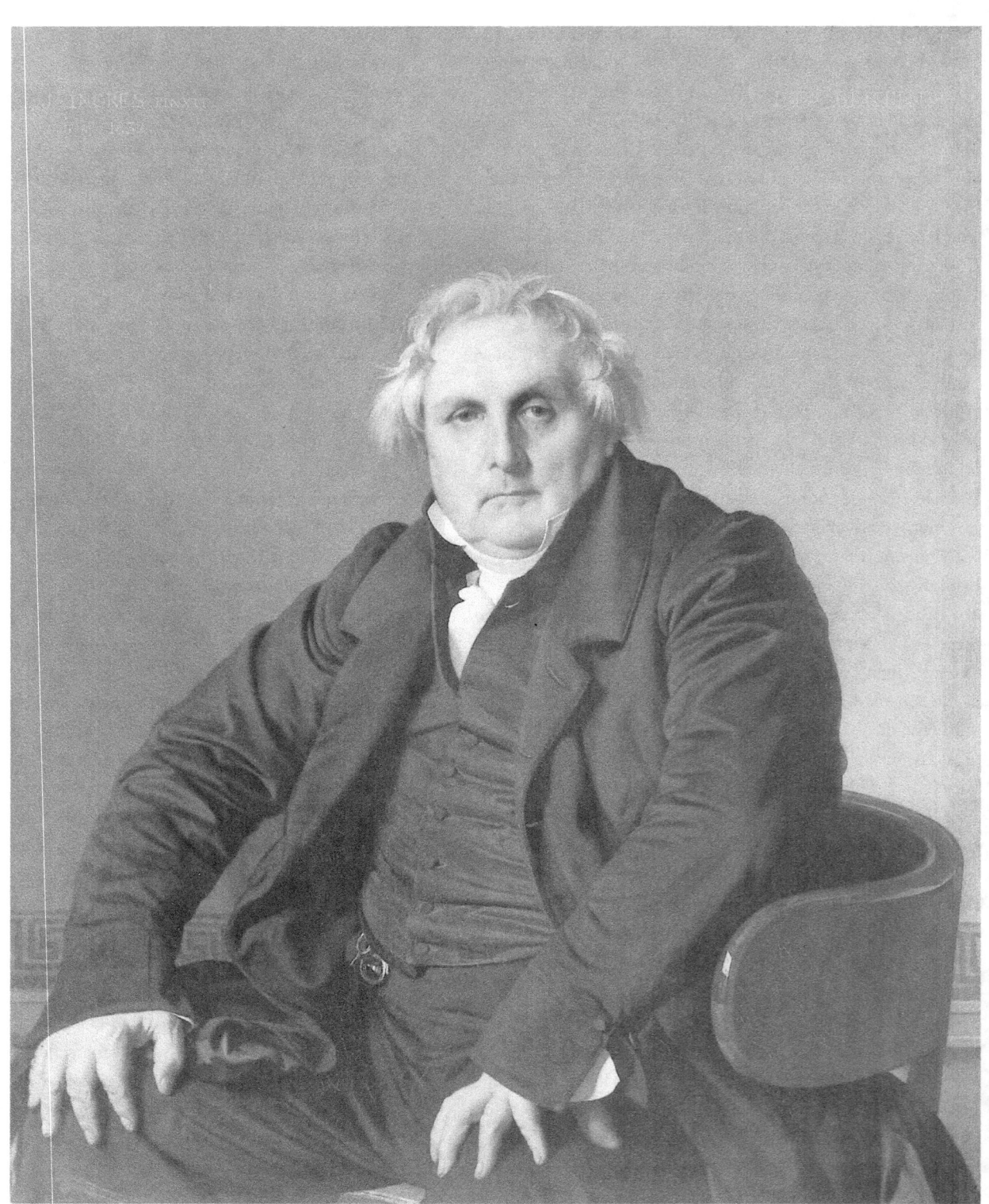

with elbows held slightly forward; head turned and tilted as if weighing the merits of an argument.

The resulting picture projects an uncanny sensation of intellectual energy held momentarily in check, a sensation reinforced by a pictorial rigor that compresses the sitter's corpulent frame into a shallow space close to the picture plane. The wiry silhouette of Bertin's rumpled greatcoat and his unruly shocks of gray hair are etched in sharp relief against a blank wall of medium-brown. Bertin is wedged between this background and the front plane of the picture. He seems both too large for the highly polished mahogany chair and inexplicably confined by its curved back that wraps around him to close the picture at the far right. Miraculously, Bertin's material presence survives this logic of spatial compression, because Ingres described every fold of cloth, every strand of hair, every bit of sagging flesh and physical quirk with an almost manic precision (note the wart in the corner of Bertin's right eye).

The work's virtuoso rendering was the main reason for its great public success at the Salon of 1833. Gustave Planche wrote of the crowd pressing to see Bertin's portrait:

Without knowing why, without even remotely suspecting the countless historical and critical questions attached to this important work, it [the crowd] allows itself to be captured by the charm of truthfulness: it studies, according to its abilities, details of the head that are rendered with such a prodigious conscientiousness; it examines attentively, with an almost childish joy, the reality of fabrics and the chair's projection into space; it marvels before the posture at once so simple and so powerful; it does not tire of gazing at the eyes and lips, so full of attention and speech.[77]

Ingres's own students, who believed their mentor to be the last refuge of high style idealism, were shocked by the work's slavish imitation of nature. "I'll tell you that I was knocked out, baffled, beaten up when I saw the portrait of M. Bertin," wrote Louis Lacuria to Hippolyte Flandrin; "when I saw

FIGURE 114. Jean-Auguste-Dominique Ingres, *Portrait of Louis-François Bertin*, 1832. Oil on canvas. Paris, Musée du Louvre, inv. RF1071 (116 × 95 cm). Photo: © RMN/Art Resource, NY/ © Christian Jean.

that full and complete submission to nature, that absolute self-denial of the painter, that brush so completely subdued, I could hardly believe it."[78] Even some professional critics, who regularly chastised Ingres for showing so little sensitivity to the effects of color, were forced to admit that when Ingres "comes up with the right tone he surpasses, to my mind, all those who would be colorists. . . . The frock coat and vest of M. Bertin, if one looked at them separately from the head, would make everyone say: the painter who did that is a colorist."[79] What was it about making the portrait of Bertin that produced such a dramatic turn in the painter's reputation?

When discussing the picture, a critic for *L'Artiste* described Bertin as "the distinguished gentleman who created by himself everything about the political newspaper."[80] His comment suggests that Bertin's public persona impacted contemporary evaluations of Ingres's portrait. A few pages later, *L'Artiste* heralds Ingres as the only man "to make an original portrait using the head of a bourgeois from our epoch. . . . He took this bourgeois as the most elevated type of the class he stands for, he impressed upon him all the most striking and least vulgar characteristics that personify this class, and we got the portrait of M. Bertin."[81] For this critic, there was a significant link between Bertin's career as a newspaperman and the visual evidence, wrested by Ingres from his appearance, that defined salient characteristics of the sitter's social class: shrewdness, attention to materials, the unidealized transcription of facts. By contrast, Théophile Gautier regretted "in seeing this drawing so above reproach, that it was not applied to quite a different subject. So much purity and exactitude in the fold of a vest and a frock coat, which could not be otherwise without being less true, strike us as useless expenditures."[82] At the Salon of 1833 Gautier believed Ingres had wasted his talent by deploying too much art on a subject of too little importance. Twelve years later, on the occasion of Ingres's retrospective at the Universal Exposition of 1855, Gautier completely reversed his earlier assessment:

No one has made portraits better than he [Ingres]. To the external likeness of the model he joins an internal likeness; beneath the physical portrait he makes the moral portrait. Isn't an entire epoch revealed in this splendid pose of M. Bertin de Vaux [sic], supporting—like a bourgeois Caesar—his handsome and strong hands on his powerful knees with the authority of intelligence, of wealth, and a justifiable self-confidence? What a well-balanced mind! What a lucid and masculine gaze![83]

Gautier now celebrates the exact fit between Bertin's external appearance and his moral fiber. How to explain this dramatic change of mind?

In 1839, between Gautier's two reflections upon the portrait of Bertin, a new instrument—the daguerreotype—was announced (see Chapter Eight). By 1855 technical improvements made it possible to record the exact look of a sitter, and at a sufficiently low cost, for portraiture to be accessible to nearly everyone. It is no surprise that Gautier now accepts photographic exactitude as the fundamental premise of painted portraiture. Does this mean that Ingres's picture of Bertin anticipated in some way the triumph of photographic representation as the preferred mode of bourgeois self-representation?[84] That would ascribe to Ingres a prophetic role in the history of photographic technology diametrically opposed to his avowed reverence for the tradition of painting. Another reading might ascribe the eruption of an obsessive pictorial exactitude, when facing the leading newspaperman of 1830s Paris, to Ingres's ill ease about pitching his picture to Bertin's mass culture public—a reaction akin to Lucien's discomfort when he moved from cenacle to newsroom. A minute glint of light opens a door to this understanding of the work's uncanny literalism.

It is said that one of Ingres's assistants repainted five or six times, and at the master's insistence, a tiny reflection of a window on the shiny mahogany of Bertin's chair.[85] Why would such a small detail be so important? The reflection of some *thing* implies its existence some *where*. A reflected window means that Ingres imagined an unseen but actual window relative to the fictive space of his picture. Yet the depicted space refuses to open in a predictable or ordinary manner. Ingres cramped his sitter uncomfortably between wall and picture plane, and wedged him into the peculiar confines of the chair itself. Where, exactly, is Bertin? Nothing indicates that he is posed in the artist's studio, nor does he seem to be installed comfortably at home. Ingres resolutely indexed Bertin's physical presence with a relentlessly

exact description, but his place in the world at large is referenced only elliptically by that tiny reflection of a window.

Perhaps this is all one should expect, for Ingres approached the world of journalism warily, as an unknown quantity ruled by fickleness and fashion. "But who knows," he wrote in 1841, "if this public and this press, so eager to avenge me today, won't give in to the caprice of taste and fortune? One has completely chased the divine Glück from the Opera, one has cursed the divine Raphael and also Racine—yes Racine! And, in the end, so many other examples!"[86] Anne Martin-Fugier describes the milieu over which Bertin presided with tenacity, as "a space shared by young socialites who lived as dandies, and young people from nowhere who adopted the dandy's style and sometimes managed to penetrate high society."[87] For Balzac, journalism was a world of shifting identities, uncertain origins, and ephemeral wealth perfectly at odds with a painter who saw himself going it alone to "confront the ignorant, selfish, and surly masses."[88] Ingres's concession to this world without substance could not be more carefully weighed: the liminal allusion of a tiny reflection on a piece of furniture that was so freighted with meaning as to require several repaintings.

Are we endowing an incidental detail with too much symbolic resonance? Consider another of Ingres's most famous portraits, the comtesse Louise-Albertine d'Haussonville (Fig. 115). Close looking reveals that a small glint of light on a pair of opera glasses placed on the mantle is the reflection of a window precisely rendered as four separate panes. But if a similar reflection on Bertin's chair erupts anomalously within the no-man's land of compressed spatial geometry described by his portrait, an unseen window is relatively easy to imagine beyond the left frame of the d'Haussonville picture. Ingres provides many subsidiary clues about the spatial container in which the comtesse stands. Most apparent is the large mirror, which not only reveals the sitter's chignon of braids held in a tortoise shell comb, but also alludes to the fullness of space around her. The comtesse leans against a mantle arranged diagonally into the picture. She stands between matching armchairs that flank the fireplace: one barely edges into the lower right corner of the picture; the other is tucked into a corner of the room at left center. Alerting us in this way to the location of one of the room's corners suggests there are

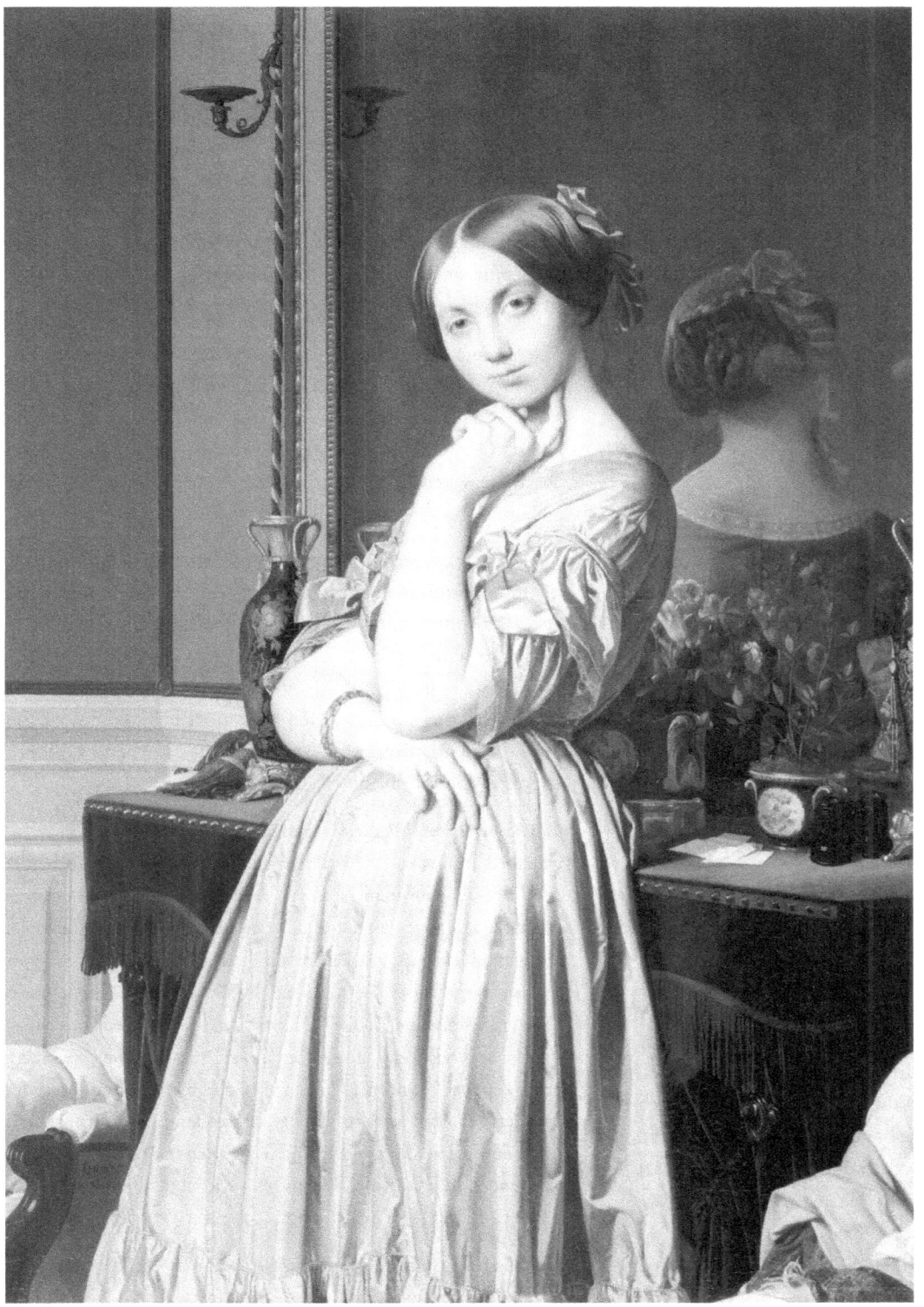

FIGURE 115. Jean-Auguste-Dominique Ingres, *Portrait of the comtesse d'Haussonville*, 1845. Oil on canvas. New York, The Frick Collection, inv. 1927.1.81 (131.8 × 92 cm). Photo: © The Frick Collection, New York.

others. It is thus perfectly plausible for an unseen window to exist off-image at the extreme left. In this case, the even and clear light that floods the comtesse to cast strong shadows from her left arm, and patterns the folds of her dress, makes good sense. So does the tiny reflection visible upon her opera glasses. Louise d'Haussonville inhabits a coherent space filled with objects that reveal her good taste: cobalt blue vases in a fashionable Chinese manner; Sèvres porcelain flowerpots; an expensive cashmere shawl dropped on the chair at the lower right; a fireplace decorated in the newest style with a blue velvet valence and matching curtains.

Ingres claimed a place in his sitter's world by signing and dating the picture on the chair to her left—a gesture quite unlike the hieratic signature he inscribed in the upper left corner of Bertin's portrait. In fact, the painter was very welcome in Louise d'Haussonville's social circle. They first met in the summer of 1840, when she and her husband visited the French Academy at Rome during the final months of Ingres's tenure as director. At that time, Ingres was showing his recently completed picture of *Antiochus and Stratonice* (now in the Musée Condé at Chantilly) to a small number of select visitors. In her memoirs of the trip to Italy, Louise describes in detail the painting and registers her admiration for the queen who "has paused at the doorway of the bedroom; she turns away gracefully while resting her chin on her hand; she makes a little pout that seems to indicate a slight embarrassment. Sadness and compassion can be read in her eyes."[89] Several years later, when Ingres took up the commission to paint the comtesse, he posed her with one hand to her chin in homage to the figure of Stratonice she had so admired at their first meeting. Théophile Thoré immediately recognized this insider reference in 1846 when he remarked that "the pose of Mme d'Haussonville is nearly the same as that of Stratonice."[90] Ingres returned to Paris from Rome in the spring of 1841, and the d'Haussonvilles returned a few months later. The painter was a dinner guest at the d'Haussonville's house on the rue Saint-Dominique—heart of the aristocratic faubourg Saint-Germain—in early 1842, about the time he was first asked to paint the comtesse.

There is no doubt that Louise d'Haussonville belonged to the social elite of Paris: she was married to a young vis-count, was the daughter of the duc de Broglie (a high-ranking official in the government of Louis-Philippe), and was the granddaughter of Madame de Staël. She frequented the political salon of Adolphe Thiers (see Chapter Three), where her brother remembered that she "was all the more remarked upon since my sister, then in the full brilliance of her beauty and having an independent nature not exempt from the spirit of contradiction, expressed in no uncertain terms various contrary opinions."[91] The comtesse also hosted a successful salon of her own, as described by a friend in a letter to her brother:

You have no idea of the brilliance of your sister's *Thursdays*. The *Mondays* are no less glorious. About half past eight your father says, "so much the better, no one will come," and at ten o'clock one suffocates and is suffocated: lawmakers, army and navy, royal court, Supreme Court. Nevertheless, everyone talks and it's not at all boring.[92]

Ingres plunged into the swim of Parisian social life upon his return from Rome. He was obsessed with cultivating the very best contacts and was incredibly successful: an invitation to dinner with the king in May of 1841 was followed in June by a great banquet hosted by the marquis de Pastoret, for which the guest list included "the most lofty names of the intellectual aristocracy."[93] Writing to his old friend Gilibert, Ingres reveled in his newfound prestige:

You know Paris. Well! it's raining down on me and I'm overwhelmed. Just when I think I'm able to reach the edge of the whirlpool, I find myself immersed even deeper into it. All my hours, all my minutes are accounted for, all my evenings start off with dinners engaged in advance. . . . I must admit that it is quite flattering to see tears wept before my works, and by all the delicate good minds: "You are number one today!" I'm told. And I see my envious rivals, spiteful and ridiculous, at my feet. . . . All that and the convincing proof of what I'm worth compared to the moderns: my position; the most beautiful works of the day; consequently a fortune, natural result of these works; honored and recognized in the highest circles; surrounded by a crowd of friends who cherish and respect me; influential, if I want, in many things.[94]

Ingres and Louise d'Haussonville surely crossed paths in the best salons of aristocratic Paris. Small wonder that he signed his name to her portrait as if belonging to the world in which she lived and moved.

Ingres apparently agreed to paint the comtesse in the spring of 1842, for he mentions a rough sketch in a June letter written to Gilibert. His work was unexpectedly interrupted in July when the duc d'Orléans—one of the painter's most important patrons and heir to the throne—was killed in a carriage accident. Ingres was kept busy by commissions for several portraits of the deceased prince and designs for the windows of a funerary chapel at Dreux. When the painter returned to his portrait of Louise d'Haussonville in early 1845 she was both more mature and more refined than when he had first sketched her in 1842. He restarted the picture from scratch, taking great pains to locate the comtesse in an appropriately refined context worthy of her station in life. Shortly after completing the work he reported to Gilibert with evident relief that "the portrait of Madame d'Haussonville has already elicited a frenzy of approbation, first of all from the duc de Broglie, from his family, and from his many friends of the social elite."[95] Whether or not Louise's husband liked the picture was apparently of secondary importance, for the public that mattered to Ingres was the sitter's illustrious father and his well-placed friends.

Ingres depicted the comtesse wearing a short-sleeved, scoop-neck gown with a gathered and ruffled skirt appropriate for evening social events. The steely blue color accords well with the cool tones of the setting and provides a visual context for the tonic note of red silk ribbon in her hair. In some early sketches for the picture Ingres wrapped a cashmere shawl around his sitter's shoulders. For the final version he preferred to relegate the shawl's bright colors of lemon yellow and Pompeian red to the lower right corner—a decision that allowed him to emphasize the long curve of his sitter's neck. Quite unlike his ruthlessly objective analysis of Bertin, Ingres augmented the natural beauty of the comtesse by giving her the nearly perfect oval face, large and penetrating eyes, and small, slightly pouty mouth that was the ideal of feminine beauty in 1840s Paris. Thiers reportedly said to Louise that "M. Ingres must be in love with you to have painted you like that."[96]

Ingres also situated the comtesse at the center of a network of social relationships quite unlike the anonymous environment of Bertin's portrait. The tassel of a corded bellpull (visible running along the edge of the mirror) lies on the mantle to index the servants Louise might summon when needed. A handful of calling cards dropped on the mantle to the right—some with turned down corners to indicate a visitor called while the comtesse was out—are evidence, as Edgar Munhall has written, "of Mme d'Haussonville's social responsibilities, for paying visits to one's friends and leaving cards was a daily ceremony for Parisians of her class."[97] Ingres knew well and valued highly the practices of this milieu. His picture includes multiple references to its social ceremonies, and he placed the comtesse fully at ease in their midst.

Let us return to the opera glasses placed on the mantle near Louise d'Haussonville. The comtesse wears an evening dress, so we might assume that the sun has set. The reflected image of a bright window on the body of the opera glasses is at best anachronistic, but this only underscores its importance. Why bother painting that tiny reflection?[98] The four small squares of light not only attest to the sitter's social space, they also draw our attention to the opera glasses themselves. They reference the comtesse's love for the theater and allude to a nearly invisible narrative in the picture. Edgar Munhall was the first to suggest that the comtesse found the calling cards in the front entry and left them on the mantle of her boudoir while making her way to the bedroom.[99] Her passage through space explains her casual drop of the cashmere shawl and fine lace handkerchief onto a chair at the right. She has just hung her small evening bag of blue silk from the gilt-bronze handle of the vase at the extreme right edge of the picture, a gesture easily coupled with leaving the opera glasses and calling cards just below. All of which suggests that the comtesse has just returned home from an evening of theater or opera. Ingres could barely acknowledge—much less represent—the hostile and fickle world of journalism in which Bertin was at home. By contrast, Ingres's achievement with his portrait of the comtesse was to inscribe his sitter in a specific social milieu and to situate her character in the cultural panorama of mid-century Paris. Louise d'Haussonville was a woman of strong opinions: she reflects upon the evening's performance or conversation with a gesture and pose that signal—as in the portrait of Marie d'Agoult (Fig. 110)—a working intellect. What had she seen this evening? Whom did she applaud? Those questions form the centerpiece of our next section.

Going Out: *Hernani* and the Demise of Classical Theater

I was present with my mother at the opening performance of Hernani, *and I was deeply moved. Mlle Mars impressed me terribly, and we sobbed, my mother and I, so hard during the final scenes that by the end of the evening my mother's eyes ached, and we promised each other that night, returning home by carriage, never again to speak ill of Victor Hugo or Mademoiselle Mars.*

—Louise d'Haussonville[100]

25 February 1830! That date remains written in blazing letters on the bedrock of our past: the date of the first performance of Hernani! *That evening determined our life! We received there the impetus that still drives us after so many years, and that keeps you moving right to the end of your career. A lot of time has passed since then, and yet our astonishment is always the same.*

—Théophile Gautier[101]

It is hard to imagine that Louise d'Haussonville and Théophile Gautier could be writing about the same evening in February 1830 when Victor Hugo's *Hernani* opened at the prestigious Comédie-Française. For the former, it was an evening of tears induced by the triple suicide of the final scene (Fig. 116), and a memorable performance by Mademoiselle Mars, one of the troupe's leading stars (Fig. 124). For the latter, it was one of those crucial turning points in life that remained both beacon and inspiration for an entire career. The opening night of *Hernani* has been rightly described as "the most famous and influential theatrical event in France in the nineteenth century."[102] Yet our citations suggest very dissimilar experiences coexisted that night. Are those differences simply products of individual temperaments? If not, what were the cultural stakes at risk?

Our two witnesses saw *Hernani* from physically different vantage points. Louise and her mother followed the performance from premium seats in the loges that were the do-

main of wealthy or aristocratic patrons. By contrast, Gautier cheered the play from the parterre—the pit in front of the stage fitted up with simple benches—in the company of his bohemian friends. They had been enlisted by Hugo to serve as the play's claque, that peculiar Parisian phenomenon of seats distributed to friends of the playwright or members of the cast whose job was to ensure that applause would fill the auditorium on opening night. Hugo took no chances: rather than hiring a professional claque he summoned "the romantic youth, full of fervor and made fanatic by the preface to *Cromwell*." Hugo's troops turned out in extravagant costumes inspired by the paintings of Rubens and Velázquez. "Satin, velvets, braids, ornamental frogs, fur trimmings," recalled Gautier, who stood out in his vest of bright red worn with green slacks, "were as good as a black suit with tails."[103] By the time Louise and her mother arrived for the curtain at seven o'clock, Gautier and his friends had been in the theater for five hours, for they arrived when the doors opened at two o'clock in order to claim space in the unreserved seating of the parterre.

Anticipation ran high all around. The next day the government's official newspaper, *Le Moniteur universel*, reported that "from six o'clock, even though the play would start only at seven, the auditorium of the Comédie-Française was filled with a crowd eager to assist at the first performance of the drama of *Hernani*. . . . When the curtain rose the room was jammed."[104] Gautier describes the moment colorfully:

It was enough to cast your eyes on this public to convince yourself that this was no ordinary performance; to see that two systems, two parties, two armies, even two civilizations—this is not an exaggeration—were faced off, cordially detesting each other the way one mutually loathes in literary grudges, wanting only battle and ready to pounce on the other side. The general mood was hostile, elbows were turned out, the brawl waited only for the least contact to burst out, and it was not hard to see that this long-haired young man found that clean-shaven gentleman disastrously idiotic and would not conceal his personal opinion for very long.[105]

For Gautier, clear lines of battle were drawn between the long-haired romantics like himself who supported Hugo, and the bald-headed academics and classicists who had come

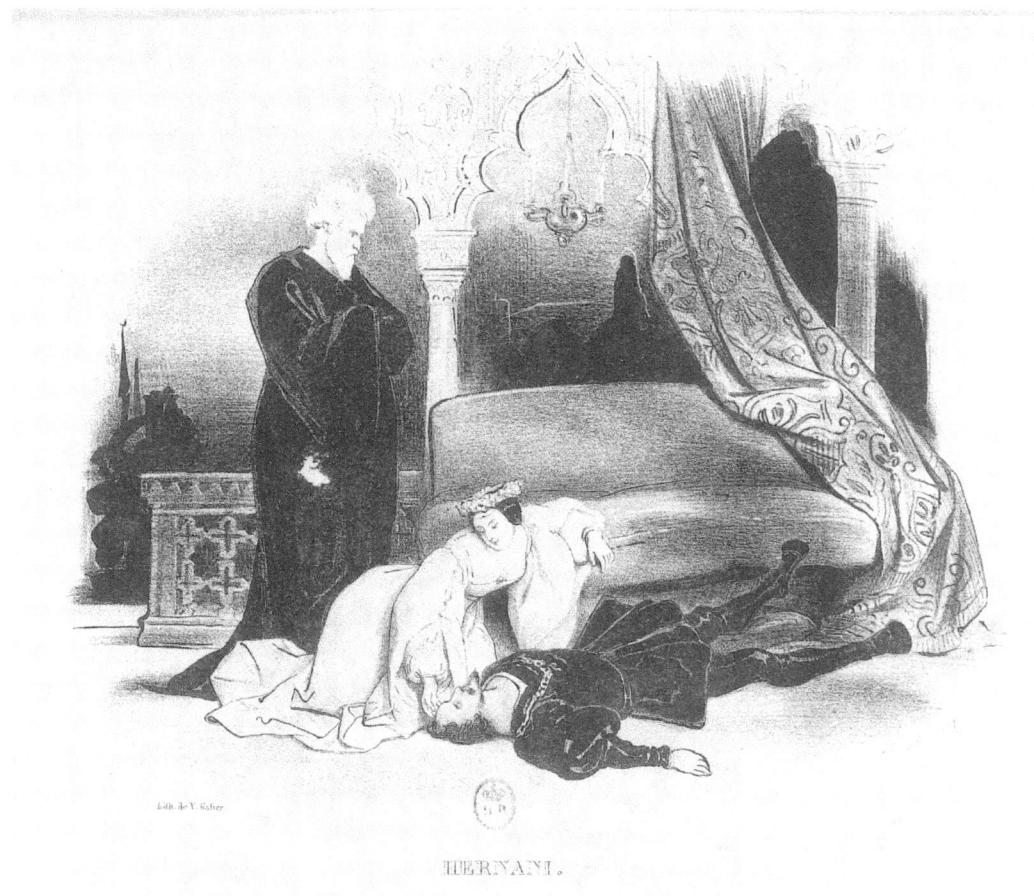

FIGURE 116. Achille Devéria, *Hernani (Act V, scene 6): The Death of Hernani*, 1830. Lithograph. Paris, BnF, Estampes, inv. Dc 178 d rés (4) (21 × 23.5 cm). Photo: BnF, Paris.

to mock *Hernani* (Fig. 117). Needless to say, those lines were not so apparent from the loge of Louise or, at best, they paled in contrast to the tears she shed with her mother.

What did the audience see that evening? Hugo's *Hernani* is a sprawling drama drawn from the annals of Spanish history. The date is 1519. Following Hugo's belittling of the unities of time and place in his preface to *Cromwell* (see Chapter Five), the action occurs over a period of several months in Saragossa, in the mountains of Aragon, and at Aix-la-Chapelle. As suggested by the play's epigraph *tres para una* [three for one], the plot is driven by the love of three men for one woman, the young and beautiful Doña Sol de Silva: in one corner of this triad is Don Carlos, the young king of Spain; in the second is Don Ruy Gomez de Silva, aging uncle and tutor of the young woman who wants to marry her; finally, there stands the dashing young outlaw Hernani, whom Doña Sol loves. Don Carlos and his troops are systematically hunting down Hernani's band of outlaws. They trap Hernani in the castle of Don Ruy Gomez de Silva, where he has come to visit Doña Sol. When Don Ruy Gomez hides Hernani and refuses to reveal him, Don Carlos takes Doña Sol hostage to punish her uncle's insolence. Hernani thus owes his life to Don Ruy Gomez: he swears—on the head of his dead father—to kill the king for having taken Doña Sol by force. Their pact is sealed when Hernani gives the old man his hunting horn and promises, whenever Don Ruy Gomez

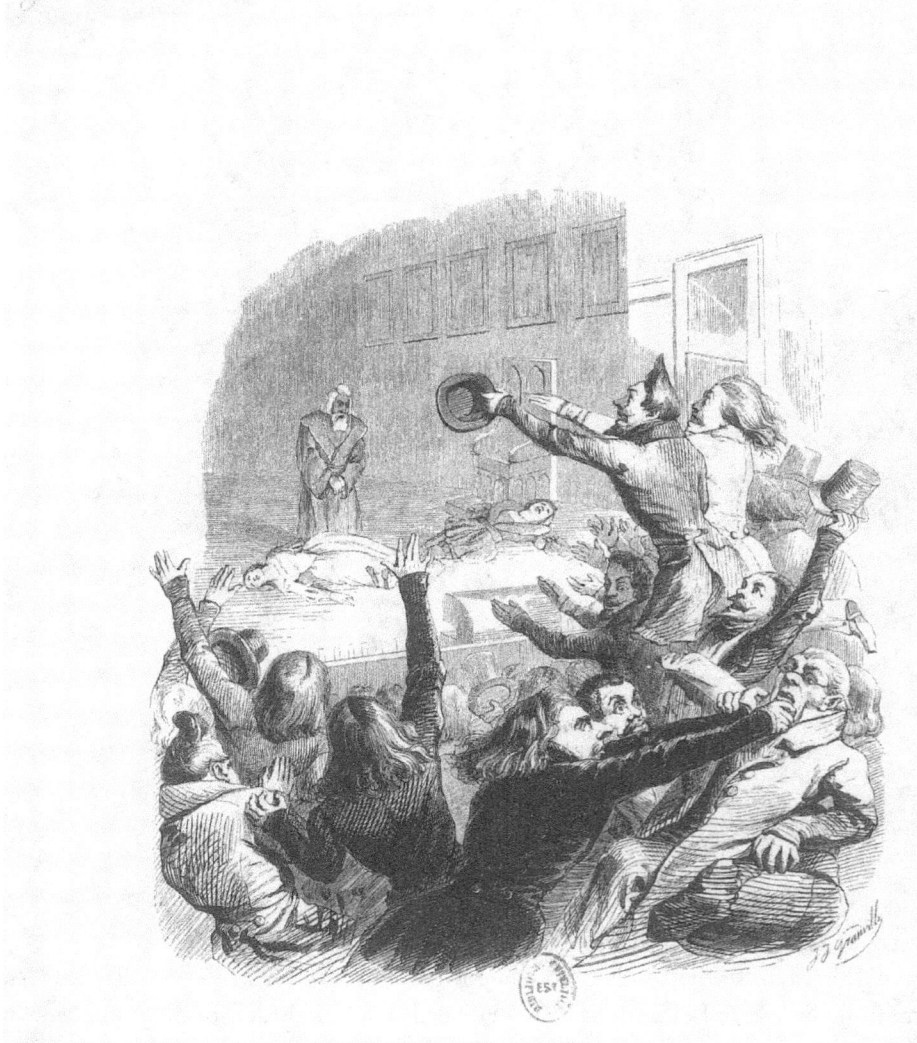

LEC ROMAINS ÉCHEVELÉS À LA 1ʳᵉ REPRÉSENTATION D'HERNANI.

Si le drame avait eu six actes, nous tombions tous asphyxiés.

might sound the horn, to end his life as a gesture of gratitude for the protection he has been given.

The scene then shifts to Aix-la-Chapelle, where the leaders of Christian Europe have gathered to select a successor to Maximilian, recently deceased leader of the Holy Roman Empire. Don Carlos, burning with ambition to be elected emperor, addresses a long soliloquy before the tomb of Charlemagne asking for guidance from the spirit of the Empire's founder. A group of nobles, including Hernani and Don Ruy Gomez, have also assembled near the tomb of Charlemagne, but their purpose is to assassinate Don Carlos. At the moment Hernani obtains the right to strike the fatal blow—and thus fulfill his oath to Don Ruy Gomez—three cannon shots announce that the king of Spain has been elected Emperor Charles Quint. The new emperor emerges from hiding to confront the plotters: to some he offers new titles; to others clemency; soon there remains only a handful of conspirators. Naturally, Hernani is among them. Hernani then reveals he is really Jean d'Aragon, whose father had been unjustly executed—and his lands seized—by King Ferdinand of Spain, the father of Don Carlos. Hernani's motive for wanting to kill Don Carlos thus becomes an affair of family honor. Don Carlos weighs his options in a tense moment of deliberation: he unexpectedly pardons Hernani, restores to him the titles and lands of Aragon, and gives him permission to marry Doña Sol. The play seems headed for a happy ending except for the bitter disappointment of Don Ruy Gomez de Silva, who has been denied his own happiness with the young woman.

The final act of *Hernani* unfolds in the Aragon family palace at Saragossa, for which Hugo specified a decor of rigorously unclassical architecture with "Moorish arcades" and a view of the "gothic and Arab arches" of the main building.[106] It is the wedding day of Jean d'Aragon (Hernani) and Doña Sol. The city is brightly illuminated, fountains play in the gardens, and the crowd of masked guests is brilliant in dress and conversation. There is one false note: "among the flowers, the women, the clothes of many colors, this specter, standing against a railing, who stains the masquerade with his black domino" (act 5, sc. 1). No one can guess who is hidden behind the mask of this figure in black, but speculation

vanishes as the happy newlyweds bid their guests farewell and prepare to enter their nuptial chamber. Doña Sol, overcome by the day's festivities and her own happiness, hesitates for a moment. The newlyweds are speaking when the sound of a hunting horn breaks the still of the night. Hernani is thrown into a panic, for he realizes that Don Ruy Gomez has come to claim his part of their oath.

Doña Sol knows nothing of the oath, so she responds innocently to the sound of the hunting horn: "Don Juan, that harmony fills the heart with joy." He replies in a fury: "Call me Hernani! Call me Hernani! I have not yet finished with that deadly name!" (act 5, sc. 3). He sends Doña Sol to look for a small box in his room. During her absence the mysterious figure in black appears onstage, echoing the words of Hernani's promise to die whenever the hunting horn is sounded. The stranger offers Hernani the choice of dagger or poison; he chooses the latter. In a moment of weakened resolve, Hernani begs for a delay of one day so that he might sleep in the arms of his bride. The stranger refuses, reminding Hernani that he swore on the head of his father. Suddenly Doña Sol returns with the box presumed to contain a deadly potion. The figure in black unmasks himself to reveal Don Ruy Gomez. Doña Sol tries to dissuade Hernani from suicide by arguing the only oath that matters is the marriage vow he has just made to her. Her words fall on deaf ears, for Hernani is ever more determined to execute his oath of honor. Doña Sol grabs the vial of poison she has brought and, in a gesture of sublime defiance, she drinks half and hands the vial to Hernani with the memorable retort:

Don't complain about me, I saved your part
You wouldn't have left me mine in the same way,
You! You don't have the heart of a Christian wife.
You don't know how to love like Silva.
But I drank first and am calm about it—Go on!
Drink if you want! (act 5, sc. 6)

Hernani drinks his part. The concluding moments of the play, as rendered in Achille Devéria's lithograph of 1830 (Fig. 116), consist of the newlyweds slowly dying in one another's arms while expressing their deep love left deplorably unconsummated. Faced with the spectacle of their double death and mutual affection, Don Ruy Gomez de Silva kills himself at the curtain's fall. Small wonder that Louise and her mother sobbed through this final scene until their eyes hurt.

IT IS EASY TO FORGET that the heart-wrenching finale of *Hernani* was a novelty at the Comédie-Française in 1830. Productions on that prestigious stage typically relegated to the wings disturbing events like deaths, and actors tended not to engage in extended pantomime. Emphasis was placed on the stylish declamation of an author's text rather than the dramatic representation of action—a minimalism that was often admired by English visitors to Paris. "The dignity and gravity of the drama are rigidly preserved," remarked Henry Milton about the Comédie-Française in 1815; "no adventitious ornaments are resorted to, and an Englishman, filled with ideas of the levity of the French, and their love of gaiety, is astonished when first he witnesses the deep impression which tragic acting produces on the audience, and the profound attention and decorum which are preserved."[107] By contrast, Parisians increasingly viewed the highly wrought language and bare-bones scenography of the Comédie-Française as shopworn and outdated. They had become accustomed to the dramatic stagings, special effects, and seemingly natural acting of the small theaters clustered along the boulevard du Temple.

As early as 1803 Julien-Louis Geoffroy, the preeminent theater critic of his day, sounded a warning: "Today, the great arena of activity for our dramatic poetry seems to be the boulevard. Each month sees a masterpiece bloom upon this new Parnassus, while our most exalted theaters, struck by a disgraceful barrenness, live off their former glory."[108] By far the most popular spectacles on the stages of the boulevard du Temple were melodramas—hybrid performances that combined segments of music or dance interspersed with pantomimes or scenes spoken in plain prose or even coarse slang. The acknowledged master of melodrama was René-Charles Guilbert de Pixérécourt, whose *Coelina ou l'Enfant du mystère* of 1800 made his fame: it was presented three hundred eighty-seven times in Paris, more than one thou-

sand in the provinces, and translated into English, German, and Dutch. For more than three decades Pixérécourt produced a steady stream of new melodramas, although most were written in less than three weeks and predictably formulaic. Pixérécourt's usual cast of characters included a tyrant or traitor, a victim, a hero devoted to defend law, justice or love, and a simpleton [niais] associated with the hero whose role was to "loosen up the audience, to provoke unforeseen complications, and sometimes to bring about a providential denouement."[109] Keeping this comic figure continuously on stage boldly mixed the genres of drama kept strictly distinct at the Comédie-Française.

A melodrama's separation of spoken scenes with interludes of comedy, ballet, and music undermined the unities of time, space, and narrative held dear by defenders of classic drama. The omnipresent niais, who invariably spoke a lowbrow, vulgar dialect that purposely mocked the high style of tragic verse, appealed to a broader, if less sophisticated, audience. Most important, Pixérécourt was among the first to realize that a simple plot could obtain phenomenal public success if supported by a meticulously orchestrated staging built around impressive changes in décor, careful attention to historical details of costume and setting, and at least one special effect of thrilling complexity. Pixérécourt and his technicians developed new types of stage structures and elaborate machinery to produce an expanded range of scenic effects: from several floors of underground rooms in the *Mines de Pologne* (1803) to a flood of simulated water that swept the heroine off stage at the end of *La Fille de l'exilé* (1819).

Joseph-Abraham Fleury, a leading comic actor at the Comédie-Française during the Empire, recorded with regret the odd relationship between the most prestigious theater of Paris and its emerging boulevard competitors:

The ladies of the new France are the instigators. They have their annual subscriptions with us, where they come for one or two hours to show off their diamonds; but their theaters of preference are on the boulevards. They have to go at least three times a week for fifty cents worth of catastrophes, fires, and carnage.[110]

Napoléon himself had little time for melodramas, which he called "tragedies for parlor maids."[111] He was loathe to see

Parisians, including high-ranking members of his imperial aristocracy, flocking to the privately owned theaters of the boulevard du Temple while the national theaters, which received lavish government subsidies, played to empty houses. Napoléon believed the root cause of the problem was too much competition, so he set about to regulate the situation. A decree of 8 June 1806 established four principal theaters for Paris and granted them exclusive rights over specific genres: the Théâtre de l'Empereur (Comédie-Française) for the "classical" repertoire; the Théâtre de l'Impératrice (Odéon) for new works; the Opéra and Opéra-Comique for their respective specialties. Secondary theaters, which were limited to twelve in number, could stage works within any genre if they paid a royalty to the principal theater owning rights to that genre. Existing theaters were obliged to prove their financial stability or close down. No new theaters could be opened without Napoléon's personal consent.

Within six months it became clear that the new regulations were having little or no effect. "The imperial theaters will have to close this summer if the current number of theaters holds good," warned a report to Napoléon in April of 1807; "what are the consequences of this huge number of performances? The public and the actors are mutually corrupted, and the leading theaters of Paris, whose superiority is recognized by all of Europe, will soon be no more than boulevard spectacles."[112] The Emperor's advisors were convinced that boulevard theaters were draining off the audience for serious drama with lowbrow spectacles of dubious moral worth. Napoléon took action again on 8 August 1807 with a decree that fixed at eight the maximum number of theaters authorized to operate in Paris. These included the four imperial theaters endorsed by the decree of 1806 and only four boulevard theaters of long history: the Gaité and Ambigu-Comique, which were restricted to staging melodramas, pantomimes, harlequinades, and other farces; the Variétés and Vaudeville, which were limited to popular musicals, parodies, and peasant plays with music based on well-known songs.

Despite Napoléon's best efforts to force Parisian theater patrons to forsake the boulevards for more highbrow dramatic forms, historians generally agree that his draconian measures failed miserably for several reasons. First, the new law implic-

itly sanctioned melodrama as a serious dramatic form by reserving for it two of the city's best stages and simultaneously eliminating competitors. Second, closing so many theaters greatly increased pressure on writers of all genres to retool their activities within the government's limitations: many began to experiment with the creation of new spectacles, such as reviews of contemporary history that became a staple of the Vaudeville. Finally, by formalizing a distinction between the serious drama or dance of the national theaters and the lowbrow forms performed on the boulevard, Napoléon polarized the public's choices. But he could not dictate its behavior. Writing in 1810, Madame de Staël remarked on the growing rift between elite culture and the general public:

In France, our most beautiful tragedies do not interest the people. On the pretense of a taste too pure and a sentiment too delicate to tolerate certain emotions, art is divided in two: bad plays contain touching predicaments poorly expressed; good plays admirably depict situations that are cold thanks to too much seriousness.[113]

This cultural split ensured that the national theaters still struggled to make ends meet while boulevard theaters enjoyed an immense popularity and increased profitability.

THE ONE BRIGHT STAR at the Comédie-Française was François-Joseph Talma (Fig. 123), arguably the most renowned tragedian in Paris and a personal favorite of Napoléon. Talma's loyal fans could be counted upon to fill the house and boost the troupe's revenue. His fame was well established before the Revolution, when he pioneered costume reform at the Comédie-Française by wearing archaeologically correct attire designed by Jacques-Louis David in the 1789 production of Voltaire's *Brutus*. Talma remained attached to the principles of historical accuracy and natural gestures. For the revival of *Hamlet* in 1804 he wore a black costume based on sixteenth-century models, and his acting style broke so clearly with the troupe's usual restraint that the critic Julien-Louis Geoffroy feared for the future of tragedy itself:

What does one go to see in *Hamlet*? Well drawn characters? No, because the play has no character except a madman and a visionary.

Situations well contrived and really pathetic? No, because the only situation in the play is the scene between Hamlet and his mother, as improbable as it is horrible. Then it must be Talma's miming that draws the curious; his distorted features, his wild eye, his quivering voice, his gloomy, sepulchral tone, his taut, muscular frame, his tremblings, his convulsive passion. If to please an audience one must indulge in fits of frenzy, what actor, however noble, natural and restrained, will not appear insipid and cold? True tragic declamation, all the fine shades of feeling and passion, all the techniques of an actor's expression will no longer be felt and no will no longer delight . . . and that will be the end of tragedy.[114]

Nonetheless, *Hamlet* was the only production to turn a profit during the financially disastrous season of 1804—a success that depended almost entirely upon Talma's controversial interpretation.

Talma brought to the stage of the Comédie-Française a style of acting influenced by his long-standing admiration for English theater formed during the 1780s while living in London with his father. He was also a friend of the great tragic actor John Kemble. Writing from Paris in 1815, Henry Milton summarized somewhat incredulously the general outline of Talma's English influence:

We had heard from several quarters that Talma . . . had introduced great alteration in the style of acting, all borrowed from the English. This information was requisite, as certainly we never should have suspected the honour done to our country. These alterations were explained to us, as consisting in the substitution of nature, ease, and propriety, for the formality and stateliness of their former manner. . . . For my own part, I am convinced that in spite of all the improprieties in what they term the old school of acting, the performance of Racine's tragedies would have delighted me, had I seen them before this anglicized manner had been attempted.[115]

Talma's enormous personal prestige made it possible for him to experiment with innovations of costume or gesture without fearing the wrath of hostile audiences or critics like Milton. When playing the part of Néron in the 1814 production of Racine's *Britannicus*, Talma astonished his fans by performing a pantomime of boredom—tracing the patterns of his robe, adjusting its folds, playing with the arm of his chair—during Agrippina's long speech of the fourth act.

After Napoléon's final defeat at Waterloo Talma found himself in the odd position of being the most prominent actor of the Comédie-Française but no longer in official favor. Talma's close association with Napoléon made him suspect in the eyes of aristocrats returned to power by the Bourbon Restoration, even though Louis XVIII awarded him an annual pension of thirty thousand francs. Talma tried to retire from the Comédie-Française in 1817, but his colleagues in the troupe realized that losing him would drastically reduce the theater's receipts, so they stalled his retreat by quibbling over details. In 1821, for the production of Étienne de Jouy's *Sylla*, Talma produced a double surprise. The play was in rehearsals when word arrived in Europe of Napoléon's death in exile on the island of Saint Helena (5 May 1821). Talma was determined to render homage to the man who had lead France in great exploits and had been one of his most ardent admirers. On opening night he astounded the house by appearing in a wig that emulated Napoléon's celebrated lock of forehead hair (Fig. 11) and, in the words of Herbert Collins, "still more amazing, as he acted he recalled the tone, the stance, the gestures of the late Emperor. The effect was prodigious. Before the very eyes of the parterre the dead Emperor stalked, commanded, raged. It was as if Austerlitz had wiped out Waterloo."[116] That was not all. In a crucial scene Sylla experiences a dream in which he is terrified by the ghosts of his many victims. He awakens with awestruck remorse. If the scene were to be played realistically, Sylla must lie in bed; never, in the history of French tragedy, had such an indecorous attitude been assumed on stage. Not only did Talma welcome the challenge of this unorthodox performance, but his interpretation received rave reviews that only exacerbated the professional jealousies between himself and other members of the troupe.

The staging of *Sylla* was no less surprising than Talma's performance. Jouy's play made full use of the width and depth of the stage, including an elaborate décor designed by Pierre-Luc-Charles Cicéri that evoked the forum of ancient Rome. For the first time ever a tragedy at the Comédie-Française included actual crowd scenes. "There are two fine scenes in the fourth and fifth acts," reported the *Journal de Paris* with enthusiasm; "in rendering Sylla's dream Talma displays a terrifying power. Finally, at the play's climax, the abdication scene presents an imposing spectacle which could not fail to assure brilliant success for the piece."[117] When this critic applauds the evening's "spectacle" he signals that productions at the venerable Comédie-Française were reluctantly embracing the thrilling stage practices popularized and perfected by theaters along the boulevards.

This tendency was institutionalized in July 1825 when the government of Charles X named Baron Isidore Taylor as Royal Commissioner responsible for overseeing the financially troubled Comédie-Française and its troupe of quarrelsome actors. Taylor's selection is a milestone because his prior experience in Paris theater was limited to a short stint of directing the Théâtre du Panorama-Dramatique on the boulevard du Temple. He moved quickly to combat the dwindling box office receipts of the Comédie-Française, and he generalized the type of theatrical spectacle that proved so popular in boulevard theaters. Taylor's first production was *Léonidas*, a play written by his friend Michel Pichat and inspired by the heroic stand of ancient Greeks against the Persians at the Pass of Thermopylae. The story resonated with contemporary attention to the modern Greeks' struggle for independence against Turkey (see Chapter Five and Fig. 78). Taylor spared no expense to ensure the critical success of *Léonidas*. Cicéri, with whom Taylor had worked at the Théâtre du Panorama-Dramatique, designed three new sets that evoked the local color and historical circumstances of the setting. A completely new wardrobe was designed with an eye towards archaeological exactitude, and a new musical score was written expressly for the production. Taylor's goal was to dazzle the eye as much as the mind, and the success of his gamble became clear on opening night (26 November 1825). "Never had anything like that been seen at the Théâtre-Français in terms of decorations, costumes, and staging," recalled Alexandre Dumas; "as the curtain rose for each act there were shrieks and a stomping of feet."[118] Talma was thrilled by the scenic innovations of the theater's new director. At the banquet in honor of Pichat's triumph, Talma threw himself into Taylor's arms and exclaimed: "My friend, you are the savior of the Comédie-Française!"[119] Talma's energetic endorsement legitimated Taylor's innovations before skeptical members of the usually squabbling troupe.

Not everyone shared Talma's enthusiasm for Taylor's stagecraft. Pierre Victor complained in 1827: "Taylor does not understand that more rehearsals are needed to play a role at the Comédie-Française than at the Panorama-Dramatique . . . When the scenery is finished the performance goes on!"[120] This critical polemic was not simply a question of style or expense. Essential distinctions were at stake between highbrow theater and commonplace competitors, as this warning from Alexandre Duval makes clear:

If the Théâtre-Français, by the quackery of scene changes, the whimsy of costumes, the scorn of unities, the novelistic bombast stolen from melodramas, or the affectation of humor, continues to approximate the spectacles of the boulevards, everyone will end up regretting that fine time when its performances left only passages of eloquence in the memory of people with taste.[121]

Resistance during the late 1820s to Baron Taylor's program of moving the Comédie-Française closer to its boulevard competitors establishes the ground against which we must read Théophile Gautier's description of the opening night of *Hernani* as a cultural showdown. Gautier wants us believe that "two systems, two parties, two armies, even two civilizations . . . were faced off, cordially detesting each other the way one mutually loathes in literary grudges." He never suggests that the nature of art is at stake. The opening performance of *Hernani* engaged more than the aesthetics of confrontation championed by Gautier. Rather, it was symptomatic of a turning point in the history of French theater when the usual distinctions between high and low culture were no longer so sharply drawn.

Ironically, the censors of Charles X's government understood more clearly than Gautier the implications of producing Hugo's play on the stage of the Comédie-Française:

However extensive my analysis, it gives only an imperfect idea of the singularity of this conception and the flaws of its execution. It seemed to me a web of absurdities to which the author tries vainly to ascribe a high-minded character, but which are only trite and often coarse. This play has an abundance of improprieties. The king often expresses himself like a bandit, the bandit treats the king like an outlaw. The daughter of a Spanish noble is only a shameless libertine with neither dignity nor decency, etc. Nevertheless, in spite of so many major faults, our opinion is not only that there is no harm in authorizing the staging of this play, but also that it is politically wise not to strike a single word of it. It is good that the public sees how far the human spirit can wander when set free from all rules and propriety.[122]

The committee of censors realized that *Hernani* would define a moment when popular theater fully occupied the domain of high culture. They optimistically believed audiences would recognize its errors and lapses of good taste. Hugo and Taylor were gambling the reputation of the Comédie-Française that the censors were wrong, and they ended by winning handsomely, for the box office spoke more loudly than words. *Hernani* was a sensation that even its actors could not fathom. "The house is full," noted Joanny (who played Don Ruy Gomez de Silva) in his journal, "and the catcalls redouble furiously. There is some kind of contradiction implied in this: if the play is bad, why does one come? if one comes so eagerly, why does one hiss and boo?"[123] Perhaps Joanny was too close to the play to see that *Hernani* was more than a spectacular financial success. It was an entirely new kind of spectacle in which the elaborate décors of Cicéri and sumptuous costumes designed by Louis Boulanger established new standards for staging that were lavishly praised, even by Taylor's detractors. A hostile critic for the royalist and conservative *Corsaire* set the tone when he decried Hugo's literary style but grudgingly admitted "the staging is the only thing that merits unqualified praise: the costumes and the sets do credit to M. Taylor and to those who helped him on this occasion."[124] Joanny, who was trained to respect the author's text above all else, failed to see that crowds flocked to *Hernani* for an experience of spectacle in which the actors and their lines had become bit players in a larger scheme of affect.

NEARLY IDENTICAL TRANSFORMATIONS were occurring across town at the Opéra, which ended the 1820s more than one million francs in debt. In March 1830 a royal commissioner was named, similar to Taylor at the Comédie-Française, to put the Opéra's financial house in order. The appointee was Louis Véron, a former medical doctor who had founded the influential *Journal de Paris*. Véron often dipped into his considerable personal fortune to ensure the success of a production, for his ambitions were grand:

When you can make use of a vast theater having fourteen layers of stage depth, an orchestra of more than eighty musicians, a chorus of nearly eighty men and women, eighty dancers not counting children, and a crew of sixty stagehands to work the scenery, the public expects and requires great things of you.[125]

Véron hired Charles-Edmond Duponchel, an architect trained in the historicist and archaeological manner of Lassus and Viollet-le-Duc (see Chapter Four), to design the scenic machinery that would fulfill Véron's vision for the Opéra's stage.[126] Duponchel introduced a host of technical innovations that were considered as daring as they were expensive: running water so that fountains on stage would actually spray; gas jets for special effects of lighting behind the scenery; so-called English trapdoors that made it possible for characters to appear and disappear as if by magic; mobile curtains so that scenery could be changed on the fly without interrupting the action.

Duponchel's stagecraft wizardry was backed up by Pierre-Luc-Charles Cicéri, one of the most renowned stage designers of his generation. Cicéri had begun his long career during the Empire and was named chief decorator of the Opéra in 1810. In 1812 Napoléon awarded him the title of *peintre d'Empereur*. His career survived several changes in government: he was named *peintre du Roi* by Louis XVIII; he designed the robes and decors for the coronation of Charles X held at the cathedral of Reims in 1825; he designed the sets for *Hernani* at the Comédie-Française in 1830. During the 1820s Cicéri teamed up with Louis-Jacques-Mandé Daguerre—best-known as the inventor of daguerreotypes (see Chapter Eight)—to produce stunning optical illusions for the Diorama. Already in 1828 the team of Duponchel and Cicéri had created an onstage eruption of Mount Vesuvius for the opera *Muette de Portici* that became an overnight sensation. Above all, Cicéri was a professional who ignored the divide between highbrow and lowbrow productions. His workshop produced stage sets for the Opéra and Comédie-Française alongside fabulous decors for boulevard theaters like the Porte Saint-Martin and the Théâtre du Panorama-

Dramatique (where he had worked with Taylor). In the words of Marie-Antoinette Allévy,

[Cicéri] united an expertise of the scene-painter, who knew how to use the mechanical resources of the theaters of his day, with the craft of painter that his training in Bellangé's studio had developed. Therein lies the true nature of this *transformation* of theatrical set design during the nineteenth century: with Cicéri, the stage-set becomes a picture.[127]

It was only in 1831, for *Robert le Diable*, that Duponchel and Cicéri enjoyed the full financial backing of Véron, who was determined to make his first production as director of the Opéra a spectacle that would set new standards. The libretto was written by Eugène Scribe and Casimir Delavigne, with music by Giacomo Meyerbeer and choreography by Jean Coralli. The most spectacular scene of the opera—a ballet in the third act where debauched nuns rise from their graves in a frenzied dance that drives Robert to take the devil's talisman—was supposed to be set in a fantastic Olympus of classical décor. Duponchel, fully aware of contemporary enthusiasm for gothic architecture spawned by the success of Hugo's *Notre-Dame de Paris* (see Chapter Four), proposed instead a medieval cloister strewn with funerary monuments. Véron was immediately taken by the idea and gave carte blanche to his designers for the sets: the final cost of building Cicéri's cloister (Fig. 118) surpassed forty-three thousand francs.

True to his interest in archaeological accuracy, Duponchel sent Cicéri to Arles to see the cloister of Saint-Trophime. Cicéri also studied the perfectly preserved cloister at Montfort-l'Aumaury near Paris. He fused these two existing monuments into an imaginary locale: to the left, a deep perspective view of a dark, covered gallery; at the right, a screen of tall, double-columned arcades and triforium that affords a view of the graveyard. Gas jets, used for the first time at the Opéra in the battens and behind the scenes, produced a powerful illusion of moonlight shaped by the architectural latticework into pools of brightness that punctuate the pervasive gloom. Cicéri's lithograph of the stage set (Fig. 118) both captures this dramatic juxtaposition of light and dark and records Duponchel's liberal use of English trapdoors through which figures rise onto the stage from below. Coralli's choreography called for the nuns—dressed in costumes of white designed to be "part monastic robe, part shroud"—to appear as if rising from the dead, and to float through the cloister's evocative spaces.[128]

When *Robert le Diable* opened on 21 November 1831, Meyerbeer protested to Véron that "you have no faith in the success of my music, you are looking for a success of staging."[129] But the composer's complaint was drowned out by accolades for the team of Véron-Duponchel-Cicéri from critics like Théophile Gautier, who exclaimed: "For the magic, the impression, and the indeterminate thrill of an unknown world, the nun's cloister in *Robert le Diable* is as good as the music, to which it adds the mysterious depth of its arcades."[130] A few weeks later Frédéric Chopin, who was not a great fan of Meyerbeer's music, left the Opéra praising the spectacle and its effect on the composer's reputation:

If there ever was to be some splendor in the theater, I don't know if it could match the level of *Robert le Diable*. . . . It's the masterpiece of the new school, in which the devils (an immense chorus) sing in the pipes and souls rise from the grave . . . in groups of fifty and sixty, in which the theater is a diorama where, at the end, you see the interior of a church . . . lighted, with monks and the faithful on benches . . . never, anywhere, has one done anything like this. Meyerbeer is immortalized![131]

Gautier and Chopin, like most of those who saw *Robert le Diable*, were especially impressed by the spectral appearance of lapsed nuns who tempt Robert with wild, bacchanal-like dancing until he grasps the devil's talisman to seal his fate. Leading these temptresses in gauzy white was a virtuoso ballerina named Marie Taglioni.

Virtuosi: The Imagery of Genius

From her début with the Paris Opéra in July of 1827, Marie Taglioni drew critical attention for the unusual elegance of her dancing. Writing in response to her appearance in Anatole Petit's adaptation of *Le Sicilien*, a critic for *Le Constitutionnel* sketched the qualities that would become Taglioni's signature:

[Mlle Taglioni] is tall and thin; the undulations of her body, at once slender and rounded, are quite in harmony with the movements of

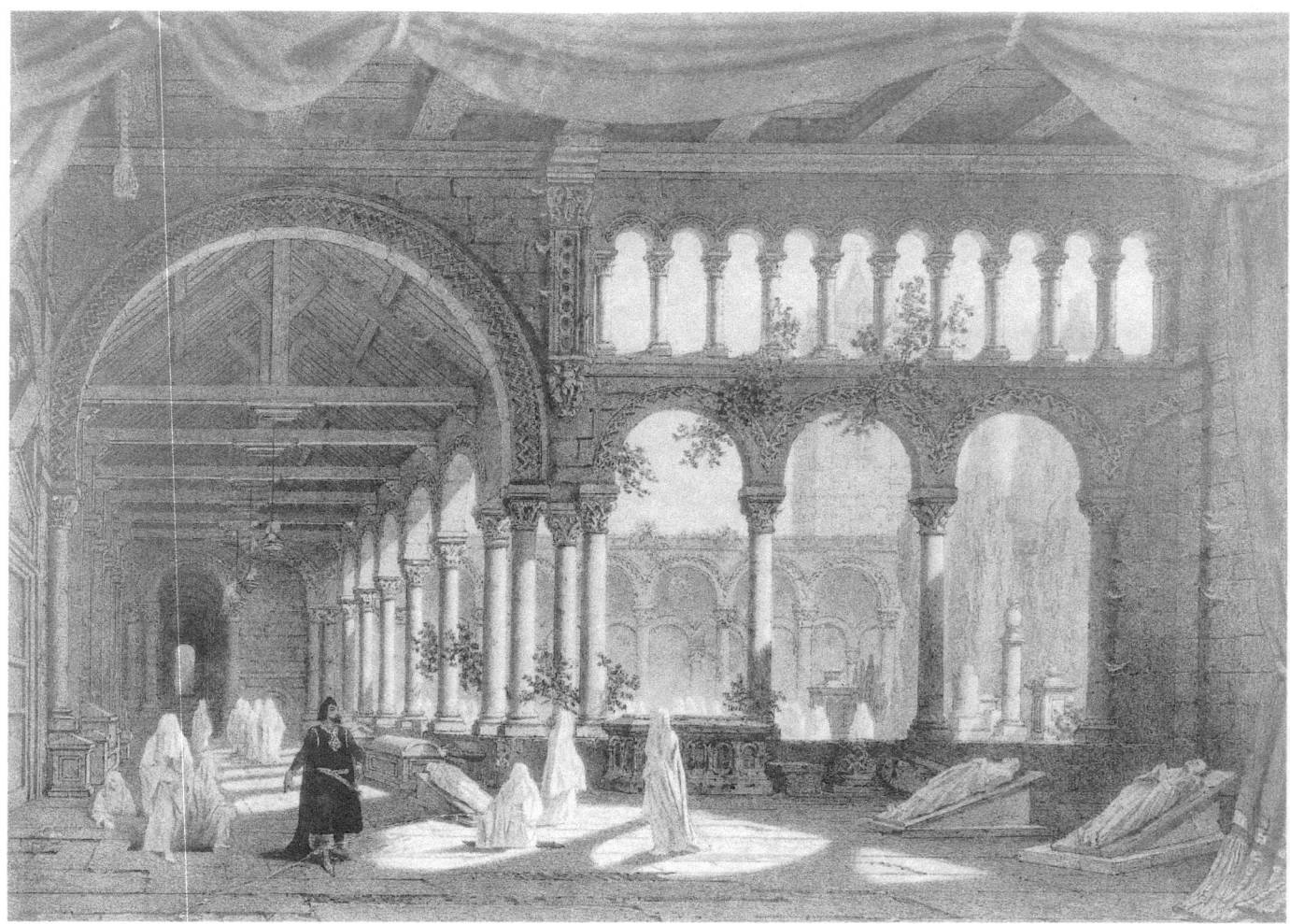

FIGURE 118.   Pierre-Luc-Charles Cicéri, *The Cloister of Sainte-Rosalie* (second set for Act III of *Robert le Diable* by Meyerbeer), 1831. Lithograph with watercolor. Paris, Bibliothèque-Musée de l'Opéra, inv. Scènes estampes, Robert le Diable, no. 29 (35 × 42.5 cm). Photo: BnF, Paris.

her neck, her head, her arms, her legs and her feet; the general effect is supple and graceful; however, this is not the grace with which we are acquainted; it has an air of originality, of strangeness even, without being wild or countrified. Mlle Taglioni's features present a type of beauty which has nothing in common with that of France; her big eyes, wide-opened and somewhat staring, hold the spectators charmed and spellbound. The occupants of the stalls at the Opéra have lost the habit of, but not the taste for, novelties; they

stamped with joy. . . . I have seldom witnessed such brilliant débuts in dancing.[132]

A few weeks later, at the time of her last appearance of the season, the same critic remarked that Taglioni exudes "a kind of modesty and artlessness which makes them beyond price; and then her dances are new; we have seen no one dance as she does."[133] After one of her début performances a young architect named Charles-Edmond Duponchel—future designer of special effects for the Opéra—expressed his admiration with a gesture that would become customary: he threw a bouquet of flowers onto the stage.

The critical terms that recur in comments about Marie Taglioni's début—her fluidity and grace marked by a certain strangeness, her beauty that is slightly out of norm, her artlessness that is nonetheless new—bracket the essential qualities of contemporary thinking about virtuosity. Charles Rosen, musicologist and virtuoso in his own right, discusses the impact of Franz Liszt's *Études*, written in the 1830s, using a vocabulary nearly identical to that employed by critics when describing Marie Taglioni's stage presence:

Played with a certain elegance, these pages are both dazzling and enchanting. The real invention concerns texture, density, tone color, and intensity—the various noises that can be made with a piano—and it is startlingly original. The piano was taught to make new sounds. These sounds often did not conform to an ideal of beauty, either Classical or Romantic, but they enlarged the meaning of music, made possible new modes of expression. On a much larger scale, Liszt did for the piano what Paganini had done only a few years previously for the violin.[134]

The migration of stunning stage techniques from boulevard theaters to the Comédie-Française and the Opéra coincides exactly with a rage in Paris for virtuosi like Taglioni, Liszt, and Paganini. Audience demands for thrilling spectacle fueled an expanded understanding of what constitutes personal artistry. Susan Bernstein has argued that the center of this new aesthetic was an emphasis on the performative qualities of virtuosity:

It is obstinately grounded in materiality and singularity. The virtuoso performance can never be dissociated from the time and space of its occurrence; it takes place in a foundational relationship to its instrument and is constituted by the physical contact with the stage, the audience, and the ambiance. The figure of the virtuoso emerges through the material details of clothing, personal appearance and charisma, name, fame and money.[135]

Like Rosen, Bernstein is writing about musical virtuosi, but her points are equally appropriate to the ballet, where the dancer's instrument is literally his or her body, and where individual performances—especially before the invention of photography—were irretrievably situated in a specific time and place. For Bernstein, "the virtuoso is a sociohistorical figure that emerges within the confines of a specific history of music, of the economics and politics of entertainment and spectacle, and of journalism."[136] We have traced several contours of those intersections in Parisian culture of the early 1830s. It makes perfect historical sense that the era of dance virtuosi was inaugurated at this time by Marie Taglioni in *The Sylphide* of 1832—a performance that remains even today intimately connected with her name and fame (Fig. 119).

The scenario for *The Sylphide* was adapted by Adolphe Nourrit from a stage work originally written by Charles Nodier (see Chapter Eight). Nourrit was a tenor who sang the lead in *Robert le Diable*: it is generally believed that he adapted Nodier's text especially for Marie Taglioni, his stage partner in that operatic triumph. The choreography was arranged by Marie's father, Philippe, and the score was composed by Jean-Madeleine Schneitzhoeffer. Cicéri designed stage sets that included the optical illusion of a rocky landscape seen through a screen of trees, a complex lighting scheme employing gas jets, and a daring ascension of the star using a system of invisible wires. Every aspect of the production, remarks André Levinson, was designed to provide "frequent opportunities for the appearance of the favourite virtuoso of the public."[137] This goal of showcasing Taglioni's talent also motivated a dramatic costuming innovation. Dancers at the Opéra usually wore pleated tunics of a vaguely Greek inspiration. The painter Eugène Lami invented for Taglioni the modern tutu: its inverted bell shape frees the legs for springing and jumping, while its narrow waist and bared shoulders optimize presentation of the dancer's physique and arm movements. Henceforth, the virtuoso ballerina's entire range of body motion and agility would be the focus of audience attention.

The Sylphide is set in Scotland—a locale popularized by Walter Scott's novels—where picturesque peasants live amidst the romantic wilds of dense forests. James, a peasant boy danced in 1832 by Marie's brother, is supposed to marry a young woman named Effie, but he is haunted by visions

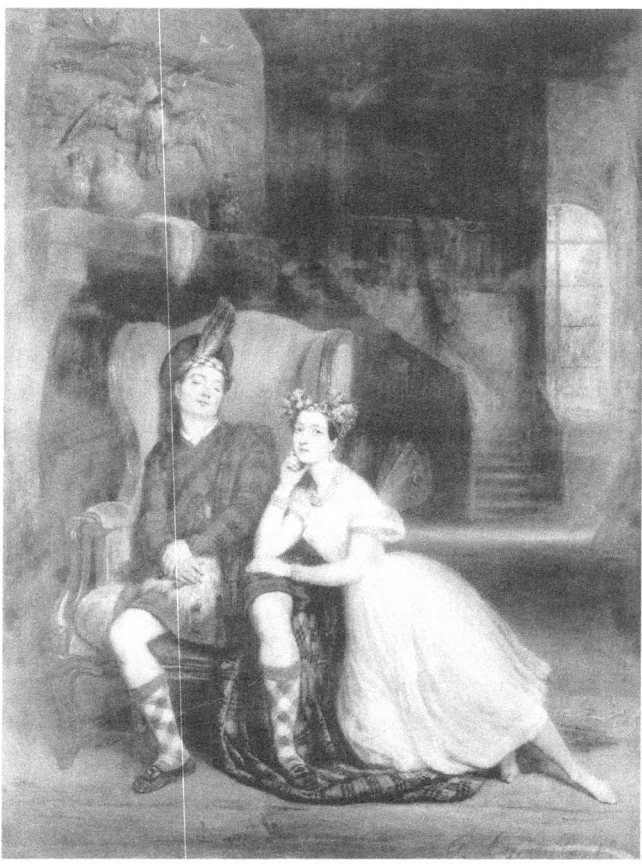

FIGURE 119.   François-Gabriel-Guillaume Lepaulle, *Marie Taglioni and her Brother Paul in* La Sylphide, 1834. Oil on canvas. Paris, Musée des Arts décoratifs, inv. 34532 (128.5 × 96.5 cm). Photo: © Photothèque UCAD/Laurent-Sully Jaulmes.

of the Sylphide—a pale, fragile spirit who lives in the forest. This elusive spirit appears only three times in the first act: at the curtain rise, where she places a kiss on the lips of James while he sleeps (Fig. 119), and twice flitting amongst the mortals on stage, invisible to all but James. In the dancing of the second act, set deep in the woods and accompanied by spirits like herself, Taglioni literally spread her wings to display the range and breadth of her talent in breathtaking *jetés* and *équilibres sur la pointe*. James inadvertently kills the Sylphide when he attempts to capture the fragile creature with a magic

scarf given to him by an evil witch. In the end, the Sylphide's body is whisked away by her kindred spirits, leaving James to suffer forever from remorse and a broken heart.

Virtuosi like Marie Taglioni presented a special kind of problem for the visual arts because the ephemeral qualities of physical presence and performative impact transfer only reluctantly to painting and sculpture. Consider one of the most famous pictures of Taglioni, the 1834 painting by François-Gabriel-Guillaume Lepaulle (Fig. 119). Lepaulle essentially avoids the problem of portraying Taglioni's extraordinary dancing by rendering the ballet's opening scene where the Sylphide approaches James to plant a kiss on his lips. He records Taglioni's distinguishing physical features— her long neck and large eyes, slender waist and long, expressive arms—but nothing of the "revolution in the order of ideas" described by André Levinson, in which "dancing becomes a transcendental language, charged with spirituality and mystery—a celestial calligraphy."[138] In short, the picture offers little more than a costume portrait of the dancer and her brother in their most famous roles.

A similar challenge faced artists who attempted to capture the diabolic energy of Niccolò Paganini, the most renowned violin virtuoso of the period. He had established his European fame with a triumphant series of concerts in Milan during 1813. Paganini's reputation was well known in Paris, although he did not play in the French capital until March of 1831. Parisian musicians knew some of Paganini's written works—notably his very difficult *Caprices*—but most found them inexplicable and unplayable. People were eager to see if the violinist could live up to his reputation and actually play his music. Moreover, Paganini's personal mythology— his reckless lifestyle, many lovers, and even stories of having spent time in jail for murder—fueled public curiosity and excitement about his visit to Paris. In an unplanned stroke of luck, Paganini's arrival in late February of 1831 coincided almost exactly with Véron's appointment as director of the Opéra. *Robert le Diable* was not slated to open until November; Véron planned to refurbish the Opéra's auditorium during the interim. Paganini's friend, the composer Gioacchino Rossini, suggested to Véron that the violinist's Parisian concerts would attract huge crowds and generate good box office receipts with very few expenses. Véron agreed: Paganini was scheduled to play ten concerts in the Opéra on Wednesdays and Sundays over the course of five weeks. The first concert was set for 9 March.

Paganini did not disappoint Véron. On opening night the Opéra was filled with the cream of Parisian society, including members of Louis-Philippe's court and the diplomatic corps, aristocrats and dandies, and all of the city's leading music critics. There was also on hand a band of enthusiastic romantics that included Théophile Gautier, Jules Janin, Charles Nodier, Alfred de Musset, George Sand, Heinrich Heine, Eugène Delacroix, and Franz Liszt. Joseph-Louis d'Ortigue left a vivid sketch of Paganini's singular and sinister appearance:

He is dressed in black, his suit coat buttoned all the way to the chin, the face pale and elongated, half in his tie, a *rictus* that toys with the unmoving wrinkles that furrow his face, a wide and prominent forehead, flowing hair, two eyes that roll in their dark sockets and cast lightning bolts into the audience, a silly smile that seems to defy the world with a mocking contempt.[139]

Ludwig von Boerne, writing for the *Frankfurter Zeitung*, painted for his readers a similar picture of Paganini's stage presence on opening night:

When Paganini stepped out on the stage—even before he began to play—he was welcomed with thunderous applause . . . but you should have seen how awkward he was! He swayed back and forth like a drunken man. His own feet got in his way and he kicked out with them, threw his arms up in the air and then in the other direction; stretched them out towards the wings and supplicated heaven, earth, and all mankind for help in his great need. . . . He was the most magnificent lout that Nature ever invented. Someone ought to have painted him.[140]

What of the performance? Even a jaded listener like François-Henri Blaze, music critic for the *Journal des Débats*, admitted that he "could not sleep all night from agitation" and he urged his readers:

Sell all that you possess; pawn everything, but go hear him! . . . This is the most astounding, the most surprising, the most marvelous, the most miraculous, the most triumphant, the most unheard-of, the most unique, the most extraordinary, the most incredible, the most unexpected, that one can imagine! . . . In a dream Tartini saw a devil playing a diabolic sonata—that devil was surely Paganini![141]

Among the artists in attendance that night, Eugène Delacroix took up von Boerne's challenge to paint the violinist. He eventually made a small and very dark picture of the strangely twisted, spectral figure of Paganini playing (Fig. 120), but he was virtually alone in braving the task of visualizing the virtuoso in the throes of his creative frenzy. Although a brisk traffic in Paganini imagery accompanied the excitement of his visit to Paris, few artists dared to wrestle with the problem of how to render the Italian's astonishing—even frightening—stage presence. More common were anecdotal subjects inspired by the sensational aspects of Paganini's murky past, of which the lithograph designed by Louis Boulanger that depicts him practicing the violin in prison is an example (Fig. 121).

A popular myth held that Paganini killed his mistress (or her lover, depending upon the version) while living in Lucca, and that he perfected his astonishing musical technique under Satan's tutelage during his incarceration for the crime. Responding to this tale, Boulanger included a spectral hand that seems to guide the violinist's fingering. Paganini was surely aware of such stories, but he had never before faced them so directly as in Paris: according to his own account, he came upon a group of people crowding around the window of a print-seller's shop during a walk along the boulevard des Italiens. Boulanger's lithograph was on display. Shocked to see himself depicted in jail, Paganini was even more taken aback when members of the group recognized him as the depicted person and began to comment on how much he had changed since those days. Suddenly he realized that "the thing was taken seriously by those whom you call, I think, rubbernecks [badauds]," and he suggests—in a letter to the journal *L'Artiste* protesting the lithograph—that he would be willing to supply other stories to fuel the fantasy of enterprising artists.[142]

L'Artiste compounded Paganini's irritation by publishing a reproduction of Boulanger's lithograph. In his complaint to the editor, Paganini discredits the entire story by pointing out that if he had served an eight-year prison sentence before

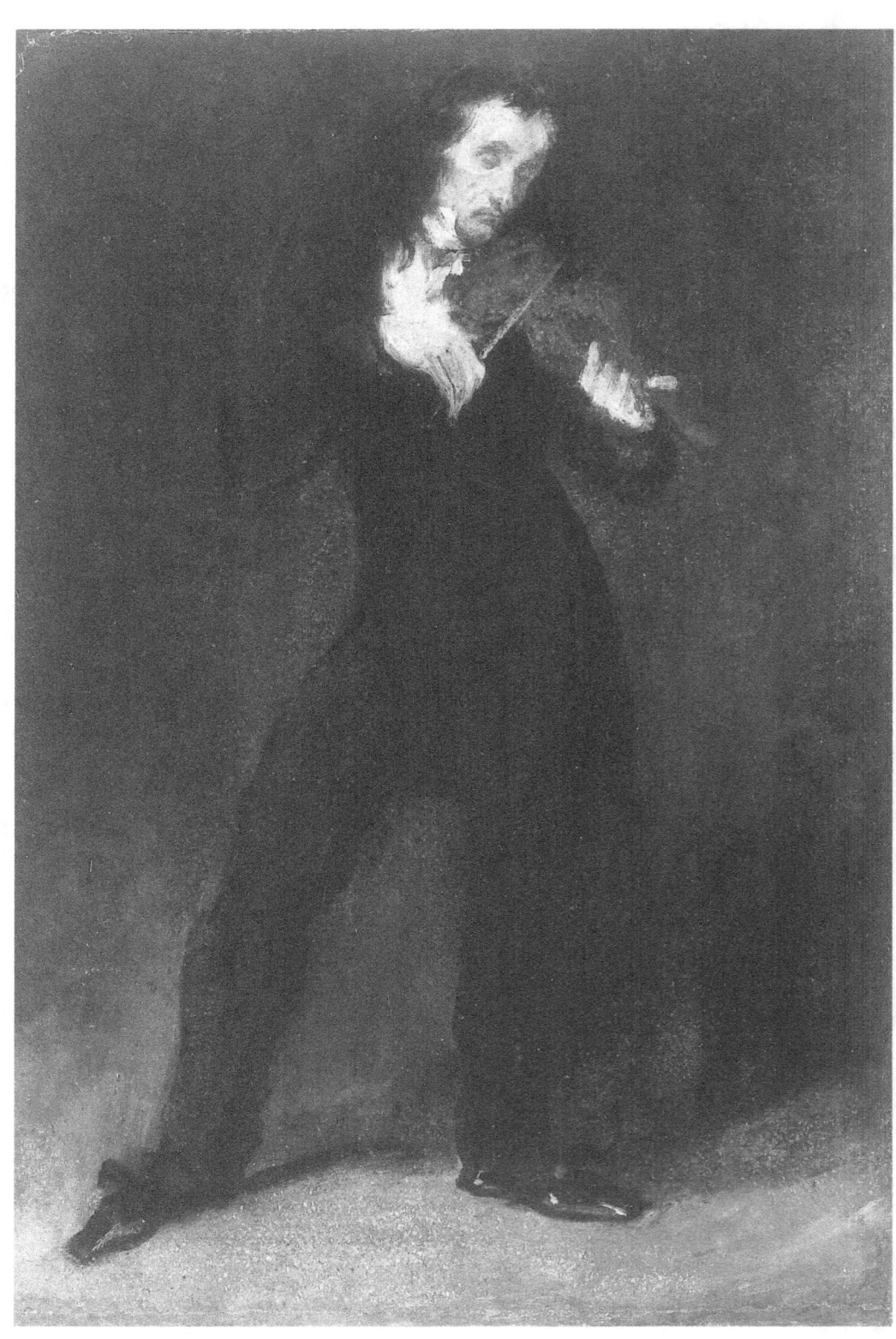

FIGURE 120. Eugène Delacroix, *Niccolò Paganini*, ca. 1832. Oil on cardboard on wood panel. Washington DC, The Phillips Collection, inv. 487 (44.7 × 30.1 cm). Photo: Courtesy of The Phillips Collection, Washington DC.

beginning his professional life (at age fourteen) he would have been seven years old at the time of the alleged murder! Even more interesting is Boulanger's reply, which *L'Artiste* published alongside Paganini's complaint. The painter is obviously trying to extricate himself from a charge of slander. The salient part of his defense is that the idea to represent Paganini in prison was directly related to the impossibility of rendering the violinist's appearance on stage:

Paganini came to Paris: enthusiasm was universal; I saw him, I heard him, and it was one of the most beautiful moments of my life. However, I did not have the pleasure of catching sight of the devil dressed as an English admiral upon his shoulder. . . . No, Sir, I did not see that, but rather an extraordinary man and an astonishing artist, whose mere countenance made a deep impression on my soul, and who fascinated me with his handsome head filled by art with divine fire. . . . Looking at that pale forehead marked by sadness, I wondered if some fatal destiny had not crushed this burning soul with its iron hand to make him pay for having received such a big share of talent that he now stands out as so much better than the rest; if some bitter memory did not cast a gloom over that stern countenance.[143]

Not finding any visible marks that might betray the depth of Paganini's genius, Boulanger was struck by a conceit that neatly combined literary history with hearsay:

Then, into my mind came that moving figure of Tasso, seated sadly upon the stone of a prison cell, alone with his lofty thoughts, sublime, radiant in the gloom: consequently, all of that got vaguely mixed up with what I had heard about Paganini's imprisonment— the grounds of which I knew nothing at all—that to my mind made him look even greater. Yes, I said to myself, this is what happens to genius! Unrecognized for a long time, often oppressed, and sometimes finally repaid for so much hardship by universal acclaim! Enviable fate![144]

Boulanger takes full responsibility for making the lithograph (he could hardly deny its authorship since his initials are on the plate). Yet he denies trafficking in cheap gossip. Rather, he claims the violinist's virtuoso performance incited a meditation on genius that led his thoughts, when mixed with vague rumors about Paganini's life, to Torquato Tasso.

A wanderer and philanderer of Renaissance Italy certainly as notorious as Paganini himself, Tasso had been locked up in a madhouse at Ferrara and forbidden to write. He was a stereotype of persecuted genius dear to the young romantics of Paris, witness Delacroix's commentary of 1819:

That man was so unlucky! One is filled with indignation against those worthless protectors who oppressed him under the pretense of shielding him from his enemies, and who deprived him of his precious manuscripts! How many tears of rage and indignation he must have shed upon seeing that in order to be more certain of seizing them he was accused of madness and creative impotence.[145]

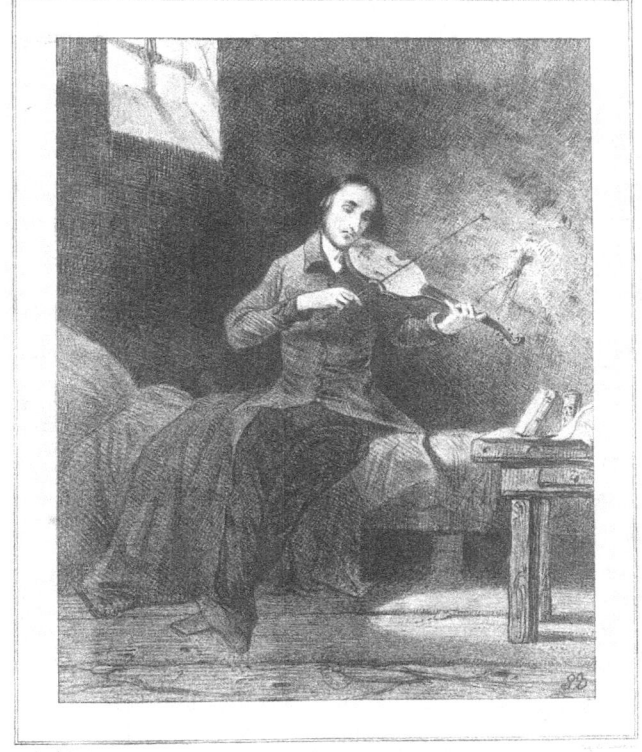

FIGURE 121. Louis Boulanger, *Paganini in Prison*, 1831. Lithograph published in *L'Artiste*, I (1831), p. 144. Paris, BnF, Estampes, inv. N2 "Paganini." Photo: BnF, Paris.

The lesson of Boulanger's tortured self-explanation is that he could not visualize the fleeting presence and performative strangeness of Paganini's concert. Less willing or able than Delacroix to wrestle directly with the demonic side of Paganini's talent, Boulanger shunned the subjective affect that is the essence of a virtuoso's magic in favor of narrative, anecdote, and literary allusion.

Among those deeply moved by Paganini's début performance in Paris was the nineteen-year-old Franz Liszt. Liszt was still suffering the effects of his thwarted love for a young aristocratic pupil, Caroline de Saint-Cricq, whose father put an end to the couple's romance on the grounds that a pianist was an unsuitable match. In the words of Alan Walker, Paganini's concert "electrified" Liszt: "He locked himself away and practiced for ten, twelve, sometimes fourteen hours a day. His aim was very simple. He wanted to do for the piano what Paganini had done for the violin; he drove himself mercilessly to conquer the keyboard's last remaining secrets."[146] Liszt emerged from this self-inflicted regime of practice and discipline a changed player. Writing about one of Liszt's recitals, Heinrich Heine inscribed the pianist in a diabolical world of conjuring powers every bit as strange as those attributed to Paganini:

For I must admit to you that, however much I love Liszt, his music does not have a pleasant effect on my state of mind, all the more so because I see ghosts which others only hear; and that, as you know, with every sound the hand strikes on the piano, the corresponding figure [Klangfigur] rises up in my mind—in short, the music becomes visible to my inner eye. My very understanding still trembles in my head when I remember the concert where I last heard Liszt play.[147]

Clara Schumann reacted similarly to a concert by Liszt in Vienna a few years later. "We have heard Liszt," she wrote; "he can be compared to no other virtuoso. He is the only one of his kind. He arouses fright and astonishment. His attitude at the piano cannot be described—he is original—he grows somber at the piano."[148] What bound Liszt and Paganini together was the dark strangeness, even frightening power of their performances.

Could this power be rendered visually? The question was faced by Henri Lehmann in 1840 when painting his well-known portrait of Liszt now in the Musée Carnavalet (Fig. 122). Eyewitness accounts of Liszt's concerts describe a physical transformation of the pianist's features that became increasingly visible as he played:

It was if an electric current went through the hall when Liszt entered. . . . He bowed and sat down at the piano. The first impression I had of his personality was the expression of great passion in his wan face. He seemed to me a demon, nailed fast to the instrument from which music poured out—the notes came from his blood, from his thoughts. . . . But as he played, so the demonic disappeared. I saw the pale face take on a more noble and more beautiful expression; the divine soul shone from his eyes and out of every feature—he was handsome, transformed by spirit and passion.[149]

This "more noble and more beautiful expression" is probably what Josef Danhauser was hoping to achieve with his picture of Liszt playing for his friends (Fig. 108). By contrast, Lehmann completely avoided the issue by choosing not to focus on Liszt the performer: although we might recognize "great passion in his wan face," there are no direct references to indicate that Lehmann's sitter is a pianist. Liszt is posed before a wall of somber greenish-gray articulated by shallow moldings that discreetly reframe his upper body within the image. Dressed entirely in black, Liszt stands with arms folded across his chest. We see his body almost as a profile, but he turns his head to look directly out of the picture and to rivet us with an unflinching gaze. The intense psychological confrontation between subject and viewer situates Lehmann's portrait amongst the pictures of artists already discussed (Figs. 112 and 113); while such imagery certainly pertains to Liszt as an artist, it signals little of his musical genius and nothing of his technical virtuosity.

A harsh raking light from the left isolates the pianist's head and left hand within the otherwise somber visual field to model crisply his thick eyebrows, fine aquiline nose, thin lips, long brown hair, and slender fingers. The lack

FIGURE 122.   Henri Lehmann, *Portrait of Franz Liszt*, 1840. Oil on canvas. Paris, Musée Carnavalet, inv. P 1683 (140 × 87 cm). Photo: © PMVP/Pierrain.

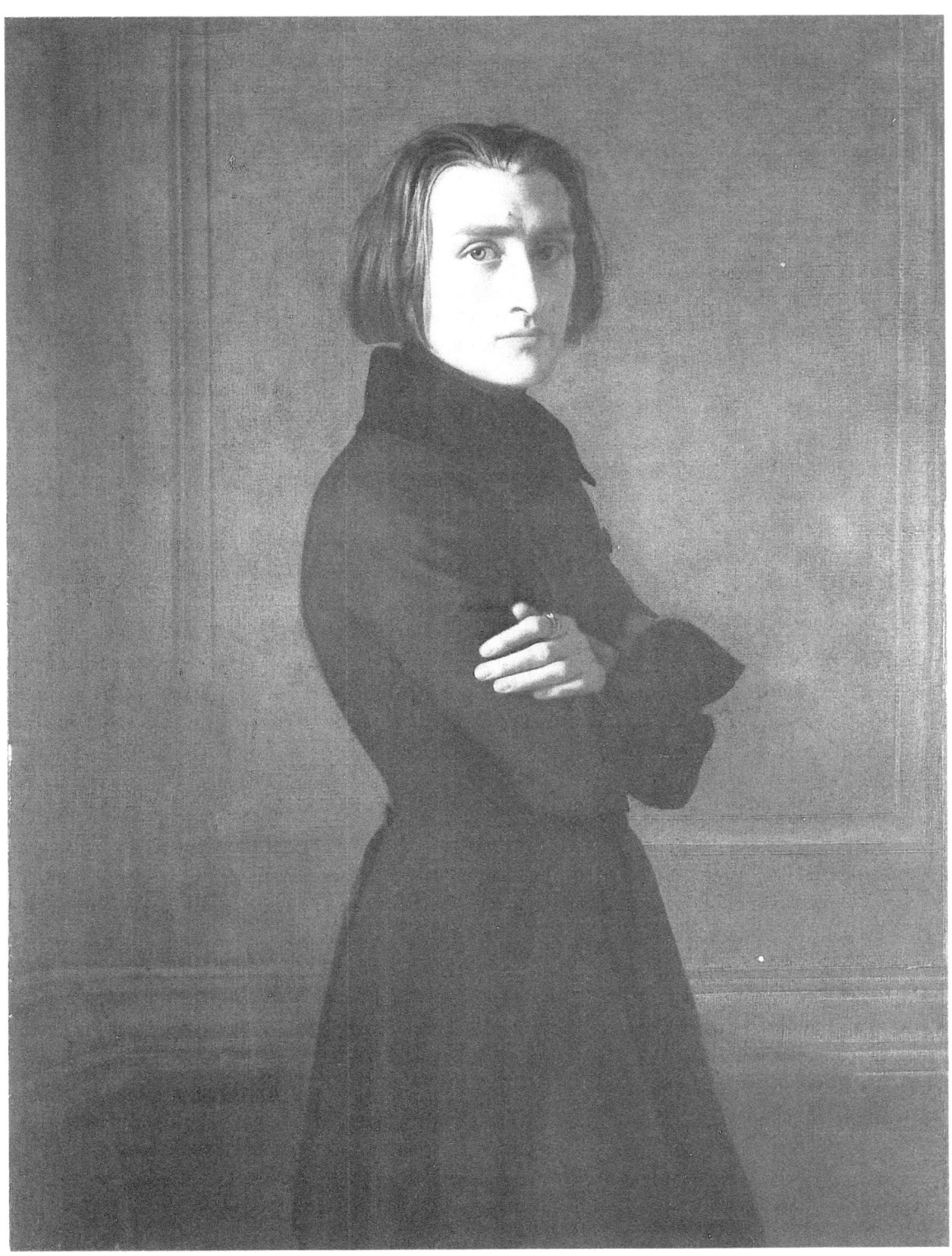

of luminary diffusion is such that the bright right side of Liszt's face almost detaches itself visually as a profile from the darker left side. This visual splitting of the face is close in spirit to Chassériau's manner of rendering himself a few years earlier (Fig. 113), and is a conceit often used by Lehmann's teacher Ingres to suggest psychological complexity (Fig. 155).[150] Lehmann adapted this device to index the fascinating duality of Liszt's talent: an exterior of detached cool shrouding the intense inner spirit that was the wellspring of his almost frightening music. Paradoxically, Lehmann's failure to manage this contrast provoked Théophile Gautier to be quite severe with the picture. "There is an affectation of wasting away and harshness in it," complained Gautier.

The head of Liszt is livelier, less petrified; restlessness and rapture disturb his physiognomy with nervous trembling; he has a look of inspiration and violence not at all conveyed by the calm painting of M. L[ehmann]; one doesn't recognize in it the passionate, very human improviser who is said to box with the piano more than he plays it.[151]

Gautier wanted to see more of the quivering, living spirit of performance—qualities that test the limits of painting and probably exceed the range of Lehmann's powers of visual representation.

In a passage from his famous "Artwork" essay of 1936, Walter Benjamin observed that "the cult of the movie star, fostered by the money of the movie industry, preserves not the unique aura of the person but the 'spell of the personality,' the phony spell of a commodity."[152] Benjamin was writing about cinematic celebrities of the twentieth century, but his point is no less valid for virtuosi of the nineteenth: although the phenomenon of a Taglioni, a Paganini, or a Liszt was surely rooted in actual technical ability, the extreme fame enjoyed by each was something entirely new. Heinrich Heine, a German living in and writing about Paris a century before Benjamin, was no less attuned to the emerging impact of mass media upon stardom. Heine believed "the triumphal strains of the piano virtuosi are characteristic of our time and give veritable witness to the victory of machine over spirit. Technical ability, the precision of an automaton, identification with the stringed wood, the

resounding instrumentalization of human beings, is now praised and celebrated as the highest thing of all."[153] The disappearance of self into instrument, which Benjamin would later call the loss of a performer's "unique aura," did not liquidate fame. On the contrary: Heine recognized that Paris served virtuosi

as a kind of announcement pillar on which their fame can be read in colossal letters. I say, their fame can be read here, for it is the Parisian press that makes them known to the gullible world, and those virtuosi understand with the greatest virtuosity the exploitation of the journals and the journalists.[154]

A century before Benjamin wrote about movie stars, Heine sensed that fame in Romantic Paris was being manufactured as a cult and marketed as a commodity by what Bernstein calls "the calculated and bought manipulation of the report of it."[155]

None of the pictures of virtuosi discussed thus far attempts to work within these new conditions of popular fame; rather, they try to frame it with the expected ambitions of portrait painting. Paradoxically, an image that comes closest to operating within the systemic logic of Heine's "announcement pillar" is the visually unremarkable picture of Talma painted in 1822 by François-Édouard Picot (Fig. 123). Stripped of anecdotal mythologies and allusions of genius, Talma is depicted in what talent agencies now call a head shot—half length, evenly lighted, looking casually towards the viewer. Talma wears a costume, but it is impossible to determine which of his many roles he has assumed for the painter. He affirms his professional life as an actor of the Comédie-Française, and does so without fanfare. In fact, Picot donated his picture to the theater at Talma's death in 1826, where it hangs today among the gallery of personalities who have performed on that famous stage. But the picture also had an important secondary existence, for it was engraved in 1824 when Talma was still alive, and lithographed in 1827, a year after his death. Which means his image—as fixed by Picot—circulated widely and in places where the actual picture would never be seen. Mechanically reproduced versions not only recorded Talma's appearance, they also ensured that the Talma phenomenon—his fame—would occupy continu-

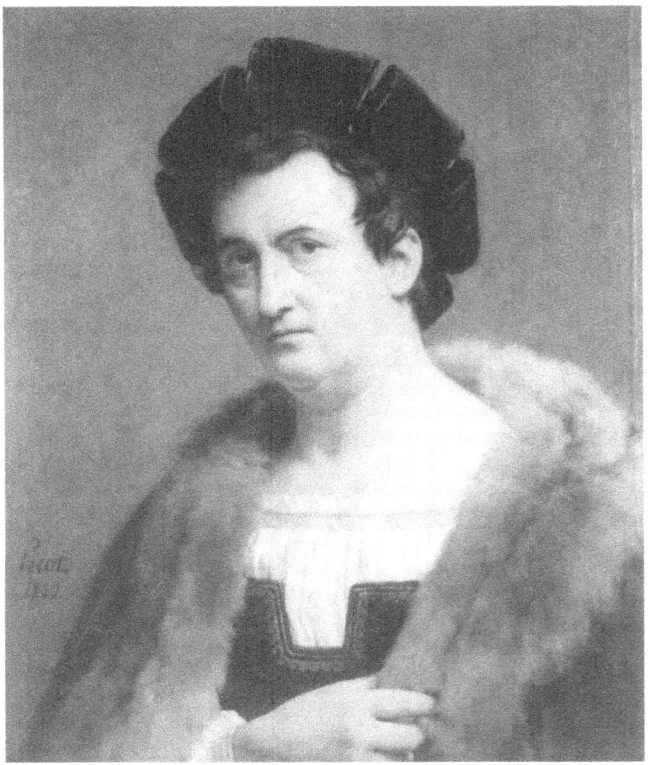

FIGURE 123.   François-Édouard Picot, *Portrait of François-Joseph Talma*, 1822. Oil on canvas. Paris, Collections de la Comédie-Française, inv. I 220 (68 × 58 cm). Photo: © Collections de la Comédie-Française/Jean-Loup Charmet.

ously the "announcement pillar" of Paris from the time of his triumph in *Léonidas* to the frenzied excitement of his last performances.[156] This multiplication of iconic imagery, and the possibility of owning his effigy, simultaneously brought Talma closer to his admirers and personalized his appeal. The attraction of Picot's picture depends less upon rendering a wealth of detail than the viewer's memories of seeing Talma on stage: there are as many "Talmas" as the number of Talma fans. Here, a system of representation displaces the traditional privileges of a single image, precisely because the system makes room for imaginative re-creations of the virtuoso's ephemeral performativity that the single picture cannot capture. To enable this imaginative play is not only

an historical achievement of Parisian artistic culture around 1830, it is also profoundly modern.

Nowhere are the implications of this dispersed, systemic mode of representation more apparent than in the lifelong sculptural project of Pierre-Jean David d'Angers, who expressed his conviction, in a letter to Goethe, that "sculpture, by its endurance and its religious character, so to speak, has a completely different mission to fulfill; that above all it should devote itself to representing models of greatness."[157] Beginning in 1815, while still a fellow at the Villa Médicis in Rome, and over the course of four decades, David d'Angers produced almost five hundred portrait medallions in bronze: his 1835 *Mademoiselle Mars* is a characteristic example (Fig. 124).[158] The majority of David's medallions were modeled directly from life, except for those sitters—notably political figures from the history of France—who were no longer alive. David first sketched his subjects in wax and used the sketch to prepare a finished work in plaster. Master molds were then prepared for casting in bronze. Nearly all of David's subjects are rendered in profile, a format he preferred because "the profile is in touch with other beings; it will avoid you, it does not look at you. The full face, by making you see several features, is more difficult to analyze, whereas the profile view is a single unit."[159] He worked in relief for its legibility, crisp contours, and control of light. "Bas-relief is a form of writing," he remarked, "these are the archives of an epoch."[160] Adopting a standard format flattens differences in time and space among many sitters and repositions them as elements of equal importance within a system of meaning produced by the collection as a whole.

The ambition of David d'Angers was to "give to posterity the features of distinguished men of our time," although the medallion of Mademoiselle Mars makes it clear that women also had a place in his pantheon.[161] One might simply conclude that he was committed to a realist art, but that misses the larger ambition of his project. The medallion of Mademoiselle Mars, for example, was made in 1835 when the actress was fifty-seven years old, yet David gave her a youthful look with hair pulled high onto her head and adorned with a garland of flowers. Such details were not incidental. David believed that "hair, pulled up high on the head, lends an air

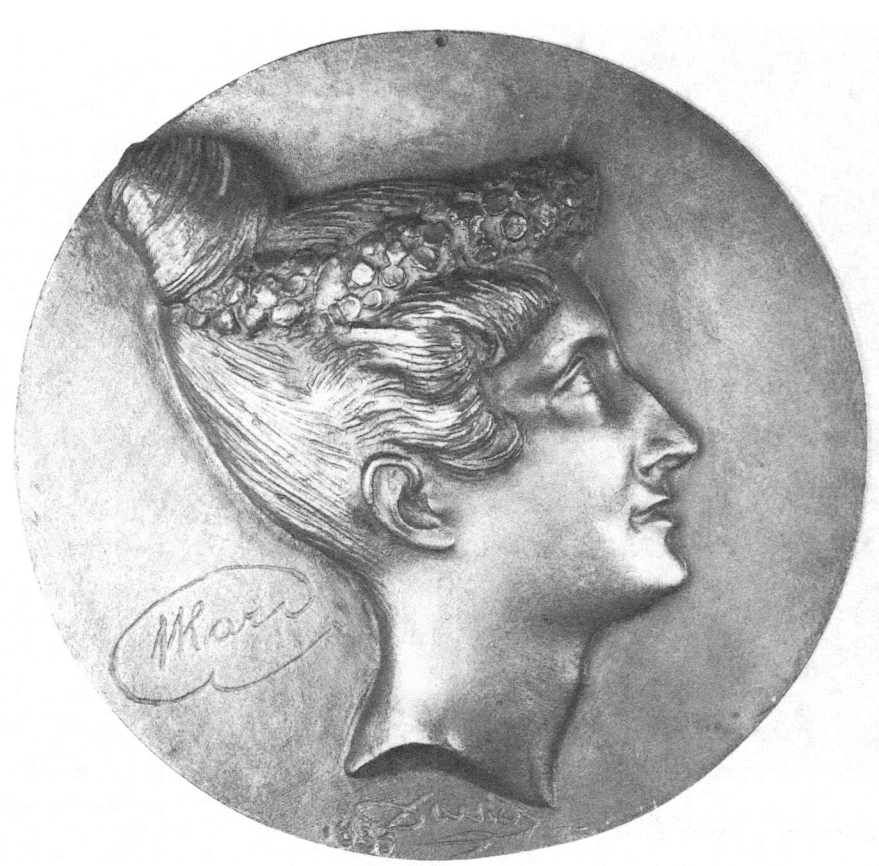

of youthfulness and modesty. When the chignon hangs down the back of the head and onto the neck, it is a sign of disorder and dissolution."[162] His medallion employs a visual shorthand for youthfulness to render the marvel that contemporaries felt before the undiminished stage presence of Mademoiselle Mars—an effect made even more poignant by the effects of aging. Frances Trollope experienced that sense of the marvelous during a performance of *Tartuffe* in 1835:

That the eye should follow with such unwearied delight every look and movement of a woman, not only old—for that does sometimes happen in Paris—but one known to be so from one end of Europe to the other, is certainly a singular phenomenon. Yet so it is: and could you see her, you would understand why, though not how, it is so. There is still a charm, a grace, in every movement of Made-

moiselle Mars, however trifling and however slight, which instantly captures the eye, and forbids it to wander to any other object—even though that object be young and lovely.[163]

Even if David d'Angers could not resist coaxing from the appearance of his sitters an ideal presence, his goal was not an ideal of beauty, but rather an ideal of character. He was deeply interested in the contemporary science of phrenology, which attempted to correlate physical appearance with personality and character traits. David's library included books by the founders of phrenology—Franz Joseph Gall and Johann Kaspar Lavater—and his notebooks are filled with observations about how physiognomy interacts with mental activity. "When the soul is busy with great philosophical thoughts," he wrote about Goethe in 1830, "it seems that nature senses all the importance of the brain's work; thus, the muscles of the neck become powerful helpers, the head leans straight forward, and one discerns the tensed muscles."[164] In another entry he remarks to himself that "nature put lumps on the skull of certain men and seemed to mark them with the words: 'You here will do such and such a thing; you over there some other thing.' There are some people upon whose foreheads one sees very few lumps; such cases are nature's spoiled children, for they do what they want."[165] Small wonder that David preferred a profile view, for it is the most economical way to record the different forehead contours where nature was thought to have marked genius.

The sitters of David's medallions were often identified by reproducing their signature: that of Mademoiselle Mars is etched just to the left of her neck (Fig. 124). The signatures are often taken to be signs of authenticity that second the artist's seemingly realist style. Keeping in mind David's remark that "bas-relief is a form of writing," his decision to reproduce idiosyncratic bits of handwriting assumes a role more affective than documentary. A signature is above all a mark of performativity, the trace of a person's having been there. In this sense it does signal to viewers that the sitter approves of his or her image. But signatures for David were also performances of a person's character and age. "Calm and timid men have an orderly handwriting," he remarked in 1830; "the letters are all the same size, while passionate men have a handwriting of different sizes."[166] A few years later he returned to the subject:

When one starts out in life, you sign your name carefully. It seems that you want to distinguish yourself by decency and tidiness, all that is found in the well-ordered letters of your name. As one advances in life, you sign with impudence; only when writing to a person whom you esteem does your signature recover the naïve proprieties of youth.[167]

To judge from the signature of Mademoiselle Mars, which is both graphic in its flourish and carefully inscribed, the actress is no longer young, but she nonetheless respects her reader/viewer—which is exactly what one might expect from the leading lady of the Comédie-Française.

Within the seemingly repetitive format of the portrait medallion, where David inscribes traits of character upon a subject's profile, the signature gives voice to the sitter rather than the artist. This distinction is made graphic by the juxtaposition of David's own signature upon the face of the medallion. David d'Angers did not want the medallions to become his personal interpretations of famous people, but visual traces of their existence—a bit like the documents of an archive. He wanted the unique character of each sitter to address viewers directly and he strove to minimize his own editorial comments: "one leaves to posterity an atrocious lie by analyzing the traits of great men," he complained; "it's as if an historian altered the lived exploits of remarkable men. Artists are the historians of traits."[168] In an extraordinary move to ensure the independent existence of his medallions, David gave the master molds to his favorite bronze founder, along with permission to make as many copies as he wished. Writing after her husband's death, Madame David explained his rationale:

My husband, who dreamed above all of making accessible to everyone the features of illustrious men, of whom he had been so happy to form his collection of contemporaries, and who wanted at the same time to be helpful to his founder, gave him the models without reserving any legal rights himself, and asked him only to sell them at a price low enough to fulfill his intentions.[169]

By this unusual arrangement, the medallions were liberated economically from David's intervention, just as their expression was liberated, by the codings of phrenology, from his personal interpretation of a sitters' renown. Cut free in this double sense, David's medallions do approach the independence of historical documents.

At the same time, a medallion only seventeen centimeters in diameter must be experienced at close range and held in one's hands. It is physically and materially a very personal object. Especially in the case of medallions representing people still alive (like Mademoiselle Mars), the uniformity of their size and presentation elicited particularization by a viewer's private experiences, impressions, or memories of the person represented. A medallion is both molded object and a "mold" into which lived content must be poured. Its unique affect depends less upon the representation of a face than a performative fleshing out in the viewer's mind. In this way, David's medallions participate fully in the aesthetics of the fragment—a recurring theme in the art of these years that was practiced overtly by David's friend and contemporary Auguste Préault (Fig. 86). Despite the superficial classicism of its format and the seeming realism of its style, David's collection of famous people is perhaps the best representative of an imaginative, truly Romantic form of portraiture that is also thoroughly modern for its embrace of mechanical reproduction and systemic cultural meaning.

FOR LOUISE D'HAUSSONVILLE, the medallion of Mademoiselle Mars might bring to life that evening in February 1830 when *Hernani* opened at the Comédie-Française; for Frances Trollope it might elicit memories of *Tartuffe* in 1835: both are valid portraits of the actress. Works of art develop multiple or conflicted readings when the elite spaces and educated audiences of high culture no longer control the production of meaning. In this chapter we have traced the steady erosion of elite culture under the pressure of lowbrow but thrilling forms that appealed across the social spectrum. David's medallions—like melodramas and virtuosi, bohemians and hack writer journalists—slipped across the defensive borders of insider cliques and highbrow cenacles to circulate in the social spaces, and among the heterogeneous publics, of the city at large. Development of these urban spaces, and the new patterns of cultural life within them, are the topics of our next chapter.

CHAPTER 7

A New Paris

What really delights me are the boulevards: this movement everywhere; these boutiques; this happy and restless people who take life much more lightly than others like us; this people whose pleasant-sounding voice amazes me. The boulevards must be, in summer, the most charming thing in the world.

We returned by way of the Marché des Innocents with its superb fountain, the grain market, and the other market pavilions. This whole quarter is ghastly, but quite singular to visit. The incredible movement, the dense population, the stench of rotting fish, the cries, the mud, the gutters, the carts blocking the narrow streets all form a picture very different from the beautiful Paris of the boulevards.

—Charles de Clary-Aldringen[1]

PRINCE CLARY-ALDRINGEN came to Paris in 1810 at the time of Napoléon's second marriage. A young Austrian aristocrat with family ties to the new empress, Clary-Aldringen was invited to the best parties and the most lavish balls. He also explored the less glamorous parts of Paris in the company of colleagues his own age who shared his enthusiasm for the hustle and bustle of the city's streets and the allure of its shop windows. In letters to his mother the prince described with remarkable detail his impressions. "You cannot imagine the magic of the boutiques and shops of Paris," he wrote on 9 April, "and it is very true that the bargains on certain items and the temptations surpass every expectation. The boutiques along the rue Vivienne, the boulevards, the rue Richelieu, and so on, constantly slow you down."[2] Clary-Aldringen records, in a manner both fresh and direct, the full spectrum of street life in Romantic Paris. The sharp contrast between his observations in the epigraph to this chapter sketch the most glaring of the city's extremes: on one hand, the open spaces, carnivalesque gaiety, and charm of the boulevards; on the other,

the overcrowded, dirty, and chaotic streets of the old central core. Like any great city, Paris offered a fascinating range of experiences to visitors who braved the streets with open eyes and curious minds. Unique to Paris during these years was the development of an urban space and a sociability that defied class, professional, and political affiliations. This chapter will sketch the contours of that development.

From Street to *Passage*

Nearly every visitor to early nineteenth-century Paris remarked on the boulevards, which were justly famous as among the most distinctive features of the city. "The boulevards are now merely very spacious streets, with avenues of trees at the sides," explained Richard Boyle Bernard to his readers; "formerly they were the boundaries of the city. They form a fashionable promenade for the Parisians, and abound with horsemen and carriages more than any other quarter of the town."[3] A few years earlier, during the Peace of Amiens, the English author of *Paris as it was and as it is* marveled at the animated street life and range of attractions offered by the boulevards:

Here, on each side, is assembled every thing that ingenuity can imagine for the diversion of the idle stroller, or the recreation of the man of business. Places of public entertainment, ambulating musicians, exhibitions of different kinds, temples consecrated to love or pleasure, Vauxhalls, ball-rooms, magnificent hotels, and other tasteful buildings, &c. Even the coffee-houses and taverns have their shady bowers, and an agreeable orchestra. Thus, you may always dine in Paris with a band of music to entertain you, without additional expense.[4]

Open space was the most salient characteristic of the boulevards, which were comprised of a wide roadway for carriage traffic and broad, tree-lined sidewalks for pedestrians. This expanse of space also encouraged street performers or peddlers to set up their stalls, and for shops to extend the allure of their displays into the open air.

Far different, as Clary-Aldringen noted, were the teeming sections of the inner city, especially around Les Halles (the central market) where there were no sidewalks. Pedestrians were forced to make their way along narrow streets with one eye on charging carriages and the other on an unsavory gutter at the center of the roadway. Landowners usually placed stout barricades [bornes] at the corners of courtyard entrances to prevent carriage wheels from smashing the door frames. These bornes jutted slightly into the roadway, thus offering a tiny refuge where pedestrians might escape a speeding carriage. Merchants, however, liked to set up displays in front of their shops to attract customers, often extending them well into the street and obliging pedestrians to risk the center of the roadway. By 1805 accidents were so common that Napoléon began to take note: "To the extent that shop displays have been moved forward," he wrote to the Minister of the Interior, "the bornes that used to be found on the street corners of Paris, and which protected pedestrians from carriages, are no longer useful. It will be necessary to organize their replacement with projections sufficiently deep to protect people from the large number of carriages."[5] Nonetheless, proper sidewalks remained the exception in Imperial Paris, and the streets of the city's center core remained genuinely hostile environments for pedestrians.

The Englishman John Scott, visiting Paris in 1814 after Napoléon's first abdication, was struck by the poor walking conditions when compared to those of his native London:

The streets are dirty and uncomfortable for walkers, to a degree which an inhabitant of London, who has not seen them, can scarcely imagine. There is, in general, no pavement by the edges of the streets, to protect those who walk from the carts and carriages. The appearance of the people, making their way, as they can amongst a crowd of fiacres, cabriolets, &c.—driving in a harum-scarum manner, which an English coachman would pronounce to be contrary to all reason,—is very strange to an English visitor.[6]

Gilbert-Joseph Chabrol, who served as Prefect of Paris under both the Empire and the Bourbon Restoration, lamented this sorry state in 1819:

The capital of France, which is adorned with wonderful monuments and has so many useful institutions, offers to those crossing it on foot only an excessively difficult, or even dangerous, pathway that seems to have been designed exclusively for the movement of carriages. One has been content to set up, in a small number of streets of sufficient width, some elevated sidewalks covered with ordinary paving stones. Frequently interrupted by carriage entrances, these offer only a long and tiresome sequence of stepping down and stepping up.[7]

None of these problems disappeared overnight. Only in the middle 1820s did sidewalks begin to become commonplace in Paris. Frances Trollope remarked on the improvement with evident pleasure at the time of her visit in 1835:

To those who knew Paris a dozen years ago, when one had to hop from stone to stone in the fond hope of escaping wet shoes in the Dog days—tormented too during the whole of this anxious process with the terror of being run over by carts, fiacres, concous, cabs, and wheelbarrows;—whoever remembers what it was like to walk in Paris then, will bless with an humble and grateful spirit the dear little pavement which, with the exception of necessary intervals to admit of an approach to the portes-cochère of the various hôtels, and a few short intervals beside, which appear to have been passed over and forgotten, borders most of the principal streets of Paris now.[8]

The gradual appearance of sidewalks was an important step in reducing the physical danger of walking the streets of

Paris. By contrast, the much-maligned gutters at the center of the roadway presented a spectacle of rubbish that English visitors, accustomed to the relative cleanliness of London, could not fathom. Frances Trollope's comments are characteristic:

On the subject of that monstrous barbarism, a gutter in the middle of the streets expressly formed for the reception of filth, which is still permitted to deform the greater portion of this beautiful city, I can only say, that the patient endurance of it by men and women of the year one thousand eight hundred and thirty-five is a mystery difficult to understand. It really appears to me, that almost the only thing in the world which other men do, but which Frenchman cannot, is the making of sewers and drains. After an hour or two of very violent rain last week, that part of the place Louis-Quinze [place de la Concorde] which is near the entrance to the Champs-Élysées remained covered with water.[9]

Centerline gutters had long been recognized as a problem. Lateral gutters were tested in 1811 along a section of the rue Saint-Honoré, but the idea was abandoned because—without curbings and sidewalks—overflow from even a modest rain poured into the shops on street level.

The idea of lateral gutters was revived during the middle 1830s, about the time of Trollope's visit, although moving them to the edges of the roadway—and close to the sidewalks—offered little solace to pedestrians walking the old and narrow streets of the city's center. Delphine de Girardin, who wrote a weekly column about Parisian life for *La Presse* between 1836 and 1848, deplored the so-called improvements:

It is no longer possible to circulate on the streets and boulevards. On rainy days, lakes of mud stop you on every side . . . and besides, the invention of gutters near the sidewalks is disastrous for any elegant stroll. Certainly, you can go out, but on condition that you go nowhere. The slightest cabriolet that passes spatters you from head to foot, sparing not even your hat. Hurry home, madame, your very pretty dress is now mud-lamé, and everyone is looking at you with smiles. Go home: you will make no visits today.[10]

Lateral gutters will keep a properly graded roadway from flooding, but without sufficiently wide sidewalks they posed new and constant threats to those on foot. Only with the broad new streets built during the Second Empire did Paris receive the combination of wide sidewalks and underground sewers that eliminated most of the physical hazards to the city's pedestrian traffic.

Long years of experience with speeding carriages, flooded roadways, and mud splatters certainly affected how Parisians used their streets. A young medical student, newly arrived from the provinces in 1810, wrote home about an ersatz practice that appeared during rainstorms:

Only a very small number of sewers existed. After heavy storms there were quarters that became impossible to traverse. There were torrents, truly impassable rivers. All communications were interrupted, even for carriages. The neighborhood messengers were equipped with planks of wood—a kind of mobile bridge—that they threw over these rivers when it was possible to do so, and one paid a toll to cross.[11]

Precisely this entrepreneurial initiative is the subject of Louis-Léopold Boilly's *The Downpour*, painted about 1805 (Fig. 125). A passing shower has flooded the narrow street, turning it into a sea of suspicious-looking mud. A plank with wheels, manned by a roughly dressed character, offers relatively dry passage to those willing to pay a toll. A woman with an umbrella and shopping basket drops a coin into the man's hand. He ignores her to stretch his arm in the direction of what appears to be a wealthy family already crossing his little bridge. The husband in breeches and top hat seems to reply to the man's entreaty with a gesture of his own that Susan Siegfried interprets as "a firm gesture of refusal, partly directed as a moral lesson to his children."[12] Siegfried assumes that the wealthy family is refusing to pay the poor man's toll. In this case, Boilly's painting might be a critique of the uneasy relationships among social classes who have been thrown together in the public space of the street.

On the other hand, madame clearly clutches a purse along with her little lap dog. There is no reason to believe that she has refused to pay the family's toll. In this scenario, her husband's gesture is not one of refusal, but rather an encouragement directed to his daughter. The young girl looks warily at the mud and the plank, seemingly unconvinced that she

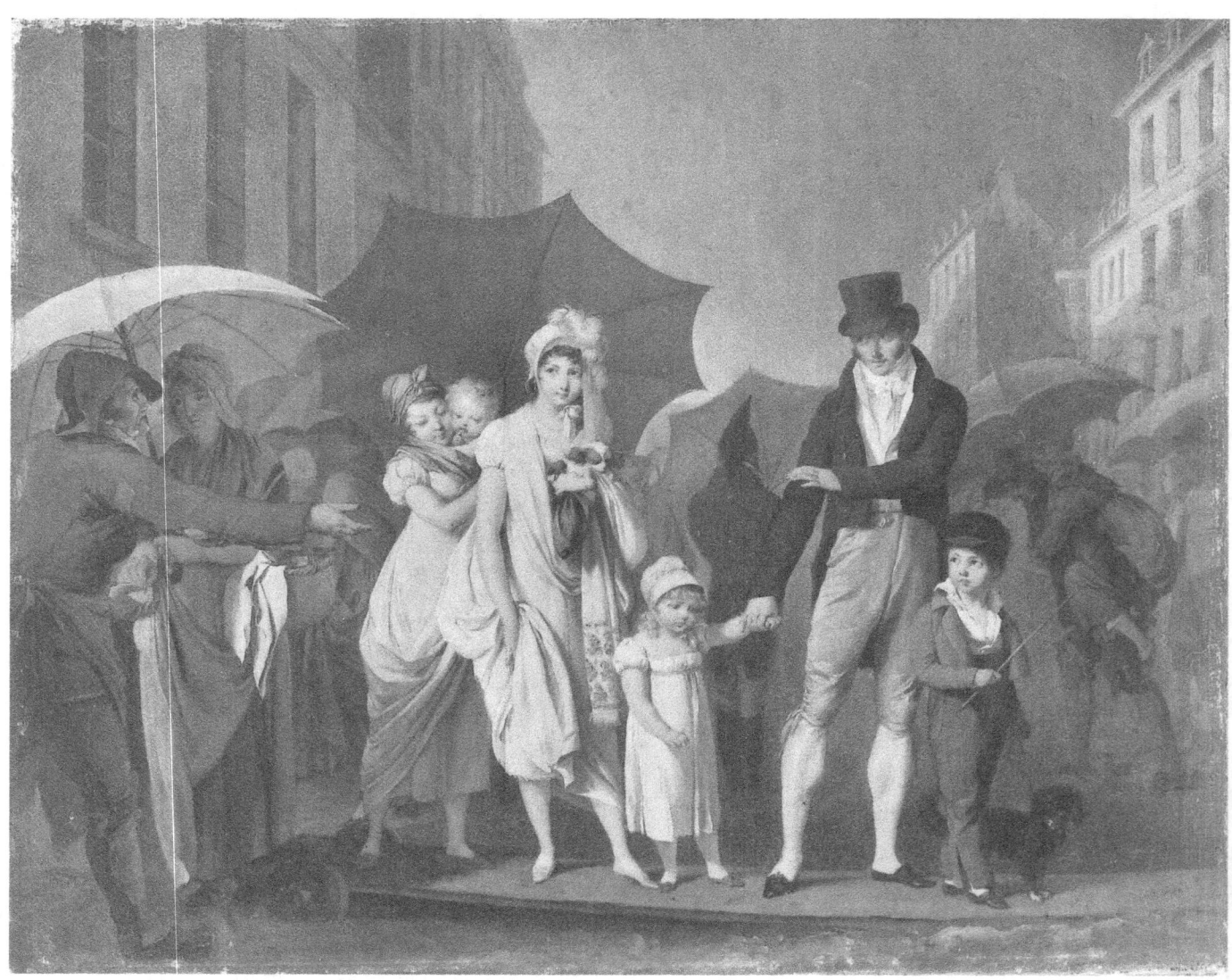

FIGURE 125.   Louis-Léopold Boilly, *The Downpour or "Passez-Payez"*, ca. 1805. Oil on canvas. Paris, Musée du Louvre, inv. RF2486 (32.5 × 40.5 cm). Photo: © RMN/Art Resource, NY/© Daniel Arnaudet.

will be spared a splash. Her distress underscores the entire family's incongruous presence on the little bridge, for they are singularly out of place and visually uncomfortable in this milieu. Boilly spaced his figures across the bridge and bathed them in a revealing light to make vivid the nearly absurd vulnerability of their delicate shoes and white stockings when confronting the vicissitudes of the muddy street. Contem-

porary viewers familiar with the hazards of walking in Paris on a rainy day surely recognized the comic aspect of Boilly's image. Decked out in flowing dresses and fancy breeches, the family's hesitant march across the plank presents a stark contrast to the physicality with which an old man carries a woman piggyback through the mud in the right background. Certainly Boilly's family is out of its element and ill at ease, but his image generates a further question: where in central Paris might such characters feel more at home?

That question leads directly to public spaces offering alternatives to the inhospitability of Parisian streets. One of the most popular and notorious of these was opened in 1786 by the duc d'Orléans, who owned the palace and gardens of the Palais-Royal. The duke was one of the richest men in France, but his famously spendthrift lifestyle required ever larger revenues. He had the idea to convert the garden of his palace—centrally located near the Louvre, the Comédie-Française, and the financial district—into an area of mixed use that would generate a steady income from rents. The project, designed by the architect Victor Louis, called for the garden to be enclosed by an elegant open arcade of cut stone. Shops were to occupy the ground floor with upper stories devoted to clubs, restaurants, and residences. The arcades would offer a promenade protected from traffic and the elements, while the enclosed garden would become a haven of open space, light, and air in the very center of town. The entire complex was imagined as a kind of refuge from both urban life and law, since it was to be built on private property and the duc d'Orléans forbade policemen from entering the garden.

Three of the four wings were finished by 1786, but the Palais-Royal project proved to be highly speculative and very expensive. The contractor ran out of cash while laying foundations for the fourth side. He finished the job early by erecting cheap, hangar-like buildings of wood fitted with three rows of commercial stalls separated by two alleys (Fig. 126).

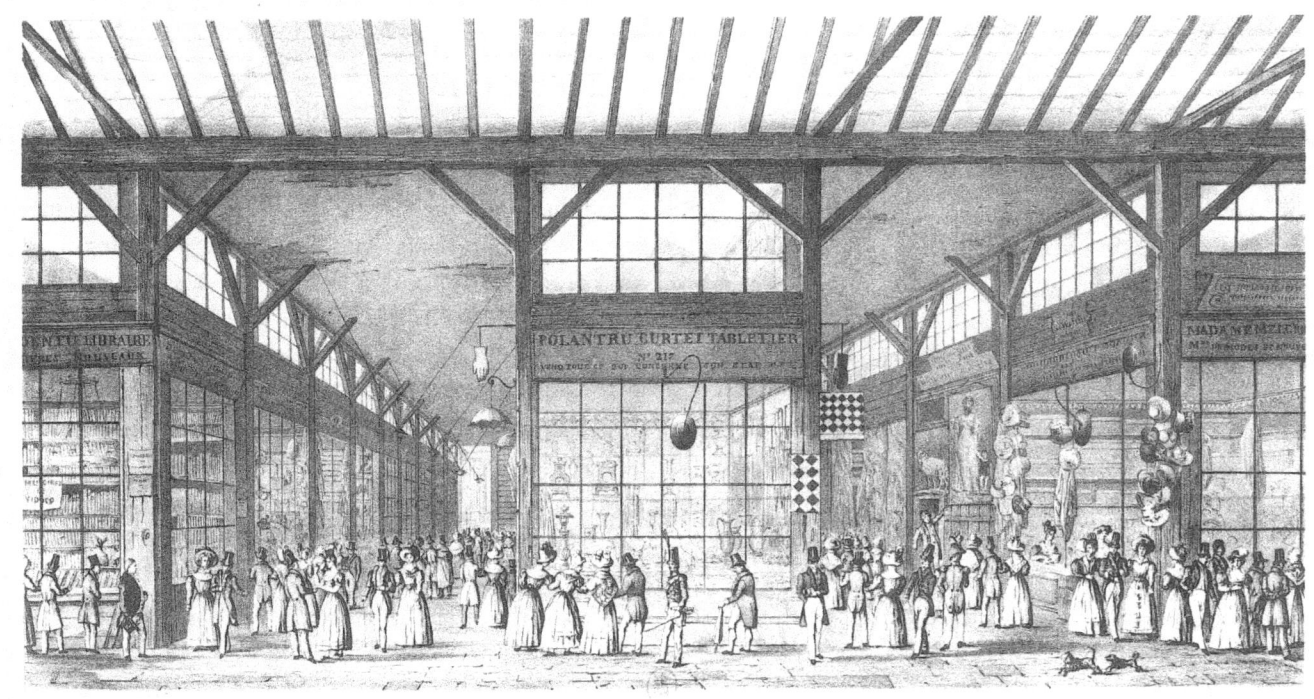

FIGURE 126.   Pierre-François Léonard Fontaine (designer) and Charles Gavard (engraver), *The Galerie Vitrée and the Galeries de Bois at the Palais-Royal*, before 1828. Engraving. Paris, BnF, Estampes, inv. Va 231c (11.7 × 22 cm). Photo: BnF, Paris.

Light entered via a row of windows running along the roof-line. The floor was bare earth. These temporary structures—known throughout Europe as the *Galeries de Bois* [wooden galleries]—were designed as short-term expedients, but they remained fixtures of the Paris landscape until 1828, when they were demolished by the son of the duc d'Orléans, the future King Louis-Philippe. Paradoxically, the Palais-Royal project quickly proved to be more lucrative than anyone had dreamed possible: the galleries were earning fifty-four thousand francs a year by 1792. Rents skyrocketed because Parisians flocked to the protected space to walk, meet, shop, and gawk without fearing weather, rushing carriages, or flying mud. A wood-frame extension, added to the Galeries de Bois in 1790, included the architectural refinement of large glass windows mounted in the roof and at each end under the pitch. This addition became known as the Galerie Vitrée [glassed gallery]; it was one of the first enclosed spaces in Paris to benefit from overhead natural light.[13]

Because the Palais-Royal was not under police jurisdiction, it soon became the preferred haunt of gamblers, prostitutes, idlers, and political agitators. Most famously, the two days of public unrest that culminated in an attack upon the Bastille on 14 July 1789 began with a fiery speech delivered by Camille Desmoulins in the garden of the Palais-Royal. "This garden, including its purlieus, presents, morning and evening, nothing but hordes of stock-jobbers, money-brokers, gamblers, and adventurers of every description," remarked an Englishman in November 1801; "the females who frequent it, correspond nearly to the character of the men; they are, for the greater part, of the most debauched and abandoned class."[14] Such notoriety was no deterrent: the Palais-Royal remained a magnet for Parisians and a must see for tourists throughout the political turmoils of Revolution, Empire, and Restoration.

A typical guide to the city, published in 1806 when much of Europe was literally ruled from Paris, tried to explain the global enticements of this unusual locale:

The Palace of the Tribunat is for Paris what Paris is for the rest of the world. All the arts are present there as if in their proper domain. They multiply themselves under a thousand seductive forms. There,

luxury lays out all its means and pleasure all its colors. It is the warehouse of all the goods of the universe, the meeting place of all the men who live in it. The galleries offer a perpetual fair. It is a hustle and bustle, a coming and going, and noise![15]

There was a new kind of attraction at work in the galleries of the Palais-Royal, one capable of seducing even the most resistant visitors. The moralistic English tourist just cited, for example, could not stay away for long. Three days after disparaging the habitués of the garden, he was back and speaking rather differently:

No small advantage to the shopkeepers established here is the chance custom, arising from such a variety of trades being collected together so conveniently, all within the same inclosure. A person resorting hither to procure one thing, is sure to be reminded of some other want, which, had not the article presented itself to his eye, would probably have escaped his recollection; and, indeed, such is the thirst of gain, that several tradesmen keep a small shop under these piazzas, independently of a large warehouse in another quarter of Paris.[16]

Today we recognize that the new and even thrilling attraction of the Palais-Royal was its astonishing collection of goods, and the experience of a thoroughly modern impulse buying that simply did not exist anywhere else. Merchants in galleries of the Palais-Royal adapted to this dynamic by inventing the business practice of fixed prices clearly marked on tags. "You walk in, and if any article strikes your fancy, you examine it at your ease," marveled our Englishman; "you consider the materials, the workmanship, and lastly the price, without being hurried by a loquacious shopkeeper into a purchase which you may shortly regret."[17] The galleries of the Palais-Royal not only protected clients from weather, traffic, and mud, they also nurtured consumer habits of browsing and window-shopping that are now taken for granted.

The fully covered Galeries de Bois instantiated a new type of urban space. Neither street nor market, they mixed commerce with entertainment and rich with poor in a single locale. Yet the Galeries de Bois occupied only a part of the Palais-Royal garden, and so they fostered two distinct architectural experiences: inside, one was immersed in the exhilarating spectacle of luxury goods and passersby; outside, they looked like any run-down market building. "An innovation was incontestably present there," writes Bertrand Lemoine, "but the point of reference remained the traditional city. It still lacked that ambiguity between the 'interiority' of a covered space established in the heart of a city block, and the 'exteriority' that the principle of an organized street gives to a covered passage."[18] The differences in space, function, and experience between the Galeries de Bois and a structure like the passage des Panoramas (Fig. 127), which first opened in 1800, rest on issues of quality rather than degree. Comparing these two structures entails imagining a new kind of urban space.

The passage des Panoramas was built on what Lemoine calls an *îlot*: literally the little island of open land formed by the backyards of buildings facing the streets surrounding a normal city block. The parcel of land used for the passage des Panoramas was the former garden of the hôtel de Montmorency, an eighteenth-century mansion confiscated during the Revolution. The courtyard doorway of the old hôtel became the entryway to the *passage* [arcade] on the rue Feydeau: it was common practice to reuse some part of the original building in this way. The new structure, which extends the length of the former garden, is a straight, street-like walkway covered by a roof and lined with shops. The roof, as shown in a gouache of 1807 (Fig. 127), was punctuated by skylights to allow for a good deal of natural light and fresh air. Workrooms and apartments were installed behind and above the shops. John Pinkerton noted in 1806 that "the new passage of the Panorama, leading from near the theatre Feydeau to the Boulevards is also an useful and agreeable improvement, being well paved, with sky lights above, and neat shops on either side."[19] Pinkerton hit upon one of the reasons for the phenomenal success of this particular arcade: it offered pedestrians a protected promenade from the busy commercial area near the Palais-Royal and the financial center of the Bourse, temporarily housed in the former convent of the Filles-Saint-Thomas (see Chapter Three), to the boulevards. The name of the arcade refers to its direct link to one of the city's newest attractions, the double panorama opened by the Americans William Thayer and Robert Fulton in 1799.

The little picture attributed to Philibert-Louis Debucourt (Fig. 127) suggests several novelties of the arcade that were not possible at the Palais-Royal. First is a reversal of the sensations associated with inside and outside. Being inside the arcade feels like being outside on a street, since the aligned facades, natural light, and good paving provide a walking experience previously imaginable only in the open air. The peculiar part is that one never sees the exterior of an arcade, except for its narrow entryway on the street. It has no principal facade other than that of its central core, and that becomes visible only upon entering. The picture also alludes to the wide range of goods and services available in the arcade. The Restaurant Dehodencq offers "coffees, ice creams, substantial lunches" [cafés, glaces, déjeuners à la fourchette]. The gourmet shop at the lower right proposes wild game and oranges. A sign at the very top of the image indicates a corridor connecting to the nearby Théâtre des Variétés. The prominent lantern signals that the passage des Panoramas was lighted at night. "You see that it is not deserted during the day," reported one writer in 1818; "there is often a crush of people when night falls. Women seeking romantic adventures are everywhere plentiful, and they add even more to the enticement of young men to the place."[20] Like nocturnes at the Palais-Royal, the night crowd was looking for more in the arcade than material goods.

Because of its prime location and diversity of shops the passage des Panoramas remained one of the most popular arcades in Paris. Louis Montigny, writing in 1826, took his readers on a detailed tour to point out some of its attractions: the well-known Café Véron; a sweet shop called La Duchesse de Courlande, which offered "throughout the year, and especially during the cold of winter, the most beautiful fruit"; the stationery shop Susse, which remains even today one of the city's most prestigious; a tea seller; a merchant of truffles and other gourmet treats; coffee shops; glove shops; bootmakers; hair salons; silversmiths; and the shop of the famous pastry chef Félix, inventor of lemon babas [babas au citron].[21]

Montigny also notes in passing, as if hardly worth mention, that "a gathering of artisans was essential in this place. I took note of their setup: brushes, English wax, and *La Gazette*."[22]

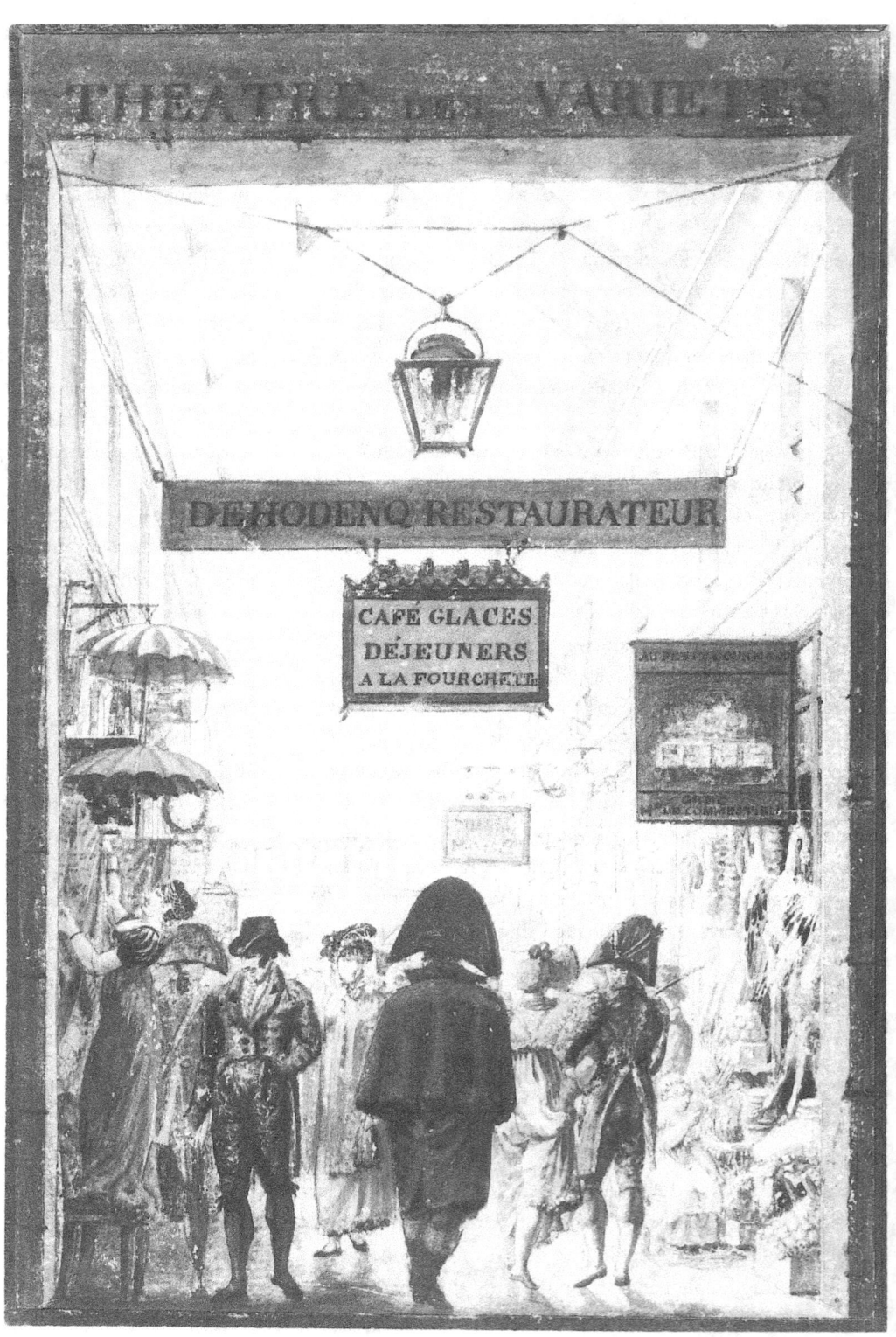

This is an elliptical reference to the mud-removing shop [salon de décrottage] that was a service found in virtually every arcade. "I must say a word here about life in the arcades, favored haunt of strollers and smokers, theater of operations for every kind of small business," wrote Ferdinand von Gall in 1845; "in each arcade there is at least one cleaning establishment. In a salon that is as elegantly furnished as its intended use permits, gentlemen sit upon high stools and comfortably peruse a newspaper while somebody busily brushes the dirt off their clothing and boots."[23] The existence of mud-removing shops underscores how much the space of an arcade, and one's appearance in it, imposed norms essentially unlike those of the street. The street was a place of mud and pedestrian terror. The arcades were different: one dressed for this public interior and deposited the mud of the street with the *décrotteur*. Walking the arcades became a practice of leisure that was, in the words of Walter Benjamin, directed to fundamentally different ends than the scurryings of street life:

Trade and traffic are two components of the street. Now, in the arcades the second of these has effectively died out: the traffic there is rudimentary. The arcade is a street of lascivious commerce only; it is wholly adapted to arousing desires. Because in this street the juices flow to a standstill, the commodity proliferates along the margins and enters into fantastic combinations ... the *flâneur* sabotages traffic. Moreover, he is no buyer. He is merchandise.[24]

Benjamin weaves together three qualities that characterize the new urban spaces of the arcades: the pervasive presence of commodities; the production of desires to consume them; the flâneur who does not buy, but becomes part of the spectacle. Benjamin argues that existence of the third is intimately bound up with the other two. Who or what is a flâneur?

Far too much has been written about the flâneur to summarize in a few pages, but it is safe to say that no figure was more closely identified with life in Romantic Paris.[25] Auguste de Lacroix, writing in *Les Français peints par eux-mêmes* of 1841, characterized the flâneur as specifically French and Parisian:

Without question, the flâneur is native and inhabitant of a vast city, most certainly of Paris. In fact, there is only one great city

that could serve as theater for his ceaseless explorations, and only the most nimble and witty people on earth could have produced *without knowing it* this kind of philosopher who seems to exercise instinctively an ability to seize everything in a single glance and to analyze it in passing. The flâneur is essentially national: different, in this sense, from celebrities in general, who are in every country, and especially different from the *tourist*, who observes on the run. No doubt the flâneur also likes movement, diversity, and crowds, but he is not tormented by an irresistible need for locomotion. He willingly delimits his domain, provided that he finds there daily food for his spirit, and—thanks to a wonderful insight—he knows how to harvest ever more incredible riches from this vast field of observation that the vulgar only reap on the surface. ... We won't even admit that the flâneur exists anywhere except Paris.[26]

Lacroix lays out the central themes of this mythic figure: incessantly exploring, philosophically engaged, capable of analyzing on the run from a first glance. The flâneur is glad to be French, has no ambition to "see everything" like a tourist, and savors aspects of everyday things that others fail to see. Discernment was the flâneur's most important quality. It produces intoxication from the most mundane experiences, as Balzac graphically describes:

Oh! to wander in Paris! Delightful and delicious existence! To flâne is a science, a gastronomy of the eye. To stroll is to vegetate; to flâne is to live. ... To flâne is to take pleasure, to collect flashes of wit, to admire sublime scenes of unhappiness, of love, of joy as well as graceful or grotesque portraits, to thrust one's attention into the depths of a thousand lives: when young, it means wanting everything and owning it all; when old, it means living on the life of young people and espousing their passions.[27]

Both Lacroix and Balzac emphasize the importance of vision to the modus operandi of the flâneur. Lacroix locates "an ability to seize everything in a single glance" deployed in a "vast field of observation." Balzac attributes to the flâneur "a gastronomy of the eye" that directs "attention into the depths of a thousand lives." Modern sociologists of the city, such as Georg Simmel and Louis Wirth, have argued that the elevation of sight over other senses was historically determined by the increasing density of urban life. Wirth explained in a seminal essay of 1938:

> The close physical contact of numerous individuals necessarily produces a shift in the mediums through which we orient ourselves to the urban milieu, especially to our fellow men. Typically, our physical contacts are close but our social contacts are distant. The urban world puts a premium on visual recognition. We see the uniform which denotes the role of the functionaries and are oblivious to the personal eccentricities that are hidden beneath the uniform. We tend to acquire and develop a sensitivity to a world of artefacts and become progressively removed from the world of nature.[28]

Walter Benjamin, a contemporary of Wirth, heroized the flâneur's presence—moving restlessly amidst the proliferation of commodities in the arcades—as a kind of sabotage. For Benjamin, the flâneur does not see things instrumentally like a consumer, and he cares little about actually owning goods. The flâneur simply shares the space of the arcades with the products on display in the shops, and so becomes—for those who really are consumers—one component among many in the spectacle of merchandise. The flâneur escapes vulgarity by becoming a self-conscious object of desire for the vulgar.

There is another way to read the enigma of the flâneur's fascinated indifference to the dialectics of desire established in the arcades between consumers and things for sale. Whether or not genuine flâneurs actually existed, contemporaries needed a *myth* of the flâneur, someone who reveled in the techniques of mass marketing but was able to resist their power. Why is this? The flâneur's imagined resistance suggests the new tools of marketing had limits. Further development was thus justified, even if that eventually eliminated traditional forms of face-to-face bartering and merchandising. Mythologizing the flâneur's detached, purely visual interest in the spectacle of commodities promoted the idea of its aesthetic value, validated engaging its effects, and veiled its true purpose, which Benjamin identified correctly as "wholly adapted to arousing desires." The flâneur's dispassionate detachment masquerades as a critical position, but is actually and inextricably implicated in the new order of commerce.[29]

The trajectory of an architecture supporting this new order can be sketched by comparing the passage des Panoramas (Fig. 127) to the Galerie Vivienne, built in 1823–1826 on designs by the architect François-Jacques Delannoy (Fig. 128). By day, the most immediate difference is that the interior of the Galerie Vivienne is bathed in an intense, even light thanks to a roof constructed entirely of small panes of glass held by strips of iron. "Such grandeur in this construction!" exclaimed the authors of *Nouveaux Tableaux de Paris* in 1825. "How gracefully are erected these transparent vaults! How simple and in good taste are these ornamental details!"[30] Arches of wood and masonry subdivide the principal space into a series of equal-sized bays, a regularity that calls attention to the modular structure of the interior facade. Far from the architectural cacophony of city streets, the storefronts of the Galerie Vivienne are rigorously ordered by a repetition of design elements in strict alignment—an order that promotes the illusion of passing from one temptation to the next with the visual ease and emotional detachment of a flâneur.

Most visitors enter the Galerie Vivienne on the rue des Petits-Champs, the portal closest to the Palais-Royal, where they immediately encounter a large, fairly wide, and brightly lighted space. Contemporaries were impressed by the spatial drama of the experience. "I saw with some regret that one went in and out along the rue Neuve-des-Petits-Champs with difficulty, since the large doorway of the building happens to be placed in an area where there is always a considerable crowding of carriages," remarked one guidebook; "but, once inside, I was delighted."[31] Proceeding along the main axis, the space narrows sharply where the porch of an existing structure was reused, but is followed by the surprise of a rotunda (about seven meters in diameter) covered by a hemisphere of iron-framed glass. Delannoy inserted this circular space to blunt perception of a slight shift in axis required by the odd parcels of land upon which the arcade was built. The rotunda opens onto the principal gallery (Fig. 128), which is longer but slightly narrower than the first segment. A third passage opens from the right of this main space towards the rue de la Banque. Continuing along the main axis, visitors descend a few steps to enter a rectangular, glass-roofed room, from which a fourth segment, also covered in glass, opens

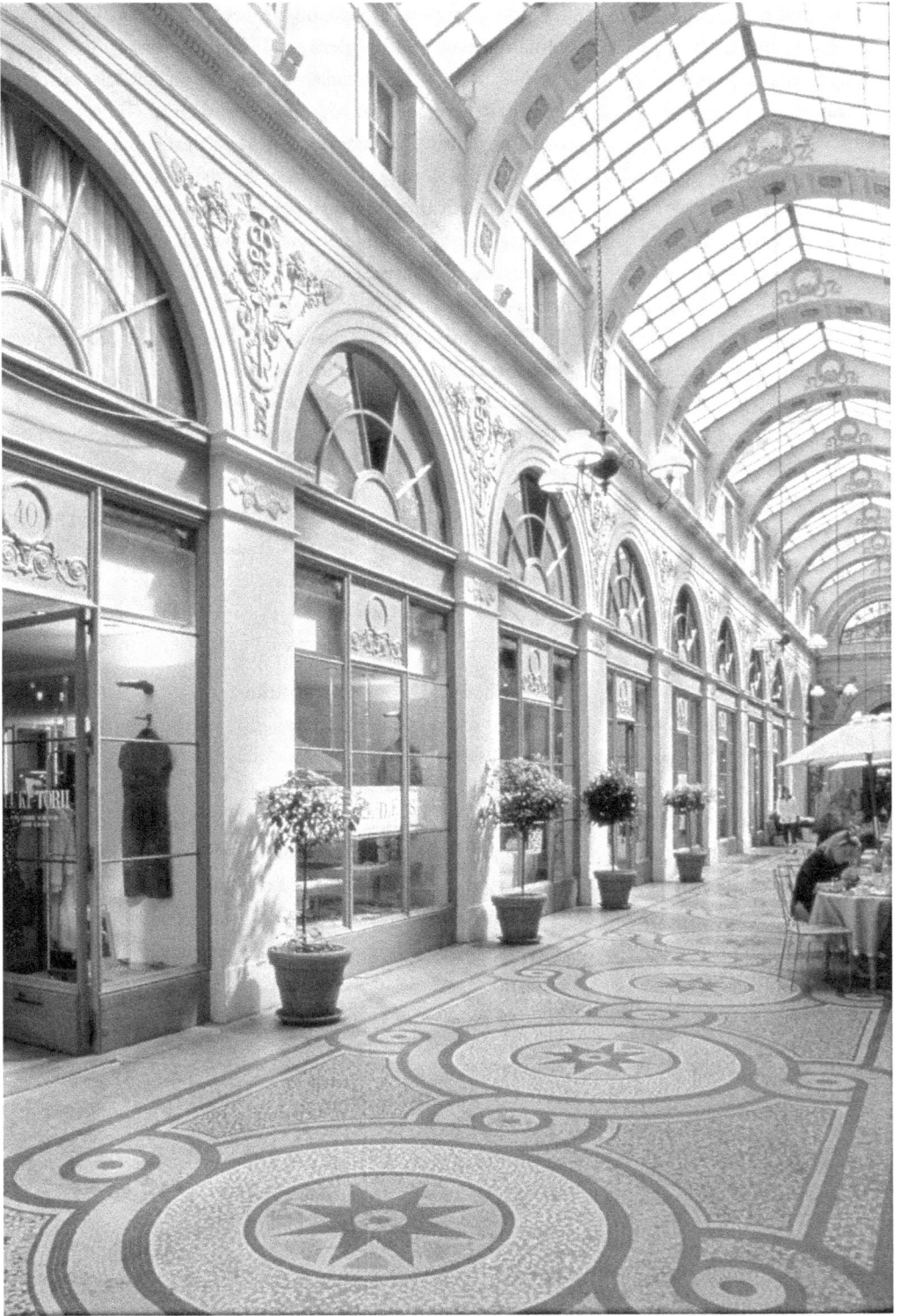

FIGURE 128. François-Jacques Delannoy, *The Galerie Vivienne*, 1823–1826. Contemporary photograph. Paris. Photo: © Centre des monuments nationaux, Paris/Pascal Lemaître.

to the left onto the rue Vivienne. The overall impression, as noted in a Paris guidebook of 1828, is "more like a series of rooms of different size and construction than a passage."[32] Quite unlike the passage des Panoramas, where a single, unbroken space is lined with shops of various décors and styles, the Galerie Vivienne is a series of distinct spatial experiences held together by the even, almost shadowless light, the modular regularity of its architectural forms, and the serialized design of an exquisite mosaic floor executed by an Italian named Faccina.

Glass was the principal component of the roof at the Galerie Vivienne. It was also used lavishly throughout the interior spaces. Individual storefronts consist almost entirely of large panes of glass, and the half-circle bay of the mezzanine above each storefront was treated as an elegant window with radiating mullions. Where windows were not appropriate or possible, mirrors were set into wall panels to produce an effect of transparency that privileges seeing and heightened visual effects. The extensive use of glass and mirrors underscores a further difference between arcades of the 1820s, such as the Galerie Vivienne, and earlier arcades. At the passage des Panoramas, as visible at the extreme right of our illustration (Fig. 127), many shops were open to passersby. By the middle 1820s, improved production techniques and lowered cost of plate glass meant that shops could be physically enclosed yet remain visually open to outsiders. Antoine Caillot, writing in 1827 about the Galerie Véro-Dodat, was impressed by the arcade's complex orchestration of purely visual effects. He recognized that they stimulated consumer desire by transforming simple strollers into elements of the spectacle itself:

The exterior is decorated with pilasters, strips of gilt copper, large glass windows that give free reign to every bit of daylight, and between which narrow, full-height mirrors make it easy for passersby to look at themselves from head to toe. The inside of these boutiques corresponds to the brilliance of their outsides: everything perfectly lighted by hydrogen gas. . . . They hide nothing that might arouse the desires of buyers.[33]

Arcades introduced ordinary people to a flâneur's restless curiosity: they were proving grounds for the design of complete shopping environments, and for techniques of display that remain the basis of modern retail merchandising.

Nightfall in the arcades ushered in an entirely different kind of experience that verged on the magical. "The art of the dazzling illusion is here developed to perfection," remarked Karl Gutzkow about the arcades he visited in 1842; "through mirrors extending along walls, and reflecting rows of merchandise right and left, these establishments all obtain an artificial expansion, a fantastical magnitude, by lamplight."[34] Like all the arcades built during the 1820s, the Galerie Vivienne was illuminated after dark by gas jets installed along its passageways and inside its shops. In the evening, the flicker of artificial light across the myriad surfaces of glass and mirror produced an environment of affect that fascinated contemporaries:

When the torrents of blazing gas stream across the windows, tint with purple the pallid countenance of women, give to copper the burnish of gold, and change glass crystal into diamonds—is when these little nothings, these toys, these expensive trifles of a thousand shapes and colors that wealthy indulgence tosses imperiously to the obedience of its favorites, gleam with a magic brilliance.[35]

The alchemical scope of such transformations was fully understood to be both ephemeral and fleeting, but even a self-conscious awareness of their artificiality could not dispel the spectacle's mesmerizing power.

The architectural structure of arcades like the Galerie Vivienne incarnated and valorized the privileging of sight that was an essential quality of the flâneur's mythic lifestyle. It also instantiated a precarious social situation. Already in 1796, Sébastien Mercier noted this when writing about the galleries of the Palais-Royal:

The jewelry boutiques are always numerous and dazzling, as if neither poverty nor misfortune existed. One sees only watch chains—half in pearls, half in diamonds—hanging among watches designed to display the day of the month. Those who have barely enough money to buy a loaf of bread look at these precious jewels, separated from their hands by only a transparent sheet of glass, and yet this fragile barrier is respected religiously.[36]

Mercier's window-shoppers, for all their misery, accepted their place in the economic hierarchy of society and respected the "fragile barrier" of the window pane. Thirty years later, Heinrich Heine witnessed a similar kind of temptation, but he worried the transparent barrier might one day be shattered by people driven to violence when the spectacle of goods becomes irresistible. He also recognized that a flâneur's mild amusement was secretly implicated in the emerging order of commerce:

At this moment, as we approach the new year and the day of gift-giving, the merchant's boutiques outdo themselves by the variety of their costly displays. The sight of these marvels can provide the leisurely flâneur a most agreeable distraction. If his brain is not completely empty, a few ideas might even come to him while gazing upon the multicolored profusion of objects of art and luxury displayed behind the gleaming glass windows of the shops, and also perhaps by casting a glance at the public standing there at his sides. The faces of the public are so solemn, so suffering, so unattractive, so impatient, and so menacing that they form a grim contrast to the objects they contemplate with gaping mouths. This contrast is so dreadful that terror sometimes leads us to see these men suddenly raise up their clenched fists to shatter all these gaudy and glittering playthings of the fashionable world, and to smash ruthlessly and mercilessly the fashionable world itself![37]

If the flâneur dares to measure the distance between the glittering spectacle of goods and the economic realities of those standing nearby, if he gives up for a moment the ambition of simply killing time and starts to think, amusement will darken to a concern for the stability of the entire system.

Naturally, business interests driving the quickening pace of commerce discouraged such moments of reflection. For these early years of mass marketing, the flâneur embodied an exemplary attitude of delight in the display of goods, a role model of discernment for consumers whose habits and attitudes were not yet fully formed. Writers aligned with commerce and the marketplace celebrated the status quo—and the flâneur's amusement—with remarks like these of Anaïs de Raucourt in 1833:

This exteriorized life, this world in full sail, this commerce in looks, talk, compliments exchanged on the run, this ambulatory sociability is above all what characterizes our great city. . . . Only in Paris do you find a huge population spilling onto the street at every hour, circulating without hurry or worry, using itself as amusement and spectacle, whirling endlessly in an agreed upon space where all the classes mix, where diverse fortunes rub shoulders with one another, where equality allows only for differences in weight, where the rule of incognito is always respected.[38]

The Galerie Vivienne, and the many other arcades erected upon similar principles of marketing and design, were the most conspicuous of the "agreed upon spaces" where this social idyll of class harmony was played out.

The arcades built in Paris during the 1820s were all products of private enterprise. In the case of the Galerie Vivienne, the moving force was a notary named Marchoux who lived at 6, rue Vivienne. Marchoux recognized the potential of a real estate speculation in his own backyard. He purchased the house he had been renting, another at 4, rue des Petits-Champs that included a small garden, and a third building that straddled 5 and 7, rue de la Banque. These three properties met one another inside the block: the Galerie Vivienne was built upon this collection of oddly shaped, contiguous parcels. Similar piecemeal real-estate transactions informed the construction of virtually every Parisian arcade. They document graphically that the arcades represented a new hybrid of urban space: built on private property and not subject to city regulations, they were nonetheless open to the public like a street; their enclosed spaces and the luxury of their decorations gave them the look and feel of a domestic interior. Geographically, the arcades also defined a new terrain, since the regular facades, good lighting, and mud-free environment of these thoroughfares appeared only in the oldest parts of town on parcels of land seized during the Revolution. They were islands of modernity embedded within the urban fabric of the past. The historical importance of the arcades, according to Bertrand Lemoine, is that "they worked like urban laboratories in which new social practices were tried out; consequently they played intensely on the register of novelty and fashionability."[39] Ultimately, the fruits of these first experiments to construct new spaces within the city migrated to more outlying areas where land was abundant and whole streets could be designed from scratch. We turn next to considering some of those projects.

Remapping the Urban Fabric

Everywhere you see only scaffolds erected, ladders hanging, and building materials piled up; armies of workers hew stone, slake lime, crush plaster, square oak beams, and practice these different tasks with an almost continuous activity; as if by magic, elegant and spaciously laid-out houses rise from this confusion; even the Parisian, had he been away for a while, would scarcely recognize his own quarter.

—*Le Moniteur universel* in 1824 [40]

During the political turmoil of the Revolution, very little new construction was begun in Paris. The deplorable state of the economy, including skyrocketing inflation, severely disrupted channels for the distribution of capital and materials. Price controls and the constant threat of foreign military invasion inhibited investors. The Revolution seized so many buildings—churches, church property, private houses and lands of aristocrats who fled the country or were condemned to death—that much of the need for new buildings in Paris was filled by recycling existing structures. Alexandre Lenoir, for example, installed the Musée des Monuments français in the former cloister of the Petits-Augustins, while the church of Saint-Geneviève became a Panthéon to honor the nation's heroes (see Chapter Three). The economic situation improved little during the Consulat and Empire, since fifteen years of nearly constant warfare drained the nation's financial reserves and discouraged private speculation. It is true that Napoléon initiated massive public works projects with new streets, aqueducts, and monumental buildings (see Chapter Three), but his main concern was less to modernize the capital than to make it the administrative and ideological center of the Empire. Thus, the rue de Rivoli was zoned to prevent businesses from generating noises, odors, or wastes that might upset the up-market calm of the new street (Fig. 30). Although there was a brief burst of private building activity in 1801 during the Peace of Amiens, it was only after Napoléon's final defeat, and a prosperity born of peace, that private investors begin to build within Paris. By 1824 the city hummed with construction. Some of it, notably the arcades, occurred in the oldest parts of town. There was also expansion into open areas and the construction of entirely new neighborhoods. Where were these areas, and

what did they offer Parisians hoping to escape the city's crowded center?

Paris at the end of the Empire was still quite compact, even though its population had grown from about 547,000 in 1804 to more than 700,000 in 1817.[41] Most of these people were concentrated in the small kernel of land bounded by what are now called the inner boulevards on the right bank of the Seine and within the Latin Quarter across the river. A city map from 1842 by Levasseur and Toussaint (Fig. 129) records clearly this concentration within the inner arc of the right bank boulevards and the maze of small streets on the left bank just below the largest island (the Cité). Population density within this core area rose more sharply than the numbers suggest and placed great strain on an already outdated infrastructure.

The slightly irregular larger circle of the Paris city limits on the map is the Farmers-General tax wall, which was built during the 1780s. It marks the administrative limits of the city at mid-century: farm products, building materials, wine, and other items were taxed at gateways in the wall before they could enter Paris proper. Between the inner, densely settled core of Paris and the administrative limits of the tax wall lay an expanse of no-man's land that was very sparsely populated. On the left bank, visible in the lower-left sector of the 1842 map, one finds large areas committed to the École Militaire and the Invalides veterans hospital—each with important esplanades—but adjacent areas exhibit only a spare network of widely spaced streets. This is the faubourg Saint-Germain, where elegant, freestanding private houses [hôtels] occupied large lots with spacious gardens. It was the preferred neighborhood of aristocratic families, such as the d'Haussonvilles (see Chapter Six), described by Anne Martin-Fugier:

During the Restoration all the hôtels in the faubourg Saint-Germain were reoccupied. The rue Saint-Dominique alone counted twenty-five hôtels, some of which had been built in the seventeenth and eighteenth centuries. Nobles of the Empire and favorites of the new regime rubbed shoulders with the old aristocracy. It is during this time that the faubourg Saint-Germain, previously famous for the beauty of its buildings and the charm of its gardens, began to have "inhabitants of quality" as its main characteristic.[42]

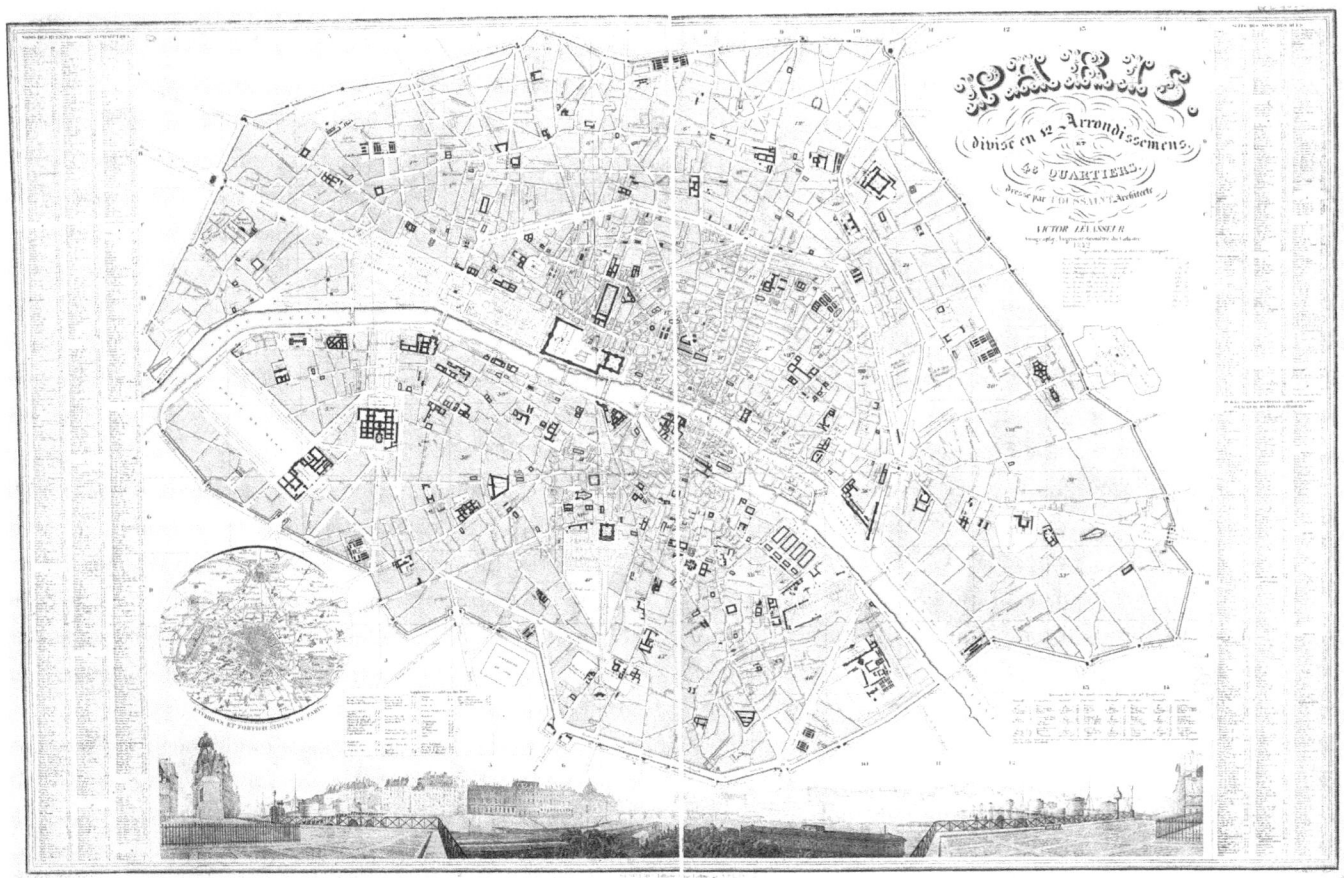

FIGURE 129.   Victor Levasseur and Toussaint, *Map of Paris showing the Twelve Arrondissements and Location of the Thiers Fortifications*, 1842. Engraving. Paris, BnF, Cartes et Plans, inv. Ge C 7050 (112 × 74.5 cm). Photo: BnF, Paris.

In this part of town, multistory apartment buildings that would increase population density were not welcome. Neither were those newly rich [nouveaux riches] who could afford luxury houses but lacked the family credentials essential for acceptance into the rarefied social milieu of the faubourg Saint-Germain.

Across the Seine, to the north of the Champs-Élysées and the boulevards, lay a vast arc of land comprised of open fields, swamps, and former church properties confiscated during the Revolution. There were also a number of pleasure gardens—usually built on property taken from nobles executed during the Terror—with exotic names like Idalie, Tivoli, the hameau de Chantilly, or Paphos that, in the words of Antoine Caillot, "made one forget the names of their ill-fated owners."[43] By the time Caillot was writing in 1827 much of this land was already under development, and he deplored the results:

When the Marbeuf, Beaujon and Tivoli gardens, the vast plain of Mousseau, this huge tract of land between the rue des Martyrs and the rue Larochefoucault, and the immense plain of Saint-Lazare are all covered with houses, how will air penetrate into the faubourgs and especially the quarters of the city located between the boulevards and the river? . . . Only a few years ago, before you left the city, you already benefited from the pleasant view of swamps and gardens that extended into the far distance; today, you pass glumly between two walls or two wooden barriers that block you from seeing the rural things that your eyes formerly liked to explore.[44]

Despite Caillot's complaint, the 1842 map of Paris reveals that real-estate development north of the boulevards had not slowed (Fig. 129). Most of the terrain between the tax wall and the inner boulevards is criss-crossed by networks of new streets. One of the areas lamented by Caillot was the "huge tract of land between the rue des Martyrs and the rue Larochefoucault" adjacent to the parcel where the Nouvelle Athènes quarter was built in 1820 and occupied by artists, actors, and writers (see Chapter Six). Caillot also regretted the loss of "the immense plain of Saint-Lazare," which is visible at the very top of the map and distinguished by a long street that runs diagonally towards the upper right. The plan for this development (Fig. 130), approved by King Charles X in 1825, lays out the Saint-Lazare project in great detail and allows us to understand how these new neighborhoods [nouveaux quartiers] reinvented the look and feel of Paris.

The most infamous and lasting rebuilding of Paris occurred later, during the 1850s and 1860s, under the direction of George Haussmann and Napoléon III. Their draconian restructuring was supported by municipal bonds, direct subventions from the central government, and concessions made by the city to private speculators. By contrast, Haussmann's immediate predecessors as Prefect of Paris— Gilbert-Joseph Gaspard Chabrol and Claude-Philibert de Rambuteau—followed a more fiscally conservative line. Under their direction, undeveloped lands between the tax wall and the boulevards were sold outright to speculators, with the idea that neither potential profits nor possible risks should upset the city's finances. "It is hoped that speculation investments and corporate interest will come to the aid of the administration," remarked Chabrol in 1822 when outlining his budget for that year.[45] In exchange for the right to develop the lands sold to them, developers accepted

strict conditions established by Chabrol and his planners. Buyers were obliged to give back to the city the rights-of-way for future streets, which meant that substantial parts of any parcel were immediately removed from further development. The new streets had to conform to a set of explicit standards: roadways at least ten meters wide; sidewalks of flat paving stones [dalles] installed along both sides of the street; streetlights placed at regular intervals. "One begins to perceive the benefit of these constructions," reported Chabrol in 1825; "one can estimate that 3000 meters of sidewalks have been constructed in Paris in only one year."[46] Builders were also required to pave the new streets. When it became clear that this was often done in haste and with poor materials, the regulations were rewritten: development companies were held responsible for a street's original paving and for the first complete repaving that might be needed. The goal for streets in the new quarters was to emulate the qualities that made arcades in the center of Paris so popular with pedestrians: a place to walk safely, a minimum of mud, and good lighting.

How were Chabrol's abstract guidelines translated into stone and asphalt? The plan for a Nouveau Quartier Poissonnière provides several important indices (Fig. 130). The bulk of the land involved in this project had belonged to the Lazarite order before the Revolution. It comprised an area bounded by the rue du Faubourg-Poissonnière, the rue du Faubourg-Saint-Denis, the Farmers-General tax wall, and the rue de Paradis (roughly the rectangle on the plan within which a church and circular crossing are projected). Seized during the Revolution and converted to a prison in 1793, this large parcel was sold in 1821 to a consortium that included three banks (André-Cottier, Moisson-Devaux, and Laffitte), the duc de Bassano, the architect Auguste Constantin (who was also an investor in the Nouvelle Athènes project), and a speculator named Lenoir. The group assembled sufficient capital to purchase the Lazarite land along with parcels connecting the rue du Faubourg-Saint-Denis to the rue du Faubourg-Saint-Martin. The idea was to construct a long, broad, and straight avenue from the heart of the new neighborhood to a passage in the tax wall at the Porte de Pantin. According to a description printed on the plan (Fig. 130), this main thoroughfare "will be 1550 meters long and 19.5 meters wide" (more than twice the minimum width), and "lined by wide sidewalks and planted trees." Another street, running almost perpendicular to the principal artery and passing behind the proposed church, connects the new neighborhood to a portal in the tax wall at the boulevard Poissonnière. The owners were required to cede "the site needed to extend the rue Hauteville to the new street and to form, at the meeting-point, a circular space with a radius of at most 50 meters."[47] This extension promised a commercial and visual link between the new neighborhood and the older sections of the city to the south (Fig. 131). Finally, a royal ordinance of 31 March 1825 called for construction of a new church for the parish of Saint-Vincent-de-Paul that would anchor the center of the quartier with a monumental religious edifice.

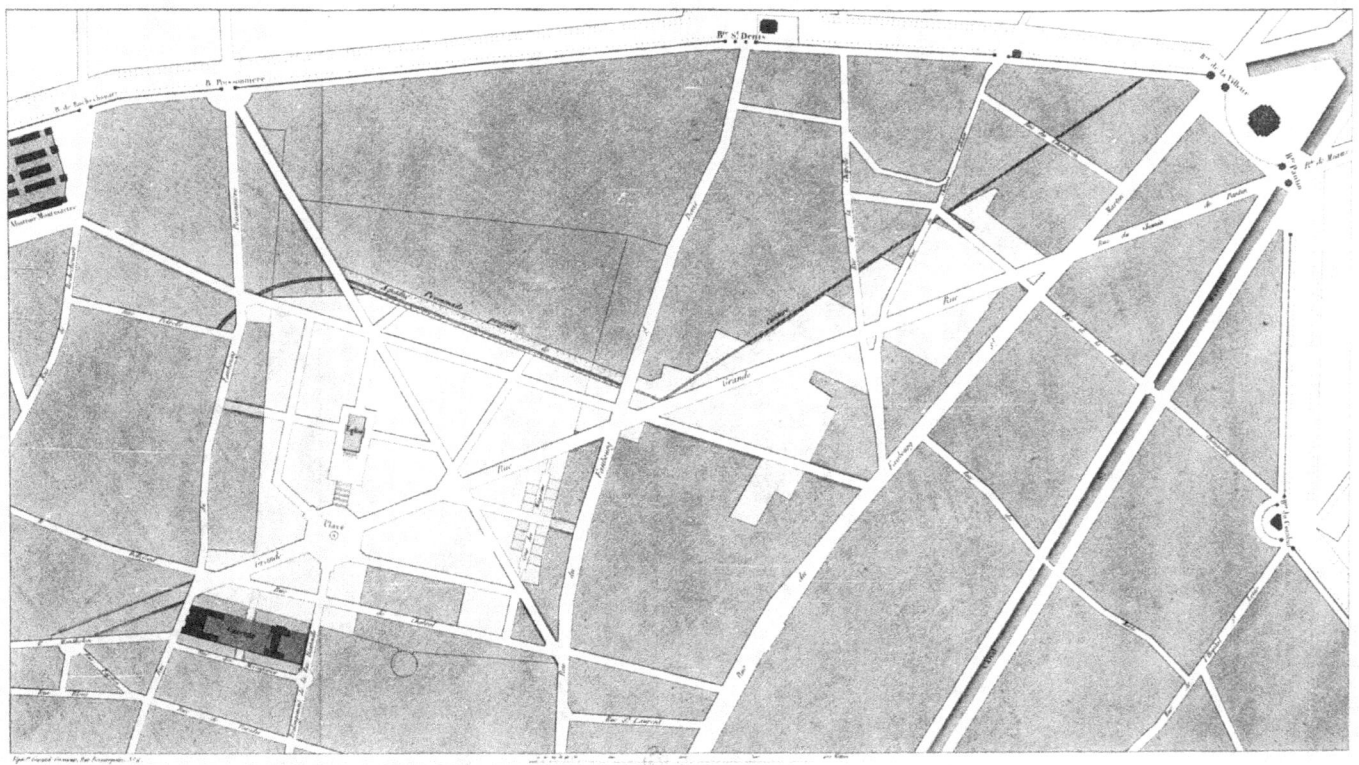

FIGURE 130.   Anonymous, *Plan of the Nouveau Quartier Poissonnière*, ca. 1824. Engraving. Paris, BnF, Estampes, inv. Va 288 (1). Photo: BnF, Paris.

FIGURE 131. *The church of Saint-Vincent-de-Paul seen from the rue d'Hauteville*, planned 1824. Anonymous photograph, ca. 1908. Paris, BnF, Estampes, inv. Va 289 (5). Photo: BnF, Paris.

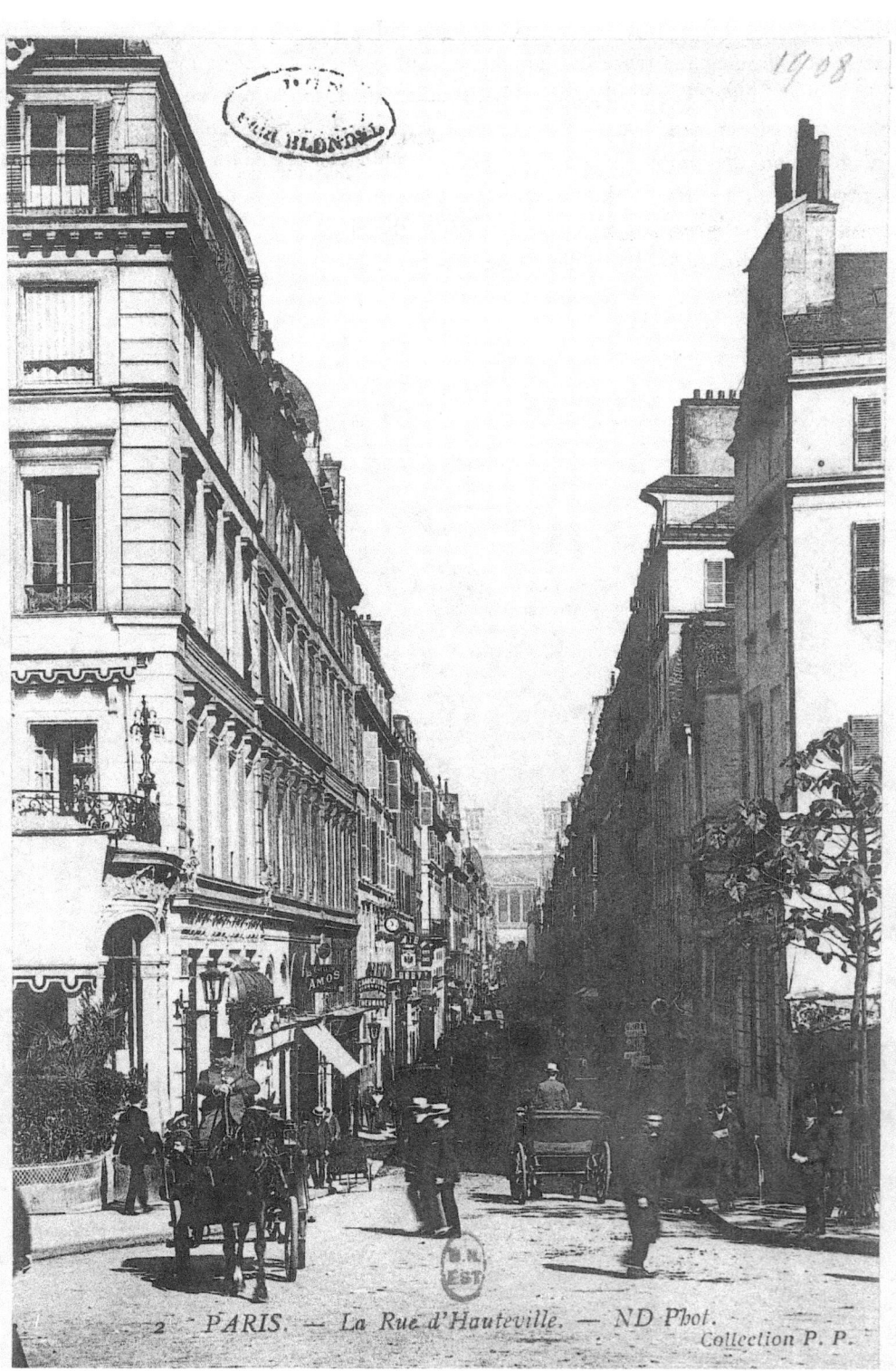

2 — PARIS. — La Rue d'Hauteville. — ND Phot.
Collection P. P.

Laying out an addition to the fabric of Paris almost from scratch necessarily raises the question: what is a quartier [neighborhood]? Bernard Rouleau proposes a reasonable working definition:

In reality, a quarter is first defined by the fact that it has a center of activity, often a business street of food shops—better yet a market street—but this could also be a square: that is, a crossroads [carrefour] with or without commercial activity. In any case, it is the nearly unique point of attraction for a population within a limited urban perimeter.[48]

Individual sectors organized around nodes of activity must be linked to neighboring sectors if the city is to be more than a mosaic-like collection of parts. Rouleau directs our attention to "the arrangement of streets relative to one another, but also their differences in width and the average type of their buildings; consequently, to the very origin of the roadway, the epoch of its formation, or of its final urbanization."[49] Larger, more animated streets are the arteries that connect one quartier to the next; smaller, more quiet streets form the heart of a neighborhood. In those parts of a city where the streets have existed for centuries, the differences may be very slight. Historic quartiers are often marked by an insularity born of shared habits and customs isolated from the city at large, a situation described by Louis Wirth:

Diverse population elements inhabiting a compact settlement thus tend to become segregated from one another in the degree in which their requirements and modes of life are incompatible with one another and in the measure in which they are antagonistic to one another. Similarly, persons of homogenous status and needs unwittingly drift into, consciously select, or are forced by circumstances into, the same area. The different parts of the city thus acquire specialized functions. The city consequently tends to resemble a mosaic of social worlds in which the transition from one to the other is abrupt.[50]

The planners of new projects in Paris during the 1820s realized that starting with a clean slate was an occasion to defeat the mosaic or patchwork model.[51] The historical importance of projects like the Nouveau Quartier Poissonnière is that the new spaces were consciously and physically connected to the older parts of town. Planners were guided, in the words of François Loyer, by an "utterly new conception of urban space"[52] that strove to develop an awareness of the development's placement within the urban fabric without destroying the sensation of a quartier. How was this achieved?

The project of 1825 proposes an armature of through streets that criss-cross the neighborhood and link it both to existing streets and to the gateways of the tax wall (Fig. 130). These intersect to produce major points of attraction that define the spatial character of the new quartier: a circular carrefour in front of the church; a star burst intersection behind it; a series of openings where the main diagonal street cuts across new and existing roadways. Smaller residential streets were slated to be laid out inside the areas delimited by these major arteries although, in fact, a large part of the project's northern sector eventually became the station and rail yard of the Gare du Nord. A hierarchy of streets was imagined from the beginning with a spine of avenues that connects the quartier to the larger urban fabric and simultaneously defines the smaller, more intimate scale of its residential sections.

Relating the new quartier to the city at large was an important consideration when siting the new church of Saint-Vincent-de-Paul. The developers were obliged to give back to the city enough land for an extension of the rue Hauteville to the new church (Fig. 131). The resulting perspective, which provides a direct visual link between the inner boulevards of old Paris and the architectural centerpiece of the new quartier, was much appreciated by Théophile Gautier:

This church is sited in an extremely successful way; it is preceded by a vast space and faces a street that runs into the boulevard to form, from each end, a charming perspective. A hillock a bit more than twenty-five feet tall serves as base. The architect made good use of this arrangement of the terrain: skillfully arranged ramps and wide, convenient staircases connect the street square to the square in front of the church, and they rise in a quite monumental manner, although perhaps a bit too cheerfully and gracefully for a building so severe as a Christian temple. But the parti pris is original and the statement is new: we will not quibble with M. Hittorff on that point.[53]

Gautier recognized the value of the reciprocal link between old and new Paris. He also recognized an attention to dramatic effect when siting the church—upon a hillock much higher than the street and carrefour—like a jewel set into the city (Fig. 132).[54] Elevated in this way, the church and its façade emerge as the identifying sign of the new quartier amidst the historical monuments of Paris.

The church of Saint-Vincent-de-Paul is the work of two architects. A design was prepared in 1824 by Jean-Baptiste Lepère, but construction was halted in 1828 by a general financial crisis with only the foundations of the building completed. When work resumed in 1831 Lepère, who was already seventy years old, passed control of the project to his son-in-law, Jacques-Ignace Hittorff. Lepère's original design called for a basilica with a temple front. His plan was much criticized as stylistically cold and too expensive to build, especially his idea for a single and very tall bell tower above the apse end of the church. Hittorff retained the basilica floor plan dictated by the foundations already in place, but

he modified the elevation using a combination of historical and national sources. The main screen of the façade became a twin-tower project inspired by Italian Renaissance models that architectural historians have long recognized as gesturing in the direction of Trinità dei Monti, the French church in Rome perched above the Spanish Steps that Hittorff admired when he was a student in Italy during 1822–1824.[55] The façade also echoes the towers and colonnade of Saint-Sulpice just across the Seine. A deep porch emulating a Greek temple, complete with Ionic colonnade supporting a sculpture-laden pediment, is the centerpiece of the ensemble.

Hittorff's use of an Ionic order for the porch of Saint-Vincent-de-Paul reaffirms the choice made by Lepère in 1824, perhaps with his son-in-law's advice. Hittorff's redesign deployed the same order throughout the colonnade of the first floor interior. A more elaborately carved Corinthian order

FIGURE 132. Jacques-Ignace Hittorff and Jean-Baptiste Lepère, *New Church of Saint-Vincent-de-Paul*, 1824–1844. Lithograph by Jean-Baptiste Arnout (1844). Paris, BnF, Estampes, inv. Va 288 (4). Photo: BnF, Paris.

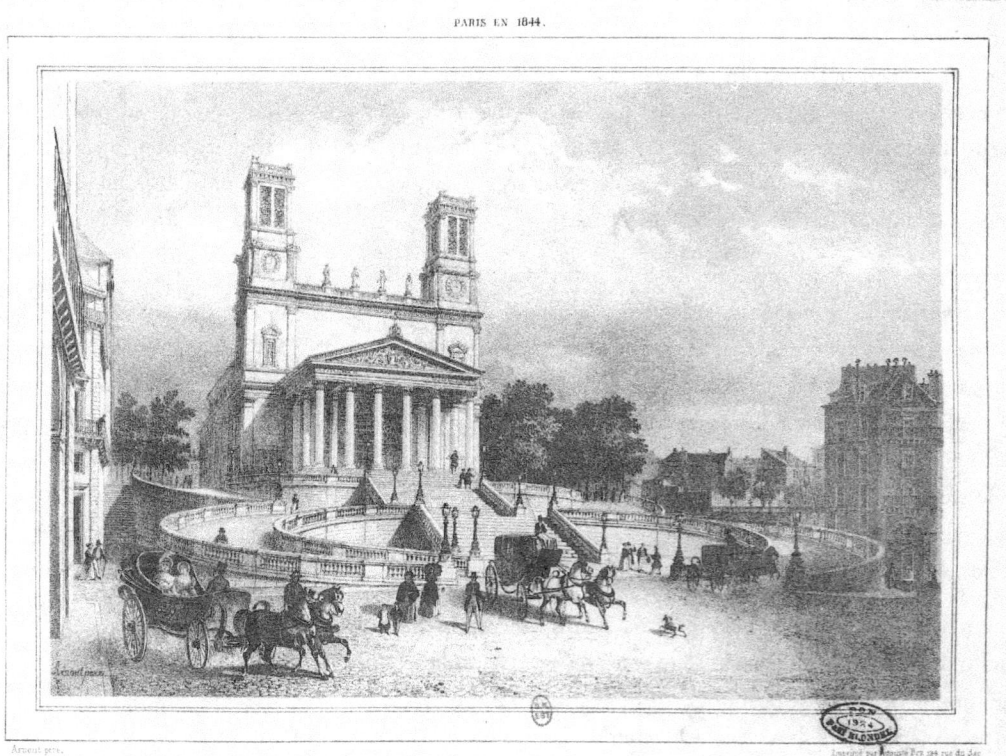

PARIS EN 1844.

VUE DE LA NOUVELLE ÉGLISE ST VINCENT DE PAUL.

was specified for the upper tribunes of the nave. It was unusual for an architect to enlist the tall and slender Ionic order as principal support for an entire building. Hittorff defended himself against critics by citing the archaeological evidence he compiled at Silenus during a trip to Sicily in 1824. Contrary to conventional architectural wisdom, Hittorff concluded that "the Greeks did not take up the progressive importance of the architectural orders, either in relation to their respective use with one another or with regard to the nature of the monuments, the way that Vitruvius presents it."[56] He also believed the Ionic order was essentially a Greek form, thus making it a more pure and expressive prototype for contemporary architects than the Corinthian order, which was based on Roman models derived second-hand from the Greeks.

In an article of 1834, written at the time of his redesign for Saint-Vincent-de-Paul, Hittorff championed the use of different orders as "one of many ways of nuancing the character of buildings." He deplored the fact that most of his colleagues "forgo these means by adopting Corinthian columns nearly everywhere, and by copying Roman architects—in this case as in many others—with more partiality than reasoning."[57] Without specifically citing the church of Saint-Vincent-de-Paul, Hittorff develops the architectural context of classical facades in Paris by discussing virtually all of the important extant examples: from the Panthéon (Fig. 45) to the Church of the Madeleine (visible in the background of Fig. 54); from the Bourse (Fig. 33) to the colonnade added by Bernard Poyet to the river facade of the National Assembly in 1806 (visible at the extreme right of Fig. 53). Hittorff implicitly situates his innovative use of the Ionic order for Saint-Vincent-de-Paul within an established system of Parisian monumental architecture. His church, which is both anchor and point of reference for an entirely new quartier, is thus linked by formal vocabulary and dramatic siting to the city at large. Mobilizing allusion and memory, the church locates the new neighborhood symbolically within the urban space of Paris, just as the network of principal arteries linked the new quartier physically to the central core and the tax wall gateways.

None of this seems terribly innovative today. Viewed historically, urban theorists of the 1830s and 1840s were just beginning to articulate a concept of urban space that transcends a quartier.[58] In 1843 Hippolyte Meynadier opened his proposal for urban renewal with the remark: "This study is concerned with a system of new and large lines of communication planned for the city of Paris, and with examining and selecting the most favorable sites for its monuments of art or administration that are to be constructed or rebuilt." Meynadier argued that planners laying out new streets should "always have a straight line in front of you." He wanted major monuments to stand clear of surrounding buildings so as to maximize "the space and air that support life as well as increase the stature of stone."[59] All of this looks forward to the 1850s and the vast urban projects of Baron Haussmann. It also summarizes nearly two decades of attention to the existence and integrity of urban space that guided the planning of Chabrol and Hittorff in the Nouveau Quartier Poissonnière. Their experiments on the ground clarified the thinking of urban theorists on the need to balance the practical demands of function and utility against the aesthetic and symbolic meanings of the built environment. They shaped in stone and asphalt the working raison d'être for the broad boulevards and dramatic perspectives that characterize Paris of the Second Empire.

NEIGHBORHOODS laid out on unbuilt land could offer a range of new housing options, the most important being apartment buildings. François Loyer has shown that a key element in the economic viability of apartment projects is the width of a lot. "When lots were less than a dozen meters wide," he notes, "it was difficult to build more than a single apartment per floor since, according to tradition, three rooms had to overlook the street (the living room, the master bedroom, and a cabinet, giving a total width of over ten meters)."[60] In the oldest parts of town, where lots seldom exceeded eight meters, it was not practical to construct new apartment houses. By contrast, wider lots were the norm in neighborhoods like the area opened in 1824 around the present-day church of Notre-Dame-de-Lorette (Fig. 133). Whole blocks were built as apartment buildings. The effect was to change both the character of the street and the rhythm of life in the quartier.

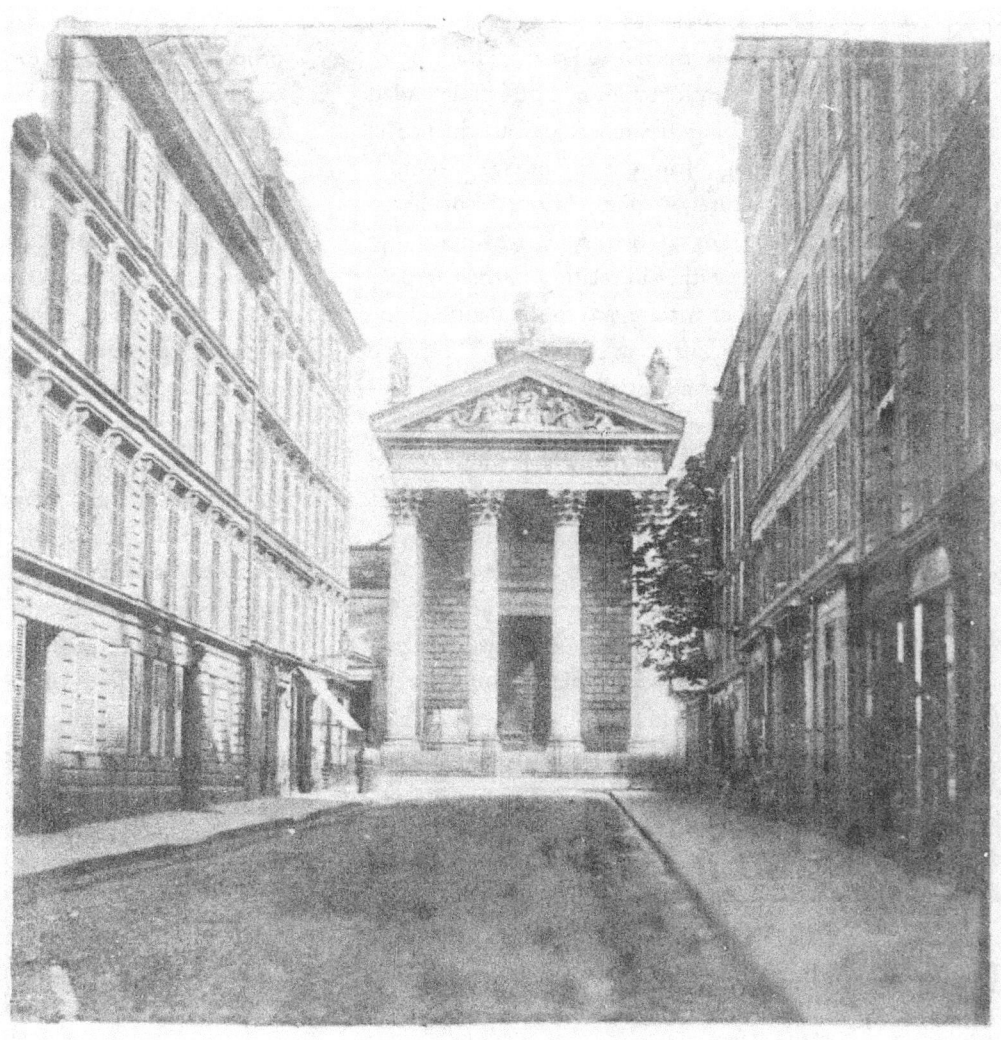

The typical 1820s apartment building consists of a ground floor devoted to shops, rising to four or five stories of residential housing. The best apartments faced the street and occupied an entire floor. Smaller or less desirable units were built at the back of the lot with access via an inner courtyard. Streetside windows were generous and regularly spaced. Sculptural decoration was kept simple to minimize costs. The facades of these apartment buildings project what François Loyer calls a "grid or checkerboard pattern" quite unlike the odd dormers and vertical accents of structures in the old parts of town. "The Restoration building," writes Loyer, "used a very elaborate graphic network of cornices, cordons, and sometimes frames around the window openings in vertical bays linking the stories together. Geometrical and abstract, this graphic system replaced the tradition of ornament."[61] All these qualities are apparent in the apartment buildings built along a section of the rue Laffitte about 1825 (Fig. 133). This street also reveals a related development: apartment buildings were designed and sized to match their neighbors, while a spare use of ornament tended to relate them formally. A strong horizontal movement running the length of the street characterized the new quartiers, which lent them an air of homogeneity—critics called it monotony—comparable to earlier projects like the rue de Rivoli (Fig. 30). The new structures consciously eschewed the cacophony of size and shape that characterizes the streets of old Paris.

Signs of modernity in these new neighborhoods included qualities of propriety, restraint, and rational order—precisely the qualities manifest in the arcades built at exactly the same time in the center of town (Fig. 128). An architecture of control was palpable in the formal homogeneity of new streets and was associated at the time with a specific class. "The tastes of the bourgeois are worthy of comment," wrote Théophile Gautier in 1836; "instead of loving what is beautiful, well-made, elegant, witty, or poetic, he prefers everything that is ugly, common, prosaic, and stupid. What charms him in architecture are whitewash and green shutters."[62] The implications of Gautier's sarcasm become clear when aligned with François Loyer's perceptive observations about the preferred architectural detailing of 1820s streets:

The charm of certain Restoration neighborhoods in Paris (notably, around Saint-Georges) is almost exclusively due to the insistent presence of outdoor shutters that unify the various facades into a coherent decorative system based on graphism and horizontality. Intentionally banal, the use of outdoor shutters as a decorative device thrust the building into anonymity and thereby linked it even more strongly to the whole formed by a street or neighborhood.[63]

The impression of anonymity produced by repeating these banal architectural forms was historically grounded in evolving ideas about the street as a public space to be shared by all citizens regardless of age, class, or gender.

The corollary of such architectural principles is the cultivation of a personal anonymity, usually achieved in public by the ubiquitous black suit, preferred costume of bourgeois men. Baudelaire wrote vividly about this mode of dress in 1846:

And yet, doesn't this outfit, so often victimized, have its own beauty and built-in charm? Isn't it the required dress of our epoch, suffering and carrying on its black and scrawny shoulders the symbol of perpetual mourning? Mind you: not only do the black suit and overcoat have their political beauty, which is the expression of universal equality, but also their poetic beauty, which is the expression of a public soul. . . . A livery of uniform desolation attests to equality; as for those eccentrics, who were easily singled out by distinct and intense colors, they now make do with nuances of design and cut more often than hue.[64]

Baudelaire realized that generalized uniformity eventually incites nonconformists to adopt a new and more focused attention to details. His characterization of the dialectic between group and personal identity was the starting point for Richard Sennett's discussion of "the fear of involuntarily disclosing character" that he takes to be a master theme of life in Paris of the 1820s and 1830s.[65] It is especially apparent in the writings of Balzac. For Sennett, the shift from clearly legible representations of one's self to a self-presentation of sameness was driven by the advent of machine-made clothes. Ready-to-wear garments fostered a cult of miniaturized signals and new anxieties about appearing in public:

As people's personalities came to be seen in their appearances, facts of class and sex thus became matters of real anxiety. The world of immanent truths is so much more intense and yet so much more problematical than the public world of the *ancien régime* in which appearances were put at a distance from oneself. In the coffeehouse, in the theater, in one's clothing, the facts of social standing were so suspended or so stated, even if false, that they needn't of necessity raise questions in a social situation. A man might or might not be what his clothes proclaimed, but the proclamation was clear. . . . The compulsive attention to detail, the anxiety for facts which has since come to obsess us in so many ways, was born of this anxiety about what appearances symbolize.[66]

The anxiety described by Sennett was associated with being in public and on the streets. Similar habits of attention migrated effortlessly from people encountered on the sidewalk to the urban context of those encounters. Like their black-suited inhabitants, the new streets wore a cloak of architectural sameness. A persistent horizontal regularity encouraged people to look ahead and to keep moving. Repetitive facades sharpened attention to detail by offering few bold gestures of identifying texture. Like the arcades, the new quarters of

Paris constructed wary, visually discerning inhabitants constantly in motion.

If contemporaries were fascinated with the figure of the flâneur, it was because his modus vivendi was keenly attuned to the exigencies of this new environment. He represented a role model adjusted to cope with the psychological demands of negotiating the evolving urban space. Women, as Sennett notes, were not so free to adopt the flâneur's roving eye:

How was a respectable woman to set herself off from a loose one, let alone a fallen woman, if the resemblance was so close? How could she, presumably innocent and pure, pick up the knowledge to guide her? There arose out of this dilemma a need to pay great attention to details of appearance and to hold oneself in, for fear of being read wrong or maliciously; indeed, who knew, perhaps if one gave off miniature signals of being loose, one really was. . . . One's only defense against such a culture was in fact to cover up, and from this came the stony feminine fear of being seen in public.[67]

Even one's street address could be the subject of malicious interpretation. Consider the apartments erected around the church of Notre-Dame-de-Lorette during the 1820s (Fig. 133). New buildings tend to remain damp until their plaster walls have completely cured. Thus, according to Maurice Alhoy, new apartments were usually rented at special terms:

A completed apartment was awarded without charge for six months to women bold enough to risk the rheumatisms produced by the tears of drying plaster. After wiping away these above-mentioned tears for two terms, you entered the class of renters paying by the quarter. The occupants, too proud to submit to this yoke, went to look in the house next door for other tears to dry. In this struggle with new plaster, the Lorettes were true Jeanne Hachettes. . . . In the space of four years some of these heroines have changed their place of residence—or rather their bivouac—sixteen times.[68]

Many such renters were young women who were also kept mistresses or prostitutes, so that the term *lorette* (from the name of the quartier) came to be used for loose women in general.[69] No respectable woman—regardless of what she was wearing—dared to walk unaccompanied in that part of town.

The story is but one example of how new patterns of social fragmentation emerged within the city's fabric from a matrix of architecture, history, and cultural practices. The terms governing these new relationships between individuals and their environment defined an urban space that was modern because it seemed to be constructed ad hoc and did not respect established hierarchies of class or prestige. A protean and malleable social space encouraged and shaped development of restaurants and mass transit, shopping habits and the public appreciation of art. Self-consciousness of what it means to be urban remains an important and lasting legacy of cultural life in Romantic Paris.

TWO FURTHER DEVELOPMENTS altered decisively a remapping of Paris during the 1830s and 1840s. Chabrol preferred to rely on private speculators and capital to fund the most expensive projects of urban renewal. Claude-Philibert de Rambuteau, who became Prefect in 1833, tended to follow this conservative fiscal policy and to avoid deficit spending whenever possible. Rambuteau described his priorities as "constantly absorbed by important public works, adjusted to the city's resources, without compromising the future nor interrupting attention to the unexpected expenses with which circumstances could burden the city at any moment."[70] For street planning, Rambuteau's preferred tactic was simply to declare the intent of widening a thoroughfare: any new buildings must be set back from the existing roadway a certain distance (usually about fifteen feet). The problem is that old buildings are demolished and completely replaced only rarely, so the process of widening an entire block—although costing the city nothing—might take decades or even centuries to be completed.

Rambuteau fully realized that conditions of trade and movement in parts of central Paris had become unmanageable. A group of prominent citizens living around Les Halles, the main marketplace, presented a petition to the Prefect in 1834 calling for a roadway twenty feet wide to connect the church of Saint-Eustache to the rue Francs-Bourgeois and thus relieve the permanent traffic jams in their neighborhood. Four years later, after scaling down the width of the proposed street to thirteen feet, a royal decree of "public utility" (5 March 1838) authorized Rambuteau "to acquire, whether by mutual agreement or by means of expropriation . . . the buildings or parts of buildings that must be taken over in order to clear a trajectory for the new street."[71] The project was relatively modest in scale, but eventually cost nine million francs, entailed destroying seventy-seven houses, and took six years to finish. Such numbers underscore the huge expense of cutting through existing neighborhoods.

The completed street—named Rambuteau after the Prefect—is a landmark in the history of Paris because it was the first attempt to cut a new route through a densely populated area (Fig. 134). "The opening of the rue Rambuteau proved to be a turning point," remarks François Loyer; "it showed the city fathers that they absolutely had to think big and build more and wider streets through the saturated center."[72] In 1841, when the rue Rambuteau was still under construction, the government of Louis-Philippe adopted laws to generalize the practice of expropriating land for instances of public utility (Law of 3 May 1841). A legalized concept of common good, lodged in the idea of a shared urban space first articulated in the new quartiers and covered arcades of the 1820s, came to define the needs and the architecture of the modern city. Although Baron Haussmann and Napoléon III eventually effected the most radical transformation of nineteenth-century Paris, they worked with the legal tools, theoretical principles, and symbolic language inherited from the age of Chabrol, Rambuteau, and the flâneur.

A final chapter in the building of new Paris was also a product of the 1840s and involved direct intervention of the state. No adult Parisian of the time could forget that Paris had been overrun by enemy soldiers in 1814 after the collapse of Napoléon's army. Many still remembered bitterly that the city was forced to capitulate because it had no coherent system of defense. In 1833 the government of Louis-Philippe proposed building a ring of freestanding forts around Paris at some distance from the old Farmers-General tax wall, but the plan foundered when political opponents pointed out that cannons mounted in such a fashion could also be turned against rebellious Parisians. Opposition leaders threatened to take to the streets in protest. The government was forced to back down and to suspend work on the forts,

but the idea did not die. A commission was named in 1836 to revisit the plan, and in 1839 it recommended building forts connected by a continuous wall. No further action was taken at that time. History and fate soon intervened.

Adolphe Thiers, who played a large role in the arts (see Chapter Three), returned to power as head of the cabinet in February 1840. Two months later Thiers successfully negotiated with England for the return to Paris of Napoléon's body (Fig. 54). The event generated a great outpouring of nationalist fervor and sentimental nostalgia for the Empire. France's cordial relations with England soured over the summer when Thiers moved aggressively and secretly to support Méhémet-Ali, the pasha of Egypt, in his struggle with the Ottoman emperor for control of Syria. Lord Palmerston, Prime Minister of England, learned of Thiers' secret negotiations with Méhémet-Ali. He enjoined Russia, Prussia, and Austria to form an alliance with Britain against Egypt and, by extension, against France (15 July 1840).

Word of Palmerston's treaty spread like wildfire in Paris. It seemed that the old alliance responsible for Napoléon's defeat was newly reincarnated against the government of Louis-Philippe. "Here, bad news arrives in quick succession," wrote Heinrich Heine from Paris on 27 July; "but the latest and worst of all—the coalition of England, Russia, Austria, and Prussia against the pasha of Egypt—has produced here, as much in the government as among the people, a joyous, warlike enthusiasm rather than consternation."[73] Even the politically conservative *Journal des Débats* owned by Louis-François Bertin (Fig. 114) warmed to the war fever. "The treaty is an insolence that France will not tolerate; her honor forbids it," exclaimed an editorial on 29 July. Two days later the paper returned to the charge by declaring: "France will not back down. . . . France cannot back down, because that would be to accept her place among second-rate powers. . . . She must prepare for war."[74] Thiers was more than willing to comply. He proposed a massive buildup of arms and men. He also resuscitated the project to fortify Paris with a new wall and a bracelet of heavily armed forts. Thiers was strongly supported by Louis-Philippe and the royal princes, all of whom believed the military position of Paris must be strengthened. A royal ordinance of 10 September 1840 authorized immediate construction of the forts and

FIGURE 134. *The rue Rambuteau*, built 1838–1845. Anonymous photograph, ca. 1906. Paris, BnF, Estampes, inv. Va 245a. Photo: BnF, Paris.

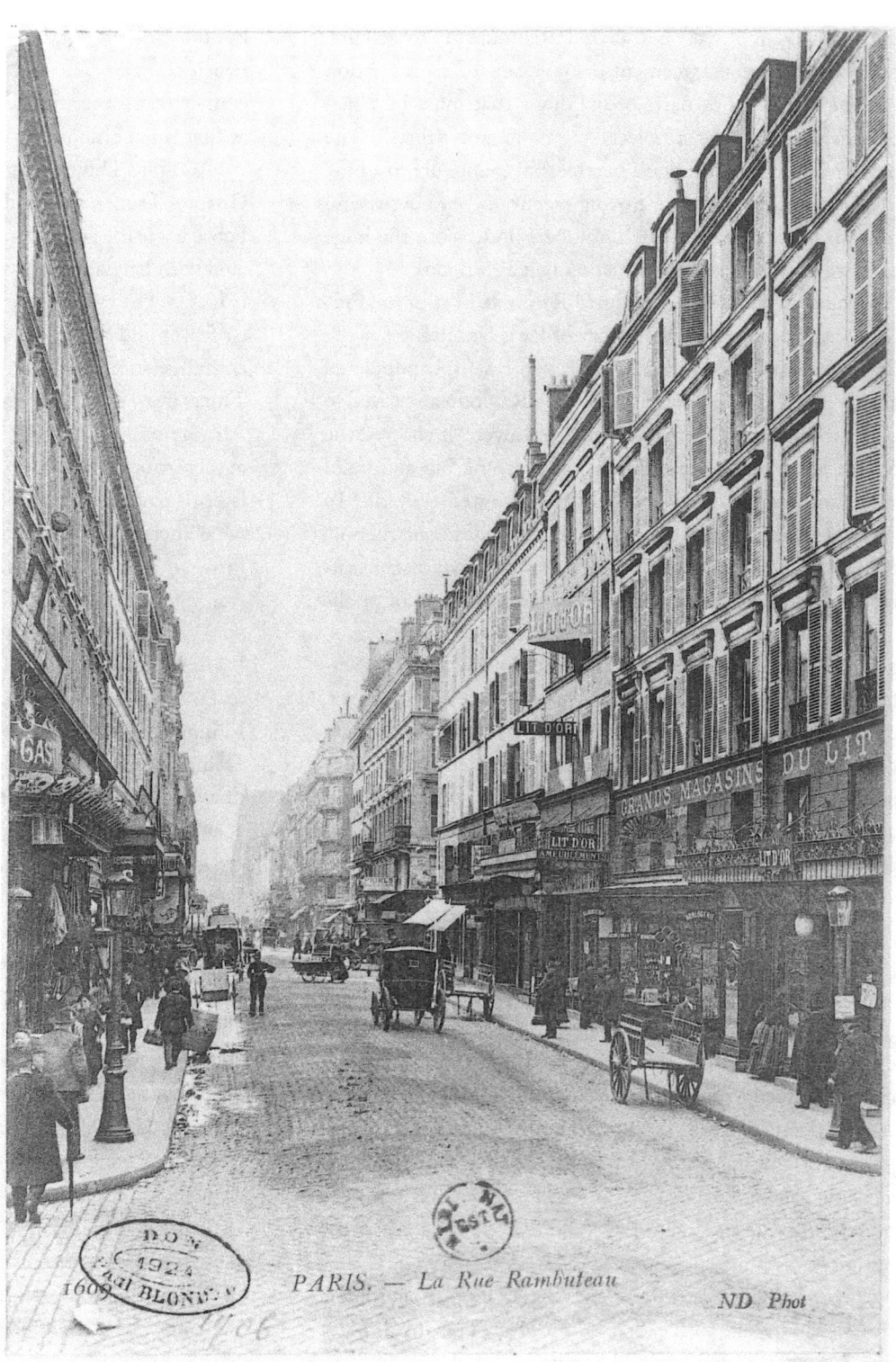

PARIS. — *La Rue Rambuteau*

ND Phot

wall, locating them far enough from the old Farmers-General tax wall to protect central Paris from enemy cannon fire. The final emplacement of this new wall is marked on the inset of the 1842 map (Fig. 129).

This large project required special state funding and it spurred a lively debate in both houses of the legislature. A measure was passed on 3 April 1841 to allocate 140 million francs for "an enclosure fortified by bastions and terraces, with ten meters of reinforced escarpment and exterior casemates." The project also called for clearing a zone 250 meters wide around the outside perimeter of the new wall. Importantly, the terrain between the new fortifications and the old tax wall did not become part of the city proper. Small communities inside the new line of defense—Auteuil, Passy, Montmartre, la Villette, Bercy, and others—remained exempt from paying municipal taxes on food, building materials, and other staples. Rambuteau resisted pressure to annex these new areas because he believed

Paris should be the elder sister of the suburbs, all the more generous because the latter increasingly assists the former every day. A part of business and industry—workers, artisans, employees of every grade—come to the suburbs in search of a more affordable life, and they have no less right to an administrative solicitude.[75]

The wall, thirty-four kilometers long, and bristling with sixteen forts, was not completed until 1846, well after the conflict with England over the Middle East had subsided.

War with England and her allies was avoided, but a legacy of that tense moment remains today. Exempt from the high taxes of Paris proper, the villages between the two walls developed rapidly during the 1840s and 1850s. Philippe Vigier describes it as "a veritable demographic explosion" in which the population of some communities more than doubled.[76] One of the boldest gestures of Second Empire Paris was to annex all of the territory inside the 1841 wall and to demolish the old tax wall. In so doing, the land surface of Paris more than doubled, its population increased by almost four hundred thousand, and the city assumed the physical size and shape that has changed very little since.

Like so much of modern Paris, traces of the past emerge from layers of building and years of development. The roughly circular scar left by the old tax wall became the trajectory for a network of outer boulevards designed by Haussmann that remains an essential part of the present-day city. The fortifications built by Thiers were not demolished until 1919. The empty strip of no-man's land known as the *zone* was sold back to the city and eventually became parks, low-income housing blocks, and the roadbed of a bustling autoroute known today as the boulevard Périphérique. In this way, the physical geography of Romantic Paris continues to shape present-day experience of the capital. Less visible, but no less real, are the daily habits and patterns of sociability developed by nineteenth-century Parisians for living in the new urban spaces of their city. These intangible aspects of life in Paris will be our next topic.

The Spectacle of City Life

Today, there are restaurants for every social class—for princes, dukes, marquis, barons, generals, politicians, men of letters, judges, lawyers, bankers, stock-market speculators, gamblers, working people, merchants, students, and even those living on small fixed incomes—ranging from a forty-franc gold piece to the modest sum of one franc and fifty centimes. The aristocracy and the haughty have come down into the courtyards where the dishes of the principal restaurants are prepared.

—Antoine Caillot[77]

Modern cities count thousands of restaurants, but in 1827 Antoine Caillot singled out the range and number in Paris as a marvel worthy of note. Restaurants as we know them were not inventions of the nineteenth century, but they were relatively new to Paris. The first restaurants serving food prepared on the premises—even the word *restaurant*—only appeared about 1765 in connection with an establishment opened on the rue des Pouliès by a man called Boulanger.[78] A guidebook of 1797 recounts the tale of Boulanger's claim to fame:

In addition to the fact that Boulanger sold broths, one could find something to eat at his place but, because he was not officially a caterer, he could not serve stews. As replacement he offered salted poultry, fresh eggs, etc. and served them on little marble tables without tablecloths. Other restaurant owners started businesses that imitated his.[79]

The number and types of restaurants in Paris mushroomed by the turn of the century. Alexandre Grimod de la Reynière, one of the first chroniclers of modern French cuisine, attributed much of this growth to aftereffects of the French Revolution:

By ruining all the old landowners, the Revolution put all the good cooks on the street. From then on, to use their talents, they made themselves into merchants of good food under the name of *Restaurateur*. . . . This revolution in cooking, and the wealth of these clever restaurant-owners, stems from two further causes: the craze for imitating English customs (because the English, as one knows, almost always eat at the pub), and that sudden inundation of legislators without a place of residence who, ultimately setting the tone, led all the Parisians to cabarets by their example.[80]

Grimod claimed there were fewer than one hundred restaurants in Paris before 1789. When he was writing in 1803 they numbered about five hundred. Twenty-five years later, Caillot estimated that more than three thousand restaurants in Paris served approximately sixty thousand people per day.[81]

Restaurants represented a new category of social space, different from both the truly public spaces of street or spectacle and the private realm of domestic life. Many deals of business, politics, and marriage were arranged around a table of conviviality. Antoine Caillot exclaimed in 1827:

Restaurant owners, you don't know what you are worth. Learn to recognize the extent of your importance in society. With your lunches, you are the regulators of opinion, of finance, of family interests, of votes at the Institute, and sometimes maybe even votes in the elected Chamber. You guarantee the success of authors and increase, by your influence over the dramatic arts, the pleasures of the stage. Everything in our lovely France rolls across your tables and around your bottles.[82]

Caillot underscores the importance of lunch [déjeuner]. Indeed, growth in the restaurant industry marched hand in hand with a major readjustment of Parisian eating habits. Before the Revolution, it was customary to have a very light meal upon rising, a main meal in early afternoon, and a light supper during the evening, usually between five and ten o'clock. Beginning in the 1790s, and due in large part to the upheavals in social and political life brought about by the Revolution, the main meal was pushed further into the afternoon or early evening. This left a large block of time—and many hungry stomachs—at midday.

Over the course of only a few years, a second déjeuner became the norm. It was novel for its timing and its substance. In 1803 Grimod de la Reynière reported: "it is true that one takes only a single real meal, which begins about six o'clock and lasts until nine. But this meal is preceded by two lunches [déjeuners], of which the second—called *à la fourchette*—is respectably robust."[83] Grimod's term for the midday meal refers to the fact that it consisted of dishes substantial enough to be eaten with a fork [fourchette]. The term entered common usage: a sign for the restaurant Dehodencq in the passage des Panoramas advertises *déjeuners à la fourchette* (Fig. 127); at least one English visitor to Paris in 1803 remarked that the restaurant on the terrace of the Tuileries Palace offered "breakfast à l'anglaise or à la fourchette, that is in the most substantial manner in the French fashion."[84] What was this French fashion? According to Jean-Paul Aron, the midday meal was both an innovation and highly stylized. Hot dishes, such as soups, roasts, and vegetables, were generally not admitted. By contrast, oysters, cold cuts, sausages of many varieties, and pastries were items of preference. The *déjeuner à la fourchette* was served simply without courses and usually taken in a restaurant. Finally, at least early in the century, women were almost always excluded.[85] The protocols of lunch established and furthered the notion that restaurants were social spaces both different from one's private life and yet not entirely public: if guests were not intimate friends they were nonetheless linked by shared professional or financial interests.

The shift to eating at midday reset old patterns of Parisian life by creating new forms of professional sociability. It also threw into question established distinctions between restaurants and cafés. As midday meals became increasingly widespread and lucrative, cafés not officially licensed to serve food began to offer lunches. Lawsuits were occasionally filed by owners of legitimate restaurants, but it was clear that existing laws presumed a separation of tasks ever more blurred by contemporary practice. The circular reasoning of a case in

1830 is characteristic of this confusion: the Tribunal d'Instance ruled that café owners would be allowed to serve *déjeuners à la fourchette* if they could prove it was customary for them to do so. Henry-Melchior de Langle, an historian of Paris cafés, points out that "the transformation of a café into a restaurant often passed through this intermediary phase of a café offering lunches à la fourchette."[86] He cites several instances from the 1820s in which large and elaborately decorated cafés were transformed into some of the city's leading restaurants. This uneasy relationship and shifting ground between restaurants and cafés registers changes in the habits of leisure and entertainment in Romantic Paris.

Cafés were fixtures of Parisian life much before restaurants. Coffee was introduced to France by Soliman Aga Mustapha Raca, who was appointed ambassador to the court of Louis XIV in 1669 by Mahomet IV, the sultan of Turkey. By the end of the seventeenth century there were many specialized establishments in Paris serving coffee, liqueurs, herbal preparations, chocolates, preserves of fruit, sorbets, and ice creams. The most famous of these—both for the luxury of its setting and the quality of its coffee—was the Café Procope founded in 1686. It remains a fixture of the Left Bank. The number of cafés increased throughout the eighteenth century. "There are an infinite number of cafés in Paris," remarked a German diplomat in 1726, "so many that sometimes one finds ten, twelve, or more in the same street; some of these are highly esteemed and are often visited by princes and other notables."[87] The most popular cafés—the Café de Foy, the Café des Anglais, the Café des Arts, and the Café du Caveau—were all situated in or around the Palais-Royal and close to the Comédie-Française.

An elaborate décor was an essential component of the most famous Parisian cafés of the early nineteenth century. "The cafés are more embellished, more brilliant, and doubtlessly more elegant than cabarets ever were," remarked Joseph Lavallée in 1803; "they are decorated with mirrors, crystal chandeliers, marbles, and paintings, while the owners and their wives are decked out like people with pensions of 50,000 livres."[88] Luxury settings came to be associated, especially in the minds of foreigners, with a specifically French and Parisian type of café. "The principal coffee houses here are fitted up with taste and elegance," reported a typical English visitor about 1802; "large mirrors form no inconsiderable part of their decoration. There are no partitions to divide them into boxes. The tables are of marble; the benches and stools are covered with Utrecht velvet. . . . In the evening they are lighted by quinquets in a brilliant manner."[89] Even more astonishing to English visitors was the presence of Parisian women in the cafés: "A stranger to *French manners*," wrote Richard Bernard in 1815, "is surprised at seeing ladies of respectability frequenting coffee-houses and taverns, which they do as a matter of course—so powerful are the habits in which we have been educated."[90]

Philibert-Louis Debucourt's engraving of the Café Frascati in 1807 conveys both the setting and the clientele characteristic of the principal cafés of the time (Fig. 135). Frascati was housed in a hôtel on the boulevard des Italiens that had been confiscated during the Revolution. It comprised several rooms and a small garden. Debucourt shows only the vestibule, which was renowned for its architectural details *à l'antique*, its lavish use of mirrors, and a replica of the Medicis Venus that is visible in the center background of the print. Arcades flanking the statue open onto a suite of six rooms that John Dean Paul described as "most splendidly lighted and furnished with mirrors, the rooms all opening onto a garden full of illuminated orange and acacia trees, and fancifully arranged with grottoes, temples, and walks, and the gay effect of the coloured lamps, and the company, recall to the imagination the fables of Arabian nights."[91] Frascati was understandably one of the most popular night spots of the period.

English tourists in Paris were obsessed with visiting only those places where good company assembled. Frascati received a telling mix of reviews. The Englishman just cited observed that Frascati "is esteemed to have the best company of any public space in Paris, but the slovenliness of the men, though contrasted with the most beautiful women, elegantly dressed, entirely takes away the tasteful appearance of a place of public entertainment."[92] A few nights later the same English gentleman returned to Frascati, "where we breathed the reviving cool night air, tasting delicious ice and fruits under the orange and acacia trees, whilst the

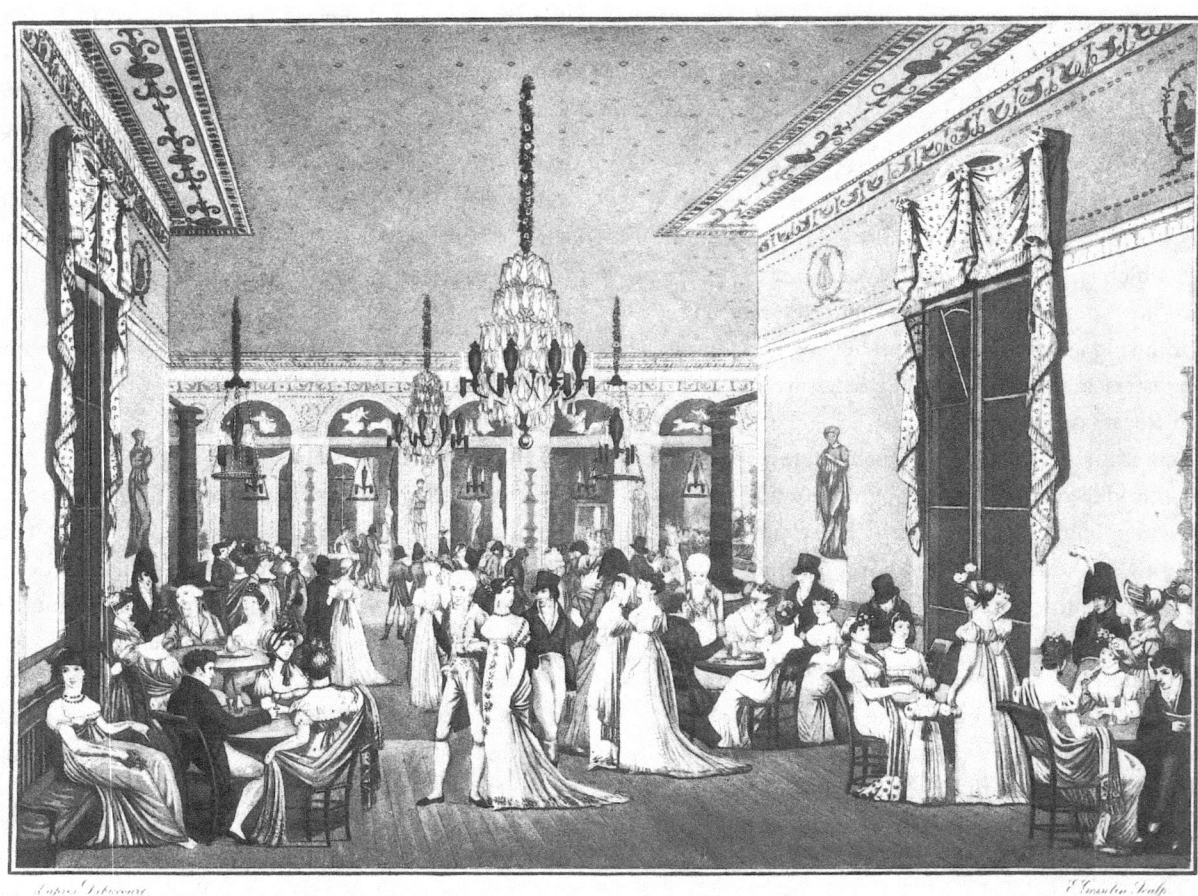

Frascati.

FIGURE 135.   Philibert-Louis Debucourt, *Café Frascati*, 1807. Colored etching with aquatint. Paris, Musée Carnavalet, inv. TOPO GC 012 D (32.3 × 39.8 cm). Photo: © PMVP/Degraces.

most elegant and beautiful women were spreading all the snares of grace and beauty, to amuse those who were wise, and entrap those who were unwary."[93] By contrast, Ann Plumptre maintained that "Frascati is frequented by the best company, and is much resorted to after the theater to conclude the evening."[94] John Carr agreed with her: he was struck by the fact that even though Frascati charged no entrance fee, "no improper intruder has yet appeared,

a circumstance which may be accounted for by the awe which well bred society ever maintains over vulgarity." He too marveled that "in the course of an hour, the astonished, and admiring stranger may see here three thousand females of the first beauty and distinction in Paris."[95] Most interesting about these reports is not their disagreements, but the recognition that Frascati offered a novel experience of social mixing that was virtually unknown in contemporary

English culture. Nor was this unique to Frascati. A similar mix of class and gender was the norm at other places of entertainment, such as the pleasure gardens of Tivoli and the Hameau de Chantilly. It was also the norm in the most prestigious restaurants. Véry, a restaurant on the terrace of the Tuileries Palace, was described by John Carr with a mixture of wonder and delight:

On the ground floor the house is divided into three long and spacious apartments, opening into each other through centre arches, and which are redoubled upon the view by immense pier glasses at each end. The first room is for dinner parties, the next for ices, and the third for coffee. In the middle is a flying staircase, lined on each side with orange trees, all of which are admirably painted after the taste of Herculaneum, and are almost lined with costly pier glasses. My fair countrywomen would perhaps be a little surprised to be told, that elegant women, of the first respectability, superbly dressed for the promenade, dine here with their friends in the public room, a custom which renders the scene delightful, and removes from it the accustomed impressions of grossness.[96]

Visitors from other cultures recognized that Parisians of both sexes regularly practiced forms of sociability in which the pleasures of seeing and being seen in public were materialized and redoubled by an impressive use of mirrors.

The point is germane to what Richard Sennett describes as the modern, public, and anxious self-awareness of personality.[97] Modern personality does not conform to models established by family background or social conventions. This was the domain of English tourists who worried about good company in the cafés of Paris. Nor does modern personality assume that a person's true self transcends appearances. Rather, it is constructed by the self-conscious expression of feelings in public arenas that are conducive to the observation and judgment of others. Such places include the cafés, restaurants, and pleasure gardens of early nineteenth-century Paris where a novel sociability both fascinated and bewildered English visitors. Modern personality emerged and flourished within the same historical matrix of urban spaces and social visibility haunted by the flâneur, but with several significant differences. If the flâneur cultivates emotional detachment, isolated mobility, and an exterior of seamless in-

scrutability, personality assumes that appearances offer clues to private feelings that can and must be orchestrated. The mythic flâneur of nineteenth-century Paris embodied and validated discernment before the flood of consumer products. Personality, by contrast, was a public performance of self that mimicked in small the thrilling examples of virtuosi like Paganini, Taglioni, and Talma that so fascinated their contemporaries (see Chapter Six).

Not every café or restaurant in Paris boasted the luxurious décor and upper class clientèle of Frascati or Véry. Most cafés were modest establishments where perfectly ordinary people gathered to drink and talk, read newspapers, and warm themselves in winter. Writing in 1802 about these simple coffeehouses, an English traveler noted, with a characteristic attention to social hierarchies, that

they are, in general the rendezvous of the idle, and the refuge of the needy. This is so true, that a frequenter of a coffeehouse scarcely ever lights a fire in his own lodging during the whole winter. . . . No person who wishes to be respected thinks of lounging in a coffeehouse, because it not only shews him to be at a loss to spend his time, which may fairly be construed into a deficiency of education or knowledge, but also implies an absolute want of acquaintance with what is termed good company.[98]

Bellangé's watercolor of 1824 records the humble appearance of such places and the types of people who frequented them (Fig. 136). An elderly man dozes over his newspaper near the warmth of a stove. He seems to be part of an entirely masculine world. The image emphasizes material simplicity and the languid passing of time. Small wonder that our Englishman assumed regular customers of such coffeehouses are indolents who lack the discernment to recognize or to keep good company.

By contrast, modern historians argue that coffeehouses were essential to the development of bourgeois sociability in nineteenth-century Paris.[99] Central to this thesis is a distinction between two types of social gathering: on one hand, salons that were predominately intellectual, intimate, and included both men and women (see Chapter Six); on the other, clubs [cercles] where professional or business colleagues met in semi-public places without the company of women. Social

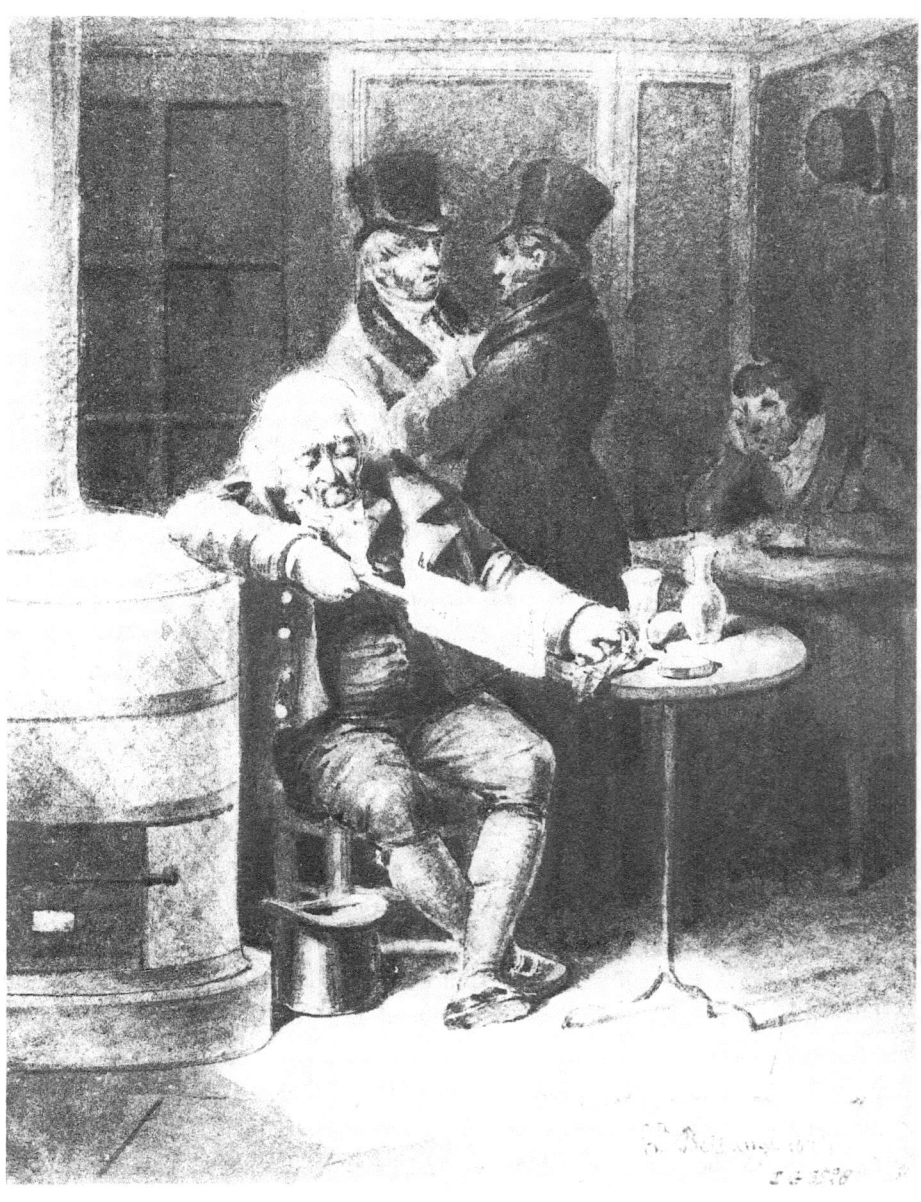

spaces conducive to clubs (cafés, pleasure gardens, reading rooms) existed from the early years of the century, but the specter of political unrest—first under Napoléon and then during the Restoration—kept them under close police surveillance. Groups seeking permission to meet in these locales were regularly refused. "The purely social meeting for relaxation, reading, and gambling," writes Maurice Agulhon, "was met by specialists of the Bourbon police with a hostility that was justly carried over from Napoleonic times. They were afraid that the conversation would be political."[100] Since everyone knew that coffeehouses were watched, Bellangé's watercolor of 1824 (Fig. 136) probably does not overstate the lethargy that reigned in most of them during the Bourbon Restoration.

The Revolution of 1830 (see Chapter Two) inaugurated a period of rapid growth in the number of clubs for at least two reasons. First, the new government lifted sanctions against organizations meeting in public. Second, the spaces and habits of café culture became an acceptable part of political life. Charles de Rémusat, a Liberal politician who served the July Monarchy for many years, recalled that "in the breakup of Parisian society that followed the July Revolution, the closure of some houses and the contraction of certain fortunes gave a new look to the world of elegance: it left sitting rooms for public spaces."[101] This move from private to public spaces brought two important corollaries: intellectual discussions migrated from mixed companies of men and women (salons) to groupings that were almost exclusively male (cafés); the "contraction of certain fortunes" mentioned by Rémusat fostered a sociability based more on shared professional interests than similarities of economic class or social background. The model usually invoked when founding a cercle in 1830s Paris was the gentleman's club common in London. "The English club, where there are only members, is an egalitarian institution," remarks Agulhon; "moreover, one that can be founded—in theory—by people who are certainly well-to-do, but not necessarily rich. Thus, for the time, the club was doubly revolutionary or, if you prefer, doubly bourgeois."[102] If cercles were imported from England and signaled allegiance to a bourgeois ideal of culture, salons continued the tradition of elite sociability rooted in pre-Revolutionary France.

The rise of clubs in Parisian cultural life registers the emergence of a social space sited in the public arena of cafés but restricted in membership to men with shared interests. Business and politics intermixed freely in this ambience, ideas were exchanged across distinctions of class or generation, and opinions were formed in conversations over the latest edition of daily newspapers. It was also a world of journalists and bohemians where identities and personalities were fashioned and reworked in response to immediate needs (see Chapter Six). Writing in 1848 about the Constituent Assembly elected after the overthrow of Louis-Philippe (see Chapter Two), Alexis de Tocqueville trenchantly characterized the origins of his newly empowered colleagues of the radical left-wing party:

They spoke a jargon that was not exactly *unschooled* French nor that of *savants*, but it retained defects of both, for it was full of vulgarities and ambitious expressions. A continuous stream of insulting or humorous catcalls was heard coming from the benches of the Mountain; at the same time, there was a huge number of jeers and maxims that alternated between a very bawdy tone and a splendid manner. Obviously, these characters belonged no more to the world of *cabarets* than of *salons*; I believe they polished their manners in the halfway house of cafés and nourished their wit only on *newspaper literature*.[103]

Tocqueville recognized that many politicians of 1848 were formed by a sociability—neither common nor elitist—registered in a political language that mixed street-smart slang [argot] with academic French.

Social historians have shown that the Parisian bourgeoisie taking shape during the first half of the nineteenth century needed to distinguish its interests and ambitions from those both higher and lower on the social scale. Louis Wirth points out that such distinctions are hard to make in large urban centers because "there is little opportunity for the individual to obtain a conception of the city as a whole or to survey his place in the total scheme."[104] Anxieties about losing one's identity in the unpredictable flux of urban life were common in Paris near mid-century. Here is the *Journal des Débats* in 1847:

The bourgeoisie is not a class, it's a position; one acquires this position, one loses it. Work, savings, and ability bestow it; vice, extravagance, and laziness cause it to be lost. The bourgeoisie is so unlike a class that its doors are open to everyone, both to leave as well as to enter.[105]

Anxieties of identity propelled the hostility directed against Gustave Courbet's pictures of country folk in 1850 (see Chapter Five). The same worry explains why the loosely joined groups that gathered and talked in the cercles of Paris cafés—arenas of a stable sociability that were neither populist nor elitist—became catalysts for shaping the self-image, political base, and ideology of the Parisian bourgeoisie.

A second quality of nineteenth-century bourgeois culture is related to the flux and uncertainties of urban life. Richard Sennett writes of the "dignity of the bourgeoisie."[106] Against the uncertainties of an economy fueled by speculation, against the fear of fraud, bankruptcy, and personal ruin, against a chaotic marketplace flooded by machine-made goods (see Chapter Eight), the bourgeoisie erected the myth of a stable home "to force the family as a group into a life of rigid propriety."[107] Central to this myth was the nuclear family: an intimate, tightly knit group of parents and children shielded from the vagaries of the outside world. This protected, mythic space supposedly encouraged each family member to develop his or her personality. It was also a place of concealment where women especially were sheltered from the unforeseen dangers of public life. The triumph of the nuclear family, including the sheltering of respectable women, hastened the demise of those luxury cafés and pleasure gardens where English tourists had previously noted the number and beauty of Parisian women among the crowds. Frascati lost its garden in 1824 when the rue Vivienne was extended to the boulevard. The Café des Mille Colonnes was reported to be almost always empty. The gardens of Tivoli were demolished in 1826 to make way for the new Europe quartier.

The structure of self-defense implied by the nuclear family did not allow bourgeois women the same level of access to public spaces as bourgeois men. Women's fashions in Paris of the 1830s and 1840s reflected this asymmetry. Dresses with long sleeves, lowered hemlines, and high necks were worn over tightly laced corsets. Hair was modestly covered by a bonnet. The unspoken purpose of this attire was to ensure that when a bourgeois woman appeared in public no detail would suggest she was anything less than physically fresh and morally respectable. By contrast, bourgeois men moved freely outside the family home and congregated in semipublic spaces of masculine sociability. Their social ramblings often included the detour described by Jean-Paul Aron:

In this way, at the very moment when bourgeois order asserts itself and its values—respectability of the house, integrity of the family, sweetness of domestic intimacy—are affirmed, French society contrives some escape routes. From the beginning of the century, the restaurant took its place—with a good rating of credibility—

among the sanctuaries of initiative and freedom. Soon it will go even further by accommodating little sitting rooms and private dining rooms, an elegant transition from liberty to licentiousness.[108]

Aron isolates a second reason why *déjeuners à la fourchette* almost never included women: they were both venues for business and arenas of masculine escape from bourgeois domesticity.

Restaurants of the early nineteenth century tended not to welcome families, but by 1825 Louis Montigny could report that they were the preferred site for "matters of private interest, love affairs, business deals, affairs of state" and, on occasion, included the company of women.[109] As a parallel development, the *déjeuner à la fourchette* became a less stylized meal with a more casual pacing that allowed for conversation, to which respectable women were invited. Lunches acquired the ambience of what Aron calls an "intimate diversion."[110] Jean-Robert Pitte further remarks on the effects of this transition around 1830: "there is, on the part of both customer and restaurant-owner, an obvious desire for ostentation, and a growing rivalry over the number and rarity of dishes and wines offered by the menus."[111] Newly enriched professionals, speculators, and business leaders came to regard dining in public—whether at midday or increasingly in the evening—as a form of conspicuous consumption that announced personal success.

Pressured by these shifts in taste and habits, many older cafés were converted to full-service restaurants with the goal of creating environments that combined personal comfort with public spectacle. One of the most noteworthy of these transformations involved the Café Hardy, which was centrally located on the corner of the rue Laffitte and the boulevard des Italiens. Hardy was famous for its *déjeuners à la fourchette*, including "the best kidneys in the capital" according to Grimod de La Reynière's guidebook for 1803.[112] Grimod said the café's profitability owed much to its prime location, for which Madame Hardy reportedly paid twenty thousand francs of key money [pots de vin] when renewing her lease. During the middle 1820s Café Hardy was patronized by stock speculators from the nearby Bourse. At Hardy, according to Louis Prudhomme, "one determines the rise and fall of government securities; there, a negotiation passes through ten or twelve hands while lunch *à la fourchette* is being prepared."[113] The fortunes of Café Hardy began to decline with the advent of evening dining as a form of conspicuous consumption. Luncheons remained the staple of its business but it was unable to attract a dinner clientèle comparable to its lavishly decorated competitors on the boulevard—notably the Café Riche, the Café des Anglais, and the Café de Paris. Madame Hardy sold the business in 1836 for a handsome profit, but her successors failed to stem its demise: Café Hardy was bankrupt within a few years.

The entire building was demolished in 1839 and rebuilt with great attention to luxurious details. "A house in gold with some embellishments in stone," reported one journalist; "it shines so brightly in the sunlight that you can't look at it.

The windows consist of a single pane of glass set into a gold frame and decorated with broad gilt balconies."[114] This glittering new building came to be known popularly as the Maison d'Or [House of Gold]. A restaurant called La Maison Dorée was opened on the ground floor corner where the Café Hardy had once held forth (Figs. 137 and 138). The Maison Dorée, according to a journalist writing in the 1880s, "inaugurated, in one sense, the reign of magnificent cafés where paintings, mirrors, gold, and luxurious furnishings attract and dazzle the eye. . . . Its opening was a Parisian happening."[115] The elaborate ironwork balconies and architectural detailing of the building's facades (Fig. 137) were carried through to the spacious interior, where diners discovered carved columns and coffered ceilings, wall paintings and large mirrors, multiple

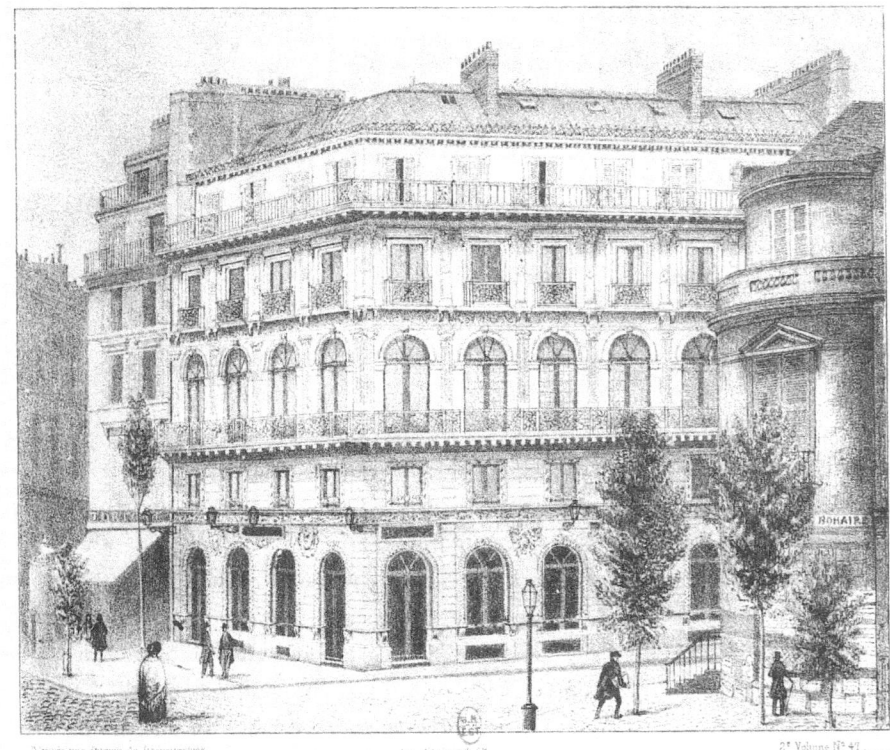

CITÉ DES ITALIENS, CONSTRUITE PAR VICTOR LEMAIRE.

LA SYLPHIDE

Journal de Mode, de Littérature et de Beaux-Arts

Direction Cité des Italiens N.1

FIGURE 137. Lemaire and Rouillard (architect and sculptor), *The Maison Dorée (boulevard des Italiens)*, 1839. Lithograph, ca. 1846. Paris, BnF, Estampes, inv. Va 285 (9). Photo: BnF, Paris.

FIGURE 138. Lemaire
and Rouillard (architect
and sculptor), *Interior of
Restaurant Maison Dorée*,
1839. Lithograph, ca. 1846.
Paris, BnF, Estampes, inv.
Va 285 (9). Photo: BnF, Paris.

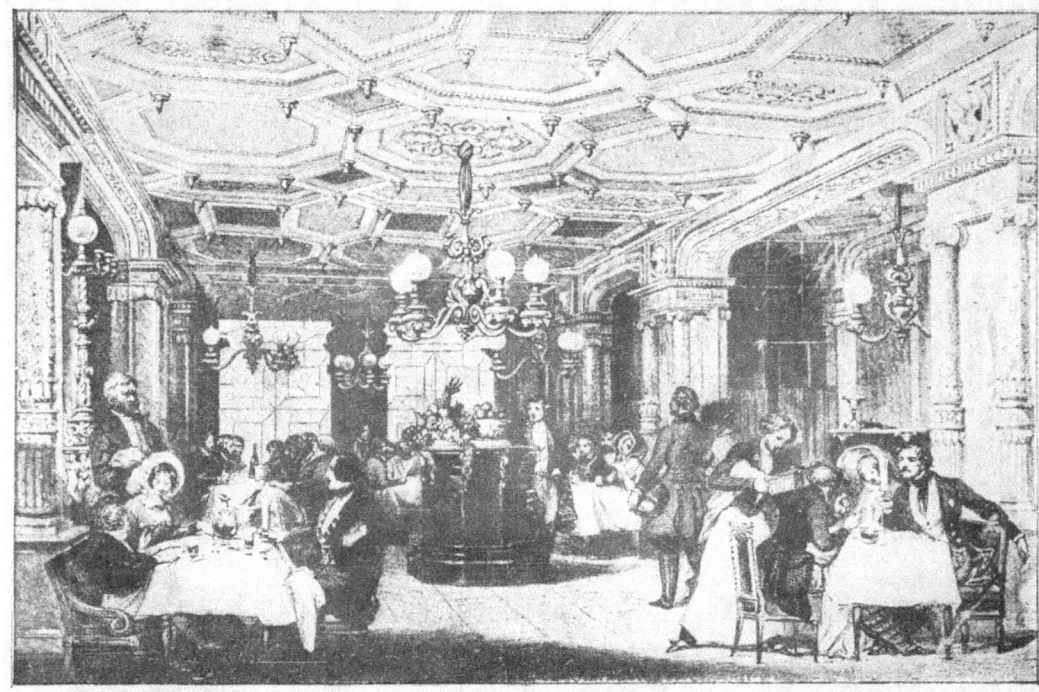

LE RESTAURANT DE LA MAISON D'OR.

chandeliers and wall sconces (Fig. 138).[116] The effect was an ambience of well-lighted and well-appointed luxury worthy of a fine and expensive meal. Gustave Flaubert's description of the Maison Dorée in *L'éducation sentimentale* renders vividly the restaurant's material excess:

One passed into a room magnificently lighted and too large for the number of guests. Cisy had purposely selected it for its pomp. A vermeil centerpiece, loaded with flowers and fruit, stood at the center of a table covered with silver plates, following the old French fashion: hors d'oeuvres dishes, filled with salt fish and spices, formed a border all around; pitchers of rosé wine chilled on ice stood at intervals; five glasses of different height were lined up before each plate, along with things whose use was unknown, thousands of ingenious eating utensils. . . . A chandelier and candelabras illuminated the apartment hung with red damask. Four servants dressed in black stood behind the leather chairs. The guests exclaimed with admiration at this spectacle, especially the private tutor.[117]

Frédéric Moreau (Flaubert's character) was invited in 1846 to a glittering private dinner at the Maison Dorée. Cisy (the hostess) ordered elaborate table decorations to impress her guests. Although our print of the dining room does not include such extraordinary measures (Fig. 138), it does suggest that even the restaurant's everyday service—the china and silver, glassware and staff—offered a high level of elegance. Many women, modestly wearing shawls and bonnets, are depicted among the diners.

La Maison Dorée was one of the first establishments to combine all the elements of a modern luxury restaurant: a rich décor, an expansive menu of rich cuisine, and an attentive staff. Its level of appointments set the standard for other Parisian restaurants. In 1843 Frédéric Soulié observed that the nearby Café de Paris was suffering because "the Maison Dorée restaurant has begun to undermine its base."[118] Maison Dorée offered a stage for gathering one's personal circle of intimates in a semi-public space. The business of catering to the fashion among well-to-do bourgeois Parisians for dining in public became one of the city's major attractions. "There is no doubt that the Parisian public has never dined out more willingly than it does now," reported a food critic in 1854; "the home-cooked meal is abandoned from one day to the next. One strives to leave the intimate and petty little circle. Every Sunday and on holidays, under the slightest pretext, the cook is dismissed and given time off until evening."[119] Today, the custom of dining out and the industry supporting it are so identified with city life that we tend to forget how much our contemporary pleasure depends upon patterns of sociability first established in the restaurants of Romantic Paris.

The City as Stage

In the city, society must depend on art to end mystification, to tell a truth which men and women can otherwise arrive at only by an often faulty process of deduction from miniaturized clues. That is to say, the relation between the audience and this art form began to be one of dependence. The theater was doing for them that which in the modern capital they could not do easily for themselves. The divisions between mystery, illusion, and deception on the one hand and truth on the other were in the mid-nineteenth century drawn into a peculiar form: authentic life, which requires no effort of decoding, appeared only under the aegis of stage art.

—Richard Sennett[120]

In his landmark study of the changes in public life during the nineteenth century, Richard Sennett draws attention to the cultural role of representations on the stage. Once alerted to the involuntary nature and meaning of clues passed in daily contacts, and thus to a projection of personality beyond immediate control, individuals adopt a defensive stance of public impassivity. Sennett describes the motives behind this process of self-defense:

A century ago, perhaps a whole class of people did experience a psychic disaster because of their attempts to ignore or suppress their impulses. But the reason they attempted to do this was logical. This was their way of coping with the confusion of public and private life. If once an emotion is clearly felt it is involuntarily shown even to strangers, then the only way to shield oneself is to try to stop feeling.[121]

Paradoxically, this systematic camouflage of personality created the longing for an arena where the physical signs of self-expression might be read unambiguously. According to Sennett, the stage was such an arena, a place where the "desire for believable and true appearances . . . first surfaced as a demand for accuracy in historical costuming."[122] The great tragic actor Talma spearheaded an early use of historically accurate costumes and gestures at the Comédie-Française in Paris, but his efforts were modest when compared to the thrilling tableaux and historical accuracy of melodramas played on the boulevard theaters of Paris (see Chapter Six).

Theatrical performances were ideal places to practice self-restraint. Audiences believed they were watching transparent representations of personality or character. They knew in advance what to expect since explanatory program notes usually sketched the plotline. The practice of lowering house lights to focus audience attention on the stage, accompanied by proscriptions against talking to one's neighbors, formalized the discipline and self-restraint that was expected of respectable audiences. Sennett remarks that "the rules for passive emotion which people used in the theater they also used out of it, to try to comprehend the emotional life of a milieu of strangers."[123] Louis-Léopold Boilly's picture of 1819, *Free Entrance to the Théâtre Ambigu-Comique* (Fig. 139), offers a rich gloss of Sennett's didactic exchange between art and life. The most striking aspect of Boilly's image is the unrestrained crush of people pushing and shoving their way into a theater. The size of the crowd attests to the popularity of boulevard melodramas—a poster announces *Les Macchabées ou la Prise de Jérusalem* by Cuvelier and Chaudezon. How might this unruly mass of human energy speak to contemporaries about passive emotion or self-restraint?

The anecdotal visual interest of Boilly's crowd and its transparent legibility were two qualities singled out by critics at the Salon of 1819. "How these common folk, these avid fans of melodrama, push forward," exclaimed Gustave Jal.

I am grateful to M. Boilly for this revel; I'm not talking about the painting. How could I talk about it? Do I have time to see if the drawing is stiff, if the coloring is garish? No, I'm far too interested in the success of this young girl who pushes to be the first to enter.[124]

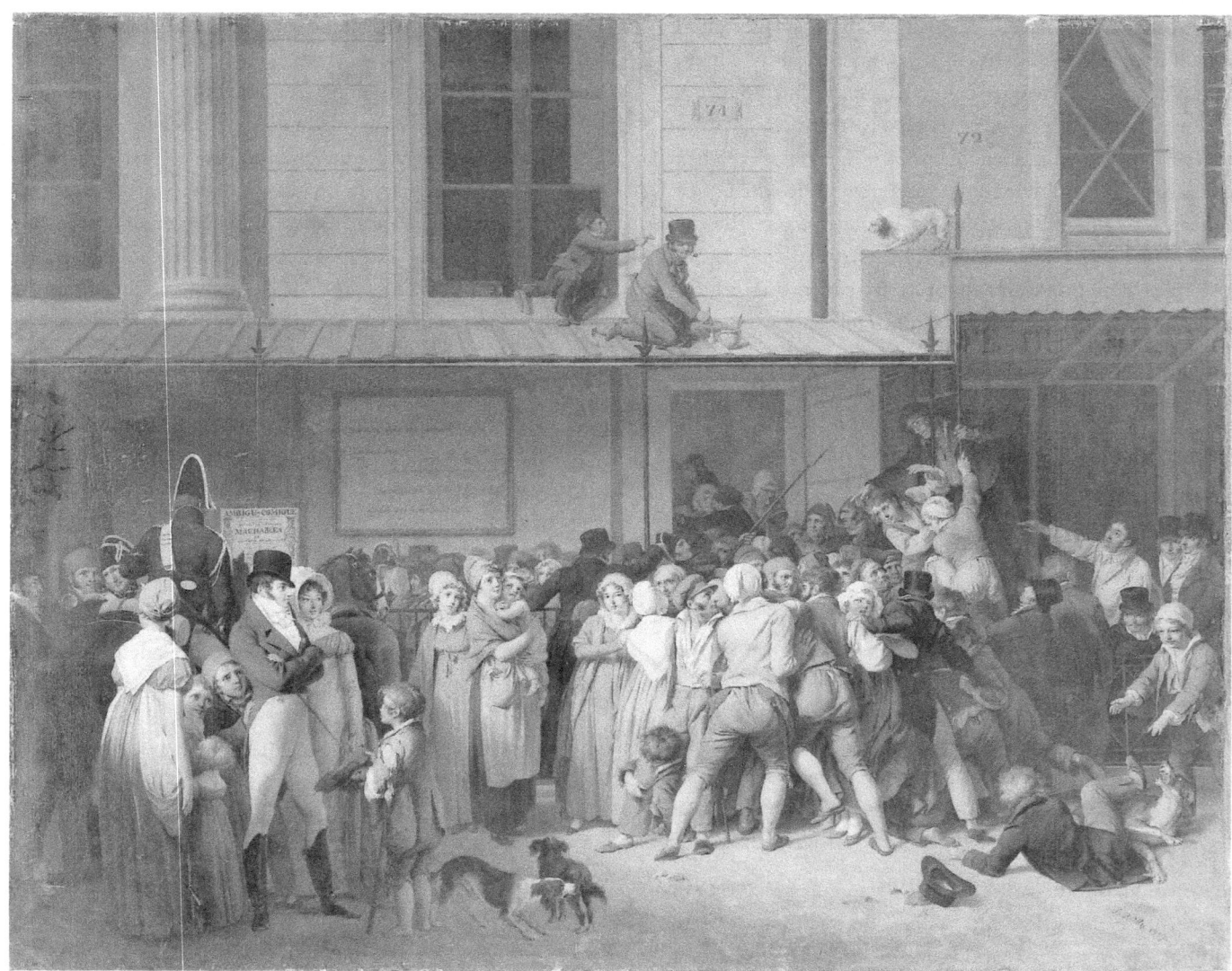

FIGURE 139.   Louis-Léopold Boilly, *Free Entrance to the Théâtre Ambigu-Comique*, 1819. Oil on canvas. Paris, Musée du Louvre, inv. RF2682 (66.6 × 80.5 cm). Photo: © RMN/Art Resource, NY/© René-Gabriel Ojeda.

Jal was so taken by the picture's illusion of truth to nature that its formal qualities were of little interest. He went on to question, however, the presence of "this handsome man wearing a red ribbon [i.e., the Legion of Honor]" and ended by hoping he would disappear: "That he should leave this spot, then, for he bothers me as much as his pretty, hard-hearted wife; these two characters spoil this nice little scene that I think I'm seeing from my window through the lens of my telescope." Another critic remarked that the work "is lacking neither effect nor even less truthfulness. The costumes, the expressions are all there in nature." He also singled out "the young man and woman who take part in the spectacle from the outside, by following with their eyes an undulating movement that would be foolhardy to approach too closely."[125]

The two figures annoying both of these writers stand near the left edge of the picture. They are clearly from a different social and economic class than those pressing to enter the theater: he wears breeches and boots, a fine white shirt under his waistcoat, and a top hat; she is a respectable lady completely covered by long dress, gloves, and bonnet. This well-dressed couple, who ignore the young boy in rags begging before them, participate in the spectacle of the scene vicariously and from a distance. They remain emotionally impassive before the vivacious grimaces of those they watch. They are masters of their emotions and their beings. Boilly literally stages for that couple the spectacle of lower class Parisians clamoring to enter the Ambigu-Comique. By extension, he also stages it for gallery viewers who are assumed to be the couple's social equals. Viewers of the picture participate in the melee vicariously—optically, and from a distance clearly established by the empty foreground.

Contemporary critics actually called the pushing and shoving of Boilly's picture a *spectacle.* The word underscores an unspoken but insistent distinction between "us" and "them" assumed by both painter and image. Jal, who wished the fancy couple would disappear, candidly imagined himself seeing the work "from my window through the lens of my telescope," a rigorously optical and spatially separate vantage point from which passive observation is the only possible attitude. Susan Siegfried argues with good reason that Boilly "presented a quite new visual frame of reference. His subjects became spectacles, scenes composed for display."[126] Her point is borne out by the later history of *Free Entrance to the Théâtre Ambigu-Comique.* The picture was purchased by the duchesse de Berry for her private gallery. Although the duchesse was known for her interest in troubadour pictures and new forms of furniture (see Chapter Four), she certainly did not buy the Boilly as a gesture of solidarity with the motley crowd pushing into the theater. The persons with whom the duchesse presumably identified were singled out in a catalogue entry for the work written in 1822 by the curator of her collection:

But, for the observer who studies the morals, character, and animated physiognomy of the human species, the most curious spectacle is

not always inside a theater; one often finds it at the door. There, guile struggles against force, politeness against rudeness, gentleness against violence. . . . There, all the passions are excited and the emotions they engender follow one another with unbelievable speed. M. Boilly . . . has caught in his picture all these movements, all these varying nuances, with as much wit as accuracy. You recognize the place and the characters in action; you hear their cries, their songs, their expressive curses; but you avoid this clamor, and you take your place alongside this smiling young woman and the elegant man who accompanies her. . . . You applaud, with her, the gibes of the rabble . . . and this applause returns to the painter who deployed such a genuine talent in this charming page.[127]

Here, in schematic form, is an outline of Sennett's complex relationship between public life and theater. The duchesse de Berry's curator assumes he is speaking to and for those who "avoid this clamor," those who stand for "politeness against rudeness" and "gentleness against violence." He identifies himself, his patron, and his readers with the well-dressed young couple. He conflates the woman's restrained amusement before the unruly crowd with the viewer's present pleasure of seeing the picture itself. Yet any outward expression of the young lady's response—she does *not* applaud in the picture—must be imagined: in public a respectable personality remains hidden behind a facade of impassive silence.

By mid-century, according to Sennett, it was de rigueur to "sneer at people who showed their emotions at a play or concert" because "restraint of emotion in the theater became a way for middle-class audiences to mark the line between themselves and the working class."[128] As might be expected, Boilly painted a sequel to *Free Entrance to the Théâtre Ambigu-Comique* in which a group of commoners, crowded into the gallery of the theater, demonstrate a full range of personal reactions to the drama they watch.[129] He also painted a very similar scene—probably conceived as a pendant—representing a bourgeois audience (Fig. 140). A woman has fainted in response to the performance. Everyone's attention shifts abruptly to the woman's involuntary loss of composure: the foreground figures literally turn their backs to the stage; an old man prepares some smelling salts. A man just behind the afflicted woman looks calmly at her rather than through his opera glass. Boilly sets up a didactic contrast between the adult calm of this onlooker and a young boy's expression of panic. The lesson is simple: we learn over time how to discipline our emotions.

The little drama of the woman's faint occupies the picture's compositional center. Boilly cleverly recorded the surrounding architecture as a frame-within-the-frame that truncates the viewer's visual field. The corner figures, who hang over the front edge of the loge, fix by their attention and spatial arrangement the picture's physical center. The narrative clarity of *The Effect of a Melodrama* masks a secondary effect at work in the image, for the viewer is assumed to be close enough to see the loge yet separated from it by an open space. Like Jal's imagined view of *Free Entrance to the Théâtre Ambigu-Comique*, viewers must imagine themselves witnessing the faint—perhaps through an opera glass—from the proximate distance of a facing loge. Boilly designed the image to ensure that viewers would be impassive spectators ultimately exonerated from taking any action. Yet the picture's rigorous frontality, and the alignment of its center with the principal vantage point—we look across space exactly to the woman's face—incite identification with the characters crowding around. These formal adjustments tend to collapse the emotional and social differences separating viewers from the afflicted woman and her companions. We worry, like the old man with the smelling salts, about reviving the victim and returning her to consciousness so that her embarrassing and involuntary display of self might be erased in a return to impassive normalcy. The picture forces viewers to adopt a distanced, optical relationship to the physiological response that ought to be suppressed in the theater but that seems to have surprised this overly sensitive woman.

FIGURE 140.   Louis-Léopold Boilly, *The Effect of a Melodrama*, ca. 1830. Oil on canvas. Versailles, Musée Lambinet, inv. 83.2.1 (32.5 × 41.2 cm). Photo: © RMN/ Art Resource, NY/© Philipp Bernard.

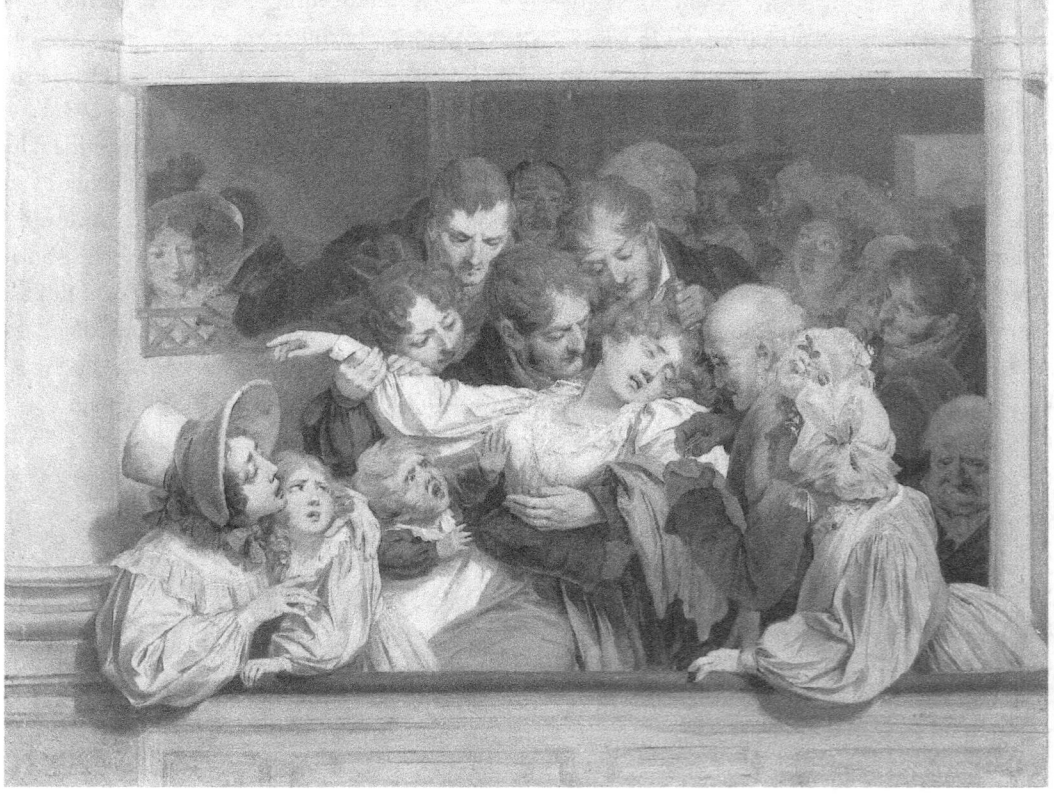

The image is both a lesson in bourgeois self-discipline and a warning about what women should be allowed to see.

Boilly's scenes of incidents inside and outside the theater instantiate a myth that certain viewers are able to look up and down the social scale without threatening their emotional detachment. A formal expression of this idea is the indeterminate distance at which Boilly locates viewers from the principal action, along with sufficient foreground clues to suggest that the intervening space cannot be bridged. Susan Siegfried points out that Boilly places viewers "partly in the scene while being able to view it pleasurably as spectacle," thus locating them in that "indeterminate positioning of the spectator . . . integral to the bourgeois ideology of universal access and social unity."[130] This placement corresponds to the passive silence of bourgeois withdrawal sketched by Richard Sennett. It also implies the power to move through the spectacle of people and things without being touched by them. "By means of the spectacle," writes Guy Debord, "the ruling order discourses endlessly upon itself in an uninterrupted monologue of self-praise. The spectacle is the self-portrait of power in the age of power's totalitarian rule over the conditions of existence. The fetishistic appearance of pure objectivity in spectacular relationships conceals their true character as relationships between human beings and between classes."[131] Debord is discussing developments of the twentieth century, but his point pertains to those decades of the nineteenth century when the Parisian bourgeoisie emerged as the dominant class within the city's social and economic life, and when a myth of "universal access and social unity" was produced to mask the facts of social and economic domination.

Reference to the "fetishistic appearance of pure objectivity" offers a timely return to Boilly's pictures. They presume and construct "spectacular relationships" between viewers and subjects by mobilizing an astonishing illusion of direct transcription and a seemingly objective truth to nature. Gustave Jal was so riveted by the spectacle of the crowd in *Free Entrance to the Théâtre Ambigu-Comique* (Fig. 139) that he could not be bothered to talk about the picture's drawing or color. The play of space, light, and expressions in *The Effect of a Melodrama* (Fig. 140) contributes to the viewer's

pleasure of reading effortlessly and transparently the clues of inner life written legibly on each character's physiognomy. Both pictures present a society within the reach of sensibility and understanding. Neither challenges the viewer's identity or limits—a politeness of distance that respects the bourgeois code of impassive observation. In a short autobiography prepared near the end of his life, Boilly emphasized, to use the words of Susan Siegfried, "self-reliance and industry."[132] Siegfried interprets Boilly's text as "a relatively precocious expression of the vision of the self-made man," an early example of an artist who thought of himself as a bourgeois. How that view of the world became art is manifest in Boilly's two pictures, where a balance of proximity and distance is both emotionally passive and historically grounded.

The peculiarity of Boilly's formulation is clarified by comparing *The Effect of a Melodrama* (Fig. 140) to *The Fifth Act at the Gaîté*, a later lithograph of a nearly identical subject by Honoré Daumier (Fig. 141). Daumier also uses the theater's architecture to frame his figures, but not to center and anchor them in the visual field; rather, a single column opening to spaces at each side suggests this is a fleeting image snapped incidentally from a larger whole. Daumier's theater, writes Ségolène Le Men, "is one of lost moments and unexpected centerings of attention, not so much dedicated to the time of the representation as to that of the spectator or, even more, of the spectacle."[133] The loge is seen from slightly off center, which accounts for its skewed rendering and explains why all the figures look towards the viewer's right, presumably in the direction of the stage. Moreover, our vantage point is slightly higher than the people we see, since we are able to look into the loge and to penetrate its depth. We have access to all of the figures and to the range of their responses: from a child sleeping in boredom to the wet handkerchiefs of the women nearby; from the stupefied daze of the foreground man to the look of consternation on his colleague just behind. All this is observed from a position both too close at hand and out of synch with the framing architecture. Unlike Boilly's orderly spectacle, it is hard to imagine ourselves in a similar loge exactly facing the one we see.

Daumier's lithograph situates us in a completely invented space that is simultaneously visual and textual. Although he

FIGURE 141.   Honoré Daumier, *The Fifth Act at the Gaîté* from *Tout ce qu'on voudra* (plate 28), 1848. Lithograph. Paris, BnF, Estampes, inv. Dc 180b rés (34) (36.1 × 27.3 cm). Photo: BnF, Paris.

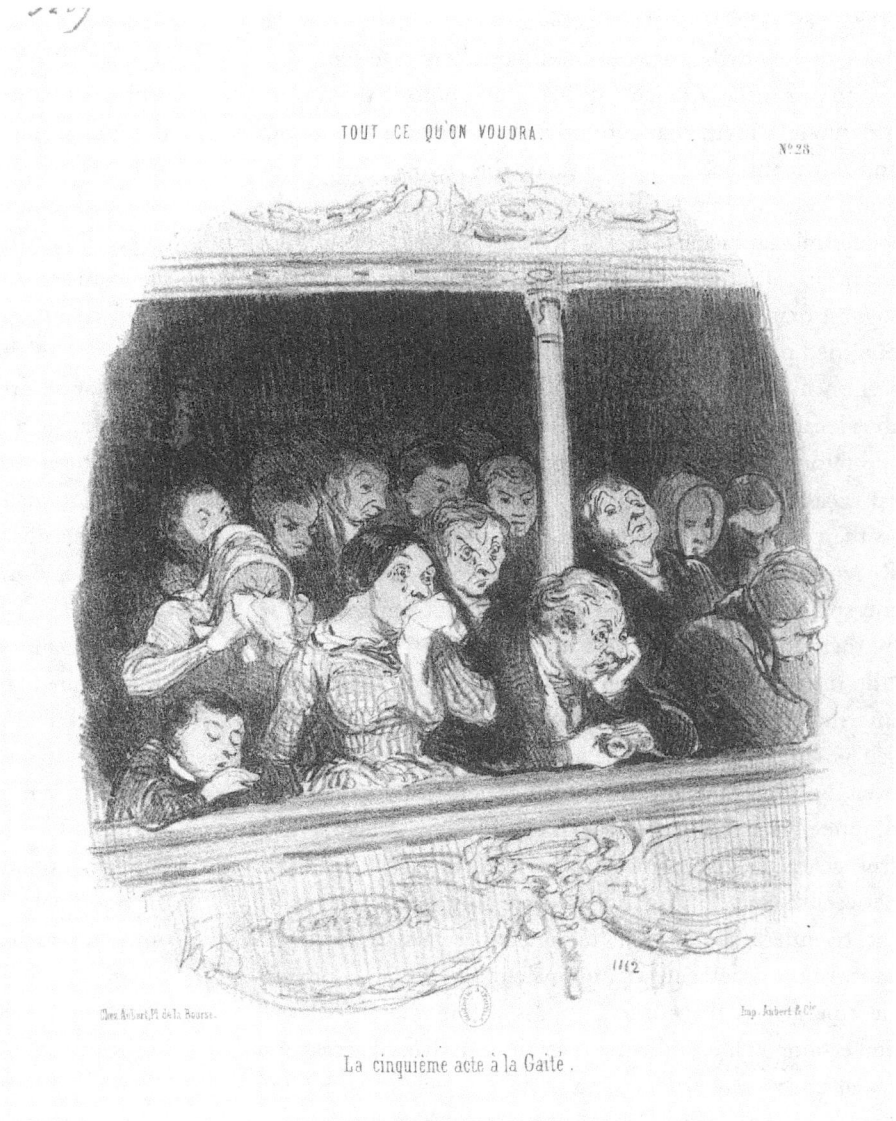

seldom composed his own captions, Daumier was certainly aware that the finished ensemble of image, title, and caption would disrupt the smooth mechanics of pictorial illusion. His manner of drawing contributes to this effect: the wiry, quick rhythms of his hand—fully apparent in *The Fifth Act at the Gaîté*—elide figures with one another or into the ground of black space, and link them visually to descriptive elements like the balcony decorations. Léon Rosenthal remarked long ago that the technical demands of lithography "singularly furthered the development of drawing. It made drawing more flexible, it encouraged the search for a summary, elliptical, synthetic rendering. . . . Ardent, colorful, powerful, rich in signification, Daumier's drawing style has the exceptional strength that conveys authority."[134] Being led to recognize the artist's voice in the material of representation, or to realize that the vantage point disrupts illusionism, forces viewers to acknowledge that the image eschews passive transcription in order to comment critically upon the depicted subject. Daumier mobilizes a critical edge where Boilly fostered neutral observation. These pictorial differences suggest diverging views of middle class life. If Boilly consciously aligns himself and his art with the bourgeoisie of Paris, where does Daumier call home?

DAUMIER WAS BORN IN MARSEILLES, the son of artisan parents: his father was a glazier and framemaker; his mother a seamstress. Daumier's father moved to Paris in 1815 to launch a new career in literature. His family followed the next year, but the father's literary career never took off. The family was poor and frequently moved when rent came due. Formal schooling for the three children was out of the question. The future artist was educated on the streets of Paris, especially while working as a notary's errand boy. By chance, one of his father's early literary patrons was Alexandre Lenoir, founder of the Musée des Monuments français (see Chapter Four). Lenoir took young Honoré under his protection, gave him drawing lessons, and encouraged him to study the masters in the Louvre.

Daumier learned early the relatively new printing technique of lithography, which had been discovered about 1798 by a German named Aloys Senefelder. Lithography differs importantly from engraving or etching. In those older processes, plates are prepared by gouging the image into a metal printing surface with tools or acid. By contrast, lithographic designs are drawn directly with a grease pencil on a prepared slab of limestone. When the stone is moistened with water and inked, the oil-based ink adheres to the greasy areas of design but not to the undrawn wet areas. When pressed against a sheet of paper only the design is transferred. Thus, lithography is a fluid and direct process that responds to the movements and pressure of the artist's hand. It produces a nuance of line, a broad range of grays, and powerful contrasts of black and white. Lithography is also faster and cheaper

than other types of print imagery, since artists work right on the printing surface rather than passing their designs to craftsmen for transfer to a printing plate. Lithographs can be printed in large numbers to further reduce the price of each sheet. Lithographic stones can be ground down for reuse after an edition has been completed. All of these factors made lithography an ideal medium for rendering current events, and for circulating a greater number of images than any competing visual form before the advent of photography (see Chapter Eight). Indeed, the violinist Niccolò Paganini discovered in 1831, much to his displeasure, the power of lithography to shape public opinion (see Chapter Six).

Daumier became a master of lithography. Within a few years he was supporting himself, his parents, and his siblings by producing illustrations for books and journals. He also drew a group of powerful political images for which he became justly famous (Fig. 157). Most of Daumier's political work was published in the early 1830s for projects sponsored by Charles Philipon (Fig. 156), whose print shop in the passage Véro-Dodat was a center of left-wing political activity after the Revolution of 1830. Daumier was one of Philipon's most controversial designers: in 1832 he spent six months in prison for a scathing caricature of King Louis-Philippe as Gargantua. Yet Daumier lived simply. "What more do I need?" he explained; "two fried eggs in the morning, and in the evening a herring or a cutlet. To that add a glass of Beaujolais, some tobacco for my pipe, and anything more would be superfluous."[135] About 1841 he moved to the quai d'Anjou on the Cité near the geographic center of Paris, but a neighborhood that remained something of an isolated enclave for lack of connecting bridges. Théodore de Banville has left a vivid account of Daumier's spare workspace in the attic of his building along the quai:

It is impossible to imagine a place less luxurious, more severely bare, from which all ornaments were rigidly proscribed. On the walls, painted in a quiet clear gray, nothing was hung except an unframed lithograph of the *Pariahs* by Préault, the notorious group refused by the Salon jury in the first skirmishes of Romanticism. A square, black stove in varnished sheet-iron, some benches set against the wall, some stuffed portfolios spilling over with sketches so that they could no longer be closed—that is all one saw in the large studio, bright and light, except for the little table on which Daumier worked his stones.[136]

The subject matter of Daumier's art was fully committed to Paris and to Parisians, yet he preferred to live at the margins of the city's social whirl and urban glitter.

Nonetheless, Daumier was not a hermit. He moved in the circle of writers and poets around Charles Baudelaire, who lived next door, and he socialized with artists and critics like Corot (Fig. 98), Barye (Fig. 90), Courbet (Fig. 101), and Champfleury in the nearby Brasserie Andler. His vision was informed by the life of bohemian Paris and sustained by the curiosity of a flâneur roaming the streets, theaters, and public spaces of the city. Daumier's friends and milieu were not those of bourgeois Paris. His fragmented, ironic, and politically committed way of seeing and recording the city has little in common with Boilly's pretensions of unfettered vision, emotional detachment, and upbeat social unity. The two men came from and spoke to very different constituencies. One place where their otherwise separate worlds might intersect was the annual exhibition of contemporary art known as the Paris Salon. It was the art world's equivalent of the new urban spaces where schools, genres, and aesthetic theories were defined, displayed, and debated before an avid and ever more heterogeneous public.

THE SALON regularly attracted large crowds of diverse visitors—numbers astonishing even by today's standards of blockbuster museum exhibitions. About forty thousand people drawn from all walks of life visited the Salon of 1846 each week, with crowds on Sundays running as high as eight thousand.[137] This in itself was not new: Thomas Crow has shown that eighteenth-century Salons brought together Parisians of every social class, and that finely dressed aristocrats regularly rubbed elbows with ordinary workers in the galleries of the Louvre.[138] The vast crowds drawn to the artistic booty of the Musée Napoléon during the Empire also comprised a social mix that visitors to Paris—especially from England—frequently noted and admired (see Chapter Three). But writers and critics of the late 1840s sensed that something about the annual exhibitions had changed. Gustave Planche complained in 1847 that "the taste for large works, the taste for grand style weakens from day to day. Apart from a few rare exceptions, the Salon is more a bazaar than a passionate struggle among sincere talents who are completely devoted to study, understanding, and the expression of beauty."[139] In the long introduction to his own booklet about the 1847 Salon, Théophile Thoré blamed the state of affairs on a shift at the core of French culture:

But he who accepts, without reflection, the domination of material things houses tyranny in his own heart, because he gives up everything that constitutes mankind: intelligence, heroism, ideal passion. I would rather be condemned to the king's galleys with a warm and gallant heart than be a millionaire in Paris with the instincts of a moneylender.... What grim fatalism has snapped all the poetic strings of the human soul, sensitive like aeolian harps to the open air, to keep only a metal wire? That's where France is now.... Art in general has become an industry instead of a passion for artists, a luxury instead of an inspired and religious cult for the public.[140]

Thoré, like Planche, deplores the fact that artworks are made and exhibited, discussed and bought as if only merchandise produced by yet one more industry. He blames the increased willingness of people to be dominated by material things. Without actually naming a culprit, Thoré points his finger at the materialist preoccupations of the bourgeoisie.

Baudelaire was more direct. His collection of essays on the 1846 Salon (see Chapter Six) was addressed to the bourgeois of Paris and acknowledged—with a certain irony—that a profound change was reorganizing the old order of art appreciation: "Some are savants, others owners: one glorious day will come when savants will be owners and owners savants. Then, your power will be complete and no one will protest it. While waiting for this supreme harmony, it's fair that those who are only owners long to become savants."[141] Baudelaire recognized the political and economic power of the Parisian bourgeoisie. He cleverly reserved for himself the critical task of enlightening them in matters of art. We might question Baudelaire's sincerity, but he at least pretended to believe that the bourgeoisie was not lost to the arts, a point he had argued with gusto in 1845:

And first of all, with regard to that impertinent term *bourgeois*, we announce that we in no way share the prejudices of our great *artistic* colleagues who, for several years, have done their best to anathematize this inoffensive being who would ask nothing more than to like good painting, if these gentlemen knew how to make him understand it, and if artists would show some to him more often.[142]

One of Baudelaire's "great artistic colleagues" was Jules Champfleury, whose own review of the 1846 Salon disparaged the pretentious posturings of *le bourgeois* before works of art.

Champfleury specifically contrasted such pretensions to the naïve but earnest intuitions of *le peuple*. After relating the comments of "a heavy and brutish wine merchant" who expressed great admiration for the work of Delacroix, he asks rhetorically:

Doesn't this conversation prove that a commoner is worth more than a bourgeois, in the sense that someone told him "Delacroix is a great painter!" and he firmly believed it? Moreover, the bourgeois, whose artistic sense is even less well-developed than the commoner, has a mania for discussion. He hopes to prove that he *knows*. He exclaims: "Delacroix doesn't know how to draw." And since he can't understand this painting he runs away, he's afraid.[143]

Champfleury raised the critical stakes by suggesting that art appreciation depends less upon competence or initiation (which was Baudelaire's point) than personal sincerity, which he believed intersects issues of class and power. Champfleury was not alone. Many critics of the late 1840s felt that the balance of power in aesthetic matters had shifted. They recognized that bourgeois viewers now played a pivotal role in making or breaking the reputations of working artists. The corollary, much disparaged in the critical press, was that artists increasingly thought of themselves as producers of goods for the market.

François-Auguste Biard's *Four o'clock at the Salon* summarizes several contemporary stereotypes of the bourgeois viewer (Fig. 142). Biard's painting was a must see at the Salon

of 1847, where Thoré remarked with some dismay that "M. Biard is forever gathering an impenetrable crowd in front of his *Four o'clock at the Salon*."[144] Most of the viewers in that compact mass were probably attracted by the picture's comic appeal, which was described by A.-H. Delaunay in one of the many guide books produced for the Salon's viewing public:

Although M. Biard has given up, bit by bit, the type of painting that made his name so popular and gave rise to so many genuine smiles, he has not completely renounced it. *Four o'clock at the Salon* is an excellent caricature of the present in which red outfits, gathered together at the extreme left of the long gallery, begin to cry out with a Stentor-like voice that will one day make the walls of the Museum crumble, like the one that fell at Jericho long ago to the sound of a less discordant music: *Gentlemen, we are closing*. Nothing so amusing as the astonishment, the fear, and the smiles of neighbors surprised without warning by this tremendous cry coming all at once from twenty mouths almost as big as the place du Carrousel. A comic scene of perfect naturalness.[145]

Delaunay's focus on the comedy of closing the Louvre at the end of the day does not exhaust the work's historical interest, because the guards occupy only a small part of the image. Equally important is Biard's rendering of the crowd's social diversity. At the left, a group of young, long-haired bohemians, dressed in black and wearing extravagant scarves, react with exaggerated gestures of consternation and brooding to the works on view. Just behind this trio, and with his back to the wall, stands a bearded, hatless man in a worker's blouse. To his right are three men in suits and top hats who could pass for critics or connoisseurs. At the extreme right, between two of the bellowing guards, a slightly stooped older man in black (perhaps a priest) focuses intently upon a printed sheet, which is probably a guide to the exhibition similar to the one just cited. This man prefers to read explanations about the pictures on view than to look at them. Finally, at the center of the work, a gaggle of respectable women in shawls and bonnets mutually admire a large picture. One of them (perhaps mother of the startled young girl) raises a hand to blunt the voice of the leading guard. She stretches to touch with her other hand the shoulder of a dandyish fop in a white wig. This figure, the only one who looks out of the painting

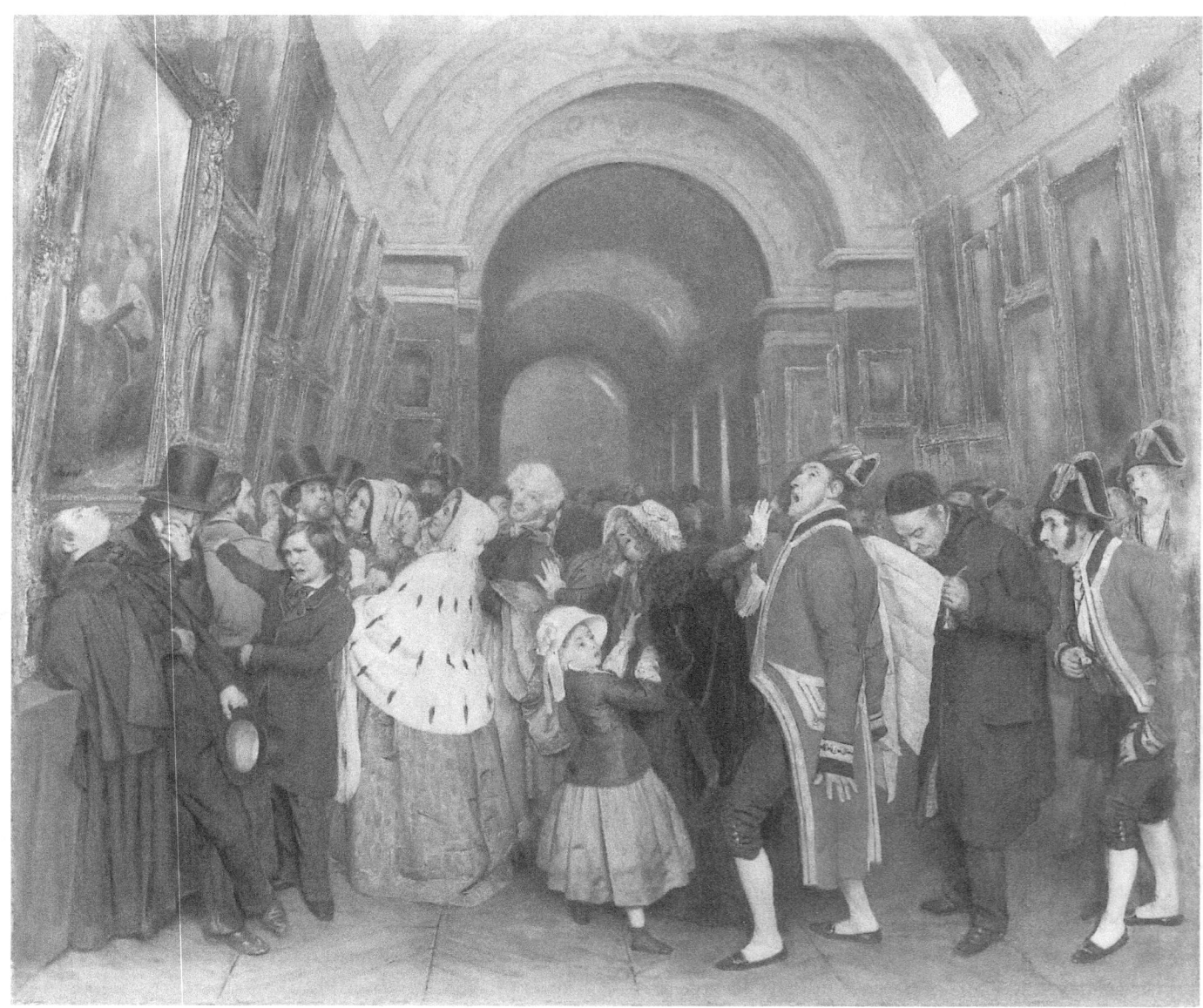

FIGURE 142.   François-Auguste Biard, *Four o'clock at the Salon (Closing Time)*, 1847. Oil on canvas. Paris, Musée du Louvre, inv. RF2347 (57 × 67 cm). Photo: © RMN/Art Resource, NY/© Daniel Arnaudet.

towards the viewer, is himself depicted within the picture being admired by the ladies. Biard records the full range of personalities and classes frequenting the galleries of the Paris Salon with an emotional passivity that refuses to comment on the expertise of any one group relative to another.

The visual structure of Biard's image is identical to that of Boilly from almost thirty years earlier (Fig. 139). Both feature a slice of empty space between the viewer and the depicted crowd, even though we seem to share their world and to view them from approximately the same height. The result, already noted in Boilly's picture, is the vague sensation of being both part of the assembly and physically removed from it. This reserve of psychologically separate proximity invests the viewer with a visual mastery that unifies a social field that is actually fragmented and diverse. The crowd becomes an unthreatening spectacle subject to a mastering bourgeois gaze. Biard's painting does differ from the Boilly in at least one important respect. Boilly's crowd is held at a greater psychological distance thanks to the bourgeois couple who both regard the people impassively and present viewers with intervening templates for their own behavior before the picture. Biard provides no such intermediaries. Viewers are situated in close proximity to the crowd without role models for evaluating what they see.

There is, however, one important exception: the central figure surrounded by admiring women who acknowledges the viewer's presence, and is simultaneously represented within a picture hanging on the gallery wall. His doubled appearance proposes a different kind of cultural model, a person who arranges to appear *as art* at the same time that he appears in public as a *viewer* of art. There is more at stake here than comic vanity. Biard articulates graphically that works of art have the power to transform persons into commodities, and to circulate those commodities before the public in ways likely to elicit discussion—perhaps even admiration and praise. The dandy in the Louvre, to paraphrase Guy Debord, figures a celebrity status open to anyone sufficiently rich to commission art; that is, possessing *"power* and *leisure*—the power to decide and the leisure to consume which are the alpha and omega of a process that is never questioned."[146] In fact, one of the most prestigious markers of material success in mid-century Paris was to appear at the Salon in the guise of a painted portrait (see Chapter Six).

Critics often complained that servicing the industry of portraiture was ruining French painting. "You have to admit that painters of modern portraits are the most miserable of men," remarked Théophile Gautier in 1837; "never before in history has dress been so contrary to the development of the visual arts. . . . Painters who take up this disagreeable occupation of representing us in duplicate are compelled to copy with a scrupulous exactitude: we are not extraordinarily beautiful, but surely we could be a little less horrible."[147] Yet the number of portraits exhibited at the Salon continued to grow exponentially, from 500 in 1841 to 673 in 1844. This statistical rise near mid-century is usually ascribed to the pretensions of newly rich patrons. A parallel surging market for small pictures—especially landscapes and scenes of genre—can be related to the modest size of bourgeois apartments. But artists were not simply victims of the economic system, for they also knew how to make it work. "I hope to do a lot of portraits," remarked Théodore Chassériau in 1840, "to make myself known first of all, and then to earn some money in order to gain the necessary independence that will allow me to fulfill the duties of a history painter."[148] Serious young painters were perfectly willing to enter the flourishing industry of making portraits in order to buy themselves a future of artistic freedom.

The cultural prestige of portraits was surely driven by the symbolic value, which belongs to no particular social formation, of placing oneself before the public eye. The astonishing trajectory of portraiture in Romantic Paris cannot be fully explained by economic forces or class allegiances. Nor do artists align themselves neatly into camps: Baudelaire opened his essay on the Salon of 1845 by suggesting that "bourgeois" should not be used disparagingly since, after all, "there are plenty of bourgeois among artists."[149] Boilly, Biard, and Chassériau are three examples among many that support his claim. Finally, museums and art galleries are far from radical spaces: for a person to appear on the walls of the Louvre remained a conservative gesture enacting known cultural values. The question is whether ambitions of respectability fully account for the pronounced spike in desire to be presented within the established, high culture arena of the Paris Salon. That would be a materialist history of an expanding, social climbing bourgeoisie constantly lusting after cultural power. By contrast, a history of culture might read a contemporary demand for the certainties of portraiture as a reaction to the unsettling experience of truly radical venues of self-presentation that forced people to appear without framing structures or established values. Among the most unorthodox, unpredictable, and modern of such social situations was riding the omnibus.

The Self in Motion

The idea to equip Paris with vehicles of public transport has a long history. A service offering passage for five sous along established routes through the city was first established in 1662. The carriages on these routes, according to Maxime du Camp, "[were] almost exclusively reserved for the bourgeoisie; a few nobles occasionally showed up in them, but . . . with regard to the common people, as one said at the time, it was strictly out of the question."[150] This early bus service lasted only about fifteen years. The most surprising part of the story is that few attempts were made to replace it for more than two centuries. As late as 1819 the Prefect of Police refused to approve requests for establishing a system of public transportation serving the boulevards and the quais of the Seine on the grounds that their frequent stops would unduly block traffic. Only in 1828, after the feasibility of carriages had been proved in Bordeaux (1827) and Nantes (1826), was the Entreprise Générale des Omnibus allowed to circulate on the streets of Paris. Soon there were one hundred carriages serving fixed stations and following pre-ordained routes according to a regular schedule.

Omnibus: the word itself was new. Maxime du Camp, like so many other commentators of his day, fully approved its layered complexity of meaning:

The name is a masterpiece. It is simultaneously easy to remember, peculiar because of its exotic origin, and it contains a complete definition. Indeed, the new coaches were for everyone; that fact ought to ensure their success and end up making them essential to the population.[151]

The first carriages were designed to carry twelve passengers and were drawn by three horses. They soon proved too small, too unwieldy to maneuver in the narrow streets of Paris and—despite their immediate popularity—unable to turn a profit. Longer and more narrow models were designed with fourteen places and a fifteenth jumpseat [strapontin]. Two horses were the preferred locomotion. Within a few years many other companies openly competed with the Compagnie Générale des Omnibus, each with distinctly decorated vehicles and fanciful names: an 1839 guide to Paris lists fifteen lines, including Favorites, Dames Blanches, Citadines,

Hirondelles, Béarnaise, Écossaises, and Gazelles.[152] This profusion might have become unmanageable were it not for the transfer [correspondance], an important innovation begun about 1834 that allowed passengers to pay their fare on one line and to switch to another line for free when continuing a single journey. The transfer, remarked Maxime du Camp, "is why you can go from Bercy to the porte Maillot [i.e., completely across Paris] for only 30 centimes; it's hard to cover distances like that for less money."[153] Anyone who has ridden today's Paris Métro will recognize that *strapontins* and *correspondances* are features of public transportation that did not disappear with the horse-drawn carriages of the omnibus.

The practical and economic advantages of riding the omnibus were certainly reasons for its commercial success. But the new transport was equally fascinating for the novelty of its experience—a social dimension that informs images like the lithograph of Victor Ratier based on a drawing by Fournier (Fig. 143). Here, the omnibus is not depicted as a thing seen from the outside. Nor is the image exactly a view of the interior. Rather, the viewer is assumed to be a rider seated at the center of a bench identical to and facing the one depicted. The print offers a visual catalogue of the various expressions elicited by the conductor's calculation that one more body ought to fit. It engages the fact that a trip on the omnibus implied contact with a mix of ages, genders, and social types—all cramped together and eyeing one another from their tiny piece of the bench. The experience not only inspired visual artists; it also seemed to incarnate city life in a way that writers like Louis Huart found worthy of comment:

Is our life anything more than a trip in the omnibus? Like omnibus travelers, we all arrive from *who knows where*; we take our place next to those already settled into theirs; we make a few acquaintances among the people traveling with us. If they get off along the way, their recollection is soon erased from our memory by other travelers who come to take their place; next, in the omnibus as in the world at large, we step on each other's feet because the ranks are everywhere tightly compacted and we try to make our way without thinking of our neighbors; finally, when the omnibus arrives at its station at the end of the journey, all of these travelers coming *from who knows where* disperse and disappear to go *who knows where*.[154]

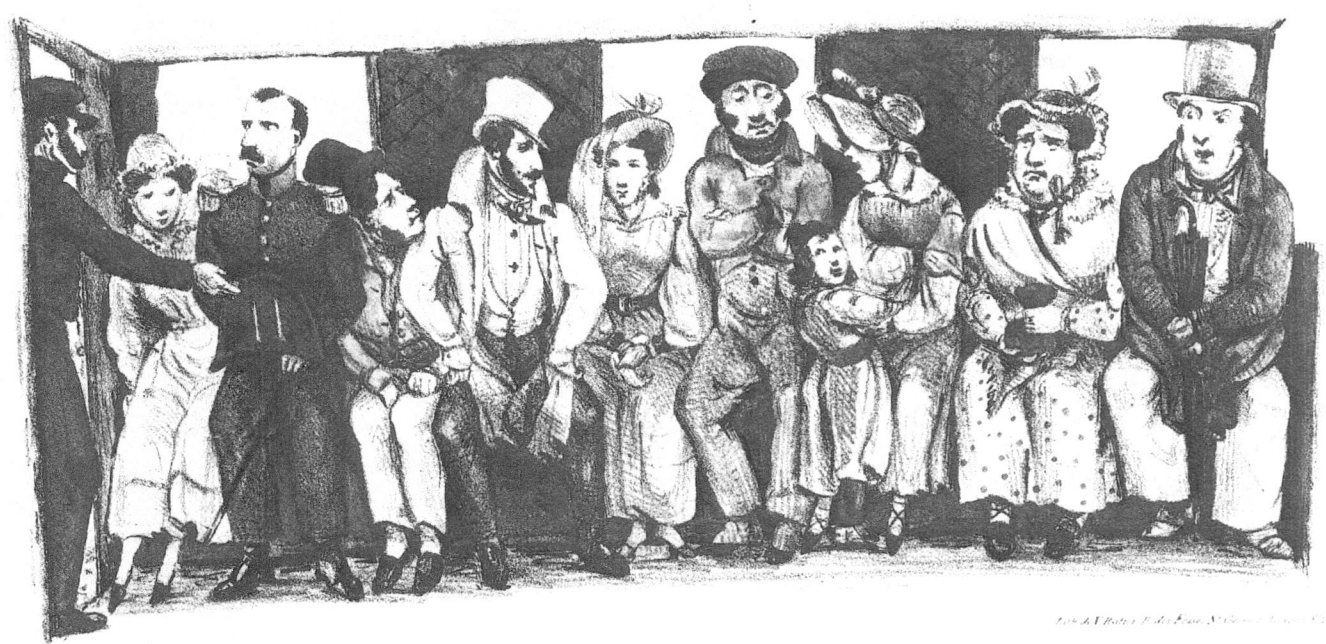

Un banc d'Omnibus.

Trois, six et trois...... huit, encore une place! serrez-vous Messieurs et Dames.

FIGURE 143.   Victor Ratier (after Fortuny de Fournier), *A Sample of Parisian Life: Seat on the Omnibus from the Madeleine to the porte Saint-Martin*, ca. 1830. Colored lithograph. Paris, Musée Carnavalet, inv. Moeurs PC 066 bis/4 (35 × 27 cm). Photo: © PMVP/Toumazet.

Uncertainty about those with whom one travels is the kernel of Huart's little allegory. Most voyagers were coming from unknown regions and headed for equally unknown destinations, so that the time and space shared in the omnibus were functions of a completely chance encounter. "Here more than anywhere else in the city Parisians were objects to each other," concludes Richard D. E. Burton; "contacts, such as they were, were fleeting and 'segmental' in character and, in general, the omnibus furnished an image of a thoroughly atomized and divided society."[155] Upon this atomized field, deprived of markers indicating social or economic rank, Parisians appeared to one another in a novel and suspiciously

indeterminate guise. Like the flip side of a coin, the contemporary explosion in high culture modes of self-representation developed in reaction to a progressive flattening of hierarchies in urban life. Dining in a luxury restaurant or displaying oneself on the walls of the Louvre were rearguard attempts to affirm personal prestige in a public sphere increasingly defined by collective experiences like the omnibus.

Ratier's lithograph focuses precisely on the spectacle of those directly across from us. It offers no clues as to who is crowding us left or right. No eye contact establishes an emotional link with those we see. The print forces us to look straight ahead and to suppress every awareness of our immediate physical state. It instantiates an omnibus frame of mind that was much remarked by contemporaries. "Regular omnibus riders, regardless of sex, are somber, silent creatures, concentrating on themselves," reported the author of *Paris-en-Omnibus* of 1854; "the omnibus makes them timid and misanthropic. . . . They sit next to one another without speaking."[156] Yet this self-imposed isolation could break down at certain moments, as noted by a German visitor to Paris in 1839:

The driver stops and you mount the few steps of the convenient little staircase and look about for a place in the car, where benches extend lengthwise on the right and the left, with room for up to sixteen people. You've hardly set foot in the car when it starts rolling again. . . . You reach calmly into your wallet and pay the fare. If you happen to be sitting reasonably far from the conductor, the money travels from hand to hand among the passengers; the well-dressed lady takes it from the workingman in the blue jacket and passes it on. This is all accomplished easily, in routine fashion, and without any bother.[157]

Of key interest in this account is the willingness of omnibus riders to engage in minimal forms of social exchange with strangers when it was a question of facilitating the journey itself. This is especially true when the exchange involved money rather than conversation. Everyone understood that the omnibus offered a product—an inexpensive and relatively fast access to distant parts of Paris. Climbing aboard meant adopting the comportment of nearly inanimate consumers linked together by nothing more than a desire to make the voyage and an ability to pay the fare (in this respect the omnibus paved the way for railway travel). Huart fashioned the omnibus ride as an allegory of life. It was also a microcosm of the implicit social leveling and strictly economic hierarchy of consumer culture.

The success of the omnibus registers an enormous shift in the way Parisians thought about themselves and their city. Its banalization of urban travel "drastically changed the thousand-year relationship between time and distance that had existed up to then," remarks François Loyer; "for the first time in its history, Paris exceeded the scale of walking distance; there is a clear connection between the opening of the first parcels of land outside the walls, beginning in 1824, and the birth of the omnibus four years later."[158] Loyer is right to link the development of new neighborhoods like the Nouveau Quartier Poissonnière to the rediscovery of the omnibus after two centuries of neglect. The ease of travel to outlying areas of town was surely a practical factor in settling them. There is also a symbolic linkage between these two developments. The new sections of Paris were designed on a scale that sited monuments at the end of visual perspectives (Fig. 131), produced streets with a horizontal coherence (Fig. 133), and reminded inhabitants of their place in an urban fabric larger and more complex than traditional ideas of a geographically limited and functionally insular quartier. The omnibus made it possible for many classes of people to imagine themselves living within an urban framework larger than their immediate surroundings, to imagine themselves as part of a mobile and cosmopolitan culture, to actually use on a daily basis those parts of Paris barely visible at the end of a long perspective.

TODAY it would be hard to convince weary commuters, jammed into the trams of the Paris Métro, that their experience was once pursued as a thoroughly modern experience. Yet riding the omnibus made the thrill of random diversity—central to the flâneur's carefully crafted lifestyle—accessible to everyone. The duchesse de Berry reportedly liked to ride them incognito and rumors of her adventures only added to the cachet of traveling by omnibus.[159] Public acceptance of the omnibus mirrored the breakdown in social hierarchies characteristic of commercial spaces designed to serve clients from every walk of life. Inhabitants of Romantic Paris learned to live in their city with an enlarged sense of geographic reach and greater expectations for its urban spectacle. Soon the arcades, with their narrow corridors of tiny shops tucked into old neighborhoods, were abandoned in favor of open-plan stores designed to entice consumers with affordable products of every sort. This change of heart, and its impact upon the visual arts, provides the setting for our next chapter.

·◡· CHAPTER 8

Art and Industry

Constance Pillerault was the head clerk of a dry goods store called The Petit Matelot, *the first of such shops that have since opened in Paris with any number of painted signs, floating banners, balancing displays full of shawls, ties arranged like castles of playing cards, and a thousand other commercial seductions, fixed prices, decorative strips of cloth, posters, illusions and optical effects taken to such a level of perfection that shop windows have become commercial poems. The low prices on all these so-called "novelties" at* The Petit Matelot *gave it an unheard-of popularity in one of the least favorable parts of Paris for commercial fashionability.*

—Honoré de Balzac[1]

ÉSAR BIROTTEAU, the principal character in Balzac's novel of the same name, first spies the woman he would marry in the doorway of *The Petit Matelot*, herself an attraction among the many others on view in the store. Balzac's description of her workplace captures the material and visual splendor that were essential components of a new kind of retailing in Paris: the dry goods store [magasin de nouveautés], where shopping was as much an adventure for the senses or an occasion for flirting as a commercial exchange. Being a head clerk [premier commis] in a small perfume shop on the rue Saint-Honoré, Birotteau had never seen such a place, "because the small businesses of Paris are fairly unacquainted with one another," but he was so taken by the beauty of Constance—and so incited by the spectacle of her setting—that "he entered *The Petit Matelot* in a fury to buy six linen shirts."[2] Birotteau is a character of old Paris who seldom wandered from his immediate quartier—he lived virtually next door to the perfume shop where he worked—who suddenly discovers the new Paris of commerce and splendor. He is emblematic of a generation of Parisians becoming accustomed to living a more wide-ranging and public life than

ever before (see Chapter Seven). Motivating this shift in daily patterns was a frenzy not unlike that with which Birotteau threw himself into *The Petit Matelot*: the allure of abundant goods at reasonable prices made possible by the introduction of industrial materials and mechanized techniques of production. This chapter will sketch the dynamics of that commercial exchange and outline its impact on the traditions of art and art-making in Romantic Paris.

Architecture and Commerce

Many aspects of the magasin de nouveautés that attracted Birotteau had long been part of Parisian merchandising.[3] Fixed prices were common before 1800 in many of the shops in the Galeries de Bois at the Palais-Royal (Fig. 126), a practice much appreciated by customers for its lack of sales pressure and freedom to browse at will (see Chapter Seven). The "thousand other commercial seductions" that astonished Birotteau could also be found in the Galeries de Bois, with its "variety of trades being collected together so conveniently, all within the same inclosure," or laid out in the "dazzling illusion" of the arcades, whose mirrors "extending along the walls, and reflecting rows of merchandise right and left" incited customers to buy things they might not have realized they needed or wanted.[4]

What was new about the magasin de nouveautés was that these effects were not incidental, but part of an ever more finely wrought merchandising scheme that was clearly evident by 1843:

In the past, boutiques stocked novelties; then came the stores; but today in Paris these stores have become immense bazaars. When you go into one, it's almost like walking through a city: spacious rooms on the ground floor decorated with luxury and elegance; counters in a Renaissance style, mirrors everywhere; a parquet that is colored, waxed, and polished, and rugs spread over the paths you should take.[5]

Every aspect of the new stores—from layout and design to stocking and staffing—was programmed to maximize a customer's desire to spend money. Window displays along the street offered the prospect of even greater discoveries inside, even if, as Frédéric Soulié noted in 1834, the promise was sometimes unfulfilled:

Attracted by the coquetry of so much beautiful merchandise, you go into the store that I'm talking about, hoping to find behind this glittering parade of fabrics a splendid assortment of everything. Futile belief! If something pleased you, it has to be taken down from the display: everything is there; the shelves hold only what is old, worn out, ordinary.[6]

Once inside, customers discovered a sales floor arranged by specialized departments, each with its particular sales staff. "To understand fully the layout of these stores," complained Soulié, "requires nothing less than a map, like the novels of [Walter] Scott."[7] Illustrating his point, Soulié takes his reader on a fictive tour of the Maison Delille.[8] First, a small room devoted to printed fabrics—indian dyes, whites, calicots, mousselines, batistes—that opens onto "a succession of vast sitting rooms, where a crowd of men measure you on the spot with three quick gestures." Walking from salon to salon introduces increasingly expensive goods: from coats and sweaters, through scarves and morning dresses, to satins, silks, and cashmeres—the latter subdivided into good-qual-

ity domestic products and extravagantly expensive imported items. Should a woman decide to have a dress made in satin or velour, she is invited to preview the look of the material by candlelight in a specially equipped room, because "to judge properly the reflections of satin or velour in a sitting room, you must see them as they will appear, and this room is lighted like a ballroom." To complete a purchase clients are led to an upstairs room where the "shelves of wood . . . counters of oak" of the sales floor give way to "magnificent mahogany armoires and counters, mirrors, giltwork, splendid wall hangings." Soulié's little tour demonstrates that the real innovation of the magasin de nouveautés was to make spending money an adventure, regardless of the purchase.

Prosper Lafaye's 1845 view of the Magasins Saint-Joseph on the rue Montmartre (Fig. 144) corroborates Soulié's description of the Maison Delille in almost every detail. The point of view is from under a relatively sombre arcade looking into a large, multi-story space that appears to be bathed in light entering from windows set into the ceiling vaults. Prestigious architectural forms—columns, vaults, and pillars—are used in complex combinations to project a monumentality usually associated with a museum or official public building. Display cases of cloth and other goods are arranged throughout the main floor, each with a sales counter and several clerks [commis] who, as became the custom in the 1840s, tend to be well-dressed young men. By contrast, most of the customers are women; it was no secret that storeowners recognized the advantage of having well-groomed and courteous young men attend to every wish of their female clients. "Princesses or bourgeois ladies," asked Balzac in a short story of 1844, "how could you not trust this nice-looking young man, cheeks soft as velvet and colored like a peach, candor in his eyes, dressed almost as well as your . . . cousin, and endowed with a voice as soft as the fleece that he unfolds for you?"[9] Since fixed prices meant there was little room for bargaining, the role of a commis was mainly to encourage customers with flattery. This little game of flirting became a major element in the adventure of shopping, and was doubly attractive because respectable women had few occasions for personal contact with men outside their immediate circle of family and personal friends (see Chapter Seven).

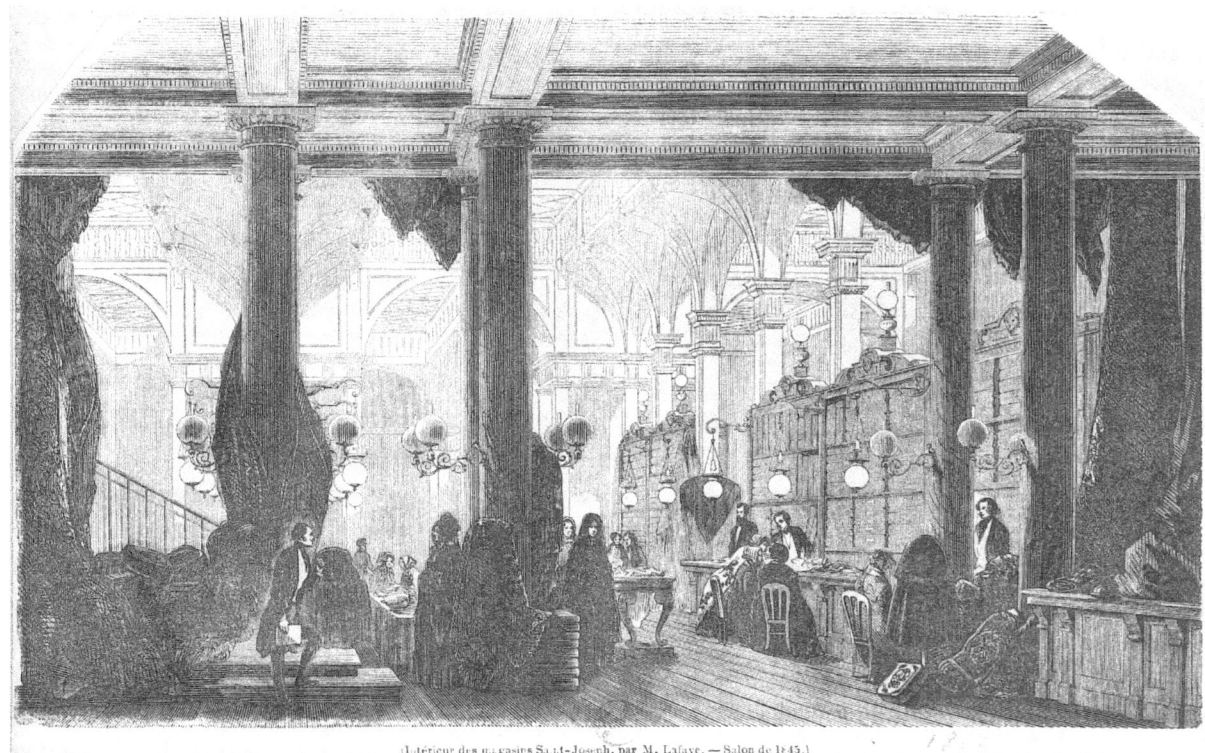

(Intérieur des magasins Saint-Joseph, par M. Lafaye. — Salon de 1845.)

FIGURE 144.   Prosper Lafaye, *Interior of the Magasins Saint-Joseph on the rue Montmartre*, 1845. Woodblock engraving. Paris, BnF, Estampes, inv. Va 240a fol. Photo: BnF, Paris.

Originally, magasins de nouveautés dealt mainly in dry goods: the fabrics, accessories, and articles related to clothing and fashion. By the very nature of this commerce, the stores were linked to ideas and objects thought to be new or in the latest taste. Every store claimed to offer the most up-to-date selection of goods; in fact, they competed for customers on the basis of very small differences in stock. The greatest variations among magasins de nouveautés concerned price and customer service—claims that were easily adapted to printed advertisements of the sort that first began to appear in Paris newspapers near the end of 1827.[10] It is no accident that the success of low-cost newspapers financed by advertising, such as *La Presse* founded by Émile de Girardin in 1836 (see Chapter Six), coincides chronologically with the commercial pressure for magasins de nouveautés to mount adver-tising campaigns vaunting the arrival of new merchandise, announcing the opening of new showrooms, or promising that "women will be charmed by the extraordinary luxury of the collections and the moderate pricing."[11] Auguste Luchet already understood this reciprocal relationship in 1834:

I really believe that commercial advertising, as it now exists, is a cre-ation of the dry goods salesman. I challenge anyone to find—in all the luxurious humbug of two-sous publications, four-franc news-papers or histories of France in bronze—an expedient, a scheme, or a ruse that had not circulated in a handbill of the magasins de nouveautés.[12]

More important, established patterns of Parisian merchan-dising were transformed by this competition for volume sales to a wide public. The piecework sales, protected prices, and face-to-face bargaining of traditional shopkeepers seemed destined for extinction. "Every day marks a new invasion of the big stores," observed Luchet; "the contagious spread of bronzes and mirrors has reached the provinces. The boutique is everywhere in decline and buries itself: soon it will have disappeared. Many people think it is already dead."[13]

Expansion of magasins de nouveautés coincides with the growing acceptance of relatively inexpensive ready-to-wear clothing produced by factories in standard sizes rather than cut-to-fit by individual tailors. Making a garment from scratch takes time, and tailors often sold their work on credit, so that the usual transaction for a new dress or suit coat required patience on the part of both buyer and seller. By contrast, ready-to-wear garments offer instant gratification to customers and instant return on investment to sellers, who are paid in cash on the spot. Speed on both sides of the transaction fosters future sales: customers looking for the next new thing will return to the store; owners with cash to buy fresh stock will have new merchandise to offer them.

Ready-to-wear clothes for sale in the magasins de nouveautés launched the fashion industry's business cycle of constantly renewed desires—a point that Frédéric Soulié did not fail to equate with the foibles of modernity itself:

Today, the dry goods salesman, who provides old lace, gives new life to ungainly fabrics, and covers a woman with thin, second-hand rags in two days, represents admirably our age, which is quick to make shabby things, casting about in the past for ideas that are all mixed up today, and creating nothing but old rags of literature, painting, and government: nothing permanent, from the form of sovereign power to that of a lady's cap; nothing lasting, from the throne to a shawl of embroidered tulle. Damask and epic poetry come from the same time; two-sous literature and six-franc dresses were born on the same day.[14]

Soulié believed that chasing after "shabby things" creates not only a new kind of commerce, but also a commercial space of novel social equality. The magasin de nouveautés, he wrote, "is no longer a sanctuary, it's a hall. From the woman with a named peerage to the working girl, everyone draws from the same well her wardrobe and her accessories. There,

the banker and the stocky commoner buy their seductions at a fixed price for cash."[15] In the contest for volume sales, magasins de nouveautés opened their doors to every kind of customer. They filtered clients according to budgets by arranging the selling floor into a labyrinth of specialty departments. Yet the magasin de nouveautés gave the impression of being a hall open to people from every walk of life and, in this respect, a truly modern space in the city akin to restaurants, newly designed quartiers, and public transports (see Chapter Seven).

A century after Soulié was writing, Sigfried Giedion drew attention to the functional overlaps among magasins de nouveautés, markets, railroad stations, and exhibition halls. Each of these architectures strives to provide the greatest possible freedom for the circulation of goods or customers, offers a clear layout organized according to the specific needs of each space, and makes maximum use of natural light.[16] With the advent of gas lighting for interior spaces (visible in Fig. 144), the risk of fire became a major concern. Architects were enjoined to design new buildings as fire-resistant as possible. All of these parameters recommended a construction of cast iron and glass for the magasins de nouveautés. Bertrand Lemoine notes that cast-iron elements "found their first applications in fitting-up stores. Indeed, a simple pole of cast iron—doubled or quadrupled if necessary—could support the weight of an entire facade or interior wall, and this, in turn, justified opening windows on the street, and both opening up and lighting the interior space of the shop."[17] The development of iron cross-beams further enhanced the fireproofing of a building's skeleton and allowed for open interior spaces rising several floors without recourse to heavy masonry piers. Charles-Louis-Gustave Eck, in an important treatise on modern building techniques written in 1841, acknowledged that "by their slender diameter, cast-iron columns deprive the shops of far less light than stone pylons, and they also make it possible to have a much larger area of useable floor space on the ground floor."[18] Eck recognized that cast iron offered a transparency not possible with cut stone, but he worried that "owners often sacrifice the solidity of their buildings to the lure of a large revenue" by building spans too tall or too wide for the physical characteristics of cast iron.

Iron was, of course, a modern manufactured material whose physical characteristics were only beginning to be explored. "In France," remarks Eck, "use of this metal becomes increasingly prevalent because, especially in recent years, one has come to appreciate fully the superiority of lightweight and fireproof systems of construction."[19] The use of iron quickly altered the basic premises of architectural design, as suggested by Guillaume-Abel Blouet's treatise of 1847:

Based on the progress that has already been made in the use of iron as an element of construction, it seems certain, given the wide range of combinations to which this material lends itself, that it has been called upon to bring about a revolution in the art of building—a revolution, one must admit, that has already begun. It behooves architects to guide this revolution well so it does not degenerate into excess by using iron wrongly.[20]

Blouet, like Eck before him, worried that iron would be used improperly by builders not formally trained in architecture. He called on professional architects to embrace the new material and thus prevent its misuse. In fact, the most adventurous early uses of iron were not designed by architects, but were fabricated by metalwork contractors [entrepreneurs de serrurerie] with experience in working iron to make locks, hinges, and other kinds of metal fittings. The best examples of their handiwork, the iron-framed glass roofs of Parisian arcades (Fig. 128), were relatively modest in scale.

Large structures, by contrast, required a technical ability backed up by a good understanding of statics to achieve, in the words of Eck, "the analysis of forces, whose solution is summed up in the word equilibrium . . . the action of equalizing the force between two bodies that act on one another."[21] Mathematics, which is the essential tool for such an analysis, acquired a new prestige when applied to framing materials whose high tensile strength and compact mass nearly approximated the purity of geometric curves drawn in space. "The significance of iron," writes Giedion, "is to condense high potential stress into the most minimal dimensions. If a comparison is permitted, iron suggests both muscular tissue and skeleton in a building. Iron opens the spaces. The wall can become a transparent glass skin."[22] Fully transparent walls would not be designed for a magasin de nouveautés

until the construction of Bon Marché in the 1860s, but examples of utilitarian structures from the 1830s demonstrated what could be achieved when architects fully exploited industrial materials—iron in its various forms (cast, rolled, or wrought) and panes of glass—that were designed and assembled with the rigor of mathematics. One of the most impressive of these structures in all of Europe was the greenhouse designed in 1833 by Charles Rohault de Fleury for the Jardin des Plantes that opened to the public in 1837 and quickly became a fixture in the Paris cityscape (Fig. 145).

According to the 1832 edition of Quatremère de Quincy's *Dictionnaire historique d'architecture*, a greenhouse is a "simple utilitarian object of agriculture or gardening," although if built as part of a larger garden it can "offer the architect an incentive for a successful arrangement of the exterior, and whose interior might provide a promenade or a refuge from seasonal inclemencies."[23] Quatremère admitted that during the winter months a greenhouse "sometimes produces an illusion and a sensation that contrasts agreeably with that of the season," but he believed this quality was due more to the contrast of environments and foliage than to the architecture itself. By contrast, Théophile Gautier's enthusiastic reaction to the greenhouse in the Jardin des Plantes was all about its architecture:

The new greenhouses are truly an airy and transparent palace in which you see neither pillars, nor buttresses, nor any other kind of support. One might call it a soap bubble blown by some childish, small giant. The light plays on and passes through these clear walls as if through empty space, and yet the most violent wind would press its knees with all its force against these fragile walls without bending them. So carefully has M. Rohaut calculated the forces of resistance, that these ramparts, which are less than one-twelfth of an inch thick, would withstand as much as heavy walls of stones and cement; yet inside there is not one buttress, not one support.[24]

Gautier focuses upon the nearly immaterial chassis that supports the structure, the torrent of light through walls that seem not to exist, and the magical paradox of solidity achieved with iron and calculations rather than stone and mass. A few lines later he remarks that the system of iron frames holding glass panes, "by taking up much less

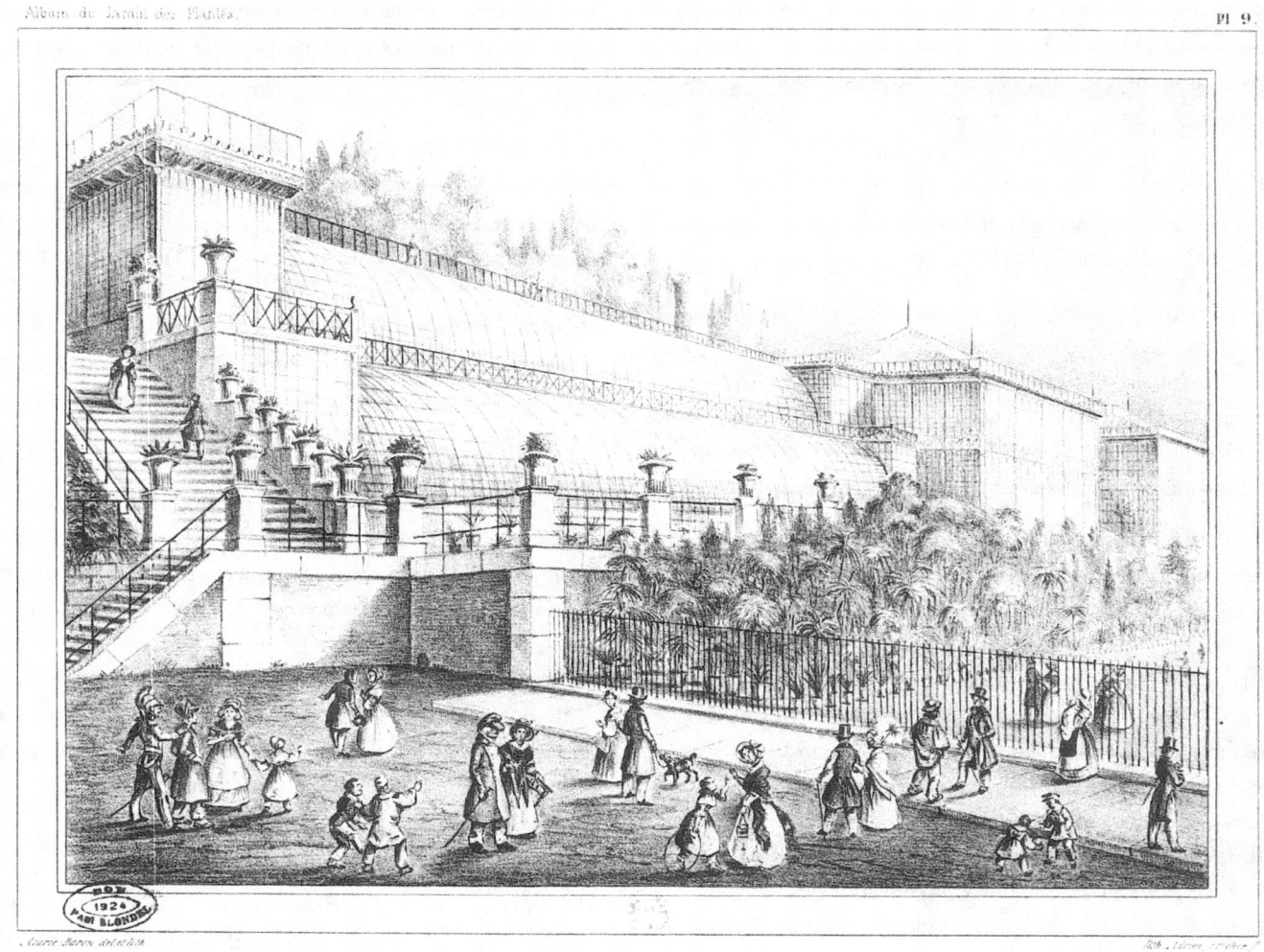

FIGURE 145.   Charles Rohault de Fleury, *Greenhouses at the Jardin des Plantes*, 1833. Lithograph by Acarie Baron from *Album du Jardin des Plantes* (1838). Paris, BnF, Estampes, inv. Va 257b. Photo: BnF, Paris.

space than wooden chassis, allows the sun's rays to penetrate more easily." He also observes that the wall of glass arched into a half-circle (visible at the far left of Fig. 145) is "much more elegant than the tilted flat plane with which greenhouses are usually constructed." In his appreciation of Rohault's greenhouse, Gautier articulates the functional advantages of iron and glass, and recognizes those materials have engendered breathtaking new spaces that seem to defy gravity.

Rohault de Fleury was perfectly conscious of this novelty.[25] He traveled to England before starting work on the Jardin des Plantes to study techniques of design and construction, along with the systems of heating and ventilation perfected by British architects. Nothing he saw in England rivaled the scale he was planning for Paris. Each of his two main pavilions, where the tallest tropical trees are grown, is a simple box—twenty meters long, twelve meters wide, and fifteen meters tall—capped by a roof of sheet metal carried on cast-iron columns at the perimeter and eight freestanding interior columns. Three of the exterior walls are simply panes of glass held in frames of iron. The fourth abuts a building in which Rohault installed mechanical systems for heating, ventilation, and rainmaking. The two main pavilions are connected by an iron-arch service bridge. Galleries extend laterally from each pavilion for about sixty meters. These galleries, built against an embankment to protect them from the north wind, consist of two curved vaults in iron and glass: one springs from ground level; the second rises from vaults supporting the first. The combination produces the stepped, rounded space free of supports that so impressed Gautier. The great technical innovation of Rohault's greenhouse was to design each wing as a single, continuous volume divided only by "glass partitions that allow for sorting the vegetation according to the temperature and humidity they need without depriving the eye of this long sequence of glass panes."[26] The result was both practical and, as Gautier reported, visually dramatic: "The formal variety of the large and small pavilions and the long curving greenhouses, by projecting transparent masses—one above the other—crowned by the beautiful green trees of the labyrinth, produces some effects of picturesque perspective to which the sunlight adds a remarkable brilliance."[27] This admirable play of light, space, and transparency would not have been possible—nor even imaginable—without the industrial materials of iron and glass.[28]

Gautier was among those who celebrated the formal inventions of this architecture born of industry. Writing in 1850, and surely with structures like the Jardin des Plantes in mind, he predicted:

For a long time one has looked, without success, for a way to create a completely new architecture. . . . Success will not come by torturing paper with impossible forms, but by making use of the new materials provided by modern industry. . . . The use of cast iron allows for and requires many new forms, like those you see in railway stations, in suspension bridges, or the vaults of the Wintergarden, whose construction would be otherwise impossible.[29]

Not everyone shared Gautier's enthusiasm. Professional architects were far more circumspect about the future of new materials. Gottfried Semper, a German architect writing in 1849 about the newly opened Wintergarden in Paris, did grant that its spaces produced a magical effect, especially during a concert:

The effect of the garden is very beautiful in sunlight, but it shows itself to greatest advantage in the moonlight, when it is reflected in the spouting water and makes dark shadows on the softly shimmering lawn, while the gentle sound of a horn resonates from the gallery. You think you have been transported into a dream world, surrounded by the whispering of elves and elemental spirits.[30]

Nonetheless, Semper was not ready to accept iron and glass as a substitute for the traditional materials of architecture. To his mind, doing so would replace artistry with simple technology:

It will still be some time before iron (and metal in general), which is just coming into its own as a building material, is technically mastered so perfectly that it can claim respect and appreciation as an artistic element of fine architecture alongside stone, brick, and wood.[31]

Semper was willing to admit that iron-frame construction "in buildings of a practical purpose—such as protective roofs of a great span, especially in the train sheds of railway stations—gives a satisfying impression."[32] Yet he warned against introducing it into monumental architecture because "wherever else it is put to use reminds one, often in a disturbing way, of every cold, drafty, and exposed railroad space, and it makes every cozy or festive ambiance impossible."[33]

As an example of the unpleasant side effects created by visible iron-frame architectural components, Semper cites Henri Labrouste's Bibliothèque Sainte-Geneviève (Fig. 146), a building nearing completion at the time of his stay in Paris:

A peculiar illustration of this allegation is the new Sainte-Geneviève Library in Paris, a building of great interest that is considered the most significant achievement of the latest republican period, but whose architect, Mr. Labrouste, thought it proper to use an iron-truss roof, unhappily visible and painted green, by the way. The library room, which also serves as reading room, lacks the cozy seclusion so necessary to serious study and pleases almost no one.[34]

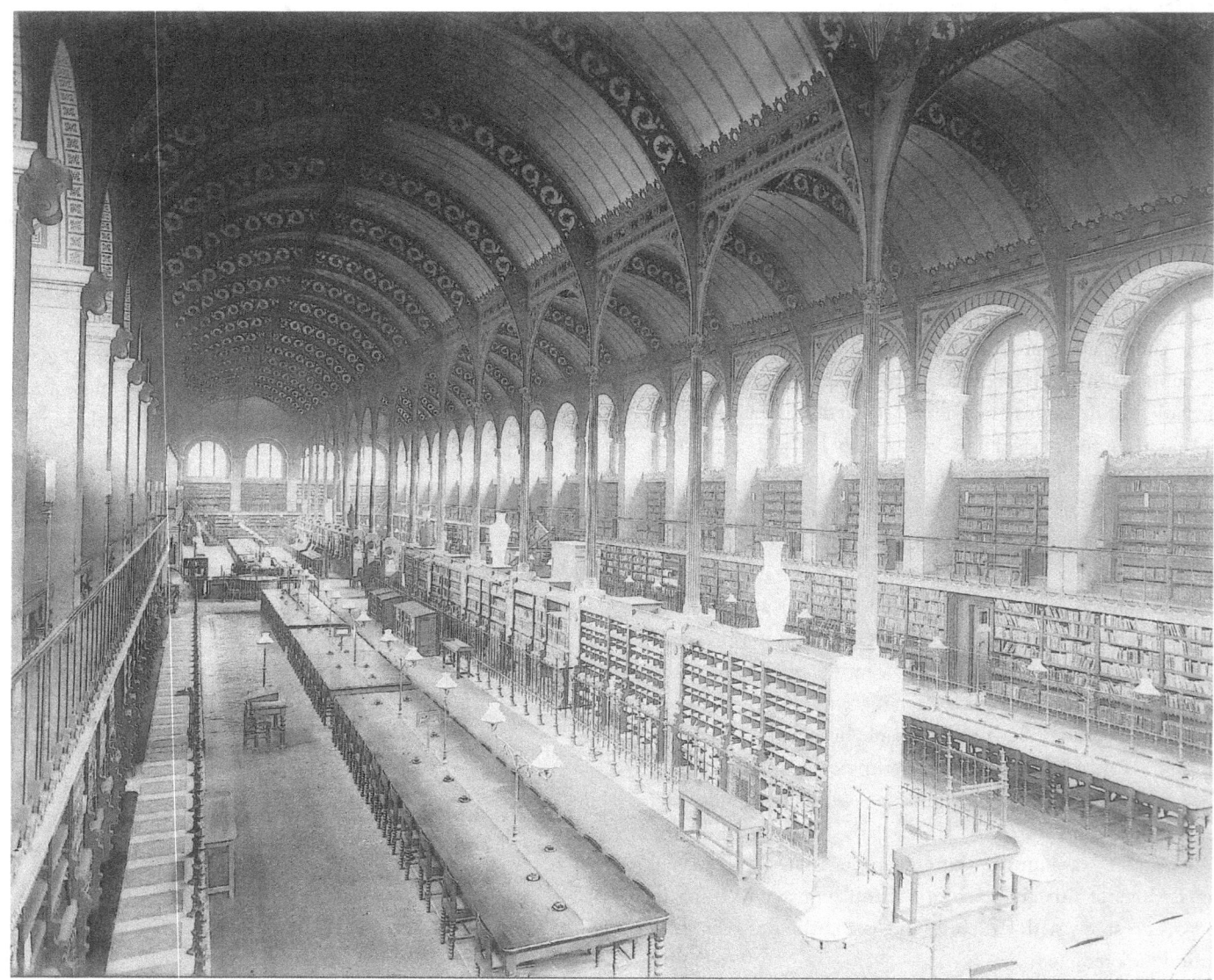

FIGURE 146.   Henri Labrouste, *Reading room of the Bibliothèque Sainte-Geneviève*, 1843–1850. Photograph taken before 1901. Paris. Photo: Roger Viollet, Paris/© ND-Viollet.

Semper had fled Germany after his involvement in the botched revolution of 1848 at Dresden. He was eager for Labrouste's library to be the emblem of a new republican era opened in France by the overthrow of Louis-Philippe (see Chapter Two). But his training and sensibility as an architect could not condone the unadorned presence of cast-iron elements in the library's main reading room. He concluded that the inherent strength of cast-iron materials actually precludes revealing their use:

Architecture, which works its effects upon the spirit through the organ of sight, must have nothing to do with this quasi-invisible material whenever it is a question of the effects of mass rather than light embellishments. Serious architecture could and should use metal in rods for the grill-work of fencing or graceful mesh-work, and make it visible as the most propitious building material, but not use it for girders carrying great weight, as the support for a building, or as the keynote of a motif.[35]

Paradoxically, hindsight has completely reversed Semper's assessment, for the Bibliothèque Sainte-Geneviève is now recognized as one of the first truly modern buildings in the history of French architecture. "Labrouste's chief accomplishment in this library," concludes Sigfried Giedion, "rests in the manner in which the iron construction is balanced in itself, so that it puts no stress on the walls. The achievement of just such a hovering equilibrium became the chief task for engineers in the second half of the nineteenth century."[36] Architectural historians since Giedion have softened somewhat this single-minded focus on the ironwork frame of the Bibliothèque Sainte-Geneviève by reminding us that Labrouste's library is replete with nonfunctional and non-ferrous forms. In fact, the most interesting questions today about this landmark building of mid-century Paris concern the coexistence of these two aspects in a single structure.

SEMPER BELIEVED the immateriality of iron must not be visible in buildings where the goal was to produce a monumental effect. Like many of his contemporaries, he felt the mass of a building should form a single unit with the symbolic and stylistic components of its decoration to achieve the convincing, almost theatrical display of space required of monumental architecture. Labrouste took just the opposite position. His design for the Bibliothèque Sainte-Geneviève deliberately juxtaposes iron and stone to undermine any possibility of producing the seamless effect Semper took for granted. Upon entering the library, visitors immediately confront robust masonry piers supporting seemingly fragile arches of ironwork—a material incongruity that was quite disconcerting to contemporary eyes:

Next, because of the way these two very different materials—stone and iron—are set side by side and joined, the pylon seems heavy and the arch scrawny. There is something shocking about seeing

so much energy spent on supporting so little. We know perfectly well all the objections that could be raised about the comparative strength of each of these materials. But one must not forget that everything true is not always beautiful: what is materially solid and sufficient might not satisfy our eyes very well. One sees and senses before reasoning, and does so more quickly than one deduces. In any case, after having calculated the sturdiness mathematically, one must then calculate no less exactly the impression that the form should produce. This rule has not been sufficiently observed in the detail we have just pointed out.[37]

Upstairs in the reading room (Fig. 146), a deep masonry arcade appears to be the useless deployment of mass supporting little more than a filigree of iron trusses. Indeed, the two types of materials and two building systems could *only* be juxtaposed, for the ironwork structure—bolted together and independently stable—actually exerts no force against the exterior masonry walls. Rather than camouflaging this structural discontinuity, Labrouste, in the words of David van Zanten, "even tries to impress this disturbing fact on us by supporting the iron trusses where they meet the girdling masonry wall by nothing more than the slightest corbels. . . . The skeletalized but nonetheless thick and stable stone viaduct enclosing the space supports nothing more than its own weight."[38]

More than a display of architectural antics, Labrouste's configuration of the library responds to some serious practical considerations. The deep arcade that circles the reading room, for example, both opens the walls to natural light and diffuses the sun's direct rays so that the space is bright without glare, filled with an even light conducive to reading and concentration. The ironwork frame of the room's walls and vaults—supported by a central spine of cast-iron columns erected upon a substructure of iron girders and sheet metal flooring—responds to the fact that the Bibliothèque Sainte-Geneviève was the first Parisian library open in the evenings and lighted by gas lamps. The pervasive use of iron from foundation to roof offered a level of fireproofing not possible with other structural materials. Finally, as Labrouste pointed out when replying to criticism of his plan before the Conseil des Bâtiments Civils, modular components of the library's iron frame were to be fabricated off-site while masonry elements were being built in situ, thus shortening the project's construction time and overall cost.[39]

Labrouste was encouraged to experiment by a lack of compelling precedents for the type of building he was commissioned to design. The famous libraries of antiquity, remarked Quatremère de Quincy in his architectural dictionary of 1832, were mentioned by Vitruvius, although he said "nothing of their construction, their form, nor their layout." Rather, Vitruvius limited his comments "to recommending that libraries be turned toward the rising sun" in order to benefit from the morning light, and to shield books from the intense brightness and heat of the midday sun.[40] Except for a few instances—notably Michelangelo's Medici Library and the Library of Saint Mark built by Sansovino in Venice—Quatremère felt that the architecture of modern libraries offered "nothing specially adapted to the character and decorum of a library. It is only a large space whose interior has been adapted to its new purpose."[41] Even in Paris, home of more libraries than any other city of Europe, Quatremère complained that "most of these literary monuments offer only the idea of a vast storehouse of books. Thus far, the arts have done nothing to embellish these temples of science and genius."[42] Labrouste's brief at the Bibliothèque Sainte-Geneviève was not simply to imagine an artistic shell appropriate to a library, but also to invent a type of building that would become the model for future libraries.

The Bibliothèque Sainte-Geneviève, which had been housed since 1624 on the upper floor of the former Génovéfain abbey (today the Lycée Henri IV), was more a study hall than a research library. It was heavily patronized by students from nearby colleges who came to consult materials they could not afford to buy.[43] The library's users and use articulated a social space not unlike the arcades and magasins de nouveautés, the restaurants and cafés, or even the omnibus of modern Paris: although students came to study—rather than to shop, socialize, or travel—they were a heterogeneous group that the building needed simply to service, not to order hierarchically. Writing in 1867, Théodore de Banville recognized the novelty of the library's mission and praised Labrouste, who

did not want to be inspired by the monuments of another age when building a monument whose use is precise and particular; those who

think that the nineteenth century has the right to exist like its predecessors will not have the courage to accuse him of a crime. . . . M. Labrouste sacrificed everything to specialized suitability and made a library that is not afraid of looking like a library.[44]

Labrouste actually referred to the new building as a study library [bibliothèque d'étude]. His practical goal was to accommodate several hundred readers (including their frequent comings and goings), and to provide service facilities for the library staff to deliver and reshelve books efficiently.[45]

Despite Labrouste's seemingly modest mission, François Barrière was right to remark that "it's the first time in Paris, I think, that a building has been constructed with the exclusive and specialized purpose of storing books."[46] Proceeding in a manner that now seems perfectly logical, but was thought novel at the time, Labrouste placed a rectangular reading room above the primary book storage areas—a move that maximized the room's size within the building's allotted footprint, minimized the distance between the books in storage and the reading areas, and lifted the room sufficiently high to ensure good light from all sides. Patrons enter the library through a nearly unadorned doorway cut into the center of the building's long street facade, pass straight through a rather dark vestibule to a staircase that splits to each side, and then return to the center axis before entering the open and bright space of the reading room where they are invited to turn either right or left. Two tiers of bookshelves, installed in the arcades under the windows, surround the reading room. Additional bookcases—installed along the center spine of iron columns—originally divided the room into two long and narrow spaces (Fig. 146).[47] Entering the library performs a passage that is both physically and intellectually illuminating: from the sombre vestibule of the ground floor, readers discover the light of day and a place of enlightenment (reading) literally surrounded by books.

Labrouste's elegantly functional solution at the Bibliothèque Sainte-Geneviève became almost immediately the model cited in architectural treatises. Writing in the 1850s, Léonce Reynaud endorses a simple rectangular plan as the most practical and cost-effective, insists that libraries stand free from other buildings, and recommends that they be iron-framed to reduce the risk of fire. He concludes that "there is an advantage to raising the main rooms of a library above the ground floor, both to provide them with a sufficient amount of light and to protect them from the effects of humidity."[48] Reynaud specifically mentions the new Bibliothèque Sainte-Geneviève as embodying all of these qualities. He also dedicated a long section to the new library when discussing recent developments in iron-frame construction, calling Labrouste "one of our most distinguished architects, and one of the men of our day in which a feeling for form is most developed."[49] Contemporaries recognized that functionality was a key term in the library's design equation.

If Labrouste hoped to respond to Quatremère's claim that the arts had failed to "embellish these temples of science and genius," the library's decorative program should second its structural innovations. Labrouste's working method is revealing in this regard. He was appointed architect of the Bibliothèque Sainte-Geneviève in 1838, and he presented a first proposal for the new building in December of the following year. His plans were approved by the Conseil des Bâtiments Civils within a month, but the project was shelved until 1842 due to lack of funding. Labrouste's project was submitted to the Chamber of Deputies for approval and funding in 1843. Construction began in August of that year. The foundation and masonry components were finished by November 1846. In the meantime, Labrouste designed the ironwork flooring, and in September 1846 he began to elaborate the exposed ironwork and vaults of the reading room. Only in late 1847, when all the structural parts of the building were designed and executed, did Labrouste turn his attention to a decorative program for the library's facade (Fig. 147). Neil Levine points out that Labrouste's working process assumed his task was

the *decoration of construction*. This contravened the classical belief in appearance as reality, wherein the process of design was seen as the *construction of decoration*. The classical ideal of apparent formal homogeneity was replaced by the reality of structural differentiation. The classical belief in the inherent content of apparently consistent forms was replaced by a discursive application of forms that could only take on adherent meaning in context.[50]

The building's chronology reveals Labrouste's lack of interest

in unifying architectural mass to decoration—a unity that architects like Semper took for granted.

IN HIS IMPORTANT STUDY of this twist in the practice of architecture, Levine suggests that the rupture between structure and decoration manifest in the Bibliothèque Sainte-Geneviève was grounded in "a new consciousness of history, which undermined the classical illusion of a naturally based coherence of form and content."[51] His point tallies with contemporary views that history itself must be written from the ground up—from the myriad details of every life—rather than shaped from some preconceived notion of progress (see Chapter Three). It also tallies with Victor Hugo's attack upon the classical unities of time and place in his notorious preface to *Cromwell* (see Chapter Five). Labrouste's rejection of the classical orders at the Bibliothèque Sainte-Geneviève was taken to be a statement in stone as radical as Hugo's experiments on stage: "Certain men," wrote Achille Hermant, "feeling in part the absurdity of covering our land with buildings that were only ridiculous copies of ancient monuments, rebelled early on against this deplorable practice. . . . M. Henri Labrouste is one of the instigators of these new ideas."[52] Finally, like the disfigured classical unities of Hugo's *Hernani* that so shocked critics in 1830, the look of Labrouste's building struck many observers as more than a little odd (Fig. 147). "And the effect of the exterior!" exclaimed François Barrière in the *Journal des Débats*; "you have to get used to the exterior effect; it looks unusual; a moment of thought explains it. Since, finally, one was building a library for books, it had to be made for their use."[53] Barrière, who was generally favorable to the new building, inadvertently put his finger on the problem by recognizing that the look of the Bibliothèque Sainte-Geneviève was shaped by its mission of holding books. Why did Labrouste believe a visible rupture between structure and decoration was essential to the idea of a library? Addressing that question means returning to Victor Hugo's epic novel, *Notre-Dame de Paris*.

Hugo's interest in architecture ran deep: from his concern to preserve the great cathedrals of French medieval culture to

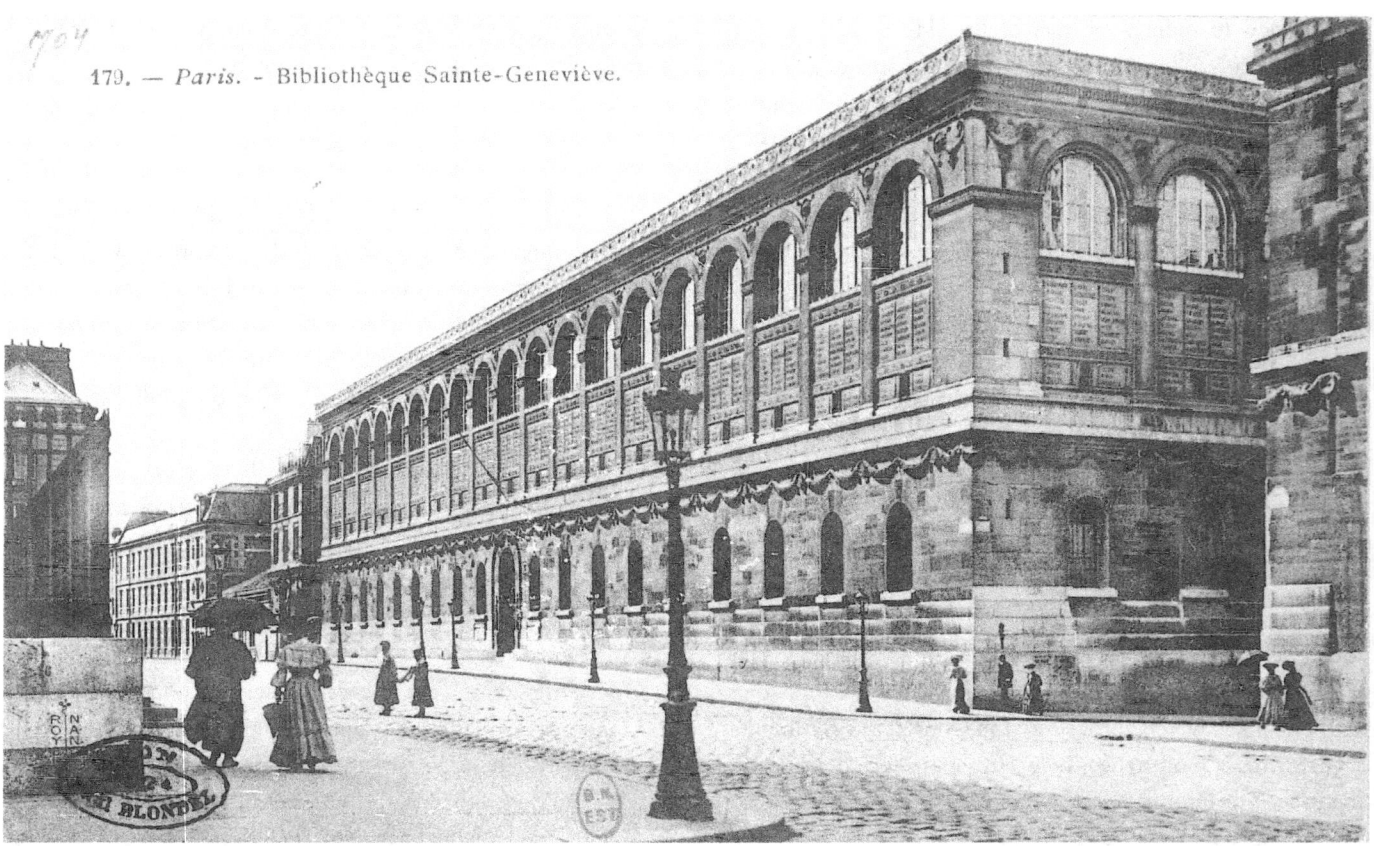

179. — *Paris*. - Bibliothèque Sainte-Geneviève.

FIGURE 147.   Henri Labrouste, *Exterior façade of the Bibliothèque Sainte-Geneviève*, 1843–1850. Anonymous
photograph, ca. 1904. Paris, BnF, Estampes, inv. Va 260f. Photo: BnF, Paris.

his scorn for contemporary "bastard buildings with the ridiculous pretension of being Greeks or Romans in France, but which are neither Roman nor Greek."[54] A chapter for *Notre-Dame de Paris* was a meditation on the future of architecture: although not included in the novel's first editions of 1831, the chapter was inserted into the so-called definitive edition of 1832. Hugo claimed the missing pages had been temporarily lost. Levine has shown that Hugo actually gave the text on architecture—written in late 1831—to Henri Labrouste, asking the architect for advice on certain technical questions and for critical comments on its content.[55]

The chapter in question is called "Ceci tuera cela" [This will kill that]. It includes an argument on the relationship between building and writing so complicated and rambling that Hugo felt obliged to introduce it with an excuse to his readers. His decoding of the chapter's cryptic title involves sweeping generalizations based on

a philosophical point of view, no longer just that of a priest, but also of a savant and an artist. It was the premonition that by changing its form human thought was going to change its mode of expression, that the fundamental idea of each generation would no longer be written with the same materials and in the same manner, that the book of stone—so solid and durable—was going to yield to the book of paper—even more solid and more durable. From this point of view, the vague phrase of the archdeacon had a second sense: it meant that one art was going to dethrone the other. It implied that the printing house will kill architecture.[56]

Hugo's main argument probably interested the young Labrouste, for it positioned architecture historically as the most enduring, the most expansive, and the most ambitious form of human expression:

Masonry emerged by plunging headlong into the task on every side. This accounts for the huge number of cathedrals that covered Europe, a number so incredible that one scarcely believes it, even after having it verified. All the material forces, all the intellectual forces of society converged on the same point: architecture. In this way, under the pretext of building churches to God, art was expanded into magnificent proportions.[57]

In stark contrast to the imposing presence and permanence of architecture, handmade manuscripts offered only "precarious immortality" that could be permanently effaced by "a torch and a Turk," whereas "to demolish the built word would require a social revolution, an earthly revolution."[58]

For Hugo, Gutenberg's invention of the printing press and moveable type was exactly that revolution:

Human thought discovers a way of immortalizing itself that is not only more durable and more robust than architecture, but also simpler and easier. Architecture is dethroned. . . . The invention of the printing press is the greatest event in history. It is the mother of all revolutions.[59]

Moreover, it set in motion a profound paradox. Although books are seemingly more fragile than stone and mortar, Hugo claims that mechanized printing gave to ideas an immortality that buildings could no longer match:

In printed form, thought is more imperishable than ever; it is ephemeral, elusive, indestructible. It mixes with air. In the days of architecture, it took itself for a mountain and powerfully grabbed hold of a century and a place. Now it takes itself for a flock of birds, scatters to the four winds, and simultaneously occupies every point in air and space. . . . From the solid that it was, thought becomes undying. It passes from duration to immortality. You can demolish a physical mass, but how do you eradicate ubiquity?[60]

The printed book, which "is made so quickly, costs so little, and can go so far," now attracts the best efforts of the human spirit, and does so at the expense of architecture. "The printed book, this worm gnawing at the building," he writes, "sucks it dry and devours it. The edifice is stripped, it loses its leaves, it wastes away before our very eyes."[61] In a final jab at stalwarts like Quatremère de Quincy who would keep architecture alive by imitating antiquity, Hugo declared that contemporary architecture "is petty, impoverished, worthless. It no longer expresses anything, not even the memory of past art. A pitiful studio beggar, it drags itself around from copy to copy."[62] Hugo's analysis of the death rattle of architecture before the power of the printed book was both historical—the decline dates from the moment of Gutenberg's invention—and structural—the printed book is a standardized industrial form that takes the imprint of whatever idea is set into its lines of type.

In a note left amongst his working papers for *Notre-Dame de Paris*, Hugo implies that the physical form of a printed book is unaffected by its contents because "words are not things."[63] Although his conclusions about the state of contemporary architecture were generally pessimistic, Hugo did not deny that it might still have "a beautiful monument here and there, an isolated masterpiece," but he was quick to add: "if, by chance, architecture gets back on its feet, it will no longer be the master. It will be subject to the rule of literature, who previously took it away from architecture."[64] How might Henri Labrouste, Hugo's friend and reader, respond to this withering criticism with a building designed to house books? One way would be to acknowledge openly Hugo's "rule of literature" by refusing to compete with the printed book, by embracing it as a design model, and by imprinting the idea of library onto a formal structure shaped by the materials of industry and the exigencies of function.

In fact, Labrouste donned Hugo's straitjacket to elaborate an entirely new architectural form. From his first sketches for the building, put down in haste on the back of a letter dated 1838, Labrouste was committed to the idea of a prominent central spine running the length of his reading room.[65] Levine suggests that Labrouste's predilection for a central spine derives from his reconstruction of the Hera I temple at Paestum, which had created a scandal in 1828–1829, and from his acquaintance with the restoration of the refectory at the Abbey of Saint-Martin-des-Champs by his friend Léon Vaudoyer.[66] Certainly these material precedents were capable of sparking the architect's imagination. But the idea of a spine for the building—especially one built of regularly repeated, industrially created iron components—must also be read as a metaphor for the spine of a book, the structural core of those industrially produced, printed texts that the library was destined to house.

That book spines were on Labrouste's mind is suggested by the decoration of his building's three visible facades (Fig. 147). For the areas of blank wall defined by the masonry arcade—below the large windows of the reading room—Labrouste specified inscribing, in red block letters and in chronological order, the names of eight hundred ten authors and writers. His list began with Moses, guardian of the tablets and thus a kind of librarian, and it ended with the Swedish chemist Jean-Jacques Berzelius, who worked for many years in Paris before his death in 1848. The names are arranged under each arcade in three vertical columns separated by carved vertical bands, and they are divided horizontally into two panels of unequal size— the upper panel being about twice the height of the lower panel. The center sections of each lower panel do not contain names; rather, they are punctuated by a single small window to light the passageways, hidden within the walls, that connect the reading room to the ground-floor storage areas. In a published letter to César Daly about the Bibliothèque Sainte-Geneviève, Labrouste related the names etched on the outside of his building to the books stored exactly behind:

On the building's facade, in the part of the upper story corresponding to the interior shelves containing the books, are inscribed in large characters the names of the principal authors or writers whose works are preserved in the library. This monumental catalogue is the principal decoration of the facade, just as the books themselves are the most beautiful ornament of the interior.[67]

The close correspondence between Labrouste's placement of names on the exterior facade, and the two levels of books lin-

ing his reading room on the interior (Fig. 146), was not lost on contemporaries. François Barrière remarked in the *Journal des Débats* that "the names of philosophers, poets, historians, savants from every century," were placed in the "quite wide broad between the ground-floor windows and the forty arched openings that light the interior." He concluded with an apt metaphor: "Their works on the inside, their names on the outside, just like the title of a good work is put on the spine of the volume."[68]

Labrouste's text-laden surface was not universally appreciated. "We deplore the large number of inscriptions that cover this facade," complained Achille Hermant in 1851; "an inscription only decorates in a satisfactory manner when it fills consistently and bluntly the space allotted to it. Close by there are words; from afar it should be an embroidery of the stone."[69] Several years later, Théodore de Banville echoed this assessment by remarking: "the idea of engraving the stone with the names of illustrious poets and savants from every age was good, and could provide a felicitous decorative motif; but it was executed far too naïvely, like a page of writing."[70] Both writers disparage the fact that Labrouste handled the facade as if a page of printed text. Yet that was exactly his point: not to rival the printed book with a fantasy of timeless architectural values, but to embrace its structure with a directness appropriate to architecture in the age of mechanized printing.

The library displays a rigorous modularity intimately related to its structure of pre-fabricated, industrial iron components: on the facade, with a repetition of nearly planar forms and rows of letters, as if printed on the surface by a rotary press; on the interior, with a central spine of identical, cast-iron columns and iron-frame trusses that support the whole. In both instances, Labrouste materialized Hugo's dictum that modern architecture "submit to the rule of literature" promulgated by "the printing press, that giant machine that pumps without rest all of society's intellectual sap."[71] Indeed, the compact, boxy appearance of Labrouste's library is nearly overshadowed by its immediate neighbor, the church of Sainte-Geneviève (Fig. 45).

Soufflot's grand statement of highly plastic sculptural forms—temple front, hovering dome, and monumental

Corinthian order—was newly enriched by David d'Angers' sculptural allegory honoring the great men of French history (see Chapter Three). By its enormous scale, monumental presence, and historical allusions, Soufflot's building announces an importance fully consonant with the cavernous spaces of its interior. It was also the type of building that Hugo pitied as the emblem of architecture's demise:

Michelangelo . . . had a final idea, a desperate idea. This titan of art piled the Pantheon on top of the Parthenon and made Saint Peter's in Rome. A great work that deserved to remain unique, the last novelty of architecture, the signature of a giant artist at the foot of the colossal stone register that was closing. Michelangelo dead, what did this miserable architecture that outlives itself do to the statement of ghost and shadow? It took Saint Peter's from Rome and both copied it and parodied it. It's a craze. It's a pity. Every century has its Saint Peter's of Rome; the seventeenth has Val-de-Grâce, the eighteenth has Sainte-Geneviève. . . . Insignificant legacy, the last drivel of a decrepit great art that lapses into infancy before dying.[72]

By contrast, the Bibliothèque Sainte-Geneviève advertises almost nothing of itself—but says much of its contents—with its odd combination of inscribed names and plastically hesitant architectural forms. The building appears to enact Hugo's image of the printed book: "this worm gnawing at the building, sucks it dry and devours it. The edifice is stripped, it loses its leaves, it wastes away before our very eyes."[73]

Labrouste referred to the columns of names on the facade of his library (Fig. 147) as a "monumental catalogue." His term purposefully identifies the building as a tool for negotiating what Hugo described as the colossal edifice of printed books constantly under construction since Gutenberg, like a "second Tower of Babel of the human species."[74] An old adage says one cannot tell a book by its cover: in the course of their trajectory from the street to the desks of the reading room, users of the Bibliothèque Sainte-Geneviève discover a spaciousness and light—not announced with fanfare but functionally implemented by the materials of industry—where they might devise their individual wanderings within Hugo's edifice of printed books. In a parallel manner, the meaning of the decorative program draped over the structure of Labrouste's

library is also driven by user choice. The facade really is a catalogue from which we are free to choose. It is not a monolithic statement to which we must submit. Like the display windows of the arcades, the merchandise racks of the magasins de nouveautés, or the multi-page menus of contemporary restaurants, the Bibliothèque Sainte-Geneviève configures a relationship among individuals—and with commodities—in a public arena, yet it does not force a choice upon them. In this context, the modernity of Labrouste's library rests less upon visible ironwork than its frank articulation of open and equal access to the world of ideas—a function shaped by industrial materials, and announced without the fanfare of symbols or allegories from the past.

Affordable Luxuries

Labrouste's shocking juxtaposition of industrially fabricated iron and manually worked stone in the Bibliothèque Sainte-Geneviève vividly schematizes debates about the relationship between art and industry in Romantic Paris. By contrast, large segments of the English economy had been converted to processes of mass production well before 1800 to fill a demand for low-cost products among working-class consumers with rising disposable incomes. The result was a flood of machine-made goods in which quality was often sacrificed to price. In France, and especially in Paris, the shift to large-scale mechanized production of cheap goods did not occur until the second half of the nineteenth century, mainly because Parisian consumers before mid-century tended, in the words of Patrick O'Brien and Caglar Keyder, to be people "with higher incomes, with greater discrimination and concern for quality and style than the typical consumers of British manufactured goods."[75] Rosalind Williams paints a similar picture when describing 1830s Paris as "on the eve of the consumer revolution. . . . The lower ranks of the bourgeoisie were asserting their right to live like the upper classes. . . . The more general status of 'living nobly' was as attractive as ever." This situation fueled "a growing domestic market for handmade but relatively inexpensive goods (machine made goods were even less expensive, but failed to convey the desired prestige) that imitated aristocratic styles from the past."[76] Bourgeois consumers in Romantic Paris tended to shop for products of traditional quality and taste rather than the lowest possible price.

Historical evidence suggests a key factor shaping the buying habits of Parisian consumers was the fact that French women usually controlled the family budget and were the principal decision makers about most domestic purchases. This state of affairs was so taken for granted that Flora Tristan, writing in 1840 from London, was shocked by the situation she discovered across the Channel:

A woman in England is still in no way mistress of the home, the way she is in France. She is even almost a stranger to it. The husband keeps the money and the keys. He is the one who pays bills, hires or fires domestics, orders dinner each evening, invites guests. He alone determines the children's future. In a word, he deals with everything by himself. . . . Between this extreme dependence, this respect of English women for the wishes of their *lord and master*, and the informality, the active interest of French women towards their husbands, lies the entire space separating contemporary French culture from that of Saint Louis.[77]

An important part of a French woman's education was to train for her future domestic responsibilities. Practical manuals published during the 1820s and 1830s regularly exhorted young women to learn that

true good taste consists of selecting things that are useful, well-adapted, durable, and that have, above all, a clearly established connection to each other. I think this agreement is an essential part of what the English mean by the word *comfortable*. It pleases the eye and produces a kind of peace of mind.[78]

Emphasis on good taste was often cited as the defining strength of French design and production, as summarized by Jules Burat in 1844:

Taste has always been a distinctive character of French industry, and if we still lag behind England in certain technical processes, if we are unable to fabricate certain items at such low prices, at least we have been able to give most of our manufactured products the invaluable advantage of making them sought after for their form, independent of their price. Let us know how to preserve these tra-

ditions with care, so useful are they to the circulation of French products.[79]

Manufacturers of mid-century France sought to incorporate new industrial processes into traditional forms of manual production rather than replacing skilled human labor with machines. They preferred a cohabitation synonymous with the contemporary hybrid of art and industry deployed by Labrouste when designing the Bibliothèque Sainte-Geneviève.

This blend of artisanal concerns for quality and industrialized fabricating techniques is especially apparent in the revolution that swept the silversmith industry during the early 1840s. In 1839 Moritz-Hermann Jacobi, a German researcher working in Russia on improvements to storage batteries, discovered by accident that the decomposed metal of the positive terminal (he was using copper) could be deposited on any surface able to carry the battery's negative charge. Jacobi announced his finding in a letter of July 1839 to Michael Faraday, who brought it to the attention of his English colleagues, including Thomas Spencer. Even before learning of Jacobi's research, Spencer had drawn identical conclusions about the potential for electroplating thin coatings of precious metals onto nonferrous metallic objects. One year later the English silversmith George Richard Elkington patented an industrial process for gold and silver plating using electrolysis. He soon discovered that adding a small quantity of carbon sulfur to a bath of silver salts would yield a surface of shiny (rather than matte) silverplate at a fraction of the cost of solid silver.

The Parisian goldsmith Charles-Henri Christofle quickly recognized the potential of Elkington's process. In 1842 Christofle purchased the right to exploit Elkington's patent in France for a period of ten years and began to produce pieces of fine silverplate (Fig. 148). Christofle's insight was soon rewarded: the firm's gross sales rose from 680,000 francs in 1844 to more than two million francs in 1847. The jury of the 1844 Exposition des produits de l'industrie awarded Christofle's company a double gold medal—one for the firm's excellence in traditional metalwork and jewelry and a second "for the manufacturing application of the galvanic processes of gold and silver plating."[80] National importance of this new industry was acknowledged that same year by King Louis-

Philippe: he named Christofle a Chevalier in the Legion of Honor and paid a personal visit to the firm's workshops. The king also commissioned a complete silverplate service for forty people destined to be used in the royal palace.[81]

A large part of Christofle's success derived from the fact that the electrolytic process ensured an even distribution of plated metal, regardless of an object's shape. Moreover, one can measure exactly the amount of precious metal deposited by simply weighing what remained of the source. Christofle was careful to certify accurately the precious metal content of each piece, thus guaranteeing its value. The teakettle made about 1843 (Fig. 148) is a good example of the marriage of science and art achieved by the Christofle firm. The work consists of large surfaces of smooth metal plated to a shining brilliance with little handwrought incising or engraving. Smaller elements of cast metal were welded to the large forms by skilled metalworkers: for example, the sculpted feet and scrollwork supports of the stand, and the arabesque of handles. The assembly was plated by electrolysis with virtually no further human intervention beyond final polishing. Yet the finished work retains the elegance and aura of a handwrought piece, and its price—while certainly not cheap—remained within the range of middle-income budgets. "So let women be very glad," exclaimed the *Gazette des Femmes* about the new process of electrolytic plating in 1845; "henceforth, steel place-settings, those crude instruments, will no longer be able to invoke the excuse of thrift. . . . Henceforth, silver and vermeil stop being a luxury, and no longer call for tying up sizeable amounts of capital."[82]

A parallel assimilation of industrial techniques to the traditions of luxury, hand-crafted production began about 1825 in the workshops of the two principal manufacturers of lead crystal glassware in France: Baccarat (Fig. 149) and Saint-Louis (Fig. 150). Both firms were founded in the 1760s and encouraged by the government of Louis XV on the grounds that France should produce high-quality glassware able to compete in world markets with that of Venice, Bohemia, and England. After three decades of prosperity, both companies fell victim to the political and economic turmoil of the Revolution and the continuous wars under Napoléon. Baccarat went bankrupt in 1806, was sold, and was forced to lay off

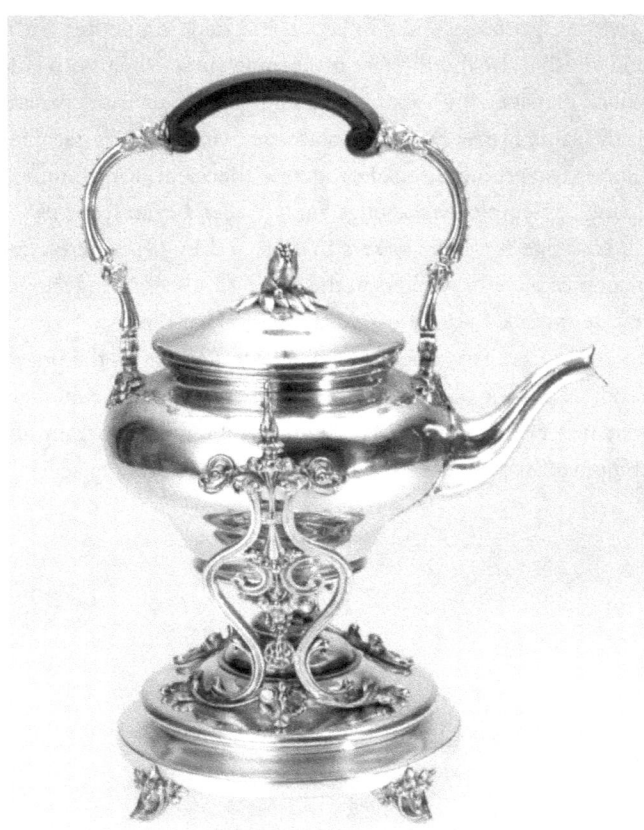

FIGURE 148.   Charles-Henri Christofle & Company, *Teakettle with Stand*, ca. 1843–1844. Silverplate and ebony. Saint-Denis: Musée Bouilhet-Christofle, inv. 43. Photo: © Musée Bouilhet-Christofle.

three-quarters of its workers. Saint-Louis produced glass during the Revolution, but was confiscated in 1798 as national property because the owners had emigrated. The firm was sold to a group of investors from Metz who operated it with a much reduced staff. After Napoléon's final defeat in 1815, the two glassmakers managed to regroup: Baccarat was bought in 1816 by Aimé-Gabriel d'Artigues, former director of Saint-Louis during the middle 1790s, who returned the firm to profitability by 1822; Saint-Louis was reorganized in 1829 when, in concert with Baccarat, it bought or absorbed several small factories. By 1832 Baccarat and Saint-Louis so fully dominated the French market that they were able to regulate prices and product lines in order to avoid competing with one another. In the interest of keeping intact their corps of skilled glassworkers—many of whom spent their entire career in the same firm—French crystalware manufacturers became leaders in corporate social programs. Baccarat, for example, opened an employee's savings bank in 1821, began free medical coverage for glassworkers in 1827, and by 1835 offered an insurance plan for workers in the cutting and engraving shops that reimbursed wages lost during periods of illness.

In this industry where a firm's greatest asset was the practiced teamwork of its skilled artisans, industrial techniques were never expected to replace years of apprenticeship training and practical expertise. Nonetheless, the 1820s brought several

important technical innovations that, like electrolytic plating at Christofle, increased output without sacrificing attention to hand-crafted detail. One of the most important of these was invented in 1824 by Ismaël Robinet, an employee of Baccarat. The Robinet compressed air pump, which is still in use, is a tool to form simple pieces of molten glass for which the special skills of a master glassblower are not required, thus freeing the master for more demanding tasks. At about the same time, techniques for molding molten glass—originally developed in the United States to simulate cheaply the effects of hand cutting—were brought to France and adapted to making high-quality lead crystal. The firm of Saint-Louis was the first to introduce a pressurized molding process that produced larger

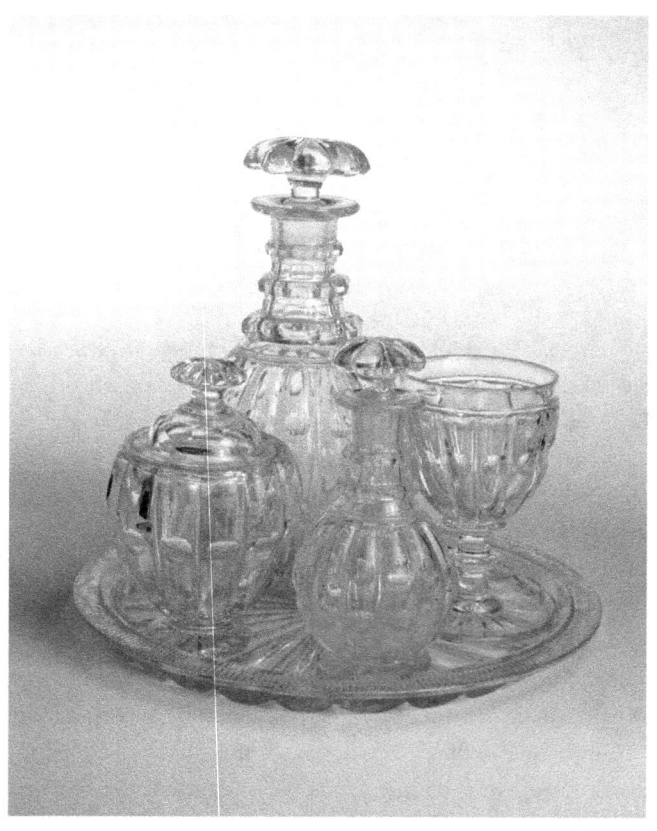

FIGURE 149.   Baccarat & Company, *Nightstand Water Service*, ca. 1831. Molded crystal with additional recutting. Paris, Musée Baccarat (platter diam: 27.6 cm). Photo: © Musée Baccarat.

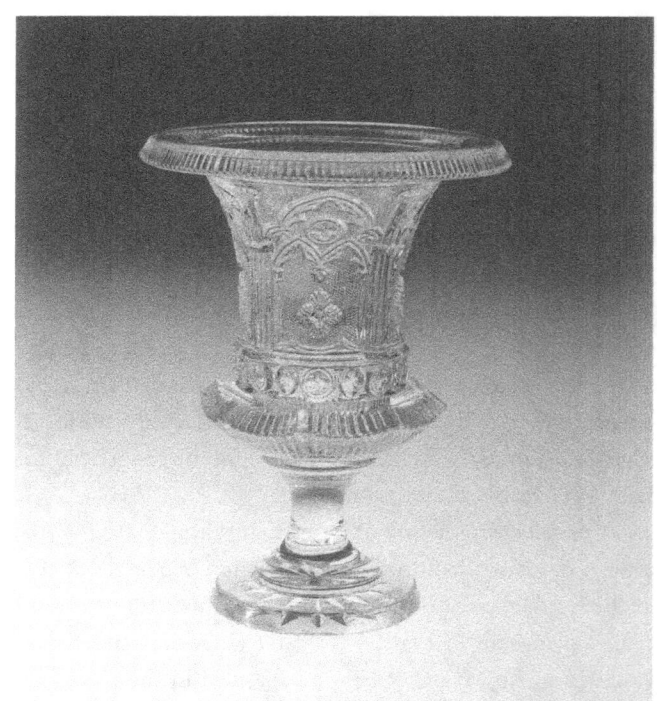

FIGURE 150.   Cristalleries de Saint-Louis, *"Medicis" Vase with Gothic Decoration*, ca. 1840. Pressed glass. New York, Cooper-Hewitt, National Design Musuem, Smithsonian Institution, Gift of Cristalleries de Saint-Louis (1988-108-1), inv. 1988-108-1. Photo: Cooper-Hewitt, National Design Museum, Smithsonian Institution/John Parnell.

and more complex shapes than those made by hand (Fig. 150)—the innovation received a gold medal at the 1834 Exposition des produits de l'industrie.[83] Machinery also entered the cold workrooms where crystalware was typically cut and finished by craftsmen seated at individual stations who turned their cutting wheels by using a pedal mechanism. In 1824 Baccarat opened a new workshop in which one hundred cutting wheels were turned simultaneously by hydraulic power harnessed from the Meurthe River. In the words of Jean-Louis Curtis, "like the Robinet air pump, the new invention offered two interconnected and complementary advantages: it greatly reduced the artisan's work and it raised production."[84]

A Baccarat bedside water service made about 1831 demonstrates how this combination of new technologies affected the design of crystalware (Fig. 149). The individual pieces are molded crystal, which yields hefty, rounded forms of thick glass—characteristics that the duchesse d'Angoulême admired in the Baccarat table service she bought in 1828 and described as "stable, robust, balanced, perfect."[85] The bulging, vertical bands [bambous] comprising the main body of each element were then hand-cut on a wheel to produce a register of reverse-refracting disc shapes [pontils]. Small star-shaped patterns were engraved under the pedestal of each piece, while a large matching star was cut into the underside of the platter. The Baccarat water service—like the Christofle teakettle (Fig. 148)—combines large surfaces of "mechanically" shaped luxury material (molded lead crystal) with areas of detail that could only be executed by skilled hands. The result, as Jules Burat remarked in 1844, was a synthesis of art and industry both aesthetically remarkable and affordable:

While molding improved its products using pressure or pistons, cutting, for its part, expanded its domain: the use of mechanical processes brought about not only greater savings, but also a greater perfection of consistency and polish. One produced these beautiful prismatic cuttings, created by broad ribs, that give crystal such brilliant reflections, and that molding can only partially imitate. The combination of molding and cutting once again made it possible to obtain rich effects at a low price.[86]

Baccarat and Saint-Louis adapted industrial processes during the 1820s that brought quality and good design to an ex-

panded number of clients by reducing costs and increasing production without sacrificing craftsmanship. Achieving this goal was commonly understood to be essential to the nation's well-being. During the course of a much-publicized visit to the Baccarat factory in September 1828, King Charles X reportedly said that "the prosperity of a factory and the well-being of a country depend upon ordinary things, and success consists of putting useful, elegant, and moderately priced items within the reach of the greatest number of consumers."[87] With this official discourse in favor of industries like Baccarat, Charles X embraced a vision of consumer goods shared by contemporaries like Madame Pariset, whose advice to the future mistresses of French bourgeois households encouraged attention to reasonable prices without relinquishing demands for lasting quality, usefulness, and good taste.

Implementing industrial techniques and mechanized processes might threaten over time craft-oriented products like metalworking or glassmaking. But there was at least one domain where their application made possible a flowering unlike anything previously imagined. Parisian publishers had long produced some of the most well-designed, expertly printed, and beautifully bound books in all of Europe. Yet they had not achieved what has been called "an intimate and profound harmony between the pages of text and the image or ornamentation that symbolizes its thought, clarifies the action of its dramatic episodes, and emphasizes the sentiments that emerge from it."[88] Close interaction between text and visual imagery on the pages of a printed book required new technologies all along the production chain. The remarkable aspect of the first decades of the nineteenth century was a confluence of these developments to produce such a thorough transformation of the printing process that it has sometimes been called "the second revolution of the book."[89] Of seminal importance was a dramatic change in the manufacture of paper, which had been produced since the time of Gutenberg in single sheets from a paste obtained by processing pieces of old cloth. Rag paper was not replaced by wood pulp until much later in the nineteenth century, but already in 1799 Nicolas-Louis Robert patented a process for making paper in a continuous roll. The first plant in France to use the new technology opened in 1816. Alongside the possibility of delivering paper continuously to a printing press—rather than one sheet at a time—came experimentation with the design of the press itself. The basic mechanics of printing had changed very little over the centuries. Two separate movements were required to print a page: one to ink the form holding the type, a second to press the form solidly against the paper. The Stanhope press of 1795, which became widely used throughout Europe, effected both movements with a single pass and, because the press was constructed entirely of cast iron rather than wood, it was both faster and more precise than most of its competitors. But even with its mechanical improvements, the Stanhope did not alter the two-step premise of printing established by Gutenberg.

Early experiments to use a roller for inking the type spawned the idea that the entire press could be reconfigured using rotating cylinders—one for inking and a second to press the paper against the type—and that their respective movements could be coordinated by means of a gear mechanism. The continuous motion of such a press, fed by a continuous supply of paper on rolls, held the promise of great improvements in productivity. Two German engineers, Friedrich Koenig and Andreas Bauer, unveiled the first completely mechanical press in 1813. The event is a landmark in the history of printing, because integrating all the moving parts of a press also meant it was possible to drive it with a single source of power. Within a year the London *Times* was being printed on a steam-powered version of the Koenig-Bauer press. By contrast, mechanical presses were adopted slowly in Paris because master printers believed the new machines threatened their livelihood. The earliest examples of the new presses were installed in Paris about 1823, but not without resistance: during the Revolution of 1830 (see Chapter Two) workers took advantage of the momentary chaos to destroy six mechanical presses belonging to the Imprimerie Nationale. Such acts of violence were both too late and too isolated to stem the tide of mechanization that flooded the print shops of Paris. By 1833 the *Magasin Pittoresque* was printing one hundred thousand eight-page copies per week on two mechanical presses powered by steam.[90]

Print runs of the sort achieved by the *Magasin Pittoresque* were made possible by a second technical revolution in the printing process perfected about the same time. One of the most labor-intensive aspects of printing was the actual setting of type into the forms that went to press. The type itself was expensive. Large print shops might own many thousands of individual characters, but even with huge inventories they were obliged to print long texts in parts so that type could be recycled for use on later pages. A second printing meant resetting the entire text page by page—an expense that few books could justify economically. One way around this problem, first developed by the Scottish printer William Ged in 1739, was to make a negative plaster mold [matrice] from a form of set type, and then use this mold to cast (usually in lead or tin) a positive [cliché] that reproduced the set type in a single block of metal able to go to press. Ged's process, which came to be known as stereotype, simultaneously freed up individual characters for re-use and fixed a page permanently so that it might be reprinted later without recourse to resetting each word. Since multiple copies of the positive cliché were easy to cast, a single print job could be set up on several presses at once, greatly reducing the printing time of any given work. Stereotype printing was widely adopted in Europe during the last decade of the eighteenth century. It was introduced into France about 1795 by the printer Firmin Didot, who first used molded plates to publish the logarithmic tables of Callot. Within a few years, Didot adopted the stereotype process for publishing new works, and he began to produce clichés of literary texts in the public domain—for example, the works of Racine, Molière, and Voltaire—which he sold to other printers who actually produced the volumes. The result was a dramatic increase in the number of books printed each year: from slightly more than one thousand volumes in 1800 to more than eight thousand in 1826.[91]

Didot also introduced into France the process of end-grain woodblock engraving, a technique perfected about 1775 by the Englishman Thomas Bewick of Newcastle. Bewick's method, which entails incising a relief of the desired image onto a block of boxwood cut across the grain, was technically related to copperplate engraving—indeed, some of the burins or cutting tools were identical for the two processes. But the great advantage of end-grain woodblocks was that because the design emerged in relief, they could be placed into press forms alongside rows of type. With the advent of stereotype printing, woodblock images and letters could be molded as part of a single cliché, making it possible for the first time in history to print both text and images on the same page with a single pass of the press. The results, as Michel Melot remarks, were utterly new:

Once engraved, the end-grain woodblock was treated like a typographic block and formed a mosaic with it, allowing the first newspaper-like page layouts in which text and image, intimately joined together, play a curious double language: reinforcing one another, but also contradicting or clarifying each other when the image does not say enough or the text says too much. . . . In books, the end-grain woodblock made it possible for the image to infiltrate the text, to grow roots or branches in it, and to transform the space of reading into a space of spectacle.[92]

Didot was the first Parisian printer to recognize the economic and aesthetic significance of integrating words and images in this way. He brought to Paris in 1817 the Englishman Charles Thompson. Himself a student of Bewick, Thompson trained a whole generation of French woodblock engravers—including Henri-Désiré Porret, Louis-Henri Brévière, Pierre-François Godard, Jacques-Adrien Lavieille, and Hippolyte Lavoignat—who produced a great flood of illustrated books in Paris during the 1830s and 1840s.

The visual synthesis and semantic interplay of words and images, central to the parameters of the new art and championed by Victor Hugo in his writings and drawings (see Chapter Six), became technically possible on a large scale by the middle 1820s. In the words of Jean Adhémar and Jean-Pierre Seguin, "a literary movement, sketched out for nearly a century, found gathered together—at the very moment it reached maturity—all the necessary conditions for its expression."[93] The single most important visual consequence of the confluence between new printing technologies and contemporary aesthetic concerns was a proliferation of visual imagery within books: from full-page illustrations in editions designed for a luxury market (Fig. 152) to small works nestled within the pages of mass-market volumes (Fig. 153). Coupled with experiments using new forms of illuminated capitals and margin decorations, books became more visually complex than ever before. The most conspicuous component of this heightened visuality was the vignette.

What is a vignette? Strictly speaking, it is simply an illustration, but is distinguished from other forms of printed imagery by a peculiar relationship to the typography of the surrounding page (Figs. 151, 153). Printed literally alongside words by means of woodblock engravings cast in the same stereotype block as the text itself, vignettes are usually unframed; rather, they bleed at the edges so that the space of the image is not delimited but simply disperses into the page itself. Where printed words establish an opacity of the page (since we tend not to imagine words hanging in mid-air), vignettes—which invariably depict something or someone in space—puncture that opacity in surprising ways. The effect is described succinctly by Charles Rosen and Henri Zerner:

The vignette is not a window because it has no limit, no frame. The image, defined from its center rather than its edges, emerges from the paper as an apparition or a fantasy. The uncertainty of contour often makes it impossible to distinguish the edge of the vignette from the paper: the whiteness of the paper, which represents the play of light within the image, changes imperceptively into the paper of the book and realizes, in small, the Romantic blurring of art and reality.[94]

Charlet's vignette of Napoléon crossing the Saint-Bernard Pass (Fig. 153) illustrates the mechanics of this blurring: on one hand, the whiteness of the snow becomes the page supporting the text; on the other, reading the associated paragraph forces us to traverse Charlet's visualization, thus closing the circuit of our attention and setting it in motion once again.

Writing in 1883, Jules Champfleury recalled the speed and insistence with which vignettes became an integral part of nearly every publishing venture:

In the heydays between 1830 and 1840 scarcely any creative work appeared without vignettes. Authors went on about them in their prefaces; criticism itself was disarmed before the image. A book was not made whose publisher, selecting his illustrators, would not vaunt them in his prospectus. You had to be irritable or annoyed by the passing fashion to deny yourself this décor.[95]

Vignettes have a long history in book publishing, but prior to the 1820s they were expensive and used sparingly. "Before 1830 one scarcely thought about illustrating books," remarked Georges Duplessis in 1857; "a few vignettes commissioned from an engraver by a thrifty publisher constituted a book's most beautiful embellishment, and often only one given its high price: it placed before the reader's eyes only one scene of the novel or only a single historical event."[96] All that changed, in the words of a reviewer at the 1844 Exposition de l'industrie française, when French typography adopted "the woodblock vignette, neglected for two centuries, and—thanks to this adornment that now presents graceful designs for each page of a book—the example of luxury joined to low prices became possible."[97]

It is no accident that both Champfleury and Duplessis cite 1830 as opening the great era of illustrated books in France, for that was the year in which the firm Delangle frères published *Le Roi de Bohème et ses sept châteaux*.[98] Written by Charles Nodier—avid bibliophile, head of the Arsenal Library, author of *La Sylphide*, and close friend of Victor Hugo (see Chapter Six)—the book was both a pastiche and a spoof of Laurence Sterne's *Tristram Shandy*, whose story about the king of Bohemia is never finished. In Nodier's version, however, the narrative thread is not so much broken off as never begun, for the text consists of voices, reveries, and lists of words that challenge the very notion of syntax. It ends abruptly when the author observes that he has used up his allotted supply of ink and paper. Even more remarkable was the book's layout and typography. Nodier specified pages where several kinds and sizes of typeface were juxtaposed or set in pictographic formations. His typographic experimentation was seconded by fifty woodblock vignettes designed by Tony Johannot and engraved by Henri-Désiré Porret. Where prior use of woodblock engraving still treated the imagery as if separate from the text, the great novelty of Nodier's creation was, to cite Simon Jeune, "the extreme flexibility of the page layout—a systematic rejection of vignettes at the top or bottom of pages. The fifty engravings are strewn through the text with an obvious whimsy. But, in fact, the author's intentions are grasped and highlighted with as much respect as ingenuity."[99] Ironically, where the book's prescient exploration of the cognitive

terrain between words and images demonstrated vividly the affective potential of vignettes, the project was a financial disaster and forced the publisher into bankruptcy.

Nodier's *Roi de Bohème* proved that copious illustrations were technically possible. There remained the problem of amortizing expenses to make the finished work accessible and profitable: with book prices varying from fifteen to one hundred francs, depending upon the quality of paper, even simple publications remained beyond the budget of most middle-income families. Not surprisingly, the final piece in the mosaic of factors fostering the great explosion of French illustrated books was an idea borrowed from the periodical press. In 1833 the *Magasin Pittoresque* began to appear weekly in the form of an eight-page booklet [livret] priced at only two sous (about one-tenth of a franc). That same year a monthly, *Le Musée des familles, lectures du soir*, began publication at ten sous. Both of these works, and others like them, featured long articles and works of literature serialized over several numbers. They were also illustrated with woodblock prints.

Some critics grasped immediately the threat to elite culture presented by this new development. Raoul de Croy deplored the appearance of the *Magasin Pittoresque* in the columns of the prestigious *Journal des Artistes*:

Huge revolution! Immense conquest! The fine arts [Beaux-Arts] are going to become as popular as the journal carrying that name. Public exhibitions will no longer be yearly, they will be daily; there will be a museum every day, not at the Louvre . . . but in your own house, in my house, in Pontoise, in Quimper, in Brive-la-Gaillarde like in Paris.[100]

Publishers, on the other hand, realized that joining new printing technologies to the strategies of sales and distribution practiced by the periodical press could open a huge market for illustrated books because large print runs reduced dramatically the cost per copy. Alexandre Paulin pioneered the new formula in 1835 by publishing a serialized edition of Alain René le Sage's *Histoire de Gil Blas de Santillane*, illustrated with woodblock vignettes designed by Jean-François Gigoux and an introductory essay by none other than Charles Nodier (Fig. 151).[101] The book's prospectus prom-

CHAPITRE III

APRÈS QUEL DÉSAGRÉABLE INCIDENT DON ALPHONSE SE TROUVA AU COMBLE DE SA JOIE, ET PAR QUELLE AVENTURE GIL BLAS SE VIT TOUT À COUP DANS UNE HEUREUSE SITUATION.

Nous poussâmes gaiement jusqu'à Bunol, où, par malheur, il fallut nous arrêter. Don Alphonse tomba malade : il lui prit une grosse fièvre, avec des redoublements qui me firent craindre pour sa vie. Heureusement il n'y avoit point là de médecins, et j'en fus quitte pour la peur. Il se trouva hors de danger au bout de trois jours, et mes soins achevèrent de le rétablir. Il se montra très-sensible à tout ce que j'avois fait pour lui ; et,

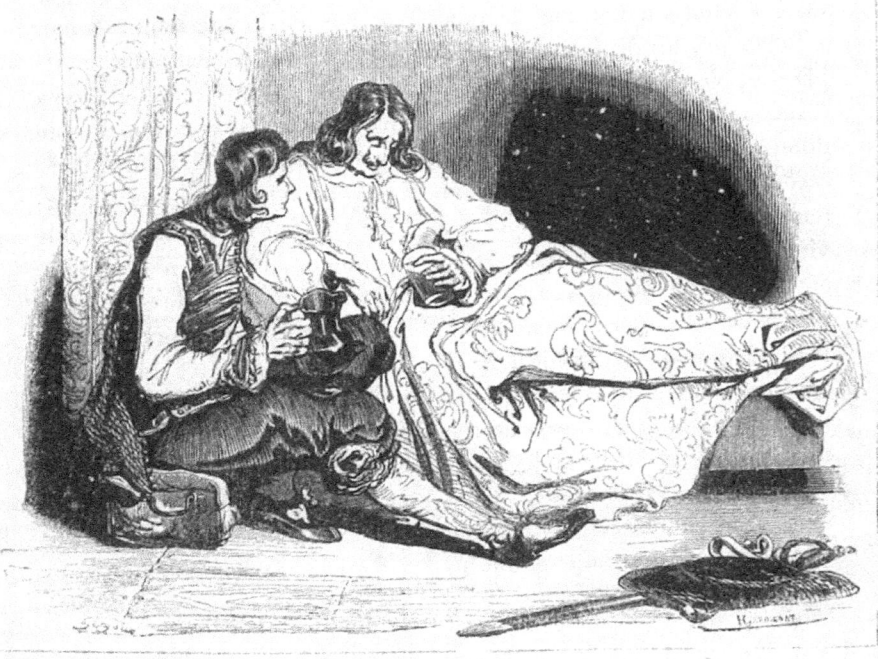

FIGURE 151. Jean Gigoux and H. Lavognat, Page from Paulin edition of *Histoire de Gil Blas* (Book VI, Chapter III), 1835. Woodblock engraving and type. Stanford, Stanford University Libraries, inv. 843.5 L62gn (25.4 × 16.5 cm). Photo: © Davey Hubay.

ised a large volume—five hundred vignettes and lavish page ornamentations—for purchase over fifty weeks at five sous, or one-quarter franc, per week. The total cost of the volume would be less than fourteen francs.[102] Customers were assured that each weekly installment [livraison] would contain four or five large vignettes plus subsidiary ornamentation. Paulin's volume eventually included six hundred vignettes, yet the total price remained a modest fifteen francs. More than fifteen thousand copies were sold.

Both Paulin and Gigoux earned tidy sums from the *Gil Blas* project. More important, its success demonstrated the livraison marketing technique was a viable alternative to traditional publishing practices. There were two interconnected reasons for this: first, a steady flow of income from weekly sales of the livraisons provided the capital to pay engravers, printers, and supplies for producing subsequent segments; second, at the end of the project Paulin owned a complete set of stereotype plates from which he could publish further editions of the entire volume by expending no more than the material costs of printing. The livraison form of marketing transformed publishers into speculators willing to take on book projects with only partial capitalization. If sales revenues failed to materialize, the project could be dropped with a relatively small loss of capital and a few disgruntled customers. Speculation produced incentives to make the arrival of each livraison an event in itself, so that publishers were soon promising a wealth of images with each installment. Finally, livraison marketing eventually affected the way authors wrote their texts, because publishers encouraged them to produce more or less complete episodes that would fit within the pages of a single installment.

Publishers [éditeurs] became key players in the production of illustrated books. Previously they assumed the material costs of making a book (editing the manuscript, setting the type, printing the pages) and passed it to booksellers [libraires] for distribution. Now they combined both roles and controlled the entire chain of production from author to reader: *éditeurs-libraires* (as they were often called) chose or commissioned texts, hired illustrators, selected typefaces and paper, enlisted the best printers, and sold the completed livraisons directly to subscribers. Writing in 1839,

Léon Curmer, one of the most successful of these entrepreneurs, summarized the new speculative character of his profession:

Today bookselling has acquired a different importance, owing to the profession of *Publisher* that has come to be established in its midst since the introduction of illustrated books. . . . The publisher, intelligent intermediary between the public and all the workers who cooperate in preparing a book, should be familiar with every detail of the latter's work; master of a reliable taste, attentive to the preferences of the public, he sometimes has to sacrifice his own feelings to those of the greatest number so as to succeed in making acceptable, imperceptibly and by calibrated concessions, what true artists of a more refined taste approve and want. This profession is more than a craft, it has become a difficult art to practice, but one that amply makes up for its troubles with intellectual pleasures at every moment.[103]

Curmer was eminently qualified to describe the multifarious tasks of publishing, for he had just brought to market one of the most ambitious and beautifully executed illustrated books of the nineteenth century: a luxury edition of two texts by Jacques-Henri Bernardin de Saint-Pierre, *La Chaumière indienne* and *Paul et Virginie* (Fig. 152).

Bernardin de Saint-Pierre, a naturalist and friend of Jean-Jacques Rousseau, originally published *Paul et Virginie* in 1788 as an appendix to the third edition of his *Études de la Nature*. Set on the island of present-day Mauritius, where the author had spent his military service, it is the story of two island adolescents whose childhood friendship becomes a chaste love that thrives in a setting of lush vegetation and the unspoiled beauty of their island home. Virginia leaves the island for France when the death of an aunt holds the prospect that she might inherit a fortune. She dies tragically in a shipwreck at the story's end—within sight of the island and witnessed by Paul—when returning to her family and her beloved. Alongside lessons in the manner of Rousseau about the evils of civilization, Bernardin de Saint-Pierre provides lavish descriptions of the island's unusual plant life, its unpredictable and violent weather, and its profoundly uncivilized state. At one point, for example, Paul and Virginia become lost not far from their homes, in

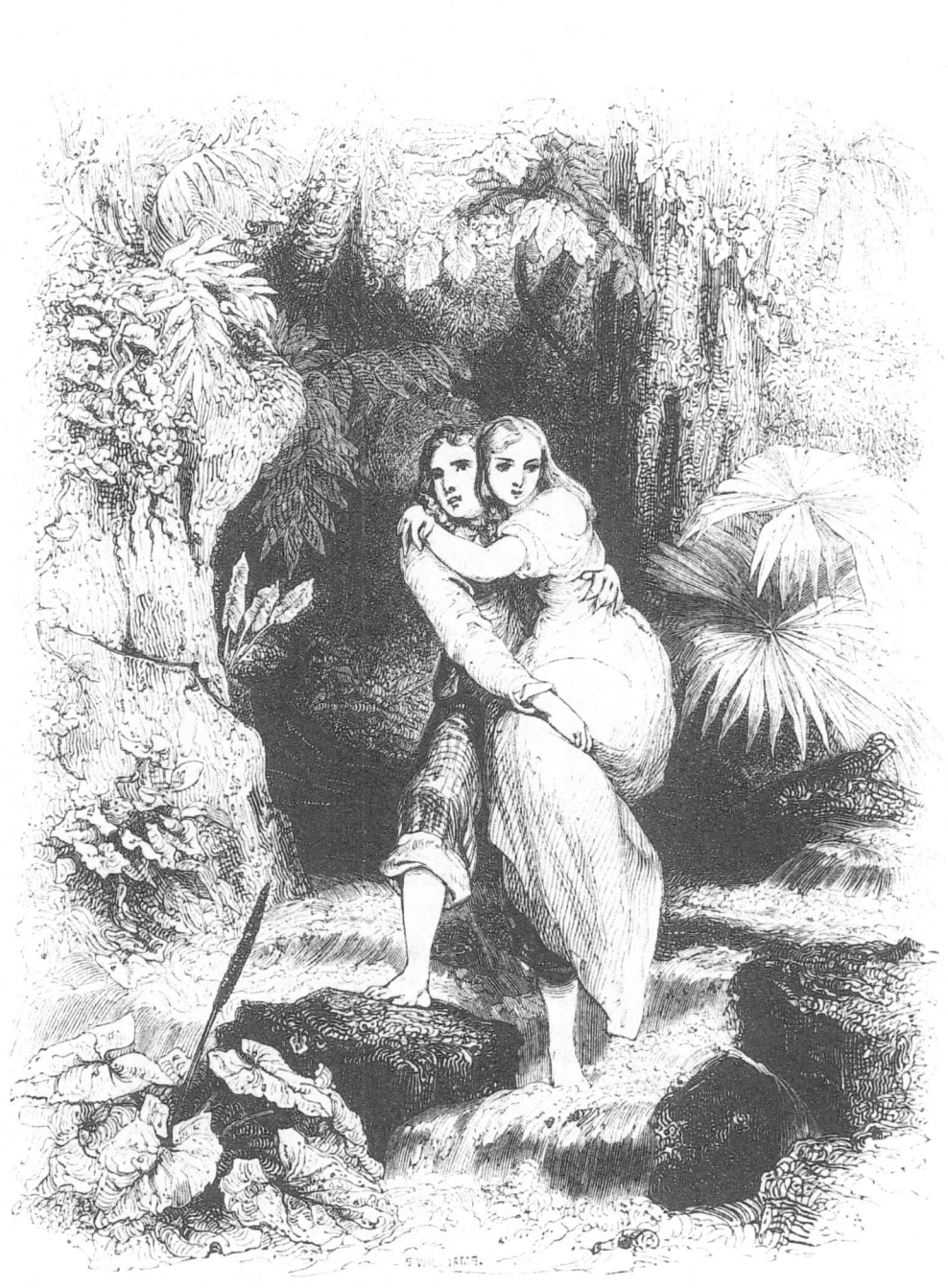

FIGURE 152. Tony Johannot and François-Louis Français, engraved by Samuel Williams, *Le Passage du Torrent* from Curmer edition of *Paul et Virginie*, 1838. Woodblock engraving. Berkeley, University of California, Bancroft Library, inv. Z239.2.C86 1838s (approx. 26.5 × 17 cm). Photo: Courtesy of the Bancroft Library, University of California-Berkeley.

a part of the island "covered by forests" and "so little known, even today, that many of its rivers and mountains are not yet named."[104] They reach a river that "ran frothing across a bed of rocks," with a sound that "frightened Virginia; she did not dare to put her feet into it to make the crossing." Paul is obliged to "take Virginia on his back and, loaded down in this way, to cross the river's slippery rocks in spite of its tumultuous waters."

Like most of the illustrations in Curmer's volume, the full-page woodblock engraving of this episode (Fig. 152) was the joint effort of two artists: Tony Johannot, who rendered Paul's transport of Virginia as a more intimate encounter than suggested by the workman-like language of the text, and François-Louis Français, who drew the pictorial surround of rocks and vegetation. One of the aims of Curmer's project was to combine a conscientious rendering of the island's unusual plant life with the sentimental attractions of its story, a goal clearly laid out in the book's prospectus:

Many of the bushes and plants named by Bernardin de Saint-Pierre are completely unknown to most readers; we have done the most conscientious research to offer an exact picture of the tropical vegetation. M. Théodore Descourtilz, long familiar with the treasures of this very diverse natural world, has drawn, especially for us, birds of elegant and supple shapes and the plants they like. While trying to give a suitable value to natural history, it will only be an essential accessory to the touching scenes of the novel. M. Tony Johannot has reproduced with a fresh superiority of sentiment all of the work's dramatic parts and, by a fortunate partnership, the crayon of M. Français has framed these charming compositions in the sites and the vegetation of the region.[105]

The complete volume contains twenty-nine full-page woodblock engravings, seven steelplate engravings, and a colored map of the island all printed on China paper. The text is interspersed with more than four hundred fifty vignettes. Curmer enlisted many artists to produce this imagery: along with Johannot and Français were Paul Huet, Eugène Isabey, Ernest Meissonier, Charles Marville, Charles-Émile Jacque, and Louis Steinheil. The woodblocks were cut by some of the best contemporary engravers, including the Frenchmen Lavoignat, Brévière, Porret and, from England, Orrin Smith,

C. Gray, and the trio of Mary Anne, Samuel and Thomas Williams. The high standards of quality set by Curmer can be inferred from his costs of producing the original edition of ten thousand copies: he paid more than twenty-eight thousand francs to the designers of its plates and vignettes, over thirty-two thousand francs to woodblock engravers, nearly eleven thousand francs to steelplate engravers, and more than thirty thousand francs to his printer. By contrast, Curmer spent a paltry three-hundred-eighty francs for the rights to publish Bernardin de Saint-Pierre's texts![106]

Paul et Virginie was produced over the course of fifteen months, at the rate of two livraisons per month, beginning in October 1836: each livraison was priced at 1 franc 25 centimes in Paris and 1 franc 50 centimes when mailed to the provinces. A Parisian could own the entire volume for 37.50 francs, while its price elsewhere was 45.00 francs. Despite the huge sums of capital tied up in the project, Curmer estimated that he cleared a profit of about eighty thousand francs, although his return on investment was achieved very slowly—nearly four thousand copies of the original edition remained unsold as late as 1845. Making books had clearly become an industry of long-term financial speculation.

A very small edition (about twenty copies) of *Paul et Virginie* was printed entirely on China paper and offered to wealthy connoisseurs and collectors of fine books able to spend three hundred francs for a single volume. In an ultimate demonstration of the same spirit, Curmer's own copy of the book—unique for being printed on fine parchment paper and richly bound in red leather—was further enhanced by having all the original drawings for the printed illustrations and vignettes glued onto separate overleafs at the appropriate places. On a sheet at the front of this unique testament to the artistry and good taste of publishing in 1830s Paris, Curmer penned a long homily to his book that celebrates its importance as both aesthetic object and product of industry:

Thanks to you, my dear book, I studied letterpress printing and I was fortunate enough to make it progress a bit at a time when it was believed to be at the outer limits of perfection. I led papermaking into a new direction; I effected a revolution in the handling of letterpress ink; wood engraving had not dared to do what it did for this book. But also, what drawings! . . . France was the land of your birth, my beloved book, and you provoked the envy of England, Germany, Spain, Italy, and the Far East—all of whom wanted to have you with your new finery in their own language. . . . Now, follow your destiny! When I leave this earth, where you will have a long career to travel before we find ourselves meeting in the same dust, may God accompany you along with my wishes, may you fall into the hands of a long dynasty of intelligent connoisseurs who appreciate you and put you in the spotlight that you deserve, may they preserve you with love![107]

By any criterion Curmer's *Paul et Virginie* represents the high end of book publishing in Romantic Paris. Its marriage of art and technology produced a luxury book well beyond the aesthetic range of a truly mass-market audience, even at its relatively modest price.

By contrast, a richly illustrated edition of the *Mémorial de Sainte-Hélène*, published by Ernest Bourdin in 1842, is characteristic of how the technology perfected by Curmer transformed the look and feel of books aimed at the widest possible public (Fig. 153).[108] The *Mémorial de Sainte-Hélène* was written by Emmanuel de Las Cases, an intimate of Napoléon who shared the first seventeen months of the Emperor's final exile on the desolate South Atlantic island of Saint Helena. Las Cases was deported by the British for trying to smuggle letters back to Europe, but during his stay he kept a daily journal of his conversations with Napoléon—including the Emperor's reflections on his downfall and insights about the great moments of Empire. The notebooks of Las Cases were confiscated by the British when he was deported in late 1816, but were returned to him after Napoléon's death (5 May 1821). Las Cases published the first edition of the *Mémorial* in 1823 to great excitement. A second edition was immediately announced, an English version appeared simultaneously, and German translations were soon published in both Stuttgart and Dresden.

The eyewitness, first-person accounts of Las Cases convinced sympathetic readers of the physical, material, and psychological trials suffered by Napoléon at the hands of his British jailors. The text tended to support French suspicions that England had treated its captive as a common criminal rather than a prisoner of war who had nobly sur-

rendered his sword. Furthermore, in his conversations with Las Cases, Napoléon did not hesitate to have the last word in shaping his legacy: he repeatedly wrapped himself in the mantle of liberal idealism and downplayed the harsh realities of military dictatorship. Finally, publication of the *Mémorial* awakened a powerful nostalgia for the great adventure of Empire (discussed in Chapter One), and fueled a market for sympathetic retrospective images, including the lithographs of Charlet (Fig. 14).

When Bourdin decided to produce a relatively cheap but lavishly illustrated edition of the *Mémorial de Sainte-Hélène*, he enlisted Charlet as principal designer. Like any good speculator, Bourdin wanted to combine the historical allure of the text with the cultural recognition of Charlet, whose fame was built—quite literally—on the imagery of Napoleonic France. Nor was the timing of Bourdin's publishing venture fortuitous, for he planned the project to take advantage of the huge public outpouring of pro-Bonapartist sentiment that swept France in the wake the Emperor's posthumous return to France in December of 1840 (Fig. 54). Bourdin's marketing savvy is evident in the prospectus circulated to announce his edition:

It is simultaneously a history, a poem, a legend, a chronicle; there is everything you could want in this last monument of imperial royalty battling misfortune; above all, in these pages, written in big letters, is the name of FRANCE. It is the most French book ever written at any time. . . . Our national treasure Charlet, that unaffected, easy-going, inspired, often sublime painter, appears with five hundred fresh and wonderful drawings. . . . The new publication, which wants to be linked to a solemn anniversary among all those announced by history, will begin on the 15th of this month, day of the return to Paris of the hero's remains.[109]

Bourdin planned to publish one hundred sixteen livraisons, at the rate of about two per week, each comprised of either eight or sixteen pages and about five or six engravings. Each livraison was priced at thirty centimes, which meant that the entire two-volume set, including twenty full-page illustrations and more than seventeen hundred pages, could be had for less than thirty-five francs. Subscribers who paid in advance for the first twenty livraisons would receive, free

« donné ce qui ne lui appartient pas : quel diable de présent ! » Cependant Duroc avait été payer le maître du bâtiment ; il en tenait la quittance de vente qu'on remit à l'homme. Dès qu'il commença à comprendre, sa joie fut jusqu'au délire ; il fit des folies. La somme était encore à peu près la même que ci-dessus. « Ainsi, disait l'Empereur, on voit « que les désirs des hommes ne sont pas aussi immodérés qu'on le « pense, et qu'il est plus facile de les rendre heureux qu'on ne croit ; càr « assurément ces deux hommes trouvèrent le bonheur. »

Napoléon répétait souvent des traits de la sorte ; en voici un écrit sous sa dictée : il s'agit du passage du Saint-Bernard , avant la bataille de Marengo.

« Le Consul montait, dans le plus mauvais temps, le mulet d'un ha- « bitant de Saint-Pierre, désigné comme étant le mulet le plus sûr de « tout le pays. Le guide du Consul était un grand et vigoureux jeune

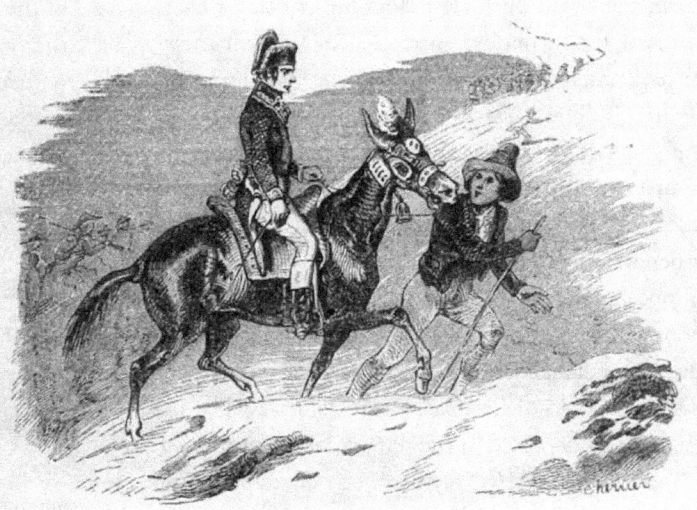

« homme de vingt-deux ans, qui s'entretint beaucoup avec lui, en s'a- « bandonnant à cette confiance propre à son âge et à la simplicité des « habitants des montagnes. Il confia au Premier Consul toutes ses pei- « nes, ainsi que les rêves de bonheur qu'il faisait pour l'avenir. Arrivé « au couvent, le Premier Consul, qui jusque-là ne lui avait rien témoi- « gné, écrivit un billet et le donna à ce paysan pour le remettre à son « adresse. Ce billet était un ordre qui prescrivait diverses dispositions,

of charge, "a very beautiful bronze medal of Napoléon engraved by our illustrious M. Bovy and made especially for this edition." Bourdin's marketing strategy was handsomely rewarded: his edition of the *Mémorial* sold more than twenty-two thousand copies. Surely the book's modest price was a factor in this success, as were its generally high production values that included good quality paper, fairly careful printing, and an attractive design that used a double fillet to frame each page and its attendant engravings.

Enlisting Charlet was a masterful idea, for his huge popular reputation rested not only upon memorable renderings of Napoleonic France but also a plain-spoken charm that many likened to Molière and La Fontaine: "The language in which he expresses himself is not that of sublime men," remarked Delacroix in his well-known essay on Charlet, "but his imagery is as penetrating as their prose or verse. He never disguises, *he never embellishes*. He is merciless with affectation and false sensibility. He adopts the language of no humanitarian clique."[110] The immediate appeal of Charlet's unaffected imagery is nowhere more evident than in the vignette he designed to accompany an anecdote about Napoléon's generosity (Fig. 153). According to the Emperor's version of the episode, as recorded by Las Cases, the young peasant who lent his mule to the general—and who guided him across the Saint-Bernard Pass—was immediately rewarded with a house and a piece of land.[111] Charlet extrapolated from this story an image of Napoléon trundling through a snowy landscape astride the sure-footed mule. Charlet's vignette anchors the tale with a flat-footed literalism that resonates widely, since most readers would regard the page while remembering official imagery of that event as recorded and made famous by Jacques-Louis David in 1801 (Fig. 1). Far from the charging horse, the implacable calm, and the heroic drive of David's picture, Charlet's little image seems to speak with a veracity that reinforces the text's claim to transcribe faithfully the Emperor's words. Here, in the pages of a book adorned by humble woodblock images, French readers discovered a Napoléon of human scale that David and his colleagues had concealed behind a rhetoric of politics and power.

In the context of efforts by Louis-Philippe's government to inscribe the memory of Empire upon the public monuments of Paris (see Chapter Three), it is no surprise that Bourdin's edition sold well. The illustrated *Mémorial* encouraged individual readers to rehabilitate Napoléon with a gesture of sentiment rather than politics—a displacement rehearsed nationally when the Emperor's body was returned to Paris and solemnly enshrined under the dome of the Invalides. A few years later, the same sentimental attachment to the Emperor's memory would become a major factor in electing Bonaparte's nephew to the presidency, an investiture that opened the door to the coup-d'état of 1852 and launched the Second Empire (see Epilogue). Without diminishing the importance of political intrigue and powerful interests in that story, one must recognize that the widespread distribution and plain-spoken appeal of low-cost, illustrated books like Bourdin's edition of the *Mémorial* paved the way for that unexpected return of Bonapartism to the center of French political life.

Re-Producing Art

Under our fickle and rainy sky, in those gardens where it is often so cold, we can scarcely understand these completely naked marble statues, we suffer their pain, and we are sometimes tempted to give them half our coat. But the day when [sculpture] found a place on the velvets of our console tables, the day it took charge of the smallest details of our interior, then it was truly welcome in our midst; it became our constant companion and, at the present time, we cannot understand how we were able to do without it for so long. That's how I explain the presence of the Susse company in the Galeries of Industry: it has made a veritable industry out of art.

—Jules Janin[112]

In his review of the 1839 Exposition des produits de l'industrie, Jules Janin spends considerable time discussing why sculpture has become more of an everyday art than ever before. Essential to this shift is what can be called the domestication of sculpture: although it was historically a large-scale, expensive, and fundamentally public art, Janin recognized that small-scale sculptures had become necessary accents for the tasteful decoration of private interiors. Like the confluence of several industrial technologies that led to the production of affordable illustrated books during the 1830s, new patterns of collecting and marketing sculpture were fueled by advancements in technology that made it possible to re-scale and reproduce three-dimensional works of art. They also generated new questions about the legal rights and responsibilities of doing so.

Foremost among the new technologies, and displayed to great interest at the 1839 exhibition, was a machine—invented and patented by Achille Collas in 1836—for mechanically reproducing sculptures. Simple in principle, albeit mechanically complex, the Collas machine consisted of a tracing needle linked to a cutting stylus, a rigid support to hold both the original sculpture and a plaster blank, and a system of gears. Turning a crank moved the tracing needle across the surface of the original sculpture and transferred its movements to the cutting stylus, where they were repeated at a preset scale to carve the blank. Collas displayed the capabilities of his machine at the exhibition of 1839 with a reduced copy of the *Venus de Milo* that Janin found incredibly compelling:

So! M. Collas has known how to do for the *Venus of Milo* what the printing press did for Homer's poem. He has popularized it; he has put it within everyone's reach. He has not made one of those messed-up, horrible, sickening copies that plaster workers peddle on their heads and sell to village innkeepers as the *Apollo Belvedere* or the *Venus of Milo*; he has made a lifelike image of this great marble.[113]

Janin was not alone in his admiration. The exhibition jury recognized that the *Venus de Milo* "would open the field that had been conquered by engineering in the long-respected domain of statuary sculpture" and awarded Collas a silver medal, an honor that was repeated in 1844.[114] The commercial potential of the Collas machine was immediately apparent; Janin drew a timely comparison with daguerreotypes and summarized its future significance for the history of collecting:

The process of M. Collas is as inexorable as M. Daguerre's sunlight; its glance is as sure, its hand is as skillful. Now, do I have to tell you all the consequences of an invention like this? Here's what it does:

the Musée du Louvre is no longer at the Louvre; the museum of Rome, Naples, or Florence is no longer only in Naples, Florence, or Rome. The masterpieces of statuary are everywhere reproduced much better than engraving, reproduced by a force as powerful for human thought as the printing press. . . . Thanks to it, we will soon have the most beautiful museum that a prince ever imagined, we will be able to gather together in our residences masterpieces selected from all the museums of Europe.[115]

By the end of 1839 Collas had joined with a silversmith named Ferdinand Barbedienne to form a company specializing in sculptural reproductions that eventually became one of the foremost bronze foundries of nineteenth-century Paris.

If the Collas machine made possible the production of reduced-scale, high-quality plaster models from large and well-known sculptures, the perfection of sand-casting techniques during the middle 1830s made it feasible to reproduce those models in the prestigious material of bronze. Sand casting involves taking a mold of a master model using fine-grained sand, drying the mold with heat, and removing the model. The reassembled mold is then filled with molten bronze, but is destroyed when extracting the cast. The salient economic characteristic of sand-casting is preserving the master model that is used to make many replicas of the relatively cheap sand molds. There are, however, two important drawbacks to sand-casting: fine details are not rendered very precisely; it is very difficult to cast complex pieces with appendages extending in several directions. The first of these problems was addressed by extensive touch ups to the casts with a process called chasing. The second was usually circumvented by cutting the original model into pieces and casting it as separate parts. Individually cast parts were then remounted by skilled employees of the foundry. The small bronze statuette of *Innocence*, designed by Charles Cumberworth around 1840 (Fig. 154), is an example of a founder's master-model cut into parts—the head and base are separate pieces held in place by removable pins.

Secondary reworkings of a completed cast were often deplored by critics as fatal shortcomings of the sand-casting process. The synopsis written by Jules Burat in 1844 is typical:

Today, the system of casting adopted without exception is sand-casting. The sculptor produces his model; a mold of it is made in prepared sand into which molten metal is poured. But this operation is not done all at once: it is carried out, like plaster casting, by dividing a model into parts, arranged so that each of them can be freed from the mold. As a result of this, you only obtain related parts that must be joined together, mended, and polished so as to recompose the model given by the sculptor. It is a question of putting back into place the arms, hands, heads, parts of the torso, etc. with a perfect precision, with a profound sentiment for art, to make a whole from it all. . . . Thus, in general, one gets much more of the work of mounters or finishers than of the creative artist.[116]

Burat and others were bothered by the fact that finished replicas displayed a great deal of handiwork by someone other than the original artist. He argued for a return to the time-honored process of lost-wax casting in which the original wax model is melted away by the molten metal (hence "lost"). Complicated models can be cast in one piece using the lost-wax technique, and it is a much more reliable recorder of finely worked details than sand-casting. Burat's main point was that the technique does not require extensive remounting and chasing. The principal drawback of the lost-wax process is precisely destruction of the original model. One could—as Burat suggested—make multiple wax models from a single plaster mold, but each wax master would have to be retouched by the artist before casting. For Burat this was a desideratum, insofar as every bronze would then be a direct record of the artist's hand rather than the work of anonymous craftsmen and variable talents. Indeed, Burat's objections to sand-casting anticipate by nearly a century Walter Benjamin's belief that "the whole sphere of authenticity is outside technical—and, of course, not only technical—reproducibility."[117] By calling for a return to lost-wax techniques, and attending to whose hand details the cast, Burat champions creative authenticity and obscures a burning legal question that complicated the industrialized reproduction of bronze sculptures: who actually owns the design?

The statuette of *Innocence* (Fig. 154) is a reminder that a foundry's inventory of master models constituted an important capital investment. The piece bears the marks of two Parisian foundries—Quesnel (partially effaced) and Leblanc. Cumberworth's sculpture was shown by Quesnel at the 1844

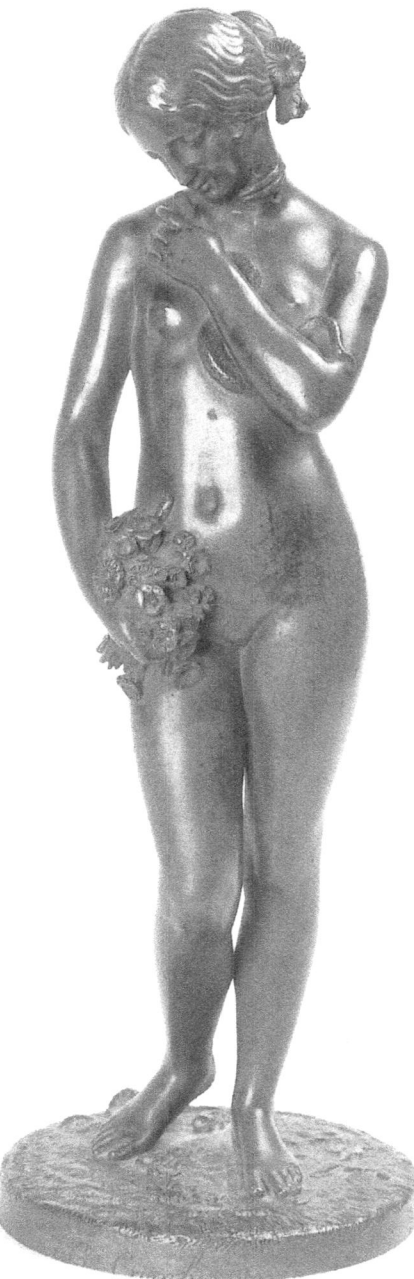

FIGURE 154.   Charles Cumberworth (designer) with E. Quesnel and Charles Leblanc (bronze casters), *Innocence*, ca. 1840. Bronze cast in parts. Paris, Musée du Louvre, Département des Sculptures, inv. RF4274 (30 × 10.5 × 10.5 cm). Photo: © RMN/Art Resource, NY/© Christian Jean.

Exposition de l'industrie française.[118] The firm apparently went out of business about 1849, which is the same year that Leblanc started operations.[119] The material evidence of the statuette supports a plausible business history: when Quesnel liquidated his business he sold a number of his master models to Leblanc, who engraved his own name into the base and produced additional replicas for sale. One presumes that the artist—Cumberworth—was not consulted in these negotiations between foundries, and that he did not share in the profits Leblanc continued to generate from the ongoing reproduction of his original design.

Issues of ownership and authorial rights emerged as topics of much discussion during the fall of 1839, when the copyright law was under revision. As originally drafted, the new law would allow artists to sell the rights to reproduce a work of art without giving up ownership of the work itself, but if they sold the original work the rights to reproduce it would pass to the new owner. Artists were alarmed by this wording, for it undermined the principle that the intellectual property of a work exists separately from its material manifestation. That separation, well-established in France since 1793, guaranteed an artist's rights over the concept of a work, even if the work itself was no longer in his or her possession. The new law took, in the words of a contemporary, "a view exactly opposite of the old law. The latter seemed to have wanted to protect the artist against the buyer; the former favors the buyer at the expense of the artist; it condemns him to a forced spoliation; it deprives him forever of future possibilities."[120] Under the proposed revisions, Cumberworth relinquished all rights to his rendering of *Innocence* (Fig. 154) when he sold the master model to Quesnel, and Quesnel could pass those rights to Leblanc without consulting Cumberworth. As Albert Vaunois points out in his study of this debate, "for the first time in a legislative work, one sees a sprouting of the idea that the right of reproduction is a privilege, a favor granted by the law, an exceptional right, and from which the term literary *property* is excluded."[121] More than a nuance of language, the proposed law disconnected making a work from the issue of who owned the rights to reproduce it; contractual agreements among owners would establish and control the rights of reproduction.

The Chamber of Peers passed the measure and forwarded it the Chamber of Deputies, where it was discussed during the spring of 1841. Alphonse de Lamartine was appointed to head a study group, but he deeply disappointed artists when he presented an eloquent brief supporting the proposed revisions. "At last the interests of the Civil List have prevailed!" exclaimed the editors of *L'Artiste*; "far be it from us any thought of questioning in the slightest the conscience and good faith of M. de Lamartine and his honorable colleagues; they were fooled, therein lies all the mystery."[122] The author's reference to the Civil List is not incidental, because these same months witnessed a court battle over artistic rights instituted by the widow of the painter Antoine-Jean Gros (Figs. 4, 7, and 9).

Madame Gros, joined by the engraver Vallot, claimed her right under the law of 1793 to reproduce certain of her husband's pictures that had been bought by the government. Her goal was to prevent the Civil List from marketing works in the royal collections as line engravings produced by the diagraphe—a mechanical drawing device perfected by Charles Gavard.[123] Madame Gros was twice denied cause by he Cour de Cassation de Paris, but the case split the magistrature. It also aroused public suspicion that the government was trying to change the copyright law so as to give itself carte blanche to profit from the many works of art it had bought or commissioned. "We repeat it quite loudly so that no one does not know," proclaimed *L'Artiste*, "what's at stake here is the Civil List; one wants to try out a gradual plundering of artists to profit only it; it alone will be called upon to exploit the benefits of the new law."[124]

The Chamber of Deputies seemed on the verge of passing the copyright revisions when the legislators suddenly performed a remarkable about-face: they diluted the most offensive article concerning rights of reproduction, and then rejected outright the totality of the new measure by a slim majority of ten votes. The editors of *L'Artiste* could scarcely believe their good fortune. "The law concerning ownership of works of science, literature, and art has been rejected at the Palais-Bourbon, after the most strange and unbelievable ups and downs," they reported; "the law is thus *buried*, according to the expression normally used in daily newspapers."[125]

Defeat of revisions to the copyright law in 1841 did not eliminate the underlying problem of how to regulate the relationship between the creator of a work of art and the industrialist who multiplies it for sale and profit. "It is especially when industry feels the need to call on art for help that it must be kept at a distance and its limits fixed," wrote Étienne Blanc in the midst of the parliamentary debates.[126] Artists, for their part, were beginning to realize that greater profits could be earned from selling rights of reproduction than from selling the originals. Léopold Robert received four thousand francs for his picture of *Pilgrims returning from the Feast Day of the Madonna dell'Arco* (Fig. 91), but his profits from the engraving of the picture ran to the hundreds of thousands.[127] Jean-Auguste-Dominique Ingres sold the *Grande Odalisque* (Musée du Louvre) to Count Pourtalès-Gorgier in 1819 for twelve hundred francs, but he obtained twenty-four thousand francs in 1825 for the rights

to publish a lithograph based on the picture (Fig. 155). At about the same time, Ingres marketed the rights to several of his most famous paintings, which ensured, in the words of Henry Lapauze, "material difficulties would be finished for good."[128]

The shift in thinking about an artist's rights of reproduction provoked by the debates of 1841 was reflected in an important change of policy for the 1844 Exposition des produits de l'industrie française. Janin had celebrated the appearance of the Susse firm at the 1839 exhibition because "it has made a veritable industry out of art" and brought sculpture into the home. Susse and his competitors functioned as editors—similar to book publishers like Curmer—who organized, capitalized, and marketed editions of sculpture but did none of the actual work themselves. It was for precisely this reason that such firms were not allowed to exhibit in 1844. *L'Artiste*, which had taken a strong stance against the

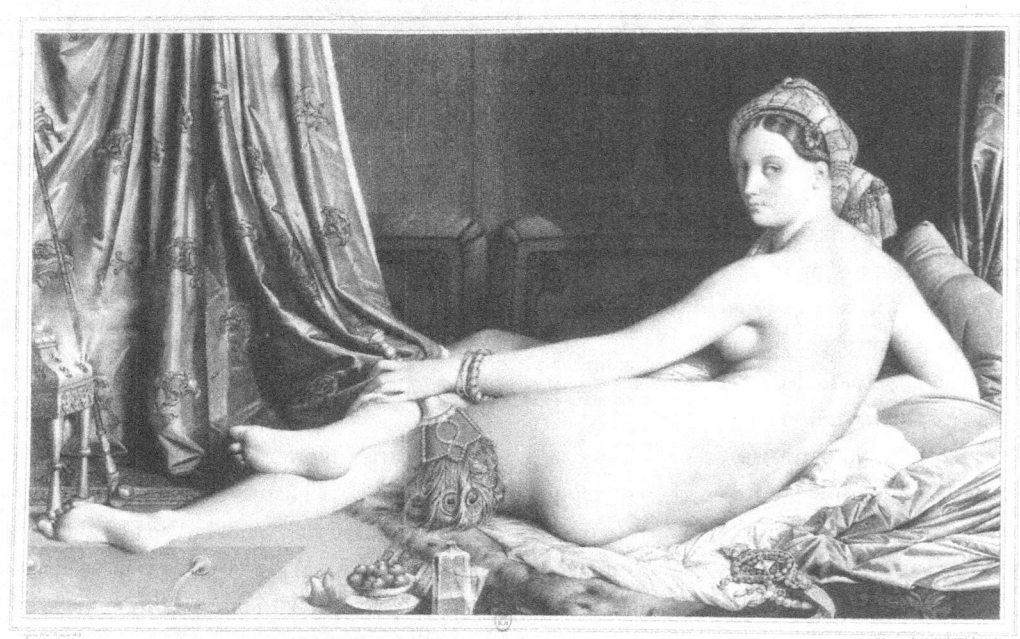

FIGURE 155. Jean-Pierre Sudré (after Ingres), *La Grande Odalisque*, 1826. Lithograph. Paris, BnF, Estampes, inv. Dc 94a fol (1). Photo: BnF, Paris.

proposed legislation of 1841, approved the new policy and called for even stricter enforcement:

One other thing struck us while examining the objects admitted to the industrial exposition. We saw the name of a certain number of merchants, who have never dealt with fabrication, joined to objects that are often very remarkable. This would be ridiculous if it weren't odious. What! because you bought, and sometimes even for a very low price, the work of another gives you the right to sign it with your own name? . . . We will return in due course to these bold encroachments of right, and we will refute them every time we notice them, but it's a scandal to which we wanted to draw public attention starting today.[129]

The exhibition jury tried to stay out of the legal fray and remain focused on the industrial processes involved in making bronze reproductions. Their aim was to reward the expertise of the best examples—witness this excerpt from the jury's final report:

Although openly doing justice to the importance of the artist who cooperates with his talent in making good bronzes, let us not forget here to bring out the participation of the manufacturer, whose discretion is entrusted with a work he must reproduce in all its original purity. This situation is vital to an industry in which art is essential because a bad bronze, even a second-rate one, is only a vanity that good sense and good taste dismiss.[130]

Deliberations of the 1844 exhibition jury reveal a confusion about how to adjudicate the conflicting claims of manufacturer and artist—a confusion that cannot be separated from the complex aesthetics of Romanticism itself. Janin's enthusiasm for the intimate and personal experience of a small-scale version of *Venus de Milo* parallels the one-on-one appeal of books lavishly illustrated with vignettes that anchor and personalize the reader's experience. Yet the Romantic cult of genius (see Chapter Six) marshaled respect for the artist's creative act, something industrial processes of reproduction tended to compromise. What appears to have happened, in the words of Jacques de Caso, is that artists "began to regard the unique piece as separated from its progeny, the series; this new attitude allowed the artist to accept *exemplaires* as reminders, reflections almost of the original work, coexisting with the originals on different artistic and commercial levels."[131] De Caso situates acceptance of these new attitudes in the early 1840s.

THE COMPETING CLAIMS that defined the terms for discussing sculptural reproductions did not exist in a vacuum. A nearly identical intersection of issues informed the reception of lithographic imagery in Paris of the 1820s. Although early examples of lithography were shown at the Salon of 1817 as industrial products [produits de l'industrie], contemporaries sensed that the new technology did not sit easily within established pictorial categories and would not remain a tool of servile reproduction:

The new art is no rival of the old; its lot is to favor graphic improvisation and to render drawing literally. But since drawing is not able to reproduce painting, lithography has no greater power. . . . To give an idea of color, of light, of chiaroscuro, of general harmony, the painter will always need the engraver. Only a line engraving is capable of translating a painting.[132]

Critics understood that lithographic images possessed an aesthetic dimension outside the range of traditional engravings. This is because lithographs reproduce the artist's hand directly, without the intervention of a professional engraver:

The artist executes a drawing on a stone; the stone serves as engraved plate. The impression on the paper is the drawing itself, reflected in the counter-proof, like a mirror. The print is, so to speak, autographic: it was formed by the hand of the master; it differs in no way from the original; it is itself an original.[133]

Time and again the early literature on lithography uses the metaphor of a mirror to explain the medium's autographic character. Thus, a special committee organized by the Institut reported in 1816: "The artist . . . sees with surprise his own work multiplied as if by magic, without the intermediary of a foreign hand . . . without missing the least line or the faintest mark, almost as accurately as an image repeated by a mirror."[134] Jules de Resseguier, writing about the Exposition des produits de l'industrie of 1823, pointed out "the lithographs, or rather the drawings, because lithography is drawing it-self. There you find the hand, the pencil, the thought of the author: this is not at all a faithful copy; to our eyes it is the echo of the model; it is a mirror that reflects and multiplies the original."[135] By the middle 1820s, the autographic qual-ity of lithography—its ability to translate directly an artist's invention and expression—was fully exploited by Delacroix in his suite of illustrations to *Faust* (Fig. 102), and pushed to an extreme in Boulanger's pictorial response (Fig. 104) to the poetry of Victor Hugo (see Chapter Six).

For some observers, the embrace of lithography by Ro-mantic artists was no surprise, because the medium encour-aged the formal bravura and lack of finish cultivated by the new school of painters:

The triumph of lithography resides in the rough sketch [ébauche], and what genius lies in the sketch? Here, it's not a question of me-ticulously traveling along all the contours of the body to enclose them in a pure, continuous, and regular line. Each form is indicated by a line that is blunt, but sure and summary. Everything is stated rather than elaborated: a few broad and strong hatchings replace the beautiful, carefully shaded surfaces of engraving, and they confront the masses of light abruptly, without transition. Yet these rapid and incomplete expressions are enough for the sensitive and practiced eye . . . and it takes much pleasure in these sketches, more than in the most complete finish.[136]

A few months after Adolphe Thiers wrote these lines, Ingres returned in triumph to Paris at the Salon of 1824 with his *Vow of Louis XIII* (Fig. 79), a picture he described as defining the high ground of "my principles, which are true, in order to stop the invasion of the Barbarians" (see Chapter Five). Ingres was flush with public acclaim, and newly decorated with the Legion of Honor awarded personally by the king (Fig. 82). He was hailed as the champion of tradition. He alone might be able to retrieve the new mass medium of lithography from the clutches of barbarism. As if testing the possibilities, Ingres personally executed a small lithograph of his *Grande Odalisque* in 1825 that was subsequently printed by François Delpech.[137]

The large and ambitious lithographic project Ingres en-trusted to Jean-Pierre Sudré the following year was some-thing more (Fig. 155). The *Grande Odalisque* was one of the painter's most famous compositions, and the idea of produc-ing a lithograph of its sinuous linear forms flies in the face of current wisdom that linked lithography to Romanticism. Ingres and Sudré set out to prove that the autographic qual-ity of lithography, when managed with care and principles, could serve the elevated style and pure line of the Grand Tradition. Ingres, who firmly believed that "all of painting is in drawing at once strong and fine," worked up a large vari-ant of his picture in a pen-and-ink drawing of pure line to serve as Sudré's model.[138] Sudré mustered all of his technical force to mimic with his lithographic crayon the finely nu-anced tonal range and carefully inscribed draftsmanship that were Ingres's personal remedies for the visual extravagances of Delacroix, Boulanger, and their friends.

Strictly speaking, Sudré's lithograph does not reproduce Ingres's picture, for it exhibits several discrepancies from the original, including a basin with running faucets at the lower left and a still-life in the center foreground. These variations are not due to Sudré's creative license, but were prescribed by Ingres in the drawing he prepared for the lithographer. In other words, Ingres started from the assumption that the lithograph was an entirely *new* creation. The variations he authorized remind us, as Marjorie Cohn has written, of his "refusal to allow prints after his paintings to be simply what they purported to be, reproductions."[139] The lithograph re-mained close enough to Ingres's original concept to warrant a large reproduction fee, and it was certainly marketed as a reflection of the *Grande Odalisque*. But Ingres apparently wanted to short-circuit—perhaps even deny—the possibil-ity of technical reproduction by ensuring that the print was not a copy, but rather a variant *coexisting* with his original. Ingres managed to have it both ways: his reputation and his pocketbook profited from the lithograph's expanded market; the authenticity and unique existence of his origi-nal picture—what Walter Benjamin would one day call its aura—remained intact.[140]

Ingres's project turned out to be less retrograde than it first appears. Michael Twyman observes that lithography was rapidly being transformed from "a miraculous method of multiplying drawings to a graphic process in its own right with its own system of working. It was no longer concerned with reproducing the essentially linear marks left by pen or chalk on the stone, but was trying to establish a tonal system of drawing."[141] By 1830 it had become so common to reproduce paintings lithographically that engravers realized their livelihood was in danger. One journal reported that engravers had formed a Société d'encouragement pour la gravure as a measure of self-protection:

Given the present set of circumstances, engraving certainly needs large-scale support. If the discovery of lithography deprived engraving of the lowliest kinds of activity and forced it to make people feel its superiority for important works, we must admit that lithography has, at the same time, established a dangerous competition for the art of the burin, and considerably limited both the number of its productions and the scope of its business.[142]

Ingres was listed among the founding members of this new group. The point is that he played both ends against the middle to secure for himself a place in the brave new world of technical reproduction, and to ensure his share of the financial bounty that came with selling copyrights. Lithography did eventually eclipse engraving as the preferred method for reproducing paintings. By 1834 official reports praised lithography for rendering to the fine arts "an immense service by delivering at low cost the pure and faithful copies of pictures that copperplate engraving would have priced much higher."[143]

Images of the Everyday

What became of the astonishing autographic immediacy of lithography that was so celebrated in its early years? The article of 1824 by Adolphe Thiers cited above is again relevant, for it was written at a decisive moment in the history of lithography when the future of the medium pointed in two very different directions. For some, the high road charted by Ingres and Sudré with their project to push lithography into the business of reproducing works of art was the future. For others, the low road was more promising, because the autographic force of lithography could be used by talents like Daumier to disseminate highly personal and powerfully opinionated commentaries on the facts and foibles of contemporary existence

(see Chapter Seven). Thiers—eminent historian, prominent political figure, and patron of the arts (see Chapter Three)—found this second path far more interesting:

The discovery of lithography brought about a true revolution. The ease with which artists seize the crayon themselves, quickly toss onto the stone the idea that has struck them, and then deliver these quick sketches to an even quicker press has led them to let nothing escape that is striking, to fix all the images that cross their mind, to seize all the fleeting views that nature offers to them. The posture of a body, the countenance of a head, an eccentric face, a scene of characteristic habits, a popular or military prank, they have reproduced all of these with a wonderful rapidity. Each of their impressions—rendered with boldness, coarseness, the truth of first reaction—comes to us without the intermediary of a cold and insensitive engraver. It's the master's drawing itself—flung onto the stone and infinitely reproduced by the lithographic press—that has been passed on to us with all the genius of the original: its touch, its omissions, its expression, its spirit.[144]

According to Thiers, lithography encouraged artists to be more attentive to modern life by making possible a swift and direct move from first-hand experience to highly personalized renderings. Moreover, lithographic images circulated in new ways and were appreciated in public spaces that were decidedly democratic:

The loves or quarrels of the people, the exaggerations of our fashions, our dress, our foibles, our faces, even certain events parodied or travestied with wit, have all been reproduced by the frivolous and caustic crayon of our young artists. The public gathered in front of the streetside shops, and looked carefully at the many lithographs decorating them with the deep pleasure given by a happy and piquant truth, a truth easy to understand, a truth taken from the public's immediate surroundings and often borrowed from itself. How many classes, how many social ranks sometimes blended together before a charming caricature of Charlet or Horace Vernet! How many men—differing in dress, habits, and spirit—stopped together before a light-hearted sketch and, despite their diverse tastes, smiling nonetheless at the same subject, with the same feeling of pleasure and laughter![145]

Thiers could be describing the animated discussion of images rendered by Charlet in his lithograph of 1819 (Fig. 14), or the lively sidewalk reaction to Boulanger's lithograph of

Paganini (Fig. 121), which so upset the violinist that he wrote a note of protest to *L'Artiste* (see Chapter Six). In hindsight, many of the subjects mentioned in passing by Thiers eventually did circulate in the visual culture of Paris thanks to the medium of lithography. But even so politically savvy an observer as Thiers could not have predicted the degree to which lithographic caricatures became, by virtue of their expressive potential and sheer number, a political force of unimagined power.

Thiers was writing in 1824 when most printed imagery was strictly censored. The press laws of March 1822 were based on an unusual asymmetry between written and visual materials: while abolishing many restrictions on the printed word, they stipulated that "no engraved or lithographed drawings can be published, sold or exhibited without prior authorization from the government."[146] This two-tiered treatment of print media generated considerable debate at the time, but the general feeling was that visual images were more dangerous than words. The government's reasoning was summarized by the Minister of the Interior in 1829:

Engravings or lithographed images act immediately upon the imagination of the people, like a book which is read with the speed of light; if it wounds modesty or public decency the damage is rapid and irremediable. It is then extremely important to forbid all that breathes a guilty intention in this regard.[147]

The immediate and lasting impression of visual imagery was rendered even more dangerous by the highly personal and autographic process of lithography. Conservative critics repeatedly attacked its visual extravagances and proclivity to caricature. In May of 1829 the *Journal des Artistes* complained about the number of

ugly sketches to which we are treated by certain draftsmen, victims of that highly vaunted facility, who use lithographic processes as they like. . . . The lithographic press, in the twinkling of an eye, flings a hundred autographic prints at us all along the quays and boulevards; in order not to see them, you have to be blind or cover your eyes.[148]

Slightly more than a year later, in its issue of 25 July 1830, the same journal grudgingly admitted that lithography "has come to offer the draftsman the means of conveying to the public his witty scribblings and satiric caricatures without the aid of an intermediary," so that "caricature took off so quickly that the shortest engraving processes were unable even to challenge the speed of drawing on stone." The author goes on to worry that "the majority of our caricaturists seem ready to embark on a false path, offering us comic exaggerations that are as monstrously drawn as they are badly conceived."[149] Two days later, the Revolution of 1830 threw Paris into a state of temporary anarchy and chased Charles X from the throne (see Chapter Two).

Among the most important reforms wrought by the July Revolution was the end of censorship. Where Charles X had tried to curtail press freedom, Article Seven of the 1830 Charter stated that "Frenchmen have the right to publish and to have printed their opinions, while conforming to the laws" and guaranteed that "censorship can never be reestablished."[150] In early October, when the legislature took up formal revision of the press laws, the old distinction between opinions expressed by printed texts and those expressed by printed images was dropped. Caricatures and other visual images were no longer bound by any kind of censorship. The flood-gates opened to an enormous circulation of visual materials. First and foremost among those to exploit the cultural and political power of lithography freed of its shackles was Charles Philipon. He founded in October 1830 *La Caricature*, a weekly journal of political satire that always included at least one lithograph. The journal made its debut on 4 November.

It was not long before the government of Louis-Philippe began to worry about the unleashed power of caricatures. The law of 10 December 1830, for example, forbid "the posting of any writings, engravings, or lithographs dealing with political news or themes, except those emanating from governmental authority, in any street or other public space." Philipon went on the attack: he published a caricature called *Les bulles de savon* [Soap Bubbles] on 24 February 1831 that depicted Louis-Philippe blowing bubbles from a *mousse de juillet*—each bubble represented a promise made after the July Revolution that had since been rescinded. The print was seized and Philipon was brought to trial in May 1832. Philipon was acquitted after pointing out that since 1830 the lithographic press was supposed to enjoy the same freedom of expression as print media. He took up the banner of freedom for visual expression with a vengeance, and dedicated *La Caricature* to safeguarding its existence:

La Caricature has made France understand the influence that artists obtained long ago in England. The power of this kind of opposition was unknown before the July Revolution because censorship, abolished for the printed press, still existed for prints and lithographs. So we revealed this power by striking the enemies of our liberties or the deserters and laggards of our camp with a previously unknown weapon. Our blows have struck with strength and precision, but we are called to higher destinies: one day we will be the boogeyman of the big kids who play at quasi-government before our eyes. Aided by our good comrades, supported by our subscribers, and prodded by the harassment of the public ministry, we will soon attain the goal of our mission, without allowing ourselves to be intimidated by the obstacles, nor even by the anonymous threats with which one has wanted to honor our efforts.[151]

Philipon's polemic makes clear that he fully realized the extent to which visual images—especially via the expressive and autographic medium of lithography—constituted a new cultural force. His intransigence was tantamount to declaring war against the government. Over the course of the next several years he and his collaborators were dragged repeatedly into court for publishing images found to be insulting to the king and his government, or outright seditious.

Nowhere was Philipon's ability to orchestrate the power of caricature more vividly demonstrated than during a second trial for a print of Louis-Philippe as a "replasterer" published in June 1831. Philipon argued, in the words of James Cuno, "that while his depiction of the mason was indeed intended to *refer* to the King, it was significant that he had not *described* him: nowhere in the image or accompanying text was the mason *identified* as the King, the mason simply resembled him."[152] To support his claim that issues of resemblance are independent of the person to whom they refer, Philipon produced the now-famous set of four drawings that move ineluctably from a passable rendering of Louis-Philippe's face to that of a pear (Fig. 156). He argued that if the government's case is valid, then people could be arrested

for insulting the king by simply drawing a pear.[153] Philipon lost the case—he was sentenced to six months in prison and fined two thousand francs—but his image of the pear stuck in the public mind and became almost overnight a universally accepted visual shorthand for the king. "The pear is still the standing popular joke in the satiric press and caricatures," wrote Heinrich Heine in March 1832; "the pear, as I said, has become a standing joke, and hundreds of caricatures in which it is seen have been put up everywhere."[154]

The pear's stinging success only served to stiffen the government's resolve to punish its inventor. In late July of 1832 Philipon reported to the readers of *La Caricature*:

Twenty seizures, six judgments, three condemnations, more than 6,000 francs in fines, thirteen months in prison, enough persecutions to require a guarantee of 24,000 francs, all within a year, is indisputable proof of the power's profound hatred for us.[155]

Philipon's inventory of legal harassment was part of a plea for yet another scheme linked to the production of images with a political agenda. His plan was to offer each month a large-scale, politically inspired lithograph by creating "an association destined to form a reserve of cash for us to pay the costs of lawsuits that might be brought against us in the future. We summon to this association all the friends of *La Caricature*, all citizens who think we have served the cause of liberty with some power and some courage, all those who want also to defend it."[156] Philipon called his new venture the Association Mensuelle.

It is significant that Philipon's sales pitch was both political and aesthetic: although the subjects of his monthly prints would be motivated by contemporary issues related to the struggle for freedom of the press, the prints themselves were to be published on good quality paper. Philipon also promised to "efface the stones three months after their first printing."[157] This means the prints would be limited in number

---

FIGURE 156.   Charles Philipon, *Sketches made at the Session of 14 November (Cour d'Assises)* from *La Caricature* (24 November 1831), 1831. Lithograph. Paris, BnF, Estampes, inv. N2 "Louis-Philippe". Photo: BnF, Paris.

Croquades faites à l'audience du 14 nov.
(Cour d'Assises)

Si, pour reconnaître le monarque dans une caricature, vous
n'attendez pas qu'il soit désigné autrement que par la ressemblance,
vous tomberez dans l'absurde. Voyez ces croquis informes, auxquels j'aurais
peut-être dû borner ma défense :

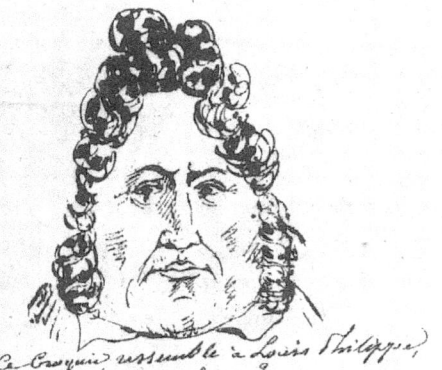

Ce Croquis ressemble à Louis Philippe,
vous condamnerez donc?

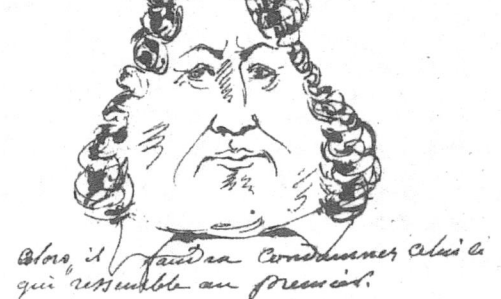

Alors, il faudra condamner celui-ci
qui ressemble au premier.

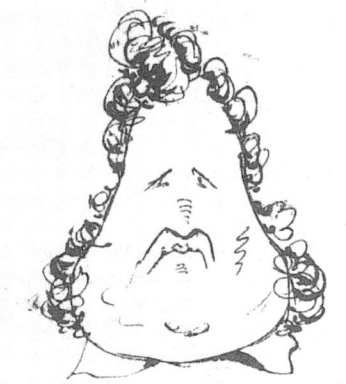

Puis condamner pour cet autre
qui ressemble au second...

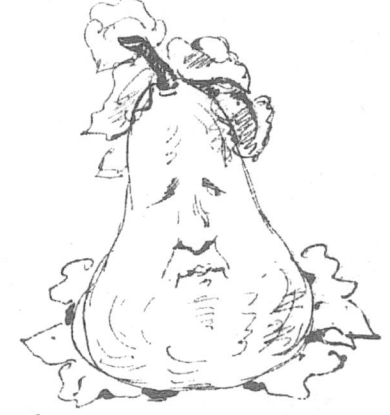

Et enfin, si vous êtes conséquents,
vous ne sauriez absoudre cette poire
qui ressemble aux croquis précédens.

Ainsi, pour une poire, pour une brioche, et pour toutes les têtes
grotesques dans lesquelles le hazard ou la malice aura placé cette
triste ressemblance, vous pourrez infliger à l'auteur cinq ans de prison
et cinq mille francs d'amende !?!

Avouez, Messieurs, que c'est là une singulière liberté de
la presse !!

(procès du journal La Caricature)   Ch. Philipon

and eventually worth more as collector's items—as works of art—than as political statements. Ségolène Le Men correctly assesses the innovations of Philipon's Association Mensuelle in the history of publishing:

The Association Mensuelle seemed, in this way, to be a new and original kind of publication, founded on the complicity of the public summoned to militate in its favor, and imposed upon Philipon by circumstances in the course of a constantly intensifying buildup of the conflict between the friends of a free press and those of the government; this publication had something of both the not-for-sale edition reserved for subscribers . . . and the limited editions of engravings that will enjoy growing favor right to the present day.[158]

Philipon's simultaneous attention to the rhetorical force and the material value of his monthly prints reveals a profoundly modern understanding of the shift in register and power—what Walter Benjamin later called "exhibition value"—that emerges when it becomes possible to reproduce an *original* work of art in great numbers.[159] "We revealed this power by striking the enemies of our liberties or the deserters and laggards of our camp with a previously unknown weapon," Philipon had written in 1832, about the political muscle of *La Caricature* that was already apparent in April of 1831. The two-tiered marketing strategy he developed for the Association Mensuelle demonstrates that he was beginning to understand how to focus the power of that weapon with ever greater precision.

In his 1936 discussion of exhibition value, Walter Benjamin suggests that picture magazines illustrated by photographs tended to make captions obligatory. "It is clear that they have an altogether different character than the title of a painting," he wrote; "the directives which the captions give to those looking at pictures in illustrated magazines soon become more explicit and more imperative in the film."[160] In fact, the prescriptive captions that Benjamin linked to early twentieth-century photomagazines were already practiced with a high level of sophistication by Philipon, who wrote and published lengthy explications for each lithograph issued by the Association Mensuelle. Ségolène Le Men argues that Philipon invented an entirely new genre in which his texts "are henceforth an integral part of the Association Mensuelle" whose publications "must be approached as a series of

mixed compositions that link the text and the image." She demonstrates that Philipon's explications went far beyond simply naming the lithograph's subject:

Indeed, if the argument and the drawing of a work necessarily precede its creation, the "explication" depends, to the contrary, upon the lithograph; it is metalinguistic by nature, and it is anchored in the plate it analyzes by very visible marks that linguists call *shifters*: terms that serve to bind the text to its referent (in this case the lithograph) such as demonstratives, phrases of presentation . . . verbs of visual perception . . . or complements of place.[161]

One print published by the Association Mensuelle—the last it issued before being dissolved—tested the semantic limits of Philipon's dialectic between printed image and textual explication. Rather than guiding reader/viewers through *La Rue Transnonain, le 15 avril 1834* by Honoré Daumier (Fig. 157), Philipon's caption invites mute contemplation of its specter of death:

This lithograph is horrible to see, as horrible as the dreadful act it relates. A murdered old man, a dead woman, the cadaver of a man riddled with wounds lying on the body of a poor little child whose skull is split open. This is certainly neither a caricature nor a satire, but a bloody page of our modern history, a page drawn by a vigorous hand and dictated by a noble indignation. In this drawing, Daumier has risen to great nobility, he has made a picture that will be neither less esteemed nor less durable for being painted in black on a sheet of paper. For those who have suffered it, the butchery of the rue Transnonain will be an indelible stain; the drawing we are citing will be the medal struck at the time to perpetuate the memory of this victory over fourteen old men, women, and children.[162]

Philipon neither names the victims nor tells the story of their fate, for he assumes that his public was fully conversant with their tale of death on the morning of 14 April 1834. He attends to aesthetic qualities of the image—its seriousness, its vigorous handling, its timelessness—embodied in the modest materials of printer's ink and paper. In this case, his words purposely fall short so that the image might speak with greater authority.

The bluntness of Philipon's assertions about the print ("this is certainly neither a caricature nor a satire, but a bloody

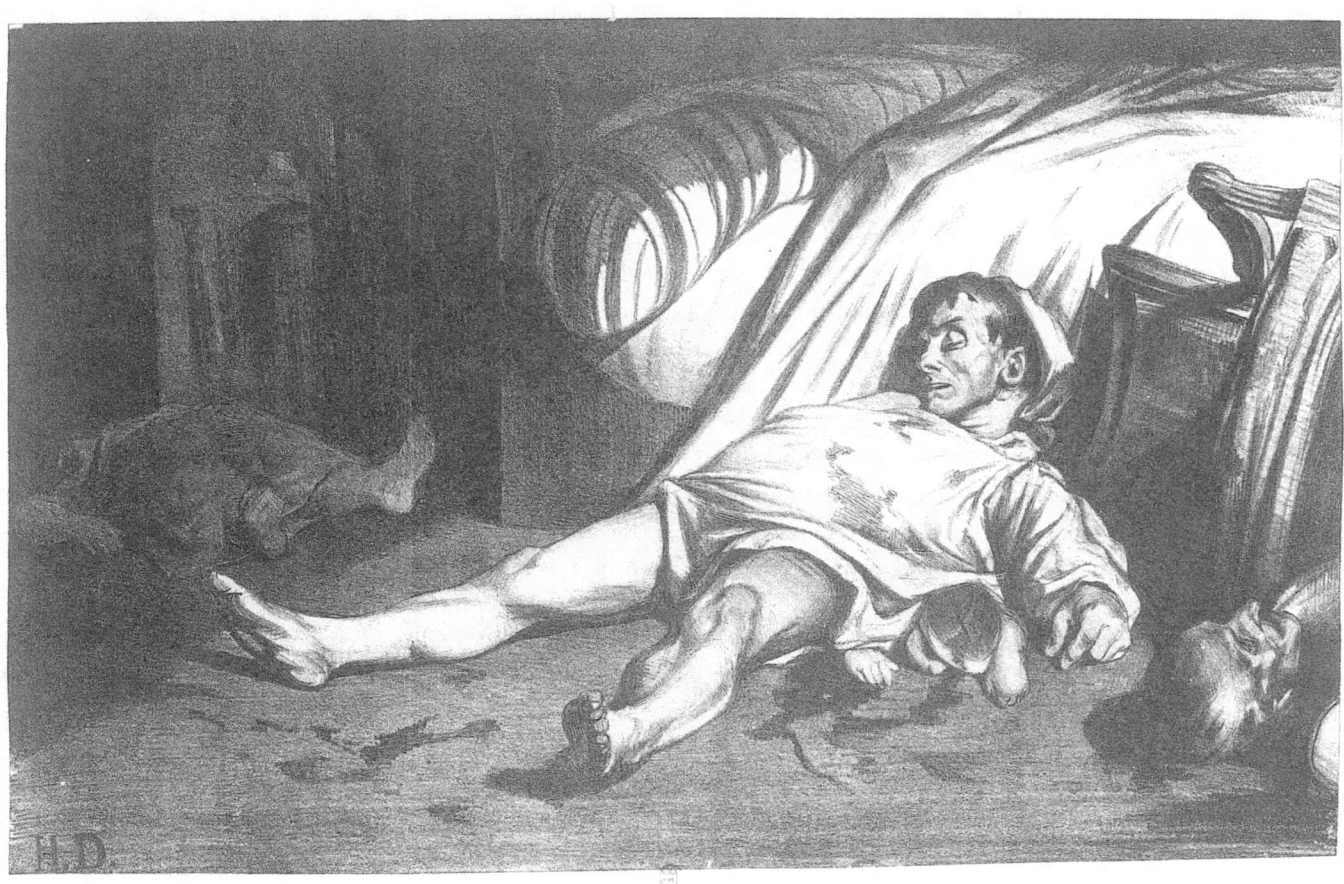

FIGURE 157. Honoré Daumier, *Rue Transnonain, 15 April 1834*, 1834. Lithograph. Paris, BnF, Estampes, inv. AA3 rés "Daumier" (29 × 44.5 cm). Photo: BnF, Paris.

page of our modern history") second its pictorial qualities: the extraordinary contrast of saturated blacks against stark whites; the emphatically drawn contours; the wide range of sombre grays achieved by reworking the trace of the lithographic crayon with several kinds of tools and rags. The gloomy shadows and suggestive staging of telling details—disheveled bed, overturned chair and chamberpot, young child crushed under the weight of a man's body—evoke, in the words of Baudelaire writing later, the sinister paradox of "a huge struggle and a great noise. . . . In this cold garret there is nothing but silence and death."[163] To fully appreciate the unusual reticence

of Philipon's language, or the palpable paradox that affected Baudelaire, means entering the media battle of contested facts within which Daumier designed his print.

Rumors had circulated in Paris for weeks that republican opponents of Louis-Philippe's government were planning an uprising in working-class parts of town timed to coordinate with similar revolts all across France. The government responded proactively by amassing nearly forty thousand troops in and around the capital and arresting most of the opposition leaders. Barricades appeared in the Marais on 13 April. Troops moved into position during the night and quickly overran the small pockets of resistance presented by the somewhat disorganized street fighters. They dismantled a barricade erected near the corner of the rue Transnonain and the rue de Montmorency. About five o'clock in the morning of 14 April, a group of soldiers from the 35th Regiment entered the house at 12, rue Transnonain. They were searching for what they believed to be snipers firing from windows of the upper floor.

What happened next is the salient question. Fourteen people were killed, but that number is about the only point of agreement amongst conflicting accounts—including eyewitness testimonies gathered by relatives of some victims—that were avidly published by newspapers opposed to the government. A front page article in the 15 April edition of *Le National de 1834* reported "massacred" inhabitants and "horribly mutilated" cadavers; more details were published the next day on the "butchery of the rue Transnonain."[164] By contrast, most newspapers allied with the government simply chose not to mention the rue Transnonain in their pages. Nearly a month passed before the *Journal de Paris* published a letter signed by C. de Failly—supposedly a lieutenant of the 35th Regiment—who tried to explain the actions of his colleagues and to counter the reports of wanton killing.[165] According to his account, a young woman named Annette Besson died in an exchange of gunshots when soldiers, entering her second-floor apartment, fired "in a confused manner; unfortunately, a woman was struck."[166] Few people were convinced by Failly's whitewash.

Many of the most gruesome details of the rue Transnonain incident were collected and published in an incendiary little booklet written by the left-wing politician Alexandre-Auguste Ledru-Rollin.[167] He cites eyewitnesses who claim there were no arms in the apartment, and that Mademoiselle Besson, reacting to the murder of an elderly man, "dashed from an adjoining room to run to his aid. . . . A soldier turned around to face her, thrust his bayonet into her below the jaw and, in this position, unleashed a rifle shot whose explosive force flung parts of her head all over the wall."[168] Ledru-Rollin's graphic version of Besson's death was eventually supported by the coroner's report. His booklet dwells upon the many discrepancies between official and first-hand accounts,

but the point is that his text popularized a sensationalist, politically radicalized version of the events distinctly at odds with the government's story. Charles Philipon staked out his position in the matter by announcing the appearance of Ledru-Rollin's booklet as "a brochure that offered an irrefutable repudiation of the royal words," and by printing excerpts from it in *Le Charivari*, his daily newspaper.[169] He was not alone: sales of Ledru-Rollin's *Mémoire* were so brisk that a second edition was announced by *Le Charivari* less than two weeks after the initial publication.[170]

It is generally assumed that Daumier drew his lithograph of the *Rue Transnonain* (Fig. 157) in late July or early August of 1834; in other words, exactly contemporary with the appearance of Ledru-Rollin's booklet and of Philipon's support for its version of the incident. About Daumier's place in the debate as to what really happened on 14 April there is little doubt, for his print dwells on the nightmarish scattering of bodies and indiscriminate spilling of blood. No soldiers are depicted—Daumier does not give us a narrative—and the caption of his print specifies a date of 15 April. Is the seemingly incorrect date merely an unfortunate printer's mistake? That is not likely, given the charged subject. Rather, Daumier focused on the consequences of the episode by presenting a horrifying still-life [nature morte] of death, whose dark spirit and frightening, matter-of-fact exposition of corpses can be quite appropriately compared to Goya's *Disasters of War*. Shifting the time frame brings together Daumier's print and the mood of Ledru-Rollin's chilling description of his visit to the room where several men, women, and children had been killed:

As for me, I will never in my life forget the shiver that ran through my limbs when I entered this bedroom for the first time, preceded by the widow Pajot. The light was beginning to fade; with a finger she pointed out to me the tracks, the spatters of blood marking the walls. Then, suddenly, in a voice broken with sobs: "It's here," she exclaimed, "that the villains killed my child, my poor baby."[171]

For Daumier to stage the incident in this way—dwelling on its aftermath rather than its unfolding in time—was a savvy strategy to avoid government censors. Since the *Rue Transnonain* does not explicitly depict the massacre or pass judgment on the army, it could not be officially suppressed.

Nonetheless, police agents worked hard to acquire as many individual prints as possible, and they confiscated the printing stone from Philipon so no further copies could be made.

In the aftermath, as Philipon had predicted, the government of Louis-Philippe reneged on the pledge written into the Charter of 1830 that censorship was forever abolished. It took steps to curtail the growing power of lithographic imagery: a law of 1834 imposed a tax on prints, and mandated that each impression be stamped to certify payment of the fee. Philipon complained bitterly about this provision, which defaced his carefully printed lithographs and destroyed their exhibition value. To no avail. Philipon informed his patrons in August 1835 that "the tax department having raised the pretence of slapping a stamp on these drawings that would mess them up and soak up the earnings," the Association Mensuelle was suspending publication.[172]

During these months of mounting government pressure to control the lithographic medium, the Minister of the Interior was none other than Adolphe Thiers, the same public figure who, ten years earlier, championed the promptitude and verve with which lithographers "fix all the images that cross their mind . . . seize all the fleeting views that nature offers to them." Reacting in September 1835 to a failed but bloody attempt in July to assassinate Louis-Philippe, the government proposed even stricter forms of censorship, including pre-publication approval of printed images that was a direct throwback to legislation of the 1820s specifically abolished in 1830. When Liberals tried to soften the proposal by allowing certain exceptions, Thiers led the charge for rigor. The irony is that the autographic character of lithography was now used to argue—somewhat disingenuously—that censoring prints did not violate the Charter's guarantee of press freedom:

Let the illustrator write his thought, let him publish it in that form, and as in that manner he addresses only the *mind*, he will encounter no obstacle. It is in that sense that it was said censorship could never be reestablished. But when opinions are converted into *acts* by the presentation of a play or the exhibit of a drawing, one addresses people gathered together, one speaks to their eyes. That is more than the expression of an opinion, that is a *deed*, an *action*, a *behavior*, with which article seven of the Charter is not concerned.[173]

The reactionary political climate of 1835 ensured passage of the new laws. Thiers addressed circulars to prefects all across France in which he counseled them to be lenient with pre-existing imagery when it was a matter of hand-made images, castings, or printed cloth and wallpaper. By contrast, he ordered a strict enforcement of pre-publication censorship on all mass-produced images such as engravings, lithographs, prints, or emblems "multiplied by printing."[174] For all practical purposes, politically charged imagery was regulated out of business by the new laws.

Philipon saw the handwriting on the wall: during debate of the so-called September Laws, he closed down *La Caricature* and refocused *Le Charivari* on less inflammatory forms of social satire, including "drawings of everyday life, caricatures of habits, scenes of the theater, fashion drawings, historical landscapes, portraits of actors, actresses, writers, artists, diplomats, newly elected deputies, big-time villains, princes, all those who—rightly or wrongly—occupy a moment of public attention."[175] The September Laws obliged Daumier and his colleagues to follow their friend and patron in his detour from political subjects to the world of social distractions. Over the course of the next decade Daumier produced several series of lithographs for the pages of *Le Charivari* in which the foibles and follies of modern life were both scrutinized and travestied: these include "Caricaturana," where the famous character of Robert Macaire was first introduced (1836–1838); a second series of "Robert Macaire" (1840–1842); "Moeurs conjugales" (1839–1842); "Émotions parisiennes" (1839–1841); and "Les gens de justice" (1845–1848). Between May 1846 and June 1849 he drew "Les Bons Bourgeois," a series that both celebrates and parodies the social class whose virtues Baudelaire praised—somewhat tongue-in-cheek—in the introduction to his review of the 1846 Salon (see Chapter Six).

One of the latter images, *Look my dear, it's my portrait* (Fig. 158) registers the ability of lithography to mass-produce timely topics in the popular press. It also acknowledges the challenge presented by daguerreotypes, the new imaging technology that swept Paris at this time. Daumier represents the return from Paris of a provincial to his hometown. Unpacking a trunk of articles brought from the capital, he unearths a daguerreotype portrait of himself, which he presents with

2132

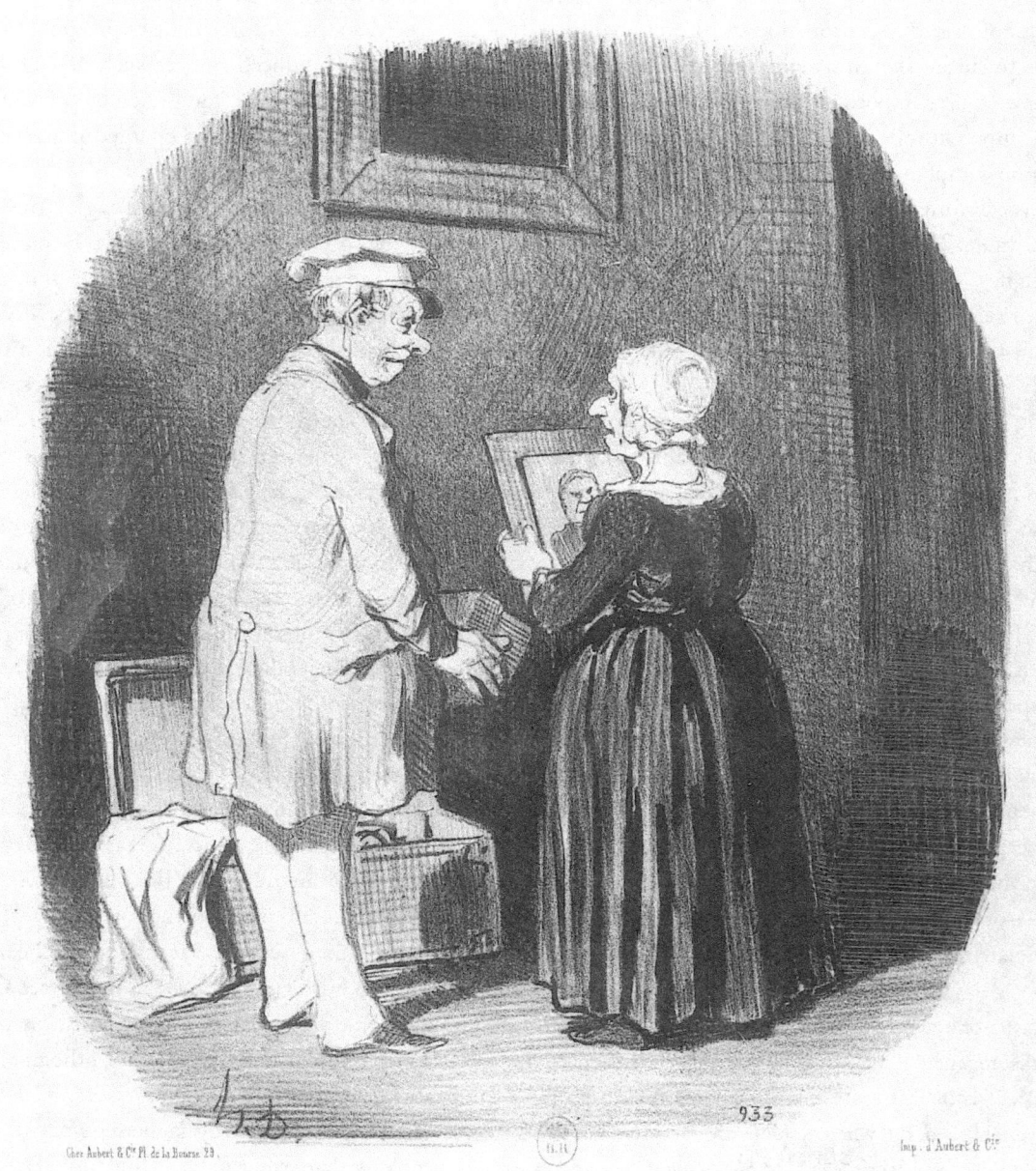

933

Chez Aubert & C°ie Pl. de la Bourse. 29.

Imp. d'Aubert & C°ie

– Tiens ma femme v'la mon portrait au Daguerreotype que je te rapporte de Paris.....
– Pourquoi donc est-ce que tu n'as pas aussi fait faire le mien pendant que tu y etais.... égoïste va!....

some pride to his wife. She replies, "so why didn't you also have mine done while you were there? Egoist!" The comic exchange can be read two ways: Madame obviously does not realize that a sitter must be physically present before the apparatus to make a daguerreotype; her husband's emphasis upon Paris as the origin of his portrait alludes to the development of a new visual marketplace in the capital. "The daguerreotype was born in Paris," remarked the authors of *La Grande Ville* in 1844, "it made its first tests in that city, and even if its success has now become European, this has not stopped cultivation of Daguerre's admirable invention in Paris; on the contrary, it seems to have earned burgher rights there." The authors further remark that visitors to Paris, like Daumier's provincial bourgeois, "don't want to leave without having tried out this invention: some because they think that everything is done better in this city than elsewhere; others because they are delighted to be able to say later on, 'I had my daguerreotype portrait done in Paris.'"[176] How did Paris emerge as the world's center of this new imaging technology?

Daguerre's Moment

For those who are not insensitive to national glory, who know that a nation does not shine over other nations with a greater brilliance than by having made the greatest advances for civilization; for such people, we say, the process of M. Daguerre is a great discovery. It is the beginning of a new art in the midst of an old civilization, one that will be epoch-making and will be retained as a glorious title. Should it be obliged to go to posterity escorted by ingratitude? Rather, let it arrive as radiant testimony of the patronage that the Chambers, the Government of July, and the entire country award to great discoveries.

—Joseph-Louis Gay-Lussac[177]

For centuries artists enlisted simple versions of the camera obscura as a drawing aid.[178] A fully enclosed box with a pinhole in one side will form an image inside the box of whatever

stands before the pinhole. Mounting a window of ground glass opposite the pinhole makes the image visible from outside the box so that it might be traced onto a sheet of paper. If the pinhole is replaced by a lens, one can adjust the size and sharpness of the image formed on the glass. Variants of this device were used regularly by artists to determine the contours and masses of complex subjects, especially landscapes.

There was also a long history of unsuccessful experiments to capture images seen on the ground glass without recourse to manual tracing. For many years chemists (or more properly alchemists) knew that certain compounds—including silver mixed with chloride, silver nitrate, and bitumin of Judea—darkened when exposed to light. In 1802 two Englishmen, Humphry Davy and Thomas Wedgewood, demonstrated a process for copying paintings on glass, and for making silhouettes of objects, by exposing them to sunlight on paper treated with silver nitrate. But Davy and Wedgewood were never able to stop the process and fix the image to prevent it from blackening completely over time.

About 1814 Joseph-Nicéphore Niépce, a Frenchman living near the town of Châlons-sur-Soâne, began to explore ways of capturing a camera obscura's image upon different types of metal. Niépce, who was trained as a lithographer, coated his plates with a varnish of bitumin of Judea dissolved in lavender oil—a mixture that hardens when exposed to light. His goal was to produce plates in relief that could be used for printing multiple examples without the intervention of an engraver. Niépce's process involved exposing the plates in a camera obscura and then washing away the unhardened (unexposed) areas of varnish to yield a slightly bumpy surface. In early 1827 Niépce reported in a letter to a friend that he had fixed images on varnished pewter plates—etched in a solution of weak acid after exposure in his camera obscura—that must count as the world's first photographs, even if they required ten or more hours of exposure.[179] At the end of the same letter, Niépce asks his friend if he knows a man called Daguerre. The stranger has been informed "I don't know how about the subject of my experiments," and has written to ask for a sample print "although he doubts that one could be completely happy with the shadows using this engraving process." Niépce was both curious and suspicious about Daguerre. "I

FIGURE 158.   Honoré Daumier, *Look my dear, it's my portrait* from *Les Bons Bourgeois* (plate 28), 1846. Lithograph. Paris, BnF, Estampes, inv. Dc 180j fol (13) (24.8 × 21 cm). Photo: BnF, Paris.

will not hide from you," he wrote to his friend, "that such an incoherence of ideas was good grounds for surprise, to say the least"; he asked his correspondent to "tell me if you know M. Daguerre personally and what you think of him."[180] It turns out that Louis-Jacques-Mandé Daguerre (Fig. 161) had learned of Niépce's work from the Paris optician Charles Chevalier, who was making lenses for both men.

Daguerre was more showman than scientist or inventor. He was well known in Paris for the dramatic combination of illusionist scenery and special lighting effects mounted in the spectacles of the Diorama (see Chapter Six). Historians of photography generally agree that Daguerre had made little progress with photographic techniques at the time he first contacted Niépce. His overture was motivated by the prospect of learning quickly from Niépce's storehouse of experience accumulated over the course of a decade. In December of 1829, after much hesitation on Niépce's part, the two men signed a formal agreement to pool their knowledge for a period of ten years. They agreed to share any profits that might be derived from perfecting Niépce's discovery that, in the terms of the contract, "consists of the spontaneous reproduction of images received in the camera obscura."[181] Niépce revealed to Daguerre "the principle upon which his discovery is based" and supplied him with all of his research notes; Daguerre passed to Niépce "the principle upon which the improvement he brought to the camera obscura is based." Research continued on both sides for several years without much headway. In 1831 Daguerre encouraged Niépce to abandon bitumin of Judea in favor of silver iodide, which yielded a surface far more sensitive to light, but it seems that Niépce obtained only mediocre inverse (negative) images in which light tones appeared dark and dark tones light.[182]

Niépce's unexpected death in July 1833 did not deter Daguerre. He continued to experiment using copper plates laminated with silver that he exposed to iodine vapors to produce a very thin, light-sensitive coating of silver iodide. Over the course of the next four years Daguerre made three key discoveries. The first two were interrelated and seem to have been almost accidental: as early as 1833 he correctly surmised that images were actually produced very quickly on the surface of silver iodide, even if not visible to the naked eye; he

also concluded that some kind of after-treatment was needed to reveal them. According to legend, it was some time in 1835 that Daguerre casually placed an exposed plate in a closed cupboard along with a number of chemical jars, only to find later that it registered a perfectly legible image. By a process of elimination he was able to discern that vapors emanating from some mercury in the cupboard were responsible for the transformation.[183] Daguerre eventually realized that submitting an exposed plate to mercury vapors developed the latent images because the airborne mercury molecules adhered only to those areas in the plate affected by light, not to the areas of shadow. Two more years of trial and error passed before Daguerre discovered that plunging a developed plate into a warm solution of ordinary kitchen salt chemically dissolved the silver iodide not affected by exposure in the camera obscura, and thus fixed the image by making it insensitive to further effects of light.[184] Because the registering of light and dark operated on the level of molecules—that is, very small, individual units—Daguerre's images recorded extremely fine detail, especially if a high quality lens was attached to the camera obscura (Fig. 159).

Isidore Niépce inherited his father's interest in the deal with Daguerre. Writing in November of 1837, he celebrated the fact that his partner was making prints with only four minutes of exposure. He eventually accepted that many differences existed between his father's process and that of his colleague. But it was not always so. In June of 1837, after showing young Niépce some early successful prints, Daguerre pressed for major modifications of their business relationship, including admission that his process, which reproduced objects "sixty or eighty times more quickly" than Niépce's process, was essentially a new invention. Daguerre also insisted that "this new process will carry only the name of Daguerre."[185] Young Niépce refused at first to sign the revised contract, but financial considerations eventually brought him around to Daguerre's point of view. By November he grudgingly acknowledged that Daguerre's process was so superior to his father's "that certainly no one familiar with the two processes would want to use the old one."[186]

Whatever their squabble over how to name the invention or inscribe its authorship, both men realized the immedi-

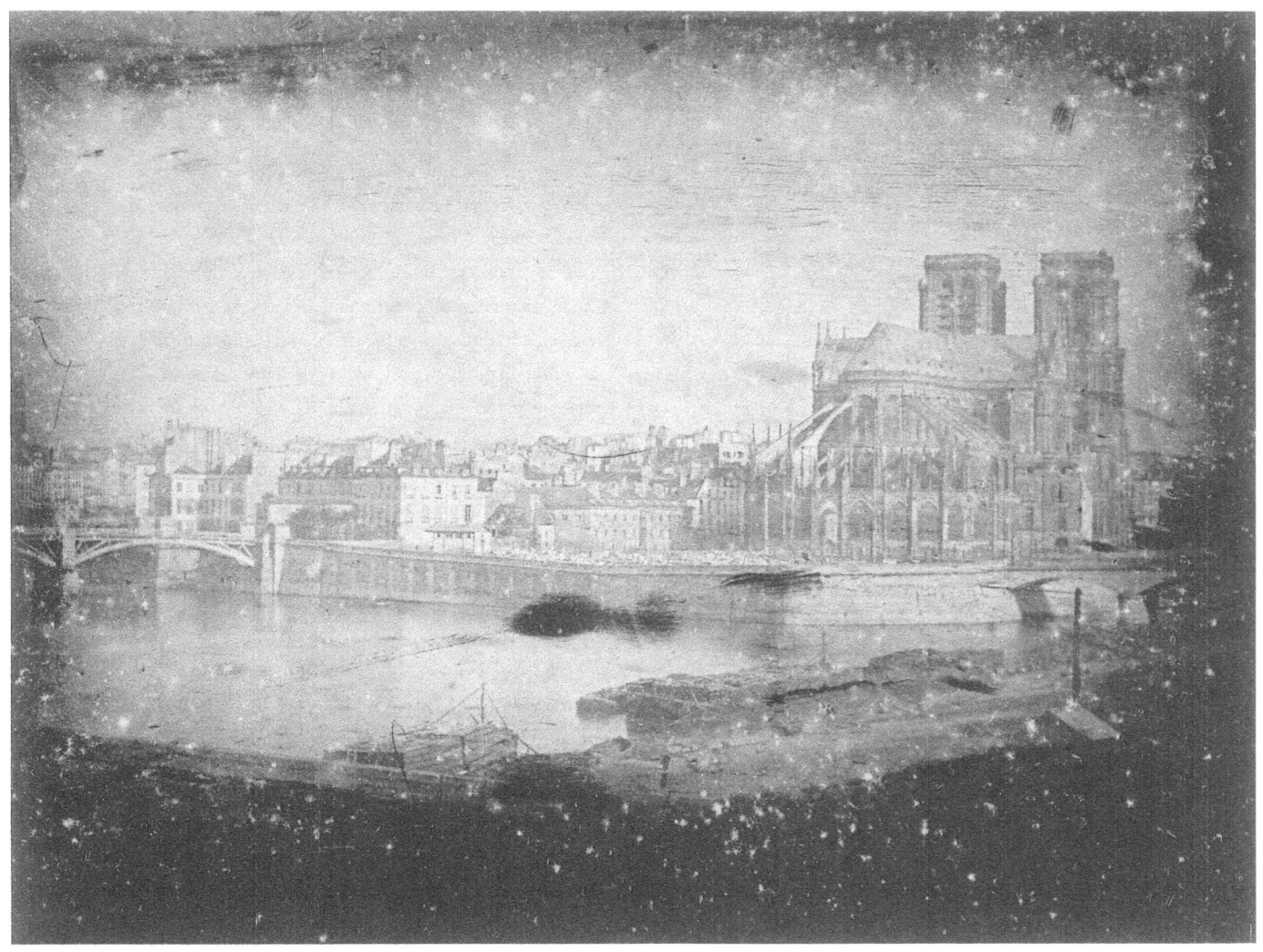

FIGURE 159.   Louis-Jacques-Mandé Daguerre, *Île de la Cité with Notre-Dame*, ca. 1839. Daguerreotype.
Austin, Gernsheim Collection, Harry Ransom Humanities Research Center, The University of Texas at
Austin (15.4 × 22.1 cm). Photo: Harry Ransom Humanities Research Center.

ate problem was that the secret of daguerreotypes was not a single device they could protect with patents. Rather, it was a process of discrete steps using well-known materials and instruments—none of which were particularly difficult to duplicate. If Daguerre and Niépce simply announced their findings, others could easily produce images following the same procedures and it would be virtually impossible for the partners to extract any profit from their years of research. Their first scheme was to publish details of the process by subscription at one thousand francs apiece, and to limit the number of subscribers to four hundred. When an initial round of subscriptions—held from 15 March to 15 August 1838—failed to attract sufficient supporters, a second launch was planned for 15 January 1839. This time Daguerre prepared advertising flyers, planned an exhibition of about fifty daguerreotype plates and, with the hope of gaining their support, invited a group of distinguished personalities from the sciences and arts to see his prints. Daguerre's guest list included François Arago, Jean-Baptiste Biot, and Alexander von Humboldt, the painter Paul Delaroche (Fig. 88), and Alphonse de Cailleux, a curator at the Louvre.[187] François Arago—eminent astrophysicist, permanent secretary of the Académie des Sciences, and elected member of the Chamber of Deputies—reacted even more positively to the demonstration than Daguerre expected. Arago was convinced the new imaging technology promised such great benefits to science, industry, and the arts that it should not be held privately by a few individuals.

Arago revealed the existence of daguerreotypes to the prestigious Académie des Sciences of Paris in an address of 7 January 1839. Without divulging the technical secrets of Daguerre and Niépce, Arago announced his intent to seek national compensation for the two men so that France might "nobly endow the entire world with a discovery that can contribute so much to progress in the arts and sciences."[188] Arago's presentation catalyzed the interest of previously skeptical Parisians: "One is also very interested in the invention of M. Daguerre," wrote Delphine de Girardin in her column for 12 January, "and nothing is more amusing than the explanation of this wonder given in all seriousness by our parlor scientists."[189] A report on Arago's speech, published in the *Journal des Artistes*, describes Daguerre's discovery as "certainly one of the most phenomenal of our century," and goes on to say that "owing to the fantastic element of its results, it naturally had to encounter a large number of unbelievers before the stately speech of M. Arago came to give it solemn confirmation."[190] Enhanced by the personal prestige and institutional endorsement of Arago's presentation before the Académie, Daguerre's discovery shifted almost overnight from an interesting experimental curiosity to a major achievement of the century.

Arago had not actually demonstrated the daguerreotype process, nor had he shown his audience any specimens. Those who wanted to judge for themselves were obliged to visit Daguerre's laboratory. Time and again the reports of contemporary visitors are filled with admiration for the images and, in particular, for their seemingly boundless ability to render detail (Fig. 159). This excerpt from *Le Commerce* is a characteristic example:

There was an admiring exclamation for each picture placed before our eyes. What a fine line! What an understanding of chiaroscuro! What delicacy! What finish! How soft is this fabric! What projection in these carved reliefs and sculptures in the round! Here's a crouching *Venus* seen from different points of view: how these foreshortenings are rendered! It's the statue itself, a veritable trompe-l'oeil. All of this is admirable; but, we ask, who guarantees that this is not the work of some clever draftsman? Who tells us that we are not being shown some bistre or sepia washes? By way of reply, M. Daguerre puts a magnifying glass in our hand. Then we perceive the tiniest folds of cloth, the lines of a landscape invisible to the naked eye. Using an opera glass, we bring the background closer: in the mass of constructions, accessories, and imperceptible random events that make up this view of Paris taken from the pont des Arts we distinguish the smallest little details, we count the paving stones, we see the dampness left by the rain, we read the sign of a shop. All the threads of the luminous fabric have passed from the object to the image.[191]

The American inventor Samuel F. B. Morse, in Paris at the time to file a patent for his electro-magnetic telegraph, could not pass up visiting Daguerre to see what he called "one of the most beautiful discoveries of the age." A letter of 9 March to his brother, later published in the *New York Observer*, registers his astonishment before the ability of daguerreotypes to render nearly imperceptible details:

But the exquisite minuteness of the delineation cannot be conceived. No painting or engraving ever approached it. For example: In a view up the street, a distant sign would be perceived, and the eye could just discern that there were lines of letters upon it, but so minute as not to be read with the naked eye. By the assistance of a powerful lens, which magnified fifty times, applied to the delineation, every letter was clearly and distinctly legible, and so also were the minutest breaks and lines in the walls of the buildings, and the pavements of the streets.[192]

Another visitor, the German scientist Alexander von Humboldt, wrote in late February to the painter Carl Gustav

Carus about an exchange with Daguerre before one of his prints:

I was able to see an interior view of the Louvre courtyard with its many relief sculptures.—Straw had just been spread on the quay. Do you see it in the picture?—No. Daguerre handed me a magnifying glass and I saw twigs of straw in every window pane.[193]

One of the most comprehensive published responses to Daguerre's invention was written by Jules Janin in late January 1839 for *L'Artiste*. Janin expressed unbridled enthusiasm for daguerreotypes. He also placed them in a larger cultural context of social mechanization, including their relationship to the sculpture duplicating device invented by Collas that he deeply admired:

We are living in a remarkable time; these days, we no longer dream of making anything by ourselves. On the contrary, we look with unequalled perseverance for ways to reproduce things for us and in our place: steam has multiplied the number of workers fivefold; before long, the railroads will double this transient capital called life; gas has replaced the sun; at this moment one is attempting endless tests to find a pathway through the air. . . . Just the other day, another man of genius . . . M. Collas, invented a wheel by means of which he reproduced the Venus of Milo with a wonderful and incredible truthfulness. Here now, with this coating spread on a plate of copper, M. Daguerre replaces drawing and engraving.[194]

Like most of his colleagues, Janin was deeply impressed by the daguerreotype's power of transcription, which he understood not as a means of stopping time but of transcending it:

The drawing skill of the greatest masters has never produced a drawing like this. If the whole is admirable, the details are infinite. Just think about it: the sun itself, now introduced as the all-powerful agent of an entirely new art, produces these incredible works. This time, it is no longer the hesitant look of a man who has a view of shadow and light from a distance, it is no longer his trembling hand that reproduces upon a loose sheet of paper the changing scene of this world that the void sweeps away. . . . No human hand can draw like the sun; no human look can plunge so deeply into these streams of light, this profound darkness. We have seen the greatest monuments of Paris reproduced in this manner—this

time Paris will really become the eternal city. We have seen the cobblestones of the Grève, the water of the Seine, the sky covering Sainte-Geneviève, and in each of these masterpieces there was the same divine perfection.[195]

Janin's utopian view of Paris as a space of historical monuments is not new (see Chapter Three) but, as we shall see, an enormous paradox lies at the heart of his belief that daguerreotypes will crystallize the imagery of Paris as the eternal city (Figs. 42 and 45).

Exposure times to make a daguerreotype in 1839 varied from three to about twenty minutes. Most city views required at least ten minutes to register on the plate. This meant that anything—or anyone—moving across the visual field was not recorded. Samuel Morse noted immediately this unusual effect of emptying the city: "Objects moving are not impressed," he remarked to his brother; "the Boulevard, so constantly filled with a moving throng of pedestrians and carriages, was perfectly solitary, except for an individual who was having his boots brushed."[196] Several of Daguerre's prints were exhibited in Vienna during August, where a local critic singled out this odd visual effect in a view of Notre-Dame (perhaps similar to Fig. 159):

The second, presenting the cathedral of Notre-Dame, has the dimensions of a miniature landscape, but seen in a very bare and lifeless way, for it is divested of any sort of staffage. Now this emptying out can be explained by assuming the device can only reproduce fixed objects. But, if this be the case, it still remains a mystery that no gaps or smudges are produced in the picture by moving objects: for example, men or groups of carriages and so on, some of which only traverse the square slowly and, in any spot depicted here, would clearly be replaced by new ones so that, in truth, they are to be considered as continually present. How might this be? Since I heard this question asked all around during many visits to the council rooms of the Royal and Imperial Academy, and since no one was able to answer it, which could hardly be otherwise considering the strangeness of the issue, I am surely permitted to raise it here as well, and herewith respectfully invite some art-loving experts to offer a short reply to it.[197]

Morse the scientist understood why the moving figures were not recorded. Ordinary viewers in Vienna could not imagine how moving people or things actually present on the street left no trace in the image.

The most interesting aspect of this erasure of life was its apparent unimportance to Janin and his Parisian contemporaries, for it elicited almost no comment. Janin does note that one daguerreotype offers "something a little more obscure than the rest," but he goes on to explain that a bird passed through the visual field at the time of the exposure and left its phantom trace on the image.[198] By contrast, people on the streets of Paris—for the most part ordinary workers, housewives, idlers, or peddlers—were easily forgotten by critics in their enthusiasm for being able to count the paving stones or to read infinitesimal street signs. Writing about these first pictures of the city, Shelley Rice reminds us that more was at stake than a technical process:

> The early camera apparatus recorded only what *endured*. This "mirror of nature" could reflect only a slow-time universe from which human activity was excluded. . . . We can look at the pictures and see that the artists themselves were struggling with questions much more complex than the "mirror of nature" analogy would allow. They were struggling to define their city in images—over a decade before Baron Haussmann would do so in fact.[199]

The empty spaces, good lines of sight, and tranquil cityscapes of Daguerre's prints were seemingly factual representations of old Paris seen through the aesthetic and social aspirations of new Paris—the elegant arcades (Fig. 128), new quartiers (Fig. 133), and wide streets (Fig. 134) under construction at the same time (see Chapter Seven). Janin's "eternal city" was an imaginary space of bourgeois values waiting to be built.

The very materials of Daguerre's process, as André Rouillé points out, restricted the early attraction and distribution of daguerreotypes to the upper strata of society: expensive, semi-precious plates of copper and silver; an artisanal procedure of carefully polishing and cleaning the plates before exposure; the specialized equipment for sensitizing and developing the plates; the fragile images that were easily smudged or scratched; the small size that demanded close viewing; most important, the fact that each print was unique.[200] A social and economic complicity subtends the early and enthusiastic reception of Daguerre's invention by an elite of savants and artists, politicians and businessmen. This same elite rallied to support Arago's project for awarding stipends to Niépce and Daguerre in exchange for making the process public and generally accessible. According to the proposal of 14 June worked out between the Minister of the Interior and the two inventors, Niépce would receive an honorarium of four thousand francs per year, and Daguerre six thousand; in the event of death, their respective widows would receive half those amounts.[201]

Arago presented a long report supporting the indemnity to the Chamber of Deputies on 3 July 1839. He argued the newness of Daguerre's invention, its ease of use, and its potential value to the arts, science, and industry.[202] Arago enlisted the advice of friends and colleagues like the painter Paul Delaroche when preparing this important address. Speaking for the fine arts, Delaroche wrote to Arago that Daguerre's process "completely satisfies art's every need. . . . Nature is reproduced . . . not only with truth, but with art. . . . M. Daguerre's wonderful discovery is an immense service rendered to art."[203] Arago enumerated a host of practical applications for the new technology that must have come from similar advisors in other fields: its value as a recorder of hieroglyphs; its potential for advancing the study of light; its usefulness to astronomers in their attempts to measure the size of the universe; its potential role in physiology and medicine, especially when used in conjunction with microscopes; he even suggested that meteorologists would benefit from the camera's different sensitivity to morning and evening light. Arago requested, and received, the support of the Chamber of Deputies for the proposal. The daguerreotype was sanctioned officially by the elite social formations most likely to benefit from its application.

Four weeks later Joseph-Louis Gay-Lussac, a renowned scientist and member of the peerage, spoke in favor of the indemnity before the Chamber of Peers. He reiterated most of Arago's points, but added an appeal to national pride that positioned France as donor of an entirely new form of art to the world.[204] The shift of symbolic register is significant, for it demonstrates how much the place of French culture, learning, and prestige had become allied with the new technology—especially in light of claims filed in late January 1839 by the Englishman William Henry Fox Talbot, who felt he was the true inventor of photography. With the stakes raised to a national level, it is no surprise that the measure was approved by the Peers with only three dissenting votes. Louis-Philippe signed the measure into law on 7 August 1839.

Niépce and Daguerre now had to fulfill their part of the bargain by revealing the secrets of the daguerreotype process. It was decided the announcement would be made under the dome of the Institut, at a joint meeting of the Académie des Sciences and the Académie des Beaux-Arts, on 19 August 1839. Excitement ran high. According to the *Journal des Artistes*, crowds began to fill the building well before the appointed hour of three o'clock:

Consequently, already in the morning the crowd squeezed into the gallery and hallways of the Institute; with curiosity and with a kind of fear and joy, one waited for the moment of being initiated into this secret of a marvelous discovery that would enrich art and especially science. A profound silence prevailed during the entire time that M. Arago spoke and, upon returning home, everyone wanted to try it out.[205]

Daguerre was scheduled to make the presentation that day, but he claimed a sore throat prevented him from speaking—many people believed it was stage fright—so Arago took over at the last minute.[206] He rehearsed many of the points made in his address of 3 July before the Chamber of Deputies, but now presented the special devices used in the various steps and exhibited three sample prints.

Arago tended to veer into complicated scientific explanations that made the process appear fairly complex; paradoxically, the perceived complexity actually assuaged those who criticized the government's support.[207] An example of this peculiar rebound effect is the editorial about-face of the *Journal des Artistes*. In late June, just before Arago presented his proposal to the Chamber of Deputies, a journalist for the magazine remarked:

Reproducing nature mechanically can be a useful thing, but it will never be an intelligent operation whose products could bear any comparison with what the taste, the skill, the genius of an artist would trace. . . . May the government launch this new branch of industry into the public domain only when it will be very certain of the benefits that can be drawn from it: without this, it will be a stone detached from the temple of the arts, good for finishing off those who still work there by crushing them.[208]

By contrast, and based upon Arago's detailed description of mid-August, the same journal completely reversed its opinion and tone:

This wonderful process is not so simple as had been said. . . . We are happy to announce that the daguerreotype is not, as one might fear, simply an ingenious mechanism; it's a splendid invention that can be useful and helpful only to those having some basic knowledge of art, of physics, of chemistry. It's a wonderful assistant to talent; it is not what might be commonly called an instruction manual. This is why we now say: the invention of M. Daguerre is wonderful! It inscribes his name in the annals of artistic history.[209]

But where the *Journal des Artistes* was consoled to learn that daguerreotypes were not for everyone, Jules Janin reported to readers of *L'Artiste* that Arago's revelation was deeply disappointing:

The good Athenians of Paris who, the day before, had bought the secret and thought they paid a fair price for it, were all disappointed when they realized that, at least until some further notice, this particular secret was not within their capabilities. . . . In place of the very simple apparatus—easily transportable and not expensive—that they expected, the public met with a series of incredible experiments, infinite details, and meticulous precautions.[210]

The differences between how critics of the two leading art journals of Paris reviewed Arago's presentation are revealing: for one, technical difficulty and the need for "some basic knowledge of art" retrieved the process from industry and placed it among highbrow culture and artistic genius; for the other, the same difficulties deflated expectations that industry and science had finally opened image-making to a wide public with neither training nor talent. Yet both critics locate Daguerre's process—product of a novel intersection of industry and the visual arts that obviated the artist's autographic touch—in the breach between elite cultural expectations and middlebrow cultural aspirations.

Daguerre was dismayed by Janin's pessimistic account of the difficulties in making a daguerreotype, especially in light of the journalist's prior enthusiasm. He invited Janin and some friends to watch him make a print. In a follow-up article, Janin admits he was thoroughly shocked to learn that "this operation, which seem nearly impossible when recounted by M. Arago, is very easy and very simple when executed by M. Daguerre"; he advises readers to look again at his original article but to ignore his "conclusions about the innumerable difficulties of the operation."[211] Janin also reports that Daguerre is launching a comprehensive publicity campaign that will include public demonstrations in a room of the Palais d'Orsay provided by the Ministry of the Interior. Finally, near the end of August, Daguerre published at the government's expense a booklet that contained the speeches of Arago and Gay-Lussac along with a detailed explanation of his process: within a year his booklet went through thirty-two editions and was translated into eight languages.

The public relations campaign seems to have worked. Parisians scrambled to try their hand at making daguerreotypes. Contemporary reports tell of optical shops besieged by customers seeking lenses and pharmacies doing a brisk trade in iodine and mercury. The mania for daguerreotypes was parodied in December 1839 by Théodore Maurisset's lithograph for Philipon's newly revived *La Caricature* (Fig. 160).[212] Amongst the thrilling modern inventions noted in Janin's first laudatory article—railways and steamships enlisted to deliver examples of Daguerre's camera around the world, gas lamps, and a hot-air balloon from which one photographs birds in flight—there are less optimistic spectacles: a falling tightrope walker caught in mid-air and gallows for rent to unemployed engravers. The landscape sprouts hundreds of Daguerre's devices pointed in all directions, along with signboards offering different types of photographic prints. Hawkers sell the newest, most improved equipment and processes. At the upper right, a group of people dance around an altar in the shape of a large camera while the artist-sun, at the upper left, uses a reflector to intensify his image-making

light over the entire scene. Prominently occupying the center of the image is the "Maison Susse Frères," a leading merchant of mechanically reproduced bronzes who now offers daguerreotype gifts for the New Year [Étrennes daguerréotypiennes pour 1840]. "Look, here comes the sublime discovery," remarked the commentator of *La Caricature*; "the famous Susse himself has gone over to the enemy—him, the Maecenas of statuettes—and despair kills these poor artists. They hang themselves: you see them hanging!"

The lower right corner of Maurisset's comic cityscape registers an obsession underpinning much of the early interest in daguerreotypes: the possibility of making portraits. A panel announces an "apparatus for daguerreotype portraits," which is really a machine, replete with clock attached to body clamps via gears and levers, to immobilize sitters during the ten or more minutes of exposure before the camera. It was nearly impossible to make daguerreotype portraits in 1839, but the idea was on everyone's minds. In the social order of 1830s Paris, where self-made careers and reputations were displacing the old hierarchies of inherited privilege, attention to the details of one's appearance was critical for establishing social identity (see Chapter Seven). The same practice of attention to detail explains why the little booklets called *physiologies*—pocket-sized guides to the physical traits of various social types—were all the rage.[213] If the principal task of modern portraiture was to inventory such socially telling details with a high order of specificity, Daguerre's invention held the promise of recording the entire range of personal traits—from physical features to mode of dress—that construct social identity, and to do so quickly, cheaply, and accurately. "Does the daguerreotype do portraits?" was the question raised among the deputies and peers to whom Arago and Gay-Lussac addressed their remarks when presenting the government's project to purchase Daguerre's process.[214]

Arago replied that Daguerre promised to "deliver to the public all the improvements by which he might further enrich his photographic methods." He underscored the importance of that promise by noting that "it will take only a very small improvement before M. Daguerre will manage to make portraits of living people using his procedures."[215]

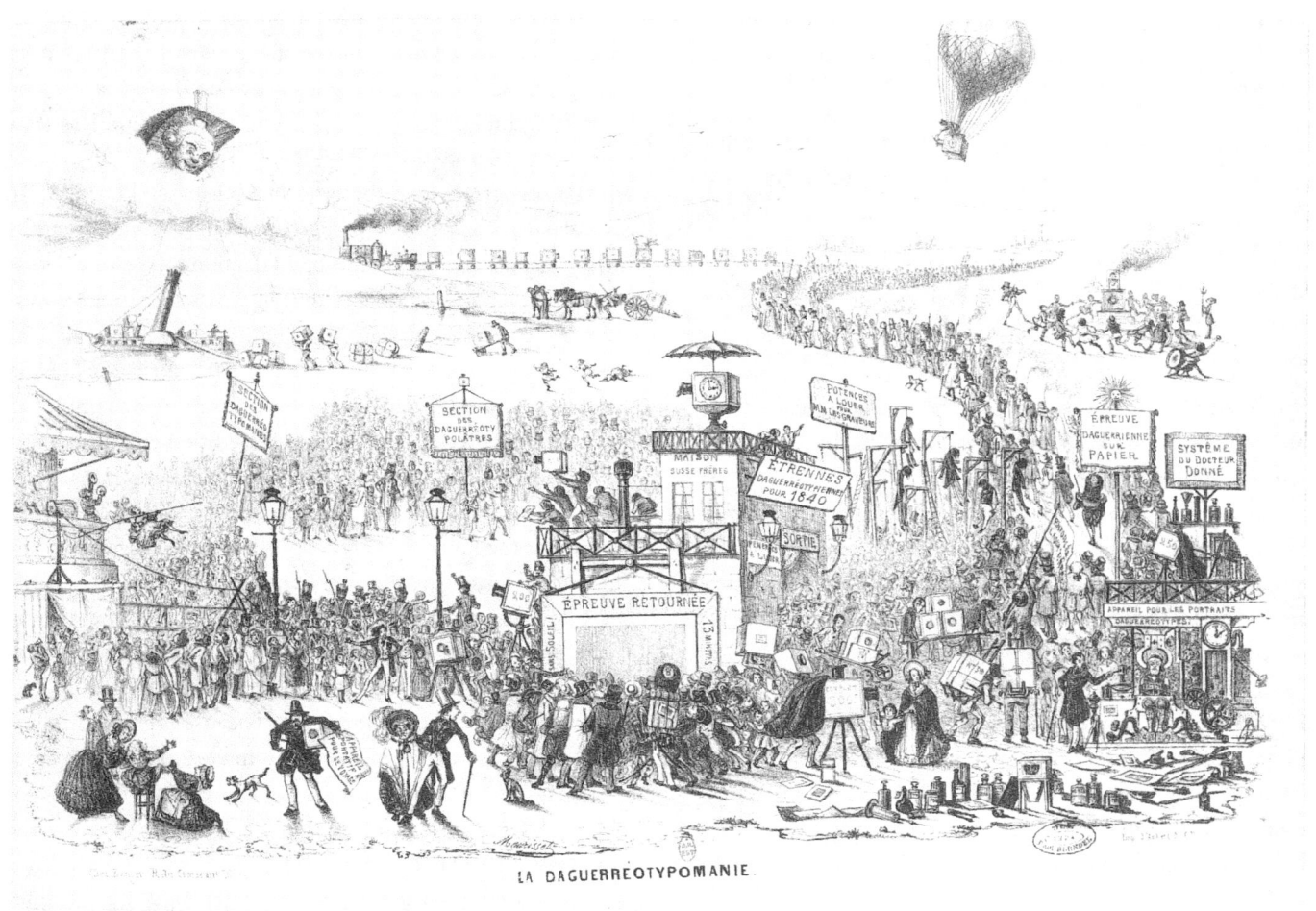

FIGURE 160.   Théodore Maurisset, *La Daguerréotypomanie*, 1839. Lithograph. Paris, BnF, Estampes, inv. Ad 1112/ fol (1) (26 × 35.7 cm). Photo: BnF, Paris.

Gay-Lussac's speech to the Chamber of Peers included assurances that "the problem of its application to portraiture is nearly sorted out; the difficulties that remain to be solved are moderate and leave no doubt about the success."[216] Jules Janin similarly reassured his readers:

M. Daguerre hopes very much that before long he will also manage to achieve a portrait without needing to have a prior portrait by M. Ingres. He is already busy inventing a machine that will help the subject to remain perfectly still; because, such is the power of this re-lentless reproducer, the daguerreotype, that it reproduces in the same instant the glance, the frown, the least forehead wrinkle, the slightest curl of moving hair.[217]

Janin invokes the painted portraits of Ingres to link the quality of unvarnished realism admired in pictures like Bertin (Fig. 114) to the unflinching mechanical rendering of Daguerre's invention. These and other references to portraiture as something that will soon happen, register the strong market pressure for a detailed photographic rendering of personal identity. André Rouillé points out that achieving the goal of portraiture quickly shifted the social domain of daguerreotype imagery:

The daguerreotype is no longer the exclusive privilege of the upper levels of society, but serves for the middle tiers of the bourgeois hierarchy as a record expressing various social successes, however modest they might be. It can do it so well that its technical characteristics make it, for the period, the most rapid image, the easiest to obtain, and thus the best buy; above all, the image exhibits eloquently, and with no possible question, the highest fidelity.[218]

Within a few years, provincial bourgeois visiting Paris were able to demonstrate their station in life by having a portrait made in Paris (Fig. 158).

Once the secrets of Daguerre's process became public knowledge, users and experimenters were quick to make technical improvements with the aim of reducing exposure times to the point that portraits would be practical. In early 1840 the Parisian optician Charles Chevalier introduced an improved set of lenses that could be adjusted for close or distant subjects, thus optimizing the amount of light transferred to the plate and reducing exposure times. The following year a four-part lens built in Germany by Peter Friedrich Voigtländer, based on designs by Josef Max Petzval, corrected most of the distortions and curvatures usually produced when focusing on a subject close at hand, yet its image was sufficiently bright to make daguerreotype prints in about seventy-five seconds. Hippolyte Fizeau discovered in March 1840 that dipping fixed daguerreotypes into a weak solution of gold chloride left a thin layer of gold on the plate that both enhanced its contrasts and protected its surface from all but the most aggressive abrasions. Fizeau's discovery made it possible for daguerreotypes to be transported and handled more freely, the way one would expect to treat a portrait. Finally, the most important advance in chemistry was announced almost simultaneously during the course of 1840–1841 by several far-flung researchers: Franz Kratochwila and the Natterer brothers in Vienna, John Goddard in London, and Antoine-François Claudet in Paris. They collectively discovered that treating the prepared, light-sensitive plate with vapors of bromine or chlo-

rine before exposure greatly enhanced sensitivity. Open-air portraits could be made in the shade—sparing sitters from squinting in strong light—with exposures between five and twelve seconds. Pictures in full sunlight required less than four seconds to register an image.

Portraiture quickly became big business. The optician Nicolas Lerebours and his partner Marc-Antoine Gaudin, who were among the first to build daguerreotype devices especially for portraits, report that in 1841 some London studios were grossing fifteen-hundred francs per day.[219] By the time that Daguerre sat for the portrait taken by E. Thiesson in 1844 (Fig. 161), the mechanics of portraiture had improved even further: according to the 1842 edition of the booklet published by Gaudin and Lerebours, "portraits are made in the shade, in a quarter or half second, depending on the intensity of the light."[220] At this speed, as demonstrated by the picture of Daguerre, the sitter can assume a pose of natural ease and the camera registers what are, in effect, the fleeting facial movements of attention and expression. "One realizes that with this speed portraits have a delightful appearance," remarked Gaudin and Lerebours, "because it lets you reproduce many thousands of physiognomic expressions without stiffness."[221]

The technical advances of these early years, driven in large part by the desire to make daguerreotypes a tool of portraiture, also produced important secondary effects upon the medium as a whole. When Gaudin first reported the use of bromine vapors to the Académie des Sciences in 1841, he clearly grasped the dual implications of an increased sensitivity to light:

The *instantaneous* prints [instantanées], so to speak, that I present to the Academy were obtained without using a continuation glass, even though one of them was subjected to light rays for only $1/19$ of a second. It's a view of the Pont Neuf in which you clearly see carriages and pedestrians in motion. The other prints are portraits that required from $1/4$ to $3/4$ of a second of light rays, according to the brightness of the day. As you will see, these portraits are completely

---

FIGURE 161.   E. Thiesson, *Portrait of Louis-Jacques-Mandé Daguerre*, 1844. Daguerreotype. Paris, Musée Carnavalet, inv. PH 00172 (9 × 7 cm). Photo: © PMVP.

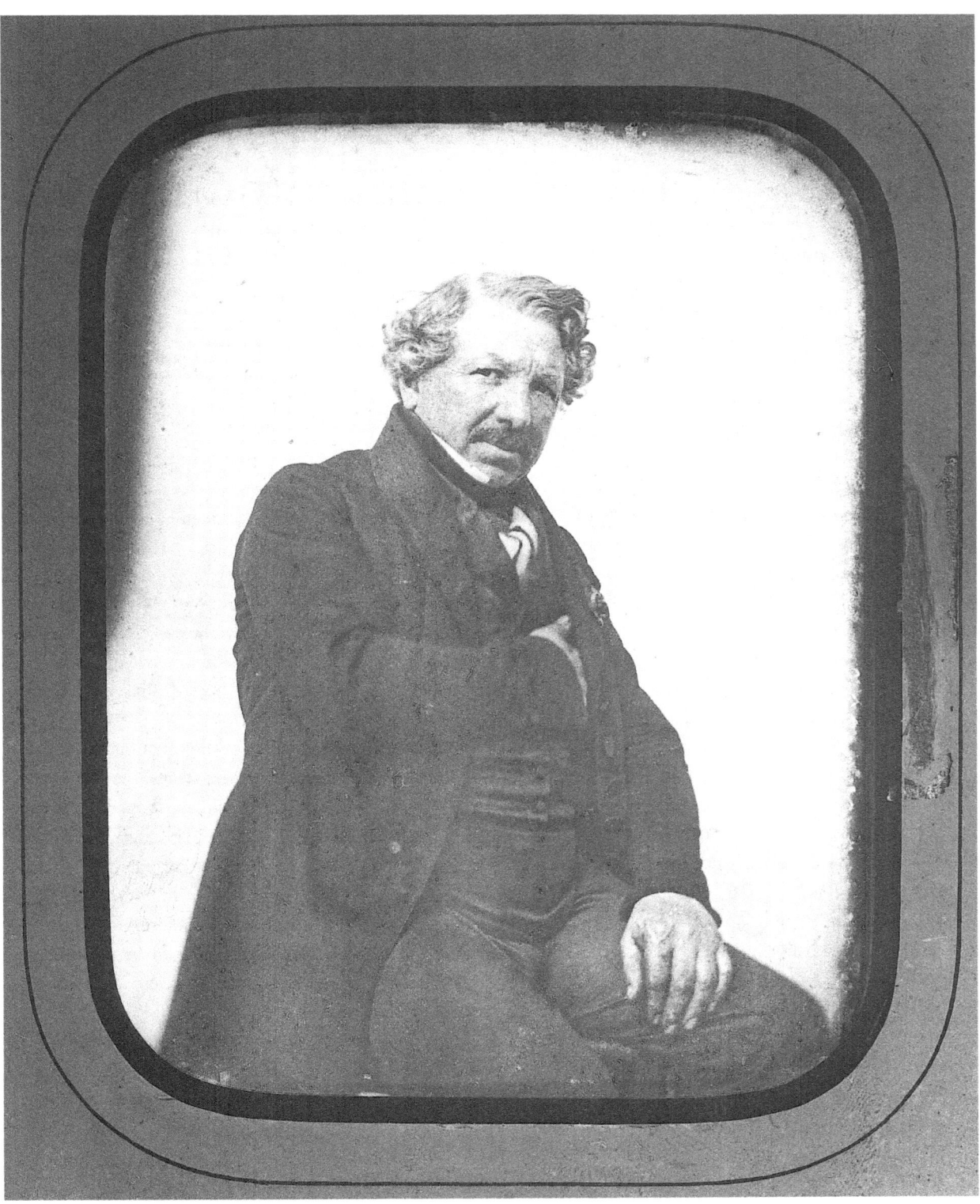

different from those made with a longer time, due to their superior rendering of life, expression, and likeness.[222]

Instantanées—Gaudin's word for this new type of city view (Fig. 162)—entered the critical literature during the summer of 1841. According to *L'Artiste*, the term was used specifically for images of "groups of people in action, views of the Pont-Neuf with carriages and pedestrians in motion; delightful portraits in which you no longer find the stiffness or dryness of the first daguerreotype portraits."[223] Today snapshots are taken for granted, but in 1841 Gaudin's pictures of the Pont-Neuf in which moving people are visible were sufficiently novel to be presented to the Académie des Sciences as curious achievements of the newest photographic technology.

Compared to the first images of Paris made by Daguerre (Fig. 159), *instantanées* gave back to the streets of Paris their life and animation (Fig. 162). In 1839, after looking at the first of Daguerre's prints, Jules Janin believed daguerreotypes would make Paris "really the eternal city" by emptying it of all but its most enduring markers—the monuments of history—rendered with the "divine perfection" that only the sun could achieve. By contrast, *instantanées* brought to the fore a different Paris—a city of continuous change, bustling activity, and a never-ending spectacle of energy and movement. This Paris is not, and cannot be, captured once for eternity; on the contrary, its ever-changing face calls for many and repeated photographs. A survey conducted by the Chambre de Commerce of Paris in 1847–1848 registered fifty-six daguerreotype portrait-makers in the capital employing forty-eight full-time workers and twenty-seven seasonal additions—an industry that generated more than 346,000 francs of annual revenue.[224] Three years later, in its summary of photography at the Exposition des produits de l'industrie français for 1849, *La Lumière*, a new journal dedicated to photographic news, estimated that one hundred thousand daguerreotype prints were made each year—not counting the many thousands of unsuccessful attempts—and that "the industry has found large outlets from sales in France, and exports even to America, for chemical substances, as have factories and metal polishers in the fabrication of plates, opticians and cabinet-makers in putting together devices, and the makers

of cardboard and frames in a host of combinations."[225] Paris had emerged as the veritable center of a global industry in the traffic of images.

THE DAGUERREOTYPE BOOM could not last. Daguerre's process, although much enhanced since its announcement in 1839, was a mature technology by about 1845. Improvements could be made in the several steps required to develop an image, but there was no way to duplicate a print short of taking another image and repeating the entire process. Hippolyte Fizeau developed a system for converting daguerreotypes into plates suitable for printing, but his method was complicated, necessarily destroyed the original image, and was soon abandoned. The future of photography lay elsewhere, and is still viable today in the form of positive prints on paper made from negatives that can be used many times. The basic principal was known since 1834, when Henry Fox Talbot began printing paper negatives on light-sensitive paper, but his images were no match for the remarkable detail and high resolution of daguerreotypes. During the later 1840s, and as the result of several different avenues of experiment, paper prints came to rival those qualities and eventually dethroned the daguerreotype.

Negatives were the first part of the equation to be greatly improved. This was achieved in three stages. The first opened about 1847 with Louis-Désiré Blanquart-Evrard. He dipped paper first in potassium iodide, then in silver nitrate, and exposed it while still wet and semi-transparent—a method called calotype already explored by Fox Talbot in 1841. When the exposed sheet was developed in a solution of gallic acid, the image appeared in negative and could be printed positive any number of times. Calotype negatives were hampered, however, by poor image definition that did not compare to the high resolution of daguerreotypes. The second stage of improving negatives involved using glass as support. Claude-Félix Abel Niépce de Saint-Victor, nephew of Daguerre's original partner, demonstrated in October 1847 a glass negative coated with a layer of beaten egg whites into which potassium iodide was mixed. The plate was sensitized with silver

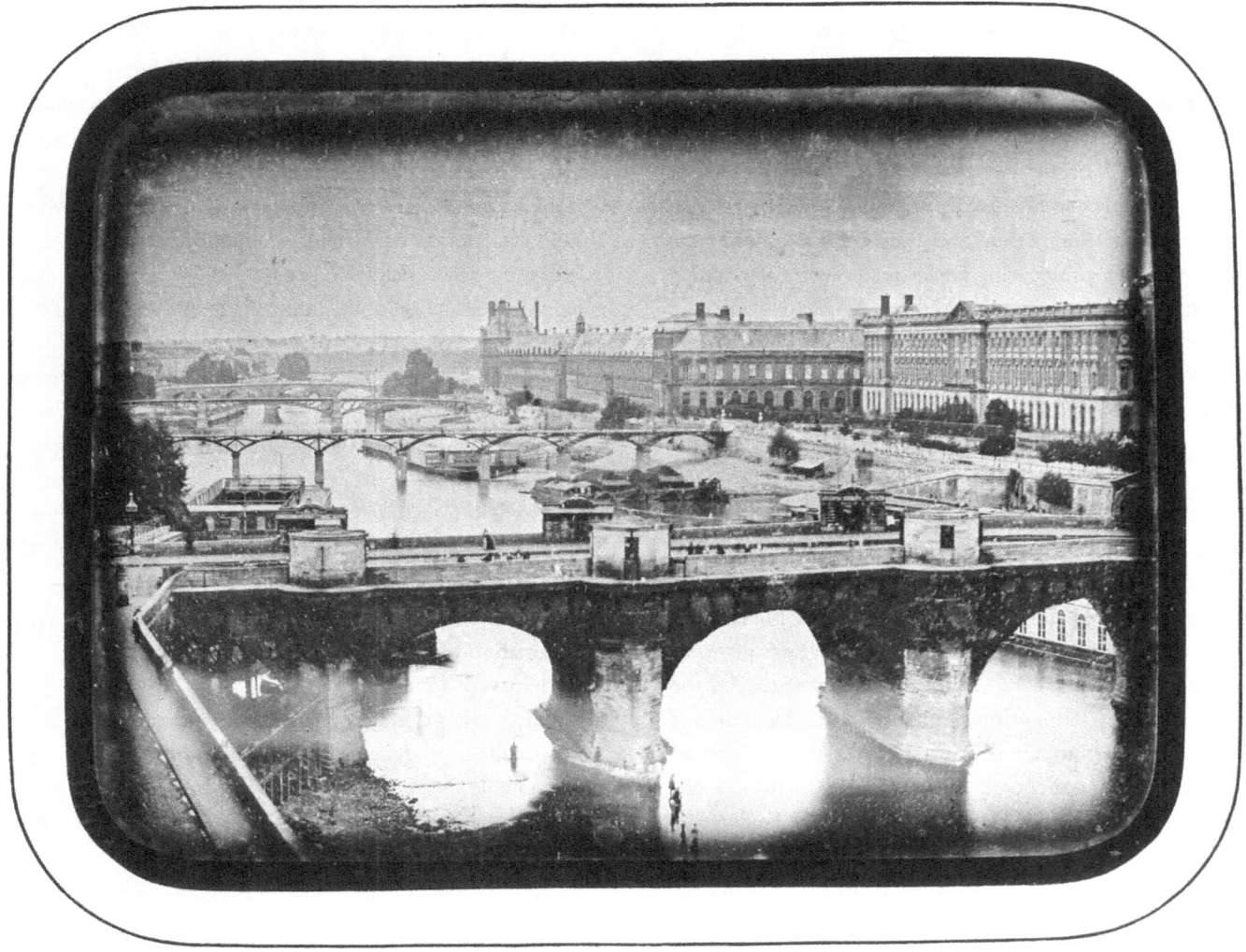

FIGURE 162.   Anonymous, *The Pont-Neuf and the Louvre*, ca. 1845–1850. Daguerreotype. Herning, Collection of the Danish Musuem of Photography, inv. 148-00-696 (7.4 × 12 cm). Photo: Courtesy of the Danish Museum of Photography.

nitrate just before exposure, and developed in a bath of gallic acid. Niépce de Saint-Victor's system, now known as albumen negatives, produced an image almost as sharp as daguerreotypes but its exposure times were long—five to fifteen minutes—making it not useful for portrait photography. Finally, in 1851, Frederick Scott Archer perfected a method of coating glass with collodion—a solution of cotton powder and ether alcohol that forms a glutinous substance and dries clear—into which silver salts were dissolved. The result was a clear, light-sensitive layer, firmly bonded to the glass and impervious to water or alcohol. Archer's plates were highly responsive to light and easily developed in a bath of gallic acid. Louis-Frédéric Mayer and Pierre-Louis Pierson, photographic historians writing in 1862, looked back on this development of

1851 as decisive, concluding that "the use of collodion virtually delivered the final blow to photography on plates."[226]

Paper printing processes also improved during the late 1840s, with the most significant breakthrough occurring in 1851—a technical conjuncture with collodion plates that all but finished off daguerreotypes. Louis-Désiré Blanquart-Evrard imagined an industry of printing photographic images on the order of five or six thousand a day.[227] He adopted a new tactic for making prints using paper treated with silver chloride. Rather than exposing the paper to the negative until the image became visible, he discovered that a short exposure—only about a minute—would suffice if the treated paper was itself developed in gallic acid, washed twice in hyposulfite of soda to fix the image, and washed thoroughly in clear water.[228] In the course of reviewing Blanquart-Evrard's treatise for *La Lumière*, Francis Wey concluded by saying "this wonderful discovery constitutes the creation of an industry."[229]

There have been many changes in procedures and chemicals since then, but today's chemical processes for treating photographic film and prints do not differ greatly from those in place by 1851. The advent of this technology eclipsed the daguerreotype by joining image quality to the capability of producing great numbers of prints from a single negative. The speed of daguerreotype *instantanées* had driven a demand for more images—more portraits, more landscapes, more views of Paris and other cities—by shifting the subject of interest from space to action, from monuments to movement. Daguerre's process created the need—but was unable to fulfill the demand—for images of the world in motion. Thus, photographic historians tend to consider daguerreotypes a dead end in the history of images. Other reasons cited for their demise are familiar: semi-precious materials of copper-silver plates; a process of several discrete steps performed in a specific order with an artisan-like attention to detail; a unique, unreproducible image.

Looking forward in the history of photography, it is clear that daguerreotypes were doomed to extinction. Looking back across the intersections of art and industry discussed in this chapter, Daguerre's process emerged from a Parisian culture that valued artisanal workmanship in the face of industry, preferred solid quality to low price, and celebrated the rare or unusual as a way of transcending the common and ordinary. Similar principles guided Christofle and Baccarat in their efforts to incorporate new industrial processes into traditional forms of manual production, incited magasins de nouveautés to maintain personalized service while offering a wide selection of machine-made dry goods, and drove the business of making mass-produced books illustrated with hand-cut woodblock engravings. They also championed the autographic quality of lithography and shaped the thorny debate about an artist's ownership of the rights to reproduce a work of art. Taking a broad view means recognizing the uniquely Parisian affinities between the modern yet artisanal process of Daguerre, and the seeming paradox of Labrouste's Bibliothèque Sainte-Geneviève—built coincident with the heyday of daguerreotypes—that cloaks an armature of industrial iron in an edifying storyboard of hand-carved stone.

The golden age of daguerreotypes was closed by the arrival of mass-produced photographic prints in 1851, a year also notable for the coup-d'état by which Louis-Napoléon Bonaparte and his cronies launched the Second Empire (see Epilogue). Karl Marx saw Bonaparte's rise to power as the opening of an era in which "industry and commerce, thus the interests of the middle class, should prosper under a government as strong as a greenhouse."[230] We might read his comment as referring ironically to the underlying fragility of Bonaparte's government, except that contemporaries were thrilled by the effortless strength of Rohault de Fleury's greenhouses for the Jardin des Plantes. What Marx saw clearly is that the greenhouse was the architecture of the future, and that big business and rapid industrialization would sweep the engaging, hand-wrought anachronisms of Romantic Paris into the dustbin of history.

Epilogue

He's a bit of a crook and a lot of rogue. You always sense in him the poor prince of industry who lived by his wits in England; his current prosperity, his triumph—both his empire and his puffing up—amount to nothing; this purple mantel drags on worn boots. Napoléon-le-Petit: nothing more, nothing less.

—Victor Hugo[1]

THESE SCATHING LINES were written by Hugo during the summer of 1852 in Brussels, where he had fled the consequences of Louis-Napoléon Bonaparte's coup-d'état of 2 December 1851. Deliberately selecting the anniversary of his uncle's great victory at Austerlitz to dispense with the Second Republic, Bonaparte dissolved the National Assembly, stationed heavily armed troops in all the principal squares and boulevards of the capital, and arrested more than seventy-five legislators and political leaders. Posters prepared in great secrecy were plastered throughout the city to announce Bonaparte's intentions, to proclaim a state of siege in and around Paris, and to promise a general election to ratify his extraordinary actions. Hugo and a number of left-wing colleagues from the National Assembly tried to arrest the march of this offensive by appealing directly to the people with a counter-proclamation that pulled no punches: "Louis-Napoléon is a traitor. He has stolen the Constitution. He has perjured himself. He is an outlaw."[2] The flyer urged Parisians to rise up in mass against the coup. Hugo's name figured prominently among the signatures on this call to arms.

Police loyal to Bonaparte seized many of these posters before they could be distributed. Moreover, it was painfully apparent to Hugo that the general population was not willing to resist the coup-d'état. He ventured into the heart of the faubourg Saint-Antoine—the capital's historic bastion of republican support—to visit a wine merchant named Auguste whose life he had saved during the civil insurrections of June 1848 (see Chapter Two). Auguste confirmed what Hugo already suspected:

That, in fact, one did not care much about the Constitution—that one loved the Republic, but that the Republic was "preserved"—that in all this one saw clearly only one thing: the canons ready to fire grapeshot—that one remembered June 1848—that Cavaignac did a lot of harm—that the women were hanging onto the men's shirts to prevent them from going to the barricades.[3]

A dispirited Hugo left Auguste for another rendezvous with his political colleagues, but Bonaparte's police were tracking their movements, forcing the group to move surreptitiously from meeting to meeting. Hugo's own house was under police surveillance and—like most of his friends—he spent

379

the first night of the new regime on the sofa of a distant acquaintance. He learned later that a police commissioner had confronted his wife during the night with a warrant for his arrest.

Without entering into the details of Bonaparte's carefully crafted putsch, a few salient episodes must be mentioned: the first flurries of armed resistance inspired by the incendiary flyer published by Hugo and his allies; the bounty of twenty-five thousand francs offered by Bonaparte for the capture of Hugo dead or alive; the barricades built during the night of 3 December that were swept away at dawn by troops with orders to take no prisoners and to leave no survivors; the fusillade on the afternoon of 4 December against unarmed civilians gathered in the boulevard Montmartre that left hundreds dead and a trail of blood destined to haunt Bonaparte's regime to the very end. Hugo was forced to run for his life, and to hide a trunk of unpublished manuscripts that included drafts of what would eventually become *Les Misérables*. He finally escaped Paris on 11 December aboard the night train to Brussels using the passport of a typesetter named Lanvin whom he had once befriended. One of the most famous men in France reached Belgium without incident early on the morning of 12 December: a long exile had begun.

Why might Bonaparte's coup-d'état and Hugo's exile serve as epilogue to a history of Romantic Paris? The answer requires unraveling how the two men's lives were intertwined. To begin, one must return to the politics of mid-1848, to the first presidential election of the Republic in December, and to Hugo's undivided support for the candidacy of Louis-Napoléon Bonaparte. Hugo was elected to the National Assembly in the complementary voting of early June 1848 after failing at his first attempt in April. His campaign unfolded against a background of mounting tension that eventually led to the workers' uprising of 24–26 June, its merciless repression, and the emergence of the general Louis-Eugène Cavaignac as virtual dictator (see Chapter Two). In this uncertain social climate, Hugo ran as a moderate republican with a conservative agenda. He was attached to the idea of a republic, but was completely out of phase with the political goals and ambitions of the far Left. Hugo explained his

political vision in a carefully worded campaign statement of 26 May:

[the Republic] will build power on the same footing as liberty, that is, on law; it will subordinate force to intelligence; it will disband rioting and war, those two forms of barbarism; it will make order the law of citizens, and peace the law of nations; it will live and be radiant; it will expand France and conquer the world; in a word, it will be the majestic embracing of the human species before a satisfied God.[4]

A few days later, the candidate was challenged by a member of the audience at a political rally to say "I am neither a red republican, nor a white republican, but a tricolored republican." Hugo replied:

Do you know why I don't cry out in a loud voice "I am a republican"? Because far too many people shout it. Do you know why I have a kind of modesty and misgiving about making this parade of republicanism? Because I see people who are in no way republican making more noise than you who are sure of your convictions. There is one thing about which I would challenge anyone: a feeling for democracy.[5]

In his pre-election statements Hugo—like many of his contemporaries—juggled a commitment to the still-fragile democratic order established by the revolution of February 1848 against two very different threats: on one hand, the masses of urban and rural poor who might implement the democratic values of equality and justice by toppling the Republic under a red banner of socialism; on the other, a loose coalition of religious conservatives, middle and upper class professionals, and old-money aristocrats who so feared the specter of a socialist upheaval that they were leaning towards a form of monarchy under the Bourbon flag of white. Therein lies the deeper sense of that trenchant question: was he a red, white, or tricolored republican? Hugo hedged his reply. He was elected nonetheless. On 10 June Hugo took his seat in the assembly among a group of conservatives known as "the party of order."

The biggest surprise of the June election was the success of Louis-Napoléon Bonaparte. He was swept into the assembly by voters in Paris and three outlying departments (Yonne, Charente-Inférieure, and Corsica). Bonaparte was living in

London and seemed to come from nowhere, especially because the Bonaparte clan was officially banned from France by a law of 1832. The provisional government duly ordered Bonaparte's arrest if he tried to enter the country to claim his seat in the National Assembly. Many pundits believed the ban was already a moot point, since the assembly agreed on 2 June 1848 to discuss allowing the Bonapartes to return. Debate on the issue was postponed until after the June elections. In the meantime, Louis-Napoléon Bonaparte scored such impressive electoral victories that it seemed impossible to prevent him from taking office. Oddly enough, parliamentary debate about dropping the ban—a position supported by conservatives and strongly opposed by Alphonse de Lamartine and other leaders of the provisional government—interested Victor Hugo very little: he neither spoke during the debate nor left any trace among his personal notes to indicate that he took the matter seriously. The law of 1832 banning the Bonapartes was eventually revoked on 13 June by a right-wing majority of which Hugo was part, but the vote was interpreted mainly as a political gesture to punish Lamartine for opening his government to members of the far Left. No one seemed to take seriously the threat of a Bonaparte revival.

As it turned out, the newly elected Bonaparte deflated the whole issue with a letter from London in which he resigned from the assembly in the name of "order and the support of a wise, great, and intelligent republic."[6] Bonaparte decided to wait for a more propitious moment, wisely cloaking his resignation in a conservative rhetoric that Victor Hugo could and did approve. Three months later, Bonaparte was re-elected to the assembly by five departments, garnering more than one hundred thousand votes in Paris alone. This time he was free to claim victory. He returned to France quietly, using an incognito to cross the frontier and booking a suite at the Hôtel du Rhin on the place Vendôme under an assumed name.

Like many French citizens, Hugo was curious about this young man with the famous name. He recorded in his journal an anecdote about the hotel owner's surprise to learn the identity of his mysterious guest. He also registered the rumor about Mademoiselle George's chat with Bonaparte, during which he admits to spending a lot of time contemplating the Vendôme Column (see Chapter Three).[7] Hugo

was very attentive to the newcomer's dress, accent, and reception on the day of his first appearance in the legislative chamber: "He mounted the speaker's platform. He read from a crumpled piece of paper in his hand. One listened to him with a profound silence. He pronounced the word *compatriots* with a foreign accent. He looks like Lockroy [an actor at the Théâtre-Français]. When he was done, a few voices shouted *Long live the Republic!*"[8] Hugo's first impression of Louis-Napoléon was not very favorable.

The poet's thinking began to evolve during the fall of 1848 as the presidential campaign heated up. He was resolutely opposed to the candidacy of Alexandre-Auguste Ledru-Rollin, a leader of the far Left who had penned the inflammatory account of the rue Transnonain massacre in 1834 (see Chapter Eight). But Hugo was no less opposed to Louis Cavaignac, the candidate preferred by most moderate republicans. The general had emerged as virtual dictator of France under the provisions of a state of emergency enacted during the June uprising. Many observers, including Hugo, believed that Cavaignac was preparing a coup-d'état supported by the military even before the election. Among the candidates Hugo might support for president, only one seemed close to fulfilling his aspirations for the Republic: Louis-Napoléon Bonaparte.

For his part, Bonaparte certainly knew the famous lines, written by Hugo in October 1830 during the heyday of Romanticism, that praised extravagantly the column of the place Vendôme (Fig. 48) and celebrated the grandeur of his uncle:

Oh! quand il bâtissait, de sa main colossale,
Pour son trône, appuyé sur l'Europe vassale,
Ce pilier souverain,
Ce bronze, devant qui tout n'est que poudre et sable,
Sublime monument, deux fois impérissable,
Fait de gloire et d'airan.
Quand il le bâtissait, pour qu'un jour dans la ville
Ou la guerre étrangère ou la guerre civile
Y brisassent leur char,
Et pour qu'il fît pâlir sur nos places publiques
Les frêles héritiers de vos noms magnifiques,
Alexandre et César!

[Oh! when he built, with his huge hand
For his throne, supported by vassal Europe,
This sovereign pillar,
This bronze, before which all is but powder and sand,
Sublime monument, twice imperishable,
Made of glory and bronze.
When he built it, so that one day in the city
Either foreign or civil wars
Would wreck their chariots on it,
And so that it would make jealous in public
The flimsy heirs of your magnificent names,
Alexander and Caesar!][9]

Bonaparte surely realized, in the words of Alain Decaux, that if he "carried a magic name . . . it was by way of Hugo that the French glorified it."[10] Near the end of October 1848 the candidate paid a surprise visit to Hugo's new apartment in the rue de La Tour-d'Auvergne, both to silence the rumors of intrigue swirling around his bid for the presidency and to emphasize the nobility of his intentions. Hugo's short account of this meeting, eventually published in *Histoire d'un Crime*, is certainly skewed by his later enmity for Bonaparte, but most historians agree he did not alter dramatically the tenor of the candidate's monologue:

Does one assume that I would restart Napoléon? There are two men that a very ambitious person can take as models: Napoléon and Washington. The one is a man of genius, the other a man of virtue. It's ridiculous to say to yourself, "I will be a man of genius," but it's honest to say "I will be a man of virtue." . . . My name, the name Bonaparte, will be on two pages in the History of France: on the first, there will be crime and glory; on the second, integrity and honor. And maybe the second will be as good as the first. Why? Because if Napoléon is greater, Washington is better. Between the guilty hero and the good citizen, I pick the good citizen. That's my ambition.[11]

Bonaparte was no fool. He framed respect for the glory of his uncle with the crime of 18 Brumaire (see Chapter One), and aligned himself with the sober virtue of George Washington rather than the reckless genius of the Emperor. In so doing, Bonaparte appealed to the multi-faceted complexity

of Hugo's enthusiasm for the young man's name—a complexity shared, it turns out, by millions of French voters.

Bonaparte's suggestion that France could aspire to greatness without revisiting the adventure of Empire was a fusion of ideals and ambitions that Hugo was inclined to endorse. Already in 1847, well before the fall of Louis-Philippe's government or the parliamentary wranglings following the elections of June 1848, Hugo supported the idea of allowing the Bonaparte family to return to France. In an address to the Chamber of Peers he evoked the benefits of remembering Napoléon with a turn of phrase that became famous:

As far as I'm concerned, in seeing the deterioration of moral sense, the highest positions overrun by the most base passions, in seeing the miseries of today, I dream about the great things of the past and, now and then, I'm tempted to say to the Chamber, to the press, to all of France: Look, let's talk a bit about the Emperor, it will do us a lot of good![12]

Hugo's speech of 1847 did not signal the beginning of a tendency to mask problems of contemporary France by looking back in time to imperial grandeur and the charisma of Napoléon. On the contrary, just such a retreat into past glory informed government cultural policy under the July Monarchy in a range of public projects: restoring Napoléon's effigy to the Vendôme Column (Fig. 50); including him on the pediment of the Panthéon (Fig. 47); returning his remains to Paris (Fig. 54).

Official manifestations gave rise to popular revivals, from lavishly illustrated histories of Napoléon's life (Fig. 153) to the *Revue de l'Empire*—a periodical founded in 1842 by a pro-Bonaparte journalist named Charles-Édouard Temblaire. Temblaire originally advertised his publication as an "impartial echo of all the glories of the Consulate and Empire," whose ambition was "purely historical," but it soon became an organ of Bonapartist propaganda.[13] The complexity of Napoleonic sentiment during these years is revealed in the history of Temblaire's journal, whose subscribers included King Louis-Philippe and his sons, most of the former generals of the Empire who were still alive, and many members of the Bonaparte family including Louis-Napoléon Bonaparte. At the time that Temblaire launched his publication, Bonaparte was imprisoned in the Château de Ham, where he was serving a life sentence for leading a botched attempt to overthrow the government of Louis-Philippe. Paradoxically, Temblaire was allowed to publish extracts from the political writings of the young Bonaparte, along with a number of his letters. Simultaneously patronized by the king and a mouthpiece for his prisoner, the *Revue de l'Empire* exemplifies the political and symbolic cross-currents that shaped the collective memory of Napoléon and the Empire in mid-century France—a complexity that Louis-Napoléon Bonaparte knew very well how to exploit.

That complex blend of history, sentiment, and politics enveloped the conception, execution, and inauguration of François Rude's *Napoléon awakening to Immortality* (Fig. 163). Rude's sculpture was commissioned by Claude Noisot, a veteran of the imperial army and fervent acolyte of the Emperor who had followed his hero into exile on the island of Elba in 1814. Noisot and Rude first became acquainted about 1840, when the veteran was introduced to the group that gathered in the evenings at Rude's studio on the rue d'Enfer to swap stories and talk of art. Noisot regaled his new friends with tales of his exploits in the service of Napoléon that, in the words of Louis de Fourcaud, "restored in Rude a balance between republican sympathies and the liberal imperialism of 1814."[14] During the summer of 1845 Rude and his family vacationed in the wine country of Burgundy close to the town of Fixin where Noisot owned a small plot of land overlooking the valley. Noisot revealed to the sculptor his dream of erecting a monument to Napoléon "that would remind my eyes of my emperor."[15] Noisot wanted neither the official Napoléon who had ruled France as a despot, nor the caricatural little corporal placed atop the Vendôme Column by Louis-Philippe (Fig. 50). He dreamed of a work that would elicit the charismatic leader he knew first-hand from his years in the army: the Napoléon of brilliant victories, grand ideas, and enduring glory—the Napoléon of legend.

Noisot offered to provide the land and the funds to cast a monument in bronze; Rude agreed to design the sculpture for free. Never mind that Rude's most famous work was the *Departure of the Volunteers in 1792* (Fig. 44), a subject inspired by the effervescent republicanism of that fateful year (see Chapter

Three), or that he would go on to design a tomb for Godefroy Cavaignac—hero of the radical Left—immediately after the monument to Napoléon. For an artist of liberal tendencies to throw himself into a commission dedicated to the memory of Napoléon was no more unusual, in the complex political situation of France on the eve of the 1848 revolution, than the basically conservative Hugo of 1847 exhorting his colleagues in the Chamber of Peers to "talk a bit about the Emperor." Everyone flirted with the Napoleonic legend, even Louis-Philippe's government, because, in the words of Frédéric Bluche, "[it] allowed the warmongers to transfer their thirst for glory to an idealized past, and the July Monarchy to practice a more pacifist policy in the present and into the future."[16]

Rude set to work upon his return to Paris. The evolution of his thinking about Noisot's project traces vividly the unstable social meaning of the Napoleonic legend in the minds and spirits of the time. His first plan was to depict the hero dead: half-nude, stretched out on a platform of rock (symbol of the island of Saint Helena), and guarded by an eagle (symbol of the Empire). But this solution was worrisome for its suggestion that the Empire outlived the Emperor, an idea at odds with Rude's republican political beliefs. How to distinguish between the despotic Emperor and the military genius so admired by Noisot? Rude's solution was to shift the work's meaning from history to allegory. He adopted the dramatic image of Bonaparte rising in death from captivity towards the heavens and immortality. Obviously, key historical details could not be ignored: Napoléon wears the corporal's uniform, bicorne hat, and sword sanctified by the visual culture of his legend. Rude borrowed the originals of these essential attributes actually worn at Austerlitz from comte Louis-Joseph-Narcisse Marchand, who had served as Napoléon's personal valet. By contrast, Rude invented the conceit of wrapping Bonaparte in a large, shroud-like bivouac blanket, which so exaggerates the hero's physical mass that the monument's base now seems impossibly small. Gravity itself appears to be thwarted as Bonaparte—eyes closed, but crowned by laurel leaves inscribed with the sites of his earliest victories in Italy—rises with an energy that bursts his chains to lift him from the craggy rocks and crashing waves of his island prison. Napoléon also leaves behind the shattered body of an

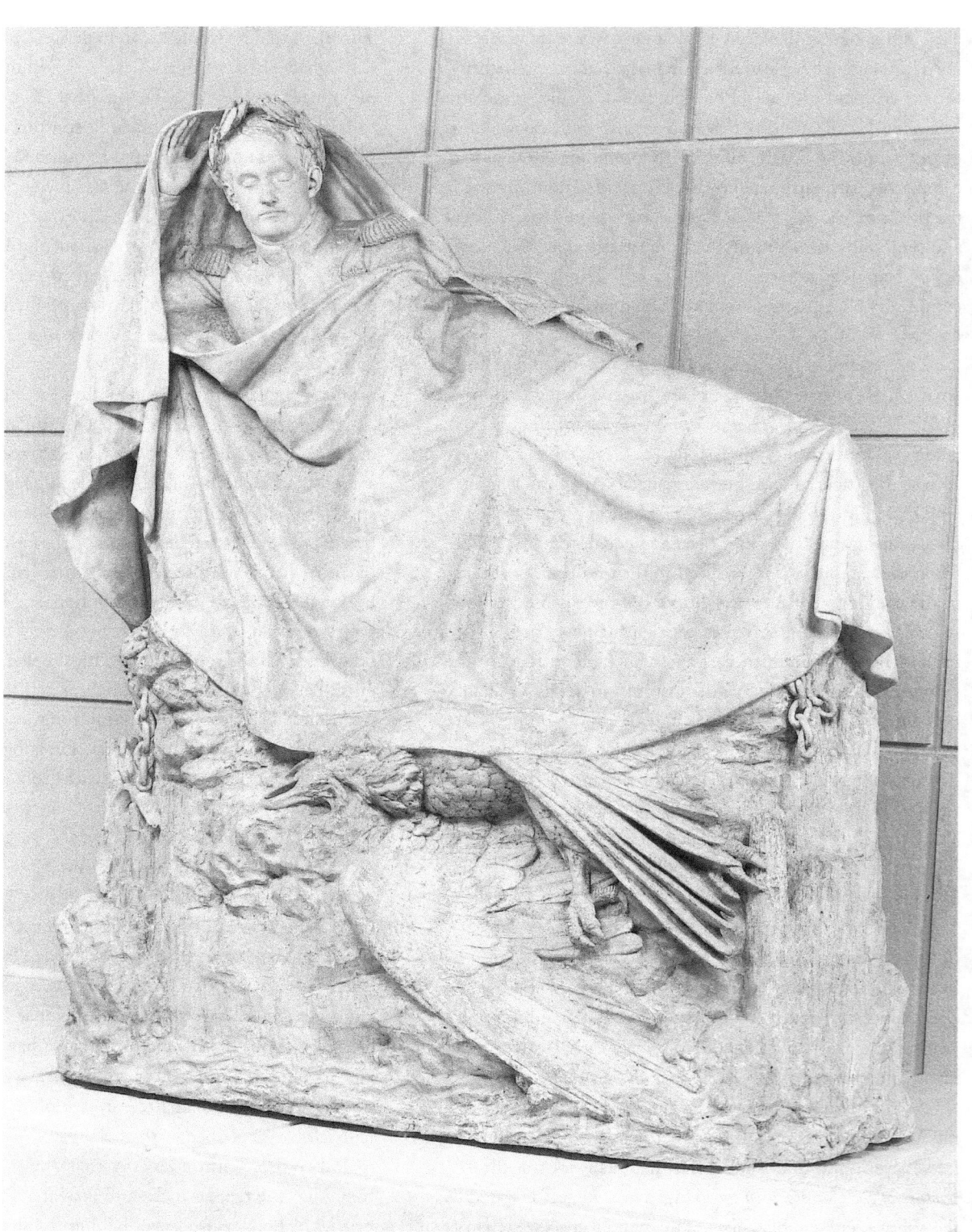

hoped to see. His text was reprinted in full on the newspaper's front page, along with an extensive editorial commentary.[25] Bonaparte cloaked himself in respectability and the fame of his name, stating explicitly that he was not "an ambitious man who dreams sometimes about empire and war, sometimes about applying subversive theories. . . . After four years, I will make it a point of honor to leave my successor with the power consolidated, liberty intact, a real progress accomplished." Echoing the language of restrained ambitions he used to convince Victor Hugo of his good intentions, Bonaparte portrays himself as devoted to social order, a faithful executor of the Assembly's will, and a respectful servant of the constitution. He concludes with a set of campaign promises crafted to attract voters across a wide political spectrum, yet sufficiently vague to avoid contradictions. The editors of *L'Événement* reacted to Bonaparte's statement with unbridled enthusiasm:

From the summit of this idea—that everything great is possible with the French people—Louis-Napoléon Bonaparte has been able to dominate and to judge the entire situation in a few quick overviews. His serious manifesto, calm and liberal, completely marked by love for the people and devotion to order, will rally to the young and worthy heir of the greatest name of our annals all the moderate and serious spirits who want to arm the first president of the Republic with a calm force.[26]

Daily praise followed in subsequent numbers of *L'Événement*. By 2 December the newspaper's endorsement was crystal clear:

So, let's take on Louis-Napoléon, let's arm him, if possible, with the authority of all our votes, let's surround him with our good will, let's help him in every way, through him let's support France, which he will represent both by election and by birth, by the choice of the people and by the choice of God.[27]

This editorial counted Victor Hugo amongst a group of eminent men [hommes supérieurs] supporting Bonaparte's candidacy for president.

It is unlikely that Hugo wrote every political column published by *L'Événement*, but it is certain that the newspaper's editorials were synchronized with his evolving opinion of the candidate. Hugo's first reaction to seeing and hearing Bonaparte in the National Assembly was a comparison to an actor from the Comédie-Française. By 19 November he came away from a dinner party with a frankly favorable impression of the candidate: "Louis Bonaparte is distinguished," he noted; "cold, gentle, intelligent with a certain degree of deference and dignity, a Germanic look, black moustache, no resemblance at all to the Emperor."[28] Even here, in his private notes of an evening's entertainment, the poet searched in vain for a glimpse of the Emperor whose fame had inspired so much of his own verse.

Like millions of French voters, Hugo ultimately settled for the name. An article published in *L'Événement* on the day of the presidential election, and usually ascribed to Hugo himself, exhorted French voters to place their trust in a name recognized by all:

With a name, people, with a name that you love, with the name of Napoléon, you can drive out the unclean demons assailing you. Act so that France will again be the first of nations, that thought will be reborn, that business will revive, that industry will flourish, that employment will reappear, that real prosperity will replace false liberty![29]

The overheated rhetoric was hardly necessary. It was clear, even before the votes were counted, that Bonaparte had won massively. On 13 December *L'Événement* celebrated "the triumph of our candidate and our cause. . . . Thus far, Paris and the provinces have given the immense majority to the Emperor's nephew, to Louis-Napoléon Bonaparte."[30] Bonaparte's success actually outstripped the most optimistic predictions of his advisors: among the slightly more than 7.3 million voters, Bonaparte was chosen by over 5.4 million; just under 1.5 million voters preferred Cavaignac; four other candidates split the remaining four hundred thousand votes.

The biggest loser of the day was Lamartine, the poet-politician abandoned by Hugo and *L'Événement* in their enthusiasm for the nephew of Napoléon. Lamartine had been the single most influential voice in the chaotic days following the February revolution. He was a leader of the provisional government. It was Lamartine who threatened to arrest Bonaparte in early June if he tried to claim his seat in the National Assembly. Lamartine's influence evaporated during the June days of civil war (Fig. 27) when général Cavaignac was invested with sweeping powers under the state of emergency. Lamartine returned briefly to center stage during late summer and fall of 1848 at the time of parliamentary discussions about the new constitution. He argued brilliantly and successfully for a single-house legislature and for direct election of the president by universal suffrage. Flush with these legislative triumphs, Lamartine believed he could eke out a victory for the presidency over the ephemeral front-runner Cavaignac. "If the president is appointed by the country and within the next two months, I will be named, be sure of it," wrote Lamartine to the comte de Circourt in early October.[31] Lamartine's spurt of resurgent popularity proved to be short-lived. A few days after *L'Événement* refused to endorse him, Lamartine realized the futility of his candidacy. "Everything points to Bonaparte or Cavaignac," he wrote on 4 November; "I don't believe in Bonaparte in spite of all the fuss. . . . I will have a few philosophical votes here and there, not many all together, except in my own department and in Paris."[32]

Like most Liberals, Lamartine did not fathom the ground swell of support for Bonaparte—fueled by an aggressive, systematic, and thoroughly modern use of print media. He was stung by receiving fewer than eighteen thousand votes. "This country is becoming lunatic!" he exclaimed to Marie d'Agoult (Fig. 110) shortly after the election; "A hat without a head for a symbol! . . . You must die nobly or forever hide the word Frenchman on your forehead, in exile!"[33] A few weeks later, Hugo visited Lamartine at home and found him "whitened, stooped over since February, looking ten years older in ten months," but "calm, smiling, and sad." Hugo remarks that Lamartine "took his defeat seriously" and explained it starkly: "I have nothing to say, universal suffrage shouted me down [m'a conspué]."[34]

Against the background of this electoral shock to French political life, Théodore Chassériau took up the theme of *Sappho at Leucadia* (Fig. 164), a subject he first painted in 1846. Chassériau was a longtime friend of the Lamartine's: his splendid, half-length pencil portrait of the

politician—dated 1844 and dedicated to Madame Lamartine—is a visual testament to the intimacy of their relationship.[35] Two years later, Chassériau presented Madame Lamartine with a watercolor of Sappho leaping into the sea from the cliffs of Leucadia.[36] In this first rendering of the Sappho story, Chassériau echoes the concentrated self-absorption and stoic determination of Gros's famous picture of 1801 (Fig. 4): gripping her kithara tightly, one foot already in mid-air, Sappho throws herself into the abyss. Chassériau's heroine, like that of Gros's picture, is victim of her emotions, but she nonetheless remains capable of acting resolutely in a willful, final gesture of self-immolation. By contrast, Chassériau's later work of 1849 (Fig. 164) stages a dramatically different ethic. Sappho sits at the edge of a cliff, seemingly lost in thought while gazing blankly into space. The heavy limbs of her body, and its weighty nestling into a corner of the rocky ledge, are a far cry from the airborne liberation made famous by Gros. Chassériau's *Sappho* of 1849 appears to be struggling with her inner self, although her emphatic gesture of gripping the rock as if to stand convinced at least one critic that "the struggle has ended."[37] A second picture of Sappho, also painted by Chassériau in 1849 but now lost, depicted her body tossed by waves onto the beach.[38] Neither version championed the act of willful self-determination that critics had called "romantic" in 1801; rather, Chassériau focused in 1849 on the story's agonizing prologue and grisly aftermath.

Why might the tale of Sappho's mortal leap resonate with Chassériau at this time? The suicide of Sappho, which comes from Ovid's *Héroïdes* and has nothing to do with the great lyric poetess from the island of Lesbos, was a popular theme for artists and writers throughout the nineteenth century.[39] It is generally believed that Chassériau's turn to the subject, coupled with the dedication of his 1846 watercolor to Madame Lamartine, was inspired by reading Lamartine's

---

FIGURE 164.   Théodore Chassériau, *Sappho at Leucadia*, 1849 (shown at the 1850–1851 Salon). Oil on wood panel. Paris, Musée d'Orsay, inv. RF3886 (27.5 × 21.5 cm). Photo: © RMN/Art Resource, NY/© Franck Raux.

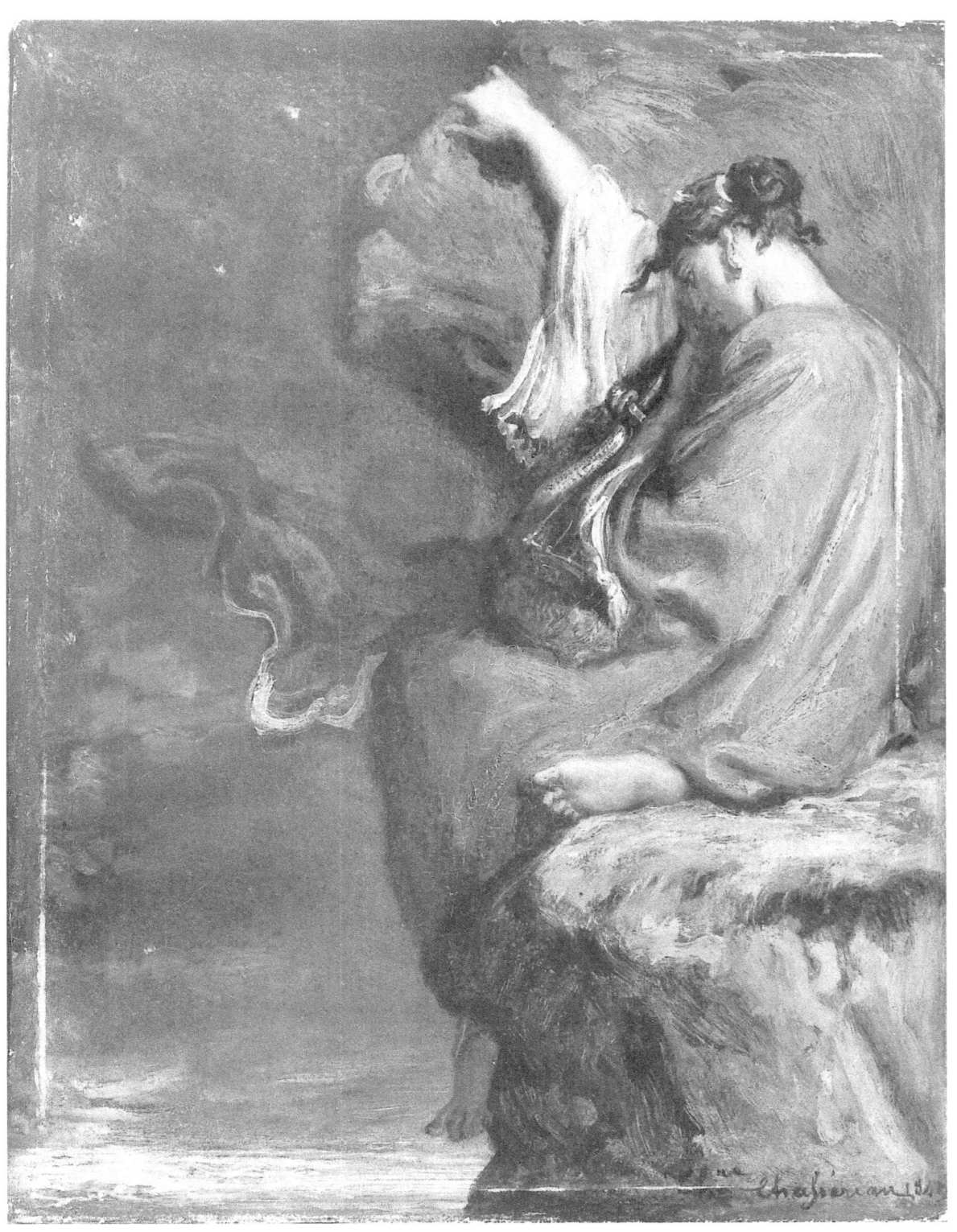

"Sapho," first published in the collection *Nouvelles Médita-tions Poétiques* of 1823.[40] Lamartine's heroine describes her many efforts to attract the attention of Phaon, her pleasure at seeing him at the gymnasium or the theater, and her verses that failed to move him:

Je composai pour lui ces chants pleins de douceur,
Ces chants qui m'ont valu les transport de la Grèce:
Ces chants, qui des Enfers fléchiraient la rigueur,
Malheureuse Sapho! n'ont pu fléchir son coeur,
Et son ingratitude a payé ta tendresse!

[I composed for him these odes full of tenderness,
These odes that earned me the transports of Greece:
These odes that would soften the harshness of Hell,
Unhappy Sappho! were unable to soften his heart,
And his ingratitude rewarded your tenderness!][41]

Sappho recites a long litany of things she would have done for Phaon if Venus had deigned to instill love in his heart. She would have lived happily as a slave in Phaon's house simply to be near her beloved. Now she wants only to de-stroy all evidence of her unrequited passion. The resolve of Lamartine's Sappho wavers for a moment. What if the gods were to lead Phaon to the shore where he would "gaze upon Sappho atop the fatal rock, in tears, wandering, disheveled, / Striking the desolate bank with futile sobs, / Still burn-ing for him." Would he not "be sorry for his long injustice?" Would he not "stop me at the edge of the abyss?" Sappho fantasizes salvation, only to be caught short by the reality of her solitude:

Oh! qu'entend-je? . . . écoutez . . . du côté de Lesbos
Une clameur lointaine a frappé les échos!
J'ai reconnu l'accent de cette voix si chère,
J'ai vu sur le chemin s'élever la poussière!
O vierges! regardez! ne le voyez-vous pas
Descendre la colline et me tendre les bras? . . .
Mais non! tout est muet dans la nature entière,
Un silence de mort règne au loin sur la terre:
Le chemin est désert! . . . Je n'entends que les flots.

[Oh! What do I hear? . . . listen . . . coming from Lesbos
A distant clamor has struck the echoes!
I recognized the accent of that voice so dear,
I saw that dust was rising on the path!
O virgins! Look! Don't you see him
Coming down the hill and offering me his arms? . . .
But no! All of nature is still,
A deathly silence reigns from afar across the land:
The path is deserted! . . . I hear only the waves.][42]

Sappho strives to hear—or to hallucinate—the sounds that might signal a reprieve from her deadly despair. They do not materialize. Lamartine's text makes clear that Sappho jumps from the cliff: "Neither Cupid's arrows, nor some stroke of fate, / Miserable Sappho, were able to save your life!"

Chassériau's painting dwells upon the heroine's state of attention—an emphatic rendering of her ear visualizes the poetic moment—as if straining to hear the sounds that might shake her resolve. It does not figure Sappho's demise as an act of pure will, but the consequence of events she could not control. The analogue would be Lamartine awaiting results of the presidential election. Chassériau's picture—inspired by Lamartine's tale of a woman spurned by the one she loves— begs to be read as an allegory of Lamartine himself in 1849. Shouted down [conspué] in the presidential election by the universal suffrage he had personally championed, Lamartine felt his only recourse before the country's lunacy was "to die nobly or forever hide the word Frenchman on your forehead, in exile!" He imagines a political death for himself not unlike Sappho's own.

Hugo, by contrast, should have been pleased with the electoral outcome since his preferred candidate won a huge mandate. But his notes from January 1849 already reveal an awareness that Bonaparte's grandeur was a chimera. "The first month of the presidency is over," he wrote on 22 January, "enthusiasm has dropped off . . . popularity has completely disappeared. One sees, little by little, Louis Bonaparte coming back down to earth." Near the end of his entry Hugo ridi-cules Bonaparte's cabinet as "impoverished, sickly, discredited, shaken, powerless, worthless." He asks: "What's going to happen? When nothing comes from the power, something comes from the country."[43] Hugo's anxiety about the future becomes palpable in the pages of his notes from the spring of 1849 where rumors of plots, insurrections, and civil unrest regularly disrupt his narrative. "Those are the kinds of worries we are living with" are the words he added in April to one rumor that promised an uprising of sixty thousand armed insurgents.[44]

The quickly evolving social context prompts an enlarged reading of Chassériau's *Sappho* (Fig. 164). Beyond an allegory of Lamartine's stinging defeat by Bonaparte, her clinging to the rocks at the edge of an abyss is emblematic of the entire generation of Romantics at mid-century. Hugo and Lamartine, two of the literary leaders of that generation, were disillusioned and disappointed by the turn of political events, albeit for very different reasons. Within months Eugène Delacroix—the most prominent visual artist of the Romantics—bluntly recorded his own disenchantment in the pages of his journal:

The pressing need in which he [Meyerbeer] thought he had to do something better or different from what had been done, in short to change things, made him lose sight of the eternal laws of taste and logic that govern the arts. These Berlioz, these Hugo, all these so-called reformers, have not yet managed to abolish all the ideas we are talking about; but they convinced everyone it was possible to do other than true and reasonable things. The same for politics.[45]

We will probably never know for whom Delacroix cast his vote in the presidential election of 1848, but his comments suggest he believed the state of French politics was no more healthy than the state of French art. His view hardened with time—witness this entry from February 1850:

I am beginning to take a sudden disliking to the Schuberts, the dreamers, the Chateaubriands, the Lamartines, etc. Why will all of this blow over? Because it's not true. . . . The emotions of the *Meditations* are false, as are those of the same author's *Raphael*. This vagueness, this perpetual sadness touches no one. It's the school of sickly love.[46]

Delacroix's newly felt scorn for the "school of sickly love" is remarkable. He deplores the poetry of Chateaubriand and Lamartine—two of the founding figures of the Romantic school—even though he had been one of its leading painters. To judge from the collective discouragement that reigned by 1850, Lamartine's political failure dropped the curtain on the lofty ambitions of Romantics to change the world. The stage was set for the arrival of here-and-now Realists like Millet and Courbet (Figs. 100 and 101).

What about Victor Hugo? What trajectory led him from mildly disappointed backer of Bonaparte in January 1849 to political exile in 1852? Hugo became convinced that Louis-Napoléon Bonaparte lied during the campaign when he promised "after four years . . . to leave my successor with the power consolidated, liberty intact, a real progress accomplished." He believed Bonaparte perjured himself at the inauguration when he promised to uphold the constitution.[47] The Constitution of 1848 limited the president to one four-year term, although a person could serve another, non-consecutive term at a later date. In early 1851 Bonaparte's backers initiated a move to amend the constitution so that their man might stand for re-election at the end of 1852.[48] Hugo was among those strongly opposed to this transparent effort to extend the president's mandate. On 17 July 1851, in a memorable address to the National Assembly, he unmasked Bonaparte's dynastic ambitions without mincing words:

What! . . . because, a thousand years after [Charlemagne], there came another genius who picked up this sword and this scepter and stood tall over the continent, who made gigantic history whose dazzling spectacle still lingers on, who put the French Revolution in chains and unleashed it in Europe, who gave to his name the resounding synonyms of Rivoli, Iéna, Essling, Friedland, Montmirail! What! because, after ten years of immense glory—an almost mythic glory by dint of its grandeur—he, in turn, dropped in exhaustion this scepter and this sword that had accomplished so many colossal things, you, you arrive, you, you want to pick them up after him, the way he had picked them up, him, Napoléon, after Charlemagne, and take in your little hands this scepter of titans, this sword of giants! To do what? What! After Auguste, little Auguste? What! because we have had Napoléon-le-Grand, we must have Napoléon-le-Petit![49]

With this last phrase the legislative chamber erupted in what the official recorder described as an "inexpressible turmoil." For Hugo to use the spiteful title of Napoléon-le-Petit was a dramatic oratorical gesture that marked a turning point in his assessment of Louis-Napoléon. Hugo publicly distinguished between the grandeur of the first Napoléon, whom he never ceased to admire, and the pretensions of the nephew. The sobriquet stung Bonaparte deeply and he did not forget: one of his orders, drawn up in secrecy before the coup-d'état, was that the poet must be captured dead or alive. Hugo's response was to flee France.

Hugo's party won the battle not to revise the constitution but ultimately lost the war. The only option for Bonaparte to hold power was the illegal use of force he deployed on 2 December. But the interesting part of the ultimate break between Hugo and Bonaparte is the fact that the poet did not see it coming. At an official dinner shortly after Bonaparte's inauguration, when still on friendly terms with the president he had helped to elect, Hugo noted with some amusement:

One of the more unusual features and atypical facts of the situation is this man, to which one can say and does say at the same time and from every side at once: prince, highness, sir, seigneur, and citizen. Everything happening now leaves its mark pell-mell on this person with many objectives.[50]

He writes as though he has discovered something new about Bonaparte's shifting, chameleon-like identity in the role of president.

Had Hugo paid more attention to the lowbrow, pro-Bonaparte imagery circulated by colporters in the villages and back roads of France, he might have been less surprised. Consider the colored woodblock print published in 1848 by the Pellerin firm of Épinal (Fig. 165). It is a kind of image seldom studied in the cenacles of literary Paris. As one might expect, Bonaparte places one hand on a copy of the "Constitution de la République," and he wears a tricolor sash to signify his respect for the duties and office of president. Bonaparte's right hand is not placed exactly over his heart but is tucked into his vest. The print references obliquely a characteristic gesture of Emperor Napoléon codified by both image and legend (Figs. 11 and 50). The accompanying text, which is a thumbnail sketch of the president's life, dwells upon his years of exile and his many writings. It glosses over Bonaparte's early forays into social philosophy. It nearly exonerates him of any wrong-doing in two unsuccessful attempts at a coup-d'état with the words: "the ventures at Strasbourg and Boulogne, so little understood and considered so diversely; devised by a young man from the depth of his exile and led with resolve, they at least attest to exceptional depth and inordinate courage." The Pellerin print overlays visual clues and narrative rhetoric in a pell-mell of meanings analogous to what Hugo had witnessed at dinner in 1848.

The print also suggests that Bonaparte's election fulfills a destiny set in motion by his birth to the brother of Napoléon-le-Grand. The visual rhetoric of a thick swag of drapery to Bonaparte's left, the richly carved chair with elaborate upholstery, and the allusions to monumental architecture situate the new president in a setting of great pomp. On the background wall hangs the image of an image: David's famous picture of 1801, *Bonaparte crossing the Saint-Bernard Pass* (Fig. 1). That work celebrated David's new-found enthusiasm for the young general who had just grabbed power in a coup-d'état (see Chapter One). When, far from the capital, the humble Pellerin print fantasized the space of political power in Paris, the artist of Épinal inserted—like a secret thought of the president himself—the galloping effigy of an earlier Bonaparte on the road to absolute dictatorship. Had Hugo looked closely at works like this, he would have realized that men and women all across France were ready and eager to embrace the thinly disguised, imperial ambitions of the new president.

We can imagine why he did not, for the Pellerin print is both symptom and indictment of the poet's legacy. If there was a Napoléon-le-Petit for Hugo to mock and to flee, it was because he had drawn, with the power of his talent and the aspirations of his generation, the haunting, larger-than-life figure of Napoléon-le-Grand. Hugo quickly realized that the myth shriveled with reincarnation, but the paradoxes of his

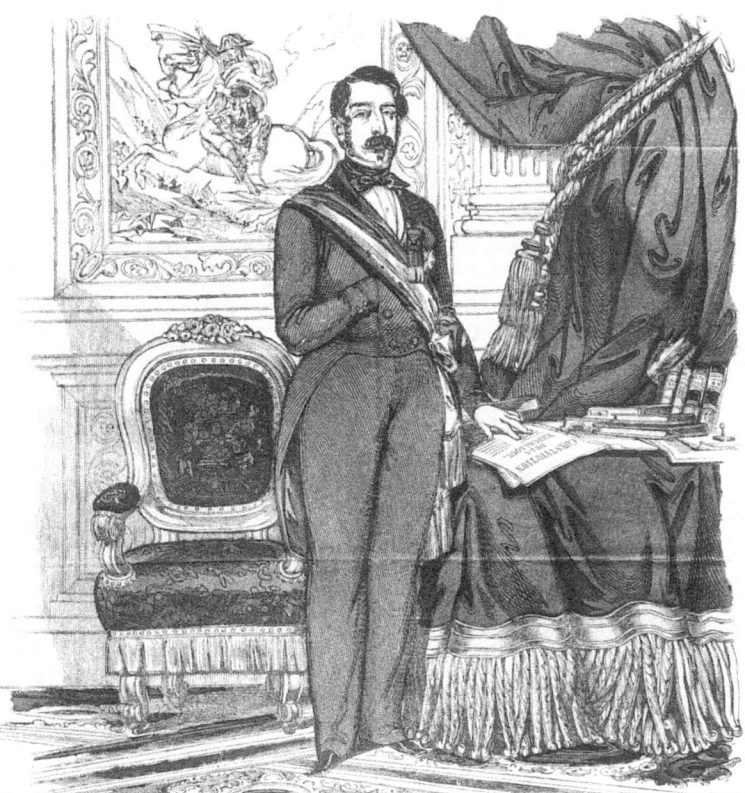

LOUIS-NAPOLÉON BONAPARTE,
REPRÉSENTANT DU PEUPLE,
Président de la République française.

FIGURE 165. Jean-Charles Pellerin & Company, *Louis-Napoléon Bonaparte, Representative of the People, President of the French Republic*, 1848. Colored woodblock print. Paris, BnF, Estampes, inv. Collection de Vinck, no. 15374 (31.6 × 29.9 cm). Photo: BnF, Paris.

thinking at mid-century lived on in the time-warp of his exile. Two decades later Hugo finally returned to his beloved Paris. It was a city without Bonaparte, a city devastated yet again by the ravages of civil war. He was wary of what he might find:

Je vois en même temps le meilleur et le pire;
Noir tableau!
Car la France mérite Austerlitz, et l'empire
Waterloo.
J'irai, je rentrerai dans la muraille sainte,
Ô Paris!
Je te rapporterai l'âme jamais éteinte
Des proscrits.

[I see at once the best and the worst;
Black picture!
Because France deserves Austerlitz, and the empire
Waterloo.
I will go, I will reenter the holy wall,
Oh Paris!
I will bring back to you the never extinguished soul,
Of exiles.][51]

Hugo reached back in time to express his mixture of dread and excitement with the language and imagery of a practiced habitué of Romantic Paris. A city, he would soon discover, that was no more.

Abbreviations

The following abbreviations are used throughout the Captions, Notes, and Bibliography.

BnF	Bibliothèque nationale de France
BnF, Cartes et Plans	Bibliothèque nationale de France, Département des Cartes et Plans
BnF, Estampes	Bibliothèque nationale de France, Département des Estampes et de la Photographie
BnF, Imprimés	Bibliothèque nationale de France, Département des Livres imprimés
COARC	Conservation des Oeuvres d'Art Religieuses et Civiles
ENSBA	École nationale supérieure des Beaux-Arts
LACMA	Los Angeles County Museum of Art
PMVP	Photothèque des Musées de la Ville de Paris
RMN	Réunion des musées nationaux
SSPL	Science and Society Picture Library
UCAD	Union Centrale des Arts décoratifs

Notes

Notes to Introduction

1. Jules Michelet, "Février 1839," *Journal*, 3 vols., ed. Paul Viallaneix (Paris: Gallimard, 1959), 1, 291.

2. Henri Lefebvre, *La production de l'espace* (Paris: Anthropos, 2000 [1974]). Despite its somewhat heavy-handed literalism, references in the text are to *The Production of Space*, trans. Donald Nicolson-Smith (London: Blackwell, 1991).

3. Lefebvre, *The Production of Space*, 73.

4. Ibid., 94.

5. Among the "mathematicians" Lefebvre names Descartes, Spinoza, Leibniz, Newton and his followers, and Kant. His group of "discursive" thinkers of space includes Sartre, Foucault, Blanchot, and Derrida (see ibid., 1–4).

6. Ibid., 26.

7. Ibid., 86.

8. "Inasmuch as they deal with socially 'real' space," remarks Lefebvre, "one might suppose on first consideration that architecture and texts relating to architecture would be a better choice than literary texts proper" (ibid., 15).

9. Ibid., 33.

10. Ibid.

11. It would be disingenuous not to acknowledge early on the impact of the writings and example of Walter Benjamin upon my research for this book. My attempts to sidestep an integrated theoretical perspective, along with my preference for plausibility over some mirage of truth, have less to do with an affection for "postmodern" pluralism than a deep admiration for the ambitions of Benjamin's unfinished *Passagen-Werk*. I certainly cannot claim to equal Benjamin's vast understanding of nineteenth-century Paris, but I have tried to keep before me the brief sketch of his goal: "Method of this project: literary montage. I needn't *say* anything. Merely show. I shall purloin no valuables, appropriate no ingenious formulations. But the rags, the refuse—these I will not inventory but allow, in the only possible way, to come into their own: by making use of them" (Benjamin, *The Arcades Project* [N1a,8], 460).

12. Lefebvre, *The Production of Space*, 33.

13. Ibid.

14. My thinking on this issue has been much affected by Certeau, *L'Écriture de l'histoire*, especially Part I, and this despite Lefebvre's low regard for Certeau's linguistic and structuralist approach to the theory of writing history.

15. Lefebvre, *The Production of Space*, 70.

16. It is also why daguerreotypes are such fascinating cultural artifacts, for the process consists of regular and repeatable acts and gestures but produces a unique, unrepeatable image. It is precisely because daguerreotypes occupied such an intermediate state that they were doomed to quick extinction (see Chapter Eight).

17. Lefebvre, *The Production of Space*, 49.

18. Ibid.

19. Ibid., 75.

20. See the canonical texts on the problems of definition by Lovejoy, "On the Discrimination of Romanticisms," and Lovejoy, *The Great Chain of Being*, 288–314. See also Honour, *Romanticism*, 11–55.

21. Lefebvre, *The Production of Space*, 54.

22. Ibid., 290.

23. Ibid.

Notes to Chapter 1

1. Bonaparte, *Correspondance*, 6, no. 4398, letter to the diplomat Beytz.

2. Thiébault, *Mémoires*, 2, 57.

3. Cited in Thompson, *Napoleon*, 136.

4. Delécluze, *Louis David*, 201–4.

5. Lajer-Burcharth, *Necklines*, esp. chap. 3.

6. Delécluze, *Louis David*, 232–33.

7. Guégan, "Orgie noire," 289–91, and O'Brien, *After the Revolution*, 49–51.

8. Cited in New York and Detroit, *French Painting 1774–1830*,

467. The word *romantique*, redefined in the 1798 fifth edition of the dictionary of the Académie Française, came to be associated with just the cluster of qualities found in Gros's picture: "Usually said of places, of landscapes that remind the imagination of the descriptions of poems and novels." See Charlton, "French Romantic Movement," 15.

9. Staël, *De la Littérature*, 163.

10. Ibid., 164.

11. Hemmings, *Culture and Society*, 118.

12. Cited in ibid., 119.

13. Cited in New York and Detroit, *French Painting 1774–1830*, 467.

14. Cited in ibid., 468.

15. Chateaubriand, *Mémoires d'outre-tombe*, 2, 12.

16. Staël, *De la Littérature*, 310–11.

17. Bonaparte, *Correspondance*, 15, no. 12585, dated 15 May 1807.

18. Thompson, *Napoleon*, 182.

19. Cited in Lefebvre, *Napoleon*, 1, 182.

20. *Archives Nationales*, F21 2, pièces 2 and 3, dated 8 and 22 Thermidor Year XI. These documents relate to repairs made to the Tennis Court building prior to its occupation by Gros. The revolutionary calendar dates correspond roughly to 26 July and 9 August 1803.

21. *Archives Nationales*, AFIV 1050, dossier 1, pièce 6, letter dated Jour 2 Complémentaire Year XII from Denon to Bonaparte. The letter is reprinted in Mollaret and Brossolet, "A propos des 'Pestiférés de Jaffa,'" 270–71. Near the end of this letter Denon remarks: "I have given all my attention to give the Salon a decoration and a dignity like it has never had; it is large, varied, interesting, and for two months will occupy the idle curiosity of Parisians."

22. *Archives Nationales*, AFIV 1049, dossier 2, pièce 8, memo from Denon to Bonaparte dated 7 Ventôse Year XII (27 February 1804). At the banquet held in Gros's honor, Denon offered a toast "to those who furnish such grand subjects to history painters and to the painters worthy of transmitting such actions to posterity." His little speech was reported in a letter to the editor of the government's "official" newspaper ("Beaux-Arts: Au Rédacteur," *Le Moniteur universel*, 26 September 1804).

23. "Salon de l'an XII: No. 1 (M. Gros)," *Journal des Débats*, 3 Vendémiaire XII (25 September 1804).

24. "Salon de l'an XII: No. 2," *Le Publiciste*, 24 Vendémiaire XII (16 October 1804): 3.

25. Grigsby, "Rumor, Contagion, and Colonization," 22–24.

26. Le Normand, *Memoirs of the Empress Josephine*, 2, 32–33.

27. *Archives Nationales*, O2 847, no. 63, 2 Pluviose XIII (22 January 1805), payment to Gros for 15,629.72 francs. The document includes two important items of information: that the picture "had been commissioned by Her Majesty the Empress" and that payment was "approved" on 19 Nivôse XIII. This second date corresponds to the approval in Napoléon's correspondence, where we find that he authorized payment "To M. Gros, for the painting of *The Plague at Jaffa*, commissioned by Her Majesty the Empress without having set the price, something which should never be done, the sum of 16,000 francs, which will not satisfy the vanity of this artist, given the extravagant price of the picture of *Phaedre* by Guérin" (Bonaparte, *Correspondance*, 10, no. 8266, dated 9 January 1805). Incidentally, Napoléon often complained about the high prices paid for works of art. By contrast, David O'Brien published an undated letter from Gros to the painter Guérin that reports Bonaparte personally dictated the subject of *Jaffa* in the presence of Joséphine and others, from which O'Brien concludes that it is "entirely in keeping with Bonaparte's character, however, to attribute the art administration's budgetary problems to Josephine's extravagance" (O'Brien, "Antoine-Jean Gros in Italy," 659 and note 68). We have no evidence that Gros's letter was ever sent to Guérin, nor does it disprove the archival trail cited above; indeed, it might itself be questioned as a gesture of professional self-promotion by Gros to give Guérin the impression that he is on intimate terms with Bonaparte. Nonetheless, Darcy Grigsby asserts that O'Brien "cleared up the ambiguity regarding the commission" and dismisses the evidence of Joséphine's role, mainly because her highly sexualized reading of the image depends importantly upon it being a male initiative (Grigsby, *Extremities*, 66, note 9).

28. Cited in Partridge, *French Romantics' Knowledge*, 38.

29. Young, *Night Thoughts*, 54–55.

30. Ibid., 62.

31. Chateaubriand, *Atala, René, Les Abencérages*, 97.

32. Ibid., 98.

33. Ibid., 99.

34. Cited in New York and Detroit, *French Painting 1774–1830*, 633.

35. Letter dated 15 February 1807 from Larrey to his wife, cited in Triaire, *Napoléon et Larrey*, 247.

36. Bonaparte, *Correspondance*, 14, no. 11.988, letter dated 11 March 1807 to Joséphine.

37. Bonaparte, *Correspondance*, 14, nos. 11.847 and 12.160, letters dated 21 February 1807 and 25 March 1807 to Cambacérès.

38. The complete text of Denon's cover letter and program are reprinted in Griener, "L'Art de persuader," 9 and 20–21.

39. Denon's cover letter specified "the picture will be the same size as that of the hospital at Jaffa and the price will be 16,000 francs." On the competition see Griener, "L'Art de persuader," and Gerstein, "Le regard consolateur."

40. O'Brien, *After the Revolution*, chap. 5 for an overview.

41. "Notice descriptive du concours de 1807, destinée aux artistes," reprinted in Griener, "L'Art de persuader," 9.

42. Anonymous, *Le nouvel Observateur au Musée Napoléon*, 10.

43. Cited in Clay, *Romanticism*, 289.

44. Cited in Lefebvre, *Napoleon*, 2, 56–57.

45. Girodet's entire poem in honor of *Jaffa* is reprinted in Mollaret and Brossolet, "A propos des 'Pestiférés de Jaffa,'" 271–73.

46. *Archives Nationales*, O2 843, letter dated 11 March 1809 from Denon to Daru.

47. Bonaparte, *Correspondance*, 5, no. 3538.

48. Ibid., no. 3527.

49. Ibid., no. 3539.

50. *Archives Nationales*, AFIV 1050, dossier 6, pièce 7, letter dated 11 November 1810 from Denon to Napoléon.

51. Guizot, "Salon de 1810," 81–82.

52. *Archives Nationales*, O2 845, undated memo from Chanal to Denon.

53. Letter dated 20 September 1811 from David to Douglas, published in Tait, "Duke of Hamilton's Palace," 401, no. 1.

54. Letter dated 8 May 1812 from David to Douglas, published in ibid., no. 3.

55. Letter dated 8 May 1812 from David to Douglas, published in ibid.

56. Delécluze, *Louis David*, 347.

57. The following pictures were listed in the catalogue of the 1812 Salon: Albert-Paul Bourgeois, *Clemency of His Majesty the Emperor towards an Arab Family* (no. 139); Guillaume-François Colson, *Clemency of the Emperor towards an Arab Family* (no. 219); André-Jean Despois, *An Act of Charity of His Majesty the Emperor* (no. 309); Jacques-Augustin Pajou, *Clemency of His Majesty the*

Emperor towards Mademoiselle Saint-Simon (no. 692); Alexandre Veron-Bellecourt, *The Emperor visiting the Invalides Hospital, 11 February 1808* (no. 958).

58. Letters dated 19 April and 19 July 1812 from Pierre-Théodore Suau to his father, published in Mesplé, "David et ses élèves toulousains," 100–101.

59. Cited in Madelin, *Catastrophe de Russie*, 358.

60. Letter dated 30 April 1813 from David to Douglas, published in Tait, "Duke of Hamilton's Palace," 402, no. 11. David's replica is now a promised gift to the Musée du Louvre; its convoluted history is summarized in Paris, Musée du Louvre, *Jacques-Louis David*, 474, no. 206.

61. Cited in Bertier de Sauvigny, *Bourbon Restoration*, 9–10.

62. Chateaubriand, *Mémoires d'outre-tombe*, 2, 531–32.

63. Clément, *Géricault*, 74.

64. Cited in Hemmings, *Culture and Society*, 83.

65. From a manuscript written by the artist and cited by Clément, *Géricault*, 249.

66. J. B. Henri Savigny and Alexandre Corréard, *Naufrage de la frégate la* Méduse *faisant partie de l'expédition du Sénégal en 1816* (Paris: chez Hocquet, 1817). A second French edition was published in February 1818, and an English translation appeared the same year in London. All the details about this booklet are summarized in Bazin, *Théodore Géricault*, 6, 89–91.

67. *Le Moniteur universel* (10 September 1816): 1024, cited in Eitner, *Géricault's Raft*, 9.

68. Bazin, *Théodore Géricault*, 6, 14–51, and Eitner, *Géricault's Raft*, 22–39.

69. Letter dated 2 November 1819 from Delacroix to Felix Guillarmardet, published in Delacroix, *Lettres intimes*, 105.

70. Gault de Saint-Germain, *Choix des productions de l'art les plus remarquables exposés au Salon de 1819*, cited in Eitner, *Géricault's Raft*, 42.

71. Letter from Géricault cited in Eitner, *Géricault's Raft*, 53.

72. The sitter's identity is carefully traced in Bazin, *Théodore Géricault*, 6, 28–29.

73. The other lithographs depict a cart overloaded with wounded soldiers, and a defiant artilleryman who threatens to blow up himself and a cart of gunpowder if the Russians approach. See Bazin, *Théodore Géricault*, 5, nos. 1467 and 1493.

74. Cited in Hemmings, *Culture and Society*, 133.

Notes to Chapter 2

1. Chateaubriand, *Mémoires d'outre-tombe*, 2, 13–14.

2. Nora, "Entre Mémoire et Histoire," xix.

3. Gérard, *La Révolution française*, 33. My discussion is based upon Gérard's account for the period 1800–1850.

4. Lady Morgan, *France*, 1, 324.

5. Charles Percier and Pierre-François-Léonard Fontaine, *Description des cérémonies et des fêtes qui ont eu lieu pour le mariage de S.M. l'empereur Napoléon avec S.A.I. Madame l'archiduchesse Marie-Louise d'Autriche* (Paris: P. Didot, 1810).

6. Clary-Aldringen, *Trois mois à Paris*, 99–100.

7. Bertier de Sauvigny, *The Bourbon Restoration*, 379.

8. Vidler, *Ledoux*, 209.

9. For illustrations of all the toll gates see ibid., 215–17.

10. Agulhon, "Imagerie civique et décor urbain," 107.

11. Planche, "Salon de 1833," 197.

12. The complicated history of the Vendôme Column is discussed in Chapter Three.

13. Lacroix, *Histoire politique, anecdotique et populaire*, 3, 247.

14. The program for this ceremony was published in *Le Moniteur* (6 December 1804).

15. Guizot, "Salon de 1810," 87–88.

16. Géricault's listing is found on folio 54 of the notebook now in the Art Institute of Chicago. For a photograph of the page see Bazin, *Théodore Géricault*, 3, 239, no. 959.

17. The day's program was published in *Le Moniteur* (17 September 1814).

18. An unfinished oil painting of Louis XVIII reviewing troops at the Champ-de-Mars is now in a private collection, but it differs significantly from the watercolor and seems to have been less directly inspired by any one ceremony. For a reproduction of this work see Bazin, *Théodore Géricault*, 3, 239, no. 960.

19. Letter begun on 17 August 1830 and continued on 4 September from Delacroix to Charles de Verninac, published in Johnson, "Eugène Delacroix and Charles de Verninac," 516–17.

20. Letter dated 12 October 1830 from Delacroix to his brother, cited in Johnson, *The Paintings of Eugène Delacroix*, 1, 146.

21. Jal, *Salon de 1831*, 40.

22. Farcy, "Salon de 1831—Deuxième Article," 347.

23. Planche, *Salon de 1831*, 108–9.

24. Stendhal, *Vie de Henri Brulard*, 23.

25. Marx, "The Defeat of June 1848," 304.

26. Tocqueville, *Recollections*, 136.

27. Ibid., 142.

28. Letter dated 22 October 1890 from Meissonier to Stevens, reprinted in Hungerford, "Meissonier's *Souvenir de guerre civile*," 288.

29. For a color reproduction see Lyon, Musée des Beaux-Arts, *Ernest Meissonier*, 180, no. 95.

30. Louis Peisse, "Salon de 1850: VII," *Le Constitutionnel* (2 March 1851): 1.

31. Sabatier-Ungher, *Salon de 1851*, 56.

Notes to Chapter 3

1. Daunou, *Cours d'études historiques*, 7, 168–69.

2. Staël, *Considérations sur les principaux événemens*, 2.

3. Barante, *Mélanges historiques et littéraires*, 2, 43.

4. Ibid., 126–27.

5. J.D. [Jules Desnoyers], "Introduction: But et Plan du Bulletin," vi (reprinted in Leterrier, *Le XIXe siècle historien*, 177). About the société, see Theis, "Guizot et les institutions de mémoire," 1585–88.

6. Paul (1814), *Party of Pleasure*, 52.

7. Berry, *Journals and Correspondence* (4 April 1802), 2, 178.

8. Milton, *Letters on the Fine Arts*, 2–3.

9. Berry, *Journals and Correspondence* (15 March 1802), 2, 133.

10. Cited in Gould, *Trophy of Conquest*, 31.

11. Milton, *Letters on the Fine Arts*, iii–iv.

12. Letter dated 7 May 1796 from the Directory government to Bonaparte, cited in Boyer, "Les responsabilités de Napoléon," 243.

13. Gould, *Trophy of Conquest*, 40.

14. Quatremère de Quincy, *Le préjudice*, 20.

15. Bonaparte, *Correspondance*, 2, no. 1509, dated 19 February 1797. See also Quynn, "The Art Confiscations."

16. Chaptal, *Souvenirs*, 269–70.

17. Cited in Boyer, "Les responsabilités de Napoléon," 248–49.

18. Paris, Musée du Louvre, *Dominique-Vivant Denon*, sections V–IX on Denon's role at the Louvre.

19. Letter dated 3 Thermidor XI (22 July 1803) from Cambacérès to Denon, cited in Lanzac de Laborie, *Paris sous Napoléon*, 8, "Spectacles et Musées," 257.

20. Forbes, *Letters from France*, 1, 411–12.

21. Ibid., 238.

22. "The pictures, exhibited in the Saloon of the Louvre, have infinitely the advantage of those in the Great Gallery; the former apartment being lighted from the top; while in the latter, the light is admitted through large windows, placed on both sides, those on one side facing the compartments between those on the other; so that, in this respect, the masterpieces in the Gallery are viewed under very unfavourable conditions" (Anonymous, *Paris as it was*, 174). Museum administrators were aware of the problem, and over time part of the Grande Galerie was fitted with skylights, so that in 1815 Henry Milton could note: "Towards the upper end of the room, where the finest Italian pictures are placed, windows in the roof have been introduced, and the light is excellent" (Milton, *Letters on the Fine Arts*, 24).

23. "The poor arrangement is especially unfavorable to the Capitoline Venus, placed not far from the Apollo Belvedere, against a wall and protected by a railing; you know, of course, that it is the back of the statue—which is a far better piece of sculpture than the Medici Venus—that is the most splendid part. Many statues, notably the Apollo, have bases that are too high: the feet are at the height of the viewer's eyes, so that you cannot see their divine forms except from well below" (Reichardt, *Un hiver à Paris*, 43–44).

24. Plumptre, *A Narrative*, 33.

25. Ibid.

26. Reichardt, *Un hiver à Paris*, 45.

27. Paul (1814), *Party of Pleasure*, 55.

28. Anonymous, *Paris as it was*, 183.

29. Paul (1814), *Party of Pleasure*, 38–40.

30. Babeau, *Les Anglais en France*, 4.

31. Milton, *Letters on the Fine Arts*, 27.

32. Ibid., 10.

33. Ibid., 95.

34. Letter dated 23 September 1815 from Wellington to Viscount Castlereagh, reprinted in Gould, *Trophy of Conquest*, 131–35.

35. Milton, *Letters on the Fine Arts*, 178; Gould, *Trophy of Conquest*, 122.

36. Milton, *Letters on the Fine Arts*, 180.

37. Gould, *Trophy of Conquest*, 130.

38. Berry, *Journals and Correspondence* (5 May 1816), 3, 97.

39. Las Cases (1823), *Mémorial de Sainte-Hélène*, 5, 181.

40. In a note of 9 February 1811 to Marthe-Camille de Montalivet, Minister of the Interior, Napoléon listed his four priorities for the city: an increased supply of water (to be obtained by diverting the Ourcq River); a new grain market; new slaughterhouses outside the city limits; a new market for wine (Bonaparte, *Correspondance*, 21, no. 17.340).

41. Clary-Aldringen, *Trois mois à Paris*, 57.

42. Pinkerton, *Recollections of Paris*, 1, 366.

43. The Constituent Assembly, the Legislative Assembly, and the National Convention had met respectively in a room of the Manège between the fall of 1789 and May of 1793, when a larger auditorium was completed on the ground floor of the Tuileries Palace. It was at the Manège that the monarchy was outlawed, and where the Committee of Public Safety was founded: the latter eventually became the principal tribunal of the Terror.

44. Bonaparte, *Correspondance*, 21, no. 17.252, dated 30 December 1810; Chateaubriand, *Mémoires d'outre-tombe*, 2, 485.

45. Milton, *Letters on the Fine Arts*, 203.

46. Plumptre, *A Narrative*, 54.

47. Cited in Duplomb, *Ponts de Paris*, 37.

48. Ariès, *L'homme devant la mort*, 2, 215 and discussion 215–50.

49. Ibid., 215.

50. Trollope, *Paris and the Parisians*, 1, 134–36.

51. Cited in Rochebouët, "La Bourse," 131.

52. *Archives Nationales*, AFIV 230.

53. Bonaparte, *Correspondance*, 14, no. 11.353, dated 2 December 1806.

54. Ibid., no. 11.445, dated 12 December 1806.

55. Cited in Silvestre de Sacy, *Brongniart*, 150.

56. Fontaine, *Journal*, 1, 366 (8 June 1813).

57. Ibid., 380 (24 December 1813).

58. Chaudonneret, *L'état et les artistes*, chap. 2.

59. *Archives du Louvre*, *AA 18, 175, cited in Chaudonneret, "Permanence et Innovation," 535.

60. *Archives du Louvre*, T6 (2 December 1830), cited in Chaudonneret, "Permanence et Innovation," 535.

61. Gustave Planche, "Salon de 1833: Dernière Article," *Revue des Deux Mondes*, 2e série, 2 (15 April 1833): 192.

62. *Journal des Artistes* (25 March 1838), cited in Rosenthal, *Du Romantisme au Réalisme*, 313.

63. Planche, "Salon du Roi," 765.

64. Letter dated 15 February 1838 from Delacroix to Charles Rivet, published in Delacroix, *Lettres*, 141.

65. *Archives Nationales*, F21 584, letter dated 31 August 1838 from Montalivet, Minister of the Interior, to Delacroix announcing the commission and a fee of 60,000 francs reprinted in Sérullaz, *Les peintures murales de Delacroix*, 53.

66. Letter dated 9 January 1848 from Delacroix to the journalist Théophile Thoré, who published it along with his review of the decorations in *Le Constitutionnel* (31 January 1848); reprinted in Sérullaz, *Les peinture murales de Delacroix*, 66–68.

67. Johnson, *Paintings of Delacroix*, 5, 35–36.

68. *Le National* (4 March 1836), cited in Rosenthal, *Du Romantisme au Réalisme*, 304.

69. Johnson, *Paintings of Delacroix*, 5, 70, where the journal of de Planet describes Delacroix's work on *Lycurgus consults the Pythia*, and a letter from Lassalle-Bordes reports the final retouching.

70. Letter dated 21 November 1839 from Hippolyte Flandrin to Auguste Flandrin, cited in Flandrin, *Hippolyte Flandrin*, 80, no. 1.

71. Grégoire, *Itinéraire de l'Artiste*, 75.

72. Ibid., introduction.

73. Grégoire, *Notice explicatif*, afterword.

74. Schmit, *Nouveau manuel complet*, 183.

75. Gautier, "Coupole de la Madeleine," 276.

76. Ibid., 278.

77. Thiers, *Discours Parlementaires*, 6, 657 (2 May 1845).

78. Montalembert, "Atteintes portées à la liberté religieuse (14 January 1845)," in *Oeuvres*, 2, 19.

79. De Maîstre, *Du Pape*, 2, 121.

80. Ibid., 1, 384.

81. Ibid., xxxiv and 2.

82. Montalembert, "De l'art religieux en France," 614–15.

83. Ibid., 599–609.

84. Montalembert, "De la peinture chrétienne en Italie à l'occasion du livre de M. Rio," in *Oeuvres*, 6, 78–162.

85. Ibid., 83

86. Rio, *De la poésie chrétienne*, 160–204.

87. Letter dated 13 May 1842 from the Préfecture de la département de la Seine, Commission des Beaux-Arts to Chassériau, cited in Bénédite, *Chassériau*, 1, 178. The changes made by Chassériau to his sketch are discussed idem, 178–83.

88. Cited in Bénédite, *Chassériau*, 1, 199. The entire text of Gautier's article is reprinted idem, 189–200.

89. Planche, "Peinture Monumentale," 160. The four figures are (from left to right): Abbot Morard, who rebuilt the church of Saint-Germain-des-Prés in the tenth century after the Norman invasions; Pope Alexander III, who dedicated a new choir in 1163; Saint Benedict, founder of the abbey's order; and Robert II, King of France, who financed much of Morard's rebuilding campaign (Saint-Germain-des-Prés, *Histoire et description par un vicaire de la paroisse*. Paris: Librairie Catholique Perisse frères, nd).

90. Planche, "Peinture Monumentale," 157.

91. Ibid.

92. Amaury-Duval, *Journal de voyage*, unpublished manuscript written in 1836 (Musée Autun: Archives de la Société éduenne), cited in Foucart, *Le renouveau*, 213.

93. Rio, *De la poésie chrétienne*, 198.

94. Montalembert, "De la peinture chrétienne en Italie," in *Oeuvres*, 6, 105.

95. Troche, *Mémoire historique*, 35, note 1.

96. *Archives Nationales*, F19 5603, cited in Driskel, *Representing Belief*, 22. It is said that Marie-Amélie, wife of Louis-Philippe and a fervent Catholic, personally intervened to reopen and restore the church—standing directly across from the Louvre—because its state of disrepair distressed her greatly. That it is one of the very few parish churches in Paris to benefit from direct government (rather than municipal) support lends credence to the story of the Queen's intervention (Troche, *Mémoire historique*, 16–18 and 37).

97. Troche, *Mémoire historique*, 33–34.

98. Ibid., 41 and 44.

99. Heine, *De la France*, 135–36 (25 March 1832).

100. Guizot, *Mémoires*, 2, 374 (address of 13 September 1830).

101. Fourcaud, *Rude*, 175.

102. *Archives Nationales*, F13 1030 (report of 30 December 1832 submitted by Bouet to the Minister of the Interior), cited in Fourcaud, *Rude*, 194.

103. Thiers first published his spirited, ten-volume account of the French Revolution between 1823 and 1827, and it went through four editions by 1834. His romanesque style strikes us today as somewhat extravagant, but it was the standard history of the French Revolution throughout the 1830s.

104. Fourcaud, *Rude*, 196, and summary of documents, 468–75.

105. Letter dated 3 August 1833 from Thiers to Etex, cited in Etex, *Souvenirs d'un artiste*, 199.

106. Buloz, "Chronique de la Quinzaine," 380.

107. Anonymous, *Détails curieux sur les fêtes*, np.

108. Buloz, "Chronique de la Quinzaine," 381.

109. *Le Moniteur universel*, no. 94 (4 April 1791): 385–86.

110. Deming, "Le Panthéon révolutionnaire" and associated catalogue entries.

111. Berry, *Journals and Correspondence* (7 November 1802), 3, 202–3.

112. Report submitted by Quatremère de Quincy, cited by Deming, "Le Panthéon révolutionnaire," 127.

113. Ozouf, "Le Panthéon," 155.

114. Berry, *Journals and Correspondence* (7 November 1802), 3, 202.

115. *Le Moniteur universel*, no. 53 (22 February 1806): 209. The decision seems to have been made a few days earlier: see Bonaparte, *Correspondance*, 12, no. 9797, note to Champagny dated 12 February 1806.

116. *Archives Nationales*, F13 1141, letter dated 9 April 1814 from Baltard to the Minister of the Interior, cited in Bergdoll, "Le Panthéon / Sainte-Geneviève," 194.

117. Cited in Bergdoll, "Le Panthéon / Sainte-Geneviève," 194–95.

118. "The inscription *aux grands hommes la patrie reconnaissante*, replaced on the pediment of the Panthéon on July 29th, disappeared during the night of Saturday–Sunday of August 15th," reported one journal; "The citizens have immediately put it back in place" (*Journal des Artistes*, 2, no. 8 [22 August 1830]: 136).

119. *Le Moniteur universel*, no. 239 (27 August 1830): 971.

120. Cited in McWilliam, "David d'Angers and the Pantheon Commission," 429.

121. The commission was awarded to David on 16 November 1830, and he officially accepted on 8 December. See the documents in *Archives Nationales*, F13 207, F13 1145, F21 578, 33 API (carton 2).

122. Cited in McWilliam, "David d'Angers and the Pantheon Commission," 428.

123. Fortoul, "Fronton du Panthéon," 314.

124. Planche, "Le Fronton du Panthéon," 415–16.

125. David d'Angers, MS 1872 (Bibliothèque municipale d'Angers), cited in McWilliam, "David d'Angers and the Pantheon Commission," 433.

126. Letter dated 13 June 1837 from the duchesse de Dino to the baron de Barante, cited in Thureau-Dangin, *Histoire de la Monarchie de Juillet*, 3, 206.

127. David d'Angers, MS 1872 (Bibliothèque municipale d'Angers), cited in McWilliam, "David d'Angers and the Pantheon Commission," 433–35.

128. A.D.L., "Le fronton du Panthéon," *La Gazette de France* (8 September 1837), cited in McWilliam, "David d'Angers and the Pantheon Commission," 437.

129. Pastoral letter dated 8 September 1837 from Monseigneur de Quelen, cited in McWilliam, "David d'Angers and the Pantheon Commission," 437.

130. *Le Journal de Paris* (6 August 1837), cited in McWilliam, "David d'Angers and the Pantheon Commission," 438.

131. Guizot, *Mémoires*, 2, 71.

132. Excerpt from Edgar Quinet, "Le Panthéon," *Paris: guide par les principaux écrivains et artistes de France* (Paris: 1868), reprinted in Paris, *Le Panthéon*, 316–20.

133. Paul (1814), *Party of Pleasure*, 50.

134. A few years later, in 1806, Napoléon wrote point blank to Cardinal Fesch, his ambassador to Rome, that "I am Charlemagne, because like Charlemagne I have united the crown of France with that of Lombardy and my empire borders on the Orient." Bonaparte, *Correspondance*, 11, no. 9656, dated 7 January 1806.

135. Ibid., 9, no. 7145 (1 October 1803).

136. Note from Napoléon to Champagny, ibid., 12, no. 9831, dated 17 February 1806.

137. Champagny to Napoléon, cited in Hénard, "Les trois statues de la colonne," 354

138. Bergeret, *Lettres d'un artiste*, cited in Biver, *Paris de Napoléon*, 168.

139. Clary-Aldringen, *Trois mois à Paris* (25 June 1810), 384–86.

140. "Journal d'un prisonnier anglais," cited in Biver, *Paris de Napoléon*, 173.

141. Song written by Paul-Émile Debraux and cited in Biver, *Paris de Napoléon*, 175.

142. Victor Hugo, "À la Colonne (9 Octobre 1830)," in *Les Chants du crépuscule*, 196.

143. Hugo, "To the Napoleon Column," in *Selected Poems*, 171–72.

144. "Rapport au Roi" dated 8 April 1831, *Le Moniteur universel*, no. 101 (11 April 1831): 761.

145. "Ministère du commerce et des travaux publics: arrêté," *Le Moniteur universel*, no. 105 (15 April 1831): 801.

146. Seurre's original sculpture now belongs to the Musée de l'Armée in Paris, where it is installed on a balcony overlooking the central courtyard of the Invalides.

147. Saint-Chéron, "La statue de Napoléon," 241–42.

148. Trollope, *Paris and the Parisians in 1835*, 1, 7–8.

149. *Archives parlementaires de 1787 à 1867* (Paris: 1867–), 48, 115, cited in Leith, *Space and Revolution*, 119.

150. Bonaparte, *Correspondance*, 19, no. 15.662, dated 15 August 1809.

151. Conversation recorded in Percier and Fontaine, *Résidences de Souverains*, and cited in Biver, *Paris de Napoléon*, 213.

152. Berry, *Journals and Correspondence* (14 July 1818), 3, 171.

153. Ibid.

154. Chateaubriand, "Compiègne Avril 1814," *Oeuvres*, 7, 42.

155. *Le Moniteur universel*, no. 21 (21 January 1816): 77.

156. Ibid., no. 49 (18 February 1816): 181.

157. Discussed in Porterfield, *Allure of Empire*, chap. 1.

158. Pinkerton, *Recollections of Paris*, 1, 493.

159. Champollion-Figeac, *L'Obélisque de Louqsor*, ix.

160. Lenoir, *De l'Obélisque de Louqsor*, 12.

161. Breton, "Histoire de la place de la Concorde," 12.

162. Chateaubriand, "Le vingt-un janvier mil huit cent quinze," *Oeuvres*, 7, 271; Chateaubriand, "Lettre au directeur de *l'Artiste*," *L'Artiste*, 1 (1831): 133–34.

163. Lacordaire, *Sainte Marie-Madeleine*, 225–26.

164. Bonaparte, *Correspondance*, 12, no. 10.235, dated 14 May 1806.

165. Ibid., 17, no. 14.414, dated 26 October 1808.

166. Ibid., 18, no. 14.599, dated 21 December 1808.

167. Lanzac de Laborie, *Paris sous Napoléon*, 2, "Administration, Grands Travaux," 260–61; Ledoux-Lebard, "Les projets de fontaines," 42–47.

168. Hugo, *Les Misérables*, 133. Hugo's novel was published in 1862, but its action and his description of the elephant are set in 1832.

169. *Archives Nationales*, F13 1243 (27 March 1824), cited in Biver, *Paris de Napoléon*, 206.

170. *Archives Nationales*, F21 579, letter dated 8 October from the Minister of Public Works to the Minister of the Interior, cited in Ledoux-Lebard, "Les projets de fontaines," 49.

171. Paris, Musée Carnavalet, *Juillet 1830*, no. 227.

172. *Le Moniteur universel*, no. 188 (7 July 1831): 1183.

173. Letter dated 5 December 1831 from Duc to a friend, cited in Hautecoeur, *Histoire de l'architecture classique en France*, 6, 52.

174. Anonymous, *Description exacte et détaillée de la colonne de Juillet*, 3; *Le Moniteur universel*, no. 171 (20 June 1833): 1728.

175. *Le Moniteur universel*, no. 253 (10 September 1833): 2064.

176. Anonymous, "Monument de Juillet," *L'Artiste*, 6 (1833): 49.

177. Ibid.

178. Heine, *De la France*, 57.

179. *Le Magasin Pittoresque* (1840), cited in Stirling, *Histoire et description de la colonne de Juillet*, 8.

180. Cited in Stirling, *Histoire et description de la colonne de Juillet*, 7.

181. Agulhon, *Marianne au combat*, 21–53.

182. Rémusat, *Mémoires*, 3, 400–401.

183. Hugo, *Notre-Dame de Paris*, 84–85.

Notes to Chapter 4

1. Michelet, *Histoire de la Révolution française*, 8, 41.

2. Chastel, "La notion de patrimoine," 1442.

3. On the museum see McClellan, *Inventing the Louvre*, 155–97; Poulot, "Alexandre Lenoir"; Benoît, *L'art français sous la Révolution et l'Empire*, 119–23; Lanzac de Laborie, *Paris sous Napoléon*, 8, 330–64.

4. *Archives Nationales*, F17 1036 (3), cited in McClellan, *Inventing the Louvre*, 162.

5. *Archives Nationales*, F17 1280A (5), "Rapport sur le dépôt des monumens . . . et sur la nécessité de rétablir les monumens des arts, pour leur conservation," cited in McClellan, *Inventing the Louvre*, 164.

6. Albert Lenoir, *Archives du Musée des Monuments français*, 1, 22, and 34.

7. Cited in McClellan, *Inventing the Louvre*, 165.

8. Mercier, "Sur le dépôt des Petits-Augustins," 474.

9. Ibid., 476.

10. Lenoir, *Description historique*, (AN VIII), 6.

11. Ibid., (AN XI), 22–23.

12. Berry, *Journals and Correspondence* (25 March 1802), 2, 152.

13. Blanvillain, *Le Pariséum*, 122, cited in Poulot, "Alexandre Lenoir," 1530.

14. Lenoir, *Description historique* (AN VIII), 161.

15. Quatremère de Quincy, *Considérations morales*, 56–57.

16. Forbes, *Letters from France*, 405–7.

17. Reported in the *Journal de l'Empire* (27 April 1807).

18. Richard, *Mes Souvenirs*, cited in Chaudonneret, *Richard et Révoil*, 64. The marriage of Valentina Visconti, daughter of the Duke of Milan, to Louis d'Orléans in 1389 provided the basis for later French claims to lands in northern Italy.

19. Richard's original eventually ended up in Russia and has recently been acquired by the Hermitage Museum, inventory GJ-10608. An unfinished variant of Richard's picture was acquired in 2003 by the Musée National du Châteaux de Malmaison et de Bois–Préau, inventory MM.2003.20.1.

20. Paris, BnF, Estampes, *Collection Deloynes*, 26, no. 698, 845–46, cited in Pupil, *Style Troubadour*, 125.

21. Madame de Staël's comment may be apocryphal, since it is reported by Richard in his unpublished memoirs; passage cited in Chaudonneret, *Richard et Révoil*, 65.

22. The story was recorded in the *Histoire de Saint-Louis* of Jean de Joinville, who lived from 1224 to 1319. Cited from New York, *The Age of Revolution*, 587.

23. Vict. F. . . . , "Salon de Peinture," *Le Mercure de France*, 34 (October 1808): 368.

24. Miel, *Essai sur les Beaux-Arts*, 290.

25. The definitive text on Joséphine's collection and taste is Pougetoux, *La Collection de peintures de l'Impératrice Joséphine*, especially 15–65.

26. Paul (1814), *Party of Pleasure*, 94.

27. In 1968 the two pictures entered the collection of the Musée du Petit-Palais in Paris as part of the Dutuit bequest, inventory numbers 1164 and 1165.

28. It is often said this episode was inspired by the *Histoire du roy Henry le Grand*, first published by Hardouin de Beaumont de Péréfixe in 1661; see Pupil, *Style Troubadour*, 425–26 and 470–81. In fact, the story does not appear in that source, but seems to have been taken from Bellavoine, *Mémorial pittoresque de la France*, 19–22.

29. Chaudonneret, *Richard et Révoil*, 134–35.

30. Lebrun de Charmettes, *Histoire de Jeanne d'Arc*, 73–74.

31. Illustrated in Deschamps, *Empire*, 46–49.

32. Clary-Aldringen, *Trois mois à Paris*, 6.

33. Berry, *Journals and Correspondence* (10 April 1802), 2, 191.

34. Plumptre, *A Narrative*, 1, 193–94.

35. Carr, *The Stranger in France*, 97.

36. Pinkerton, *Recollections of Paris*, 202.

37. *Archives Nationales*, O3 1985, letter dated 16 April 1817 from Thierry de Ville d'Avray of the Garde-Meuble to the comte de Pradel, administrator of the Maison du Roi, cited in Samoyault-Verlet, "Louis XVIII," 43.

38. Discussed and illustrated in Samoyault-Verlet, "Louis XVIII," 48 and fig. 7.

39. Arizzoli-Clémentel, "Les soieries de Lyon," 23.

40. *Archives Nationales* O3 2001, letter dated 26 May 1823, cited in Samoyault-Verlet, "Louis XVIII," 48.

41. *Archives Nationales*, O3 2003, letter dated 3 July 1824 to commission the new bed and washstand, cited in Samoyault-Verlet, "Louis XVIII," 49.

42. The bed is still owned by the Mobilier National, inventory GME 6633. It is reproduced and discussed in Paris, *Un âge d'or des arts décoratifs*, 189–90.

43. The box is now in a private collection. For a reproduction and discussion see ibid., 197–98.

44. Sèvres, Archives de la Manufacture Nationale de Sèvres, inv. no. D§10 1848 No 7(1er). See New York, *Sèvres Porcelain Manufactory*, 260, cat. 70.

45. Waquet, *Les Fêtes Royales*, 147, 153, and 177.

46. Hugo, *Notre-Dame de Paris*, 354.

47. Letter from Planche to Hugo cited in Léon, *La Vie des Monuments français*, 108.

48. Wright, *Painting and History during the French Restoration*, esp. chap. 3 and 132–44.

49. Thierry, *Lettres sur l'histoire de France*, 73–74.

50. Cited in Léon, *La Vie des Monuments français*, 113.

51. Delécluze, *Souvenirs de soixante années*, 501.

52. Balzac, *La Peau de chagrin*, 148.

53. Lafaye's picture, the gothic predilections of Marie d'Orléans, and the redecoration of her study are discussed at length in Paris, Musée du Louvre, *Marie d'Orléans*, 164–227.

54. *Archives Nationales* 300 AP IV 158, "Récit anonyme de la vie de la princesse Marie," cited in Paris, *Un âge d'or des arts décoratifs*, 260.

55. Paris, Musée du Louvre, *Marie d'Orléans*, 64–101.

56. Ibid., 146–61.

57. Michelet, *Histoire de France (Livres V–IX)*, 310–12.

58. Letter dated 4 September 1824 from Barante to the comte de Sainte-Aulaire; published in Barante, *Souvenirs*, 3, 214.

59. Summerson, *Architecture in Britain*, 510.

60. An extant watercolor by Auguste Garneray now in a private collection depicts the interior of this neo-gothic décor. It is reproduced and discussed in Pradère, "Du style troubadour au style Boulle à l'hôtel d'Osmond," 73.

61. On the forming and maturation of ideas about the uses of history among the generation of architects active in France during these decades see Bergdoll, *Léon Vaudoyer*, chaps. 3 and 4.

62. Samoyault-Verlet, "L'ameublement des palais royaux sous la Monarchie de Juillet," 230–32.

63. Ibid., 232.

64. Hugo, *Notre-Dame de Paris*, 88.

65. Cited in Fermigier, "Mérimée et l'inspection des monuments historiques," 1606.

66. De Lassus and Viollet-le-Duc, "On the Restoration of the Cathedral of Notre-Dame de Paris," 280.

67. Ibid., 286.

68. Viollet-le-Duc, "Restauration," 14.

69. Foucart, "Viollet-le-Duc et la restauration," 1630.

70. Carlier, *Les Anciens Monuments*, 2, 474.

71. Deseine, "Opinion sur les musées," 279–80.

72. Rodin, *Les cathédrales de la France*, 144.

Notes to Chapter 5

1. Chauvin, *Salon de mil huit cent vingt-quatre*, 22–23.

2. Article in *L'Ami de la religion et du roi*, 32 (1822), cited in Spitzer, *French Generation of 1820*, 47.

3. Chauvin, *Salon de mil huit cent vingt-quatre*, 14.

4. Lauvergne, *Souvenirs de la Grèce*, 125.

5. Paris, Salon de 1824, *Explication*, 52, no. 450.

6. In an entry dated "Saturday May 1823" he wrote: "I have decided to make for the Salon some scenes of the *Massacre at Chios*" (Delacroix, *Journal*, 1, 32).

7. Entry dated 12 January 1824 in Delacroix, *Journal*, 1, 45.

8. Voutier, *Mémoires du colonel Voutier*, 251.

9. Entry dated 8 October 1822 in Delacroix, *Journal*, 1, 17.

10. Entry dated 26 January 1824 in ibid., 50.

11. Fraser, *Delacroix, Art and Patrimony*, 39–77, argues that Delacroix's picture was motivated less by politics than a secret complicity with contemporary ideas about family values and paternal authority in Restoration France. Fraser's reading of *Chios* as "a consensus painting" that "calls forth a feeling of pity toward another in need of help" is consonant with the larger project of affect I describe here.

12. Stendhal, "The Salon of 1824," 107.

13. Landon, *Salon de 1824*, 54.

14. M . . . , *Salon de 1824*, 5.

15. Ibid.

16. Stendhal, "The Salon of 1824," 107.

17. M . . . , *Salon de 1824*, 5.

18. Ibid., 5–6.

19. Y., "Salon de 1824," *Le Globe* (28 Sept 1842), cited in Johnson, *Paintings of Delacroix*, 1, 88.

20. Chauvin states unequivocally a few lines later in the passage cited: "I call . . . romantic the *Massacre of Chios*" (Chauvin, *Salon de mil huit cent vingt-quatre*, 23).

21. Flocon and Aycard, *Salon de 1824*, 16.

22. Fraser, *Delacroix, Art and Patrimony*, 78–93.

23. Piron, *Eugène Delacroix*, 66.

24. Cited by Silvestre, *Histoire des artistes vivants*, 1–2.

25. Ingres copied his response to the Prefect into a letter dated 3 June 1821 to his friend Jean-François Gilibert, published in Boyer d'Agen, *Ingres d'après une Correspondance inédite*, 78.

26. Bazin, *Histoire de France sous Louis XIII*, 1, iii–iv.

27. Letter dated 15 July 1821 from Ingres to Gilibert, published in Boyer d'Agen, *Ingres d'après une Correspondance inédite*, 80.

28. Stendhal, "The Salon of 1824," 114, and M . . . , *Salon de 1824*, 150.

29. Passages drafted by Ingres to the Minister of the Interior, copied into a letter dated 20 April 1821 to Gilibert, published in Boyer d'Agen, *Ingres d'après une Correspondance inédite*, 69–70.

30. Letter dated 12 November 1824 from Ingres to Gilibert, published in Boyer d'Agen, *Ingres d'après une Correspondance inédite*, 120–21.

31. M . . . , *Salon de 1824*, 130.

32. Ibid.

33. Stendhal, "The Salon of 1824," 105.

34. Anonymous, *Revue des productions*, 39.

35. Jal, *L'Artiste et le philosophe*, 95.

36. Pillet, *Une Matinée au Salon . . . de 1824*, 34.

37. M . . . , *Salon de 1824*, 307–8.

38. Citations from Spitzer, *French Generation of 1820*, 136.

39. Spitzer, *French Generation of 1820*, 136.

40. Letter dated 26 April 1828 to Charles Soulier, published in Delacroix, *Correspondance générale*, 1, 217.

41. Ibid.

42. Fraser, *Delacroix, Art and Patrimony*, chap. 4, argues that the work's themes of royal death and failed masculine authority crystalize a "political imaginary" considered threatening to Bourbon family rule. Her reading is plausible but largely ignores the intersection with Victor Hugo that motivates my interpretation.

43. Paris, Salon de 1827, *Explication*, 2e Supplément, no. 1630.

44. Silvestre is cited in Johnson, *The Paintings of Eugene Delacroix*, 1, 117.

45. Louis Vitet, "Salon de 1827," *Le Globe* (8 March 1828), cited in Spector, *Delacroix: The Death of Sardanapalus*, 81.

46. Jal, *Esquisses, croquis, pochades*, 312–13.

47. Letter dated 8 February 1828 to Charles Soulier, published in Delacroix, *Correspondance générale*, 1, 211.

48. Letter dated 3 April 1829 to Victor Pavie, published in Hugo, *Oeuvres Complètes de Victor Hugo: Correspondance*, 1, 453–54.

49. Documents cited in Johnson, *The Paintings of Eugène Delacroix*, 1, 119.

50. He ordered white lead, Naples yellow, yellow ochre, cobalt blue, peach-black, Van Dyck red, and burnt sienna. See his orders to Madame Haro dated 29 October 1827 and 16 December 1827, published in Delacroix, *Correspondance générale*, 1, 200 and 207.

51. Letter dated 24 September to Victor Pavie, published in Hugo, *Oeuvres complètes de Victor Hugo: Correspondance*, 1, 444. Hugo's handwritten title page for the manuscript of *Cromwell* also carries the remark that "I wrote the preface in October 1827" (reproduced in Hugo, *Cromwell – Hernani*, frontispiece).

52. Hugo, *Cromwell – Hernani*, 15.

53. Ibid.

54. Ibid., 20.

55. Ibid., 27.

56. Ibid., 28.

57. Ibid., 32.

58. Étienne Delécluze, "Exposition au Louvre," *Journal des Débats* (21 March 1828), cited in Jobert, *Delacroix*, 83.

59. Chesneau, *Peintres et statuaires romantiques*, 98.

60. Ballads VIII and XIII are dedicated to Boulanger and were accompanied by an explanatory note in the 1828 edition. See Hugo, *Odes et Ballades – Les Orientales*, 326, 352, and 383.

61. "M. Coutain gave me the craving to do a Mazeppa," wrote Delacroix in his journal on 14 March 1824. "I am hesitating for some time between Mazeppa, Don Juan, Tasso, and a hundred others," he lamented on 11 April. He jotted down yet a third idea on 11 May: "Mazeppa cursing those who strapped him to his steed, with the château of Palatin destroyed to its foundations" (Delacroix, *Journal*, 1, 60, 73, and 100).

62. Anonymous, *Examen du Salon de 1827*, 31.

63. Gautier, *Histoire du Romantisme*, 226–27.

64. Jal, *Esquisses, croquis, pochades*, 342.

65. Béraud, *Annales de l'école française*, 169.

66. The text of "Mazeppa" is reprinted in Hugo, *Odes et Ballades – Les Orientales*, 733–37.

67. Bürger et al., "Jean Du Seigneur, statuaire," 86.

68. The phrase "eine edle Einfalt und eine stille Grösse," is from Winckelmann, "Gedanken über die Nachahmung der Griechischen Werke," 43. For the lasting impact of Winckelmann's formulation of 1755, see Potts, *Flesh and the Ideal*, 1–10.

69. "Salon de 1831: Sculpture," *L'Artiste*, 1 (1831): 313.

70. Extract from the "Ode à Duseigneur" by Théophile Gautier, originally published in the *Mercure de France* (1831) and reprinted in Bürger et al., "Jean Du Seigneur, statuaire," 72–76.

71. Benoît, *La Sculpture romantique*, 52.

72. Letter dated April 1867 from Préault to Théophile Gautier, reprinted in Paris, Musée d'Orsay, *Auguste Préault*, 285.

73. Janin, "Salon de 1833: Sculpture," 141–42 and 153–54.

74. Paris, Salon de 1834, *Explication*, 193, no. 2124.

75. Théophile Gautier, "Salon de 1834," *La France industriel* (April 1834): 22.

76. Préault submitted two works to the Salon of 1833—*Misery* and *Famine*—that took urban poor as their subjects. At least one critic suggested that Préault was making "republican" art: see Jean-Barthélémy Hauréau, "Variétés-Revue des Arts-Salon," *La Tribune politique et littéraire* (3 May 1833), 4. On the possible political motives of Préault's *Slaughter*, see Boime, *Hollow Icons*, 46–53.

77. Gautier, "Salon de 1834," *La France industriel* (April 1834): 22.

78. Manuscript note in the Bibliothèque Municipale of Angers (fonds Robert David), cited in de Caso (1988), *David d'Angers*, 97.

79. Silvestre, *Histoire des artistes vivants*, 294.

80. Tardieu, *Salon de 1833*, 42–43.

81. Jal, *Salon de 1833*, 342–43.

82. Laviron and Galbacio, *Le Salon de 1833*, 22–24.

83. Planche, "Salon de 1834," in *Études sur l'école française*, 1, 237–38.

84. Paris, Salon de 1834, *Explication*, 52, no. 503.

85. Bann, *Paul Delaroche*, 124.

86. Planche, "Salon de 1834," in *Études sur l'école française*, 1, 241.

87. Hunt, *Pre-Raphaelitism*, 1, 130; Meisel, *Realizations*, 238.

88. Decamps, *Salon de 1834*, 31.

89. Rosen and Zerner, *Romanticism and Realism*, 121.

90. Rosenthal, *Du Romantisme au Réalisme*, 205 and 207.

91. Ibid., 202–3.

92. Wright, *Painting and History*, chap. 4.

93. Amaury-Duval, *L'Atelier d'Ingres*, 101.

94. Manuscript report from Delaroche to François Arago, published in full by Cromer, "Une Pièce historique," 114–18.

95. Fabien Pillet, "Salon de 1834," *Le Moniteur universel* (10 March 1834), cited in Ziff, *Delaroche*, 130.

96. Barye's *Tiger Hunt* is now in the Walters Art Gallery, Baltimore (inv. no. 27.176), reproduced in Baltimore, Walters Art Gallery, *Untamed: The Art of Antoine-Louis Barye*, 113, cat. 28. For the most recent analysis of the centerpiece see Leroy-Jay Lemaistre, "The *Surtout de Table* of the Duc d'Orléans."

97. *Arch. Nat.*, 300 API 2394, 1840.

98. Janin, "Salon de 1833: Sculpture," 143.

99. Undated letter from Delacroix to Barye marked "Saturday," in Delacroix, *Correspondance générale*, 1, 225. Joubin assigned this letter to October 1828, but new research has shown it must have been written on 19 June 1829: see Loffredo, "Des recherches communes de Barye et Delacroix."

100. Hugo, *Cromwell – Hernani*, 33.

101. Joinville, *Vieux Souvenirs*, 190–91.

102. The arrangement and use of the *surtout* must be conjectured from extant inventories made before the pieces were sold off in separate lots. The most important publications, based upon all the available archives, are Isabelle Leroy-Jay Lemaistre, "Des Sculpteurs et des bronziers," and "The *Surtout de Table* of the Duc d'Orleans."

103. Hugo, *Odes et Ballades – Les Orientales*, 616.

104. Planche, "Salon de 1837," in *Études sur l'école française*, 2, 55.

105. Reported by Lami, *Dictionnaire des sculpteurs*, 1, 71.

106. Stendhal, "The Salon of 1824," 112.

107. Letter dated 19 April 1822 from Robert to Navez, reprinted in Gassier, *Léopold Robert*, 298.

108. Letter dated 25 September 1823 from Robert to Navez, reprinted in Gassier, *Léopold Robert*, 308.

109. *Brigands dans les montagnes de Terracina*, no. 1099; *Une vieille femme disant la bonne aventure à une jeune fille de Sonnino*, no. 1100; *Une jeune religieuse recevant la bénédiction d'une abbesse*, no. 1101; *Procession de religieux dans l'église de Saints Côme et Damien*, no. 1102.

110. Stendhal, "The Salon of 1824," 112.

111. Neuchâtel, *Léopold Robert et les Peintres de l'Italie romantique*, 47.

112. Cited in Gassier, *Léopold Robert*, 158. Seven years later Heinrich Heine opened his remarks about Robert with an identical question: "Is he an historical or a genre painter? I seem to hear from the masters of the guilds of Germany. Unfortunately, I cannot evade this question" (reprinted in Holt, *Triumph of Art for the Public*, 307).

113. Letter dated 25 September 1825 from Robert to his brother Aurèle and his mother, reprinted in Gassier, *Léopold Robert*, 172. Robert used the word *enfoncer* to describe how his rivals must be treated.

114. Gassier, *Léopold Robert*, 172–73.

115. Jal, *Esquisses, croquis, pochades*, 459.

116. *Le Moniteur universel* (1 March 1828): 255.

117. Said, *Orientalism*, 3.

118. Entry dated 27 February 1824 in Delécluze, *Impressions romaines*, 175.

119. Hugo, *Odes et Ballades – Les Orientales*, 620.

120. Letter dated 23 October 1827 from Robert to his family, reprinted in Gassier, *Léopold Robert*, 320.

121. Lenormant, "Salon de 1831," reprinted in *Les artistes contemporaines*, 2, 63–64.

122. Ibid., 65.

123. Entry dated 1 April 1832 in Delacroix, *Journal*, 1, 145.

124. Entry dated 11 May 1824 in ibid., 99.

125. Charles Cournault, "La Galerie Poirel au Musée de Nancy,"

Courrier de l'Art, 2, no. 41 (12 October 1882), cited in Johnson, *The Paintings of Eugène Delacroix*, 3, 166.

126. The Louvre watercolors are reproduced in Johnson, *The Paintings of Eugène Delacroix*, 3, 166–67, figs. 37–39.

127. Johnson, *The Paintings of Eugène Delacroix*, 3, 167.

128. Gustave Planche, "Salon de 1834," in *Études sur l'école française*, 1, 219.

129. Letter from Cournault cited in Jobert, *Delacroix*, 147.

130. Daguerre de Hureaux, *Delacroix*, 176.

131. Melman, *Women's Orients*, 59–63.

132. Suzanne Rodin Pucci, "The Discrete Charms of the Exotic: Fictions of the Harem in Eighteenth-Century France," in Porter and Rousseau, *Exoticism in the Enlightenment*, 150.

133. Melman, *Women's Orients*, 63.

134. Ibid., 102.

135. Ibid., 136. For an extended and insightful comparison between the accounts of Lady Montagu's *Letters* and Charles de Secondat Montesquieu's *Lettres persanes*, see Lowe, *Critical Terrains*, 30–74.

136. Melman, *Women's Orients*, 113.

137. Ibid., 122.

138. Pardoe, *The City of the Sultan*, 2, 98–9.

139. Shelton, *Ingres and his Critics*, chap. 1.

140. Montauban, Musée Ingres, Inventory 867.2029. For a reproduction see Vigne, *Dessins d'Ingres*, 406.

141. Excerpt from Lady Montagu's *Letters* copied by Ingres into Notebook 9, cited by Vigne, *Ingres*, 222.

142. Théophile Gautier in *Le Moniteur universel* (14 July 1855), reprinted in Gautier, *Critique d'art*, 273.

143. Baudelaire, "The Museum of Classics at the Bazar Bonne Nouvelle," reprinted in Holt, *Triumph of Art for the Public*, 457.

144. Letter dated 25 August 1840 from Ingres to Charles Marcotte, cited in Delaborde, *Ingres*, 237. The picture is dated 1839 but Ingres continued to work on it until August of 1840.

145. Letter dated 17 December 1840 from Ingres to Édouard Gatteaux, cited in Delaborde, *Ingres*, 238–39.

146. "Introduction au Salon de 1846," in Thoré, *Salons de T. Thoré (1844–1848)*, 250–51 and 240.

147. Nochlin, "Imaginary Orient," 37–38.

148. Théophile Gautier, "Salon de 1841," *La Revue de Paris* (28 April 1841), reprinted in Holt, *Triumph of Art for the Public*, 375.

149. An example would be Clodion's small terra-cotta group (58 cm) of a *Bacchante playing a Tambour* now in the Philadelphia Museum of Art.

150. *Le Moniteur universel* (6 September 1844): 2591.

151. Balzac, *Illusions perdues*, 177–78.

152. Ibid., 183.

153. Ibid., 687.

154. Green, *Spectacle of Nature*, 59.

155. Ibid., 106.

156. Lazare Carnot, "Mémoire adressé au Roi en juillet 1814," reprinted in Stewart and Desjardins, *French Patriotism*, 158. Also see the discussion of *la patrie* after Waterloo in Einecke, "Beyond Seeing," 62–68.

157. Félibien, *Entretiens*, 310–11. See also Vincent Pomarède, "Realism and Recollection," in Washington DC, *In the Light of Italy*, 89–105.

158. Roger de Piles, *Cours de peinture par principes* (1708), cited in Puttfarken, *Roger de Piles' Theory of Art*, 48.

159. Watelet and Lévesque, *Dictionnaire des arts*, 4, 8–9.

160. Valenciennes, *Élémens de perspective pratique*, 381–82.

161. Ibid., 479.

162. The very fine collection of oil studies painted by Valenciennes in Italy during the 1780s (now in the Louvre) was not "discovered" so to speak until 1930, when princesse Louise de Croÿ bequeathed it to the museum. The entire lot, bought in 1819 by de Croÿ's ancestors at the artist's estate sale, had not been seen in public for more than one hundred years. In 1973 a second batch of Valenciennes's oil sketches, these done in Brittany, appeared on the market. See Lacambre, *Les Paysages de Pierre-Henri Valenciennes*.

163. *Archives de l'Institut*, 5E9, cited in Grunchec, *Le Grand Prix de Peinture*, 339, n. 32.

164. Deperthes, *Théorie du Paysage*, 210.

165. Ibid., 144 and 157.

166. Constable, *Correspondence*, 6, 87–88. The two other pictures acquired by Arrowsmith were *View on the Stour near Dedham* (now in the Huntington Library at San Marino, CA) and a *View near London, Hampstead Heath*.

167. Bermingham, *Landscape and Ideology*, 136. See also London, Tate Britain, *Constable: The Great Landscapes*, 128–61.

168. Stendhal, "The Salon of 1824," 109.

169. Letter dated 17 December 1825 from Constable to John Fisher, reprinted in Holt, *From the Classicists to the Impressionists*, 117.

170. Jal, *L'Artiste et le philosophe*, 292–93.

171. Stendhal, "The Salon of 1824," 109.

172. Letter dated 17 December 1825 from Constable to John Fisher, reprinted in Holt, *From the Classicists to the Impressionists*, 116.

173. New York, Metropolitan Museum of Art, *Corot*, cat. no. 61.

174. Louis Viardot, "Salon de 1835," *Le National de 1834* (5 April 1835), cited in New York, Metropolitan Museum of Art, *Corot*, 157.

175. Lenormant, "L'École française en 1835," reprinted in *Beaux-Arts et Voyages*, 1, 114.

176. Victor Schoelcher, "Salon de 1831," *L'Artiste*, 2 (1831): 1.

177. Green, *Spectacle of Nature*, 80–98, where the term "extended promenades" is introduced on 83.

178. Ibid., 87.

179. Thoré, "Salon de 1847," reprinted in Thoré, *Salons de Th. Thoré*, 459.

180. "Lettre à Béranger" [preface to Salon of 1845], reprinted in Thoré, *Salons de Th. Thoré*, 104–5.

181. Théophile Thoré, "Salon de 1848," in Thoré, *Salons de Th. Thoré*, 559.

182. Ibid., 565.

183. Louis Veuillot, "Situation morale des compagnes," *L'Univers* (29 May 1849), cited in Clark, *Image of the People*, 86.

184. Adolphe Blanqui, "Les populations rurales de la France," *Annales provençales d'agriculture* (1851), cited in Clark, *Image of the People*, 88.

185. Report of 21 December 1849, cited in Clark, *Image of the People*, 97.

186. Albert de la Fizelière, "Salon de 1851," *Le Siècle* (15 April 1851), cited in Clark, *Absolute Bourgeois*, 94.

187. Auguste Desplaces, "Salon de 1851," *L'Union* (29 January 1851), cited in Clark, *Absolute Bourgeois*, 94.

188. A. Dauger, "Salon de 1851," *Le Pays* (9 February 1851), cited in Clark, *Image of the People*, 145.

189. The emptiness of this front and center space before the picture with "nowhere to stand outside the painting" is cause for a lengthy meditation on the beholder's "quasi-corporeal" absorption in Fried, *Courbet's Realism*, 111–47.

190. Clark, *Image of the People*, 115.

191. Undated letter (probably February–March 1850) from Courbet to Champfleury, reprinted in Courbet, *Letters*, 93.

192. Letter dated 31 July 1850 from Courbet in Dijon to Francis Wey in Paris, reprinted in Courbet, *Letters*, 99.

193. Théophile Gautier, "Salon de 1850–51," *La Presse* (15 February 1851), reprinted in Gautier, *Critique d'art*, 135.

194. Claude Vignon, *Salon de 1850–51*, cited in Clark, *Image of the People*, 141.

195. Louis Peisse, "Salon de 1850–51," *Le Constitutionnel* (8 January 1851), cited in Clark, *Image of the People*, 134.

Notes to Chapter 6

1. Gautier, *Histoire du Romantisme*, 5.

2. The diminutive distinguished Gautier's friends from the more prestigious groups who gathered around Victor Hugo, Charles Nodier, or Pierre-Jean de Béranger.

3. Entry dated 28 February 1824 in Delacroix, *Journal*, 1, 54.

4. Letters dated 27 June 1825 and 1 August 1825 from Delacroix to Pierret, reprinted in Delacroix, *Correspondance générale*, 1, 161–69.

5. Note dated Wednesday September 1827 from Delacroix to Hugo, reprinted in Delacroix, *Correspondance générale*, 1, 198.

6. "What is striking and characteristic in the nineteenth-century theater," writes Martin Meisel, "is that its dramaturgy was pictorial, not just its *mise en scène*, and that such pictorialism was strongest in what were regarded as its most 'dramatic' genres" (Meisel, *Realizations*, 39).

7. Letter dated 18 June 1825 from Delacroix to Pierret, reprinted in Delacroix, *Correspondance générale*, 1, 159–61.

8. Entry dated 29 June 1855 in Delacroix, *Journal*, 2, 349.

9. "Above all, it was the production of a dramatic opera on *Faust*, which I saw in London in 1825, that prompted me to make something on that subject," recalled Delacroix in 1862 (letter dated 1 March 1862 from Delacroix to Philippe Burty, reprinted in Delacroix, *Correspondance générale*, 4, 303–5).

10. The notebook used by Delacroix, into which he copied passages of *Faust* alongside some of his first ideas for how to illustrate them, now belongs to the Bibliothèque d'Art et d'Archéologie, Fondation Jacques Doucet in Paris (Manuscript 250).

11. *Faust*, tragédie de M. de Goethe, traduite en français par M. Albert Stapfer, Ornée d'un portrait de l'auteur et de dix-sept

dessins d'après les principales scènes de l'ouvrage et exécutés sur pierre par M. Eugène Delacroix (Paris: chez Ch. Motte, 1828).

12. Letter dated 18 June 1825 from Delacroix to Pierret, reprinted in Delacroix, *Correspondance générale*, 1, 160.

13. Eckermann, *Conversations with Goethe*, 172–73.

14. Goethe's review appeared in *Über Kunst und Altertum*, 6 (1827), cited (and translated) in Trapp, *Attainment of Delacroix*, 145. Evidence that Delacroix knew of Goethe's praise comes from a letter of 1836 to Théophile Thoré: "there appeared in 1828 a suite of lithographs based on Goethe's *Faust*, published with a new translation in a luxury edition. Goethe reviewed this publication with special praise in the journal of literature and art that he himself edited" (letter dated 18 January 1836 from Delacroix to Thoré, reprinted in Delacroix, *Correspondance générale*, 1, 406–9).

15. Letter dated 8 February 1862 from Delacroix to Philippe Burty, reprinted in Delacroix, *Correspondance générale*, 4, 304.

16. Paris, *Un âge d'or des arts décoratifs*, no. 158, 305–6, and Paris, *Mélancolie*, no. 246, 462. Our illustration is the larger version of *Satan* cast in 1850 (79 cm tall) now in the Los Angeles County Museum of Art.

17. Heine, *Religion and Philosophy in Germany*, 99. Also see the discussion in Honour, *Romanticism*, 257–58.

18. Entry for 1 June 1824 in Delacroix, *Journal*, 1, 107.

19. Cited from a note published with "La Légende de la Nonne" in the 1828 edition, reprinted in Hugo, *Odes et Ballades – Les Orientales*, 383.

20. Cited from "La Ronde du Sabbat," reprinted in Hugo, *Odes et Ballades – Les Orientales*, 359–64.

21. Baudelaire, *Salon de 1845*, 158.

22. Letter dated 2 October 1842 from Gustave Planche to Paul Huet, cited in Séché, *Cénacle de Joseph Delorme*, 2, 128–29.

23. "Rêves," which is Ode XXV of the collection *Odes et Ballades*, is reprinted in Hugo, *Odes et Ballades – Les Orientales*, 294–300. The lines reproduced by Huet in the Salon catalogue are excerpted from Hugo's first vignette:

Trouvez-moi, trouvez-moi
Quelque asile sauvage
Quelque abri d'autrefois,
. . . .
Trouvez-le-moi bien sombre,
Bien calme, bien dormant,

Couvert d'arbres sans nombre,
Dans le silence et l'ombre,
Caché profondément.

[Find for me, find for me
Some wild refuge
Some tree of old,
. . . .
Find one for me very dark,
Very calm, very sleepy,
Sheltered by a great many trees,
In silence and shadow,
Deeply hidden away.]

Huet edited out several intervening lines, including references to a river port and a country house, in order to synchronize the poetry with his image of nature purified of all but the specter of Gothic spires against the sky. For discussion of Huet's picture, see Miquel, *Paul Huet*, 68–69, and Einecke, "Beyond Seeing," 42–49.

24. Planche, "Salon de 1831," in *Études sur l'école française*, 1, 96.

25. Victor Schoelcher, "Salon de 1831," *L'Artiste*, 1 (1831): 272.

26. Huet, *Paul Huet (1803–1869)*, 95.

27. Letter dated 29 May 1802 from Constable to John Dunthorne in Constable, *Correspondence*, 2, 31–32.

28. Planche, "Salon de 1831," in *Études sur l'école française*, 1, 97.

29. Victor Schoelcher, "Salon de 1831," *L'Artiste*, 1 (1831): 210.

30. Burty, *Paul Huet*, 51.

31. Cited from Victor Hugo's letter to the editor of the *Journal des Débats* (published July 1824), reprinted in Hugo, *Odes et Ballades – Les Orientales*, 564.

32. Letter dated 18 September 1839 from Hugo to Adèle, reprinted in Hugo, *Alpes et Pyrénées*, 201–2.

33. The excerpt is from the fifth stanza of "À Mes Odes," reprinted in Hugo, *Odes et Ballades – Les Orientales*, 96.

34. Gaudon, "Souvenir de . . . ," 165.

35. Focillon, "Les dessins de Victor Hugo," 199.

36. Baudelaire, *Salon de 1846*, 121.

37. Gautier, "Monographie du Bourgeois Parisien," *Revue du XIXe siècle* (25 September and 2 October 1836), reprinted in Gautier, *Paris et les Parisiens*, 444.

38. Nerval, "Les Filles du Feu: Sylvie," in *Oeuvres Complètes*, 3, 538.

39. Gautier, *Histoire du Romantisme*, 50.

40. Ibid.

41. Ibid.

42. Seigel, *Bohemian Paris*, 10–11.

43. Murger, *Scènes de la Vie de Bohème*, 64.

44. "Cinq étages du monde Parisien," the best-known image of the vertical arrangement of social classes in nineteenth-century Paris, was published in Texier, *Tableau de Paris*, 1, 65.

45. Balzac, *Illusions perdues*, 227.

46. Sand, *Histoire de ma vie*, 4, 77–78.

47. Ibid., 81.

48. Letter dated 20 December 1832 from George Sand to Jules Boucoiran, reprinted in Sand, *Correspondance*, 1, 234–35.

49. François Thiollet, *Choix de maisons et d'édifices publics de Paris et de ses environs*, 2nd ed. (Paris: Bancé, 1838), cited in Paris, *La Nouvelle Athènes*, 23.

50. Letter dated 15 March 1841 from Balzac to Madame Hanska, reprinted in Balzac, *Lettres à l'Étrangère*, 1, 553.

51. Ernest Chesneau, "Les petits romantiques," *Le Constitutionnel* (14 March 1865), cited in Rosenthal, "Jules-Robert Auguste," 145.

52. Sand, *Histoire de ma vie*, 4, 405.

53. Balzac, *Illusions perdues*, 233.

54. Murger, *Scènes de la Vie de Bohème*, 212.

55. Lecture delivered on 21 April 1830, cited in McWilliam, *Dreams of Happiness*, 76–77.

56. Hippolyte Carnot, "Discours sur les beaux-arts," *L'Organisateur* (25 December 1830), cited in McWilliam, *Dreams of Happiness*, 62.

57. Enfantin cited by McWilliam, *Dreams of Happiness*, 105.

58. Letter dated 2 July 1830 from Michel Chevalier to E. Humann, cited in McWilliam, *Dreams of Happiness*, 105–6.

59. Letter dated 26 April 1832 from Pol Justus to Charles Duveyrier, cited in McWilliam, *Dreams of Happiness*, 109.

60. Reported on 9 December 1830 by Alfred de Vigny, *Journal d'un poète*, cited in McWilliam, *Dreams of Happiness*, 118.

61. Émile Barrault, "Prédication du 27 novembre," in *Religion saint-simonienne* (1831), cited in McWilliam, *Dreams of Happiness*, 119.

62. "Portrait de Mme Dudevant (George Sand)," Salon of 1839, no. 331. The picture, which was cut down to an oval by Solange, the daughter of George Sand, is now in Paris at the Musée Carnavalet, inventory P1945 (86 × 65 cm). See Bruson and Leribault, *Peintures du Musée Carnavalet*, 124.

63. George Sand reportedly dictated the text to Maurice Sand, her son, who recopied it onto the back of the fan. The manuscript text, today in a private collection, is reprinted in Paris, *George Sand: Visages du Romantisme*, 52, no. 225.

64. The characters at the left side (from left to center) are Luigi Calamatta, Maurice Sand, Charles Didier, Emmanuel Arago, Count Albert Grzymala, and Pierre Bocage. To the right side (from right to center) are Charpentier, a friend of Sand's called M. de Bonnechose, Solange Sand (as a lion), Michel de Bourges, and Enrico Marliani (playing the guitar).

65. On 2 March 1838 Balzac wrote to Eva Hanska about his stay at Nohant: "It's with respect to Liszt and Mme d'Agoult that she [Sand] gave me the subject for the *Galériens*, or *Amours forcés*, that I will write because, in her situation, she can't do it. Be sure to keep this a secret." Reprinted in Balzac, *Lettres à Mme Hanska*, 1, 587. Balzac eventually published his novel in 1839 under the title of *Beatrix*.

66. Baudelaire, *Salon de 1846*, 157.

67. "Never, perhaps, have there been more portraits at the Salon than this year," remarked Gustave Planche in 1831. "This is really very easy to understand. In fact, it would be unwise to undertake vast compositions on the off chance of selling them without being pretty sure in advance where they will go; wanting to venture too much all at once and right away often sets you up for bitter disappointments" (Planche, "Salon de 1831," reprinted in *Études sur l'école française*, 1, 32). The argument that portraiture flourishes when large commissions vanish was a commonplace among Salon critics throughout the 1830s and 1840s.

68. Letter dated 21 March 1839 from Stendhal to Madame Jules Gaulthier, reprinted as "The Salon of 1839" in Stendhal, *Stendhal and the Arts*, 122–23.

69. Maurice Alhoy, "Les séances de l'atelier," *Musée pour Rire* (1839), cited in Rosenthal, *Du Romantisme au Réalisme*, 23.

70. Sarah Maza's recent attempt to prove "that the French bourgeoisie did not exist" is mainly an attack upon the straw-man bourgeois invented by Karl Marx (Maza, *Myth of the French Bourgeoisie*, 5). Her account of the 1820s and 1830s—notably the writings of Thierry, Guizot, and Royer-Collard—admits the term was used "in something close to [its] familiar modern meaning," but she enlists some tortuous reasoning to prove only that "none of the Resto-

ration's politicians and historians actually formulated the definition of the bourgeoisie which has been the standard one since Marx" (Maza, *Bourgeoisie*, 157). The yield of Maza's argument, especially for the decades under discussion, seems both overvalued and a distortion of the textual evidence.

71. Planche, "Salon de 1838," in *Études sur l'école française*, 2, 132–33.

72. Entry dated 18 July 1850 in Delacroix, *Journal*, 1, 391.

73. Jules Janin, "Être artiste!" *L'Artiste*, 1 (1831): 9–10.

74. Balzac, *Illusions perdues*, 241.

75. Ibid., 242.

76. Ibid., 382–83.

77. Planche, "Salon de 1833," in *Études sur l'école française*, 1, 207.

78. Letter dated 10 December 1832 from Louis Lacuria to Hippolyte Flandrin, published in Hardouin-Fugier, "Monsieur Ingres vu par Louis Lacuria 1832–1838," 44.

79. Lenormant, "Salon de 1833," in *Les artistes contemporaines*, 2, 164.

80. Anonymous, "Salon de 1833," *L'Artiste*, 5 (1833): 130.

81. Ibid., 154.

82. Gautier, "Salon de 1833," *La France littéraire* (1833), reprinted in Gautier, *Critique d'art*, 259.

83. Gautier, *Le Moniteur universel* (12 and 14 July 1855), reprinted in Gautier, *Critique d'art*, 275.

84. Rosenblum, "Ingres's Portraits and Their Muses," 6.

85. In 1897 a ceramicist named Ovide Scribe wrote to Jules Momméja, curator of the Musée Ingres in Montauban, that "this chair was painted by Duthanofer, a well-known ornamental painter of the time. The master made him redo this point of light five or six times, never finding the curtain sufficiently detailed" (cited in Vigne, "Ingres and Co.," 531).

86. Letter dated 2 October 1841 from Ingres to Jean-François Gilibert, reprinted in Boyer d'Agen, *Ingres d'après une Correspondance inédite*, 304.

87. Martin-Fugier, *La vie élégante*, 371.

88. Letter dated 15 March 1831 from Ingres to Jean-François Gilibert, reprinted in Boyer d'Agen, *Ingres d'après une Correspondance inédite*, 227.

89. Louise d'Haussonville, *Voyage à Rome en 1840* (unpublished ms.), cited in Munhall, *Ingres and the Comtesse d'Haussonville*, 76, note 16.

90. Thoré, "Introduction au Salon de 1846," reprinted in Thoré, *Salons de T. Thoré*, 253.

91. Broglie, *Mémoires*, 2, 14.

92. Letter dated 28 January 1844 from Doudan to Albert de Broglie, reprinted in Doudan, *Mélanges et Lettres*, 2, 4–5.

93. Alphonse-Jean Laurent, "La Cène de M. Ingres pour faire pendant à celle de Leonardo da Vinci," *Le Charivari* (18 June 1841), cited in Tinterow, "Paris, 1841–1867," 354.

94. Letter dated 2 October 1841 from Ingres to Jean-François Gilibert, reprinted in Boyer d'Agen, *Ingres d'après une Correspondance inédite*, 302–3.

95. Letter dated 27 July 1845 from Ingres to Jean-François Gilibert, reprinted in Boyer d'Agen, *Ingres d'après une Correspondance inédite*, 379.

96. Letter of June 1845 from Ingres to Charles Marcotte, cited in Blanc, *Ingres: Sa vie et ses ouvrages*, 144–45.

97. Munhall, *Ingres and the Comtesse d'Haussonville*, 94.

98. Even if, as Georges Vigne suggests, the accessories (including the glint of light) were painted by Armand Cambon, there is no reason to doubt that Ingres directed what should be included and with what level of detail (Vigne, "Ingres and Co.," 538).

99. Munhall, *Ingres and the Comtesse d'Haussonville*, 86 and 93.

100. Louise d'Haussonville, *Mémoires* (unpublished), cited in Munhall, *Ingres and the Comtesse d'Haussonville*, 127.

101. Gautier, *Histoire du Romantisme*, 99.

102. Halsall, *Victor Hugo and the Romantic Drama*, 77.

103. Gautier, *Histoire du Romantisme*, 102.

104. *Le Moniteur universel*, no. 57 (26 February 1830): 227.

105. Gautier, *Histoire du Romantisme*, 113.

106. For the stage directions see Hugo, *Cromwell – Hernani*, 632.

107. Milton, *Letters on the Fine Arts*, 234.

108. Julien-Louis Geoffroy, *Journal des Débats* (17 January 1803), cited in Descotes, *Le public de théâtre*, 219.

109. Lanzac de Laborie, *Paris sous Napoléon*, 8, 183.

110. Joseph-Abraham-Bernard *dit* Fleury, *Mémoires de Fleury de la Comédie-Française, 1757 à 1820*, 6 vols. (Paris: Dupont, 1836–38), 6, chap. 4, cited in Descotes, *Le public de théâtre*, 222.

111. Lecomte, *Napoléon et le monde dramatique*, 74.

112. *Archives Nationales*, F7 4333, cited in Lanzac de Laborie, *Paris sous Napoléon*, 8, 143–44.

113. Staël, "De l'Art dramatique," in *De l'Allemagne*, 2, 253–54.

114. Julien-Louis Geoffroy, *Journal des Débats* (19 March 1804), cited in Collins, *Talma*, 158.

115. Milton, *Letters on the Fine Arts*, 232.

116. Collins, *Talma*, 321.

117. *Journal de Paris* (28 December 1821), cited in Collins, *Talma*, 323.

118. Dumas, *Souvenirs dramatiques*, 1, 394.

119. Mirecourt, *Le baron Taylor*, 63.

120. Victor, *Mémoire contre le baron Taylor*, 65.

121. Duval, *Charles II*, xlvi–xlvii.

122. "Rapport du Comité du Théâtre Français sur *Hernani*, drame en cinq actes et en vers, signé par MM. Brisant, Chéron, Laya et Sauvo," dated 23 October 1829, cited from Hugo, *Cromwell – Hernani*, 714.

123. Entry dated 5 March 1830 in Joanny's journal, cited from Hugo, *Cromwell – Hernani*, 728.

124. *Le Corsaire* (13 March 1830), cited in Allévy, *La mise en scène en France*, 96.

125. Véron, *Mémoires d'un bourgeois de Paris*, 3, 180.

126. In 1832 this same Duponchel, a longtime friend of Eugène Delacroix, would recommend that the painter accompany the comte de Mornay to Morocco (see Chapter Five).

127. Allévy, *La mise en scène en France*, 54.

128. Levinson, *Marie Taglioni*, 40.

129. Note from Meyerbeer to Véron cited in Barbier, *À l'Opéra au temps de Rossini et de Balzac*, 104.

130. Cited by Pressouyre, "Les spectacles parisiens et la redécouverte du Moyen-Âge," 129.

131. Letter dated 12 December 1831 from Chopin to Titus Woyciechowski, reprinted in Chopin, *Correspondance*, 1, 45–46.

132. *Le Constitutionnel* (28 July 1827), cited in Levinson, *Marie Taglioni*, 21.

133. *Le Constitutionnel* (13 August 1827), cited in Levinson, *Marie Taglioni*, 22-23.

134. Rosen, *The Romantic Generation*, 492.

135. Bernstein, *Virtuosity*, 11.

136. Ibid., 11–12.

137. Levinson, *Marie Taglioni*, 46.

138. Ibid., 42.

139. Ortigue, *Le balcon de l'Opéra*, 262–63.

140. Cited in Courcy, *Paganini*, 2, 15.

141. Cited in ibid., 15. For a gloss on the satanic aspects of Paganini's persona, many related to imagery of the cholera epidemic, see Athanassoglou-Kallmyer, "Blemished Physiologies."

142. Paganini's letter to the editor was published in *L'Artiste*, 1 (1831): 159–60. He sent an almost identical version of the same letter to the *Revue Musicale*, where it was published on 21 April 1831.

143. *L'Artiste*, 1, (1831): 160–61.

144. Ibid.

145. Letter dated 22 September 1819 from Delacroix to Jean-Baptiste Pierret, reprinted in Delacroix, *Correspondance générale*, 1, 54.

146. Walker, "Liszt's Musical Background," 45.

147. Heine, "Über die französische Bühne," 301.

148. Letter dated 12 April 1838, cited in Litzmann, *Clara Schumann: Ein Künstlerleben*, 1, 199.

149. Impressions of a concert played by Liszt in Hamburg during 1840, cited from Andersen, *A Visit to Germany*, 34–35.

150. Marrinan, "Picasso as an 'Ingres' young Cubist," 756–63. Among twentieth-century artists, Picasso most frequently employed this kind of split face/head, as in his *Studio with Plaster Head* of 1925 or the famous *Girl before a Mirror* of 1932 (both in the collection of The Museum of Modern Art, New York).

151. Gautier, "Salon de 1840," *La Presse* (20 March 1840), cited in Paris, *Les années romantiques*, 414.

152. Benjamin, "The Work of Art in the Age of Mechanical Reproduction," 231.

153. Heine, *Lutèce* (20 Mars 1843), 305.

154. Ibid.

155. Bernstein, *Virtuosity*, 79.

156. Consider these numbers: on 1 June 1826 Talma played in *Léonidas* to a full house and box office receipts of 2,657 francs; the next night was *Iphigenia* without Talma and receipts of 245 francs; on 3 June Talma returned to the stage in *Charles VI* and the box office reported 2,704 francs! (Cited from Collins, *Talma*, 364–65).

157. Letter dated 27 April 1830 from David d'Angers to Goethe, cited in Saint-Rémy-lès-Chevreuse, *Aux Grands Hommes*, 59.

158. All of David's medallions are now catalogued in Reinis, *The Portrait Medallions of David d'Angers*. The medallion of Mademoiselle Mars is no. 306 of the catalogue.

159. Entry in notebook seven used by David d'Angers in 1829–1830, reprinted in Bruel, *Les carnets de David d'Angers*, 1, 65.

160. Entry in notebook thirty-three used by David d'Angers in 1838, reprinted in Bruel, *Les carnets de David d'Angers*, 2, 32.

161. Cited in Reinis, *The Portrait Medallions of David d'Angers*, xxiv.

162. Entry in notebook nine used by David d'Angers in 1830, reprinted in Bruel, *Les carnets de David d'Angers*, 1, 91-92.

163. Trollope, *Paris and the Parisians in 1835*, 1, 13.

164. Entry in notebook nine used by David d'Angers in 1830, reprinted in Bruel, *Les carnets de David d'Angers*, 1, 85.

165. Entry in notebook seven used by David d'Angers in 1829–1830, reprinted in Bruel, *Les carnets de David d'Angers*, 1, 72.

166. Entry in notebook nine used by David d'Angers in 1830, reprinted in Bruel, *Les carnets de David d'Angers*, 1, 89.

167. Entry in notebook seventeen used by David d'Angers in 1831–1832, reprinted in Bruel, *Les carnets de David d'Angers*, 1, 199.

168. Entry in notebook three used by David d'Angers in 1828, reprinted in Bruel, *Les carnets de David d'Angers*, 1, 30.

169. Letter dated 28 December 1863 from Emilie David to the comte de Las Cases, cited in de Caso, *David d'Angers: Sculptural Communication*, 8.

Notes to Chapter 7

1. Letters dated 1 April and 6 April 1810 from Charles de Clary-Aldringen to his mother, reprinted in Clary-Aldringen, *Trois mois à Paris*, 54 and 102.

2. Letter dated 9 April 1810 from Clary-Aldringen to his mother, reprinted in Clary-Aldringen, *Trois mois à Paris*, 112.

3. Bernard, *A Tour through some parts of France*, 58.

4. Letter dated 3 December 1801, cited in Anonymous, *Paris as it was*, 1, 305.

5. Bonaparte, *Correspondance de Napoléon*, 10, no. 8405, memo dated 9 March 1805 from Napoléon to Jean-Baptiste Nompère de Champagny, Minister of the Interior.

6. Scott, *A Visit to Paris in 1814*, 173–74.

7. Chabrol, *Recherches statistiques sur la ville de Paris*, 2, 16, cited in Lanzac de Laborie, *Paris sous Napoléon*, 2, 97.

8. Trollope, *Paris and the Parisians*, 1, 243–44.

9. Ibid. 81.

10. "Le courrier de Paris, 11 April 1840," reprinted in Girardin, *Lettres parisiennes du vicomte de Launay*, 1, 655–56.

11. Poumiès de la Siboutie, *Souvenirs d'un médecin de Paris*, 82; Lanzac de Laborie, *Paris sous Napoléon*, 2, 105.

12. Siegfried, *The Art of Louis-Léopold Boilly*, 89.

13. The passage Feydeau, opened in 1791 near the present-day Bourse, also featured a roof inset with panes of glass. It was destroyed in 1824 when a street perpendicular to the main facade of the Bourse was cut through the area (see Chapter Three).

14. Anonymous, *Paris as it was*, 1, 193.

15. Villiers, *Manuel de voyageur à Paris*, 148.

16. Anonymous, *Paris as it was*, 1, 201.

17. Ibid., 202.

18. Lemoine, *Les passages couverts en France*, 15.

19. Pinkerton, *Recollections of Paris*, 1, 523.

20. Collin de Plancy, *Voyages de Paul Béranger dans Paris*, 1, 279.

21. Montigny, "Le passage des Panoramas," in *Le provincial à Paris*, 1, 158–72.

22. Ibid., 166–67.

23. Gall, *Paris und seine Salons*, 2, 22–23.

24. Benjamin, *The Arcades Project*, 42.

25. The classic study of the flâneur is Walter Benjamin's chapter in *Charles Baudelaire: A Lyric Poet in the Era of High Capitalism*, 35–66. See also Burton, *The Flâneur and His City*; Ferguson, *Paris as Revolution*; Frisby, "The Flâneur in Social Theory."

26. Lacroix, "Le flâneur," 65–66.

27. Balzac, *Physiologie du mariage*, 903.

28. Wirth, "Urbanism as a Way of Life," 55.

29. My gloss on Benjamin's account of the flâneur is clearly indebted to Guy Debord, *The Society of the Spectacle*, especially 39. Debord writes that "the individual who in the service of the spectacle is placed in stardom's spotlight is in fact the opposite of an individual, and as clearly the enemy of the individual in himself as of the individual in others. In entering the spectacle as a model to be identified with, he renounces all autonomy in order himself to identify with the general law of obedience to the course of things." Debord's comment is germane to any consideration of why the flâneur emerged as a figure of such great interest in the 1820s.

30. Pain and Costa de Beauregard, *Nouveaux Tableaux de Paris*, 1, 36.

31. Ibid.

32. Béraud and Dufey, *Dictionnaire historique de Paris*, 2, 696.

33. Caillot, *Mémoires pour servir à l'histoire des moeurs et usages des Français*, 2, 219–20.

34. Gutzkow, *Briefe aus Paris*, 1, 225.

35. Luchet, "Les Passages," 112.

36. Mercier, *Le Nouveau Paris*, 381.

37. Heine, *Lutèce* (11 December 1841), 208–9.

38. Raucourt, *L'époque sans nom*, 2, 141–42.

39. Lemoine, *Les passages couverts en France*, 55.

40. Article from *Le Constitutionnel*, cited in *Le Moniteur universel*, no. 251 (7 September 1824): 1221.

41. Figures taken from an 1829 report published in *Recherches statistiques sur la Ville de Paris et le département de la Seine*, cited in Pronteau, "Construction et Aménagement des Nouveaux Quartiers de Paris," 8, note 4.

42. Martin-Fugier, *La vie élégante*, 109.

43. Caillot, *Mémoires pour servir à l'histoire des moeurs et usages des Français*, 1, 383.

44. Ibid., 385–86.

45. Report dated 24 August 1822 from *Budget pour la Ville de Paris pour 1822*, cited in Pronteau, "Construction et Aménagement des Nouveaux Quartiers de Paris," 9.

46. Report dated 15 July 1825 from *Budget pour la Ville de Paris pour 1826*, cited in Pronteau, "Construction et Aménagement des Nouveaux Quartiers de Paris," 16.

47. Royal ordonnance of 27 November 1822, cited in Pronteau, "Construction et Aménagement des Nouveaux Quartiers de Paris," 21.

48. Rouleau, *Le tracé des rues de Paris*, 11.

49. Ibid., 13.

50. Wirth, "Urbanism as a Way of Life," 55.

51. Thinking about the city as an interconnected, organic whole was already ingrained in much urban theory of the eighteenth century: see Papayanis, *Planning Paris before Haussmann*, 13–61.

52. Loyer, *Paris Nineteenth Century*, 73.

53. Théophile Gautier, "L'église de Saint-Vincent-de-Paul," *La Presse* (3 November 1844), reprinted in Gautier, *Paris et les Parisiens*, 105–8 (citation 107).

54. Donald Schneider suggests that the "dramatic, though not entirely Baroque conception" of the siting "is the fruit of Hittorff's training in ceremonial décor and theater design" (Schneider, *Hittorff*, 1, 315).

55. "Barely into the street, we had before us the Piazza di Spagna, and with it the fountain with its little boat, the extraordinary play of water, the ramps, terraces, and steps leading to Trinità dei Monti," exclaimed Hittorff in a letter dated 31 January 1823 to Joseph Lecointe, cited in Hammer, *Jakob Ignaz Hittorff*, 155–56.

56. Hittorff, "De l'architecture chez les grecs, ou restitution complète du temple d'Empédocle dans l'acropole de Sélinonte," 272. Some years later, in the full publication of his Sicilian findings, Hittorff dared to conclude: "One generally accepts that the Doric order gave birth to the Ionic order; however, the Ionic order at Silenus counters this theory; its capital, which brings to mind a wooden support with a large span, created for utilitarian reasons, bears little resemblance to a modified Doric capital" (Hittorff, *Restitution du Temple d'Empédocle à Sélinonte*, 1, 442 note 1).

57. Hittorff, "Considérations sur l'église de la Madeleine," 356.

58. Papayanis, *Planning Paris before Haussmann*, chaps. 2–4.

59. Meynadier, *Paris sous le point de vue pittoresque et monumental*, 1 and 4.

60. Loyer, *Paris Nineteenth Century*, 91.

61. Ibid., 94.

62. Théophile Gautier, "Monographie du bourgeois parisien," *Revue du XIXe Siècle* (25 September and 2 October 1836), reprinted in Gautier, *Paris et les Parisiens*, 441–53 (citation 444).

63. Loyer, *Paris Nineteenth Century*, 96.

64. Baudelaire, *Le Salon de 1846*, 180–81.

65. Sennett, *The Fall of Public Man*, 159.

66. Ibid., 167–68.

67. Ibid., 166–67.

68. Alhoy, *Physiologie de la Lorette*, 101–2. Also see Paris, Musée Renan-Scheffer, *La Nouvelle Athènes*, 43–45, and Dumas, "Lorettes," passim.

69. According to tradition, the term was first used by Nestor Roqueplan for "the pretty sinners who, around 1840, were almost all housed behind the church of Notre-Dame-de-Lorette, thanks to a special set of circumstances" (cited from Larousse, *Le Grand Dictionnaire universel du XIXe Siècle*, 14, 680). Roqueplan is also cited as inventor of the term in Alhoy, *Physiologie de la Lorette*, 15.

70. Rambuteau, *Mémoires du comte de Rambuteau*, 291.

71. Royal decree of 5 March 1838, cited in Pinon, "Quelques percées avant le Second Empire," 32.

72. Loyer, *Paris Nineteenth Century*, 117.

73. Heine, *Lutèce* (27 July 1840), 99.

74. Cited in Thureau-Dangin, *Histoire de la Monarchie de Juillet*, 4, 234.

75. Rambuteau, *Mémoires du comte de Rambuteau*, 368.

76. Vigier, *Nouvelle Histoire de Paris*, 242–43; Rouleau, *Paris: Histoire d'un espace*, 329–36.

77. Caillot, *Mémoires pour servir à l'histoire des moeurs et usages des Français*, 1, 357.

78. In a recent history of Parisian restaurants, Rebecca Spang dismisses the story of Boulanger as fitting "neatly with the late twentieth-century sense of France primarily as an exporter of savory luxury goods and tightly argued, hair-splitting *explications de texte*," but without basis in the archives. I am less ready than Spang to dispatch the story as pure construct, and find her counter-arguments no more convincing than the original tale (Spang, *Invention of the Restaurant*, 9–10).

79. Mésangère, *Le voyageur à Paris*, 3, 88.

80. Grimod de la Reynière, *Almanach des Gourmands*, 163–64.

81. Caillot, *Mémoires pour servir à l'histoire des moeurs et usages des Français*, 1, 358.

82. Ibid., 361.

83. Grimod de la Reynière, *Almanach des Gourmands*, 162.

84. Anonymous, *Paris as it was*, 1, 119.

85. Aron, *Le mangeur du XIXe siècle*, 44.

86. Langle, *Le petit monde des cafés et débits parisiens*, 30.

87. Nemeitz, *Séjour de Paris*, 1, 111.

88. Lavallée, *Lettres d'un mameluck*, 384.

89. Anonymous, *Paris as it was*, 2, 156.

90. Bernard, *A Tour through some parts of France*, 58.

91. Paul (1802), *Journal of a Party of Pleasure to Paris*, 41.

92. Ibid.

93. Ibid., 67.

94. Plumptre, *A Narrative*, 1, 80.

95. Carr, *The Stranger in France*, 138–39.

96. Ibid., 80–81.

97. See the discussion above and Sennett, *The Fall of Public Man*, 150–54.

98. Anonymous, *Paris as it was*, 2, 154–55.

99. Agulhon, *Le Cercle dans la France bourgeoise*, esp. 51–57; Vigier, *Nouvelle Histoire de Paris*, 504–6.

100. Agulhon, *Le Cercle dans la France bourgeoise*, 27.

101. Rémusat, *Mémoires de ma vie*, 3, 13–14.

102. Agulhon, *Le Cercle dans la France bourgeoise*, 29.

103. Tocqueville, *Souvenirs*, 107.

104. Wirth, "Urbanism as a Way of Life," 57.

105. *Journal des Débats* (17 December 1847), cited in Daumard, *La bourgeoisie parisienne*, 246.

106. Sennett, *The Fall of Public Man*, 140.

107. Ibid.

108. Aron, *Essai sur la sensibilité alimentaire*, 17.

109. Montigny, *Le provincial à Paris*, 2, 119.

110. Aron, *Essai sur la sensibilité alimentaire*, 45.

111. Pitte, *Gastronomie française*, 170.

112. Grimod de la Reynière, *Almanach des Gourmands*, 183; Fosca, *Histoire des Cafés de Paris*, 41.

113. Prudhomme, *Voyage descriptif et historique de Paris*, 2, 185–86.

114. Article by Jacques Boulenger, cited in Courtine, *La Vie Parisienne*, 158.

115. *Le Courrier Français* (18 August 1899), cited in Courtine, *La Vie Parisienne*, 176.

116. Prints such as these beg to be read with a certain indulgence, because publishers frequently reused visual materials and simply changed captions. For example, our illustration was published as a view of the interior of the Maison Dorée restaurant, but a virtually identical image appeared in 1846 as a view of the restaurant Les Trois Frères Provençaux, itself very close to a watercolor by Eugène Lami now in a private collection. See Paris, Musée du Louvre, *Marie d'Orléans*, fig. 54 and catalogue no. 66. The best one can say about this family resemblance is that certain standards for a "luxury" restaurant were fulfilled by the image—regardless of the locale actually depicted.

117. Flaubert, *L'éducation sentimentale*, 250.

118. Soulié, "Restaurants et Gargotes," 10.

119. Anonymous, "Paris-Restaurant," 84.

120. Sennett, *The Fall of Public Man*, 176.

121. Ibid., 173–74.

122. Ibid., 174.

123. Ibid., 212.

124. Jal, *L'ombre de Diderot*, 78–79.

125. Kératry, *Lettres sur le Salon de 1819*, 78.

126. Siegfried, *The Art of Louis-Léopold Boilly*, 133.

127. Bonnemaison, *Galerie de Son Altesse Royale Madame, Duchesse de Berry*, 2, n.p [Boilly].

128. Sennett, *The Fall of Public Man*, 206.

129. *A Loge on a Day of Free Entrance* is an oil on canvas now in the Musée Lambinet at Versailles, inventory 87.7.1 (32.5 × 41.7 cm). See Gendre, *Peintures du Musée Lambinet*, no. 46.

130. Siegfried, *The Art of Louis-Léopold Boilly*, 136–37.

131. Debord, *The Society of the Spectacle*, 19.

132. Siegfried, *The Art of Louis-Léopold Boilly*, 20. Boilly's autobiography is discussed idem, 18–20.

133. Le Men, "Daumier et le théâtre," 27.

134. Rosenthal, *Du Romantisme au Réalisme*, 355.

135. Cited in Vincent, *Daumier and His World*, 80.

136. Banville, *Mes Souvenirs*, 173–74.

137. *La Mode*, no. 8 (16 March 1846): 483, cited by Allemand-Cosneau, "Le Salon à Paris de 1815 à 1850," 116.

138. Crow, *Painters and Public Life in Eighteenth-Century Paris*, 79–133.

139. Planche, "Le Salon de 1847," 366.

140. Thoré, *Le Salon de 1847*, xi–xiii.

141. Baudelaire, *Le Salon de 1846*, 121.

142. Ibid., 142.

143. Champfleury, "Salon de 1846," 16.

144. Thoré, *Le Salon de 1847*, 28.

145. Delaunay, *Catalogue complète du Salon de 1847*, 17.

146. Debord, *The Society of the Spectacle*, 39.

147. Gautier, "Variétés: Salon de 1837," *La Presse* (18 March 1837): 2.

148. Letter dated 23 November 1840 from Chassériau to his brother Frédéric, cited in Chevillard, *Un peintre romantique*, 48.

149. Baudelaire, *Le Salon de 1845*, 142.

150. Camp, "Les Omnibus," 72.

151. Ibid., 73.

152. Marchant, *Le nouveau Conducteur de l'étranger à Paris en 1839*, 21–30.

153. Camp, "Les Omnibus," 74.

154. Huart, "Les voitures publiques," 178.

155. Burton, *The Flâneur and His City*, 42.

156. Anonymous, "Paris-en-Omnibus," 54–55.

157. Letter dated 31 March 1839 from Eduard Devrient, reprinted in Devrient, *Briefe aus Paris*, 61–62.

158. Loyer, *Paris Nineteenth Century*, 107.

159. Poumiès de la Siboutie, *Souvenirs d'un médecin de Paris*, 194.

Notes to Chapter 8

1. Balzac, *César Birotteau*, 59.

2. Ibid., 60

3. For an overview of magasins de nouveautés, see: Miller, *The Bon Marché*, 21–27; Hautecoeur, *Histoire de l'architecture classique en France*, 6; Perrot, *Les dessus et les dessous*, 93–99.

4. Anonymous, *Paris as it was*, 1, 201; Gutzkow, *Briefe aus Paris*, 1, 225.

5. Anonymous, "Magasins de nouveautés," 1, 241.

6. Soulié, "Marchands de nouveautés," 152.

7. Ibid., 154.

8. Ibid., 154–62.

9. Balzac, *Gaudissart II*, 849.

10. Marcel Gaillot points out that a sharp rise in advertisements was related to the steep increase of postage rates imposed by the government of Charles X in December 1827: newspapers made room for revenue-producing announcements in order to offset the costs without raising subscription rates beyond the budgets of most readers (Gaillot, *La publicité à travers les âges*, 92–97).

11. Advertisement for the magasin de nouveautés "La Ville de Paris," *La Gazette des Femmes*, 3, no. 123 (14 October 1843): 16.

12. Luchet, "Les Magasins de Paris," 245; also see Gaillot, *La publicité à travers les âges*, 97–111.

13. Luchet, "Les Magasins de Paris," 240.

14. Soulié, "Marchands de nouveautés," 151.

15. Ibid., 152.

16. Giedion, *Building in France*, 117.

17. Lemoine, *L'Architecture du Fer*, 43.

18. Eck, *Traité de l'application du Fer*, 2, 9.

19. Ibid., 7.

20. Blouet, *Supplément au Traité théorique*, 2, 21–22.

21. Eck, *Traité de l'application du Fer*, 2, 45.

22. Giedion, *Building in France*, 101.

23. Quatremère de Quincy, *Dictionnaire historique d'architecture*, 1, 460.

24. Gautier, "Feuilleton," *La Presse* (12 May 1837), reprinted in Gautier, *Paris et les Parisiens*, 55.

25. "A minister, an enlightened protector of the arts who gave a powerful boost to public works," wrote Rohault de Fleury about his charge from Adolphe Thiers, "wanted the greenhouses of the Museum to be worthy of the great institution of which they would be part, and would overlook nothing to achieve this end" (Rohault de Fleury, *Muséum d'histoire naturelle*, 4).

26. Ibid.

27. Ibid.

28. The range of iron components used in the greenhouses is detailed in ibid., plates VII and IX.

29. Théophile Gautier, "Feuilleton de La Presse: Exposition des manufactures nationales de Porcelaine, Vitraux et Émaux de Sèvres," *La Presse* (1 June 1850): 1.

30. Semper, "Der Wintergarten zu Paris," col. 520.

31. Ibid., col. 521.

32. Ibid., col. 522.

33. Ibid., col. 521; also see the discussion of Sokratis Georgiadis in his introduction to Giedion, *Building in France*, 7–9.

34. Semper, "Der Wintergarten zu Paris," col. 521.

35. Ibid.

36. Giedion, *Space, Time, and Architecture*, 221. Giedion's book was first published in 1941, but he had formulated his view about the importance of Labrouste's library as early as 1928: see Giedion, *Building in France*, 107–9.

37. Hermant, "La Bibliothèque Sainte-Geneviève," 130–31.

38. van Zanten, *Designing Paris*, 96.

39. Cited in ibid., 89.

40. Quatremère de Quincy, *Dictionnaire historique de l'architecture*, 1, 201.

41. Ibid., 202.

42. Ibid., 203.

43. Laborde, *De l'organisation des bibliothèques dans Paris*, 28.

44. Banville, "Le Quartier Latin et la Bibliothèque Sainte-Geneviève," 1358–59.

45. Henri Labrouste, "Bibliothèque de Sainte-Geneviève: Projet d'un bâtiment à ériger sur l'emplacement de l'ancienne prison de Montaigu et destiné à recevoir la bibliothèque de Ste. Geneviève," *Archives Nationales* F21 1362 (December 1839), fasc. 1 (cited in Levine, "The Book and Building," 155 and note 181).

46. Barrière, "Feuilleton: Embellissemens de Paris," 1.

47. The reading room has long since been altered. Our illustra-tion is a vintage photograph of the room's original layout.

48. Reynaud, *Traité d'architecture*, 2, 386–87.

49. Ibid., 1, 461–64 and plate 73.

50. Levine, "The Romantic Idea," 332.

51. Ibid., 328

52. Hermant, "La Bibliothèque Sainte-Geneviève," 129.

53. Barrière, "Feuilleton: Embellissemens de Paris," 1.

54. Victor Hugo, "Guerre aux démolisseurs! (1825)," 153. The passage is discussed in Levine, "The Book and the Building," 140. Levine's article is essential reading for any interpretation of Labrouste's decorative program for the Bibliothèque Sainte-Geneviève.

55. Levine, "The Book and the Building," 142–48.

56. Hugo, *Notre-Dame de Paris*, 142.

57. Ibid., 146.

58. Ibid., 148.

59. Ibid.

60. Ibid.

61. Ibid., 149.

62. Ibid., 149–50.

63. "Reliquât: Notre-Dame de Paris," Bibliothèque Nationale, MS n.a.fr 13378, no. 133/24, folio 424, reprinted in Hugo, *Notre-Dame de Paris – Les Travailleurs de la Mer*, 553.

64. Hugo, *Notre-Dame de Paris*, 151.

65. Letter dated 28 November 1838 from Auguste Bossel de Saint-Martin to Labrouste, MS 3911 (Paris: Bibliothèque Sainte-Geneviève), cited in Levine, "The Romantic Idea," 338 and note 36.

66. Levine, "The Romantic Idea," 338

67. Labrouste, "À M. le Directeur de la Revue d'Architecture," col. 383.

68. Barrière, "Feuilleton: Embellissemens de Paris," 1.

69. Hermant, "Bibliothèque Sainte-Geneviève," 130.

70. Banville, "Le Quartier Latin et la Bibliothèque Sainte-Geneviève," 1358.

71. Hugo, *Notre-Dame de Paris*, 151 and 153.

72. Ibid., 150.

73. Ibid., 149.

74. Labrouste, "À M. le Directeur de la Revue d'Architecture," col. 383; Levine, "The Book and the Building," 167; Hugo, *Notre-Dame de Paris*, 153.

75. O'Brien and Keyder, *Economic Growth in Britain and France*, 162.

76. Williams, *Dream Worlds*, 49–50.

77. Tristan, *Promenades dans Londres*, 267–68.

78. Pariset, *Manuel de la Maîtresse de Maison*, 22.

79. Burat, *Exposition de l'industrie française*, 2, 3.

80. Cited in the entry "Christofle" in Paris, *Un âge d'or des arts décoratifs*, 518, and Dion-Tenenbaum, "1844," 422.

81. The service was valued at more than 46,000 francs (*Archives Nationales*, O4 2239B).

82. Anonymous, "Economie domestique à l'usage des Femmes," 16.

83. Dion-Tenenbaum, "1834," 281, and Ingold, *Saint Louis*, 67–69.

84. Curtis, *Baccarat*, 53.

85. Cited in ibid., 55

86. Burat, *Exposition de l'industrie française*, 2, 18.

87. Cited in Curtis, *Baccarat*, 55.

88. Calot, Michon, and Angoulvent, *L'art du livre en France*, 148, and the discussion in Bassy, "Le texte et l'image."

89. Barbier, "L'industrialisation des techniques," 56, and Barbier, "Les innovations technologiques," 545–51.

90. Melot, "Le texte et l'image," 289.

91. Bellos, "La conjoncture de la production," 552–57. Similarly, Adhémar and Seguin note that the number of printed pages passed from about 47 million in 1814, to nearly 81 million by 1820, and to more than 144 million pages in 1826 (Adhémar and Seguin, *Le livre romantique*, 11 and 21).

92. Melot, "Le texte et l'image," 298.

93. Adhémar and Seguin, *Le Livre romantique*, 11.

94. Rosen and Zerner, *Romanticism and Realism*, 81–84.

95. Champfleury, *Les Vignettes romantiques*, 4.

96. Duplessis, "Les graveurs sur bois contemporains," 372.

97. Burat, *Exposition de l'industrie française*, 2, 3.

98. Charles Nodier, *Histoire du roi de Bohème et de ses sept châteaux* (Paris: Delangle, 1830).

99. Jeune, "Le Roi de Bohème et ses sept châteaux" (1980), 201.

100. Croy, "Les magasins pittoresques à deux sous," 281.

101. *Histoire de Gil Blas de Santillane* par Le Sage, vignettes par Jean Gigoux et "Notice sur Gil Blas" par Charles Nodier (Paris: Chez Paulin, 1835).

102. Brivois, *Bibliographie des ouvrages illustrés*, 257–58.

103. Curmer, *Note présenté*, 3 and 25.

104. Bernardin de Saint-Pierre, *Paul et Virginie* (1964), 101.

105. Cited from the prospectus for *Paul et Virginie* republished in Brivois, *Bibliographie des ouvrages illustrés*, 391.

106. The figures are cited in Brivois, *Bibliographie des ouvrages illustrés*, 395–96.

107. Reprinted in ibid., 394–95, and Vicaire, *Manuel de l'amateur de livres*, 7, cols. 58–59 (with several orthographic errors).

108. Emmanuel de Las Cases, *Le Mémorial de Sainte-Hélène*, suivi de Napoléon dans l'exil par MM. O'Meara et Antommarchi, et de l'Historique de la translation des restes mortels de l'Empereur Napoléon aux Invalides, 2 vols. (Paris: Ernest Bourdin, 1842).

109. "Prospectus" bound with the first volume of the 1842 edition of *Le Mémorial de Sainte-Hélène*, in the collection of the Bibliothèque Nationale de France, côte 4-Larrey-106(1).

110. Delacroix, "Charlet," 241.

111. Las Cases, *Le Mémorial de Sainte-Hélène* (1842), 182–83.

112. Janin, "Exposition des produits de l'industrie: Deuxième article," 36.

113. Janin, "Exposition des produits de l'industrie: Premier article," 22. Very similar enthusiasms are echoed by the anonymous author of "La *Vénus de Milo* et les réductions de M. Achille Collas," *L'Artiste*, 2e sér., 7 (1841): 159–61, which might also have been written by Jules Janin.

114. *Exposition des produits de l'industrie française en 1839: Rapport du Jury Central*, 3 vols. (Paris: L. Bouchard-Huzard, 1839), 3, 193–94; *Exposition des produits de l'industrie française en 1844: Rapport du Jury Central*, 3 vols. (Paris: Fain et Thunot, 1844), 3, 228–29.

115. Janin, "Exposition des produits de l'industrie: Premier article," 22.

116. Burat, *Exposition de l'industrie française*, 2, 27.

117. Benjamin, "The Work of Art," 220.

118. See the lithograph "Bronzes de Quesnel et C^{nie}" in Burat, *Exposition de l'industrie française*, 2, n.p.

119. Metman, "La petite sculpture," 206–7 and 200. Also see Bann, *Parallel Lines*, 35–37.

120. Ladet, "De la propriété en matière d'art," 71.

121. Vaunois, *De la notion du droit naturel*, 144.

122. Anonymous, "Beaux-Arts," *L'Artiste*, 2e sér., 7 (1841): 190.

123. For a description and schematic of Gavard's mechanical drawing device see Gavard, *Notice sur le Diagraphe*.

124. Anonymous, "Beaux-Arts," *L'Artiste*, 2e sér, 7 (1841): 190.

One finds similar suspicions repeated throughout the coverage of the legislative debate in the pages *L'Artiste* during 1841.

125. Ibid., 245.

126. Étienne Blanc, "À M. le Directeur de *l'Artiste*," *L'Artiste*, 2e sér., 7 (1841): 133.

127. Vaunois, *De la notion du droit naturel*, 294.

128. Lapauze, *Ingres*, 246, and Cohn, "Introduction," 20.

129. Laviron, "Exposition des produits de l'industrie," 266.

130. *Exposition des produits de l'industrie française en 1844: Rapport du jury central*, 3 vols. (Paris: Fain et Thunot, 1844), 3, 29–30.

131. Caso, "Serial Sculpture," 4.

132. Miel, *Essai sur les Beaux-Arts*, 420–21.

133. Ibid., 415.

134. Institut Royal de France, "Rapport sur la lithographie," 24.

135. Resseguier, "Moeurs: Un samedi au Louvre," 46.

136. Thiers, "De la lithographie," 48.

137. An example now belongs to the Musée Ingres in Montauban, inventory number *réserves* 110a (32.7 × 49.7 cm). It is reproduced and discussed in Rome, *Le Retour à Rome de Monsieur Ingres*, 265–67. Also see Bann, *Parallel Lines*, 66.

138. Montauban, Musée Ingres, inventory number 867.1197 (32.4 × 49.2 cm). Ingres's aphorism is cited in Delaborde, *Ingres*, 126. About Ingres's drawing for Sudré, see Schwarz, "Ingres Graveur," 337–40, Bann, *Parallel Lines*, 149–50, and Condon, "The Grande Odalisque."

139. Cohn, "Introduction," 20.

140. "That which withers in the age of mechanical reproduction is the aura of the work of art," remarks Benjamin; "this is a symptomatic process whose significance points beyond the realm of art. One might generalize by saying: the technique of reproduction detaches the reproduced object from the domain of tradition. By making many reproductions it substitutes a plurality of copies for a unique existence" (Benjamin, "The Work of Art," 221).

141. Twyman, *Lithography 1800–1850*, 121.

142. Anonymous, "Société d'encouragement pour la Gravure," 52.

143. Dupin, "Lithographie," 376–77.

144. Thiers, "De la lithographie," 46.

145. Ibid., 46–47.

146. Cited in Goldstein, *Censorship of Political Caricature*, 109–11.

147. Circular to prefects dated 8 September 1829 from the Minister of the Interior, cited in ibid., 3.

148. Y . . . , "De la facilité," 329.

149. C.V., "Gravure et Lithographie," 61.

150. Cited in Goldstein, *Censorship of Political Caricature*, 120.

151. *La Caricature*, no. 26 (28 April 1831): cols. 199–20.

152. Cuno, "The Business and Politics of Caricature," 102.

153. Philipon's drawing, "Croquades faites à l'audience du 14 novembre (Cour d'Assises)," appeared in *La Caricature*, no. 56 (22 December 1831), was reprinted in the issue of 26 January 1832, and reworked for *Le Charivari* in 1834.

154. Heine, "Französische Zustände: Artikel V," 122.

155. *La Caricature*, no. 90 (26 July 1832): cols. 715–16.

156. Ibid.

157. *La Caricature*, no. 84 (23 August 1832).

158. Le Men, "Ma muse, ta muse s'amuse," 67.

159. Benjamin, "The Work of Art," 225–26.

160. Ibid., 226.

161. Le Men, "Ma muse, ta muse s'amuse," 68–74.

162. *La Caricature*, no. 204 (2 October 1834), reprinted in Paris, *Daumier, 1808–1879*, 177.

163. Baudelaire, "Quelques caricaturistes français," 264.

164. "Événemens de Paris," *Le National de 1834* (15 April 1834): 1, and "Nouveaux détails sur la boucherie de la rue Transnonain," *Le National de 1834* (16 April 1834): 1.

165. *Journal de Paris*, no. 2868 (8 May 1834): 2. The letter from de Failly was originally addressed to the editor of *Le National de 1834*, who refused to print it. The *Journal de Paris* published the letter as the voice of "an officer of the 35th Regiment who indignantly dismisses the slanders of which his regiment has been victim," and the editors reproached *Le National* for its overtly partisan reporting of the episode. Naturally, *Le National* replied in print to this accusation: *Le National de 1834* (9 May 1834): 2.

166. *Journal de Paris*, no. 2868 (8 May 1834): 2.

167. Alexandre-Auguste Ledru-Rollin, *Mémoire sur les événements de la Rue Transnonain*, dans les journées des 13 et 14 avril 1834 (Paris: Guillaumin, 1834).

168. Ibid., 17–18.

169. *Le Charivari*, 3e année, no. 215 (4 August 1834).

170. Ibid., no. 220 (18 August 1834).

171. Ledru-Rollin, *Mémoire sur les événements de la Rue Transnonain*, 22–23.

172. Box advertisement in *Le Charivari*, 4e année, no. 243 (31 August 1835): col. 7.

173. Jean-Charles Persil, Minister of Justice, cited in Goldstein, *Censorship of Political Caricature*, 2.

174. *Archives Nationales*, F18 2342, circulars to prefects of the departments dated 23 September, 7 October, and 9 October 1835, cited in Goldstein, *Censorship of Political Caricature*, 153.

175. "Aux abonnés du *Charivari* et de la *Caricature*," *Le Charivari*, 4e année, no. 235 (23 August 1835).

176. Anonymous, "La Daguerréotype," 193.

177. Joseph-Louis Gay-Lussac, "Rapport fait à la Chambre des Pairs, séance du 30 Juillet 1839," reprinted in Daguerre, *Historique et Description*, 31–35 (citation is 35).

178. Two recent and controversial studies of these and related practices are Hockney, *Secret Knowledge*, and Steadman, *Vermeer's Camera*. Hockney's book, in particular, generated considerable discussion at the time of its publication.

179. Letter dated 2 February 1827 from Nicéphore Niépce to the engraver Augustin-François Lemaître, reprinted in Rouillé, *La Photographie en France*, 25–28 (citation is 27). On the relationship between Niépce, Lemaître, and Daguerre, see Bann, *Parallel Lines*, 89–103.

180. Letter dated 2 February 1827 from Nicéphore Niépce to Augustin-François Lemaître, reprinted in Rouillé, *La Photographie en France*, 25–28 (citation is 28).

181. "Traité provisoire" between Niépce and Daguerre, dated 14 December 1829, reprinted in Rouillé, *La Photographie en France*, 29–30.

182. Letters dated 24 June 1831, 8 November 1831, 29 January 1832, and 3 March 1832 from Niépce to Daguerre, reprinted in Daguerre, *Historique et Description*, 53–56.

183. Daguerre himself was never very clear on how these discoveries came to pass, and some photographic historians dismiss the story of the cupboard as a fable: Potonniée, *Histoire de la découverte*, 170; Gernsheim and Gernsheim, *Daguerre*, 71–72; Gernsheim, *Origins of Photography*, 42.

184. About the middle of March 1839, after Sir John Herschel reported to the Royal Society of London on the superior fixing powers of hyposulfite of soda, Daguerre switched from kitchen salt to this more effective solution (Potonniée, *Histoire de la découverte*, 170–72).

185. "Traité définitif" between Isidore Niépce and Daguerre,

dated 13 June 1837, reprinted in Niépce, *Historique de la découverte improprement nommé Daguerréotype*, 52–54.

186. Letter dated 1 November 1837 from Isidor Niépce to Daguerre, reprinted in Daguerre, *Historique et Description*, 56.

187. Gernsheim and Gernsheim, *Daguerre*, 79–81, reproduces a translation of Daguerre's advertising flyer, of which only one surviving copy is known to exist (today in the collection of the George Eastman House in Rochester, New York). This apparently unique example is reproduced in Paris, *Paris et le daguerréotype*, 22.

188. Arago, "Séance du lundi 7 janvier 1839," 6.

189. Girardin, "12 Janvier 1839," in *Lettres parisiennes du vicomte de Launay*, 1, 383–90 (citation is 389).

190. Anonymous, "Découverte faite par M. Daguerre," *Journal des Artistes*, 13e année, 1, no. 2 (12 January 1839): 21–22.

191. "Feuilleton: Découverte de M. Daguerre," *Le Commerce*, no. 13 (13 January 1839): 1

192. Samuel F. B. Morse, *New York Observer* (20 April 1839), reprinted in Gernsheim and Gernsheim, *Daguerre*, 89–90.

193. Letter dated 25 February 1839 from Alexander von Humboldt to Carl Gustav Carus, reprinted in Recht, *La Lettre de Humboldt*, 9–12.

194. Janin, "Le Daguerotype," 148.

195. Ibid., 146.

196. Samuel F. B. Morse, *New York Observer* (20 April 1839), reprinted in Gernsheim and Gernsheim, *Daguerre*, 89–90.

197. Review signed Karl Preyßner, *Allgemeinen Theaterzeitung* (31 August 1839), reprinted in Frank, *Vom Zauber alter Licht-Bilder*, 24–25 and 28 (citations are 25 and 28).

198. Janin, "Le Daguerotype," 148.

199. Rice, *Parisian Views*, 7 and 10.

200. Rouillé, *L'Empire de la photographie*, 37–42 and 46–48.

201. "Projet de Loi," reprinted in Daguerre, *Histoire et Description*, 5.

202. Arago, "Rapport fait à la Chambre des Députés."

203. Arago cited only fragments of the memo from Delaroche in his speech, but the whole text is reprinted and translated in Buerger, *French Daguerreotypes*, 7.

204. Gay-Lussac, "Rapport fait à la Chambre des Pairs."

205. Anonymous, "Procédé du Dagerrotype," 113–14.

206. "But you will see that M. Daguerre would not dare to demonstrate by himself this admirable process that he has handed

over to France," reported Jules Janin. "Once again, the inventor of the daguerreotype placed himself in the learned and kindly shadow of M. Arago who, in this whole business, has served as tutor and godfather" (Jules Janin, "La Description du Daguérotype," 277).

207. Arago, "Séance du lundi 19 août 1839."

208. Croy, "Le Daguerrotype," 410–11.

209. Anonymous, "Procédé du Dagerotype," 114.

210. Janin, "La Description du Daguérotype," 282.

211. Janin, "Le Daguérotype: Nouvelle Expérience," 2.

212. "Daguerréotypomanie," *La Caricature* (8 December 1839). Maurisset's image has been much discussed in the literature on early photography, beginning with Potonniée, *Histoire de la découverte*, 190. For a detailed analysis of Maurisset's lithograph see Ewer, "Théodore Maurisset's 'Fantaisies.'" The long commentary originally published by *La Caricature* is reprinted in Paris, *Paris et le daguerréotype*, 11.

213. According to James Cuno, between 1835 and 1841 the Maison Aubert alone published thirty-two different *physiologies* comprising about 160,000 volumes, approximately three-quarters of the more than 220,000 circulating in Paris at the time (Cuno, "The Business and Politics of Caricature," 111, and Lhéritier, "Les Physiologies"). Nathalie Preiss has described the period 1840–1845 as "the physiological epidemic," estimating that more than 325,000 examples were printed in Paris alone (Preiss, *Les Physiologies en France*, 147–55).

214. Mayer and Pierson, *La Photographie considérée comme art et comme industrie*, 45–46.

215. Arago, "Rapport fait à la Chambre des Députés," 29.

216. Gay-Lussac, "Rapport fait à la Chambre des Pairs," 33.

217. Janin, "Le Daguerotype," 148.

218. Rouillé, *L'Empire de la photographie* 39.

219. Contrary to what many modern historians have written, the authors do not claim to have taken personally fifteen hundred portraits: see Gaudin and Lerebours, *Derniers perfectionnements* (1841), 42–43.

220. Gaudin and Lerebours, *Derniers perfectionnements* (1842), 52.

221. Ibid.

222. Gaudin, "Séance du lundi 11 octobre 1841."

223. Anonymous, "Des nouveaux procédés de la photographie," 245.

224. "Fabricants de portraits au daguerréotype," reprinted with analysis in Rouillé, *La Photographie en France*, 82-86.

225. Anonymous, "Rapport du Jury Central," (1851), 10.

226. Mayer and Pierson, *La Photographie considérée comme art et comme industrie*, 83.

227. "Supposing a well set up factory," wrote Blanquart-Evrard in 1851, "one model can furnish two to three hundred prints a day, and one could very easily clear five to six thousand prints by working thirty models a day" ("Lettre de M. Blanquart-Evrard," 37).

228. Blanquart-Evrard, *Traité de photographie sur papier*.

229. Wey, "Publications héliographiques," 99.

230. Marx, *Le Dix-huit Brumaire*, 136.

Notes to Epilogue

1. Hugo, *Napoléon-le-Petit*, 178.

2. Hugo, "Le 2 décembre 1851," 300.

3. Hugo, *Histoire d'un Crime*, 371.

4. Hugo, "Victor Hugo à ses concitoyens, 26 mai 1848," 107.

5. Hugo, "Séance des cinq associations d'art et d'industrie, 29 mai 1848," 117.

6. Cited in Pierre, *Histoire de la République de 1848*, 1, 350.

7. Hugo, "Louis Bonaparte Incognito," 414. The editors of Hugo's complete works published these fragments without a date, but Henri Guillemin proposes dating them to the period of Bonaparte's return to Paris. See Guillemin, *Victor Hugo: Souvenirs personnels*, 104–6.

8. Hugo, "Assemblée Nationale," 388.

9. Hugo, "À la Colonne" in *Les Chants du crépuscule*, 194.

10. Decaux, *Victor Hugo*, 704.

11. Hugo, *Histoire d'un Crime*, 1, 274.

12. Hugo, "La famille Bonaparte, 14 juin 1847," 92.

13. *Revue de l'Empire* (1842), cited in Bluche, *Bonapartisme*, 253.

14. Fourcaud, *Rude*, 274.

15. Cited in ibid., 292.

16. Bluche, *Bonapartisme*, 225.

17. Thoré, *Salon de 1846*, 196.

18. Hugo, "À la Colonne" in *Les Chants du crépuscule*, 194.

19. Cited in Fourcaud, *Rude*, 302.

20. Cited in ibid., 303.

21. *Spectateur de la Côte-d'Or* (25 September 1847), cited in Fourcaud, *Rude*, 305.

22. Juin, *Victor Hugo*, 2, 120–21.

23. *L'Événement* (27 October 1848): 1.

24. *L'Événement* (28 October 1848): 1.

25. "Louis-Napoléon Bonaparte à ses concitoyens," *L'Événement* (28 November 1848): 1.

26. *L'Événement* (28 November 1848): 1.

27. *L'Événement* (2 December 1848): 1.

28. Hugo, "Assemblée Nationale," 393–94.

29. "Au Peuple!" *L'Événement* (10 December 1848): 1.

30. "L'élection du président de la République," *L'Événement* (13 December 1848): 1.

31. Letter from Lamartine to the comte de Circourt, published in Lamartine, *Correspondance*, 4, 287, no. DCCCCXXXVI.

32. Letter dated 4 November 1848 from Lamartine to Monsieur Dargaud, published in Lamartine, *Correspondance*, 4, 291–92, no. DCCCCXLI.

33. Letter from Lamartine to the comtesse d'Agoult, published in Lamartine, *Correspondance*, 4, 297–98, no. DCCCCXLVII.

34. Hugo, "Chez Lamartine," 421.

35. Paris, Musée du Louvre, inventory number RF-5222 (31.5 × 22.7 cm), reproduced in Prat, *Dessins de Théodore Chassériau*, 1, 438–39, no. 1071.

36. Paris, Musée du Louvre, inventory number RF-24388 (37 × 22.8 cm), reproduced in Prat, *Dessins de Théodore Chassériau*, 1, 77, no. 52.

37. Sabatier-Ungher, *Salon de 1851*, 41.

38. A drawing in the Louvre, inventory number RF-25970 (47.5 × 30.8 cm), seems to have been a working study for the painting that disappeared in World War II. Reproduced in Prat, *Dessins de Théodore Chassériau*, 1, 266, no. 572.

39. The two Sapphos were frequently blurred or confused by writers of the time, witness Émile Deschanel's "Études sur l'Antiquité: Sappho et les Lesbiennes" of 1847. See also Guégan, "Orgie Noire."

40. Lamartine, "Sapho: Élégie Antique," in *Oeuvres Poétiques Complètes*, 113–18.

41. Ibid., 115.

42. Ibid., 117.

43. Hugo, "Notes sur la situation," 8–9.

44. Ibid., 22–23.

45. Entry dated 23 April 1849 in Delacroix, *Journal*, 1, 290.

46. Entry dated 14 February 1849 in ibid., 340.

47. Hugo opens *Napoléon-le-Petit* with the ceremony of Louis-Napoléon's oath before the National Assembly on 20 December 1848; breaking that oath is the continuous leitmotif of Hugo's searing condemnation of the coup-d'état. See Hugo, *Napoléon-le-Petit*, 5–9.

48. Writing to Madame de Flahault on 23 February 1851, Auguste de Morny was blunt: "You must now understand what chance the President has got of being re-elected. In my opinion he has none, and the solution of the matter must be extra-legal. . . . So, either the Assembly must declare by a majority of three-quarters of its members that the Constitution can be revised, or else there will be a fight—and one side or the other must be beaten. . . . My idea is that the revision having been refused, the Assembly will find itself so unpopular that it will have to disappear—followed by the curses of the country. But in any case it must have a violent ending" (Lansdowne, *Secret of the Coup d'État*, 125–26).

49. Hugo, "Révision de la Constitution," 257.

50. Hugo, "Le Premier Dîner," 413.

51. Hugo, "Au moment de rentrer en France," 5. This poem, inserted as preface to the 1870 edition of *Les Châtiments*, was written by Hugo in Brussels, six days before his return to Paris.

Bibliography

In the interest of economy and ease of use, discursive comments and references to secondary literature have been kept to a minimum in the Notes. Reviews published in contemporary serials are cited fully in the Notes. All the other works consulted when preparing the text are listed in the Bibliography. Numbers in brackets after each entry signal the chapter or chapters in which the citation has played an especially important role in shaping the present exposition.

Anonymous. "Des nouveaux procédés de la photographie." *L'Artiste*, 2e sér., 8 (1841): 244–45. [08]

———. *Description exacte et détaillée de la colonne de Juillet*. Paris: Veuve Demoraine & Bonequin, 1841. [03]

———. *Détails curieux sur les fêtes qui vont avoir lieu à l'Arc de Triomphe de la Barrière de l'Étoile, les 28 et 29 juillet 1836*. Paris: Imprimerie de Chassaignon, 1836. [03]

———. "Économie domestique à l'usage des Femmes: Les services de table dorés." *La Gazette des Femmes* 4 (March 1845): 15–16. [08]

———. *Examen du Salon de 1827* (Novembre et Décembre), seconde partie. Paris: chez Roret, 1828. [05]

———. "Juridiction Artistique." *Journal des Artistes*, 17e année, 2 (17 September 1843): 184–85. [08]

———. "La Daguerréotype." In *La Grande Ville: Nouveau tableau de Paris*. 2 vols. Paris: Marescq, 1844, 1: 193–204. [08]

———. *Le nouvel Observateur au Musée Napoléon ou Réflexions d'un amateur sur l'exposition de l'an 1801*. Paris: Aubry, 1808. [01]

———. *Lettres impartiales sur les expositions de l'an XIII*. Paris: BnF, Collection Deloynes, 31, no. 873. [01]

———. "Lithographie à la Manière Noire." *L'Artiste* 2 (1831): 213–14. [06]

———. "Magasins de nouveautés." In *La Grande Ville: Nouveau tableau de Paris*. 2 vols. Paris: Marescq, 1844, 1: 241–50. [08]

———. "Monument de Juillet." *L'Artiste* 6 (1833): 49–50. [03]

———. *Paris as it was and as it is*; or a Sketch of the French Capital in a series of letters written by an English Traveller during the years 1801–1802 to a Friend in London. 2 vols. London: C & R Baldwin, 1803. [03] [07] [08]

———. "Paris-en-Omnibus." In *Les Petits-Paris*, par les auteurs des Mémoires de Bilboquet. 5 vols. Paris: Alphonse Taride, 1854–1855, 3, fasc. 13. [07]

———. "Paris-Restaurant." In *Les Petits-Paris*, par les auteurs des Mémoires de Bilboquet. 5 vols. Paris: Alphonse Taride, 1854–1855, 1, fasc. 5. [07]

———. "Procédé du Dagerrotype." *Journal des Artistes*, 13e année, 2 (25 August 1839): 113–17. [08]

———. "Rapport du Jury Central de l'Exposition des produits de l'industrie française." *La Lumière* 1 (23 February 1851): 9–10. [08]

———. *Revue des productions les plus remarquables de nos Beaux-Arts exposées au Salon du Louvre en 1824, par une société de gens de lettres et d'artistes*. Paris: Sétier-Delaunay, 1824. [05]

———. "Société d'encouragement pour la Gravure." *Journal des Artistes*, 4e année, 1 (17 January 1830): 52–53. [08]

Adhémar, Jean and Jean-Pierre Seguin. *Le livre romantique*. Paris: Éditions du Chêne, 1968. [08]

Agoult, Marie d', Franz Liszt, and Henri Lehman. *Une Correspondance romantique: Madame d'Agoult, Liszt, Henri Lehman*. Ed. Solange Joubert. Paris: Flammarion, 1947. [06]

Agulhon, Maurice. *Le Cercle dans la France bourgeoise 1810–1848*. Paris: Armand Colin, 1977. [07]

———. "Fêtes spontanées et fêtes organisées à Paris en 1848." In *Fêtes de la Révolution*. Eds. Jean Ehrard and Paul Viallaneix. Paris: Société des études robespierristes, 1977: 243–77. [03]

———. "Imagerie civique et décor urbain." In *Histoire vagabonde*. 2 vols. Paris: Gallimard, 1988, 1: 101–36. [02]

———. *Marianne au combat: L'imagerie et la symbolique républicaine de 1789 à 1880*. Paris: Flammarion, 1979. [01] [03]

———. "Paris: La traversée d'est en ouest." In *Les Lieux de Mémoire*, sous la direction de Pierre Nora. 3 vols. Paris: Gallimard-Quarto, 1997, 3: 4589–4622. [03]

Alhoy, Maurice. *Physiologie de la Lorette*. Paris: Aubert & Lavigne, n.d. [1841]. [07]

Allemand-Cosneau, Claude. "Le Salon à Paris de 1815 à 1850." In Paris, *Les années romantiques*, 106–27. [07]

Allen, James Smith. *Popular French Romanticism: Authors, Readers, and Books in the 19th Century*. Syracuse NY: Syracuse University, 1981. [08]

Allévy, Marie-Antoinette. *La mise en scène en France dans la première moitié du dix-neuvième siècle*. Paris: E. Droz, 1938. [06]

Amaury-Duval, Eugène-Emmanuel. *L'Atelier d'Ingres*. Paris: Charpentier, 1878. Reprint. Paris: Bibliothèque Dionysienne–Éditions G. Crès, 1924. [05] [06]

Andersen, Hans Christian. *A Visit to Germany, Italy, and Malta, 1840–1841*. Trans. Grace Thornton. London: Peter Owen, 1985. [06]

Arago, François. "Rapport fait à la Chambre des Députés, séance du 3 Juillet 1839." Reprinted in Daguerre, *Histoire et Description*: 9–29. [08]

———. "Séance du lundi 7 janvier 1839: Fixation des images qui se forment au foyer d'une chambre obscure." *Comptes rendus des séances de l'Académie des sciences* 8 (January–June 1839): 4–7. [08]

———. "Séance du lundi 19 août 1839: Le Daguerréotype." *Comptes rendus des séances de l'Académie des sciences* 9 (July–December 1839): 250–67. [08]

Ariès, Philippe. *L'homme devant la mort*. 2 vols. Paris: Seuil, 1977. [03]

Arizzoli-Clémentel, Pierre. "Les soieries de Lyon sous la Restauration et la Monarchie de Juillet." In Paris, Galeries nationales du Grand Palais, *Un âge d'or des arts décoratifs*: 22–23. [04]

Arnaud, René. *Le 2 décembre*. Paris: Hachette, 1967. [EP]

Aron, Jean-Paul. *Essai sur la sensibilité alimentaire à Paris au 19e siècle*. Paris: Armand Colin, 1967. [07]

———. *Le mangeur du XIXe siècle*. Paris: Robert Laffont, 1973. [07]

Athanassoglou-Kallmyer, Nina. "Blemished Physiologies: Delacroix, Paganini, and the Cholera Epidemic of 1832." *Art Bulletin* 83 (December 2001): 685–710. [06]

———. *French Images from the Greek War of Independence, 1821–1830*. New Haven: Yale University, 1989. [05] [06]

Aubry, Octave. *Le Second Empire*. Paris: Fayard, 1938. [02]

Babeau, Albert. *Les Anglais en France après la Paix d'Amiens*. Paris: Plon, Nourrit, et Cie, 1898. [03]

Baldensperger, Fernand. *Le Mouvement des idées dans l'émigration française*. 2 vols. Paris: Librairie Plon, 1924. [01]

Baltimore, Walters Art Gallery. *Untamed: The Art of Antoine-Louis Barye*, exhibition catalogue. Eds. William R. Johnston and Simon Kelly. Baltimore: The Walters Art Gallery, 2006. [05]

Balzac, Honoré de. *César Birotteau*. In *La Comédie humaine*. 12 vols. Ed. Pierre-Georges Castex. Paris: Gallimard-Pléaide, 1976–1981, 6: 35–312. [08]

———. *Gaudissart II*. In *La Comédie humaine*. 12 vols. Ed. Pierre-Georges Castex. Paris: Gallimard-Pléaide, 1976–1981, 7: 847–56. [08]

———. *Illusions perdues*. Paris: Gallimard-Folio, 1974. [05] [06]

———. *La Peau de chagrin*. Ed. and Intro. Madeleine Ambrière. Paris: Imprimerie Nationale, 1982. [04]

———. *Lettres à l'Étrangère*. 4 vols. Paris: Calmann-Lévy, 1899. [06]

———. *Lettres à Mme Hanska*. 4 vols. Ed. Roger Pierrot. Paris: Les éditions du Delta, 1967–1971. [06]

———. *Physiologie du mariage*. In *La Comédie Humaine*. 12 vols. Ed. Pierre-Georges Castex. Paris: Gallimard-Pléaide, 1976–1981, 11: 903–1205. [07]

Bann, Stephen. "Ingres in Reproduction." *Art History* 23 (December 2000): 706–25. [08]

———. *Parallel Lines: Printmakers, Painters and Photographers in Nineteenth-Century France*. New Haven: Yale University, 2001. [08]

———. *Paul Delaroche: History Painted*. London: Reaktion Books, 1997. [05]

Banville, Théodore de. "Le Quartier Latin et la Bibliothèque Sainte-Geneviève." In *Paris-Guide par les principaux écrivains et artistes de la France*. 2 vols. Paris: Librairie Internationale, 1867, 2: 1349–1363. [08]

———. *Mes Souvenirs*. Paris: G. Charpentier, 1882. [07]

Barante, Prosper de. *Mélanges historiques et littéraires*. 3 vols. Paris: Ladvocat, 1835. [03]

———. *Souvenirs* publiés par son petit-fils. 8 vols. Paris: Calmann-Lévy, 1890–1901. [04]

Barbier, Frédéric. "L'industrialisation des techniques." In Martin et al., *Histoire de l'édition française*, 3: 56–67. [08]

———. "Les formes du livre." In Martin et al., *Histoire de l'édition française*, 2: 570–85. [08]

———. "Les innovations technologiques." In Martin et al., *Histoire de l'édition française*, 2: 545–51. [08]

Barbier, Patrick. *À l'Opéra au temps de Rossini et de Balzac*. Paris: Hachette, 1987. [06]

Barrière, François. "Feuilleton: Embellissemens de Paris." *Journal des Débats* (31 December 1850): 1–2. [08]

Barrière, Théodore and Henri Murger. *La Vie Bohème, pièce en cinq actes, mêlée de chants*. Paris: Michel Lévy, 1849. Reprint. Paris: Calmann-Lévy, 1989. [06]

Bassy, Alain-Marie. "Le texte et l'image." In Martin et al., *Histoire de l'édition française*, 2: 140–61. [08]

Baudelaire, Charles. *Le Salon de 1845*. Ed. André Ferran. Toulouse: Aux Éditions de l'Archer, 1933. [06] [07]

———. *Le Salon de 1846*. Ed. David Kelley. Oxford: Clarendon Press, 1975. [06] [07]

———. "Quelques caricaturistes français." In *Curiosités Esthétiques*. Intro. Jean Adhémar. Lausanne: L'Oeil, 1956: 256–77. [08]

———. *Salons and Other Exhibitions*. Ed. and Trans. Jonathan Mayne. London: Phaidon, 1965. [05]

Bausset, Louis-François-Joseph. *Mémoires anecdotiques sur l'intérieur du palais de Napoléon, sur celui de Marie-Louise, et sur quelques événemens de l'Empire, depuis 1805 jusqu'en 1816*. 4 vols. Paris: A. Levasseur, 1829. [03]

Bazin, Anaïs de Raucou. *Histoire de France sous Louis XIII*. 4 vols. Paris: Chamerot, 1840. [05]

Bazin, Germain. *Théodore Géricault: étude critique, documents, et catalogue raisonné*. 6 vols. Paris: Bibliothèque des Arts, 1987–1994. [01] [02]

Beale, Arthur. "A Technical View of Nineteenth-Century Sculpture." In *Metamorphoses in Nineteenth-Century Sculpture*, exhibition catalogue. Ed. Jeanne L. Wasserman. Cambridge MA: Fogg Art Museum / Harvard University, 1975: 29–55. [08]

Bechtel, Edwin de T. *Freedom of the Press and L'Association Mensuelle: Philipon Versus Louis-Philippe*. New York: The Grolier Club, 1952. [08]

Bellavoine, M. L. *Mémorial pittoresque de la France, ou Recueil de toutes les belles Actions, Traits de Courage, de Bienfaisance, de Patriotisme et d'Humanité arrivées depuis le règne de Henri IV jusqu'à nos jours*. Paris: chez l'auteur et Didot le jeune, 1786. [04]

Bellos, David. "La conjoncture de la production." In Martin et al., *Histoire de l'édition française*, 2: 552–57. [08]

———. "Naissance de la stéréotypie." In Martin et al., *Histoire de l'édition française*, 2: 546. [08]

Bénédite, Léonce. *Théodore Chassériau: Sa vie et ses oeuvres*, manuscrit inédit publié par André Dezarrois. 3 vols. Paris: Braun, 1931. [03]

Benge, Glen F. *Antoine-Louis Barye: Sculptor of Romantic Realism*. University Park PA: Pennsylvania State University, 1984. [04] [05]

Benjamin, Walter. *Charles Baudelaire: A Lyric Poet in the Era of High Capitalism*. Trans. Harry Zohn. London: Verso-NLB, 1973. [07]

———. *The Arcades Project*. Trans. Howard Eiland and Kevin McLaughlin. Cambridge MA: Belknap Press–Harvard University, 1999. [IN] [07]

———. "The Work of Art in the Age of Mechanical Reproduction." In *Illuminations*. Ed. Hannah Arendt. Trans. Harry Zohn. New York: Schocken, 1969: 217–51. [06] [08]

Benoît, François. *L'art français sous la Révolution et l'Empire*. Paris: 1897. Reprint. Geneva: Slatkin-Magariotis Reprints, 1975. [04]

Benoît, Luc. *La Sculpture romantique*. Paris: Renaissance du Livre, 1928. [05] [06]

Béraud, Antoine-Nicolas. *Annales de l'école française des Beaux-Arts*. Paris: Pillet, 1827. [05]

Béraud, Antoine-Nicolas and Pierre-Joseph Dufey. *Dictionnaire historique de Paris contenant la description détaillée de ses places, rues, quais, promenades, monumens et édifices publics, de ses établissemens publics en tout genre*. 2nd ed. 2 vols. Paris: J.-N. Barba, 1828. [07]

Bergdoll, Barry. "Le Panthéon / Sainte-Geneviève au XIXe siècle: La monumentalité à l'épreuve des révolutions idéologiques (1806–1885)." In Paris, *Le Panthéon*: 175–233. [03]

———. *Léon Vaudoyer: Historicism in the Age of Industry*. New York / Cambridge MA: The Architectural History Foundation / MIT, 1994.

Bergeron, Louis. *France under Napoleon*. Trans. R. R. Palmer. Princeton: Princeton University, 1981. [01]

———. "Paysages de Paris." In *Paris: Genèse d'un paysage*. Ed. Louis Bergeron. Paris: Picard, 1989: 262–91. [07]

Bermingham, Ann. *Landscape and Ideology: The English Rustic Tradition, 1740–1860*. Berkeley: University of California, 1986. [05]

Bernard, Richard Boyle. *A Tour through some parts of France, Switzerland, Savoy, Germany, and Belgium.* London: Longman, Hurst, Rees, Orme, and Brown, 1815. [07]

Bernardin de Saint-Pierre, Jacques-Henri. *Paul et Virginie.* Ed. Pierre Trahard. Paris: Garnier Frères, 1964. [08]

Bernstein, Susan. *Virtuosity of the Nineteenth Century: Performing Music and Language in Heine, Liszt, and Baudelaire.* Stanford: Stanford University, 1998. [06]

Berry, Mary. *Extracts from the Journals and Correspondence of Miss Berry from the year 1783 to 1852.* 2nd ed. 3 vols. Ed. Lady Theresa Lewis. London: Longmans, Green, & Co., 1866. [03] [04]

Bertier de Sauvigny, Guillaume de. *Nouvelle Histoire de Paris: La Restauration, 1815–1830.* Paris: Hachette, 1977. [07] [08]

———. *The Bourbon Restoration.* Trans. Lynn M. Case. Philadelphia: University of Pennsylvania, 1966. [01] [02]

Bezucha, Robert J. "The Renaissance of Book Illustration." In University of Missouri-Columbia, Museum of Art and Archaeology, *The Art of the July Monarchy: France 1830 to 1848,* exhibition catalogue. Columbia MO: University of Missouri, 1990: 192–213. [08]

Bhabha, Homi. "Of Mimicry and Man: The Ambivalence of Colonial Discourse." *October* 28 (Spring 1984): 125–33. [05]

———. "The Other Question: Difference, Discrimination and the Discourse of Colonialism." In *Literature, Politics, and Theory: Papers from the Essex Conference, 1976–1984.* Ed. Francis Barker. London: Methuen, 1986: 148–72. [05]

Bierman, John. *Napoléon III and His Carnival Empire.* New York: St. Martin's, 1988. [EP]

Biver, Marie-Louise. *Le Paris de Napoléon.* Paris: Plon/Éditions d'Histoire et d'Art, 1963. [03]

Blair, Claude. *L'Argenterie: Art et Histoire.* Trans. Paul Cox, Thierry Detienne, and Roselyne Saignes. Paris: Flammarion, 1989. [08]

Blanc, Charles. *Ingres: Sa vie et ses ouvrages.* Paris: Vve J. Renouard, 1870. [06]

Blanc, Louis. *Révolution française: Histoire de Dix Ans.* Nouv. éd. 5 vols. Paris: Félix Alcan, 1878. [03]

Blanquart-Evrard, Louis-Désiré. "Lettre de M. Blanquart-Evrard." *La Lumière* 1 (13 April 1851): 37–38. [08]

———. *Traité de photographie sur papier.* Intro. Georges Will. Paris: Roret, 1851. [08]

Blanvillain, J. F. C. *Le Pariséum, ou Tableau actuel de Paris.* 2nd ed.

Paris: Frères Piranesi, 1807. [04]

Blouet, Guillaume-Abel. *Supplément au Traité théorique et pratique de l'art de bâtir de Jean Rondelet.* 2 vols. Paris: F. Didot, 1847–1848. [08]

Bluche, Frédéric. *Le Bonapartisme: Aux origines de la droite autoritaire, 1800–1850.* Paris: Nouvelles Éditions Latines, 1980. [01] [02] [05] [08] [EP]

Boime, Albert. *Hollow Icons: The Politics of Sculpture in Nineteenth-Century France.* Kent OH: Kent State University, 1987. [05]

Bonaparte, Napoléon. *Correspondance de Napoléon Ier,* publiée par l'ordre de l'Empereur Napoléon III. 32 vols. Paris: Imprimerie Impériale, 1858–1870. [01] [02] [03] [07]

Bonnemaison, Féréol de. *Galerie de Son Altesse Royale Madame, Duchesse de Berry,* sous la direction de M. le chevalier Bonnemaison. 2 vols. Paris: J. Didot, 1822. [07]

Bordes, Philippe. "Le recours à l'allégorie dans l'art de la Révolution française." In *Les Images de la Révolution Française.* Ed. Michel Vovelle. Paris: La Sorbonne, 1988: 243–49. [03]

Boudon, François. "Visconti et le décor urbain: Les fontaines parisiennes." In Paris, Délégation à l'action artistique de la Ville de Paris, *Louis Visconti:* 78–100. [03]

Bouilhet, Henri. *Les Origines et les progrès de la Galvanoplastie, conférence faite devant la Société d'encouragement pour l'industrie nationale.* Paris: Madame Vve Bouchard-Huzard, 1866. [08]

Bowie, Karen, ed. *La modernité avant Haussmann: Formes de l'espace urbain à Paris, 1801–1853.* Paris: Éditions Recherches, 2001. [03] [07]

Boyer, F. "Le Sort sous la Restauration des tableaux à sujets napoléoniens." *Bulletin de la Société de l'histoire de l'art français,* année 1966 (1967): 271–81. [01]

———. "Les responsabilités de Napoléon dans le transfert à Paris des oeuvres d'art de l'étranger." *Revue d'histoire moderne et contemporaine* 11 (1964): 241–62. [03]

Boyer d'Agen [pseud. Auguste-Jean-Boyé]. *Ingres d'après une Correspondance inédite.* Paris: H. Daragon, 1909. [05] [06]

Brès. *Arc de triomphe des Tuileries,* érigé en 1806, d'après les dessins et sous la direction de MM. C. Percier et P-F-L Fontaine, architectes, dessiné, gravé et publié par Normand fils, avec un texte explicatif par M. Brès. Paris: Normand fils, 1828. [03]

Bressler, Fenton. *Napoleon III: A Life.* London: Harper-Collins, 1999. [EP]

Breton, Ernest. "Histoire de la place de la Concorde à Paris (1748–1840)." Extrait du *Journal de l'Institut historique*. Paris, 1840 [BnF Lk7 7588]. [03]

Brimont, Béatrice de. "La duchesse de Berry: Un Amateur illustre sous la Restauration." *L'Estampille: L'Objet d'art* 255 (February 1992): 60–72. [04]

Brivois, Jules. *Bibliographie des ouvrages illustrés du XIXe siècle, principalement des livres à gravures sur bois*. Paris: L. Conquet, 1883. [08]

Bro de Comères, Colonel. *Mémoires*. Ed. Henry Bro de Comères. Paris: Plon-Nourrit, 1914. [01]

Broglie, Charles-Jacques-Victor-Albert de. *Mémoires*. 2 vols. Paris: Calmann-Lévy, 1938–1941. [06]

Brongniart, Alexandre. *Plans du Palais de la Bourse de Paris, et du Cimetière Mont-Louis en six planches*, par Alexandre-Théodore Brongniart, architecte. Paris: l'Imprimerie de Crapelet, 1814. [03]

Brooklyn, The Brooklyn Museum. *Courbet Reconsidered*, exhibition catalogue. Brooklyn: The Brooklyn Museum, 1988. [05]

Bruel, André. *Les carnets de David d'Angers*. 2 vols. Paris: Plon, 1958. [06]

Brunel, Georges. "La peinture religieuse: Art officiel et art sacré." In Paris, *Les années romantiques*, 46–75. [03]

Bruson, Jean-Marie and Christophe Leribault. *Peintures du Musée Carnavalet: Catalogue sommaire*. Paris: Éditions des musées de la Ville de Paris, 1999. [06]

Bryson, Norman. *Vision and Painting: The Logic of the Gaze*. New Haven: Yale University, 1983. [01]

Buerger, Janet. *French Daguerreotypes*. Chicago: University of Chicago, 1989. [08]

Buloz, F. "Chronique de la Quinzaine: 31 juillet 1836." *Revue des Deux Mondes* 7 (1836): 378–84. [03]

Burat, Jules. *Exposition de l'industrie française: année 1844*. 2 vols. Paris: Challamel, 1844. [08]

Bürger, W. [pseud. Théophile Thoré] et al. "Jean Du Seigneur, statuaire." *Revue Universelle des Arts (Paris)* 23 (1866): 69–110. [05]

Burton, Richard D. E. *The Flâneur and His City: Patterns of Daily Life in Paris, 1815–1851*. Durham: University of Durham, 1994. [07] [08]

Burty, Philippe. *Paul Huet: Notice biographique et critique*. Paris: J. Claye, 1913. [06]

C.V. "Gravure et Lithographie: Aperçu des travaux contemporains." *Journal des Artistes*, 4e année, 2 (25 July 1830): 57–62. [08]

Cabanis, André. *La Presse sous le Consulat et l'Empire*. Paris: Société des études robespierristes, 1975. [01]

Cadier, Jean-Marc. "*Les Voyages Pittoresques et Romantiques dans l'ancienne France* du Baron Taylor." *Revue de la Bibliothèque Nationale* 49 (Summer 1991): 56–63. [05]

Caillot, Antoine. *Mémoires pour servir à l'histoire des moeurs et usages des Français*. 2 vols. Paris, 1827. Reprint. Geneva: Slatkine-Megariotis, 1976. [07]

Calot, Frantz, Louis-Marie Michon, and Paul-Joseph Angoulvent. *L'art du livre en France des origines à nos jours*. Paris: Librairie Delagrave, 1931. [08]

Camp, Maxime du. "Les Omnibus." In *Paris: ses organes, ses fonctions, et sa vie jusqu'en 1870*. Paris, 1873. Reprint. Monaco: G. Rondeau, 1993: 72–78. [07]

Carlier, Achille. *Les Anciens Monuments dans la civilisation nouvelle*. 4 vols. Paris: Les Pierres de France, 1945. [04]

Carlson, Marvin. "*Hernani*'s Revolt from the Tradition of French Stage Composition." *Theatre Survey* 13 (May 1972): 1–27. [06]

———. *The French Stage in the Nineteenth Century*. Metuchen NJ: Scarecrow, 1972. [06]

Carr, John. *The Stranger in France, or A Tour from Devonshire to Paris*. London: J. Johnston, 1803. [03] [04] [07]

Carteret, Laurent. *Le trésor du Bibliophile romantique et moderne, 1801–1875*. 4 vols. Paris: L. Carteret, 1927. [08]

Caso, Jacques de. *David d'Angers: L'avenir de la mémoire*. Paris: Flammarion, 1988. [05]

———. *David d'Angers: Sculptural Communication in the Age of Romanticism*. Trans. Dorothy Johnson and Jacques de Caso. Princeton: Princeton University, 1992. [03] [05] [06]

———. "Serial Sculpture in Nineteenth-Century France." In *Metamorphoses in Nineteenth-Century Sculpture*, exhibition catalogue. Ed. Jeanne L. Wasserman. Cambridge MA: Fogg Art Museum/Harvard University, 1975: 1–27. [08]

Castelot, André. *L'histoire à table*. Paris: Perrin, 1972. [07]

———. *Napoléon Bonaparte*. Paris: Perrin, 1984. [01]

Certeau, Michel de. *L'Écriture de l'histoire*. Paris: Éditions Gallimard, 1975. [IN]

Champfleury, Jules. *Les Vignettes romantiques: Histoire de la littérature et de l'art 1825–1840*. Paris: E. Dentu, 1883. [08]

———. "Salon de 1846." In *Oeuvres Posthumes de Champfleury: Salons 1846–1851*. Intro. Jules Troubat. Paris: Alphonse Lemerre, 1894: 3–82. [07]

Champollion-Figeac. *L'Obélisque de Louqsor transporté à Paris*. Paris: Firmin-Didot, 1833. [03]

Chaptal, Jean-Antoine-Claude. *Mes Souvenirs sur Napoléon*, publiées par son arrière-petit-fils Le Vte An. Chaptal. Paris: E. Plon, Nourrit, 1893. [03]

Charlton, Donald G. "Prose Fiction." In *The French Romantics*. 2 vols. Ed. Donald G. Charlton. Cambridge UK: Cambridge University, 1984, 1: 163–203. [01]

———. "The French Romantic Movement." In *The French Romantics*. 2 vols. Ed. Donald G. Charlton. Cambridge UK: Cambridge University, 1984, 1: 1–32. [01]

Chastel, André. "La notion de patrimoine." In *Les Lieux de Mémoire*, sous la direction de Pierre Nora. 3 vols. Paris: Gallimard-Quarto, 1997, 3: 1433–1469. [04]

Chateaubriand, François-René de. *Atala, René, Les Abencérages, suivis du Voyage en Amérique*. Paris: Firmin Didot, 1853. [01]

———. *Mémoires d'outre-tombe*. 2nd ed. 2 vols. Ed. Maurice Levaillant. Paris: Flammarion, 1949–1950. [01] [02] [03]

———. *Oeuvres complètes de Chateaubriand*. 12 vols. Paris: Garnier, 1929–1938. [03]

Chaudonneret, Marie-Claude. *L'état et les artistes: De la Restauration à la Monarchie de Juillet, 1815–1830*. Paris: Flammarion, 1999. [03]

———. *Fleury Richard et Pierre Révoil, la peinture troubadour*. Paris: Arthena, 1980. [04]

———. "Permanence et Innovation: Le Musée du Louvre dans les années 1820." In *Hommage à Michel Laclotte*. Eds. Pierre Rosenberg, Cécile Scailliérez, and Dominique Thiébaut. Paris/Milan: Réunion des musées nationaux/Electa, 1994: 532–37. [03]

Chauvin, Auguste. *Salon de mil huit cent vingt-quatre*. Paris: Pillet, 1825. [05]

Chénique, Bruno. "Géricault: Une Vie." In Paris, *Géricault*: 261–308. [01]

Chesneau, Ernest. *Peintres et statuaires romantiques*. Paris: Charavay frères, 1880. [05]

Chevillard, Valbert. *Un peintre romantique: Théodore Chassériau*. Paris: Alphonse Lemerre, 1893. [07]

Chopin, Frédéric. *Correspondance de Frédéric Chopin*. 3 vols. Ed.

and Trans. Bronislas Édouard Sydow. Paris: Richard-Masse, 1953–1960. [06]

Clark, Timothy J. *Image of the People: Gustave Courbet and the 1848 Revolution*. Princeton: Princeton University, 1982. [05] [06]

———. *The Absolute Bourgeois: Artists and Politics in France, 1848–1851*. Princeton: Princeton University, 1982. [02] [05] [07]

Clary-Aldringen, Charles de. *Trois mois à Paris, lors du mariage de l'Empereur Napoléon Ier et de l'Archiduchesse Marie-Louise*. Paris: Plon-Nourrit, 1914. [02] [03] [04] [07]

Clay, Jean. *Romanticism*. Trans. Daniel Wheeler and Craig Owen. Secaucus NJ: Chartwell, 1981. [01] [06]

Cleary, Richard L. *The Place Royale and Urban Design in the Ancient Régime*. New York: Cambridge University, 1999. [03]

Clément, Charles. *Géricault; étude biographique et critique*. 3rd ed. Paris: Didier, 1879. Reprint. Paris: L. Lapet, 1973. [01]

Cohen, Jean-Louis and André Lortie. *Des fortifs au périf: Paris, les seuils de la ville*. Paris: Éditions du Pavillon de l'Arsenal/Picard, 1992. [07]

Cohn, Marjorie B. "Introduction." In Louisville, *Ingres—In Pursuit of Perfection*: 8–33. [08]

Collin de Plancy, Jean-Auguste-Simon. *Voyages de Paul Béranger dans Paris d'après 45 ans d'absence*. 2 vols. Paris: Lerouge & Dalibon, 1819. [07]

Collins, Herbert F. *Talma: A Biography of an Actor*. New York: Hill and Wang, 1964. [06]

Condon, Patricia. "The Grande Odalisque." In Louisville, *Ingres—In Pursuit of Perfection*: 126–28. [08]

Constable, John. *John Constable's Correspondence*. 6 vols. Ed. R. B. Beckett. London: H.M. Stationery Office, 1962–1968. [05] [06]

Constantin, Marc. *Histoire des Cafés de Paris*. Paris: Desloges, 1857. [07]

Copart (Mademoiselle). "La vie, l'oeuvre, le catalogue raisonné de l'oeuvre sculpté de Jean Duseigneur." M.A. Thesis, Paris IV (Institut d'art et d'archéologie). Paris: Université de Paris-Sorbonne, 1980. [05]

Corbin, Alain. "Paris—Province." In *Les Lieux de Mémoire*, sous la direction de Pierre Nora. 3 vols. Paris: Gallimard-Quarto, 1997, 2: 2851–2888. [05]

Courbet, Gustave. *The Letters of Gustave Courbet*. Ed. and Trans. Petra ten-Doesschate Chu. Chicago: University of Chicago, 1992. [05]

Courcy, Geraldine de. *Paganini the Genoese*. 2 vols. Norman OK: University of Oklahoma, 1957. [06]

Courtine, Robert. *La Vie Parisienne: Cafés et restaurants des Boulevards, 1814–1914*. Paris: Perrin, 1984. [07]

Cromer, G. "Une Pièce historique: L'Original de la note du peintre Paul Delaroche à Arago au sujet du Daguerréotype." *Bulletin de la Société Française de Photographie et de Cinématographie*, 3e sér., 18 (1930): 114–18. [05]

Crow, Thomas E. *Painters and Public Life in Eighteenth-Century Paris*. New Haven: Yale University, 1985. [07]

Croy, Raoul de. "Le Daguerrotype: A propos du projet de loi de la Chambre des Députés." *Journal des Artistes*, 13e année, 1 (30 June 1839): 409–11. [08]

———. "Les magasins pittoresques à deux sous." *Journal des Artistes*, 7e année, 2 (3 November 1833): 281–83. [08]

Cummings, Frederick. "Boothby, Rousseau, and the Romantic Malady." *Burlington Magazine* 110 (December 1968): 659–66. [01]

Cuno, James B. "The Business and Politics of Caricature: Charles Philipon and La Maison Aubert." *Gazette des Beaux-Arts* 106 (October 1985): 95–112. [08]

———. "Charles Philipon and the Maison Aubert: The business, politics, and public of caricature in Paris, 1820–1840." Ph.D. Diss., Harvard University. Ann Arbor: University Microfilms, 1985. [07]

Curmer, Léon. *Note présenté à MM. les membres du Jury central de l'Exposition des produits de l'industrie française sur la profession d'éditeur*. Paris: A. Everat, 1839. [08]

Curtis, Jean-Louis. *Baccarat*. Paris: Éditions du Regard, 1991. [08]

Cuzin, Jean-Pierre. "François-Joseph Heim (1787–1965): Peintre d'esquisses." *Bulletin de la Société de l'histoire de l'art français*, année 1991 (1992): 199–217. [05]

Daguerre de Hureaux, Alain. *Delacroix*. Paris: Hazan, 1993. [05]

Daguerre, Louis-Jacques-Mandé. *Historique et Description des procédés du Daguerréotype et du Diorama*. Paris: Lerebours et Susse Frères, 1839. [08]

Darnis, Jean-Marie. *Les Monuments expiatoires du supplice de Louis XVI et de Marie-Antoinette*. Paris: Union parisienne de l'imprimerie, 1981. [03]

Daudet, Ernest. *Louis XVIII et le duc Decazes, 1815–1820*. Paris: Plon, 1899. [01]

Daumard, Adeline. *La bourgeoisie parisienne de 1815 à 1848*. Nouv. éd. Paris: Albin Michel, 1996. [07] [08]

Daunou, Pierre-Claude-François. *Cours d'études historiques*, publié par Taillandier. 20 vols. Paris: Didot, 1842–1845. [03]

de Luna, Frederick A. *The French Republic under Cavaignac, 1848*. Princeton: Princeton University, 1969. [02]

De Maître, Joseph. *Du Pape*. 2nd ed. 2 vols. Lyon/Paris: chez Rusand, 1821. [03]

Debord, Guy. *The Society of the Spectacle*. Trans. Donald Nicholson-Smith. Cambridge MA: MIT, 1995. [07]

Decamps, Alexandre. *Le Musée—Revue du Salon de 1834*. Paris: Abel Ledoux, 1834. [05]

Decaux, Alain. *Victor Hugo*. Paris: Perrin, 1984. [EP]

Delaborde, Henri. *Ingres: sa vie, ses travaux, sa doctrine*. Paris: Henri Plon, 1870. [05] [08]

Delacroix, Eugène. "Charlet." *Revue des Deux Mondes*, 23e année, 2e pér., 37 (1 January 1862): 234–42. [08]

———. *Correspondance générale d'Eugène Delacroix*. 5 vols. Ed. André Joubin. Paris: Librairie Plon, 1935–1938. [05] [06]

———. *Journal de Eugène Delacroix*. 3 vols. Ed. André Joubin. Paris: Plon, 1932. [05] [06] [EP]

———. *Lettres de Eugène Delacroix (1815 à 1863)*. Ed. Philippe Burty. Paris: A. Quantan, 1878. [03]

———. *Lettres intimes*. Ed. Alfred Dupont. Paris: Gallimard, 1954. [01]

Delaunay, A-H. *Catalogue complète du Salon de 1847*. Paris: Au Bureau du Journal des Artistes, 1847. [07]

Delécluze, Étienne-Jean. *Impressions romaines*. Ed. Robert Baschet. Paris: Boivin, 1942. [05]

———. *Louis David: son école et son temps*. Nouv. éd. Notes by Jean-Pierre Mouilleseaux. Paris: Macula, 1983. [01]

———. *Souvenirs de soixante années*. Paris: Lévy frères, 1862. [04]

Delestre, J. B. *Gros: sa Vie et ses Ouvrages*. Paris: Vve Jules Renouard, 1868. [01]

Delorme, Jean-Claude and Anne-Marie Dubois. *Passages couverts parisiens*. Paris: Parisgramme, 1996. [07]

Delteil, Loys. *Le Peintre-Graveur illustré*. 32 vols. Paris, 1925. Reprint. New York: Collector's Edition/de Capo, 1968. [07]

Deming, Mark. "Le Panthéon révolutionnaire." In Paris, *Le Panthéon*: 97–150. [03]

Deperthes, Jean-Baptiste. *Théorie du Paysage*. Paris: Lenormant, 1818. [05]

Deschamps, Jules. "Sur la légende de Napoléon." In *Bibliothèque de la Revue de littérature comparée* 73. Paris: Champion, 1931. [01]

Deschamps, Madeleine. *Empire*. New York: Abbeville, 1994. [04]

Deschanel, Émile. "Études sur l'Antiquité: Sappho et les Lesbiennes." *Revue des Deux Mondes*, nouv. sér., 19 (1 July 1847): 330–57. [EP]

Descotes, Maurice. *Le public de théâtre et son histoire*. Paris: Presses Universitaires de France, 1964. [06]

Deseine, Louis-Pierre. "Opinion sur les musées où se trouvent tous les objets d'art qui sont la propriété des temples consacrés à la religion catholique (1801)." In *Notices historiques sur les anciennes académies royales de peinture, sculpture de Paris, et celle d'architecture; suivies de deux écrits qui ont déjà été publiés, et qui ont pour objet la restitution des monumens consacrés à la religion catholique*. Paris: Le Normant, 1814: 233–312. [04]

Desnoyers, Jules [J.D.]. "Introduction: But et Plan du Bulletin." *Bulletin de la Société de l'histoire de France* 1 (1834): i–xiv. [03]

Devrient, Eduard. *Briefe aus Paris*. Berlin: Jonas, 1840. [07]

Dion-Tenenbaum, Anne. "1834: L'exposition des produits de l'industrie." In Paris, *Un âge d'or des arts décoratifs*: 280–81. [08]

———. "1844: L'exposition des produits de l'industrie." In Paris, *Un âge d'or des arts décoratifs*: 422–23. [08]

Doudan, Ximénès. *Mélanges et Lettres*. 4 vols. Eds. Silvestre de Sacy and Alfred-Auguste Cuvillier-Fleury. Paris: Calmann-Lévy, 1878. [06]

Driskel, Michael. "Eclecticism and Ideology in the July Monarchy: Jules-Claude Ziegler's Vision of Christianity at the Madeleine." *Arts Magazine* 56 (May 1982): 119–28. [03]

———. *Representing Belief: Religion, Art and Society in Nineteenth-Century France*. University Park PA: Pennsylvania State University, 1992. [03]

Drouard, Nathalie. "François Biard: Peintre-Explorateur." M.A. Thesis, Paris IV (Institut d'art et d'archéologie). Paris: Université de Paris-Sorbonne, 1990. [07]

Dumas, Alexandre. "Lorettes." In *La Grande Ville*. 2 vols. Paris: Marescq, 1843, 2: 345–67. [07]

———. *Souvenirs dramatiques*. 2 vols. Paris: Michel Lévy, 1868. [06]

Duncan, Carol. "Ingres's *Vow of Louis XIII* and the Politics of the Restoration." In *Art and Architecture in the Service of Politics*. Eds. Henri Millon and Linda Nochlin. Cambridge MA: MIT, 1978: 80–91. [05]

Dupain, S. *Notice historique sur le pavé de Paris*. Paris: Charles de Mourgues, 1881. [07]

Dupêchez, Charles F. *Marie d'Agoult, 1805–1876*. Paris: Perrin, 1989. [06]

Dupin, Baron Charles. "Lithographie." In *Rapport du jury central sur les produits de l'industrie exposés en 1834*. 3 vols. Paris: Imprimerie Royale, 1836, 1: 376–78. [08]

Duplessis, Georges. "Les graveurs sur bois contemporains." *L'Artiste*, nouv. sér., 1 (23 August 1857): 372–74. [08]

Duplomb, Charles. *Histoire générale des Ponts de Paris*. Paris: J. Mersch, 1911. [03]

Duval, Alexandre-Vincent. *Charles II, ou le labyrinthe de Wodstock, comédie en trois actes . . . précédée d'une notice sur l'état actuel des théâtres et de l'art dramatique in France*. Paris: Barba, 1828. [06]

Duval, Amaury. *Les Fontaines de Paris, anciennes et nouvelles; ouvrage contenant soixante planches dessinées et gravées au trait par M. Moisy*. Paris: Firmin Didot, 1812. [03]

Eck, Charles-Louis-Gustave. *Traité de l'application du Fer, de la Fonte, et de la Tôle dans les constructions civiles, industrielles, et militaires*. 2 vols. Paris: Carilian-Goeury et Vor Dalmont, 1841. [08]

Eckermann, Johann Peter. *Conversations with Goethe in the Last Years of His Life*. Trans. S. M. Fuller. Boston: James Munroe, 1852. [06]

Eder, Josef-Maria. *History of Photography*. 3rd ed. Trans. Edward Epstean. New York: Columbia University, 1945. Reprint. New York: Dover, 1978. [08]

Einecke, Claudia. "Beyond Seeing: The Somatic Experience of Landscape Painting in Mid-Nineteenth-Century France." Ph.D. Diss., University of Missouri-Columbia, 1994. [05] [06]

Eitner, Lorenz. *Gericault, His Life and Work*. London: Orbis, 1983. [01]

———. *Géricault's Raft of the Medusa*. London: Phaidon, 1972. [01]

Erlande-Brandenburg, Alain. "Paris: La restauration de Notre-Dame." In Paris, *Viollet-le-Duc*: 72–76. [04]

Escholier, Raymond. *Daumier et son monde*. Nancy: Berger-Levrault, 1965. [08]

Etex, Antoine. *Les souvenirs d'un artiste*. Paris: Dentu, 1877. [03]

Etlin, Richard. *The Architecture of Death: The Transformation of the Cemetery in Eighteenth-Century Paris*. Cambridge UK: Cambridge University, 1984. [03]

Ewer, Gary W. "Théodore Maurisset's 'Fantaisies': *La Daguerréotypomanie.*" *Daguerreian Annual* (1995): 135–45. [08]

Farcy, Charles. "Peinture et Sculpture: Salon de 1831—Deuxième Article." *Journal des Artistes et Amateurs*, année 5, 19 (8 May 1831): 343–53. [02]

Félibien, André. *Entretiens sur les Vies et sur les Ouvrages des plus excellens Peintres anciens et modernes.* Trévoux: Impr. de S.A.S, 1725. Reprint. Farnborough: Gregg P., 1967. [05]

Ferguson, Priscilla Parkhurst. *Paris as Revolution: Writing the 19th-Century City.* Berkeley: University of California, 1994. [03] [07]

Fermigier, André. "Mérimée et l'inspection des monuments historiques." In *Les Lieux de Mémoire*, sous la direction de Pierre Nora. 3 vols. Paris: Gallimard-Quarto, 1997, 3: 1599–1614. [04]

Fisher, H. A. L. *Bonapartism: Six Lectures delivered in the University of London.* Oxford: Clarendon Press, 1908. [08]

Flandrin, Louis. *Hippolyte Flandrin: Sa vie et son oeuvre.* Paris: H. Laurens, 1902. [03]

Flaubert, Gustave. *L'éducation sentimentale.* In *Oeuvres.* 2 vols. Eds. Albert Thibaudet and René Dumesnil. Paris: Gallimard-Pléiade, 1952, 2: 1–457. [07]

Flocon, F. and M. Aycard. *Salon de 1824.* Paris: Leroux, 1824. [05]

Focillon, Henri. "Les dessins de Victor Hugo (1914)." In Picon and Bargiel, *Victor Hugo Dessins*: 199–205. [06]

Fontaine, Pierre-François. *Arc de Triomphe du Carrousel édifié par Percier et Fontaine architectes*, gravé d'après leur dessins par Louis-Pierre Baltard, précédé d'un aperçu sur les monuments triomphaux rédigé par Fontaine et d'une notice sur l'arc du Carrousel tirée presque entièrement de ses mémoires manuscrits. Paris: Jules Claye, 1875. [03]

———. *Journal, 1799–1824.* 2 vols. Paris: ENSBA, 1987. [03]

Forbes, James. *Letters from France written in the years 1803 and 1804, including a particular account of Verdun, and the situation of the British captives in that City.* 2 vols. London: J. White, 1806. [03] [04]

Fortoul, Hippolyte. "Fronton du Panthéon." *La Nouvelle Minerve* (10 September 1837). In Paris, *Le Panthéon*: 313–16. [03]

Fosca, François. *Histoire des Cafés de Paris.* Paris: Firmin-Didot, 1934. [07]

Foucart, Bruno. *Le renouveau de la peinture religieuse en France (1800–1860).* Paris: Arthena, 1987. [03]

———. "Viollet-le-Duc et la restauration." In *Les Lieux de Mémoire*, sous la direction de Pierre Nora. 3 vols. Paris: Gallimard-Quarto, 1997, 1: 1615–1643. [04]

Fourcaud, Louis de. *François Rude Sculpteur: Ses oeuvres et son temps.* Paris: Librairie de l'art ancien et moderne, 1904. [03] [05] [EP]

Frank, Hans. *Vom Zauber alter Licht-Bilder: Frühe Photographie in Österreich, 1840–1860.* Vienna: Molden, 1981. [08]

Frankfurt-am-Main, Städtische Galerie. *Eugène Delacroix: Themen und Variationen, Arbeiten auf Papier*, exhibition catalogue. Frankfurt-am-Main: Städtische Galerie im Städelschen Kunstinstitut, 1987. [05] [06] [08]

Fraser, Elisabeth. *Delacroix, Art and Patrimony in Post-Revolutionary France.* Cambridge UK: Cambridge University, 2004. [05]

Fried, Michael. *Courbet's Realism.* Chicago: University of Chicago, 1990. [05]

Friedlaender, Walter. *David to Delacroix.* New York: Schocken Books, 1968. [01]

———. "Napoleon as Roi Thaumaturge." *Journal of the Warburg and Courtauld Institutes* 4 (1940–1941): 139–41. [01]

Frisby, David. "The Flâneur in Social Theory." In *The Flâneur.* Ed. Keith Tester. London: Routledge, 1994: 81–110. [07]

Frizot, Michel, André Jammes, Paul Jay, and Jean-Claude Gautrand. *1839: La photographie révélée*, exhibition catalogue. Paris: Centre Nationale de la Photographie / Archives Nationales, 1989. [08]

Fureix, Emmanuel. "La ville coupable: L'effacement des trace de la capitale révolutionnaire dans le Paris de la Restauration, 1814–1830." In *Capitales culturelles, capitales symboliques: Paris et les expériences européennes, XVIIIe–XXe siècles.* Eds. Christophe Charle and Daniel Roche. Paris: Publications de la Sorbonne, 2002: 25–43. [03]

Furet, François and Denis Richet. *The French Revolution.* Trans. Stephen Hardman. New York: Macmillan, 1970. [07]

G***, Alfred. *Notice Historique sur la Place du Carrousel et l'arc de triomphe*, d'après Dulaure. Paris: A. Coniam, 1828. [03]

Gaehtgens, Thomas W. *Napoleons Arc de Triomphe.* Göttingen: Vandenhoeck und Ruprecht, 1974. [02]

Gaillot, Marcel. *La publicité à travers les âges.* Paris: Hommes et Techniques, 1955. [08]

Galassi, Peter. *Corot in Italy: Open-Air Painting and the Classical-Landscape Tradition.* New Haven: Yale University, 1991. [05]

Gall, Ferdinand von. *Paris und seine Salons*. 2 vols. Oldenburg: Schulzesche, 1844–1845. [07]

Gassier, Pierre. *Léopold Robert*. Neuchâtel: Ides et Calendes, 1983. [05]

Gaudibert, Pierre. "Delacroix et le romantisme révolutionnaire." *Europe* 41 (April 1963): 4–21. [02] [03]

Gaudin, Marc-Antoine-Augustin. "Séance du lundi 11 octobre 1841: M. Gaudin écrit relativement à des nouvelles modifications qu'il a introduites dans les procédés photographiques." *Comptes rendus des séances de l'Académie des sciences* 13 (July–December 1841): 832–33. [08]

———. *Traité pratique de photographie: Exposé complet des procédés relatifs au Daguerréotype*. Paris: J.-J. Dubochet, 1844. [08]

Gaudin, Marc-Antoine-Augustin and Nicolas-Marie-Paymal Lerebours. *Derniers perfectionnements apportés au Daguerréotype*. 2nd ed. Paris: Lerebours et Susse, Novembre 1841. [08]

———. *Derniers perfectionnements apportés au Daguerréotype*. 3rd ed. Paris: Lerebours et Susse, 1842. [08]

Gaudon, Jean. "La lettre et l'esprit." In Paris, *La Gloire de Victor Hugo*: 511–25. [06]

———. "Souvenir de. . . ." In *Victor Hugo et les images*. Eds. Madeleine Blondel and Pierre Georgel. Dijon: Ville de Dijon / Aux Amateurs du Livre, 1989: 153–67. [06]

Gautier, Théophile. "Coupole de la Madeleine." In *Les Beaux-Arts en Europe*. 2 vols. Paris: Michel Lévy, 1856, 2: 276–85. [03]

———. *Critique d'art: Extraits des salons (1833–1872)*. Ed. Marie-Hélène Girard. Paris: Séguier, 1994. [05] [06]

———. *Histoire du Romantisme suivie de Notices Romantiques et d'une Étude sur la poésie française, 1830–1868*. 2nd ed. Paris: Charpentier, 1874. [05] [06]

———. *Paris et les Parisiens*. Ed. Claudine Lacoste-Veysseyre. Paris: La Boîte à Documents, 1996. [06] [07] [08]

———. "Variétés: Salon de 1837." *La Presse* (18 March 1837): 2–3. [07]

Gavard, Charles. *Notice sur le Diagraphe*. 2nd ed. Paris: Mme Huzard, 1831 [BnF V-40018]. [08]

Gay-Lussac, Joseph-Louis. "Rapport fait à la Chambre des Pairs, séance du 30 Juillet 1839." In Daguerre, *Historique et Description*: 31–35. [08]

Geiger, Monique. "Victor Hugo et Louis Boulanger." In *Victor Hugo et les images*. Eds. Madeleine Blondel and Pierre Georgel. Dijon: Ville de Dijon–Aux Amateurs du Livre, 1989: 29–41. [06]

Geist, Johann Friedrich. *Arcades: The History of a Building Type*. Trans. Jane O. Newman and John H. Smith. Cambridge MA: MIT, 1983. [07]

Gendre, Catherine. *Peintures du Musée Lambinet à Versailles: Catalogue sommaire*. Paris/Versailles: Somogy éditions d'art / Musée Lambinet, 2005. [07]

Geneva, Musée d'Art et d'Histoire. *Statues de Chair: Sculptures de James Pradier (1790–1852)*, exhibition catalogue. Geneva: Musée d'Art et d'Histoire, 1995. [05]

Gérard, Alice. *La Révolution française, mythes et interprétations*. Paris: Flammarion, 1970. [02]

Gernsheim, Helmut. *The Origins of Photography*. 3rd ed. London: Thames & Hudson, 1982. [08]

Gernsheim, Helmut and Alison Gernsheim. *L. J. M. Daguerre: The History of the Diorama and the Daguerreotype*. 2nd ed. New York: Dover, 1968. [05] [08]

Gerstein, Marc. "Le regard consolateur du grand homme: Le concour pour la *Bataille d'Eylau*." In Paris, *Dominique-Vivant Denon*: 321–31. [01]

Giedion, Siegfried. *Building in France—Building in Iron—Building in Ferro-Concrete*. Trans. J. Duncan Berry. Intro. Sokratis Georgiadis. Leipzig, 1928. Reprint. Santa Monica CA: The Getty Center for the History of Art and the Humanities, 1995. [08]

———. *Space, Time, and Architecture: The Growth of a New Tradition*. 5th ed. Cambridge MA: Harvard University, 1967. [08]

Girardin, Delphine de. *Lettres parisiennes du vicomte de Launay*. 2 vols. Ed. Anne-Marie Fugier. Paris: Mercure de France, 1986. [07] [08]

Godechot, Jacques. *The Counter-Revolution: Doctrine and Action, 1789–1804*. Trans. Salvator Attanasio. London: Routledge & Kegan Paul, 1972. [01]

———. *The Taking of the Bastille*. Trans. Jean Stewart. London: Faber & Faber, 1970. [07]

Goldstein, Robert Justin. *Censorship of Political Caricature in Nineteenth-Century France*. Kent OH: Kent State University, 1989. [08]

Gould, Cecil. *Trophy of Conquest: The Musée Napoléon and the Creation of the Louvre*. London: Faber & Faber, 1965. [01] [03]

Graña, César. *Bohemian Versus Bourgeois: French Society and the*

French Man of Letters in the Nineteenth Century. New York: Basic Books, 1964. [06]

Granet, Solange. "Le monument à Louis XVI de la place de la Concorde." *La Revue des Arts* 6 (December 1956): 238–40. [03]

Green, Nicholas. *The Spectacle of Nature: Landscape and Bourgeois Culture in Nineteenth-Century France.* Manchester: Manchester University, 1990. [05]

Grégoire, Joseph-Amable. *Itinéraire de l'Artiste et de l'Étranger dans les églises de Paris,* ou état des objets d'art commandés, depuis 1816 jusqu'en 1830, par l'administration de cette ville. Paris: chez l'auteur, 1833. [03]

———. *Notice explicatif des objets d'art qui décorent la nouvelle église Notre-Dame-de-Lorette.* Paris: chez l'auteur, 1837. [03]

Griener, Pascal. "L'Art de persuader par l'image sous le Premier Empire." *L'écrit-voir* 4 (1984): 8–21. [01]

Grigsby, Darcy Grimaldo. *Extremities: Painting Empire in Post-Revolutionary France.* New Haven: Yale University, 2002. [01] [05]

———. "Orients and Colonies: Delacroix's Algerian Harem." In *The Cambridge Companion to Delacroix.* Ed. Beth S. Wright. Cambridge UK: Cambridge University, 2001: 69–87. [05]

———. "Rumor, Contagion, and Colonization in Gros's 'Plague-Stricken of Jaffa' (1804)." *Representations* 51 (Summer 1995): 1–46. [01]

Grimod de la Reynière, Alexandre-Balthazar Laurent. *Almanach des Gourmands.* Paris: Maradan, 1803. [07]

Grunchec, Philippe. *Le Grand Prix de Peinture: Les concours des Prix de Rome de 1797 à 1863.* Paris: École Nationale Supérieure des Beaux-Arts, 1983. [05]

Guégan, Stéphane. "Orgie noire: terreur et mélancolie au Salon de 1801." In Paris, *Mélancolie:* 284–94. [01] [EP]

Guerrini, Maurice. *Napoleon and Paris: Thirty Years of History.* Trans. Margery Weiner. London: Cassell, 1970. [01]

Guillemin, Henri. *Le coup du 2 décembre.* Paris: Gallimard, 1951. [EP]

———, ed. *Victor Hugo: Souvenirs personnels 1848–1851.* Paris: Gallimard, 1952. [EP]

Guillerme, Jacques. "Le Panthéon: Une matière à controverse." In Paris, *Le Panthéon:* 151–73 [03]

Guizot, François. "Salon de 1810." In *Études sur les Beaux-Arts en générale.* Nouv. éd. Paris: Librairie Académique Didier, 1851: 3–100. [01] [02]

———. *Mémoires pour servir à l'histoire de mon temps.* 8 vols. Paris: Michel Lévy, 1858–1867. [03]

Gusman, Pierre. *La Gravure sur bois en France au XIXe siècle.* Paris: Albert Morance, 1929. [08]

Gutzkow, Karl. *Briefe aus Paris.* 2 vols. Leipzig: F. U. Brodhaus, 1842. [07] [08]

Halsall, Albert W. *Victor Hugo and the Romantic Drama.* Toronto: University of Toronto, 1998. [06]

Hammer, Karl. *Jakob Ignaz Hittorff: Ein Pariser Baumeister, 1792–1867.* Stuttgart: Anton Hiersemann, 1968. [07]

Hardouin-Fugier, Elisabeth. "Monsieur Ingres vu par Louis Lacuria 1832–1838." *Bulletin du Musée Ingres* 55–56 (December 1985): 39–55. [06]

Hargrove, June. *The Statues of Paris: An Open-Air Pantheon.* Antwerp: Mercatorfonds, 1989. [03]

Harper, Mary J. "The Poetics and Politics of Delacroix's Representation of the Harem in *Women of Algiers in their Apartment.*" In *Picturing the Middle East: A Hundred Years of European Orientalism.* New York: Dahesh Museum, 1996: 53–65. [05]

Harrisse, Henry. *Louis-Léopold Boilly, Peintre, dessinateur, et lithographe: Sa vie et son oeuvre 1761–1845.* Paris: Société de propagation des Livres d'Art, 1898. [07]

Hautecoeur, Louis. *Histoire de l'architecture classique en France.* 6 vols. Paris: A. et J. Picard, 1948–1967. [03] [07] [08]

Heine, Heinrich. *De la France.* Paris: Eugène Renduel, 1833. [03]

———. "Französische Zustände: Artikel V (25 März 1832)." In *Heinrich Heine Säkularausgabe: Werke, Briefwechsel, Lebenszeugnesse.* 27 vols. Berlin/Paris: Akademie-Verlag / CNRS, 1970, 7: 115–27. [08]

———. *Lutèce: Lettres sur la vie politique, artistique, et sociale de la France.* Paris: M. Lévy, 1861. Reprint. Paris/Geneva: Slatkine, 1979. [06] [07]

———. *Religion and Philosophy in Germany (1834).* Trans. J. Snodgrass. Boston: Beacon Press, 1959. [06]

———. "Über die französische Bühne." In *Heinrich Heine Werke.* 4 vols. Frankfurt-am-Main: Insel, 1968, 3: 238–303. [06]

Hemmings, Frederick W. J. *Culture and Society in France, 1789–1848.* Leicester: Leicester University, 1987. [01]

———. *The Theatre Industry in Nineteenth-Century France.* Cambridge UK: Cambridge University, 1993. [06]

Hénard, Robert. "Les trois statues de la colonne." *Revue des études napoléoniennes* 1 (May 1912): 349–72. [03]

Herbert, Robert. "Baron Gros's Napoleon and Voltaire's Henri IV." In *The Artist and Writer in France: Mélanges Jean Seznec.* Oxford: Clarendon Press, 1974: 52–75. [01]

Hermann, Wolfgang. *Gottfried Semper: In Search of Architecture.* Cambridge MA: MIT, 1984. [08]

Hermant, Achille. "La Bibliothèque Sainte-Geneviève." *L'Artiste,* 5e sér., 7 (1 December 1851): 129–31. [08]

Hillairet, Jacques. *Dictionnaire historique des rues de Paris.* 2nd ed. 2 vols. Paris: Les Éditions de Minuit, 1963. [03] [07]

———. *La rue de Richelieu.* Paris: Minuit, 1966. [07]

Hittorff, Jacques Ignace. "Considérations sur l'église de la Madeleine." *Journal des Artistes et Amateurs,* 8ème année, 1 (18 May 1834): 353–59; 21 (25 May 1834): 366–75; 22 (1 June 1834): 384–87. [07]

———. "De l'architecture chez les grecs, ou restitution complète du temple d'Empédocle dans l'acropole de Sélinonte." *Annali dell'Instituto di corrispondenza archeologica* 2 (1830): 263–84. [07]

———. *Restitution du Temple d'Empédocle à Sélinonte, ou L'architecture polychrome chez les Grecs.* 2 vols. Paris: Firmin Didot, 1851. [07]

Hockney, David. *Secret Knowledge: Rediscovering the Lost Techniques of the Old Masters.* New York: Viking Studio, 2001. [8]

Hofer, Paul. *Delacroix's Faust.* Cambridge MA: Harvard University, 1964. [06]

Holt, Elizabeth Gilmore, ed. *From the Classicists to the Impressionists: Art and Architecture in the 19th Century.* New Haven: Yale University, 1986. [05]

———. *The Triumph of Art for the Public, 1785–1848.* Princeton: Princeton University, 1983. [05]

Honour, Hugh. *Romanticism.* New York: Harper & Row, 1979. [IN] [06]

Houssaye, Arsène. *1815.* 21st ed. 3 vols. Paris: Perrin, 1895–1905. [01]

Houx-Marc, Eugène. *Physiologie de la Galerie Vivienne et des Deux Pavillons.* Paris: E. de Soye, 1851. [07]

Huart, Louis. "Les voitures publiques." In *Nouveau Tableau de Paris au XIXe siècle.* 7 vols. Paris: Mme Charles-Béchet, 1834–1835, 4: 161–81. [07]

Hubert, Gérard. "L'art français au service de la Restauration: À propos des épaves de l'arc du Carrousel conservées au Louvre." *La Revue des Arts* 5 (December 1955): 209–16. [03]

Huchard, Viviane. "Les portraits de David: la nature et l'âme." In Saint-Rémy-lès-Chevreuse, *Aux Grands Hommes*: 59–69. [06]

Huet, Paul. *Paul Huet (1803–1869), d'après ses notes, sa correspondance, ses contemporains.* Ed. René Paul Huet. Paris: Librairie Renouard–H. Laurens, 1911. [06]

Hugo, Victor. *Alpes et Pyrénées.* In *Oeuvres Complètes de Victor Hugo: En Voyage.* 2 vols. Paris: Imprimerie Nationale / Ollendorff, 1910, 2: 171–439. [06]

———. "Assemblée Nationale." In *Oeuvres Complètes de Victor Hugo: Choses Vues.* 2 vols. Paris: Imprimerie Nationale / Ollendorff, 1913, 1: 379–400. [EP]

———. "Au moment de rentrer en France (31 août 1870)." In *Oeuvres Complètes de Victor Hugo: Poésie.* 14 vols. Paris: Imprimerie Nationale / Ollendorff, 1910, 4: 5–8. [EP]

———. "Chez Lamartine." In *Oeuvres Complètes de Victor Hugo: Choses Vues.* 2 vols. Paris: Imprimerie Nationale / Ollendorff, 1913, 1: 421. [EP]

———. *Cromwell – Hernani.* In *Oeuvres Complètes de Victor Hugo: Théâtre.* 6 vols. Paris: Imprimerie Nationale / Ollendorff, 1912, 1. [05] [06]

———. "Guerre aux démolisseurs! (1825)." In *Oeuvres Complètes de Victor Hugo: Philosophie.* 2 vols. Paris: Albin Michel / Imprimerie Nationale / Ollendorff, 1934, 1: 153–56. [08]

———. *Histoire d'un Crime.* In *Oeuvres Complètes de Victor Hugo: Histoire.* 2 vols. Paris: Imprimerie Nationale / Ollendorff, 1907, 1: 265–458, and 2: 1–187. [EP]

———. "La famille Bonaparte, 14 juin 1847." In *Oeuvres Complètes de Victor Hugo: Actes et Paroles.* 3 vols. Paris: Imprimerie Nationale / Ollendorff, 1937, 3: 91–95. [EP]

———. "Le 2 décembre 1851." In *Oeuvres Complètes de Victor Hugo: Actes et Paroles.* 3 vols. Paris: Imprimerie Nationale/Ollendorff, 1937, 1: 299–303. [EP]

———. "Le Premier Dîner: 24 décembre 1848." In *Oeuvres Complètes de Victor Hugo: Choses Vues.* 2 vols. Paris: Imprimerie Nationale / Ollendorff, 1913, 1: 408–13. [EP]

———. *Les Chants du crépuscule.* In *Oeuvres Complètes de Victor Hugo: Poésie.* 14 vols. Paris: Imprimerie Nationale / Librairie Ollendorff, 1909, 2: 173–308. [03] [EP]

———. *Les Misérables.* In *Oeuvres Complètes de Victor Hugo:*

Romans. 9 vols. Paris: Imprimerie Nationale / Albin Michel, 1942, 3–6. [03]

———. "Louis Bonaparte Incognito." In *Oeuvres Complètes de Victor Hugo: Choses Vues.* 2 vols. Paris: Imprimerie Nationale / Ollendorff, 1913, 1: 414. [EP]

———. *Napoléon-le-Petit.* In *Oeuvres Complètes de Victor Hugo: Histoire.* 2 vols. Paris: Imprimerie Nationale / Ollendorff, 1907, 1: 5–201. [EP]

———. "Notes sur la situation." In *Oeuvres Complètes de Victor Hugo: Choses Vues.* 2 vols. Paris: Imprimerie Nationale / Ollendorff, 1913, 2: 5–24. [EP]

———. *Notre-Dame de Paris.* In *Oeuvres Complètes de Victor Hugo: Romans.* 9 vols. Paris: Imprimerie Nationale / Ollendorff, 1904, 2. [03] [04] [08]

———. *Notre-Dame de Paris – Les Travailleurs de la Mer.* Ed. Jacques Seebacher et Yves Gohin. Paris: Gallimard–Pléiade, 1975. [08]

———. *Odes et Ballades – Les Orientales.* In *Oeuvres Complètes de Victor Hugo: Poésie.* 14 vols. Paris: Imprimerie Nationale / Ollendorff, 1912, 1: passim. [05] [06]

———. *Oeuvres Complètes de Victor Hugo: Correspondance.* 4 vols. Paris: Albin Michel, 1947. [05]

———. "Révision de la Constitution: 17 juillet 1851." In *Oeuvres Complètes de Victor Hugo: Actes et Paroles.* 3 vols. Paris: Imprimerie Nationale / Ollendorff, 1937, 1: 236–66. [EP]

———. "Séance des cinq associations d'art et d'industrie, 29 mai 1848." In *Oeuvres Complètes de Victor Hugo: Actes et Paroles.* 3 vols. Paris: Imprimerie Nationale / Ollendorff, 1937, 1: 108–20. [EP]

———. *Selected Poems.* Trans. Henry Carrington. Philadelphia: George Barrie & Son, 1897. [03]

———. "Victor Hugo à ses concitoyens, 26 mai 1848." In *Oeuvres Complètes de Victor Hugo: Actes et Paroles.* 3 vols. Paris: Imprimerie Nationale / Ollendorff, 1937, 1: 106–7. [EP]

Hungerford, Constance Cain. "Meissonier's *Souvenir de guerre civile.*" *Art Bulletin* 61 (June 1979): 277–88. [02]

Hunt, William Holman. *Pre-Raphaelitism and the Pre-Raphaelite Brotherhood.* 2nd ed. 2 vols. New York: E. P. Dutton, 1914. [05]

Ingold, Gérard. *Saint Louis: De l'art du verre à l'art du cristal de 1856 à nos jours.* Paris: Hermé, 1998. [08]

Institut Royal de France, Académie des Beaux-Arts. "Rapport sur la lithographie, et particulièrement sur un recueil de dessins lithographiés par M. Engelmann." In Johnson, *French Lithography:* 23–27. [08]

Jal, Augustin. *Esquisses, croquis, pochades ou tout ce qu'on voudra sur le Salon de 1827.* Paris: A. Dupont, 1828. [05]

———. *L'Artiste et le philosophe, entretiens critiques sur le Salon de 1824.* Paris: Ponthieu, 1824. [05]

———. *Salon de 1831: Ébauches critiques.* Paris: Dénain, 1831. [02]

———. *Salon de 1833: Les Causeries du Louvre.* Paris: Charles Gosselin, 1833. [05]

Jal, Gustave. *L'ombre de Diderot and le Bossu du Marais, dialogue critique sur le Salon de 1819.* Paris: chez Coréard, 1819. [07]

Jammes, Isabelle. *Blanquart-Evrard et les origines de l'édition photographique française.* Geneva: Droz, 1981. [08]

Jamot, Paul. "Goethe et Delacroix." *Gazette des Beaux-Arts,* 6e sér., 8 (July–December 1932): 279–98. [06]

Janin, Jules. "Exposition des produits de l'industrie: Premier article." *L'Artiste,* 2e sér., 3 (1839): 17–23. [08]

———. "Exposition des produits de l'industrie: Deuxième article." *L'Artiste,* 2e sér., 3 (1839): 33–39. [08]

———. "La Description du Daguérotype." *L'Artiste,* 2e sér., 3 (1839): 277–83. [08]

———. "Le Daguérotype." *L'Artiste,* 2e sér., 2 (1839): 145–48. [08]

———. "Le Daguérotype: Nouvelle Expérience." *L'Artiste,* 2e sér., 4 (1 September 1839): 1–3. [08]

———. "Salon de 1833: Sculpture." *L'Artiste,* 5 (1833): 141–43 and 153–55. [05]

Jeune, Simon. "Le Roi de Bohème et ses sept châteaux, livre-objet et livre-ferment." In *Charles Nodier:* Colloque du deuxième centenaire (Besançon Mai 1980). *Annales littéraires de l'université de Besançon* 253. Paris: Les Belles-Lettres, 1981: 199–210. [08]

———. "Le Roi de Bohème et ses sept châteaux." In Martin et al., *Histoire de l'édition française,* 3: 296–97. [08]

Joannides, Paul. "Some English Themes in the Early Work of Gros." *Burlington Magazine* 117 (December 1975): 774–85. [01]

Jobert, Berthélémy. *Delacroix.* Paris: Gallimard, 1997. [02] [05]

Johnson, Dorothy. *Jacques-Louis David: Art in Metamorphosis.* Princeton: Princeton University, 1993. [02]

Johnson, Lee. "Eugène Delacroix and Charles de Verninac: An Unpublished Portrait and New Letters." *Burlington Magazine* 110 (September 1968): 511–18. [02]

———. *The Paintings of Eugène Delacroix: A Critical Catalogue*, 6 vols. Oxford: Clarendon Press, 1981–1989. [02] [03] [05] [06]

Johnson, W. McAllister. *French Lithography: The Restoration Salons, 1817–1824*. Kingston Ontario Canada: Agnes Etherington Art Centre, 1977. [08]

Joinville, François-Ferdinand-Philippe d'Orléans, prince de. *Vieux Souvenirs de Mgr le Prince de Joinville, 1818–1848*. Ed. Daniel Meyer. Paris: Mercure de France, 1970. [05]

Juin, Herbert. *Victor Hugo*. 3 vols. Paris: Flammarion, 1984–1986. [EP]

Jürgensen, Knud Arne and Ann Hutchinson Guest. *Robert le Diable: The Ballet of the Nuns*. Amsterdam: Gordon and Breach, 1997. [06]

Kahn, Jean-François. *L'extraordinaire métamorphose, ou cinq ans de la vie de Victor Hugo, 1847–1851*. Paris: Seuil, 1984. [EP]

Kant, Emmanuel. *Foundation of the Metaphysics of Morals* and *What Is Enlightenment?* 2nd ed. Trans. Lewis White Beck. New York: Macmillan, 1990. [01]

Karénine, Wladimir. *George Sand: Sa vie et ses oeuvres*. 4 vols. Paris: Plon-Nourrit, 1912. [06]

Kaufmann, Ruth. "François Gérard's 'Entry of Henry IV into Paris': The Iconography of Constitutional Monarchy." *Burlington Magazine* 1173 (December 1975): 790–802. [03]

Kératry, Auguste-Hilarion, comte de. *Annuaire de l'école française de peinture, ou Lettres sur le Salon de 1819*. Paris: Maradan, 1820. [07]

Kerr, David S. *Caricature and French Political Culture, 1830–1848*. Oxford: Clarendon Press, 2000. [08]

Klahr, Douglas. "Le Développement des rues parisiennes pendant la Monarchie de Juillet." In Bowie, *La modernité avant Haussmann*: 217–30. [03] [07]

Kolb, Marthe. *Ary Scheffer et son temps, 1795–1858*. Paris: Boivin, 1937. [03] [06]

Kris, Ernst. *Psychoanalytic Explorations in Art*. New York: International Universities, 1952. [08]

Laborde, Léon de. *De l'organisation des bibliothèques dans Paris, Huitième Lettre: Étude sur la construction des bibliothèques*. Paris: A. Franck, 1845. [08]

Labrouste, Henri. "À M. le Directeur de la Revue d'Architecture." *Revue Générale de l'Architecture et des Travaux Publics* 10 (1851): cols. 382–84. [08]

Lacambre, Geneviève. *Les Paysages de Pierre-Henri Valenciennes, 1750–1819*, exhibition catalogue. *Dossiers du Musée du Louvre*, 11. Paris: Musée du Louvre, 1976. [05]

Lacordaire, Henri-Dominique. *Sainte Marie-Madeleine*. 3rd ed. Paris: Librairie Poussielgue Frères, 1872. [03]

Lacroix, Auguste de. "Le flâneur." In *Les Français peints par eux-mêmes: Encyclopédie morale du dix-neuvième siècle*. 4 vols. Paris: L. Curmer, 1841, 3: 65–72. [07]

Lacroix, Paul. *Histoire politique, anecdotique et populaire de Napoléon III, empereur des Français et de la dynastie napoléonienne*. 4 vols. Paris: Du Four, Mulat et Boulanger, 1853. [02]

Ladet, U. "De la propriété en matière d'art." *L'Artiste*, 2e sér., 7 (1841): 71–74 and 111–12. [08]

Lagarrigue, Louis. *Cent Ans de transports en commun dans la région Parisienne*. 2 vols. Paris: Firmin-Didot, 1956. [07]

Lajer-Burcharth, Ewa. *Necklines: The Art of Jacques-Louis David after the Terror*. New Haven: Yale University, 1999. [01] [02]

Lamartine, Alphonse de. *Correspondance de Lamartine*, publiée par Mme Valentine de Larmartine. 2nd ed. 4 vols. Paris: Hachette, Furne, Jouvet, 1881. [EP]

———. *Oeuvres Poétiques Complètes de Lamartine*. Ed. Marius-François Guyard. Paris: Gallimard-Pléiade, 1963. [EP]

Lambeau, Lucien. *Histoire des Communes annexées à Paris en 1859: Charonne*. 2 vols. Paris: Ernst Leroux, 1916–1921. [03]

Lami, Stanislas. *Dictionnaire des sculpteurs de l'école française au dix-neuvième siècle*. 4 vols. Paris: E. Champion, 1914–1921. [05]

Landon, Charles P. *Annales du Musée et de l'École moderne des Beaux-Arts: Salon de 1824*. Paris: Ballard, 1824. [05]

Langle, Henry-Melchior de. *Le petit monde des cafés et débits Parisiens au XIXe siècle: Évolution de la sociabilité citadine*. Paris: Presses Universitaires de France, 1990. [07]

Lansdowne, Henry William Edmund. *The Secret of the Coup d'État*; unpublished correspondence of Prince Louis Napoleon, MM. de Morny, de Flahault, and others. Ed. Earl of Kerry. Intro. Philip Guedalla. New York: G. P. Putnam's Sons, 1924. [EP]

Lanzac de Laborie, Léon. *Paris sous Napoléon*. 8 vols. Paris: Plon-Nourrit, 1905–1913. [03] [04] [06] [07]

Lapauze, Henry. *Ingres: Sa vie et son oeuvre*. Paris: Georges Petit, 1911. [08]

Larousse, Pierre. *Le Grand Dictionnaire universel du XIXe siècle*. 24 vols. Paris: 1876. Reprint. Nîmes: C. Lacour, 1991. [07]

Las Cases, Emmanuel de. *Le Mémorial de Sainte-Hélène.* 2 vols. Ed. André Fugier. Paris: Garnier, 1961. [02] [08]

———. *Le Mémorial de Sainte-Hélène.* 8 vols. Paris: chez l'auteur, 1823. [03]

———. *Le Mémorial de Sainte-Hélène,* suivi de Napoléon dans l'exil par MM. O'Meara et Antommarchi, et de l'Historique de la translation des restes mortels de l'Empereur Napoléon aux Invalides. 2 vols. Paris: Ernest Bourdin, 1842. [08]

Lassus, Jean-Baptiste de and Eugène-Emmanuel Viollet-le-Duc. "On the Restoration of the Cathedral of Notre-Dame de Paris." In *The Architectural Theory of Viollet-le-Duc: Readings and Commentary.* Ed. M. F. Hearn. Cambridge MA: MIT, 1990: 279–88. [04]

Lauvergne, Hubert. *Souvenirs de la Grèce pendant la campagne de 1825, ou Mémoires historiques et biographiques.* Paris: chez Avril de Gastel, 1826. [05]

Lavallée, Joseph. *Lettres d'un mameluck, ou Tableau moral et critique des moeurs de Paris.* Paris: chez Capell, 1803. [07]

Lavedan, Pierre. *Histoire de l'urbanisme à Paris.* 3rd ed. Paris: Hachette, 1993. [03]

———. *Nouvelle Histoire de Paris: Histoire de l'urbanisme à Paris.* 2nd ed. Paris: Hachette, 1993. [07]

Laviron, Gabriel. "Exposition des produits de l'industrie." *L'Artiste,* 3e sér., 5 (28 April 1844): 265–67. [08]

Laviron, Gabriel and Bruno Galbaccio. *Le Salon de 1833.* Paris: Abel Ledoux, 1833. [05]

Lazare, Félix and Louis Lazare. *Dictionnaire administratif et historique des rues et monuments de Paris.* 2nd ed. Paris: Au Bureau de la Revue Municipale, 1855. [03] [04] [07]

Le Hallé, Guy. *Les fortifications de Paris.* Le Coteau: Horvath, 1986. [07]

Le Men, Ségolène. "Daumier et le théâtre." In *Honoré Daumier: Scènes de vie et vies de scène.* Ed. Julian Zugazagoitia. Milan: Electa, 1998: 22–27. [07]

———. "L'édition illustrée, un musée pour lire." In Paris, *La Gloire de Victor Hugo:* 527–68. [06]

———. "La vignette et la lettre." In Martin et al., *Histoire de l'édition française,* 3: 313–27. [08]

———. "Les frontispices des éditions illustrées." In *Victor Hugo et les images.* Eds. Madeleine Blondel and Pierre Georgel. Dijon: Ville de Dijon–Aux Amateurs du Livre, 1989: 233–47. [06]

———. "'Ma muse, ta muse s'amuse . . .': Philipon et l'Association Mensuelle (1832–1834)." *Cahiers de l'Institut d'histoire de la presse et de l'opinion* 7 (1983): 63–135. [08]

Le Normand, Mademoiselle M. A. *Historical and Secret Memoirs of the Empress Josephine.* 2 vols. Trans. Jacob M. Howard. Philadelphia: A. Hart, 1852. [01]

Lebrun de Charmettes, Philippe-Alexandre. *Histoire de Jeanne d'Arc, surnommée la Pucelle d'Orléans.* Paris: A. Bertrand, 1817. [04]

Lecomte, Louis-Henry. *Napoléon et le monde dramatique, étude nouvelle d'après des documents inédits.* Paris: H. Daragon, 1912. [06]

Ledoux-Lebard, Guy. "Les projets de fontaines pour la place de la Bastille et la fontaine à l'éléphant." *Archives de l'art français,* nouv. pér., 24 (1959): 37–56. [03]

Ledru-Rollin, Alexandre-Auguste. *Mémoire sur les événements de la Rue Transnonain, dans les journées des 13 et 14 avril 1834.* Paris: Guillaumin, 1834. [08]

Lefebvre, Georges. *Napoleon.* 2 vols. Trans. Henry F. Stockhold. New York: Columbia University, 1969. [01]

Lefebvre, Henri. *La production de l'espace.* 4th ed. Paris: Anthropos, 2000 [1974]. [IN] [03] [07] [08]

———. *The Production of Space.* Trans. Donald Nicolson-Smith. London: Blackwell, 1991. [IN]

Leith, James. *Space and Revolution: Projects for Monuments, Squares, and Public Buildings in France, 1789–1799.* Montreal: McGill–Queen's University, 1991. [03]

Lelièvre, Pierre. *Vivant Denon.* Paris: Picard, 1993. [01]

Lemoine, Bertrand. *L'Architecture du Fer: France XIXe siècle.* Paris: Champ Vallon, 1986. [08]

———. *Les passages couverts en France.* Paris: Délégation à l'action artistique de la Ville de Paris, 1989. [07]

Lenoir, Albert. *Archives du Musée des Monuments français.* 3 vols. Paris: E. Plon–Nourrit, 1883–1897. [04]

Lenoir, Alexandre. *De l'Obélisque de Louqsor.* Paris: P. Baudouin, n.d [BnF Lk7 7566]. [03]

———. *Description historique et chronologique des monumens de sculpture réunis au Musée des Monumens français.* Paris: chez l'auteur, AN VIII [1800]. [04]

———. *Description historique et chronologique des monumens de sculpture réunis au Musée des Monumens français.* 7th ed. Paris: chez l'auteur, AN XI [1803]. [04]

Lenormant, Charles. *Beaux-Arts et Voyages, précédés d'une lettre par M. Guizot.* 2 vols. Paris: M. Lévy, 1861. [05]

———. *Les artistes contemporaines.* 2 vols. Paris: Alexandre Mesnier, 1833. [05] [06]

Léon, Paul. "L'Église de la Madeleine." *Revue des Deux Mondes,* nouv. sér., 7e année, 11 (1 June 1954): 405–26. [03]

———. *La Vie des Monuments français.* Paris: A. et J. Picard, 1951. [04]

Leroy-Jay Lemaistre, Isabelle. "L'Ascension du bronze." In Paris, *Un âge d'or des arts décoratifs*: 281–85. [06] [08]

———. "Des Sculpteurs et des bronziers." In Paris, *Le Mécénat du duc d'Orléans*: 128–45. [05]

———. "The *Surtout de Table* of the Duc d'Orleans." In Baltimore, *Untamed: The Art of Antoine-Louis Barye*: 26–41. [05]

Leterrier, Sophie-Anne. *Le XIXe siècle historien: Anthologie raisonnée.* Paris: Belin, 1997. [03]

Levine, Neil. "The Book and the Building: Hugo's Theory of Architecture and Labrouste's Bibliothèque Sainte-Geneviève." In *The Beaux-Arts and Nineteenth-Century French Architecture.* Ed. Robin Middleton. London: Thames and Hudson, 1982: 138–73. [08]

———. "The Romantic Idea of Architectural Legibility: Henri Labrouste and the Neo-Grec." In *The Architecture of the École des Beaux-Arts.* Ed. Arthur Drexler. New York: The Museum of Modern Art, 1977, 325–416. [08]

Levinson, André. *Marie Taglioni.* Trans. Cyril W. Beaumont. London: 1930. Reprint. London: Dance Books, 1977. [06]

Lhéritier, Andrée. "Les Physiologies." In Martin et al., *Histoire de l'édition française,* 3: 380–81. [08]

Litzmann, Berthold. *Clara Schumann: Ein Künstlerleben.* 3 vols. Leipzig: Breitkopf & Haertel, 1923–1925. Reprint. Hildesheim / New York: Georg Olms, 1971. [06]

Loffredo, François-Raphaël. "Des recherches communes de Barye et Delacroix au laboratoire d'anatomie du Muséum d'histoire naturelle." *Bulletin de la Société de l'histoire de l'art français,* 1982. Paris: Jean Schemit, 1984: 147–57. [05]

London, Tate Britain. *Constable: The Great Landscapes,* exhibition catalogue. London: Tate Publishing, 2006. [05]

Los Angeles, LA County Museum. *The Romantics to Rodin: French Nineteenth-Century Sculpture from North American Collections,* exhibition catalogue. Eds. Peter Fusco and Horst W. Janson.

Los Angeles: Museum Associates of Los Angeles County Museum of Art, 1980. [06]

Louisville, J. B. Speed Museum. *Ingres—In Pursuit of Perfection: The Art of J.-A.-D. Ingres,* exhibition catalogue. Eds. Patricia Condon, Marjorie B. Cohn, and Agnes Mongan. Louisville KY: The J. B. Speed Art Museum, 1983. [08]

Lovejoy, Arthur O. "On the Discrimination of Romanticisms (1923)." In *Essays in the History of Ideas.* Baltimore: Johns Hopkins University, 1948: 228–53. [IN]

———. *The Great Chain of Being: A Study of the History of an Idea.* Cambridge MA: Harvard University, 1936. [IN]

Lowe, Lisa. *Critical Terrains: French and British Orientalists.* Ithaca: Cornell University, 1991. [05]

Loyer, François. *Paris Nineteenth Century: Architecture and Urbanism.* Trans. Charles Lynn Clark. New York: Abbeville, 1988. [07]

Lucas-Dubreton, Jean. *France de Napoléon.* Paris: Librairie Jules Tallandier, 1981. [01]

———. *Le Culte de Napoléon, 1815–1848.* Paris: A. Michel, 1959. [01] [08] [EP]

Luchet, Auguste. *L'art industriel à l'Exposition Universelle de 1867.* Paris: Librairie Internationale, 1868. [08]

———. "Les Magasins de Paris." In *Le Livre des Cent-et-Un.* 15 vols. Paris: chez Ladvocat, 1834, 15: 237–68. [08]

———. "Les Passages." In *Nouveau Tableau de Paris au XIXe siècle.* 7 vols. Paris: Mme Charles-Béchut, 1834–1835, 6: 97–113. [07]

Lyon, Musée des Beaux-Arts. *Ernest Meissonier: Rétrospective,* exhibition catalogue. Lyon/Paris: Musée des Beaux-Arts de Lyon / Réunion des musées nationaux, 1993. [02]

M. . . . *Revue critique des productions de Peinture, Sculpture, Gravure, exposées au Salon de 1824.* Paris: J. G. Dentu, 1825. [05]

Madelin, Louis. *La Catastrophe de Russie.* Paris: Librairie Hachette, 1949. [01]

———. *The Consulate and Empire.* Trans. E. F. Buckley. London: William Heinemann, 1934. [01]

———. *La France à l'apogée de l'Empire.* Paris: Hachette, 1970. [01]

———. *La Nation sous l'Empereur.* Paris: Hachette, 1948. [01]

Mallbrave, Harry Francis. *Gottfried Semper: Architect of the Nineteenth Century.* New Haven: Yale University, 1996. [08]

Mansel, Philip. *The Court of France, 1789–1830.* Cambridge UK: Cambridge University, 1988. [01]

Marchant, François-Marie. *Le nouveau Conducteur de l'étranger à Paris en 1839*. 20th ed. Paris: Moronval, 1839. [07]

Marie, Aristide. *Le Peintre-poète Louis Boulanger*. Paris: H. Floury, 1925. [06]

Marix-Spire, Thérèse. *Les Romantiques et la musique: Le cas de George Sand*. Paris: Nouvelles Éditions Latines, 1954. [06]

Marrinan, Michael. "Literal/Literary/'Lexie': history, text, and authority in Napoleonic painting." *Word&Image* 7 (July–September 1991): 177–200. [01]

———. *Painting Politics for Louis-Philippe: Art and Ideology in Orléanist France, 1830–1848*. New Haven: Yale University, 1988. [02] [03] [05] [07] [08] [EP]

———. "Picasso as an 'Ingres' young Cubist." *Burlington Magazine* 119 (November 1977): 756–63. [06]

———. "Schauer der Eroberung: Strukturen des Zuschauens und der Simulation in den Nordafrika-Galerien von Versailles." In *Bilder der Macht/Macht der Bilder: Zeitgeschichte in Darstellungen des 19. Jahrhunderts*. Eds. Stefan Germer and Michael F. Zimmermann. Munich/Berlin: Klinkhardt & Biermann, 1997, 267–96. [05]

Martin, Henri-Jean, Roger Chartier, and Jean-Pierre Vivet, eds. *Histoire de l'édition française*. 4 vols. Paris: Promodis, 1982–1986. [06] [08]

Martin, Marc. "Journalistes parisiens et notoriété (vers 1830–1870): Pour une histoire sociale du journalisme." *Revue historique* 266 (July–September 1981): 31–74. [06]

Martin, Odile and Henri-Jean Martin. "Le monde des éditeurs." In Martin et al., *Histoire de l'édition française*, 3: 159–215. [08]

Martin-Fugier, Anne. *La vie élégante, ou la formation du Tout-Paris 1815–1848*. Paris: Fayard, 1990. [06] [07]

Marx, Karl. *Le Dix-huit Brumaire de Louis-Bonaparte*. Paris: Éditions Sociales, 1976. [08]

———. "The Defeat of June 1848." In *Marx and Engels: Basic Writings on Politics and Philosophy*. Ed. Lewis S. Feuer. New York: Doubleday-Anchor, 1959, 281–307. [02]

Mayer, Louis-Frédéric and Pierre-Louis Pierson. *La Photographie considérée comme art et comme industrie: Histoire de sa découverte, ses progrès, ses applications, son avenir*. Paris: L. Hachette, 1862. [08]

Mayer, Ralph. *A Dictionary of Art Terms and Techniques*. New York: Thomas Y. Crowell, 1969. [07]

Maza, Sarah. *The Myth of the French Bourgeoisie: An Essay on the Social Imaginary, 1750–1850*. Cambridge MA: Harvard University, 2003. [06] [07]

McClellan, Andrew. *Inventing the Louvre: Art, Politics, and the Origins of the Modern Museum in Eighteenth-Century Paris*. Cambridge UK: Cambridge University, 1994. [03] [04]

McCoubrey, John. "Gros's 'Battle of Eylau' and Roman Imperial Art." *Art Bulletin* 43 (June 1961): 135–39. [01]

McKendrick, Neil. "Home Demand and Economic Growth: A New View of Women and Children in the Industrial Revolution." In *Historical Perspectives: Studies in English Thought and Society*. Ed. Neil McKendrick. London: Europa, 1974: 152–210. [08]

———. "The Commercialization of Fashion." In *The Birth of a Consumer Society: The Commercialization of Eighteenth-Century England*. Eds. Neil McKendrick, John Brewer, and John Harold Plumb. London: Hutchinson, 1982: 34–99. [08]

———. "The Consumer Revolution." In *The Birth of a Consumer Society: The Commercialization of Eighteenth-Century England*. Eds. Neil McKendrick, John Brewer, and John Harold Plumb. London: Hutchinson: 1982, 9–33. [08]

McWilliam, Neil. "David d'Angers and the Pantheon Commission: Politics and Public Works under the July Monarchy." *Art History* 5 (1982): 426–46. [03]

———. *Dreams of Happiness: Social Art and the French Left, 1830–1850*. Princeton: Princeton University, 1993. [05] [06]

———. "Opinions professionnelles: Critique d'art et économie de la culture sous la Monarche de Juillet." *Romantisme* 71 (1991): 19–30. [06]

Meisel, Martin. *Realizations: Narrative, Pictorial, and Theatrical Arts in Nineteenth-Century England*. Princeton: Princeton University, 1983. [05] [06]

Mellon, Stanley. *The Political Uses of History*. Stanford: Stanford University, 1958. [03]

Melman, Billie. *Women's Orients: English Women and the Middle East, 1718–1918*. London: Macmillan, 1992. [05]

Melot, Michel. "Le texte et l'image." In Martin et al., *Histoire de l'édition française*, 3: 287–311. [08]

Mercier, Sébastien. *Le Nouveau Paris*. Paris: Fuchs, C. Pougens, C.-F. Cramer, AN VII [1798]. Reprint. Paris: Mercure de France, 1994. [07]

————. "Sur le dépôt des Petits-Augustins, *dit*: Le Musée des Monumens français." *Paris pendant l'année 1797* 15 (14 October 1797): 473–75. [04]

Mésangère, Pierre-Antoine Leboux de la. *Le voyageur à Paris, tableau pittoresque et moral de cette capitale.* 3 vols. Paris: Chaignieau & Devaux, 1797. [07]

Mesplé, Paul. "David et ses élèves toulousains." *Archives de l'art français,* nouv. pér., 24 (1969): 90–102. [01]

Metman, Bernard. "La petite sculpture au XIXe siècle: Les éditeurs." *Archives de l'art français,* nouv. pér., 30 (1989): 175–218. [08]

Meynadier, Hippolyte. *Paris sous le point de vue pittoresque et monumental, ou Éléments d'un plan générale d'ensemble de ses travaux d'art et d'utilité publique.* Paris: Dauvin & Fontaine, 1843. [07]

Michelet, Jules. *Histoire de France (Livres V–IX).* In *Oeuvres Complètes.* Ed. Paul Viallaneix. Paris: Flammarion, 1975, vol. 5. [04]

————. *Histoire de la Révolution française.* 9 vols. Paris: A. Lacroix, 1877–1880. [04]

————. *Journal.* 3 vols. Ed. Paul Viallaneix. Paris: Gallimard, 1959. [IN]

Miel, Edmé-François-Antoine-Marie. *Essai sur les Beaux-Arts et particulièrement sur le Salon de 1817, ou examen critique des principaux ouvrages d'art exposés dans le cours de cette année.* Paris: Pélicier, 1817–1818. [04] [08]

Miller, Michael B. *The Bon Marché: Bourgeois Culture and the Department Store, 1869–1920.* Princeton: Princeton University, 1981. [08]

Milton, Henry. *Letters on the Fine Arts written from Paris in the year 1815.* London: Longman, Hurst, Rees, Orme & Brown, 1816. [03] [06]

Miquel, Pierre. *Paul Huet: De l'aube romantique à l'aube impressionniste.* Paris: Éditions de la Martinelle, 1962. [06]

Mirecourt, Eugène de. *Le baron Taylor.* Paris: J.-P. Roret, 1854. [06]

Mollaret, H. and J. Brossolet. "A propos des 'Pestiférés de Jaffa' de A. J. Gros." *Koninklijk Museum voor Schone Kunsten-Antwerpen* (Jaarboek 1968): 263–307. [01]

Moncan, Patrice de. *Les passages couverts de Paris.* Paris: Éditions du Mécène, 1995. [07]

Montalembert, Charles-René de. "De l'art religieux en France." *Revue des Deux Mondes,* 4e sér., 12 (1 December 1837): 592–617. [03]

————. *Oeuvres de M. le comte de Montalembert.* 9 vols. Paris: J. Lecoffe, 1860–1868. [03]

Montigny, Louis. *Le provincial à Paris: Esquisses des moeurs parisiennes.* 3 vols. Paris: l'Advocat, 1825. [07]

Mora, Edith. *Sappho: Histoire d'un poète et traduction intégrale de l'oeuvre.* Paris: Flammarion, 1966. [01] [EP]

Morgan, Lady Thomas Charles. *France.* 2 vols. New York: James Eastburn, 1817. [02]

Morrissey, Robert. "Charlemagne." In *Les Lieux de Mémoire,* sous la direction de Pierre Nora. 3 vols. Paris: Gallimard-Quarto, 1997, 3: 4389–425. [03]

Motte, Charles. "Lithographie à la Manière Noire: Au Directeur de *l'Artiste*." *L'Artiste* 2 (1831): 238–39. [06]

Mouilleseaux, Jean-Pierre. *Mazeppa: variations sur un thème romantique,* exhibition catalogue. Rouen: Musée des Beaux-Arts, 1978. [05]

Munhall, Edgar. *Ingres and the Comtesse d'Haussonville,* exhibition catalogue. New York: The Frick Collection, 1985. [06]

Münster, Westfälisches Landesmuseum für Kunst und Kulturgeschichte. *La Caricature: Bildsatire in Frankreich 1830–1835 aus der Sammlung von Kritter,* exhibition catalogue. Göttingen: Kunstgeschichtliches Seminar der Universität Göttingen, 1980. [08]

Murger, Henri. *Scènes de la Vie de Bohème.* Ed. Paul Ginisty. Paris: 1851. Reprint. Paris: Garnier, 1912. [06]

Nemeitz, Joachim-Christoph. *Séjour de Paris, c'est-à-dire, instructions fidèles pour les voiageurs.* 2 vols. Leiden: Jean van Abconde, 1727. [07]

Nerval, Gérard de. *Oeuvres Complètes.* 3 vols. Eds. Jean Guillaume and Claude Pichois. Paris: Gallimard-Pléiade, 1993. [06]

Neuchâtel, Musée des Beaux-Arts. *Léopold Robert et les Peintres de l'Italie romantique,* exhibition catalogue. Neuchâtel: Musée des Beaux-Arts, 1983. [05]

New Haven, Yale University Art Gallery. *Prints of Eugène Delacroix,* exhibition catalogue. New Haven: Yale University Art Gallery, 1977. [05] [06] [08]

New York, Bard Graduate Center for Studies in the Decorative Arts. *The Sèvres Porcelain Manufactory: Alexandre Brongniart and the Triumph of Art and Industry, 1800–1847,* exhibition catalogue. New York: Bard Graduate Center for Studies in the Decorative Arts, 1997. [04]

New York, Frick Collection. *Clodion Terracottas in North American Collections*, exhibition catalogue. New York: The Frick Collection, 1984. [05]

New York, Metropolitan Museum of Art. *Corot*, exhibition catalogue. New York: The Metropolitan Museum of Art, 1996. [05]

———. *Portraits by Ingres: Image of an Epoch*, exhibition catalogue. New York: The Metropolitan Museum of Art, 1999. [06]

New York, Metropolitan Museum of Art, and Detroit, Institute of Arts. *French Painting 1774–1830: The Age of Revolution*, exhibition catalogue. New York/Detroit: The Metropolitan Museum/Institute of Arts, 1975. [01] [04]

Newman, Edgar Leon. "L'image de la foule dans la Révolution de 1830." *Annales historiques de la Révolution française* 52 (1980): 499–509. [02]

———. "What the Crowd Wanted in the French Revolution of 1830." In *1830 in France*. Ed. John Merriman. New York: New Viewpoints, 1975: 17–40. [02]

Niépce, Isidore. *Historique de la découverte improprement nommé Daguerréotype*. 1841. Reprint. La Courneuve: OFMI/Garamont, 1972. [08]

Nochlin, Linda. *The Body in Pieces: The Fragment as a Metaphor of Modernity*. London: Thames and Hudson, 1994. [06]

———. "The Imaginary Orient." In *The Politics of Vision: Essays on Nineteenth-Century Art and Society*. New York: Harper & Row, 1989: 33–59. [05]

Nora, Pierre. "Entre Mémoire et Histoire." In *Les Lieux de Mémoire*, sous la direction de Pierre Nora. 3 vols. Paris: Gallimard, 1984, 1: i–xlii. [02]

Nouty, Hassan el. *Théâtre et pré-cinéma: Essai sur la problématique du spectacle au XIXe siècle*. Paris: A.-G. Nizet, 1978. [05]

O'Brien, David. *After the Revolution: Antoine-Jean Gros, Painting, and Propaganda under Napoléon*. University Park PA: Pennsylvania State University, 2006. [01] [03]

———. "Antoine-Jean Gros in Italy." *Burlington Magazine*, 137 (October 1995): 651–660. [01] [03]

O'Brien, Patrick and Caglar Keyder. *Economic Growth in Britain and France, 1780–1914: Two Paths to the Twentieth Century*. London: George Allen & Unwin, 1978. [08]

Ortigue, Joseph-Louis d'. *Le balcon de l'Opéra*. Paris: Renduel, 1833. [06]

Ozouf, Mona. *Festivals and the French Revolution*. Trans. Alan Sheridan. Cambridge MA: Harvard University, 1988. [02]

———. "Le Panthéon." In *Les Lieux de Mémoire*, sous la direction de Pierre Nora. 3 vols. Paris: Gallimard-Quarto, 1997, 1: 155–78. [03]

Pailleron, Marie-Louise. *George Sand: Années glorieuses*. 2 vols. Paris: Bernard Grasset, 1942. [06]

Pain, Joseph and Joseph-Henri Costa de Beauregard. *Nouveaux Tableaux de Paris, ou Observations sur les moeurs et usages des Parisiens au commencement du XIXe siècle*. 2 vols. Paris: Pillet, 1828. [07]

Papayanis, Nicholas. *Planning Paris before Haussmann*. Baltimore: Johns Hopkins University, 2004. [03] [07]

Pardoe, Julia. *The City of the Sultan and Domestic Manners of the Turks in 1836*. 2 vols. London: H. Coburn, 1837. [05]

Paris, Bibliothèque Nationale. *George Sand: Visages du Romantisme*, exhibition catalogue. Paris: BnF, 1977. [06]

Paris, Caisse Nationale des Monuments Historiques et des Sites. *Le Panthéon: Symbole des révolutions*, exhibition catalogue. Paris/Montreal: Caisse Nationale des Monuments Historiques et des Sites/Centre Canadien d'Architecture/Picard, 1989. [03]

Paris, Délégation à l'action artistique de la Ville de Paris. *Le Mécénat du duc d'Orléans 1830–1842*, exhibition catalogue. Ed. Hervé Robert. Paris: Délégation à l'action artistique de la Ville de Paris, 1993. [04] [05] [06]

———. *Louis Visconti, 1791–1853*, exhibition catalogue. Paris: Délégation à l'action artistique de la Ville de Paris, 1991. [03]

Paris, Galeries nationales du Grand Palais. *Chassériau: Un autre romantisme*, exhibition catalogue. Paris: Réunion des musées nationaux, 2002. [EP]

———. *Daumier, 1808–1879*, exhibition catalogue. Paris: Réunion des musées nationaux, 1999. [08]

———. *Géricault*, exhibition catalogue. Paris: Éditions de la Réunion des musées nationaux, 1991. [01]

———. *Gustave Courbet, 1819–1877*, exhibition catalogue. Paris: Éditions des musées nationaux, 1977. [05]

———. *La Gloire de Victor Hugo*, exhibition catalogue. Paris: Éditions des musées nationaux, 1985. [06]

———. *La Sculpture française au XIXe siècle*, exhibition catalogue. Paris: Éditions de la Réunion des musées nationaux, 1986. [02] [03]

———. *Les années romantiques: La peinture française de 1815 à 1850*, exhibition catalogue. Paris: Éditions de la Réunion des musées nationaux, 1995. [03] [05] [06]

———. *Mélancolie: Génie et folie en Occident*, exhibition catalogue. Paris: Éditions de la Réunion des musées nationaux / Gallimard, 2005. [01] [04] [05] [06] [EP]

———. *Un âge d'or des arts décoratifs, 1814–1848*, exhibition catalogue. Paris: Réunion des musées nationaux, 1991. [04] [05] [06] [08]

———. *Viollet-le-Duc*, exhibition catalogue. Paris: Éditions de la Réunion des musées nationaux, 1980. [04] [05] [06]

Paris, Hôtel de Sully. *Le "Gothique" retrouvée avant Viollet-le-Duc*, exhibition catalogue. Paris: Caisse Nationale des Monuments Historiques et des Sites, 1979. [06]

Paris, Musée Carnavalet. *Alexandre-Théodore Brongniart 1739–1813*, exhibition catalogue. Alençon: Imprimerie Alençonnaise, 1986. [03]

———. *De la place Louis XV à la place de la Concorde*, exhibition catalogue. Alençon: Imprimerie Alençonnaise, 1982. [03]

———. *Hittorff: Un Architecte du XIXe siècle*, exhibition catalogue. Alençon: Imprimerie Alençonnaise, 1986. [03]

———. *Juillet 1830*, exhibition catalogue. Alençon: Imprimerie Alençonnaise, 1980. [03]

———. *Le Palais-Royal*, exhibition catalogue. Paris: Paris-Musées, 1988. [02]

———. *Paris et le daguerréotype*, exhibition catalogue. Paris: Paris-Musées, 1989. [08]

Paris, Musée d'Orsay. *Auguste Préault, sculpteur romantique (1809–1979)*, exhibition catalogue. Paris: Réunion des musées nationaux / Gallimard, 1997. [05]

———. *Le corps en morceaux*, exhibition catalogue. Paris: Éditions de la Réunion des musées nationaux, 1990. [05] [06]

Paris, Musée de la Musique. *L'Invention du sentiment: Aux sources du Romantisme*, exhibition catalogue. Paris: Réunion des musées nationaux / Musée de la Musique, 2002. [01] [06] [EP]

Paris, Musée du Louvre. *Achille-Etna Michallon*, exhibition catalogue. *Dossiers du Musée du Louvre*, no. 43. Paris: Réunion des musées nationaux, 1994. [05]

———. *Dominique-Vivant Denon: L'oeil de Napoléon*, exhibition catalogue. Paris: Réunion des musées nationaux, 1999. [01] [03]

———. *Jacques-Louis David, 1748–1825*, exhibition catalogue. Paris: Éditions de la Réunion des musées nationaux, 1989. [01]

———. *La griffe et la dent: Antoine-Louis Barye (1795–1875), sculpteur animalier*, exhibition catalogue. *Dossiers du Musée du Louvre*, no. 51. Paris: Éditions des musées nationaux, 1996. [05]

———. *Marie d'Orléans 1813–1839: Princesse et artiste romantique*, exhibition catalogue. Paris: Musée du Louvre Éditions, 2008. [04] [07]

———. *Théodore Rousseau*, exhibition catalogue. Paris: Réunion des musées nationaux, 1967. [05]

Paris, Musée Renan-Scheffer. *La Nouvelle Athènes: Le quartier Saint-Georges de Louis XV à Napoléon III*, exhibition catalogue. Paris: Musées de la Ville de Paris, 1984. [06] [07]

Paris, Musée Rodin. *Le faubourg Saint-Germain: La rue de Varenne*, exhibition catalogue. Paris: Délégation à l'action artistique de la Ville de Paris, 1981. [07]

———. *Le faubourg Saint-Germain: La rue Saint-Dominique*, exhibition catalogue. Paris: Délégation à l'action artistique de la Ville de Paris, 1984. [07]

Paris, Salon de 1824. *Explication des Ouvrages de Peinture, Sculpture, Gravure, Lithographie et Architecture des Artistes vivans*, exposés au Musée Royal des Arts, le 25 août 1824. Paris: C. Ballard, 1824. [05]

Paris, Salon de 1827. *Explication des Ouvrages du Peinture, Sculpture, Gravure, Lithographie et Architecture des Artistes vivans*, exposés au Musée Royal des Arts, le 4 Novembre 1827. Paris: Ve Ballard, 1827. [05]

Paris, Salon de 1834. *Explication des Ouvrages de Peinture, Sculpture, Architecture, Gravure et Lithographie des Artistes vivans*, exposés au Musée Royal, le 1er Mars 1834. Paris: Vinchon, 1834. [05]

Pariset, Madame. *Manuel de la Maîtresse de Maison, ou Lettres sur l'économie domestique*. 3rd ed. Paris: Audot, 1825. [08]

Partridge, Eric. *The French Romantics' Knowledge of English Literature, 1820–1848*. Paris: Édouard Champion, 1924. [01]

Paul, John Dean. *Journal of a Party of Pleasure to Paris in the month of August 1802*. London: Cadell & Davis, 1802. [07]

———. *Journal of a Party of Pleasure to Paris in the month of August 1802*. 3rd ed. London: T. Cadell and W. Davies, 1814. [03] [04]

Peltre, Christine. *Orientalism in Art*. Trans. John Goodman. New York: Abbeville, 1998. [05]

———. *Théodore Chassériau*. Paris: Gallimard, 2001. [EP]

Percier, Charles, and Pierre-François-Léonard Fontaine. *Description des cérémonies et des fêtes qui ont eu lieu pour le mariage de S.M. l'empereur Napoléon avec S.A.I. Madame l'archiduchesse Marie-Louise d'Autriche*. Paris: P. Didot, 1810. [02]

———. *Résidences de Souverains. Parallèle entre plusieurs résidences de Souverains de France, d'Allemagne, de Suède, de Russie, d'Espagne et d'Italie*. Paris: chez les Auteurs, 1833. [03]

Perrot, Philippe. *Les dessus et les dessous de la bourgeoisie: Une histoire du vêtement au XIXe siècle*. Paris: Arthème Fayard, 1981. [07] [08]

Petit, Anatole. *Le Sicilien, ou l'Amour peintre*, ballet-pantomime en 1 acte. Paris: Barba, 1827. [06]

Picon, Geneviève and Réjane Bargiel. *Victor Hugo Dessins*. Paris: Gallimard, 1985. [06]

Pierre, Victor. *Histoire de la République de 1848*. 2 vols. Paris: E. Plon, 1878. [EP]

Pillement, Georges. *Paris en fête*. Paris: Bernard Grasset, 1972. [02]

Pillet, Fabien. *Une Matinée au Salon, ou Les Peintres de l'école passés en revue: Critique des Tableaux et Sculptures de l'Exposition de 1824*. Paris: Delaunay, 1824. [05]

Pimienta, Robert. *La propagande bonapartiste en 1848*. Paris: Édouard Cornély, 1911. [EP]

Pinkerton, John. *Recollections of Paris in the years 1802–3–4–5*. 2 vols. London: Longman, Hurst, Rees, & Orme, 1806. [03] [04] [07]

Pinkney, David H. *Napoleon III and the Rebuilding of Paris*. Princeton: Princeton University, 1972. [07]

Pinon, Pierre, "A travers révolutions architecturales et politiques, 1715–1848." In *Paris: Genèse d'un paysage*. Ed. Louis Bergeron. Paris: Picard, 1989: 147–215. [07]

———. "Entreprises et Financements." In *Paris-Haussmann: Le pari d'Haussmann*. Eds. Jean des Cars and Pierre Pinon. Paris: Éditions du Pavillon de l'Arsenal / Picard, 1991: 102–6. [07]

———. "Les conceptions urbaines au milieu du XIXe siècle." In *Paris-Haussmann: Le pari d'Haussmann*. Eds. Jean des Cars and Pierre Pinon. Paris: Éditions du Pavillon de l'Arsenal / Picard, 1991: 44–50. [07]

———. "Quelques percées avant le Second Empire." In *Paris-Haussmann: Le pari d'Haussmann*. Eds. Jean des Cars and Pierre Pinon. Paris: Éditions du Pavillon de l'Arsenal / Picard, 1991: 25–32. [07]

Piron, Achille. *Eugène Delacroix, sa vie et ses oeuvres*. Paris: Claye, 1865. [05]

Pitte, Jean-Robert. *Gastronomie française: Histoire et géographie d'une passion*. Paris: Fayard, 1991. [07]

Planche, Gustave. *Études sur l'école française (1831–1852)*. 2 vols. Paris: Michel Lévy frères, 1855. [02] [05] [06]

———. "Le Fronton du Panthéon." *Revue des Deux Mondes*, 4e sér., 11 (15 August 1837): 410–34. [03]

———. "Le Salon de 1847: La peinture." *Revue des Deux Mondes*, nouv. sér., 18 (17 April 1847): 354–66. [07]

———. "Le Salon du Roi." *Revue des Deux Mondes*, 4e série, 10 (15 June 1837): 752-767. [03]

———. "Peinture Monumentale: MM. Eugène Delacroix et Hippolyte Flandrin." *Revue des Deux Mondes*, nouv. sér., 15 (1 July 1846): 148–61. [03]

———. *Salon de 1831*. Paris: Pinard, 1831. [02]

———. "Salon de 1833." In Planche, *Études sur l'école française*, 1: 173–232. [02]

Plumptre, Ann. *A Narrative of a Three Years' Residence in France, principally in the southern departments, from the year 1802 to 1805*. 3 vols. London: Richard Taylor, 1810. [03] [04] [07]

Poletti, Michel and Alain Richarme. *Barye: Catalogue raisonné des sculptures*. Paris: Gallimard, 2000. [05]

Pommier, Edouard. "Idéologie et Musée à l'époque révolutionnaire." In *Les Images de la Révolution française*. Ed. Michel Vovelle. Paris: La Sorbonne, 1988: 57–78. [03]

Porter, Roy and G. S. Rousseau, eds. *Exoticism in the Enlightenment*. Manchester: Manchester University, 1990. [05]

Porterfield, Todd B. *The Allure of Empire: Art in the Service of French Imperialism, 1798-1836*. Princeton: Princeton University, 1998. [03]

Potonniée, Georges. *Daguerre, peintre et décorateur*. Paris: Paul Montel, 1935. Reprint. Paris: Jean-Michel Place, 1989. [08]

———. *Histoire de la découverte de la photographie*. Paris: Paul Montel, 1925. Reprint. Paris: Jean-Michel Place, 1989. [08]

Potts, Alex. *Flesh and the Ideal: Winckelmann and the Origins of Art History*. New Haven: Yale University, 1994. [05]

Pougetoux, Alain. *La Collection de peintures de l'Impératrice Joséphine*. Paris: Éditions de la Réunion des musées nationaux, 2003. [04]

Pouillet, Eugène. *Traité théorique et pratique de la Propriété Littéraire et Artistique et du droit de représentation*. Paris: Imprimerie et Librairie Générale de Jurisprudence, 1879. [08]

Poulot, Dominique. "Alexandre Lenoir et les musées des monuments français." In *Les Lieux de Mémoire*, sous la direction de Pierre Nora. 3 vols. Paris: Gallimard-Quarto, 1997, 3: 1515–1543. [04]

Poumiès de la Siboutie, François-Louis. *Souvenirs d'un médecin de Paris*. 3rd ed. Paris: Plon-Nourrit, 1910. [07]

Pradère, Alexandre. "Du style troubadour au style Boulle à l'hôtel d'Osmond." *Connaissance des Arts* 472 (June 1991): 72–83. [04]

Prat, Louis-Antoine. *Dessins de Théodore Chassériau*. 2 vols. Paris: Éditions de la Réunion des musées nationaux, 1988. [EP]

Preiss, Nathalie. *Les Physiologies en France au XIXe siècle: Étude historique, littéraire et stylistique*. Mont-de-Marsan: Éditions InterUniversitaires, 1999. [08]

Pressouyre, Léon. "Les spectacles parisiens et la redécouverte du Moyen Âge." In Paris, Hôtel du Sully, *Le "Gothique" retrouvée avant Viollet-le-Duc*: 128–29. [06]

Pronteau, Jeanne. "Construction et Aménagement des Nouveaux Quartiers de Paris (1820–1826)." *Histoires des Entreprises* 1 (November 1958): 8–32. [07]

Providence, Brown University, List Art Center, Bell Gallery. *All the Banners Wave: Art and War in the Romantic Era, 1792–1851*, exhibition catalogue. Providence: Brown University Department of Art, 1982. [01]

Prudhomme, Louis. *Voyage descriptif et historique de Paris: Miroir fidèle de cette capitale*. Nouv. éd. 2 vols. Paris: chez l'auteur, 1825. [07]

Pulver, Jeffrey. *Paganini: The Romantic Virtuoso*. London: 1936. Reprint. New York: Da Capo, 1970. [06]

Pupil, François. *Le Style Troubadour*, ou la nostalgie du bon vieux temps. Nancy: Presses Universitaires de Nancy, 1985. [04]

Puttfarken, Thomas. *Roger de Piles' Theory of Art*. New Haven: Yale University, 1985. [05]

Quatremère de Quincy, Antoine-Chrysostôme. *Considérations morales sur la destination des ouvrages de l'art*. Paris: Crapelet, 1815. [04]

———. *Dictionnaire historique d'architecture*. 2 vols. Paris: Librairie d'Adrien le Clère, 1832. [08]

———. *Le préjudice qu'occasionneroient aux Arts et à la Science, le déplacement des monumens de l'art de l'Italie, le démembrement de ses Écoles, et la spoliation de ses Collections, Galeries, Musées, &c.* Paris: Desenne, Quatremère, AN VI [1796]. [03]

Quentin-Bauchart, Pierre. *Lamartine: Homme Politique*. 2 vols. Paris: Plon-Nourrit, 1903. [EP]

Quynn, Dorothy M. "The Art Confiscations of the Napoleonic Wars." *American Historical Review* 50 (April 1945): 447–60. [01] [03]

Rabreau, Daniel. "L'arc de triomphe: de la gloire au sacrifice." In Paris, *La Sculpture française au XIXe siècle*: 162–77. [02]

Rambuteau, Claude-Philibert Barthelot, comte de. *Mémoires du comte de Rambuteau publiées par son petit-fils*. Ed. and Intro. Georges Lequin. Paris: Calmann-Lévy, 1905. [03] [07]

Ratcliffe, Barrie. "Visions et (révisions) des dynamiques de la croissance urbaine dans le Paris de la première moitié du XIXe siècle." In Bowie, *La modernité avant Haussmann*: 41–55. [07]

Raucourt, Anaïs de [pseud. M. A. Bazin]. *L'époque sans nom: Esquisses de Paris 1830–1833*. 2 vols. Paris: Alexandre Messier, 1833. [07]

Ray, Gordon N. *The Art of the French Illustrated Book, 1700–1914*. 2 vols. New York: The Pierpont Morgan Library, 1982. [06] [08]

Recht, Roland. *La Lettre de Humboldt: Du jardin paysager au daguerréotype*. Paris: Christian Bourgois, 1989. [08]

Reichardt, Johann-Friedrich. *Un hiver à Paris sous le Consulat, 1802–1803*, d'après les lettres de J.-F. Reichardt. Ed. A. Laquiante. Paris: E. Plon, Nourrit, 1896. [03]

Reid, Donald. *Paris Sewers and Sewermen: Realities and Representations*. Cambridge MA: Harvard University, 1991. [07]

Reinis, J. G. *The Portrait Medallions of David d'Angers*. New York: Polymath, 1999. [06]

Rémusat, Charles de. *Mémoires de ma vie*. 5 vols. Ed. Charles Pouthas. Paris: Plon, 1958–1967. [03] [07]

Rémusat, Madame Claire de. *Memoirs of the Empress Josephine*. 2 vols. Trans. Mrs. Cashel Hoey and John Lillie. New York: P. F. Collier, 1910. [01]

Resseguier, Jules de. "Moeurs: Un samedi au Louvre—Septembre 1823—Exposition des produits de l'industrie." *La Muse française* (1823–1824). In Johnson, *French Lithography*: 46. [08]

Reynaud, Jean-Pierre. "Le contour et l'infini." In *Victor Hugo et les images*. Eds. Madeleine Blondel and Pierre Georgel. Dijon: Ville de Dijon/Aux Amateurs du Livre, 1989: 213–22. [06]

Reynaud, Leonce. *Traité d'architecture*. 4 vols. Paris: Librairie pour l'Architecture, 1860. [08]

Rhodes, Solomon A. *Gérard de Nerval, 1808–1855*. New York: Philosophical Library, 1951. [06]

Ribeiro, Aileen. *Ingres in Fashion: Representations of Dress and Appearance in Ingres's Images of Women*. New Haven: Yale University, 1999. [06]

Rice, Shelley. *Parisian Views*. Cambridge MA: MIT, 1997. [08]

Richard, Fleury-François. *Mes Souvenirs*. Manuscript written 1847–1850. Private Collection. [04]

Rio, Alexis-François. *De la poésie chrétienne dans sa matière et dans ses formes*. Paris: Debécourt, 1836. [03]

Rochebouët, Beatrice de. "La Bourse, Genèse et Construction." In Paris, *Brongniart*: 118–67. [03]

Rodin, Auguste. *Les cathédrales de la France*. Paris: A. Colin, 1914. [04]

Rohault de Fleury, Charles. *Muséum d'histoire naturelle: Serres chaudes*. Paris: chez l'auteur, 1844. [08]

Rome, Académie de France à Rome. *Le Retour à Rome de Monsieur Ingres: Dessins et peintures*, exhibition catalogue. Rome: Fratelli Palombi, 1993. [08]

Rosen, Charles. *The Romantic Generation*. Cambridge MA: Harvard University, 1995. [06]

Rosen, Charles and Henri Zerner. *Romanticism and Realism: The Mythology of Nineteenth-Century Art*. New York: Viking, 1984. [05] [08]

Rosenblum, Robert. "Ingres's Portraits and Their Muses." In New York, *Portraits by Ingres*: 3–23. [06]

———. *Transformations in Late Eighteenth-Century Art*. Princeton: Princeton University, 1974. [01]

Rosenthal, Donald A. "Jules-Robert Auguste and the Early Romantic Circle." Ph.D. Diss., Columbia University, New York, 1978. [06]

Rosenthal, Léon. *Du Romantisme au Réalisme: Essai sur l'évolution de la peinture en France de 1830 à 1848*. Paris, 1914. Reprint. Paris: Macula, 1987. [03] [05] [06] [07]

———. *La peinture romantique: Essai sur l'évolution de la peinture française de 1815 à 1830*. Paris: Albert Fontemoing, 1901. [06]

Rosenthal, Michael. *Constable: The Painter and His Landscape*. New Haven: Yale University, 1983. [05] [06]

Rouillé, André. *L'Empire de la photographie: Photographie et pouvoir bourgeois, 1839–1879*. Paris: Le Sycomore, 1982. [08]

———. *La Photographie en France—Textes et Controverses: Une Anthologie, 1816–1871*. Paris: Macula, 1989. [08]

Rouleau, Bernard. *Le tracé des rues de Paris*. Paris: Presses du CNRS, 1988. [07]

———. *Paris: Histoire d'un espace*. Paris: Seuil, 1997. [07]

Rozelaar, Louis. "Le Mémorial de Sainte-Hélène et le Romantisme." *Revue des études napoléoniennes*, 18e année, nouv. sér., 29 (October 1929): 203–26. [02] [08]

Rubin, James Henry. "Oedipus, Antigone, and Exiles in Post-Revolutionary French Painting." *Art Quarterly* 36 (Autumn 1974): 141–71. [01]

Sabatier-Ungher, François. *Salon de 1851*. Paris: Librairie phalanstérienne, 1851. [02] [EP]

Saddy, Pierre. *Henri Labrouste, architecte 1801–1875*, exhibition catalogue. Paris: Caisse Nationale des Monuments Historiques et des Sites, 1976. [08]

Said, Edward W. *Orientalism*. New York, 1978. Reprint. New York: Vintage Books, 1979. [05]

Saint-Chéron, Alexandre de. "Beaux-Arts: La statue de Napoléon." *L'Artiste* 5 (1833): 241–43. [03]

Saint-Guilhem François de and Klaus Schrenk. *Honoré Daumier: L'oeuvre lithographique*. 2 vols. Paris: Arthur Hubschmid, 1978. [07] [08]

Saint-Rémy-lès-Chevreuse, Fondation de Coubertin. *Aux Grands Hommes: David d'Angers*, exhibition catalogue. Saint-Rémy-lès-Chevreuse: Fondation de Coubertin, 1990. [06]

Samoyault-Verlet, Colombe. "L'ameublement des palais royaux sous la Monarchie de Juillet." In Paris, *Un âge d'or des arts décoratifs*: 230–34. [04]

———. "Louis XVIII: L'ameublement des châteaux royaux à l'époque de la Restauration." In Paris, *Un âge d'or des arts décoratifs*: 42–49. [04]

Sand, George. *Correspondance*. 4th ed. 6 vols. Paris: Calmann-Lévy, 1883. [06]

———. *Histoire de ma vie*. 4 vols. Paris: Calmann-Lévy, 1893–1912. [06]

Sandoz, Marc. *Théodore Chassériau, 1819–1856: Catalogue raisonné des peintures et estampes*. Paris: Arts et métiers graphiques, 1974. [EP]

Santa Barbara, University Museum. *The Cult of Images: Baudelaire and the 19th-Century Media Explosion*, exhibition catalogue. Santa Barbara: Regents of the University of California, 1977. [08]

Savigny, J. B. Henri and Alexandre Corréard. *Naufrage de la frégate la Méduse faisant partie de l'expédition du Sénégal en 1816.* Paris: chez Hocquet, 1817. [01]

Say, Léon. "Bertin aîné et Bertain de Veaux." In *Le Livre du Centenaire du Journal des Débats, 1789–1889.* Paris: E. Plon, Nourrit, 1889: 14–47. [06]

Schlenhoff, Norman. "Baron Gros and Napoleon's Egyptian Campaign." In *Essays in Honor of Walter Friedlaender.* New York: NYU Institute of Fine Arts, 1965: 152–64. [01]

Schmit, Jean-Philippe. *Nouvel manuel complet de l'architecte des monuments religieux,* ou Traité d'application pratique de l'archéologie chrétienne à la construction, à l'entretien, à la restauration et à la décoration des églises. 2 vols. Paris: Roret, 1859. [03]

Schmoll gen. Eisenwerth, J. Adolf, ed. *Das Unvollendete als künstlerische Form.* Berne: Francke, 1959. [06]

Schneider, Donald David. *The Works and Doctrine of Jacques Ignace Hittorff, 1792–1867.* 2 vols. New York: Garland, 1977. [07]

Schwartz, Vanessa R. *Spectacular Realities: Early Mass Culture in Fin-de-Siècle Paris.* Berkeley: University of California, 1998. [07]

Schwarz, Heinrich. "Ingres Graveur." *Gazette des Beaux-Arts,* 6e pér., 54 (December 1959): 329–42. [08]

Scott, Barbara. "The Duchess of Berry as a Patron of the Arts." *Apollo* 124 (October 1986): 345–53. [04]

Scott, John. *A Visit to Paris in 1814;* being a review of the Moral, Political, Intellectual, and Social Condition of the French Capital. 4th ed. London: Longman, Hurst, Rees, Orme, and Brown, 1816. [07]

———. *Paris Revisited in 1815, by way of Brussels.* Boston: Wells and Lilly, 1816. [01]

Séché, Léon. *Le Cénacle de Joseph Delorme: Victor Hugo et les artistes.* 2 vols. Paris: Mercure de France, 1912. [06]

Seigel, Jerrold. *Bohemian Paris: Culture, Politics, and the Boundaries of Bourgeois Life, 1830–1930.* New York: Viking Penguin, 1986. [06]

Semper, Gottfried. "Der Wintergarten zu Paris." *Zeitschrift für praktische Baukunst* (1849): cols. 515–26. [08]

Senefelder, Aloys Johann Nepomuk Franz. *The Invention of Lithography.* Trans. Julius. W. Muller. Munich: Thienemann, 1818. Reprint. Sewickley PA: GATF Press, 1998. [07]

Sennett, Richard. *The Fall of Public Man.* New York: Alfred A. Knopf, 1977. [07] [EP]

Sensier, Alfred. *Souvenirs de Th. Rousseau.* Paris: Léon Techener, 1872. [05]

Sérullaz, Maurice. *Les peintures murales de Delacroix.* Paris: Les Éditions du Temps, 1963. [03]

Seyd, Felizia. *Romantic Rebel: The Life and Times of George Sand.* New York: Viking, 1940. [06]

Shelton, Andrew Carrington. *Ingres and his Critics.* Cambridge UK: Cambridge University, 2006. [05]

———. "Ingres Versus Delacroix." *Art History* 23 (December 2000): 726–42. [05]

Shroder, Maurice Z. *Icarus: The Image of the Artist in French Romanticism.* Cambridge MA: Harvard University, 1961. [05] [06]

Siegfried, Susan. *The Art of Louis-Léopold Boilly: Modern Life in Napoleonic France.* New Haven: Yale University, 1995. [07]

Silvestre de Sacy, Jacques. *Alexandre-Théodore Brongniart, 1739–1813.* Paris: Plon, 1940. [03]

Silvestre, Théophile. *Histoire des artistes vivants.* Paris: E. Blanchard, 1855. [05]

Sinnreich, Ursula. "Delacroix's Faust-Illustrationen." In Frankfurt-am-Main, *Eugène Delacroix:* 56–65. [06]

Soulié, Frédéric. "Marchands de nouveautés." In *Nouveau Tableau de Paris au XIXe siècle.* 6 vols. Paris: Mme Charles-Béchet, 1834–1835, 2: 147–65. [08]

———. "Restaurants et Gargotes." In *La Grande Ville.* 2 vols. Paris: Marescq, 1843, 2: 5–24. [07]

Spang, Rebecca L. *The Invention of the Restaurant: Paris and Modern Gastronomic Culture.* Cambridge MA: Harvard University, 2000. [07]

Spector, Jack J. *Delacroix: The Death of Sardanapalus.* New York: Viking, 1974. [05]

Spitzer, Alan B. *The French Generation of 1820.* Princeton: Princeton University, 1987. [05]

Staël, Anne-Louis-Germaine de. *Considérations sur les principaux événemens de la Révolution française.* 3 vols. Paris: Delaunay, 1818. [03]

———. *De l'Allemagne.* 4 vols. Paris: Hachette, 1958. [06]

———. *De la Littérature considérée dans ses rapports avec les institutions sociales.* Paris: Maradan, 1800. Reprint. Paris: G. Charpentier, 1887. [01]

Steadman, Philip. *Vermeer's Camera: Uncovering the Truth behind the Masterpieces.* Oxford: Oxford University, 2001. [8]

Stendhal [pseud. Marie-Henri Beyle]. *Stendhal and the Arts.* Ed. and Trans. David Wakefield. London: Phaidon, 1973. [05] [06]

———. "The Salon of 1824." In *Stendhal and the Arts.* Ed. David Wakefield. London: Phaidon, 1973: 88–121. [05]

———. *Vie de Henri Brulard.* Ed. and Intro. Victor Del Litto. Grenoble: Glénat, 1988. [02]

Stewart, H. F. and Paul Desjardins. *French Patriotism in the Nineteenth Century (1814–1833),* traced in contemporary texts. Cambridge UK: Cambridge University, 1923. [05]

Stirling, Julien. *Histoire et description de la colonne de Juillet et de la place de la Bastille.* Paris: H. Champion, 1914. [03]

Summerson, John. *Architecture in Britain, 1530–1830.* 5th ed. Harmondsworth: Penguin Books, 1969. [04]

Tait, A. A. "The Duke of Hamilton's Palace." *Burlington Magazine* 125 (July 1983): 394–402. [01]

Tardieu, Ambroise. *Annales du musée et de l'école française moderne: Salon de 1833.* Paris: Pillet, 1833. [05]

Ténot, Eugène. *Paris en décembre 1851: Étude historique sur le coup d'état.* Paris: Armand le Chevalier, 1868. [EP]

Texier, Edmond. *Tableau de Paris.* 2 vols. Paris: Paulin et Le Chevallier, 1852–1853. [06]

Theis, Laurent. "Guizot et les institutions de mémoire." In *Les Lieux de Mémoire,* sous la direction de Pierre Nora. 3 vols. Paris: Gallimard-Quarto, 1997, I: 1575–1597. [03]

Thiébault, baron général Paul-Charles-François. *Mémoires du Général Thiébault.* Paris: E. Plon, Nourrit, 1894. [01]

Thierry, Augustin. *Lettres sur l'histoire de France.* Nouv. éd. Paris: Garnier, [1866]. [04]

Thierry, Jules and Gustave Coulon. *Notice historique de l'arc de triomphe de l'Étoile.* Nouv. éd. Paris: J. Thierry, Rosselin, 1842. [03]

Thiers, Adolphe. "De la lithographie et de ses progrès." *La Pandore* 259 (30 March 1824) and 263 (3 April 1824). In Johnson, *French Lithography:* 46–48. [08]

———. *Discours Parlementaires,* publiés par M. Calman. 16 vols. Paris: C. Lévy, 1879–1889. [03]

Thomasseau, Jean-Marie. *Le mélodrame.* Paris: Presses Universitaires de France, 1984. [06]

———. "Le Mélodrame et la Censure sous le Premier Empire et la Restauration." *Revue des Sciences Humaines* 162 (1976): 171–82. [01]

Thompson, Christopher W. *Victor Hugo and the Graphic Arts, 1820–1833.* Geneva/Paris: Librairie Droz, 1970. [06]

Thompson, J. M. *Napoleon Bonaparte.* Oxford & New York: Basil Blackwell, 1988. [01]

Thoré, Théophile. *Le Salon de 1846, précédé d'une lettre à George Sand.* Paris: Alliance des Arts, 1846. [EP]

———. *Le Salon de 1847, précédé d'une lettre à Firmin Barrion.* Paris: Alliance des Arts, 1847. [07]

———. *Salons de T. Thoré (1844–1848).* Intro. W. Bürger. Paris: Librairie internationale, 1868. [05] [06]

Thureau-Dangin, Paul. *Histoire de la Monarchie de Juillet.* 4th ed. 7 vols. Paris: Plon-Nourrit, 1905–1909. [03] [05] [07] [08]

Tilby, Michael. "'Telle main veut tel pied': Balzac, Ingres and the Art of Portraiture." In *Artistic Relations: Literature and the Visual Arts in Nineteenth-Century France.* Eds. Peter Collier and Robert Lethbridge. New Haven: Yale University, 1994: 111–29. [06]

Tinterow, Gary. "Paris, 1841–1867." In New York, *Portraits by Ingres:* 351–77. [06]

Tocqueville, Alexis de. *Recollections.* Trans. George Lawrence. Garden City NJ: Doubleday, 1970. [02]

———. *Souvenirs.* Nouv. éd. Ed. Luc Monnier. Paris: Gallimard, 1942. [07]

Trapp, Frank Anderson. *The Attainment of Delacroix.* Baltimore: Johns Hopkins, 1971. [06]

Triaire, Paul. *Napoléon et Larrey.* Tours: Alfred Mame, 1902. [01]

Trianon, Henry. "Nouvelle Bibliothèque Sainte-Geneviève." *Illustration: Journal Universel* (10 January 1851): 29–30. [08]

Tristan, Flora. *Promenades dans Londres: ou L'aristocratie et les prolétaires anglais.* Ed. François Bédarida. Paris: H.-L. Delloye, 1840. Reprint. Paris: François Maspero, 1978. [08]

Troche, Nicholas-Michel. *Mémoire historique et critique sur la chapelle de la Sainte Vierge de l'église royale et paroissiale de Saint-Germain-l'Auxerrois à Paris.* Paris: Paul Dupont, 1848. [03]

Trollope, Frances. *Paris and the Parisians in 1835.* 2 vols. Paris: A. and W. Galignani, 1836. [03] [06] [07]

Tscherny, Nadia and Guy Stair Santy. *Romance and Chivalry: History and Literature Reflected in Early Nineteenth-Century French Painting,* exhibition catalogue. New York/London: Stair Sainty Maththiesen/Matthiesen Fine Art, 1996. [01] [04] [05] [06]

Tudesq, André-Jean. *L'élection présidentielle de Louis-Napoléon Bonaparte, 10 décembre 1848*. Paris: Armand Colin, 1965. [EP]

Tulard, Jean. "Le retour des Cendres." In *Les Lieux de Mémoire*, sous la direction de Pierre Nora. 3 vols. Paris: Gallimard-Quarto, 1997, 2: 1729–1753. [03]

———. *Napoleon: The Myth of the Saviour*. Trans. Teresa Waugh. London: Weidenfeld and Nicolson, 1984 [01]

———. *Nouvelle Histoire de Paris: La Révolution*. Paris: Hachette, 1989. [07]

———. *Nouvelle Histoire de Paris: Le Consulat et l'Empire, 1800–1815*. Paris: Hachette, 1970. [01] [07]

Turner, Jane, ed. *The Dictionary of Art*. 34 vols. London: Macmillan, 1996. [06]

Twyman, Michael. *Lithography, 1800–1850: The Techniques of Drawing on Stone in England and France and Their Application in Works of Topography*. London: Oxford University, 1970. [06] [07] [08]

Ubersfeld, Anne. "Hugo metteur en scène." In *Victor Hugo et les images*. Eds. Madeleine Blondel and Pierre Georgel. Dijon: Ville de Dijon/Aux Amateurs du Livre, 1989: 169–83. [06]

Valenciennes, Pierre-Henri. *Élémens de perspective pratique, à l'usage des artistes, suivis de réflexions et conseils à un élève sur la peinture, et particulièrement sur le genre de paysage*. Paris: Desenne-Duprat, AN VIII [1800]. Reprint. Geneva: Minkoff Reprint, 1973. [05]

van Zanten, David. *Building Paris: Architectural Institutions and the Transformations of the French Capital, 1830–1870*. Cambridge UK: Cambridge University, 1994. [03]

———. *Designing Paris: The Architecture of Duban, Labrouste, Duc and Vaudoyer*. Cambridge MA: MIT, 1987. [08]

Vanier, Henriette. *La Mode et ses métiers: Frivolités et luttes des classes, 1830–1870*. Paris: Armand Colin, 1960. [08]

Vauchez, André. "La Cathédrale." In *Les Lieux de Mémoire*, sous la direction de Pierre Nora. 3 vols. Paris: Gallimard-Quarto, 1997, 3: 3109–3140. [04]

Vaulchier, Claudine de. "Saint-Vincent-de-Paul entre réminiscences et l'invention, 1824–1844." In Paris, *Hittorff*: 111–51. [07]

Vaunois, Albert. *De la notion du droit naturel chez les romains; De la propriété artistique en droit français*. Paris: Moquet, 1884. [08]

Vauthier, G. "L'arc de triomphe en 1810." *Revue des études napoléoniennes*, 2 (July–December 1913): 466–70. [02] [03]

Venard, Marc. "La grande cassure (1520–1598)." In *Histoire de la France religieuse, II: Du Christianisme flamboyant à l'aube des Lumières*. Ed. François Lebrun. Paris: Seuil, 1988: 249–81. [05]

Véron, Louis. *Mémoires d'un bourgeois de Paris*. 7 vols. Paris: Gonet, 1855. [06]

Vicaire, Georges. *Manuel de l'amateur de livres du XIXe siècle*. 8 vols. Paris: A. Rouquette, 1910. [08]

Victor, Pierre. *Mémoire contre le baron Taylor*. Paris: Ponthieu, 1827. [06]

Vidler, Anthony. *Claude-Nicolas Ledoux*. Cambridge MA: MIT, 1990. [02]

Vigier, Philippe. *Nouvelle Histoire de Paris: Paris pendant la Monarchie de Juillet, 1830–1848*. Paris: Hachette, 1991. [07]

Vigne, Georges. *Dessins d'Ingres: Catalogue raisonné des dessins du Musée de Montauban*. Paris: Réunion des musées nationaux/Gallimard, 1995. [05]

———. *Ingres*. Trans. John Goodman. New York: Abbeville, 1995. [05] [06]

———. "Ingres and Co.: A Master and His Collaborators." In New York, *Portraits by Ingres*: 523–42. [06]

Villiers, P. *Manuel de voyageur à Paris, ou Paris ancien et moderne*. Nouv. éd. Paris: chez Delaunay, 1806. [07]

Vincent, Howard P. *Daumier and His World*. Evanston: Northwestern University, 1968. [07]

Viollet-le-Duc, Eugène-Emmanuel. "Restauration." In *Dictionnaire raisonné de l'architecture française*. 10 vols. Paris: B. Bance/A. Morel, 1854–1868, 8: 14–34. [04]

Visconti, Ludovic-Tullius-Joachim. *Fontaines monumentales construites à Paris et projetées pour Bordeaux*, publié par Léon Visconti. Paris: Firmin Didot, 1860. [03]

Voutier, Olivier. *Mémoires du colonel Voutier sur la guerre actuelle des Grecs*. Paris: Bossange frères, 1823. [05]

Walker, Alan. *Franz Liszt*. 2 vols. New York: Alfred A. Knopf, 1983. [06]

———. "Liszt's Musical Background." In *Franz Liszt: The Man and His Music*. Ed. Alan Walker. London: Barrie & Jenkins, 1970: 36–78. [06]

Walton, Whitney. "'To Triumph before Feminine Taste': Bourgeois Women's Consumption and the Hand Methods of Production in Mid-Nineteenth-Century Paris." *Business History Review* 60 (Winter 1986): 541–63. [08]

Waquet, Françoise. *Les Fêtes Royales sous la Restauration, ou l'Ancien Régime retrouvée*. Paris: Arts et métiers graphiques, 1981. [04]

Washington DC, National Gallery of Art. *In the Light of Italy: Corot and Early Open-Air Painting*, exhibition catalogue. Washington DC: National Gallery, 1996. [05]

Watelet, Claude-Henri and Pierre-Charles Lévesque. *Dictionnaire des arts de peinture, sculpture, et gravure*. 5 vols. Paris: L. F. Prault, 1792. [05]

Waugh, Nora. *The Cut of Women's Clothes, 1600–1930*. London: Faber & Faber, 1968. [07]

Wey, Francis. "Publications héliographiques: Traité de photographie sur papier par M. Blanquart-Evrard." *La Lumière* 1 (27 July 1851): 99–100. [08]

Wiegand, Wilfried. *Frühzeit der Photographie, 1826–1890*. Frankfurt-am-Main: Societäts-Verlag, 1980. [08]

Williams, Rosalind H. *Dream Worlds: Mass Consumption in Late Nineteenth-Century France*. Berkeley: University of California, 1982. [08]

Winckelmann, Johann Joachim. "Gedanken über die Nachahmung der Griechischen Werke in der Malerei und Bildhauerkunst." In *Kleine Schriften, Vorreden, Entwurfe*. Ed. Walter Rehm. Berlin: de Gruyter, 1968: 27–59. [05]

Wirth, Louis. "Urbanism as a Way of Life (1938)." In *Urbanism in World Perspective: A Reader*. Ed. Sylvia Fleis Fava. New York: Thomas Y. Cromwell, 1968: 46–63. [07]

Wright, Beth Segal. *Painting and History during the French Restoration: Abandoned by the Past*. Cambridge UK: Cambridge University, 1997. [02] [04] [05] [06]

Wright, Beth Segal, ed. *The Cambridge Companion to Delacroix*. Cambridge UK: Cambridge University, 2001. [02] [05]

Y. . . . "De la facilité." *Journal des Artistes*, 3e année, 1 (17 May 1829): 318–20. [08]

Yaffe, Ann G. "Delacroix as Printmaker." In New Haven, *Prints of Eugène Delacroix*: 5–15 [06]

Young, Edward. *The Complaint: Or, Night Thoughts*. Hartford: S. Andrus, 1847. [01]

Zeldin, Theodore. *France 1848–1945: Taste and Corruption*. Oxford: Oxford University, 1980. [08]

Zerner, Henri. "La gravure sur bois romantique." *Médecine de France* 150 (1964): 17–32. [08]

Ziff, Norman D. *Paul Delaroche: A Study in Nineteenth-Century French History Painting*. New York: Garland, 1977. [05]

Index

The authorized representative in the EU for product safety and compliance is:
Mare Nostrum Group
B.V Doelen 72
4831 GR Breda
The Netherlands

www.ingramcontent.com/pod-product-compliance
Lightning Source LLC
Chambersburg PA
CBHW080901170526
45158CB00008B/1956